The Works of Edmund Spenser

A Variorum Edition

THE PROSE WORKS

LONDON: GEOFFREY CUMBERLEGE
OXFORD UNIVERSITY PRESS

THE WORKS

OF

EDMUND SPENSER

A Variorum Edition

EDITED BY

EDWIN GREENLAW
CHARLES GROSVENOR OSGOOD
FREDERICK MORGAN PADELFORD
RAY HEFFNER

Baltimore
THE JOHNS HOPKINS PRESS

Copyright 1949, The Johns Hopkins Press

Printed in the United States of America
by J. H. Furst Company, Baltimore, Maryland

SPENSER'S PROSE WORKS

RUDOLF GOTTFRIED
Special Editor

Baltimore
THE JOHNS HOPKINS PRESS
1949

TO THE MEMORY
OF
RAY HEFFNER
WHO ORIGINALLY UNDERTOOK TO EDIT
THE TEXT OF SPENSER'S PROSE

PREFACE

In 1805 Sir Walter Scott, reviewing Todd's achievements as an editor of Spenser, was careful to note that scholarship had not as yet done justice to the poet's prose. The complete text of the Spenser-Harvey correspondence might well have been republished, and the most important of the prose works had suffered from neglect of another kind: " it was chiefly in that very curious and interesting tract, the View of the State of Ireland, that Spenser required the aid of a commentator to elucidate his positions as a historian and antiquary, and very frequently to correct his answers. Hardly any picture is more interesting than that of the poet reviewing at once with fear and with some degree of respect, the manners of the rude natives by whom he was surrounded; and it is a shame to literature that nothing has been added worth noticing to what Sir James Ware has long since said on so curious a subject."

Before Scott's criticism had been met, however, there was to be an even longer interval. In 1912 the complete text of the correspondence was finally republished, but without commentary. In 1934 Professor W. L. Renwick brought out an edition of the *View* which provided far more commentary than any of its predecessors had done; but, superior though it was to them, it still left the field open for a variorum edition of the *View* as well as of the shorter writings in prose.

Subsequently, with the intention of adding such an edition to the *Works* of Spenser published by the Johns Hopkins Press, Professor Ray Heffner, assisted by Miss Dorothy E. Mason, gathered variants from eleven manuscripts of the *View* and transcribed a twelfth, the Ellesmere MS, which was to serve as the basic text of the dialogue. For this material, which the General Editors sent me after Professor Heffner's death in 1942, it would be hard to exaggerate my indebtedness. It does not lessen the debt to add that Professor Heffner is not responsible for the use I have made of his material.

In financing the visits to American, English, and Irish libraries which the preparation of this volume made necessary, I have repeatedly taken advantage of the generosity of Indiana University; and the assistance of the American Council of Learned Societies likewise made it possible for me to go abroad in the summer of 1947. I am very happy to record my gratitude to these institutions.

PREFACE

To the owners of the books and manuscripts I have used I am indebted in many ways, of which it is possible to acknowledge only the more important. Mrs. Ray Heffner has graciously afforded me the opportunity to examine the unpublished papers of her husband. Carl H. Pforzheimer and Arthur A. Houghton, Jr., have granted ready access to some of their rarest volumes. And permission to publish from manuscript material, as well as to read in the great collections of Elizabethan books which several of them contain, has been generously given by the Henry E. Huntington Library; the Folger Shakespeare Library; the Trustees of the British Museum; the Public Record Office; his Grace the Archbishop of Canterbury and the Ecclesiastical Commissioners (for the Lambeth Library); Gonville and Caius College, Cambridge; the University Library, Cambridge; the Bodleian Library; the National Library of Ireland; and the Library of Trinity College, Dublin.

I wish also to make acknowledgment to the following for permission to quote from the publications listed under each:

George Allen and Unwin, Ltd.
   Constantia Maxwell, *Irish History from Contemporary Sources (1509–1610)*.

Edward Arnold and Company.
   W. L. Renwick, *Edmund Spenser*.

George Banta Publishing Company.
   Guy Andrew Thompson, *Elizabethan Criticism of Poetry*.

G. Bell and Sons.
   Thomas Seccombe and J. W. Allen, *The Age of Shakespeare*.
   Edmund Spenser, *Poetical Works*, ed. John Payne Collier.

Ernest Benn, Ltd.
   George Sigerson, *Bards of the Gael and the Gall*.

British Museum.
   Standish O'Grady and Robin Flower, *A Catalogue of Irish Manuscripts in the British Museum*.

Cambridge University Press.
   B. E. C. Davis, *Edmund Spenser*.
   Modern Language Review.
   Sir Philip Sidney, *The Complete Works*, ed. Albert Feuillerat.

Chatto and Windus.
   Poem Book of the Gael, ed. Eleanor Hull.

PREFACE

Clarendon Press.
    J. B. Black, *The Reign of Elizabeth*.
    Dictionary of National Biography.
    Lucian of Samosata, *The Works*, trans. H. W. and F. G. Fowler.
    Elizabethan Critical Essays, ed. G. Gregory Smith.
    A New English Dictionary on Historical Principles.
    Review of English Studies.

The Controller of His Britannic Majesty's Stationery Office.
    Calendar of the Carew MSS.
    Calendar of the State Papers, Ireland.
    Historical Manuscripts Commission, Salisbury MSS.

Cork University Press.
    Pauline Henley, *Spenser in Ireland*.
    Alfred O'Rahilly, *The Massacre at Smerwick (1580)*.

E. P. Dutton and Company.
    Émile Legouis, *Spenser*.

Encyclopaedia Britannica, Inc.
    Encyclopaedia Britannica.

Harper and Brothers.
    R. W. Church, *Spenser*.

Houghton Mifflin Company.
    Edmund Spenser, *The Poetical Works*, ed. Francis J. Child.
    Edmund Spenser, *The Complete Poetical Works*, ed. R. E. Neil Dodge.

Irish Text Society.
    Geoffrey Keating, *The History of Ireland*, ed. and trans. David Comyn.
    Tadhg Dall mac Cairbre O'Huiggin, *Bardic Poems*, ed. and trans. Eleanor Knott.

Jackson, Son and Company, Successors.
    William Lithgow, *The Rare Adventures and Painefull Peregrinations*.

Longmans, Green, and Company, Inc.
    P. W. Joyce, *A Social History of Ancient Ireland*.

Modern Language Association of America.
    Publications of the Modern Language Association.

Oxford University Press, London.
: Edmund Spenser, *Poetical Works*, ed. J. C. Smith and Ernest de Selincourt.

Oxford University Press, New York.
: Ralph M. Sargent, *At the Court of Queen Elizabeth*.

G. P. Putnam's Sons.
: H. R. Fox Bourne, *Sir Philip Sidney*.

W. L. Renwick.
: Edmund Spenser, *A View of the Present State of Ireland*, ed. W. L. Renwick.

G. Routledge.
: *Ireland under Elizabeth and James I*, ed. Henry Morley.

Shakespeare Head Press.
: Gabriel Harvey, *Marginalia*, ed. G. C. Moore Smith.

John Sherratt and Son.
: Fynes Moryson, *Shakespeare's Europe*, ed. Charles Hughes.

Robert M. Smith.
: *Shakespeare Association Bulletin*, ed. Robert M. Smith.

Quotations from H. S. V. Jones, *A Spenser Handbook*, have been reprinted by permission of Appleton-Century-Crofts, Inc.; from *The Cambridge History of English Literature*, George Saintsbury's *History of English Prosody*, and Edmund Spenser's *Works* (ed. J. W. Hales and Richard Morris), by permission of the Macmillan Company, Publishers.

The personal good offices which have forwarded this volume include such various services as giving information or encouragement, providing the physical accommodations for research, and apprising the editor of his mistakes. Without specifying the nature of each debt, I wish to express my gratitude to Miss Dorothy E. Mason and Dr. James G. McManaway of the Folger Shakespeare Library; Miss Mary Isabel Fry and Dr. Herbert C. Schulz of the Henry E. Huntington Library; Miss Emma H. E. Stephenson of the Yale University Library; Miss Irene J. Churchill of the Lambeth Library; Dean Fernandus Payne, Professor Verne B. Schuman, and Professor Aubrey Diller of Indiana University; Professor D. D. Griffith of the University of Washington; Professor John L. Lievsay of the University of Tennessee; Professor Roland M. Smith of the University of Illinois; Dr. Marshall W. S. Swan of the American Swedish Historical Museum; Mr. Donald Goodchild of the American Council of Learned

PREFACE

Societies; Miss Harrison of the Carl H. Pforzheimer Company; and Messrs. C. W. Dittus and Harold E. Ingle of the Johns Hopkins Press.

Although the name of my private secretary is not available for publication, I may mention two others whose assistance has long outrun any ability of mine to thank them. Professor Charles G. Osgood, who has given laborious hours, not only to reading and proofreading, but to patiently advising a sometimes recalcitrant editor, may congratulate himself on having effected many notable improvements in this book; and it would also have been a much poorer production if it could not have drawn, as it so constantly has done, upon the friendship and the wisdom of Professor Alexander C. Judson.

R. B. G.

TABLE OF CONTENTS

	PAGE
TEXT:	
Spenser's Letters	1
Axiochus	19
A View of the Present State of Ireland	39
A Brief Note of Ireland	233
COMMENTARY:	
Spenser's Letters	249
Axiochus	269
A View of the Present State of Ireland	278
A Brief Note of Ireland	430
APPENDICES:	
I. Letters: Harvey's Letters and the Preface "To the Cvrteovs Buyer"; the Earthquake; the Areopagus and English Versifying; Publication and Reception; the Identity of E. K.	441
II. Axiochus	487
III. A View of the Present State of Ireland: General Criticism; the Date and Place of Composition; the Text; Smerwick; Prefatory Matter from Ware's Edition, 1633	497
IV. A Brief Note of Ireland	533
V. Verse in Spenser's Prose	538
BIBLIOGRAPHY	539
INDEX	547
MAP OF IRELAND	40

SPENSER'S LETTERS

A Note on the Text

The correspondence of Spenser and Gabriel Harvey originally appeared in a quarto volume which was divided into two sections and had two separate title pages, (1) *Three Proper, and Wittie, Familiar Letters* and (2) *Two Other, Very Commendable Letters*, both title pages dated 1580; the letters in the second section were written earlier than those in the first section. In the present edition it has been decided to discard the organization of the quarto: the letters have been numbered according to the dates at which they were written rather than according to their occurrence in the quarto; and Spenser's letters (I and III) are printed here, with his other prose pieces, while Harvey's letters (II, IV, and V) and the preface of the first section are reserved for Appendix I A. The printer's device on the last page is the only part of the original volume which has been omitted.

Except in the case of a few obvious misprints, the text which follows reproduces that of the original quarto of 1580. The extant copies of the quarto have been collated, and in the textual footnotes their readings are distinguished as follows:

Q^1 the Henry E. Huntington Library copy.
Q^2 the British Museum copy.
Q^3 the Bodleian Library copy.
Q^4 the Carl H. Pforzheimer copy.
Q^5 the Arthur A. Houghton copy, from a photostat in the Folger Shakespeare Library.
Q^6 the Folger Shakespeare Library copy.

Q indicates a reading common to all six copies.

In addition, a selection of variants is given from the following reprints, in whole or in part, of the correspondence:

Fr Abraham Fraunce, *The Arcadian Rhetorike* (London, 1588), sig. C4r.

R *A Poetical Rhapsody* (1602), ed. Hyder E. Rollins (Cambridge, Massachusetts, 1931), 1. 233.

F Edmund Spenser, *The Works* (London, 1679), sigs. A2r–A4v.

Hu Edmund Spenser, *The Works*, ed. John Hughes (London, 1715), 6. 1745-58.

T Edmund Spenser, *The Works*, ed. Henry J. Todd (London, 1805), 1. xvii-xxix, xxxiii-xxxix.

H *Ancient Critical Essays upon English Poets and Poësy*, ed. Joseph Haslewood (London, 1815), 2. 255-303.

Ch Edmund Spenser, *The Poetical Works*, ed. Francis J. Child (Boston, 1855), 5. 381-92.

Co Edmund Spenser, *The Works*, ed. J. Payne Collier (London, 1862), 1. clvii-clxvii.

- *M* Edmund Spenser, *Complete Works*, ed. R. Morris (London, 1869), pp. 706-10.
- *G1* Edmund Spenser, *The Complete Works in Verse and Prose*, ed. Alexander B. Grosart (London, 1882-1884), 9. 257-78.
- *G2* Gabriel Harvey, *The Works*, ed. Alexander B. Grosart (London, 1884-1885), 1. 1-107.
- *Sm* *Elizabethan Critical Essays*, ed. G. Gregory Smith (Oxford, 1904), 1. 87-122.
- *D* Edmund Spenser, *The Complete Poetical Works*, ed. R. E. Neil Dodge (Cambridge, Massachusetts, 1908), pp. 768-73.
- *Se* Edmund Spenser, *The Poetical Works*, ed. J. C. Smith and Ernest de Selincourt (London, 1912), pp. 609-43.

¶ TVVO OTHER,
very commendable Let-
ters, of the same mens vvri-
ting: both touching the foresaid
Artificiall Versifying, and cer-
tain other Particulars:

*More lately deliuered vnto the
Printer.*

IMPRINTED AT LON-
don, by H. Bynneman, dvvelling
in Thames streate, neere vnto
Baynardes Castell.
Anno Domini. 1 5 8 0.
Cum gratia & priuilegio Regiæ Maiestatis.

[LETTER I]

❧ To the Worshipfull his very singular good friend, Maister G. H. Fellow
of Trinitie Hall in Cambridge.

Ood Master *G.* I perceiue by your most curteous and frendly Letters your good will to be no lesse in deed, than I always esteemed. In recompence wherof, think I beseech you, that I wil spare neither speech, nor wryting, nor aught else, whensoeuer, and wheresoeuer occasion shal be offred me: yea, I will not stay, till it be offred, but will seeke it, in al that possibly I may. And that you may perceiue how much your Counsel in al things preuaileth with me, and how altogither I am ruled and ouer-ruled thereby: I am now determined to alter mine owne former purpose, and to subscribe to your aduizement: being notwithstanding resolued stil, to abide your farther resolution. My principal doubts are these. First, I was minded for a while to haue intermitted the vttering of my writings: leaste by ouer-much cloying their noble eares, I should gather a contempt of my self, or else seeme rather for gaine and commoditie to doe it, for some sweetnesse that I haue already tasted. Then also me seemeth the work too base for his excellent Lordship, being made in Honour of a priuate Personage vnknowne, which of some yl-willers might be vpbraided, not to be so worthie, as you knowe she is: or the matter not so weightie, that it should be offred to so weightie a Personage: or the like. The selfe former Title stil liketh me well ynough, and your fine Addition no lesse. If these, and the like doubtes, maye be of importaunce in your seeming, to frustrate any parte of your aduice, I beeseeche you, without the leaste selfe loue of your own purpose, coun-

2 G. H.] Gabriel Harvey *Hu*   4 G.] G. H. *F* Gabriel Harvey *Hu*   12 your . . . things] *in all things your counsel FHu*   15 farther] former *Hu*   16 are] *were FHu*
18 a] *om. Co*   23-4 weightie a Personage] *great a person FHu*   24 stil] *om. FHu*
26 in]to *Co*   27 selfe loue . . . purpose,] *self-love, . . . purpose FHu*

5

cell me for the beste: and the rather doe it faithfullye, and carefully, for
that, in all things I attribute so muche to your iudgement, that I am euer-
more content to adnihilate mine owne determinations, in respecte thereof. 30
And indeede for your selfe to, it sitteth with you now, to call your wits,
and senses togither, (which are alwaies at call) when occasion is so fairely
offered of Estimation and Preferment. For, whiles the yron is hote, it is
good striking, and minds of Nobles varie, as their Estates. *Verùm ne
quid durius.* 35

I pray you bethinke you well hereof, good Maister *G.* and forthwith
write me those two or three special points and caueats for the nonce,
De quibus in superioribus illis mellitissimis, longissimisque Litteris tuis.
Your desire to heare of my late beeing with hir Maiestie, muste dye in
it selfe. As for the twoo worthy Gentlemen, Master *Sidney*, and Master 40
Dyer, they haue me, I thanke them, in some vse of familiaritie: of whom,
and to whome, what speache passeth for youre credite and estimation,
I leaue your selfe to conceiue, hauing alwayes so well conceiued of my
vnfained affection, and zeale towardes you. And nowe they haue pro-
claimed in their ἀρείῳ πάγῳ, a generall surceasing and silence of balde 45
Rymers, and also of the verie beste to: in steade whereof, they haue by
authoritie of their whole Senate, prescribed certaine Lawes and rules of
Quantities of English sillables, for English Verse: hauing had thereof
already greate practise, and drawen mee to their faction. Newe Bookes
I heare of none, but only of one, that writing a certaine Booke, called 50
The Schoole of Abuse, and dedicating it to Maister *Sidney*, was for hys
labor scorned: if at leaste it be in the goodnesse of that nature to scorne.
Suche follie is it, not to regarde aforehande the inclination and qualitie
of him, to whome wee dedicate oure Bookes. Suche mighte I happily
incurre, entituling *My Slomber*, and the other Pamphlets, vnto his honor. 55
I meant them rather to *Maister Dyer*. But I am, of late, more in loue
wyth my Englishe Versifying, than with Ryming: whyche I should haue
done long since, if I would then haue followed your councell. *Sed te
solum iam tum suspicabar cum Aschamo sapere: nunc Aulam video egre-
gios alere Poëtas Anglicos.* Maister *E. K.* hartily desireth to be com- 60
mended vnto your Worshippe: of whome, what accompte he maketh,

---

31 sitteth] fitteth Q^a *Sm*   33-8 For . . . . *tuis.*] *om. FHu*   33 the] *om. Co*   39 in] *of FHu*
41 vse of] *use and FHu*   42 for] *to FHuCo*   43 leaue] leave to *CoM*   45 ἀρείῳ πάγῳ]
SmSe ἀρειωπαγῶ *Q* ἀρειωπάγῳ *FHuMG1G2D* ἀρειωπαγῳ *THCo* ἀρειοπάγῳ *Ch*   47 authoritie]
THChCoMG1G2SmDSe   authotie *Q*   Authority *FHu*   47 Lawes and rules] *Rules and
Laws FHu*   49 and] *and almost FHu*   49 to] *into FHu*   52-3 scorne . . . . it,]
scorn such folly) Is it F   scorn such Folly.) Is it *Hu*   53 aforehande] *before hand FHu*
54 Bookes.] *Books? FHu*   55 vnto] *to FHu*   56 of late] *om. FHu*   57 my] *om. FHu*
58-60 Sed . . . Anglicos.] *om. FHu*   61 vnto] *to FHu*

LETTER I

youre selfe shall hereafter perceiue, by hys paynefull and dutifull Verses of your selfe.

Thus muche was written at Westminster yesternight: but comming this morning, beeyng the sixteenth of October, to Mystresse *Kerkes*, to haue it deliuered to the Carrier, I receyued youre letter, sente me the laste weeke: whereby I perceiue you otherwhiles continue your old exercise of Versifying in English: whych glorie I had now thought shoulde haue bene onely ours heere at London, and the Court.

Truste me, your Verses I like passingly well, and enuye your hidden paines in this kinde, or rather maligne, and grudge at your selfe, that woulde not once imparte so muche to me. But once, or twice, you make a breache in Maister *Drants* Rules: *quod tamen condonabimus tanto Poëtae, tuaeque ipsius maximae in his rebus autoritati*. You shall see when we meete in London, (whiche, when it shall be, certifye vs) howe fast I haue followed after you, in that Course: beware, leaste in time I ouertake you. *Veruntamen te solùm sequar, (vt saepenumerò sum professus,) nunquam sanè assequar, dum viuam*. And nowe requite I you with the like, not with the verye beste, but with the verye shortest, namely with a fewe *Iambickes*: I dare warrant, they be precisely perfect for the feete (as you can easily iudge) and varie not one inch from the Rule. I will imparte yours to Maister *Sidney*, and Maister *Dyer*, at my nexte going to the Courte. I praye you, keepe mine close to your selfe, or your verie entire friendes, Maister *Preston*, Maister *Still*, and the reste.

Iambicum Trimetrum.

VNhappie Verse, the witnesse of my vnhappie state,
  Make thy selfe fluttring wings of thy fast flying
  Thought, and fly forth vnto my Loue, whersoeuer she be:
Whether lying reastlesse in heauy bedde, or else
  Sitting so cheerelesse at the cheerfull boorde, or else
  Playing alone carelesse on hir heauenlie Virginals.
If in Bed, tell hir, that my eyes can take no reste:
  If at Boorde, tell hir, that my mouth can eate no meate:
  If at hir Virginals, tel hir, I can heare no mirth.
Asked why? say: Waking Loue suffereth no sleepe:

67 otherwhiles] *om. FHu*   69 onely ours heere] ours *FHu*   69 at] in *Co*   70-118 Truste . . . . mouth.] *om. FHu*   78 requite I] to requite *Co*   88 *Thought*] Thoughts *Fr*   thoght printed at end of previous line *R*   92 my] mine *R*   93 eate no meate] taste no food *R*

Say, that raging Loue dothe appall the weake stomacke:
Say, that lamenting Loue marreth the Musicall.
Tell hir, that hir pleasures were wonte to lull me asleepe:
Tell hir, that hir beautie was wonte to feede mine eyes:
Tell hir, that hir sweete Tongue was wonte to make me mirth. 100
Nowe doe I nightly waste, wanting my kindely reste:
Nowe doe I dayly starue, wanting my liuely foode:
Nowe doe I alwayes dye, wanting thy timely mirth.
And if I waste, who will bewaile my heauy chaunce?
And if I starue, who will record my cursed end? 105
And If I dye, who will saye: this was, Immerito?

I thought once agayne here to haue made an ende, with a heartie *Vale*, of the best fashion: but loe, an ylfauoured myschaunce. My last farewell, whereof I made great accompt, and muche maruelled you shoulde make no mention thereof, I am nowe tolde, (in the Diuels name) was thorough 110 one mans negligence quite forgotten, but shoulde nowe vndoubtedly haue beene sent, whether I hadde come, or no. Seing it can now be no otherwise, I pray you take all togither, wyth all their faultes: and nowe I hope, you will vouchsafe mee an answeare of the largest size, or else I tell you true, you shall bee verye deepe in my debte: notwythstandyng, thys other 115 sweete, but shorte letter, and fine, but fewe Verses. But I woulde rather I might yet see youre owne good selfe, and receiue a Reciprocall farewell from your owne sweete mouth.

Ad Ornatissimum virum, multis iamdiu nominibus clarissimum, G. H. Immerito 120

sui, mox in Gallias nauigaturi,

εὐτυχεῖν.

SIc malus egregium, sic non inimicus Amicum:
Sicque nouus veterem iubet ipse Poëta Poëtam,
Saluere, ac caelo post secula multa secundo 125
Iam reducem, caelo mage, quàm nunc ipse, secundo
Vtier. Ecce Deus, (modò sit Deus ille, renixum

103 *thy*] my *R*   108 *an*] my *Co*   117 *yet*] om. *CoM*   119 *Ad*] *FHu* resume at this point
123-239 *SIc . . . . charissime.*] om. *Sm*   123 *non*] no *Co*

Qui vocet in scelus, et iuratos perdat amores)
Ecce Deus mihi clara dedit modò signa Marinus,
Et sua veligero lenis parat Æquora Ligno, 130
Mox sulcanda, suas etiam pater Æolus Iras
Ponit, et ingentes animos Aquilonis—
Cuncta vijs sic apta meis: ego solus ineptus.
Nam mihi nescio quo mens saucia vulnere, dudum
Fluctuat ancipiti Pelago, dum Nauita proram 135
Inualidam validus rapit huc Amor, et rapit illuc.
Consilijs Ratio melioribus vsa, decusque
Immortale leui diffissa Cupidinis Arcu.
Angimur hoc dubio, et portu vexamur in ipso.
Magne pharetrati nunc tu contemptor Amoris, 140
(Id tibi Dij nomen precor haud impune remittant)
Hos nodos exsolue, et eris mihi magnus Apollo.
Spiritus ad summos, scio, te generosus Honores
Exstimulat, maiusque docet spirare Poëtam,
Quàm leuis est Amor, et tamen haud leuis est Amor omnis. 145
Ergo nihil laudi reputas aequale perenni,
Praeque sacrosancta splendoris imagine tanti,
Caetera, quae vecors, vti Numina, vulgus adorat,
Praedia, Amicitias, vrbana peculia, Nummos,
Quaeque placent oculis, formas, spectacula, Amores 150
Conculcare soles, vt humum, et ludibria sensus.
Digna meo certè Haruejo sententia, digna
Oratore amplo, et generoso pectore, quam non
Stoica formidet veterum Sapientia vinclis
Sancire aeternis: sapor haud tamen omnibus idem. 155
Dicitur effaeti proles facunda Laërtae,
Quamlibet ignoti iactata per aequora Caeli,
Inque procelloso longùm exsul gurgite ponto,
Prae tamen amplexu lachrymosae Coniugis, Ortus
Caelestes Diuûmque thoros spreuisse beatos. 160
Tantùm Amor, et Mulier, vel Amore potentior. Illum
Tu tamen illudis: tua Magnificentia tanta est:
Praeque subumbrata Splendoris Imagine tanti,
Praeque illo Meritis famosis nomine parto,

131 *sulcanda*] sulcando T   *fulcanda* HCo   138 *diffissa*] FHuTChG2   *diffessa* QHCoMG1DSe   147 *imagine tanti,*] imagine, tanti FHuT   155 *idem.*] idem G1
156 *Dicitur*] Discitur Co   158 *exsul*] exul Hu   158 *gurgite ponto,*] gurgite, ponto FHuT
161 *potentior. Illum*] potentior, Illum; FHuT   163 *Imagine tanti,*] imagine, tanti FHuT

Caetera, quae Vecors, vti Numina, vulgus adorat, 165
Praedia, Amicitias, armenta, peculia, nummos.
Quaeque placent oculis, formas, spectacula, Amores,
Quaeque placent ori, quaeque auribus, omnia temnis.
Nae tu grande sapis, Sapor at sapientia non est:
Omnis et in paruis benè qui scit desipuisse, 170
Saepe supercilijs palmam sapientibus aufert.
Ludit Aristippum modò tetrica Turba Sophorum,
Mitia purpureo moderantem verba Tyranno
Ludit Aristippus dictamina vana Sophorum,
Quos leuis emensi male torquet Culicis vmbra: 175
Et quisquis placuisse Studet Heroibus altis,
Desipuisse studet, sic gratia crescit ineptis.
Denique Laurigeris quisquis sua tempora vittis,
Insignire volet, Populoque placere fauenti,
Desipere insanus discit, turpemque pudendae 180
Stultitiae laudem quaerit. Pater Ennius vnus
Dictus in innumeris sapiens: laudatur at ipse
Carmina vesano fudisse liquentia vino.
Nec tu pace tua, nostri Cato Maxime saecli,
Nomen honorati sacrum mereare Poëtae, 185
Quantamuis illustre canas, et nobile Carmen,
Ni stultire velis, sic Stultorum omnia plena.
Tuta sed in medio superest via gurgite, nam Qui
Nec reliquis nimiùm vult desipuisse videri,
Nec sapuisse nimis, Sapientem dixeris vnum. 190
Hinc te merserit vnda, illinc combusserit Ignis.
Nec tu delicias nimis aspernare fluentes,
Nec serò Dominam, venientem in vota, nec Aurum
Si sapis, oblatum, (Curijs ea, Fabricijsque
Linque viris miseris miseranda Sophismata: quondam 195
Grande sui decus ij, nostri sed dedecus aeui:)
Nec sectare nimis. Res vtraque crimine plena.
Hoc bene qui callet, (si quis tamen hoc bene callet)
Scribe, vel invito sapientem hunc Socrate solum.

170 *scit*] sit *Hu*   172 *Sophorum*] Sororûm *FHu*   173 *Tyranno*] tyranno; *ChG2* tyranno: *DSe*   174 *Aristippus*] Aristippum *FHu*   175 *Quos*] Quod *CoG1*   176 *altis*] actis *FHuT*   178 *Denique*] Denque *H*   180 *discit*] dicit *T*   181 *quaerit.*] quaerit *FHu*   181 *Pater*] *FHuTChCoMG1G2DSe* Paeter *QH*   182 *in*] om. *FHuT*   182 *ipse*] ipsa *CoG1*   183 *liquentia*] *HChCoMG1G2DSe* liquentio *Q* loquentia *FHuT*   186 *Quantamuis*] Quantumvis *T*   187 *Stultorum*] *MG1G2DSe* Sultorum *QHCo* stultorum *FHuTCh*   190 *dixeris vnum.*] dixeris; unum *FHuT*   193 *Aurum*] Aurum. *G1*   194 *oblatum*] *FHuTChG2D* ablatum *QHCoMG1Se*

LETTER I

Vis facit vna pios: Iustos facit altera: et altra   200
Egregiè cordata, ac fortia pectora: verùm
Omne tulit punctum, qui miscuit vtile dulci.
Dij mihi, dulce diu dederant: verùm vtile nunquam:
Vtile nunc etiam, ô vtinam quoque dulce dedissent.
Dij mihi, (quippe Dijs aequiualia maxima paruis)   205
Ni nimis inuideant mortalibus esse beatis,
Dulce simul tribuisse queant, simul vtile: tanta
Sed Fortuna tua est: pariter quaeque vtile, quaeque
Dulce dat ad placitum: saeuo nos sydere nati
Quaesitum imus eam per inhospita Caucasa longè,   210
Perque Pyrenaeos montes, Babilonaque turpem,
Quòd si quaesitum nec ibi invenerimus, ingens
Æquor inexhaustis permensi erroribus, vltrâ
Fluctibus in medijs socij quaeremus Vlyssis.
Passibus inde Deam fessis comitabimur aegram,   215
Nobile cui furtum quaerenti defuit orbis.
Namque sinu pudet in patrio, tenebrisque pudendis
Non nimis ingenio Iuuenem infoelice, virentes,
Officijs frustra deperdere vilibus Annos,
Frugibus et vacuas speratis cernere spicas.   220
Ibimus ergo statim: (quis eunti fausta precetur?)
Et pede Clivosas fesso calcabimus Alpes.
Quis dabit interea conditas rore Britanno,
Quis tibi Litterulas? quis carmen amore petulcum?
Musa sub Oebalij desueta cacumine montis,   225
Flebit inexhausto tam longa silentia planctu,
Lugebitque sacrum lachrymis Helicona tacentem.
Harueiusque bonus, (charus licet omnibus idem,
Idque suo merito, prope suauior omnibus vnus,)
Angelus et Gabriel, (quamuis comitatus amicis   230
Innumeris, geniûmque choro stipatus amaeno)
Immerito tamen vnum absentem saepe requiret,
Optabitque, Vtinam meus hîc Edmundus adesset,
Qui noua scripsisset, nec Amores conticuisset,
Ipse suos, et saepe animo, verbisque benignis   235
Fausta precaretur: Deus illum aliquando reducat. etc.

200 *altra*] alt'ra *TCh*   alter'a *G2*   203 *nunquam*] nunque *Co*   205 *aequiualia*] aequalia *TChG2*   209 *Dulce*] Ducle *H*   209 *dat*] da *FHu*   212 *Quòd*] Qod *H*   216 *cui*] qui *CoG1*   222 *Clivosas*] *FHuDSe* Clibosas *QHCoMG1* clivosas *TCh* cliuosas *G2*   224 *petulcum?*] petulcum! *FHuTHChCo*   225 *desueta*] deserta *FHu*   228 *bonus*] bonos *Hu*   228 *idem,*] idem) *FHuT*   229 *vnus,)*] unus *FHuT*   232 *absentem*] absentum *G2*   233 *hîc*] his *FHuT*   236 *etc.*] om. *Hu*

Plura vellem per Charites, sed non licet per Musas.
Vale, Vale plurimùm, Mi amabilissime Harueie, meo cordi, meorum omnium longè charissime.

I was minded also to haue sent you some English verses: or Rymes, for a farewell: but by my Troth, I haue no spare time in the world, to thinke on such Toyes, that you knowe will demaund a freer head, than mine is presently. I beseeche you by all your Curtesies, and Graces, let me be answered, ere I goe: which will be, (I hope, I feare, I thinke) the next weeke, if I can be dispatched of my Lorde. I goe thither, as sent by him, and maintained most what of him: and there am to employ my time, my body, my minde, to his Honours seruice. Thus with many superhartie Commendations, and Recommendations to your selfe, and all my friendes with you, I ende my last Farewell, not thinking any more to write vnto you, before I goe: and withall committing to your faithfull Credence the eternall Memorie of our euerlasting friendship, the inuiolable Memorie of our vnspotted friendshippe, the sacred Memorie of our vowed friendship: which I beseech you Continue with vsuall writings, as you may, and of all things let me heare some Newes from you. As gentle *M. Sidney*, I thanke his good Worship, hath required of me, and so promised to doe againe. *Qui monet, vt facias, quod iam facis*, you knowe the rest. You may always send them most safely to me by *Mistresse Kerke*, and by none other. So once againe, and yet once more, Farewell most hartily, mine owne good *Master H.* and loue me, as I loue you, and thinke vpon poore *Immerito*, as he thinketh vppon you.

Leycester House. This .5. of *October* .1579.

Per mare, per terras,
Viuus, mortuusque,
Tuus Immerito.

237-9 *Plura .... charissime.*] *om. FHu*   240 I] *preceded by heading* POSTSCRIPT. *FHu Sm resumes at this point*   240 also ... you] *with these to have sent you also FHu*
240 or Rymes] *om. FHu*   241-3 to ... presently.] *om. FHu*   249 vnto] *to FHuT*
253 writings] *Writing FHu*   255 required] *desired FHu*   255-6 and .... rest.] *om. FHu*
257 most] *om. FHu*   258 So once] *FHuTHChCoMG1G2SmD*   Soonce *QSe*   259 H.] Harvey *FHu*   260 vppon you] *on you FHu*   261 5] 16 T   261 1579] *FHuTChMG1G2SmDSe* 2579 *QHCo*   262-4 *Per ... Immerito.*] *om. FHu*

¶ THREE PROPER,
and wittie, familiar Letters:
lately paſſed betvvene tvvo V-
niuerſitie men: touching the Earth-
quake in Aprill laſt, and our Engliſh
reſourmed Verſifying.

*With the Preface of a wellwiller
to them both.*

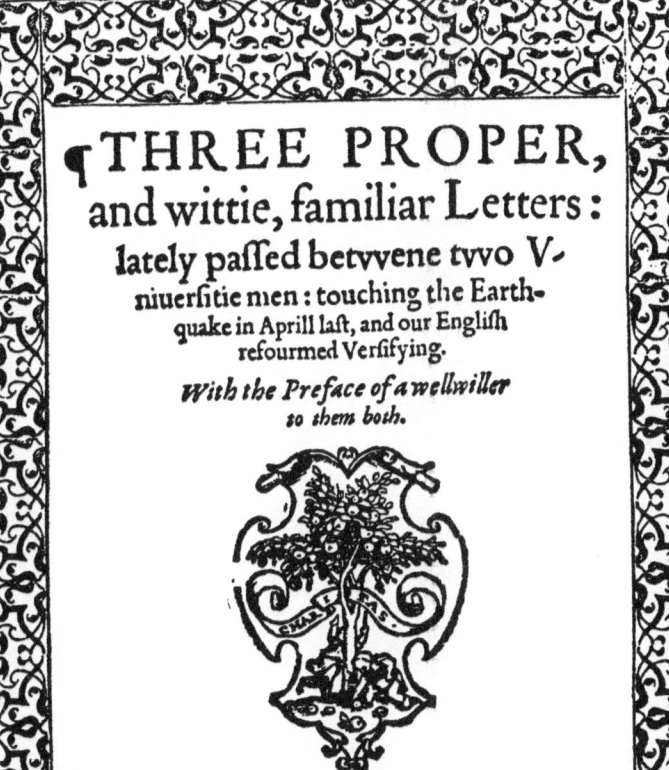

IMPRINTED AT LON-
don, by H. Bynneman, dvvelling
in Thames ſtreate, neere vnto
Baynardes Caſtell.
Anno Domini. 1 5 8 0.
Cum gratia & priuilegio Regiæ Maieſtatis.

Three proper wittie fami-
liar Letters, lately passed be-
twene two Vniuersitie men, tou-
ching the Earthquake in April last,
and our English reformed Versifying.

[LETTER III]

To my long approoued and singular
good frende, Master *G. H.*

*Ood Master H.* I doubt not but you haue some great important matter in hande, which al this while restraineth youre Penne, and wonted readinesse in prouoking me vnto that, wherein your selfe nowe faulte. If there bee any such thing in hatching, I pray you hartily, lette vs knowe, before al the worlde see it. But if happly you dwell altogither in *Iustinians* Courte, and giue your selfe to be deuoured of secreate Studies, as of all likelyhood you doe: yet at least imparte some your olde, or newe, Latine, or Englishe, Eloquent and Gallant Poesies to vs, from whose eyes, you saye, you keepe in a manner nothing hidden. Little newes is here stirred: but that olde greate matter still depending. His Honoure neuer better. I thinke the *Earthquake* was also there wyth you (which I would gladly learne) as it was here with vs: ouerthrowing diuers old buildings, and peeces of Churches. Sure verye straunge to be hearde of in these Countries, and yet I heare some saye (I knowe not howe truely) that they haue knowne the like before in their dayes. *Sed quid vobis videtur magnis*

2 *G. H.*] Gabriel Harvey *Hu*   3 *H.*] Harvey *FHu*   4 al] *at FHu*   4 while] *time FHu*   6-7 nowe faulte] *are now faulty FHu*   8 al] *om. FHu*   9 happly] *happily FHu*   11 all] *om. T*   11 some] *some of FHu*   12-3 from . . . hidden.] *om. FHu*   19 their] *these FHu*   19-20 *Sed . . . Philosophis?*] *om. FHu*

15

Philosophis? I like your late Englishe Hexameters so exceedingly well, that I also enure my Penne sometime in that kinde: whyche I fynd indeede, as I haue heard you often defende in worde, neither so harde, nor so harshe, that it will easily and fairely, yeelde it selfe to oure Moother tongue. For the onely, or chiefest hardnesse, whych seemeth, is in the Accente: whyche sometime gapeth, and as it were yawneth ilfauouredly, comming shorte of that it should, and sometime exceeding the measure of the Number, as in *Carpenter*, the middle sillable being vsed shorte in speache, when it shall be read long in Verse, seemeth like *a lame Gosling, that draweth one legge after hir:* and *Heauen*, beeing vsed shorte as one sillable, when it is in Verse, stretched out with a *Diastole*, is like *a lame Dogge that holdes vp one legge.* But it is to be wonne with Custome, and rough words must be subdued with Vse. For, why a Gods name may not we, as else the Greekes, haue the kingdome of oure owne Language, and measure our Accentes, by the sounde, reseruing the Quantitie to the Verse? Loe here I let you see my olde vse of toying in Rymes, turned into your artificial straightnesse of Verse, by this *Tetrasticon.* I beseech you tell me your fancie, without parcialitie.

> *See yee the blindefoulded pretie God, that feathered Archer,*
>   *Of Louers Miseries which maketh his bloodie Game?*
> *Wote ye why, his Moother with a Veale hath coouered his Face?*
>   *Trust me, least he my Looue happely chaunce to beholde.*

Seeme they comparable to those two, which I translated you *ex tempore* in bed, the last time we lay togither in Westminster?

> *That which I eate, did I ioy, and that which I greedily gorged,*
>   *As for those many goodly matters leaft I for others.*

I would hartily wish, you would either send me the Rules and Precepts of Arte, which you obserue in Quantities, or else followe mine, that *M. Philip Sidney* gaue me, being the very same which *M. Drant* deuised, but enlarged with *M. Sidneys* own iudgement, and augmented with my Obseruations, that we might both accorde and agree in one: leaste we ouerthrowe one an other, and be ouerthrown of the rest. Truste me, you will hardly beleeue what greate good liking and estimation Maister *Dyer*

---

20 late] *om. FHu*   20 exceedingly] *om. FHu*   22 in] the *Co*   23 that] *but that FHu*
24 or] *and FHu*   25 yawneth] *Orig.* pawneth *Sm*   28 shall] *should FHu*   30 out] *om. FHu*   33 else] *om. FHu*   34 the Quantitie] that Quantitie *G1G2*   35-45 Loe .... others.] *om. FHu*   42-3 Seeme ... Westminster?] *om. T*   46-51 I ... rest.] *om. T*   46 and Precepts] *or Principles FHu*   47 mine, that] *those which FHu*   50 accorde and agree] *agree and accord FHu*   51-6 Truste ... for] *om. FHu*

had of youre *Satyricall Verses,* and I, since the viewe thereof, hauing before of my selfe had speciall liking of *Englishe Versifying,* am euen nowe aboute to giue you some token, what, and howe well therein I am able to doe: for, to tell you trueth, I minde shortly at conuenient leysure, to sette forth a Booke in this kinde, whyche I entitle, *Epithalamion Thamesis,* whyche Booke I dare vndertake wil be very profitable for the knowledge, and rare for the Inuention, and manner of handling. For in setting forth the marriage of the Thames: I shewe his first beginning, and offspring, and all the Countrey, that he passeth thorough, and also describe all the Riuers throughout Englande, whyche came to this Wedding, and their righte names, and right passage, etc. A worke beleeue me, of much labour, wherein notwithstanding Master *Holinshed* hath muche furthered and aduantaged me, who therein hath bestowed singular paines, in searching oute their firste heades, and sourses: and also in tracing, and dogging oute all their Course, til they fall into the Sea.

O Tite, siquid, ego,
Ecquid erit pretij?

But of that more hereafter. Nowe, my *Dreames,* and *dying Pellicane,* being fully finished (as I partelye signified in my laste Letters) and presentlye to bee imprinted, I wil in hande forthwith with my *Faery Queene,* whyche I praye you hartily send me with al expedition: and your frendly Letters, and long expected Iudgement wythal, whyche let not be shorte, but in all pointes suche, as you ordinarilye vse, and I extraordinarily desire. *Multum vale. Westminster. Quarto Nonas Aprilis* 1580. *Sed, amabò te, Meum Corculum tibi se ex animo commendat plurimùm: iamdiu mirata, te nihil ad literas suas responsi dedisse. Vide quaeso, ne id tibi Capitale sit: Mihi certè quidem erit, neque tibi hercle impunè, vt opinor, Iterum vale, et quàm voles saepè.*

Yours alwayes to commaunde

IMMERITO.

---

55 what,] *om. Sm*   56 at conuenient leysure] *om. FHu*   58 very] *om. FHu*   59 rare] new *FHu*   60 first] *om. FHu*   61 that] *om. FHu*   61 also] *om. FHu*   62 this] his *FHu*   63-70 and their . . . . hereafter.] *om. FHu*   66-7 their . . . all] *om. T*   71 (as . . . Letters)] *om. FHu*   72 hande] *TChCoMG1G2SmDSe* haude *QH* hand *FHu*   76 *Westminster*] *om. FHu*   76-82 Sed . . . . IMMERITO] *om. FHu*   77 amabò] amato *T*   79 Mihi] Mih Q^3Q^6

Postscripte.

I take best my *Dreames* shoulde come forth alone, being growen by meanes of the Glosse, (running continually in maner of a Paraphrase) full as great as my *Calendar.* Therin be some things excellently, and many things wittily discoursed of *E. K.* and the Pictures so singularly set forth, and purtrayed, as if *Michael Angelo* were there, he could (I think) nor amende the best, nor reprehende the worst. I know you woulde lyke them passing wel. Of my *Stemmata Dudleiana,* and especially of the sundry Apostrophes therein, addressed you knowe to whome, muste more aduisement be had, than so lightly to sende them abroade: howbeit, trust me (though I doe neuer very well,) yet in my owne fancie, I neuer dyd better: *Veruntamen te sequor solùm: nunquam verò assequar.*

AXIOCHUS

A Note on the Text

Except in the case of a few obvious misprints, the following text reproduces that of the original quarto edition of the *Axiochus* (1592). In the textual footnotes the surviving copies of this edition are indicated as

Q^1 the Frederick M. Padelford copy, as reproduced in facsimile (Baltimore, 1934).

Q^2 the Carl H. Pforzheimer copy.

Q indicates a reading common to both copies. It may be added that a collation of the two copies reveals no real evidence that the text was corrected during printing; the apparent differences are probably due to faulty type or to blurred reproduction in the facsimile of Q^1.

Axiochus.
A moſt excellent Dialogue,
written in Greeke by *Plato* the Phy-
loſopher: concerning the ſhortneſſe and vncer-
tainty of this life, with the contrary ends of
the good and wicked.
(∴)

Tranſlated out of Greeke by
Edw. Spenſer.

*Heereto is annexed a ſweet ſpeech or Oration,
ſpoken at the Tryumphe at White-hall before her
Maieſtie, by the Page to the right noble Earle
of Oxenforde.*

AT LONDON,
Printed for Cuthbert Burbie, and are
to be ſold at the middle ſhop in the Poultry,
vnder S. Mildreds Church.
Anno. 1592.

To the Right Worshipfull

Maister *Benedic Barnam*, Esquire, Alderman and Sheriffe of this honorable Citty of London: health and happinesse.

Orshipfull Sir, I am bold (by way of dedication) to giue yee this excellent Dialogue of *Plato* the Phylosopher, for two reasons. The first, that so singuler a worke, doone by a Heathen man, might as wel florish in our vulgare speech, as of long time it hath doone both in Greeke and Latine.

The seconde, that your countenaunce might shaddowe it from reprochefull slaunders, which common censures too lightly bolt out against the best endeuours. But concerning the speciall matter, to wit, my presumption, without first acquainting yee heere-with: thus I protect my selfe. My familiarity with yee in your younger yeeres, when sometimes wee were Schollers together, and my present ioy, to see ye so happie a succeeder both in your Fathers vertues, place, and Office: imboldened mee to shew a remembrance of the one, yet reuerently, and gladnes of the other as well becommeth me.

If in thys small gift, ye make acceptance both of the one and other, yee shall declare no lesse then each one well discernes in ye, and ioy him that euery way is at your commaund.

2 Al-] Al Q^1 20 in] iu Q^1

To the Reader.

THis Dialogue of Axiochus, *gentle Reader, was translated out of Greeke, by that worthy Scholler and Poet, Maister* Edward Spenser, *whose studies haue and doe carry no mean commendation, because their deserts are of so great esteeme.*

If heerein thou find not the delightfull pleasures his verses yeeldeth, yet shalt thou receiue matter of as high contentment: to wit, comfort in the verie latest extremitie. For his sake then be kind in acceptance heereof, and doe him the right he very well deserueth.

Axiochus of
Plato, or a Dialogue
of Death, being both short
and very Elegant.

Socrates. Clinias. Axiochus.

AS I went one day to my common schoole *Cynosargus*, and being in the waye by *Elizeus*, I might heare the voice of one calling aloude to me, *Socrates*. And turning me about to see whence it came, I saw *Clinias Axiochus* his sonne, together with *Damon* the Musitian and *Charmides*, the sonne of *Glauco* running hastely toward *Callirrhoe*, whereof the one was a Maister and professor of the Arte of Musicke, and the other by means of great familiarity and acquaintance, did both loue him, and also was of him beloued; whereupon I thought good, leauing my ready way, to go meet them, that I might the sooner vnderstand his meaning. Then *Clinias* bursting out in teares, O *Socrates* (quod he) now is the time when thou maist shew forth thy long fostered and famous wisedome, for my father is euen nowe taken with a grieuous disease, and drawing neere (as it seemeth) to his end, is therwithall grieuously troubled, and greatly disquieted. Howbeit, heeretofore hee was so farre from the feare of death, as that he was wont pleasantly to scoffe and scorne at those which vsed to portraict the Image of death, painting him with a dreadfull countenance and a griesly face. Wherefore I beseech thee O *Socrates*, to go and comfort my father as you were wont to doo: for so the rather being strengthened with your good counsaile, he shall bee able without any grudging or fainting to passe through the way of all flesh, and I with the rest of his friends and kinsmen will maintaine the yearely memory of that his good end.

Socrates.

O *Clinias* I will not denie thy so reasonable a request, specially concerning such a matter, as to deny it were great vnkindnes and discourtesie:

6 *Cynosargus*] *Lynosargus* Q

to grant it, perteyneth both to godlinesse and charitie. Let vs therefore speede vs to him: for if thy father be in so sore taking, there needeth speedines and great hast.

Clinias.

O *Socrates*, I am sure that my father, assoone as hee but beholdeth you, will be much better at ease: for his fitte and panges of his sicknesse vse oftentimes to surcease and be asswaged.

Socrates.

But that we might the sooner come to him, we tooke the way, which lieth beside the town wall by the Gardeins) for his dwelling was hard by the gates which lyeth toward the *Amazons* piller: whither wee comming, found *Axiochus* (which by this time was come to himself againe) being indeed somewhat strong in his body, but very weake and feeble in his minde, and resting altogether comfortlesse: often tossing him, and tumbling vp and downe in his bed, fetching deepe and dolefull sighes, with aboundant streames of trickling teares, and wailefull wringing of his handes: whome beholding, O *Axiochus* quoth I, what meaneth this? where bee now those haughtie and couragious words, wherewith thou wast wont to scorne and despise death? where bee those thy dayly and continuall prayses of vertue and goodnesse vanished? where also is now that thy vnspeakeable stoutnesse, wherewith thou wast woont to confirme thy selfe and strengthen others: for like as a cowardly champion, which at the first comming forth as to the skirmish, with stately steps and a vaunting visage, dooth soone after cast away his Target, and taketh him to flight: euen so seemest thou now, when there is need most of al to flinch. Hast thou no more regarde of thy diuine and excellent nature, that sometime wast a man of so good life and calling, so obedient to reasons rule? and if there were nothing els, yet should it be sufficient to mooue thee, that thou art an *Athenian* borne: and lastly should mooue thee that common saying, which is worne in all mens mouths; That this our life is a Pilgrimage, which when we haue ended with perfect measure and stedfast trauell: it behoueth vs with like constancy of minde, and ioyfulnes of spirit, and as it were singing a merry Paean, to enter into the purposed place of rest. But thus to languish in dispaire and tender-harted out-cries, behauing thy selfe like a froward Babe, in thee is neither regard of thy wisedome, nor respect of thy age.

56 al] al, ?

Axiochus.

True indeed O *Socrates*, and that which thou sayest, me seemeth right: But it commeth to passe I knowe not how, that when I drawe neere vnto present daunger, than those great and stout-hearted wordes which I was wont to cast at death, doo closely flit away and downe are trodden vnderfoote. And then that Tormentor feare, the messenger of dreaded daungers, dooth sundrye wayes wound and gall my grieued minde, whispering continually in mine eare that if I bee once depriued of this worldly light, and bereft of goods: I shall like a rotten blocke lye in the darkesome deapth, neither seene nor heard of any, beeing resolued into dust and wormes.

Socrates.

O *Axiochus* thy talke is very foolish, for reasoning thus without reason, and seeking to make some sence of senceles wordes, thou both dost and sayest cleane contrary to thy selfe, not marking, how at one time thou dost both complaine for the lacke of sence which thou shalt haue: and also art greatly vexed for the rotting of thy carrion Carcasse, and despoyling of thy former delights: as if by this death thou shouldest not passe into another life, or shouldest be so despoyled of all sence and feeling, as thou wert before thou wast first brought into this world. For euen as in those yeares when *Draco* and *Callisthenes* gouerned the common wealth of *Athens*, thou then wast vexed with no euil, for in the beginning thou wast no such as to whome euill might chance: so likewise when thou hast ended this state of mortalitye thou shalt no more be afflicted, for thou shalt not be in such case as that any euill can touch thee. Wherefore shake off and cast away all these trifles and worldly baggage, thus waying in thy minde, that when the frame of this earthly building is dissolued, and the soule being singled, is restored to his naturall place: this bodye which is then left an earthly masse and an vnreasonable substance, is then no more a man. For we are a soule, that is to say, an immortall creature, beeing shut vp and inclosed in an earthly dungeon. Wherewithall nature hath clothed vs, and charged vs with many miseries, so that euen those things which seeme pleasant to vs and ioyfull, are indeed but vaine and shadowed, beeing mingled and wrapped in many thousand sorrowes, and those also which vse to breede vs sorrowe and heauines, are both sodaine, and therefore more hardely auoyded, and also perdurable, and therefore the more painefull and wearisome. Such be diseases and inflammation of

77 seene] feene *Q¹*   91 afflicted] afslicted *Q¹*

the sences: Such bee inward griefes and sickenesses, through which it
cannot choose but that the soule must bee also diseased, since that beeing
scattered and spread through the powres and passages of the body, it
coueteth the vse of that open and kinde heauen out of which it was deriued,
and thirsteth for the wonted company and surpassing delights of that
aeternall fellowship; whereby it is euident, that the passage from life,
is a change from much euill to great good.

Axiochus.

Since therefore O *Socrates* thou deemest this life so tedious and troublesome, why doost thou still abide in the same? beeing as thou art a man of so great wisedom and experience, whose knowledge reacheth farre aboue our common sence, and beyond the vsuall reason of most men.

Socrates.

Thou *Axiochus* doost not report rightly of me: for thou iudgest as the common people of *Athens*, that because you see I am giuen to seeke and search out many things, therefore I know somewhat. But to say the truth, I would hartely wish, and would the same account in great parte of happinesse, if I knew but these common and customable matters: so farre am I from the knowledge of those high and excellent things. For these things which I nowe declare, are the sayinges of *Prodicus* the wise man: some of them beeing bought for a pennye: some for two groats, and other some for foure: For that same notable man vsed to teach none without wages, hauing alwaies in his mouth that saying of *Epicharmus*, One hand rubbeth another: giue somewhat, and somewhat take. And it is not long sithence, that he making a discourse of Philosophye in the house of *Callias* the sonne of *Hipponicus*, such and so many things he spake against the state of life: that I also account life in the number of those thinges which be of lesse waight. And euer since that time O *Axiochus*, my soule gaspeth after death, daily longing to die.

Axiochus.

What then was said of *Prodicus*?

110 aeternall] aerernall Q

AXIOCHUS

Socrates.

Marrie I will tell you, as they come to my minde. For what parcell (quod he) of our life is not full of wretchednes? dooth not the babie euen taken from the mothers wombe, powre out plenty of teares, beginning the first step of life with griefe? neither afterward hath it once any breathing or resting time from sorrow, being either distressed with pouertie, or pinched with colde, or scortched with heate, or payned with stripes: and whatsoeuer it suffereth, vtter once it cannot, but onely with crying dooth show his minde, hauing no voice but that alone to bewray his griefe: and hauing through many woes waded to seauen yeares of age, he is yet afflicted with greater griefes, being subiect to the tyranny of the Schoolemaister and Tutor. And as his yeares encreased, so is the number of his guides and gouernours encreased, being afterwards in the handes of Censors, Philosophers and Capitaines. Soone after being waxen a stripling he is hemmed in with greater feare, namely of Lyceum, of the Academie, of the Schoole of games, of Rulers, of Roddes: and to shut vp all in one worde, of infinite miseries. And all the time of his youth is spent vnder ouer-seers which are set ouer him by the *Areopagits* from which labours young men beeing once freed, are yet ouer-layde with greater cares and more weightie thoughts, touching the ordering of his state and trade of life: which also if they be compared with those that followe, all these former troubles may seeme but childish and indeed babish trifles. For herevpon dooth a troope of euils accrew, as be the exploites of warfare, the bitternesse of wounds, the continuall labour, skirmishes: and then closely creepeth on olde Age, in which are heaped all the harmes that pertaine to mankinde, whether of weakenesse as naturall, or of paine as being externall. And but if one betimes restore his life as a dew debt to death: Nature euer waiting as a greedy vsurer, taketh paynes aforehand, snatching and pulling from this man his sight, from that his hearing, from som both two senses. And if any fortune longer then commonly is seene in this life to linger, Nature weakening hir powres, dooth loose, lame, and bow downe all partes of his body, but they whose bodies in old age long flourisheth in minde, as the saying is, become twise children. And therfore the gods, knowing what is most expedient for men, those whome they most deerely loue, do soonest take out of this vale of wretchednes. And for this cause *Agamedes* and *Trophonius*, when they had built a Temple to *Pythius Apollo*, desiring of the god therefore to grant them the best rewarde that might be giuen, soone after when they layde them downe to rest, neuer rose againe.

Likewise *Cleobis* and *Biton*, the sonnes of the *Argiue* Nunne, when their mother had made hir praier to *Iuno*, that to her sonnes for their great godlines might be giuen some singuler gift (for that they when her yoake of Oxen were not readily to bee found at the time of sacrifice, themselues being yoaked in the charriot, drew their mother to the Temple) vpon this their mothers request, the two sonnes the next morning were found dead. It were too long in this place to reherse the testimonies of Poets which in their diuine poesies do diuinely bewaile and lament the miseries of mans life, I will nowe onely in place of many, recite the witnesse of one, being most worthie of memorie, which thus saith,

> *How wretched a thred of life haue the gods spun,*
>   *To mortall men that in this race of life do run.*

And againe:

> *Of all that in the earth are ordained by nature,*
> *Than man, is not to bee found*
>   *a more wretched creature.*
> But of *Amphiaraus* what saith the Poet?
> *Him loued highest* Iupiter *and Apollo deare,*
>   *yet could he not reache to his eldest yeare.*
> *What thinkest thou of him*
>   *that taught the childe to crie:*
> *When first the Sunne bright day,*
>   *he seeth with tender eye.*

But I will let them passe, least contrarye to promise, I seeme to discourse at large, and that in the alleadging of forraine witnesses. What trade of life I pray you is there, or what occupation, of which you shall not find many that complaine and greatly mislike of their present affaires. Let vs ouerrunne the companies of Artificers and craftsmen, which continually labour from night to night, and yet hardly able to find them necessaries to liue, by bewayling theyr bare estate, and filling their nightwatchings with sorrow and teares. Let vs els suruew the life of Marriners and Seafaring men, which make a hole through so many dangers, and which as *Bias* said, are neither in the number of the liuing nor yet of the dead, for man being borne to abide vpon the earth, dooth as it were a creature of a double kinde, thrust himselfe into the maine sea, and wholy put his life into the hands of fortune. But the life of husbandmen will some say is pleasant, and so in deed it is: but haue they not a continuall ranckling gall, euer

186 *run*] *rnn* Q   192 *loued*] *loned* Q¹   204 liue, by] liue by, ?

breeding new cause of greefe and disquiet, sometime by reason of drought, sometime because of raine, otherwhile for scortching, oft through blasting, which parcheth the vntimely eare oftentimes, because of importunate heate or vnmeasurable colde, miserably weeping and complaining. But aboue all, that honourable state of gouernement and principallitie (for I let passe many other things and wrap them vp in silence) through how many dangers is it tossed and turmoiled, for if at any time it haue any cause of ioye, it is like vnto a blowne blister or a swelling sore, soone vp, and sooner downe: oftentime suffering a foule repulse, which seemeth a thousand times worse then death it selfe. For who at any time can be blessed, that hangeth vpon the wauering will of the witlesse many? And albeit the Magistrate deserue fauour and praise, yet is he but a mocking stocke and scoffe of the comminalty, being soone after, outcast, hissed at, condemned, and deliuered to a miserable death. For where I praye thee O *Axiochus*, (thee I aske that art in office in the commonwealth) dyed that mightie *Miltiades?* where that victorious *Themistocles?* where that valiant *Ephialtes?* where finally those noble kings and glorious Emperours, which not long a goe flourished in the commonwealth. As for my selfe, I could neuer be brought to beare office in the Cittie: for I neuer accounted it as a worthie and lawdable thing to be in authority together with the madding multitude.

But *Theramenes* and *Calixenus* of late memorie appointing vnder them certaine Magistrates, condemned certaine guiltlesse men, not hearing their causes to vndeserued death. Onelye withstood them you, and *Triptolemus*, of thirty thousand men which were gathered in the assemblie.

Axiochus.

It is as thou sayest *Socrates*, and since that time I haue refrained my selfe from the stage: neither hath any thing euer to mee seemed of greater waighte, then the gouerning of the common-wealth, and that is well knowne to them which are in the same office. For thou speakest these things, as hauing out of some high loft onely ouerlooked the troubles and tempests of the common-wealth, but we know the same more assuredly, hauing made proofe therefore in ourselues, for the common people indeede ô freend *Socrates* is vnthankefull, disdainefull, cruell, enuious, and vnlearned, as that is gathered together of the scumme and dregs of the rascall route, and a sorte of idle losels: whome hee that flattereth and feedeth is much worse himselfe than they.

228 those] thse *Q*   244 ô freend] our freends *Q*

Socrates.

Since therefore O *Axiochus*, thou doost so greatly disallow that opinion, which of all other, is counted most honest and liberall; what shall we iudge of the other trades of life? shall wee not thinke that they are likewise to bee shunned: I remember that I once heard *Prodicus* say; that death pertayneth neither to the liuing nor to the dead.

Axiochus.

How meane you that, *Socrates*?

Socrates.

Mary thus; that death toucheth not them that are, and as for those that are departed out of this life, are now no more, and therfore death now toucheth them not: for thou art not yet dead, neither if thou decease, shall it concerne thee, for thou shalt then haue no more. Therefore, most vaine is that sorrow which *Axiochus* maketh, for the thing which neyther is present, nor shall euer touch *Axiochus* himselfe. And euen as foolish is it, as if one should complaine and be afraid of *Scylla*, or the Centaures, which were monsters, of Poets broode, which neyther now belong to thee, nor to thy liues end shall appertaine; for feare is conceyued of such things as be: but of such things as be not, what feare can there be?

Axiochus.

Truely *Socrates*, you haue fetched these things, out of the riche and most aboundant Storehouse of your woonderfull wisedome: And thereof riseth that your mildenesse and lightnesse of speech, which you vse to allure the mindes of yoong men to vertue. But the losse of these worldly commodities, dooth not a little vexe and disquiet my minde; albeit these reasons, which now to my great good liking you haue alledged, seeme to mee much more allowable, than those which late you vsed; for my minde is not carryed away with error through the entisement of your words, but perceiueth them well, neither doe those things greatly mooue my minde, which onely haue a colour and shadowed showe of truth, being set out with flanting pride, and glory of words, but yet truth haue they none.

258 are now] they are now ?

Socrates.

Thou art farre wide *Axiochus*, and reasonest vnskilfully, ioyning the feeling of euill, with the wante of good things, forgetting thy selfe that then thou shalt bee in the number of the sencelesse dead. For him indeed which is bereft of all good things, dooth the contrary force of euill things greatly vexe. But he which hath no being, can take nor feele nothing, in place of those things whereof he is despoiled. Then by what reason can any griefe bee conceyued of that thing, which breedeth no sence nor perseuerance of any thing which hurteth. For if in the beginning O *Axiochus*, thou didst not, though indeed in vayne, ioyne sence and feeling to death, most vnwisely, thou shouldest neuer had cause to feare death. But now thou doest confound thy selfe, and speakest contrarie to thy selfe, oft fearing that thou shalt bee depriued of soule and sence together, and oft thinking, that with thy sence thou shalt feele that thing, whereof there is no sence nor feeling. And to this purpose do all those excellent and notable reasons of the soules immortalitie tend.

For it is not the weake nature of mortall man, to raise himselfe to the fulfilling of such high and haughtye matters, as to despise the ramping rage of wilde beasts, to ieopard himselfe in the wastefull sea, to builde Cities, and them with lawes and pollicie to establish: to looke vp into heauen, and marke the course of the Starres; and the wayes of the Sunne and Moone, with their risings and setting, to consider their eclipses, their spaces, their making of the nights and dayes alike, their double conuersions, to behold the order of the windes, the seauen watrie starres, of winter, of summer, of stormes, with the violent rage of whirlewindes, and as it were these labours of the world, to deliuer to posteritie, vnlesse in our mindes there were a certaine diuine spirit and vnderstanding, which could comprehend and reach vnto the supernaturall knowledge of so great matters.

Wherefore nowe O *Axiochus*, thou art not in the way to death, but to immortality, neither shalt thou (as thou didst seeme right now to feare) bee bereft of all good, but shall hereby enioy true and perfect good: Neither shalt thou perceiue such durty pleasures as are these, beeing mingled with the puddle of this sinfull body, but most pure and perfect delight being deuoid of all contagious trouble. For beeing loosed and deliuered out of the darkesome dungeons of this body, thou shalt passe to that place where is no lacke nor complaint, but all things full of rest, and deuoid of euill. Moreouer there is calme and quiet liuing without all

291 shalt] shalt. Q^1

knowledge of vnrest, peaceable and still occupied in beholding the course and frame of Nature, and studying Philosophy, not to please the idle ignorant and common sort, but with vpright and vndeceiuable truth.

Axiochus.

O *Socrates* with this thy gladsome speech thou hast now brought mee into a cleane contrary minde, for so farre am I nowe from dread of death, that I am euen set on fire and burne with desire thereof. And that I may stay my selfe in the steppes of them which are counted workemasters of speech, I will say thus much more excellently, Now I begin to behold those high matters, and doo ouerlooke that aeternall and heauenly course of things, hauing now raysed vp my selfe out of my weakenes, and being as it were renued and refreshed of my former malady.

Socrates.

If you demaunde of mee another reason, and signe of the soules immortality, I will tell you what the wise man *Gobrias* shewed me: He saide that at what time *Xerxes* conuayed his huge Army into *Greece*, his Grandfather which was of the same name, was sent into *Delos* to defende that Iland in which were two Gods borne. In the same Iland that his Grandfather learned out of certaine brasen Tables which *Opis* and *Hecuergus* had brought out of the Northerne Countries, That the soule after time it is dissolued from the body passeth into a certaine darkesome place, a Coast that lyeth vnder the earth wherein is *Plutoes* Pallace no lesse than *Iupiters* kingdome: For the earth being equally ballanced in the middest of the world, and the compasse thereof beeing round as a ball, that the one halfe Sphere thereof is allotted to the higher Gods, and the other halfe to the infernall powres; betwixt whom there is such kindred and allyance, that some bee brothers, and other some brothers children. But the entry of the way which leadeth to *Plutoes* kingdome is fenced with iron gates, and fastened with brasen bolts: which when a man hath opened, he is entertained of the Riuer *Acheron*; next which is *Cocytus*: which flouds being ouerpassed, hee must come before *Minos* and *Rhadamanthus*, the merciles Iudges: which place is called the plain of Truth where the Iudges sit examining euery one that commeth thither how he hath liued, and with what trade or manner of life hee hath inhabited his mortall body, with whom there is no place for lies; nor refuge for excuses. Then they which in their life time were inspired and led with a good Angell, are receiued

341 Gods] God *Q*¹

into the houshold of the blessed, where all seasons flowe with abundance
of all fruits, where from the siluer springs doo calmely run the Christall
streames, where the flourishing medowes are cloathed with chaungeable
Mantles of glorious colours, where are famous Schooles of renowmed
Philosophers, goodly companies of diuine Poets, trim sorts of Dauncers,
heauenly Musicke, great banquets furnished with costly cates, Tables
abounding with all bounty, delights without all care, and pleasures with-
out all paine: For the Inhabitants thereof are neither touched with force
of cold, nor payned with excesse of heate, but the moderate Aire breatheth
on them mildly and calmely, being, lightned with the gentle Sunnebeames.

In this place, and in the Elysian fields, they which haue taken holy orders
are highly aduanced and reuerenced, dayly ministring the vnsearcheable
rytes of Religion. Wherefore then shouldest thou doubt but to be made
partaker of the same honor, being one of the seede of that heauenly race:
It is an old saying and rightly reported, that *Hercules* and *Bacchus* going
downe to hell, they were instituted in holly orders, and that they were
emboldned to goe thither of the Goddesse *Eleusina*. But they which being
wrapped in wickednes haue led an vngodly life, are snatched vp by the
Furies, and by them carried through the lowest hell into deepe darkenes
and vtter confusion, where the place and abode of the wicked is, and
where the three score daughters of *Danaus* dwell, whose punishment is
continually to fill a sort of bottomlesse vessels, where also is to bee seene
the vnquencheable thirst of *Tantalus*, the gnawen Entrailes of *Titius*,
and the endles stone of *Sisiphus*, whose end beginneth a newe labour.
There bee they rent of wilde beasts, continually scorched with burning
Lamps, pained with all kind of torments, and afflicted with endlesse pen-
nance. These thinges I remember that I haue heard *Gobrias* tell; but you
Axiochus may iudge of them as you list. Only this I know and assuredly
hold fast, that euery mans minde is immortall and passing out of this life
feeleth no griefe nor sorrowe. Wherefore O *Axiochus* whether thou be
carryed into those highest Pallaces or lower Vawts, needes must it bee that
thou shalt bee blessed because thou hast liued well and godly.

Axiochus.

Minding to haue said something vnto thee (O *Socrates*) I am impeached
with bashfull shame: For so farre am I now from the horror and dread
of death, that I continually couet the time thereof: So hath thy heauenly
and comfortable speeches pierced and relieued my faint heart. And nowe
loath I this life, and scorne the delights thereof, as that shall from hence-

forth passe into a better abode. And now by my selfe alone will I recount these thy notable sayings, but I pray thee (O *Socrates*) after noone resort to me againe.

Socrates.

I will doo as you say, and now will I returne to walk in my school *Cynosargus* from whence I was hither called.

FINIS.

396 *Cynosargus*] *Lynosargus Q*

A VIEW OF THE PRESENT STATE OF IRELAND
A Note on the Text

A manuscript in the Henry E. Huntington Library supplies the basic text of the *View* which is published in this volume. The Huntington MS, officially known as Ellesmere 7041 and here designated *E*, is reproduced with no other alterations than the following: all abbreviations, except in the case of numbers, of proper names, and of words abbreviated in modern usage, are spelled out; and all marginalia, as well as many of the deleted words, are omitted.

The most important part of the material in the footnotes is derived from three texts:

- *C*   Gonville and Caius College, MS 188.221.
- *R*   Bodleian Library, MS Rawlinson B 478.
- *W*   *The Historie of Ireland* (Dublin, 1633), ed. Sir James Ware.

Wherever the wording of *C*, *R*, or *W* differs from that of *E*, except in the use of *you* for *ye* and *ye* for *you*, the difference is recorded; but in spelling and punctuation only those differences which have some conceivable interest are recorded. If the initials of more than one text appear after a variant, the variant reproduces the spelling of the first text cited, not necessarily that of any other text.

Less frequently the footnotes make use of the following manuscripts:

- *A*   British Museum, Additional MS 22022.
- *D1*   Cambridge University Library, MS Dd. 10. 60.
- *D2*   Cambridge University Library, MS Dd. 14. 28(1).
- *F*   Folger Shakespeare Library, MS 6185.
- *G*   Bodleian Library, Gough MS, Ireland 2.
- *H1*   British Museum, Harleian MS 1932.
- *H2*   British Museum, Harleian MS 7388.
- *Ho*   the Arthur A. Houghton MS.
- *L*   Lambeth Palace, MS 510.
- *N*   National Library of Ireland, MS 661 (Gurney MS).
- *P*   Public Record Office, State Papers 63. 202, Pt. 4, item 58.
- *T*   Trinity College, Dublin, MS E.3.26.

The variants selected from these manuscripts are limited to numbers, to proper names, to unusual words, to certain mechanical features, and to the omission or addition of extended passages.

Among the footnotes there are likewise a few readings, marked *?*, which rest on nothing more secure than editorial guesswork.

A vewe of the present state of Irelande.
discoursed
by way of a dialogue
betweene
Eudoxus and Irenius.
E. S.

f. 1ʳ

A viewe of the presente state of Irelande discoursed by waye of a diologue betwene *Eudoxus and Irenius*

Eudox: But if that Countrie of Irelande, whence youe latelye come be so goodlie and Comodious a soyle as yee reporte I wonder that no course is taken for the turninge theareof to good vses, and reducinge that salvage nacion to better gouerment and Cyvilitye/

Iren: Mary soe theare haue byne diuerse good plottes devised and wise Councells cast allreadye aboute reformacion of that realme, but they saie yt is the fatall destinie of that Lande that no purposes whatsoeuer are mente for her good, will, prosper or take good effecte, which wheather it proceed from the *very Genius* of the soile, or influence of the starres, or

5

10

1-3 A ... Irenius] A vewe of the present state of Ireland, discoursed by waie of a dialogue betwene *Eudoxus and Irenius*. CD1HoLP   A viewe *of the presente Estate of Irelande discoursed by waye of a Dialogue betweene Eudoxius, and Irenius* D2   A *veiwe of the present estate of Ireland discoursed by way of a dialogue between Eudoxius and Irenis./* F   A *View of the Present State of Ireland; by way of Dialogue*. G   A viewe of the present state of: Ireland discoursed by waie of dialogue betwene Eudorus: and Iremus / H1   A View of the present state of Irelande discoursed by way of a dialogue betweene *Eudoxus* and *Irenaeus* [*badly faded*] A   A veiwe of the present state of Ireland discoursed by waye of Dyalogue—betwene *Eudoxus* and *Irenius* N   *Veiwe of the present* state of Irelande discoursed by waye of a *Dialogue* Betweene *Eudoxus:* and *Irenius* by Mʳ Edw: Spencer gentleman H2   A vewe of the presente state of Ireland discoursed by waye of a dialogue betwene *Eudoxus* and *Irenius*. 1596. by Ed: Spenser gentleman R   [*words torn away*] *by waie of a Diologue betwene Endoxus and Irenius/.* T   A VIEW OF THE STATE OF IRELAND, Written Dialogue-wise betweene *Eudoxus* and *Irenaeus*, By *Edmund Spenser* Esq. in the yeare 1596. W   *Separate titles*: *Irelands Survey or A Historical Dialogue and View of* ancient and modern times wherein is discoursed the Ancient Originalls of the Irish Nation, And the severall Conquests made of them, And of their first reduceing to Christianitie, Also the Antiquity of their Letters, Characters, and Learning./ *Together with their Tenures and Ancient and Modern Laws and Customes to them only particular.*   Their Habitts Armes Soldiers and manner of Fights Lyveings and evill Usages: Also how they use and bestow their Church Liveings./   And the Authors opinion out of long employment and experience there how that Realme may be reduced to Obedience and Civillity.   And yeild a great Revenue to the State of England./ With many other matters and things both pleasant profitable and worthy Observation to the Iudicious Reader./ G   The state *of Ireland*. 1597. *by* E. S.   A dialogue between *Eudoxus* and *Irenius*. Anno Eliz. 39. N   A vewe *of the state of Ireland*. [*repeated in modern hand on separate leaf*] P   A discourse touching the present state of Ireland wrytten dialoug wise by mʳ Edmunde Spenser./   Anno 1596 R   A VIEW OF THE STATE OF IRELAND, Written dialogue-wise betweene *Eudoxus* and *Irenaeus*, By EDMUND SPENSER Esq. in the yeare 1596. W   *Additional note*: This booke was written by Edmund [*corrected from* Edward] spencer clarke of the province of Mounster in Ireland in anno 1596. C   4 Eudox:] Eudoxius G   Eudorus H1   Endox: *throughout* T   4-5 But ... reporte] I have often heard you report of the goodness and Commodious Soyle in the Realme of Ireland from whence you lately came. But if Ireland be so excellent Riche and Commodious a soyle as you report it to be. G   4 come] came RW   4 be] *last letter worn off* C   bee of W   6 salvage] *om.* W   8 Iren:] Irenaeus A   *no new paragraph* C   10 whatsoeuer] *last four letters worn off* C   whatsoever which W   11 will,] will CRW   11 or] and R   12 *Genius*] Genus Ho   12 influence] *last two letters worn off* C

43

that Allmighty god hathe not yeat Appointed the tyme of her reformacion or that he reserueth her in this vnquiet state still, for some secrete skourge, which shall by her Come vnto Englande it is harde to be knowen but yeat muche to be feared//

Eudox. Surelye I suppose this but a vaine Conceipt of simple men, which iudge thinges by theire effectes and not by theire causes, ffor I woulde rather thinke the Cause of this evell which hangeth vppon the Countrie, to proceed rather of the vnsoundnes of the Counsells and Plottes, which youe saie haue bynne often tymes laied for her reformacions or of faintnes in followinge and effectinge the same, then of anye suche fatall Course or appointment of god as youe misdeeme, but it is the manner of men that when they are fallen into anye Absurditye or theire accions succede not as they woulde they are readye allwaies to impute the blame theareof vnto the heavens, soe to excuse theire owne follies and imperfeccions. So haue I allsoe harde it often wished (even of some whose greate wisdome in opinion shoulde seme to iudge more soundlye of so weightye a Consideracion, that all that Lande weare a sea poole, which kinde of speache is the manner rather of desperate men farre driven to wishe the vtter rvine of that which they Cannot redresse then of graue Councellours which oughte to thinke nothinge so harde but that thoroughe wisdome maye be mastred and subdued, since the Poet sayeth that the wiseman shall rule even over the starres, muche more over the earthe, for weare it not the parte of a desperate Phisicion to wishe his diseased patient dead rather to Applye the beste endevours of his skill for his recouerye | But since wee are so farr entred, let vs I praye youe a little devise of those evills by which that Countrie is helde in this wretched Case, that it cannot as youe saie be recured, And if it be not painefull to youe tell vs what thinges duringe your late Continvance theare youe observed to be moste offensive, and Impeachefull vnto the good rule and gouernement theareof. *Iren*: Surelye

15 vnto] *last two letters worn off C* 16 feared//] feared *C* 18 causes] *last letter worn off C* 19 vppon the] vppon that *CRW* 20 rather of] rather vpon *R* 21 her] the *W* 21 reformacions] reformacion *CRW* 22 and] *last letter worn off C* 22 Course] Cause *G* curse *HoT* 22-3 or appointment] or appoint= *C* appointed *W* 23 as youe misdeeme,] (as youe misdeme) *C* 24 when] *last letter worn off C* 25 readye allwaies] alwayes readie *W* 26 imperfeccions.] ymperfeccons, *R* 27 allsoe ... wished] heard it often wished also *W* 27 wished] *last letter worn off C* 27 wisdome] wisedomes *W* 28 seme] *last letter worn off C* 28-9 Consideracion, that] Consideracion) that *with last two letters worn off C* consideracon) that *RW* 32 but] *last letter worn off C* 32 maye] it may *W* 34 not the] *last three letters worn off C* 35 Phisicion] Phicion *R* 35 dead] *om. C* 35 rather] rather then *RW* 36 endevours] endevor *CW* 37 a little] *om. R* 37 evills] evill *C* 38 as youe saie] (as you say) *W* 39 tell] to tell *R* 40 observed] obserued, *R* 41 Impeachefull vnto] greatest impeachment to *W* 41 the] *om. C* 41 Iren:] *new paragraph CRW Irenis. and new paragraph F*

Eudoxus. the evills which youe desire to be recounted are verye manye and allmoste Countable with those which weare hidden in the baskett of *Pandora.* But since youe so please I will out of that Infinite numbre, reckon but some that are moste Capitall and Commonlye occurrent bothe in the liefe and Condicions of private men And allsoe in the menage and publike affaires and policye The which youe shall vnderstande to be of diuerse natures as I observed them, for some of them are of verye great antiquitye and longe Continvance, Others more late and of lesse enduraunce; Others dailye growinge and increasinge Continvallye as the evill occacions are everye daie offered/

Eudox. Tell them then I praye youe in the same order that youe haue now rehearsed them, ffor theare cane be no better methode then this which the verie matter it selfe offereth, And when youe haue reckoned all the evills let vs heare your opinion for redressinge of them. After which theare will perhaps of it selfe appeare some reasonable waie to settle a sounde and perfecte rule of gouernement by shvnninge the former euills and followinge the offered good, The which method we maye learne of the wise Phisicions which firste require that the maladye be knowne thoroughlie and discouered, afterwardes doe teache to cure and redresse the same, And Lastelie do prescribe a diet with streighte rules and orders to be daylie observed for feare of relapse into the former disease or fallinge into some more daungerous then it.

Iren. I will then accordinge to your advicement beginne to declare the evills which seme to be moste hurtefull to the Common weale of that Lande, And firste those which I saide weare moste anciente and longe growen | And they allsoe are of three kindes, the firste in the Lawes the seconde in Customes, the laste in religion/

Eudox: why *Irenius.* cane theare be anye evill in the lawes cane the thinges which are ordeyned for the good and safety of all, turne to the evill and hurte of them? This well I note bothe in that state and all

42 *Eudoxus*] *Eudoxius when unabbreviated throughout* H2   Eudorus *when unabbreviated throughout* H1   44 so] *om.* W   46 And] as W   46 menage and] meane age of C   menage of R   managing of W   49 longe] *om.* W   50 as] by W   50 the] there CW   51 are] which are W   52 then] *om.* R   55 for] for the W   55 them.] them C   them, R   them: W   56 of] if C   60 doe] to W   60 teache] teache howe CRW   60 the same] it CRW   61 rules] rule W   62 more] other more CRW   65 be] me CRW   65 weale] well C   66 which I saide] (I say) which W   67 allsoe are] are also R   67 kindes] sorts W   68 Customes,] Customes, and W   69 *Eudox:*] *no new paragraph* G   69 *Irenius.*] *Irenaeus when unabbreviated throughout* AW   Irenis *when unabbreviated through-out first half* F   69 lawes] lawes. R   lawes, W   69 cane the] can W   70 good and safety] saiftye and good R   71 them?] them: CR   71 note] wote CRW   71 all] in all CRW

other, that weare they not Conteyned in dewtye with feare of lawe which restraineth offences, and Inflicteth sharpe punishment to misdoers no man shoulde enioye anye thinge euerye mans hande would be againste another, Therefore in findinge faulte with the Lawes I doubte me youe shall muche ouershote your selfe and make me the more dislike your other dislikes of that gouernment

Iren: The Lawes *Eudoxus*. I doe not blame for themselves knowinge rightwell that all Lawes are ordayned for the good of the Common weale and for repressinge of licenciousnes and vice, but it falleth out in Lawes no otherwise then it dothe in Phisicke, which was at firste devised and is yeat dailye mente and mynistred for the healthe of the patiente, but neuerthelesse we often see that either thoroughe Ignoraunce of the disease or vnseasonablenes of the time or other accidentes comminge betwene, in steade of good it worketh hurte and out of one evill throweth the patient into manye miseries, So the lawes weare at firste intended for the reformacion of Abuses and peaceable Continvance of the Subiecte, but are sithence either disanulled or quite prevaricated thoroughe Change and Allteracion of tymes, yeat are they good still in themselues, But to that Comon wealthe which is ruled by them they worke not that good, which they shoulde and somtymes allsoe perhaps that evill which they woulde not

Eudox wheather doe youe meane this by the Comon lawe of the realme or by the Statute Lawes and Actes of parlamentes/.

Iren: Surelye by them bothe for even the Comon Lawe beinge that which *William of Normandye* broughte in with his Conquest and laied vpon the necke of Englande thoughe it perhaps fitted well with the state of Englande then beinge and was readilye obeyed thoroughe the power of the Commaundour which had before subdued the people vnto him and made easye waye to the setlinge of his will yeat with the state of Irelande peradventure it dothe not so well agree beinge a people alltogeather stubborne
f. 2ᵛ and | vntamed, or if it weare euer tamed yeat now latelye havinge quite

---

74 thinge] thing; *W*   74 another,] another; *R*   an other. *W*   75 me] *om. C*   77 gouernment] governement: *C*   gouerment:/ *R*   government. *W*   78 Iren:] *no new paragraph G*   79 rightwell] *om. R*   79 ordayned] ordeyned *with last letter worn off C*   79 weale] wealth *R*   80 licenciousnes] Licensiousious *C*   81 otherwise] *last two letters worn off C*   81 at] att the *C*   82 healthe] good health *C*   83 thoroughe] *last two letters worn off C*   84 vnseasonablenes] vnseasonable meate *C*   thorough unseasonablenesse *W*   86 miseries,] miseries: *R*   miseries. *W*   86 at] att the *C*   87 peaceable] *last three letters worn off C*   87 Subiecte] subiectes *R*   89 to] in *W*   91 perhaps] *om. W*   91 not] not./ *C*   nott:: / *R*   not. *W*   92 Eudox] *no new paragraph G*   92 lawe] lawes *RW*   92 of the] of that *W*   94 Iren:] *no new paragraph G*   94 Lawe] lawes *R*   96 it perhaps] perhaps it *W*   98 vnto] to *R*   99 setlinge] settinge *R*   100 alltogeather] very *W*   101 euer] once *R*   101 havinge] haue *R*

A VIEW OF THE PRESENT STATE OF IRELAND 47

shaken of theire yoke and broken the bondes of theire obedience, ffor Englande before thentraunce of the Conquerour was a peaceable kingedome And but latelye envred to the milde and godlye gouernement of Kinge Edwarde surnamed the Confessour, besides now latelye growen vnto a loathinge and detestacion of the vniust and tiranous rule of Harolde an Vsurper, which made them the more willinge to accepte of anye reasonable Condicions and order of the new victor thinkinge surelye that it coulde be no worse then the latter, and hopinge well it woulde be as good as the former, yeat what the profe of the firste bringinge in and establishinge of those Lawes was. was to manye full bitterlye made knowen, But with Irelande it is farr otherwise, for it is a nacion ever Acquainted with warrs thoughe but Amongest themselves, and in theire owne kinde of milytare discipline trayned vp even from theire youthes which they haue neuer yeat bynne taughte to laye aside nor made to learne obedience vnto the Lawe scarselye to knowe the name of Lawe but insteade theareof haue allwaies preserued and kepte theire owne lawe which is the *Brehon* Lawe./

Eudox, what is that which youe call the *Brehon* lawe it is a worde to vs alltogeather vnknowen./

Iren: It is a certaine rule of righte vnwritten but deliuered by tradicion from one to another in which often tymes theare appeareth greate shewe of equitye in determyninge the righte betwene partie and partie but in manye thinges repugninge quite to godes lawe and mans, as for ensample in the Case of murther. The *Brehon* that is theire Iudge will Compounde betwene the murderer and the friendes of the partie murdered which prosecute the Accion that the malefactour shall give vnto them or to the Childe or wife of him that is slaine a recompence, which they call an *Iriach* by which vile lawe of theires manye murders are amongest them made vp and smothered, And this iudge beinge as he is Called the Lordes

---

102 yoke] yokes *C*   102 bondes] bandes *CR*   103 before ... Conquerour] (before ... Conqueror) *W*   103 a peaceable] an vnpeaceable *R*   104 envred] *corr. of* entred *E* entred *R*   104 godlye] goodlye *CW*   105 Kinge] *om. W*   105 surnamed] surnamed *C*   105 vnto] into *W*   108 that it coulde] yt would *R*   109 latter] Later *C*   110 of the] of *W*   111 was.] was, *CRW*   113 milytare] miletaree *CRW* 114 even] ever *W*   115 the Lawe] Lawe *C*   Lawes *W*   117 Brehon] Brehoone *A* 118 *Eudox*,] *no new paragraph G*   118 Brehon] Breehoone *A*   118 lawe] lawe: *R* law, *W*   118-9 it ... vnknowen./] *om. R*   118 to] vnto *W*   119 vnknowen./] unknowne? *W*   120 Iren:] *no new paragraph G*   120 certaine] *om. W*   123 to] bothe to *CW*   from *R*   124 murther. The] murder *C*   murther: The *R*   murder, the *W* 124 Brehon] Brehoon *A*   128 Iriach] Breaghe *A*   Iriach. *C*   Eriach: *W*   128 vile] vilde *W*   128 are amongest them] amongest them are *W*   129 smothered] smoothed *C*

Brehon adiudgeth for the moste parte a better share vnto his Lorde, That is the Lorde of the soile or the heade of that sept and allsoe vnto him selfe for his iudgement a greater porcion then vnto the plaintifs or parties greued/ |

Eudox: This is a moste wicked Lawe indede but I truste it is not now vsed in Irelande since the Kinges of England haue had the Absolute dominion theareof and established theare owne lawes theare/ *Iren*: Yes trewlie for theare are manye wide Countries in Irelande in which the lawes of Englande weare neuer established nor anye acknowledgement of subieccion made, and allsoe even in those which are subdued and seme to acknowledge subieccion yeat the same *Brehon* lawe is privilye practized amongeste themselves, By reason that dwellinge as they doe whole nacions and septes of the Irishe togeather without anye Inglishman amongest them they maye doe what they liste and Compounde or alltogeather Conceale amongest themselves theire owne Crimes of which no notice cane be had by them which woulde and mighte amende the same by the rule of the lawes of Englande/

Eudox. what is this which youe saie? And is theare anye parte of that realme or anye nacion thearein which haue not yeat bynne subdued to the Crowne of Englande, did not the whole realme vniuersallie accepte and acknowledge our late Prince of famous memorye *Henrye* the Eighte theire onely kinge and Leige Lorde.

Iren: yeas verelye in a Parlament houlden in the tyme of Sr Ant^h St Leger then Lorde Deputye, All the Irishe Lordes and principall men came in and beinge by faire meanes wroughte thearevnto Acknowledged kinge *Henrye* for theire soueraigne Lorde reservinge yet (as some saye) vnto themselves all theire owne former priviledges and seigniories inviolate

Eudox. Then by that Acceptaunce of his soueraignety they allsoe accepted of his lawes whye then shoulde anye other lawes be now vsed amongeste them/

---

130 *Brehon*] *Brehoon* A   132 greater] greate R   132 the] *om*. C   132 or] *last letter worn off* C   134 *Eudox*:] *no new paragraph* CG   134 This] That R   135 Kinges] kinges *with last three letters worn off* C   136 *Iren*:] *new paragraph* CRW   137 are] be CW   137 Irelande] *last three letters worn off* C   137 in which] which W   138 nor] *last letter worn off* C   in, nor W   140 subieccion] subiection, R   140 *Brehon*] *Brehoone* A   140 privilye practized] illy practised C   practised W   141 amongeste] among W   147 *Eudox*.] *no new paragraph* G   147 saie?] saie, CR   149 Englande,] Ingland/ C   Englande: R   England? W   150 Eighte] viijth *for* CW   151 Lorde.] Lord? W   152 *Iren*:] *no new paragraph* G   152 St Leger] *Sentleger* A   S^t largar F   St Legar R   Sellinger T   156 inviolate] inviolate./ C   invyolate:/ R   inviolate. W   157 *Eudox*.] *no new paragraph* G   158 his lawes] his Lawes: C   his lawes, R   his lawes. W   159 them/] them::/ R   them? W

Iren: Trewe it is that theareby they bounde themselues to his lawes and obedience, and in case it had bynne followed vppon them, (as it shoulde haue bene) And a gouernement thearevppon presentlye setled amongest them agreable thearevnto they shoulde haue byne reduced to perpetuall Civilytie and Contayned in Continvall dewtye | But what bootes it to breake a Colte And to let him streighte rune loose at random, So weare this people at firste well handeled and wiselye broughte to acknowledge Alleigiance to the Kinges of Englande, but beinge straighte left vnto themselues and theire owne inordinate life and manners they eftsones forgote what before they weare taughte and soe sone as they weare out of sighte by themselues shoke of theire bridles and began to Colte anewe more licentiouslye then before//

Eudox. It is greate pittye that so good an oportunitye was omitted and so happie an occacion forslacked that mighte haue bred the eternall good of that lande, but doe they not still acknowlledge that submission//

Iren. Noe they doe not for nowe the heires and posteritye of them which yealded the same, are (as they saie) either ignorante theareof or do willfullye denye or stidfastly disavowe it.

Eudox. Howe cane they soe doe iustlie? Dothe not the Acte of the parent in anye lawfull graunte or Conveyaunce binde his heires for euer thearevnto, Since then the Ancestours of these that now live yelded themselus then subiectes and Leigemen shall it not tye theire children to the same subieccion./

Iren: They saie noe for theire Auncestors had not estate in anye theire Landes, Segniories or hereditamentes longer then duringe theire owne lives, as they Alleadge, ffor all the Irishe doe houlde theire Lande by *Tanistrye* which is saie they, no more but a personall estate for his life tyme that is *Tanist.* by reason that he is admitted thearevnto by eleccion of the Countrie

160-1 lawes and] *om. C*   161 vppon] against *R*   161-2 (as . . . bene)] as . . . ben *CW* as . . . bene) *R*   162 presentlye] *om. W*   163 amongest] among *W*   165-6 random,] randome: *R* randome. *W*   166 this] these *W*   167 acknowledge] *last two letters worn off C*   172 is] is a *W*   173 bred] beene *W*   173-4 of that] of the *W*   174 submission//] submission *C* submission? *W*   176 yealded] yeilded, *R*   176 (as they saie)] as as they saye *C* 177 it] *om. C*   178 iustlie?] iustlye, *CR*   178 parent] *corr. of* Parlment *E*   179 his] their *W* 179-80 thearevnto,] therunto; *C* therevnto? *RW*   180 Since] Sith *W*   180 these] those *W*   182 subieccion./] subieccion? *W*   183 had] had had *R*   183 not] noe *CRW*   185 Lande] Landes *R*   186 saie they,] to saye they have *C* to saye *R* (say they) *W*   187 *Tanist.*] *Tanistih A*   tamist, *C*   *Tanist: R*   *Tanist, W* 188 Countrie] Cuntry/. *C*   Countrye: *R*   Countrey. *W*

Eudox: what is this youe Call *Tanist* and *Tanistrye* They be names and tenures neuer harde of or knowen to vs

Iren: It is a Custome amongest all the Irisherie that presentelye after the deathe of anie theire Chief Lordes or Captaines they doe presentlye asemble themselues to a place generallie appointed and knowne vnto them to Choose another in his steade, wheare they doe nominate and electe for the moste parte not the eldest soonne nor anie of the Children of theire Lorde deceased but the next to him of bloode, that is the eldest and worthiest as Comonlye the nexte brother vnto him if he haue anye or the nexte Cozen germaine or soe forthe as any is elder | In that kindred or sept., And then nexte to him do they Chose the nexte of blood to be Tanist, whoe shall nexte succede him in the saide Captenrye if he live thearevnto

Eudox. Doe they vse anie Ceremonye in this eleccion. ffor all barbarous nacions are Comonlye greate observours of Ceremonyes and Supersticious rites.

Iren. They vse to place him that shalbe theire Captaine vppon a stonne allwaies observed for that purpose and placed Comonlye vppon a hill, In manye of the which I haue sene the fote of a man formd and engraven, which they saie was the measure of theire firste Captaines fote wheareon he standinge receaueth an othe to preserue all the former aunciente Customes of the Countrye inviolable, And to deliuer vpp the succession peaceablye to his Taniste and then hathe a wande deliuered vnto him by some whose proper office that is, after which discendinge from the stonne he turneth himself rounde thrise forwarde and thrise backwarde.

Eudox: But howe is the Tanist Chosen/

Iren: They saie he setteth but one foote vppon the stone and receaueth the like oathe the Captaine did

Eudox: Haue youe euer harde what was the occacion and firste beginninge

---

189 this] this which *CW* 189 *Tanist*] *Tanistih A* *Tamist C* 189 *Tanistrye*] *Tamistry? C Tanistry? W* 190 tenures] termes *CRW* 190 or] nor *CW* 190 to] vnto *C* 190 vs] vs. *RW* 191 Irisherie] Irishmen *C* Irishe *RW* 192 anie] any of *W* 193 them] them and *C* 195 theire] the *W* 198 germaine] *om. W* 199 they] these *R* 199 of] of the *RW* 200 Tanist] *Tanistih A* 201 thearevnto] therunto./ *C* therevnto. *RW* 202 vse] not use *W* 202 eleccion.] election? *W* 206 observed] reserued *RW* 207 manye of the] some of *W* 207 the fote of a man] *om. W* 207 engraven] Ingraved *C* graven *R* ingraven a foot *W* 209 receaueth] receive *W* 209 the] *om. C* 209 former aunciente] auncient former *W* 211 Taniste] *Tanistih A* 212 is,] is. *C* 213 backward.] backwarde *C* 214 Tanist] *Tanistih A* 214 Chosen/] chosen *C* chosen: *R* chosen? *W* 216 oathe] oathe that *CW* 216 did] ded. *CW* did: *R*

A VIEW OF THE PRESENT STATE OF IRELAND 51

of this Custome, for it is good to knowe the same and maye perhaps discouer some secret meaninge and intente thearein verye materiall to the state of that gouernement/

Iren: I haue harde that the beginninge and Cawse of this ordinaunce amongest the Irish was speciallye for the defence and maintenaunce of theire lande in theire posteritye and for excludinge all innovacion or alienacion theareof vnto Straungers and speciallye to the Englishe, ffor wheare theire Captaine dyeth if the Segniorye shoulde discende to his Childe and he perhaps an infante anie other mighte perhaps stepp in betwene and thruste him out by stronge hande beinge then vnable to defende his righte or to withstand the force of a forrener And therefore they doe apointe the eldest of the kinne to haue the Segniory for that he Comonlye is a man of stronger yeares and better experience to mainteigne the inheritance and to defend the Countrie either againste the nexte borderinge Lordes | which vse Comonlye to encroche one vppon another as eache one is stronger, or againste the Inglishe which they thinke lye still in waighte to wipe them out of theire Landes and Territories And to this ende the Taniste is allwaies readye knowen If it shoulde hapen the Capteine soddenlye to die or to be slaine in battle or to be out of the Countrie to defende and kepe it from all suche doubtes and daungers, ffor which Cause the *Tanist* hathe allsoe a share of the Countrie allotted vnto him and Certaine Cuttinges and spendinges vppon all the Inhabitantes vnder the Lorde/

Eudox. When I heare this worde Tanist it bringeth to my remembraunce which I haue read of *Tania* that it shoulde signifye a province or Seigniorye as *Aquitania*. *Lusitania*. and *Britania* The which some do thinke to be derived of *Dania* that is from the Danes but I thinke amisse. But sure it semethe that it came auntientlye from those Barbarous nacions that ouerranne the worlde which possessed those dominions whereof they are now so Called, And so it maye well be That from thence the firste originall of this worde *Tanist and Tanistry* came And the Custome theareof hathe sithence As manye others else bene Contynewed, But to that generall subieccion of the Lande wheareof we formerlye spake me semes, that this Custome or tenure Cane be no barre nor Impeachement seyinge that in

218 Custome,] custome? W   223 lande] Landes CW   224 speciallye] especiallye R
225 wheare] when CRW   225 to] vnto R   226 anie other mighte] another W
226 perhaps stepp] peradventure stepp CW   227 and thruste] or thrust CW   and
thurste R   235 Taniste] Tanistih A   237 suche] om. C   237 daungers,] dangers. W
239 all] om. C   241-302 Eudox....iuste] om. F   241 heare] heard W   241 Tanist]
Tanistih A   242 which] what CRW   243 as] om. R   243 Lusitania.] blank
space H2   243 do] om. W   244 to] to to R   244 Dania] Diana Ho   244 I thinke]
I thincke, R   247 be] om. C   248 Tanist] Tanistih A   250 spake] spake, RW
250 semes,] semes CRW   251 seyinge] seeinge CRW

open Parliament by theire saide Acknowledgement they wayved the bennefitt theareof and submitted themselves to the ordinaunce of theire newe Soueraigne/

Iren: yea but they saie as I earste tolde youe that they reserued theire titles Tenures and seigniories holle and sounde to themselves and for proffe alleadge that they haue euer sithence remayned to them vntouched, So as now to alter them shoulde they saie be a greate wronge/

Eudox what remedye is theare then or meanes to avoide this Inconveniaunce for without firste Cuttinge of this daungerous Custome it semeth harde to plante anye sounde ordinaunce or reduce them to a Civill gouerment, | Since all theire ill Customes are permitted vnto them/

Iren: Surelye nothinge harde, ffor by this Acte of Parliament wheareof we speake nothinge was given to Kinge Henrye which he had not before from his Auncestors, but onelye the bare name of a Kinge. ffor all other absolute power of Principalitye he had in himselfe before derived from manye former Kinges his famous progenitours and worthie Conquerours of that lande The which sithence they firste Conquered and by force subdued vnto them, what neded afterwardes to enter into anye suche idle termes with them to be Called their king when as it is in the power of the Conquerour to take vpon him self what title he will ouer his dominnions Conquered, ffor all is the Conquerours as *Tully* to *Brutus* saieth Thearefore me semes in steade of so greate and meritorious a service as they boste they performed to the Kinge In bringinge all the Irishe to acknowledge him for theire Leige, they did greate hurte to his title and haue lefte a perpetuall gall in the minde of that people, who before beinge absolutelye bounde to his obedience are now tyed but with tenures wheras bothe theire lives theire Landes and theire Libertis weare in his fre power to appointe what tenures what lawes, what Condicions he woulde ouer them, which weare all his, againste which theare coulde be no resistaunce, or if theare weare he mighte when he woulde establishe them with a stronger hande/

Eudox: Yea. but perhaps it semed better vnto that noble Kinge to bringe them by theire owne accorde to his obedience and to plante a peaceable

252 wayved] wayed *C*   253 ordinaunce] benefite *W*   257 alleadge] alledged *R*   257 sithence] synce *C*   258 shoulde they saie] they saye should *R*   should (say they) *W*   259-60 Inconveniaunce] inconvenience? *W*   262 ill] evill *R*   265 from] for *C*   268 lande] Lande. *CW*   269 neded] neede *C*   neede he *R*   270 as] om. *W*   272 *Brutus*] last letter worn off *C*   272 saieth] saithe, *CR*   saith. *W*   272-3 Thearefore] And therfore *R*   273 me semes] (me seemes) *W*   275 to] vnto *CRW*   276 that] the *W*   277 tenures] corr. of termes *E*   termes *CRW*   277 wheras] wheras ells *CW*   280 his,] his. *C*   280 no] noe rightfull with last two letters worn off *C*   noe rightfull *RW*   280 resistaunce] assistance *R*   282 noble] last two letters worn off *C*

gouernment amongest them then by suche violente meanes to plucke them vnder. Nether yeat hathe he theareby loste anye thinge that he formerlie had, for havinge all before absolutelye in his owne power it remaynethe so still vnto him/ he havinge neither forgiven nor forgone anye thinge thereby vnto them, but havinge receaued somthinge from them, that is a more voluntarye and loyall subieccion, So as her maiestie maye yeat when it shall please her alter anye thinge of those former ordinaunces or appointe other Lawes that maye be more for theire owne behofe and for the good of that people

Iren: not soe. for it is not so easye nowe that thinges are growen into an habit and haue theire certaine Course to Change the Chanell and turne theire streames another waye. ffor they maye haue now a Coulorable pretence to | To withstande suche innovacion havinge accepted of other lawes and rules allreadye/

Eudox. But youe saie they doe not accepte of them but delighte rather to leane to theire oulde Customes and *Brehon* lawes thoughe they be muche more vniuste and allsoe more inconveniente for the Comon people, as by your late relacion of them I gathered, As for the Lawes of Englande they are surelye moste iuste and moste Agreable bothe with the gouernement and withe the nature of the people, How falls it out then that youe seme to dislike of them as not so mete for that realme of Irelande/ and not onelye the Comon Lawe but also the statutes and Actes of Parlament which weare speciallye provided and intended for the onlye benefite theareof/

Iren: I was aboute to haue tolde youe my reasone thearein but that your selfe drewe me away with other questions. ffor I was shewinge youe by what meanes and in what sorte the Positive Lawes weare firste broughte in and establyshed by the Norman Conquerour which weare not by him devised nor applied vnto the state of the realme then beinge nor as it mighte best be (as shoulde by lawgivers principallye be regarded) but weare indede the verie Lawes of his owne Countrye of *Normandye* the Condicion whereof how farr it differeth from this of Englande is apparante to euerye leste iudgemente/ But to transfer the same lawes for the

285 thinge] *last two letters worn off* C   287 vnto him] *om.* R   287 havinge] having thereby W   288 havinge] have C   289 subieccion,] subjection. W   290 those] these C   291 more] more bothe CRW   291 theire] her CW   292 people] people/ C people.://R   people. W   293 into] unto W   296 To] *om.* CRW   296 innovacion] invocasion R   innovations W   299 Brehon] Brehoon A   299 muche] *om.* W   300 inconveniente] vnconvenient R   301 gathered,] gatherid C   have gathered. W   302 and] F *resumes at this point*   303 people,] people C   people. W   303 out] *om.* CW 306 speciallye] especiallie C   307 theareof/] thereof? W   308 that] that yow R 309 youe] *om.* C   310 in] by W   312 it] yet W   314 Normandye] Normandie. W 315 is] it is C

governinge of the realme of Irelande was muche more inconveniente and vnmete for he founde a better advantage of the time then was in the plantinge of them in Irelande and followed the execucion of them with more severitye and was allso presente in persone to ouerloke the magis- trates and to ouerawe the Subiectes with the terrour of his sworde and Countenaunce of his maiestie, But not soe in Irelande, for they weare otherwise affected and yeat doe soe remayne soe as the same Lawes me semes Cane ill fitt with theire disposicion or worke that reformacion that is wished: for lawes oughte to be fashioned vnto the manners and Con- dicion of the people to whom they are mente and not to be imposed vnto them accordinge to the simple rule of righte for then as I saie in steade of good they maie worke ill, and perverte iustice to extreame inustice; for he that woulde transfer the lawes of the *Lacedemonians* to the people of *Athens* shoulde finde a greate absurditye | And inconvenience, ffor those lawes of *Lacedemonians* weare devised by Licurgus as moste proper and best agreeinge with that people whom he knewe to be inclyned allto- geather to warrs and thearefore whollye trayned them vp even from theire Cradles in armes and militare exercises Cleane Contrarye to the institucion of *Solon*. whoe in his Lawes to the *Athenians* laboured by all meanes to temper theire warlike Courages with swete delightes and learninge and sciences so that as muche as the one excelled in armes thother exceded in knowledge, The like regarde and moderacion oughte to be had in Tem- peringe and menaginge of this stubborne nacion of the Irishe to bringe them from theire delighte of licentious barbarisme vnto the loue of goodnes and Civilitye/

Eudox. I Cannot see how that maie better be then by the discipline of the Lawes of Englande, ffor the Inglishe weare at firste as stoute and warlike a people as ever weare the Irishe And yeat yee see are now broughte vnto that Civilytie that no nacion in the worlde excelleth them in all goodlye Conuersacion and all the studies of knowledge and hvmanitye/

Iren. what they now be bothe youe and I see verye well but by how manye thornye and harde waies theye are Come thearevnto by how manye

319 Irelande] *correction of* Englande *E* England *R*   320-1 magistrates] *Magnates Ho*
321 to] *om. C*   321 the Subiectes] these subjects *W*   323 affected] effected *R*   323 doe soe remayne] not so remaind *R*   323-4 me semes] (me seemes) *W*   325-6 Condicion] conditions *W*   326 vnto] vppon *CRW*   327 as] (as *W*   327 saie] said *CR*   said) *W*
329 woulde transfer] transferres *W*   331 *Lacedemonians*] Lacedimonia *C*   *Lacedemon RW*
334 militare] militaree *CRW*   335 *Solon.*] Solon *C* Solon, *RW*   336 and learninge] of Learninge *CRW*   338 knowledge,] knowledge. *W*   340 delighte] delightes *C*
341 Civilitye/] Ciuilitie *C*   342 see how that] howe they *C*   343 at] att the *C*
344 weare] *om. W*   344 vnto] to *R*   345 goodlye] godlye *R*   346 the] *om. R*

A VIEW OF THE PRESENT STATE OF IRELAND 55

Civill broiles by howe manye tumvltuous rebellions, that even hazarded often times the whole saftye of the kingedome maye easelye be Considered All which they neuerthelesse fairelye ouercame by reason of the Continvall presence of theire Kinge whose onelye persone is often times in steade of an Armye to Contayne the vnrvlye people from a thowsande evill occasions which that wretched kingedome is for wante theareof daylye Carryed into, The which when soe they make heade no lawes no penalties Cane restraine but that they doe in the violence of that furye treade downe and trample vnderfoote all bothe divine and hvmaine thinges and the lawes themselues they doe speciallye rage at and rend in peces as moste repugnaunte to theire libertye and naturall fredome which in theire madnes they affecte./ |

f. 6ᵛ *Eudox.* It is then a verye vnseasonable time to pleade lawe when swordes are in the handes of the vulgare or to thinke to retayne them with feare of punishmentes when they loke after libertye and shake of all gouernement/

Iren: Then soe it is with Irelande Continvallye/ *Eudoxus.* for the sworde was neuer yeat out of theire hand but when they are wearye with warrs and broughte downe to extreame wretchednes then they Creepe a little perhaps and sue for grace till they haue gotten newe breathe. and recouered theire strength againe So as it is in vaine to speake of plantinge of lawes and plottinge pollicies till they be alltogeather subdued

Eudox. weare they not soe at the firste Conqueringe of them by Strangbow in the time of K. Henrye the Seconde? was theare not a thorowe waye then made by the sworde for the ymposinge of the Lawes vppon them, and weare they not then executed with suche a mightye hande as youe saie was vsed by the Norman Conquerour, what odds is theare then in this Case why shoulde not the same lawes take as good effecte in that people as they did heare beinge in like sorte prepared by the sworde, and broughte vnder by extremitye. And why shoulde it not Continewe in as good force and vigour for the Contayninge of the people/

Iren. The Case yeat is not like but theare appeareth greate odds betwene them for by the Conquest of Henrye the Seconde trewe it is that the Irishe

---

349 hazarded] hazzard *CR*   350 Considered] Considered, *R* considered: *W*   352 theire] the *R*   352 often times] oftymes *C*   354 that] this *W*   354 is . . . theareof] is for want therof is *C*   for want thereof is *W*   355 into,] into. *W*   355 when soe] whensoever *W*   355 soe they] they so *R*   360 affecte] effect *R*   364 *Eudoxus.*] om. *R*   364 the] om. *C*   365 with] of *W*   367 breathe.] breathe *C* breath *RW*   368 theire] om. *R*   368 of lawes] lawes *W*   369 plottinge] plottinge of *R*   369 pollicies] pollicie *W*   369 subdued] subdued/ *C*   subdued:/: *R*   subdued. *W*   370 of them] om. *C*   370 Strangbow] *Strongbowe W*   371 Seconde?] seconde *C*   372 them,] them? *W*   373 executed] excluded *Ho*   373 a] om. *R*   374 Conquerour,] Conquerour? *W*   375 Case] Case, *CR*   case? *W*   377 extremitye.] extreamity? *W*   377 it] they *CW*   378 people/] people? *W*   379 appeareth] apperes *R*

weare vtterlye vanquished and subdued so as no enemy was able to houlde vp heade againste his power in which theare weakenes he broughte in his lawes and setled them as now they theare remayne/ like as William the Conquerour did; soe as in thus muche they agree but in the reste that is they Chiefeste they varye/ ffor to whom did kinge Henrye the seconde ympose those lawes, not to the Irishe for the moste parte of them fledd from his power into desertes and mountaynes leavinge the wide Countrie to the Conquerour whoe in theire steade eft sones placed Inglishemen whoe possessed all the lande and did quite shutt out the Irishe or the moste parte of them. And to those new Inhabitantes and Colonies he | 390

f. 7ʳ he gave his Lawes, to weet the same lawes vnder which they weare borne and bredd the which it was no difficultye to place amongeste them beinge formerlye well envred therevnto, vnto whom afterwardes theare repaired diuerse of the pore distressed people of the Irishe for succour and relief of whom suche as they thoughte fitt for labour, and industriouslye disposed as the moste parte of theire baser sorte are; they receaued vnto them, as theire vassalls but scarselye vouche safed to imparte vnto them the bennefitt of those lawes vnder which themselves lived; but euerie one made his will and Comaundement a lawe vnto his owne vassall, Thus was not the lawe of Englande euer properlye applied vnto the Irishe nacion as by a purposed plott of gouernement, but as they Coulde insinvate and steale themselves vnder the same by theire humble Carriadge and submission/

Eudox Howe Comes it then to passe that havinge bynne once soe lowe broughte and thoroughlye subiected they afterwardes lifted themselves so strongelye vp againe and sithence doe stande soe stifflye againste all rule and gouernment:/

Iren: They saie that they Continved in that lowlinesse vntill the tyme that the division of the Twoe howsses betwene Lancastre and Yorke arose for the Crowne of Englande At which time all the greate Inglishe Lordes and gentlemen which had greate possessions in Irelande repaired ouer hither into Englande some to succour theire frindes here and to strenghthen theire partie for to obtaine the Crowne others to defende theire Landes and possicions here againste suche as hovered after the same vppon hope of the Allteracion of the kingedome and successe of that side which they favored and affected, Then the Irishe whom before they had banished into the

---

383 William] *Abilliam T*   384-5 is they] is the *CW*   is in the *R*   386 lawes,] Lawes *C*   389 the lande] their lands *W*   391 he] *om. CRW*   392 no difficultye] not deffyculte *R*   393 envred] *corr. of* entred *E*   entred *R*   393 theare] they *W*   396 are;] are, *CW*   are *R*   399 and Comaundement] a comaundment and *R*   399 vassall,] vassall: *W*   402 humble] *om. C*   404-5 themselves ... vp] up themselves so strongly *W*   405 soe] *om. R*   406 gouernment:/] gouerment *R* government? *W*   408 of] betwene *CRW*   408 Twoe] *om. R*   408 betwene] of *CRW*   411 some] *om. R*   413 possicions] possessions *CRW*   413 here] *om. R*   415 affected,] effected, *R*   affected. *W*   415 before they] they before *CR*

mountaines where they lived onelye vppon white meates as it is recorded, seinge now the Landes so dispeopled and wekened came downe into all the plaines adioyninge and thence expellinge those fewe Englishe that remayned repossessed them againe, since which they haue remayned in them and growinge greater haue broughte vnder them manye of the Englishe | which weare before theire Lordes, This is one of the occasions by which all those Countries which lyinge neare vnto anye mounttaines or Irishe desertes had bynne planted with Englishe weare shortelye displanted and loste; as Namelye in *Mounster* all the Landes adioyninge vnto Slewlogher, Arlo and the bog of Allon, In Connaghte all the Countries borderinge vppon the Cullvers Moneroo and Orourks Countrie, In Leinster all the landes neighboringe vnto the mountaines of Glanmalor vnto Shillelah vnto the Briskelah and Polmonte In vlster all the Countries neare vnto Tirconell Tirowne and ffertellah and the Skottes.

Eudox. Surelye this was a greate violence but yeate by your speache it semethe that onelye the Countries and valleis neare adioyninge vnto those mountaines and desertes weare thus recouered by the Irishe, But howe comes it nowe that we see allmoste all that realme repossessed of them; was theare anie more suche evill occacions growinge by the troubles of Englande; or did the Irishe out of these places soe by them gotten breake further and stretche themselues out thoroughe the whole lande/ But now for oughte that I Cane vnderstande theare is no parte but the bare Englishe pale in which the Irishe haue not greatest footinge/

Iren: Bothe out of these smalle beginninges by them gotten neare the

417 seinge] salinge *C*   417 the] there *CRW*   417 Landes] *om. R*   417 all] *om. C*
419 which] which tyme *R*   421 Lordes,] lordes: *C*   Lordes. *RW*   421 is] was *CW*
423 or] or or *C*   423 had] which had *R*   424 loste;] lost. *W*   425 Slewlogher]
Slewloghir A   Cloughbougher *D1*   Sleveloughar *D2*   Slevloughar *F*   Slewloghen *H2*
Slowlougher *L*   Sleuloghen *N*   Slewlougher *R*   Sleloughar *T*   425 Allon] *Allone A*
Allen H2   425 Connaghte] *Cannaugh F*   426 vppon] vpp *C*   426 Cullvers]
blank space *A*   Culuer *P*   Calners *T*   Curlues *W*   426 Moneroo] blank space *A*
Moneroe *H2*   Monrroo *L*   Moneror *N*   Monerio *P*   Mointerolis *W*   426 Orourks]
Oriorke is *A*   Orarkes *F*   Oroncks *G*   Courkes *H1*   427 Leinster] Lymster *T*   427 landes]
bandes *C*   427 neighboringe] bordering *W*   427 Glanmalor] *Glaunmaleerih A*   Glanmullo *D1*
Glan Malor *D2F*   Glamalour *H2*   Glamnaloe *Ho*   Glanmallo *RL*   Glamnalor *T*
428 Shillelah] blank space *A*   Shillebah *CH2*   Shelleglagh *D1*   shellelaugh *D2*   Shillelagh
H1Ho   Shellelagh *R*   428 Briskelah] blank space *A*   Briskelaughe *D2F*   Brisklagh *RLN*
Briskelagh *T*   Brackenah *W*   428 Polmonte] blank space *A*   Polemonte *D2*   Dolemont *F*
Polmonti *H1*   Polmone *H2*   Poulmonte *RL*   Pollemont *T*   429 Tirconell] blank space *A*
Tyroonell *G*   Tironell *H2D1N*   429 Tirowne and] blank space *A*   Tyrone *W*
429 ffertellah] blank space *A*   Fortellagh *D1*   Fertzlaugh *F*   ffertellaz *Ho*   ffertellagh *R*
fertlagg *T* om. *W*   431-9 that ... beginninges by them gotten] *om. D1*   431 Countries
and valleis] Countrye and Valley *R*   433 them;] them, *C*   them. *R*   them? *W*
435 these] those *CW*   436 But] for *CW*   437 Cane] cannott *C*   438 not]
not the *W*   439 Bothe] But *W*   439 neare] *D1 resumes at this point and places* Ireni:
in margin   neare to *W*

mountaines did they spredd themselves into the inlande and allsoe to theire 440
further advantage theare did other like vnhappie accidentes happen out of
Englande which gaue harte and good oportunitye to them to regaine theire
olde possessions. ffor in the raigne of kinge Edward the iiijth thinges
remayned yeat in the same state that they weare after the late breakinge
out of the Irishe which I spake of. And that noble Prince begane to caste 445
an eye vnto Irelande and to minde the reformacion of thinges theare run
amisse, for he sente ouer his brother the worthie Duke of Clarence whoe
havinge married the heire of Lacie and by her havinge all the Earldome of
Vlster and muche in meathe and in mounster verye Carefullie wente aboute
f. 8^r the redressinge of all those late evills | And thoughe he Coulde not 450
beate out the Irishe againe by reason of his shorte Continvance yeat he did
shutt them vp within those narrow Corners and glennes vnder the moun-
taine foote in which they lurked by buildinge stronge houldes vppon euerie
border and fortefyinge all passages, Amongest the which he builte the
Castle of Clare in *Thomond* of which Countrie he had the inheritaunce 455
and of Mortimors Landes adioyninge which is now by the Irishe Called
Killalow/ and so kepte them from breakinge anie further, But the times
of that good Kinge growinge allsoe troblesome did let the thoroughe
reformacion of all thinges And thearevnto sone after was added another
fatall mischief which wroughte a greater Callamatye then all the former, 460
ffor the saide Duke of Clarence then Lord Lieftennante of Irelande was by
practize of evill personnes aboute the kinge his brother Called thence awaie
and sone after by sinister meanes was Cleane made awaie/ Presentlye
after whose deathe all the Northe revoltinge did set vp Oneale for theire
Captaine beinge before that of smalle power and regarde and theare arose 465
in that parte of Thomonde one of the Obriens Called Murrogh en ranagh,
that is Morrice of the fearne or waste wilde places whoe gatheringe vnto
him all the relikes of the discontented Irishe eftsones surprised the saide

440 inlande] Inland Countrye *R*   443 iiijth] seconde *CP*   446 vnto] vnto vnto *C*
448 Lacie] V*lster AH2NT*   the L: Lacye *G*   the Earle of *Vlster WP*   450 all] *om. R*
452 glennes] glynnes *W*   452-3 mountaine] mountaines *W*   453 they lurked] *inserted between lines and deleted after* Killalow *E om. CR*   they lurked, and so kept them from break-ing any further *W*   454 Amongest] (Amongst *R*   454 builte] repaired *W*   455 Clare] *blank space A*   455 Thomond of] Tomond *A*   Thamond *C*   Toomunde he *D2*   Tormond, in *F*   456 by the Irishe] (by the *Irish*) *W*   457 Killalow/] *blank space A*   Killalowe) *CR*   Billalowe *P*   457 and... further] *om. W*   457 and so] they lurked and *CR*   457 them] *om. R*   458 allsoe] *om. R*   461 Lieftennante] Lieutenant *W*   462 thence] there *R*
463 awaie/] away. *W*   464 vp] vpp, *R*   464 Oneale] Oneales *H2*   466 Thomonde] Tomond *A*   Thamond *C*   Toomonde *D2*   Tarmound *F*   466 Obriens] *Orbiens* Ho
466 Murrogh] *blank space A*   Murroh *H1*   466 en ranagh] *blank space A* en Ramugh *F*
enranugh *G*   Enranah *H1*   Enranog *H2*   *en ranash P*   467 Morrice] *Morie G*   murrogh *N*
467 fearne] *blank space A*   Ferme *D2*   Feroune *F*   farme *RLD1*   fenne *GT*

A VIEW OF THE PRESENT STATE OF IRELAND 59

Castle of Clare burnte and spoiled all the Englishe theare dwellinge and in shorte space possessed all that Countrie beyonde the river of Shenan and neare adioyninge whence shortelye breakinge forthe like a sodaine Tempest he ouerran all monster and Connaght breakinge downe all the houldes and fortresses of the Englishe defacinge and vtterlye subvertinge all Corporate townes that weare not strongelye walled, ffor those he had noe meanes nor engines to overthrowe neither in deed woulde he staye at all aboute them but spedelye rann forwarde Countinge his suddennesse his moste advantage That he mighte overtake the Englishe before they coulde fortifye or f. 8ᵛ gather themselves togeather, Soe in shorte space he | he Cleane wyped out manye greate Townes, As firste Insheginn then Killalow before Called Clarriforte afterwardes Thurles Mourne Buttevant/ and manye others whose names I Cannot remember and of some of which theare is now no memorye nor signe remayninge: vppon reporte wheareof theare flocked vnto him all the scum of Irishe out of all places; that ere longe he had a mightye Armie and thence marched forthe into Leinster wheare he wroughte greate outrages wastinge all the Countrie wheare he wente; ffor it was his pollicye to leave no houldes behinde him but to make all plaine and waste In the which he sone after Created him selfe kinge, and was Called kinge of all Irelande. which before him I doe not reade that anie did so generallye but onely Edwarde le Bruce/

Eudox what was theare euer anie generall kinge of all Ireland I never harde it before but that it was allwaies whilste it was vnder the Irishe divided into fower and somtimes into five kingedomes or dominions. But this Edwarde le Bruce, what was he that he coulde make himselfe kinge of all Irelande/

Iren. I woulde tell youe incase youe woulde not Challenge me anone for 495
forgettinge the matter which I had in hande that is the inconveniaunce
and vnfittnes which I suppose to be in the lawes of the Lande

Eudox Noe surelye I haue no cause for neither is this impertinente thearevnto for sithence youe did set your Course (as I remember) in your firste
parte to treate of the evills which hindereth the peace and good orderinge 500
of that lande amongest which that of the inconveniaunce in the lawes was
the firste which yee had in hande this discourse of the ouerrunninge and
wastinge of the realme is verye materiall thearevnto. for that it was the
beginninge of all the other evills which sithence haue afflicted that lande
and opened a waie vnto the Irishe to recouer theire possession and to beate 505
out the Englishe which had formerlie wonne the same and besides it will
give a | greate Lighte bothe vnto your seconde and thirde parte which
is the redressinge of those evills and plantinge of some good forme of
Pollicye thearein, by renewinge the remembrance of those occasions and
accidentes by which those ruines hapened and layinge before vs the ensam- 510
ples of those times to be Compared with ours and to be bewared by those
which haue to doe in the like. Therefore I praye youe tell them vnto vs
and as for the pointe wheare youe lefte I will not forgett afterwardes to
Call youe backe againe therevnto:

Iren. This Edwarde le Bruce was brother of Rob̄te le Bruce whoe was 515
kinge of Skotlande at suche time as kinge Edwarde the Seconde Raigned
heare in England and bare a moste malicious and spitefull minde againste
kinge Edwarde doinge him all the scathe that he could and Anoyinge his
terretories of Englande whilste he was trobled with Civill warrs of his
Barrons at home He allsoe to worke him the more mischief sente ouer his 520
saide Brother Edwarde with a power of Skottes and Redshankes into Irelande wheareby the meanes of the lacies and of the Irishe with whom they
Combyned they gote footinge and gatheringe vnto him all the scattorlinges and outlawes out of all the woodes and mountaines in which they
longe had lurked marched forthe into the Englishe pale which then was 525

495 incase] yf in case *R*   495 anone] om.*R*   497 suppose] supposed *RW*   497 Lande] Lande./. *C*   land:: *R*   Land. *W*   499-500 remember) . . . parte] remember . . . part) *W*   500 hindereth] hindered *W*   501 in] of *R*   502 yee] he *C*   504 all the] om. *R*   506 the same] the the same *C*   507 your] the *W*   508 forme of] forme or *W*   509 those] these *W*   511 with] to *W*   511 and] om. *C*   511 bewared] *corr. of* rewarded *E*   rewarded *CR*   warned *W*   regarded *Ho*   512 haue] shall have *CRW*   512 like.] leike, *CR*   515 *Iren.* . . . Rob̄te le Bruce] *om. and no new paragraph P*   515 Edwarde le] Edward Lee *R*   515 brother] the brother *CR*   515 Rob̄te le] K. Robt Lee *R*   518 that] om. *R*   520 home] home/ *C*   home: *R*   home. *W*   522 wheareby] where by *CRW*   522 the meanes] meanes *R*   523 gote] gave *W*   523-4 scattorlinges and] scatterlins of *R*

A VIEW OF THE PRESENT STATE OF IRELAND 61

Chieflye in the Northe from the pointe of Donluce and beyonde vnto
Dublin havinge in the middest of her Knockfergus Belfast *Armage and
Carlingforde* which are now the moste outboundes and abandoned places
in the Englishe pale, And inded not Counted of the Englishe pale at all:
ffor it stretcheth now no further then dundalke towardes the Northe, 530
Theare the saide Edwarde Le Bruce spoiled and burnte all the oulde
Englishe pale puttinge to the sworde all the Englishe inhabitantes and
sacked and raced all Citties and Corporate Townes no lesse then murro or
f. 9ᵛ renagh of whom I earste tolde youe ffor he | wasted *Belfast, Greene
Castle Kelles Beltalbot Castletowne newton* and manye other verye good 535
Townes and stronge houldes he rooted out the noble familye of the
Audlies and Talbottes the dutches the Chamberlaines the maundevills and
the Salvages thoughe of the Lo Salvage theare remaine yeat one heire that
is now a verye poore gentelman dwellinge in the Ardes and Comminge
lastelye to dondalke he theare made himselfe kinge and raigned by the 540
space of one whole yeare by the name of Edwarde Kinge of Irelande vntill
that Kinge Edwarde of Englande havinge sett some quiet in his affaires
at home sente ouer the Lọ Iohn Brenningham to be generall of the warrs

526 Donluce] *blank space A*   Dunlace *D1D2L*   Donlace *FH1H2*   Don Luce *G*   Dun-
luce *R*   527 Belfast] *blank space A*   527 Armage] Armagh *CRW*   528 Carlingforde]
Cartingforde *CD2FH1Ho*   Carlingsone *D1*   Carlargford *G*   528 outboundes] one
boundes *C*   529 in the Englishe] *last four letters worn off C*   529 inded . . . pale]
some noe parte thereof *R*   530 Northe,] North: *R*   North. *W*   531 the saide]
they said *R*   531 Le] lee *R*   532 puttinge . . . Englishe] *om. W*   533 lesse] lesse
noe lesse *R*   533-4 or renagh] *blank space A*   en ranaghe *C*   Euranagh *H1*   en Ranagh *RW*
in Ranagh *T*   534-5 Belfast . . . newton] *blank space A*   534-5 Greene . . .
Castletowne] Greene, Castle Relles, Beltalbot castle, Tome *F*   534-5 Greene Castle]
Grenecastle *C*   Greene-Castle *W*   Greene, Castell *Ho*   535 Kelles] Keills *D1*   Kellos *GP*
Kiells *L*   535 Beltalbot] Bellturbut *W*   535 newton] Newtowne *R*   536 houldes]
holdes, *W*   536 familye] families *CRW*   537 Audlies] Andleyes *R*   Arodeleyes *N*
537 and Talbottes] the Talbottes *CR*   Talbotts *W*   537 the dutches] the Tutchites *CRL*
the Touchettes *D1H2A*   the Tutchetts *D2FH1N*   the Tutchittes *GHo*   the Tewchetts *T*
Tuchets *W*   537 the Chamberlaines the] *Chamberlaines W*   the Chamberlames the *N*
538 Salvages] Savages out of Ardes *WP*   538 of] *om. C*   538 Lọ Salvage] Salvages *HoP*
538 remaine] remaineth *W*   538 one] an *CRW*   539 verye] *om. W*   539 gentelman]
Gentleman of very meane condition, yet *W*   539 in] at *R*   539 the Ardes] *blank space A*
540 kinge] Kinge. *R*   540 by] *om. W*   541-7 by . . . they] havinge overthrowne his
brother Robert *Le Bruce* in a feilde at   hee eftsoones sent over Hugh de Lacy,
whome hee beefore vppon somme occasion of his enimyes, had imprisoned and disgraced,
and appointed Generall, in those warres againste Edwarde *Le Bruce*. who incounteringe him
and his Scottes, and his Iryshe beesydes *Dundalke* was therat firste by him discomfited, but yet
saved him selfe and his people throwghe his wyse goverment from anye great losse. ffor as
hee was a man of excellent Courage, so hee was verye well experienced beefore in all the
manners and kinde of fight of the Iryshe. nevertheleese soone after the recomfortinge of his
people hee gaue battayle againe to the saide *Ed le Bruce* nere to *Athboy*, where hee ouer-
threwe him, and prosecuted him selfe so cloaselye and so sharplye that hee forced him to flye
still beefore him vntill hee *P*   541 by the name . . . Irelande] *om. W*   541 Kinge of]
Kinge of of *R*   542 Kinge Edwarde] Edward King *W*   543 Brenningham] Brem-

againste him whoe incountringe him neare to dundalke overthrewe his Armye and slewe himself and presentlye followed the victorye so hottlye vppon his Skottes that he suffered them not to breathe or gather themselves togeather againe vntill they came to the seacoste, notwithstandinge all the waie as the fledd they for verye rancour and despighte in theire returne vtterlye Consumed and wasted whatsoeuer they hadd before lefte vnspoilled soe that of all Townes and Castles fortes bridges and habitacions he lefte not anye sticke standinge nor anye people remayninge for those fewe which yeat survived fled from his furye further into the Englishe pale that now is. thus was all that goodlye Countrye vtterlye wasted and lefte desolate as yeat it remayneth to this daie which before had bynne the Chiefe ornament and bewtye of Irelande for that parte of the Northe somtyme was as populous and plentifull as anye parte in Englande And yealded vnto the Kinges of Englande (As yeat appeareth by good recordes) Thirtye Thowsande markes of olde money by the yeare besides manye thowsandes of hable men to serve them in theire warrs And sure it is, it is a moste bewtifull and swete Countrie as | anye is vnder heaven, seamed thoroughe out with manye goodlye rivers replenished with all sortes of fishe moste aboundantlye sprinckled with manye swete Ilandes and goodlye lakes like little Inlande seas, that will carye even shipps vppon theire waters, adorned with goodly woodes fitt for buildinge of howsses and shipps so comodiously as that if some princes in the worlde had them they they woulde sone hope to be Lordes of all the seas and ere longe of all the worlde Allsoe full of verye good portes and havens openinge vppon Englande and Skotlande as invitinge vs to Come vnto them to see what excellente Comodities that Countrye Cane afforde; besides the soile it self moste fertile fitt to yealde all kinde of fruite/ that shalbe committed thearevnto And Lastlye the heavens moste milde and temperate thoughe somwhat more moyste then the partes towardes the weste/

Eudox. Trewlye *Irenius* what with your praises of the Countrye and what

megham *A* Bremecham *H2* Bremingham *RFGHoT* Birmingham *W* 545 himself and] him. Also hee *W* 546 his] the *W* 546 breathe] staye *R* 547 seacoste,] Seacoast. *W* 548 as the] as they *CR* that they *W* 548 they] om. *RW* 548-9 in theire returne] then *R* in their returne they *W* 549 Consumed and wasted] waisted and consumed *R* 550 that] as *W* 550 Townes and] Townes *W* 550-1 habitacions] Inhabitancions *C* 551 he] they *W* 551 sticke] stoke *C* 552 yeat] om. *C* 552 his] their *W* 553 is.] is, *CR* 554-9 and . . . warrs] om. *WP* 554 as yeat it] and as yett *R* 556 somtyme] sometymes *C* 557 (As] as *R* 558 Thowsande] thowsandes *C* 558 besides] besyde *R* 559 thowsandes] thowsand *R* 559 theire] the *C* 559 And] om. *R W and P resume at this point* 559-60 is, it is] is yett *CRW* 560 and swete] om. *C* 561 seamed] being stored *W* 561 thoroughe out] thorought *C* 562 aboundantlye] abundantly, *CW* aboundantlie: *R* 562 manye] verie manie *CRW* 564 fitt] even fit *W* 566 they] om. *CRW* 567 worlde] worlde, *CR* world: *W* 568 and Skotlande] Scotland *R om. W* 570 thearevnto] therinto *CR* 572 more]

with your discourse of the lamentable desolacion theareof made by those Ragtaile Irishe Skottes youe haue filled me with a greate Compassion of theire Callamities that I do muche pittye the swete lande to be subiecte to soe manye evills, as everye daie I see more and more throwne vppon her and doe halfe begine to thinke that it is (as ye saide at the beginninge her fatall misfortune aboue all Countries that I knowe to be thus miserablye Tossed and turmoylled with these variable stormes of affliccions. But since we are thus farr entred into the Consideracion of her mishapps tell me, Haue there bynne anye more suche Tempestes as yee terme them whearein she hathe thus wretchedlye bene wrecked/

f. 10ᵛ *Iren.* manye more god wott haue theare bynne in which her | Principall partes haue bene rente and torne a sunder but none that I Cane remember so vniuersall as these, and yeat the Rebellion of Thomas fz Garret did wellnighe stretche it selfe into all partes of Irelande, But that which was in the tyme of the gouernement of the Lorde Graie was surely no lesse generall then all these, for theare was no parte free from the Contagion but all Conspired in one to Caste of theire subieccion to the Crowne of Englande Neuerthelesse thoroughe the moste wise and valiant handlinge of the righte noble Lord it gott not that head which the former evills founde, for in them the realme was lefte like a shippe in a storme amiddest all the raginge surges vnruled and vndirected of anye, ffor they to whom shee was Comitted either fainted in theire labour or for sooke theire Chardge, But he like a moste wise Pilott kepte her Course Carefullye and helde her moste strongelye even againste those roringe billowes that he safelye broughte her out of all, so as longe after even by the space of xij or xiij yeares shee rod at peace thoroughe his onelye paines and excellent endurance how euer envye liste to batter againste him/ But of this we shall haue more occasion to speake in another place, nowe if youe please let vs retorne againe into our firste Course/

last letter worn off C   574 your discourse of] *om. R*   575 Ragtaile Irishe Skottes] ragtailes in Scotland *R*   *Scottes W*   575 Ragtaile] ragtayle *with last two letters worn off C*
576 the] that *CRW*   577 everye daie] *om. W*   577 throwne] to bee layde *W*
578 beginninge] begynninge) *RW*   579 all] all other *W*   580 affliccions] affliction *W*
581 me,] me *CR*   583 hathe] have *C*   583 wrecked/] wracked. *C*   wracked::/ *R*   wracked? *W*   584 manye] Manie manie *C*   Verie many *R*   584 more] moe *R*
584 her] *om. W*   585 rente and] *om. R*   585-6 that . . . remember] (as . . . remember] *W*
586 these] this *W*   586 fz] *blank space P*   587 Garret] Gerrald *A*   587 wellnighe] willingelie *R*   587 it] her *C*   588 Graie] *inserted between lines E om. CP*   589 these] those *W*   591 Englande] England, *R*   England. *W*   592 of the] of that *RW*
592 that] the *W*   596 like . . . Pilott] (like . . . Pilote,) *W*   597 moste] nose *CR*
597 even] *om. R*   598 safelye broughte her] brought her safely *CR*   599 xiij] xiij whole *CW* 14 *GP*   600 endurance] endurance. *R*   600 batter] bluster *A*   blatter *CRWD2FHoP*   blutter *LD1*   601 in another place] at another tyme *R*   601 place,] place. *W*   601 nowe] *om. R*   601-2 if youe please] yf it please yow *R*   (if you please) *W*
602-778 againe . . . . falleth] to the case howe it often fallethe out, *P*   602 into] unto *W*

Eudox Trewlye I ame verye glad to heare your iudgement of the gouernement of that honorable man soe soundlye. for I haue indede harde it often times maligned and his doinges depraved of some whom I perceaued did 605 rather of malicious minde or private grevaunce seke to detracte from the honour of his deds and Councells then of anye iuste Cause, But he was neuertheles in the iudgement of all wise and good men defended and mainteyned and now that he is dead his imortall fame survivethe and

f. 11ʳ florisheth in the mouthes of all the people that | even those which 610 did backebite him are Choked with theire owne fenim and breake theire galls to heare his soe honorable reporte/ But let him reste in peace and turne we to our more troublous matters of discourse of which I ame righte sorye that ye make so shorte an ende and Covet to passe ouer to your former purpose; ffor theare be manye other partes of Irelande (which as 615 I haue harde) haue bene no lesse vexed with the like stormes then these of which youe haue treated/ As the Countrie of the Birnes and Tooles neare dvblin with the insolent outrages and spoiles of Pheagh mᵃ Hugh The Cuntries of Carlo Wexforde and Waterforde of the Cavenaghes The Countries of Leix killkenny and killdare of the mores The Countries of 620 Offalye meathe and longeford of the Conhoures the Countries of weastmeathe Cavan and Louthe of the Orelies the kellies and manye others So as the discoursinge of them shoulde besides the pleasure which shoulde redounde out of your Historye be allsoe verye profitable for matter of pollicye 625

Iren. All these which ye haue named and manye moe besides oftentimes haue (I righte well knowe) And yeat often doe kindle great fires of tumul-

---

604 indede] *om. W*   605 depraved] repraved *C*   605 whom] whoe *CRW*   605 I perceaued] I perceaue *R* (I perceive) *W*   608 iudgement] Iudgmentes *R*   608 wise and good] good and wise *W*   610 all the] all those *C*   all *W*   611 Choked] checked *W*   611 fenim] venyme *C*   vennom *RW*   613 troublous] troublesome *W*   615 purpose] purposes *W*   615 (which] which (as *C*   which *RW*   615 as] *om. W*   616 harde)] heard *W*   617 of which ... treated] which you have treated of *W*   617 Countrie] Countries *W*   617 Birnes and Tooles] *blank space A*   617 Birnes] Bornes *F*   Bryans *G*   Brans *H2*   617 Tooles] *Tales Ho*   618 Pheagh] *Feugh A*   *Phragh F*   *Pheab T*   618 mᵃ] *in Ho*   618 Hugh] *last letter worn off C*   619 Carlo] *Katerlagh A*   *Carle D2*   Earle *and blank space F*   *Carles Ho*   Catherlagh *W*   619 Wexforde] *Waxford D2*   619 Waterforde of] *Waterford, by W*   620 Leix] *Leyse A*   *Leis H2N*   620 of the mores] by the *O Moores W*   620-1 Countries of Offalye] Counties of Offalie *CR*   621 meathe and] *om. A*   Mertheland *G*   and *W*   621 longeford] *Loungfoord A*   Langforde *RGL*   621 of the Conhoures] of the *Conhue F*   by the *Connors W*   621 Countries] Counties with last letter worn off *C*   Counties *R*   622 Cavan and] *Cavanand G*   Catoun and *LD1*   622 of the Orelies] of the *ollelies F*   of the *Orleys G*   by the *O Relyes W*   622 kellies] *Kelles D1H2L*   Kellied *G*   623 them shoulde] them *W*   623 which shoulde] which would *W*   624 your] their *W*   624 matter] matters *CW*   625 pollicye] pollicie: *R*   policy. *W*   626 these] *om. C*   this *W*   626 moe] more *W*   627 (I] I *W*   627 knowe)] knowen) *R*   knowne *W*   627 And ... doe] to *R*

tuous trobles in the Countries borderinge vppon them, All which to reherse shoulde rather be to Cronicle times then to searche into the reformacion of abuses in that realme and yeat verye nedefull it wilbe to Consider them and the evills which they haue often stirred vp that some redresse thereof and provencion for the evills to Come maye thearby the rather be devized/ But I suppose we shall haue a fitter oportunitye for the same when we shall speake of the particuler abuses and enormities of that governement which wilbe nexte after those generall defectes and inconveniaunces which I saide weare in the Lawes Customes and religion

f. 11ᵛ *Eudox.* Goe to then in godes name and followe the Course | which yee haue proposed to your selfe for it fitteth beste I muste Confesse with the purpose of our discourse declare your opinion as yee begunne/ aboute the lawes of that Realme what Incommoditye yee haue conceyved to be in them Chieflye in the Comon lawe which I woulde haue thought moste free from all suche dislike/

Iren. the Comon Lawe is (as I before saide) of it selfe moste rightefull and verye Conveniente I suppose for the kingedome for which it was firste devized for this I thinke (as it semes reasonable that out of the manners of the people and abuses of the Countrye for which they weare invented theye toke theire firste beginninge: ffor els they shoulde be moste vniuste, for no lawes of man, accordinge to the straighte rule of righte, are iuste, but as in regarde of the evills which they prevente and the safetye of the Comon weale which they provide for/ As for ensample in the trew ballauncinge of Iustice, It is a flatt wronge to punishe the thoughte or purpose of anye before it be acted, ffor trewe Iustice punisheth nothinge but the evill acte or wicked worde, yeat by the lawes of all kingedomes it is a capitall Cryme to devize or purpose the deathe of the kinge The reasone is for that when suche a purpose is effected it shoulde

628 trobles] broyles *W* 628 them,] them. *W* 629 times] *om.* C 629 the] *om. W* 631 often] *om.* R 632 provencion] prevention *CRW* 632 for] of *W* 632 the rather] rather *W* 634 that] the *W* 635 those] these *W* 636 religion] relidgion: *R* Religion. *W* 637 then] them *RW* 637 in] a *W* 638 proposed] purposed *R* promised *W* 639 discourse] discourse. *CW* 639 begunne] began *W* 640 that] the *RW* 640 yee] he *C* 642 suche] *om.* C 642 dislike/] dislyk *R* dislike. *W* 643 before saide] saide before *W* 644 I suppose] (I suppose) *W* 645 I thinke] (as) (I thinke) as *W* 645 reasonable] reasonable) *CR* 645-6 the manners of the] your manners of your *W* 646 the Countrye] your Countrey *W* 647 toke] take *W* 647 ffor] or *W* 648 accordinge ... righte] (according ... right) *W* 650 ensample] example *RW* 651 in the] in your *W* 652 acted] *corr. of* enacted *E* enacted *CRW* 653 yeat] that *W* 654-5 the kinge] the kinge, *C* the Kinge: *R* your King: *W* 655 is effected] effected *C*

be to late to devize of the punishmente thereof and shoulde turne that Common weale to more hurte by suche losse of theire Prince, then suche punishment of the Malefactours coulde remedye. And therefore the lawe in that Case punisheth his thoughte, for better is a mischief then an inconvenience. Soe that *Ius Politicum* thoughe it be not of it selfe iuste yeat by applicacion or rather necessitye is made iuste And this onelye respecte makethe all lawes iuste: Now then if those Lawes of Irelande be not likewise applied and fitted for that realme they are sure verye inconvenient

Eudox: youe reason strongelye but what vnfittnes do ye finde in them for that realme? shewe vs some particulers: |

Iren. The Comon Lawe appointeth that all trialls aswell of Crymes as titles and rightes shalbe made by verdite of A Iurye Chosen out of the honestest and moste substantiall frehoulders/ Nowe all the ffrehoulders of that realme are Irishe which when the cause shall fall betwene an Inglisheman and an Irishe, or betwene the Quene and anye ffrehoulder of that Countrye they make no more scruple to passe againste the Inglishman or the Quene thoughe it be to straine theire oathes then to drinke milke vnstrained, soe that before the Iurye goe togeather it is all to nothinge what theire verdite wilbe, The Triall heareof haue I soe often sene that I dare Confidentlye avouche the abuse thereof yeat is the lawe of it selfe/ (as I saide good) and the firste institucion theareof beinge given to all Inglishemen verye rightefull, but now that the Irishe haue stepped into the romes of the Inglishe whoe are now become soe hedefull and provident to kepe them out from hence forthe that they make no scruple of Conscience to passe againste them it is good reason that either that course of the lawe for trialls be altered or other provision for Iuryes be made/

Eudox: In sothe *Irenius* youe haue discouered a pointe worthe the Consideracion, ffor hereby not onely the Englishe subiecte findethe no indif-

---

656 be] then be *W*   656 of the punishmente] om. *W*   656 that] the *W*   657 Common weale] Common-wealth *W*   657 hurte ... losse] losse by the death *W*   658 coulde remedye] *inserted between lines R* om. *CRW*   659 his] the *W*   659 is] it is *C*   659-60 inconvenience.] inconvenience, *CR*   660 *Ius Politicum*] in pollicie *D1*   this politick Law *G*   *Ius politicui H2*   *Ius Politian Ho*   Ius Pollicium *RL*   660 of it] of his *C*   661 is] it is *W*   662 lawes] lawe *R*   662 iuste:] iuste, *C*   662 those] these *W*   663 inconvenient] inconvenient: *C*   inconvenient.. *R*   inconvenient. *W*   665 realme?] Realme *C*   realme, *RW*   667 A] om. *R*   668 honestest] honest *W*   668 all] most of *W*   669 betwene] betwixt *W*   670 Inglisheman ... Irishe] Irishe man and an Englishe *R*   671 Countrye they] Countie, that *R*   671-2 the Inglishman or] an Englishman, and *W*   673 vnstrained,] vnstrayned. *W*   673 it is] is it *C*   674 theire] the *W*   674 wilbe,] wilbe *C*   shall be. *W*   674 heareof] thereof *R* om. *W*   674 haue I] I have *C*   675 thereof] hereof *C*   676 (as ... good)] (as I said) good *W*   677 rightefull] rightfully *W*   678 romes ... soe] very roomes of your English, wee are now to become *W*   679-81 to ... made] in Iuryes *W*   679 out] forth *R*   682 discouered] discoversed *W*   682 worthe] worthy *W*

ferencye in decidinge of his Cause be it neuer so iuste, but allso the Quene as well in all pleas of the Crowne as allsoe in all inquiries for excheates, landes attainted, wardeshipps, concelmentes and all suche like is abused and excedinglye endamaged.

Iren: yee saye verye trew, for I dare vndertake that this daie theare are more attainted Landes concealed from her maiestie then shee now hathe possessions in all Irelande And that is no small Inconvenience, ffor besides that shee looseth soe muche lande as shoulde turne her to greate profitt shee besides looseth so manye good subiectes which mighte be assured to her as those landes woulde yealde Inhabitaunce and livinge vnto/

Eudox: But does that people, saie youe, make no more | Conscience to periure themselues in theire verdittes and to damne theire soules/

Iren. not onelye soe in theire verdites but allsoe in all other theare dealinges speciallye with the Englishe they are moste willfullye bente for thoughe they will not seme manifestlye to doe it yeat will some one or other subtill headed fellow amongest them picke some quirke, or devise some evacion wheareof the rest will lightelye take houlde, and suffer them selves easelye to be led by him, to that themselues desired: ffor in the moste apparante matter that maie be the leaste question or doubte that cane be moved will make a stoppe vnto them and put them quite out of the waie. Besides that of themselues they are for the moste parte so cautelous and wily headed speciallye beinge men of so small experience and practize in lawe matters that youe woulde wonder whence they borrowe suche subtilties and slye shiftes/

Eudox: But me thinkes this inconvenience mighte be muche helped in the Iudges and Chiefe maiestrates which haue the Chosinge and nominatinge of those Iurours if they woulde haue Care to appointe either moste Englishemen or suche Irishemen as weare of the soundest disposicion. ffor noe doubte but some theare be incorruptible.

684 allso] *om. W*   685 in all inquiries] for all inquiries *R*   in inquiries *W*   685 excheates,] excheat *R*   686 attainted,] *last two letters worn off C*   attainted *R*   687 excedinglye] that excedingelie *R*   687 endamaged] dammaged *W*   688 that] that at *RW*   689 now hathe] hath now *W*   690 that] it *W*   691 that] that, *W*   691 her to] to her *W*   692 to] unto *W*   693 Inhabitaunce] inhabytantes *RW*   693 vnto/] vnto *R*   694 does] doth many of *W*   694 saie youe] (say you) *W*   694 youe,] yow: *R*   695 and to] and *W*   695 soules/] soules? *W*   697 speciallye] especially *W*   698-9 some . . . other] one or other some *C*   699 picke] put *W*   700 evacion] subtill evasion *R*   700 lightelye take houlde] take hold lightly *C*   700 houlde] holde of *R*   703 cane] may *W*   703 a] *om. R*   704 waie.] waie *C*   waye: *R*   704 they . . . parte] (for the most part) they are *W*   705 speciallye] especiallye *RW*   708 helped] holped *R*   710 Care] dared *W*   711 or] and *W*   711 disposicion] iudgment and disposition *W*   712 incorruptible.] incorruptable *R*

Iren: Some theare be in dede as youe saie, but then woulde the Irishe partie Crye out of parcialitye and Complaine he hathe not iustice, he is not vsed as a subiecte he is not suffered to haue the free bennefite of the lawe 715 And these outcries the magistrates theare doe muche shunne as they haue Cause since they are so redelye herkened vnto heare, Neither cane it indede allthoughe the Irishe partie woulde be Contente to be so compassed that suche Englishe freehoulders which are but fewe and suche faithe full Irishemen which are indede as fewe, shall allwaies be Chosen for trialls 720 ffor beinge soe fewe they shoulde sone be made wearye of theire freehoulde and therefore a good Care is to be had by all good occacions to increase theire number and to plante more by them, But weare it soe that the Iuries coulde be picked out of suche Choice men as yee desire theare woulde neuerthelesse be as badd Corrupcion in the triall for the | 725
f. 13ʳ ffor the evidence beinge broughte in by the base Irishe people wilbe as deceiptefull as the verdittes, ffor they Care muche lesse then the others what they sweare, and sure theire Lordes maye Compell them to saie anye thinge, ffor I my selfe haue harde when one of that base sorte which they Call Churles beinge Challendged and reproued for his false oathe hathe 730 answeared confidentlye that his Lorde Comaunded him, And that it was the leaste thinge that he Coulde doe for his Lorde to Sweare for him, soe inconscionable are these Comon people and soe little feelinge haue they of god or theire owne soules healthe//

Eudox It is a moste miserable Case But what helpe then cane theare be in 735 this, ffor thoughe the mannour of the triall shoulde be altered yeat the profe of euerie thinge muste nedes be by testimonyes of suche persons as the parties shall produce which if they shall bee corrupte how cane theyre ever anie lighte of the truethe Appeare? what remedye is theare for this evill, but to make heavye lawes and penalties againste periurours? *Iren*: 740 I thinke sure that will doe small goode: ffor when a people are inclyned to anye vice or haue no touche of Conscience nor sence of theire evill doinge it is bootles to thinke to restraine them by anye penalties or feare

---

713 Some] Some summe *R*   713 in dede] *om. C*   714 hathe not] hath no *W*   715 subiecte] subiecte/ *C*   subiect, *RW*   717 so] *om. W*   717 herkened] heakened *C*   717 it] it bee *W*   718 partie] parte *R*   718 Contente] so contented *W*   720 allwaies] alwaies *with last letter worn off C*   721 sone] *om. W*   721-2 freehoulde] free-houldes *W*   724 Iuries] Iurors *W*   724 theare] this *W*   726 ffor the] *om. CRW*   726 evidence] evidences *C*   726 by the] by *C*   726 base] baser *W*   727 verdittes] verdict *W*   727 then] then then *R*   728 sweare] Answere *C*   729 I] *om. R*   729 that base] the baser *W*   729-30 which ... Churles] (which ... Churles) *W*   730 hathe] haue *R*   731 that it] it *W*   732 that] *om. CR*   734 healthe] good *CRW*   736 this,] this? *W*   736 triall] tryalls *W*   737 by] by the *W*   737 testimonyes] *last four letters worn off C*   testimony *W*   738 bee] *om. CR*   739 ever] *om. R*   739 the] *om. R*   739 Appeare?] appere *C*   appeare, *RW*   740 periurours?] periurors *C*   periurors::/ *R*   Iurors. *W*   740 *Iren*:] *new paragraph CRW*   741 are] be *W*   743 doinge] doings *W*   743 them] *om. C*

A VIEW OF THE PRESENT STATE OF IRELAND 69

of punishment, but either the occacion is to be taken awaye or a more vnderstandinge of the righte and shame of the faulte is to be imprinted: ffor if that *Licurgus* shoulde haue made it deathe for the *Lacedemonians* to steale. they beinge a people which naturallye delighted in stealthe, or if it shoulde be made a Capitall Cryme for the fflemminges to be taken in drunkennesse theare shoulde haue bene fewe *Lacedemonians* sone lefte, and fewer fflemmynges. So ympossible it is to remove anye faulte soe generall in a people with Terrour of Lawes or moste sharpe restraintes

Eudox: what meanes maie theare then be to avoide this inconvenience. ffor the Case sure semes verie harde./

Iren: we are not yeat come to that pointe to devize remedies for the evills but onelye haue now to recounte them, of the which this which I haue tolde youe is one defecte in the Comon lawe/ |

f. 13ᵛ *Eudox*: Tell vs then I praye youe further haue youe anye more of this sorte in the Common lawe.

Iren: By rehearesall of this I remember me allsoe of another like which I haue often oberued in trialls to haue wroughte greate hurte and hinderaunce And that is the Excepcions which the Comon lawe alloweth to a felon in his triall, for he maye haue as youe knowe xxxvj excepcions peremtorye againste the Iurours of which he shall shewe no Cause and as manye as he will of suche as he Cane shewe Cawse, By which shifte theare beinge as I haue shewed youe suche small store of honest Iurymen he will either put of his triall or drive it to suche men as perhaps are not of the soundest sorte, By whose meanes if he Canne acquite himselfe of the Crime as he is likely then will he plague suche as weare broughte to be firste of his Iurye and all suche as made anye partie againste him and when he Coms forthe, will make theire Cowes and garrons to walke if he doe no other mischief to theire persons

Eudox: This is a slye devise but I thinke mighte sone be remedied but we

745 and] or *R*   745 is] *om. W*   746 that] *om. R*   747 steale.] steale *R*   steale, *W*
749 sone] then *W*   750 fewer] few *W*   750 fflemmynges.] fflemminges *CR*   *Flemmings now. W*   751 restraintes] restraintes. *CW*   752 then be] be then *W*   753 Case] cause *R*   753 sure] *om. W*   753 harde./] hard? *W*   754 *Iren*:] *no new paragraph H2*
754 that] the *W*   754 the] *om. C*   755 this which] this that *R*   756 in] of *C*
757-8 *Eudox*: . . . lawe.] *om. H2*   757 I praye youe] (I pray you) *W*   758 lawe.] Lawe, *C*   Law? *W*   759 me] *om. RW*   761 Excepcions] exception *C*   761 to] *om. W*
762 as youe knowe] (as you know) *W*   762 xxxvj] 56. *W*   763 peremtorye] peremtortye *C*   763-4 and . . . Cawse] *om. W*   764 suche] such, *R*   765 as . . . youe] (as . . . you) *W*   765 shewed] *last two letters worn off C*   766 suche] so *W*
766 perhaps] (perhaps) *W*   767 the soundest] soundest *C*   768 Crime] Cryme *with last two letters worn off C*   768-9 to be firste] first to be *CRW*   770 will] he will *W*   771 other] *last letter worn off C*   771 mischief] harme *W*   771 persons]

muste leave it a while with the reste in the meane tyme doe youe goe forwarde with others

Iren: Theare is another no lesse inconveniente then this which is for the triall of Accessaries to felonye, ffor by the Comon lawe the Accessarie cannot be proceded againste till the Principall haue receaued his triall Nowe the Case often falleth in Irelande that a stelthe beinge made by a rebell or an Outlawe the stollen goodes are Conveyed to some other husbandeman or gentellman which hathe well to take to and livethe moste by the receipte of suche stelthes, wheare theye are founde by the owner and handled, whearevppon the partie perhaps is apprehended and Comitted to gaole or put vppon suerties till the sessions; at which time the owner preferringe a bill of Inditement proveth sufficiently the stealthe to haue bynne Comitted vppon him by suche an Outlawe and to haue bene founde in the possession of | of the prisoner againste whom neuertheles no Course of lawe cane proceed nor triall cane be had for that the principall theffe is not to be gotten notwithstandinge that he likewise standeth perhaps indicted attonce with the receyvour beinge in rebellion or in the woodes wheare peradventure he is slaine before he can be gotten and soe the receivour cleane acquited and dischardged of the Cryme, By which meanes the Theves are greatlye encoraged to steale and theire maynteiners emboldened to receaue theare stealthes knowinge howe hardely they Cane be broughte to anye triall of lawe/

Eudox: Truely this is a greate inconvenience and a greate Cause as youe saie of the mayntenaunce of Theves knowinge theire receyvours allwaies readye. for woulde theare be no receivours theare woulde be no theves, But this me semes mighte easelye be provided for by some Acte of Parlament that the receyvour beinge Convicted by good proffes mighte receaue his triall without the principall/

Iren: Youe saie verye trew *Eudoxus*: but that is allmoste impossible to be Compassed. and hearein allso youe discouer another imperfeccion in the Course of the Comon lawe and firste ordinaunce of the realme for yee knowe that the saide parliment muste Consist of the peres gentlemen

persons./ *C*   persons: *R*   persons. *W*   773 with] to *W*   773 reste] rest. *W*
773 meane tyme] meane-while *W*   773 tyme] tyme, *R*   773 youe] *last two letters worn off C*
774 forwarde] forwards *W*   774 others] others/. *C*   others. *W*   775 Theare is]
There *R*   775 inconveniente] inconvenience *W*   775 for] *om. W*   776 Accessarie]
Accessaryes *CW*   777 triall] tryall, *C*   tryall: *R*   tryall. *W*   778 the Case] to the case,
how it *W*   778 falleth] falleth out *W*   778 in] *P resumes at this point*   779 other]
om. RW   780 and] and yette *CRW*   782 handled] hanted *C*   782 perhaps is]
is perhaps *W*   783 time] *om. R*   784 sufficiently] suffycient *R*   786 of of] óf *CRW*
787 Course] cause *R*   788 standeth] standing *W*   789 rebellion] rebells *C*   790 can be gotten]
is taken *R*   791 Cryme,] crime. *W*   794 of lawe] *om. C*   795-6 as youe saie]
(as you say) *W*   797 woulde theare be] were there *W*   798 me semes] (me seemes) *W*
800 principall/] principall *C*   801 that] this *C*   804 the peres] peres *C*

freehoulders and Burgesses of that realme it self, Nowe these beinge perhaps themselves or the moste parte of them as maye seme by theire stiffe withstandinge of this Acte, Culpable of this Cryme or favorers of theire friendes which are suche by whom theire kitchens are somtymes amended, will not suffer anye suche statute to passe yeat hathe it oftentymes bene attempted And in the tyme of Sr Iohn Perrott verye earnestlye I remember, labored but by no meanes, coulde be effected And not onely this but manye other like which are as nedefull for the reformacion of that realme/ |

Eudox: This allsoe is surelye a greate defecte but we maye not talke youe saie of the redressinge of this vntill our seconde parte come which is purposelye appointed therevnto Therefore procede to the recountinge of more suche evills yf at leaste youe haue anie more/

Iren: Theare is allsoe a greate inconvenience which hathe wroughte greate damage bothe to her maiestie and to that Comon wealthe thoroughe Closse and Coullorable conveyaunces of the Landes and goodes of Traytors felons and fugitives And when one of them mindeth to goe into rebellion he will Convaye awaye all his Landes and Lordeshipps to feffees in truste wheareby he reserveth to himselfe but a state for terme of liffe which beinge determined either by the sworde or by the halter theire Lande streight Cometh to their heire and the Quene is defrauded of the intente of the lawe which laied that grevous punishement vppon Traytours to forfeite all theire Landes to the Prince to the ende that men mighte be the rather terrefyed from Comittinge Treasons, for manye which woulde little esteme of theire owne lives yeat for remorse of theire wives and Children shoulde be withhelde from that haynous Cryme, This appeared plainlye in the late Earle of desmonde, for before his breakinge forthe into open rebellion he had Conveyed secretlye all his Landes to feffees of truste in hope to haue Cutt of her maiestie from the escheate of his Landes

Eudox: yea but that was well ynoughe avoided for the Acte of Parlament which gave all his Landes to the Quene did (as I haue harde) Cutt of and frustrate all suche Conveyaunces as had anye time by the space of xij

805 self,] self *C* self. *RW* 806-7 as . . . Acte] (as . . . Acte) *CRW* 809 passe] Passe: *C* passe, *R* passe. *W* 810 Perrott] Parratt *G* Parott *R* 811 I remember] (I remember) *W* 811 by . . . coulde] could by no meanes *W* 812 other] others *C* 815 youe saie] (you say) *W* 815 of this] of of this *R* 816 therevnto] therunto, *CR* thereunto. *W* 817 of more] of moe *R* 817 more/] more *C* 819 maiestie] maiestes *R* 821 And] As *CRW* 824 Lande] lands *W* 825 their] the *R* 827 Landes] Lande *C* 827 be the rather] the rather be *W* 828 Comittinge] Comitted *C* 829 shoulde] would *W* 830 Cryme,] Cryme *C* crime. *W* 833 maiestie] maiesties *C* 833 Landes] landes. *CW* landes: *R* 835 did (as . . . harde)] (did as . . . hard *R* 836 anye]

yeares before his rebellion bene made within the Compasse wheareof that fraudulent feffment and manye other the like of his Accomplicies and fellow traytours weare Contayned

Iren: Verye trewe but howe hardelye that Acte of Parlament was wronge out of them, I cane wittnes and weare it to be passed againe, I dare vndertake woulde | never be Compassed, But weare it soe that suche Actes mighte easelye be broughte to passe againste traitours and felones yeat weare it not an endles trouble that no traytour nor felon shoulde be attainted But a Parlament muste be Called for bringinge his Landes to the Quene which the Comon lawe giveth her

Eudox: Then this is no faulte of the Comon lawe but of the persons which worke this fraude to her maiestie

Iren: yeas marye for the Comon Lawe hathe lefte them this bennefitt wheareof they make advantage and wreste to theire badd purposes, So as they are theareby the bolder to enter into evill accions knowinge that if the worste befall them they shall lose nothinge but themselves whearof they seme surelye verye Careles like as all barbarous people are, as Cesar in his Comentaries saith verye fearlesse of death

Eudox: But what meane youe of fugitives herein or how doeth this Concerne them

Iren: yeas verye greatlie for ye shall vnderstand that theare be manye ill disposed and vndewtifull persons of that realme like as in this pointe there are allsoe in this realme of Englande to manye which beinge men of good inheritance are for dislike of the religion or daunger of the lawe into which they are rvnne or discontent of the presente gouernement fled beyonde the Seas wheare they live vnder princes that are her maiestes professed enemyes and Converse and are Confederate with other Traytours and fugitives which are theare abidinge, The which neuerthelesse haue

the bennefitt and proffittes of theire Landes heare by pretence of suche 865
Colorable Conveyaunces theareof formerlye made by them to theire privye
friendes heare in truste whoe | secretelye doe sende ouer vnto them
the saide revenewes whearewith they are theare mayntayned and enhabled
againste her maiestie

Eudox: I doe not thinke that theare be anye suche fugitives which are 870
relieved by the profitt of theire Landes in Englande, for theare is a
streighter order taken And if theare be anye suche in Irelande, it weare
good that it weare likewise loked vnto for this evill maye easelye be
remedied But proceed/

Iren: It is allsoe inconvenient in that realme of Irelande that the wardes 875
and mariadges of gentelmens Children shoulde be in the disposicion of
anie of those Irishe lordes as now theye are by reason that theire landes
are helde by knightes service of those Lordes, by which meanes yt Comethe
to passe that those saide gentlemens children beinge thus in the warde of
those Lordes are not onelye theareby broughte vp lewdelye and Irishe like 880
but allsoe for euer after soe bounden to theire services as that they will run
with them vnto anye disloyall accion/

Eudox This grevance *Iren*: is allsoe Complained of in Englande, but
howe Cane it be remedied since the service muste followe the Tenure of
the Landes and the landes weare given awaie by the kinges of Englande 885
to those Lordes when they firste conquered that realme, And to saie truethe
this allsoe woulde be some preiudice to the Prince in her wardeshipps/

Iren: I doe not meane this by the Princes wardes but by suche as fall into
the handes of Irishe Lordes for I Coulde wishe and this I woulde enforce
that all those wardeshipps weare in the Pinces disposicion | ffor then 890
it mighte be hoped that she for the vniuersall reformacion of that Realme,
woulde take better order for the bringinge vp of those wardes in good
nourture and not suffer them to Come into so bad handes; and thoughe
these thinges be allreadie passed awaie by her Progenitours former grauntes
vnto those saide Lordes, yeat I Coulde finde a waye to remedye a great 895
parte theareof, as heareafter when fitt time servethe shall appeare, And

abiding. *W*   865 bennefitt] benefits *W*   866 to] unto *W*   867 secretelye] privily *W*
867 doe] *om. R*   869 maiestie] maiestie./. *C*   maiestie: *R* Majestie. *W*   873 that]
om. W   874 remedied] remedied, *C*   remedyed: *R* remedied. *W*   875-940 *Iren*:
.... enforced/] *om. with two and a quarter pages blank C om. with most of one page blank P*
875 in that] in the *RW*   878 are] bee *W*   878 Lordes,] Lordes as now they *R*   Lords. *W*
878 Comethe] comes *W*   879 saide gentlemens children] Gentlemen *W*   881 bounden]
bound *W*   881 as that] *om. W*   882 vnto] into *RW*   884 remedied] remedied? *W*
884 Tenure] tennor *R*   887 wardeshipps] wardshipp *R*   888 wardes] ward *R*   889 of]
of the *R*   889 woulde] could *W*   890 Pinces] princes *RW*   892 the ... of]
bringing up *W*   893 thoughe] although *W*   896 servethe] serves *W*

since we are entred into speache of suche grauntes of former princes to sundrie persones of that Realme of Irelande, I will mencion vnto youe some other of like nature to this and of like inconvenience by which the former kinges of Englande passed vnto them a greate parte of theire prerogative which thoughe then it weare well intended and perhaps well deserued of them which receaued the same, yeat now suche a gapp of mischiefe lyethe/ open theareby as I Coulde wishe weare well stopped, Of this sorte are the grauntes of Countye Pallantines in Irelande, which thoughe at firste weare graunted vppon good Consideracion when they weare firste Conquered, for that those landes laie then as a verye border to the wilde Irishe, subiecte to Continewall invacion, so as it was nedefull to giue them greate priuiledges to the defence and thinhabitance theareof, yeat now that it is no more a border, nor frontierd with enemies why shoulde suche priviledges be anie more continewed

Eudox: I woulde gladlie knowe what ye Call a Countye Pallantine and whence it is so Called/

Iren: It was as I suppose firste named Palatine of a pale, as it weare a pale and defence to theire inner landes so as now it is Called the Englishe pale, And thereof allso is a Palsgrave named that is an Earle Palcatine/ | Others thinke of the Latine Palare that is to forrage or outrunne because those marchers and borderers vse Comonlye so to doe, So as to haue a Countie Pallatine is in effecte but to haue a priviledge to spoile the enemies borders adioyninge. And surelye so it is vsed at this daie as a priviledged place of spoiles and stealthes: for the Countye of Tipperarye which is now the onelye Countye Palatine in Irelande is by abuse of some bad ones made a receptacle to robb the reste of the Countries aboute it by meanes of whose priviledges none will followe theire stealthes, so as it beinge scituate in the verye lapp of all the lande is made now a border which howe inconveniente it is let euerie man iudge. And thoughe that righte noble man that is the Lorde of the libertye, do paine him selfe all that he maie to yealde equall iustice vnto all, yeat Cane there not but

898 that] this *W* 900 former] om. *R* 901 weare] was *W* 903 lyethe/] lyeth *R* lyes *W* 903 as] that *W* 903 wishe] wish it *W* 903 well] om. *R* 903 stopped,] stopped. *W* 904 Countye] the Countie *R* Counties *W* 904 Pallantines] palatines *WD2FGH1HoT* Pallentynes *RD1LN* 907 was] is *R* 908 to the] for the *W* 908 and thinhabitance] of the inhabytantes *RW* 909 it] om. *R* 909 nor] but *R* 910 continewed] contynewed:/ *R* continued? *W* 911 Pallantine] Pallentine *RLD1* palatine *WD2FGH1HoLNT* 912 is] om. *W* 913 as I suppose] (I suppose) *W* 913 Palatine] Pallantine *H2* Pallentine *D1* 913 weare] were of *R* 914 theire] the *R* 914 inner] inward *W* 914 landes] landes. *R* 914 now] om. *W* 915 thereof allso] therefore *W* 915 that is] om. *W* 915 Palcatine/] *Palantine G* Palentyne *RAD1LN* Palatyne, *H1D2FH2HoT* Palatine. *W* 916 Palare] word *Patere F* 917 doe,] doe. *W* 918 Pallatine] Pallentyne, *R* 918 but] om. *W* 920 Tipperarye] Typparie *H1* Typperare *H2* 921 Palatine] Pallantyne *H2* palentine *A* 922 Countries] Counties *W* 924 scituate] siituate *W* 924 lapp] Topp *R* 926 of the] of that *R* 927 that] om. *W*

greate abuses lurke in so inwarde and absolute a priviledge, the Consideracion wheareof, is to be respected Carefullie for the nexte succession, And muche like vnto this graunte theare are allsoe other priviledges graunted vnto moste of the Corporacions theare that they shall not be bounde to anie other gouernement then theire owne, that they shall not be Chardged with anie garrissons, that they shall not be travelled forthe of theire owne franchises, that they maie buy and sell with theves and rebells, that all amerciamentes and fines which shalbe imposed vppon them shall come vnto themselues, All which thoughe at the time of theire firste graunte they weare tollerable and perhaps reasonable, yeat now are moste vnresonable and inConveniente/ But all these will easelie be cutt of with the superiour power of her maiestes prerogative againste which her owne grauntes are not to be pleaded nor enforced/ |

Eudox now trulye *Irenius* ye haue (me semes) verye well handled this pointe towchinge inconveniences in the Comon lawe theare, by youe observed, and it semeth that youe haue had a mindefull regarde vnto the thinges that maye Concerne the good of that realme And if yee Can aswell goe thoroughe with the Statute lawes of that lande I will thinke youe haue not loste all your time theare, Therefore I praye youe now take them to youe in hande and tell vs what ye thinke to be amisse in them:

Iren: The Statutes of that realme are not manye and thearefore we shall the sooner run thoroughe them. And yeat of those fewe theare are sundrie impertinente and vnnessessarye the which perhaps thoughe at the time of the makinge of them weare verye nedefull, yeat now thoroughe Change of time are Cleane antiquated and alltogeather idle As that which forbideth anye to weare theire beardes all one the vpper lipp and none vnder the Chinn And that which putteth awaie, saffron shirtes and smockes. And that which restrainethe vsinge of guilte bridles and pittorels, And that which appointed to the recorders and Clarkes of dublin and drodagh to take but ijd for the Copie of a plainte and that which Comaundeth bowes and arrowes, and that which makethe that all Irishe men which shall con-

verse amongest the englishe shalbe taken for spies and so punished and
that which forbidethe persons not ameanable to lawe to enter and dis- 960
traine in the landes in which they haue title, and manie other the like I
coulde rehearse/////

Eudox: These trulye which ye haue repeated seme verye ffrivolous and
fruitles for by the breache of them little damadge or inconvenience canne
Come to the Comon wealthe; neither indede if anye transgresse them shall 965
he seme worthie of punishment scarse of blame savinge but for that they
abide by the names of lawes But lawes oughte to be suche as that the
kepinge of them shoulde be greatlye for the behofe of the Comon weale
and the violatinge of them shoulde be verye haynous and sharpelye pun-
ishable, But tell vs of some more weighty dislikes in the statues then these, 970
and that maye more behooffullye importe the reformacion of them/ |

f. 17ᵛ *Iren.* Theare is one or Two statutes which make the wrongefull distreyn-
inge of anye mans goodes againste the forme of Comon lawe to be felonye,
The which statutes seme surelye to haue bene at firste mente for the greate
good of that realme and for restrayninge of a foule Abuse which then 975
raigned Comonlye amongest that people, and yeat is not alltogeather
laied aside, that when anye one was indebted to another he woulde firste
demaunde his debt and if he weare not paied he woulde streighte goe and
take a distresse of his goodes or Cattells wheare he Coulde finde them to
the valewe, the which he woulde kepe till he weare satisfied And this the 980
simple sorte as they Call them dothe Comonlye vse to doe yeate thoroughe
Ignoraunce of his misdoinge or evill vse that hathe longe setled amongest
them, But this thoughe it be sure moste vnlawfull, yeat surelye me semes
to harde to make it deathe, since theare is no purpose in the partie to steale
the others goodes or to Conceale the distresse but dothe it openlye for the 985
moste parte before wittnesses And againe the same Statutes are so slacklye
penned and besides that later of them is vnsenciblye Contrived that it scarse
Carryeth anye reason in it, that theye are often and verye easelye wrested
to the fraude of the subiecte, as if one goinge to distreine vppon his owne

shall *R*   959 amongest] amonge *RW*   959 englīshe] *Englishmen F*   960 forbidethe]
forbids *W*   960 not] *om. W*   961 which] the which *R*   961 title] little *R*   961 I]
which I *R*   966 for] *om. C*   967 the names] that name *W*   970 statues] states *CR*
statutes *W*   971 maye] maye bee *R*   971 behooffullye importe] behouefull, imparte *R*
972 wrongefull] wrongfull *with last two letters worn off C*   973 felonye,] fellony. *W*
974 greate] *om. W*   978 demaunde] demaund demaund *C*   979 or] and *C*   979 Cattells]
Chattles *H2AD2GNT*   cattell *W*   980 the which] which *RW*   980 this] *om. C*
981 sorte] Chorte *C*   Churle *RW*   981 as ... them] (as ... him) *CW*   (as ... him, *R*
981 doe] doe, *RW*   983 me semes] (me seemes) *W*   987-8 and ... it,] (besides
... yt) *CW*   987 that later] that latter *GL*   the latter *H2*   the letter *N*   the later *W*
987 is] is so *RW*   987 it] is *C*   989 owne] *om. R*

A VIEW OF THE PRESENT STATE OF IRELAND 77

lande or tenemente wheare lawfullye he maye yeat if in doinge theareof 990
he trassgresse the leaste pointe of the Comon lawe he streighte Comitteth
ffelonye, Or if one by another occasion take anye thinge from another As
boyes vse somtimes to Capp one another the same is streighte felonye,
This is a verye harde Lawe/

Eudox: Neuerthelesse the evill vse of distreyninge another mans goodes 995
youe will not denye but is to be abolished and taken awaye/

Iren: It is soe but not by the takinge awaye the subiecte withall, for that
is to violente a medicine: speciallye this vse beinge permitted and made
lawfull to some and to other some deathe. As to moste of the Corporate
f. 18ʳ Townes theare it is graunted by theire Charter that | They maye 1000
everye man by himself without an officer (for that weare more Tollerable)
for anie debte distreine the goodes of anye Irishe beinge founde within
theire libertye or but passinge thoroughe theire Townes. And the firste
permission of this was for that in those times when that graunte was made
the Irishe weare not amenable to lawe, soe as it was not safetye for the 1005
townes man to goe to him forthe to demaunde his dett nor possible to
drawe him into lawe, soe that he had leave to be his owne Baylliffe to arrest
his saide dettours goodes within his owne franchise, The which the Irishe
seinge, thoughte it as lawfull for them to distreine the Townes mans good
in the Countrye wheare the founde it, And so by ensample of that graunte 1010
to Townesmen they thoughte it lawfull and made it a vse to distreine one
anothers goodes for smalle debtes And to saye truethe me thinkes it harde
for euerye trifflinge dett of ij or iijˢ to be driven to lawe, which is so farr
from them somtymes to be soughte, for which me thinkes it an heavye ordi-
naunce to give deathe, especiallye to a rude man that is ignoraunte of lawe 1015
and thinketh a Common vse or graunte to other men a lawe for himself.

Eud: Yea but the Iudge when it Cometh before him to triall maye easelye
decide this doubte and laye open the intente of the Lawe by his better
discrecion/

991 trassgresse] transgresse *CRW*   992-3 Or . . . felonye,] *om. R*   992 by another]
by any other *W*   993 felonye,] fellony. *W*   995 the] that *W*   995 another] of another *W*
996 is] it is *CW*   997 by the] by *CRW*   999 and . . . some] *om. C*   999 deathe.]
deathe, *CR*   1000 Townes] townes, *R*   1002 debte] debte to *RW*   1002 Irishe]
Irisheman *D2FN*   1006 forthe] for *C*   1006-7 to drawe] drawe *R*   1008 franchise,]
franchese. *W*   1008 Irishe] Irisheman *D2F*   1009 good] goodes *CW*   1010 the founde]
they founde *CRW*   1010 by] *om. R*   1011 a] an *R*   1011 one] on *W*   1013 trifflinge]
tryfline *R*   1014 thinkes] thinketh *W*   1014 it] yt were *R*   1014 an heavye] too
heavy an *W*   1016 thinketh] thinketh that *W*   1016 men] men, is *W*   1016 himself.]
him self, *C*   1017 Eud:] *added in margin in different hand E om. and no new paragraph C*

Iren: yea but it is daungerous to leave the sence of a lawe vnto the reasone or will of the Iudge whoe are men and maye be miscaried by affeccions and manye other meanes But the lawes oughte to be like stonye tables playne stedfaste and vnmoveable. Theare is allsoe suche another statute or twoo which ordeyne coignye or Liuerye to be treasone, no lesse inconvenient then the former, beinge as it is penned, howeuer the firste purpose theareof weare expediente for thereby now no man cane goe vnto anye other mans howse for lodginge nor to his owne Tennantes house to take victuall by the waye notwithstandinge that theare is no other meanes, for him to haue | Lodginge nor horsemeate nor manns meate, theare beinge no Innes, nor non otherwise to be boughte for money but that he is endaungered to the statute of treasone when soeuer he shall happen to fall out with his Tenante or that his saide hoste liste to Complaine of greevance As oftentimes I haue sene them verye malicyouslye doe thorowe the leaste provocacion

Eudox: I doe not well knowe, but by gesse what they doe meane by theise Tearmes of *Coigny* and *Liuery* Therefore I praye youe explaine them

Iren: I knowe not wheather the wordes be Inglishe or Irishe but I suppose them rather to be ancient Englishe for the Irishe men Cane make no derivacion nor analoge of them; what Liuerye is we by Comon vse in Englande knowe well ynoughe namely that is Allowinge of Horsemeat as they Comonlye vse the worde in stablinge as to kepe horses at Liuerye the which worde as I ghesse is derived of liveringe or deliveringe forthe theire nightlye foode, Soe in greate howses the liverye is saide to be served vp for all nighte that is theire Eveninges allowance of drinke, And liuerye is allsoe Called the vpper garment which a servingeman weareth so Called as I suppose for that it was deliuered and taken from him at pleasure Soe it is apparante that by the worde Liuerye is theare mente horsemeate, like as

---

1020 a] the *W* 1021 affeccions] effeccons *R* 1022 the] *om. C* 1022 like] like to *CR*
1023 vnmoveable.] imoveable, *CR* 1024 ordeyne] *inserted between lines E* make *CRW*
1024 coignye] *Coygne A* *Coigine H2* Coigne *LD1* *Cognie N* 1024 or] and *W*
1025 the firste] the the firste *C* 1026 vnto] into *W* 1026-7 anye other mans] anothers *R*
another mans *W* 1028 meanes,] meanes *RW* 1028-9 for him] *om. C* 1029 Lodginge
nor] lodginge or *R* 1031 to the] to that *R* by that *W* 1031 of] for *W* 1034 provocacion] provocacion:/ *C* provocations:/ *R* provocation. *W* 1035 they] ye *RW*
1036 *Coigny*] *Coygne A* Coigne *LD1* *Cognie N* 1036 Liuery] Lyuerye, *RW*
1036 them] them:/ *R* them. *W* 1038 rather to be] to bee rather *W* 1039 nor]
or *R om. W* 1039 analoge] *blank space P* anolie *R om. W* 1039 them;] them, *CR*
1039 what] what, *C* 1039-40 in Englande] doe *R* 1040 namely] *om. R* 1040 is
Allowinge] it is allowance *CRW* 1041 they Comonlye] comonlye they *R* 1041 stablinge]
stabline *R* 1042 as] *om. W* 1042 forthe] for *C* 1043 foode,] foode: *W* 1044 of]
for *W* 1045 vpper] proper *R* 1045 garment] *written small as if inserted in space
left blank E* *blank space C* weede *W* 1045-6 as I suppose] (as I suppose) *W*
1046 and] at *R* 1046 pleasure] pleasuer./ *C* pleasure: *RW* 1047 worde] wordes *R*

by *Coigny* is vnderstoode manns meate, But whence the worde is derived is verye harde to tell, Some saye of Coyne for that they vsed Comonlye in theire *Coignies* not onelye to take meate but Coyne allsoe and that that takinge of money was speciallye mente to be prohibited by that Statute: But I thinke rather, that this worde *Coigny* is derived of the Irishe The which is a Comon vse amongest the Irishe Landelordes to haue a Comon spendinge vppon theire Tennantes, for all theire Tennantes beinge Comonlye but Tennantes at will they vse to take of them what victualls they liste, for of victells they | weare wonte to make small reckoninge neither in this was the Tennante wronged for it was an ordinarye and knowne Custome, and his Lorde Comonlye vsed so to Covennant with him, which if at anye time the tenant disliked he mighte frelye departe at his pleasure, But now by this statute the saide Irishe Lorde is wronged for that he is Cutt of from his Customarye services of the which this was one besides manye other of the like as Cuddie Cossherie, Bonnaaght, Sragh, forehin and suche others the which I thinke at firste weare Customes broughte in by the Englishe vppon the Irishe the which weare never wonte and yeat are loathe to yealde anye Certaine rente but onlye suche spendinges, for theire Comon sayinge is *Spende me and defende me*

Eudox: Surelye I take it as youe saie that thearein the Irishe Lorde hathe wronge since it was an antiente Custome and nothinge Contrarye to lawe, for to the willinge theare is no wronge done, And this righte well I wott that even heare in Englande theare are in manye places as lardge Customes as that of *Coigny* and Liverye, But I suppose by your speache that it was the firste meaninge of the statute to forbide the violent takinge of victells vppon other mens tennantes againste theire wills which surelye is a greate outrage and yeat not so greate me semes as that it shoulde be made Treasone, ffor Consideringe that the nature of Treasone is Concern-

1048 *Coigny*] Coign *D1*   Coygine *H2*   the word *Coigny WA*   1049 verye] *om. W*
1049 tell,] tell *C*   tell: *RW*   1049 of] *om. C*   1049 Comonlye] Comodytie *R*
1050 *Coignies*] Coygnes *H2*   Coignes *LD1*   Coignice *T*   1050 that that] that *CW*
1052 rather] *om. C*   1052 that] *om. W*   1052 *Coigny*] Coygne *H2*   Coigne *D1*
Coggnic *T*   1052 Irishe] Irish. *W*   1053 is a] is *R*   1053 the Irishe Landelordes]
Land-lords of the *Irish W*   1053 Landelordes] landholders *C*   1054 vppon theire]
vpon theire, *R*   1055 they] the *C*   1055 victualls] victuall *R*   1057 an] an an *R*
1060 saide] *om. R*   1062 Cuddie] Cuddeehih *A*   Enddie *G*   1062 Cossherie]
Cosshirh *A*   Cossheire *C*   Ensherie *G*   1062 Bonnaaght] Bonnaght *C*   Boomaught *D2*
Boomaght *F*   Bundaght *G*   Bonnaught *H2AN*   Bonnagh *RD1*   1062 Sragh] *blank space A*
om. D2F   Stragh *H2Ho*   Stiragh *N*   Shragh *T*   Shrah *W*   1063 forehin] *blank space A*
ffrehin *D1*   fforehim *G*   Brehim *H2*   Fehin *Ho*   Brehin *N*   Sorehin *W*   Fonichin *T*
1063 I thinke] (I thinke) *W*   1063 at . . . Customes] were customes at first *W*
1064 broughte] brought brought *C*   1064 the which] for they *W*   1066 sayinge]
sayinge, *R*   1066 *defende me*] defende me../. *C*   defende me: *R*   defend me. *W*
1067 Lorde] Lord, *R*   1069 And] And, *C*   1070 heare in] herein *C*   1072 of the]
of that *C*   1072 statute] state *R*   1074 me semes] (mee seemes) *W*

inge the royall estate or persone of the Prince or practizinge with his enemyes to the derogacion and daunger of his Crowne and dignitye it is hardelye wrested to make this Treasone, But as youe erste saide, *Better a mischiefe then an Inconvenience*

Iren: Another statute I remember which havinge bene an | Aunciente Irishe Custome is nowe vppon Advizement made an Englishe Lawe and that is Called the Custome of kincongishe which is that everye heade of every septe and everye Chiefe of everye kindred or familye shoulde be answeareable and bounde to bringe forthe euerye one of that kindred or sept vnder him at all times to be iustified when he shoulde be required or Chardged with anye treason felonye or other haynous Cryme,

Eudox: Whye surelye this semes a verye necessarye lawe for Consideringe that manye of them be suche Losels and scatterlinges as that they Cannot easelye by anye Sheriffe, Constable, Bayliffe or other ordinarye officer be gotten when they are Challendged for anye suche facte this is a verye good meanes to gett them to be broughte in by him that is the heade of the septe or Chiefe of that howsse whearefore I wonder what iuste excepcion ye Cane make againste the same

Iren: True *Eudoxus* in the pretence of the good of this Statute yee haue nothinge erred, for it semethe verye expediente and necessarye, But the hurte which Comes theareby is greather then the good, ffor whilste everye Chief of a septe standethe so bounde to the lawe for everye man of his blodd or septe that is vnder him, *inclusive* everye one of his septe is put vnder him, and he made greate by the Comaundinge of them all, ffor if he maye not commaunde them then that lawe dothe wronge that bindeth him to bringe them forthe to be Iustifyed, And if he maye Comaunde them then he maye Comaunde them aswell to ill as to good, Heareby the Lordes and Captaines of Countries the principalles and heades of septes are made stronger whom it shoulde be a moste speciall care in policye to

---

1078 as . . . saide] (as . . . said) *W*   1079 *Inconvenience*] Inconvenience/ *C*   Inconuenienc: *R*   inconvenience. *W*   1081 Irishe] Englishe *H2AGN*   1081 an Englishe] a *W*   1081 Englishe] Irishe *H2AGN*   1082 kincongishe] Kincorgishe *D1*   Kinconglish *F*   Kingcongishe *N*   Kincougish *RL*   Kin-cogish *WA*   1083 or] of *C*   1084-6 answeareable . . . Cryme,] required *R*   1084-5 answeareable . . . shoulde be] *om. Ho*   1084-5 kindred or sept] sept and kinred *W*   1085 him] it *W*   1086 Cryme,} Cryme/: *C*   crime. *W*   cryme/≡/ Done or Commytted by any of his allyes or householde *Ho*   1087 Whye] Why? *W*   1089 Sheriffe] shreif *C*   1092 of the] or of the *R* of that *W*   1093 iuste] deepe *R*   1093 same] same: *C*   same:/ *R* same. *W*   1094 *Eudoxus*] Edox: *R*   1096 Comes] cometh *CW*   1097 a] *om. C*   1097 man] man that is *R*   1098 him, *inclusive*] him inclusiue *R*   1098-9 *inclusive* . . . him] *om. W*   1099 and he] he is *W*   (*Faults escaped*)   1100 bindeth] bindeth that bindeth *C*   1102 good,] good. *W*   1103 Countries] the Countryes *R*   1103 principalles] principall *W*   1103 heades]

weaken and to set vpp and strengthen diuerse of his vnderlinges againste
which whensoeuer he shall | Offer to swarve from duetye maye be
hable to bearde him; ffor it is verye daungerous to leave the Commaund
of soe manye as some septes are, beinge v or vj thowsand persones to the
will of one man whoe maye leade them to what he will as he him selfe
shalbe inclyned

Eudox: In verye dede *Irenius* it is verye daungerous especiallye seinge
the disposicion of those people not allwaies inclynable to the best; And
therefore I houlde it no wisdome to leave vnto them to muche Comaunde
over theire kindred but rather to withdrawe theire followers from them
as muche as maye be and to gather them vnder the Comaunde of lawe by
some better meane then this Custome of kincongish The which worde I
woulde be gladd to knowe what it namelye signifieth for the meaninge
theareof I seme to vnderstande reasonable well

Iren: It is a worde mingled of Englishe and Irishe togeather so as I ame
partelye led to thinke that the Custome theareof was firste Englishe and
after warde made Irishe, ffor suche another lawe they had heare in Eng-
lande as I remember made by kinge *Alured* that everye gentelman shoulde
Continuallye bringe forthe his kindred and followers to the lawe so kin
is Englishe and *Conghish* signifyethe *Affinitye* in Irishe/

Eudox: Sithe then that we haue thus reasonablie handled the inconveni-
ences in the Lawes let vs now passe vnto your seconde parte which was
as I remember of the Abuses of Customes in which me semes ye haue a
faire Champian laide open vnto youe, in which yee maye at lardge stretche
out your discourse into manye swete remembraunces of Antiquityes from
whence it semeth that the Customes of that nacion proceeded |

Iren: Indeed *Eudoxus* youe saie verie trewe for all the Customes of the
Irishe which I haue often noted and Compared with that I haue redd
woulde minister occacion of a moste ample discourse of the firste originall

heade *C*   1105 againste] against him *RW*   1108 thowsand] hundreth *F*   1110 shalbe] is *R*
1110 inclyned] inclyned./. *C*   inclined. *W*   1111 especiallye] *om. W*   1112 not] is not *W*
1116 kincongish] *Kingonlish F*   *Kinconglishe H1*   Kingcoingishe *N*   *Kin-cogish. WA*
1118 reasonable] reasonablye *CW*   1118 well] well: *CR*   well. *W*   1121 after warde]
afterwardes *RW*   1121 made] *om. R*   1122 Alured] *Alfred F*   *Alarand H2*   Alarad *N*
1123 Continuallye] *om. W*   1123 lawe] lawe, *CR*   Law. *W*   1124 *Conghish*]
Cogish A   *Coughish CD1*   Cougish *L*   1124 signifyethe] *om. W*   1125 *Eudox*:]
inserted above line C   1125 that we] wee that *W*   1126 your] the *W*   1127 as] *om. W*
1130 of] from *C*   1130 proceeded] proceeded./. *C*   procede *R*   proceeded. *W*
1131 *Eudoxus*] End: *D1*   1132 often] verie often *R*   1133 a] *om. R*   1133 firste]

of them and the Antiquitye of that people which in trueth I doe thinke
to be more antiente then moste that I knowe in this eande of the worlde,
so as if it weare in the handlinge of some man of sounde iudgement and
plentifull readinge it woulde be moste pleasante and profitable But it
maye be we maye at some other time of metinge take occacion to treate
theareof more at lardge, heare onelye it shall suffice to tuche suche
Customes of the Irishe as seme offensive and repugnante to the good
government of that realme

Eudox: ffollowe then your owne Course for I shall the better Contente
my selfe to forbeare my desire now in hope that yee will as youe saie some
other time more aboundauntlye satisfie it

Iren: Before we enter into the treatye of theire Customes it is firste nede-
full to Consider from whence they firste spronge, ffor from the sundrie
manners of the nacions from whence that people which now is Called
Irishe weare derived some of the Customes which now remaine amongest
them haue bene firste fetched; and sithence theare Continved amongest
them: ffor not of one nacion was it peopled as it is but of sundrie people
of different Condicions and manners But the Chiefest which haue firste
possessed and inhabited it I Suppose to be Scithians which at suche time
as the Northern nacions ouerflowed all Christendome Came downe to the
sea Coste wheare inquiringe for other Contries abroade and gettinge
intelligence of this Countrye of Irelande fyndinge shippinge Conveniente
passed over hither and Arived in the Northe parte thereof | whiche
is now Called Vlster which firste inhabitinge and afterwarde stretchinge

om. *W* 1134 doe] om. *W* 1135 knowe] do knowe *C* 1139 lardge,] large. *W*
1141 realme] realme./ *C* realme: *R* Realme. *W* 1143 desire] desyre, *R* 1143-4 some . . .
more] om. *R* 1144 it] om. *C* yt:/ *R* it. *W* 1145 treatye] treatise *R* 1146 firste]
om. *R* 1147 now is] are nowe *R* 1148 derived] deuided *R* 1149 firste] om. *R*
1149 fetched] fetche *C* 1149 sithence theare] since they haue bene *R* 1150 it peopled]
that people *R* 1151 Chiefest] cheif *R* 1152 Scithians which] *Scythians*.

Eudox. How commeth it then to passe, that the *Irish* doe derive themselves from *Gathelus* the *Spaniard*?

Iren. They doe indeed, but (I conceive) without any good ground. For if there were any such notable transmission of a Colony hether out of *Spaine*, or any such famous conquest of this Kingdome by *Gathelus* a *Spaniard*, as they would faine believe, it is not unlikely, but that the very Chronicles of *Spaine*, (had *Spaine* then beene in so high regard, as they now have it) would never have omitted so memorable a thing, as the subduing of so noble a Realme to the *Spaniard*, no more then they doe now neglect to memorize their conquest of the *Indians*, specially in those times, in which the same was supposed, being nearer unto the flourishing age of learning and Writers under the *Romanes*. But the *Irish* doe heerein no otherwise, then our vaine *Englishmen* doe in the Tale of *Brutus*, whom they devise to have first conquered and inhabited this Land, it being as impossible to proove, that there was ever any such *Brutus* of *England*, as it is, that there was any such *Gathelus* of *Spaine*. But surely the *Scythians* (of whom I earst spoke) *W* Harvard copy; for " England " read " Albany " in Osgood copy; " in some copies, for *Albany*, read either *Albion* or *England* " *W* (Faults escaped)
1153 Northern] Northen *C* 1156 over] om. *W* 1156 hither] thither *RW* 1157 after-

themselves forthe into the lande as theire numbers increased named it all of themselues Scuttenlande which more brieflye is Called Scuttlande or Scotlande

Eudox: I wonder *Irenius* wheather ye run so farr astraye for whilste we talke of Irelande me thinkes yee ripp vpp the Originall of Scottlande But what is that to this

Iren: Surelye verye muche; for Scotlande and Irelande are all one and the same/

Eudox That semeth more straunge. ffor we all knowe righte well that they are distinguished with a great sea rvnninge betwene them or els theare are two Scottlandes

Iren: Neuerthemore are theare two Scottlandes, but twoe kinde of Scotts theare weare indede as ye maye gather out of *Buckhanan* the one Irin or Irishe Scottes the other Albin Scottes for those Scuttes or Scithians arrived as I saide in the Northe partes of Irelande whence some of them afterwardes passed ouer into the nexte Coaste of *Albyne* now Called Scottlande, which after muche troble they possessed and of themselves named it allsoe Scuttlande. But in processe of time as is Comonlye sene in the denominacion, part prevailed in the whole, for the Irishe Scottes puttinge awaie the name of Scottes weare Called onelie Irishe and the *Albyne* Scottes leavinge the name of *Albyne* weare Called/ onelye scottes. Therefore it Comethe that of some wrighters Irelande is Called *Scotia Maior* and that which now is Called Scotlande is named *Scotia Minor*

warde] afterwardes *RW*   1159 Scuttenlande] *Scutterland AHo*   Scutten—*land F*   1159 or] of *R*   1160 Scotlande] Scotland. *RW*   1161-5 Eudox: ... same/} *om. A*   1161 *Irenius*] (*Irenaeus*) *W*   1161 wheather] whither *C*   1162 me] my *C*   1163 this] this? *CW* this:/ *R*   1164 all] *om. R*   1167 with] with with *C*   1168 Scottlandes] Scotlandes: *C Scotlands. W*   1169-95 two .... agree] twoe: for this which is nowe Called Irelande was ancientlye called Scotlande at which time that which is nowe Scotlande was Called *Albin*. ffor in all ancient Authors Irelande is commenlye Called *Scotia maior*. but in processe of time longe after that the *Scythians* or *Scottes* had possessed the lande, the came into the west (as the Iryshe Cronicles make mention, a certayne people out of Spayne: which inhabited all the west partes of Mounster and Conaght which whether theye were Spaniardes or no it is verye harde to coniecture. *P*   1169 kinde] kyndes *RW*   1169 Scotts] Scotes, *R*   1170 theare] *om. W*   1170 as] (as *W*   1170 Buckhanan] Bucanan *D2* Buchanan *FHo* Buckanon *H2*   Buchanam, *R*   Buchanan) *W*   1171 Scuttes] Scotes *RW*   Cuttes *T*   1171 or] are *W*   1171 Scithians] *Schythians A*   1172 as I saide] (as I suppose *R* (as I said) *W*   1172 Irelande] the Ilande *R*   1172 whence] *inserted between lines E om. C*   where *RW*   1172-3 afterwardes] after *W*   1173 ouer] *om. RW*   1173 *Albyne*] Albany *T*   1174 after muche troble] (after much trouble) *W*   1175 it] *om. W* 1175 allsoe] *om. RW*   1175 Scuttlande] Scotland *RW*   1175 as ... sene] (as ... seene) *W*   1175 as] as it *C*   1175 sene in] sene *with in inserted between lines E* sene *CRW*   1176 denominacion,] denominacon of the *R*   dominion of the *W*   1176 prevailed] prevaileth *W*   1178 Called/] called *CRW*   1178 scottes.] Scottes, *R*   1179 Comethe] commeth thence *W*   1179 Irelande] that Iland *R*   1180 Called] named *R*   1180 is named] is called *R om. W*   1180 *Minor*] minor/. *C*   minor. *W*

Eudox I doe now well vnderstande your distinguishinge of the Two sortes of Scottes and two Scottlandes howe that this which is now Called Irelande was antientlye Called Irin and afterwardes of some written Scutlande And that which is now Called Scotlande was formerlye Called *Albyne* before the Comminge of the Scuts thether | But what other nations Inhabited the other parte of Irelande

Iren: After this people thus planted in the Northe or afore (for the certeintye of times in thinges so farr from all knowledge Cannot be iustlie avowched) Another nacion Comminge out of spaine Arrived in the weste partes of Ireland and findinge it waste or weakelye inhabited possessed it whoe wheather they weare native *Spaniards*, or *Gaules* or *Africans* or *Goths* or some other of those Northeren nacions which did ouerspred all Christendome it is vnpossible to be affirmd, onelye some naked Coniectures maye be gathered, But that out of Spaine certeinlye they Came that doe all the Irishe Cronicles agree

Eudox: ye do verye boldely *Irenius* adventure vppon the historye of so anciente times and leane to Confidentlye vnto those Irishe Cronicles which are moste fabulous and forged in that out of them ye dare take in hande to laye open the originall of a nacion soe antique as that no monument remaynethe of her beginninge and inhabitinge heare speciallye havinge bene allwaies without Lettres but onely bare tradicion of times and remembraunces of bardes which vse to forge and falsefye euerie thinge as they liste to please or displease anie man///

Iren: Trewlye I muste Confesse I doe soe, But yeat not so absolutelye as ye doe suppose do I hearein relye vppon those Bardes or Irishe Cronicles, thoughe the Irishe themselues thoroughe theire Ignorance in matters of Learninge and deper iudgement doe moste Constantlye beleve and Avouch theym, But vnto them besides I add myne owne readinge and out of them bothe togeather with comparison of times likenes of manners and Cus-

1182 is now] now is *W*   1183 Irin] *Erin W*   1183 Scutlande] Scotland *RW*
1184 is now] now is *W*   1185 Scuts] *Scythes W*   1185 nations] nation *W*   1186 parte] partes *RW*   1186 Irelande] Ireland. *C*   Ireland:/ *R*   Ireland? *W*   1187 or afore (for] (or before) for *W*   1187 afore] before *R*   1190 partes] parte *RW*   1190 waste or] waste. *R*   1191 wheather] whither *CR*   1191-2 *Africans* or *Goths*] *Goathes* or *Africans N*   1192 other] *om. R*   1193 vnpossible] ympossible *RW*   1193 be affirmd] affirme *CRW*   1195 agree] agree:/ *C*   agree. *W*   1196 *Eudox*:] *P resumes at this point*   1196 adventure] venture *R*   1196 historye] histories *RW*   1196 so] *om. RW*   1197 vnto] on *W*   1199 a] such a *W*   1200 remaynethe] remaines *W*   1200 and] and first *W*   1200 heare] there *R om. W*   1200 speciallye] especially *W*   1201 allwaies] in those times *W*   1201 tradicion] tradytions *RW*   1205 doe suppose] suppose *R*   suppose. *W*   1205 do I] I doe *RW*   1205 those] *om. C*   1205 Cronicles] Chroniclers *W*   1207 deper] deepe *RW*   1208 theym] *inserted between lines E om. C*   1208 myne] my *R*   1209 with] without *R*   1209 likenes] like-

tomes Affinytie of wordes and names properties of natures and vses resem- 1210
blaunces of rightes and Ceremonies monimentes of Churches and Tombes
and manie other like circumstances I doe gather a likelyhode of truethe,
not certainlye affirminge anye thinge but by Conferringe of times nacions
f. 22ʳ languages | monimentes and suche like I doe hunte out a probabilitye
of thinges which I doe leaue vnto your Iudgement to beleeue or refuse, 1215

wise W   1210 natures] nature C   1211 rightes] rites W   1213 affirminge] affirminge, R
1213 nacions] om. RW   1214 languages] language W   1214 probabilitye] probalitie C
1215 doe] om. CRW   1215 vnto] to W   1215-1330 your . . . . from] the iudgement
of the reader to beeleeue or refuse: but where yee saye theye haue alwayes been without
lettres, yee are therin surelye muche deceved. ffor it is certaine that Irelande hathe had the
vse of lettres verie ancientlye, and longe beefore Englande: in so muche that in the tyme of
                    the Saxons were glad to sende into Irelande for lerned men for their
instruccion: amongest which was sent ouer vnto them *Patricius* commenlye called St *Patricke*:
who comminge into Englande broughte with them the knowlege of letters, and therin
Instructed the *Brytons*. Nowe from the Scythians or Scottes of Irelande they had them not:
for theye were alwayes barbarous and without lettres. Therfore theye had them from the
Africans, whoe were always lettered and muche resemblinge the Iryshe, which nowe increas-
inge in number and in strengthe had beaten the Scottes out of all the westerne partes in to the
northe: for the Sowtherne and Easterne partes were formerlye possessed and peopled of the
Britons and Galls.

Eudox: Doe you then saye that all Irelande was peopled firste of the Scithians, and after-
wardes of the Africans, and from no other nation? This is Contrarie to their owne Cronicles:
for they saye that it was rather peopled by the Spaniardes: and that one Gathelus a Spaniarde
with his brotheren aryvinge heare did firste inhabit it.

Ireni: I did not saye that it was planted onlie of the Scithians and Africans, but princi-
pallye. for that from them twoe cheifelye, I suppose the originall of the Iryshe was derived.
But I am not ignorant that it was inhabited also by sundrye other nations: but yet onlye in
parte, as moste of the Sowtherne Coaste was possessed of the Galls, as maye appeare by somme
of their ancient names beinge Called
which were nations of the Gallye as yee maye reade in   lykewise the
Easterne Coaste and parte of the Sowthe towardes Englande I suppose to haue been peopled
from the Brittons, the which I gather hearbye: for that manye wordes of the Iryshe almoste
are verye Welshe at least Brytyshe (for the Welshe it selfe as I suppose to bee muche
changed from the olde Brytyshe) as fyre is in Welshe Tane: in Iryshe Tuinnye: an heigh
lande in Welshe and Iryshe Tarbert: and Curve Cosh eribord, is bothe Welshe and Iryshe.
also it appearethe by our cronicles, and other olde recordes that Edgar kinge of the Brytons
had vnder his obedience all the Islandes in the northe even to   And lykewise
kinge Arthure had service and homage of them, in which appearethe that Irelande was con-
tained and is also to bee gathered that it receved muche people out of Brytanye, as maye bee
proved bye somme of their names: namelye the Brins the Tooles, the
and manie other, as in his place shalbee shewed. Moreouer I am of opinion that Irelande
receved muche people afterwarde from the Saxons, havinge subdued the Britons. for it is
vsuallye in the Conquest of anye Countrye that manie of the Conquerours doe plant them
selves in the lande of the Conquered. And it is also to bee gathered by verie manie wordes
of Irishe beeinge almost mere Saxon: as for example Marh in Saxon is a horse, marrah in
Iryshe is a horseman, and   to ryde in Iryshe is *gemanus* and so in saxon,
or a commen person. all which thenceforthe tradinge and lyvinge together (the Countrie
beeinge wyde enoughe for them all) grewe in tracte of tyme in to one people. But as for that
idle opinion which somme of them are redye to take vpp of their inhabitinge by Spaniardes,
bothe rather discouer an affeccion to the Spanishe insolencie [inso *repeated at page division*]
and a minde geeven to newefanglenesse then anie shadowe of truthe. ffor yf ther were anie
suche notable transmission of a Colonie hither out of Spayne, or anie suche famous Conquest

Neuerthelesse theare be some verye anciente Aucthours which make mencion onelye of these thinges and some moderne which by Comparinge of them withe the experience of the presente time and theire owne reasone doe open A windowe of great lighte vnto the reste that is yeat vnseene as namelye of the elder, *Caesar, Strabo, Tacitus, Ptotolomie, Plinie, Solinnus,* 1220 *Pomponius Mela and Berosus,* of the later *Vincentius, Æneaes Syluius, Lluddus, and Buckhanan,* of all which I do give moste Credite vnto *Buckhanan,* for that he himselfe beinge an Irishe Scott or Pict by nacion and beinge verye excelentlye learned and Industrious to seke out the truethe of these thinges Concerninge the Originall of his owne people hathe bothe 1225 set downe the Testimonies of the Ancientes truelye, and his owne opinion withall verye reasonablye, thoughe in some thinges he doe somwhat folter. Besides the Bardes and Irishe Cronicles themselues thoroughe desire perhaps of pleasinge to muche, or ignorance of Artes and purer learninge, they haue Clouded the truethe of those times, yeat theare remaynethe 1230 amongest them some relickes of the trewe Antiquitye thoughe disguised, which a well eyde man maye happelye discouer and finde out/

of this kingdome by Gathelus a Spaniarde, as theye woulde fayne beeleive, it is not vnlykelie but that the verie Cronicles of Spaine, had Spaine then been in so heigh regarde, as theye nowe haue it, woulde not haue omitted so memorable a thinge, as the subduinge of so noble a Realme, to the Spaniarde, no more then theye doe nowe neglect to memorize their Conquest of the Indians: speciallie in those times, in which the same was supposed, beinge nearer vnto the floryshinge age of learninge and Wryters vnder the Romans. But the Iryshe doe hearin no otherwise then our vayne Englyshemen doe in the tale of Brutus, whome they devise to haue firste conquered and inhabited this lande, it beeinge as impossible to prove that ther euer was anie suche Brutus of Albanye, as it is, that ther anie suche Gathelus of Spaine. But hearin theye shewe their great lightnes, which beeinge a barbarous and salvage nation, woulde faine fetche them selves from Spaine Lyke as wee and the French also woulde from the Troians: wherin theye muche deceive them selves in their reckninge. for *P*
1215 refuse,] refuse. *W*   1216 which] that *W*   1217 onelye] *om. RW*   1217 these] those *R*   1217-8 of them] them *W*   1218 the experience . . . time] the presente tymes experience *R* present times, experience *W*   1219 windowe of great] greate windoe of *C*
1220 elder] oulder *R*   elder times *W*   1220 *Strabo*] Strabe *H2*   1220 *Ptotolomie*] *om. A*   Ptolomae *C*   Ptolimie *D1*   Ptolamjus *G*   Ptolome *H1D2F*   Potolonis *H2*   Ptolomei *Ho*   Ptolomis *N*   Ptolomie *RWAL*   Ptolimeus *T*   1220 *Plinie*] Plinius *H1FHo*   Pline *H2*   Plimus *T*   1220 *Solinnus*] Solinas *G om. RWAD1H2LN*   Solnius *T*   1221 *Pomponius Mela*] Pompeius Melo *A*   Pompeius mela *CGH2LN*   Pomponius, Mela *F*   Pompeus, Mela *R*   Pomponis. Mesa *T*   1221 *Berosus*] Beresas *H2*   1221 later] latter *R*   1221 *Vincentius*] Nincen *T*   1221 *Æneaes Syluius*] *Æneas, Syluius CL*   1222 *Lluddus, and*] Luiddus. *T*   Luidus *W*   1222 *Buckhanan*] Buchanam *D1*   Buckanan *H2*   Buchanan *N*   Buchanan *WD2FH1HoT*   1222-3 of . . . *Buckhanan*] *om. W*   1223 *Buckhanan*] Buchanan *FD2H1HoT*   Buckanan *H2*   Buckhaname *N*   Buckhanam *R*   1223 for] *om. R*   1223 Pict] Pick'e *D2*   Picke *G*   Pike *RLD1*   1225 these] all *W*   1226 Testimonies] testimony *W*   1226 Ancientes truelye] Auncientes truthe *C*   1227 withall] together withall *W*   1227 doe] doth *RW*   1227 folter.] folter, *C*   flatter: *R*   flatter. *W*   1228 Cronicles] Chronicles *W*   1228 thoroughe] thoughe thorowe *CRW*   1228-9 perhaps of pleasinge] of pleasinge perhapps *RW*   1229 or] and *RW*   1229 ignorance] ignorances *W*   1229 Artes] arte *R*   1229 purer] pure *R*   1230 Clouded] concluded *R*   1230 times] lines *W*   1230 remaynethe] appearethe *R*   appeares *W*   1231 amongest] among *W*   1232 which] with *R*

Eudox How Cane theare be anie truethe in them at all since the ancient nacions which firste inhabited Irelande weare alltogeather destitute of Lettres muche more of learninge by which they mighte leave the veritye of thinges written, And those Bardes Comminge allsoe so manye hundred yeares after Coulde not knowe what was done in former ages nor deliuer certeintye of anye thinge but what they finde out of theire owne vnlearned heades// |

Iren: Those Bardes indeed as *Caesar* wrighteth deliuer no certaine truethe of anie thinge neither is theare anye houlde to be taken of anye Antiquitye which is receaued by tradicion since all men be lyars and many lye when they will, But yeat for the Ancientnes of the wrighten Cronicles of the Irishe give me leave to saye somthinge not to iustifye them but to shewe that some of them mighte saye truethe/ ffor wheare ye saie that the Irishe haue allwaies bene without Lettres yea are thearein muche deceaued ffor it is Certaine that Irelande hathe had the vse of lettres verye Ancientlye and longe before Englande//

Eudox: Is it possible? howe Comes it then that they are so barbarous still and so vnlearned beinge soe olde schollers: for Learninge, as the Poet saiethe, *Emollit mores nec sinit esse feros* whence then I praye youe Coulde they haue those Lettres

Iren: It is harde to saie for wheather they at theire firste Comminge into the Lande or afterwardes by tradinge with other nacions which had Lettres learned them of them or devized them amongest themselues it is verye doubtefull But that they had Lettres ancientlye it is nothinge doubtefull ffor the Saxons of Englande are saide to haue fetched theire Lettres and learninge and learned men from the Irishe and that allsoe appearethe by the liknesse of the Character for the Saxon Character is the same with the Irishe Nowe the Scythians never, that I Cane reade of olde, had Lettres amongest them, Therefore it semeth that they had them from that nacion

---

1235 leave] learn ? *Morris* 1238 finde] fayned *CRW* 1238 owne] *om. W*
1238 vnlearned] *om. C* 1240 as] *om. RW* 1240 deliuer] delivered *W* 1241 houlde] certaine hold *RW* 1242 receaued] rereceyued *R* 1242 many] maye *CR* 1243 will, But] will but, *R* wil, *W* 1243 for the] for *R* 1243 Ancientnes] antiquities *W*
1243-4 the Irishe] Ireland *RW* 1245 that the] the *W* 1249 possible?] possible, *CR*
1249 so] soe so *R* 1249-50 barbarous . . . vnlearned] unlearned still *W* 1250 schollers:] schollers? *W* 1250-1 as . . . saiethe] (as . . . saith) *W* 1251 *Emollit*] *Emollet H2*
1251 *feros*] *feros: W* 1251 I praye youe] (I pray you) *W* 1252 they] yow *R*
1252 Lettres] lettres/. *C* lettres::/ *R* letters? *W* 1253 wheather] whither *C* 1255 them of] of *C* 1255 themselues it] themselves, *W* 1256 it] *om. W* 1257 fetched] *om. RW*
1259 Saxon] Saxons *RW* 1260 Irishe] Irishe, *R Irish. W* 1260 that] as *RW*
1260 reade] reade, *W* 1260 olde,] old *W* 1261 Therefore] for *R* 1261 from that]

which Came out of Spaine, ffor in Spaine theare was (as *Strabo* wrighteth) lettres ancientlye vsed | wheather broughte vnto them by the *Phenitians* or the *Persians* which (as it appeareth by him) had some footing theare, or from *Marsiles* which is saide to haue bene inhabited firste of the Grekes and from them to haue had the Greke Character, of which Massilians it is written that the Gaules learned them firste and vsed onelye for the furtheraunce of theire trades and private businesses ffor the Gaules as is stronglye to be proved by manye anciente and verye authenticall writers did firste inhabite all the Sea Coastes of Spaine even vnto Cales and the mouthe of the Streightes and peopled allsoe a greate parte of Italye which appeareth by sundrie Citties and Havens in Spaine Called of them *Portugalia Gallecia Galdumo*

and allsoe by sundrie nacions thearein dwellinge which yeat reserued theire owne names of the Gaules as the

Praesamarci Tamaricj, Nerij, and diuerse others All which *Pomponius Mela* beinge him selfe a Spanyarde, yeat saieth to haue descended from the *Celtie* of ffraunce. wheareby it is to be gathered that that nacion which Came out of Spaine into Irelande weare ancientlye Gaules and that they broughte with them those Lettres which they had learned in Spaine firste into Irelande the which some allsoe saye doe muche resemble the olde Phenitian Character beinge likewise distinguished with pricke and accentes as theire ancient   But the further enquirie heareof nedethe a place of longer discourse then this our shorte Conference/

from the *RW*   1262 (as *Strabo* wrighteth)] as, (Strabo writeth *R*   1263 wheather] whither *C*   1263 vnto] into *CR*   1263-4 *Phenitians*] Venecians *H2*   1264 *Persians*] Percians *GH2*   Parsians *R*   1264 (as] as *C*   1265 *Marsiles*] Marseilles *A*   Mersiles *CHo*   Marsells *D1*   Marcelles *G*   *Marsellre H1*   *Marsilis H2*   Mareides *T*   *Marsellis W*   1265 firste of] by *RW*   1266 which] the which *R*   1266-7 Massilians] marsellians *D1*   Marcelianes *G*   *Mersilians Ho*   marsilianns *RWD2FH1H2LN*   Massihoois *T*   1267 written] said, *RW*   1267 Gaules] Grekes *C*   1267 vsed] used them *W*   1268 businesses] buysiness *C*   busynesse *RW*   1269-70 as . . . writers] (as . . . writers) *RW*   1269 is] it is *C*   1269 verye] om. *W*   1270 Coastes] cost *R*   coast *W*   1270 Cales] Cadiz *H1D2F*   Cades *Ho*   1272 Citties and Havens] havens and cities *W*   1273 of] from *W*   1273 them] them, as *RW*   1273 *Portugalia*] Portingallia *RF*   1273 *Galdumo*] Galduvium *D2*   Galduciū *F*   Galdum *H2AGT*   Galdamon *Ho*   Galdiū *N*   Galduū *R*   Galdunum *W*   1273-4 *blank space*] om. *CRW*   1274 allsoe] om. *C*   1274 yeat] yet haue *RW*   1275 reserued] received *W*   1275-6 *blank space*] Regni *G*   Rhegine *RD1H2NT*   Rhegni *WA*   1276 *Praesamarci*] Praesamerici *C*   Presamaria *D1*   Praesamarchi *D2*   Samarchi *F*   Presamarsi *GT*   Ptesamarei *H2*   Presamariae *N*   Presamarie *RL*   Presamarei *WA*   1276 *Tamaricj*, Nerij*] Nerii. Framarici *D2*   Neri and Framarici *F*   1276 *Tamaricj*] Tamarite *A*   Tamaritie *D1*   Tramarici *H1Ho*   Tamaritiae *N*   Tamariti *RL*   Tamari *W*   1276 *Nerij*] Cineri *W*   1276 others] others. *RW*   1276-7 *Pomponius*] Pomp: *D2*   *blank space F*   Pompeius *G*   Pompeus *R*   1278 *Celtie*] Celtics *A*   Coltie *C*   Colcies *D1*   Celta *D2F*   Celtae *H1*   Celties *H2G*   Colties *RLNT*   Celts *W*   1278 ffraunce.] france, *RW*   1280 had] om. *C*   had anciently *W*   1281 the which] which *W*   1282 Phenitian] *Phornitian D2*   Phunician *T*   1282 accentes] accent *RW*   1283 theire] theires *RW*   1283 ancient] auncien *C*   ancientlie *RW*   1283 *blank space*] om. *CRW*   1283 heareof] thereof *R*

A VIEW OF THE PRESENT STATE OF IRELAND 89

Eudox. Surelye ye haue shewed a great probabilitye of that which I had thoughte ympossible to haue byne proved, But that which ye now saie that Irelande shoulde haue bene peopled with the Gaules semeth muche more strange, ffor all theire Cronicles do saie that the Weste and Southe was possessed | And inhabited of Spanniardes and *Cornelius Tacitus* allsoe dothe strongelye affirme the same All which ye muste either overthrowe and falsifye or renounce your opinion

Iren: Neither so nor so: for these Irishe Cronicles as I saide vnto youe beinge made by vnlearned men and wrightinge thinges accordinge to the apparaunce of the truethe which they Conceaue doe err in the Circumstances not in the matter, ffor all that came out of Spaine, they, beinge no dilligente searchers into the differences of nacions, supposed to be Spaniardes and soe Called them, But the grounde worke theareof is neuerthelesse (as I erste saide) trewe and certaine howe euer they thoroughe ignoraunce disguise the same or thoroughe theire owne vanitye whilste they woulde not seme to be ignoraunte doe thearevppon builde and enlarge manye forged histories of theire owne Antiquitye which they deliuer to fooles and make them beleve them for trewe. As for ensample that firste of one *Gathelus* the sonne of *Cecrops* or *Argus* whoe havinge married the kinge of Egeiptes daughter Thence sayled with her into Spaine and theare inhabited; Then that of Nemed and his ffower sonnes whoe Comminge out of *Scithia* peopled Irelande and inhabited it with his sonnes Twoe hundred and fiftene yeares till he was ouercome of the Geauntes dwellinge then in Irelande And at laste quite banished and roted out, After whome twoe hundred yeares the sonnes of one *Dela* beinge Scithians arrived heare againe and possessed the wholle lande of which the yongest called *Slanius* in the ende made himself *monarch*. Lastlye of the | ffower sonnes of *Milesius* kinge of Spaine which Conquered that Lande from the *Scythyans* and

1288 theire] the *W*   1288 Cronicles] Cronicles, *R*   1289 Spanniardes] Spain *C*
1289-90 allsoe dothe] dothe alsoe *CW*   1290 either] om. *W*   1291 or] or else *W*
1291 opinion] opinion:/ *R*   opinion. *W*   1292 these] the *RW*   1292 as . . . youe]
(as I shewed you) *W*   1294 Conceaue] conceyued *RW*   1295 they,] (they *RW*
1296 nacions,] the nations) *W*   1298 (as . . . saide)] om. *W*   1298 erste saide)]
said *R*   1298 thoroughe] through theire *R*   1299 theire owne] om. *W*   1302 beleve
them] believe *W*   1302 trewe.] true, *C*   true; *W*   1302 ensample] exsample *R*
1303 one] all one *R*   1303 *Cecrops*] *Ceroppes C*   *Cecrosus* D2*F*   Cirops *G*   secrops *N*
Cecroys T   1303 *Argus*] Arosus *G*   *Argos RW*   1304 Egeiptes] Aegistes *C*   Aegiptes *H1*
Egeps *L*   Egipps *R*   Egistes *T*   Egypt his *W*   1304 Thence . . . Spaine] blank space *C*
1304-5 blank space] om. *RW*   1305 Nemed] Memed *G*   Named *H1*   Nemodus *T*
Nemedus *W*   1306 ffower] om. *W*   1306 *Scithia*] Scythia Cominge out of Scythia *R*
1307 his] his ij *R*   1307 fiftene] fyftye *RW*   1307 till] vntil *W*   1308 at] at the *W*
1310 blank space] om. *CRW*   1310 heare] there *RW*   1311 *Slanius*] Slenius AD2*F*
Slauyius D1   Slamius *G*   Stanius H1   1312 *monarch*.] monnarch *R*   1312 of the]
the *C*   1312 *Milesius*] Melesius H2   Nilesius *T*   1313 that] the *W*

inhabitinge it with Spanniardes called it of the name of the yongest *Heberius Hibernia* All which are in truethe meare fables and verye Milesian lyes as the Latine proverbe is, for nether was there euer suche a kinge of Spaine called milesius nor anye suche Colonie state with his sonnes as they faine that Cane euer be proved But yeat vnder these tales yee maye in a manner see the truethe lurke, ffor *Scythians* heare inhabitinge they name And doe speake of Spaniardes, wherby appeareth that bothe those nacions heare inhabited: But wheather verye Spanniardes (as the Irishe greatlye affecte) ys no waies to be proued:

Eudox. whence Comethe it then that the Irishe doe soe greatlye Covet to fetche themselues from the Spaniardes since the oulde Gaules are a more anciente and muche more honorable nacion

Iren: Even of a verye desire of Newfainglenes and vanitye: for beinge, as they are nowe accounted the moste barbarous nacion in Christendome they to avoide that reproche woulde derive themselues from the Spanniardes whom they now see to bee a verye honorable people and nexte borderinge vnto them/ But all that is moste vaine for from the Spaniarde that nowe is or that peaple that nowe inhabites *Spayne* they no waies can prove themselues to discende neither shoulde it indede be greatlye glorious vnto them, ffor the Spaniarde that now is, is come from as rude and salvage nacions, as theare beinge | As it maye be gathered by Course of ages and view of theire owne historye (thoughe they thearein labour muche to ennoble themselues) scarse anye dropp of the oulde Spannishe blodd lefte in them ffor all Spaine was firste Conquered by the Romaines and filled with Collonies from them which weare still increased and the native Spanniarde still Cutt of; Afterwarde the Carthaginians in all the longe *Punick* warrs havinge spoiled all Spaine and in the ende subdued it whollye to

1314 inhabitinge] inhabited *W*   1314 called] and called *W*   1314 of the name] *om. R*
1315 *Heberius*] Heberus *CH1H2N*   Hiberous *D1*   Hiberius *D2FG*   Heberous *RL*   Itiberius *T*
Hiberus *W AHo*   1315 Hibernia] Hebernia *H2*   Itibernia *T*   1315 meare] *om. W*   1316 as
...is,] (as...ys) *R*   1316 Latine] later *W*   1316 nether...euer] was there never *R*
never was there *W*   1317 milesius] Nilesius *T*   1317 state] seate *C*   seated *RW*
1320 doe speake of] put *W*   1320 of] *om. C*   1321 those] these *W*   1321-2 (as...
affecte)] as...affect, *W*   1322 affecte)] effecte, *R*   1322 waies] waye *R*   1325 nacion]
nacion./ *C*   nacion:/ *R*   nation. *W*   1326-8 beinge...woulde] they *W*   1328-9 Spanniardes] Spanyard *R*   1329 whom...see] as seeing them *W*   1329 nexte] neere *W*
1330 the] *P resumes at this point*   1330 Spaniarde] *Spaniards W*   1331 is] are *W*
1331-3 or...now is] *om. R*   1331 inhabites] inhabite *W*   1331 waies] waie *C*
1331 can] *inserted between lines E om. C*   1332 indede] *om. W*   1334 theare] they
there *C*   they, there *RW*   1334 it] there *W*   1335 labour] laboure, *R*   1336 scarse]
havinge scarse *R*   1339 Afterwarde] Afterwardes *RW*   1339 Carthaginians] Carthagnians *C*
1339-41 in...themselues] vnder Hanniball and Asdruball havinge wonne all that Countrye *P*
1340-1 havinge...themselues] (having...themselues) *W*   1340 to] vnto *W*

A VIEW OF THE PRESENT STATE OF IRELAND 91

themselves did (as it is likelye rote out all that weare affected to the Romaines And lastelye the Romaines havinge againe recouered that contrye and beate out Hanniball; did doubtles cutt of all that had favored the Carthagineans so that betwixte them bothe too and fro, theare was scarse a native Spaniarde lefte but all inhabited of Romaines; All which Tempestes of troubles beinge overblowne theare longe after arose a newe storme more dreadfull then all the former which ouerrann all Spaine and made an infinite Confusion of all thinges That was the Comminge downe of the *Gothes* the *Hunnes* and the *Vandales*, And Lastelie all the nacions of *Scithya* which like a mountaine floudd did ouerflowe all Spaine and quite drowne and washe away what ever relickes theare weare lefte of the land bred people yee and of all the Romaines to The which Northerne nacions findinge the Complexcion of that soile and the vehemente heate theare farr differinge from theire natures toke no felicytye | in the Countrie but from thence passed over and did spred themselves into all Countries in Christendome of all which theare is none but hathe some mixture and sprinclinge yf not thoroughe peopleinge of them And yeat after all these the mores and Barbarians breakinge over out of Africa did finallye possesse all spaine or the moste parte theareof And treade downe vnder theire foule heathenishe fete what euer litle they founde theare yeat standinge the which thoughe afterwardes they weare beaten out by *fferdinando* of *Arraggon* and Elizabeth his wiffe yeat they weare not so clensed but that thorogh the mariages which they had made and mixture with the people of the lande duringe theire longe Continvance theare they had lefte no pure dropp of Spannishe blodd no nor of Romayne nor Scithian So that of all nacions vnder heaven I suppose the Spaniarde is the moste mingled moste vncertaine and moste bastardlie, wherefore moste foolishelye do the Irishe thinke to enoble themselues by wrestinge theire ancestrye from the Spaniarde whoe is vnhable to derive him selfe from anye Certeine

1341 (as] as *W*   1341 likelye] likely) *CR*   1343 Hanniball;] *Anniball AG* Hanniball *CRW* Hanniall *H1*   1343 had] *om. W*   1348 thinges] thinges, *R*   things; *W*   1349 *Hunnes*] blank space *HoP*   1349 and the] and *CR*   1350 floudd] fledd *C*   1351 drowne and washe] drownde and washt *RW*   1351 what ever] whatsoever *W*   1351 weare] was *W* 1352 to] too. *W*   1353 Complexcion of that] nature of the *W*   1353 and the] and *C* 1354 theare] thereof *W*   1354 natures] constitutions *W*   1354 the] that *W*   1356 in] of *W* 1357 and] or *W*   1357 thoroughe] throughe *CR*   throughly *W*   1358 these] those *R* 1358 and] and the *W*   1359 treade downe] did tread *W*   1360 theire] the *C*   1360 foule] *om. W*   1360 fete] foote *C*   1360-1 theare yeat standinge] yet there standing. *W* 1361 afterwardes] afterward *R*   after *W*   1362 *Arraggon*] *Arggon C*   1362 Elizabeth] Isabell *A*   1365 nor of] more then of *W*   1365 nor Scithian] nor of *scythian C*   nor Scythan. *R*   or of *Scythian. W*   1366 I suppose] (I suppose) *W*   1367 mingled] mingled, and *W*   1367 and moste bastardlie] *om. W*   1368 theire] the *C*   1368 ancestrye] Auncientry *W*   1369 Certeine] Certeine/. *C*   nacion certaine, *R*   in certaine. *W*

Eudox: youe speake verye sharpelye *Irenius* in dishonour of the Spaniarde whome some other boaste to be the onelye brave nacion vnder the skye/

Iren: Soe surelye he is a verye brave man neither is that which I speake anye thinge to his derogacion ffor in that I saide he is a mingled people is noe dispraise for I theare is no nacion now in Christendome nor muche farther but is mingled and Compounded with others, for it was a singuler providence of god and a moste admirable purpose of his wisdome to drawe those Northerne heathen nacions downe into these Cristian partes wheare they mighte receaue Christianitye and to mingle nacions so remote so miraculouslye to make as it weare one kindred and bloud of all people and eache to haue knowledge of him *Eudox*: Neither haue youe sure anie more | dishonoured the Irishe for youe haue broughte them from verye greate and anciente nacions as anie weare in the worlde howe euer fondlye they affecte the Spanishe ffor bothe the Scithians and the Gaules weare two as mightye nacions as ever the worlde broughte forthe, But is theare anie token denominacion or moniment of the *Gaules* yeat remayninge in Irelande as theare is of the Scithians

1370 dishonour] dispraise *W*   1371 other] others *W*   1371 nacion] soldyer *R*   1371 the skye] skye *R*   1372-3 which ... thinge] any thing which I speake *W*   1373 people] people it *CW*   1373-5 is noe ... mingled] *om. R*   1374 I] I thincke *CW*   1376 admirable] admirall *C* admirall *corrected to* admirable *W* (*Faults escaped*)   1377 those] these *C*   1377 these] those *W*   1378 remote so] remote *W*   1379 kindred and bloud] blood and kindred *W* 1380 him] him/ *C* him: *R* him. *W*   1380 *Eudox*:] *new paragraph CRW*   1383 Spanishe] Spanyard *R*   1383-1451 ffor .... Subieccion/] *Ireni*: I knowe theye doe so: but it is moste vainlye: for by that which I haue heard of some of good iudgment in Irelande, and by that which I my selfe haue observed, it shoulde rather seeme that all those families which you name are descended of the Africans (as I earste shewed you. ffor Maccartye, seemes to haue Come from that was from a Carthaginian: as the worde it selfe seemes to beewraye. for it is in Iryshe written Maccarthaye: Mac, signifiethe a sonne: and Carthaye beeinge almoste verie Carthage: for *y*: and *g*: at in moste languages Changable letters, as in Englyshe *yeue* and *geeue*. *yate* and *gate*: *foryett* and *forgett*.

Eudox: This trulye is a pretye observation. but whence Comes *Odriscoll*?

Ireni: *Dursica* also was a name amongest the Carthaginians, as yee maye reade of one so named, that valientlye served vnder Asdruball in the first Punicke warres, which hathe a great resemblance with Driscall: and is the verye same, but changinge a letter. And as for Osullivant, it maye seeme that hee was first descended ether from the olde Sullaine, or so called of comminge from the Levant sea, as it were Sullevant

Eudox: Since ther is nothinge of this vnlykelye, and yet nothinge but lykelyehoodes: But what of Brourke and Oflahartye?

Ireni: Orourk surelye commes of Rodoricke which some saye is a Spanishe name: and it maye well bee that his ancestor was a Spaniarde: and also that some spaniardes came over with the other Africans, to flye from those troblous times: but it is ancientlye a Scithians name: also as you maye reade in Olaus magnus. and yet all this notwithstandinge, it maye bee that somme partes of the west were inhabited by the Spanishe: as namelye when the Moores invaded the kingdome of Granado and Portugall it is certaine that manie of them fled from the furye of that tyme, and forsakinge their owne Countrye went into other partes: and it might bee came into Irelande, where theye planted, and sythence continewed. but that theye were generallye peopled from Spaine is moste fonde and absurde. *P*
1383 bothe the] both *W*   1383 and the] and *W*   1386 the Scithians] the *Scithians*./ *C*

A VIEW OF THE PRESENT STATE OF IRELAND 93

Iren: yea surelye verye manye for theare is firste in the Irishe language manye wordes of *Galles* remayninge and yeat dailye vsed in Comon speache//

Eudox: whye? what was the Gallishe speache? Is theare anye parte of it still vsed amongest anye nacion 1390

Iren: the *Gallish* speache is the verye *Brittish* the which was generallye vsed heare in all Britany before the Comminge in of the Saxons and yeat is retained of the welchemen the Cornishemen and the *Britones* of ffraunce, thoughe time workinge alteracion of all thinges and the tradinge 1395
and enterdeale with other nacions rounde aboute haue Chaunged and greatlye altered the dialect theareof, but yeat the originall wordes appeare to be the same. As whoe that liste to reade in Cambden and *Buckanan* maye se at large. Besides theare be manye places as havens hills townes and Castells which yeat beare name from the *Galles* of the which *Buck*- 1400
hanan rehearsethe aboue three hundrethe in Scottlande, and I Cane I thinke recounte neare as manye in Irelande. Moreover theare be of the olde *Galles* Certaine nacions yeat remayninge in Irelande which Retaine the olde denominacions of the *Gaules* As the menapij the *Cancij* the venti and others: By all which and manye others verye manye probabilities which 1405
this shorte Course will not suffer to be laied forthe it appearethe that the
f. 26ʳ Chiefe inhabitantes in Irelande weare *Galles* | Comminge thither firste out of *Spayne* and afterwardes from beside Tanais wheare the *Gothes* the *Hunnes* and the *Getes* sate downe they allsoe beinge as it is saide of some) anciente *Galles* And lastlie passinge out of Gallia it selfe from all 1410

Scythians:/ *R* the *Scythians*? *W*   1387-8 for . . . manye] *om. W*   1388 of] of the *W*
1390 whye?] whie *C*   Whie, *R om. W*   1390 Gallishe] Gaules *H2*   1390 speache?]
speache *C*   speech, *W*   1391 amongest] among *W*   1391 nacion] nation: *C* nation? *W*
1392 the *Gallish*] *Gallish C*   1392 was] was verie *CW*   1393 Britany] *England D2F*
Bryttaine *RWGH2LN*   1393 in of] of *CW*   1394 welchemen] Walshman *A*   1394 the
Cornishemen] and Cornishmen *C*   Cornishmen *W*   1395 alteracion] the alterarion *W*
1398 same.] same, *CRW*   1398 that] hath *W*   1398 Cambden] Cambon *C*   1398 and]
or *R*   1398 *Buckanan*] Buckanam *R*   Buchanan *WD2FHo*   1399 large.] large, *C*
1400 name] the names *W*   1400-4 of . . . . Gaules] *om. A*   1400-1 Buckhanan]
Bucaknan *H2*   Buchanan *WD2FHo*   1401 aboue three hundrethe] 200 *G*   above 500. *W*
1401 hundrethe] hundred *CR*   1401 I thinke] (I thinke) *W*   1402 Irelande.] Ireland *C*
1402-3 Moreover . . . Irelande] *om. W*   1403 *Galles*] Gallees *C*   1403 Retaine]
corr. of detaine *E*   detaine *CR*   1404 denominacions] denomination *W*   1404 menapij]
Manapij *A*   Menavij *F*   Menasy *T*   1404 the *Cancij*] the *Cauci CGHo*   the *Canci*
RAD2FH1   the *Coenci T*   Cauci *W*   1404 the venti] the Pentj *D1*   the *vente F*
Venti *W*   1405 which and] which *C*   1405 manye others] manye other *CRW*   1405 verye
manye] verie reasonable *CR*   reasonable *W*   1405-6 which this . . . forthe] (which . . .
forth) *W*   1407 Irelande] the Iland *LD1*   1408 out of] from *R*   1408 afterwardes]
after *W*   1408 beside] besides *W*   1408 Tanais] Tannis *C*   Tunnis *D1Ho*   Thamis *D2F*
Tanius *RL*   Tania *T*   1408 Gothes] Goathes *AN*   Goates *H2*   1409 Hunnes] Hamnes *H2*
Hunneis *N*   1409 Getes] Geathes *A*   Gets *F*   1409 allsoe] all so *R*   1409-10 as . . .

the seacostes of Belgia and *Celtica* into all the Southerne Costes of Ire-
lande which they possessed and inhabited wheare vppon it is at this daie
amongest all the Irishe a Comon vse to Call anye strange inhabitante
theare amongest them Gald that is discended from the *Gaules*

Eudox: This is verye likelye, for even so did the *Gaules* ancientlye pos- 1415
sesse and people all the Southerne Costes of our *Brytaine* which yeat
retaine theire olde names as the *Belgae* in *SommersetShire Wilshire* and
parte of *Hamshire*, *Atrebatij* in *Berkshire Regni* in *Sussex* and *Surrey* with
manye others Nowe thus farr then I vnderstande your opinion that the
Scythyans planted in the Northe partes of Ireland, the Spaniarde (for soe 1420
we will call them what euer they weare that Came from Spaine) in the
weste, the *Gaulles* in the Southe, So that theare now remayneth onelye the
Easte partes towardes Englande which I woulde be gladd to vnderstande
from whom ye thinke they weare peopled

Iren: Marye I thinke from the *Brittanes* themselues of which thoughe 1425
theare be little footinge now remayninge by reasone that the Saxons
afterwardes and Lastelye the Englishe drivinge out all the firste inhabi-
tantes theareof did possesse and people it themselues Yeat amongest the
Tooles the Brins the Cavanaghes and other nacions in Leinster there is
some memorye of the Britons remayninge As the Tooles are called of the 1430
olde Brittishe worde *Tol* that is an hillye Countrie, The Brins of the |
f. 26ᵛ Brittishe worde Brin That is woddye And the Cavanaghs of Caune that

some)] (as . . . some) *CW*   (as . . . said) of some *R*   1411 seacostes] Sea-coast *W*
1411 *Celtica*] Celcia *H2*   1413 all] *om. CW*   1413 strange] stranger *W*   1414 Gald
. . . discended] *om. C*   1414 Gald] *Gaull AG*   Galdes *D2F*   Gaules *H1*   1414 *Gaules*]
Gaules/ *C*   Gaules:/ *R*   Gaules. *W*   1415 the] those *CW*   these *R*   1416 and
people] *om. W*   1416 of our] from *C*   1417 *Belgae*] Belgi *A*   Belga *CGHoR*   Belge *H2*
Belgia *LD1N*   Belgee *T*   1417 *SommersetShire*] Sommetshire *C*   1417 *Wilshire*]
Wiltshire *D1D2FGHoLT*   1418 *Hamshire*] hampshire *AD2FHoNT*   1418 *Atrebatij*]
Arebatij *D2*   Atnouatu *T*   1418 with] and *W*   1419 others] others, *CR*   others. *W*
1419 then] *om. R*   1420 partes] part *W*   1420 Spaniarde] *Spanierds CW*   1421 will]
om. W   1422 Southe,] South. *R*   1422 now] *om. C*   1422 onelye] *om. W*   1423 partes]
parte *R*   1424 whom] whence *W*   1424 ye] you doe *W*   1424 they weare peopled]
they were peopled./ *C om. R*   them to be peopled. *W*   1425 *Iren:*] *no new paragraph L*
1425 I thinke] *om. R*   1425 from] of *W*   1426 Saxons] Saxons; *R*   1427 all the
firste] the *W*   1428 themselues] themselves. *W*   1429 Brins] Brines *D1L*   Birnes *F*
Bryens *G*   Bruins *H1*   Bryeines *H2*   Birns, or Brins *W*   1429 Cavanaghes] Conaaghes *D2*
Connaughs *F*   Catianages *H2*   Cauanghes Ho   Cauanaghes *T*   1429 nacions] nacons
nacons *R*   1430 Britons] Brittaines *G*   1430 remayninge] remayning. *W*   1430 Tooles]
Tooleis *D2*   1430 are called] *inserted between lines and deleted after* worde *E om. CR*
1431 worde] worde are called *C*   word is called *R*   1431 *Tol*] Tooll *D1*   1431 an hillye]
a hill *W*   1431 Brins] Birnes *D2*   Birne *F*   Bryens *G*   Bremes *H2*   1432 Brin]
Brine *T*   1432 woddye] woode *W*   1432 Cavanaghs] Conaughes *D2*   Connaughs *F*
Cauanghes Ho   Cananaghes *T*   1432 Caune] Cann *D2*   Caane *G*   Canur *T*   the word

A VIEW OF THE PRESENT STATE OF IRELAND 95

is stronge So that in these three people the verye denominacion of the olde *Britons* dothe still remayne, Besides when anye flyethe vnder the succour or proteccion of anye againste an enemye he Criethe vnto him Cummericke that is *Britone* helpe, for the Britone is Called in his owne Language *Cumeraigh*. ffurthermore to proue the same; Irelande is by *Diodorus Siculus* and by *Strabo* Called Britannia And a parte of greate Britaine. ffinallye it appearethe by good recorde yeat extante that kinge Arthur and before him Gurgunt had all that Ilande in his Allegiance and Subieccion. Hearevnto I Coulde ad manie probabilitis of the names of places personnes and speaches as I did in the former but they shoulde be to longe for this place and I reserue them for another And thus ye haue hard my opynion how all that realme of Irelande was firste peopled and by what nacions

        After all which the Saxons succedinge did whollye subdue it vnto themselves for firste Egfride K: of the Northumbs did vtterlye waste and subdue it As Appearethe out of Bedas Complainte againste him And afterwardes kinge Edgar broughte it vnder his obedience as appearethe by an ancient recorde in which is written that he subdued all the Islandes of the Northe even vnto Norwaye and theire kinges did bringe into his Subieccion/

Eudox: This rippinge vp of Ancestries is verye pleasinge vnto me and indede savorethe of good conceite and some readinge withall. I see hearebye howe profitable travell and experience of forren nacions is to him that will applie them to good purpose Neither indede woulde I haue thoughte that anye suche Antiquities coulde haue bene avowched for the Irishe that makethe me the more to longe to see some other of your obseruacions which yee haue gathered | out of that Countrye and haue erste halfe promised to put forthe. And sure in this minglinge of nacions appearethe as youe earste well noted, A wonderfull providence and pur-

Caune *W*   1433 denominacion] Denominations *C*   1434 dothe] doe *W*   1434 remayne,] remayne *C*   remaine. *W*   1435 or] and *CW*   1435 Cummericke] *Cummurreeih A* Camerick *H2T*   comericke *WD2F*   1436 *Britone*] in Bryttaine *H2*   in the Brittish *W* 1436 his] their *W*   1437 *Cumeraigh.*] *Cumeraig, CHo* Commerauge *D1* *Camerage H2 Comeraige GD2F* Cummerouge *L* Cumrage *N* Cummeraige, *R Comeroy. W*   1437 same;] same *CR* same, *W*   1437 Diodorus] *Diadorus H2* Brodorrus *T*   1438 *Strabo*] Strabb *RL* Strau *T*   1438 Britaine] Brittany *C*   1440 before] after *corrected to* before *W* (*Faults escaped*)   1440 Gurgunt] Bargunt *D2F* Gurguntius *G* Gurgwint *H1* Gargant *T*   1440 in his] under their *W*   1440 Subieccion.] subieccion *C* subjection, *W* 1442 for] in *C*   1443 place] *om. W*   1443 hard] had *W*   1444 that] the *R* 1444 Irelande] *om. R*   1444 nacions] nacion *R* nations. *W*   1444-5 *blank space*] *om. CRW* 1445-6 did ... themselves] subdued it wholly to themselves. *W*   1446 the Northumbs] the Northumberlandes *AH2* Northumbs *CH1* the Nothumbers *D2* the Northumbers *FGHo* Northumb *RLD1* Northumberland *WNT*   1447 Bedas] Bede is *A* Beda his *G* Bedus *T* 1448 afterwardes] after him *W*   1448 Edgar] Edgard *C* Edward *T*   1449 is] it is founde *CRW*   1450 Norwaye] noway *F*   1450-1 theire ... bringe] brought them *W* 1452 *Eudox*:] *P resumes at this point*   1452 vp of Ancestries] of Auncestors *W*   1453 withall.] withall *C* withall, *R*   1455 woulde I] I would *C*   1457 Irishe] Irishe, *RW*   1460 as ...

pose of Allmightye god that stirred vp the people in the farthest parte of the worlde to seke out these regions so remote from them and by that meanes bothe to restore theire decayed habitacions and to make himself knowen to the heathen But was theare I praye youe no more generall impeoplinge of that Ilande then firste by the *Scythyans* which ye saie weare the Scottes and afterwardes by the Spaniardes besides the *Gaules Britons* and *Saxons*

Iren: yeas theare was another and that the laste and the greatest which was by the Englishe when the Earle Strangbowe havinge Conquered that Lande delivered vp the same vnto the handes of Henrye the Second then kinge, whoe sente ouer thither greate store of gentlemen and other warlicke people amongest whom he distributed the Lande And settled suche a stronge Colonye thearein as neuer since coulde with all the subtill practises of the Irishe be roted out but abide still a mightye people of soe manye as remayne Englishe of them

Eudox: what is this that ye saie of soe manye as remayne Englishe of them? why? are not they that weare once Englishe abidinge Englishe still./

Iren: no for the moste parte of them are degenerated and growen allmoste meare Irishe yea and more malitious to the Englishe then the verye Irishe themselves/

Eudox: what heare I? and is it possible that an Englisheman broughte vp naturallye in suche swete Civilytie as Englande affordes can finde suche likinge in that barbarous rudenes that he shoulde forgett his owne nature and forgoe his owne nacion? howe maie this be? or what I praye youe maye be the Cause heareof?

Iren: Surelye nothinge but the firste evill ordinaunce and institucion of that Comon wealthe But thereof nowe is heare | no fitt place to speake leaste by the occacion theareof offeringe matter of a longe discourse we

noted] as ... noted) *C* (as ... noted) *RW* 1461 farthest] furtheste *CW* 1461 parte] parts *W* 1462 these] those *C* their *W* 1463 theire] the *R* 1465 impeoplinge] employing *W* 1466 afterwardes] afterward *W* 1466 Spaniardes] *corr. of Africanes E Africans CR* 1467 Britons] *om. C* 1467 Saxons] saxons./ *C* Saxons:/ *R* Saxons? *W* 1468 the laste and the] last and *W* 1469 Strangbowe] Stranbowe *N* Strongbowe *T* 1470 vnto] into *W* 1470 Henrye] Kinge Henrye *D2F* 1472 the Lande] *om. C* 1475 them] them./ *C* them. *W* 1476 this] *om. R* 1477 them? why?] them, whie *CR* 1477 abidinge] *om. W* 1478 still./] still *C* still::/ *R* still? *W* 1479 the moste parte] some *W* 1480 meare] nere *R* 1480 yea] *om. C* 1480 verye] *om. W* 1481 themselves/] them selfes *R* 1482 I?] Iren: *D1* 1483 naturallye] *om. W* 1483 Englande] England, *R* 1483 can] *inserted between lines E om. C* coulde *R* should *W* 1485 nacion?] nation *C* nation, *W* 1485 be?] bee, *W* 1485 I praye youe] (I pray you) *W* 1486 heareof?] therof. *C* hereof:/ *R* thereof? *W* 1488 nowe is heare]

A VIEW OF THE PRESENT STATE OF IRELAND

mighte be drawen from this that we haue in hande namelye the handlinge of Abuses in the Customes of Ireland

Eudox: In truethe *Irenius* ye doe well remember the plott of your firste purpose But yeat from that me semes ye haue muche swarved in all this longe discourse of the firste inhabitinge of Irelande for what is that to your purpose??

Iren: Trulye verye materiall for if ye marked the Course of all that speache well it was to shewe by what meanes the Customes that now are in Ireland beinge some of them indede verie strange and allmoste heathenishe weare firste broughte in And that was as I saide by those nacions from whom that Countrie was firste peopled, for the difference of manners and Customes dothe followe the difference of nacions and people The which I haue declared vnto youe to haue bene Three speciall, which seated themselues heare to witt firste the Scithian then the *Gaules* and lastelye the Englishe notwithstandinge that I ame not Ignorante that theare weare sundrie other nacions which gote footinge in that Lande of the which theare yeat remayne diverse greate families and septes of whom I will allsoe in theire proper places make mencion../

Eudox: ye bringe your selfe *Iren*: verye well into the waye againe notwithstandinge that it semethe ye weare never out of the waye, But now that ye haue passed thoroughe those Antiquities which I Coulde haue wished not so sone ended, begine when yee please to declare what Customes and manners haue bene derived from those nacions to the Irishe and which of them yee finde faulte withall |

Iren: I will then beginne to Counte theire Customes in the same order that I counted theire nacions and firste with the Scithian or Scottishe manners Of the which theare is one vse amongest them to kepe theire Cattell and to live themselves the moste parte of the yeare in *Bollyes* pasturinge vppon the mountaine and waste wilde places and removinge still to freshe lande as they haue depastured the former The which appearethe plaine to be the manner of the Scithians As ye maye reade

here is *W* 1490 handlinge] handlinges *C* 1491 Ireland] Ireland/. *C* Irelande:/ *R* Ireland. *W* 1493 me semes] (me seemes) *W* 1495 purpose??] purpose. *C* 1499 as] *om. C* 1500 of] in *W* 1501 people] people. *W* 1502 declared] declared, *R* 1502 vnto] to *W* 1502 Three] foure *G* 1502 speciall] especially *W* 1503 heare] there, *R* 1503 Scithian] *Scithians CAD2FT* 1503 Gaules] *Gals F* Gaules then the Spanish *G* African *P* 1504 Englishe] *English. W* 1505 other] *om. W* 1508 againe] *om. C* 1509 semethe] semeth that *RW* 1511 ended] in deed *C* 1511 yee please] it please youe *C* 1513 withall] withall/. *C* withall::/ *R* withall. *W* 1514 then beginne] begin then *W* 1515 Scithian] *Scithians CD2F* 1516 manners] manners. *W* 1517 yeare] yeares *R* 1517 Bollyes] Boolies *W* 1518 mountaine] mounteines *C* 1519 to] to the *C* 1519 freshe] *Irish F* 1519 former] former dayes, *R* former. *W*

8

in *Olaus Magnus* and *Io: Boemus* and yeat is vsed amongest all the Tartarians and the people aboute the *Caspian* sea which are naturallie Scithians to live in Herdes As they Call them beinge the verye same that the Irishe *Bollyes* are drivinge theire Cattell Continuallye with them and fedinge onelye on theire milke and white meates/ 1525

Eudox: what faulte Cane ye finde with this Custome for thoughe it be an olde Scithian vse yeat it is verye behoofull in this Countrye of Irelande wheare theare are greate mountaines and waste desertes full of grasse that the same shoulde be eaten downe and norishe manye thowsandes of Cattell for the good of the whole realme which Cannot me thinke well be anye 1530 other waye then by kepinge those *Bollyes* as theare ye haue shewed./

Iren: But by this Custome of Bolloyinge theare growe in the meane time manye greate enormityes vnto that Comon wealthe for firste if theare be any outlawes or loose people (as they are never without some) which live vppon stealthes and spoile, they are evermore succored and finde reliefe 1535 onelye in those Bollies beinge vppon the waste places, wheares els they shoulde be driven shortelye to sterve or to Come downe to the townes to f. 28ᵛ steale reliefe wheare by one meanes or other they | they woulde sone be Caughte: besides suche stealthes of Cattell as they make they bringe Comonlye to those *Bollyes* wheare they are receaued readilye and the 1540 Thiefe Harbored from daunger of Lawe or suche officers as mighte lighte vppon him. Moreouer the people that live thus in these Bollies growe thereby the more Barbarous and live more licentiouslye then they Could in townes vsinge what meanes they liste and practisinge what mischiefs and villanies they will either againste the gouernement theare generallye 1545 by theire Combinacions or againste private men whom they maligne by stealinge theire goodes or murderinge themselves; for theare they thinke themselues haulfe exemted from lawe and obedience and havinge once tasted fredome doe like a steare that hathe bene longe out of his yoke grudge and repine ever after to Come vnder rule againe 1550

1521 *Olaus*] *Oleus A*   1521 *Io: Boemus*] *Io. Bennus A*   *Ioh̄is Bormus D2*   *Io: Boru F*   *Io: Bohemus H1*   1522 Tartarians] *Tarturians Ho*   1522 *Caspian*] *Caspia D1*   *Caspiā L*   1524 *Bollyes*] *Boolies W*   1525 milke and] *om. R*   1525 meates/] meates *C*   1526 Custome] custome? *W*   1527 it is] is it *W*   1529 thowsandes] thowsand *R*   1530 me thinke] (me thinks) *W*   1531 *Bollyes*] *Boolies W*   1531 as theare] there, as *W*   1532 Bolloyinge] Bollyng *R*   Boolying *W*   1532 growe] grewe *R*   1533 manye] maye *R*   1534 loose] losse *R*   1534 (as . . . some)] as . . . some *R*   1535 vppon] vpon the *R*   1535 spoile] spoyles *CW*   spoyled *R*   1536 those] these *W*   1536 Bollies] *Boolies W*   1536 the] those *C*   1536 wheares] wheras *CW*   where *R*   1537 or to] or *C*   1538 steale] seeke *RW*   1538 other] another *R*   1538 they they] they *CRW*   1539 Caughte:] Caught *C*   1539 make they] *om. R*   1539 make] make. *and blank space C*   1540 Comonlye] continvallie *C*   1540 *Bollyes*] *Boolies*, being upon those waste places *W*   1540 receaued readilye] readily received *W*   1542 him.] him, *C*   1542 live thus] thus live *W*   1542 these] those *W*   1543 Could] would *R*   1544 meanes] manners *W*   1545 generallye] *om. W*   1549 bene] beinge *C*   1550 againe] againe: *C*   againe:/ *R*

A VIEW OF THE PRESENT STATE OF IRELAND

Eudox: By your speache *Irenius* I perceaue more evill Come by this vse of Bollies then good by theire grazinge and therefore it maye well be reformed but that muste be in his due Course. doe youe procede to the nexte.

Iren: They haue another Custome from the *Scythyans* that is the wear- inge of mantells and longe glibbes which is a thicke Curled bushe of haire hanginge downe over theire eyes and monstrouslye disguisinge them which are bothe verye bad and hurtefull

Eudox: doe ye thinke that the mantle cometh from the *Scythyans* I woulde surelye thinke otherwise, ffor by that which I haue red it appeareth that moste nacons in the worlde antientlye vsed the mantle ffor the Iewes vsed it as yee maye read of *Elyas* mantle of   The Chaldees allso vsed it as ye maie reade in *Diadorus* The Egiptians likewise vsed it as ye maye reade in *Herodotus* and maye be gathered by the discripcion of *Berenice* in the greke Comentaries vppon *Callymachus* The Greekes allso vsed it auncientlye as appeares | by venus mantle lyned with Starrs, thoughe afterwardes they Chaunged the forme thereof into theire Clokes called *Pallia* as some of the Irishe allso vse and the Ancient Latines and Romaines vsed it as yee maye Reade in Virgill whoe was a verye greate *Antiquary* that *Evander* when *Æneas* Came to him at his feaste did entertaine and feaste him sittinge one the grounde and lyinge one mantles In soe muche as he vsethe the verie worde *mantile* for a mantle *mantilia sternunt* soe that it semethe that the mantle was a generall habit to moste nacions and not proper to the Scithians onelye as ye suppose

Iren: I Cannot denye but Ancientlye it was Comon to moste and yeat

againe. *W*   1551-2 this vse of] these *R*   1552 Bollies] Boolies *W*   1553 Course.] Course *CR* course, *W*   1555 *Iren:*] no new paragraph *T*   1558 hurtefull] hurtfull.. *C* hurtfull:/ *R* hurtfull. *W*   1559 *Scythyans*] *scithians*, *C*   Scythians? *RW*   1561 in] of *W*   1562 *Elyas*] Samuells mantle, Elias *G*   1562 mantle of *blank space*] Mantle, etc. *W*   1562 Chaldees] *Chaldaeans AF*   Caldees *CGT*   Caldeyes *D1*   Caldean *H2*   Caldeans *N* Caldies *RL*   1563 allso vsed it] vsed it also *C*   1563 *Diadorus*] Dyodorus, *R* Dyodrus *T*   Diodorus. *W*   1563 Egiptians] *Agytians T*   1564 *Herodotus*] Herodus *RLD1Ho*   1564 and] om. *C*   1564 discripcion] decypline *R*   1565 *Berenice*] Berne *A* Berence *H2N*   1565 Comentaries] Commentary *W*   1565 *Callymachus*] Cathimachus *H2* Carthimacus *N*   Callymachus, *R*   Callimachus. *W*   1566 vsed] nsed *W*   1566 appeares] appeareth *RW*   1566 venus] *Vonus T*   1567 Starrs] blank space *C*   1568 and the] and *C*   1569 vsed] also vsed *R*   1570 *Antiquary*] Antiquarye *C*   Atiquarie *R* Antiquary. *W*   1571 sittinge] om. *R*   1572 mantles] Mantles. *W*   1572 mantile] mantili *D1*   mantilia *N*   Mantell *P*   1572-3 a mantle] a mantle/: *C*   a mantle, *R* a Mantle. *W*   1573 mantilia sternunt] Humi mantilia sternunt. on line by itself *W* 1573 mantilia] followed by "humi" which is deleted *E*   Mantilia hmi *C*   Mantilia humi *RAD1D2FGH1H2HoLN*   humi mantilia *P*   1573 sternunt] corr. of steruunt *E*   steruunt *CR* struunt *H1*   1574 suppose] suppose./ *R*   suppose. *W*   1575 but] but that *W*

sithence disvsed and laied awaie But in this Latter age of the worlde since the decaie of the Romaine Empire it was renewed and broughte in againe by those Northern nacions, when breakinge out of theire Colde Caves and frozen habitacion into the swete soile of *Europe* they broughte with them theire vsuall weedes fitt to shilde the Coulde and that Continvall froste to which they had bene at home envred The which yeat they lefte not of by reasone that they weare in perpetuall warrs with the nacions whom they had invaded but still removinge from place to place Carried allwaies with them that weede as theire house theire bed and theire garment, and Comminge Lastelye into Irelande they founde theare more speciall vse thereof by reasone of the rawe Colde climate from whom it is now growen into that generall vse in which that people now haue it, Afterwarde the Africanes succedinge yeat findinge the like necessitye of that garment Continved the like vse theareof/

Eudox: Since then the necessitie theareof is so Commodious as ye alleadge that it is in steade of howsinge beddinge and Cloathinge what reason haue youe then to wishe so necessarye a thinge Caste of//

Iren: Because the Comoditye dothe not Countervaile | The discomoditie ffor the inconveniences which thearby do arise are muche more manye, for it is a fitt howsse for an outlawe a mete bedd for a Rebell and an Apte cloake for a thefe, ffirste the Outlawe beinge for his manye Crymes and villanies banished from the Townes and howses of honeste men and wanderinge in waste places far from daunger of lawe maketh his mantle his howsse and vnder it Couerethe him self from the wrathe of heaven from the offence of the earthe and from the sighte of men. when it raynethe it is his pentise, when it blowethe it is his Tent, when it frezethe it is his Tabernacle. In sommer he cane weare it Lose, in winter he Cane wrapp it Closse. at all times he Cane vse it, never heavye neuer Cumbersome. Likewise for a Rebell it is as serviceable, ffor in his warr that he makethe (yf at leaste it deserve the name of warr, when he still flyethe from his foe and lurketh in the thicke woods and straighte passages,

---

1576 Latter] later *CW*   1577 Romaine] romaye *C*   1578 those Northern] these Northen *C*   1579 habitacion] habitations *W*   1579 *Europe*] *Enry T*   1581 bene at home] att home bene *CRW*   1582 whom] where *R*   1585 into] into, *R*   1586 the] that *C*   1587 it,] it. *W*   1587 Afterwarde] Afterwardes *C*   After whom *W*   1588 Africanes] *Gaules W*   1588 like] little *R*   1592 wishe] wyshe, *R*   1592 of//] off? *W*   1593 *Iren:*] *no new paragraph N*   1596 an] *om. R*   1596 thefe,] thiefe. *W*   1600 men.] men *C*   men, *R*   1601 pentise,] pentise *C*   pent-house; *W*   1602 Tabernacle.] tabernacle *C*   tabernacle, *R*   1602 Lose,] Loose *C*   1603 Closse.] close *C*   close, *RW*   1603-4 Cumbersome.] Cumbersome, *C*   1604 his] *om. C*   1605 warr,] warre) *CW*

A VIEW OF THE PRESENT STATE OF IRELAND 101

waytinge for Advantages) it is his bedd yea and allmoste all his hous-
houlde stuffe, for the wood is his house againste all weathers and his
mantle is his Cave to slepe in Thearein he wrappeth himself rounde and
ensconceth himselfe strongelye againste the gnattes which in that Contry
doe more Annoye the naked rebells whileste they kepe the woodes and
doe more sharpelye wounde them then all theire enemyes swordes or
speares which cane seldome Come nighe them, yea and often times theire
mantle servethe them when they are neare driven beinge wrapped aboute
theire lefte arme in steade of a Targett for it is harde to Cutt thoroughe
it with a sworde besides it is lighte to beare, lighte to throwe awaie, and
beinge as they then Comonlye are naked it is to them all in all. Lastlie for
a Thefe it is so hansome as it maye seme it was firste invented for him,
ffor vnder it he Cane Clenlye Convaye anye fitt pillage that | Comethe
handesomelye in his waie, and when he goethe abroade in the nighte on
freebotinge it is his beste and sureste friende for lyinge as they often doe
two or three nightes togeather abroade to watche for theire bootye with
that they Cane pretelye shroude themselues vnder a bushe or a banke side
till they maye Convenientlye doe theire errande, And when all is done he
Cane in his mantle passe thoroughe anye Towne or Companye beinge Closse
hooded ouer his heade as he vsethe from knowledge of anie to whom he
is endangered. Besides all this he or anie man els that is disposed to
mischief or villanye maye vnder his mantle goe privilye armed without
suspicion of anye Carrye his heade pece his skeane or pistoll if he please
to be allwaies in a readines. Thus necessarie and fittinge is·a mantle for a
badd man. and surelye for a bad huswif it is no lesse Conveniente for
some of them that be these wanderinge weomen Called of them *monashul*
It is haulfe a wardrope for in sommer ye shall finde her arayed Comonlye
but in her smocke and mantle to be more readye for her lighte services
In winter and in her travell it is her Cloake and safegarde and allsoe a
Coverlett for her Lewed exercises. And when she hathe filled her vessell
vnder it she maye hide bothe her burden and her blame. yea and when
her bastarde is borne it serues in steade of all her swadlinge cloutes, her

warr). R   1607 Advantages)] advantages, CRW   1607 all] as W   1609 Cave] couch W   1609 in] in, C   in: R   in. W   1609 himself] his self R   1610 ensconceth] coucheth W   1610 that] *corr. of the* E   the CR   1616 it with] with W   1616 sworde] sworde, RW   1616 beare, lighte] beare C   1617 as . . . are] (as . . . are) W   1617 then] *om.* W   1617 all.] all C   all, R   1619 Cane] may W   1620 on] in W   1623 pretelye] prattelie R   1623 banke side] banckes syde C   backsyde R   1624 done] over W   1626 hooded] whoded C   1627 endangered.] indaungered C   endangered, R   1627 all] *om.* W   1628 privilye] privilie, R   1630 in a] in W   1632 these] *om.* W   1632 monashul] *corr. of monashut* E   Beantoolhe [*or* Beantoolne?] A   Monashut CRD2H1H2   HoLN   Monhashatt D1   Monashitt G   1634 for her] for the R   1634 services] services, C   seruices: RW   1636 exercises] exercise CRW   1637 maye] can CRW   1637 blame.] yea and] blame yea C   1638 all her] *om.* W   1638 swadlinge] swadlinges C   1638-9 her mantells, her Cradles, with which others are vainlye Combred. And as for all other good weomen which love to doe but little worke howe hansome it is to lye in and slepe and to louse them selues in the sunshine they that haue bene but a while in Irelande Can well wittnesse, Sure I ame that yee will thinke it verye vnfitt for good huswiffe to stirre in or to busie herselfe aboute her huswifrye in sorte as they shoulde. These be some of Thabuses for which | I woulde thinke it mete to forbidd all mantells/

Eudox. O evill minded man that havinge reckoned vp soe manye vses of a mantell will yeat wishe it to be Abandoned Sure I thinke diogenies dishe did neuer serve his master for more turnes notwithstandinge that he made his dishe his Cupp his cap his measure his waterpott, then a mantle dothe an Irishe man: But I see they be all to bad intentes and therefore I will ioyne with youe in abolishinge it, But what blame laye youe to the glibbe Take hede I praye youe that youe be not to busye thearewith for feare of your owne blame seinge our Inglishemen take it vp in suche agenerall fassion to weare theire haire so vnmeasurable longe that some of them excede the Irishe glibbes//

Iren: I feare not the blame of anye vndeserved mislikes but for the Irishe glibbes I saye that besides theire salvage brutishnes and loathly filthines which is not to be named they are fitt maskes as a mantle is for a thiefe for whensoeuer he hathe rune himself in to that perill of lawe that he will not be knowen he either Cuttethe of his glibbe quite by which he becommethe nothinge like himselfe, or pulleth it so lowe downe over his eyes that it is verye harde to discerne his thevishe Countenaunce And therefore fitt to be trussed vp with the mantle

Eudox: Trulye these three Scithian abuses I houlde moste fitt to be taken awaye with sharpe penalties and sure I wonder howe they haue bene kepte this Longe notwithstandinge so manye good provicions and orders as haue bene devized for that people

Iren the Cause theareof shall appeare to youe heareafter but let vs now

mantells ... Combred] *om. RW*   1641 and to] or to *CRW*   1641 louse] loose *C*
1642 wittnesse,] witnes. *CW*   witnesse *R*   1643 for] *inserted between lines E om. C*
for a *W*   1643 huswiffe] huswyves *R*   1644 sorte as they] such sort as she *W*
1644 shoulde.] should, *C*   1647 a mantell] mantles *R*   1647 yeat] ye *C*   yee yett *R*
1647 Abandoned] abandoned, *CR*   abandoned! *W*   1647 diogenies] *diogines C*   Diogenes his *GP*   1648 for] *inserted between lines E om. CR*   1649 made] made it *W*   1649 Cupp his cap] Cupp, *R*   1650 an Irishe man] not Irishemen *with last three letters hidden in binding C*
1650 all] most *W*   1652 glibbe] Glibb: *C*   glibb, *R*   glibbe? *W*   1652 I praye youe] (I pray you) *W*   1654 vnmeasurable] vnmeasurablie *CR*   immeasurably *W*   1655 the] the longest *CRW*   1656 mislikes] dislikes *W*   1657-8 I ... named] *om. W*   1657 loathly] *om. R*   1658 are] are as *W*   1661 pulleth] puttethe *C*   1662 Countenaunce] countenance. *W*   1663 mantle] mantle/. *C*   mantle:/ *R*   Mantle. *W*   1664 moste] *om. R*   1666 this] thus *CRW*   1667 people] people/. *C*   people: *R*   people. *W*

goe forwarde with our Scithian Customes of which the nexte that I haue to treate of is theire manner of the raisinge there crye in theire conflictes and | And at other troblesome times of vprore The which is verye naturall *Scythyan* as ye haue red in *Diodorus Siculus* and in *Heroditus* describinge the manner of the *Scythyans* and *Parthians* Comminge to give the Charge at theire battells at the which it is saide that he came runninge with a Terrible yell and Habbub, as if heaven and earthe woulde haue gone togeather which is the verye Image of the Irishe Hubub which theire kerne vse at theire firste encounter. Besides the same Herodotus wrighteth that they vsed in theire battles to Call vppon the names of theire Captaines or Generalls and somtimes vppon theire greatest kinge deceased As in that Battle of *Tomyris* againste *Cirus* which Costome to this daie manifestlie appearethe amongeste the Irishe for at theire ioyninge of Battell they likewise Call vppon theire Captaines name or the worde of his Auncestours As they vnder *Oneale* crye *Landargabo*, that is the bloddie hande which is *Oneles* badge. they vnder Obrien Call which is   And to theire ensample the olde Englishe allsoe which theare remaynethe haue gotten vp theire cryes Scithyanlike as *Cromabo* and *Butlerabo* And hearein allso lyethe open another verye manifest profe that the Irishe be Scithes or Scotts for in all theire incounters thei vse one verye Comon worde Cryinge *Farragh Ferragh* which is a Scottishe worde to wete the name of one of the firste kinges of Scotlande Called *Ferragus* or *Fergus*, which foughte against the Pictes As ye maye reade in *Buckanan de Rebus*

1669 Customes] customes. *W* 1669 which] *om. R* 1669 nexte] next the next *C* 1670 is theire] is the *RW* 1670 the] *om. W* 1670 there] the *CW* 1670 crye] *corr. of* ioye *E* ioye *CR* 1671 And] *om. CRW* 1671 troblesome times] troblesomes *R* 1672 haue red] maye read *RW* 1672 and in] and *R* 1673 *Parthians*] Persians *A* Percians *H2* Perthians *R* 1674 theire] *om. W* 1674 at the] at *W* 1674 that he] that they *CW* they *R* 1675 and Habbub] *om. W* 1675 Habbub] hubbabowe *A* h *and blank space C* hollowe *G* hubbabye *H2N* *blank space P* hubbuble *Ho* Hubbubbe *RD1D2FL* 1676 Hubub] *Hubbabowe A* hubab *C* hubbubs *D2* hubbaby *H2N* hubbuble *Ho* 1677 encounter.] encounter, *C* 1679 kinge] Kings *W* 1680 *Tomyris*] Tomoris *F* Temyries *T* Thomyris *W* 1683 worde] name *R* 1683 Auncestours.] Auncestours. *W* 1683 Oneale] Onrale *H2* 1683 Landargabo] Layarrigabowe *A* Oandragabo *P* Launderg-abo *W* 1684 Oneles] Onrales *H2* 1684 badge.] badge *C* 1684-5 Call *and blank space*] call *Laun-laider W* 1685 which is *and blank space*] that is, the strong hand *W* 1687 *Cromabo*] the Geraldins Croumabowe *A* Coremabo *F* cremabo *H1* 1687 *Butlerabo*] the Butlers Bulteaurabowe *A* Butterabo *F* 1687 hearein] here *W* 1688 verye] *om. W* 1688 be] ar *R* 1688 Scithes] Scithians *G* 1689 one] *corr. of* our *E* our *C* 1690 *Farragh Ferragh*] Farrih. Farrih. *A* fferrah: ferrah *H1* Ferragh, ferrogh *LD1* Ferragh ferragh *RW* 1691 the] theire *R* 1691 *Ferragus* or *Fergus*] Forgus or Feragus *D1* Fergus or Ferragus *RAD2FHoL* Feragus *T* 1692 Pictes] Pickes *R* 1692 Buckanan] Buckanon *H2* Buckanam *RLD1* Buchanan *WD2FHo* 1692 de Rebus] de hebris *D1L* dorebus *T*

Scoticis But as others write it was longe before that the name of theire Chief Captaine vnder whom they foughte againste the Africanes the which was then so fortonate vnto them that ever sithence they haue vsed to Call vppon his name in theire Battells/

f. 31ᵛ *Eudox*: Beleve me this Observacion of yours *Irenius* | ys verye good and delightefull far beyonde the blinde Conceipte of some whoe I remember haue vppon the same worde *Ferragh* made a verye blunte Coniecture as namelye, mr *Stannihurst* whoe thoughe he be the same Contryman borne that shoulde searche more nerely into the secrete of these thinges yeat hathe straied from the truethe all the heavens wide (as they saie) for he thearevppon groundethe a verye grosse ymaginacion that the Irishe shoulde discende from the *Ægiptians* which Came into that Ilande firste vnder the leadinge of one *Scota* the daughter of *Pharao* wherevppon they vse (saiethe he) in all theire battells to Call vppon the name of *Pharao* crynge *Ferragh Ferragh*. Surelye ye shoote wide one the bowe hand and verye farr from the marke, for I woulde firste knowe of him what Anciente grounde of Aucthoritye he hathe for suche a sencelesse fable, and if he haue anye of the rude Irishe bookes as it maye be he hathe yeat me semes a man of his Learninge shoulde not soe lightelye haue bene Carried awaie with olde wyves tales from approvaunce of his owne reasone. ffor wheather *Scota* be like an Egiptian worde, or smacke of anye Learninge or iudgement let the Learned Iudge. But his *Scota* rather Comes of the greke *Scotos* that is darkenes which hathe not let him see the lighte of the truethe

Iren: youe knowe not *Eudoxius* howe well mr *Stan*: Coulde see in the darke perhaps he hathe owles or Catts eyes but well I wote he seethe not well the verye lighte in matters of more weighte. But as for *Ferragh*: I haue tolde youe my Coniecture onelye and yeat thus muche I haue more
f. 32ʳ to prove a liklyhode that theare be yeat at this daie in Irelande | manye Irishe men Chieflye in the Northern partes called by the name of *Ferragh*.

1693 *Scoticis*] *Scotihs* F   1693 others] other *C*   1693 before] before, *R*   1695 sithence] since *C*   1697 Beleve] Betwene *C*   1697 of yours] your *R*   1698 far] for *C*   1698-9 I remember] (I remember) *W*   1699 *Ferragh*] *Farrih* A *fferiagh* G *Farrah* H1   1699 made] haue made *R*   1702 hathe] haue *R*   1705 one] *om. R*   1705 *Scota*] *Scotia* T   1705 *Pharao*] *Pharaho* H2   1705-6 wherevppon . . . *Pharao*] *om. R*   1707 *Ferragh Ferragh*.] *Farrih. Farrih.* A *Feragh. Feragh.* C *ferrah, ferrah* H1H2 *Ferragh Ferragh, R*   1707 ye] he *CRW*   1707 shoote] shott *R*   shootes *W*   1710 hathe] hath, *W*   1710-1 me semes] (me seemes) *W*   1711 a] that a *W*   1713-4 *Scota* . . . iudgement] it be a smack of any learned iudgment, to say, that *Scota* is like an *Egyptian* word *W*   1714 of] vpon *R*   1715 *Scotos*] *Scotes* D1H1 σκότος F *Scotas* T σκότος *W*   1716 truethe] trueth/. *C* truth. *W*   1717 *Eudoxius*] *Eudox*: *R* *Eudoxus* *W*   1717 *Stan*:] *Stanhurst* H2 *Stannih*: *R* *Stanyhurst* T   1718 darke] darke, *RW*   1719 *Ferragh*] *Farrih* A *fferrage* G *ferrah* H1   1720 youe] *om. W*   1720 thus] this *C*   1720 I haue] *om. C*   1722 Irishe] English *A*   1722 Chieflye . . . partes] (chiefly . . . parts) *W*   1722 in the] in *C*   1722 *Ferragh*] *Farreels* A *Ferrah* H1 *Farragh* R

A VIEW OF THE PRESENT STATE OF IRELAND 105

But let that nowe be This onelye for this place sufficethe that it is a worde vsed in theire Comon Hububs the which with all the reste is to be abolished for that it discouerethe an affectacion of Irishe Captenrye, which in this Platforme I endevour speciallie to beate downe Theare be other sortes of Cryes allsoe vsed amongeste the Irishe which savor greatlye of the *Scythyan* Barbarisime as theire Lamentacions at theire burialls with despairefull outcries and ymoderate waylinges the which mr *Stanihurst* mighte allsoe haue vsed for an Argument to proue the *Egiptians* ffor so in scripture it is mencioned That the Egiptians lamented for the deathe of *Ioseph*. Others thinke this Custome to Come from the Spaniardes for that they do so inmeasurablye likewise bewaile theare dead But the same is not proper spannishe but Alltogeather heathenishe broughte in firste thither eyther by the *Scythyans* or by the *Moores* which weare *Africanes* but longe possessed that Countrye, for it is the manner of all pagans and *Infidells* to be intemperate in theire waylinges of theare dead for that they had no faithe nor hope of salvacion, And this is Custome allsoe is speciallye noted by *Diodorus Siculus* to haue bene in the *Scythyan* and is yeat amongeste the Northerne Scottes//

Eudox: This is sure an ill Custome allsoe but yeat dothe not soe muche Concerne Civill reformacion as abuse in religion.

Iren: I did not rehearse it as one of the Abuses which I thoughte moste worthie of reformacion but havinge | made mencion of Irishe Cryes I thoughte this manner of Crynge and howlinge not impertinente to be noted as vncivile and Scithianlike. ffor by these oulde Customes and other like Coniecturall circumstances the discentes of nacions canne onelye be proued wheare other monimentes of wrightinges be not remayninge

Eudox Then I praye youe whensoeuer in your discourse youe mete with them by the waye doe not shunn but bouldlye tuche them for besides theire

---

1723 be] be, *CR* be: *W*   1724 Hububs] *Hubbobowe A*   Hubbub *GD1LT*   1724 with ... reste] (with ... rest) *W*   1726 downe] downe, *CR* down. *W*   1727 allsoe] all so *R*   1727 amongeste] among *W*   1727 of the] of *R*   1729 ymoderate] imorderate *C*   1729 *Stanihurst*] Stanhurst *H2*   1730 the] them *RW*   1730-1 ffor ... Egiptians] which *R*   1732 *Ioseph*.] Ioseph *C*   1733 so] *om. W*   1733 inmeasurablye] immeasureablie *RW*   1733 dead] deed *C*   1734 firste thither] thither first *W*   1735 or by] or *RW*   1735 which] that *W*   1735 but] and *W*   1736 all] the *C*   1738 this is] this ill *CRW*   1739 *Scythyan*] scythians *CRW*   1740 Scottes//] Scottes *R* Scots at this day, as you may reade in their Chronicles. *W*   1741 sure] *om. R*   1741 ill] evill *R*   1742 religion.] religion *CR* 1744 worthie] worth *R*   1745 Crynge] lewd crying *W*   1746 noted as] *corr. of* not as *E* not *C*   1746 Scithianlike] *Scithians* like *R*   1748 wrightinges] wrytinge *R*   1748 be] are *W*   1748 remayninge] remayninge: *C* remayninge:/ *R* remayning. *W*   1749 I praye

greate pleasure and delighte for theire Antiquitye they bringe allsoe greate proffitte and helpe vnto Civilytye//

Iren: Then sithe youe will haue it soe I will heare take occasion since I latelye spake of theire manner of Cryes in Ioyninge battaile to speake also somwhate of the manner of theire Armes and array in theire battaile with other Customes perhaps worthe the notinge. And firste of theire armes and weapons Amongeste which theire broade swordes are proper *Scythyan* for suche the *Scythes* vsed Comonlye As ye maye reade in *Olaus magnus*.

And the same allsoe the olde Scottes vsed as ye maye reade in *Buckhanan* and in *Hector Boethius* and in *Ia: de Breȳ*. wheare the pictures of them are in the same forme expressed. Allsoe theire shorte bowes and little quivers with shorte bearded Arrowes are verye *Scythyan* as ye maye reade in the same *Olaus* And the same sorte bothe of bowes quiuers and Arrowes are at this daie to be sene Comonlie Amongest the Northerne Irishe whose Scottishe bowes are not paste Three quarters of a yarde longe with a stringe of wreathed hempe slacklie bente and whose Arrowes are not muche aboue haulfe an ell longe | Tipped with stele heades made like Comon broade arrowes heades but muche more sharpe and slender that they enter into an armed man or horss moste Cruelye notwithstandinge that they are shott forthe weakly. moreouer theire longe broade shieldes made but of wicker rodds which are Comonlye vsed amongest the saide Northerne Irishe but specially of the Scottes are broughte from the Scithians as ye maye reade in *Olaus magnus Solynus* and others/ Likewise theire goinge to battell without armour on theire bodies or heades but trustinge onelye to the thicknes of theire glibbes the which they saie will somtimes beare of a good strocke is mere salvage and *Scythyan* as ye maye se in the saide Images of the olde *Scythes* or Scottes sett forthe by *Herodianus* and others, Besides theire Confused kinde of marche in heapes without anie order or array, theire Clashinge of swordes togeather, theire fiers Comminge vppon theire enemyes and theire manner of fighte, resemblethe alltogeather that which is reade in

youe] (I pray you) *W*   1751 allsoe] *om. C*   1754 Ioyninge] ioyning of *W*   1755 in theire] in *CRW*   1756 worthe] worthy *W*   1756 the] *om. C*   1758 *Scythes*] Scythians *H2*   1759 *blank space*] *om. CRW*   1760 *Buckhanan*] Buckanam *D1L* Buchanam *R*   Buchanan *WD2FHo*   1760 Hector ... Breȳ.] *added in different hand E blank space CRD2FH1HoL   other and blank space D1*   Hector Boetius *G*   Silvius *P* Hector Boetius *and in flattesbury T*   Solinus *W om. H2AN*   1760-1 *blank space*] *om. W* 1761 expressed.] expressed *C*   1763 are] *om. C*   1765 Irishe] *Irish-Scots W*   1767 muche] *om. R*   1767 ell] elne *CR*   1768 arrowes] Arrow *W*   1768 muche] many *R*   1769 an armed] a *W*   1770 weakly.] weakelye, *CR*   1771 of] with *W*   1772 specially] especially *W*   1772 are] and *R*   1773-4 *Olaus ... others*] *blank space P*   1773 *magnus*] Magus *Ho*   1774 others/] others *R*   1774 *blank space*] *om. RW*   1775 onelye] *om. W* 1776 they saie] (they say) *W*   1776-7 salvage and] *om. W*   1778 *Herodianus* and others] *blank space P*   1778 others,] others *CR*   others. *W*   1780 Comminge] rvnninge *RW*

A VIEW OF THE PRESENT STATE OF IRELAND 107

all histories to haue bene vsed of the Scithians. By which it maye allmoste infallible be gathered togeather with other Circumstances that the Irishe are verye *Scottes* or *Scythes* originallye thoughe sithens intermingled with manye other nacions repayringe and ioyninge vnto them. And to these I maie allso add another verye stronge Coniecture which Comethe to minde that I haue often obserued theare amogest them, that is certaine religious Ceremonies which are verye supersticiouslye yeat vsed amongest them the which are allsoe written by sundrie Aucthours to haue bene obserued amongest the *Scythyans*, by which it maye verye vehementlie be presumed that the nacions weare ancientlye all one. ffor Herodetus as I remember in his treatise of *Homere* endevoringe to searche out the truethe what Countrimann Homere was prouethe it moste strongelye (as he thinkethe) that he was an *Ætolian* borne, for that in discribinge a sacrifyce of the *Grekes* he omitted the burninge of the Chinebone called ὀφυν the which all the other *Grecians* save onelye the *Ætolians* doe vse to burne in theire sacrifices, Allso for that he maketh the entralls to be rosted on five spittes | The which was the proper manner of the *Ætolians* whoe onelie of all the nacions and Countries of *Grecia* vsed to sacrifice in that sorte wheare as all the reste of the *Grekes* vsed to roste them vppon three spittes, by which he inferrethe necessarilie that *Homere* was an *Ætolian*. And by the same reasone maie as I reasonablie Conclude that the Irishe are discended from the *Scythyans* for that they vse even to this daie some of the same ceremonies which the *Scythyans* auncientlye vsed As for exsample ye maye reade in Lucian in that swete *Dialouge* which is intituled *Toxaris* or of frendshippe that the Common oathe of

1785

1790

1795

f. 33ᵛ

1800

1805

1782 all] *om. W*   1782 Scithians.] *scythians CR*   1782 maye] maye bee yt maye *R*
1783 infallible] infallablye *CRW*   1785 these] the vse *R*   1786 verye] *om. W*   1786 to] to my *CRW*   1787 amogest] amongest *CRW*   1787 certaine religious] Certe religious and *C*
1788 supersticiouslye] superstitious *R*   1791 Herodetus] *corr. of* Plutarche *E*   Plutarche *CRWAD1D2FH1H2HoNP*   Plutarchs *L*   Herastus *G*   1791 as I remember] (as I remember) *W*   1792 Homere] *Homero Ho*   Homeste *LD1*   1793 (as he thinkethe)] as he thincketh *R*   1794 Ætolian] Aolian *C*   Italyan *H2LD1*   Chian *P*   Itollian *R*
Æolian *WD2FHoT*   1794-7 discribinge . . . spittes] *blank space P*   1794 discribinge] distributinge of *R*   1795 burninge . . . Chinebone] chinbone *H2AN*   chyne bone *H1D2F*   *blank space RLD1*   loyne *W*   1795 Chinebone] *Cherubine Ho*   1795 called ὀφυν] *om. WAG*   1795 ὀφυν] ὀφύν *C*   Oxe *H2*   οφιχο *Ho*   οφχε *N*   *blank space RD1D2FH1LT*
1796 all] withall *R*   1796 Grecians] Greekes *H1H2N*   1796 save . . . doe] (saving the Æolians) *W*   1796 Ætolians] Æolians *CHoT*   Aolians *D2F*   Etolians *H1*   Italyans *H2L*
Italian *D1*   1797 sacrifices] sacryfice *R*   1797-1802 Allso . . . Ætolian] *om. G*
1797 maketh] makes *W*   1798 *blank space] om. CRW*   1798 The] *om. W*   1799 Ætolians] Aolians *C*   Chians *P*   Æolians *WD2FHoT*   1799 and Countries] *om. W*   1799 Grecia] Gretia *LD1*   1800-1 in . . . spittes] *blank space P*   1800-1 wheare . . . spittes] *om. W*
1800 Grekes] Graecyans *D2F*   1801 Homere] Homero *Ho*   1802 an Ætolian] *corr. of* a Chian *E*   a Chian *CP*   an Italyan *H2D1*   an Æolian *WD2FHoT*   1802 as I] I as *CRW*
1803-4 even . . . daie] (even . . . day) *W*   1803 even to] into *C*   1804 Scythyans] Scithes *T*   1805 vsed] used. *W*   1805 Lucian] *Lucan A*   Lucane *H2N*   *blank space RLD1*
1806 Toxaris] Toxaxis *RAD1D2GH2LNT*   Texaxis *C*   Toxuris *H1*   Toxuxis *Ho*

the *Scythyans* was by the sworde and by the fire, for that they accompted these Two speciall divine powers which should worke vengeaunce on periurours, so do the Irishe at this daie when they goe to anie battell saye Certaine praiers or Charmes to theire swordes makinge a Crosse theare- with vppon the earthe and thrustinge the pointe of theire blades into the grounde, thinkinge thearby to haue the better successe in fighte. Allsoe they vse to sweare Comonlie by theire swordes. likewise at the kindelinge of the fire and lightinge of Candles they saie Certaine prayers and vse some other supersticious rites which shewe that they honor the fire and the lighte ffor all these Northerne nacions havinge bene vsed to be anoyed with muche Colde and darkenesse are wonte therefore to haue the fire and the sonne in great veneracion. like as Contrariwise the *moores* and *Egiptians* which are muche offended and greued with extreame heate of the sunne doe everie morninge when the sunne arisethe fall to Cursinge and banninge of him as theire plague and Chiefe scourge. Allsoe the *Scythyans* vsed when they would binde anie solempe vowe or Combinacion to drinke a bowle of blodd togeather vowinge thearby to spende theire laste blodd in that quarrell, And even so do the wilde Scottes as ye maie reade in *Buchannan* and some of the Northern Irishe likewise. ye maye also reade in the same booke in the tale of *Arsacomas* that it was the manner of the *Scythyans* when anie one of them | was heavilye wronged and woulde assemble vnto him anye forces of people to ioyne with him in his revenge to sitt in publique place for certaine daies vppon an oxehide to whiche theare woulde resorte all suche personnes as beinge disposed to take armes woulde enter into his paie or ioyne with him in his

1807 *Scythyans*] Scythians, *R*   1807 accompted] accounted, *R*   1808 these] those *CRW*
1808 Two] two. two *C*   twoe two *R*   1808-9 on periurours,] or periurous *C*   on the perjurers. *W*   1809 anie] om. *W*   1811 pointe] points *W*   1812 better] bitter *C*
1812 fighte.] fighte, *CR*   1813 to sweare Comonlie] commonly to sweare *W*   1813 swordes.] swordes, *CR*   1813-21 likewise . . . . scourge.] om. *WP*   1814 the . . . of] om. *R*
1815 honor] *corr. of* haue *E*   haue *C*   1815 and the] and *C*   1816 these] those *CR*
1818 veneracion.] veneracion *C*   veneracion, *R*   1819 *Egiptians*] Ethiopians *G*   1819 with] *followed by* muche *which is deleted E*   with muche *CR*   1820 arisethe] Riseth *CR*
1821 scourge.] scourge, *CR*   1821 Allsoe] *W and P resume at this point*   1822 Combinacion] combination amongst them *W*   1825 *Buchannan*] Buckanan *A*   Buckanon *H2*   Buchan *Ho*
Buckhenam *L*   Buckhanam *R*   1825 Irishe] *Irish. W*   1825 likewise] *om. C*   Likewise at the kindling of the Fire, and lighting of Candles, they say certaine prayers, and use some other superstitious rites, which shew that they honour the Fire and the light: for all those Northerne Nations having beene used to be annoyed with much colde and darkenesse, are wont therefore to have the Fire and the Sunne in great veneration; like as contrarywise the *Moores* and *Egyptians* which are much offended and grieved with extreame heat of the Sunne, doe every morning when the Sunne ariseth, fall to cursing and banning of him as their plague. *W*   same except " lykewise. Lykewise " *for* " Likewise "; " the candels " *for* " Candles "; *and* " Aethiopians " *for* " Egyptians " *P*   1825 ye] as yee *W*   1826 *Arsacomas*] *Arsecomas A Arsacomus CD1   Arsachomas D2   Arsoconias N   Arsocomas H2   Arsaconus P   Arsacomes T*
1829 sitt in] sytte in in *R*   1829 publique] some publique *CRW*   1831 paie] Armes

A VIEW OF THE PRESENT STATE OF IRELAND 109

quarrell And the same ye maye likewise reade to haue bene the Anciente manner of the wilde Scottes which are indede the verye naturall Irishe, moreouer the *Scythyans* vsed to sweare by theire kinges hande as *Olaus* shewethe And so do the Irishe vse now to sweare by theire Lordes hande and to forsweare it houlde it more Cryminall then to sweare by god. Allso the Scithians saide that they weare once euerie yeare turned into wolues and so it is written of the Irishe Thoughe mr *Camden* in a better sence do suppose it was a disease Called *lycanthropia* so named of the wolfe. And yeat some of the Irishe doe vse to mak the wolfe theire gossip. The Scithians allso vsed to sethe the fleshe in the hide And so do the northe Irishe yeat The *Scythians* likewise vsed to   the blodd of the beaste livinge and to make meate theareof And so doe the Irishe still in the Northe. manie suche Customes I Coulde recounte vnto youe as of theire olde manner of marryinge of buryinge of davncinge of singinge of feastinge of Cursinge thoughe Christians, haue wyped out the moste parte of them, by resemblaunce wheareof it mighte plainelye appeare to youe that the nacions are the same but that by the reckoninge of these fewe which I haue tolde vnto youe I finde my speache drawen out to a greater lengthe then I purposed   Thus muche onelye for this time I hope shall suffise youe to thinke that the Irishe are aunciently reduced from the *Scythyans*/

Eudox Surelye *Iren*: I haue in these fewe wordes hearde that from youe which I woulde haue thoughte had bene ympossible to haue bene spoken of times so remote and Customes soe anciente with delighte, wheare of I was all that while as it weare entraunced and Carried so far from my selfe as | as that I ame now righte sorie that yee ended so sone/ But I marveile muche howe it Comethe to passe that in soe longe Continewance of time and manye ages come betwene yeat anie iott of those olde Rites and supersticious Customes shoulde remayne amongest them/

Iren: It is no Cause of wonder at all for it is the manner of all barbarous

would enter into his paye *R*   1833 Irishe,] Irishe *C*   Irishe: *R*   *Irish.* *W*   1834 as] as, *R*   1834 *Olaus*] Oleus *L*   1835 now] now vse *R*   1836 forsweare it] forsweare yt and to forsweare yt *C*   1836 god.] god, And *C*   god, *R*   1837 euerie] a *W*ᶠ   1838 *Camden*] Campden *P*   Cambden *R*   1839 do] doth *W*   1839 a] *om. R*   1839 *lycanthropia*] *corr. of* Hicanthropia *E*   Hicantropia *C*   Hicanthropia *RD1D2H1H2HoLN*   1840 gossip.] gossip, *C*   1841 allso vsed] used also *W*   1842 northe Irishe yeat] Northerne *Irish.* *W*   1842 Irishe] Irishe, *CR*   1842 likewise] *om. W*   1842 *blank space*] boyle *R*   draw *W*   1844 still . . . Northe] in the North still *W*   1844 Northe.] Northe *W*   north, *R*   1846 Christians,] Christians *CW*   christianitie *H1G*   Christianlie *T*   1847 resemblaunce] resemblance, *RW*   1847 appeare] appeare, *R*   1850 purposed] purposed, *C*   purposed: *R*   purposed. *W*   1851 reduced] deduced *CRW*   1853 in . . . hearde] heard in these few words *W*   1854 woulde] could *R*   1855 delighte,] delight *CRW*   1855 wheare of] whereof, *R*   1856 as] (as *W*   1856 so] *om. R*   1857 as as] as *CRW*   1859 manye] so many *W*   1859 come] came *C*   1859 anie] not anie *C*   1861 of all] of all the *C*   1861 all barbarous] many *W* nacions to be verye superstitious and dilligent observers of olde Customes and Antiquities which they receaue by Continvall tradicion from theire parentes by recordinge of theire bardes and Cronicles in theire songes and by dailye vse and ensample of theire elders/

Eudox: But haue youe I praye youe obserued anie suche Customes amongest them broughte likewise from the Spaniardes or Gaules as these from the *Scythyans* that maye sure be verye materiall to your firste purpose

Iren: Some perhaps I haue, and who that will by this occacion more dilligentlye marke and Compare theire Customes shall finde manye more/ But theare are fewer I thinke remayninge of the Gaules or Spanniardes then of the Scithians by reason that the partes which they then possessed lyinge vppon the Coastes of the westerne and Southern sea weare sithens Continvallye visited with Straungers and forreine people repairinge thither for Trafficke and for fishinge which is verye plentifull vppon those Costes for the trade and enterdeale of seacost nacions one with another workethe more Civilitye and good fashions/ then the inland dwellers:/

which are seldome sene of forrenours. yeat some of suche as I haue noted I will recounte vnto youe And firste I will for the better Creditt of the reste shewe youe one out of theire Statutes Amongest which it is enacted that no mann shall weare his bearde only vppon the vpper lipp like muschachios shavinge all the rest of his Chinne And this was the Ancient manner of the Spanniardes as yeat it is of all the mahometans to Cutt all theire beardes Closse saue onelye theire mvschachios which they weare longe And the Cause of this vse was for that they beinge bred in a hote Countrie founde muche haire on theire faces and other partes to be noyous vnto them ffor which Cawse they did cutt it moste awaie like as
f. 35ʳ Contrarilye all other nacions | broughte vpp in Colde Countries do vse to norishe theire haire to kepe them the warmer which was the Cawse that the *Scythyans* and Scottes wore glibbes as I shewed youe to kepe theire

1864 in theire] and *C*   1866 I praye youe] (I pray you) *W*   1867 these] those *R*
1868 *Scythyans*] *Scithians*? *RW*   1869 purpose] purpose./ *C* purpose. *W*   1872 I thinke] *om. W*   1872 of . . . Spanniardes] *om. C*   1873 they then] they *R*   1874 Coastes] Coaste *CRW*   1875 Continvallye] *om. W*   1878 then . . . dwellers:/] *blank space C*
1878 then] in them, then in those that dwell neere *H1*   all sea men beeinge more naturallye desirous of new fashions then amongest *P*   (all Sea men being naturally desirous of new fashions,) then amongst *WG*   1878 dwellers] folks *G* folke *WP*   1878-9 *blank space*]
om. RW   1881 Amongest] among *W*   1882 weare] weare, *R*   1882 vppon] on *CW*
in *R*   1883 like muschachios] *om. W*   1883 the rest of] *om. W*   1885 Cutt] cut off *W*
1885 onelye theire] onelie *R*   1886 this] the *C*   1886 a] *om. C*   1888 ffor] *om. R*
1891 wore] ware *C* weare *R*   1891 as . . . youe] (as . . . you) *W*

heads warme and longe beardes to defende theire faces from Coulde from them allsoe I thinke Came safron Shirtes and Smockes which was devised by them in those hott Countries wheare saffron is verye Comon and rife for Avoidinge of that evill which Comethe by muche sweatinge and longe wearinge of lyninen. Allso the weomen amongest the old Spaniardes had the chardge of all houshoulde affaires bothe at home and abroade (as Boemius wrightethe thoughe now these spaniardes vse it quite otherwise And so haue the Irishe weomen the truste and Care of all thinges bothe at home and in the feildes. Likewise rounde leather Targettes is the Spannishe fashion whoe vsed it for the moste parte painted which in Ireland they vse allsoe in manie places Colloured after theire rude fashion. moreouer theire manner of theire weomens ridinge of the wronge side of the horse (I meane with theire faces towardes the righte side as the Irishe vse is as they saie olde Spannishe and as some saie *Africane* for amongest them the weomen (they saie) vse so to ride, and to ride a Crosse, Allso the depe smocke sleves hanginge to the grounde which the Irishe weomen vse they saie was olde Spannishe and is vsed yeat in Barbarye and yeat that should seme rather to be an olde Englishe fashion for in Armorye the fashion of the *manche* which is given in Armes by manye beinge in dede nothinge els but a sleve is fashioned muche like to that sleve. And that knightes in Ancient times vsed to weare theire mistresses or loves sleve vppon theire Armes Appearethe by that is written of Sr Launclot that he wore the sleve of the faire maide of Asterothe in a Tvrney wheareat Quene *Guenover* was muche displeased/

Eudox: your Conceite is verye good and well fittinge for thinges so far from Certeintye of knowledge and learninge onelie vppon Likelyhodes

1892 Coulde] Coulde, CR   cold. W   1893 I thinke] (I thinke) W   1895 of] om. W
1895 by] om. R   1896 lyninen.] lynnen, C   Linnen: W   1897 at] om. R   1898 Boemius]
Bormus D2F   Bohemius H1   Bennyus H2   Baenius N   Bohemus P   Boemus W
1898 wrightethe] writeth) W   1898 these] the W   1900 feildes.] feilde CW   feyldes, R
1901 for . . . parte] (for . . . part) W   1902 in] om. C   1902 fashion.] fashion, C
1903 theire manner] the manner W   1903 ridinge of] ridinge on CRW   1904 (I] I CRW
1904 towardes the] towarde theire R   1905 is] yt, C   1905 as they saie] (as they say) W
1905 as some] some W   1906 the] the the R   1906 saie)] saye R   1906 so] *inserted between lines and deleted after* and E om. R   1906 and to ride] and soe to ryde C om. RW
1906 a Crosse,] acrosse: C   acrosse,, R om. W   1907 sleves] sleive CRW   1907 hanginge
. . . grounde] om. W   1908 they saie] (they saye) R   1909 Englishe] Irishe R
1910 manche] march F   Maunche G   1913 Armes] Armes as CRW   1913 is] which is W
1914 he wore] wonne C   he ware R   1914 Asterothe] Asteloth W   1915 Guenover]
Grenvver C   Gournouer F   Guynever G   Guenora H2AN   Gneinarr T   1915 displeased/]
displeased R   1916 verye] om. W   1916 and] om. R   1916 far] far growne W

and Coniectures But haue youe anie Customes remayninge from the *Gaules* or *Brittons*

Iren: I haue obserued a fewe of either and whoe will better searche into them maye finde more And firste the profession of theire Bards was as (*Caesar* wrightethe) vsuall amongest the *Gaules* and the same was allso Comon amongeste the Brittons and is not yeat alltogeather lefte | of the Welche which are theire posteritye. ffor all the fashions of the Gaules and Brittons as he tistifyethe weare muche like; The longe dartes Came allso from the Gaules as ye maye reade in the same *Caesar* and in *Iohn Boemus* likewise the saide *Boemus* wrighteth that the *Gaulles* vsed swordes a handfull broade and so do the Irishe nowe Allsoe that they vsed longe wicker shildes in Battell that shoulde Cover theire whole bodies and soe doe the Northern Irishe. But because I haue not sene suche fashioned Targettes vsed in the Southerne partes but onelye amongest those Northern people and Irishe Scottes I do thinke that they weare broughte in rather by the Scithians then by the Gaules. Allsoe the Gaules vsed to drinke theire enemyes blodd and to painte themselues therewith So allsoe they write that the owlde Irishe weare wonte And so haue I sene some of the Irishe doe but not theire enemyes but friendes blodd as namelye at the execucion of A notable Traitour at Limericke Called murrogh Obrien I sawe an olde woman which was his foster mother take vp his heade whilste he was quartered and sucked vp all the blodd rvnninge theareout Sayinge that the earthe was not worthie to drinke it and thearewith allso steped her face, and breste and torne heare Crynge and shrikinge out moste terrible/

1919 *Brittons*] Brittons: *CR* Brittaines? *W*   1921-2 as (*Caesar*] as *Cesar C* (as *Cesar RW*   1924 of the Welche] of, by the walshe *R*   off, with the *Welsh W*   1924 Welche] Welshmen *GF*   1924 fashions of] fashions of of *C*   1925 Gaules and] *om. R*   1925 like;] like, *CR*   1925 dartes] dearth *R*   1926 *Caesar*] Ceaser *H2AL*   Ceasar *D1*   1927 *Iohn Boemus*] *Jhon Boenius H1*   I. Bormus *D2F*   Io: Benius *H2AN*   Io: Bohemus *P*   *Iohn Boemus, R*   Io: *Boemus . W*   1927 likewise . . . *Boemus*] *om. R*   1927 saide *Boemus*] sayd *Benius H2AN*   said Bormus *D2F*   Boemius *G*   said *Boenius H1*   said Io: Bohemus *P*   same Iohn *Boemus T*   said Io: *Boemus W*   1927 vsed] vsed, *R*   1928 nowe] nowe, *CR*   now. *W*   1928 that] *om. W*   1930 because] *om. W*   1932 those] the *W*   1933 Gaules.] Gawles, *CR*   1934 and to] and *W*   1935 therewith] therwith, *CR*   therewith. *W*   1936 friendes] theire frindes *W*   1937 blodd] blood. *W*   1937 Limericke] lamericke *C*   Climbricke *D1*   Lunerick *Ho*   Lymbricke *R*   1938 murrogh] *Murrogho A*   1938 Obrien] *obrein A*   O Brein *H2*   1939 take] toke *CR*   1940 rvnninge] that runne *W*   1941 torne] torned her *C*   tare her *R*   tore her *W*   1942 and shrikinge out] out and shreekinge *W*   1942 shrikinge] shickinge *C*   1942 terrible] terriblye *CRW*   1942 *blank space*] four

f. 36ʳ *Eudox.* Yee haue verye Well run thoroughe suche Customes as the Irishe haue derived from the firste olde nacions which inhabited that Lande Namelye the Scythians the Spanniardes the Gaules the Brittons, It now remayneth that youe take in hande the Customes of the old Englishe which are amongest the Irishe of which I do not thinke that ye shall haue muche to finde faulte with anie Consideringe that by the Englishe moste of the olde badd Irishe Customes weare abolished and more Civill fashions broughte in theire steade/

Iren: youe thinke otherwise *Eudox*: then I doe, for the the Chiefest abuses which are now in that realme are growen from the Englishe and the Englishe that weare are now muche more Lawles and Licentious then the verie wilde Irishe, so that as muche Care as was then by them had to reforme the Irishe so muche and more muste now be vsed to reforme them so muche time dothe alter the manners of men/

fifths of page blank C   blank space one inch long H1   turne over leafe followed by blank page L   blank space six inches long P   turne over leife and page blank except for words here should bee nothing R om. AD1D2FGH2HoNTW   1944 that] the W   1945 the Brittons,] and the Brittaines. W   1947 muche] much cause W   1948 anie] om. W 1950 in] vpp in R   1951 Iren:] no new paragraph N   1951 the the] the CRW   1953 the Englishe that weare] some of them W   1953 Lawles] lawles. C   1954 verie] om. C 1955 Irishe] Englishe LD1   1955 muche and] and much W   1956 them] them, W

Eudox: That semethe verie strange which youe saie that men shoulde so muche degenerate from theire firste natures as to growe wilde/

Irenius Soe muche Can libertie and ill example doe

Eudox: What libertye had the Englishe theare more then they had heare at home? weare not the Lawes planted amongest them at the firste and had they not Gouernours to Curbe and kepe them still in awe and obedience

Iren They had, but it was for the moste parte suche as did more hurte then good, for they had governours for the moste parte of themselues and Comonlie out of the Two families of the *Geraldines* and the *Butlers* bothe Aduersaries and Corrivals one againste the other, whoe thoughe for the moste parte they weare but deputies vnder some of the kinges of Englandes sonnes and Bretheren or other neare kinsemen whoe weare the kinges Lieftennantes yeat they swayed soe muche as they had all the Rule and the others but the title, Of which Butlers and Geraldines Albeit I muste Confesse theare weare verye brave and worthie men, as allsoe of other the Peares of that realme made Lorde deputies and Lordes Iustices at sundrie times, yet thorowe greatnes of theire late Conquestes and seigniories they grewe insolente and bente bothe that regall Aucthoritye | And allsoe theire private powers one againste another to the vtter subuercion of themselues and strenghtheninge of the Irishe againe. This ye maye reade plainelie discouered by a Lettre written from the Cittezens of Corke out of Irelande to the Earle of Shrewsburye then in England and remayninge yeat vppon recorde bothe in the Towre of Englande and allso Amongest the Cronicles of Irelande whearein it is by them Complained that the Englishe Lords and gentlemen whoe then had greate possessicions in Irelande begane thoroughe pride and insolencie to make private warrs one againste another And when either parte was weake they woulde wage

---

1958 wilde/] wilde *R*   1959 example] examples *W*   1959 doe] doe: *R* doe. *W*
1960 then] then, *C*   1961 home?] home *C*   1962 obedience] obedience./ *C*   obedience? *W*
1964 of] om. *C*   1965 and the] and *W*   1965 *Butlers*] Butlers, *R*   1966 one] on *R*
1966 other,] other. *W*   1966 thoughe] thought *C*   1967 they weare] om. *C*   1968 and] om. *CRW*   1969 Lieftennantes] lieutenantes *CW*   Livetennantes *R*   1969 soe] om. *C*
1970 title,] title. *W*   1970 Geraldines] Garaldines *with last two letters worn off C*
1970-1 I muste Confesse] (I must confesse) *W*   1971 theare] they *R*   1972 the] om. *C*
1972 Lordes] Lo: *W*   1973 at . . . Conquestes] om. *R*   1974 bente bothe] euill bente, both against *R*   1976 againe.] againe, *CR*   1978 Shrewsburye] shrewisbury *with last two letters worn off C*   Shrowsburye *H2N*   Shrasburye *L*   1979 Englande] London in Engl: *T*   London *WD1GHoL*   1980 Amongest] among *W*   1980 Irelande] Ireland. *W*
1980-2 wheareín . . . Irelande] om. *R*   1981 possessicions] possessions *CW*   1983 either]

A VIEW OF THE PRESENT STATE OF IRELAND 115

and drawe in the Irishe to take theire partie by which meanes they bothe greatlie encouraged and enhabled the Irishe which till that time had bene shutt vp within the mountaines of Slewlogher and weakened and dishabled themselues in so muche that theire Revenewes weare wonderfullie empaired and some of them which are theare reckoned to haue bene hable to haue spente xij or xiiij hundred poundes per annum of olde rente (that I may saie noe more) besides theire Comodities of Crekes and havens were now scarse hable to dispende the thirde parte ffrom which disorder and thoroughe other huge Callamities whiche haue Come vppon them thereby they are nowe growen to be allmoste as lewde as the Irishe I meane of suche Englishe as weare planted aboue towarde the weste. for the Englishe pale hathe preserved it thoroughe nearenesse of the State in reasonable Civillitye but the rest which dwelte Aboue in *Connaught and Mounster* which is the sweteste Soile of Irelande and some in Leinster and

f. 37ʳ vlster are degenerate | degenerate and growen to be as verye Patchokes as the wilde Irishe yea and some of them haue quite shaken of theire Englishe names and put on Irishe that they mighte be alltogeather Irishe/.

Eudox: Is it possible that anye shoulde so far growe out of frame that they shoulde in so shorte space quite forgett theire Countrie and theire owne names that is a moste daungerous *Lethargie* muche worse then that of *messala Corvinus* whoe beinge a moste learned man thorowe sicknes forgott his owne name But cane youe counte vs anye of this kinde

Iren: I Cannot but by reporte of the Irishe themselves who reporte that the *macmahons* in the Northe weare auncientlye Englishe to witte discended from the fzvrsula which was a noble familye in Englande and that the same apearethe by the significacion of theire Irishe names. Likewise that the *macswines* now in Vltster weare antientlye of the *Veres* of

thother *R*   1984 take] *blank space C*   1985 enhabled] enhabited *R*   1986 mountaines] Mountaine *R*   1986 Slewlogher] *Slevelougher D2F   Slewtogher Ho*   1989 xiiij hundred] xiij *CD1*   1300. *W*   1990 (that ... more)] that ... more *R*   1991 parte] part. *W*   1992 other] theire *R*   1993 nowe ... lewde as] almost now growne like *W*   1993 Irishe] Irishe, *R*   1994 towarde] towardes *RW*   1995 hathe] haue *C*   1995 it] it self *CRW*   1995 the] there *CR*   1996 dwelte] dwell *R*   1996 Aboue] *om. W*   1996 *Connaught*] Connagh *RHo*   1996 *and*] and in *W*   1997 sweteste] sweerest *W*   1997 Leinster] Lemster *C   Levister F*   1998 degenerate degenerate] Degenerate *CRW*   1998-9 and ... Irishe] *om. W*   1998 Patchokes] Rakehells *D2   Puthaks F   Pachockes Ho*   Patchookes *P* Patchcockes *RGL*   2003 names] names: *CW*   names, *R*   2004 *messala*] Messila *RN* 2004 *Corvinus*] Corrinius *N   Carvinas R*   2005 forgott] forgat *W*   2005 name] name, *CR* 2005 kinde] kinde/ *C*   kynde::/ *R*   kinde? *W*   2006 Cannot] can not speake *R*   2006 that] *om. C*   2007 *macmahons*] Marmahons *D2F*   Macmagons *P*   Macmaghons *RD1*   2008 fzvrsula] Fitzursuale *F*   ffits Ursualaes *G*   ffityvr *Sulas H2N*   Vrsulaes *P*   fz Vrsulas *RD2Ho   Fitz Vrsula's W*   2009 names.] names: *W*   2010 *macswines*] macsomes *H2   Macksweins Ho*

Englande but that they themselues for hatred of the Englishe so disguised theire names./

Eudox: Coulde they euer Conceaue anye suche divillishe dislike of theire owne naturall Contries as that they woulde be ashamed of her name and bite at the dug from which they sucked liffe/

Iren: I wote well theare shoulde be none, but proude hartes doe often times like wanton Coltes kicke at theire mothers as we reade *Alcibiades* and *Themistocles* did whoe beinge banished out of *Athens* fledd vnto the kinge of *Asia* and theare stirred him vp to warr againste theire Countrie in which warrs they themselues weare Chieftaines. So they saie did these *machswines* and *macmahons* or rather *Veres* and *fzursvlies* for private dispite turne themselues againste Englande ffor at suche time as *Robert Vere E.* of Oxforde was in the Barrons warrs againste K. Richarde the Seconde, thoroughe the malice of the peeres banished the realme and proscribed, he with his kinseman *fzvrslie* fledd into Irelande wheare beinge prosecuted and afterwardes in Englande put to deathe his kinsemen theare remayninge behinde in Irelande rebelled and Conspiringe with the Irishe did quite caste of | theire Englishe name and Allegeance since which time they haue ever soe remayned and haue still sithens bene Counted mere Irishe. the verye like is allso reported of the *makswines*, m̄ *mahons* and *mackshahies* of mounster how they likewise weare ancientlye Englishe and olde followers to the Earles of desmonde vntill the Raigne of K. Edwarde the iiij^th at which time the Earle of desmonde that then was Called Thomas beinge thorowe false subornacion as they saie of the Quene for some offence by her againste him Conceaved brought to his deathe at Tredagh moste vniustlye notwithstandinge that he was a verye good and sounde subiecte to the kinge, thearevppon all his kinsemen of the Geraldines which then was a mightie familye in mounster in revenge of that huge wronge rose into Armes againste the kinge and vtterlye renounced and forswore all obedience to the Crowne of Englande to whom the saide *mackswynes mackshehies* and *mackmahons* beinge then servantes and followers did the like and haue sithens ever so Continved And with them they saye all the people of mounster wente out and manye other of them which weare mere Englishe thenceforthe ioyned with the Irishe againste the kinge and termed themselues verye Irishe takinge on them Irishe habittes and Customes which coulde neuer since be cleane wyped awaye but the Contagion thearof hathe remained still amongest theire posterities Of which sorte they saie be moste of the Surnames which end in an. as *Hernan shinan mangan etc* the which now accounte themselues naturall Irishe. Other great howses theare be of the olde Englishe in Irelande which thoroughe licentious Conuersinge with the Irishe or marryinge and fosteringe with them or lacke of mete nourture or other suche vnhappye occacions haue degendred from theire antiente dignities are now growne as Irishe as Ohanlans breeche, (as the proverbe theare is) of which sorte theare are two moste pittifull ensamples | Aboue the reste, to witt the Lo. Bremingham, whoe beinge the moste anciente Baron I thinke in Englande is now waxen the moste Salvage Irishe naminge him selfe Irishlike, maccorishe. and the other is the great mortimer whoe forgettinge how greate he was once in Englande or Englishe at all is nowe become the moste barbarous of them all and is Called *macnemarra* and not muche better then he, is the olde *Lò Courcie* whoe havinge lewdlye

saie] (as they say) *W*   2036 Tredagh] *Drogheda A*   Tredaughe *D2*   Tredath *F*   Tredach *G*   Tradagh *R*   2037 to] *om. R*   2039 vtterlye] vtterlie, and vtterlie *R*   2040 forswore] forsooke *W*   2041 mackswynes] Macksweins *Ho*   2041 mackshehies] Mᵃshetries *D2F*   mackshelies *G*   Machohes *H2*   Mackheheis *Ho*   Macshethies *P*   mᵃ Shehirs *T*   2041 mackmahons] Marmahons *F*   2041 beinge] *om. R*   2042 sithens ever] ever sithence *W*   2043 they saye] (they say) *W*   2043 wente out] *om. C*   wente *R*   2045 againste ... Irishe] *om. R*   2047 thearof] *om. W*   2048 posterities] posterityes. *W*   2048 they saie] (they say) *W*   2049 in an.] in an *C*   in, an *R*   in *an, W*   2049 Hernan] Harman *C om. LD1*   Herman *D2F*   Heenam *R*   2049 shinan] Shiman *LD1*   2049 mangan] *corr. of* mangnan *E*   Mangnan *C*   Magan *F*   margan *H1*   Manan *T*   Mungan *WGP*   2050 Irishe.] Irishe, *CR*   2050 olde] *om. W*   2051 thoroughe] though *R*   2052 and] or *W*   2053 degendred] degenerated *W*   2054 are] and are *RW*   2054 Ohanlans] Ohantas *D1*   ohankans *G*   Ohalans *H1D2F*   Ohoalans *Ho*   Ohalandes *T*   2054 (as ... is)] as ... is. *W*   2055-63 of .... quite Irishe] *om. W*   2056 Bremingham] Breningham *CG*   Birmingham *D1*   Brenigham *H1*   Bremecham *H2AN*   2058 Irishlike] Irishe, like *R*   2058 maccorishe] blank space *A*   Nicorishe *D1*   Norcorish *L*   Noccorishe *RD2FH2Ho*   mᵃ Corish *T*   2058 is the] is the other is the *R*   2058 mortimer] Mortimers *A*   2060 macnemarra] Macknihmarrih *A*   Macnemorrah *GT*   Macnencarra *N*   2061 Courcie] Caircye *D2*   Caurcy *F*

wasted all the Landes and Seigniories that he had and aliened them vnto the Irishe is himselfe now growen quite Irishe

Eudox: In truethe this which youe tell is a moste shamefull hearinge and to be reformed with moste sharpe Censures in so greate personages to the terrour of the meanour for wheare the Lordes and Chief men wax so barbarous and bastardlike what shalbe hoped of the pesantes and base people And hearby sure we haue made a faire waye vnto your selfe to laye open the abuses of theire evill Customes which ye haue now nexte to declare The which no doubt but are verye bad and barbarous beinge borrowed from the Irishe as theire apparrell theire language theire ridinge and manye other the like

Iren: ye Cannot but thinke them sure to be verye brute and vncivill for weare they at the beste that they weare of olde when they weare broughte in they shoulde in so longe an alteracion of time seme verye straunge and vncouthe for it is to be thoughte that the vse of all Englande was in the Raigne of Henrye the Seconde when Irelande was firste planted withe Englishe verye rude and barbarous so as if the same shoulde be now vsed in Englande by anye it would seme worthie of sharpe Correccion and of new lawes for reformacion but it is but even the other daye since Englande grewe Civill Therefore in Countinge the evill Customes of the Englishe theare I will not haue regarde wheather the beginninge theareof | weare Englishe or Irishe but will haue respecte onelye to the inconvenience theareof. And firste I haue to finde faulte with the Abuse of language that is for the speakinge of Irishe amongest the Englishe which as it is vnnaturall that anye people shoulde love anothers language more then theire owne soe is it verye inConvenient and the Cause of manye other evills//

Eudox: It semethe straunge to me that the Englishe shoulde take more delighte to speake that language then theire owne wheareas they shoulde (me thinkes) rather take scorne to acquainte theire Tounges thereto for it hathe bene ever the vse of the Conquerour to despise the Language of

---

Conrrye Ho Courrie RLD1 Couryer T 2062 vnto] to *C* 2063 himselfe] himself also *CR*
2063 quite Irishe] quite Irishe./ *C* quite Irishe:: *R* 2064 *Eudox*:] *W resumes at this point*
2065 moste] *om. C* most most *R* 2066 wheare] if *W* 2066 Lordes] lorde *C*
2066-7 wax ... bastardlike] degenerate *W* 2067 bastardlike] bastardlie *C* 2067 base] baser *W* 2068 we] yow *RW* 2068 waye] *om. R* 2070 and barbarous] *om. W*
2071 theire language] theire theire language *R* 2072 like] like./ *C* like:/: *R* like. *W*
2073 thinke] hold *W* 2073 brute and] *om. W* 2075-6 straunge and vncouthe] uncouth and strange *W* 2076-8 was ... Englishe] (was ... *English*) *W* 2077 firste] *om. W*
2079 Englande] England: *R* 2080 but it] for it *W* 2081 Civill] Civill, *C* Civill: *RW*
2081 Englishe] Englishe, *R* 2082 not] *om. R* 2085 amongest] among *W* 2085 it is] yt *R*
2087 is it] it is *W* 2087 other] there *R* 2090-1 they shoulde (me] (they should me *C*
2091 thinkes)] thinckes *R* 2092 it] it it *C* 2092 bene ever] ever beene *W* 2092 despise

A VIEW OF THE PRESENT STATE OF IRELAND 119

the Conquered and to force him by all meanes to learne his. So did the Romaines allwaies vse in soe muche that there is allmoste no nacion in the worlde but is sprinckled with theire language It weare good thearefore (me thinkes) to searche out the Originall Cause of this evill for the same beinge discouered a redresse theareof wilbe the more easlyer prouided, ffor I thinke it verye strange that the Englishe beinge soe manye and the Irishe soe fewe as they then weare left the fewer shoulde drawe the more vnto theire vse.

Iren: I suppose that the Chief Cause of bringinge in the Irishe language amongest them was speciallye theire fosteringe and marryinge with the Irishe The which are two moste daungerous infeccions for firste the Childe that suckethe the milke of the nurse muste of necessitye learne his firste speache of her, the which beinge the firste that is envred to his tounge is ever after moste pleasinge vnto him In so muche as thoughe he afterwardes be taughte Englishe yeat the smacke of the firste will allwaies abide with him and not onelye of the speche but allsoe of the manners and Condicions for besides that younge Children be like Apes which will affecte and ymitate what they see done before them speciallye by theire nurses whom they love so well, they moreouer drawe into themselues togeather with theire sucke even the nature and disposicion of theire nurses |

f. 39ʳ ffor the minde followethe muche the Temparature of the bodye and allsoe the wordes are the Image of the minde So as they procedinge from the minde the minde must be nedes affected with the wordes So that the speache beinge Irishe the harte muste nedes be Irishe for out of the abundance of the harte the tonge speakethe. The nexte is the marryinge with the Irishe which how daungerous a thinge it is in all Comon wealthes appearethe to euerye simpleste sence and thoughe some great ones haue perhaps vsed suche matches with theire vassalls and haue of them neuerthelesse raysed worthie Issue, as *Telamon* did with *Tecmessa, Alexander the* greate with *Roxane* and Iulius Cesar with Cleopatrie

Yeat the exsample is so perilous as it is not to be adventured for in steade of those fewe good I Coulde Counte

the] dispose his *R*   2093 his.] his, *CR*   2094 no] in a *R*   2095 language] language, *R* language. *W*   2096 thinkes] seemes *W*   2096 Cause] course *R*   2096 this] the *C* his *R*   2097 wilbe . . . easlyer] will the more easily be *W*   2097 easlyer] easlie *C* easielie *R*   2098 I thinke] (I thinke) *W*   2098 verye] were *R*   2103 The] om. *R* 2105 that is] om. *W*   2106 ever] om. *R*   2106 he] om. *C*   2108 allsoe] om. *R* 2109 that] the *R*   that, *W*   2109 like] lyke, *R*   2110 speciallye] especially *W*   2114 they] the *R*   2115 the minde must] must *C*   2115 be nedes] needes be *W*   2115 affected] effected *R*   2115 wordes] words. *W*   2117 speakethe.] speaketh, *C*   2120 perhaps] om. *R*   2121 *Tecmessa*] *Tecmesia G   Tormessa* H1   *Termessa* H2AN*Ho   Tocmissa* RLD1 *Ternisia* T   *Termessa corrected to Tecmessa W*   (*Faults escaped*)   2122 and . . . Cleopatrie] added in different hand E   blank space C   2122 Iulius Cesar] Antonye *P*   2122 Cleopatrie] cleopatre *L*   *Cleopatra* WD1D2Ho   2122-3 blank space] om. *RW*   2124 Coulde]

vnto them infinite manye evill And indede how cane suche matchinge but bringe forthe an evill race seinge that Comonlye the Childe takethe moste of his nature of the mother besides speache manners inclynacion which are for the moste parte agreable to the Condicions of theire mothers for by them they are firste framed and fashioned soe as what they receaue once from them they will hardelye euer after forgoe: Therefore are those Two evill Customes of fosteringe and marryinge with the Irishe moste Carefullye to be restrained for of them two the Thirde that is the evill Custome of Language which I speake of Chieflye procedethe//

Eudox: But are theare not Lawes allreadye provided for avoidinge of this evill.///

Iren: yeas I thinke theare be but as good neuer a whitt as neuer the better for what doe statutes availe without penalties or lawes without Charge of execucion? for soe theare is another like lawe enacted againste wearinge of Irishe Apparrell | But neuerthemore it is obserued by anie or executed by them that haue the Chardge ffor they in theire private discrecions thinke it not fitt to be forced vppon the pore wretches of that contrye which are not worthe the price of Englishe apparell nor expediente to be practized againste the habler sorte by reason that the bare Contrye (saye they) dothe yealde no better and weare theare better to be had yeat these weare fitter to be vsed as namelye the mantle in travellinge because theare be no Innes wheare mete beddinge maye be had soe that his mantele serues him thearefore for a bed, The Leather quilted Iacke in iurneyinge and in Campinge for that it is fittest to be vnder his shirte for anie occasion of sodaine service as theare hapen manye to Couer his thinne breche on horesbacke The greate linnen rowle which the weomen weare to kepe theare heades warme after Cuttinge theire haire which they vse in anye sicknes Besides theire thicke foulded Lynnen shirtes theare longe sleved smockes theire haulfe sleved Coates theire silken fillettes and all the reste they will devise some Coller for either of necessitye or of Antiquitye or of Comlinesse/

would *C* 2125-6 but ... race] succeede well *W* 2127 inclynacion] and inclynation *W* 2128 for the ... parte] (for ... part) *W* 2129 as] *om. C* 2129 what] *om. R* 2129 once] any thinge *R* 2130 forgoe:] forgoe, *C* 2130 those] these *CRW* 2130 Two] *om. W* 2131 moste] more *C* 2132 that ... evill] evill that is the *W* 2133 which ... of] (which ... of,) *W* 2133 speake] spake *CRW* 2134 not] noe *C* 2134 provided] appointed *R* 2135 evill.///] evill? *W* 2137 for ... availe] *om. C* 2138 execucion?] execution, *CR* 2139 Irishe] the *Irish W* 2139 it is] is it *W* 2143 againste] amongest *C* 2143 bare] *om. RW* 2144 dothe] doe *R* 2146 mete] meate or *R* 2146 maye] might *R* 2147 thearefore] then *CRW* 2147 bed,] bed. *W* 2148 iurneyinge] Iorninge *R* 2148 shirte] shirte of male *R* shirt of Male, and *W* 2149 to] and to *CR* 2149-50 thinne breche] trouse *W* 2150 horesbacke] horsbacke, *CR* horsebacke. *W* 2152 sicknes] sicknes, *CR* sickenesse. *W* 2154 Coller] coullor, *R*

Eudox: But what Collour soeuer they alleadge me thinkes it not expedient that the execucion of a lawe once ordayned shoulde be lefte to the discrecion of the officer But that without parcialytie or regarde it shoulde be fullfilled aswell on Englishe as Irishe/

Iren: But they thinke this precisenes in reformacion of Apparrell not to be so materiall or greatlye pertinente/

Eudox: yeas surelye but it is ffor mens Apparell is Comonlye made accordinge to theire Condicions and theire Condicons are often times gouerned by theire garmentes ffor the persone that is gowned is by his gowne putt in minde of gravetye and allsoe | Restrained from lightenes by the verye vnaptnes of his wede Therefore it is written by *Aristotle* that when *Cirus* had ouercome the Lidians that weare a warlike nacion and devised to bringe them to a more peaceable liffe he Chaunged theire Apparrell and musicke And in steade of theire shorte warlike Coate cloathed them in longe garmentes like weomen and in steade of theire warlike musicke appointed to them certaine Lascivious layes and loose gigs by which in shorte space theire mindes weare so mollified and abated that they forgate theire former firesnes and became moste tender and effeminate wheareby it appeareth that theare is not a litle in the garment to the fashioninge of the minde and Condicions But be these which youe haue described the fashions of the Irishe Wede/

Iren: Noe all these which I haue rehearsed to youe be not Irishe garmentes but Englishe, for the quilted leather Iacke is olde Englishe for it was the proper wede of the horsemen as ye maye reade in *Chaucer* wheare he describeth: S*r* *Thopas* apparrell and armour when he wente to fighte againste the Geaunte which Checklaton is that kinde of gilden leather with which they vse to imbrother theire Irishe Iackes and theare likewise by all that discripcion ye maye see the verye fashion and manner of the Irishe horsmen moste livelye set forthe in his longe hose, his Rydinge shoes of Costelye Cordwaine his hacqueton and his habericion with all the rest thearevnto belonginge

2158 officer] Iudge, or Officer *W*   2159 on] on the *C*   2161 pertinente/] pertinent *CR*
2163 are] *om. C*   2166 vnaptnes] aptnes *R*   2166 wede] weed, *CR* weed. *W*   2167 and] *om. R*   2169 And] are *R*   2169 Coate] Coates *R*   2170 weomen] wyves *R*   2170 warlike] *om. C* warlike, *R*   2172 so] *om. R*   2172 forgate] forgott *CRW*   2175 be] by *C*   2176 Wede/] weedes/. *C* weedes:?: *R* weedes? *W*   2179 horsemen] horseman *CRW*   2179 wheare] when *W*   2180 describeth:] discribeth *CRW*   2180 *Thopas*] Sethopas *D1*   Tapas *G* *Thepas Ho*   *Thesias T*   2180 when] as *W*   2181 the] the, *R*   2181 which Checklaton] in his robe of Shecklaton, which *W*   2181 Checklaton] Checklation *P*   *Ehecklaton T*   2181 gilden] guilded *W*   2182 vse] doe vse *C*   2182 imbrother] embroder *C*   Imbroader *R* imbroyder *W*   2182 Iackes] Iackets *W*   2184 horsmen] horseman *W*   2184 livelye] truely *W*   2184 forthe] out *R*   2184 Rydinge] *blank space C om. R*   2185 hacqueton] hacquelon *T*   2185 habericion] haberion *CRW*   2186 belonginge] belonginge/. *C*

Eudox: I surelye thoughte that that manner had bene kindelye Irishe for it is farr differinge from that we haue nowe as allso all the furniture of his horsse his stronge brasse bitt his slydinge Raynes his Shanke pillion without stirrops | his manner of mountinge his fashion of ridinge his Chardginge of his speare aloafte aboue hande the forme of his Speare/

Iren: Noe sure they be native Englishe and brought in by the Englishemen firste into Irelande neither is the same yet Counted an vncomelye manner of Ridinge for I haue hearde some great warriours saie that in all the services which they had sene abroad in forreine Contries they neuer sawe a more Comlye horseman then the Irisheman, nor that Commethe one more bravelye in his Chardge neither is his manner of mountinge vnsemelye thoughe he lacke Stirrops but more readye then with stirrops for in his gettinge vp his horse is still goinge whereby he gaynethe waie and therefore the stirrope was Called soe in scorne as it weare a staire to gett vpp beinge derived of the olde Englishe worde *Sty*. which is to mounte/

Eudox: It semethe then that ye finde no faulte with this manner of Ridinge. whye then woulde youe haue the quilted Iacke layed awaye?

Iren I woulde not haue it laied awaie but the abuse theareof to be put awaie for beinge vsed to the end that it was framed that is to be worne in warr vnder a shirte of male it is allowable as allso the shirte of mayle and all his other furniture but to be worne daylie at home and in Townes and Civill places it is a rude habitt and moste vncomelye seminge like a players painted Coate

Eudox: But it is worne they saie likewise of Irishe footemen howe do youe allowe of that for I should thinke it verye vnsemelye

Iren: Noe. not as it is vsed in warr for it is then worne likewise of a footeman vnder a shirte of mayle the which footeman they Call a *Galloglasse*

belonginge:/ R   belonging. W   2187 that that] that the W   2187 kindelye] *om*. W
2191 his speare] speare R   2191 hande] head W   2193 yet] *om*. CW   2193 Counted] accounted W   2193 an] and C   2195 the] these R   2196 horseman] man W
2200 soe in] from R   2201 of] out of R   2201 *Sty*.] sty C *Sty*, RW   2201 is to] is to get up, or W   2202 mounte/] mount./. C   mount R   2203 Ridinge.] Rydinge C   rydinge, RW   2204 quilted] gylded R   2204 awaye?] awaye./. C   awaye:/ R
2205 woulde . . . it] doe not wish it to be W   2205 it] that R   2208 and in] as in R
2210 Coate] Cote. CW   coate: R   2211 they saie likewise] likewise they saye C   2211 they saie] (they say) W   2211 likewise] *om*. R   2211 footemen] footemen, RW   2212 that] that? W   2212 verye] were R   2212 vnsemelye] vnsemelye./ C   vnseemelie: R   unseemely. W   2213 Noe.] Noe CR   No, W   2213 then worne] worne then W   2213 likewise] likewise likewise R   2213-4 a footeman] footmen W   2214 vnder . . . footeman] *om*. R   2214 a shirte] their shirts W   2214 footeman] footmen W   2214 *Galloglasse*]

A VIEW OF THE PRESENT STATE OF IRELAND 123

f. 41ʳ the which name | dothe discouer him to be allsoe Aunciente Englishe ffor *Gallogla* signifies an Englishe servitour or yeoman And he beinge so armed in a longhe shirte of mayle downe to the Caulfe of his legge with a longe broade Axe in his hande was then *Pedes gravis armaturae,* and was in steade of the armed foteman that now wearethe a Corslett then before the Corslett was vsed or allmoste invented

Eudox. Then him belike ye likewise allowe in your streight reformacion of old Costomes/

Iren: Bothe him and the kerne allsoe (whome onelye I toke to be the proper Irishe soldiour Cane I allowe soe that they vse that habitt and Costome of theires in the warrs onelye when they are led forthe to service of theire Prince, and not vsually at home and in Civill places And besides doe they laie aside the evill and vild vses which the Galloglasse and kerne doe vse in theire Comon trade of life

Eudox: What be those/

Iren: marye these be the moste loathelye and barbarous tradicions of anye people I thinke vnder heaven for from the time that they enter into thet Course they doe vse all the beastlye behavour that maye be The oppress all men they spoile aswell the subiecte as the enemye they steale they are Cruell and bloddye full of revenge and delightinge in deadlye execucion licentious swearers and blasphemours Comon ravishers of weomen and murderers of Children

Eudox: These be moste villanous Condicions: I marveile then that they be euer vsed or Imployed or allmoste/ suffered to live what good cane theare be in them/

Iren: yeat sure they are verye valiante and hardye for the moste parte

---

gallowe glasse *D2* Gallowglasoe *F* Galloyglash *G* Galloglasses *W* 2215 him] them *W* 2215 to be allsoe] also to be *W* 2216 ffor . . . Englishe] *om. R* 2216 *Gallogla*] Gallogle *A* Gallowgla *D2* Gallowglase *F* Galoglaa *P* 2217 his] the *R* 2218 *armaturae*] Armature *CHo* Armatura *N* 2218-9 and . . . Corslett] (and . . . Corslet,) *W* 2219 then] *om. W* 2220 was] were *CR* 2220 invented] invented. *CW* invented: *R* 2221 likewise] also *R* 2222 Costomes] Customes *CRW* 2223 *Iren*:] *om. D1* 2223 toke] take *W* 2224 soldiour] souldyor, *R* Souldier) *W* 2224 they vse] the vse of *C* 2225 Costome] custome *CRW* 2225 to] to the *CRW* 2226 vsually] *corr. of* vsuall *E* vsuall *CR* 2227 they] *om. CRW* 2227 and vild] wylde *R* and wilde *W* 2227 kerne] Kerne: *R* 2228 Comon] evill *R* 2228 life] lief./. *C* lyfe:::/ *R* life. *W* 2229 those/] those?/ *C* those? *W* 2230 these] those *CRW* 2230 loathelye and barbarous] barbarous and loathly *W* 2230 tradicions] Condicions *CRW* 2231 I thinke] (I thinke) *W* 2232 be] bee, *W* 2232 The] They *CW* to *R* 2234 full] full, *R* 2234 delightinge] delight *R* 2234 in] *added in margin E om. C* 2234 execucion] execution, *R* 2236 Children] Children./ *C* children. *W* 2237 These] Those *R* 2237 Condicions:] Condicions *C* Condycions, *RW* 2237-8 they be euer] ever they bee *R* 2238 live] lyve, *R* live; *W* 2239 be] then be *C* bee then *R* 2239 them/] them? *W* 2240 hardye] hardie, *W*

greate endurers of Colde Labour honger and all hardnesse verye active and stronge of hande verye swifte of foote verye vigilaunte and circumspecte in theire enterprises verye presente in perills verye great scorners of deathe/

Eudox Trulye by this that ye saie it semes the Irishe man is a verye brave soldier

f. 41ᵛ *Iren*: yea surelye even in that rude kinde of service he | he bearethe himselfe verye Coragiouslye but when he Comethe to experience of service abroade and is putt to a pece or a pike he makethe as worthie a souldiour as anye nacion he metethe with But let vs I praye youe turne againe to our discourse of evill Customes amongest the Irishe/

Eudox: me semes all this which youe speake of concerneth the Customes of the Irishe verye materiallye for theire vses in warr are of no small importance to be Considered as well to reforme those which are evill as to Confirme and Continewe those which are good but followe youe your owne Course and shewe what other theire Customes ye haue to dislike of

Iren: Theare is amongst the Irishe a certen kinde of people Called Bardes which are to them in steade of Poets whose profession is to sett fourthe the praises and dispraises of menne in their Poems or Rymes, the which are hadd in soe highe regard and estimation amongest them that none dare displease them for feare to runne into reproch throughe their offence, and to be made infamous in the mouthes of all men/ ffor the verses are taken vpp with a generall applause and vsuall songe att all feastes and meetinges by certeine other persons whose proper function that is which also receive for the same great Rewardes and reputation besides/.

Eudox: Doe you blame this in them which I would otherwise haue thought to haue bene wourthie of good accompt, and rather to haue bene mainteyned and augmented amongest them, then to have bene misliked, ffor I have Redd that in all ages Poets have bene in speciall reputacion and that me seemes not without great Cause for besides theare sweete invencions and most wittie they haue allwaies vsed to sett fourthe the praises of the

2241 hardnesse] hardnesse, *R*   2244 Trulye] Surelie *R*   2244 semes] semes that *CW*
2245 soldier] soldier/. *C* souldyer, *R* Souldier. *W*   2246 surelye] trulie *R*   2246 even] om. *CW*   2246 he he] hee *CRW*   2248 and] or *W*   2249 I praye youe] (I pray you) *W*
2251-6 *Eudox*: . . . . *Iren*:] Eudoxus deleted and rest om. *A*   2251 semes] thinkes *W*
2252 of the] amongst the *R*   2255 of] of./ *C* of:/ *R* of. *W*   2256-71 *Iren*: . . . . badd] *second handwriting E*   2256 Theare] *A resumes at this point*   2256 Bardes] the bardes *R*   2258 and] or *W*   2258 menne in] men, Noe: *R*   2261 ffor the] for their *CRW*   2262 vsuall songe] vsuallie sounge *RW*   2262-3 feastes and meetinges] feastmetinges *R*   2263 which] who *W*   2264 besides] beside *C* amongst them *W*
2267 misliked] disliked *RW*   2268 bene] bene hadd *CR*   2269 me seemes] (mee thinkes) *W*   2270 wittie] wittye layes *CRW*   2270 haue] are *R*   2270 praises of

good and virtuous and to beat downe and disgrace the badd and vicious so that manye braue yonge mindes haue oftentimes thoroughe hearinge the prayses and famous *Eulogies* of worthie men sunge and reported vnto them bene stirred | vpp to affecte like Comendacions and so to strive vnto the like desertes So they saie that the Lacedemonians weare more excited to desire of honour with the excellente verses of the poete *Tyrteus* then with all the exhortacions of theire Capitaines or authoritye of theire rulers and magistrates//

Iren: It is moste trewe that suche poetes as in theire wrightinges doe labour to better the manners of men and thoroughe the swete bayte of theire numbers to steale into the yonge spirites a desire of honour and vertue are worthie to be had in greate respecte, But these Irishe Bardes are for the moste parte of another minde and so farre from instructinge yonge men in morrall discipline that they themselues doe more deserue to be sharpelye discipled for they seldome vse to Chose out themselues the doinges of good men for the argumentes of theire poems but whom soeuer they finde to be moste Licentious of life moste bolde and lawles in his doinges moste daungerous and desperate in all partes of disobedience and rebellious disposicion him they set vp and glorifye in theire Rymes him the praise to the people and to yonge men make an example to followe/

Eudox: I marvaile what kinde of speaches they can finde or what face they Cane put one to praise suche lewde persones as live so lawleslye and licentiouslye vppon stealthes and spoiles as moste of them doe or howe Cane they thinke that anie good minde will applaude or approve the same/

Iren: Theare is none so bad *Eudox*: But that shall finde some to favour his doinges but suche licencious partes as these tendinge for the moste parte to the hurte of the Englishe or mayntenaunce of theire owne lewd libertie they themselues beinge moste desirous theareof do moste allowe besides this evill thinges beinge decte and suborned with the gaye attire of goodlye wordes maye easelye deceaue and Carrye awaie the affeccion of a yonge minde that is not well stayed but desirous by some bolde adventure to make profe of himselfe | for beinge (as theye all be) broughte

the] *om. R* 2271 and vicious] *return to first handwriting E* 2271 vicious] vitious. *W*
2272 hearinge] the hearinge *CR* 2273 the] of *C* 2273 *Eulogies*] *Eclogies H1* 2274 like] the like *W* 2274 so] *om. C* 2275 vnto] to *W* 2275 desertes] desertes, *R* deserts. *W*
2275 saie] *om. C* 2276 excited] enclyned *R* 2276 *Tyrteus*] *Tyrreus A Tyrus H2 blank space Ho Tyrrens N* 2277 authoritye] aucthorities *R* 2279 poetes] Potes *C*
2279 wrightinges] wrightinge *CR* 2280 of men] *om. R* 2282 are worthie] *om. R*
2285 discipled] disciplined *C* disciplined *W* 2285 out] vnto *CRW* 2286 argumentes] ornamentes *R* 2289 Rymes] Rithmes *W* 2289 the] they *CRW* 2290 and to] and *C*
2290 followe/] follow *W* 2292 lewde] bad *W* 2294 or approve] *om. R* 2295 that] *om. W* 2296 partes] persones *D2F* poetes? 2298 allowe] allowe. *CW* allowe, *R*
2299 this] these *R* this, *W* 2299 suborned] attired *W* 2301-2 adventure] adventures *W*

vp idlye without awe of parentes without preceptes of masters without
feare of offence not beinge directed nor ymployed in anye Course of life
which maye Carrye them to vertue will easelye be drawen to followe suche, 2305
as anye shall set before them for a younge minde Cannot reste and if he
be not still busied in some goodnes he will finde himself suche busines as
shall sone busie all aboute him. In which if He shall finde anie to praise
him and to give him encouragement, as these Bardes and rymers doe for
litle rewarde or a share of a stollen Cowe then waxeth he moste insolente 2310
and haulfe mad with the loue of himselfe and his owne lewde deds And
as for wordes to sett forthe suche Lewdnes it is not harde for them to give
a goodlye glose and painted shewe thearevnto borrowed even from the
prayses which are proper vnto vertue it selfe As of a moste notorious
Thiefe and wicked outlawe which had lived all his lief time of spoiles 2315
and Robberies, one of theire Bardes in his praise saide That he was none
of those Idle milkesopps that was broughte vp by the fire side/ but that
moste of his daies he spente in armes and valiante enterprises that he did
neuer eate his meate before he had wonne it with his sword that he laye
not slugginge all mighte in a Cabbyn vnder his mantle But vsed Comonlye 2320
to kepe others wakinge to defende theire lives and did lighte his Candle
at the flame of theire howses to leade him in the darkenes that the daie
was his nighte and the nighte his daie that he loued not to lye longe
owinge of wenches to yealde to him but wheare he Came he toke by force
the spoile of other mens love and lefte but lamentacion to theire louers 2325
That his musicke was not the harpe nor layes of love but the Cryes of
f. 43ʳ people and Clashinge of | Of Armour, and that finallye he died not
bewaylled of manye but made manye waile when he died that dearely
boughte his deathe doe youe not thinke *Eudoxus*? that manye of these
praises mighte be applied to men of beste deserte yeat are they all yealded 2330
to a moste notable Traytour and amongest some of the Irishe not smallye
accounted of for the songe when it was firste made and sunge vnto a

2302-3 be) broughte vp] be broght up) *W*   2303 masters] masters, and *W*   2304 not] and not *C*   2305 will] well *C*   2305 be] to be *C*   2306 and] *om. RW*   2308 him.] him *C*   him, *R*   2309 these] those *CW*   those, *R*   2309 rymers] rymers, *R*   Rythmers *W*   2309 for] for a *C*   2313 glose] *om. W*   2314 vnto] to *W*   2314 selfe] selfe. *W*   2314 of] for *C*   2315 lief] *om. R*   2316 saide] will say *W*   2317 those] the *W*   2320 slugginge all mighte] all night slugging *W*   2320 mighte] nighte *CR*   2322 flame] flames *W*   2322 howses] howses./ *C*   2323 lye] be *W*   2324 owinge] woyeinge *C*   woinge *RW*   2327 Of] *om. CRW*   ı   2327 that finallye] finally, that *W*   2328 made] *om. R*   2329 deathe] deathe, *CR*   death. *W*   2329 Eudoxus?] Eudoxus *CR*   Eudoxius: beginning new paragraph H2   (Eudoxus) *W*   2330 deserte] deserts *W*   2331 a] *om. R*   2331 Traytour] trators *R*   2332 songe] same *R*   2332 sunge] sunge and sunge *R*   2332 vnto] to *W*

persone of highe degree there was boughte as theire manner is for ffortye Coowes.

Eudox And well worthie sure/ But tell me I praye youe haue they anye Arte in their Composicions or be they anie thinge wittye or well savored as Poems should be

Iren: yea Truelye I haue Cawsed diuerse of them to be translated vnto me that I mighte vnderstande them and surelye they savored of swete witt and good invencion but skilled not of the goodlie ornamentes of Poetrye yet weare they sprinkled with some prettie flowers of theire owne naturall devise which gaue good grace and Comlinesse vnto them The which it is great pittye to see so abused to the gracinge of wickednes and vice which woulde with good vsage serue to beautifye and adorne vertue This evell Custome therefore nedethe reformacion And now nexte after the Irishe kerne me semes the Irishe horsboyes woulde Come well in order the vse of which thoughe necessitye (as times now be) doe enforce yeat in the thoroughe reformacion of that realme they shoulde be Cutt of for the Cause whye they muste nowe be permitted is the wante of Conveniente Innes for lodginge of traueilours on horsbacke and of hostelers to tende theire horses by the waye, But when thinges shalbe reduced to a better passe this nedethe speciallye to be reformed for out of the frye of these rakehellye horsboyes growinge vp in knaverye and villanye are theare kerne continallye | Supplied and mainteyned, for havinge bene once broughte vpp an Idle horsboye he will neuer after fall to labour but is onely made fitt for the halter And these allsoe (the which is one foule ouersighte) are for the moste parte broughte vp amongest Englishemen and souldiours of whom learninge to shote in a pece and beinge made acquainted with all the trades of the Englishe they are afterwards when they become kerne made more fitt to Cutt theire throates. Nexte to this theare is another muche like but muche more lewde and dishonest and that is of theire Carrowes which are a kinde of people that wander vp and downe gentelemens howses livinge onelye vppon Cardes and dice the

2333 there was] they were *R* 2333 as . . . is] (as . . . is) *W* 2333 for] om. *C*
2334 Coowes] corr. of Crownes *E* Crownes *CRW* 2335 I praye youe] (I pray you) *W*
2336 Composicions] compositions? *W* 2337 be] be/. *C* be? *W* 2340 ornamentes] argumentes? an ornament *R* 2341 sprinkled] sprinckled, *R* 2341 owne] om. *W* 2343 so] so good could *C* 2344 woulde . . . vsage] with good usage would *W* 2344 woulde] 2344 beautifye . . . vertue] adorne and beautifie vertue. *W* 2344 vertue] vertue, *R* 2346 semes] thinks *W* 2346 horsboyes] *Horseboyes* or *Guilles* as they call them *A* 2349 muste nowe] are now to *W* 2349 the] om. *W* 2353 rakehellye] rake-hell *W* 2354 once] om. *C* 2355 horsboye] horsboyes *C* 2357 ouersighte)] oversight, *R* 2357 broughte] bredd *CRW* 2357-8 Englishemen and souldiours] the Englishmen *W* 2358 a] om. *R* 2359 Englishe] Englishe) *C* 2360 throates.] throtes, *CR* 2362 is of] is *C* 2362 Carrowes] *Kearrooghs A* 2362 are] is *RW* 2363 downe] downe to *W* 2363 the] corr. of they *E* they *C*

which thoughe they haue litle or nothinge of theire owne yeat will they playe for muche money which if they winne they waste moste lightelye 2365 and if they lose they paye as slenderlye but make recompence with one stelthe or another whose onelye hvrte is not that they themselues are idle Losels but that thoroughe gamynge they drawe others to like lewdnesse and ydlenesse. And to these maye be added another sorte of like lose fellowes which doe passe vp and downe amongeste gentlemen by the name 2370 of Iesters but are indede notable rouges and partakers not onelye of manie stealthes by settinge forthe other mens goodes to be stollen but allso privie to manye traytorous practises and Common Carriours of newes with desire wheareof youe would wonder howe muche the Irishe are fed for they vse Comonlye to sende vp and downe to knowe newes and if anye 2375 mete with another his seconde worde is what newes Insomuche that heareof is toulde a prettye Ieste of a ffrenchman whoe havinge bene somtime in Irelande wheare he marked theire greate enquirye for newes and metinge afterwardes in ffraunce an Irisheman whom he knewe in |
f. 44ʳ Irelande firste saluted him and afterwardes thus merelye O Sir I praye youe 2380 (quothe he) tell me of Curtesye haue youe harde yeat anye thinge of the newes that ye soe muche enquired for in your Countrye/

Eudox: This arguethe sure in them a greate desire of innovacion and therefore these occasions which nourrishe the same are to be taken awaie as namelye those Iesters, Carrowes, *monashule* and all suche straglers for 2385 whome me semes the shorte riddance of a marshall weare meter then anye ordinaunce or prohibicion to restraine them Therefore I praye youe leave all this rablement of suche lose runnagates and passe to some other Customes/

Iren: Theare is a greate vse amongest the Irishe to make greate assem- 2390 blies togeather vppon a Rathe or hill theare to parlye (as they saie) aboute matters and wronges betwene Towneshipp and Towneshippe or one private persone and another But well I wote and trewe it hathe bene often times

---

2367 another] an other. *C*   2367 hvrte] *corr. of* harte *E* harte *C*   2371 indede] (indeed) *W*   2373 traytorous] traytors *C*   2374 fed] fledd *C*   2376 with] *om. R* 2376 is] *om. C*   2376 newes] newes? *W*   2378 somtime] sometimes *W*   2379 whom] whoe *C*   2380 thus] said thus *W*   2380 merelye] merrilie, *CW*   merelye, *R* 2380 O] *om. CR*   2381 (quothe he)] *om. W*   2381 yeat] *om. W*   2382 Countrye/] Cuntrye *C*   Countrey? *W*   2384 are to] must *W*   2385 Carrowes] *Kearrooghs A* 2385 *monashule*] *corr. of* monashite *E* Beantooilhs *A* Monashite *CH1HoR* Morashitte *D1* Monashites *D2* Mooashites *F* Monashute *GP* Monashits *H2N* Morashite *L* Monashhis *T* Mona-shutes *W* Mona-shules *Todd* morashites *Morley*   2386 me semes] (me thinkes) *W*   2386 anye] an *W*   2387 them] them. *CW* them, *R*   2387 I praye youe] (I pray you) *W*   2388 suche lose] *om. W*   2388 some] *om. W*   2390 amongest] amonge *R*   2392 matters] matters matters *C*   2392 one] on *C*   2393 and another] or an other *C*   2393 and trewe]

aproued that in these metinges manye mischiefs haue bene bothe practised and wroughte ffor to them doe Comonlye resorte all the scum of lose people wheare they maye frelye mete and Conferr of what they liste which else they Coulde not doe without suspicion or knowledge of others Besides at those parlies I haue diuerse times knowen that manye Englishemen and other good Irishe subiectes haue bene villanouslye murdered by movinge one quarrell or another amongest them, for the Irishe neuer come to those Rathes but armed wheather on horse or fote which the Englishe nothinge suspectinge are then Comonlye taken at advantage like shepe in the pinfoulde/

f. 44ᵛ *Eudox*: It maye be. *Iren*: that abuse maye be in those | metinges But these rounde hills and square bawnes which youe see soe strongelye trenched and throwne vp weare (they saie) at firste ordeyned for the same purpose that people mighte assemble themselves theareon And therefore Ancientlye they weare Called *Folkmotes* that is a place for people to moote or talke of anie thinge that Concerned anie difference betwene parties and Towneshipps which semethe yeat to me verye requisite/

Iren: ye saie verye Trewe *Eudox*. the firste makinge of these hye hills was at firste indede to verye good purpose for people to mete but howe euer the times when they weare firste made mighte well serue to good accacions as perhaps they did then in Englande yeat things beinge since alltered and now Irelande muche defferinge from that state of Englande the good vse that then was of them is now turned to abuse. ffor those Hills whereof ye speake weare as ye maye gather by readinge apointed for two speciall vses and builte by two seuerall nacions The one is those which youe Cale *Folkmotes* the which weare builte by the Saxons as the worde bewraieth for it signifyethe in Saxon metinge of folke or people and these are for the moste parte in forme fowre square well entrenched

that trewe *R*   2394 aproued] proved *W*   2394 these] their *W*   2394 haue bene bothe] hathe bothe bene *C*   2395 lose] the *W*   2396 frelye] om. *W*   2397 others] others, *CR* others. *W*   2397-8 Besides at] Beside *C*   2398 those] these *CRW*   2398 parlies] meetings *W*   2398 diuerse times knowen] knowne divers times *W*   2399 other] om. *W*   2400 amongest] against *W*   2401 horse] horsebacke *R*   2401 or] or on *RW*   2402 then] the *C*   2402 advantage] tagge *R*   2402 the] a *C*   2404 be.] be *CRW*   2404 Iren:] (*Irenaeus*) *W*   2404 those] these *CR*   2406 weare] we *C*   2406 saie)] saye *C* 2407 theareon] therein *W*   2408 *Folkmotes*] *Folkmothes T*   *Talk-motes* corrected to *Folkmotes W* (*Faults escaped*)   2408 for] of *W*   2409 moote] meete *RW*   2409 Concerned] Concerneth *C*   2411 *Eudox*.] *Eudox*:, *R Eudoxus*, *W*   2412 was] were *W* 2412-3 howe euer] though *R*   howsoever *W*   2414-5 yeat . . . Englande] om. *R*   2415 that] the *W*   2417-21 Hills . . . these] om. *RLD1*   2417 whereof] om. *C*   2417 as . . . readinge] (as . . . readinge) *CW*   2418 nacions] nations, *C*   nations. *W*   2418 those] that *W*   2419 *Folkmotes*] talkemottes *D2F*   *folkmothes T*   *Talk-motes* corrected to *Folkmotes W* (*Faults escaped*)   2419 the which] which *W*   2420 metinge] a meeting *W* 2420 or people] om. *W*   2421 are] *RLD1 resume at this point*   2421 entrenched]

10

for the metinge of that hundred The others that are rounde weare Caste
vpp by the danes as the names of them dothe betoken for they are Called
Deanerathes That is hills of the danes the which weare by them devised
not for parlies and treaties but apointed as fortes for them to gather vnto 2425
in troublous times when anie tvmulte arose for the danes beinge but a fewe
in Compasition of the Saxons vsed this for theire safetye They made these
smalle rounde hills soe stronglie fenced in euerie quarter of the hundred
f. 45ʳ to thende that if in the nighte | Or anie other time anye troubles Crye
or vprore should happen they mighte repair with all spede vnto theire 2430
owne forte which was appointed for theire quarter and theare remayne
safe till they Coulde assemble themselues in greter strengthe for they
weare made so stronge with one small entraunce that whosoeuer Came
thither firste weare he one or twoe or like fewe he or they mighte theare
reste safe and defende themselues againste manye till more succor came 2435
vnto them and when they weare gathered to a sufficiente number they
marched to the nexte forte and so forwarde till they mett with the perill
or knewe the occacion theareof But besides these two sortes of hills theare
weare Ancientlye diuerse others ffor some weare raised wheare theare had
binne a great Battell foughte as a memorye or Trophe thereof Others as 2440
monimentes of buriall of the Carcasses of all those that weare slaine in
anye feilde vppon whom they did throughe vp suche rounde mountes as
memoriall for them and somtimes did Caste vp greate heapes of stones
as yee maye reade in manye places of the Scripture and other whills they
did throwe vp manye rounde heapes of earthe in a Circle like a garlande 2445
or pitche manye longe stones on end in Compasse, Euerye of which they
saie betokened some worthie persone of note theare slaine and buried for
this was theire anciente Custome before Christianitye Came in amongest
them that Churchyardes weare inclosed//

trenched *R*   2422 for the metinge . . . hundred] for meeting *A* om. *W*   2422 hundred]
blank space *CR*   quarter *D2F*   people *Ho* om. *T*   2422 are] were *W*   2423 names]
name *CW*   2424 Deanerathes] Denerathes *C*   Deanes Rathes *D2F*   Danerathers *H2*
Danerathes *RAD1H1HoL*   Danezathos *T*   Danes-Rathes *W*   2425 parlies and treaties]
treaties and parlies *W*   2426 troublous] troblesome *RW*   2426 times] time *W*   2426 tvmulte]
trouble *W*   2427 Compasition] Comparison *CRW*   2427 Saxons] *Saxons* (in *England*) *W*
2427 safetye] saiftie, *RW*   2427 these] those *W*   2429 Or] or at *R*   2429 troubles]
troublous *CW* om. *R*   2432 greter] greate *R*   2434 or twoe] twoe *R*   2434 theare]
om. *R*   2435 themselues] them selfes *R*   2437 forte] fortes *R*   2438 occacion]
occasions *W*   2439 raised wheare] raysed, where, *R*   2440 foughte] om. *R*   2440 Trophe]
Trophes R   2440 thereof] therof, *CRW*   2441 buriall] Buryalls *RW*   2442 feilde] fight *R*
2442 vp] om. *W*   2443 memoriall] memorialls *CRW*   2443 for] of *W*   2444-6 as . . .
stones] om. *RLD1H2AN*   2444 as . . . Scripture] (as . . . Scripture) *W*   2444 reade]
read the like *W*   2445 manye] mane *C*   2446-7 they saie] (they say) *W*   2447 worthie]
om. *W*   2448 Christianitye] *last three letters hidden in binding C*   2449 inclosed//]

Eudox. yea haue verye well declared the originall of these mountes and greate stones encompassed, which some vainlye terme the olde Geauntes, Trivetes and thinke that those huge stones woulde not els be broughte into order or reared vp without the strenthe of Geauntes, and others as vainelye thinke that they weare neuer placed theare by mans hande or arte but onelye remayned theare so since the beginninge of the worlde and weare afterwardes discouered by the deluge and laied open as then by the washing of the waters or other like casualties | But let them dreame theire owne ymaginacions to please themselues But ye haue satisfied me muche better bothe by that I see some Confirmacion theareof in the holye writ and allso remember that I haue red in manye histories and Cronicles the like mountes and stones often tymes mencioned as in herodotus theodorus siculus and others

Iren: Theare be manye greate auctorityes I assure youe to proue the same but as for these metinges on hills whereof we weare speakinge it is verye inconueniente that anye suche shoulde be permitted speciallye in a people so evill minded as they now be and diuerslye shewe themselues

Eudox: But yeat it is verye nedefull me semes for manie other purposes as for the Countrye to gather togeather when theare is anye ymposicion to be laide vppon them the which they then all agree at suche metinges to Cutt and devide vppon themselues accordinge to theire houldinges and habilityes. so as if at those assemblies theare be anye officers as Constables Bayliffes or suche like amongeste them theare cane be no perill nor doutt of suche badd practizes/

Iren: Neuerthelesse daungerous are suche assemblies whether for Cesse or oughte els the Constables and officers beinge allsoe of the Irishe and if anye hapen theare to be of the Englishe even to them they maye proue perillous Therefore for avoidinge of all suche evill occacions they weare beste to be abolshed//

Eudox: But what is that which ye Call Cesse it is a worde sure vnvsed amongest vs heare therefore I praye youe expounde the same/

Iren: Cesse is none other but that which your selfe Called ymposicion but it is in a kinde vnacquainted perhaps vnto youe, ffor theare are Cesses of sondrye sortes One is the Cessinge of Souldiours | Vppon the Countrye, for Irelande beinge a Countrye of warr (as it is handled) and allwaies full of souldiours, they which haue the gouernment wheather they finde it the moste ease to the Queenes purse or the moste readye meanes at hand for victulinge of the Souldiours or that necessity enforcethe them thearevnto doe scatter the Armye abrode the Countrye and place them in vyllages to take theire victualls of them at suche vacante times as they lye not in Campe nor are otherwise imployed in service. Another kinde of Cesse is, the ymposinge of provicion for the gouernours housse kepinge which thoughe it be moste necessarye and be allso for avoydinge of all the evills formerlie thearein vsed latelye broughte to a Composicion yeat it is not without greate inconveniences no lesse then heare in Englande or rather muche more. The like Cesse is allsoe charged vppon the Countrye somtyme for victulinge of the soldiours when they lye in garrisone at suche times as theare is none remayninge in the Quenes store or that the same Cannot Convenientlye be Conveyed to theire place of Garrissone. But these two are not easye to be redressed when necessitye thearevnto Compelleth: but as for the former as it is not necessarye, so is it moste hurtefull and offensive to the pore Countrye and nothinge Conveniente to the Soldier himselfe, whoe duringe his lyinge at Cesse vsethe all kinde of outragies disorder and villanye bothe towardes the pore men which vittell and lodge them And allsoe to all the reste of the Countrie aboute them whom they abuse oppresse spoile and afflicte by all the meanes they Cane moste invente, ffor they will not onely not Contente themselues with suche vittells as ther hostes doe nor yeat perhaps as the place will afforde but they will haue other meate provided for them and Aquavite sente for yea and money besides laied at his Trencher which if

---

2481 but] then *W*   2483 sortes] sortes, *RW*   2483 is] *om. R*   2484 (as ... handled)] (as ... handled *C* as ... handled *R*   2486 Queenes] Quene *C*   2486 or the] or *R* 2487 for] for the *R*   2487 Souldiours] Souldiour *W*   2487 enforcethe] forceth *C* 2488 abrode] abroad in *W*   2489 in vyllages] *crowded as if added in blank space E   blank space C* in Townes *R*   2490 service.] service, *CR*   2491 Cesse] Cesse, *W*   2491 is,] is *CRW*   2492-3 for ... vsed] (for ... used) *W*   2495 more.] more *C*   2496 somtyme] sometymes *RW*   2497 as] as when *R*   2498 Convenientlye be] be conveniently *W* 2498-9 Garrissone] Garrisoninge *C*   2499 easye] easye, *R*   easily *W*   2499-2500 thearevnto] thereto *W*   2500 for] *om. R*   2500 is it] it is *C*   2502 to the Soldier himselfe] for the Souldiours themselves *W*   2502 his] their *W*   2502 vsethe] use *W*   2503 outragies] outragious *CRW*   2504 which] that *R*   2504 reste of the] *om. W*   2505 aboute] round about *W*   2505 oppresse] *om. R*   2506 moste] *om. RW*   2507 doe] doe prouide, them *R om. W*   2507-8 perhaps ... place] as the place perhaps *CW*   as the place *R* 2508 will afforde] affords *W*   2508 other] theire *R*   2509 Aquavite] aqua vita *CW* aqua vitae *R*   2509 his Trencher] their trenchers *W*

A VIEW OF THE PRESENT STATE OF IRELAND   133

f. 46ᵛ he wante then aboute the howse he walketh with the wretched | pore man and his sillye wife whoe are glad to purchase theire peace with anie thinge by which vile manner of abuse the Countrye people ye and the verye Englishe which dwell abroade and see and somtimes fele these outrages growe into greate detestacion of the soldiour and thearby into hatred of the verye gouerment which draweth vppon them suche evills And therefore this ye maye allsoe adioyne vnto the former evill Customes which we haue to reproue in Irelande/

Eudox: Truelye this is one not the leaste and thoughe the persons by whom it is vsed be of better note then the former rogishe sorte which ye reckoned yeat the faulte me semes is no lesse worthie of a marshall/

Iren: That weare a harde Course *Eudox.* to redresse euerye abuse by a marshall it woulde seme to youe verye evill surgerye to Cutt of everye vnsounde or sicke parte of the bodye which beinge by other dewe meanes recured mighte afterwardes doe verye good service vnto the bodie againe and happelye helpe to saue the wholle Therefore I thinke better that some good salve for redresse of this evill be soughte forthe, then the leaste parte suffer to perishe But heareof we haue to speake in another place nowe we will procede to other like defectes amongest which theare is one generall inconvenience which raigneth allmoste thoroughe out all Irelande and that is the Lordes of lande and ffreholders which do not theare vse to sett out theire Landes in ffearme or for terme of yeares to theire Tenantes but onelye from yeare to yeare and some duringe pleasure neither indede will the Irishe Tenant or husbandman otherwise take his lande then soe longe as he liste him selfe The reasone heareof in the Tenant is for that the Landlordes theare vse moste shamefullie to racke theire Tenantes layinge vppon him Coynie and liverye at pleasure and exacting of him besides his Covenante what he please So the pore Husbandman eyther

2510 he wante] they want *W*   2510 he walketh] they walke *W*   2511 his sillye] the syllye poore *R*   2512 thinge] thing. *W*   2513 these outrages] this outrage *W*   2514 soldiour] Souldiours *W*   2515-6 evills ... former] *om.* C   2516 adioyne] ioyne *RW*   2516 vnto] with *R*   2516 we] yee *R*   2518 is] *om. R*   2518 by] of *R*   2520 me semes] (me thinkes) *W*   2520 is] *om. R*   2521 harde] harder *W*   2522 marshall] marshall, *CRW*   2522 verye] *om. R*   2524 recured] recouered *RW*   2524 vnto] to *RW*   2525 wholle] whole, *CR*   whole: *W*   2526 for] for the *W*   2526 this] the *W*   2527 suffer] suffred *CRW*   2527 place] place, *R*   place. *W*   2528 other] the other *R*   2528 amongest] amonge *R*   2529 out] *om.* C   2530 and that] that *W*   2530 is the] is of the *C*   of *R*   2530 lande] landes *R*   2530 which] *inserted between lines E om. CRW*   2531 Landes] land *W*   2531 in] to *R*   2532 pleasure] pleasuers *C*   2533 husbandman] husband *R*   2534 him selfe] him self, *CR*   himselfe. *W*   2536 vppon him] upon them *W*   2536 Coynie] Coigne *D1*   *Coigur G*   Coygnie *L*   Cognie *N*   Cognye *P*   Coignie *R*   Coigny *WHo*   2536 of him] of them *W*   2537 besides his Covenante] (besides his Covenants) *W*   2537 please] pleaseth. *W*   2537 So] soe that *CRW*   2537 Husbandman] husbandman, *R*

dare not binde himself to him for longer terme or that he thinketh by his Continvall libertie of Change to kepe his Landelorde the rather in Awe from wronginge him And the reasone whye the Landelorde will no Longer Covennante with him is for that he daylie lokethe after Chaunge and alteracion and houerethe in expectacion of newe worldes/

Eudox: But what evill Comethe heareby to the Common wealthe or what reasone is it that anye Landelorde shoulde not sett nor anie Tenante take his lande as him selfe liste//

Iren: marye the evill which Comethe theareby is greate for by this meane bothe the landlorde thinketh that he hathe his Tenant more at Comaunde to followe him into what accion soeuer he shall enter and allsoe the Tenant beinge lefte at his libertye is fitt for euerie variable occacion of Change that shalbe offered by time and so muche allsoe the more readye and willinge is he to runne theareinn for that he hathe no suche estate in anye his holdinge no suche buildinge vppon anie ferme no suche Costes employed in fencinge or husbandinge the same as mighte with holde him from anie suche willfull Course as his Lordes cause or his owne lewde disposicion maye Carye him into All which he hathe forborne and spared soe muche expense for that he had no former estate in his Tenement but onelye a Tenante at will or litle more and soe at will maye leave it, And this inconvenience maye be reasone ynoughe to grounde anie ordinaunce for the good of a Common wealthe againste the private behoufe or will of anie Landlorde that shall refuse to graunte anye suche tenure or estate vnto his tenant as maye tend to the good of the whole realme/

Eudox. Indede me semes it is a greate willfullnes in anye suche Landelorde to refuse to make anye longer fearmes vnto theire Tenantes as maye besides the generall good of the realeme be allsoe greatlye for theire owne profitt and availe for what reasonable mann will not thinke that the tenant shalbe made muche | muche the better for the Lordes behofe yf the Tenante maye by suche meanes be drawen to builde him selfe some han-

2538 to him] *om. C*   2538 terme] tyme *R*   2538 that he] *om. W*   2539 Landelorde] landlord, *R*   2540 wronginge] wronging of *W*   2540 no] not *R*   2541 after] *om. R*   2542 worldes/] worldes *C*   2545 liste//] list *R*   list? *W*   2546 evill] evilles *RW*   2546 theareby] hereby *W*   2546 is] are *R*   2546 meane] meanes *W*   2547 Comaunde] Comandment *C*   2548 shall] will *R*   2549 variable] *om. W*   2550 offered] offreed *R*   2550-1 readye and willinge] willinge and redye *R*   2551 theareinn] therinto *C*   into the same *RW*   2551 estate] state *CW*   2552 Costes] coste *W*   2553 or] and *R*   2553 husbandinge] husbandrye *C*   husbandringe *R*   2554 from] for *R*   2554 Lordes cause] landlord *C*   2554 or] and *R*   2555 into] vnto, *R*   unto. *W*   2556 muche] much, *R*   2556 former] firmer *Ho*   firme *WGP*   2556 but] but was *CRW*   2559 a] the *W*   2560 tenure] terme *W*   2561 tenant] Tennantes *R*   2562 me semes] (me thinkes) *W*   2565 tenant] tenement *CW*   Tenement, *R*   2566 muche the] *om. CW*   the *R*   2566 yf] Y *R*   2567 suche] such good *W*   2567 selfe] self, *R*   2567-8 hansome] haue some *R*

A VIEW OF THE PRESENT STATE OF IRELAND 135

some habitacion theareon to ditche and enclose his grounde to mannour and husbande it as good farmers vse ffor when his tenantes terme shalbe expired it will yealde him in the renewinge of his Lease bothe a good fine and allsoe a better rente And allsoe it shalbe for the good of the Tenant likewise whoe by suche buildinges and inclosures shall receaue manye benefittes. ffirste by the hansomnes of his howse he shall take greate Comforte of his life more safe dwellinge and a delight to kepe his saide howse neate and Clenlye which now beinge (as they Comonlye are) rather Swynsteades then howses is the Chiefest Cause of his so bestlye manner of life and salvage Condicion lyinge and livinge togeather with his beaste in one howse in one rome and in one bed that is the cleane strawe or rather the foule dvnghill And to all those other Comodities he shall in shorte time finde a greater added that is his owne wealthe and ritches encreased and wonderfullie enlardged by kepinge his Cattell in enclosures where they shall allwaies haue freshe pasture that now is all trampled and ouerrune warme Lewre that nowe lyethe open to all weather safe beinge that now are Continvallye filtched and stollen//

Iren: youe haue well *Eudox*: accompted the Comodities of this one good ordinance amongest which this that ye named laste is not the leaste for all the other beinge moste beneficiall bothe to the Landelorde and Tenante/ this Chieflye redoundethe to the good of the whole Comon wealthe to haue the lande thus enclosed and well fenced ffor it is bothe a principall barre and empeachement vnto theves from stealinge of Cattle in the nighte and allsoe a gavle againste all Rebles | And outlawes that shall rise vp in anie numbers againste that gouernment for the thefe theareby shall haue muche adoe firste to bringe forthe and afterwardes to drive his stollen praye but thoroughe the Comon highwaies wheare he shall sone be discried and mett withall and the rebell or open enemye if anie suche shall happen either at home or from abroade shall easelye be founde when he Comethe forthe and allsoe be well encountred withall by a fewe in so streight passages and stronge enclosures. this thearefore when we Come to the reform-

```
    2568 theareon] thereof R      2568 grounde] grounde and C      2569 tenantes] tennant C
2570 yealde ... Lease] in the Renueinge of his lease yeelde him C           2570 of] om. W
2571 And ... shalbe] om. R      2573 the] his R     2573 greate] more W       2574 a] om. C
2575 (as ... are)] as ... are RW      2575-6 Swynsteades] swyne-styes W       2576 howses]
houses; W      2578 and] om. W      2578 is the] is, W      2578-9 the foule] a foule W
2579 those] these CRW          2579 shorte] sort W          2581 wonderfullie] wrongfullie C
2581 enclosures] inclosuers with last two letters worn off C      2582 allwaies] alwaies, R
2582 pasture] pastures R         2583 Lewre] coverth A    lure D2   blank space F   living G
liure H1    lien Ho    couer RD1H2LN    layer T    covert W      2585 well Eudox:] Eudoxus
well W      2586 is] it C      2587 bothe] om. W      2587 and] and the R      2587 Tenante/]
Tennant. W       2588 whole] om. RW      2592 that] om. R     the W      2592 theareby] om. C
2593 drive] drive away W        2597 allsoe] om. R        2598 enclosures.] enclosuers, C
```

inge of all these former evill Costomes is nedfullye to be remembred.
But now by this time me semes that I haue well run thoroughe the evill
vses which I haue obserued in Irelande Neuerthelesse I well wott that
manye more thearebe and infinite manye more in the private abuses of
men but these that are moste generall and tendinge to the hurte of the
Comon wealthe as they haue Come to my remembraunce I haue as brieflye
as I Coulde rehersed vnto you And therefore now I thinke best that we
passe vnto our thirde parte in which we noted inconvenienc that is in
religion/

Eudox: Surelie ye haue verye well handled these two former and if youe
shall aswell goe thoroughe the thirde likewise yee shall meritt a verye
good meede/

Iren: Little haue I to saie of Religion bothe because the partes thereof
be not manye it selfe beinge but one and my selfe haue not muche bene
conuersante in that Callinge but as lightlye passinge by I | I haue sene
or harde Therefore the faulte that I finde in religion is but one but the
same vniuersall thoroughe all that Countrye, that is that they are all
Papistes by theire profession but in the same so blindelye and brutishly
enformed for the moste parte as that ye woulde rather thinke them *Atheists*
or infidles but not one amongest a hundred knowethe anye grounde of
religion anie article of his faithe but Cane perhaps saie his pater noster
or his *Ave marye* without anie knowledge or vnderstandinge what one
worde thereof meanethe/

Eudox: This is trewelie a moste pittifull hearinge that so manye soules
should fall into the divells Iawes at once and lacke the blessed comforte

2599 these] those *W*   2599 former] *om. RW*   2599 Costomes] customes *C*   customes before menconed *RW*   2599 nedfullye] needfull *RW*   2600 me semes] (me thinkes) *W*   2601 vses] abuses *C*   2601 Irelande] Ireland, *CR*   *Ireland. W*   2601-3 Neuerthelesse . . . moste] And how beit there be many more abuses woorthye the reformation both in publicke and in private amongest yet these for that they are the more *A*   2601 well wott] will note *R*   well note *W*   2602 manye more thearebe] there be many more *W*   2602 infinite] infinitelye *CRW*   2604 wealthe] weale *CW*   2604 as . . . remembraunce] (as . . . remembrance) *W*   2605 now] *om. R*   2606 vnto] to *R*   2606 inconvenienc] *corr. of* inconveniences *E*   incoveniences *R*   inconveniences *W*   2606 is] are *W*   2607 religion/] Religion *R*   2609 aswell] doe well *R*   2612 it . . . one] (it . . . one) *W*   2612 muche bene] bene muche *CR*   2613 I I] I *CRW*   2614 harde] harde, *C*   heard: *RW*   2614 that] which *CRW*   2615 same] same is *W*   2615 thoroughe] throught *C*   through out *RW*   2615 are] be *W*   2616 and] and soe *C*   2617 for . . . parte as] (for . . . part) *W*   2617-8 ye . . . but] *om. W*   2618 a] an *CR*   2619 anie] and *R*   or any *W*   2620 marye] Marie *C*   Maria *RW*   2622-66 This . . . . Pope] *om. W*   2623 Iawes] handes *R*

of the swete Gosple and Christes deare passion Ay me how Comethe it to passe that beinge a people as they are tradinge with so manye nacions and frequented of so manye yeate they haue not tasted anie parte of those happie ioyes nor once bene lightned with the morninge starr of truethe but lye weltringe in suche spirituall darkenes harde by hell mouthe even readye to fall in yf god happelie helpe not

Iren: The generall faulte Comethe not of anie late abuse either in the people or theire priestes who Cane teache no better then they knowe nor shew no more lighte then they haue sene but in the firste Institucion and plantinge of religion in all that realme which was (as I reade) in the time of Pope *Celestine* who as it is written did firste sende ouer thither *Paladius* who theare deceasinge he afterwardes sente ouer *St Patrick* beinge by nacion a Britton whoe Conuerted the people beinge then Infidles from *Paganisme* and Christened them In which Popes time and longe before it is certaine that religion was generallie | Corrupted with theire Popishe trumperie Therefore what other Coulde they learne then suche trashe as was taughte them And drinke of that Cupp of fornicacion with which the purple Harlott had then made all nacions drunken/

Eudox. what? doe youe then blame and finde faulte with soe good an Acte in that good Pope as the reducinge of suche a greate people to Christendome bringinge so manye soules vnto Christe? yf that weare ill what is good?/

Iren: I doe not blame the Christeninge of them for to be sealed with the marke of the Lambe by what hande soeuer it be donne rightlye, I houlde it a good and gracious worke for the generall profession which they then take vppon them of the Crosse and faithe in Christe I nothinge doubte but thoroughe the powerfull grace of that mightye Saviour will worke Sallvacion in manye of them. But neuerthelesse since they drunke not from the pure springe of life but onelye tasted of suche trobled waters as weare broughte vnto them the druggs theareof haue bred greate Contagion in theire Soules the which dailye encreasinge And beinge still Augmented with theire owne lewde lives and filthie Conuersacion hathe

2624-2806 of .... imployed] *om. F*   2624 passion] passion: *R*   2628 weltringe] meltinge *R*   2629 not] not./. *C* not:/ *R*   2631 no] *om. R*   2631 they] *om. R*   2633 of] *om. R*   2633 was (as] (was as *R*   2634 *Celestine*] Colestine *H2*   Caelestine *Ho* Celestins *P   Calestine RD1LN*   2634 written] written) *C*   2634 *Paladius*] Balladius *H2* Pallidus *RLD1*   2635 ouer] over, *R*   2636 Britton] Brittayne *D2*   2639 trumperie] trumperie, *C* trumperie: *R*   2642 what?] what *CR*   2644 vnto Christe?] to Christ, *R* 2645 good?/] good: *C* good:/ *R*   2648 worke] marke *R*   2648 they] *om. R*   2650 but] but but *C*   2651 drunke] drincke *R*   2652 from] of *R*   2653 druggs] dregges *A* 2653 bred] brought *R*   2654 still] still more *CR*

now bred in them this generall disease that Cannot but onelye with verye stronge purgacions be Clensed and Carryed awaie/

Eudox: Then for this defecte ye finde no faulte with the people them selues nor with the priestes which take the Chardge of soules but with the firste ordinaunce and institucion thereof

Iren: Not soe *Eudox*: for the sinne or ignoraunce of the Priestes shall not excuse the people nor the auctoritye of the greate Pastor Peters successours shall not excuse the priestes but they shall all dye in theire sinnes for they haue all erred and gone out of the waye togeather/

Eudox But if this Ignorance of the people be suche a burthen vnto the Pope is it not a like blott to them that now houlde that place in that they which now are in the lighte them selues suffer a people vnder theire Chardge to wallowe in suche deadlie darkenes? ffor I do | not see that the faulte is Chaunged but the faultes master/

Iren: That which ye Blame *Eudox*. is not I suppose anye faulte of will in these godlye fathers which haue Chardge theareof nor anye defecte of zeale for reformacion heareof but the in Convenience of the time and troublous occacions whearewith that wretched Realme hathe Continvallye bene tormoyled. ffor instruccion in religion nedethe quiett times and ere we seke to settle a sounde discipline in the Clergie we muste purchase peace vnto the Layitye for it is ill time to preache amongest swordes and moste harde or rather impossible it is to settle a good opinion in the mindes of men for matters of Religion doubtfull which haue a doubtlesse evill opinion of ourselues for er a newe be broughte in the olde muste be removed

Eudox Then belike it is mete that some fitter time be attended that god sende peace and quietnes there in Civill matters before it be attempted in ecclesiasticall I woulde rather haue thoughte that as it is saide Correccion

2660 thereof] therof./. *C* thereof: *R*   2661 Priestes] preist *R*   2662 the greate] their great *CR*   2662 Pastor] Pastors *C*   2662-3 successours] successour *R*   2663 priestes] priest *CR*   2663 shall all] all shall *CR*   2666 is] *W resumes at this point*   2666 a like] then a little *W*   2666 houlde] held *R*   2666 that place in] the place of government *W*   2667 they] *om. C*   2667 selues] selues: *R*   2668 darkenes?] darkenesse, *CR*   darkenesse. *W*   2668-9 ffor ... master/] *om. W*   2670 I suppose] (I suppose) *W*   2671 these] those *W*   2671-2 nor ... heareof] *om. W*   2673-4 Continvallye bene] bene contynuallie *CR*   2675 the] *om. C*   2676 amongest] among *W*   2677 settle] *corr. of indecipherable word E*   persuade *C*   2678 doubtfull] doubfull *R*   2678 a doubtlesse] a doublesse *R*   doubtlesse an *W*   2679 ourselues] us *W*   2680 removed] removed./. *C* remoued: / *R* removed. *W*   2681 *Eudox*] *om. and no new paragraph H2*   2683 ecclesiasticall] Ecclesiasticall: *C* ecclesiasticall, *R* Ecclesiasticall. *W*   2683 as ... saide] (as ... said) *W*

shoulde begine at the howse of god and that the Care of the soule shoulde haue bene preferred before the Care of the bodie/

Iren: moste trewe *Eudox* the Care of the soule and soule matters is to be preferred before the care of the bodye in Consideracion of the worthines of bothe: but not in the time of reformacion for if youe should knowe a wicked persone daungerouslye sicke havinge now bothe soule and bodye sore diseased, yeat bothe recouerable, woulde ye not thinke it ill advizement to bringe the preacher before the phisicion? for if his bodie weare neclected it is like that his Languishinge soule beinge Disquieted by his diseasfull bodye woulde vtterlye refuse and lothe all spirituall Comforte, But if his bodye weare firste recured and broughte to good frame shoulde theare not then be founde best time to | Recure his soule allso: so it is in the state of a realme. Therefore as I saide it is expediente firste to settle suche a Course of gouernment theare as thearby bothe Civile disorders and allsoe ecclesiasticall abuses maie be reformed/ and amended whearto nedethe not anie suche greate distance of times as ye suppose, I require, but one ioynte resolucion for bothe that eche mighte seconde and Confirme the other/

Eudox: That we shall see when we Come theare vnto In the meane time I Conceaue thus muche as youe haue deliuered towchinge the generall faulte which ye suppose in religion, to wete that it is popishe But doe youe finde no particuler abuses thearein nor in the ministers theareof/

Iren: yeas verylye for what euer disorders ye see in the Churche of Englande yea maye finde theare and manye more, namelye grosse *Symony*: gredye Covetousnes, fleshlye incontinence, Carelesse slouthe, and generallye all disordered liffe in the Comon Clergie men. And besides all these they haue theire owne peculier enormityes for all the Irishe priestes which now enioye the Churche livinges theare are in a manner meare Laye men Savinge that parte haue taken holye orders, but otherwise they doe like laye men, goe like laye men, live like laye men, followe all kinde of

---

2684 shoulde begine] must first begin *W*   2686 *Eudox*] *Eudoxus, W*   2686 is] are *R*   2687 in] and *C*   2688 of bothe] of *inserted between lines E*   bothe *C*   thereof *RW*   2688 in] till *W*   2690 sore] greatlie *RW*   2690-1 ill advizement] evill advertizement *W*   2691 phisicion?] Phisician; *C*   Phisicion, *RW*   2695 Recure his] recover the *W*   2695 allso:] also, *R*   2696 realme.] Realme, *CR*   2696 as I saide] (as I said) *W*   2698 allsoe] *om. RW*   2698 ecclesiasticall] *last two letters worn off C*   2699 ye suppose] (you suppose) *W*   2702 theare vnto] thereto, *R*   thereunto, *W*   2703 Conceaue] consider *R*   2704 religion, to wete] relidgion to weete, *R*   2705 abuses] abuses, *R*   2705 theareof/] thereof? *W*   2707 manye] manye manie *R*   2708 incontinence] incontinency *W*   2708 and] *om. C*   2710 owne] *om. W*   2710 peculier] particuler *RW*   2710 the] *om. W*   2711 livinges theare] livings, they *W*   2711 a] *om. CR*   2712-3 Savinge ... doe like laye men] *om. R*   2712 parte] *corr. of the E*   they *CW*   2712-3 doe

husbandrye and other worldlye affaires As the Common Irishe Laye men doe. They neither reade Scriptures nor preache to the people nor minister the sacrament of Comunion But the Baptisme they doe, for the Christen, yeat after the popishe fashion and with the Popishe Latine ministracion: Onely the Take the Tithes and offeringes and gather what fruites els they maye of theire Livinges the which they Conuerte as badlye And some of them they saie paie as dewe tributes and shares of theire Livinges to theire Bishopps (I speake of those which are Irishe) as they receaue them dewelye/ |

Eudox. But is that suffered amongeste them. It is wonder but that the gouernours redresse suche shamefull abuses/

Iren: Howe Cane they since they knowe them not for the Irishe Bishopps haue theire Clergies in suche awe and subieccion vnder them that they dare not Complaine of them so as they maye doe to them what they please. for they knowinge theire owne vnworthines and incapacitye and that they are therefore still removeable at theire Bishops will yealde what pleasethe him and he takethe what pleasethe him yea and some of them whose diocesse are in remote partes somwhate out of the worldes eye doe not at all bestowe the benefices which are in theire owne donacion vppon anye but kepe them in theire owne handes and sett theire owne servantes and horsboyes to take vp the Tithes and fruites of them with the which some of them purchase greate Lands and builde faire Castles vppon the same Of which abuse if anye question be moved they haue a verye semely Coullour of excuse that they haue no worthie ministers to bestowe them vppon but kepe them soe vnbestowed for anye suche sufficiente persone as anye shall bringe vnto them/

Eudox. But is theare no Lawe nor ordinance to mete with this mischief nor hathe it neuer before bene loked into/

Iren: yes it semes it hathe for theare is a statute theare enacted in Irelande which semes to haue bene grounded vppon a good meaninge that

---

... live] doe goe, and live *W*   2714 the Common] thother *R*   other *W*   2714 Laye] om. *W*   2715 doe.] doe, *R*   2715 minister] administer *W*   2716 sacrament of] om. *W*   2716 But the] but *W*   2716 for the] for they *CRW*   2716 Christen,] Christyan *R*   christen *W*   2717 and ... ministracion] om. *W*   2717 ministracion:] ministration *C*   2718 the Take] they take *CRW*   2718 fruites] fruite *W*   2720 they saie] (they say) *W*   2723 is that] is yt *R*   2723 them.] them *C*   them, *R*   them? *W*   2724 redresse] doe redresse *W*   2725 since] since, *R*   2725 not] not? *W*   2726 Clergies] Cleargie *RW*   2728 knowinge] knowinge, *R*   2729 still] om. *R*   2729 will] will, *W*   2730 pleasethe him yea] he listeth, Yea *R*   he listeth: yea *W*   2731 diocesse] Diocesses *W*   2732 donacion] devocyon *R*   2734 the Tithes] the the tythes *R*   2734 the which] which *C*   2735 vppon] vponn them *R*   2735 same] same. *W*   2737 of] and *W*   2738 vnbestowed] bestowed *W*   2740 nor] or *R*   2740 mischief] mischeif? *RW*   2741 into/] into? *W*

whatsoeuer Englishe man beinge of good Conuersacion and sufficiencye shalbe broughte vnto anye of these Bishops and nominated vnto anye Livinge within theire diocesse that is presentlye voide that he shall without Contradiccion be thearevnto admitted before anye Irishe/ |

f. 51ʳ *Eudox*: This is surelye a verye good Lawe and well provided for this evill wheareof ye spoke but why is not the same obserued/

Iren: I thinke it is well obserued and that none of the Bishopps transgressethe the same but yeat it workethe no reformacion heareof for manye defectes firste theare are no suche sufficiente Englishe ministers sente ouer as mighte be presented to anie Bishope for anie livinge But the moste parte of suche Englishe as come ouer thither of themselues are either vnlearned or men of some badd note for which they haue forsaken Englande so as the Bishoppe to whom they shalbe presented maye iustlye reiecte them as incapable and insufficiente. Secondlye the Bishoppe himself is perhaps an Irishe man whoe beinge made iudge by that lawe of the sufficiencye of the minister maye at his owne will dislike of the Englisheman as vnworthie in his opinion and admitt of anye other Irishe whom he shall thinke more for his turne, And if he shall at the instance of Any Englisheman of Countenaunce theare whom he will not displease accepte of anye suche Englishe minister as shalbe tendred vnto him yet he will vnder hand Carrye suche an harde hande ouer him or by his officers wringe him soe sore that he will sone make him wearye of his pore Livinge Lastlye the benefices themselues are soe meane and of so small profitte in those Irishe Countries thoroughe the ill husbandrye of the Irishe people which inhabitt them that they will not yealde anie Competent mayntenaunce for anie honeste mynister to live scarsely to buy him a gowne And weare all this redressed

f. 51ᵛ as happelye it mighte be yeat what good shall anye Englishe | mynister doe amongest them by preachinge or teachinge which either Cannot vnderstande him or will not heare him or what Comforte of life shall he haue wheare his Parishioners are soe insociable, so intractable so ill affected

---

2745 these] those *CR* the *W*   2746-7 without Contradiccion] (without contradiction) *W*
2747 thearevnto admitted] admitted therunto *CRW*   2749 spoke but] speake, and *R*   speake, but *W*   2749 obserued/] observed? *W*   2750-1 transgressethe] transgresse *RW*   2751 heareof] thereof *W*   2752 defectes] defectes, *C*   respectes, *R*   defects. *W*   2755 Englande] England. *W*   2757 insufficiente.] insufficient, *C*   2759 minister] Ministers *W*   2760 anye other] an other *C*   any *W*   2761 his] his owne *C*   2763 hand] *inserted between lines E om. C*
2764 an] a *RW*   2765 Livinge] lyvinge: *R*   living. *W*   2767 which] which doe *W*
2769 live] live on *C*   liue vpon, *RW*   2770 as ... be] (as ... bee) *W*   2770 yeat] *om. C*   2770 shall] should *W*   2770 anye] anie soche *C*   2771 preachinge or teachinge] teaching or preaching to them *W*   2772 heare him] heare him? *W*   2772 life] lyf, *R*   2772 shall] *om. C*   2773 wheare] when *R*   2773 insociable,] insatiable? *W*

to him as they vsuallye be to all the Englishe or finallye how dare allmoste anye honest minister that are peacefull Civill men Comitte his safetye into the handes of suche neighbours As the bouldest Captaines dare scarselye dwell by/

Eudox: Little good then I see is by that statute wroughte howeuer well intended but the reformacion theareof muste growe higher and be broughte from a stroinger ordinaunce then the Comaundement or penaltye of a Lawe which none dare informe or Complaine of when it is broken But haue youe anye more of these abuses in the Clergie/

Iren. I Coulde perhaps reckon more but I perceaue my speache to growe to longe and these maye suffice for to iudge of the generall disorders which raigne amonge them, As for the particulers they are to manye to be reckoned for the Clergie theare (exceptinge some fewe grave fathers which are in highe place aboute the state and some fewe others which are latelye planted in theire new Colledge) are generallye badd Licentious and moste disordered/

Eudox yee haue then as I suppose gone thoroughe those three firste partes which ye proposed vnto your selfe to wete the Inconvenience which ye obserued in the Lawes in the Customes and in the religion of that Lande the which me semes yee haue so thoroughlye touched as that nothinge more remaynethe to be spoken theareof/

Iren: Not so thoroughlye as yee suppose that nothinge more Cane remayne but so generallye as I purposed that is to laye open the generall evills of that realme which do hinder the good reformacion theareof. for to accounte the particuler faultes of private men shoulde be a worke to infinite yet some theare be of that nature that thoughe they be in private men yeat theire evell reachethe to a generall hurte as the extorcion of Shiriffes sub-
f. 52ʳ shirefs, and theire Baylliffes | The Corrupcion of victellours Cessours

2774 vsuallye] usuall *W*   2774 or] and *C*   2775 honest] *om. C*   2775 minister] ministers *R*   2775 peacefull] peaceable *W*   2775 into] to *W*   2777 by/] by? *W*   2778 I see is] (I see) was *W*   2778 that] the *C*   2780 stroinger] stranger *R*   2781 none] any *R*   2782 these] those *W*   2782 Clergie/] Clargie *R*   Clergy? *W*   2783 Coulde] would *W* (*Osgood copy*)   could *W* (*Harvard copy*)   2784 for] *om. CRW*   2785 amonge] amongst *RW*   2785 them,] them; *W*   2786 exceptinge] excepte *R*   2786 some fewe] the *W*   2788 Colledge)] Colledge *C*   2790 as I suppose] (as I suppose) *W*   2790 those] these *R*   2791 proposed] purposed *R*   2791 Inconvenience] inconveniences *CRW*   2792 Lande] iand. *W*   2793 me semes] (me thinkes) *W*   2794 to] now to *R*   2794 theareof/] therof, *C*   thereof *R*   thereof. *W*   2795 more] *om. W*   2796 purposed] purpose *R* 2797 accounte] count *W*   2800 reachethe] Reachest *C*   2800-1 Shiriffes subshirefs] shreifes subshreifes *C*   Sheriffs, and their Sub-sheriffs *W*   2801 theire] *om. W*   2801 victel-

and purveyours the disorders of Senescalls Captaines and theire Souldiours and manye suche like all which I onelye name heare that theire reformacion maye be minded in place wheare it moste concernethe But theare is one verye foule abuse which by the waye I maye not omitt And that is in Captaines who notwithstandinge that they are speciallye imployed to make peace thoroughe stronge execucion of warr yeat they doe so dandle theire doinges and dallye in the service to them Comitted as if they would not haue the enemye subdued or vtterlie beaten downe for feare leste afterwarde they shoulde nede ymployment and so be dischardged of paye for which Cause some of them which are laied in garrison doe so handle the matter that they will doe no greate hurte to the enemyes yet for colour sake some men they will kill even haulf with Consente of the enemye beinge persons either of base regarde or enemyes to the enemye whose hedes eft sones they sende to the governour for Comendacion of theire great endevour Tellinge how weightye a service they haue performed by Cuttinge of suche and suche daungerous Rebells/

Eudox: Trewlie this is a prettye mockerye and not to be permitted by the gouernours/

Iren: yea but how Cane the Gouernours knowe readilye what persones those weare and what the purpose of theire killinge was yea and what will youe saie if the Captaines doe iustifye this theire Course by ensample of some of theire Gouernours whoe (vnder *Benedicite* I do tell it to youe) do practize the like sleightes in theire gouernmentes//

Eudox: Is it possible take hede what youe saie *Iren*:

Iren: to youe onelye *Eudox*: I doe tell it and that even with greate hartes griefe and inwarde trouble of minde to see her maiestie so abused by some whom they put in speciall truste of those greate affaires, Of which some beinge martiall men will not doe allwaies what they maie for quietinge of | thinges but will rather wincke at some faultes and suffer them vnpunished leaste they havinge put all things in that Assurance of peace

lours] victualls *R*   2802 disorders] disorder *C*   2803 all which] as *C*   2803 I] I will *CRW*   2804 minded] mended *W*   2806 notwithstandinge] not withstandinge thoughe *C*   2806 to] *F resumes at this point*   2808 the] theire *R*   2809-10 afterwarde] afterwardes *RW*   2811 them which] them that *RW*   2811 doe] doth *R*   2812-3 yet . . . enemye] *om. R*   2813 with] with the *W*   2815 eft sones] ofte tymes *C*   2815 to] into *CR*   2815 governour] governers *C*   2815 Comendacion] Comendacons *R*   2816 endevour] endeauors *R*   2816 Tellinge] tell *R*   2816 haue] a commendation *W*   *om. W*   2819 gouernours/] governers *C*   2820 yea] *om. W*   2820 Gouernours] Govrrnour *W*   2822 if the Captaines] of the Captaines, *R*   2823 (vnder] vnder, *R*   2823 *Benedicite*] *Benideceta T*   2823 to] vnto *C*   2824 like] light *W*   2824 sleightes] sleight *CW*   2824 gouernmentes//] govermentes *R*   governments? *W*   2825 possible] possible, *R*   possible? *W*   2825 hede] head *R*   2826 youe] yow yow *R*   2827 so] soe muche *CRW*   2828 whom they] who are *W*   2828 those greate] theire *R*   2831-2 havinge that they mighte be shoulde seme afterwardes not to be neded nor Continewed in theire gouernment with so greate a Chardge to her maiestie And therefore they doe Cvnninglye carrye theire Course of gouernment and from one hande to another doe bandye the service like a Tennis ball which they will neuer strike quite awaye for feare leaste afterwardes they should wante sporte 2835

Eudox: doe youe speake of vnder magistrates *Irenius*: or of some principall Gouernours/

Iren: I doe speake of noe particulers but the truethe maie be founde out by triall and reasonable insighte into some of theire doinges And if I shoulde saie theare is some blame heareof in some of the principall Gouernours I thinke I mighte allso shewe some reasonable profe of my speache for by that which bothe I and manye haue obserued the like mighte be gathered, As for ensample some of them seinge the ende of theire gouernment to drawe nighe and some mischiefe or troublous practize growinge vp which afterwardes maye worke troble to the nexte succedinge gouernour will not attempte the redresse or Cuttinge of theareof either for feare they shoulde Leave the realme vnquiet at the ende of theire government or that the nexte which Comethe should receaue the same to quiet and so happely wynne more praise theareof then they before And therefor they will not (As I saide) seke at all to represse that evill but will eyther by grauntinge proteccion for a time or houldinge some imparlance with the Rebell or by treatye of Commishioners or other like devises onelye smother and kepe downe the flame of the mischiefe soe as it maye not breake out in theire time of gouernment. what Comes afterwardes they Care not, or rather wishe the worste. This Course hathe bene noted in some governours | 2840 2845 2850 2855

f. 53ʳ *Eudox*: Surelye *Iren*: This if it weare trewe shoulde be worthie of an heavie iudgement But it is hardlye to be thoughte that anye Gouernour woulde soe muche either envye the good of that realme which is put into his hande or defraude her maiestie whoe trustethe him so muche or 2860

... mighte be] (having ... might) they *W*   2833 gouernment] gouermentes *RW*   2833 a] om. *C*   2833 to] of *C*   2834 theire] that *C*   2835 doe] doe, *R*   2836 quite] quiet *C*   2837 wante sporte] want. *W*   2837 sporte] sport: *C*   sporte:/ *R*   2838 doe] om. *C*   2838 of some] of *CR* om. *W*   2839 Gouernours/] Governours? *W*   2840 noe] *inserted between lines E* om. *C*   2842 saie] said *C*   2842 heareof] thereof *W*   2842 some of] om. *W*   2844-5 for ... gathered] om. *W*   2844 bothe] om. *R*   2845 seinge] seinge, *R*   2846 mischiefe or] mischiefes and *W*   2847 afterwardes] afterwarde *R*   2847 maye] might *C*   2850 which] that *W*   2852 (As I saide)] as I saye, *R*   2854 other] by other *W*   2856 government.] goverment *C*   goverment, *RW*   2857 worste.] wourse *C*   worst, *R*   2858 governours] governours./. *C*   gouernors:/ *R*   Governors. *W*   2859 *Iren*:] *Irenius henceforth where not abbreviated F*   (*Irenaeus*) *W*   2861 woulde] should *W*

A VIEW OF THE PRESENT STATE OF IRELAND 145

maligne his successour which shall possesse his place as to suffer an evill to growe vpp, which he mighte timely haue kepte vnder or perhaps to nourishe it with Colored Countenaunces or suche sinister meanes/

Iren: I doe not certainlye avouche soe muche *Eudox*: but the sequele of thinges dothe in a manner proue and plainlye speake soe muche That the Gouernours vsuallie are envious one of anothers greater glorye, which if they woulde seke to excell by better gouerninge it shoulde be a moste laudible emulacion But they doe quite otherwise. ffor this (as ye maye marke) is the Comon order of them that whoe Comethe nexte in place will not followe that Course of gouernement howeuer good which his predecessour helde, either for disdaine of himselfe, or doute to haue his doinges drowned in another mans praise, but will streighte take awaye quite Contrarye to the former as if the former thought by kepinge vnder the Irishe to reforme them the nexte by discounttinancinge the Englishe will Cvrrye favour with the Irishe and so make his gouerment seme plausible as havinge all the Irishe at his Comaunde, But he that Coms next after will perhaps followe neither the one nor thother but will dandle the one and the other in suche sorte as he will sucke sweete out of them bothe and leaue bitternesse to the pore lande, which if he that comes after shall seke to redress he shall perhaps finde suche Crosses as he shall hardlie be able to beare or doe anie good that mighte worke the disgrace of his predecessours. Ensamples heareof ye maye see in the Gouernours of late times sufficientlye And in others of former times more manifestlie, when the government of that realme was Comitted sometymes to the Geraldines, As when the | house of Yorke helde the Crowne of Englande, somtimes to the Butlers as when the house of Lancaster gott the same, And otherwhiles when an Englishe gouernour was appointed he perhaps founde enemyes of bothe, And this is the wretchednes of that fatall kingedome which I thinke thearefore was in olde time not Called amisse *Banno* or *sacra Insula* takinge *sacra* for accursed/

Eudox. I ame sorye to heare soe muche as ye reporte and now I beginne

2863 successour] successors C   2865 Countenaunces] countenance *RW*   2866 soe muche] *om. R*   2866 *Eudox*:] (*Eudoxus*) *W*   2868 greater] great *C*   2872 which] *om. C*   2873 predecessour] predecessors *W*   2873 either] *om. R*   2874 awaye] a waye *RW*   2875-6 by ... Irishe] (by ... *Irish*) *W*   2876 discounttinancinge] *corr. of* discontinvinge *E*   discontynueinge *C*   discontynewinge, *R*   2877 Cvrrye] *corr. of* Carrye *E*   carye *C*   2877 his] the *C*   2877-8 seme plausible] plausible in vewe *R*   2878 next] *om. W*   2879 dandle] dandle, *R*   2881 lande] Countrey *W*   2883 doe] to doe *C*   2883 the] *om. R*   2884 predecessours.] predecessor *C*   predecessors, *R*   2884 heareof ... see] you may see hereof *W*   2884-5 late times] late tyme *C*   2887 when the] when the, *R*   2887 helde] had *W*   2890-2 bothe, ... accursed/] both. *W*   2891 was ... time] an ould tyme was *R*   2891 *Banno*] *Ramo D1*   *Bardon F*   *Banna H1A*   *Ranno RL*   2892 *sacra* for] sacred for *H2*   2893 now I]

to Conceive somwhat more of the Cause of her Continiall wretchednes then heareetofore I founde and wishe that this inconvenience were well loked into, ffor sure me semes it is more weightye then all the former and more hardelye to be redressed in the gouernement, as a maladye in a vitall parte is more incurable then in an externall/

Iren: ye saie verye trewe, But now that we haue thus ended all the abuses and inconveniences of that governmte which was our firste parte, it followethe nexte that we passe vnto the seconde parte which was of the meanes to Cure and redresse the same which we muste labour to reduce to the firste beginninge theareof/

Eudox: Righte so. *Iren*: for by that which I haue noted in all this your discourse ye suppose that the wholle ordinaunce and institucion of that realmes goverment was bothe at firste when it was placed evill plotted and allsoe sithens thoroughe other ouersighte run more out of square to that disorder which it is now Come vnto, like as to indirecte lynes the further they are drawen out, the further they goe asunder/

Iren: I doe soe. *Eudox*: and as ye saie, so thinke that the longer that goverment thus Contineweth in the worse Case will that realme be. ffor it is all in vaine that they now strive and endevour by faire meanes and peaceable plottes to redresse the same without firste Removinge all those inconveniences and new framinge | As it weare in the forge all that is worne out of fashion, for all other meanes wilbe but loste labour, by patchinge vp one hole to make manye. ffor the Irishe doe strongelye hate and abhore all reformacion and subieccion to the Englishe by reason that havinge bene once subdued by them they weare thruste out of all theire possessions. So as now they feare that if they weare againe broughte vnder they shoulde likewise be expelled out of all which is the Cause that they hate the Englishe governement accordinge to the sayinge *Quem metuunt*

nowe *C*   2895 I] I have *C*   2895 well] *om. R*   2896 me semes] (me thinkes) *W*
2897 gouernement] governour then the gorverned *C*   gouernor then in the gouerned *RW*
2898 incurable] incurerable *R*   2901 nexte] now *W*   2901 that ... parte] *om. R*
2901 parte] part. *W*   2903 theareof/] therof *C*   2904 so.] soe *CRW*   2907 sithens]
since *R*   2907 ouersighte run] over-sights came *W*   2907 to] *om. R*   2908 further]
further that *W*   2910 soe.] soe *C*   so: *R*   see *W*   2911 goverment] gouerment, *R*
2911 Case will that] course will the *W*   2914 As it weare] (as it were) *W*   2914 that]
that, *R*   2915 but] but as *W*   2916 strongelye] strongelie, *R*   2919 possessions.]
possessions *C*   possessions, *R*   2920 likewise be] bee likewise *W*   2921 hate the] hate *R*
2921 *Quem*] *Qnem Ho*   2921 *metuunt*] metuant *FT*   2922 *oderunt*] oderant *H2T*
Oderunt, *R*   oderunt: *W*   2922 with the] with *C*   the *W*

oderunt Therefore the reformacion muste nowe be with the strengthe of a greate power//

Eudox: But me thinkes that mighte be with makinge of good lawes and establishinge of newe statutes with sharpe penalties and punishementes for amendinge of all that is presentlye amisse and not as ye suppose to beginne all as it weare anewe and to alter the whole forme of the governement, which howe dangerous a thinge it is to attempte youe your selfe muste nedes confesse and theye which haue the menaginge of the realmes wholle policye Cannot without greate Cause feare and refraine ffor all inovacion is perillous in so muche as thoughe it be meante for the better yeat soe manye accidentes and fearefull eventes maye Come betwene as that it maye hazzarde the losse of the wholle/

Iren: verye Trewe *Eudox*: all chaunge is to be shonned wheare the affaires stande in suche state as that they maie continue in quietnes or be assured at all to abide as they are. But that in the Realme of Irelande we see muche otherwise ffor everye daie we perceaue the trowbles growinge more vppon vs and one evill growinge on another, in soe muche as theare is no parte now sounde or ascerteined but all haue theire eares vprighte waytinge when the watcheworde shall Come That they shoulde all rise generallye into Rebellion and Caste away the Englishe subieccion, To which theare nowe little wantethe for I thinke the worde be all readie given and theare wantethe nothinge but oportunitye, which trewly is the deathe of one noble persone whoe beinge himself most | stedfaste to his Soueraigne Quene his Countrye Coastinge vppon the Southe sea stoppethe the ingate of all that evill which is loked for and holdethe in all those which are at his backe with the terrour of his greatnes and the Assurance of his Imoveable loyalltye And therefore where ye thinke that good and sounde lawes mighte amende and reforme thinges theare amisse, ye thinke surelie amisse. ffor it is vaine to prescribe lawes wheare no man carethe for kepinge them nor fearethe the daunger for breakinge them. But all the Realme is firste to be reformed and lawes are afterwardes to be made for kepinge and Continewinge in that reformed estate/

Eudox: Howe then doe ye thinke is the reformacion thereof to be begonne yf not by Lawes and Ordinaunces/

2922 the strengthe of] *om. R*   2923 greate] greater *CRW*   2924 with] by *CRW*   2926 as ye suppose] (as you suppose) *W*   2927 to] *om. C*   2931 thoughe] though as though *R*   2935 state] sort *W*   2938 on] vpon *RW*   2939 now] *om. R*   2939 or] nor *R*   2939 ascerteined] ascertented *C*   2939 eares] evills *C*   2940 rise] arise *CW*   2941 subieccion,] subjection. *W*   2944 Soueraigne] noble *R*   2945 Quene] Queen and *GP*   Quene, *RFH1H2HoT*   Queene, and *W*   2945 Countrye] Countrey, *W*   2947 backe] becke *W*   2948 Imoveable] most immoveable *W*   2949 theare amisse] amysse theire *R*   2950 is] is in *C*   2951 kepinge] keeping of *W*   2951 breakinge] breaking of *W*   2952 afterwardes] afterwarde *R*   2953 Continewinge] contayninge *R*   2953 in] it in *CRW*   2955 Ordinaunces/] ordi-

Iren: Even by the sworde. for all those evills muste firste be Cutt awaie by a stronge hande before anie good Cane be planted, like as the Corrupte braunches and vnholsome boughes are firste to be pruned and the foule mosse clensed and scraped awaye before the tree cane bringe forthe anye good fruite/

Eudox: did ye blame me even nowe for wishinge kerne Horsboyes and Carrowes to be cleane cutt of as too violente a meanes, and doe youe your selfe now prescribe the same medicyne? Is not the sworde the moste violent redresse that maye be vsed for anie evill//

Iren: It is soe but yeat wheare no other remedye maie be devized nor no hope of recouerie had theare muste neds this violente meanes be vsed As for that lose kinde of people which yee woulde haue Cutt of, I blamed it for that they mighte otherwise be broughte perhaps to good as namelye by this waye which I sett before youe/

Eudox: Is not your waie all one with the former in effecte which yee founde faulte with save onelye this odds that I saide by the halter and ye saie by the sworde? what difference is theare/

Iren: theare is surelie greate when youe shall vnderstande it. ffor by the sworde which I named I doe not meane | The Cuttinge of all that nacion with the sworde, which farr be it from me that euer I shoulde thinke soe desperatlye or wishe soe vncharatablie: but by the sworde I meante the Royall power of the Prince which oughte to stretche it selfe forthe in her Chiefe strengthe to the redressinge and Cuttinge of all those evills which I before blamed, and not of the people which are evill: for evill people by good ordinaunces and government maye be made good/ but the evill that is of it selfe evill will never become good./

Eudox: I praye you then declare your minde at lardge howe ye woulde wishe that sworde which ye meane to be vsed to the reformacion of all those evills/

---

nances? *W*   2956 those] these *CW*   2957 by] with *R*   2958 vnholsome boughes] the vnwholsome lawes *R*   2959 and] or *R*   2960 good] good good *R*   2961 did] Doe *R*   2961 kerne] of Kerne *W*   2962 Carrowes] *Kearrooghs A*   2962 youe] *om. C*   2963 now] *om. C*   2963 same] same as to vyolent a *R*   2963 medicyne?] medicyne, *CR*   2964 evill//] evill? *W*   2965 yeat] *om. W*   2965 devized] founde *R*   2965-6 no hope] hope *W*   2966 vsed] vsed, *R*   used. *W*   2967 that] the *CW*   2968 be broughte perhaps] perhapps be brought *RW*   2970-89 *Eudox*: . . . . subiecte/] *om. T*   2971 odds that] odes, (that *R*   2971 saide] saye *R*   2972 sworde?] sword, *W*   2972 theare/] there,:/ *R*   there? *W*   2974 doe] did *W*   2974 of] of of *CR*   off *W*   2975-6 which . . . vncharatablie] (which . . . vncharitablye) *C*   2975 euer I shoulde] I should ever *W*   2976 meante] meane *RW*   2977 selfe] *om. C*   2977-8 her Chiefe] her cheiffest *C*   the chiefest *W*   2978 of all] of of *CR*   off *W*   2980 ordinaunces]

Iren: The firste thinge muste be to sende ouer into the realme suche a strong power of men as that shoulde perforce bringe in all that Rebellious route of loose people which either doe now stande out in open armes, or in wanderinge Companies doe kepe the woodes spoilinge and infestinge the good subiecte/

Eudox: Yea speake now *Irenius* of an infinite Chardge to her maiestie to sende over suche an armye as shoulde treade downe all that standethe before them on foote and laye on the grounde all the stiffenecked people of that lande for theare is now but one Outlawe of anie greate reckoninge to wete the Earle of *Tyrone* abroade in armes againste whom ye see what huge Chardges she hathe bene at this laste yeare in sendinge of men providinge of victualls and makinge heade againste him yeat theare is little or nothinge at all done But the Quenes treasure spente her people wasted the pore Countrie trobled and the enemye neuertheles broughte into no more subieccion then he was, at list outwardlye to shewe, which in effecte is none, but rather a scorne of her power an imbouldninge of a proud Rebell and an encoragement vnto all like lewde disposed Traitours that shall dare to lifte vp theire heele | Againste theire Soueraigne Ladie. Therefore it weare harde Councell to drawe suche an excedinge Chardge vppon her, whose evente shoulde be soe vncertaine/

Iren: Trewe indede if the evente shoulde be vncertaine but the Certeintye of the effecte heareof shalbe so infallible as that no reasone can gainsaye it neither shall the Chardge of all this Armye the which I demavnde bee muche greater then soe muche as in this laste Twoe yeares warrs hathe vainlye bene expended. ffor I dare vndertake that it hathe Coste the Quene aboue Two hvndred thowsande poundes allreadie and for the presente Chardge that shee now is at theare amounteth to verye neare, Twelue thowsand poundes a monethe wherof Caste ye the accompte, yeat nothinge done. the which some yf yt had bene ymployed as it shoulde be woulde haue effected all this which I nowe goe aboute/

ordynance R   2985 the] that *CRW*   2986 as that] as *W*   2986 shoulde] shall *R* 2987 of] and *W*   2988 spoilinge] spoylinges *C*   2988 and infestinge] *om. W*   2989 subiecte] subjects *W*   2990 *Eudox*:] T *resumes at this point*   2992 on foote] vnder foote *C̄* 2994 *Tyrone*] Terrone *H1*   2999 at] or *CRW*   3000 an imbouldninge] and embouldeninge *CW*   and enboldninge *R*   3001 vnto] of *C* to *W*   3001 lewde] lewdlie *W* 3002 Ladie.] Lady, *CR*   3003 Chardge] great charge *W*   3005 Trewe] Trewe: *R* 3007 the which I demavnde] (the ... demaund) *W*   3007 the which] which *R*   3008 this] the *C* these *W*   3010 aboue] aboue: *R*   3011 that] *om. C*   3011 now is] is now *RW* 3011 amounteth] amountes *C*   3011 neare,] nere *RW*   3012 Twelue thowsand poundes] crowded as if added in blank space *E* blank space *CT*   3012 Twelue thowsand] 200 *D1* 2000 *RL*   3012 accompte] Counte *R*   3013 done.] don *C* done, *R* is done. *W* 3013 yf yt had] hadd it *CRW*   3014 which] that *R*   3014 I nowe] now I *W*

Eudox. Howe meane youe to haue it imployed but to be spente in the paye of Souldiours and provicion of victell

Iren: Righte soe but it is nowe not disbursed at once as it mighte be but drawen out into a Longe leangthe by sendinge ouer now Twentye Thowsande pounds and the nexte halfe yeare Tenn Thowsande, so as the soldiour in the meane tyme is for wante of dewe provicion of victell and good payment of his soulde starued and consumed that of a Thowsande which come ouer Lustie hable men in halfe a yeare theare are not left v^C. And yeat is the Quenes Chardge neuer a whitt the lesse, but what is not paide in presente money, is accompted in debte, which will not be longe vnpaide: ffor the Captaine halfe of whose souldiours are dead and the other quarter neuer mustred nor sene comes shortlye to demaunde payment heare, of his wholle accompte: wheare by good meanes to some greate ones, and privie sharinge withe servantes and officers of other some, he receavethe his debte muche lesse perhaps then was dewe, yeat muche more indeed then he iustelye deserved/

Eudox: I take this sure to be no good husbandrie for what muste nedes be spente as good spente at once wheare is ynoughe as to haue it drawen out into longe delayes seinge that thearby bothe the service is muche hindered and yeat nothing saved. But it maye be *Irenius* that the Quenes treasure in so greate occacions of huge disbursmentes as it is well knowen she hathe bene at latelye is nott allwaies soe readye nor so plentifull as it cane spare so greate a some togeather, but beinge paide as it is nowe some and then some it is no greate burthen vnto her nor anie great impouerishinge to her Coffers, seinge by suche delaie of time that it dailye Comethe in as faste as she poowrethe it out/

Iren: It maye be as yowe saie But for the goinge thoroughe of so honorable a Course I doubte not but if the Quenes Coffers be not so well stored/ which we are not to loke into but that the wholle realme which now (as thinges are vsed) doe fele a Continuall burthen of that wretched Realme hanginge vppon theire backes woulde for a finall riddaunce of all that

---

3015 imployed] imployed? *W*   3016 victell] victell: *CR* victualls. *W*   3017 Righte] Right, *R*   3018 now] now, *R*   3018-9 Twentye Thowsande] 120000 *H1*   3019 and the] and *CRW*   3019 Tenn Thowsande] 1000 *H1* 10000. pounds *WAHo*   3020 soldiour] said souldior *C*   3020 is] *om. W*   3020 of victell] as victuall *R*   3021 soulde] souldior *C* wages *G blank space R* due *W*   3021 starued] is starved *W*   3022 come] came *CRW* 3023 neuer . . . lesse] neuerthelesse *R*   3027 heare,] here *CR om. W*   3027 to] of *RW* 3028 sharinge] shareings *W*   3028 servantes and officers] the servauntes and officers *C* the offycers and servantes *RW*   3032 spente at] spend it at *W*   3032 to] *om. C*   3034 *Irenius*] *om. R*   3035 huge] *om. W*   3035-6 as . . . latelye] (as . . . lately,) *W*   3036 nor] *word illegible C*   3037 is nowe] is, now *R*   3038 some] *inserted between lines E om. C* 3038-9 impouerishinge] impouerishment *CW*   3040 in as] in so *R*   3040 poowrethe] parteth *W*   3041 saie] said *R*   3042 I doubte not] (I doubt not) *W*   3043 which . . . into] (which . . . into) *CRW*   3043 (as] as *CW*   3044 vsed)] vsed *W*   3045 finall]

trouble be once trobled for all and put to all theire shoulders and helpinge handes and hartes to the defrayinge of that Chardge moste gladfullie and willinglye And surelye the Chardge in effecte is nothinge to the infinite greate good which shoulde Come thearby bothe to the Queene and to all this realme generallye as when time servethe shalbe shewed/ 3050

Eudox: Howe manye men then woulde youe require to the finishinge of this which ye take in hande and howe longe space woulde youe haue them entertained/

Iren: verelie not aboue Tenn thowsande footemen and a Thowsande horsemen and all those not aboue the space of one yeare and an half, 3055 for I woulde still as the heate of the service abateth abate the nomber in paie and make other provicion for them as I will shewe youe/

f. 56ᵛ *Eudox* Surelye it semethe not muche which ye require | nor no longe time but howe woulde ye haue them vsed? woulde ye leade forthe your Armye againste the enemye and seke him wheare he is to fighte/ 3060

Iren: No. *Eudox*: that woulde not be for it is well knowne that he is a flyinge enemye hidinge him self in woodes and bogges from whence he will not drawe forthe but into some streighte passage or perilous forde wheare he knowes the Armie muste nedes passe theare will he lye in awayte and if he finde advantage fitt will daungerouslye hazard the 3065 troubled Souldiour Therefore to seke him out that still flittethe and followe him that cane hardlye be founde weare vaine and botelesse: but I woulde devide my men in garrison vppon his Country in suche places as I shoulde thinke mighte moste annoye him/

Eudox: But howe Cane that be *Iren*: with so fewe men for the enemye 3070 as ye now see is not all in one Countrye but some in Vlster some in Connaght and others in Leinster so as to plante stronge Garrisons in all these places shoulde nede manye more men then ye speake of or to plante all in one and to leaue the rest naked shoulde be but to leave them to the spoile/

small *W*   3045 all] *om. R*   3046 to all] to *C*   3047 to] too, to *C*   also to *RW*
3047 gladfullie] gladlie *C*   3049 which] that *C*   3049 and to] and *RW*   3051 then]
om. W   3051 finishinge] furnishing *W*   3052 hande] hand? *W*   3053 entertained/]
entertained? *W*   3054 Tenn thowsande] 1000 *RL*   3055 horsemen] horse *CRW*   3055 those]
these *W*   3055 one] a *W*   3055 an] a *RW*   3057 youe] *om. CRW*   3058 which]
that *R*   3059 vsed?] vsed *CR*   3059 Armye] Arny *R*   3060 is] is, *W*   3060 fighte/]
fight *R*   fight? *W*   3061 *Iren*: No. *Eudox*:] *om. and no new paragraph D1   inserted in
margin without new paragraph RL*   3061 No.] Noe *CRW*   3061 that . . . be] *om. RLD1*
3064 passe] passe, *R*   passe: *W*   3064 will he] he will *C*   3065 awayte] *corr. of*
a waye *E*   a waye *C*   waite *W*   3066 Souldiour] soldyer, *R*   Souldiour. *W*   3066 flittethe]
flyeth *R*   3068-71 in suche . . . Countrye] *om. N*   3070 *Eudox*:] *om. and no new paragraph D1*   3070 men] men? *W*   3071-2 Connaght] Connaugh *FH*o   Connagh *H1*
Connough *R*   3072 Leinster] *Lempster H1   Lemster GH2*   Lymster *N*   Leinster. *W*
3072 these] those *CW*   3073 places] places, *R*   3073 more] moe *R*

Iren: I woulde wishe the Chife power of the Armye to be garrisonde in one Countrie that is strongest and the rest vppon the rest that are weakest As for ensample the Earle of Tyrone is nowe Counted the strongest vppon him woulde I laye Eighte Thowsande men in Garrisone A Thowsande vppon feaghe m^a Hugh and the Cavanaghes and a Thowsande vppon some partes of Connaght to be at the direccion of the governour/

Eudox: I see now all your men bestowed but in what places woulde youe sett theire Garrison that they mighte rise out moste Convenientlie to service? and thoughe perhaps I ame ignorante of the places yeat I will take the mapp of Irelande before me and make myne eyes in the meane while my Scollemasters to guide my vnderstandinge to iudge of your plott/

Iren: Those eighte thowsande of vlster I woulde devide likewise into foure partes so as theare shoulde be Two thowsande footemen in everye garrisone The | The which I woulde thus place, vppon the Blacke water in some Conveniente place as highe vp to the Riuer as might be I woulde laie one Garrisone Another would I putt at Castlecliffer or Castlefin or theareaboutes so as they shoulde haue all the passages vppon the Riuer to Loghfoile The thirde I woulde place aboute fermanaghe or Bundroisse as they mighte lye betwene Connaght and Vlster to serue vppon bothe sides as occacion shalbe offered and this therefore woulde I haue stronger then anye of the reste because it shouldebe moste enforced and moste ymployed and that they mighte put wardes at Ballashaine Belick and all those passages. The laste woulde I sett aboute monohan or Belterbert, so as it should fronte bothe vppon the enemye that waie and allsoe kepe

---

3075 wishe] *om.* C   3076 and the rest] and thother *RW*   3076 are] is *W*   3077 weakest] weakest, *C*   3077 Tyrone] Terrone *RHo*   3077 Counted] accompted *W*   3077 strongest] strongeste, *CRW*   3079 feaghe] *Feughe A   Phagh* H1G   *Fragh* H2   3079 Cavanaghes] *Keuanaghs A   Carvanaghes F   Canuanashes* H2   *Cannaughs* T   3080 Connaght] *Connaughe Ho   Connagh R*   3081 in] *om.* W   3083 service?] service *CR*   3084 before] and lay it before *W*   3084 myne] my *R*   3084-5 in . . . while] (in . . . time) *W*   3087 Those] These *R*   3087 of] in *W*   3088 foure] *written above* three *E*   three *CT*   3089 The The] The *CRW*   3089 place,] place. *W*   3090 vp to] vpp *C*   vpon *RW*   3090-1 I woulde laie] *om. R*   3091 Garrisone] garison, *C*   garrison. *RW*   3091 at] a *C*   3091 Castlecliffer] *blank space A*   Castle liffer *C*   Castleliffer *R*   Castle-liffer *W*   3091 or Castlefin] *blank space A om. W*   3092 all] *om. C*   3093 Loghfoile] loghfoile, *C   Loighfocle* H1   *Loghfoyh:* H2   Laythfoyle, *RLD*1   *Logh-foyle. W*   3093 fermanaghe] *Fearnemunnaghe A   fermangh D*1   *Fermanah Ho   ffermagh RL*   3093 Bundroisse] *blank space A   Bondraise D1H1   Blundrisse G   Bondcrosse H2N   Blundroisse P   Bundroiste T*   3094 as] so as *RW*   3094 Connaght] *Connagh D1Ho   Cannaugh F   Connah H1   Comaugh L   Connaugh RD2*   3097 Ballashaine] *blank space A   Bellashame G   Ballashine LD1   Ballashame T   Ballishannon, and W*   3097 Belick] *blank space A   Belicque P*   3098 passages.] passages, *R*   3098 laste] rest *R*   3098 monohan] *blank space A   Monahoon F   Moneham H1   Monason N   Monoghan W*   3098 Belterbert] *blank space A   rather at Bellfaste and Monahan bothe D2   Bellerbert and in margin or rather at Belfast and Monahon both F   bellerberte H2   Bellarbart Ho*

A VIEW OF THE PRESENT STATE OF IRELAND 153

the Countye of Cavan and meathe in awe from passing of Straglers and outgadders from these partes whence they vse to Come forthe and often times worke muche mischief. and to euerie of these Garrisons of two thowsande fotemen I woulde haue two hundreth horsemen added for the one without the other Cane doe but litle service. The fowre garrisons thus beinge placed I woulde haue to be victelled aforehande for halfe a yeare which ye will saie to be harde Consideringe the Corrupcion and vsuall waste of victells. but why should not they be as well victelled for so longe time as the shipps are vsuallie for a yeare and somtimes two seinge it is easier to kepe them on lande then water? Theire bred I woulde haue in flower so as it mighte be baked still to serue theire necessarye wante, theire drinke also theare brewed within them from time to time, and theire beffe before hande barrelled the which maye be vsed but as it is neded, for I make no doubte but freshe victells they will somtimes purvaye themselues amongest theire enemies Crete. Herevnto woulde I likewise haue them to haue a store of hose and shoes with suche other necessaries as maye be nedefull for soldiours So as they shoulde haue no occacion to loke for Reliefe from abroade, or occacion suche | troble for theire Continuall supplie as I see and haue often proved in Irelande to be more Combrous to the deputie and daungerous to them that releive them then haulfe the leadinge of an Armie. ffor the enemyes knowinge the ordinarye waies by which theire reliefe muste be broughte them, vsethe Comonlye to drawe himselfe into the streighte passages thitherwarde and oftentimes dothe daungerouslye distresse them, Besides the paye of suche force as shoulde be sente for theire Convoye, the Chardge of the Carriages, the Rysing out of the Countrye shalbe spared, but onelie euerie haulfe yeare the supplie broughte by the deputie himself and his power whoe shall then visite and ouerloke all those Garrisons, to see what is neded to Chaunge, what is expediente and to directe what he shall beste advize

Bellterbet T *Balturbut* W   3100 Countye] Countyes W   3100 Cavan] *blank space* A *Caruan* F   3100 meathe] *corr. of* meashe E   *blank space* A   Meash CD2FHoR   3100 passinge] passage W   3100-1 and outgadders] *om.* W   3101 these] those CRW   3101-2 oftentimes] oftentimes use to W   3104 service.] service, CR   3104 thus] this C   3105 aforehande] before hand W   3107 not ... well] they not aswell be R   3109 them] victuall W   3109 then] then on R   3109 water?] water, C   water: R   water. W   3109 I woulde] would I R   3110 necessarye] *om.* R   3110 wante,] want. W   3111 drinke] Beere W   3111 allso theare] there also W   3112 before hande] aforehand C   3112 but] *om.* R   3113 freshe victells] of fresh victuall R   3114 themselues] for themselves W   3114 enemies Crete.] Enemies. W   3114 Crete.] Crete C   3114 woulde I likewise] likewise would I W   3114 likewise] also R   3115 to] *om.* CRW   3115 a] *om.* C   3117 from] *om.* C   3117 suche] of such W   3117-8 Continuall] contynewallie R   3118 more] *om.* R   3119 daungerous] daungerous and daungerous C   more dangerous R   3120 the enemyes] thenymie R   the Enemy W   3121 by] thorough the W   3123 paye] praye R   3125 Rysing out] *inserted in different hand* E   *blank space* C   exactions RW   3125 spared,] spared. W   3127 neded] needed, R   needefull W   3128 Chaunge,] change CR   3128 he] *om.* C

And these fowre garrisons issuinge forthe at suche Convenient times as they shall haue intelligence or espiall vppon the enemye will soe drive him from one side to another and tennys him amongest them that he shall finde no wheare safe to kepe his crete nor hide him selfe but flyinge from the fire into the water and out of one daunger into another that in shorte space his Crete which is his moste sustenaunce shalbe wasted with prayinge or killed with drivinge or starued for wante of pasture in the woodes and he him self broughte so lowe that he shall haue no harte nor habilitye to endure his wretchednes The which will surelie come to passe in verye shorte time, for one winters well followinge of him will so plucke him on his knees that he will neuer be able to stande vp againe/

Eudox do youe thinke then the winter time fittest for the services of Irelande how falls it then that our moste employmentes be in sommer and the Armies then led comonlye forthe/

Iren: It is surelye misconceyued for it is not with Ireland as with other Countries wheare the warres flame moste in Sommer and the hellmettes glister brightest in the faire | Sunshine. But in Irelande the winter time yealdethe best services, for then the trees are bare and naked which vse bothe to Cloathe and hide the kerne, the grounde is Cold and wett which vseth to be his beddinge, the aire is sharp and bitter to blowe thoroughe his naked sides and legges, the kine are barren and without milke which vsethe to be his onely foode. Neither if he kill them then will they yealde him fleashe nor if he kepe them will they give him fode. besides then beinge all with Calfe for the moste parte they will thoroughe muche Chasinge and drivinge Caste all theire Calfes and lose theire milke which shoulde relieve him the nexte sommer after/

Eudox: I doe well vnderstande your reasone, but by your leave I haue harde it otherwise saide of some that weare Outlawes, that in sommer they kepte themselues quiet but in winter they woulde playe theire partes, and when the nightes weare longest then burne and spoile moste so that they mighte safelye retorne before daie

Iren: I haue likewise harde and allsoe sene profe thereof trew but that was of suche Outlawes as weare either abidinge in well inhabited Countries

---

3129 these] those *W*   3129 fowre] former *R*   3130 espiall] especiallye *C*   3131 side] steade *R*   3132 kepe] kepe, *R*   3132 crete] Creete in *W*   3133 fire] fyer shall fall *CRW*   3133 space] tyme *R*   3134 moste] cheife *W*   3138 time] space *R*   3138 winters ... of] Winter well followed upon *W*   3140 thinke then] then thincke *CRW*   3141 Irelande] Ireland, *RW*   3142 forthe/] forth? *W*   3143 as] as it is *W*   3145 in the] in *C*   3145 faire] fairest *W*   3145 time] *om. RW*   3147 hide] house *CRW*   3148 bitter] bytter which vseth *R*   3150 them] them, *R*   3150 then] *om. W*   3151 give him] geive them *C*   3151 fode.] foode, *RW*   3151 then] *om. W*   3152 with] in *CR*   3152 for ... parte] (for ... part) *W*   3153 lose] loose all *R*   3154 after] *om. W*   3159 daie] daye/ *C*   daye::/ *R*   day. *W*   3160 allsoe] *om. C*   likewise *R*   3161 weare]

as in mounster or borderinge to the Englishe pale as Pheagh m̃ª Hugh the Cavanaghes the moores, the dempses the ketinges and Kellies, or suche like. ffor. for them the winter indede is the fittest time for spoillinge and robbinge because the nightes are then (as ye saide) longest and darkest and allsoe the Countries all aboute are then fullest of Corne and good provicion to be euerie wheare gotten by them but it is far otherwise with a stronge peopled enemy that possesse a wholle Countrye, ffor the other beinge but a fewe are indede privelye lodged and kepte in out villages and Corners nighe the woods and mountaines by some theire privie frindes to whom they bringe theire spoiles and stealthes and of whom theye Continvallie receaue secrete reliefe But the open enemye havinge all his Countrye wasted what by him selfe and what by the soldiour findethe then succour in no place, Townes theare are none of which he maie gett spoile they are all burnte, Cuntrye howses and fermours theare be none they be all fledd, bread he hathe none he plougheth not in Sommer, fleshe he hathe but if he kill it in winter he shall wante milke in sommer and shortlie wante liefe Therefore if they be well followed but one winter ye shall haue little worke with them the nexte Sommer/

Eudox: I doe now well perceaue the difference and do verelie thinke that the winter time is there fittest for service. withall I Conceaue the manner of your handlinge of the service to wete by drawinge sodaine draughtes vppon the enemye when he lokethe not for youe and to watche advantages vppon him as he doethe vppon youe by which streight kepinge in and not sufferinge them at anie time longe to rest I muste nedes thinke that they will sone be brought lowe and driven to greate extreamityes. All which when ye haue performed and brought them to the verye laste Cast suppose that either they will all offer to Come into youe and submitt themselves or that some of them will seke to withdrawe themselues what is your advice to doe will ye haue them received 3190

Irenius Noe But at the beginninge of these warrs and when the garrisons are well planted and fortifyed I woulde wishe proclamacion weare made generallye to come to theire knowlledge that what persons soeuer woulde within xx^ty daies absolutelye submitt themselues (exceptinge onelye the verye principall and ringeleaders should finde grace. I doubt not but 3195 vppon the setlinge of these Garrisons suche a terrour and nere Consideracion of theire perillous estate wilbe striken into moste of them that they will Covett to drawe awaie from theire Leaders And againe I well knowe
f. 59^r that the Rebells | Themselues, (As I sawe by proffe in the desmoundes warres will turne awaie all theire raskall people whom they thinke 3200 vnservicable as olde men Weomen Children and Hindes which they Call Churles which woulde onelye waste theire victells and yealde them no aide but theire Cattle they will surelye kepe awaie These therefore thoughe pollicye woulde turne them backe againe that they mighte the rather consume and afflicte the other Rebells yeat in a pittifull Comiseracion I woulde 3205 wishe them to be receaued, the rather for that this base sorte of people dothe not for the moste parte rebell of himself havinge no harte thearevnto but is of force drawen by the graund Rebells into theire accion and Carryed awaie with the violence of the streame, else he shoulde be sure to lose all that he hathe and perhaps his liefe to, the which now he Carieth 3210 vnto them in hope to enioye them theare, but he is theare by the stronge Rebells themselues sone turned out of all so that the Constrainte heareof maye in him deserue pardone. likewise if anie of theire hable men or gentlemen shall then offer to Come awaie and to bringe theire Crete with them as some no doubte maie steale them awaie privilye I wishe them allso 3215 to be receued for the dishablinge of the enemie, but withall that good assurance maye be taken for theire trewe behaviour and absolute sub-

vnto *C*   in vnto *R*   to *W*   3190 doe] doe, *RW*   3190 received] receyved: *C*   receyved:// *R* received? *W*   3191 these] those *W*   3192 fortifyed] well fortefied *C*   3192 wishe] wishe a *CRW*   3194 (exceptinge] excepting *R*   3194 onelye] also *C*   3195 principall] Principalls *W*   3195 ringeleaders] Ring-leaders) *W*   3195 grace.] grace, *CR*   3197 estate wilbe striken] state would be strucken *W*   3199 the Rebells] these Rebellions *C*   3199 in the] in *W*   3199 desmoundes] Desmond *H1*   3200 warres] warres *CR*   warres,) *W* 3200 raskall] Castle *C*   3201 vnservicable] vnseruiceable) *R*   3201-2 which ... Churles] (which ... Churles,) *W*   3203 Cattle] cattle, *R*   3203 awaie] awaye, *C*   awaye: *RW* 3204 the] be *C*   3205 a] *om. C*   3206 wishe] have *C*   3206 this] these *C*   3206 base sorte of] sort of base *W*   3207 himself] them selues *CW*   3208 is of] are by *W* 3209 streame,] streame *C*   3209 he] they *W*   3210 he hathe] they have *W*   3210 his liefe] their lives *W*   3210 to] also *R*   3210 now he Carieth] they now carry *W*   3211 vnto] with *R*   3211 he is] they are *W*   3213 him] them *W*   3213 pardone.] pardon *C* pardon, *R*   3214 gentlemen] gentlemen, *R*   3214 Crete] Cattle *W*   3217-8 submission.]

A VIEW OF THE PRESENT STATE OF IRELAND 157

mission. And that then they be not suffered to remayne anye longer in those partes no nor aboute the garrison but sente awaie into the inner partes of the realme and dispersed in suche sorte as they shall not Come togeather nor easelye retorne if they woulde. ffor if they might be suffered to remaine aboute the garrison and theare inhabite as they will offer to till the grounde and yealde A greate parte of the profitt theareof and of theire Cattell to the Coronell, whearewith they haue hearetofore | Tempted manye, they woulde as I haue by experience knowne, be euer after suche a gall and inconvenience vnto them as that theire profitt shall not recompence theire hurte, for they will privelie relieve theire friendes that are forthe, they will sende the enemye secrete advicement of all theire purposes and iournies which they meane to make vppon them, they will not allso sticke to drawe the enemye privelie vppon them yea and to betraye the forte it selfe by discouerie of all her deffectes and disadvauntages yf anie be, to the Cuttinge of all theire throates, for avoydinge wheareof and manie other inconveniences I wishe that they shoulde be Carryed far from thence into some other partes so that as I saide they Come in and submitt themselues vppon the firste Sommons. But afterwardes I woulde haue none receiued but lefte to theire fortune and miserable ende, my reasone is for that those which will afterwardes remayne without, are stoute and obstinate Rebells suche as will neuer be made dutifull and obediente nor brought to labour or civill Conuersacion havinge once tasted that licentious liffe and beinge acquainted with spoile and outrages but will euer after be readye for the like occacions so as theare is no hope of theire amendment or recouerye and therefore nedefull to be cutt of

Eudox: Surelye of suche desperate persons as will willfullie followe the Course of theire owne follie theare is no Compassion to be had, and for the others ye haue proposed a mercifull meanes muche more then they haue deserued. but what then shalbe the Conclusion of this warr for ye haue prefixed a shorte time of his Continuaunce

submission C submission, RW   3218 then they] they then R   3219 aboute] aboutes R   3219 garrison] Garrisons W   3220 shall] may W   3222 garrison] Garrisons W   3222 offer] offer: R   3224 Coronell] Collonell D2FHo   3224 they haue hearetofore] heretofore they haue C   3225 as . . . knowne] (as . . . knowne) CRW   3226 vnto] to RW   3226 shall] should R   3228 advicement] advertisement R   advertizements W   3230 not allso] also not CR   3230 privelie] om. R   3230 and to] and C   3231 her] their C the R   3231-2 yf anie be] (if any be) W   3232 throates,] throates. W   3234 as I saide] (as I say) W   3234 in] om. R   3236 ende,] ende C   end: W   3237 will] om. R   3237 afterwardes] afterwardes, R   3239 that] the R   3240 but] om. RW   3240 euer] neuer R   3241 be readye] om. C   3242 therefore] therefull R   3242 of] of:/. C   of:/ R   off. W   3243 will] om. R   3243 willfullie] om. W   3245 the] om. W   3246 then] om. R   3247 his Continuaunce] his Contynuewance: C   theire contynewance::/ R

Iren: The ende will I assure me be verye shorte and muche soner then Cane be in so great a troble (as it semethe) hoped for, Allthoughe theare should none of them fall by the sworde nor be slaine by the soldiour, yeat thus beinge kepte from manuraunce and theire Cattle from Comminge abroade by this harde restrainte they woulde quicklye Consume them-selues and devour one another The profe wheareof I sawe sufficientlye ensampled in | Those late warrs of mounster, for notwithstandinge that the same was a moste ritche and plentifull Countrye full of Corne and Cattell that ye woulde haue thoughte they Coulde haue bene able to stande longe yeat ere one yeare and a haulfe they weare broughte to soe wonderfull wretchednes as that anie stonie harte would haue rewed the same. Out of euerie Corner of the woods and glinnes they Came Crepinge forthe vppon theire handes for theire Leggs Coulde not beare them, they loked like Anotomies of deathe, they spake like ghostes Cryinge out of theire graues, they did eate the dead Carrions, happie wheare they Coulde finde them, Yea and one another sone after, in so muche as the verye carkasses they spared not to scrape out of theire graves. And if they founde a plotte of water Cresses or Shamarocks theare they flocked as to a feaste for the time, yeat not able longe to Continve thearewithall, that in shorte space theare weare non allmoste lefte and a moste populous and plentifull Countrye sodenlye lefte voide of man or beaste, yeat sure in all that warr theare perished not manie by the sworde but all by the extreamitye of famine which they themselves had wroughte/

Eudox: It is wonder that ye tell, and more to be wondered how it shoulde so shortlie Come to passe/

Iren: yeat is it moste trewe and the reasone allsoe verye readie for ye muste Conceaue that the strengthe of all that Accion is the kerne Gallow-glasse Stocagh horseman and horsboye, the which havinge bene never vsed to haue anie thinge of theire owne and now livinge vpon spoile of others make no spare of anie thinge but havocke and Confusion of all they mete with wheather it be theire owne frinds good or theire foes. And if they

its continuance? *W*   3248 will ... me] I assure mee will *R*   will (I assure me) *W*
3249 (as it semethe)] as it seemeth *W*   3249 semethe)] semeth *R*   3249 for,] for. *R*
3251 Comminge] runninge *RW*   3253 one] *om. C*   3253 another] another. *W*   3254 Those] these *W*   3254 of] in *R*   3256 Coulde] would *R*   should *W*   3257 haulfe] half that *C*   3257-8 soe wonderfull] such *RW*   3258 same.] same, *CR*   3260 Leggs] legges, *R*   3260 them,] them *C*   3260-1 loked like] looked *R*   3261 deathe,] deathe *C*   3261 spake] speak *C*   3262 eate] eate of *R*   3262 wheare] were *CRW*
3265 Shamarocks] *Thamorockes Ho*   3265 theare] they *R*   3268 or] and *W*   3271 is] is a *W*   3272 so shortlie] *om. R*   3273 yeat is it] It is *RW*   3274 Accion] Nation *RW*
3275 Stocagh] seragh *D1*   Stocags *G*   *Stocab W*   3276 livinge] being *W*   3278 good]

A VIEW OF THE PRESENT STATE OF IRELAND 159

happen to gett never so great spoile at anie time the same they waste and Consume in a trice, as naturallye delightinge in Spoile thoughe it doe themselues no good And on | And on the other side whatsoeuer they leave vnspente the Soldiour when he Comethe theare spoillethe and havockethe likewise so that betwene bothe nothinge is verie shortlie lefte. And yeat this is verye necessarye to be done for the soone finishinge of the warr and not onelie this in this wise but allsoe all those subiectes which border vppon those partes are either to be remoued and drawen awaie or likewise to be spoiled that the enemye maye finde no succour theareby for what the soldiour spares the Rebell will surelye spoile/

Eudox I doe now well vnderstande youe. But now when all thinges are brought to this passe and all filled with this rufull spectacles of soe manie wretched Carcasses starvinge, goodlie Countries wasted, so huge a desolacion and Confusion as even I that doe but heare it from youe and do picture in my minde do greatlie pittye and Comiserate, if it shall happen that the state of this miserye and lamentable image of thinges shalbe tolde and felingelye presented to her sacred maiestye beinge by nature full of mercye and Clemencye whoe is moste inclynable to suche pittifull Complaintes and will not endure to heare suche tragedies made of her people and pore subiectes as some aboute her maie insinuate, then shee perhaps for verye Compassion of suche Calamities will not onelye stopp the streame of suche violence and retorne to her wonted mildenes, but allso con them litle thankes which haue bene the Aucthors and Counsellours of suche blodye platformes So I remember that in the late goverment of that good Lo. Grey when after longe travell and manye perilous assayes he had broughte thinges allmoste to this passe that yee speake of, that it was even made readie for reformacion and mighte haue bene broughte to what her maiestie woulde, like Complainte was made againste him that he was a blodye man and regarded not the lief of her subiectes no more then dogges but had wasted and Consumed all, soe as nowe she had nothinge allmoste

goodes *RW*   3279 spoile] spoyles *R*   3279-80 waste ... in] spoyle and waste at *R*   3280 delightinge] delightfull *C*   3281 good And] good. *W*   3281 on And on] on *CRW*   3282 spoillethe and havockethe] he havokethe and spoylethe *R*   3283 bothe] them both *R*   3285 this in] in *C*   3285 all] *om. W*   3285 which] which doe *W*   3288 surelye] surely surelye *R*   3290 all] *om. C*   3290 with this] with these *CRW*   3290 spectacles] spectacles, *R*   3291 Carcasses starvinge,] carcasses starvinge *C*   carcases, starvinge *R*   3291 Countries wasted,] Countries, wasted *R*   3291 a] *om. W*   3292 as] that *W*   3293 in] yt in *RW*   3293 Comiserate,] comisserate itt, *R*   commiserate it. *W*   3294 miserye and] miserie and, and *R*   3294 thinges] thinckes *C*   3295 felingelye] feelinges *C*   3297-8 people and pore] poore people and *W*   3298 insinuate,] insinuate. *W*   3302 platformes] platformes, *C*   platformes: *RW*   3303 Lo.] Lord, *R*   3303 when] where *R*   3306 woulde,] would *C*   3307 her] ther *C*   3308 nothinge allmoste] almost nothinge *C*

lefte but to raigne in theire ashes. Eare was sone lente thearvnto, all sodenlye turned topsydeturvey, He noble Lord eftsones was blamed the | The wretched people pittied and new Councells plotted in which it was Concluded that a generall pardone shoulde be sente ouer to all that woulde accepte of it. vppon which all former purposes weare blanked, the governour at a baye and not onelye all that greate and longe Chardge which she had before bene at quite loste and Cancelled, but allso all that hope of good which was even at the dore put backe and Cleane frustrate. All which wheather it be trewe or not your selfe Cane well tell

Iren: Too trewe *Eudox*: the more the pittye for I maye not forgett so memorable a thinge. neither can I be ignorant of that perillous devise and of the wholle meanes by which it was Compassed and verye Cvnninglie Contrived by sowinge firste dissencion betwene him and another noble personage whearein they bothe at lengthe founde how notable they had bene abused, and how theareby vnderhande this vniuersall alteracion of thinges was broughte aboute, But then to late to staye the same, ffor in the meane tyme all that was formerlye done with longe labour and greate toile was (as youe saie) in a momente vndone, and that good Lord blotted with the name of a bloddye man, whom whoe that well knewe, knewe to be moste gentle affable Lovinge and temperate. But that the necessitye of that presente state of thinges forced him to that violence and allmoste Changed his verye naturall disposicion, But otherwise he was so farr from delightinge in blodd that oftentimes he suffered not iuste vengeance to fall wheare it was deserued and even some of those which weare afterwardes his accusers had tasted to muche of his mercye, and weare from the gallowes broughte to be his accusers., But his Course in dede was this that he spared not the heads and principalls of anye mischevous practize or Rebellion but shewed sharpe iudgement on them Chieflye for ensamples sake that all the meaner sorte which allso weare then generallye infected with that evill mighte by terrour theareof be reclaimd and saved if it weare possible, ffor in that last conspiracye of the Englishe pale thinke youe not that theare weare manye more guiltye then that felte the pun-

nothing *R*   3309 ashes.] ashes *C*   Ashes, *W*   3309 Eare] Eare, *R*   3310 topsydeturvey] topsye turvye *R*   3310 He] the *W*   3310-1 the The] the *CRW*   3313 it.] it *C*   yt: *R* it, *W*   3314 all] *om. C*   3316 frustrate.] frustrate, *C*   frustrate *R*   frustrated. *W* 3317 not] noe *CRW*   3317 tell] tell: *C*   tell/: *R*   tell. *W*   3322 founde] found, *R* 3322 notable] notably *CRW*   3326 saie)] saye *R*   3327 a] the *C*   3328 temperate.] temperate *C*   temperate, *R*   3329 forced] enforced *CRW*   3330 verye] *om. W*   3332 those] them *W*   3333-4 had . . . accusers] *om. R*   3335 the] *om. R*   3336 Chieflye] *om. C* 3336 ensamples] ensample *R*   3337 then generallye] generally then *W*   3339-40 possible . . . weare] *om. R*   3339 that] the *W*   3339 of] of some of *W*   3340 then] then

A VIEW OF THE PRESENT STATE OF IRELAND

ishment? or was theare anie allmoste Cleare from the same? yeat he towched onelye a fewe of speciall note, and in the triall of them allsoe to prevente the blame of Crueltye and parciall procedinge as sekinge theire blodde which he in his greate wisdome (as it semethe) did forsee woulde be obiected againste him, he for avoidinge thereof did vse a singuler discrecion and regarde for the Iurye that wente vppon theire triall, he made to be Chosen out of theire nerest kinsemen, and theire iudges he made of some theire owne fathers, of others theire vncles and dearest friendes, whoe when they Coulde not but iustlye Condempe them yeat vttered theire iudgement in aboundance of teares. And yeat he even hearein was Counted bloddye and Crvell/

Eudox: Indede so haue I harde it often heare spoken but I perceaue (as I allwaies verelye thoughte) that it was moste vniustlye, for he was allwaies knowen to be a moste iuste sincere godlie and righte noble man, far from suche sternenesse, far from suche vnrighteousnes. But in that sharpe execucion of the Spaniardes at the forte of Smerwicke I harde it speciallye noted and if it weare trewe as some reported surelye it was a greate touche to him in Honour. ffor some saie that he promised them lief, others that at leaste he did put them in hope theareof./

Iren: Bothe the one and the other is moste vntrewe for this I cane assure youe my selfe beinge then as neare as anye, that he was so far from either promisinge or puttinge in hope, that when firste theire Secretarye Called as I remember *Segnior Ieffrey*, an Italian beinge sente to treate with the Lo deputie for grace was flatlye refused and afterwardes theire Coronell named *Don Sebastian*: Came forthe to entreate that they mighte parte with theire Armours like souldiours, at leaste with theire lives accordinge to the Custome of warr and lawe of nacions, it was strongelye denied him and tolde him by the Lord deputye him self that they Coulde not iuslye pleade either Custome of war or lawe of nacions, for that they weare not anie lawfull enemyes, and if theye weare willed them to shewe by what

they *W*   3340-1 punishment?] punishment, *R*   3341 or ... same?] *om. W*   3341 same?] same, *CR*   3343 to] evene to *CRW*   3343 as] and *CW*   3344 in] as in *W*   3348 some] some of *W*   3349 vttered] he uttered *W*   3350 he even] *om. C*   3350 Counted] counted a *C*   3352 *Eudox*:] *no new paragraph L*   3352 often heare] often so *R*   heere often *W*   3352 but] and *R*   3353 thoughte] thoughe *C*   3354 allwaies] *om. C*   3355 that] *om. C*   3356 Smerwicke] Senwicke *D2F* Semnwicke [*or Senmwicke*] *H1* Stenwicke *H2N*   Senawicke *RD1HoL* Sinerwick *corrected to* Smerwicke *W* (*Faults escaped*) 3359 at] *om. W*   3359 theareof./] thereof *R*   3360 Iren:] *in middle of line without new paragraph L*   3360 the one] one *C*   3361 then as neare] as nere then *CR* as neare them *W*   3361 from either] from *R* either from *W*   3362 in] them in *W*   3362-3 Called ... remember] (called ... remember) *W*   3363 *Segnior*] Iaques *A* Sequor *CD1H1LR* Iaquas *H2N*   3363 treate] treatie *C*   3364 Coronell] Collonell *D2FHo*   3365 *Sebastian*] Sevastian *H2* Sabastian *N*   3366 Armours] Armes *W*   3366 souldiours,] soldiors *CR* 3366 at] at the *W*   3368 iuslye] iustlie *CRW*   3370 willed] hee willed *W*

f. 62ʳ Commission they | Came thither into another Princes dominions to warr whether from the Pope or the kinge of Spaine or any other. The which when they saide they had not but weare onelye adventurours that Came to seke fortune abroade and serve in warrs amongest the Irishe whoe desired to entertaine them, yt was then toulde them that the Irishe themselues as the Earle and Iohn of desmounde with the rest weare no lawfull enemies but Rebells and Traytours and therefore they that Came to succour them no better then Roges and Runnagates speciallye Comminge with no license nor Comission from theire owne kinge, so as it shoulde be dishonorable for him in the name of his Quene to Condicion or make anye termes with suche Rascalls but lefte them to theire Choise to yealde and submitte themselues or noe, whearevppon the saide Coronell did absolutelye yealde himselfe and the forte with all therein and Craved onelye mercye, which it beinge not thoughte good to shewe them bothe for daunger of themselues if beinge saved, they shoulde afterwardes ioyne with the Irishe, and allso for terrour of the Irishe, who weare muche embouldened by those forreine succours, and allso put in hope of more er longe, theare was no other waie but to make that shorte ende of them which was made Therefore moste vntrewlye and malitiouslye do these evill tonges backebite and slaunder the sacred ashes of that most iuste and honorable personage, whose leste vertue of manye moste excellente which abounded in his heroicke spirite they weare never able to aspire vnto/

Eudox: Trewlye *Iren*: I ame righte gladd to be thus satisfied by youe in that I haue often hearde questioned and yeat was neuer hable till nowe to Chocke the mouthe of suche detractours with the Certaine knowlledge of theire slaunderous vntruethes neither is the knowledge hereof impertinente to that which we formerlie had in hande I meane to the thoroughe prosecutinge of that sharpe course which ye haue set downe for the bringinge vnder of those Rebells of Vlster and Connaghte and preparinge awaie to theire perpetuall reformacion, leaste hapelie by anie suche sinister suggestions of Crueltye and to muche blodd shed All the plott mighte be
f. 62ᵛ overthrowne and all the Coste | And Labour thearein imployed be vtterlie loste and Cast awaie

---

3372 other.] other, *CW*   other *R*   3372 The which] Then *R*   3373 they had] hadd *C*   3374 and] and to *W*   3375 them,] them. *W*   3379 kinge,] King. *W*   3382 Coronell] Collonell *D2FHo*   3382 yealde] submitt *C*   3384 not thoughte good] thought good not *R*   3384 bothe] *om. W*   3384 themselues] them *W*   3386 of] to *W*   3386 weare] are *W*   3387 more] moe *R*   3387 longe,] longe *C*   3388 which] as *W*   3388 made] made, *CR* made. *W*   3391 which] that *W*   3392 spirite] spirite. *C*   3393 *Eudox*:] *Eudor. without new paragraph L*   3396 vntruethes] vntruthe *C*   3396 hereof] thereof *R*   3397 to the] for the *W*   3398 prosecutinge] persecuteinge *C*   3399 Connaghte] Connaghe *CHo*   Connagh *H1*   3399-3400 awaie to] a way for *W*   3401 mighte] mighe *C*   3403 loste and] *om. C*   3403 awaie] awaye/. *C*   awaye:/ *R*   away. *W*

Iren: ye saie moste trewe, for after that Lordes callinge awaye from thence the Two Lordes Iustices Continewed but a while of which the one was of minde (as it semed) to haue Continewed in the footinge of his predecessours but that he was Curbed and restrained, but thother was more mildelye disposed, as was mete for his profession, and willinge to haue all the pittifull woundes of that Common wealthe healed and recured, but not with that hede as they shoulde be) After whom Sr Iohn Perrott succedinge as it weare into another mans harvest founde an open waie to what Course he liste, the which he bente not to that pointe which the former governours intended, but rather quite Contrarye as it weare in skorne of the former, and a vaine vaunte of his owne Counsells, with the which he was to willfullie Carryed, for he did treade downe and disgrace all the Englishe, and sett vp and Countenaunce the Irishe all that he coulde: wheather thinkinge thearby to make them more tractable and buxome to his gouernement whearein he thought muche amisse, or privilye plottinge some other purposes of his owne as it partlye afterwards appeared. But surelye his manner of gouernement Coulde not be sounde nor holsome for that realme beinge so Contrarye to the former as it was, even as two Phisicions shoulde take one sicke bodye in hande at two sundrie times, of which the former woulde minister all thinges mete to purge and kepe vnder the bodye, thother to pamper and strengthen it suddeinlye againe, wheareof what is to be loked for but a moste daungerous relapse, that which we now see, thoroughe his rule, and the nexte after him, happened thearevnto, beinge now more daungerouslie sicke than euer before. Therefore by all meanes it muste be forsene and assured that after once entringe into this Course of reformacion, theare be afterwardes no remorse or drawinge backe, for the sighte of anie suche rufull obiectes as muste thearevppon followe, nor for Compassion of theire Callamityes, seinge that by no other meanes it is possible to recure them, and that these are not of will but of verye vrgente necessitye/ |

Eudox: Thus farr then ye haue now proceded to plante your Garrissons and to directe theire services, of the which neuerthelesse I muste nedes Conceive that theare cannot be anie Certaine direccion set downe so that they muste followe the occacions that shalbe dailye offered and dilligentlye

3406 (as it semed)] as yt seamed *R* 3406-7 predecessours] predecessor *CR* 3409 pittifull] om. *RW* 3410 that] the *R* 3410 be)] be, *CR* bee. *W* 3410 whom] when *W* 3411 as it weare] (as it were) *W* 3412 that] om. *C* 3413 intended] hadd intended *C* 3414 a] in *CW* in a *R* 3414 with the] with that *R* 3416 Countenaunce] Countennce *C* 3417 more] the more *C* 3418 whearein...amisse] (wherein...amisse) *W* 3421 beinge] it being *W* 3421 former...was,] former, for it was *C* former: for yt was *R* former. For it was *W* 3426 relapse,] relapse? *W* 3426 and] om. *C* 3430 or] nor *W* 3431 obiectes] obiect *R* 3432 recure] cure *W* 3436 direccion] dyrections *R* 3437 that]

awayted, But by your leave *Iren*: notwithstandinge all this your Carefull foresighte and provicion me thinkes I see an evill lurke vnespied that maye Chaunce to hazarde all the hope of this great service if it be not verye well loked vnto, And that is the Corrupcion of theire Captaines, for thoughe they be placed neuer soe Carefullie and theire Companies fild neuer so sufficientlye yeat maye they if they liste discarde whom they please and sende awaie perhaps suche as will willingelye be ridd of that daungerous and harde service The which well I wotte is theire Comon Custome to doe when they are laide in garrisone, for then they maye better hide theire defaultes then when they are in Campe, wheare they are Continvallie eyed and noted of all men. Besids when theire paie Commethe they will (as they vse) detaine the greatest porcions thereof at theire pleasures by an hundred shiftes that nede not heare be named, thoroughe which they often times deceaue the Soldiour Abuse the Quene and greatlye hinder the service So that let the Quene paie neuer so fullie let the muster master view them neuer so dilligentlie let the deputye or generall loke to them neuer so exactlie yeat they Can Cozen them all Therefore me semes it weare good if at leaste it be possible to make some provicion for this inconvenience/

Iren: It will surelie be verye harde but the Chiefest helpe for prevencion heareof muste be the Care of the Coronell that hathe the governement of all his garison to haue an eye to theire allteracions to knowe the number and names of the sicke soldiours and the slaine, to marke and obserue theire ranks in theire dailye risinge forthe to service, by which he Cannot easelie be abused so that he | himselfe be a man of speciall assurance and integritie. And therefore greate regarde is to be had in the Chosinge and appointinge of them. Besides I woulde not by anie meanes that the Captaines shoulde haue the payinge of their soldiours but that theare shoulde be a paye master appointed of speciall truste which shoulde paie euerye man accordinge to his Captaines tickett and the accompte of the Clerke of his Bonde ffor by this meane the Captaine will neuer seke either to

which *W*   3438 by your] by good *C*   3438 *Iren:*] *new paragraph T (Irenaeus) W*
3438 notwithstandinge] nothwithstandinge *C*   3439 me thinkes] (mee thinkes) *W*   3439 that]
and that *W*   3440 all . . . of] hope of all *C*   3441 vnto] into *W*   3442 Companies]
Capteines *C*   3444 perhaps . . . will] suche as will perhaps *CW*   such as will *R*
3445 service] servyce. *R*   3445 well I wotte] (well I wote) *W*   3448 men.] men *C*
men, *R*   3449 vse)] vse *R*   say) *W*   3449 pleasures] pleasure *CRW*   3449 an] a *W*
3451 Soldiour] Souldier, and *W*   3451 service] service. *W*   3452 fullie let] fullie, *R*
3453 them] him *C*   3454 all] all, *R*   all. *W*   3454 semes] thinkes *W*   3455 at
leaste] *om. W*   3455 some] *om. W*   3457 heareof] hereof, *R*   3457 Coronell]
Colonell *Ho*   3458 allteracions] alteration *CR*   3458 nomber] numbers *W*   3462 greate]
good *R*   3462 is . . . had] *om. C*   3463 them.] them, *C*   them *R*   3465 be . . .
master] a paymaster bee, *R*   3467 Bonde] band *CRW*   3467 meane] meanes *CW*
3467 either] *om. RW*

falsefye his alteracions nor to diminishe his Companye nor to deceive his Souldiours when nothinge thereof shalbe sure to come vnto himself but what is his owne bare paie And this is the manner of the Spanniarde whoe neuer hathe to meddle with his soldiours paye and indede skornethe the name as base to be counted his soldiours *Pagadore*. whereas the Contrarye amongest vs hathe broughte thinges in soe bad a passe that theare is no Captaine but thinkes his bande verye sufficiente if he Cane muster iijxx and stickes not to saie openlie that he is vnworthie to haue a Capteinshipp, that Cannot make it worthe vC.^{li} by the yeare the which they righte well verifye by the profe/

Eudox. Truely I thinke this a verye good meane to avoide that inConvenience of Captaines abuses. but what saie youe of the Coronell, what auctoritye thinke youe mete to be given him? wheather will ye allowe him to protecte, to safeconduit, to haue marshall lawe as they are accustomed?/

Iren: yea verelie but all these to be limitted with verie streighte instrucions. as thus, for proteccions, That they shalle haue authoritye after the firste proclamacion for the space of xx^{ti} daies to protect all that shall come in vnto them and them to sende vnto the deputie with theire saufconduit or passe to be at his disposicion, but so as none of them retorne backe againe beinge once Commen in, but be presentlie sente awaie out of the Countrye vnto the nexte Shiriffe and soe Convaied in safetye, And likewise for marshall lawe that to the souldiour it be not extended but by triall formerlie made of his Crime by a Iurye of his fellowe | Soldiours as it oughte to be and not rashelie at the will or displeasure of the Coronell as I haue sometimes sene too lightlie, And as for other of the Rebells that shall light into theire handes that they be well aware of what Condicion they bee and what holdinge they haue. ffor in the laste generall warrs theare I knewe manie good ffreholders executed by marshall lawe whose lande was thearby saued to theire heires which shoulde otherwise haue excheated

3468 Companye] Companies *R*   3469 shalbe] shall *C*   3469-70 sure . . . And] for his gaine *R*   3470 Spanniarde] spannishe Captaines *D2F*   Spanyardes Captaines *R* Spaniards Captaine *W*   3472 counted] Compted *R*   3472 soldiours] soldyers, *R*   3472 *Pagadore.*] pagadora *H2N*   Pugadore: *RLD1*   Pagadore, *W*   3472 the] as *C*   3473 in] to *CRW*   3475 stickes] sticke *R*   3476 make it] maketh *C*   3476 worthe] om. *R*   3476 by the] a *C*   3478 meane] meanes *W*   3479 abuses] abusions *CR* 3479 Coronell,] Coronell *C*   Colonell? *Ho*   Coronell? *W*   3480 him?] him, *CR* 3481 to safeconduit,] to saifconducte *R* or safe conduct, and *W*   3481 lawe] lawes *W* 3481 accustomed?/] accustomed./. *C*   accustomed:/ *R*   3483 as] *corr. of* and *E* and *C* 3483 thus] first *W*   3483-4 That . . . to] om. *R*   3483 they] hee *W*   3484 in] om. *C* 3485 vnto them] om. *W*   3485 them to] then to *C*   3485 vnto the] to the Lord *W* 3485 saufconduit] safe Conduict *C*   saif conducte *RW*   3486 retorne] turne *R*   3487 Commen] Commen, *R*   come *W*   3488 vnto] to *W*   3488 Shiriffe] shreif *C*   3489 lawe] lawes *R*   3489-90 formerlie] formally *G*   3490 made] om. *W*   3491 at] as *R* 3491 Coronell] Collonell *D2FHo*   3495-6 lande was] landes were *W*   3496 otherwise haue] have otherwise *W*   3496 excheated] escheated *W*

to her maiestie. In all which the greate discrecion and vprightnes of the Coronell himselfe is to be the Chiefest staye bothe for all those doubtes and for manie other difficulties that maye in the service happen/

Eudox: your caution is verye good. but now touchinge the Arch-Rebell himselfe I meane the Earle of Tyrone if he in all the time of these warrs shoulde offer to Come in and submitt himselfe to her maiestie woulde ye not haue him receaued givinge good hostages and sufficiente assurance of himselfe/

Iren: No marrye, for theare is no doubte but he will offer to Come in as he hathe done diuerse times allreadie, but it is without anie intente of trewe submission as theffecte hathe well shewed. neither in dede Cane he now if he woulde Come in at all nor give that assurance of himselfe that shoulde be mete. for beinge, as he is, verye subtillye headed, seinge himselfe now so far engaged in this bad accion, Canne he thinke that by his submission he Can purchase to himselfe anye safetie but that heareafter when thinges shalbe quieted these his villanies will euer be remembred? And whensoeuer he shall tread awrye (as nedes the moste righteous muste somtimes) advantage wilbe taken theareof as a breache of his pardone and he broughte to a reckoninge for all former matters. Besides howe harde it is for him now to frame himself to subieccion that havinge set once before his eyes the hope of a kingedome hathe thearevnto founde not onely | encouragement from the greatest kinge of Christendome, but allso founde greate faintenes in her maiesties withstandinge him. wheareby he is animated to thinke that his power is able to defende him and offende further then he hathe done when so he please, let euerie reasonable man iudge. But if he himselfe shoulde Come in and leave all other his accomplices without as *Odonell macmahon, mackguyre* and the reste, he muste neds thinke that then even they will er longe Cutt his throate, which

3497 maiestie.] Maiestie; *C* maiestie, *R* 3498 Coronell] Collonell *D2FHo* 3498 those] these *CR* 3501 himselfe ... Tyrone] him self, ... *Tyrone, R* 3501 Tyrone] *Terone Ho* 3504 himselfe/] himselfe? *W* 3507 trewe] true meaninge or *C* 3507 hathe] haue *C* 3508 now ... all] come nowe in att all if he would *C* 3509 verye] verily *C* 3509 subtillye] subtill *RW* 3510 engaged] enaged *C* 3510 he] you *W* 3512 will euer be] wilbe ever *CRW* 3512 remembred?] Remembred *C* remembred, *RW* 3513-4 (as ... somtimes)] as ... somtymes *CR* 3515 matters.] matters/ *C* matters, *R* 3516 for him now] now for him *W* 3516-7 set once] once sett *CRW* 3517-8 founde not onely] not onlie founde *CW* 3518 of] in *CW* 3519 maiesties] Maiestie *C* 3519 withstandinge him.] with standinge him, *CW* withstandinge, *R* 3520 able] *om. R* 3521 hathe] had *R* 3521 when so] whensoever *W* 3522 in] *om. W* 3523 Odonell] Donnell *D1 Odolor H2* Adonell *L* 3523 mackguyre] *corr. of* macknyre *E* Magueeirhe [*or* Magueeire?] *A* Macknyre *CH1HoT* Mackmire *D2* Mackuirre *F* mackuyre *RLD1* Maguire *WP*

A VIEW OF THE PRESENT STATE OF IRELAND 167

havinge drawen them all into this accion now in the middeste of theire trouble givethe them the slippe wheareby he muste nedes perceive howe ympossible it is for him to submitt himselfe But yeat if he would so doe, can he not give anye assurance of his good obedience for how weake holde theare is by hostages hathe to often bene proued,. And that which is spoken of takinge Shane *Oneales* sonnes from him and settinge them vp againste him is a verie perilous Councell and not by anie meanes to be put in profe/ for weare they let forthe and Coulde ouerthrowe him who shall afterwardes ouerthrowe them or what assurance Can be had of them It wilbe like the Tale in Aesope of the wilde horse who havinge enmitye againste the stagge came to a man to desyre his ayd against his foe, who yielding therevnto mounted vpon his back and so following the stagge ere longe slue him but then when the horsse woulde haue him alighte, he refused but kepte him ever after in his service and subieccion Suche I doubte woulde be the profe of Shane Oneales sonnes Therefore it is moste daungerous to attempte anie suche plott. ffor even that very manner of plott was the meanes by which this Traytorous Earle is now made so greate, ffor when as the laste Oneale Called Terlagh Lenagh beganne to stande vppon tickle terme this fellowe then Called Barō of Dōganō was sett vp at it weare to bearde him, and Countenaunced and strengthened by the Quene so farr as that he is now hable to kepe her selfe playe. muche like vnto a gamster that havinge loste all borrowethe of his nexte fellowe gamster that is the moste winner somwhat to mayntaine playe which he settinge vppon him againe shortlie therby winnethe all from the winner//

Eudox: was this Rebell then sett vp firste by the Quene as yowe saie and now become so vndewtifull |

3525 accion] occasion *CRW*   3526 perceive] perceaue, *R*   3527 But] *Eudoxus* But beginning new paragraph *A*   3528 not] *om. RW*   3528 assurance] good assurance *W*   3528 good obedience] obedience? *W*   3529 theare is] is there *W*   3530 Shane] Ohan *RLD1*   3530 Oneales] oneale is *A*   3532 him] *inserted between lines E om. CR*   3532 shall] should *RW*   3533 of them] of them, *C*   of them? *W*   3534 againste] with *W*   3535-6 the ... following] *inserted between lines E*   3535 foe] enimye *R*   3535 yielding] yeilded *C*   3538 kepte ... after] ever after kept him *W*   3538 service and subieccion] subjection and service. *W*   3538 subieccion] subiection, *R*   3539 Shane] Ohan *D1*   3539 Oneales] *o neale is A*   3539 sonnes] sonnes, *CR*   sonnes. *W*   3541 this] the *C*   3541 so] *om. W*   3542 as] *om. W*   3542 Terlagh] *Tyrrelaghe A*   Turlaghe *CD1LR*   *Tyrlagh D2*   *Turlough H2N*   *Torlagh HoT*   3542 Lenagh] *Renagh D2*   Kennaugh *F*   Oneale *H2AN*   Leugh *T*   Leinagh *W*   3543 tickle terme] some tickle termes *CRW*   3543 then] then, *W*   3543 Dōganō] Dungans *GP*   3544 at] as *CRW*   3545 playe.] playe *CR*   play: *W*   3547 that ... winner] *om. W*   3547 is] is nowe *C*   3548 vppon] vnto *CRW*   3549-50 *Eudox*: ... vndewtifull] *om. R*   3549 firste] at first *W*   3549 as yowe saie] (as you say) *W*   3550 vndewtifull] vnduetifull/ *C*

Iren: He was I assure youe the moste outcaste of all the Oneals then, and lifted vp by her maiestie out of the duste to that he nowe hathe wraughte himself vnto, And now he playeth like the frozen Snake whoe beinge for Compassion releived by the husbandman sone after he was warme, begane to hisse and threaten daunger even to him and his/ 3555

Eudox: He surelie then deseruethe the punishment of that snake and shoulde worthelye be hewen to peeces. But if they like not of the lettinge forthe of Shane Oneales sonnes againste him what saie yee then of that advice which I hearde was given by some to drawe in Scottes to serue againste him? howe like youe that devise?/ 3560

Iren: muche worse then the former, for who that is experienced in those partes knowethe not that the Oneales are nearelye alyed vnto the *Mackonells* of Scottlande and to the Earle of *Argile* from whence they vse to haue all theire succours of those Scottes and Redshankes? Besides all these Scottes are thoroughe longe Continvaunce entermingled and allied to all 3565 the inhabitantes of the Northe, soe as theare is no hope that they will euer be wroughte to serue faithefullie againste theire olde friendes and kinsemen. And thoughe they woulde, howe when the warrs are finished and they haue ouerthrowen him shall they themselues be put out? doe we not all knowe that the Scottes weare the firste inhabitantes of all the 3570 Northe And that those which nowe are Called Northe Irishe are indede verye Scottes which Challenge the Anciente inheritaunce and dominion of all that Countrie to be theire owne Ancientlye. This then weare but to leape out of the pan into the fire. for the Chiefeste Caveat and provicion in reformacion of the Northe muste be to kepe out the Scotts/ 3575

Eudox: Indeed I remember that in your discourse of the firste peoplinge of Irelande ye shewed that the Scithians or Scottes weare the firste that satt downe in the northe whearby it semes they maye Challenge some righte thearein. Howe Comes it then that Oneale Claymes the dominion thereof

---

undutifull? *W*   3551 *Iren*:] *om. and no new paragraph D1*   3551 I assure youe] (I assure you) *W*   3552 nowe hathe] hath nowe *RW*   3556 that] the *R*   3557 hewen] hewed *CRW*   3557 to] in *R*   3557 they] ye *CRW*   3557 of] *om. RW*   3558 forthe of] *om. R*   3558 Oneales] *o neale is A*   3558 that] the *C*   3559 I hearde] (I heard) *W*   3559 in] in the *CR*   3560 him?] him *C*   him, *R*   3560 devise?/] device/. *C*   aduise:? *R*   advice? *W*   3561 who] who is hee *R*   3562 partes] partes, and *R*   3562-3 *Mackonells*] *Mack honets D2F   Maconeales RAD1H2LN   Mac-Neiles W*   3563 whence] whom *R*   3564 Redshankes?] Redshanckes/ *C*   Redshankes, *R*   *Redshanckes*: *W*   3564 these] those *R*   3566 that] *om. R*   3568 thoughe] yf *R*   3568-9 the . . . him] they have ouerthrowne him, and the warres are finished *W*   3569 out?] owt *C*   out, *R*   3569 we] *om. R*   3571 nowe are] are nowe *CR*   3571 Called] called, *R*   called the *W*   3571 are indede] were in deed *R*   3573 all] *om. W*   3573 Ancientlye.] auncentlie, *C*   auncyentelie *R*   3573 weare] were then *C*   3574-5 provicion in] proviso in the *R*   3575 out the] out those *W*   3577 Scithians] Scythian *R*   3578 semes] seemes that *W*   3579 thearein.] therin *C*   therein, *R*   3579 Oneale] Onle *L*   *O-Neales W*

A VIEW OF THE PRESENT STATE OF IRELAND 169

f. 65ᵛ And this Earle of Tirone, Sayethe the righte is in him | I praye youe resolue me thearein for it is verie nedefull to be knowen and makethe muche vnto the righte of the warr againste him, whose successe vsethe Comonlie to be accordinge to the Iustnes of the Cause for which it is made. ffor if Tyrone haue anie righte in that Seigniorye me semes it shoulde be wronge to thruste him out Or if (as I remember ye saide in the beginninge, that Oneale when he acknowledged the kinge of Englande for his Leige Lorde and Soueraigne did (as he aleadgeth) reserue in the same submission all his Seigniories and rightes vnto himselfe it shoulde be accounted vniuste to thruste him out of the same/

Iren: ffor the righte of Oneale in the Seignorie of the Northe it is surelye none at all. for besides that the Kinges of Englande Conquered all the realme and thereby assumed and invested all the righte of that lande to themselues and theire heires and successours for euer So as nothinge was lefte in Oneale but what he receaued backe from them, Oneale himselfe neuer had anye ancient Seigniorie ouer that Countrie but what by vsurpacion and encrochement after the deathe of the Duke of Clarence he gott vppon the Englishe whose landes and possessions beinge formerlie wasted by the Scottes vnder the leadinge of *Edwarde le Bruce* as I formerlie declared vnto youe, he eftsones entered into, and sythens hathe wrongefullie deteined thoroughe the other occupacions and great affaires which the kinges of Englande sone after fell into heare at home, soe as they Coulde not intende to the recouerie of that Countrye of the Northe, nor restrayne the insolencye of Oneale, who findinge none now to withstand him Raigned in that desolacion and made him selfe Lorde of those fewe people that remayned theare vppon whom euer sithence he had Con-

f. 66ʳ tinewed his | firste vsurped power and now exactethe and extortethe vppon all men what he liste Soe that now to subdue or expell an vsurper should be no vniuste enterprize nor wrongefull warr, but a restitucion of

3580 Tirone,] Tyrone *CRW* Terone *Ho*   3580 the] that the *W*   3580 him] him, *R* him? *W*   3581 thearein] herein? *W*   3582 muche] most *R om. W*   3584 Tyrone] *Terone Ho* 3584 me semes] (me thinkes) *W*   3585 wronge] wrought *R*   3585 thruste] thust *C* 3585 remember] remember) *W*   3585 beginninge,] begyninge) *CR*   3586 that] that, *R* 3587 (as he aleadgeth)] as hee alledgeth *R*   3588 all] *om. W*   3588 it shoulde] what should it *W*   3589 vniuste] *om. W*   3589 same/] same? *W*   3590 Oneale] *Meale H2* 3591 Kinges] kinge *C*   3592 assumed and] *om. R*   3594 in] in, *R*   3595 ouer] in *R* 3596 gott] gat *R*   3598 *le*] Lo: *G*   Lee *R*   3598-9 as . . . youe] (as . . . you) *W* 3601 sone after] (soone after) *W*   3601 heare] *om. C*   3602 recouerie] recouerie to the recouerie *R*   3603 restrayne] *corr. of* restrayninge *E*   restrayninge of *C*   restrayning *R* 3603 Oneale] Onle *L*   3604 Raigned] *om. R*   3605 had] hathe *CRW*   3606 his] the *R* 3606 firste] *om. C*   3607 expell] expell, *R*   3608 enterprize] prize *R*   3608 nor] or *W*

auncient righte vnto the Crowne of Englande and a restoringe of moste iuste possessicions vnto the people of Englande from whence they weare moste vniustlie expelled and longe kepte out/

Eudox: I ame verie glade hearein to be thus satisfied by youe that I maye the better satisfie them whom I haue often harde to obiecte these doubtes and slaunderouslye to barke at the Courses which are helde againste that Trayterous Earle and his Adherentes, But now that youe haue thus setled your service for Vlster and Connaghte I woulde be glade to heare your opinion for the prosecutinge of feagh m^a Hugh whoe beinge but a base villaine and of him selfe of no power yeat so Continewallie troublethe that state notwithstandinge that he liethe vnder theire nose that I disdaine his boulde Arrogancie and thinke it to be the greateste indignitye to the Quene that maie be to suffer suche a Caitiffe playe suche Rex and by his ensample not onelie to give harte and Couragement to all suche bolde Rebells but allso to yealde them succour and refuge againste her maiestie whensoeuer they flie vnto his Comericke, wherefore I woulde firste wishe before youe enter into your plott of service againste him that youe shoulde laye open by what meanes he beinge so base firste lifted himselfe vpp to this daungerous greatenes and how he mayntainethe his parte againste the Quene and her power notwithstandinge all that hathe bene donne and Attempted Againste him And wheather allsoe He haue anye pretence of righte in the Landes he houldethe or in the warrs that he makethe for the same/

Iren: I will soe at your pleasure and since ye desire to knowe his firste beginninge I will not onelye | discouer the beginninge of his private howse but allso the Originall of all his septe of the Birnes and Tooles so farr as I haue learned the same from some of themselues and gathered the rest by readinge, This people of the Birnes and Tooles (As before I shewed vnto youe my Coniecture) descended from the ancient Britons which firste inhabited all those Easterne partes of Irelande as theire names do betoken for *Brin* in the Brittons language signifyethe woddye and *Toll* hillye which

---

3609 auncient] an Auncyent R   3609-10 and ... Englande] om. RW   3610 iuste possessicions] possessions C   3614 which] that R   3614 that] the R   3615 Adherentes] adherence R   3615 haue] om. R   3616 Connaghte] Connagh CH1Ho   Connaughs D2   3617 feagh] *Feugh A   Pheah* H1   3619 that state] the State W   3620 and] I C   3621 playe] to play W   3621 Rex] Rexe C   reakes R   3622 harte] hurte R   3622 Couragement] encorragement CRW   3622 bolde] bad W   3624 vnto] into C   3624 Comericke] *cummerreeighe A*   3624 wherefore] whereof W   3629 him] him. W   3630 Landes] lands which W   3631 same/] same? W   3632 since ... his] will further declare, not only the W   3633 I ... beginninge] om. W   3634 all his] the W   3634 Tooles] Tooleys Ho   3636 readinge,] reading R   reading: W   3636 This] The W   3636 Tooles] Tooleys Ho   3636 vnto] om. R   3637 Coniecture)] coniecture, R   3639 Brin] Birne D2F   3639 Brittons] *Brittish W*   3639 woddye ... hillye] hillye and *Tol,* hole,

A VIEW OF THE PRESENT STATE OF IRELAND 171

names it semethe they toke of the Countrye which they inhabited which is
all verye mountanye and wooddye In the which it semethe that euer sithens
the Comminge in of the Englishe with Dermotnigald they haue Con-
tinewed wheather that theire Countrie beinge so rude and mountanye
was of them despised and thoughte not worthie the inhabitinge or that
they weare receaued to grace by them and suffered to enioye theire Landes
as vnfitt for anye other yet it semethe that in some places of the same they
did put foote and fortified with sundrie Castells of which the ruines doe
theare onelye now remaine Since which time they are growen to the
strengthe that they are hable to lifte vp hande againste all that state and
now latelye thorowe the boldnes and late good successes of this feagh
m^a Hugh they are so farr imboldened that they threaten perill even to
dublin ouer whose necke they Continewallye hange. But towchinge your
demaund of this ffeaghs righte vnto that Countrye or the seigniorye which
he Claimes thearein it is moste vaine and Arrogante ffor this ye Cannot
be ignouraunte that it was parte of that which was given in inheritaunce by
Dermot m^a murrogh kinge of Leinster to *strangbow* with his daughter and
which *strangbow* gaue ouer vnto the kinge and to his heires So as the
righte is absolutelye now in her maiestie. And if it weare not yeat Coulde
it not be in this *Pheagh* but in *Obrin* whoe is the Auncienter Lorde of all
that Countrie ffor he and his Auncestours weare but followers vnto Obrien,
and his grandfather Shane m^a Tirlagh was a man of meaneste regarde
amongeste them neither havinge wealthe nor power, but his sonne Hugh
m^a Shane the father of this feagh firste begane to lifte vp his heade and
thoroughe the strengthe and greate fastenes of *Glan malour* which |

3640
3645
3650
3655
3660

valley or darke *A*   3639 Toll] Tooles *G*   Toole *W*   3640 Countrye] Countryes *W*
3641 mountanye] mountaine *R*   mountainous *W*   3641 wooddye] woody. *W*   3641 sithens]
since *W*   3642 Dermotnigald] *Deurmuid negalh A*   Dermonegald *C*   Dermongild *D2F*
Dermotingald *GP*   Dermonigle *H1*   Dermonigelle *H2*   *Dermon and blank space* Ho   Der-
mongile *N*   Dermonigile *RLD1*   Dermonigilde *T*   *Dermot ni-Gall W*   3643 mountanye]
mountaynous *RW*   3644 not worthie] not worthie, *R*   unworthy *W*   3644 that] that,
that *W*   3646 of the same] om. *C*   3647 did] have *W*   3647-8 doe theare onelye]
only doe theare *CRW*   3648 which] om. *R*   3648 the] that *CRW*   3649 all that]
all the *R*   3650 successes] successe *RW*   3650 of] of *W*   3650 feagh] *Feughe A*
Pheaff *F*   Fragh *H2*   3653 ffeaghs] *Feughe* is *A*   fferaghes *C*   Pheaffs *F*   Pheahes *H1*
Fraghes *H2*   Phenagh *P*   3653-4 or . . . Claimes] which he claimes, or the seigniory *W*
3656 Dermot] *Deurmuid A*   3656 m^a] in *H2*   3656 murrogh] Murrogho *A*   marrogh *G*
morrogh *H2*   Morrough *W*   3656 to *strangbow*] to Sranbow *L*   to Stanbowe *R*   unto
Strongbowe *WT*   3657 *strangbow*] Srangbow *L*   Strangbowe, *R*   Strongbowe *WT*
3657 vnto] to *R*   3657 to] om. *RW*   3658 absolutelye now] nowe absolutelie *C*
3659 Pheagh] *Feughe A*   Pheaff *F*   3659 Obrin] Obrien *GPD2F*   obryine *H2*   Obirne Ho
3659-60 whoe . . . Obrien] om. *R*   3659 whoe] which *W*   3659 Auncienter] auncient *CW*
3660 Obrien] *O-Brin W*   Obirne Ho   3661 m^a] in *H2*   3661 Tirlagh] Tirrelaghe *A*
Triglah *F*   Tarloghe *H2*   Turlogh *RN*   Terlagh *WG*   3663 m^a] in *H2*   3663 feagh]
Feughe A   Pheaf *F*   3664 strengthe] strenght *R*   3664 fastenes] fatnes *R*   3664 Glan

f. 67r Adioyneth vnto his howsse of *Ballinecorre* drewe vnto him manye theves 3665
and Outlawes which fledd vnto the succour of that glenne as to a Sanctu-
arye and broughte vnto him parte of that spoile of all the Countrie
thoroughe which he grewe stronge and in shorte space got vnto himself
a greate name therby amongest the Irishe, In whose footinge this his sonne
Contynewinge hathe thoroughe manie vnhappie occacions incresed his 3670
saide name and the opinion of his greatnes so that now he is becomme a
daungerous enemye to deale withall//

Eudox: Surelye I Canne Comende him that beinge of himself of so meane
Condicion hathe thoroughe his owne hardinesse lifted himself vp to that
heighte that he nowe dare front Princes And make termes with greate 3675
Potentates the which as it is to him honorable so is to them moste dis-
gracefull to be bearded of suche a base varlet that beinge but late growen
out of the dunghill beginnethe now to ouercrowe so highe mountaynes
And make himself greate protector of all Outlawes and Rebells that will
repaire vnto him. But doe you thinke that he is nowe so daungerous an 3680
enemye as he is Counted or that it is soe harde to take him downe as some
suppose/

Iren: Noe verelie, theare is no greate reckoninge to be made of him, for
had he ever ben taken in hande when the reste of the realme or at leaste
the partes adioyninge had bene quiet as the honorable gentleman that nowe 3685
gouernethe theare I meane Sr William Russell gave a notable attempt
there vnto and had as worthelye performed it yf his Course had not bene
Crossed vnhappelie, he Coulde not haue stode three monethes nor ever
haue loked vp againste a verye meane power. But now all the partes
aboute him beinge vp in a maddinge mode As the moores in Liex, the 3690
Cannavaghes in the Countie of wexforde, and some of the Butlers in the

malour] *Glanmaleeirh A*   3664 *Glan*] *Shane D1*   *Slan L*   *Ilan T*   3664 *malour*]
maclor D2F   *malous T*   3664 which] with *R*   3665 *Ballinecorre*] *Ballinecorrih A*
Ballinecarre CT   *Ballin corr D2F*   *Ballenacre H2*   *Ballincarre Ho*   *Ballynecarrie N*   Ballene-
carre *RLD1*   *Ballinecor W*   3666 that] the *R*   3667 that] the *CRW*   3668 got vnto]
gettinge to *R*   3670 incresed] inceased, *R*   3671 saide] *om. R*   3671 so] insomuch *W*
3673 meane] bace *R*   3674 hardinesse] hardnesse *R*   3674 that] the *RW*   3675 nowe
dare] dare now *W*   3676 to him honorable] honorable to him *R*   3676 so] soe it *CRW*
3677 but] but of *W*   3678 ouercrowe] overcrowe, *R*   3680 that] *om. W*   3682 suppose/]
suppose? *W*   3684-5 or . . . adioyninge] (or . . . adjoyning) *W*   3686 theare] there, *R*
3686 I . . . Russell] (I . . . *Russell*) *W*   3687 as] *om. RW*   3688 vnhappelie,]
vnhappelye: *R*   3688 not] *om. C*   3689 a verye] anie *C*   3690 a] *om. R*   3690 Liex]
Lax H1D2FHo   *Leir P*   *Lease RH2N*   *Leix WGT*   3691 Cannavaghes] *Kevanaghs A*
Cavunaghes C   *Cannaughes F*   *Cauanaghes G*   *Connaghs P*   *Cavanaghes R*   *Cananaugh T*

Countie of killkennye, they all flocke vnto him and drawe vnto his Countrye as to a stronge houlde wheare they thinke to be safe from all that prosecute them, And from thence they doe at theire pleasures breake out into all the borders adioyninge which are well peopled Countries, as the Counties of dublin, of kildare, of Satherlagh, of kilkenny, of wexforde, with the Spoiles wheareof they victell and strengthen themselues which otherwise shoulde in shorte time be starued and forpined So that what he is of him self ye maye heareby perceaue/ |

Eudox: Then by soe muche as I maye gather out of your speache the nexte waie to end the warrs with him and to roote him quite out shoulde be to kepe him from invadinge of those Countries adioyninge which (as I suppose is to be done either by drawinge of all the inhabitantes. of those nexte borders awaie and leavinge them vtterlye waste or by plantinge garrisons vppon all those frontiers aboute him that when he shall breake forthe maye sett vpon him and shorten his retorne/

Iren. ye Conceive verye rightelie *Eudox*: But for that the dispeoplinge and drawinge awaie all the inhabitantes from the Countries aboute him which ye spake of shoulde be a greate Confusion and trouble aswell for the vnwillingenes of them to leave theire possessions, as allso for placinge and providinge for them in other Countries, me semes the better Course should be by plantinge of garrisons aboute him the which whensoeuer he shall loke forthe or be drawen out with desire of the spoile of those borders or for necessitie of victell shalbe allwaies readye to intercept his goinge or Comminge

Eudox: wheare then do ye wishe those garrisons to be planted that they maie serue beste againste him and how manye in euerye garrisone/

Iren: I myselfe by reason that (as I toulde youe) I am noe marshall man will not take vppon me to directe so dangerous affaires but onelye as

Cavenaghes W Ho   3692 killkennye] *Kelkenny* F   3692 vnto his] into his W   3693 a] *om.* R   3693 that] that doe C   3696 Counties] Countye R   3696 Satherlagh] *Catherlagh* CW *Caterlough* D2F   *Katherlagh* GP   *Caterlagh* H1AT   *Karlough* H2   *Carlagh* Ho   *Carlough* RD1LN   3696 wexforde] *Waxford* H2   3698 forpined] sone pyned R   sore pyned W   3700 maye] *om.* RW   3701 quite out] out quite W   3702 of] *om.* R   3702 which (as] (which as C   which as R   3702-3 suppose] suppose) CW   3703 either] *om.* CR   3703 of all] all RW   3703 inhabitantes.] Inhabitantes CRW   3707 verye] *om.* R   3707 rightelie] hardly C   3707 that] *inserted between lines E om.* CR   3708 drawinge] dryvinge RW   3708 Countries] Countries, R   countrey W   3709 ye] hee R   3709 spake] speak C   3709 aswell] *first letter blotted* E   3711 me semes] (me thinkes) W   3712 the] *om.* W   3713 with] with the W   3714 for] for the C   3714 goinge or] *om.* R   3715 Comminge] *Comynge*/. C   cominge:/ R   comming. W   3716 those] these R   3717 garrisone/] Garrison? W   3718 I toulde youe)] *om.* R   3719 me] *inserted between*

I vnderstande by the purposes and plottes which the Lo̅ Grey whoe was 3720
well experienced in that service againste him did laye downe to the per-
formance wheareof he onelie required a Thowsande men to be laide in
fowre garrisons that is at Ballinecorre ijC footemen and fiftie horsse
which shoulde shutt him out of his greate glenne wheareto he so muche
trustethe, at knocklouh ijC footemen and 50. horsemen to answeare the 3725
Countie of Carlo, At Arclo or wicklo ij^C footemen to defende all that side,
towarde the sea. in Shillelagh C footemen which shoulde Cutt him from
the Cavanaghes and the Countye of wexforde and aboute the three Castles
fiftye horsemen, which shoulde defende all the Countye of dublin and C
footemen at Talbotes Towne which shoulde kepe him from breakinge 3730
into the Countye of kildare and be allwaies on his necke on that side, The
which garrisons so laide will so busie him that he shall neuer reste at home
f. 68ʳ nor sturr forthe abroade but he shalbe had As for his | Create they Cannot
be aboue grounde but they must nedes fall into theire hands or sterue for
he hathe no fastenes nor refuge for them. And as for his partakers of the 3735
moores Butlers and Cavanaghes they will sone leave him when they see
his fastenes and stronge places thus taken from him/

Eudox: Surelie this semethe a plott of greate reason and small difficultie
which promisethe hope of a shorte ende But what speciall direccions will
ye set downe for the services and risinges out of these garrisons/ 3740

Iren: None other then the presente occacions shall minister vnto them
and as by good espeialles wheareof theare they Cannot wante store they
shalbe drawen Continewallie vppon him so as one of them shalbe still
vppon him and somtimes all at one instante baytinge him And this I assure
my selfe will demaunde no longe time but wilbe all finished in the space 3745
of one yeare, which howe small a thinge it is vnto the eternall quietnes
which shall theareby be purchased to the realme and the greate good which

---

lines E om. C   3720 vnderstande] vnderstood *CRW*   3721 experienced] experienced *C*
3723 fowre] 6. *W*   3723 Ballinecorre] *Ballinecorrih A*   *Balin core D2*   *Balincor F*
Ballincarre H1Ho   *Ballinecarre H2T*   *Ballinecor W*   3723 horsse] horsemen *W*
3724 glenne] *Glinne A*   gleane *G*   glynne *W*   3725 knocklouh] *blank space A*   *Knock-
loghe D2FHo*   knockliugh *G*   Knocklonghe *P*   knocklough *RD1H2LNTW*   3725 horsemen]
horse *R*   3726 Carlo] *Catarlaghe A*   Carle *C*   Carly *G*   *Catherlagh W*   3726 wicklo]
Wickley H2   3726 to defende] and 50. horsemen to defend *W*   3727 towarde]
Towardes *RW*   3727 sea.] sea *C*   3727 Shillelagh] *blank space A*   Shillelah *C*
Shelaghe: H2   *Shelelagh Ho*   3728 Cavanaghes] *Cannanaughs T*   3728 wexforde]
Waxford H2   3729 the Countye of] *om. C*   3729 C] a C *C*   3730 Talbotes] *Tabbtts H2*
3731 into] out into *W*   3731 necke] necke on his necke *R*   3733 had] hadd, *CR*
had; *W*   3735 them . . . . for] them or *R*   3735 his] the *C*   3736 Cavanaghes]
Cananaughes T   3737 places] places, *R*   3742 espeialles] *corr. of* especialls *E*   especialls *C̄*
spialls *R*   3742 wheareof] wherfore *C*   3744 baytinge] bayt *R*   baytiug *W*   3744-5 I . . . selfe]
(I . . . selfe) *W*   3744 assure] assure yow *R*   3746 it is] *om. C*   3747 to the] to that *CRW*

shall growe to her maiestie shoulde me thinkes readelye drawe on her highnes to the vndertakinge of the enterprize/

Eudox ye haue verye well me semes *Iren*: plotted a Corse for the atchivinge of these warrs now in Irelande which seme to aske no longe time nor greate Chardge so as the effectinge theareof be Committed to men of sure truste and sound experience aswell in that Countrie as in the manner of those services. for if it be lefte in the hande of suche rawe Captaines as are vsuallye sente out of Englande beinge theareto preferred onelye by friendshippe and not Chosen by sufficiencye it will sone fall to grounde/

Iren: Therefore it weare mete me thinkes that suche Capteins onelye weare hearevnto imployed as haue formerlie serued in that Countrye and bene at leaste Lieftennantes vnto other Captains theare for otherwise beinge broughte and transferred from other services abroade as in ffraunce in Spaine and in the lowe Countries thoughe they be of good experience in those and haue neuer so well deserued yeat in these they will be newe to seke and before they haue gathered experience they shall buy it with greate losse to her maiestie either by hazardinge of theire Companies thoroughe ignoraunce of | the places and manner of the Irishe service or by losinge a greate parte of the time which is required hearevnto but shorte in which it mighte be finished before they haue allmoste taken out a new lesson or Cane tell what is to be done/

Eudox: youe are no good friende to new Captaines it semes *Iren* that barre them from the Creditt of this service, But to saie truethe me thinkes it weare mete that anie one before he Came to be a Captaine shoulde haue bene a soldiour for *Parere qui nescit*, nescit *imperare*/ and besides theare is great wronge done to the olde soldiour from whom all meanes of advauncement which is dewe vnto him is cut of by shufflinge in these newe Cuttinge Captaines into the places for which he hathe longe serued and perhaps better deserued. But now that ye haue thus (as I maye suppose)

3748 shall] should *W*   3748 me thinkes] (me thinkes) *W*   3750 me semes] (me thinkes) *W*   3751 these] those *W*   3751 seme] seemes *W*   3752 theareof] thereof, *R*   3752 sure] some *R*   3753 sound] some *R*   3753 that] the same *R*   3754 those] these *C*   3754 hande] handes *RW*   3755 theareto preferred onelye] thereunto onely preferred *W*   3756 to] to the *W*   3756 grounde/] grownde *C*   3757 me thinkes] (mee thinckes) *RW*   3758 hearevnto] thereunto *W*   3759 Lieftennantes] lieutennantes *C* livetennantes *R*   Leivtennants *W*   3759 other] theire *R*   3762-3 in those ... experience] *om. R*   3762 in those] *om. C*   3763 experience] *last two letters apparently cut away E*   3765 and] and in *C*   3765 service] services *RW*   3766 but] beinge but *RW*   3767 before ... allmoste] almost before they have *W*   3768 done/] done *C*   3769 Captaines] Captaines; *W*   3769 that] that yow *RW*   3770 to saie truethe] (to say truth) *W*   3771 Came] Come *CR*   3772 for] fo: *C*   3772 Parere] paree *T*   3772 nescit] nessit *H2*   3772 nescit] *inserted between lines E om. CH1H2NR*   *non dignus est T*   3772 *imperare*] imparere *R*   3773 whom] *om. R*   3774 which] (which *R*   3775 Cuttinge] *om. C*   3775 the] there *R*   3775 places] place *W*   3776 deserued.] deserved) *C*   3776 ye] *om. R*   3776 thus] thus thus *R*   3776 maye suppose)] suppose) *CW*   suppose *R*

finished all the warr, and broughte all thinges to that lowe ebb which yee spake of, what Course will ye take for the bringinge in of that reformacion which ye intend and recoueringe all thinges from this desolate estate. in which me thinkes I behoulde them now lefte vnto that perfecte establishement and new Comon wealthe which ye haue Conceived, of which so greate good maie redounde to her maiestie and An assured peace be Confirmed, for that is it whearevnto we are now to loke and doe greatlie longe for, beinge longe sithens made wearye with the huge Chardge which ye haue laied vppon vs and with the stonie endurance of soe manie Complaintes soe manye delaies soe manie dobtes and daungers as will heareof I knowe well arise, vnto the which before ye Come it weare mete me thinkes that ye shoulde take some order for the soldiour which is nowe firste to be dischardged and disposed of some waye the which if ye do not well forsee maye growe to as greate inconvenience as all this that we suppose ye haue quitt vs from by the lose leavinge soe manye thowsande souldiours which from thenceforthe wilbe vnfitt for anie labour or other trade but muste either seke service and employment abroade which maie be daungerous or els will perhaps employe themselues heare at home as maye be discomodious/

Iren: ye saie verye trewe and it is a thinge muche mislikd in this our Comon wealthe that no better Course is taken for suche as haue bene employed once in service but that | Retorninge, wheather maimed and so vnhable to labour, or otherwise thoughe wholle and sounde yeat afterwardes vnwillinge to worke, rather willinge to set the hangeman to worke/ But that nedethe another Consideracion but to this that we haue nowe in hande it is farre from my meaninge to leave the soldiour so at randome or to leave that waste relme so weake and destitute of strengthe which maye bothe defende it againste other that mighte seke then to set vppon it and allso kepe it from that relapse which I before did forecaste for it is one speciall good of this plott which I woulde devize that Sixe thowsande

3778 spake of] speake R   speake of W   3779 estate.] estate C   state, R   estate? W
3780 me thinkes] (mee thinkes) W   3781 Conceived, of] conceived of, by W   3782 to] unto W   3784 longe for] longe, for R   3785 stonie] strong W   3787 I knowe well] (I knowe well) RW   3787 well] well, C   3787 ye] wee W   3787-8 me thinkes] (me thinkes) W   3790 to as] to a R   3790 we] I W   3791 soe] of soe CRW
3791 thowsande] thowsandes C   3792 thenceforthe] henceforth R   3794 will] *om.* W
3796 *Iren:*] *Eud: D1*   3796 a] indeed a C   3796 this] *om.* R   3797 that] but C
3798 once] *om.* W   3799 thoughe] *om.* W   3800 rather] rathe C   or rather RW
3800 set . . . worke] make worke for the hangeman R   3800 hangeman to] hang-man on W
3801 But] *Ireni:* But *beginning new paragraph D1*   3801 this that] this that *and* turne to the other syd *followed by blank space of almost one page and second* that R   this which W
3804 other] others RW   3804 then] *om.* R   3805 kepe] to keepe W   3805 did] *om.* C

souldiours of these whom I haue now Imploied in this service and made thoroughlye acquainted bothe with the state of the Countrie and manners of the people shoulde henceforthe be still Continewed and for euer mayntayned of the Countrye without anie Chardge to her maiestie. and the reste that either are olde and vnhable to serue longer or willinge to fall to thrifte as I haue sene manye soldiours after the service to proue verye good husbandes shoulde be placed in parte of the landes by them wonne at suche rate or rather better then others to whom the same shalbe sett out/

Eudox Is it possible *Iren*: Can theare be anye suche meanes devised that so manie men shoulde be kepte still for her maiestes service without anie Chardge to her at all Surely this weare an exceedinge greate good bothe to her Highnes to haue so manie olde souldiours allwaies readye at Call to what purpose soeuer she list imploye them, and allso to haue that lande theareby so strengthened that it shall neither feare anye forrein invacion nor practize which the Irishe shall euer attempte, but shall kepe them vnder in Contineweall awe and firme obedience/

Iren: It is so inded And yeat this trewelye I do not take to be anie matter of greate difficultye as I thinke it will allsoe sone Appeare vnto youe And firste we will speake of the Northe parte for that the same is of moste Weighte and Importaunce, So sone as it shall appeare that the enemye is broughte downe and the stoute Rebell either Cutt of or driven to the wretchednesse that he is no longer able to houlde vp hande but will Come into anie Condicions which I assure my selfe wilbe before thende of the seconde Winter I wishe that theare be a generall proclamacion made that whatsoeuer Outlawes will frelye Come in and submitt themselues to her maiesties mercie, shall haue libertye soe to doe wheare they shall either finde that grace that they desire or haue leave to retorne againe in safetye/ Vppon which it is likelye that soe manye as survive will Come in to sewe for grace Of which whoe soe are thoughte mete for subieccion and fitt to be broughte to good maye be receaued or els all of them for I thinke that all wilbe but a verie fewe vppon Condicion and assurance that they will submit themselues absolutelye to her maiesties ordinaunce for them, by which they shalbe assured of liefe and libertie and be onelie to suche

3807 this] that *R*   3809 euer] ever be *C*   3811 that] that rest that *R*   3811 longer] any longer *W*   3811 or] are *C*   3812-3 as . . . husbandes] as . . . husbandes) *C* (as . . . husbandes) *R*   3812 the] theire *R*   3814 out/] out *R*   3815 Iren:] Irenaeus? *W*   3816 for] in *W*   3817 all] all, *R* all. *W*   3819 purpose] purposes *C* 3819 imploye] to imploye *CW*   3821 nor] nor a *C*   3821 but] but but *C*   3824 greate] om. *C*   3825 firste we will] we will first *C*   3825 moste] more *W*   3826 Importaunce,] importance. *W*   3827 to the] to that *CRW*   3828 hande] his head *W*   3829 into] in to *W*   3832 maiesties] Maiestie *C*   3833 that they] they *RW*   3833 haue leave to] om. *R*   3835 grace] grace. *C*   3835 whoe] whose *C*   3836-7 for . . . fewe] (for . . . few) *W*   3837 fewe] fewe, *R*   3839 of] of of *C*   3839 to] tyed to *CRW*

Condicions as shalbe thoughte by her mete for Contayninge them ever after in dewe obedience, To the which Condicions I nothinge doubte but that they will all moste readelye and vppon theire knees submitt themselues, by the profe of that which I sawe in mounster for vppon the like proclamacion theare they all Came in bothe tag and rag and whenas afterwarde manye of them weare denied to be receaued they bad them doe with them what they woulde for they woulde not by anie meanes retorne againe nor goe forthe for in that Case whoe will not accepte allmoste of anye Condicions rather then die of hunger and miserye/

Eudox: It is verye likelye soe. But what then is the Ordinaunce and what be the Condicions which ye will propose vnto them that that reserue vnto them an assurance of liefe and libertye/

Iren: So sone then as they haue given the best assurance of themselues which maie be required which muste be as I suppose some of theire principall men to remaine in hostage one of another and some other for the reste (for other suertye I reckon of none that maye binde them neither of wiffe nor of Children since then perhaps they woulde gladlie be rid of bothe from the famine I woulde haue them firste vnarmed vtterlie and stripped quite of all theire warlike weapons and then these Condicions set downe and made knowen | vnto them that they shalbe broughte and remoued with suche Crete as they haue remayninge into Leinster wheare they shalbe placed and haue lande given them to occupie and to live vppon in suche sorte as shall become good subiectes to labour thenceforthe for theire livinge and to applye themselues vnto honest trades of Civilitye as they shall euerye one be founde mete and hable for/

Eudox: wheare then a godes name will ye place them in Leinster or will ye finde out anie new lande theare for them that is yeat vnknowen?

Iren: Noe I will place them in all the Countrye of the Birnes and Tooles which feagh m^a Hugh hathe, and in all the landes of the Cavanaghes which are now in rebellion and all the landes which will fall to her maiestie thereaboutes which I knowe to be verye spacious and large ynoughe to Containe them beinge verie neare Twentye or Thirtye miles wide/

3841 obedience,] obedience. *W*　　3843 sawe] have seene *W*　　3844 bothe] *om. R*　　3845 afterwarde] afterwardes *RW*　　3846 for . . . anie] by noe *R*　　3850 that that] that shall *CR*　　which shall *W*　　3852 as] *om. C*　　3853 as] *om. CRW*　　3853 I suppose] (I suppose) *W*　　3854 of] for *W*　　3855 (for] for *W*　　3855 maye] they *C*　　3856 rid of] rydd *C*　　3857 famine] famine *CR*　　famine, *W*　　3859-61 broughte . . . placed] placed in *Leinster W*　　3860 as . . . remayninge] *om. C*　　3860 remayninge] *om. R*　　3860 Leinster] *Lemster Ho*　　lympster *LD1*　　lymster *R*　　3861 and to] and *R*　　3862 shall become] shalbe come *CR*　　3863 vnto] to *W*　　3865 Leinster] Limpster *D1*　　*Lemster H2*　　Lynster *RL*　　*Leinster? W*　　3866 vnknowen?] vnknowne: *C*　　vnknowen::/ *R*　　3867 them] *om. C*　　3867 in all] all in *W*　　3867 Birnes] *Brinnes A*　　Burne *C*　　Brynes *G*　　Brines *D1H2N*　　Brns *L*　　Bryns *T*　　3867 Tooles] *Tooleys Ho*　　3868 feagh] *Feugh A*　　3868 of the] of *C*　　3868 Cavanaghes] *Cannaughs F*　　*Cananaghes T*　　3870 ynoughe]

A VIEW OF THE PRESENT STATE OF IRELAND 179

Eudox: But then what will ye doe with all the Birnes the Tooles and the Cavannaghes and all those that nowe are ioyned with them/

Iren: At the same verie time and in the same manner that I make that proclamacion to them of vlster will I allsoe haue it made to these and vppon theire submission thearevnto, I will take assurance of them as of the other After which I will translate all that remaine of them into the places of the other in vlster, withall theire Crete and what els they haue lefte them the which I will Cause to be devided amongest them in some mete sorte as eche maye thereby haue somwhat to susteine himselfe a while withall vntill by his further traveill and labour of the Earthe he shalbe able to provide himselfe better/

Eudox: But will ye then give the Lande frelye vnto them and make them heires of the former Rebells So maie ye perhaps make them heires allsoe of all theire former villanies and disorders or howe els will ye dispose of them/

Iren: Not so but all the Lands I will geue vnto Englishe men whome I will haue drawne thither whoe shall haue the same with suche estates as shalbe thoughte mete and for suche rente as shall efte sones be rated/ f. 70ᵛ Vnder everye of those Englishe men will I place some of those | Irishe to be Tenantes for a Certaine rente accordinge to the quantitye of suche lande as everie man shall haue alotted to him and shalbe founde hable to welde, whearein this speciall regarde shalbe had that in no place vnder anie Lanlorde theare shalbe manie of them planted togeather but dispersed wide from theire Acquaintances and scattered farr abroad thoroughe all the Countrye, ffor that is the evill which I nowe finde in all Irelande That the Irishe dwell alltogeather by theire septes and seuerall nacions so as they maye practize or Conspire what they will wheares if theare weare Englishe shed amongest them and placed ouer them they should not be

yeanough *R*   3872 then what] what then *CR*   3872 Birnes] *Brinnes A*   Brynes *G*   Brimes *H2*   3872 Tooles] *Tooleys Ho*   3873 Cavannaghes] *Cavanages F*   *Cananag* [*rest hidden in binding*] *T*   3874 manner] verie maner *CW*   3874 make that] make that I make that *R*   3875 allsoe haue it] have it also *W*   3875 haue] have haue *C*   3876 take] take like *CRW*   3877 other] other. *W*   3877-8 After . . . other] *om. R*   3877 into] unto *W*   3878 in] *om. C*   3878 withall] with *R*   3878 Crete] Cseete *L*   3882 to provide himselfe] of him self to provide *C*   3883 then . . . Lande] give the land then *W*   3884 Rebells] rebells, *CR*   Rebells? *W*   3884 heires allsoe] also heires *W*   3884 allsoe] *om. C*   3885 all] *om. R*   3886 them/] them? *W*   3887 I will] will I *W*   3889 shall] shalbe *C*   3889 rated/] rated *C*   rated, *R*   3891 be] bee the *R*   3892 to him] vnto him *CRW*   3893 welde] weeld *RW*   3894 Lanlorde] Landlord *CRW*   3894 shalbe manie] shall remaine *R*   3894 planted] placed *W*   3895 Acquaintances] acquaintance *W*   3896 I nowe] now I *W*   3898 wheares] wheras *CRW*   3899 shed . . . ouer] well able once to sturr or to murmure but that it shoulde be knowen and they shortened accordinge to theire demerrittes/

Eudox: yee haue good reason but what ratinge of rentes meane youe? to what ende do youe purpose the same/

Iren: my purpose is to rate the rente of all those Lands of her maiestes in suche sorte vnto those Englishe men which shall take them as they maie be well hable to live thearvppon yeilde her maiestie a reasonable Chieferie and allso giue a Competente maintenaunce vnto the garrissons which shall theare be lefte amongest them. ffor those soldiours (as I tolde youe) remayninge of the former garrisons I caste to maynteine vppon the rente of those landes which shalbe excheated and to haue them devided thoroughe all Irelande in suche places as shalbe thoughte moste Conveniente and occacion maie require And this was the Course which the Romaines observed in the Conquest of Englande for they planted some of theire legions in all places Conveniente the which they Caused the Countrye to mayneteine Cuttinge vppon euerie porcion of lande a reasonable rente which they Called *Romescot* the which mighte not surchardge the tennant or freholder and defraie the payment of the garrison And this hathe bene allwaies obserued by all princes in all Countries to them newelye subdued to sett garrisons amongest them to Conteyne them in dewtye, whose burthen they made them to beare, And the wante of this Ordinaunce in the firste Conquest of | Irelande by Henrye the Seconde was the Cawse of the so shorte decaie of that gouernement and the quicke recouerye againe of the Irishe/ Therefore by all meanes it is to be provided for/ And this is it which I woulde blame (yf it shoulde not misbecome me) in the late plantinge of mounster, That no Care was had of this ordinaunce nor anie strengthe of a garrisone provided for by a Certaine Allowaunce out of all the saide Landes but onelie the presente profitt loked vnto and the safe Continvaunce thereof for euer heareafter neclected/

placed among *W*   3900 or to] or *R*   3900 but] for *C*   3902-3 *Eudox*: . . . same/] *om*. *D1*   3902 youe?] youe *CR*   you, *W*   3903 same/] same *C*   same? *W*   3904 *Iren*:] *Eud*: *D1*   3904 maiestes] maiestie *R*   3905 which] as *R*   3905 maie] shall *W* 3906 yeilde] yeildinge *R*   to yeeld *W*   3906 a] *om*. *W*   3908 theare be] be there *W* 3908 those] these *R*   3908 youe)] yow *R*   3910 thoroughe] throught *C*   3912 which] of *R*   3913 some] *om*. *R*   3916 *Romescot*] Romes cott *H2*   3917 defraie] might defray *W*   3917 payment] paie *CRW*   3918 by] in *R*   3918 subdued] sudewed *C* 3923 Irishe/] Irishe, *C*   3923-4 is it] is *W*   3924 which] that *CRW*   3924 (yf . . . me)] if . . . mee, *W*   3926 of a] of *W*   3926 garrisone] garrison, *R*   3926 for] for: *R*   3926 by a] by *C*   3927 vnto] into *W*   3928 thereof] *om*. *C*   3928 for]

A VIEW OF THE PRESENT STATE OF IRELAND 181

Eudox: But theare is a bande of Soldiours layde in mounstr to the mayntenaunce of which what ods is theare whether the Quene receivinge the Rente of the Countrie do giue paye at her pleasure or that theare be a setled allowaunce appointed vnto them out of her Allowance theare/

Iren: Theare is greate odds for now that saide rente of the Countrye is not appointed to the paie of the soldiours it is by euerye other occacion Comminge betwene Conuerted to other vses and the soldiour in times of peace dischardged and neclected as vnneccessarye, wheareas if the saide rente weare appointed and ordeyned by an establishement to this end onelie, it should not be turned to anie other, nor in troublous times vppon everye occacion her maiestie be so troubled with sendinge ouer new soldiours as she nowe is, nor the Countrie euer shoulde dare to mvtine havinge still the soldiour in theire necke, nor anie forreine enemye dare to invade knowinge here so stronge a garrison allwaies readie to receaue them

Eudox: Sithe then ye thinke this cuttinge of the paie of the Soldiour vppon the lande to be bothe the redieste waye to the soldiour and lesse troblesome to her maiestie, tell vs I praye youe how ye woulde haue the same Landes rated that bothe a rente maie rise theareout vnto the Quene and allsoe the soldiours paye which me semes wilbe harde/

Iren: firste we are to Consider how muche lande theare is in all Vlster
f. 71ᵛ that accordinge to the quantity thereof | We maie Cese the saide rente and allowance issuinge thereout/ Vlster as the ancieente recordes of that realme doe testifye dothe Conteine Nyne Thowsande ploughlandes euerie of which ploughelandes conteineth sixe score acres after the rate of xxj foote to euerie perche of the saide acre which amountethe in the wholle vnto 1240000 acres. Euerie of which plowlandes which shall excheate to her maiestie maye be rented at xlvjs viijd by the yeare which is not muche

---

om. CR   3930 receivinge] of England perceyvinge C   3932 Allowance] Landes CRW
3932 theare/] there C there? W   3933 greate] good C   3933 now] now, R   3934 appointed]
apparently added in space left blank E   blank space C   vsuallie applyed R   3934 paie]
paye paye R   3934 it is by] But yt is R   but it is by W   3934-5 euerye ... betwene]
(euerie ... betwene, R   3935 Conuerted] Coverted C   3935 soldiour] souldiers CW
3935 times] time W   3937 an establishement] a stablishment R   3938-9 not ...
maiestie] *om*. R   3940 nowe is] is now W   3940 mvtine] mutinie W   3941 enemye]
Enemie, R   3942 here] there RW   3942 stronge] strong and great W   3942 them]
him/. C him/: R   them. W   3943 thinke] thinke that W   3943 cuttinge] *apparently
added in space left blank* E   blank space C   Romescott RW   3943 Soldiour] Souldiours W
3944 soldiour] Souldiers W   3944 lesse] leaste CW   3945 I praye youe] (I pray you) W
3945 ye woulde] would you W   3946 same] said CW   3946-9 rise ... maie] *om*. R
3947 paye] receive pay W   3947 me semes] (mee thinkes) W   3949 Cese] ceasse H2
R *resumes at this point*   3950-1 as ... testifye] (as ... testifie) W   3950 recordes]
recordes, R   3951 Thowsande] thowsandes C   3952 sixe score] 120. W   3953-4 saide
... acres.] Acre, W   3953 in] to in C   3954 acres.] acres; C acres, R   3954-5 which
shall ... rented] I will rate RW   3954 to] vnto C   3955 xlvjs viijd] 40ˢ W   3955 xlvjs]

more then j^d o͞b an acre the which yearelie rente amountethe in the whole
to xviijm^{l}i. But because the Countye of Louthe beinge a parte of Vlster
and Contayninge in it vij^C and xij plowghelandes is not whollye to
excheate vnto her maiestie as the rest they havinge in all these warres
Continewed for the moste parte dewtifull thoughe otherwise a greate parte
thereof is now vnder the Rebells theare is an abatement to be made here
out of iiij^C or v^C ploughelandes as I estimate the same the which are not
to paie the wholle yearelie rente of xlvj^s. viij^d out of euerie ploughelande
like as the excheated landes doe, but yeat shall paye for theire Composicion
of Cesse towardes the mayntenaunce of the Soldiour xx^s out of euerie
ploughlande, so as theare is to be deducted out of the former Summ ij or
iij^C poundes yearelye the which maye neuerthelesse be supplied by the
rente of the fishinges which are excedinge greate in in Vlster and allsoe
by an increase of rente in the beste Landes and those that lye in the beste
places neare the seacoste the which xviijm^{l}i will defraye the entertaynement
of xv^C soldiours with some ouerplus towardes the paye of the victellers
which are to be employed in the victellinge of these garrissons/

Eudox: So then belike ye meane xv^C soldiours in garrison for Vlster to
be paide principallie out of the rente of those lands which shall theare
excheate vnto her maiestie The which wheare I praye youe will youe haue
garrizoned/

Iren: I will haue them devided into three partes that is v^C in euerye
garrison the which I will haue to remayne in | Three of the same places
wheare they before appointed to weet v^C at Strabane and aboute loghfoile
so as they maie houlde all the passages of that parte of the Countrye and
some of them be put in wardes vppon all the streightes theareaboutes
which I knowe to be suche as maye stop all passages into the Countrye on
that side. and some of them allsoe vppon the bande vp towardes logh

xls *T*   3955-6 which ... acre] *om. W*   3956 j] 3 *D2F*   3956 an] the *C*   3956 yearelie] *om. C*   3957 xviijm^{l}i] 1800^{li} *H1*   1800^l. besides 6^s. 8^d. chiefrie out of every Plow-land *W*   3958 vij^C] vij^l *RL*   3959 these] their *W*   3961-2 here out] thereout *W*   3962 iiij^C] iiij^{Cl} *RL*   3962 v^C] v^{Cll} *L*   3963 xlvj^s. viij^d] *corr. of* xls *E*   x^l vj^s viij^d *A*   xls *CD1D2FHoLNRW*   3965 Cesse] Ceasse *H2*   3965 towardes] towaudes *R*   3965 mayntenaunce of the] keeping of *W*   3965 Soldiour] Soldiers *W*   3966 ij] 200. *W*   3967 supplied] suppli- *W*   3968 fishinges] fishing *C*   3968 are] is *C*   3968 in in] in *CRW*   3970 seacoste] Sea-coast. *W*   3970 the which] The, which *R*   3970 xviijm] 1800 *D1D2*   180000. *H2*   xviijm ^{C} *L*   3971 xv^C] 15000 *Ho*   3971 some] *om. C*   3971 towardes] toward *R*   3971 victellers] victells *CR*   3972 the] *om. R*   3973 meane] meane to leave *CRW*   3973 xv^C] 15 thousand *D2*   3973 garrison] garrison, *R*   3974-5 theare excheate] be there escheated *W*   3975 vnto] to *C*   3975 maiestie] Majestie. *W*   3975 I praye youe] (I pray you) *W*   3975 haue] have them *W*   3976 garrizoned/] garrisoned? *W*   3977 Iren:] *placed beside second line of speech* H1   3978 same] said *R*   3979 before] were before *CW*   weree, before *R*   3979 Strabane] *blank space A*   Strabon *H2*   Struban *P*   Straban *RLD1*   3979 loghfoile] Loughfoyll *D2*   Loagfoile *F*   Logfoyle *H2*   Longhfoile *W*   3980 so] and so *R*   3982 suche] such, *W*   3983 side.] side *C*   syde, *RW*   3983 bande] *blank space AC*   banke *H1*   Dane *H2*   Bane *N*   Ban

A VIEW OF THE PRESENT STATE OF IRELAND 183

Sidnee as I formerlie directed Allsoe other v^C at the forte vppon logh Earne and wardes taken out of them which shalbe laide at fernnanagh at Belicke at Ballyshannō and on the streightes towardes Connaght the which I knowe doe so strongelie Comaunde all the passages that waie as that none Can passe from vlster vnto Connaght without theire leave The laste v^C shall allsoe remaine at theire forte in monoghan and some of them be drawen into wardes to kepe the keyes of all that Countrye bothe downewarde and allsoe towardes Orelies and the pale at Eniskillin some at Belterbrt some at the Blackeforde and so alonge that Riuer as I formerlye shewed in the firste plantinge of them And moreouer at euerye of these fortes I woulde haue the seate of a Towne layed forthe and encompassed, in the which I would wishe that theare should inhabitantes of all sortes as merchantes Artificers and husbandmen placed to whom theare shoulde Charters and franchises be graunted to incorporate them the which as it wilbe no matter of difficultye to drawe out of Englande persons which woulde verye gladlie be so placed so woulde it in shorte space turne those partes to greate Comoditye and bringe er longe to her maiestie muche proffitte for those places are so fit for trade and traffick, havinge moste Conveniente outgates by ryvers to the sea and ingates to the richeste partes of the lande that they woulde sone be enriched and mightelye enlarged, for the verye seatinge of the garrisons by them besides the safetie and assurance which they shall worke vnto them will allsoe drawe thither store of people and trade as I haue sene ensampled at mariburgh and Philips-

RD1D2FGHoLPTW 3983-4 logh Sidnee] *blank space A* Ploughe Sidneye *D2F* Logh Surney *H1* 3984 directed] directed/ *C* directed. *W* 3984-5 logh Earne] *blank space A* Loughhern *D2F* Logh Kearne *G* Logh Xerne *Ho* Loghkarne *LD1* Loghe Hearne *P* 3985 fernnanagh] *blank space A* fermanagh *CD2FH2RW* Farnnenagh *D1* ffarmanagh *GLP* ferman *H1* Feamanag *Ho* Fermanas *N* 3986 Belicke] *blank space A* Belack *N* Bealick *W* 3986 Ballyshannō] *blank space A* Belishanan *D2* Billishamon *H2* Ballishanne *P* Ballyshame *T* 3986 on] on all *CR* all *W* 3986 Connaght] Connagh *RHo* 3987 waie] maye *R* 3988 vnto] into *CRW* 3988 Connaght] Connagh *H1Ho* 3988 leave] leave. *W* 3989 v^C] v^C, *R* 3989 at] in *W* 3989 theire forte] the forte *C* theire fortes *R* 3989 monoghan] Moghonan *C* Manahen *D2* Monghan *H1* 3990 keyes] Kaies *W* 3990-1 downewarde] downwardes *CRW* 3991 towardes] towatdes *W* 3991 Orelies] Oreheis *D2* Orlyes Countrie *LD1* Orelies Countrie *RW* 3991 pale] pale as some *CR* Pale, and some *W* 3991 at Eniskillin] as Eniskillin *C* 3991 Eniskillin] *blank space A* Enishskellin *D2* Skellin *F* Eueskene *H2* Eviskillin *Ho* Eneskeine *N* 3992 Belterbrt] *blank space A* Belerbert *C* Bettervert *T* Belterberte *RH2* Belturbut *W* 3992 Blackeforde] blacke fort *CAD1D2FGH1H2HoLNPRTW* 3994 seate] state *R* 3996 as] of *C* or *R* 3996 placed] be placed *CW* to bee placed *R* 3997 them] them. *W* 3997 it] *om. C* 3999 gladlie] *om. C* 4001 places] places, *R* 4002 Conveniente outgates] Covenient outgages *C* 4002 by] by divers *W* 4002 partes] parte *R* 4006 ensampled] ensample *W* 4006 mariburgh] Marribrough *N* Marborough *H2* Mariborogh *W*

f. 72ᵛ towne in Leinster wheare by | Reasone of those two fortes thoughe theare weare but smalle wardes lefte in them theare are two good townes nowe growen which are the greatest staie of bothe those ij Counties

Eudox: Indede me semes Three suche Townes as ye saie woulde doe verye well in those places with the garrissons and in shorte space woulde be so augmented as they woulde be hable with little helpe to enwall themselues stronglie but for the plantinge of all the reste of the Countrie what order woulde ye take/

Iren: what other then as I saide to bringe people out of England which shoulde inhabite the same whearevnto thoughe I doubte not but greate troupes woulde be readye to run, yeat for that in suche Cases the worste and moste decaied men are moste ready to remove, I woulde wishe them rather to be Chosen out of all partes of this realme eyther by discreacion of wise men thearevnto appointed or by lott or by the drvm as was the olde vse in sendinge forthe of Collonies or suche other good meanes as shall in theire wisdome be thoughte meteste Amongeste the Chiefe of which I woulde haue the lande sett into Seigniories in suche sorte as it is now in mounster and devided into hundredes and parishes or wardes as it is in Englande and laied out into Shires as it was ancienly (viz the Countye of downe the Countye of *Autrian* the Countye of *Louthe* the Countye of *Armagh* the Countye of *Cavan*. the Countye of *Colran*. the Countye of *Monahon* the Countye of *Tyrone*. the Countye of *Fermanagh* the Countye of *Donergall* beinge in all tenn. Over all which I wishe a Lord Presidente and a Councell to be placed which maie kepe them afterwardes in awe and obedience and minister vnto them Iustice and equitye/

Eudox: Thus I see the wholle purpose of your plott for Vlster and now I desire to heare your like opinion of Connaghte/

Iren: by that which I haue allreadye saide of Vlster youe maye gather my opinion for Cannaghte beinge verye answearable vnto the former but for

4007 Leinster] lempster *L*   4008 townes] towne *C*   4009 Counties] Counties/. *C* Counties:/ *R*   Countries. *W*   4010 me semes] (me thinkes) *W*   4010 Townes] towne *C*   4012 helpe] om. *W*   4012 enwall] wall *R*   4014 take/] take? *W*   4015 as I saide] (as I said) *W*   4016 but] but that *C*   4022 meteste] meetest. *W*   4023 haue] haue/ *C*   4025 into] in *CR*   4025 (viz] vidᵗ *C*   viz: *F*   (vizᵗ) *G*   vizt *RN*   viz. *W*   4026 *Autrian*] blank space *A*   Antrian *CD1LR*   Antriam *D2*   Antram *F*   Autrim *T*   Antrim *WH2*   4026 *Louthe*] Loath *GP*   4027 *Cavan*] Canon *T*   4027 *Colran*] blank space *A*   Cotrane *F*   Colarne *T*   Colerane *W*   4028 *Monahon*] blank space *A*   Monaho *C*   Monahen *D2*   Monahand *F*   Menahon *P*   Monoghan *W*   4028 *Fermanagh*] blank space *A*   ffarmanagh *G*   4029 *Donergall*] blank space *A*   Doũgall *D2*   Dovergall *FHo* dobergall *H2*   Donnegall *W*   4029 in all] all in *C*   4029 tenn.] teir *C*   Ten: *R*   4031 equitye/] equitie *R*   4033 of] for *CRW*   4033 Connaghte] Connaghe *D1* Connagh *RHo*   4035 Cannaghte] Cannagh *D1*   Connagh *RHo*   Connaght *WF*   4035 vnto]

that the Landes which thearein shall excheate vnto her maiestie are not so entirelye togeather as that they Cane be accompted into one Summe it nedethe that | they be Considered seuerallie The province of *Connaght* containeth in the wholle (as Appearethe by the Recordes of Dublin seven Thowsande and Two hundred plowlandes of the former measure and is of late devided into Six shires or Counties, the Countye of *Clare* the Countye of *Letrim*, the Countye of *Roscaman* the Countie of *Galwaie* the Countie of *Maio* and the Countye of *Slygah*, of the which all the Countye of *Slygah* all the Countye of *Mayo* the moste parte of the Countye of *Roscaman* the moste parte of the Countie of *Listrim* a greate parte of the Countye of *Gallwaye* and some of the Countye of *Clare*/ is like to excheate to her maiestie for the Rebellion of theire presente possessiurs The which two Countis of *Sligah* and *Maio* are supposed to Containe allmoste iij^m plowlandes the rente wheareof ratablye to the former I vallewe allmoste at vj^{mli} per Annum the Countie of *Roscoman* savinge what perteinethe to the house of *Roscoman* and some other Englishe theare latelie seated is all out And therefore it is whollie likewise to excheate to her maiestie savinge those porcions of the Englishe Inhabitantes and even those Englishe doe (As I vnderstande by them) paie as muche rente to her maiestie as is sett vppon those in Vlster Countinge theire Composicion money thearewithall so as it maie rvnn all into one Reckoninge with the former two Counties, so that this Countye of *Roscoman*. Contaynethe xij^C plowlandes as it is accompted amountethe to ij^m. iij^C poundes by the yeare which with the former two Counties rente makethe aboute viij^m—vij^C poundes for the former wanted somwhat, But what the excheated Landes of the Countie

to *CW*   4036 Landes] land *R*   4036 thearein shall] shal therein *W*   4037 into] in *W*   4038 seuerallie] seuerally, *CR*   severally. *W*   4038 *Connaght*] Connagh *RHo*   4039 containeth ... wholle] in the whole containeth *W*   4039 Recordes] record *R*   4039 of Dublin] at *Dublyn*) *C*   at Dubline, *R*   of *Dublin*) *W*   4039-40 seven ... hundred] 1200 *F*   4041 Counties,] Counties. *W*   4042 *Letrim*] Leutrum *A*   Letein *D1*   Lyretrime *D2*   Liretrin *F*   Lietrim *H1*   Letrum *N*   Letrymone *T*   Leytrim *W*   4042 *Roscaman*] Roseaman *D2F*   4042 *Galwaie*] Galloweye *H2AFHo*   4043 *Maio*] Maiho *A*   4043 *Slygah*,] Slegho *A*   Slygagh, *GPF*   Sligo. *W*   4044 *Slygah*] Sleugho *A*   Sligagh, *F*   Sligath: *Ho*   Sligo, *W*   4044 *Mayo*] Maiho *A*   4045 *Roscaman*] Roseaman *D2F*   4045 *Listrim*] Leutrum *A*   lietrim *CLR*   Letein *D1*   Lirtrime *D2*   Lyretrim *F*   Letrim *GHo*   Leitrim *H2*   Leitrum *N*   Letreym *T*   Letrim *W*   4046 *Gallwaye*] Galloway *AFHo*   4047 to] vnto *CR*   4047 possessiurs] possessors. *W*   4048 *Sligah*] Sleugho *A*   Sligagh *GFP*   Sligath *Ho*   Sligo *W*   4048 *Maio*] Maiho *A*   Man *H1*   4048 Containe] containe, *R*   4049 rente] rate *R*   4050 vj^m] 7000 *D2F*   4050 Annum] annum. *W*   4050 *Roscomon*] Roseaman *D2* Roseamam *F*   4050-1 savinge ... *Roscoman*] om. *W*   4050 what] that which *W*   4051 *Roscoman*] Rosaman *D2F*   4051 other] other fewe *C*   fewe other *RW*   4052 out] one *W*   4052 to her] vnto her *C*   4053 the] om. *W*   4054 (As ... them)] (as ... them *C*   as ... them *R*   4056 rvnn all] all run *W*   4056 all] om. *C*   4057-9 so ... rente] which *D2F*   4057 *Roscoman*. Contaynethe] *Roscoman* Conteyninge *CRW*   4057 xij^C] vij^C *G*   4058 ij^m. iij^C] 2400. *WHo*   4058 iij^C] iiij^C *CR*   4059 viij^m—vij^C] viijm viijC *RLD1*   8300. *W*   4060 Countie] countyes *R*

of *Galway* and *Lyetrim* will rise vnto, is yeat vncertaine to define till survaie thereof be made for that those landes are entermingled with the Earle of *Clanricard* and others landes but it is thoughte that they be thone halfe of bothe those Counties so as they maie be Counted to the vallew of one wholle Countye which Contayneth aboue one thowsande plowlandes for soe manye the leaste Countye of them all | Comprehendeth) which makethe two thowsande poundes more that is in all x. or xj thowsande poundes thother two Counties muste remayne till theire excheates appeare The which lettinge passe yeat as vnknowen yeat thus muche is knowen and to be acounted for certaine that the Composicion of these two Counties beinge rated at xx^s euerie plowlande will amounte to aboue two thowsande poundes more. all which beinge laide togeather to the former maie be reasonablie estimated to rise vnto xiij$^{m\text{li}}$ the which somme togeather with the rente of the excheated landes in the two laste Counties which Cannot yeat be vallewed (beinge as I doubte not lesse then a Thowsande poundes more) will yealde paie largelye vnto a Thowsande men/ and theire victellers and a Thowsande poundes ouer towardes the gouernour/

Eudox: yea haue me thinkes made but an estimate of theise landes of *Connaght* even at a verye venter so as it shoulde be harde to builde anie certaintye of Chardge to be raised vppon the same/

Iren: Not alltogeather yeat vppon vncerteintis, for thus muche maie easelie Appeare vnto youe for certaine as the Composicion money of euerie plowlande amovntethe vnto for this I woulde haue youe principallye to vnderstand that my purpose is to rate all the Landes in Irelande at xx^s euerie plowlande for theire Composicion towardes the garrisson, The which I knowe in regarde of beinge freed from all other Chardges whatsoeuer wilbe readelye and moste gladlie yealded vnto, So that theare beinge in all Irelande (as appearethe by theire olde Recordes 43920 plowlandes the

---

4061 *Galway*] Galloway *AFHo*   4061 *Lyetrim*] Leutrum *A*   Letein *D1*   Lirtrime *D2*   Lyretrim *F*   Leytrim *H2*   Leitrnm *N*   Letrynne *T*   Letrim *WGHo*   4061 rise] arise *C*   4061 is] it is *C*   4063 Earle of] Earle *R*   4063 *Clanricard*] Clanricardes *W*   4063 landes] *om. R*   4063 that] *om. W*   4066 for] (for *CR*   4066 them all] all *C*   them *R*   4067 is] *om. C*   4067 all] all about *C*   4067 x. or xj thowsande] 9 or 10000 *A*   4068 poundes] poundes, *R* poundes. *W*   4069 passe] passe, *R*   4069 thus] this *CW*   4070 and] *om. W*   4071 plowlande] plowlandes *C*   4071 aboue] *om. C*   4071-2 two thowsande] iij^m *RLD1*   4072 more.] more *C*   more, *RW*   4073 to rise] *om. C*   4073 xiij$^{m\text{li}}$] xiiij$^{m\text{l}}$ poundes *R*   thirty thousand poundes *T*   4075 not] not) no *W*   4076 more)] more, *W*   4076 paie] *om. R*   4078 gouernour/] govenour/. *C*   gouernor *R*   4079 me thinkes] (me thinkes) *W*   4079 made] made, *R*   4079 theise landes of] *om. R*   4079 theise] those *CW*   4080 *Connaght*] Connagh *H1Ho*   4081 same/] same, *R*   4082 thus] this *W*   4083 for] to be *CW*   4084 to] *om. R*   4085 in] in in *W*   4086 garrisson,] Garrison. *W*   4087 regarde] regarde, *R*   4088 vnto,] unto. *W*   4089 theire] *om. C*   4089 Recordes]

A VIEW OF THE PRESENT STATE OF IRELAND 187

same shall amounte to the svmme likewise of 43920 poundes and the reste 4090
to be reared of the excheated Landes which fall to her maiestie in the saide
province of Vlster Connaghte and that parte of Leinster vnder the Rebells/
for mounster we deale not yeat withall/

Eudox: But tell me this by the waie doe youe then laye Composicion
f. 74r vppon the excheated Landes as youe doe | Vppon the reste for so me 4095
thinkes youe reckon all togeather And that sure weare too muche to paie
vij nobles out of euerie plowlande and Composicion money besides that
is xx^s out to euerie plowlande/

Iren: Noe youe mistake me I do put onelie vij nobles rente and Composicion bothe vppon euerie plowlande excheated that is xls for Composicion 4100
and vj^s viij^d for Chieferye to her maiestie/

Eudox: I doe now Conceaue youe procede then I praye youe to the
Appointinge of your garrissons in Connaghte and shewe vs bothe howe
manie and wheare youe woulde haue them placed/

Iren: I woulde haue one Thowsande laide in *Connaght* in Two garrissons 4105
namelye v^C in the Countie of *Maio* about *Clan m^a Costulaghes* which shall
kepe all *Maio* and the Burkes of *m^a Wellm. Euter*. Thother v^C· in the
Countie of *Clanriccard* aboute *Garrandough*. that they maie Containe the
Connars and the Burkes theare the kellies and *Mackmures* withall theare
aboute for that garrisson which I formerlie placed at *Loughearne* will serue 4110

recordes) *CRW*   4090 43920] 43920000. *H2AN*   4092 province] provinces *CRW*
4092 Connaghte] *Connagh H1Ho*   4092 Leinster] Limster *D1*   *Lemster H2N*   Lempster *L*
4093 for] (for *CR*   4093 yeat] om. *R*   4093 withall/] withall) *C*   4094 waie]
waye, *RW*   4095 reste] rest? *W*   4095-6 me thinkes] (mee thinkes) *W*   4096 all
togeather] alltogether *W*   4098 to] of *CRW*   4099 me] me, *RW*   4099 do] om. *R*
4102 Conceaue youe] conceaue yow: *R*   conceive you, *W*   4102 I praye youe] (I pray
you) *W*   4103 Connaghte] *Connagh H1Ho*   4104 placed/] placed? *W*   4105 laide]
om. *C*   4105 Connaght] *Connagh H1Ho*   4106 Maio] *Maiho A*   4106 Clan m^a
Costulaghes] blank space *A*   4106 m^a] in *D2FH2*   4106 Costulaghes] *Costulos H1D2FN*
Costalors H2   *Costalaghes T*   *Costilagh W*   4107 all Maio] *Maio R*   the mores *H2AÑ*
4107 Burkes] bankes *Ho*   4107 m^a Wellm. Euter] blank space *A*   Macwelling-euter *F*
4107 m^a] in *H2* om. *RLD1*   4107 Wellm.] welling *D2*   welliam *H1*   Well^{a}m *G*
Wilm̄ R   William *WNT*   4107 Euter] Enter *D1D2H1H2HoT*   Eighter *W*   4108 Clan-
ticcard] *Clarinam D2*   *Clavroinam F*   *Clanriuan H1*   *Claricand H2*   Clan Rinane *Ho*
Galway W   4108 Garrandough] blank space *A*   *Garingdough D2*   Gaurandough *G*
Garradough N   *GaranClough T*   4109 Connars] blank space *ACHoR*   McConres *P*
4109 Burkes] Burkes, *R*   4109 kellies] Killes *C*   4109 Mackmures] the and blank space *A*
the *mackmurries C*   the mackuires *D2*   the *Macknirrs F*   Mackmurries *GP*   *Macknyrrs H1*
mackquiares H2N   Mac Marreys *Ho*   mark and blank space *RL*   marke *D1*   *Mack murrs T*
Murries W   4109-10 theare aboute] them about *R*   them there-abouts *W*   4110 Loughearne]

for all occacions in the Countie of *Slygah* beinge neare adioyninge theareevnto; so as in one nightes marche they maye be allmoste in anie place theareof when nede shall require them: And like as in the former places of garrisons in vlster I wished two Corporate Townes to be planted which vnder the safegarde of that strengthe shall dwell and trade safelie withall the Countrie aboute theare soe woulde I allsoe wishe to be in this of Connah and that besides theare, another established at Athlone with a Convenient warde in the Castle theare for theire defence/ 4115

Eudox: what shoulde that nede seinge that the gouernour of *Connaght* vsethe to lie theare allwaies whose presence wilbe a defence to all that Towneshippe/ 4120

Iren: I knowe he dothe so but that is muche to be dislikd that the gouernour shoulde lie so far of in the remotest place of all the province wheareas it weare meter that he shoulde be Continewallie abidinge in the middest of his Chardge that he mighte bothe loke out alike into all places of his gouernment | And allsoe be sone at hande in anie place wheare occacion shall demaunde him for the presence of the gouernour is (as youe saide) a greate staie and brdle vnto them that are ill disposed like as I see it is well obserued in mounster wheare the dailye good thearef is Continewallie apparante, And for this Cause allsoe I do greatlie dislike the Lord deputies seatinge at dublin beinge the outest Corner in the realme and leaste nedinge the awe of his presence whereas me semes it weare fitter since his proper care is of Leinster thoughe he hathe Care of all besides generallie, that he shoulde seate himselfe aboute Athie or theareaboutes vppon the skirte of that vnquiet Countrye so that he mighte sitt as it weare at the verye maine maste of his shipp where he mighte easelye ouerloke and somtimes ouerreache the moores/ the Butlers the dempsies the ketins the 4125 4130 4135

f. 74ᵛ

blank space A Logh carne *GP* Logh Karne *Ho* 4111 *Slygah*] Slegho *A* Sligagh *F* Slygath *Ho* Sligo *W* 4112 as in] as *C* 4114 garrisons] Garrison *CR* 4114 two] iij *RAD1D2FH1H2HoLNW om. T* 4115 that] the *R* 4115 shall] should *CW* 4116 the Countrie] that Countrey *C* 4116 aboute theare] about them *CRW* 4116 of] *om. C* 4117 Connah] *Connaughte A* Connagh *CH1Ho* Cannaught *F* Connaught *G* Connoght *R* Connaght *WD2P* 4117 theare,] theare were *CRW* 4117 Athlone] *Allone A* Athlowe *F* Aghlow *Ho* Arklo *T* 4119 *Eudox:*] Iren. *W* 4119 that the] the *W* 4119 *Connaght*] Connagh *H1Ho* Connough *R* 4121 Towneshippe/] Towneshipp *R* Towneshipp? *W* 4123 all the] all that *C* 4124 he] yt *R* 4125 his Chardge] the charge *W* 4125 into] unto *W* 4127 saide)] said *R* 4128 brdle] bridle *CRW* 4128 them] those *CW* 4128 is] *om. C* 4129 thearef] therof *CRW* 4130 I do] doe I *RW* 4130 dislike] mislike *W* 4131 in] of *W* 4132 me semes] (me thinkes) *W* 4133 Leinster] Lemster *H2* 4133 hathe] have *CW* 4134 aboute] at *W* 4134 Athie] *blank space AHo* Althie *F* Atly *T* 4135 as it weare] *om. R* 4136 his] the *R* 4136 where] whence *CRW* 4137 the Butlers] *om. W* 4137 dempsies] Dempries *D2F* 4137 the ketins] *om. W* 4137 ketins] Kelmes *D1* *Kettimes D2F* Ketties *G* Ketines *L* Kettiers *P*

Connours/ Ocarroll Omoloy and all that heape of Irishe nacions which theare lie hundredes togeather without anie to ouerawe them or Containe them in dewtie for the Irishemen I assure youe feares the gouerment no longer then he is within sighte or reache/

Eudox Surelye me thinkes hearein youe obserue a matter of muche importance more then I haue hearde euer noted but sure that semes so expedient as that I wonder it hathe bene hearetofore neuer sene or omitted But I suppose the instance of the Cittizens of dublin is the greatest lett theareof/

Iren: Trewlie then it ought not so to be for no Cause haue they to feare that it will be anie hinderance for them for dublin wilbe still as it is the kaye of all passadges and transportacions out of Englande thither to no lesse profitte of those Cittizens then it now is, and besids other places will theareby receaue some bennefitt, But let vs now I praye youe Come to Leinster in the which I woulde wishe the same Course to be obserued as in vlster/

Eudox: youe meane for the leavinge of the garrissons in theire fortes, and for plantinge of Englishe in all those Contris betwene the Countie of dublin and the Countie of wexforde but those waste wilde places I thinke when they are wonne vnto her maiestie that theare is none which wilbe hastie to seke to inhabite/

Iren: yes enoughe I warrante you for thoughe the wholle trackt of the Countrie be mountaine and woddye yeat theare are manye goodlie valleis amongest them, fitt for faire habitacion to which those mountaines adioyned wilbe a greate increase of pasturage for that Countrye is a verye greate soile of Cattell and verie fit for breede, As for Corne it is nothinge naturall saue onelye Barlie and Oates and some places for Rie and therefore the larger penniworthes maie be allowed vnto them thoughe otherwise the widenes of the mountaine pasturage doe recompence the badnes of the Soile, So as I doubte not but it will finde inhabitantes and vndertakers enoughe

Kellies T   4138 Connours] *Conhurs D2F   Connars N*   4138 Ocarroll] *occorell D2F*
4138 Omoloy] *blank space A   omoley D2FH1*   4139 hundredes] hudled *CRW*   4139 ouerawe] overrule *R*   4140 Irishemen] Irishman *CRW*   4140 I assure youe] (I assure you) *W*
4142 me thinkes] me seemes *C*   mee thinges *R*   (me thinkes) *W*   4144 it ... hearetofore] that heretofore it hath bene *CW*   4144 neuer sene or] oversene or *CW*   over *R*
4145 theareof/] there *R*   4147 for them] to them *W*   4148 thither to] thitherto, *W*
4150 theareby] herebie *CRW*   4150 I praye youe] (I pray you) *W*   4151 Leinster] Lemster *H2N*   4151 as] that was *CW*   4155 wexforde] *Waxford H2*   4156 which] that *R*   4158 I warrante you] (I warrant you) *W*   4158 you] *inserted between lines E om. CR*   4158 trackt] *tracke W*   4159 mountaine] mountayny *C*   mountainous *W*
4160 habitacion] habitacions *CW*   4161 Countrye] Countrie, *R*   4161 verye] *om. W*
4162 breede,] bread,/ *R*   breed: *W*   4163 places] *om. C*   4164 vnto] to *CW*   4165 widenes] wickednesse *C*   wyldnes *R*   4166 but] but that *C*   4167 enoughe] enoughe/. *C*

Eudox: Howe muche then doe youe thinke that all those Landes which *Pheagh m^d Hugh* houldethe vnder him maye amounte vnto and what rente maie be reared theareout to the maintenaunce of the garrissons that shalbe laied theare

Iren: Trewlye it is impossible by anie to tell it And as for experience and knowlledge theareof I doe not thinke that theare was euer anie of the particulers thereof But yeat I will (if it please youe gesse theareat vppon grounde onelye of theire iudgement which haue formerlie devided all that Countrye into 2 shires or Counties namelye the Countye of *Wicklo* and the Countie of *Fernes*, The which two I see no Cause but they should whollie excheate to her maiestie All saue the Barronrye of *Arclo* which is the Earle of Ormondes anciente inheritance and hathe euer bene in his possession for all the wholle lande is the Quenes vnles theare be some graunte of anie parte theareof to be shewed from her maiestie As I thinke theare is onelye of Newcastle to Sr Henrye Harrington and of the Castle of ffernes to Sr Thomas masterson the reste beinge allmoste Thirtye miles ouer I doe suppose Cane Containe no lesse then Two Thowsande plowlandes which I will estimate at iiij^m poundes rente by the yeare The reste of Leinster beinge vij Counties to weete the | Countye of *Dublin, Kildare, Cathrlogh, Wexforde, Kilkeni*, the kinges and the Quenes Countie doe Containe in them 7400 which amountethe to so manie poundes for Composicion to the garrisson that makes in the wholle xj^m iiijC^{li} the which somme will yealde paie vnto m soldiors litle wantinge which maie be supplied out of other landes of the Cavannaghes which are to be excheated to her maiestie for the Rebellion of theire possessiours thoughe otherwise in dede they be her owne anciente demeane/

Eudox It is great reasone, but tell vs now wheare woulde youe wishe

enough:/ *R* enough. *W* 4168 then] *om. W* 4169 *Pheagh*] *Feugh A* 4171 theare] theare/. *C* there:/ *R* there? *W* 4172 anie] ayme *CRW* 4172 as] *om. CW* 4173 theareof] *om. R* 4173 euer] every *W* 4174 (if] if *CR* 4174 youe] you) *W* 4177 *Fernes*] *Hernes D1* 4177 but] but that *W* 4178 saue] but *R* 4178 Barronrye] Baronye *CRW* 4178 *Arclo*] *Sticklo F   Airlo H2* wyclo *N* 4179 Ormondes] Ormond is *A*   Wormewoodes *D1*   Ormewoodes *RL* 4182 Newcastle] Newcalse *LD1* 4182 ffernes] *Fermes D2* 4183 Thomas] Iohn *C* 4183 masterson] maisterson *CG* Mucksterson *P   Masterson, W* 4184 Cane] can not *C* 4184 then] then, *R·* 4185 the] *om. C* 4185 yeare] yere, *CR* yeare. *W* 4185 Leinster] Lemster *D1H2N* Lempster *L* 4186 Cathrlogh] *Kataraghe A   Catherlogh CR   Caterlogh Ho   Cathelagh WG* 4187 kinges] kinge *R* 4188 7400] 7400 plowlandes *RW* fower thousand seaven hundred plow landes *T* 4189 the which] which *W* 4191 Cavannaghes] *Cannanaghes T* 4192 possessiours] possessions *R* 4192 be] bee of *W* 4193 demeane/] demeane, *R* 4194 woulde youe]

A VIEW OF THE PRESENT STATE OF IRELAND 191

those garrissons to be laied wheather alltogeather, or to be dispersed in sundrie places of the Countrie/

Iren: marye in sundrie places to wete in this sorte or muche the like as maie be better advised for CC in a place I do thinke to be ynoughe for the safegard of that Countrye and kepinge vnder all sodaine vpstartes that shall seke to trouble the peace thereof therefore I wishe CC to be laied at Ballinocorr for the kepinge of all bad persons from *Glanmalour* and all the fastnes theareaboutes and allsoe Containe all that shalbe planted in those landes thenceforthe, Another CC at at knoclough in theire former place of garrison to kepe the Biskellagh and all those mountaines of the Cavannaghes/ CC more to lie at ffernes and vpwardes in wardes vppon the *Slane*. CC. to be placed at the forte of Leix to restraine the mores Ossorie and Ocurrall other CC at the forte of Offalye to Curbe the Connours Omoloys m^a Coghlan maccachegan and all those Irishe nacions borderinge theareaboutes

Eudox: Thus I see all your thowsande men bestowed in Leinster what saie youe then of meathe which is the fifte parte/

Iren: meathe which Containethe bothe eastmeathe and westmeathe and of late the Analye now Called the Countye of Longeforde is accounpted thearevnto But meathe it selfe (accordinge to the old recordes) | Contaynethe 4320 plowlandes and the Countye of Longeforde 947 which in the wholle make 5267 plowlandes of which the Composicion money will

you will *W*   4196 Countrie/] country? *W*   4197 to wete] *viz*. *W*   4199 of that] of the *R*   4200 thereof] thereof,: *R*   thereof, *W*   4200 CC] *om*. *R*   4201 Ballinocorr] *Ballinecorrih A*   Ballinorcrosse *D1*   *Balincor D2F*   *Ballincarre H1*   *Balynocores H2*   *Ballincort Ho*   Ballinocros *RLN*   Ballin *Corre T*   *Ballinecor W*   4201 *Glanmalour*] blank space *A*   *Glammalour H2*   Glamnalogh *Ho*   4202 theareaboutes] therabout *C* 4202 allsoe] alsoe to *CRW*   4203 thenceforthe,] thenceforth: 200. *R*   thenceforth. *W* 4203 at at] at *CRW*   4203 knoclough] blank space *A*   knocklouh *C*   Knoclong *P* 4204 Biskellagh] blank space *A*   Briskelagh *CD2H1PT*   Briskleighe *D1*   Briskelaghes *G* Brisklagh *RFH2HoLN*   Bracknagh *W*   4205 Cavannaghes/] Cavanaghes *CR*   Cananaghes *T* *Cavenaghes, W*   4205 ffernes] Ferenes *D1*   4205 in wardes] inward *W*   4206 *Slane*.] *Slane, CW*   *Slane R*   4206 Leix] *Lease A*   Liue *D1*   *Leire F*   4206 Ossorie] Osbrie *GP* *Ossoris H2*   *Ossarye Ho*   *vpper-Ossory W*   4207 Ocurrall] Occariall *C*   *Occorall D2F* Ocarroll *RW*   4207 other] other: *R*   4207 Connours] *Conhurs D2FH1*   O Connors *RAW* *Connorce T*   4208 Omoloys] blank space *A*   Omoleis *F*   *Oenoloys H1*   4208 m^a Coghlan] in Coyghlane *D1*   m^{o}scoghlan *D2*   in *Sleghban F*   m^c*Coghan H1*   in *Coghlan H2*   in *Coghlane L* 4208 maccachegan] blank space *A*   Maccaghegan *CT*   Maccingheian *D1*   *Machaghegan D2FHo*   Maccoghegan *GP*   Maccagehan *H1*   Maccaghergon *H2*   m^{c}cughgan *N*   Maccughegan *RL*   Mageoghegan *W*   4209 theareaboutes] therabout/. *C*   thereaboutes: *R* there-abouts. *W*   4210 thowsande] *om*. *W*   4210 Leinster] *Lemster H2*   Leinster, *W* 4211 meathe ... parte/] *Meath? W*   4211 fifte] first *R*   4213 of late] late *C* 4213 Analye] blank space *A*   *Analeg T*   4213 Longeforde] *Langforde Ho*   *Lanforde L* Langeford *RD1G*   4213 accounpted] counted *W*   4214 (accordinge ... recordes)] according ... records, *W*   4214 (accordinge] according *C*   4214-5 Contaynethe] *om*. *R* 4215 Longeforde] Langford *Ho*   langeford. *RD1G*   4215 947] 944 *D1*   4216 make] amount likewise to five thowsande two hundreth thre score and vij plowlandes to the mayntenaunce of the garrisson But because all meathe lyinge in the bosome of that kingedome is allwaies quiet enoughe it is nedeles to put anye garrisone theare so as all that Chardge maie be spared, But in the Countie of Longeforde I wishe to hundred fotemen and fiftie horsemen to be placed in some Conveniente seat betwene the Analie and the Brenie, as aboute Lough syllon or some like place of that riuer so as they mighte kepe bothe the Orelies and allso the Offeralls and all that out skirte of Eastmeathe in awe the which vse vppon euerie lighte occacion to be stirringe and havinge continewall enmitye amongeste themselues do theareby oftentimes troble all those partes the Chardge whereof beinge iiij^m iiijC and odd poundes is to be Cutt out of that Composicion money for meathe and Longeforde, The ouerplus beinge allmoste two thowsande poundes by the yeare will come in Clearelye to her maiestie/

Eudox: yt is worthe the harkeninge vnto but now that youe haue done with meathe procede I praye youe to mounster that we maie see how it will rise theare for the maintenaunce of the garrissone/

Iren: movnster Containethe by recorde at dubline 16000 plowlandes the Composicion wheareof as the reste will make 16^m poundes by the yeare out of the which I woulde haue a thowsande soldiours to be mainteined for the defence of that province the Chardge wheareof with the victellers wages will amounte to xij^m poundes by the yeare, Thother iiij^m poundes will defraie the Chardge of the Presidencie and the Councell of that province/ |

Eudox: The Reckoninge is easie but in this Account by your leave me thinkes youe are deceived for in this some of the Composicion money ye Counte the Landes of the vndertakers of that province whoe are by theire graunte from the Quene to be free from all suche ymposicions what soeuer, exceptinge theire onelye rente which is surelie ynoughe/

makes *CW*   make, *R*   4217 five ... vij] 5267. *W*   4217 hundreth] hundred *CR*
4217-8 plowlandes] poundes *RW*   4221 Longeforde] Langeford *GP*   *Langforde Ho*
4222 Analie] *blank space A*   Armalie *H2*   4222 Brenie] *blank space A*   Bremy *G*
Bryme *H2*   Bryne *Ho*   Brein *N*   4223 Lough syllon] *blank space A*   Loughsidnei *D1*
Longesillon *H1*   Longhfillon *H2*   Hugh Sillon *Ho*   Longhsildone *L*   4224 kepe] *om. R*
4224 Orelies] *Oneales RLD1H2*   4224 Offeralls] *Offoralls F*   *Oferales H2*   4225 Eastmeathe] meath *RW*   4225 in awe] *om. C*   4227 iiij^m iiijC] 1400 *F*   4400 *RLD1H2AN*
4228 money] *om. C*   4228 for] for, *R*   4229 Longeforde] *Lonfoord F*   *Langforde Ho*
4230 her] he *W*   4230 maiestie/] *followed by additional paragraph*   Iren: Mounster contayneth by record at Dubline, 1600 plowelandes *RL*   4232 I praye youe] (I pray you) *W*
4233 theare for] therefore *R*   4233 garrissone/] garrison?/. *C*   4235 16^m] 116000 *F*
4235 by the] by *C*   4236-8 out ... yeare] *om. D2*   4237 wheareof] of which *R*
4238 xij^m] 1200 *H2D1*   4238 the] *om. C*   4238 Thother] the othe *C*   4239 Chardge] Charges *R*   4239 that] the *C*   4241-2 me thinkes] (me thinkes) *W*   4243 Counte] accompt *CW*   account *R*   4243 province] province Province *R*   4245 surelie] surerlie *R*

A VIEW OF THE PRESENT STATE OF IRELAND 193

Iren: ye saie Trewe I did soe, But the same xx^s for euerie plowlande I meante to haue deducted out of that rente due vppon them to her maiestie which is no hinderaunce nor Chardge at all more to her maiestie then it now is. for all that rente which she receaues of them she puttethe forthe againe to the maintenaunce of the presidencye theare the Chardge wheareof it dothe scarselie defraye, wheareas in this accompte bothe that Chardge of the presidencie and allso of a thowsande soldiours more shalbe mainteined/

Eudox: It shoulde be well if it Coulde be broughte to that but now wheare will youe haue your thowsande men garrissoned/

Iren: I will haue C of them placed at the Baintree wheare is a moste fitt place not onelye to defende all that side of the weste parte from forrein invasion but allsoe to answeare all occacions of troubles to which that Countrie beinge so remote is verye subiecte, And surelie theare woulde allso be placed a good Towne havinge bothe a verye good haven and a plentifull fishinge and the lande beinge allreadye excheated to her maiestie, but beinge forciblie kepte from her by a Ragtaile kirne that proclaimes him selfe the Bastarde sonne of the Earle of Clarence beinge Called donell maccartie whom it is mete to foresee to cutt of: for whensoeuer the Earle shall die all whose landes after him are to Come to her maiestie, he is like to make a foule sturr theare thoughe of him self of no power yeat | Thoroughe supportance of some others whoe ly in the winde and loke after the fall of that inheritaunce: another C. would I haue placed at Castlemayne which shoulde kepe all desmond and kerrye, for it answearethe them bothe moste Convenientlye Allsoe aboute killmore in the Countye of Corke woulde I haue CC placed the which shoulde breake that neste of theues theare and answeare equallie bothe the Countye of Lyn^ricke and allsoe the Countye of Corke Another C woulde I haue lye

---

4246 Trewe] trewe in deed *R*   true, *W*   4247 that] the *R*   4249 that] the *C*   4249 receaues] receaues, *R*   4252 of a thowsande] of, 1000: *R*   4254 It] I *R*   4254 that but] that: *R*   4255 garrissoned/] garrissond *R*   garrisond? *W*   4256 will] would *CRW*   4256 Baintree] Kaintre *D1*   4256 is] it is *C*   4257 from] from from *R*   4259 theare] here *R*   4259-60 woulde allso] alsoe would *CRW*   4260 placed] planted *W*   4260 a verye] verie *R*   a *W*   4260 and a] and *R*   4262 a Ragtaile kirne] one *W*   4262 Ragtaile] roughtayle *L*   roughe tayld *D1*   4263 Clarence] *Clancare CAT*   *Clanrare F*   Clancarre *GHo*   Clanricard *H1*   Clanecarre *H2*   *Clancar RD1D2LNPW*   4264 maccartie] m^acharlie *D1*   m^a *Carter F*   in *Carlie H2*   m^a *Chartie RL*   4264 cutt of] *om. W*   4265 whose] those *CRW*   4265 after him] (after him) *W*   4265 to her] vnto hir *C*   4266 of no] noe *CW*   4268 inheritaunce:] Inherritaunce *C*   4268 would I] I would *W*   4269 Castlemayne] the Castle mayne *C*   4269 kerrye] Kyrtye *RL*   4270 bothe] *om. C*   4270 Convenientlye] convenientlye, *C*   convenientelie: *RW*   4270 killmore] *blank space A*   Kilmare *H2*   4271-3 woulde . . . Corke] *om. T*   4271 the which] which *R*   4272 bothe] both to *W*   4272 Countye] counties *C*   4273 Lyn^ricke] limericke *CD2FH1W*   Limkirk *Ho*   Lymbricke *RD1LN*   4273 Corke] Corke, *CR*   *Corke: W*

at Corke aswell to Comaunde the Towne as allsoe to be readie for anie forreine occacion, likewise at watrforde woulde I place CC for the same reasons and allsoe for other privie Cawses that are no lesse importante moreouer on this side of Arlo neare to mvskrie whirke which is the Countrye of the Bourkes aboute/ *Kilpatrick* woulde I haue CC more to be garrisoned which shoulde scoure bothe the white knightes Countrye and Arlo and muscrye Whirke by which places all the passage of theues dothe lye, which Conveye theire stealthe from all mounster downe wardes towardes Tipperar and the Englishe pale and from the Englishe pale allsoe vp into mounster whereof they vse a Comon trade, Besides that er longe I doubte the Countrye of Tipperary it self will nede suche a strengthe in it which weare good to be theare readie before the evill fall that is dailye of some expected and thus youe see all our garrissons placed/

Eudox: I see it righte well but let me I praye youe by the waie aske youe the reasone whie in those Cities of mounster namelye Waterforde and Corke ye rather placed Garrissons then in all thothers in Irelande ffor they maye thinke themselues to haue greate wronge to be so Chardged aboue all the reste/ |

f. 77ᵛ *Iren* I will tell youe those two Cities aboue all the reste doe offer an Ingate to the Spanniarde moste fittlye and allso the inhabitantes of them are moste ill affected to the Englishe gouernment and moste friendes to the Spanniarde/ But yeat because they shall not take excepcion to this that they are Chardged aboue all the reste I will allsoe laye a Chardge vppon thothers likewise, for indede it is no reasone that the Corporate Townes enioyinge greate ffranchises and priviledges from her maiestie and livinge theareby not onelye safe but drawinge to them the wealthe of all the Lande should live so free as not to be partakers of the burthen of

4275 occacion,] occasion *C*   occasion: *W*   4276 importante] importaunt, *CR* important: *W*   4277 this] the *R*   4277 Arlo neare] *Arlonerre F*   4277 Arlo] *Arls H2 Arkloe Ho*   4277 mvskrie whirke] *blank space A   Muskery quirke W*   4277 mvskrie] *Muskerie D2F   Moscrie H1   Auskrye Ho*   4278 Bourkes] *Banrkes T*   4278 aboute/] about *CRW*   4278 *Kilpatrick*] *apparently added in space left blank E   blank space ACD1H2HoLNR*   4278 woulde I] I would *W*   4279 knightes] *Knight; W*   4280 Arlo] *Alo G   Arkloe Ho*   4280 muscrye Whirke] *blank space A   Muskery quirk W*   4280 muscrye] *Muskery D2F   Muskay H2*   4280 Whirke] werkes *D1* wherkes *RH2LN*   4280 passage] passages *CRW*   4280 dothe] doe *W*   4281 all] *om. W* 4282 Tipperar] Tipperari *RW   Tipporary T*   4282 and the] and that *R*   4282-5 and from ... before] *om. F*   4283 into] vnto *W*   4283 vse] vse to make *CRW*   4283 that] that, *W*   4284 the] I the *C*   that the *W*   4284 Countrye] County *CRW*   4284 of] of, *R* 4284 it self] *om. C*   4286 our] your *RW*   4287 *Eudox*:] *Euder L*   4287 I praye youe] (I pray you) *W*   4287 aske youe] aske *R*   4288 namelye] namelie namely *C* 4289 thothers] others *W*   4291 reste] rest? *W*   4292 yow] yow, *RW*   4293-5 and ... Spanniarde] *om. W*   4294 friendes] friende *C*   4295 excepcion] exceptions *W* 4297 thothers] the other *C*   4298 enioyinge] Inioyninge *C*   4299 and] *om. C*

A VIEW OF THE PRESENT STATE OF IRELAND 195

this garrissone for theire owne saftie speciallye in this time of trouble and seinge all the reste burthened And therefore I will thus Chardge them all ratablie accordinge to theire Abillities towardes theire mayntenaunce The which her maiestie maie if shee please spare out of the Chardge of the rest and reserue towardes her other Costes or els ad to the Chardge of the Presidencye in the Northe/

Waterforde.	C	Clonmell.	x.	Dandolk	x.
Corke.	1	Cashell.	x.	Mollingar	x.
Lymerick.	l.	Fedard.	x.	Newry	x.
Galwaye	1	Kilkenny.	xxv.	Trim	x
Dinglecush.	x	Wexford.	xxv.	Ardie	x
Kinsale.	x	Tredagh.	xxv.	Kelles	x
Youghall.	x	Rosse.	xxv.	Dublin	C
Kilmallock.	x				

Summ   iiij^C—iiij^{xx} //

Eudox. It is easie Iren: to laie a Chardge vppon anye Towne but to forsee how the same maie be answeared and defraied is the Chiefe parte of good Advicement

4301 speciallye in this] especiallie in the C 4302 And therefore] (and therefore) W 4302 them all] them C 4303-4 accordinge ... maie] om. C 4304 if shee please] (if she please) W 4305 els] om. R 4306 Presidencye] Presidence R 4306 Northe/] northe: C northe. placed as if it were the first name in the following list P northe R North. W 4307-14 Waterforde....Kilmallock.—x] D2 arranges the list in two columns, eleven names in each; F in three columns, of eight, nine, and five names respectively; and H1 in three columns, of eight, eight, and six names respectively. But the order, in all three cases, is the same as in E. H2 places the list in the following form:

Waterford	100	Galwaie	50	Youghill	10		
Corke	50	Dinglelagh	10	Killmillock	10		
Limbrick	50	Kinsale	10	Clonmell	10		
Cashell	10	Molingars	10				
Federd	10	Newrye	10				
Kilkenny	25	Dundalk	10				
Wexford	25	Trym	10				
Dreodagh	25	Kells	10				
Ros	25	Dublin	100				

4307 Waterforde] Wateford F 4307 Clonmell] Colonmell F Clemmell T 4307 Dandolk] Dandalk CGP Dondalke D2FH1HoT Dundalke RD1NW 4308 Corke.—1] Corck 100 RLD1 4308 Cashell] Casthell C Cushell Ho 4308 Mollingar] Molingaire A Nolingarre F 4309 Lymerick] om. A Lymbricke RD1LN 4309 Fedard] Fetherte A Eedred LD1 Tedard D2F Hedard G Hedardo P Eederd RN Eedard T 4310 Galwaye] Galloway Ho 4310 Kilkenny.—xxv] Kilkenny 10 N 4310 Trim] Trine D1 Trin F 4311 Dinglecush.—x] Dinglecush.1 T 4311 Dinglecush] Dingellechooishe A Dinglecashe G Kinsaile LD1 4311 Ardie] Hardie D2F Hrdie H1 Ardrye LD1 Arclye P 4312 Kinsale] Dinglecushe LD1 4312 Tredagh] Drogheda A Dreddagh LD1 ffredagh P Dreodagh RN 4312 Kelles] Rells D2F 4313 Youghall] Youthall LD1 4313 Dublin—C] Dvbline 10 NT 4315 Summ] om. AF Summa LD1D2 Somma T In all W 4315 iiij^C—iiij^{xx}] om. AF 580[11] D2 v^C iiij^{xx} G 570 H2 490 LD1 CCCCCxxx T 580. W 4318 Advicement]

Iren: Surelie this Chardge which I put vppon them I knowe to be so reasonable as that it will not muche be felte/ for the porte Townes that haue bennefitte of Shippinge maie cut it easelye of theire tradinge and in Lande Townes of theire Corne and Cattell Neither doe I see but that since to them speciallie the bennefitt of peace dothe redounde that they speciallie shoulde helpe to beare the burthen of theire owne safegarde and defence As we see all the Townes of the lowe Countries doe Cutt vpon themselues an excise of all thinges towardes the mayntenaunce of the warr that is made in theire behaulfe to which thoughe these are not to be Compared in riches yet are to be Chardged accordinge to theire pouertye/

Eudox: But now that youe haue set vp these forces of souldiours and provided well as ye suppose for theire paye, yeat theare remayneth to forecaste how they maie be victelled and wheare purveiaunce theareof maye be had, for in Irelande it selfe/ I cannot se how anie thinge allmoste is to be had for them beinge allreadye so pittifullie wasted as it is with this shorte time of warr/

Iren: for the firste Two yeares indede it is nedefull that they be vittelled out of Englande thorouglye from halfe yeare to haulfe yeare aforehande All which time the Englishe pale shall not be burthened at all but shall haue time to recouer themselues And mounster allsoe nowe beinge reasonablie well stored will by that time allsoe God sende seasonable weather | be thoroughlie well furnished to supplie a greate parte of that Chardge for I knowe theare is greate plentie of Corne sente over sea from thence the which if they mighte haue sale for at home they woulde be gladd to haue money soe neare at hande speciallie if they weare straightelye restrained from transportinge of it. thearevnto allso theare wilbe a greate helpe and furtheraunce given in the puttinge forwarde of husbandrie in all mete places as heareafter shall in due place appeare/ But heareafter when thinges shall growe vnto a better strengthe and the Countrie be replennished with Corne as in shorte space it will if it be well followed, for the Countrye people themselues are greate plowghers and small

advizement./. *C* aduisement: *R*   advisement. *W*   4320-1 that haue] which haue *R*   4321 easelye of] easily off *W*   4321 in] in all *R*   4322 that] *om. W*   4323 them speciallie] them *R*   them especially *W*   4323 dothe] doe *C*   4323 they speciallie] they especially *W*   4324 helpe to] *om. RW*   4324 owne] *om. W*   4324 safegarde] saivegardes *R*   4325 Countries] Country *C*   4325 themselues] them selves, *R*   4327 made] mad *R*   4328 riches yet are] richesse yet are they *W*   4329 haue] haue thus *CW*   4330 as ye suppose] (as you suppose) *W*   4332 had] made *CRW*   4332 how . . . allmoste] almost how any thing *W*   4333 to] to to *C*   4335 indede . . . nedefull] it is needefull indeede *W*   4335 they] the *R*   4336 aforehande] afore-hand. *W*   4337 All] *om. R*   4337 but shall] but *C*   4338 time] *blank space C*   4338 allsoe nowe beinge] beinge also nowe *C*   also beinge *RW*   4339 allsoe] if *CR*   (if *W*   4339 seasonable] reasonable *R*   4339 weather] weather) *W*   4343 at] *om. CRW*   4344 of it.] it *C*   of yt, *R*   4345 in the] to the *R*   4347 vnto] into *C*   to *R*   4349-50 for . . . Corne/]

spenders of Corne/ then woulde I wishe that theare shoulde be good 4350
storehowses and magasines erected in all those greate places of garrisson
and in all greate Townes aswell for the victellinge of soldiours and shipps
as for all occacions of suddaine services as allsoe for preventinge of all
times of dearthe and scarsitye And this wante is muche to be Complained
of in Englande aboue all other Countries whoe trustinge to muche to the 4355
vsuall blessinge of the earthe doe neuer forecaste anie suche harde sesons
nor anye suche suddaine occacions as these troblous tymes maye euerye daie
bringe forthe when it wilbe to late to gather provicion from abroade and
to bringe it perhaps from far for the furnishinge of shipps or soldiours
which peradventure maie nede to be presently imployed and whose wante 4360
maie (which god forbidd) happ to hazarde a kingedome/// |

f. 79r *Eudox*: In dede the wante of these magazines of victells I haue harde often
times Complayned of in Englande and wondred at in other Countries but
that is nothinge now to our purpose/ But as for these garrissons which
ye haue now so strongelye planted thorougheout all Irelande and euerie 4365
place swarminge with soldiours shall theare be no ende of them for now
this beinge me semes/ I do see rather a Countrye of warr then of peace
and quiet which yee earst pretended, to worke in Irelande for if youe
bringe all thinges to that quietnes, which ye saide what then nedethe to
mayntaine so greate forces as youe haue Chardged vppon it/ 4370

Iren: I will vnto youe *Eudox*: in privitye discouer the drifte of my pur-
pose I meane as I tolde youe/ and doe well hope heareby bothe to settle
an eternall peace in that Countrie and allsoe to make it verie profitable
to her maiestie the which I see muste be broughte in by a stronge hande
and so Continewed till it run into a stedfaste Course of gouernment, The 4375
which in this sorte wilbe neither difficull nor daungerous for the soldiour
beinge once broughte in for the service into Vlster and havinge subdued
it and Connaghte I will not haue to laie downe his Armes anie more till
he haue effected that which I purpose That is firste to haue this generall

(for ... Corne) *C*   4350 that] *om. CR*   4351 storehowses] store of Houses *W*
4355 to the] of the *C*   4357 troblous] troblesome *R*   4359 it] *om. R*   4362 these]
those *CW*   4362 harde] *om. W*   4365 thorougheout] throught *C*   4366 them] them? *W*
4367 this] thus *CRW*   4367 me semes/] mee semeth *R*   (me thinkes) *W*   4368 pre-
tended,] pretended *CRW*   4369 that] the *R*   4369 which] that *CW*   4369 then
nedethe] need then *R*   4371-2 purpose] purpose, *W*   4372 I meane ... youe/]
(I ... yowe) *C*   4372 as ... youe/] (as ... yow) *RW*   4372 heareby] thereby *W*
4372 bothe] *om. C*   4374 by] with *W*   4374 stronge] strange *R*   4375 till] vntyll *R*
4375 run] growe *R*   4375 into] in *W*   4375 The] *om. W*   4376 wilbe neither]
will neither be *CRW*   4376 difficull] difficill *C*   defyculte *RW*   4376 daungerous]
dangerous: *R*   4378 Connaghte] Connagh *CH1*   4378 to] him to *RW*   4379 effected]
affected *R*   4379 this] a *R*

Composicion for the maintenaunce of these thorougheout all the Realme 4380
in regarde of the troblelous times and dailye daunger which is threatned
to this realme by the kinge of Spaine and theare vppon to bestowe all my
soldiours in sorte as I haue done that no parte of all that realme shalbe
able or dare to quinche, Then will I eftsones bringe in my reformacion
and thearevppon establishe suche an order of gouernement | As I maye 4385
thinke meteste for the good of that Realme which beinge once established
and all thinges put into a right waye, I doubte not but they will run on
fairelye, and thoughe they woulde euer seke to swerue aside yeate shall
they not be able without forreine violence once to Remove as youe your
selfe shall sone I hope in your owne reason readelye Conceaue which if 4390
it shall ever appeare then maie her maiestie at pleasure withdrawe some
of the Garrisson and turne theire paye into her purse, or if she will neuer
please so to doe which I woulde rather wishe then shall shee haue a nom-
ber of braue olde Soldiours allwaies readye for anye occacion that she will
employe them vnto supplyinge theire garrissons with freshe ones in theare 4395
steede the maintenaunce of whom shalbe no more Chardge to her maiestie
then nowe that Realme is, for all the Revenewe theareof and muche more
she spendethe even in the moste peaceable times that are theare (as thinges
nowe stande) and in time of warr which is once nowe sure everye vijth
yeare, she spendeth infinite treasure besides to smalle purpose/ 4400

Eudox: I perceaue your purpose but now that youe haue thus strongelye
made waie vnto your reformacion as that I see the people so humbled and
prepared that they will and muste yealde to anie ordinaunce that shalbe
given them I doe muche desire to vnderstande the same for in the begin-
ninge youe promised to shewe a meane how to redresse as well these 4405
inConveniences and abuses which youe shewed to be in that state of
gouernement which nowe standes theare as in the lawes Customes and
Religion wheareiin I woulde gladlie knowe firste wheather in steade of
those lawes ye woulde haue newe lawes made, for now for oughte that I |
I see yee maie doe what youe please/ 4410

4380 for the] for *W* 4380 thorougheout] throught *C* 4380 all] *om. R* 4381 troblelous] troublous *CRW* 4382 Spaine] *Spaine. W* 4382-5 to bestowe ... thearevppon] *om. D2* 4382 my] the *R* 4383 in] in such *W* 4383 that realme] Ireland, *R* 4384 or] to *RW* 4384 to] so much as, *R* 4384 quinche,] quich *C* quitch. *GP* quinch: *W* 4385 an order] a forme *W* 4386 established] setled *CW* 4390 I hope] (I hope) *W* 4392 the] her *R* 4392 Garrisson] garrisons *W* 4393 which ... wishe] (which ... wishe) *RW* 4394 she] shee *W* 4396 steede] steed. *W* 4397 that] the *CR* 4398 times] tyme *R* 4398-9 (as ... stande)] as ... stand. *W* 4399 time] the tyme *C* 4399 once nowe sure] now surely *W* 4399 vijth] vij *R* 4401 that] yf *R* 4402 as] and *W* 4404 them] them. *W* 4405 meane] meanes *W* 4405 as well these] well *inserted between lines E* all these *C* all those *RW* 4407 standes] standeth *R* 4409-10 I I] I *CRW*

Iren: I see *Eudox*: That youe well remember our firste purpose and do rightelie Continewe the Course theareof/ ffirste thearefore to speake of lawes since we firste begane with them I doe not thinke it Conveniente (thoughe now it be in the power of the Prince) to Chaunge all the Lawes and make newe for that shoulde brede a greate trouble and Confusion aswell in the Englishe theare dwellinge and to be planted as allsoe in the Irishe for the Englishe havinge bene trayned vp allwaies in the Englishe Gouernement will hardelie be inevrde vnto anye other, and the Irishe will better be drawen to the Englishe then the Englishe to the Irishe gouernemente, Therefore sithens we Cannot now applie Lawes fitt to the people as in the firste institucion of Comon wealthes it oughte to be we will applie the people and fitt them to the Lawes as it moste Convenientlye maye be. The lawes thearefore we resolue shall abide in the same sorte that they doe bothe Common lawe and statutes, onelye suche defectes in the Comon lawe and inConveniences in the statutes as in the beginninge we noted and as men in deeper insighte, shall advise maye be Changed by some other new actes and ordinaunces to be by a parliament theare confirmed As those of Triall of pleas of the Crowne and private rightes betwene parties, Coulorable Conveyaunces, accessaries/,

Eudox: But how will those be redressed by parlament when as the Irishe which swaie moste in parliament as youe saide shall oppose themselues againste them/

Iren: That maie now be well avoided for now that soe manye frehouldes of Englishe shalbe established they togeather with Burgesses of Townes and suche other Loyall Ireshmen as maie be preferred to be knightes of the shire and suche like will be able to bearde and to Counterpese the reste, whoe allsoe beinge now broughte more in awe will the more easelye submitt to anye suche ordinaunces as shalbe for the good of themselues and that Realme generallie/

Eudox: youe saie well for the increase of freehoulders for theire nvmbers will heareby be greatelye augmented but how shall it passe thoroughe the hier howsse which will still Consiste all of Irishe/

Iren: marye that allsoe maie be well redressed by ensample of that which I haue hearde was done in the like Case by K Edwarde the Thirde as I remember whoe beinge greatlye bearded and Crossed by the Lordes of the Clergye they beinge then | By reason of the Lorde Abbottes and others to manye and to stronge for him, so as he Coulde not for theire frowardenes order and reforme thinges as he desired was advized to directe out his writtes to certaine gentlemen of beste abilitye and truste entytelinge them therein Barrons to serue and sitt as Barrons in the nexte parliament, By which meanes he had so manye Barrons in his parliament as weare able to waighe downe the Cleargie and theire friendes The which Barrons they saie weare not afterwardes Lordes but onelye Barronettes as sundrie of them do yeat retaine the name/ And by the like device her maiestie maye now likewise Curbe and Cutt shorte those Irishe and vnrulye Lordes that hinder all good procedinges

Eudox: It semes no lesse: then for reforminge of all those inconveniente statutes which ye noted in the beginninge and redressinge of all those

A VIEW OF THE PRESENT STATE OF IRELAND

euill Customes and lastlie for setlinge sounde Relegion amongest them me thinkes youe shall not nede anie more to ouergoe those particulers againe which youe menconed nor anie other which mighte besides be remembred, but to leaue all to the reformacion of suche a parliament in the which by the good Care of the Lord deputie and Councell they maie all be amended, Thearefore now youe maie Come to that generall reformacion which youe spake of and bringinge in of that establishement of which youe saie all men shoulde be Contained in dewtie ever after without the Terrour of Warlicke forces or violente wrestinge of thinges by sharpe punishment

Iren: I will soe at your pleasure the which me semes cane by no meanes be better plotted then by | ensample of suche other Realmes as haue bene annoyed with like evills that Irelande now is and vsethe still to be, And firste in this our Realme of Englande it is manifest by reporte of the Cronicles and other ancient writers that it was greatlie infested with Robbers and outlawes which lurkinge in woodes and faste places vsed often to breake forthe into the hywaies and sometymes into smalle villages to Robb and spoile for Redresse wheareof it is written that kinge *Alured* or *Alfred* whoe then Raigned did devide the realme into shieres and the shieres into hundredes and the hundreds into Lathes or wapentackes and the wapentackes into tythinges So that Tenn Tithinges made an hvndred, And five made a Lathe or wapentacke, of which Tenn eache one was bounde for another and the eldest or beste of them whom they Called the Tithingeman or borsholder that is the eldest pledge became suertye for all the reste So that if anie one of them did starte into anye vndutifull accion the borsholder was bounde to bringe him forthe who ioyninge efte sones with all his tithinge woulde followe that lose persone thoroughe all lose places till they broughte him in/ And if all that Tithinge failed then all that Lathe was Chardged for that Tythinge and if that lathe failed then all the hun-

that *W*   4459 setlinge] settinge *R*   4459 sounde] of sound *CW*   4462 a] *om. R*
4462 in the] in *CRW*   4463 all be] be all *C*   4463 be amended,] amend, *R*   be amended. *W*
4464 now] now that *R*   4464 to] vnto *CW*   4465 that] all that *R*   4465 saie]
said *CRW*   4467 violente] vyolate *R*   4467 punishment] pvnishmentes/ *C*   punishments. *W*
4468 me semes] (me thinkes) *W*   4468-9 cane ... be] by noe meanes canbee *R*   4470 with]
with the *R*   4470 Irelande] Iland *R*   4471 our] *om. R*   4471 it] yt yt *R*   4471 the] *om. C*
4472 other] *om. W*   4472 infested] infected *R*   4473 outlawes] owlawes *R*   4473 lurkinge]
lurked *R*   4473 vsed] whence they vsed *R*   4473 often] oftentymes *R*   4475 spoile]
spoyle. *W*   4475-6 *Alfred ... Raigned*] *Aldred W*   4477 and the hundreds] *om. R*
4477 Lathes] Rapes *RAD1H2LN*   4477 or] *inserted between lines E om. CR*   4477 wapentackes and] rapentales and *H2*   Wappentages: and *Ho*   Rapentackes, and *RLD1*   4477-8 the wapentackes] Rapentales *H2*   wapentackes *R*   4478 made an] made a *CR*   make an *W*
4479 Lathe] Leighe *D1*   4481 borsholder] *Boronsholder G*   *bursoldier H1*   Burshold *H2*
Bowroughholder *LD1*   Borrougholder *R*   Borsolder *W*   4481 reste] rest. *W*   4482-3 borsholder] bowroughoulder *D1*   barsoldier *H1*   burrow holder *RLA*   Borsolder *W*   4483 him]
om. C   4484 that] the *R*   4484 all lose] all *CRW*   4485 that Tithinge] the tythinges *R*
4485 then] *om. R*   4485 that Lathe] the Tythe *RLD1*   the Lathe *G*   4486 for that]
for the *R*   4486 lathe] they *R*   4486 the] that *W*

dred was demaunded for them and if the hundred then the shiere whoe ioyninge eftsones alltogeather woulde not rest till they had founde out and deliuered in that vndewtifull fellowe which was not ameaneable to lawe And thearein it semes that that good Saxon kinge followed the Counsell of *Iethro* to *Moses*, whoe | Advised him to devide the people into hundreds and to set Captaines and wisemen of truste ouer them, which shoulde take the Chardge of them and ease him of that burthen And soe did *Romulus*, as youe maie reade, devide the Romaines into Tribes and the Tribes into Centuries or hundredes/ By this ordinaunce this kinge broughte the Realme of Englande which before was moste troblesome vnto that quiet state that no one bad persone Coulde stirr but he was straighte taken houlde of by those of his owne Tithinge and theire Borsholder whoe beinge his neighbours or nexte kinsemen weare privie to all his waies and loked narowlye into his liffe, The which institucion if it weare obserued in Irelande woulde worke that effecte which it did then in Englande and kepe all men within the Compasse of dewtie and obedience//

Eudox: This is Contrarie to that youe saide before for as I remember youe saide theare was a greate disproporcion betwene Englande and Irelande so as the lawes which weare fitting for thone woulde not fitt tother. howe Comes it then nowe that ye woulde transfer a principall institucion from Englande to Irelande/

Iren: This Lawe was made not by the *Norman* Conquerour but by a Saxon kinge at what time Englande was verie like to Irelande as it now standes. ffor it was (as I tolde youe) annoyed greatly with Robbers and outlawes which troubled the wholle state of the Realme euerie Corner havinge a

---

4487 then] theh *W*   4488 alltogeather] together *W*   4489 vndewtifull] vnlawfull *R*
4489 ameaneable] a meane able *C*   amesnable *W*   4490 thearein] herin *CRW*   4490 semes] semed *R*   4490 that that] that *R*   4491 of] of, *R*   4492 which] who *W*   4493 of them] over them *C*   4493 him] om. *W*   4494 *Romulus*] *Romilus* H2   4494 as . . . reade] (as . . . read) *W*   4495 Centuries] Centuryons *R*   4495 hundredes/] hundredes *C*   *Hundreths. W*
4495 this kinge] the king *R*   4496 the] this *RW*   4496 which . . . troublesome] (which . . . troublesome) *W*   4496-7 vnto . . . state] om. *R*   4497 that quiet] the quiete *C*
4497 he] that he *R*   4498 Borsholder] *Bursoldier H1*   burrowholder *RLD1*   4499 neighbours] neighbor *W*   4499 kinsemen] corr. of kinseman *E*   kinsman *CRW*   4499 weare] was *R*   4500 into] vnto *R*   4500 liffe,] life. *W*   4500-1 if . . . Irelande] (if . . . Ireland) *W*   4501 that] the *C*   4501 then] om. *CW*   4502 the] om. *C*   4504 youe saide] om. *R*   you said, that *W*   4504 was] was, *R*   4505 for] of *R*   4505 thone] one *W*   4505 thother.] the other *C*   the other, *R*   4506 then nowe] nowe then *CW*
4507 Irelande/] *Ireland? W*   4508 made not] not made *W*   4508 the] a *R*   4509 at] beinge at *R*   4509 it now] nowe it *CRW*   4510 (as] om. *R*   4510 youe)] yow *R*
4511 troubled] trouble *R*   4511 state of the] om. *R*   4511-2 a . . . it] in yt a Robbine

A VIEW OF THE PRESENT STATE OF IRELAND   203

Robin hoode in it that kepte the woodes and spoilled all passengers and inhabitantes as Irelande now hathe so as me semes this ordinaunce woulde fitt verye well and bringe them all into Awe/

Eudox: Then when ye haue thus tithed the Cominaltye as youe saie and set borsolders ouer them | All, what woulde yee do when ye came to the gentlemen woulde ye houlde the same Course?/

Iren: yea marrye moste speciallie for this youe muste knowe that all the Irishe allmoste boste themselues to be gentlemen no lesse then the welche for if he cane derive himselfe from the heade of anie septe as moste of them Can, (they are experte by theire bardes) then he houldethe himselfe a gentellman and thereuppon scorneth eftsones to worke or vse anie hande labour, which he saiethe is the liffe of a pesante or Churle but thence forthe becomethe either an horsboye or a Stocagh to some kerne envringe himselfe to his weapon and to his gentlemanlye trade of stealinge (as they Counte it) So that if a gentleman or anie welthie yeoman of them haue anie Children the eldest perhaps shalbe kepte in some order but all the rest shall shifte for themselues and fall to this occupacion And moreouer it is a Comon vse amongest some of theire beste gentelmens sonns that so sone as they are able to vse theire weapons they straighte gather to themselues iij or iiij stocaghes or kerne with whom wandringe a while idlie vp and downe the Countrie takinge onelye meate, he at laste fallethe into some bad accion that shalbe offered which beinge once made knowen he is thenceforthe counted a man of worthe in whom theare is Couradge whearvppon theare drawe to him manie other like lose younge men which stirringe him vp with encouragement provoke him shortlye to flatt Rebellion, And this happens not onelye in the sonns of theire gentlemen but often times allsoe of theire noble men speciallye of theire base sonns as

hood *R*   4512 the] all *R*   4513 scmes] seemeth *R*   thinkes *W*   4514 Awe/] awe *C*
one: *R*   4515 *Eudox:*] om. *H1*   4516 set] om. *R*   4516 borsolders] housholders *F*
*B*arsolders *H1*   burrowholders *RLD1*   4516 came] Come *R*   4517 gentlemen]
gentlemen, *RW*   4517 Course?/] Course/ *C*   Course: *R*   4518 speciallie] especially *W*
4519 allmoste] almost, *R*   4519 welche] *walsh H1*   Welch men *RLD1*   4520 anie] a *R*
4520 as] (as *W*   4521 (they . . . bardes)] they . . . Bardes, *CR*   they . . . Bardes) *W*
4521 are] are soe *CW*   4521 then he] and so *R*   4522 eftsones] om. *W*   4522 hande]
handy *R*   hard *WG*   4524 becomethe either] eyther becometh *R*   4524 an] om. *C*   a *R*
4524 Stocagh] *Stocagd F*   Stockughe *H2*   stocage *RLD1*   *Stocab W*   4524 envringe]
endeavoring *R*   4525 and to his] and to the *CW*   4525 gentlemanlye] generall *R*
4525-6 (as . . . it)] as . . . yt) *C om. R*   (as . . . it.) *W*   4526 that] om. *C*   4526 welthie]
worthie *R*   wealthy man *W*   4527 eldest] eldest of them *W*   4528 moreouer] om. *R*
4529 vse] *text of G ends at this point*   4529 beste] om. *W*   4530-1 to themselues]
them selues togither *C*   4531 iij or iiij] om. *R*   4531 stocaghes] *stocages D2F*
stranglers *L*   straglers *RAH2NW*   Storaghes *T*   4531 kerne] kearnes *R*   4531-2 idlie
. . . downe] up and downe idlely *W*   4531 idlie] ydle *C*   4532 takinge] taketh *C*
4532 into] unto *W*   4533 accion] *corr. of* occacicn *E*   occasion *CRW*   4537 in]
sometimes in *W*   4537 theire gentlemen] gentlemen *R*   4538 often times] om. *W*
4538 allsoe of] by *R*   4538 speciallye of] speciallye *R*   4538 theire base] them who
have base *W*   4538 base] base borne *R*

theare are fewe without some of them, ffor they are not ashamed onelye to acknowledge them but allsoe boaste of them and vse them to suche secrete services as they them selues will not be sene in, as to plague theire enemys to spoile theire neighbours, to oppresse and Crushe some of their owne too stuborne freholders which are not tractable to theire bad wills. Twoe suche | Bastardes of the L. *Roches* there are now out in mounster whom he doethe not onelye Countenance but allso priuilye maynteigne and relieue nightelye amongest his Tenantes., suche another is theare of the Earle of *Clancares* in desmounde and manye other in manye other places/

Eudox: Then it semes that this ordinance of Tythinge them by the polle is not onelye fitt for the gentlemen but allsoe for the noblemen whom I woulde haue thoughte to haue bene of soe honorable mindes, as that they shoulde not nede suche a base kinde of beinge bounde to theire Alleagiaunce who shoulde rather haue helde in and staied all others from vndewtifullnes then nede to be forced thearevnto themselues/

Iren: yeat so it is *Eudox*: But yeat because the noblemen Cannot be tythed theare beinge not manye Tithinges of them and allsoe because a Borsholder ouer them shoulde be not onely a great indignitye, but also a daunger to ad more power to them then they haue, or to make one the Comaunder of Tenn, I houlde it mete that theare weare onelye suerties taken of them and one bounde for another wheareby if anye shall swarue, his suerties shall for sauegarde of their bondes either bringe him in or seke to serue vppon him, and besides this I woulde wishe them all to be sworne to her maiestie which they neuer yeat weare but at the firste creacion: and that oathe woulde sure Containe them greatlie or the breache of it bringe them to shorter vengeaunce, for God vsethe to punishe periurie sharpelye. So I reade in the Raigne of Edwarde the seconde and allso of

A VIEW OF THE PRESENT STATE OF IRELAND 205

Henrie the vijth when the tymes weare verie broken that theare was a Corporate oathe taken of all the Lordes and best gentlemen of ffealtye to the kinge which now is no lesse nedefull because manye of them are suspected to haue taken another oathe priuilye to some bad purposes, and theare vppon to haue receaued the Sacrament and bene sworne to a priste which they thinke bindethe them more then theire Allegiaunce to theire prince or loue of theire | Countrye/

Eudox: This Tithinge of the Comon people and takinge suerties of Lordes and gentlemen I like verie well but that it wilbe vearye troblesome. shoulde it not be aswell for to haue them all booked and the Lordes and gentlemen to take all the meaner sorte vppon themselues for they are best able to bringe them in whensoeuer anye of them startethe out/

Iren: This indede *Eudox*: hathe bene hitherto and yeat is a Comon order amongest them to haue all the people booked by the Lordes and gentlemen, but it is the worste order that euer was deuised for by this bookinge of men all the inferiour sorte are broughte vnder the Comaunde of theire Lordes and forced to followe them into anie accion whatsoeuer, Now this ye are to vnderstande that all the Rebellions which youe see from time to tyme happen in Irelande are not begone by the Comon people but by the Lordes and Captaines of Countries vppon pride or willfull obstynacie againste the gouernement which whensoeuer they will enter into they drawe with them all theire people and followers which thinke themselues bound to goe with them because they haue booked them and vndertaken for them And this is the reasone that in Englande ye haue fewe suche bad occacions by reasone that the Noblemen how euer they shoulde happen to be ill disposed haue no Comaund at all ouer the Cominaltye thoughe dwellinge vnder them because euerye mann standethe vppon himselfe and buildeth his fortunes vppon his owne faithe and firme Assuraunce The which this manner of Tythinge the polls will worke allsoe in Irelande. ffor by this the people are broken into manie smalle partes like little streames that they Cannot easelye come togeather into one heade which is the principall

4567 vijth] vij *R*   4567-8 Corporate] corporall *W*   4568 taken] taken in the raignes of *Edward the Second*, and of *Henry the Seventh*, (when the times were very broken) *W*   4569 kinge] Kings *W*   4570 purposes] purpose *R*   4571 to haue] they haue *R*   4571 bene] beinge *R*   4572 they] the *C*   4574 of the] to the *W*   4575 troblesome.] troblesome *C* troblesome, *R* troblesome; *W*   4576 for] *om. R*   4577 the] *om. R*   4578 startethe] started *R*   4579 *Eudox*:] (*Eudoxus*) *W*   4581 it is] yet *W*   4583 whatsoeuer,] whatsoever. *W*   4587 againste the gouernement] *om. R*   4588 and] and such *R*   4590 in . . . occacions] yow haue fewe such badd occasions here in England *R*   4591 ill] evill *RW*   4593 because] because that *W*   4596 into] into/ *C*

regarde that is to be had in Irelande to kepe them from growinge into suche a heade and adhearinge vnto greate men/

Eudox: But yeat I Cannot well se how this cane be broughte aboute without doinge greate wronge vnto the | Noblemen theare for at the firste Conquest of that Realme those great Seigniories and Lordeshipps weare given them by the kinge that they shoulde be the stronger againste the Irishe by the multitude of followers and Tennantes vnder them All which hould theire Tenementes of them by fealtye and suche services wheareby they are by the firste graunte of the kinge made bounden vnto them and tied to rise out with them into all occacions of service And this I haue often harde that when the Lord deputie hathe raised anie generall hostinges the noblemen haue Claimed the leadinge of them by graunte from the kinges of Englande vnder the greate Seale exhibited so as the deputye coulde not refuse them to haue the leadinge of them or if they did they woulde so worke as none of theire followers should rise forthe to the hostinge/

Iren: yea saie verye trewe but will youe se the fruite of those grauntes, I haue knowen when those Lordes haue had the leadinge of theire owne followers vnder them to the generall hostinge that they haue for the same set vppon euerie plowlande within theire Countrie xls or more wheareby some of them haue gathered aboue vij or viij C poundes and others muche more into theire purse in lieu wheareof they haue gathered vnto themselues a number of lose kernes out of all partes which they haue Caryed forthe with them to whom they neuer gaue pennye of entertainement allowed by the Countrye or forced by them but let them fede vppon the Countries and extorte vppon all men where they Came. for thes people will neuer aske better entertainement then to haue a Collour of service or employment given them by which they will poll and spoile so outragiouslye as the verye enemye Cannot doe muche worse and they allsoe somtimes turne to the enemye/

Eudox: It semes the firste intente of those grauntes was againste the Irishe which now some of them vse againste the Quene herselfe But now what

4598 them] him *R*   4598 into] vnto *CW*   4600 well] *om. CW*   4600 broughte aboute] well wrought *C*   well brought *W*   4602 firste] *om. R*   4602 that] the *R*   4604 multitude] multitudes *W*   4605 of them] *om. C*   4606 by the ... kinge] (by ... King) *W*   4606 bounden] bound *R*   4607 into] vpon *R*   4608 deputie hathe] haue *R*   4609 hostinges] Ostinges *R*   4611 deputye] *Deputies W*   4611 coulde] *corr. of* woulde *E*   would *CR*   4611 they] he *R*   4613 hostinge] Ostings *R*   hostage *W*   4614 the] *om. R*   4614 those] these *R*   4616 hostinge] Osting *R*   hostings *W*   4617 set] cutt *CRW*   4617 within theire Countrie] *om. R*   4620 kernes] kerne *RW*   4621 gaue] gave any *W*   4622 but let them] *om. C*   4623 and] *om. R*   4623 Came] can *R*   come *W*   4623 thes] that *CRW*   4623 neuer] neve *C*   4625 as] that as *R*   4626 they ... turne] besydes turne them selues *R*   4626 somtimes] sometyme *C*   4629 againste] ageinst *with last*

remedye is theare for this or how Cane those grauntes of the kinges be 4630
avoided without wronginge of those Lordes which had those landes and
Lordeshipps given them/

Iren: Surelye they maie be well enoughe for moste of those Lordes since
theire firste grauntes from the kinges by whome those landes weare given
them, haue sithens bestowed the moste parte of them amongeste their kins- 4635
f. 84ᵛ folkes | As euerie Lorde perhaps in his time hathe given one or another
of his principall Castles to his yonger sonne and other to others as lardgely
and amplie as they weare given vnto him And others they haue soulde and
others boughte which weare not in theire firste graunte which now neuer-
theles they bringe within the Compasse thereof and take and exacte vppon 4640
them as theire firste demaynes all those kinde of services, yea and the verye
wilde exaccions as *Coyne* and *Liuerie* for him and suche like, by which the
pole and vtterlie vndoe the pore Tennantes and freholders vnder them.
who either thoroughe ignoraunce knowe not theire Tenures, or thoroughe
greatenes of theire new Lords dare not Challendge them: yea and some 4645
Lordes of contries allsoe, as greate ones as themselues, are now by stronge
hande broughte vnder them and made theire vassals, as for example,
Arvndell of the Stronde in the Countye of Corke whoe was ancientlye a
greate Lord and hable to spende iiijᵐ and vᶜⁱⁱ by the yeare as appearethe
by good recordes is nowe become the L *Barryes* man and doeth to him all 4650
those services which are dewe vnto her maiestie. for reformation of all
which I wishe that theare weare a Comission graunted forthe vnder the
greate Seale (as I haue sene one recorded in the olde Councell boke in
mounster it was sente forthe in the time of Sʳ wm Drewrye) vnto persons
of speciall truste and iudgement to enquire thoroughe out all Irelande 4655
(beginninge with one Countye firste and so restinge a while till the same

letter worn off C   4630 this] this? *W*   4630 those] these *R*   4634 whome] which *C*
4635 amongeste] emonste *R*   4635-6 kinsfolkes] kinsfolke *CW*   4636 in . . . given]
hath given in his time *W*   4636 or] *om. W*   4636-7 another of] other *C*   4637 sonne]
sonnes *R*   4638 amplie] as amplie *RW*   4638 vnto] to *RW*   4639 boughte] they
have bought *W*   4639 graunte] grantes *R*   4641 as] as vppon *CW*   4641 all]
of all *R*   4642 wilde] vylde Irishe *C*   wilde Irish *R*   4642 as] *om. W*   4642 Coyne]
Coigny *CW*   Cognie *R*   4642 and *Liuerie*] liuery *CW*   4642 for him] Forehin *C*   Torehin *P*
Sorebon *W*   4642 the] they *CRW*   4643 them.] them *CR*   them, *W*   4644 who]
which *CRW*   4644 knowe] knewe *R*   4644 Tenures] tennors *R*   4646 allsoe] *om. C*
4646 ones] once *C*   4647 vassals,] Vassalls. *W*   4648 Stronde] *Strowd H2A*   Stroud *N*
strand *RLD1*   Stromb *T*   4648 Corke] *Yorke H1*   4649 Lord and] Lord and and *R*
4649 hable] was able *W*   4649 iiijᵐ and vᶜ] iiiᵢ vᶜ *C*   3500 *RAD1D2FH1H2HoLNPTW*
4650 *Barryes*] Burrghs *D2*   Boroughs *F*   Bains *H2*   4651 maiestie.] maiestie *C*   maiestie, *R*
4651 all] *om. R*   4652 I wishe] *om. R*   4652 forthe] forthe in the olde Councell
with last four words underlined *P*   4653-4 (as . . . Drewrye)] as . . . Drewrie *RW*
4653-4 in mounster] of mounster *C*   in mounster, *R*   of *Mounster, W*   4654 it] that *CW*
4655 thoroughe out] throught *C*   4656 (beginninge] begynninge *RW*   4656 with] in *R*
4656 till] vntill *R*

weare setled by the verdicte of a sounde and substanciall Iurye how euerye
man houldethe his landes of whom and by what tenure so that euerie one
shoulde be admitted to shewe and exhibite what Righte he hathe and by
what services he houldethe his lande wheather in Chiefe or in Socage or
in knightes service or how els soeuer. thearevppon woulde appeare firste
how all those greate Englishe Lordes do Claime those greate services
what seigniories they vsurpe what wardeshipps they take from the Quene
what Landes of hers they Conceale and then howe those Irishe Captaines
of Countries haue encroched vppon | the Quenes freholders and Ten-
nantes how they haue translated the Tenures of them from Englishe hould-
inge vnto Irishe *Tanistrye* And defeated her maiestie of all her rightes
and dewties which are to accrewe to her thereout as wardships, liueries,
mariadges, fines of alienacions and maye other Comodities which now are
kepte and concealed from her maiestie to the valewe of lxm li by the yeare
I dare vndertake in all Irelande by that which I know in one Countye/

Eudox: This *Iren*: woulde seme a dangerous Comission and readye to
stir vp all the Irishe into Rebellion who knowinge that they haue nothing
to shewe for all these Landes which they houlde but theire swordes woulde
rather drawe them then suffer theire Landes to be thus drawne awaie from
them/

Iren Neither shoulde theire Landes be taken awaie from them nor the
vttermoste Advantages enforced againste them but this by discreacion of
the Comissioners should be made knowen vnto them that it is not her
maiestes meaninge to vse anie suche extremitye but onelye to reduce
thinges into order of Englishe lawe and make them houlde theire Landes
of her and restore to her her dewe services which they detaine out of all
those landes which weare ancientlye helde of her And that they shoulde
not onelye not be thruste out but allsoe haue estates and grauntes of theire

---

4657 setled] setled) *C*   4657 a] *om. R*   4658 landes] land *CW*   4658 tenure]
tennor *R*   4660 lande] landes *C*   4660 Chiefe or] Cheif *R*   4661 in knightes]
by knightes *CW*   in Knight *R*   4661 how els soeuer.] els soeuer, *C*   ells whatsoeuer *R*
4662 Englishe] *Irishe N*   4664 Conceale] concealed *R*   4665 of Countries] *om. R*
4666 Tenures] tennors *R*   4667 vnto] into *R*   4667 *Tanistrye*] Tanissa *D1*   *Tymistie H2*
4668 to her] vnto her *C*   4668 thereout] thereabout *R*   4669 fines] and fynes *R*
4669 and maye] and manie *CW*   with many *R*   4670 of] of, *R*   4670 lxm] fortie
Thowsand *CPTW*   4670 by the yeare] yerely *CR*   *per annum W*   4671 vndertake]
followed by blank space and second vndertake *C*   4673 into Rebellion] *om. R*   in Rebellion *W*
4674 these] those *CRW*   4674 swordes] swordes. *C*   4674 woulde] would, *R*   4675 theire]
the *W*   4675 thus] this *C*   4677 awaie] *om. C*   4678 vttermoste] utmost *W*   4678 by]
by the *R*   4682 of her] of her maiestie *R*   4682 restore] to restore *W*   4682 out]
not *R*   4682 all] *om. CRW*   4683 helde] holden *R*   4683 her] her. *W*   4684 not be]
be *CR*   4684 grauntes] graunte *C*

A VIEW OF THE PRESENT STATE OF IRELAND

landes now made to them from her maiestie so as they shoulde thence forthe holde them rightefullye which they now vsurpe moste wrongefully and yeat withall I would wishe that in all those Irishe Countries theare weare some lande reserued to her maiesties free disposicion for the better Contayninge of the reste and entermedlinge them with englishe inhabitantes and Customes that knowledge mighte still be had by them for all theire doinges so as no manner of practise or conspiracye shoulde be in hande amongeste them but notice shoulde be geven thereof by one meanes or other and theire practizes prevented/

Eudox: Trewlye neither Cane the Irishe nor yeat the Englishe Lordes think themselues wronged | nor hardlye dealte withall hearein to haue that which is indede none of theire owne at all but her maiesties absolutely given to them with suche equall Condicions as that bothe they maie be assured thereof better then they are and also her maiestie not defrauded of her righte vtterlye. for it is greate grace in a prince to take that with Condicions which is absolutelye her owne. thus shall the Irishe be well satisfied, and as for the greate men which had suche grauntes made them at first by the Kinges of Englande it was in regarde that they shoulde kepe out the Irishe and defende the kinges righte and his subiectes./ But now seinge that in steade of defendinge them they Robb and spoile them and in steade of kepinge out the Irishe they doe not onelye make the Irishe theire Tennantes in those Landes and thruste out the englishe, but allso they themselues become meere Irishe with marryinge with them fosteringe with them, and Combyninge with them againste the Quene what reasone but that those grauntes and priuiledges shoulde be either reuoked or at leaste reduced to the firste intencion for which they weare graunted for sure in mine opinion they are more sharpelye to be chasticed and reformed then the rude Irishe whiche beinge verie wilde at the firste are now become somwhat more Civill when as these from Civillitye are growne to be wilde and mere Irishe/

4685 now] new W   4686 rightefullye] Rightfullie) C   4686 moste] *om*. W   4688 free] owne free C   4689 entermedlinge] intermingling W   4690 by] of W   4690 for] of R and of W   4691 in] had in W   4693 other] another RW   4694 Irishe] English A   4694 yeat the] *om*. R   4694 Englishe] Irish A   4695 nor] or R   4696 which is indede] indeed which is R   4697 to] vnto R   4699 righte] rightly W   4699 greate] a greate RW   4699 in] with R   4699 to] *om*. R   4700 owne.] owne, CR   4701 grauntes] graunt CR   4701 them] to them W   4702 it] *om*. R   4702 that] *om*. R   4703 out] forth W   4707 they] some of W   4707 them fosteringe] them, with fosteringe W   4708 Combyninge] companiinge R   4708 what] but what R   4708 reasone] reason is there W   4709 that] *om*. R   4709 priuiledges] procedinges R   4709 or] or or R   4710 the] theire R   4711 sure] surelye R   4711 mine] my R   4711 are] were R   4712 at . . . are] is R   4713 somwhat] *om*. W   4713 these]

Iren: In dede as youe saie *Eudox*: these doe nede a sharper reformacion then the Irishe for they are muche more stubborne and disobedient to lawe and governement then the Irishe be, and more malicous againste the Englishe that dailye are sente ouer/

Eudox: Is it possible I praye youe howe Comes it to passe and what maie be the reason theareof?/

Iren: marye they saie that the lande is theires onely by righte beinge firste Conquered by theire ancestours and that they are wronged by the new Inglishemens intrudinge thearevnto, whom they Call *Sassonas* that is Englishe with as greate reproche as they woulde rate a | A dogge. And for that some of theire Auncestours weare in times paste when they weare Civill and vncorrupted deputies and Iustices of the lande, they thinke that the like aucthoritye shoulde be Comitted vnto them and the Chardge of the Realme leafte in theire hande, which for that they see now otherwise disposed and that truste not given them which theire Ancestours had they thinke themselues greatelye indignifyed and disgraced and thearby growe bothe discontente and vndewtifull/

Eudox. In truethe *Iren*: This is more then euer I harde that the englishe Irishe theare shoulde be worse then the wilde Irishe. Lorde how quicklye dothe that country alter mens natures It is not for nothinge I perceaue which I haue harde that the Councell of Englande thinke it no good policye to haue that Realme reformed or planted with englishe leaste they shoulde growe as vndewtifull as the Irishe and become muche more dangerous As appearethe by thensample of the *Lacies* in the time of *Edwarde* the seconde which ye spake of that shoke of theire Allegiaunce to theire naturall Prince and turned to the Scott devisinge to make him kinge of Irelande/

Iren Noe times haue bene without bad men But as for that purpose of

---

Englishe R   4715 saie] said C   4715 sharper] sharpe R   4716 Irishe] verie Irish CR
4716 muche] *om*. W   4716-7 and ... governement] *om*. C   4717-31 be, ... vndewtifull/] be. W   4717 againste] *om*. R   4719 Is] It R   4719 it to] that to C   4719 and] *om*. R
4719 maie] might R   4720 theareof?/] therof./. C   4721 thereof, R   4721 by] *om*. R
4722 ancestours] ancytors R   4723 intrudinge] entring R   4723 thearevnto] therinto C
4723 *Sassonas*] Alloonagh A   Sassona CD2FHoN   La: *sassona* RLD1   Sascona H1   4723 is] is in R   4724 a A] a CR   4725 for] *om*. R   4725 Auncestours] ancyetors R   4725 when] where R   4728 hande] handes R   4729 Ancestours] ancyetors R   4730 and thearby] thereby, and so R   4731 bothe] *om*. C   4731 discontente] discontented R   4732 *Eudox*.] W *resumes at this point*   4732-3 the englishe Irishe] the Englishe P   any *English* W
4733 theare] there, W   4733 wilde] *om*. W   4733 Irishe.] Irishe, CR   4734 dothe] doe C   4734 natures] natures, CR   natures? W   4734 I perceaue] (I perceive) W
4735 which] that R   4735 that] *om*. R   4737 growe as] growe so RW   4738 thensample] the ensamples W   4738 of the] of R   4738 *Edwarde*] K. *Edw*: F   4739 Allegiaunce] religion R   4740 and ... Scott] *om*. R   4740 the Scott devisinge] *Edward le Bruce* W
4740 Irelande] England D2F

A VIEW OF THE PRESENT STATE OF IRELAND 211

the Cownsell of Englande which ye spake that they shoulde kepe that
Realme from reformacion I thinke they are moste lewdelie abused for their
greate Carefullnes and erneste endevours do wittnes the Contrarye Neither
is it the nature of the Countrye to alter mens manners, but the bad mindes
of the man, whoe havinge bene broughte vp at home vnder a streighte rule
of dutie and obedience beinge allwaies restrained by sharpe penalties from
lewde behauiour, so sone as they Come thither wheare they see lawes
more slacklye tended and the harde Constrainte which they weare vsed
vnto now slacked, they growe more lose and Careles of theire duetie and
as it is the nature of all men to loue libertye So they become Libertines
f. 86ᵛ and fall to all Licentiousnes | of the Irishe, more boldlie daringe to disobaie the lawe thoroughe presumpcion of favour and freindeshippe then
anye Irishe dareth/

Eudox: then if that be soe me thinkes your late advizment was verie evill
whereby youe wished the Irishe to be sowed and sprincked with englishe
and in all the Irishe contries to haue Englishe planted amongest them for
to bringe to Englishe fashions, since the Englishe sonner drawe to the Irishe
then the Irishe to the Englishe. for as youe saide before they muste rvn
with the Streames the greater nomber will Carrye awaie the lesse, therefore me semes by this reason it shoulde be better to parte the Irishe and
Englishe then to mingle them togeather/

Iren: Not soe *Eudox*: but wheare theare is no good staie of gouernement
and stronge ordinaunces to houlde them theare indede the fewer will followe the more: but wheare theare is due order of discipline and good rule
there the better shall goe formoste and the worste shall followe. And
therefore now since Irelande is full of her owne nacion that maye not be
roted out and somwhat stored with Englishe allreadye and more to be,
I thinke it best by an vnion of manners and Conformitye of mindes to
bringe them to be one people, and to put awaie the dislikefull Conceite

---

4742 spake that] spake of that *CW*   speake, *R*   4742-3 that Realme] the realme *R*
4744 endevours] endeauor *R*   4744 wittnes] testifie *C*   4745 it] *om. R*   4745 mens]
a mans *R*   4746 the man] men *CW*   them *R*   4746 whoe] whom *R*   4748 as they]
as the *R*   4748 lawes] lawe *R*   4749 more] so *R*   4749 Constrainte] restraintes
C om. R   restraint *W*   4749 weare] are *C*   4750 duetie and] duetie, *R*   4751 become]
become flatt *CRW*   4752 all] flatt *R*   4752 of the Irishe] *om. RW*   4753 presumpcion] the presumption *W*   4754 dareth] dare *R*   4755 that] yt *R*   4755 me
thinkes] (me thinkes) *W*   4756 sprincked] sprinckled *CRW*   4756-7 englishe and]
the English *R*   4758 bringe] bringe them *CRW*   4758 sonner drawe] bee soner drawen *R*
4759 youe] I *R*   4759 they] if they *W*   4759 muste] much *R*   4760 Streames]
streame *CRW*   4760 nomber] *om. R*   4760 lesse,] lesse: *W*   4761 me semes]
(me thinkes) *W*   4761 and] then the *R*   4762 to] *om. R*   4763 Not soe *Eudox*:] *om. C*
4766 worste] wourse *C*   4767 now] *om. R*   4767 maye not] ought not to *W*   4770 them]
om. C   4770 Conceite] Conceipt *CW*   concepte *R*

bothe of thone and thother which wilbe by no meanes better then by there
enterminglinge of them, that neither all the Irishe maye dwell togeather,
nor all the Englishe, but by translatinge of them and scatteringe them in
smalle nombers amonge the Englishe, not onely to bringe them by dailye
Conuersacion vnto better likinge of eache other but allsoe to make bothe
of them lesse hable to hurte. And therefore when I Come to the Tithinge
of them, I will tithe them one with another, And for the moste parte will
make an Irishe man the Tithingeman, whereby he shall take the lesse
excepcion to parciallitye and yeat be the more tyed theareby. But when I
come to the head burroughe which is the heade of the Lathe him will
I make an Englishe man or Irisheman of speciall assurance as also when I
come to appointe the Aldermen that is the heade of the hundred him will I
surelye Chuse an | Englisheman of speciall regarde that maie be a staie
and pillowe of all the Burroughe vnder him/

Eudox: what do youe meane by your hundred and what by your Burroughe
by that which I haue red in ancient recordes of Englande, an hundred did
Containe an hundred villages or as some saie an hundred plowlandes
beinge the same whiche the Saxons called a Cantred The which Cantred as
I finde it recorded in the blacke boke of Irelande did Containe xxx *Villatas,
terre* which some call quarters of lande and euerie *Villata* Cann mayntaine
CCCC Cowes in pasture and the iiijC kowes to be devided in foure heardes
so as none of them shall Come neare other euerie *villata* Contayninge xviij
plowlandes as is theare set downe. and by that which I haue rede of a
Burroughe it signifyethe a free Towne which had a principall officer
called a headburoughe to become ruler and vndertake for all the dwellers
vnder him havinge for the same franchises and priviledges graunted

---

4771 there] thus *C*   this *RW*   4772 that] For *W*   4773-4 in smalle nombers] *om. W*
4774 amonge] amongst *CRW*   4777 of them] *om. R*   4778 an] and *C*   the *R*   4779 to] of *C*
4780 come] come, *R*   4780 burroughe] burgh *C*   4780 heade of the] *om. C*   4781 or] or an *W*
4781 speciall] noe small *R*   4782 Aldermen] Elderman *R*   *Alderman W*   4782 of the]
of that *C*   4782 hundred] Hundreth *W*   4783 Chuse] choose to be *W*   4783 Englisheman]
yrishman *H1*   4784 pillowe] pilloe *or* pillre *C*   pillour *H1H2N*   piller *RAD1D2FHoLW*
4784 Burroughe] Burroughes *R*   4785 Burroughe] Burrough, *R*   Borough? *W*   4786 which]
that *W*   4787 hundred villages] hundreth villages *W*   4788 Saxons] Saxons, *R*   4788 a]
om. W   4788 The] The The *R*   4789 it] *om. CR*   4789 boke] booke booke *C*
4789 Irelande] *preceded by the words " the Exchequer of " in brackets W*   4789-90 *Villatas,
terre*] villatasterre *C*   4789 *Villatas,*] villates *F*   villata *H2*   villatas *RW*   4790 *terre*]
terrae WD2FP   4790 mayntaine] conteyne *C*   4791 the] *om. C*   4791 heardes]
heades *R*   4792 other] another, *R*   4792 Contayninge] contayneth *R*   4792 xviij]
tenne *F*   17 *RD1H2LN*   4793 is] it is *C*   4794 had] haddeth *C*   4795 a] an *R*
4795 headburoughe] headburghe *C*   4795 all] all, *R*   4796 same] same same *R*

A VIEW OF THE PRESENT STATE OF IRELAND

them by the kinge wheareof it was Called a freburoughe of the Lawyer *Franciplegium*/

Iren: Bothe that which youe saide *Eudox*: is trewe and yet that which I saie not vntrewe for that which ye speake of devidinge the Countrye into hundredes was a divicion of the Landes of the Realme but this which I tell was of the people who weare thus devided by the poll so that a hundred in this sence signifyethe C pledges which weare vnder the Comaund and assurance of theire Allderman The which as I suppose was allsoe Called a wapentacke so named of touching the weopon or speare of their Aldermen, and swearing to followe him faithefullie and serue theire prince trewly But others thinke that a wapentacke was x hundredes or Burroughes, Likewise a burroughe is as I heare vse it and as the olde lawes still vsed it, is not a Burroughe Towne as they now Call it That is a ffranchise Towne but a main pledge of C free persons therefore Called a freburroughe or (as youe saie) *Franciplegium* for bothe in old *Saxon* signifyethe a pledge or suertye and yeat is so vsed with vs in some speches, as *Chaucer* saithe St Iohn to borrowe that is for assurance and warrantye/

Eudox I Conceaue the difference but now that youe haue thus devided the people into these Tithinges and hundredes how will ye haue them so preserued and Continewed, for people do often Chaunge theire dwellinges and some muste die whilste other some doe growe vp into strengthe and yeares and becom men/

Iren: These hundredes I woulde wishe to assemble themselues once euerie yeare with theire pledges and to presente themselues before the iustices of the peace which shalbe thearevnto appointed to be survaied and numbred to see what Change hathe happened since the yeare before and the defectes

---

4797 freburoughe] freeburghe *C* 4797 of] and of *W* 4797 Lawyer] Layers *C* Lawyers *W* 4798 *Franciplegium*] *Franciplegia* H1 *franciplegin* T 4799 saide] saie *C* 4800 speake] spake *W* 4801 of the Landes] of of the Landes *C* 4802 who] which *W* 4802 a] an *R om. W* 4802 hundred] hundreth *W* 4803 signifyethe] signifieth, *R* 4803 C] a 100. *W* 4804 Allderman] Aldermen *R* 4804 as I suppose] (as I suppose) *W* 4805 wapentacke] weopontacke *R* 4805 weopon] wapon *R* 4805 speare] sparke *R* 4805-6 Aldermen] alderman *CRW* 4807 others] others, *R* 4807 wapentacke] weopontacke *R* 4807 x hundredes] 100 *F* 10000ˢ *L* 4807-8 Burroughes,] Boroughes *C* boroghs: *W* 4808 is] *om. CRW* 4809 vsed it] use *W* 4810 ffranchise] franchist *R* franchised *W* 4810 C] a *CC* 4811 freburroughe] freeburghe *C* 4811 saie)] saye *R* 4811 *Franciplegium*] *Francisligni* H2 *franciplegin* T 4811 bothe] Borghe Ho Borth *RAD2FH2N* Borh *WH1PT* 4812 and] and yt *R* 4812 with vs] *om. R* 4813 as *Chaucer* saithe] (as *Chaucer* saith) *W* 4813 borrowe] *Borroccghe* D2 *Burrowe* H1Ho Barrow *R* Borroh *W* 4815 hundredes] Hundreths *W* 4816 do] *om. C* 4816-7 often ...doe] *om. R* 4816 dwellinges] dwelling places *W* 4817 doe] must *C* 4817 strengthe] strengthe into Strengthe *C* 4817-8 and yeares] of yeirs *CRW* 4818 becom] become// *C* and become *R* 4818 men/] men *R* 4819 wishe] *om. R* 4821 the] *om. C* 4822 defectes]

to supplie of those yonge plantes late growen vp, the which are dilligentlye to be ouerloked and viewed of what Condicion and demeanure they be so as pledges maie be taken for them, and they put into order of some tythinge, of all which alteracions notes is to be taken and bokes made thereof accordinglye/ 4825

Eudox: now me thinkes *Iren*: ye are to be warned to take heade leaste vnawares youe fall into that in Convenience which ye formerly founde fault with in others namely that by this bokinge of them youe do not gather them into a new heade and havinge broken theire former strengthe do not againe vnite them more stronglye. for euerie Allderman hivinge all this freepledges of his hundred vnder his comaund maye me thinkes if he be ill disposed drawe all his Companye into anie evill accion. And likewise by this assemblinge of them once a yeare vnto theire Alderman by theire wapentackes take hede leaste ye allso giue them occacion and meanes to practize together in Conspiracye/ 4830 4835

Iren: neither of bothe is to be doubted for theire Aldermen and head-
f. 88ʳ boroughes will not be suche men | of power and Countenaunce of them-
selues beinge to be Chosen thearevnto, as nede to be feared., neither if he weare is his hundred at his Comaunde further then his princesse service. and allsoe euerie Tithingeman maie Controll him in suche a Case. and as for the assemblinge of the hundred neither is anie daunger thereof to be doubted, seinge it is to be before a Iustice of peace or some highe constable to be thearevnto appointed So as of these Tithinges theare Cane no perill ensue but a certaine assurance of peace and greate good, for they are theareby withdrawne from theire Lordes and subiected to the prince. moreouer for the better breakinge of these heades and septes which I toulde youe was one of the greatest strengthes of the Irishe me thinkes it shoulde be verye well to renve that olde statute which was made in the Raigne of   in Englande, by 4840 4845 4850

defecte *C* defectes, and *R*   4823 those] *om. W*   4823 the] *om. R*   4825 order of some] some ordre of *C*   4826 notes] note *CR* notisse *PT*   4828 me thinkes] (me thinkes) *W*   4828 heade] heede *CW* good head *R*   4829 that] the *R*   4829 in Con-venience] inconveniencies *R*   4832 againe . . . stronglye] vnite them more strongly againe *W*   4832 hivinge] havinge *CRW*   4833 this] his *CR* these *W*   4833 me thinkes] (me thinkes) *W*   4834 ill] evill *W*   4834 anie] an *CW*   4835 vnto] vnto Vnto *R*   4835 Alderman] Ealdermen *C*   4836 wapentackes] weapontackes *R*   4836 hede] head *R*   4837 together] *om. C*   any harme *R*   4837 in] in anie *CRW*   4837 Conspiracye] conspiracyes *W*   4838 theire] the *R*   4838 Aldermen] Ealdermene *C* Elderman *R*   4838-9 headboroughes] headburghes *C*   4840 if] of *C*   4841 princesse] Princes *CRW*   4843 neither] *corr. of* muche *E* muche lesse *CRW*   4844 to be] *om. RW*   4844 a] some *W*   4845 these] those *R*   4847 the] theire *R*   4847 prince.] Prince, *CR*   4848 better] *om. R*   4848-9 I toulde youe] (I tould you) *W*   4850 be] doe *R*   4850 which] that *R*   4851 Raigne] Realme *A*   4851 blank space] *om. A* Edward the fourth *WP*   4851 Englande] *Ireland W*

A VIEW OF THE PRESENT STATE OF IRELAND 215

which it was Comaunded that wheareas all men then vsed to be Called by the name of theire septes accordinge to theire seuerall nacions, and had no surnames at all, that from thenceforthe eache one shoulde take vnto him selfe a seuerall surname ether of his trade and facultye or of some qualitye of his bodie or minde, or of the place wheare he dwelte, so as euerie one should be distinguished from thother, or from the moste parte, wherby they shall not onelye not depende vppon the heade of theire septe as now they doe but allso shall in shorte time learne quite to forgett his Irishe nacion. And hearewithall woulde I allsoe wishe all the Oes and the mackes which the heades of the septes haue taken to theire names to be vtterlye forbidden and extinguished for that the same beinge an ordinaunce as some saie firste made by Obrien for the strenghteninge of the Irishe the Abrogatinge thereof will as muche enfeable them/

Eudox: I like this ordinaunce verye well but now that ye haue thus devided and distingushed them what other order will ye take for theire manner of lief for all this thoughe perhaps it maie kepe them from disobedience and disloyaltye yeat will it not bringe them from theire Barbarisme and salvage life/

Iren the next that I will doe shalbe to appointe to euerie one that is not able to liue of his frehoulde a | Certaine trade of life to which he shall finde himself fittest and shalbe thoughte ableste, the which trade he shalbe bounde to followe and liue onely thearevppon. All trades therefore it is to be vnderstode to be of three kindes manvall, intellectuall and mixed, Thone Contayninge all suche as nede the exercise of bodely labour to the performance of theire profession, thother Consistinge onelye of the exercise of witt but dependinge moste of industrye and Carefullnes, Of the firste

4852 that] that that *C*   4852 then] that *R*   4853 to theire] to the *W*   4854 one] surname *C*   4854 vnto] upon *W*   4855 and] or *R*   4857 thother] other *CR*   4858 not depende] depende *C*   4859 shall in shorte] in *W*   4859 his] this *R*   4860 wishe] wishe, *R*   4860 Oes] Oed *F* Othes *RLD1* Les *T*   4861 mackes] *Maccu F* markes *RLD1*   4861 of the] of *CRW*   4861 taken] om. *C*   4862-3 ordinaunce] old manner *R*   4863 as some saie] (as some sayth) *R* (as some say) *W*   4863 Obrien] Obrine *F*   Obrin *RLD1*   Obrian *HoT*   4863 strenghteninge] strengthninge *CRW*   4864 them/] them *R*   4867-9 lief ... life/] life? *W*   4867 it] om. *C*   4867 them] him *C*   4869 life/] lyfe *R*   4873 thearevppon.] thervppon, *CR*   4873 it] om. *CRW*   4873 is] are *W*   4874 three] the *C*   4874-5 mixed, Thone] *mixed.* The first *W*   4875 nede the] needeth *W*   4876 profession, thother] profession. The second *W*   4876 onelye] only/ *C*   4877 witt] witt and reason, the third partly of bodelye labour and partly of witt *A* witt and reason The third sorte of bodilie labor and parte of the witt *C*   witt and reason: And the third partly of bodylie labour and partly of the witt *Ho*   wytt, and reason: the thirde, parte of bodelye labour, and parte of witt: *PD1FL*   witt and reason, the thirde parte of bodelye labour and parte of the wytt, *RD2H1H2N*   wit and reason. The third sort, part of bodily labor, and part of the wit, *W*   4877 moste] om. *R*   4877 Carefullnes,] Care-

sorte to be all handicraftes and husbandrye labor. Of the seconde be all sciences and those which are Called liberall artes Of the Thirde is marchandize and Chafferye that is buyinge and sellinge. And without all these three theare is no Comon wealthe cane allmoste Consiste or at the leaste be perfecte. But the wretched Realme of Irelande wantethe the moste principall of them That is the intellectuall Therefore in sekinge to reforme her estate it is speciallye to be loked into But bycause by husbandrie which suppliethe vnto vs all thinges necessarye for foode we Chieflye liue, therefore it is firste to be prouided for The firste thinge then that we are to drawe these new tithed men vnto oughte to be husbandrye. firste because it is the moste easelye to be learned nedinge onelye the labour of the bodye, nexte because it is moste generall and moste nedefull then because it is moste naturall, and lastlye because it is moste ennemye to warr and moste hatethe vnquietnes as the Poet saiethe/ *Bella execrata Colonis* for husbandrie beinge the nurse of thrifte and daughter of industrie and labour, detestethe all that maie worke her scathe and destroye the trauell of her handes whose hope is all her liues Comforte. vnto the ploughe therefore are all those kerne stocaghes and horsboies to be driven and made to employe that hablenes of bodye which they weare wonte to vse to thefte and villanye// | henceforthe to labour and husbandrie in the which by that time they haue spente but a little paine they will finde suche swetenes and happie Contentment that they will afterwardes hardly be haled awaie from it or drawen to theire wonted lewde life in theeverie and Rogerie. and beinge once thus envrde thervnto they are not onelye to be Countenanced and encouraged by all

fullnes *C* Carefulnes. *W* 4878 to] *om. CRW* 4878 labor.] labor *C* labour, *R* 4878 seconde be] second of *C* 4879 are] be *W* 4879 Called] called the *RW* 4879 artes] Artes/ *C* the Artes, *R* Arts. *W* 4879-80 marchandize] marchandrie *R* 4881 no] noe noe *R* 4881 Consiste] consistes *C* 4882 But the] But that *R* 4882 wretched] *om. W* 4883 intellectuall] Intellectuall, *R* intellectuall; *W* 4883 reforme] refore *R* 4884 estate] state *W* 4884 into] vnto *CRW* 4884 by] of *R* 4885 foode] food whereby *RW* 4885 liue,] live. *W* 4886 for] for. *W* 4886 then] therefore *W* 4886 are] care *R* 4887 drawe] drawe, *R* 4887 vnto] into *W* 4887 husbandrye.] husbandry *C* husbandrie, *R* 4888 easelye] easie *CRW* 4888 bodye,] Body. *W* 4889-90 generall . . . naturall] naturall *R* 4891 *Bella execrata Colonis*] *Bello execrata Colonis. written on line by itself C bella execrata colonis. printed on line by itself W* 4891 *execrata*] *execranda Ho* exerata *T* 4891 for] But *R* 4892 thrifte] thurst *C* 4892 daughter] the daunger *C* the daughter *R* 4894 Comforte.] comfort *CRW* 4894 ploughe] plough, *RW* 4895 all] *om. W* 4895 stocaghes] Stockers *H2* Stockhaghes *Ho* Stochans *LD1* Stochairs *N* Stochars *R* Stoguhes *T* 4896 weare] *om. R* 4897 *blank space*] *om. CRW* 4898 husbandrie] industry. *W* 4898 the] *om. C* 4900 afterwardes hardly] hardlie afterwardes *R* 4900 to] from *R* 4901 once thus] once *C* this once *R* 4901 envrde] enterred *R*

A VIEW OF THE PRESENT STATE OF IRELAND 217

good meanes but allsoe provided that theire Children after them maie be broughte vp likewise in the same and succede in the romes of theire fathers To which ende theare is a statute in Irelande allreadie well prouided which Comaundeth that all the sonns of husbandmen shalbe trained vp in theire fathers Trade but it is god wott verye slenderlye executed/

Eudox: But doe youe not Counte in this trade of husbandrie pasturadge of Cattell and keping of theire Cowes for that is Reckoned as a parte of husbandrie/

Iren: I knowe it is and nedefull to be vsed but I doe not meane to allowe anye of those able bodies which are able to vse bodelye labour to followe a fewe Cowes grazinge, but suche impotente persons as beinge vnable for stronge trauell are yeat able to drive Cattle to and fro to theire pasture; for this keping of Cowes is of it selfe a verye idle liffe and a fitt nurserye for a thiefe, ffor which Cause ye Remember that I disliked the Irishe manner of kepinge Bollies in Sommer vppon the mountaines and livinge after that Salvage sorte, But if they will allgates fede manie Cattle or kepe them on the mountaines let them make some Townes neare to the mountaines side wheare they maye dwell togeather with neighbours and be Conuersante in the viewe of the worlde, And to saie truethe thoughe Irelande be by nature accompted a greate soile of pasture yeat had I rather haue fewer Cowes kepte and men better manered, then to haue suche huge encrease of Cattle and no encrease of good Condicions. I woulde therefore wishe that there weare some ordinaunce made againste them that whosoeuer kepethe xx^{tie} kine shoulde kepe a ploughe goinge, for otherwise all men woulde fall to pasturadge and none to husbandrye which is a greate Cause of this dearthe now in Englande and a Cause of the vsuall stealthes in Irelande. for loke into all Countries that live in suche sorte by keping of Cattle and youe shall finde that they are bothe verie Barbarous and vncivill, and allsoe greatlye given to warr. The Tartarians the mvscovites the Norwaies, the Geates the Armenians and manye others doe wittnesse

4904 the same] that same *R*   4905 fathers] Fathers. *W*   4907 Trade] trades *W*   4907 god wott] (God wot) *W*   4908 executed] loked vnto *R*   4909 pasturadge] pasturinge *RW*   4911 husbandrie/] husbandry *C*   4912 nedefull] needfullie *CRW*   4913 those] these *R*   4914 grazinge,] grazeing. *W*   4914 suche] *om. C*   4915 to theire] the *R*   4917 thiefe,] thiefe. *W*   4917 ye Remember] (you remember) *W*   4917 that] *om. RW*   4918 of] for *R*   4918 kepinge] kepinge of *R*   4918 Bollies] *Boolies W*   4918 mountaines] mountaine *R*   4919 allgates] alwayes *R*   4919 manie] any *C*   4922 Conuersante] coversaunt *C*   4923 accompted] counted *CRW*   4925 Condicions.] Conditions, *CR*   4926 ordinaunce] ordinances *W*   4926 againste] amongst *CRW*   4926-7 whosoeuer] whatsoeuer *R*   4927 kepethe] should kepe *C*   4928 pasturadge] pasturinge *C*   4929 stealthes] stealthes nowe *R*   4931 bothe] *om. R*   4932 allsoe] as *C*   4932 warr.] warr, *CR*   4933 Norwaies] *Norwegians W*   4933 Geates] *Gotes RN Gothes W AD1H2L*   4933 Armenians] *Aruntinans A   Amenians H2N*   4933 others] other *RW*

f. 89ᵛ the same, And therefore since now we purpose to | drawe the Irishe from desire of warrs and tumultes to the loue of peace and Civillitye it is expediente to abridge theire greate Custome of heardinge and Augment theire more trade of Tillage and husbandrye, As for other occupacions and trades they nede not to be enforced to but euerie mann bounde to followe one that he thinkes him selfe aptest for for other trades of Artificers wilbe occupied for verye necessitye and Constrained vse of them, and so likewise will marchandize for the gaine thereof. But learninge and bringinge vp in liberall sciences will not Come of it selfe but muste be drawen on with straighte lawes and ordinaunces And therefore it weare mete that suche an one weare ordained that all the sonnes of Lordes, gentlemen and suche others as are able to bringe them vp in learninge shoulde be trained vp thearein from theire Childhoodes, And for that end euerye parishe shoulde be forced to kepe one pettie schollmaster adioyninge vnto the parishe Churche to be the more in viewe which shoulde bringe vp theire Children in the firste elamentes of letters. and that in euerye Cantred or baronye they shoulde kepe another able Scholmaster which should enstructe them in grammar and in the principles of sciences to whom they shoulde be Compelled to sende theire youthe to be dissiplined, whearby they will in shorte space growe vp to that Civill Conversacion that bothe the Children will loathe the former rudenes in which they weare bredd and allsoe theire parentes will even by thensample of theire younge Children perceaue the fowlenes of theire owne brutishe behaviour Compared to theires. ffor Learninge hathe that wonderfull power in it selfe that it cane soften and attemper the moste sterne and salvage nature/

Eudox: Surelye I ame of your minde, that nothinge will bringe them from theire vncivile liffe soner then learninge and discipline nexte after the knowledge and feare of god And therefore I do still expecte that yee shoulde Come thearevnto and sett some order for reformacion of Religion which is firste to be respected accordinge to the sayinge of Christe. ffirste

f. 90ʳ seke the | kingedome of heaven and the righteousnes theareof

4934 from] *om. C*   4935 warrs] warre *W*   4936 abridge] abridge, *RW*   4936 greate] *om. R*   4936 heardinge] hardening *W*   4937 more] *om. W*   4937 Tillage] tillinge *R*   4937 husbandrye,] husbandrye *C* husbandrie. *W*   4938 to be] bee *W*   4938 bounde] bound only *CR* to bee bound onely *W*   4938 one] *om. R*   4939 for for] for *C* for, ffor *R* for. For *W*   4944 one] acte *RW*   4944 Lordes] Lordes and *R*   4945 shoulde] should *C*   4946 thearein] herein *R*   4947 one] a *W*   4948 Churche] churge *R*   4949 elamentes] rudymentes *R*   4949 letters.] lettres, *CR* Letters: *W*   4949 Cantred] Countrie *RW*   4949 baronye] Barronrye *R*   4950 able] habler *C*   4953 space] time *R*   4954 the] their *W*   4955 parentes] parence *R*   4956 brutishe] *om. W*   4957 in] of *R*   4958 attemper] temper *RW*   4958 sterne] serne *C*   4962 some] downe *C*   4963 Christe.] Christe *CR* CHRIST, *W*   4963-4 ffirste seke] *Seeke first W*   4964 seke] I seeke *C*   4964 theareof]

A VIEW OF THE PRESENT STATE OF IRELAND 219

Iren: I haue in minde so to doe. But let me I praye youe firste finishe that which I had in hande wheareby all the ordinaunce which shall afterwards be set for Religion maye abide the more firmelye and be obserued more dilligently: Now that this people is thus tithed and ordered and euerie one bounde to some honest trade of liffe which shalbe particulerlye entred and set downe in the Tithinge bookes yeat perhaps theare wilbe some straglers and Rvnagates which will not of themselues come in and yealde themselues to this order, And yeat after the well finishinge of the presente warr and establishinge of the Garrissones in all stronge places of the Countrie wheare theare wonted refuge was moste I suppose theare will fewe stande out or if theare doe they will shortlie be broughte in by the eares, But yeat afterwardes leaste anie one of these should swarue or anie that is tyed to a Trade should not afterwardes followe the same accordinge to this institucion, but shoulde straggle vp and downe the Countrye or miche in Corners amongest theire frindes idelye as Carrowes, Bardes Iesters or suche like, I woulde wishe that theare weare a prouoste marshall appointed in euerie shire which shoulde Continewallye walke thoroughe the Countrye with haulfe a dozen or haulfe a skore horsemen to take vp suche lose persons as they should finde thus wanderinge whom he shoulde punishe by his owne aucthoritye with some paines as the persone shall seme to deserue, for if he be founde againe so loytteringe he maye scourge him with whipps or rodds Afterwardes if he be againe taken let him haue the bitternesse of marshall lawe, Likewise if anie reliques of thoulde rebellion be founde by him that either haue not Come in and submitted themselues to the Lawe or that havinge once come in doe breake forthe againe or walke disorderlye let them taste of the same Cupp in godes name, for it was deue to them for theire firste guilte and now beinge reviued by theire

---

therof etc. *C* thereof: *R* *thereof*. *W*   4965 I praye youe] (I pray you) *W*   4966 ordinaunce] ordynances *RW*   4966-7 shall afterwards be] shalbe afterwardes *C*   4967 firmelye] formerlye *C*   4968 dilligently:] dilligently *C* deligentelie, *R* diligently. *W*   4969 to] vnto *CRW*   4970 the] *om. R*   4970 bookes] Booke *W*   4975 theare] they *RW*   4976 leaste] if *C*   4976 these] them *W*   4977 not afterwardes] afterwardes not *CRW*   4979 miche] muche *H2* meete *P* marche *T*   4979 Carrowes] *Carrooghs A* Carrowe *R*   4979 Bardes] and Bardes *R*   4980 or] and *CRW*   4980 theare . . . marshall] a Provost *Marshall* should bee *W*   4981 thoroughe] about *W*   4982 a dozen] Dozen *R*   4982 skore] score, *R*   4984 some] soche *CRW*   4984 persone shall] persons should *R*   4984 seme] serve *C*   4985 be] be butt once soe taken ydlie Rogueinge he maie pvnnishe him more lightlie as with stockes or soche like, But if he be *CWH1* same except taken soe *for* soe taken *A* more *om. and* and *for* or *D2* taken so *for* soe taken *and* with the *for* with *and* and *for* or *F* goinge *for* Rogueinge *and* strokes *for* stockes *H2* taken *om. and* with the *for* with *Ho*   as *om. P* strookes *for* stockes *RD1LN* butt *and* soe *om. and* idle *for* ydlie *T*   4986 Afterwardes] after which *CRW*   4986 be] have *C*   4987 bitternesse] bittereste *C*   4987 marshall] the marshall *R*   4987 lawe,] lawe *R* lawe. *W*   4988 him] any *W*   4988 submitted themselues] submitteth him self *R*   4989-90 or walke] and walke *W*   4990 them] him *C*

f. 90ᵛ latter losenes let them haue theire firste desarte as | now beinge founde vnfitt to live in a Comon wealthe/

Eudox: This was a good ordinaunce but me thinkes it is all vnneccessarie Chardge and allsoe vnfitt to continewe the name or forme of anie marshall lawe when as theare is a proper officer allreadye appointed for theise turnes to wete the Shiriffe of the shiere whose peculier office it is to walke Continewallye vp and downe his Bayliwicke as ye woulde haue a marshall to snatche vp all theise Rvnagates and vnprofitable members and to bringe them to his goale to be punished for the same therefore this maye well be spared/

Iren: Not soe, me semes, for thoughe the Shiriffe haue this aucthoritye of him selfe to take vp all suche straglers and imprisone them yeat shall he not doe soe muche good nor worke that terrour in the hartes of them that a marshall will whom they shall knowe to haue power of liffe and deathe in suche Cases and speciallye to be appointed for them, Neither dothe it hinder but that thoughe it pertaine to the Shiriffe the Shiriffe maye doe thearein what he Cane and yeat the marshall maie walke his Course besides for bothe of them maie do the more good and more terrefye the idle rogue knowinge that thoughe he haue a watche vppon thone yeat he maie lighte vppon thother, But this prouisoe is nedefull to be had in this Case that the Sheriffe maie not haue the like power of liffe as the marshall hathe and as hearetofore they haue bene accustomed, ffor it is daungerous to give power of life into the handes of him which maie haue bennefitt by the parties deathe As if the saide loose lyuer haue anye goodes of his owne the Shirife is to Cease thearevppon, wheareby it hathe often come to passe that some which haue not perhaps deserued iudgement of deathe, thoughe otherwise perhaps offendinge haue bene for theire goodes sake Caughte vp and Carried straighte to the boughe, A thing indede pittifull and verye horrible Therefore by no meanes woulde I wishe the Shiriffe to haue suche aucthoritye nor yeat to imprisone that losell till the Sessions, ffor soe all the goales mighte be sone filled but to sende him to

4992 latter] later *W*   4993 a] the *CW*   4994 was] weare *CR*   4994 ordinaunce] manner *R*   4994 all] an *CRW*   4995 anie] a *C*   4996 allreadye appointed] appointed alreadie *C*   4997 Shiriffe] shreif *C*   4997 peculier] perticular *R*   4997-8 Continewallye] *om. W*   4998 downe] downe, *R*   4999 theise] those *RW*   5000 same] same, *CR* same. *W*   5002 me semes] (me thinkes) *W*   5002 Shiriffe] shreif *C*   5002 this] that *R*   5003 of] vpon *R*   5004 he not] not he *C*   5004 that] the *C*   5005 whom] when *R*   5007 but] that, but *W*   5007 Shiriffe the Shiriffe] shreif the shreif *C*   sherife *R* 5012 Sheriffe] shreif *C*   5016 his] *om. W*   5016 Shirife] shreif *C*   5016 Cease] seaze *CRW*   5016-7 often come] Come *CW*   commen ofte *R*   5017 which] whoe *CRW* 5017 perhaps] *om. W*   5020 pittifull and verye] verie pittifull and *CW*   5020 horrible] horrible, *CR*   horrible. *W*   5020 woulde I wishe] I would have *W*   5021 Shiriffe] shreif *C*   5021 to haue] have *W*   5022 the] *om. CRW*   5022 be sone] soone bee *RW*

A VIEW OF THE PRESENT STATE OF IRELAND 221

f. 91ʳ the marshall whoe eftesones findinge | him faultye shall give him mete Correccion and rid him awaye forthewith/

Eudox: I doe now perceaue your reasone well but come now to that wheareof we earste spake I meane to religion and religious men what order will ye set amongest them/

Iren: ffor Religion litle haue I to saie my selfe beinge as I saide not professed thearein, and it selfe beinge but one so as theare is but one waie thearein. ffor that which is trewe onelye is and the rest are not at all. yeat in plantinge of religion thus muche is nedefull to be obserued that it be not soughte forciblie to be impressed into them with terrour and sharpe penalties as now is the mannour, but rather deliuered and intymated with mildenes and gentlenes soe as it maie not be hated before it be vnderstode and theire professours despised and reiected. for this I knowe that the moste of the Irishe are so far from vnderstandinge the Popishe Religion as they are of the Protestantes profession and yeat dothe hate it thoughe vnknowen even for the verye hatred which they haue of the Englishe and theire gouernement Therefore it is expediente that some discrete ministers of theire owne Cuntrymen be firste sente amongeste them which by theire milde perswacions and instruccions as allso by theire sober liffe and Conuersacion maie drawe them firste to vnderstande and afterwardes to imbrace the doctrine of theire salvacion. ffor if that the ancient godlie fathers which firste Conuerted them beinge infidels to the faithe weare able to pull them from Idolatrye and Paganisme to the trewe belief in Christe as *Sᵗ Patrick* and *Sᵗ*   did, how muche more easely shall godlie teachers bringe them to the trewe vnderstandinge of that which they allredaye professe whearein it is greate wonder to see the odds which is betwene the zeale of the popishe priestes and the ministers of the gosple for they spare not to Come out of Spaine from Rome from Reymes by longe toile and dangerous travell hither wheare they knowe perill of

f. 91ᵛ deathe | Awaitethe them And no Rewarde or Riches is to be found, onelye

5025-7 *Eudox:* ... them/] *om. N*   5025 come] come we *CRW*   5026 men] men, *RW*
5027 them/] them? *W*   5028 *Iren:*] *Eudox: N*   5028 as I saide] (as I sayd) *RW*
5030 are] is *W*   5030 all.] all *C*   5031-2 it be] beinge *R*   5033 intymated] intituled *C*
5035 professours] professions *R*   5035-9 for ... gouernement] And *W*   5036 the Popishe] of people and *C*   of the popishe *R*   5037 dothe] doe they *CR*   5039 gouernement] goverment, *CR*   5040 sente] sent over *W*   5041 milde] meeke *W*   5041 by] of *C*   5042 Conuersacion] conversations *W*   5044 which...faithe] *om. R*   5044 beinge] when they were *W*   5044 infidels] Infidells, *W*   5045 pull] drawe *R*   5045 Idolatrye] infidelitie *R*   5045 Paganisme] pagannacie *H2*   pagansie *RLD1*   5045-6 to the ... did] *om. R*   5046 blank space did] Colum.ᵗ *C*   Golmithe did *D2F*   blank space *H1* Cohunt *P*   Coline *T*   Columb *WHo*   5046-7 easely shall] the *R*   5048 professe] profeste *CW*   5049 the popishe] Popishe *CRW*   5049 and the] and *R*   5051 by] and *C*   5051 travell] traveillinge *CW*   5052 or] nor *CR*   5052 Riches] Ritches, *R*

to drawe the people vnto the Churche of Rome: wheareas our Idle ministers havinge a waie for Creditte and estimacion thereby opened vnto them and havinge the livinges of the Countrye offered them without paines without perill will neither for the same nor for anie love of god nor zeale of Religion nor for all the good which they maye doe by wynninge of manye Soules to god, be drawen forthe from theire warme nestes, and theire swete loues sides, to loke out into godes haruest, which is even readie for the sickle, and all the feildes yellowe longe agoe. doubtles these good oulde fathers will I feare me Rise vp in the daie of Iudgement to Condemne them/.

Eudox. Surelye it is greate pittie *Iren*: that there are none of the ministers of Englande good and sober discreate men which mighte be sente ouer thither to teache and instructe them and that theare is not as muche Care had of theire Soules as of theire bodies for the Care of bothe lyethe vppon the Prince/

Iren: weare theare neuer so manye sente ouer they shoulde doe smalle good till one enormitye be taken from them/ that is that bothe they be restrained from sendinge theire younge men abroade to other vniuersities beyonde sea as Reymes doway Lovaine and the like and that others from abroade be restrained from Comminge to them for they lurkinge secretely in theire howses and in Corners of the Countrye doe more hurte and hinderaunce to religion with theire private perswacions then all thothers Cane doe good with theire publike instruccion/ And thoughe for these latter theare be a good statute theare ordained yeat the same is not executed, and as for the former there is no lawe for theire restrainte at all./

Eudox: I marveile that it is no better loked vnto, and not onelye this but that allsoe which I remember youe mencioned in your abuses Concerninge the profittes and Revenewes of the landes of fugitiues in Irelande which by pretence of Certaine Coullorable Convayaunces are sente continewally over vnto them to the Comfortinge of them and others againste her maiestie, for which heare in Englande theare is good order taken, And whie not then aswell in Irelande. for thoughe theare be no statute theare

richesse *W* 5053 vnto] to *R* 5053 our] some of our *W* 5055 offered] offered unto *W* 5055 paines] paines, and *W* 5056 for anie] anie *CW* 5056 zeale] hele *C* 5057 which] *om. W* 5057 maye] mighte *R* 5057-8 of manye] *om. CW* of so manye *R* 5058-9 and . . . sides] *om. W* 5059 sides] syde *CR* 5059 into] vnto *C* 5060 agoe.] agoe *C* agoe, *RW* 5060 these] those *W* 5061 oulde] ould godlie *CRW* 5061 I feare me] (I feare mee) *W* 5063 none] none chosen out *CRW* 5064 and sober] sober, and *W* 5069 taken] taken awaye, *R* 5069 them/] them *R* 5071 sea] seas *R* the Sea *W* 5071 Reymes doway] Reynes *and blank space H1* 5071 that] *om. W* 5072 from] for *CW* 5072 to] into *W* 5075 instruccion] instructions *W* 5075 latter] later *CR* 5077 for theire] for their ordre for ther *C* nor order for theire *RW* 5078 that] *om. CW* 5079 that allsoe] also that *R* 5079 mencioned] motioned *C* 5084 Irelande.] Ireland? *W*

yeat enacted therefore yet mighte her maiestie by her onelye prerogatiue 5085 seaze the fruites and profittes of those fugitives landes into her handes till they Come over to testifye theire trewe Allegiaunce/

Iren: In dede she mighte doe soe but the Cumberous times do perhaps hinder the regarde hearef and of manye other good intencions/

Eudox: But whie then did they not minde it in peaceable times/ 5090

Iren: Leaue we that to theire grauer Consideracions, but procede we forwarde. nexte Care in religion is to be builde vpp and repaire all the Ruined Churches wheareof the moste parte lie even withe the grounde, and some that haue bene latelye repaired are so vnhansomelye patched and thatched that men doe even shvn the places of the vncomelines theareof Therefore 5095 I woulde wishe that theare weare order taken to haue them builte in some better forme accordinge to the Churches of Englande. for the outwarde shewe asure your selfe dothe greatlye drawe the rude people to the reverensinge and frequentinge theareof what euer some of our late too nice foles saie that theare is nothinge in the semelye forme and Comelye order of the 5100 Churche. And for so kepinge and Continewinge them theare should likewise Churche wardens of the grauest men in the parishe be appointed as theare be heare in Englande which shoulde take the yearelie Chardge bothe heareof and allsoe of the scholehowses which I wished to be builte neare to the saide Churches, for maintenaunce of bothe which it weare mete 5105 that some smalle porcion of lande weare alotted sithe no more Mortmaines are to be loked for/// |

f. 92ᵛ *Eudox*: In dede me semes it woulde be so Conveniente But when all is done how will youe haue your Churches serued or your ministers mainteyned, since the Livinges (as youe) saide are not sufficiente to make them 5110

5085 enacted] enacted, *C* 5087 Come] came *R* 5087 Allegiaunce/] alleigeance *R* thereof *RW* 5088 In dede] I would *C* 5088 doe soe] soe doe *CRW* 5089 hearef] hereof *C* thereof *RW* 5090 then] *om. R* 5090 minde] mend *W* 5090 times/] tymes *R* times? *W* 5091 grauer] graue *RW* 5091-2 forwarde.] forward, *R* 5092 be] *om. CRW* 5092 Ruined] Ruine *R* 5093 whereof] thereof *R* 5093 withe] to *C* 5094 that] *om. R* 5094 vnhansomelye] *om. R* 5095 of] for *CRW* 5095 theareof] therof, *CR* thereof; *W* 5098 asure your selfe] (assure your selfe) *W* 5098 dothe] doe *R* 5098 rude] *om. C* 5099 theareof] thereof. *W* 5099 what] And what *CR* 5099 late] *om. R* 5100 that] *inserted between lines E om. CRW* 5101 so] the *W* 5102 grauest] greatest *R* 5103 theare] they *CW* 5104 wished] wishe *CW* 5104 builte] builded *R* 5105 to] *om. W* 5105 Churches] church *C* 5106 smalle] seuerall *R* 5106 lande] lands *W* 5106 sithe] seinge *R* 5106 Mortmaines] monnteynes *H2* 5108 me semes] (me thinkes) *W* 5109 haue your] haue his *R* 5109 or] and *W* 5109-10 mainteyned,] maintained? *W* 5110-1 since...maynntenaunce] *om. R* 5110 youe) saide] yowe said) *C* you say) *W* 5110-1 to...scarse] scarse to make them *CW*

scarse a gowne muche lesse to yelde them mete mayntenaunce accordinge to the dignitye of theire degres/ *Iren*:

Theare is no waie to helpe that but laie Two or three of them togeather vntill suche time as the Countrye growe more ritche and better inhabited, at which time the tithes and other obvencions will allsoe be more augmented and better vallewed. But now that we haue gone thoroughe all the three sortes of trades and set a Course for theire good establishement, let vs if please youe go nexte to some other nedefull pointes of other publicke matters no lesse Concerninge the good of the Comon wealthe thoughe but accidentallye dependinge on the former. and firste I wishe that order weare taken for the Cuttinge downe and openinge of all places thoroughe wodes so that a wide waye of the space of C. yardes mighte be laide open in euerye of them for the safetie of trauellers whiche vse often in suche perillous places to be Robbed and somtimes murdered Next that Bridges weare builte vppon all Riuers and all the fordes marred and spilt so as none mighte passe anie other waye but by those bridges, and euerie bridge to haue a gate and a smalle gatehowse set theareon. whereof this good will Come that no nighte stealthes which are Comonlye driven in by waies and by blinde fordes vnvsed of anie but suche like, shalbe Convaied out of one Countrye into another as they vse, but that they muste passe by those bridges, wheare they maie either be happelye encountred or easelye tracted or not suffred to passe at all by meanes of those gatehowses thereon. Allsoe that in all stretes and narrowe passages as betwene Two Boggs or thoroughe anie depe forde or vnder anye mountaine side theare shoulde be some litle fortilage or woden Castle set which shoulde kepe and | Comaunde that streighte wheareby anie Rebelles that should come into the Countrye mighte be stopped that waie or passe with greate perill/

Moreouer that all higeh waies shoulde be fenced and shutt vp on bothe sides leavinge onely xl fote breadth for passadge so as none shoulde be

5111 a gowne] gownes *W*   5111 them mete] meete *CW*   5112 degres] degree *CRW*   5112 *Iren*:] *new paragraph CRW*   5113 but] but to *CRW*   5114 growe] growe. *C* grewe *R*   5115 time] tymes *R*   5116 gone] thus gone *CRW*   5117 the three] that theire *R*   5118 if please youe] if it please yow *C*   yf yow please *R*   (if it please you) *W*   5121 downe] *om. W*   5121 places] paces *CR*   5124 murdered] murdered/. *and blank space C*   murthered, *R*   murdered. *W*   5125 all Riuers] the Rivers *W*   5126 waye] waies *R*   5127 smalle] *om. W*   5127 theareon.] thereon, *RW*   5129 anie] any, *R*   5129 shalbe] must be *R*   shall not be *W*   5130 that] *om. W*   5131 either be] bee eyther *R*   5132 tracted] tracked *RW*   5132 by] by by *C*   5133 thereon.] theron, *C* thereon *R*   5133 stretes] sleightes *R*   5135 Castle] Castle, *R*   5137 into] in *R*   5137 stopped] stopped, *R*   5137 that waie] the waye *R*   5138 *blank space*] *om. RW*

hable to passe but thoroughe the highe waies, wheareby theves and nighte Robbers might be the more easelye pursued and encountred when theare shalbe no other waie to drive theire stollen Cattell but therein as I formerlye declared:

    further that theare shoulde in sundrie Conveniente places by the highe waies be townes appointed to be builte the which shoulde be free-burouges and incorporate vnder Bailifes to be by theire inhabitantes well and strongelye entrenched or otherwise fenced with gates at eache side theareof to be shutt nightely like as theare is in manye places in the Englishe pale and all the waies aboute it to be stronglye shut vp so as none shoulde passe but thoroughe these Townes, To some of which it weare good that the priviledge of a market weare given the rather to strengthen and enhable them to theire defence for theare is nothinge dothe soner Cause Civilitye in anye Countrye then manye market Townes by reasone that people repairinge often thither for theire nedes will dailye see and learne Civill manners of the better sorte, Besides theare is nothinge dothe more staye and strengthen the Countrye then suche Corporate Townes as by profe in manye Rebellions hathe apeared in which when all the Countries haue swerued the townes haue stode faste and yealded good Reliefe to the Soldiours in all occacions of service And Lastelye theare is nothinge dothe more enriche anye Country or Realme then manye Townes for to them will all people drawe and bringe the fruites of theire trades aswell to make money of them as to supplie theire nedefull vses And the Countrymen wilbe allsoe more industrious in Tillage and rearinge all husbandrye | Comodities knowinge that they shall haue readye sale for them at these Townes. And in all these Townes shoulde theare Conveniente Innes be erected for the lodginge and harboringe of all travellers whoe are now often times spoiled by lyinge abroad in wett theached howses for wante of suche safe places to shroude themselues in/

Eudox: But what profitt shall your market Townes reape of theire market wheareas eche one maie sell theire Corne and Cattell abroade in the

---

    5141 waies] waye *R*   5144-5 *blank space*] *om*. *RW*   5145 shoulde] should bee *W* 5146 be townes] townes *W*   5146-7 freeburouges] freeburghes *C*   free burrowes *R*   free Burgesses *W*   5148 fenced] *om*. *C*   5148 at] on *W*   5150 waies] walls *C*   5150 as] that *R*   5151 these] those *CRW*   5152 a] *om*. *C*   5153 theare is] *om*. *R*   5153 dothe] doe *C*   5156 sorte,] sorte *C*   sort: *W*   5158 apeared] bene proued *R*   5158 which when all] which all when *C*   all which when *R*   5159 faste] stiffe and fast *W*   5160 service] services *CW*   5160-1 is nothinge dothe] doth nothing *R*   5161 anye] the *R*   5162 all] all the *W*   5162 fruites] fruite *R*   5164 wilbe allsoe] wilbe *C*   will also bee the *R* will also be *W*   5164 all] of all *W*   5165 that] *om*. *R*   5165 these] those *CRW* 5166 these] those *CRW*   5166 Conveniente Innes be] be convenient Innes *W*   5167 all travellers whoe] Travellers, which *W*   5168 lyinge] lodging *RW*   5168 wett theached] weake thetche *C*   weake thatch *R*   weake thatched *W*   5169 themselues] them *W* 5170 *Eudox*:] *no new paragraph R*   5170 market] market? *W*   5171 wheareas]

Countrye and make theire secrete bargaines amongest themselues as now I vnderstande they vse/

Iren: Indede *Eudox*: They doe so and theareby no small Inconvenience dothe growe to the Comon wealthe for now when anie one hathe stollen a Cowe or a garren he maye secretlye sell the same in the Countrie without privitye of anie wheareas if he broughte it to a market Towne it woulde perhaps be knowen and the theef discouered   Therefore it weare good that a streighte ordinaunce weare made that none shoulde buy or sell anie Cattell but in some open market theare beinge now market Townes euerie wheare at hande/ vppon a greate penaltye neither shoulde they likewise buy anye Corne to sell the same againe vnlesse it weare to make maulte theareof for by suche engrossinge or Regratinge we se the dearthe that now Comonly raigneth heare in Englande to haue bene Cawsed/ hearevnto allso is to be added that good ordinaunce which I remember was once proclaimed thorougheout all Irelande that all men shoulde marke theire Cattell with an open seuerall marke vppon theire flankes or Buttockes so as if they happened to be stollen they mighte appeare whose they weare, and they which shoulde buy them mighte theareby suspecte the owner and be warned to abstaine from buyinge them of a suspected persone with suche an vnknowen marke/

Eudox: Surelye these ordinaunces seme verie expedient but speciallye that of fre Townes, of which I wonder that theare is suche smalle store in Irelande and that in the firste peoplinge and plantinge theareof they weare neclected and omitted// |

Iren: They weare not omitted for theare weare thoroughe all places of the Countrie Convenient, manye good Townes seatd which thoroughe that invndacion of the Irishe which I firste tould youe of weare vtterlye wasted and defaced of which the ruines are yeat in manye places to be sene and of some no signe at all remayninge saue onelye theire bare names but theire seates are not to be founde/

when as *CW*   5173 vse/] vse *R*   5174 Inconvenience] inconvenience inconvenience *R*   5175 growe] arise *CR*   rise *W*   5176 the same] yt *CRW*   5177 to a] into the *R*   5178 discouered] discouered, *CR*   discovered. *W*   5180-1 theare . . . hande/] (there . . . hande) *CRW*   5183 theareof] therof to sell the same againe *C*   5183 or] and *CRW*   5184 Cawsed/] caused *CR*   caused. *W*   5184-5 hearevnto] here vnto, *R*   5185 is] *om. C*   5186 proclaimed] proclameth *R*   5186 Irelande] *Ireland. W*   5190 be warned] beware *C*   5190 them] of them *R*   5192 ordinaunces] evidences *R*   5193 that of] that *inserted between lines E*   of *C*   that, of *R*   5193 that theare is suche] there is so *W*   5195 omitted//] omitted *R*   5197 seatd] *last letter apparently cut off E*   5198 youe] *om. R*

Eudox: But howe Comethe it then to passe that they haue neuer since recouered nor theire habitacions bene reedefied as of the reste which haue bene no lesse spoiled and wasted/

Iren: The Cause thereof was for that after theire desolacion they weare begde by gentelmen of the kinge vnder Colour to repair them and gather the pore Reliques of theire people againe togeather of whom havinge obteyned them they weare so far from reedifyinge them as that by all meanes they haue endevored to kepe them waste leaste that beinge repaired theire Charters mighte be renewed and theire Burgesses restored to the Landes which they had now in theire possession muche like as in those olde monumentes of Abbies and religious howses we se them likewise vse to doe for which Cause it is iudged that Kinge Henrye the viijth bestowed them vppon them knowinge that theareby they shoulde neuer be hable to rise againe, And even so do these Lordes in those pore olde Corporate Townes of which I Coulde name youe diuerse but for kindlinge of displeasure Therefore as I wished manye Corporate Townes to be erected so woulde I againe wishe them to be free not dependinge vppon the service nor vnder the Comaunde of anie but the Gouernour And beinge so they will bothe strengthen all the Countrye rounde aboute them which by theire meanes wilbe the better replenished and enritched And allsoe be as Continewall holdes for her maiestie/ If the people shoulde revoulte or breake out againe, for without suche it is easye to forrune and ouercome the wholle lande, let be for ensample all those freburroughes in the lowe Countries which now are all the strengthe theareof/ These and other like ordinaunces mighte be devised for the good establishement of that Realme after it is once subdewed and reformed in which it mighte afterwardes be verye easelye kepte and mayntayned with smalle Care of the gouernour and Counsell theare appointed so as it shoulde in shorte space yeald | A plenti-

full revenewe to the Crowne of Englande which now doethe bothe sucke 5230
and Consume the treasure theareof thoroughe the vnsounde plottes and
Chaungeable orders which are dailye devized for her good yeat neuer
effectuallye prosecuted or performed

Eudox. But in all this your discourse I haue not marked anye thinge by
youe spoken towchinge the principall appointement of your officer to 5235
whom ye wishe the Chardge and performaunce of all this to be Comitted
Onelye I obserued some foule abuses by youe noted in some of the late
gouernours the reformacion wheareof they lefte of for this presente place/

Iren: I delighte not to laie open the blames of so greate magistrates to the
rebuke of the worlde And therefore theire reformacion I will not meddle 5240
with but leave vnto the wisdome of grauer heades to be Considered/
Onelye thus muche I will generallye speake heareof to satisfye your desire
that the gouernement and Chiefe magistracie I wishe to Continewe as it
doethe To weet that it be ruled by a Lord deputye or iustice for that is a
verye safe kinde of rule But thearewithall I wishe that ouer him theare 5245
weare allsoe placed a Lorde Liuetennante of some of the greatest per-
sonages in Englande suche an one I Coulde name vppon whom the ey of
all Englande is fixed and our laste hopes now rest whoe beinge entituled
with that dignitye and beinge allwaies heare residente maye backe and
defende the good Course of that gouernement againste all maligners which 5250
els will thoroughe theire Cvnninge workinge vnder hande depraue and
pull backe what euer thinge shalbe well begvn or intended there, as we
Comonlye se by experience at this daie to the vtter ruine and desolacion
of that pore Realme, And this Lieftenancye should be no discounte-
nancinge of the Lord deputye but rather a strengtheninge and mainteyn- 5255
inge of all his doinges for now the Chiefe evill in that gouernement is
that no gouernement is suffered to goe on in anie one Course but vppon

---

5230 bothe] butt *CRW*   5231 treasure] Threasurye *R*   5231 the vnsounde] the so
vnsound *C* those vnsound *RW*   5232 Chaungeable] changefull *RW*   5233 performed]
performed/. *C* performed: *R* performed. *W*   5235 principall . . . your] appointment of
the principall *CRW*   5236 Comitted] Comitted, *CR* committed: *W*   5237 obsereued]
observed *CRW*   5237 by] as *C*   5238 the] that the *C*   5238 they] ye *CRW*   5238 of]
ofte *C* om. *R*   5238 place] tyme *R*   5239 so] om. *W*   5241 grauer] greater *RW*
5241 Considered/] considered, *RW*   5242 thus] this *C*   5242 generallye speake] speake
generallie *RW*   5242 heareof] thereof *W*   5244 iustice] Iustyces *R*   5244 is] it is *W*
5245 wishe] wishe wishe *R*   5246 allsoe placed] placed *R* placed also *W*   5246 Liue-
tennante] Lieutenant *W*   5247 in] of *R*   5247 Englande] England, *W*   5247-8 suche
. . . rest] (such . . . rest) *R*   5247 an] a *W*   5247 ey] key *R*   5248 rest] rest: *C*
5249 allwaies heare] here alwayes *W*   5250 Course] cause *R*   5250 that] the *R*
5251-2 and pull backe] om. *C*   5252 what euer] whatsoever *R*   5252 thinge] thinges *R*
5252 well] om. *W*   5254 that] the *R*   5254 Lieftenancye] livetennancye *R* Leiutenancie *W*
5255-6 and mainteyninge] om. *W*   5256 doinges] doinges doinges *R*   5257 gouernement]
gouernor *RW*   5257 in] with *CRW*

A VIEW OF THE PRESENT STATE OF IRELAND 229

the leaste informacion heare of this or that, he is either stopped or Crossed and other Courses appointed him from hence which he shall rvn/ whiche how inconueniente it is, is at this howre to well felte And thearefore this shoulde be one principall in the Appointement of the Lord deputies aucthoritye that it shoulde be more ample and absolute then it is and that he shoulde haue vncomptrolled power to doe anie thinge that he with the
f. 95ʳ Advizement of the | Councell shoulde thinke mete to be done for it is not possible for the Councell heare to directe a gouernour theare whoe shalbe forced oftentimes to followe the necessitye of present occacions and to take the sodaine advantage of time which beinge once loste will not be recouered, whileste thoroughe expectinge direccion from hence (the delaies wheare of are oftentimes thoroughe other greater affaires moste irkesome) the oportunities theare in the meane tyme passe awaye and greate daunger often growethe which by suche timelye prevencion mighte easelye be stopped and this I remember is worthelye obserued by machiavell in his discourse vppon Livie wheare he Comendethe the manner of the Romaines gouernement in giuinge absolute power to all theire Consulls and gouernours which if they abused/ they shoulde afterwardes dearelie Answeare and the Contrarye theareof he reprehendethe in the states of *Venice* of florence and manye other principalities of Italye whoe vsed to limitt theire Chief officers so streightlye as that thereby some times they haue loste suche happie occacions as they coulde neuer come vnto againe, the like wheareof who so hathe bene Conuersante in the gouernement of Irelande hathe to often sene to theire greate hurte. Therefore this I could wishe to be redressed, And yeat not soe but that in particuler things he shoulde be restrained thoughe not in the generall gouernement, as namelye in this that no offices shoulde be soulde by the Lord deputye for money, nor no pardones/ nor proteccions boughte for rewarde nor no bieves taken for Captenries of Countries nor no shares of Bishopprickes for nominatinge theire Bishops nor no forfeytures nor dispensacion with penalt

5258 stopped or] stopped and *W*   5259 and] or *W*   5260 inconueniente] convenient *R*   5260 is at this howre] at this howre *C*   at this howre is *R*   5260-1 this shoulde] it should *C*   5261 Appointement] appointing *W*   5263 vncomptrolled] an vncontrowled *R*   5266 occacions] actions *W*   5267 loste] lefte *R*   5268 direccion] dyrections *R*   5268-70 (the ... irkesome)] the ... yrksome) *C*   the ... yrksome, *RW* 5269 other] *om. R*   5272 I remember] (I remember) *W*   5272 machiavell] Machievill *D2 Macheuile F*   matchavell *RL*   matcheuall *D1*   5273 discourse] discourses *CRW*   5273 Livie] blank space *T*   5274 Consulls] Councellors *W*   5275 which if they] *om. C*   5277 florence] Morence *F*   5277 principalities] principallities *with last three letters worn off C*   5277 vsed] vse *CRW*   5278 streightlye] strictly *W*   5278-9 some ... haue] they have oftentimes *W* 5278 some times] oftentymes *R*   5280 hathe] have *C*   5280 in the] in that *RW* 5281 hathe] have *C*   5281 hurte.] hurt, *CR*   hinderance and hurt. *W*   5283 the] *om. C* 5284 for money] *om. R*   5285 proteccions] protections, *R*   no protections *W*   5287 theire] of *W*   5287 dispensacion] despensations *RW*   5287-9 with ... exportacion] *om. C* 5287 penalt] pennall *RW*

statutes given to theire servantes or friendes nor no sellinge of licences for exportacion of prohibited wares and speciallye of Corne and fleshe with manie the like which nede some manner of restrainte or els verie greate truste in the honorable disposicion of the Lord deputye/ 5290

f. 95ᵛ Thus I haue *Eudox*: as brieflye as I coulde and as my remembraunce woulde serue me run thoroughe the state of that wholle Countrye bothe to let youe see what it now is and allsoe what it maie be by good Care and amendement not that I take vppon me to Chaunge the pollicye of so greate a 5295 kingedome or prescribe rules to wise men as haue the handlinge theareof but onelye to shewe youe the evill/ which in my smalle experience I haue obsereued to haue bene the Chiefe hinderaunce of the reformacion thereof and by waie of Conference to declare my simple opinion for redresse theref and establishinge a good good Course for the gouernement, which I doe not 5300 deliuer as a perfecte plott of my owne invencion to be onelye followed but as I haue learned and vnderstode the same by the Consvltacions and accions of euerye wise gouernour and Counsellour whom I haue somtymes harde treate heareof so haue I thoughte good to set downe a remembraunce of them for my owne good and your satisfaccion that who so liste to ouerloke 5305 them allthoughe perhaps muche wiser then they which haue thus advized of that estate yeat at leste by Comparison hereof maie perhaps better his owne iudgement and by the lighte of others foregoinge him maie followe after with more ease and happelye finde a fairer waie thearevnto then they which haue gone before/ 5310

Eudox. I thanke youe *Iren*: for this your gentle paines withall not forgettinge now in the shuttinge vp to put youe in minde of that which ye haue formerlye halfe promised that heareafter when we shall mete

5289 exportacion] expectacon *R* transportation *W*   5290 verie] *om. C*   5291 Lord] Lordes *C*
5291 deputye/] Deputie, *R*   5291 *blank space*] *om. C AD1D2FH1H2HoLNPRTW*   5292 Thus] new paragraph *CHoPTW*   5292 remembraunce] memorie *W*   5293 me] *om. R*   5293 run thoroughe] am thorought *C*   5294 it maie] may *R*   5296 wise] such wise *RW*   5297 evill] evills *RW*   5298 obsereued] observed *CRW*   5298 haue bene] bee *RW*   5298 thereof] *om. W*   5299 redresse] the redresse *W*   5299 theref] therof *CRW*   5300 good good] good *CRW*   5300 for] of of *C*   5300 the] that *CR om. W*   5301 as] for *R*   5301 my] myne *CRW*   5302 as] *om. C*   5303 euerye] verie *CRW*   5303 gouernour and Counsellour] governours and Counsellors *CRW*   5303 somtymes] (sometimes) *W*
5304 heareof] thereof *R*   5305 my] myne *CR*   5305 so] *om. R*   5307 estate] state *W*
5310 before/] before *R*   5313 that] *om. R*

againe vppon the like good occacion ye will declare vnto vs those your observacions which ye haue gathered of the Antiquities of Ireland////

Finis /

A BRIEF NOTE OF IRELAND

A Note on the Text

The following document is transcribed from a manuscript in the Public Record Office (State Papers 63. 202, Part 4, item 59), where it is endorsed as "*A briefe discourse of Ireland. by Spencer.*" This text is reproduced with no other alterations than the following: all abbreviations, except in the case of numbers, of proper names, and of words abbreviated in modern usage, are spelled out; and all deleted words are omitted.

A transcription of the same manuscript is printed in Alexander B. Grosart's edition of Spenser's *Works* (London, 1882-1884, l. 537-555); differences between Grosart's wording and that of the present transcription are recorded in the footnotes initialed *G*. In the British Museum Ray Heffner discovered a one-page manuscript (Harleian MS 3787, p. 184) which, under the title "*Spensers discours breifly of Ireland,*" reproduces part of the last section of *The Brief Note*; from this copy are drawn the variants initialed *H*. A few desirable corrections, marked *?*, are likewise suggested in the footnotes.

A breife note of Ireland

The kinges of England haue lands of inheritance as Lords of Ireland in good substance beside the title of the Crowne, as the

> *Erledome of vlster*
> wholly Lords of Connought Meth of foure
> partes of Leinster and four partes of Mounster.

Besides there are
{
in Ireland ------ 5530
in Leinster ----- 930
in Connought --- 900
in Mounster ---- 2100
in vlster ------- 2060
in Meth ------- 540
} townes./

There is of arrable Land in it 38640. plowlands besides Rivers meadowes bogges and woods euerie plowland conteineth 120. acres euerie acre 4. perches in bredth and 40. in length euerie perch 21. foote euerie foote 12. inches./ In *Edward* the 4.th his tyme (whoe had Ireland in his obedience) it yeelded the Crowne of England 14146.li sterling taking but a noble for a plowland./ And besides he received for Customes, fishinges and other Royalties 100000. markes yerelie paid to the Castle of *dublin* as yet appereth by recorde And had aboue this, his yerelie Rent of *Vlster*, *Connonght*, *Meth Leinster* and *Mounster* which was 22000.li sterling, More then this had they advousons of manie Churches, wards, Marriages and guift of diuers other good thinges

21 *Connonght*] Connought G

To the Queene./

Out of the ashes of disolacon and wastnes of this your wretched Realme of Ireland. vouchsafe moste mightie Empresse our Dred soveraigne to receive the voices of a fewe moste vnhappie Ghostes, of whome is nothinge but the ghost nowe left which lie buried in the bottome of oblivion farr from the light of your gracious sunshine which spredeth it selfe ouer Countries moste remote to the releeving of their destitute Calamities and to the eternall aduancement of your renowne and glorie yet vpon this miserable land being your owne iuste and heritable dominion letteth no one little beame of your large mercie to be shed either for vnworthinesse of vs wreches which no way diserue so great grace, or for that the miserie of our estate is not made knowne vnto you but rather kept from your knowledge by such as by concealement thereof think to haue their blames concealed. Pardon therefore moste gracious Soveraigne vnto miserable wreches, which without your knowledge and moste against your will are plunged in this Sea of sorrowes to make there euell case knowne vnto you and to call for tymelie redresse vnto you if yet at least any tyme be left which that your maiestie in your excellent wisdome may the better knowe how to redresse May the same vuchsafe to consider from what begining the same first sprunge and by what late euill meanes it is brought to this miserable condicion which wee nowe Complaine of./

The first cause and Roote thereof was the indirect desire of one persons privat gaine to whome your Maiestie Comitted this vnfortunat gouernment whoe whiles he fedd your expectacion with the hope of increasing this your kingdome with a newe Countie (to witt the Countie of modoham) vnder that pretence sought to enlarge his owne treasure and to infeoffe his sonnes and kinsmen in all the territorie which might neuertheles haue ben tollerated in regard some good should thereby haue come vnto you, had it not ben wrought by moste uniuste and dishonorable meanes. ffor after that he had receaved *A. B.* into your faith and proteccion promising him to make him Mc̩Mahon for 100. beefes afterwards whereas an other of his kinsemen offered 300. he vniustly tooke and honge him and in his stede invested the other wherevpon the land lordes and gentlemen of the Countrie adioyning being terrified with the face of so foule a trecherie,

42 May] May you ?   48 modoham] Monohan *G*

began eftsoones to combine themselues and to labour the Erle of Tireone vnto theire parte who neuertheles did not manifestlie adhere vnto them nor durst breake out into manifest rebellion but taking onely dislike of such bad dealing begann to finde greuance at the gouernment (as in deede vnder correction me seemes some cause he had) for first he | might feare by that example lest he might be intrapped in the like then was he by this new Countizing of the Countrie of Monohan both to loose that seignoritie which he claimed of that land and allso that seruice which he claimed of *Macmahon* who by holding nowe of your Maiestie should be ffreed from his challenge. Lastly he was by some his frendes made to beleeve (whether trulie or no god knowes) that ther was a practise privilie wrought by the deputie either against his life or libertie where vpon he kept him selfe aloofe and durst not comitt his saftie in to the handes of the gouernour yet offred still if he might haue leave to come into England freelie to iustifie him selfe before your Maiestie. which whether he so trulie meant is vncertaine yet that leave would not haue ben denied since if he had not performed it he might haue bene in tyme discouered before he had growne vnto this head that nowe he is. But so some as the rest which then were out, felt him thus wauering and doubtfully disposed they increased his offence with daily causes of dislike vntill such tyme as they might practiz with your Maiestes aduersarie the king of Spaine to drawe him to his partie and not with strong feares and vaine hopes to feede his euill humour yet all this while durst he not break out into open disloialtie but so carried him selfe as that he might make advantage of both parties either to worke his owne Condicions of peace with your Maiestie by fearing you with his enterdeale with the king of Spaine or if he could not accomplishe this to vse the same directly against you yet all this while matters might haue bene so managed as that he might well enough haue bene conteined in reasonoble termes but that some were allwaies against it who covited nothing more then to alien him from your obedience and to Minister newe matter of Ielousies still against him wherevpon he breaking at length openly fourth yet was so dauled with and so faintly prosecuted as that meeting some tyme with some good successes in fight he tooke greater hart thereby and hauing once felt his owne strength and the faintnesse of those which were sett here to followe him grewe extreamlie insolent which he allso increased through occasion of the devision of the gouernment here betwixt S:r willm Russell and S:r Iohn Norris. Of which the one being sharplie bent to prosecute him the other thought by good treaties rather wynn him to make fair warrs But by some it was thought that the

70 handes of the] *om. G*   75 some] sone *G*   79 with] with[out] *G*   92 sett] sent ?

onely purpose of Sr Iohn Norris in handling thinges after that sorte was
to obtaine the absolute gouernment to him selfe./

After which the chaunge of gouernment succeeding the death of the
noble Lō. Burrowes ensewing the sundrie alteracions of Councills and
purposes following together with the devision and partaking of those
themselues of your Councill here haue since brought thinges | to that
dangerous condicion that nowe they stand in./ ffor from this head through
tolleracion and too much temporizing the euill is spred into all partes of
the Realme and growne in to so vniuersall a contagion that nothing but a
moste violent medecyne will serue to recouer yt. ffor all the Irish of all
partes are confederated and haue generallie agreed to shake of the yoke
of there obedience to the Crowne of England, And even now the vennyme
is crept vpp hither into this Prouince of Mounster which hath hitherto
continued in reasonable good quietnes The which nowe so much as it
was later euill then the rest so much is it nowe worse then all the rest,
and become indeed amoste miserable disolacion like as a fire the longer
it is kept vnder the more violentlie it burneth when it breaketh out./.

There came vpp hither latelie of the Rebells not past 2000. being sent by
the said Traitour E: of Tyreone presently vpon whose ariveall all the
Irish rose vpp in Armes against the english which were lately planted
theire so that in fewe daies the became 5. or 6000 whereby manifestly
appereth that the were formerlie combined with them./ ffor as Capteine
Tirrell one of the cheefe leaders of them said openlie he had before his
coming vp 80. of the best lordes and gentlemens handes writing sent him
promissing him to ioyne with him heare which accordinglie they per-
formed. And going straight vppon the English as they dwelt disparsed
before they could assemble themselues spoiled them all, there howses
sacked and them selues forced to flie away for safetye, so many as they
could catch they hewed and massacred miserablie the rest leaving all
behinde them fledd with their wives and Children to such porte townes
as were next them where they yet remaine like moste pittifull creatures
naked and comfortles lying vnder the towne walls and begging aboute all
the streetes daily expecting when the last extremity shalbe lade vpon them.
Coulde your maiesties moste mercifull eyes see but some parte of the image
of these our moste ruefull calamities they would melt with remorce to se
so manie soules of your faithfull subiectes brought hither to inhabit this
your land of the which many were the last day men of good substance
and abilitie to live,. others of verie able bodies to serue your Maiestie nowe

102 thinges] *word almost illegible*   111 later] lately [less] *G*   117 the] the[y] *G*   118 the]
the[y] *G*   121 promissing] permissing *G*

suddeinly become so wretched wightes and miserable out castes of the 135
worlde as that none of the Countrie people here vouchsafeth to com-
miserate but rather to scorne and approbriouslie revile them as people
abandoned of all helpe and hope and exposed to extreme miserie./

Truelie to think that a Countrie so rich so well peopled so firmlie fenced
and fortified with so manie stronge Castles with manie faire walled townes 140
and with sea halfe walling it aboute should be suddeinlie wunne hir inhabi-
tantes banished their goods spoiled there dwelling places disolated and all
the land allmoste in a moment overunne without stroke stricken without
f. 197ᵛ bloud shedd without | enenie encounted or seene without forreine invasion
it is amoste marvelouse thing and but so wrought of god hardlie to be 145
beleeued of man being such indeede as hardlie anie historie can aford
example of the like/. And surelie should any stranger here that the Eng-
lish nation so mightie and puisant so farr a broade in a Countrie of your
owne dominion lying hard vnder the lapp of England should by so base
and Barbarous a people as the Irish so vntrained in warrs so inexperte of 150
all gouerment and good pollicies be so suddenlie troden downe and blowne
away allmoste with a blast they would for euer condemne vs not knowing
the meanes howe the same is come to passe/ Therefore it is not a misse
to consider by what meanes and euill occasions all this mischeefe is hap-
pened the rather for the better redressing thereof and avoyding the like 155
hereafter, Some think that the first plott by which the late vndertakers of
your maiestes Landes here in Mounster were planted was not well insti-
tuted nor grounded vpon sound aduisement and knowledg of the Countrie,
ffor that more care was therin taken for profitt and vtilitie then for strength
and safetie/. ffor indeed what hope was there that a sorte of husbandmen 160
trained vpp in peace placed a broade in sundrie places dispersed as your
land lye dispersed should be able to maintaine and defend themselues
against a people newlie recouered out of the relikes of rebellion and yet
practizing Armes and warlike exercises without due provision therefore
which is, that first rebelliouse people should haue bine vtterlie disarmed 165
and for euer bounde from the vse of the like hearafter and in stede thereof
be compelled vnto other more Civill trades of life which they should haue
bene settled in by such sure establishment that they should neuer haue bene
able to haue swerved from the same/.

But the devisour thereof perhapps thought that the civill example of the 170
English being sett before them and there daylie conuersing with them
would haue brough them by dislike of there owne savage life to the liking

143 overunne] overcume *G*   144 enenie] enemie *G*   144 encounted] encounte[re]d *G*
162 land] lands *?*   172 brough] brought *G*

and imbrasing of better civilitie, But it is farr other wise, for in steede of following them they flie them and moste hatefullie shune them for 2º. causes, ffirst because they haue euer bene brought vpp licenciouslie and to liue as eche one listeth which they esteeme halfe happines, So that nowe to be brought into anie better order they accompte it to be restrained of theire libertie and extreame wretchednes/. Secondlie because they naturallie hate the English, so that theire fashons they allso hate. The cause of this originall hate is for that they were Conquered of the English the memorie whereof is yet fresh among them and the desire bothe of reuenge and allso of recouerie of theire landes and daylie revived and kindled amongst them by theire lordes and Councellours for which they both hate our selues and our lawes and customes. Therefore in the first institucion should haue bene provided for that before newe building were erected the olde should haue bene plucked downe. ffor to think to ioyne and patch them both to gether in an equalitie of state is impossible and will neuer be without daunger of agreat downefall such as nowe is hapened. | Howe then? should the Irish haue ben quite rooted out? That were to bloudie a course: and yet there continuall rebelliouse deedes deserue little better/. But then when this prouince was planted they were so weake that they might haue bene framed and fashoned to anie thinge then should they haue ben disarmed for euer and stronge garrisons sett ouer them. which they should haue ben forced at there owne charges to maintaine without anie charge to your Maiestie since there disloyall dealinges were the cause thereof. which they would then haue ben moste glad to bere by which meanes your Maiestie might haue had even out of this Prouince 3. or 4000. souldiers continuallie maintained vnto you. whome youe might at all tymes haue vsed to your seruice with continuall supplie and change of newe./

And this I vndertake (vnder correction vpon all that I haue in the world) should haue bene afforded you with as litle greevance and burden of the Countrie as nowe they beare allreadie. ffor the charge which nowe this Prouince beareth what of your Maiestes Composicion what of the President his Imposicion what of Sheriffes and Cessours extorcion and other daylie bad occasions is no lesse then woulde maintaine you so great a garrison besides it is nowe exacted with the peoples great discontentment that wolde be then yeelded with verie good will when they should be sure to knowe the vttermoste of there charge/.

This at the tyme of the late placing of inhabitantes here might haue easly bene established but thoccasion was then let slipp when this Country was

182 and daylie] are daylie G

weake and waste, yet since the like is likely and must of necessitie ensue a gaine after the subdueing of this Present generall rebellion it is expedient to be minded before it be to be effected/ But in the meane season wee poore wreches which nowe beare the burden of all ouersightes power out our moste humble and pittiouse plainte vnto your moste excellent Maiestie that it may please you to caste your graciouse minde vnto the cairfull regarde of our miseries which being quite banished out of our inhabitance and the lands vpon which wee haue spent all the small porcion of our abilities in building and erecting such traides of husbandries as wee haue betaken haue nowe nothing left but to cry vnto you for tymelie aide before wee be brought to vtter distruction and our wreched liues (which onelie now remaine vnto vs be made the pray of dogges and sauage wilde beastes/.

Whereas your Maiestie as you haue hitherto made your selfe through all the worlde a gloriouse example of mercie and Clemencye and euen vnto these vile Catifes (though moste vnworthie thereof) So nowe by extending vpon them the terror of your wrath in avengement of there continuall disloyalltie and disobedience you shall | spreade the honorable fame of your Iustice and redeeme both your owne honour and allso the reputacion of your people which these base raskalls through your to longe suffrance and this so late hapened reproche shaken and endangered with all moste all Christian princes besides which you shall setle a perpetuall establishment both of peace (whereby your riches shall be much increased) and allso of great strength which may from hence be drawne both to the better assurance of this your kingdome and allso to the continuall seruice of that your Realme of England. ffor wee well hope and that is some comforte to vs in all these our miseries that God hath put this madding minde so generallie into all this rebelliouse nacion the rather to stirre vpp your Maiestie nowe to take vengance of all theire longe and lewde and wicked vsage and to make an vniuersall reformacion of all this Realme which nowe doth allmoste offer yt selfe vnto yo that may worke a perpetuall establishment of peace and good gouernment to your Maiestes great honour and no lesse profitt: So that nowe at lenght you may haue an end of wasting your treasure and people in this sorte as you haue done too longe and hindering you from more honorable atchivementes/.

Pardon therefore moste gracious Soueraigne to wreched greued wightes your true faithfull subiectes which too sharplie haue tasted of these euills to vnfoulde vnto your Maiestie the feeling of theire miserie and to seeke

225 euen] euer G   230 to] so G   231 shaken] [haue] shaken G

to impresse in your Princlie minde the due sence thereof whereby some
meete redresse may be tymelie provided therefore before wee feele and your
Maiestie hereof that which wee simple wreches see hard at hand/. But
our feare is leste your Maiestes wonted mercifull minde should againe be
wrought to your wonted milde courses and perswaded by some milde
meanes either of pardons or proteccions, this rebelliouse nacion may be
againe brought to some good conformacion which wee beseech allmightie
god to averte and to sett before your gracious eyes the iuste consideracion
howe that possiblie may be/. ffor it is not easie to thinke that they whoe
haue imbrewed them selues so deeplie in our bloud and inriched them
selues with our goods should euer trust vs to dwell againe amongste them:
or that wee should endure to liue amongst those peacablie without taking
iuste reuenge of them for all our euils, Besides they haueing once thus
shaken vs will euermore presume vpon the pride of there owne strength
which they haue nowe prooued through knowledge whereof they will be
ymboldened euer hearafter vpon the least dislike to revolte from your
obedience: And the relaps of euills your Maiestie well knowes be moste
perillouse: Moreouer howe great dishonour it shall be to protect or pardon
them which not onelie haue allwaies carried them selues vndutifully but
nowe allso in theire Common meetinges and their | Priestes preachinges
do speake so lewdlie and dishonorably of your moste sacred Maiestie that
it perceth our very soules to here it, But if your highnesse will dispose your
selfe to be inclined to any such milder dealing with them or to temporiz
any longer with pardons and proteccions as hath bene done by your gouer-
nours here then we humbly beseeche your Maiestie to call vs your poore
subiectes alltogether away from hence that at least we may die in our
Countrie and not see the horrable calamities which will thereby come vpon
all this land and from hence perhapps further as it may well be thought,
The which I humblie beseeching allmigtie god to put in your graciouse
minde as may be moste for his glorie and your owne kingdomes good we
cease not daylie to pray vnto allmightie god who keepe and maintaine
your longe prosperous reigne ouer vs in all happines

Finis./

251 hereof] here of *G*   279 who] to *G*

Certaine pointes to be considered of in the recouery of the Realme of Ireland./.

<small>Question</small> The question is whether be better and easier for hir Maiestie to subdue Ireland throughly and bring it all vnder or to reforme it and to repaire hir decayed partes/

| Of these twoe that must needes be better and also easier which may be done with less | charge
perill
tyme. |

<small>Reason</small> The assumption then is that it will be lesse charge, lesse perill and lesse spending of tyme to subdewe it alltogether then to go about to reforme it/

<small>*e of the n*</small> If you seeke to reforme it then you must retaine and saue the partes that seeme sounde and afterward recouer the partes that are vnsounde./

<small>f. 199ᵛ</small> To save and retaine the partes sounde is verie hard and allmoste vnpossible for that from them the partes vnsounde will receive both secret and open succours

| Secret | by working vnderhand trecherously |

| Open. | by milde and gentle intreaty |

| To recouer them must be | by warlike pursute
by milde and gentle intreaty |

| By gentle treatie must be either by | offering peacable condicons
abiding till they seek for peace |

To offer them is moste dishonorable and yet perhapps they will not accept yt being offered, which would be more dishonour/.

<small>282 of] om. H   283 of the Realme] om. H   284 Question] om. H   284 be] it be H   285 all] wholy H   285 and to] and H   288 needes] om. H   288 perill] lesse perill H   289 tyme] and lesse tyme H   291 Reason] om. H   291 assumption] assumpsit H   291 perill] daunger H   293-4 Proofe . . . reason] The reason is H   293 retaine] first retaine it H   294 afterward] after H   294 that are] om. H   295 vnpossible] impossible H   297 succours] succure H   299 trecherously] treacherie, and H   300-1 milde . . . intreaty] taking it forciblye H   302 be] be either H   302 pursute] pursuite or H   303 milde and] om. H   304-5 gentle . . . be] entreaty H   304 offering] offeringe them H   305 by] om. H   305 abiding] or abidinge H   305 seek] sue H   306 yet] om. H   307 being</small>

To abide till they seeke yt would be chargable and allso perillouse for they will not seeke it till they be driven to it by force.

Therefore they must needs be driven to it by force/ 310

But whether with great force or with smale force is nowe to be considered by comparing the { Charge / Perill / Tyme./ }

The lesse force seemeth lesse charge but considering the long continuance that it will rquire and the perill thereby growinge both to Ireland and 315 allso to England it selfe in suffering so great a rebellion stand so longe on foote it will in the end prooue more chargable and allso much more dangerous and yet not so effectuall/.

Resolucion Besides in so longe continuance the Countrie maladie will consume all the forces./ 320

The resolucion therefore appereth

That the greater force will finish all in one yere or 2º. yeres which the lesse will not do in 4 or 5. yeres./

Lesse chargfull is the grosse accompte

Less perillous { To the forces themselues 325 / To both the Realmes }

f. 200ʳ Lesse losse of tyme by meanes of the spedie finishing of the enterprise

Great force must be the instrument but famine must be the meane for till Ireland be famished it can not be subdued./.

But if the reformacion shall neuertheles be intemded then these propo- 330 sicions are therein to be considered and obserued/.

That there can be no conformitie of gouernment whereis no conformitie of religion/.

That there can be no sounde agreement betwene twoe equall contraries viz: the English and Irish./ 335

... dishonour] and then it wilbe mere dishonorable *H* 309 driven ... force] enforced *H* 310 driven ... force] enforced *H* 311 *But*] Nowe *H* 311 *with smale force*] small *H* 312 *nowe*] it *H* 312 *by*] and that by *H* 312 *the*] *om. H* 313 *Tyme*] and tyme *H* 314 lesse ... lesse] lest force semeth the lest *H* 316 allso to] *om. H* 316 stand] to stande *H* 319 *Resolucion*] *om. H* 319 all the] all your *H* 322 will] which will *H* 322 yere] *om. H* 324 Lesse chargfull is] is lesse chargeable in *H* 326 *To*] and to *H* 327 Lesse] and lesse *H* 328 must be the meane] the meanes *H* 330 intemded] intended *GH* 331 considered and obserued] weighed, and considered *H* 332 whereis] where there is *H* 335 and] and the *H*

That there can be no assurance of peace where the worst sorte are the stronger

That all which make the head of anie faction is to be remoued or weakened

> This will be accomplished with 10000. men in halfe a yere which els will not be performed of 3000 in 2.° yeres and the same 10000. wilbe thence presentlie ymployed to the rest of the warr./

ffor the conveyance of the portes which are to be possessed stronglie as well to let in our owne forces continuallie as to keepe out others and allsoe for the great reliefe of townes here for the rawe souldier

That the same is meetest to be begune in *Mounster* and from thence to proceede to the rest throughe *kery* and *Offalye*./

That the laying of garrisons will make but a protractiue warr vnles the Queene do first make hir selfe mistris of the feild whereunto there is necessarie a competent force of Horse/

All that the garrisons can doe is but to take prayes, but if the enemie were once broken he must be forced to scatter and then the garrisons shoulde haue good meanes of seruice vpon the broken partes

If it shall seeme that the resolucion to subdue Ireland wholly with stronge force is too blouddie and crewell the same is thus to be mittigated./

That before the great force goe forthe generall proclamacion be made that all which will come in and submitt themselues absolutelie within ten or twelue daies (the principall excepted) shall haue pardon of life onelie vpon condicion that theire bodies their landes and theire goods shalbe at the disposicion of hir Maiestie which if they refuse what reason but afterwards rigor should be extended to them that will not receive mercie, and haue vtterlie renownced there obedience to hir Maiestie/

Whereas manie of the lords of the Countrie not longe before the confederating of this rebellion procured there freeholders to take there lands of them selues by lease manie of which are since gone into rebellion/ That provision may be made for the avoyding of such fraudulent conveyances made onelie to defeat hir Maiestie of the benefitt of theire attainder./

336 worst] worser *H*   338 That ... weakened] *om. G*   338 That] And that *H*   338 make] maye be *H*   339 This] *At this point H concludes with the rhyme*

> Marke Irishe when this doth fall
> Tirone and tire all
> A Peere out of Ingland shall come
> The Irish shall tire all and some
> St Patrick to St George a horseboye shalbe sene
> And all this shall happen in ninetye nyne.

343 of the] of them ?   347 kery] *Leix* ?

COMMENTARY

Guide references are to the line numbers of the present edition.

Notes not otherwise assigned are by the Editor. Editorial comment upon notes is either included in square brackets or designated EDITOR.

The titles of books or works cited more than three or four times are omitted, and only the name of the author, with reference to volume, page, or line, is given. Citations from articles in periodicals or series are made only by reference to the volume and page of the journal. Titles can in general be found under names of authors in the Bibliography. Notes from commentaries are cited by editor's name only. Where notes on Spenser's poems are cited by line numbers only, the reference is to the commentary in the earlier volumes of the present edition.

ABBREVIATIONS

SPENSER'S WORKS

Am.	Amoretti
As.	Astrophel
Ax.	Axiochus
Bel.	Visions of Bellay
Bel. 1	Version of Bel. in Th. W.
Bel. 2	Version of Bel. in Comp.
B. N.	Brief Note of Ireland
Col.	Colin Clouts Come Home Againe
Comp.	Complaints
Daph.	Daphnaida
Ded. Epist.	E. K.'s Epistle to Harvey prefacing the S. C.
Ded. Son.	Dedicatory Sonnets in Book III, pp. 190-8
Epith.	Epithalamion
F. H.	Fowre Hymnes
F. Q.	Faerie Queene
Gen. Arg.	Generall Argument of the Whole Booke, prefacing the S. C.
Gn.	Virgils Gnat
Hub.	Mother Hubberds Tale
H. L.	Hymne in Honour of Love
H. B.	Hymne in Honour of Beautie
H. H. L.	Hymne of Heavenly Love
H. H. B.	Hymne of Heavenly Beautie
Letter I	First letter in Two Other Very Commendable Letters, 1580
Letter III	First letter in Three Proper and Witty, Familiar Letters, 1580
Mui.	Muiopotmos
Pet.	Visions of Petrarch
Pet. 1	Version of Pet. in Th. W.

Pet. 2	Version of *Pet.* in *Comp.*
Pr.	*Prologue*
Proth.	*Prothalamion*
R. R.	*Ruines of Rome*
R. T.	*Ruines of Time*
S. C., Jan., etc.	*Shepheardes Calender, January,* etc.
T. M.	*Teares of the Muses*
Th. W.	Vander Noodt's *Theatre for Worldlings,* 1569
Van.	*Visions of the Worlds Vanitie*
View	*View of the Present State of Ireland*

PERIODICALS AND COLLECTIONS

Anglia	*Anglia Zeitschrift*
Archiv	*Archiv für das Studium der Neueren Sprachen und Literaturen*
C. C. MSS.	*Calendar of the Carew Manuscripts*
C. S. P. Ir.	*Calendar of State Papers Relating to Ireland*
C. S. P. S.	*Calendar of Letters and State Papers Relating to English Affairs, Preserved Principally in the Archives of Simancas*
C. S. P. V.	*Calendar of State Papers and Manuscripts, Relating to English Affairs, Existing in the Archives and Collections of Venice*
DNB	*Dictionary of National Biography*
EHR	*English Historical Review*
ELH	*English Literary History*
HMC	*Historical Manuscripts Commission*
JCHAS	*Journal of the Cork Historical and Archaeological Society*
JEGP	*Journal of English and Germanic Philology*
JRSAI	*Journal of the Royal Society of Antiquaries of Ireland*
MLN	*Modern Language Notes*
MLQ	*Modern Language Quarterly*
MLR	*Modern Language Review*
MP	*Modern Philology*
NED	*New English Dictionary on Historical Principles*
NQ	*Notes and Queries*
PMLA	*Publications of the Modern Language Association*
PQ	*Philological Quarterly*
PRIA	*Proceedings of the Royal Irish Academy*
RES	*Review of English Studies*
SAB	*Shakespeare Association Bulletin*
SP	*Studies in Philology*
TLS	*London Times Literary Supplement*
TRIA	*Transactions of the Royal Irish Academy*
UTB	*University of Texas Bulletin*

LETTERS

GREENLAW (*PMLA* 25. 535-8) emphasizes the difference in tone between Spenser's two letters: the first is full of hope and worldly ambition; the second is concerned with purely literary matters. CALDWELL (*PMLA* 41. 571-2) places the change in tone, not between Letters I and III, but between the parts of Letter I written respectively on 5 October (119-264) and 15-16 October (1-118). HEWLETT (*PMLA* 42. 1060-5), in turn, sees no change in tone between the two parts of Letter I and doubts that Spenser's plans for travel had been dropped in the interval, since Harvey's reply on 23 October shows that he still expected Spenser to go abroad (Letter II 134-41).

JENKINS (*SAB* 19. 158-9), far from finding significant changes in tone, believes that the letters contain internal evidence of all having been concocted by Spenser and Harvey, working together in Westminster, and that none of them actually passed through the mails. [But see note on Letter I 64-7 below.]

LETTER I

16-28. GREGORY SMITH. Presumably referring to the *Shepheardes Calender*. Spenser, still hesitating to publish his poem, is doubtful of its welcome by Sidney and the common friends who were received at Penshurst and Leicester House.

17. "vttering." DODGE. Publishing, not necessarily in print.

20. "the work." DODGE. Evidently the *Calendar*.

20-1. "his excellent Lordship." TODD. The Earl of Leicester, I suppose.

DODGE. Leicester, to whom apparently, at this time, the *Calendar* was meant to be dedicated.

[For what appear to be other allusions to Leicester see Letters I 245-7, III 14-5, IV 481, V 192-4.]

21-3. If the work in question is *S. C.*, this private personage is undoubtedly the Rosalind of that volume (Child 1. xiv). Banks (*PMLA* 52. 335-7) believes that Spenser married the Rosalind of *S. C.*, who is likewise the sweetheart of Letters III 76-80; IV 6; V 110-4, 533-8. While Banks is probably right in translating "*altera Rosalindula est*" (V 536) as "she is a changed little Rosalind," *Col.* makes it difficult to believe that the sweetheart of the letters is the Rosalind of *S. C.* See *Minor Poems* 1. 651-5; Judson, *Life*, pp. 44-5; and note on Letter III 76-80.

24-5. JUDSON (*Life*, p. 62). Have we here a hint of Harvey's cooperation in its [*S. C.'s*] editing?

[If the "selfe former Title" is *The Shepheardes Calender*, is Harvey's "fine Addition" the subtitle "Conteyning twelue Æglogues proportionable to the twelue monethes," which saves the reader from confusing *S. C.* with the old *Kalender of Shepherdes?*]

31-5. At the time this letter was written, it was expected that Richard Bridgewater would resign the post of Public Orator of Cambridge; the following April, as soon as Harvey heard that the position was actually vacant, he wrote to Burghley to request it for himself (see Moore Smith, *Gabriel Harvey's Marginalia*, pp. 34-5).

34-5. "*Verùm ne quid durius.*" "But nothing more difficult [than to seek preferment from a noble]."

38. "*De quibus . . . tuis.*" "Concerning which [you have written] in that former very sweet, long letter of yours." Judson (*Life*, p. 62) believes that in their letters Spenser and Harvey found Latin "suitable for their more intimate confidences—an epistolary lowering of the voice."

39-40. CHILD (1. xiii) notes that the sentence, if "understood loosely, would lead us to believe that Spenser had even been already presented to the Queen. . . . But the most that these words will really warrant is, that he had at some time been employed as Leicester's agent on confidential business with Elizabeth."

GROSART (Spenser's *Works* 1. 68). This at least informs us that Spenser had been introduced to Elizabeth long before Sir Walter Ralegh took him to Court.

BUCK (*PMLA* 23. 85). In the fall of 1579 Spenser had an audience with the Queen. . . . The reception of the young poet was not altogether a flattering one to him. He will say nothing about it.

40-1. TODD. Sidney and Dyer appear to have been particular friends. Harvey calls them "the Castor and Pollux of poetry." In Davison's *Poetical Rapsodie*, edit. 1602, two pastoral Odes are to be found, made "by Sir P. Sidney upon his meeting with his two worthy friends, and fellow-poets, Sir Edward Dier and M. Fulke Grevill."

GREGORY SMITH. Sir Edward Dyer (*d*. 1607), courtier and poet. Sidney and Dyer are grouped together in the prefatory verses to Watson's Ἑκατομπαθία—

"Hic quoque seu subeas Sydnaei, siue Dyeri
Scrinia, qua Musis area bina patet."

EDITOR. Sidney and Dyer are mentioned together at six, or possibly seven, other places in the Spenser-Harvey letters: I 54-6, 82-3; II 43; IV 578-9 (?); V 12-9, 179-81, 269-70. Spenser also refers to Dyer in III 52-3 and to Sidney in I 50-2, 254-6; III 48-9. Harvey refers to Sidney in V 21. For Spenser's relationship to Sidney see *Minor Poems* 1. 487-90; for Harvey's, see note on Letter I 41-4.

41-4. Harvey, who met Sidney at Audley End in 1578, in his *Gratulationum Valdinensium* of the same year (lib. IIII, pp. 15-8) celebrates the young courtier in two Latin poems, totaling ninety-three lines. Nashe later asserted that Sidney, although he had originally encouraged Harvey, began with time to look askance at his pride and vanity (*Haue with You to Saffron-Walden*, 1596, sigs. S1^v–S2^r). See also Letter III 52-3.

COMMENTARY 251

44-60.   Spenser continues the subject of prosody in Letters I (67-78) and III (20-56); Harvey replies in Letters II (46-112) and V (10-55, 102-4, 412-532). See Appendix I, section C.

45.   GREGORY SMITH. Orig. ἀρειωπαγῷ. Of this *Areopagus* we know little. It was probably an informal society, perhaps unknown by that name except to one or two of its members. "Academies" were in the air; and it may be that the young writers had Baïf's recent project in mind. It has been suggested that the title was borrowed from "the Florentine Academy in the time of Lorenzo, which bore the same name" (Einstein, *Ital. Renaissance in England* (1902), p. 357), but it is more probably a direct adaptation from classical history. "Areopagites" frequently occurs in the ordinary sense. [See Letter II 42-5 and Appendix I, section C.]

47.   "their whole Senate." MACINTIRE (*PMLA* 26. 501) interprets the phrase to mean that the Areopagus had other members than Sidney and Dyer. [But Spenser seems rather to be playfully calling a group of two men a senate; and Harvey apparently understands him in this sense, Letter II 42-5.]

48-9.   SARGENT (p. 63). Dyer's part in the new versification is by no means clear: not a scrap of verse written by him in classical hexameter has been preserved. . . . Can one even be certain that Dyer ever joined in the experiment? . . . . [Spenser] fails to refer to any specific poem by Dyer. [Sidney's "greate practise," however, is witnessed by the quantitative poems in the *Arcadia*.]

49.   It is significant that *F* and *Hu* add "almost" before "drawen": in 1679 it is already incredible, or discreditable, that Spenser should for a time have favored a quantitative prosody.

50-2.   TODD. Stephen Gosson; whose book was first published in 1579. He was a preacher, and a writer of verses; noted, according to Antony Wood, for his admirable penning of pastorals; yet very severe "against Poets, Pipers, Players, and their Excusers," as he is pleased thus to class them, in his *Schoole of Abuse* and in his *Apologie* (published in the same year) for the said didactick work!
    BOURNE (p. 205). Whatever scorn Sidney may have felt he seems to have kindly kept from the knowledge of Gosson, who, in his ignorant boldness, dedicated to him in November [1579] another book, "The Ephemerides of Phialo."
    ORWEN (*MLN* 42. 574-6) believes that Spenser was wrong in assuming that Sidney scorned Gosson; but WILLIAM RINGLER (*Stephen Gosson*, pp. 36-7) shows that Sidney's interest in poetry was not generally known in 1579 and that the scorn he felt for *The Shoole of Abuse* probably became apparent to Gosson, who was not stupid, only after the publication of the Spenser-Harvey letters in mid-1580.

55.   BIRCH (p. xii) and DODGE (p. xiv) believe that "*My Slomber*" is the same work which Spenser later calls "my *Dreames*" [see Letter III 70 and note on same]; TODD, who is followed with less conviction by GREGORY SMITH, identifies "*My Slomber*" as the poem Ponsonby calls "*A senights slumber*" in

the preface of *Comp.* (1591). [For the comments of Hales, Grosart, and Buck see *Minor Poems* 2. 514-5.]

EDITOR. In 1660-1661 John Worthington and Samuel Hartlib attempted, without avail, to secure from Ireland copies of "*A senights slumber*," "*The Dying Pellicane*," and the "*Dreames*" (Worthington's *Diary and Correspondence*, ed. Crossley and Christie, 1. 259, 261, 271, 279; 2. 76, 86).

55.   "his honor." Probably Sidney, to whom reference has just been made (50-2).

56-60.   TODD. We lament the perverted taste of Spenser in this respect. But he afterwards paid little or no attention to this *versifying*. He means, by *versifying*, the unnatural adaptation of English verse to Latin prosody; of which further notice is presently taken.

58-60.   "But then I thought that you alone were wise with Ascham; now I see that the Court fosters excellent English poets."

DODGE. It was Roger Ascham who, in his *Schoolmaster*, began the crusade for the recovery of classic measures. [See *The Scholemaster*, 1570, ff. 59^v–62^r, and Harvey's references to Ascham in Letters II 79-83; V 17-20, 436-41, 481-3.]

60.   "Maister E. K." See Todd's note in *Minor Poems* 1. 645-6; Letter III 86-7; Appendix I, section E.

62-3.   CRAIK (1. 34) suggests that E. K.'s verses may be found in the Latin poem which follows in the same letter [119-236]; and this suggestion has been accepted by KUERSTEINER (*PMLA* 50. 153, 154) and JENKINS (*SAB* 20. 31) as evidence that E. K. is Spenser. [But the part of Spenser's letter which promises E. K.'s verses "hereafter" was written on 15 October, when Spenser still supposed that his Latin verses had already reached Harvey.]

62.   *Painful* in the sense of *laborious* occurs in *Hub.* 275, *F. Q.* 2. 3. 40. 9, *Am.* 32. 1, etc.

64-7.   Since 16 October, 1579, was a Friday, Harvey's letter of "laste weeke" must have been sent between 4 and 10 October; and since Spenser was surprised that it did not mention his own letter of 5 October (108-10), Harvey's letter was probably written between 7 and 10 October.

65.   GREGORY SMITH. The references to "Mistresse Kerke" in Spenser's letter have a strong circumstantial value in the argument for a real "E. K." They at least show that some one of the name was actually known to Spenser and Harvey; and it may well be that she was the mother of their College contemporary, and had received them as her son's friends at her house in London. [See Letter I 257 and *Minor Poems* 1. 645-50.]

J. C. SMITH. It is not unlikely, indeed, that the "Mistress Kerke" in Westminster, who took charge of letters for Spenser in October of this year, was E. K.'s mother and that all three were living in her house. [Note that Spenser does not imply that Mistress Kirke lived in Westminster.]

COMMENTARY 253

68. "Versifying in English." Writing of English verses in accordance with a quantitative system.

70-118. The omission of this passage by *F* and *Hu* reveals how little sympathy the neo-classical period felt for the attempt to imitate classical prosody in English.

73. TODD. Among the many publications by Drant, I have not discovered *these Rules*; which may be a subject of deep lamentation to English hexametrists, and pentametrists, atque id genus omne, unless they have been more fortunate in their search! Tanner's list of his publications is copious. Drant was of St. John's College, Cambridge, afterwards prebendary of Chichester and archdeacon of Lewes. See his character in Warton's *Hist. of Eng. Poetry*, vol. iii. p. 429.

SCHELLING (*Poetic and Verse Criticism*, p. 28) assumes that Drant was the author of a work entitled *Prosody*. [See Harvey, Letter V 20-1.] SAINTSBURY (2. 175) argues that Drant's rules actually existed since Spenser later asks for Harvey's own rules [Letter III 46-8].

GREGORY SMITH. These ["Maister *Drants* Rules"], if ever committed to writing, are not extant. The references throughout these letters, and elsewhere, do not preclude the possibility that Drant had merely conveyed his views to his friends in conversation, and had persuaded them to carry them out in their verse-making.

Thomas Drant (*d.?* 1578), Archdeacon of Lewes, is known as the author of *A Medicinable Morall*, 1566, and of *Horace his arte of Poetrie, pistles and satyrs Englished*, 1567. In neither is there any critical material. His recognition in later literary history is undoubtedly due to the allusions in these letters (especially Spenser's), and is as undoubtedly in excess of his deserts, even as a contributor to the narrow controversy about the English hexameter.

DODGE. Archdeacon Thomas Drant (died 1578) would have subjected English prosody strictly to classic law.

EDITOR. Drant's university career seems to have centered in St. John's College 1558-1569 (Venn); in 1569-1570 he was a chaplain of Archbishop Grindal's, to whom he dedicated his volume of Latin poems, *Praesvl* and *Silua* (1578?). For his connection with the Sidney group see Appendix I, section C. Spenser mentions his rules again (Letter III 48). Harvey's references to Drant in the Letters (II 91-2, 98-109; V 20-1, 414, 437) are disparaging in tone; but while he scorned "Dranting of Verses," he seems to have admired Drant's sermons, his translations of Horace, and his "aspiring spirit" (*Pierces Supererogation*, 1593, pp. 74, 191-2; *Marginalia*, pp. 173, 231).

73-4. "Which, however, I pardon in so fine a poet and for your very great authority in these matters of [Drant] himself."

77-8. "Nevertheless I shall follow only you, as I have often avowed, yet never indeed overtake you while I live." See Letter III 94.

CHURCH (p. 19) notes that Spenser's "language is extravagant, but there is no reason to think it was not genuine."

80.   "warrant." See Harvey, Letter II 109-10.

80.   "precisely perfect." See Harvey, Letter II 49, 76, 89.

82-3.   In October, 1579, the Privy Council held its meetings either at Greenwich or in the Star Chamber at Westminster (*Acts of the Privy Council*, ed. John R. Dasent, 11. 270-94). It may be assumed that the Court was staying at one or other of the palaces in these places.

84.   TODD. Preston, first of King's College, Cambridge, afterwards Master of Trinity Hall, was the author of "A Lamentable Tragedy mixed ful of pleasant mirth, conteyning the life of Cambises king of Percia, etc." which is said to have rendered the author an object of ridicule. He wrote also "A geliflower or swete marygolde, wherein the frutes of teranny you may beholde." See the *Biographia Dramatica*, Art. Preston, (Thomas) and Cambyses. See also *Bibliograph. Poetica*.

GREGORY SMITH. Thomas Preston (1537-98), Master of Trinity Hall, Cambridge, author of *Cambises* (1569).

EDITOR. Preston matriculated at Cambridge in 1553 and received the B. A. in 1557-8, the M. A. in 1561, and perhaps the LL. D. in 1576 (Venn). He and Harvey were rivals for the Public Oratorship of the University in 1579-80; and when Preston was appointed Master of Trinity Hall in 1584, Harvey was defeated in his ambition to hold that post (*Marginalia*, pp. 35, 49). In 1577 Harvey praised the abilities of Preston as an orator (*Rhetor*, sigs. 01ʳ, 02ᵛ); and he noted in his copy of Livy's *Opera* that he and Preston had read Livy together (Moore Smith, *MLR* 28. 79). E. K. Chambers (*Elizabethan Stage* 3. 469) believes that another Thomas Preston, not the Master of Trinity Hall, was the author of *Cambyses*. See Judson, *Life*, p. 40.

84.   TODD. Still, who was afterwards bishop of Bath and Wells, is believed to be the author of *Gammer Gurtons Needle*, the earliest exhibition of what "looks like a regular comedy" in our language. See *Biograph. Dram.* Art. Still, (John) and Malone's *Hist. Acc. of the Eng. Stage*. "His breeding," says Sir John Harington, "was from his childhood in good literature, and partly in musick, which was counted in those days a preparative to divinitie.—To conclude of this bishop, without flatterie, I hold him a rare man for preaching, for arguing, for learning, for living." *Briefe View of the State of the Church of England in Q. Eliz. time*, etc. edit. 1653. 12mo. p. 119.

GREGORY SMITH. John Still (?1543-1608), Bishop of Bath and Wells, and the reputed author, on very doubtful evidence, of *Gammer Gurton's Needle* (1575).

EDITOR. As a member of Christ's College 1559-1572 and the master of Trinity Hall 1577-1593 (Venn), Still must have been well known to Harvey, who praises him in his printed works (*e. g., Pierces Supererogation*, 1593, pp. 191-2). See Letter IV 400-1. Still was an uncle by marriage of the poet William Alabaster, whose *Eliseis* Spenser praises in *Col.* 400-15. See Judson, *Life*, p. 40.

85-106.   ABRAHAM FRAUNCE (*The Arcadian Rhetorike*, 1588, sig. C4ʳ) quotes

COMMENTARY 255

these lines, as by "*Immeritô: Spencer,*" to illustrate the mixture of "*Iambicke*" and "*Spondaeus.*"

TODD. Admitted into Davison's *Poetical Rapsodie*, edit. 1611. And since reprinted in Warton's *Observations on the Faerie Queene*, in Waldron's *Literary Museum*, and in Neve's *Cursory Remarks on the English Poets*.

HALES (p. xxix). Spenser of the sensitive ear wrote these lines. When the pedantic phantasy which had for a while seduced and corrupted him had gone from him, with what remorse he must have remembered these strange monsters of his creation!

SAINTSBURY (2. 173). Even in iambics—as nearly indigenous as any English foot—and even in the hands of such a poet as Spenser, the ungainly shamble of this truly "unhappy verse" curiously "witnesses" its writer's "unhappy state." [It does not seem to have occurred to Hales or Saintsbury that the tone of these lines is intentionally playful; Harvey calls them "Comicall Iambickes" in Letter II 79.]

RIX (pp. 63-4). One of the principal uses to which Spenser put the figures of rhetoric was to build out of them stanzas and larger blocks of verse, sometimes almost entire poems. . . . It is interesting to observe that in these verses, in which Spenser was interested exclusively in metrics, or form, he resorted to various rhetorical figures to provide both his framework and the material for the individual lines. The first three verses consist of an *apostrophe* to the poem itself; the other eighteen make up the scheme *carmen correlativum*. Within this figure, the first group of three lines introduces the subject matter, which has three parts: the bed, the board, and the virginals. Each of the remaining groups, or triplets, aside from carrying out the basic figure of the poem, has its own special use of *anaphora* [initial repetition] and *parison* [parallelism in both sound and sense], and the figure known as *pysma* [the use of a series of questions] also appears in the final triplet. In short, not only do these verses "varie not one inch from the Rule" of metrics; they are equally perfect from the point of view of rhetoric. The "Iambicum Trimetrum" has, of course, no poetic value whatever, but it is worth attention as showing how serviceable Spenser regarded this "art of schoole."

[For Harvey's criticism of this poem see Letter II 46-97. For commentary and detailed textual variants see *Minor Poems* 2. 509-10 and 709-10.]

87-8.   See *Minor Poems* 2. 723 on the correct position of "*Thought.*"

101.   "*kindely reste.*" See *F. Q.* 3. 1. 58. 2. *Kindly* in the sense of *natural* occurs in *Hub.* 695, *T. M.* 383, *F. Q.* 4. 10. 45. 9, etc.

106.   "Immerito." GREGORY SMITH. Spenser so signs the prefatory verses to his *Shepheardes Calender*.

115-6.   "thys other . . . Verses." The letter, containing verses, which has just arrived from Harvey (see 64-83).

119-239.   Spenser's Latin epistle may be translated, in irregular verses, as follows:

"To G. H., a man most eminent and long by many titles known to fame, good luck from his Immerito, about to sail for Gaul:

"Thus the lowliest poet greets a poet transcendent;
One who is new, a poet long known; one not unfriendly,
A friend: for whom, coming home after many a year, he   125
Wishes fair skies, still fairer than those he himself now enjoys
At departure. Lo the god (if he be really a god who
Lures the unwilling to evil and severs love that is sworn),
The sea god even now has given me manifest signs
And gently levels the waters my sail-laden ship will   130
Presently furrow; Father Aeolus even now has impounded
The great angry passionate gusts of the north wind—
All things are thus fit for my journey; only I am unfit.
For my heart, wounded I cannot tell how, has of late
Heaved on the perilous ocean, while Love, a mighty shipmaster, 135
Lashes and drives the shivering vessel hither and yon.
Cupid's nimble arrow has lightly divided
Reason, with her solider counsels, from honor immortal.
Torn between doubts, in the very port I have foundered.
"Rip these love-knots apart, you now stalwart despiser   140
Of Love quiver-armed (I pray that the gods may not allow you that name
Without payment), and you will become my stalwart Apollo.
A magnanimous spirit, I know, spurs you up to the summits
Of honor and inspires your poems with emotions more solemn
Than light-hearted love (yet not all love is light-hearted). 145
Therefore you prize nothing so much as perennial fame
Or more than the radiant vision of glory divine.
Other things which the giddy mob rabble adores as its gods—
Fat farmlands, gold, city freeholds, alliance of friends;
What gladdens the eye, pleasing forms, pageantry, paramours comely— 150
These you trample like muck and call a mocking of reason.
"Your scorn is worthy indeed of the Harvey I honor,
The orator copious, the heart that is noble; nor would
The wise Stoics of old fear to set their sanction, with seals
Everlasting, upon it. But men's tastes are not always the same. 155
The eloquent son of hoary Laërtes, howbeit an exile
Worn out with long tossing under alien quarters of heaven,
Across the wide ocean's storm-tortured waste of gray waters,
Is yet said, for his weeping helpmate's embrace, to have spurned
Immortal good fortune and the genial bed of a goddess: 160
So steadfast was Love, and a wife even stronger than he. Him
You make sport of, however: so high is your grandiose spirit.
Beside the still brighter, more radiant vision of glory
And that fame begot far and near by notable merits,
Other things which the giddy mob rabble adores as its gods— 165
Fat farmlands, gold, freeholds, cattle, alliance of friends;
What gladdens the eye, pleasing forms, pageantry, paramours comely;
Whatever flatters the ear or the palate—all these you despise.
"Sapience, great indeed though your sapience be, is not sense;
And one who can in good season make light of trivial things 170
Often will easily triumph over supercilious wisemen.

COMMENTARY

The bitter tribe of the Sophists derided and mocked Aristippus
Who softened mild words to a tyrant proud of his purple;
Aristippus scoffed at the vainglorious talk of the Sophists
Whom the thin flitting shade of a midge could cruelly torture.   175
Whoever strives to tickle the fancy of mighty patricians
Strives to be foolish, for follies ever multiply favor.
Whoever wishes, in fine, to ennoble his forehead with bands
Of the laurel and, by pleasing the people, to win their applause,
Learns to play mad and reaps the base praise which rewards   180
Ignominious nonsense. Father Ennius, although he was styled
The one wise man among thousands unwise, is also commended
For pouring out poems which flowed with delirious wine.
Nor, by your good leave, do you, O our age's great Cato,
Really deserve the sacred name of a time-honored poet,   185
However high-minded and noble the melodious verse you compose,
Unless you are willing to dote: the world is so laden with dullards.
   " But the safe road still divides the abyss through the middle,
For you would describe as a wise man only one who wished to appear
Neither too much of a fool nor a mentor shrewd beyond measure.   190
Here the wave would overwhelm, there the fire consume you.
Nor ought you to spurn voluptuous pleasures too much;
Nor a wife brought at long last to the altar; nor, if you are wise,
An offer of gold (such pitiful sophistries it were better
To leave for men worthy of pity, Curii or Fabritii, once   195
Their age's bright honor, now the dishonor of ours); nor yet seek
These pleasures too often. Either course is fraught with reproach.
He who discerns this full well (if any, indeed, well discerns this)—
Write it even though Socrates differ—only he is a wise man.
One virtue fashions devout men; another, men who are just;   200
A third, minds highly judicious and bold; but he wins
Every vote of approval who mingles use with delight.
   " Long ago the gods made me the gift of delight, but not of the useful:
O would they had given the useful, even now, along with delight.
May they, unless they too much begrudge joy among mortals   205
(And for gods the mightiest deeds are no more than the least),
Be able to yield me both use and delight at one stroke. But
Your good fortune is so large that it gives, whenever you please,
Equal portions of both, while we whose birth star was bitter
Go stalking our fortune far off through the Caucasus grim,   210
Across the rude Pyrenees, by Babylon's midden impure;
And should we not find there what is sought, we shall seek it
Beyond, comrades of Ulysses who wander the measureless ocean
On journeys ever renewed, far and wide amid waters remote;
And thence with heavy footsteps shall follow the sorrowing goddess   215
From whose search dark earth withheld his illustrious theft.
For a youth not too meagerly gifted feels it shameful to waste
His green season waiting at home, where vainly he lingers
In the ignominious twilight of duties obscure, and too late
Find the grown ear of his hope still vacant of grain.   220
We shall go then at once (who wishes me Godspeed at going?);
We shall press our worn feet up the jagged defiles of the Alps.
   " But who will meanwhile provide you with fond little letters

>   Tasting of Britain's sweet dew, or songs wanton with love?
>   Under the strange Oebalian mountain's gray forehead my muse,   225
>   Lamenting with grief unexhausted, will mourn her long silence
>   And weep solemn tears that Helicon's choirs are hushed.
>   My good Harvey (howbeit equally dear to us all,
>   And with reason, since alone almost sweeter than all of the rest),
>   Angel and Gabriel both,—though surrounded by friends   230
>   Who are countless, attended by a gracious circle of talents,
>   Yet for Immerito, the only one absent, will often inquire
>   And murmur the wish, 'Would Heaven my Edmund were here.
>   He would have written me news, nor himself have been silent
>   Regarding his love, and often, in his heart and with words   235
>   Of the kindest, would bless me. May God guide him hither once more.' Etc.
>
> If the Graces had their way, I would write more; but the Muses are unwilling. Farewell, fare very well, my sweetest Harvey, to me of all my friends by far the dearest."

121.   HUGHES (1. xi). In the Year 1579. he was sent abroad by the Earl of *Leicester*, as appears by a Copy of *Latin* Verses dated from *Leicester*-House, and address'd to his Friend Mr. *Harvey*: but in what Service he was employ'd, is uncertain.

CHURCH (p. 23). He was on the eve of starting across the sea to be employed in Leicester's service, on some permanent mission in France, perhaps in connexion with the Alençon intrigue.

MOORE SMITH (*Gabriel Harvey's Marginalia*, p. 29) believes that the break in the Spenser-Harvey correspondence from October, 1579, to April, 1580, may have been due to the poet's absence from England. LONG (*PMLA* 31. 720-3) doubts that Spenser's trip was ever seriously intended and calls attention to the light manner in which Harvey dismisses it [Letter II 134-62].

JUDSON (*Life*, p. 63). In his Latin poem that should have gone to Harvey on October 5, 1579, Spenser had remarked that the truly wise man does not postpone marriage too long, and it may well be that he was contemplating this important step at the very moment Leicester proposed the foreign journey. If we are to believe that the Spenser who was married at St. Margaret's on October 27 was the poet [see Eccles, *TLS* 30. 1053], we may conjecture that Spenser felt free to proceed with his marriage after the journey abroad had been given up.

EDITOR. No evidence that Spenser made the trip has ever come to light. During the political uncertainties of the period plans of this kind were frequently made and later dropped; for example, Harvey's plans to go to Germany in 1578 were not realized (Moore Smith, *Gabriel Harvey's Marginalia*, p. 21).

Spenser's proposed tour, if we take "*in Gallias*" literally, would include northern Italy as well as France. His later references to the Caucasus and the Pyrenees (210-1) are probably due to poetic license, although "*Babilonaque turpem*" (211) may indicate that he had some idea of going to Rome. He speaks of crossing the Alps (222) and seems, immediately afterwards, to refer to Vesuvius (225). It may be noted that Jerome Turler's *Traueiler* (1575), of which Spenser had given a copy to Harvey in 1578 (*Marginalia*, p. 173) and which Harvey

COMMENTARY

mentions in his reply to the present letter, is limited in its account of foreign parts to a full description of Naples (pp. 118-93). See note on Letter I 125-6 and Harvey's comments on the trip in Letter II 134-62 (Latin translated in Carpenter, pp. 57-8).

123-236. COLLIER (1. clxiii) calls this poem a "not very favourable" specimen of Spenser's powers in Latin verse, and CHURCH (p. 17) finds it "contemptible in its mediaeval clumsiness."

RENWICK (*Edmund Spenser*, p. 104). The one existing specimen of Spenser's Latin verse gives no high idea of his skill in the scholarly art, but the academic practice must have helped to develop his sense of metre.

[See Harvey, Letter II 112-6.]

125-6. The implication is that Harvey too plans a trip to foreign parts. In Letter II 114-5 he speaks of "that time I haue been resident a yeare or twoo in *Italy*"; but from the tone of the passage it seems clear that he is merely chaffing Spenser, who is really planning a trip to France and Italy.

134-9. The love of which Spenser speaks here and later in the same poem must have been more than a conventional pose for him. If he married Machabyas Chylde on 27 October, 1579 (Eccles, *TLS* 30. 1053), he was probably considering marriage when he wrote these lines; his sweetheart, in any case, had probably become Mrs. Spenser by 23 April, 1580, when Harvey calls her "*Domina Immerito*" (Letter V 411 and 537-8; see Bradner, *Edmund Spenser*, p. 64). For Harvey's reply to the present passage see Letter II 117-34 (Latin translated in Carpenter, p. 57).

138. CHILD. This line appears to be corrupt.

142. This refers to Apollo in his traditional rôle of savior and healer.

147-50. Hasty composition perhaps explains the repetition of these lines, with slight changes, in 163 and 165-7.

156-60. Calypso offered Ulysses immortality if he would remain with her forever (*Odyssey* 5. 129-58).

172-5. Spenser probably has in mind a passage in the *Epistles* of Horace (1. 17. 13-32) which deals with Aristippus, the Cyrenaic philosopher of the fourth century B. C. Horace does not tell precisely this anecdote; but he, like Spenser, uses Aristippus to symbolize the balanced, rational philosophy which refuses to regard pleasure as an evil in itself. In his "Aulicus" (*Gratulationum Valdinensium*, 1578, lib. IIII, p. 19) Harvey quotes a line from the same passage in the *Epistles*:

Omnis Aristippum decuit color, et locus, et res.

But Harvey seems on the whole to have thought of Aristippus as a lover of pleasure (*Letter-Book*, pp. 78, 182; *Works* 3. 108), and Nashe uses his name to typify flattery (*Works*, ed. McKerrow, 1. 7, 3. 194, 3. 346). It is significant that Spenser follows the more urbane interpretation of Horace.

181-3. See Horace, *Epistulae* 1. 19. 7-8:

> Ennius ipse pater nunquam, nisi potus, ad arma
> Prosiluit dicenda.

The belief that a poet needs wine in order to free himself from care is expressed in *S. C. Oct.* 100-14 (see also gloss on 100 and 105).

184. See Harvey, Letter II 26.

187. See Cicero, *Epistulae ad Familiares* 9. 22. 4: "Stultorum plena sunt omnia." The phrase is used as an example in William Lily's *Shorte Introdvction of Grammar* (edition of 1567, ed. Vincent J. Flynn, 1945, sig. C7ᵛ); and it is discussed by Harvey (*Pierces Supererogation*, 1593, p. 168): "The wise-man, that said without exception, *Stultorum plena sunt omnia*: might easely haue bene entreated, to haue set it downe for a souerain Maxim, or generall rule; *Asinorum plena sunt omnia.*" Spenser may also remember Erasmus, *Moriae Encomium*, cap. 62.

188-202. With the doctrine that wisdom is a mean between extremes compare Spenser's conception of continence in *F. Q.* 2.

191. Spenser's choice of wave and fire to represent opposite and equally unfortunate extremes reappears in the names of Cymochles and Pyrochles in *F. Q.* 2.

194. Manius Curius Dentatus and Gaius Fabricius Luscinus, Roman leaders of the third century B. C., were frequently cited as examples of an old-fashioned simplicity of life; Horace (*Carminum* 1. 12. 40-1) and Cicero (*Pro Plancio* 25; *In Pisonem* 24) mention them together.

197. "*crimine.*" In *F. Q.* 2. 12. 75. 9 Spenser probably uses "crime," as here, in the Latin sense of *reproach.*

202. This line, quoted from Horace, *Ars Poetica* 343, is a commonplace of Elizabethan writing. See, for example, Harvey's *Rhetor*, 1577, sig. O4ᵛ.

205. GROSART (Spenser's *Works* 1. 69). "Æquivalia" should be "aequalia."

210-1. LONG (*PMLA* 31. 723). Poetic imagination has certainly transfigured the facts.

212. GROSART (Spenser's *Works* 1. 69). "Quaesitum" should be "quaesitam." "Invenerimus" — a false quantity, *e* being short, whereas the position requires it to be long.

215-6. The reference is to Ceres, whose daughter Proserpina was stolen by Pluto, the king of the underworld.

217-20. ROLAND SMITH (*MLN* 60. 394-8) suggests that these lines probably impressed Milton as a young man, as the parallels in his sonnet "How Soon Hath Time" reveal, and that Spenser may have been one of the "more timely-happy spirits" for Milton.

218. GROSART (Spenser's *Works* 1. 69). "Non nimis," etc. — query corrupt?

224.   "*Litterulas.*" Their surviving correspondence suggests that Spenser tended to write much shorter letters than Harvey did, and here there may be a playful allusion to this difference.

225.   "*Oebalij . . . montis.*" Spenser probably refers to Vesuvius: the mother of one Oebalus was a nymph of the stream Sebeto near Naples (see note on Letter I 121). But Spenser may possibly have in mind Oebalus King of Sparta; in that case the reference would be to the mountain range Taÿgetus.

230.   "*Angelus et Gabriel.*" See Letter V 10-1.

233.   In less than a year after the publication of the anonymous *S. C.* an intelligent reader would here discover the first name of its author, since the Immerito of these letters speaks unmistakably of "my *Calendar*" (III 86).

243.   "presently." DODGE. At present.

245.   "my Lorde." JUDSON (*Life*, p. 60). Evidently Leicester. [See note on Letter I 121.]

250-3.   GROSART (Harvey's *Works* 1. xlvi). The deepened words "the eternal memory," etc., etc., occur in a letter which bubbles over with raillery even to burlesque on Spenser's part.

EDITOR. *Memory* and *friendship* are repeated in accordance with the rhetorical figure known as *antistrophe, epiphora,* or *conversio,* repetition at the end of phrases or clauses (Rix, pp. 26-7).

252.   Gabriel Harvey (*Fovre Letters*, 1592, p. 7), in criticizing *Hub.*, uses the phrase "with the good leaue of vnspotted friendshipp."

256.   "He who reminds you to do what you already do." See the last lines of Ovid's *Tristia* (5. 14. 45-6), where the rest is given:

ille monendo
Laudat et hortatu comprobat acta suo.

["By his reminder praises, and by his charge commends, your acts."]

261.   Leicester House, later known as Essex House, was on the Thames between London and Westminster, in what was known as the Liberties of the Duchy of Lancaster (John Stowe, *A Survey of London*, 1908, 2. 92). See *Proth.* 137-45. Spenser seems to have had separate lodgings in Westminster (Letters I 64; III 43, 76).

261.   TODD. He says in a former part of this letter that it was the *sixteenth* day of month. . . . The date 5 at this conclusion, in the original publication, is therefore a mistake.

HASLEWOOD (2. xx) agrees with this reasoning, while MORRIS, CHILD, GROSART, GREGORY SMITH, and DODGE query if the date should not read "16" of October. MOORE SMITH (*Gabriel Harvey's Marginalia*, p. 28) accepts the date "5 of October 1576" for both the Latin poem and the English postscript, and CALDWELL (*PMLA* 41. 574) supports 5 October, 1579, for both, with the following arguments:

1. The content of "the letter" falls into two evidently separate parts [1-118, 119-264], with a naturally corresponding separation of dates.

2. One part Spenser calls his last farewell [249]; in the other he refers to a previous miscarried (and now enclosed) letter by this identical term [108].

3. The enclosure of the letter, *faute de mieux*, at least seems to be entire.

4. In one part he apologizes for the omission of some English verses for a farewell [240-3]; in another twenty-one lines of English verse are included [85-106].

5. In one part he is in a rush of departure [240-60]; in another, he is making engagements at Harvey's leisure [74-6].

JENKINS (*SAB* 19. 159) still believes that the final date is intended to apply to the whole letter and explains the confusion as an error due to the fact that Spenser and Harvey concocted the letters together in Westminster, without sending them through the mails.

262-4. "On sea, on land, alive and dead, your Immerito."

HALES and LEE note that this letter "is in most copies signed 'E. Spenser.'"

LETTER III

1-2. GROSART (Harvey's *Works* 1. xlv-vi). The phrase "long-approved and singular good friend" was a letter-heading of the time as conventional as "your obedient servant" of to-day,—*e. g.* in the Desmond and other rebel correspondence much the same forms are found passing between men who detested each other. It was a phrase and nothing more, and might simply be adopted by Spenser *caeteris paribus*.

STARNES (*SP* 41. 183), however, believes that the verbal similarity between this phrase and that which opens E. K.'s Epistle to Harvey in *S. C.* is evidence that E. K. was Spenser.

9-13. WEBBE (sig. C4ᵛ) praises, along with Spenser, one who, "though nowe long since, seriously occupied in grauer studies, (Master *Gabriell Haruey*)," is a rare poet.

9-10. GREGORY SMITH. The clue to this is found in a letter in Harvey's *Letter-Book* addressed to Sir Thomas Smith. "Your wurship mai marvel mutch that to haue absentid mi self thus long time from you, having so great and iust occasion to resort unto you, as I haue had. But suerly, sir, mi lets and hinderances eueri wai haue bene sutch, that I could not possibly do that I purposid fully, and wuld willingly haue dun for mi better proffiting in the ciuil lawe. It were too long a thing to declare them al severally and at larg; but truly, what for sicknes and priuate busines, I could scars reade ouer thre titles in Justinian before Lent, and euer sins the beginning of Lent, at the instant and importunate request of M. Church, mi verri frend, I haue red the rhetorick lecture in the schooles; so that the prouiding for mi lecture, together with the reading to mi pupils, the doing of ordinari acts in the howse, and disputing in the schooles, haue made me so unprouidid for Justinian, that, to sai troth, I haue bene ashamid to cum unto you"

COMMENTARY

(Camden Soc. edit. pp. 176-7). [Harvey's letter, which hardly reveals his preoccupation with Justinian, was written about six years before the present letter of Spenser's; it is more significant that Harvey was elected a fellow of Trinity Hall, the home of the study of Civil Law, on 18 December, 1578, only a year and a half earlier (Moore Smith, *Gabriel Harvey's Marginalia*, pp. 21, 22). See Harvey, Letter V 190-2, 408-9 (Latin translated in Carpenter, p. 58).]

14. "that olde greate matter." JUDSON (*Life*, p. 64). Presumably the French marriage.

14-5. TODD. The Earl of Leicester.

15-20. It is possible that these three sentences on the earthquake were not in Spenser's original letter, but were inserted when it was decided to publish the volume. The date of the earthquake conflicts with that of the letter (see note on 76); and the question "*Sed quid vobis videtur magnis Philosophis?*" is suspiciously like the question "what say you Philosophers . . . to this suddayne Earthquake?" which Harvey reports to have been asked of him at a gentleman's house in Essex (Letter IV 56-7). Harvey, or whoever prepared the volume for publication, may have felt that an allusion to the earthquake in Spenser's letter would justify the very lengthy treatment of that subject by Harvey.

15-7. GREGORY SMITH. April 6, 1580. Thomas Twyne, the translator of the Aeneid, was also prompted to write *A shorte and pithie Discourse* concerning it and earthquakes generally; and Anthony Munday, too, wrote a *Short Discourse*.

EDITOR. The effects of the earthquake in London and its neighborhood are described by Churchyard immediately after the event: "the Abbey Church of Westminster, was therewith so shaken, that one of the Pinacles of the same, loste aboue one foote of his toppe, the stones whereof fel to the ground. Also the steeple in the Pallace [of Westminster] so shoke, that the bel of the great Clocke sounded therewith, as thoughe it hadde bene stricken with some hammer. Also at White Hal where hir Maiestie lieth, the great Chamber and other parts of the Court so shooke, as seemed strange to such as were present. . . . It chanced also, *Tho. Cobbed* being in the pulpit in Christes church in Newgate market, preaching to the people, sodenly the church so shooke, that out of the roofe of the same fell certayne greate stones. . . . A number being at the Theatre and the Curtaine at Hollywell, beholding the playes, were so shaken, especially those that stoode in the hyghest roomthes and standings, that they were not a little dismayed. . . . Also in Shordiche, and other places, fell Chimneis, and among others, in Filpot Lane, at Maister Alderman Osbornes fel a peece of a Chimney: likewise from the toppe of Paules Church, and other places, fel small peeces of stone, and morter from the toppes of houses" (*A Warning*, sigs. B1v–B2r).

See Twyne, sig. B3r; John Stowe, *The Annales of England*, 1601, p. 1163; Camden, *Annales*, p. 297. In the present volume see Harvey's account in Letter IV 5-452, Letter V 7-8, and Appendix I, section B. Tucker Brooke surmises that this earthquake was the one remembered by the Nurse in *Romeo and Juliet* (*Essays and Studies in Honor of Carleton Brown*, p. 256).

17-9. Stowe mentions earthquakes which occurred in the region just south of London in 1551, in Lincoln and Northamptonshire in 1563, and in the West Midlands in 1575 (*The Annales of England*, 1601, pp. 1021, 1112, 1149). Golding (sig. A4r) refers without date to "the perticular Earthquake, in the time of oure most gratious soueraigne Lady that now is, which transposed the boundes of mens groundes, and turned a Churche to the cleane contrarie situation."

19-20. "But what think you great philosophers [at Cambridge]?"

20-36. SCHELLING (*Poetic and Verse Criticism*, p. 29). There seems no little reason to doubt Spenser's seriousness as to the new venture. . . . [In this passage] he clearly shows his knowledge of the real difficulty and of its absurdity.

24-35. HALES (p. xxviii). His ear was far too fine and sensitive to endure the fearful sounds uttered by the poets of this Procrustaean creed. The language seemed to groan and shriek at the agonies and contortions to which it was subjected; and Spenser could not but hear its outcries. But he made himself as deaf as might be.

B. E. C. DAVIS (*Edmund Spenser*, p. 192). In short, until pronunciation becomes stabilised the poet may be allowed considerable licence so long as he duly respects his "numbers" or "quantities." Verse is conditioned by all the elements of sound, which include tone, stress, pitch and elision; but the unit of rhythm upon which it is grounded is temporal and not accentual. Thus, although the immediate concern of the poet is the luckless "English hexameter," the experiment focuses his attention upon a basic principle of his art.

MCKERROW (*MLQ* 4. 177), on the contrary, believes that in this passage Spenser is arguing, not for the use of the natural quantities of English as it is commonly pronounced, but for an artificial system of quantities which would cause the pronunciation of poetry to differ from that of ordinary speech.

EDITOR. One of the chief causes of the obscurity of this passage for a modern reader is the term *accent*. Willcock (*MLR* 29. 3-8) has shown that no definite prosodic meaning was given to the word by critics before Puttenham (1589); in fact, accent and quantity were not clearly distinguished. When Spenser writes that in the middle syllable of *carpenter* "the Accente" comes short of what it should be in verse, "the Accente" is obviously, not the prosodic stress, but the quantity of the middle syllable in common pronunciation.

27. Here "Number" seems to mean the length of a syllable according to classical prosody.

27-9. See Harvey, Letter V 412-71.

28. "when it shall be read long in Verse." The *e* in the middle syllable of *carpenter* is long according to the Latin rule of position since it occurs before two consonants.

29-31. See Harvey, Letter V 472-501.

30. "*Diastole.*" In Greek and Latin prosody the lengthening of a syllable naturally short. See Harvey, Letter V 485-6.

COMMENTARY 265

32.   "rough words must be subdued with Vse." THOMPSON (p. 163) interprets the phrase to mean that Spenser wishes "the adaptation of English diction to Latin prosody." [The following sentence seems to mean that Spenser wishes English quantitative prosody, like the Greek, to be free to depart from ordinary English pronunciation, rather than to control it or to be controlled by it. See MCKERROW in note on 24-35.]

32-5.   WEBBE (sig. G3v). Cannot we then as well as the Latines did, alter the cannon of the rule according to the quality of our worde, and where our wordes and theyrs wyll agree, there to iumpe with them, where they will not agree, there to establish a rule of our owne to be directed by?

PUTTENHAM (f. 3r). Why should not Poesie be a Vulgar Art with vs aswell as with the Greeks and Latines, our language admitting no fewer rules and nice diuersities then theirs?

32.   "why a Gods name." See Harvey's "now a Gods name" in Letter II 5.

33.   TODD. *Else* is perhaps a misprint for *als* or *also*.

38-41.   Harvey criticizes this poem in Letter V 102-4. For analogues see Clément Marot, "Chanson x," stanza beginning "Si Cupido doulx et rebelle" (*Oeuvres*, ed. P. Jannet, 2. 180) and Wyatt's poem "why loue is blinde" (*Tottel's Miscellany*, ed. H. E. Rollins, 1. 77; *Poems of Sir Thomas Wiat*, ed. A. K. Foxwell, 1. 57, 2. 72). The subject and manner of this quatrain connect it with Spenser's four Anacreontic epigrams which were published in the same volume as the *Amoretti* in 1595; his previous statement in 35-6 suggests that he may originally have written the quatrain as a rhymed, accentual poem and later turned it into unrhymed quantitative verse. For further commentary and textual variants see *Minor Poems* 2. 510 and 710.

42-5.   The distich is quoted in E. K.'s gloss on *S. C. May* 69 (see commentary in *Minor Poems* 1. 307, including Mustard's second note under *May* 57). If E. K.'s gloss was completed by 10 April, 1579, when he dated his Epistle to Harvey, "the last time we lay togither in Westminster" must have occurred before that date, perhaps around 20 December, 1578, when Harvey noted in his *Howleglas* that he had been with Spenser in London (*Marginalia*, p. 23). On 15 October, 1579, however, Spenser implies that his experiments with English versifying were a new departure (Letter I 56-8).

WEBBE (sig. H1v) quotes the two verses from *S. C.* and marks out the quantities of the second: "Ās fŏr thōse mănĭĕ gōōdlīĕ māttĕrs lĕ̄ft Ĭ fŏr ōthĕ̄rs."

JENKINS (*SAB* 20. 32) agrees with others that the appearance of the couplet in both E. K.'s gloss and Spenser's letter is evidence that E. K. was Spenser. [See *Minor Poems* 1. 645-50, 2. 510, and 2. 710.]

53.   TODD. Spenser, it seems, had prefixed to these satyrical verses a Sonnet. See Harvey's *Foure Letters, and certaine Sonnets*, 1592. Sign F. 3. b.

where Harvey, having given a dozen of his own hexameters, adds; "the verse is not vnknowen; and runneth in one of those *vnsatyricall Satyres*, which M. Spencer long since embraced with an overlooving Sonnet: a token of his affection, not a testimony of hys iudgement." The Sonnet is lost; as is another poem also, of which E. K. has given us a line in his notes on the sixth Eclogue of the *Shepheards Calender* [on *June* 25].

56-67. CRAIK (1.29). The marriage of the Thames and the Medway, then, was originally intended to be the subject of a poem written in hexameters or trimeter iambics. It is probable, however, that the design was never executed.

GREGORY SMITH. *Epithalamion Thamesis* is unknown.

BIRCH (1. xii), TOWRY (*The Bibliographer* 1. 129), BUCK (*PMLA* 23. 98), SPENS (notes on *F. Q.* 4. 11), and BENNETT (p. 104) identify the *Epithalamion Thamesis* as an early version of *F. Q.* 4. 11. 11-53; DE SELINCOURT (p. xx) believes this may have been the case. But OSGOOD (notes on *F. Q.* 4. 11) cites a number of excellent reasons for believing that the *Epithalamion* was quite unlike the marriage of the Thames and the Medway. [For the comments of Vallans, J. Hughes, Upton, Child, Dodge, Harper, Sandison, Hales, Case, and Flower see *Minor Poems* 2. 515 and 670-1. For Harvey's criticism see Letter V 272-5.]

63-7. HARPER (p. 11). This letter . . . proves Spenser's acquaintance with the first edition of Holinshed, 1577. The two folio volumes of that edition may even have been among the books which Spenser took with him to Ireland the very year that he wrote the letter, 1580. In the second place, it shows that Spenser had no mind, even then, to follow Holinshed slavishly.

68-9. GREGORY SMITH. Cicero, *De Senect.* i. 1. Generally *praemii*.

EDITOR. "O Titus, if I [accomplish] anything, will there be any reward?" The full quotation from *De Senectute* reads:

> O Tite, si quid ego adiuero curamve levasso
> quae nunc te coquit et versat in pectore fixa,
> ecquid erit praemi?

"Tite" is Cicero's lifelong friend, Titus Pomponius Atticus; but Cicero himself quotes the lines from Ennius, *Annales*, lib. x, where "Tite" refers to Titus Quinctius Flaminius. Harvey noted in his commonplace book (*Marginalia*, p. 108): "Aretinus, ex improuiso semper irruens perpetua Regula: Ecquid erit precij?" See Harvey's reply to Spenser's quotation in Letter V 276-305.

70. HALES (p. xxvii) and DE SELINCOURT (p. xx) are inclined to accept a connection between the *Dreames* and *Comp.* GREGORY SMITH notes that the *Dreames* seem to have been ready for press, although no copies are known, and that some have endeavored to identify this work with *Mui.* and *Bel. 2.* More recently BENNETT (pp. 114-5, 121, 232) has suggested that the *Dreames* may be a link between the visions in *Th. W.* and the vision element in *F. Q.* 1.

COMMENTARY 267

[For further comments by J. Hughes, Craik, Child, Keightley, Birch, Todd, R. W. Church, Towry, Littledale, Grosart, Buck, Sandison, Hales, and Stein see *Minor Poems* 2. 414, 511-2, 527; also *Minor Poems* 1. 241, 416, and in the Spenser-Harvey correspondence Letters III 84, IV 466-7, V 304-26. See note on Letter I 55.]

70. HALES (p. xxvii) believes that the *Dying Pellicane* is altogether lost; and GREGORY SMITH notes that it is referred to in the printer's preface for *Comp.* (1591), that it appears to have been ready for the press, but that no copies are known. [See *Minor Poems* 2. 515-6 for the comments of Buck, Carpenter, and Sandison; the *Dying Pellicane* can hardly be one of the *Dreames*, as Buck suggests, since the two works are here mentioned with a co-ordinate *and*. See Harvey, Letters IV 466-7 and V 303; for the attempt to recover this poem in the seventeenth century see note on Letter I 55.]

72-3. TODD. This is a direct proof that Spenser had begun his great poem; he desires the opinion of his friend upon it; which, as we shall presently see, was not calculated to encourage the ardour of the poet.

EDITOR. See Letter V 327-48. Harvey's depreciation of the *F. Q.* is so famous that it is usually forgotten that he wrote a poem "To the Learned Shepheard" which appears among the commendatory verses printed with the *F. Q.* in 1590, and that still later he wrote, "Is not the Verse of M. *Spencer* in his braue Faery Queene, the Virginall of the diuinest Muses, and gentlest Graces?" (*A New Letter of Notable Contents*, 1593, sig. A4ᵛ). Sidney Thomas (*MLN* 55. 418-22) believes that in his reply to the present passage Harvey was not depreciating the *F. Q.* as poetry, but attacking its general plan and the use of irrational legend as its subject matter.

76-80. "Best wishes. Westminster, 2 April, 1580. But, as I love you, my sweetheart sincerely commends herself to you, wondering that you have made no reply to her letter. Beware, I beg, lest this be fatal to you. Fatal to me it certainly will be, nor will you go unpunished, I imagine. Farewell again and as often as you wish." Harvey answers this passage by promising to write "*Domina Immerito*" as soon as possible and by assuring her that, although she has altered toward him, his love for her remains unchanged (Letter V 533-8; translation in Carpenter, p. 58, corrected by Banks, *PMLA* 52. 335-7; uncorrected translation in Galway, *TLS* 46. 372). Evidently Spenser was already married.

76. CHILD (1. xvi). The date is printed "quarto *Nonas* Aprilis" [2 April], but *Nonas* must be a mistake for *Idus* [in which case the date is 10 April], since the earthquake of the 6th of April is mentioned at the beginning of the letter.

GROSART (Spenser's *Works* 1. 70) refers to this letter as of "14th April." [The date 10 April has been generally accepted; but see note on Letter III 15-20.]

HALES and LEE observe that this letter "is without date."

84-7. See E. K.'s gloss on *S. C. Nov.* 195 and Appendix I, section E.

87-90. KUERSTEINER (*PMLA* 50. 146) believes that Spenser is saying that his own *Dreames* could not be amended or reprehended by Michel Angelo. [The reference must be to the proposed illustrations for the *Dreames*; in view of the woodcuts which had recently appeared with *S. C.*, one would like to believe that this passage is not *extra iocum*.]

90-4. TODD. This work appears, by a subsequent extract from Harvey's Letter to Spenser [Letter IV 469], to have been written in Latin. It was, no doubt, a curious and valuable description of the Earl of Leicester's genealogy; and "the sundry apostrophes therein" we may reasonably suppose to have been addressed to Sir Philip Sidney.

CRAIK (1. 30) and CHILD (1. xix) are uncertain whether this work was written in prose or verse; DODGE (p. xiv) thinks that it was probably composed in "neo-classical metre" [but Harvey calls it a Latin work]. HALES (p. xxvii), DODGE (p. xiv), BUCK (*PMLA* 23. 95), SANDISON (*PMLA* 25. 142), and DE SELINCOURT (p. xx) are agreed that the *Stemmata* was probably utilized in *R. T.*; GROSART (Spenser's *Works* 1. 97-9) thinks that the transformation of the earlier into the later work is even referred to in *T. M.* 372.

BENNETT (pp. 89-92) has suggested that the British genealogies in *F. Q.* 2. 10 and 3. 3, rather than *R. T.*, may contain material from the *Stemmata*.

ORWEN (*NQ* 190. 9-11) notes that at the close of this passage Spenser speaks of following Harvey, a remark which may mean that the *Stemmata* followed Harvey's *Gratulationes* (1578) in praising Leicester and proposing his marriage to Elizabeth. In that case the present passage, as well as the *Stemmata*, must have been written before Leicester's marriage to the Countess of Essex became known in 1579; and the passage must be an editorial insertion in the letter, which is dated "*Quarto Nonas Aprilis* 1580." [See also notes on Letter III 15-20 and 76. For additional comments by Orwen, Dodge, Collier, Child, Hales, and Stein see *Minor Poems* 2. 516, 522, 526-7, 528.]

90-2. BENNETT (p. 92). Pedigrees setting forth claims to royal blood, however remote, were always dangerous in the Tudor period. Leicester was already under a cloud for having married the Queen's second cousin. His sister was married to the Earl of Huntington, one of the chief Protestant claimants to the succession. We know that in 1580 Leicester was interested in his ancestry, perhaps because he hoped for an heir, but he would certainly object to the publication of a genealogy of the Dudleys because it would be certain to arouse jealousy and resentment.

94. See Letter I 77-8.

COMMENTARY

AXIOCHUS

DEDICATION

2. For information on Benedict Barnam see Appendix II.

TO THE READER

3. "Edward." PADELFORD. A marginal note, in the hand of H. Atterbury, reads "A mistake for Edmund."

TEXT

5. In his poetry Spenser makes only one direct reference to Socrates, in *F. Q.* 2. 7. 52. 5-9.

6. Cynosarges, a place in Athens associated with Hercules.

PADELFORD notes that "*Lynosargus*" in the original edition is a typographical error for "*Cynosargus*." [Since the Welsdalius Latin version follows the Greek in reading "*Cynosarges*," Spenser, who translates from one or other, is probably not responsible for "*Lynosargus*."]

7. "*Elizeus*" is the Ilissus, a small river.

10-1. Glaucon was the maternal uncle of Plato, and Charmides his cousin.

11. Callirrhoe, a fountain in southeastern Athens.

17. "long fostered." See "Long fostred" in *F. Q.* 1. 7. 17. 3, 4. 2. 46. 1; "fostred long" in *F. Q.* 6. 1. 8. 4; "Long time she fostred" in *F. Q.* 3. 4. 20. 4. The words do not come from the Latin of Welsdalius, which reads "*celebris*."

17-8. Spenser seems to have consulted the Greek text when he simplifies the "*specimen . . . documentumque . . . sapientiae*" of Welsdalius to "wisedome" and "*Pater . . . meus Axiochus*" to "my father."

20-1. The formula *to be so far from . . . that* also occurs in *S. C. May* 37-8; *F. Q.* 4. 9. 33. 1-2, 6. Pr. 5. 2-3, 6. 8. 26. 8-9, 6. 9. 39. 6-8; *View* 3361-2.

21. "scoffe and scorne." See "Whose scoffed words he taking halfe in scorne" in *F. Q.* 4. 2. 6. 6; "Then he would scoffe at learning, and eke scorne" in *Hub.* 832.

22. "to portraict the Image of death." See "that sad pourtraict | Of death" in *F. Q.* 2. 1. 39. 3-4; "The drearie image of sad death" in *F. Q.* 3. 4. 57. 7; "deathes owne image" in *F. Q.* 3. 12. 19. 6. The verb *to portrait* occurs in *Ded. Son.* 17. 2, *F. Q.* 4. 5. 12. 7, *Ded. Epist.* 9.

22-3. "death . . . with a dreadfull countenance and a griesly face." PADELFORD (*Axiochus*, p. 26) notes that "dreadfull" and "griesly" are favorite words with Spenser, the former occurring 170 times in his poetry, the latter 60; and he cites the following parallels: "threatned death with dreadfull countenaunce" in *F. Q.* 2. 3. 14. 2; "Full blacke and griesly did his face appeare" in *F. Q.* 4. 5. 34. 6; "for her so dreadfull face" in *F. Q.* 6. 6. 11. 1; "*Death* with most grim and griesly visage seene" in *F. Q.* 7. 7. 46. 2; "With hollow browes and greisly countenaunce" in *T. M.* 185; "With greislie countenaunce and visage grim" in *Gn.* 326; "a dreadfull countenaunce" in *Am.* 31. 6. [See also "deathes most dreadfull face" in *F. Q.* 5. 5. 31. 4.] Padelford also shows (*Axiochus*, pp. 19-20) that Spenser cannot have found the idea of this passage in any version but that of Welsdalius.

40-1.   "we tooke . . . Gardeins)." PADELFORD. This is a most interesting translation. The Greek reads: τὴν παρὰ τὸ τεῖχος ᾔειμεν, ταῖς Ἰτωνίαις. "ταῖς Ἰτωνίαις" refers to the Itonian gates, but the translators apparently did not understand the meaning of the phrase. Agricola, taking it to be the name of a street, translated the passage as follows: "ea quae circa muros cognominata est ab Itono iuimus." Ficino, followed by Belprato, translated it by "peritonios agros," apparently having in mind the pomerium, or open space left free from buildings within and without the walls of a town. Pirckheymer translated it by "Itonias," without an accompanying noun, and probably did not understand it. Welsdalius, in turn, translated it by "viam ipsius pomerii." Spenser apparently took his hint from Welsdalius, and visualizing this area from the city that he knew best, translated "ipsius pomerii" as "by the Gardeins." He seemingly placed the phrase in parentheses, but the printer carelessly omitted the first member.

42.   BURGES. The Amazon was Antiopé, as may be inferred from Pausanias i. 2. [This is not the Antiopa to whom Spenser refers in *F. Q.* 3. 11. 35. 1.]

45-6.   "comfortlesse . . . deepe and dolefull sighes." PADELFORD (*Axiochus*, p. 26) notes that "dolefull" was a favorite word of Spenser's, occurring fifty-three times in his poetry, and cites as parallels "fry in hartlesse griefe and dolefull teene" in *F. Q.* 2. 1. 58. 4; "lowd shrieks and drerie dolefull cries" in *T. M.* 172. [See also "Deepe, darke, vneasie, dolefull, comfortlesse" in *F. Q.* 1. 5. 36. 6. Spenser seems to have added "dolefull," for which there is no equivalent in the Welsdalius version; Welsdalius had added the idea of "deepe" to the Greek.]

47.   "aboundant streames of trickling teares." PADELFORD (*Axiochus*, p. 26) cites "Like April shoure, so stremes the trickling teares" in *S. C. Ap.* 7; "the trees, their trickling teares to shedde" in *S. C. June* 96; "Whose streames my tricklinge teares did ofte augment" in *S. C. Aug.* 156; "hardned more with my aboundant teares" in *F. Q.* 4. 12. 7. 5. [See also "trickling teares" in *F. Q.* 3. 7. 9. 2; the phrases *trickling stream* and *trickling streams* in *S. C. July* 81; *F. Q.* 1. 1. 41. 2, 1. 11. 48. 2; *Gn.* 228. There is no equivalent for "trickling" in the version of Welsdalius, which Spenser seems to have been using.]

47-8.   "wailefull wringing of his handes." PADELFORD (*Axiochus*, p. 27) cites "Wringing her hands, and making piteous mone" in *F. Q.* 2. 1. 13. 7; "Now wringing both his wretched hands in one" in *F. Q.* 6. 5. 4. 4; "Then gan she wofully to waile, and wring | Her wretched hands in lamentable wise" in *T. M.* 169-70. [Welsdalius writes simply, "*manuum plausu.*"]

52-3. "wherewith ... others." Spenser is not following Welsdalius, who writes, "*quod verbis nemo explicare posse videbatur.*" The Greek is translated by Burges as "not to be broken down."

54-5. "with stately steps and a vaunting visage." PADELFORD (*Axiochus*, p. 27) cites "With stately steps" in *F. Q.* 4. 3. 5. 2 and notes that *vaunt* is a favorite word with Spenser, occurring, in its different verbal forms, thirty-three times in his poetry.

61. "that common saying, which is worne in all mens mouths." See "the text is rife in euery mans mouth" in Letter IV 223.

61-2. Life is called a pilgrimage in *F. Q.* 1. 10. 61. 3 and *Daph.* 372. BURGES notes that this sentiment is Pythagorean in origin and that it is also found in Marcus Aurelius 2. 17 and Cicero, *De Senectute* 23.

65. "the purposed place of rest." PADELFORD (*Axiochus*, p. 27) cites "Vnto that purposd place I did me draw" in *F. Q.* 4. 10. 29. 3. [See also "place of rest" in *F. Q.* 4. 3. 22. 6, 6. 3. 28. 7. Welsdalius writes simply, "*vitae terminum.*"]

72-3. "downe are trodden vnderfoote." See "treade downe and trample vnderfoote" in *View* 357.

74. "grieued minde." See the same phrase in *F. Q.* 4. 12. 14. 1, *Gn.* 643; "grieued mindes" in *F. Q.* 2. 2. 23. 5. The version of Welsdalius has no equivalent for "grieued."

82. "cleane contrary." See the same phrase in *View* 334 and *Ax.* 322.

84. "carrion Carcasse." PADELFORD (*Axiochus*, p. 27) cites "carrion carcas" in *S. C. May* 258; "carrion carcases" in *F. Q.* 1. 9. 33. 5; and the phrase *carrion corse* in *F. Q.* 2. 11. 46. 2, 3. 7. 43. 5, 4. 7. 32. 4, 5. 3. 30. 5. [Welsdalius does not specify what was "rotting."]

88-9. Draco flourished around 621 B. C.

96. "earthly masse." See the same phrase in *F. Q.* 2. 9. 45. 3, 4. 5. 45. 4, 4. 9. 2. 6; *R. T.* 419. Welsdalius merely used the adjective "*terrenum.*"

100-1. "vaine and shadowed." See the phrases *vain shadows* and *shadows vain* in *F. Q.* 6. 9. 27. 5, 6. 10. 2. 7; *Hub.* 912; *Am.* 88. 6; *H. L.* 255.

108. "kinde." In the sense of *native*, if intended to translate "*cognatum*" in Welsdalius; or in its ordinary sense, perhaps associated with the physical image of the open air (see "the solace of the open aire" in *F. Q.* 1. 4. 37. 2; "th'open freshnesse of the gentle aire" in *F. Q.* 3. 8. 11. 4).

108. "heauen out of which it was deriued." See "heauen, whence she deriu'd her race" in *F. Q.* 5. 1. 11. 4; "deriu'd at furst | From heauenly seedes" in *F. Q.* 6. Pr. 3. 6-7.

115-6. "reacheth farre aboue our common sence, and beyond the vsuall reason." See "His wonder far exceeded reasons reach" in *F. Q.* 2. 11. 40. 1; "my slender reasons reach" in *R. T.* 487; "things exceeding reach of common reason" in *Van.* 1. 4; "passeth reasons reach" in *Col.* 837.

124. Prodicus, the Sophist, a contemporary of Socrates. See *Ax.* 252.

127. Epicharmus is the first Greek comic writer of whom a definite account survives; he lived in the fifth century B. C.

127-8. "One hand rubbeth another." PADELFORD (*Axiochus*, p. 27) cites "the left hand rubs the right" in *F. Q.* 4. 1. 40. 9. [See notes, Book IV, p. 172.]

129-30. Callias, the son of Hipponicus, was a wealthy profligate; at his house Plato lays the scene of the *Protagoras*, at which Prodicus was present.

139. "from the mothers wombe." See "from my mothers wombe" in *F. Q.* 2. 3. 45. 1; "in their mothers wombe" in *F. Q.* 3. 7. 48. 6; "from his mothers wombe" in *F. Q.* 6. 4. 4. 8; "out of their mothers woomb" in *R. T.* 48; "from mothers womb" in *Am.* 74. 6. Welsdalius uses the colorless phrase "*in ipso vitae exordio.*"

149. "Philosophers." Spenser's rendering of "γεωμέτραι" in the Greek and "*Mathematici*" in the Latin of Welsdalius.

156. "trade of life." This phrase is repeated, with only slight variations in three of the cases, in *Ax.* 199-200, 251, 350; *Hub.* 398; *View* 4871; *B. N.* 167.

160. "closely creepeth." See "closely creeping" in *Mui.* 403; "closely nearer crept" in *F. Q.* 3. 10. 22. 6; "So closely as he could he to them crept" in *F. Q.* 3. 10. 49. 1; "creeping closely" in *Van.* 6. 7; the phrase *creeping close* in *S. C. May* 251, *F. Q.* 1. 9. 28. 8, *Col.* 698; the phrase *close creeping* in *F. Q.* 1. 10. 25. 5, 3. 10. 44. 1.

171-4. Agamedes and his brother Trophonius were legendary builders; the present story is also told by Cicero in *Tusculanae Quaestiones* 1. 47.

172. The name of Apollo is given by Welsdalius but not in the Greek, which merely refers to "the god at Pytho [Delphi]."

175-81. Cleobis and Biton were the sons of Cydippe, a priestess of Hera at Argos. Their names, included by Welsdalius but not in the original Greek of the *Axiochus*, are given in the versions of the story written by Herodotus (1. 31) and Cicero (*Tusculanae Quaestiones* 1. 47).

185-97. HAMER (*RES* 12. 85). That he kept an eye on the Greek is, I think, proved by his putting into the crude verses . . . three, or perhaps there are four, quotations from Homer, which, in verse in the Greek text, appear as prose in the Latin text.

185-6. PADELFORD. From the *Iliad* 24. 525-6.

188-93. PADELFORD (*Axiochus*, pp. 28-9). These verses recall the youthful attempts at translation in the epigrams of *The Theatre for Worldlings*, and incline

COMMENTARY 273

one to assign the *Axiochus* a date well prior to the writing of *The Shepheardes Calender.*

188-90.   PADELFORD.   From the *Iliad* 17. 446-7.

191.   Amphiaraus, the Argive hero, was killed in the expedition of the Seven against Thebes.

192-3.   PADELFORD.   From the *Odyssey* 15. 245-6.

194-7.   PADELFORD.   From the lost *Cresphontes* of Euripides. . . . The quotation from the Greek poet is confined to "τὸν φύντα [θρηνεῖν εἰς ὅς' ἔρχεται] κακά" . . . , the question ["What thinkest thou of him that taught"] being addressed by Socrates to Axiochus. Was it through ignorance or design that Spenser construed the whole passage as a quotation, and seemingly as a part of the quotation that preceded it? [Spenser was probably misled by the line arrangement of the Greek text in the Welsdalius edition, which might easily suggest that 192-7 was a continuous quotation.]

By way of rendering the quotation, Perionius borrows Cicero's translation or elaboration of it (*Disputationes* 1. 48. 115):

> Nam nos decebat coetus celebranteis domum
> Legere, ubi esset aliquis in lucem aeditus,
> Humanae uaria uitae reputanteis mala.

Spenser's "When first the Sunne bright day, | he seeth with tender eye" suggests the "aliquis in lucem aeditus," and it is possible that Spenser likewise recalled Cicero's translation. I think it very unlikely that he knew Perionius' translation, for he gives no supporting evidence of having seen it. [The adjective *sun-bright* occurs in *S. C. Oct.* 72; *F. Q.* 1. 5. 2. 8, 1. 11. 40. 9.]

204.   "their nightwatchings." Spenser follows the Greek, not Welsdalius, who renders this: "*omnes lucubrationes, et nocturnam, quam bibunt fuliginem.*"

206.   Bias, one of the seven wise men of Greece, lived in the sixth century B. C.

215-8.   "aboue all, that honourable state of gouernement and principallitie . . . through how many dangers is it tossed and turmoiled." See Ireland's "fatall misfortune aboue all Countries that I knowe to be thus miserablye Tossed and turmoylled" in *View* 579-80.

217.   "wrap them vp in silence." See "Wrapt in eternall silence," *F. Q.* 1. 1. 41. 9.

220.   "foule repulse." The phrase occurs in *F. Q.* 2. 10. 22. 9. Welsdalius styles the repulse "*acerbam,*" *i. e., rough* or *violent.*

222.   "wauering will of the witlesse many." See "wauering wemens wit," *F. Q.* 3. 12. 26. 4. Welsdalius has no equivalent for "wauering."

223-4.   "a mocking stocke and scoffe." See "The laughing stocke of fortunes mockeries," *F. Q.* 1. 7. 43. 2; "scoffe them out with mockerie," *Hub.* 705.

227.   Ephialtes and his brother Othos were giants who, according to one tradition, attempted to set the world on fire. See *Gn.* 375-6.

228-31.   This approximates the version of Welsdalius; but BURGES translates the original Greek: "and where recently the ten army-leaders? when I did not put (the question) to the vote; for it did not seem to me a solemn act to hold office in union with a maddened mob." He comments:

> This is supposed to allude to the ten naval officers, for whose condemnation Socrates, in his character of chairman of a public meeting, refused what he had the power to do, to put the question to the vote; as he knew well that they would in the then excited state of the people be put, as six of them subsequently were, to death, for neglecting to take up the dead bodies of the Athenians, who had fallen into the sea, in the naval battle at Arginusae.

228.   "noble kings and glorious Emperours." See "Renowmed kings, and sacred Emperours," *F. Q.* 3. 3. 23. 1.

231.   "madding multitude." See "madding mynd," *S. C. Ap.* 25; "madding kiddes," *S. C. July* 87; "madding mood," *F. Q.* 5. 7. 11. 9; "madding mother," *F. Q.* 5. 8. 47. 5; "maddinge mode," *View* 3690; "madding minde," *B. N.* 237-8.

232-5.   Theramenes and Callixenus were leaders in the accusations made against the victorious generals of the battle of Arginusae in 406 B. C. (see note on 228-31); Euryptolemus, whose name Spenser follows Welsdalius in rendering as "*Triptolemus*," opposed the illegal proceedings against the generals. See Xenephon, *Hellenica* 1. 7. 4-35.

237.   "It is as thou sayest *Socrates*." See "In dede as youe saie *Eudox*:" at the beginning of a speech in *View* 4715.

244.   PADELFORD. Spenser's manuscript probably read, "ô friend Socrates," and was misunderstood by the printer. Note the Latin of Welsdalius: "Populus enim, ô chare Socrates, est ingratus."

246.   "rascall route." This phrase, in either the singular or the plural, occurs in *F. Q.* 1. 7. 35. 5, 2. 9. 15. 4, 5. 2. 54. 8, 5. 6. 29. 4. There is no equivalent for "rascall" in the Welsdalius version.

246.   "idle losels." See "idle Losels," *View* 2367-8. *Losel*, in singular or plural, also occurs in *F. Q.* 2. 3. 4. 1, 5. 3. 20. 6, 5. 3. 35. 5, 5. 6. 38. 5, 6. 4. 10. 2; *T. M.* 226, 324; *Hub.* 67, 813; *View* 1088. *Idle* is not a literal translation of "*vehementibus*" in Welsdalius or of "$\beta\alpha\iota\omega\nu$" in the Greek; but with Spenser it is a favorite term of contempt, occurring ninety times in his poetry.

246-7.   "flattereth and feedeth." See "feede the eares of fooles with flattery," *T. M.* 323. There is no equivalent for "feedeth" in the Latin of Welsdalius.

249.   "opinion." Spenser misunderstands either the Greek or the literal translation of it, "*scientiam*," in Welsdalius.

257.   Spenser probably wrote "thee," not "them"; Welsdalius reads "*te*."

COMMENTARY

263. For Scylla see *Gn.* 539-40.

268-9. "the riche and most aboundant Storehouse of your woonderfull wisedome." See "T'enrich the storehouse of his powerfull wit," *Hub.* 790.

270-1. "mildenesse and lightnesse of speech, which you vse to allure." See "allure with gifts and speaches milde," *F. Q.* 5. 1. 6. 5; "Allur'd with myldnesse," *F. Q.* 6. 3. 23. 3.

270-1. "to allure the mindes of yoong men to vertue." See "to steale into the yonge spirites a desire of honour and vertue," *View* 2281-2.

277. "a colour and shadowed showe." See "in colourd showes may shaddow," *F. Q.* 3. Pr. 3. 8; "for shadow to pretend | Some shew," *F. Q.* 6. 11. 6. 5-6; "all their showes but shadowes," *Am.* 35. 14. Welsdalius has no equivalent for "shadowed showe."

278. Spenser omits a sentence here, which Welsdalius renders: "*Morbi autem sophismatis istis non curantur, at illis cedunt quae ad animum penetrare valent.*"

296. "high and haughtye." See "highly honourd in his haughtie eye," *F. Q.* 1. 7. 16. 2; "his haughty crest so hye," *F. Q.* 2. 5. 12. 4; "the most haughtie mountaines hight," *Bel.* 2 7. 7; "haughtie words most full of highest thoughts," *Col.* 716. Welsdalius reads, "*tot tantasque.*"

296. *Ramping* is applied to wild beasts in *F. Q.* 1. 3. 5. 2, 1. 3. 41. 5, 1. 8. 12. 5, 1. 11. 37. 3.

297. "to ieopard himselfe in the wastefull sea." See "Floting amid the sea in ieopardie," *Col.* 273. The idea of "ieopard" is not in Welsdalius.

311. "durty pleasures." The phrase occurs in *H. H. L.* 220.

312. "pure and perfect." See "perfect pure," *F. Q.* 1. 7. 33. 5; "all pure perfection," *Col.* 343; "From whose pure beams al perfect beauty springs," *H. H. B.* 296. There is no equivalent for "perfect" in Welsdalius.

314. "darkesome dungeons." See "darknesse he in deepest dongeon droue," *F. Q.* 1. 7. 23. 3; "darkesome dungeon," *F. Q.* 1. 7. 51. 7.

315. "but all things full of rest." See "But stedfast rest of all things," *F. Q.* 7. 8. 2. 3. Welsdalius reads, "*omnia, nec senectuti obnoxia.*"

317-8. "course and frame of Nature." See "natures kindly course," *S. C. Nov.* 124; "course of nature," *F. Q.* 3. 2. 41. 8, 3. 4. 26. 4. Welsdalius reads simply, "*naturam.*"

328. "renued and refreshed." See "oft refreshed, battell oft renue," *F. Q.* 1. 6. 44. 3.

332. Xerxes invaded Greece in 480 B. C.

334-6. BURGES notes that the two gods were Artemis and Apollo, otherwise known, respectively, as Opis and Hecaergus. [See the description of Delos in *F. Q.* 2. 12. 13.]

337. "into a certaine darkesome place." See "in darksome place," *F. Q.* 1. 5. 27. 5; "in a darkesome lowly place," *F. Q.* 1. 10. 25. 7; "to some darksome place," *Daph.* 486.

338. "*Plutoes* Pallace." See *S. C. Oct.* 29; *F. Q.* 1. 5. 14. 8, 1. 5. 32. 3.

339. "kingdome." A mistranslation of "αὐλῆς" in the original or of "*aula*" in Welsdalius.

339-40. "the world, and the compasse thereof beeing round." See "the compast world were sought around," *R. T.* 567.

343. BURGES identifies the brothers as Zeus, Poseidon, and Pluto; the brothers' children as Minos, Aeacus, and Rhadamanthus.

344-5. "fenced with iron gates, and fastened with brasen bolts." See "neither yron barres, nor brasen locke," *F. Q.* 4. 11. 3. 3. Welsdalius has no equivalent for "brasen."

346. Acheron is described in *F. Q.* 1. 5. 33. 1-2.

346. Cocytus is mentioned in *F. Q.* 1. 1. 27. 9, 2. 7. 56. 8, 3. 4. 55. 5.

347-8. See *Gn.* 623-7, where Minos is called a "cruell Iudge."

352. "Angell." BUYSSENS (*Revue Belge de Philologie et d'Histoire* 14. 133) refers this translation of "*genius*" (Welsdalius) to Spenser's explanation of Genius in *F. Q.* 2. 12. 47-8.

354-5. "from the siluer springs doo calmely run the Christall streames." See "a Christall streame did gently play," *F. Q.* 1. 1. 34. 8; "the Christall running by," *F. Q.* 2. 12. 58. 7; "siluer streames," *F. Q.* 4. 10. 52. 5, 5. 9. 28. 8; "siluer streaming *Thamesis*," *R. T.* 2; "the siluer Springs of *Helicone*," *T. M.* 5; "a siluer Spring forth powring | His trickling streames," *Gn.* 227-8. The Welsdalius version has no equivalent for "siluer." See note on *F. Q.* 6. 10. 7. 2 in Book VI, p. 246.

355-6. "medowes are cloathed with chaungeable Mantles." See "mantled medowes," *S. C. Nov.* 128. The idea of "Mantles" is not in Welsdalius.

356-7. "famous Schooles of renowmed Philosophers." See "Through famous Poets verse each where renownd," *F. Q.* 1. 10. 54. 7; "most renowmed fame," *F. Q.* 2. 10. 73. 3; "renowmed for the Romaines fame," *F. Q.* 4. 11. 21. 6; "Renowm'd for fruite of famous progenie," *R. R.* 6. 6.

357. "goodly companies." See "goodly company" in *F. Q.* 1. 6. 31. 8, 3. 12. 23. 3.

357. "trim sorts of Dauncers." See "daunce, and trimly trace," *F. Q.* 6. 9. 42. 4.

363.   The Elysian Fields are mentioned in *S. C. Nov.* 129, *F. Q.* 4. 10. 23. 5, *R. T.* 332, *Gn.* 421.

366.   "seede of that heauenly race." See the phrase *heavenly race* in *S. C. Ap.* 53; *F. Q.* 1. 10. 8. 7, 5. 10. 1. 8; *H. L.* 112; — *heavenly seed* in *F. Q.* 2. 11. 19. 8, 3. 4. 41. 6, 4. 8. 33. 9, 4. 10. 34. 3, 7. 7. 3. 3; *R. T.* 648; *Am.* 79. 10.

367-8.   In *T. M.* 461 Calliope says, "*Bacchus* and *Hercules* I raisd to heauen." See *Minor Poems* 2. 328.

369.   "Goddesse" is apparently Spenser's addition; the reference is to the mysteries celebrated at Eleusina.

371-2.   "into deepe darkenes and vtter confusion." See "out of deepe darknesse," *F. Q.* 1. 1. 38. 1; "Deepe, darke," *F. Q.* 1. 5. 36. 6; "in deep darknes," *R. T.* 126; "deep digd vawtes, and Tartar couered | With bloodie night, and darke confusion," *Gn.* 444-5; "Of darkenes deepe," *Daph.* 20; "in deepe darknesse," *H. L.* 60.

373-4.   See *Gn.* 393-6 and *F. Q.* 1. 5. 35. 9, where Spenser mentions the "fifty" daughters of Danaus; according to the legend, forty-nine of them had slain their bridegrooms.

375-6.   Tantalus, Titius, and Sisiphus are described together in *F. Q.* 1. 5. 35. 3-6. For Tantalus see also *F. Q.* 2. 7. 57. 7-60. 9.

377.   "rent." So Welsdalius; the Greek says *licked*.

378-9.   "pained with all kind of torments, and afflicted with endlesse pennance." See *F. Q.* 1. 5. 33. 7-9:

> The house of endlesse paine is built thereby,
> In which ten thousand sorts of punishment
> The cursed creatures doe eternally torment.

See "endlesse penance," *F. Q.* 1. 5. 42. 6.

381.   "euery mans minde is immortall." See "man, that breathes a more immortall mynd," *H. L.* 103.

389.   "pierced and relieued my faint heart." Welsdalius, following the Greek, gives an entirely different idea: "*in tuam adduxit sententiam.*" Spenser uses various forms of the phrase *pierce the heart* in *F. Q.* 1. 3. 1. 8, 3. 5. 30. 9, 3. 6. 40. 5, 4. 8. 4. 9, 6. 1. 45. 3-4, 6. 4. 18. 5; *H. L.* 123; *H. H. L.* 156;—of the phrase *faint heart* in *F. Q.* 1. 7. 31. 8, 1. 9. 52. 6, 3. 8. 34. 7, 3. 10. 21. 9, 4. 10. 17. 6, 5. 3. 26. 3, 5. 7. 20. 5. See also "th'heart mote haue relieued," *F. Q.* 5. 6. 24. 8.

396.   PADELFORD notes that "*Lynosargus*" in the original edition is a typographical mistake for "*Cynosargus.*" [See note on 6.]

A VIEW OF THE PRESENT STATE OF IRELAND

3. The name *Eudoxus* was undoubtedly suggested to Spenser by Gr. ἐυδόξος, *of good repute, honored*. *Irenius*, on the other hand, can hardly come from Gr. εἰρηναῖος, *peaceful* (although a note on the Arthur A. Houghton MS translates the name as "*pacificus*"); it must be associated with *Irena*, the name for Ireland in *F. Q.* 5. 1, since Irenius is an Englishman who has spent some time in Ireland. Stanyhurst (Holinshed, vol. II, *The Description of Ireland*, pp. 14-5) quotes extensively from a Latin dialogue by Nicholas Harpsfield, called "Alan Cope," in which one of the speakers is "Irenaeus"; but it is apparent from the original dialogue (*Dialogi Sex*, 1566, pp. 431-2) that the name has nothing to do with Ireland. The Irish implication was suggested by the context in Stanyhurst, if indeed Spenser remembered the occurrence of the name there. (See R. W. Chambers in Nicholas Harpsfield, *The Life and Death of Sir Thomas Moore*, London, 1932, p. cxcvi.) The spelling "Irenaeus," found in Ware's text, appears in BM Additional MS 22022 but in no other manuscript of the *View*.

4. Spenser himself had lately come from Ireland to England when he wrote the *View* in 1596 (see Appendix III, section B); but it would be dangerous to identify the experiences of Irenius as Spenser's in every case.

9-16. RENWICK. Such pessimistic phrases were current. Deploring Grey's possible departure, Spenser's friend Ludovick Bryskett wrote to Walsingham, May 10, 1582: "What can be sayd but that the secrett Judgement of God hangeth over this soyle, that causeth all the best endeavours of those that labour the reformacion thereof to comme to naught." (*State Papers Ireland, vol.* 92, no. 29)

EDITOR. See Plomer and Cross, p. 39. Sir Henry Sidney wrote to the Privy Council of "the fatall Cursse of this Countrie"; and Walsingham wrote to Sidney, "when I caule to Mynde the cursed Destynye of that Ilande, I can not put of all Dredd" (*Letters and Memorials* 1. 95, 74). God had determined Ireland must decay, Sir Nicholas Malby informed Walsingham (*C. S. P. Ir. 1574-1585* 70. 51). John Hooker probably echoes official opinion when he speaks of "a fatall destinie, and ineuitable to euerie good gouernor in that land" and "a fatall and an ineuitable destinie incident to that nation" (Holinshed, vol. II, *The Supplie of the Irish Chronicles*, pp. 110, 153). Sir William Gerrard, however, endeavors to refute the idea "that the curse of God is light uppon that soyle, and therefore not to be reformed" (*Analecta Hibernica* 2. 97). Irenius later takes a less pessimistic view than he does here (4741-50). See also 2890-2.

12. JONES (*Spenser's Defense*, p. 206) connects the phrase "*Genius* of the soile" with the theory of geographical milieu in Jean Bodin's *Methodus ad Facilem Historiarum Cognitionem*.

17-36. Eudoxus, however, later inclines to the official pessimism (575-80, 4734-7).

20. "Plottes." MORLEY. Ground-plans. Not in a bad sense, from the French *complot*, but from English plot or plat, as in grass-plots or political platforms.

COMMENTARY

23-6. See *F. Q.* 5. 4. 28. 1-3.

33-4. RENWICK. "Commune est hodie, cui simile est illud Ptolomaei: Sapiens dominabitur astris." — Cognatus, in appendix to the *Adagia* of Erasmus, 1612.

EDITOR. Stanyhurst translates the same adage: "Planetary woorckinges thee wismans vertue represseth" (*The First Fovre Bookes of Virgil His Aeneis*, ed. Edward Arber, 1880, p. 13). Describing a conversation in which Spenser is supposed to have participated, Lodowick Bryskett writes (*A Discovrse of Civill Life*, 1606, p. 172): "we may by our free choise and voluntarily giue our selues to good or to euill, and master the inclination of the heauens, the starres, or destinie, which troubleth so much the braines of some, that in despite of nature they will needes make themselues bond being free: whom *Ptolomie* doth fitly reprehend, by saying, that the wise man ouer-ruleth the starres."

39. "recured." MORLEY. Recovered.

41 n. "impeachment." MORLEY. French *empêchement*, hindrance.

46. "menage." See *Ded. Son.* 2. 2, *F. Q.* 3. 12. 22. 3.

54-8. The *View* is actually constructed on this three-fold plan: (1) the evils, 64-2898; (2) the redressing of the evils, 2899-4400; (3) the final settlement, 4401-5291.

61. "streighte." MORLEY. Strict.

64-8. GREENLAW (*MP* 7. 194-5) believes that the text of the whole *View*, as it is set forth in the present paragraph, appears in Machiavelli's statement (*Il Principe*, cap. 3): "Ma quando si acquistano stati in una provincia disforme di lingua, di costumi e d'ordini, qui sono le difficultà, e qui bisogna avere gran fortuna e grande industria a tenerli."

JONES (*Spenser's Defense*, p. 209). Although these are topics which Machiavelli considered in the third chapter of the *Prince*, the general scheme of the Italian's work is quite different from that which Spenser has followed. Machiavelli classifies kinds of governments; Spenser, the evils of Ireland.

EDITOR. Fynes Moryson, writing between 1617 and 1620, before the *View* was printed, follows Spenser's scheme very closely (*Shakespeare's Europe*, p. 195): the Irish "will neuer be reformed in Religion, manners, and constant obedience, to our lawes, but by the awe of the sword, and by a strong hand at least for a tyme bridling them."

88. "sithence." MORLEY. The preceding form of the word since, originally two words, a preposition governing a pronoun in the dative, *sith thám*, after that. *Sith thám* then became the one word *sithen*, commonly used in the reign of Henry VIII. Taken adverbially it then came to receive a genitive suffix in further suggestion of its adverbial character, and grew to be sithenes. The *es* came to be spelt with *ce*, and as *ones*, *twies* became *once*, *twice*, so *sithenes* became *sithence*. The last change was by the speaker's common elision of *th* in the middle of a word of two short syllables, and as *other* became *o'r*, or, *sithence* became *sin'ce*, *since*.

88.   "prevaricated." MORLEY. Bent and stretched.

94-6.   RENWICK. This idea of William the Conqueror as founder of the English common law, was commonly held, though inaccurate. See Polydore Vergil, Holinshed on the reign; Camden, *Brit.* p. 152 — less absolutely stated than in his early editions.

   EDITOR. Spenser soon makes it clear (309-16) that he believed William replaced the old laws of England with Norman law. Holinshed (vol. III, *The Chronicles of England*, p. 8) says that William abrogated the ancient laws but that his successors departed from this policy; and William Harrison (Holinshed, vol. I, *The Description of England*, p. 177) still further qualifies the statement. Camden (*Britannia*, p. 89), in every edition from 1587 on, quotes Gervasius Tilburiensis to the effect that William kept some of the original English laws. William Lambard also quotes the passage from Gervasius as well as a decree of William's that all subjects obey the law of Edward the Confessor and William's additions to it (Αρχαιονομια, 1568, sigs. C1^v–C2^r, f. 125^v; *A Perambulation of Kent*, 1576, p. 5). Sir John Davies (*Discoverie*, pp. 127-8) is explicit: "our Norman Conqueror ... governed Al, both English and Normans, by one and the same Law; which was the ancient and common law of England, long before the Conquest." Spenser's error occasions a long passage in O'Flaherty (pp. 368-9).

105-7.   Holinshed (vol. I, *The Historie of England*, pp. 174-5) tells how Harold made an unjust distribution of the spoils after the battle of Stanford Bridge and mentions his responsibility for exiling the Archbishop of Canterbury.

112-7.   Ireland's reputation for warlike disorderliness dated back at least to the beginning of the sixteenth century (*State Papers, Henry VIII* 2. 11). See *Col.* 312-9.

117.   ROLAND SMITH (*JEGP* 42. 502). Ir. *brethemhan* [judge. *NED* cites "Breighoon" in Campion, p. 19, as the first occurrence of the Anglicized form; but "Breawen" appears in legal French as early as 1351 (Berry 1. 388)].

120-33.   MORLEY. Spenser was wrong in thinking that the Brehon Laws were not committed to writing. They were so called from a late English corruption of the Irish name for the old hereditary judges, "Breitheamhuin," pronounced breihoo-in, brehon. Traditions of St. Patrick say that the old laws were revised by him at the command of King Leaghaire for the omission of everything inconsistent with Christianity. No MS. now known is older than the end of the thirteenth century, but there are quotations made from the collection in the Glossary of Cormac MacCullinan, made in the ninth century. There are collections of these Laws in MS. in the libraries of the Royal Irish Academy, Trinity College, Dublin, the British Museum, the Bodleian, and elsewhere, written in the fourteenth, fifteenth, and sixteenth centuries, and they contain records of old usages, like that of compensation for the taking of life, that belong to the early civilization of both Teuton and Celt. The old collection was called the Sanchas Mor (pronounced Sanchus môr), the Great Law Compilation, and it was treasured by the people of Ireland in Spenser's time as the written code of their old National Law. A Royal Commission was appointed in 1852 to secure the accurate transcription and translation of the Brehon Laws, and four volumes have accordingly been published, the last in 1885, of Ancient Laws and Institutes of Ireland, giving the Irish text, with translations, dissertations, and indexes.

EDITOR. Of the Brehon system, already on the wane, Elizabethan writers reveal a very limited and inaccurate notion. To the accounts of Campion (pp. 18-9) and Stanyhurst, founded on Campion, (Holinshed, vol. II, *The Description of Ireland*, p. 45; *De Rebvs*, p. 37) Spenser adds a full explanation of the "Iriach" and the false statement that the Brehon Law was unwritten. Subsequently Dymmok (pp. 9-10), Davies (*Discoverie*, pp. 165-7), and Moryson (*Shakespeare's Europe*, p. 225), like Spenser, concentrate on the "Iriach," probably because it was the most striking and least defensible side of the Irish system. An Englishman at the end of the sixteenth century would have no means of discovering more than a few sensational facts about the Brehon Law: its practices were falling out of use because they were ancient and because the English Government discouraged them; and the laws themselves were written in a language too obscure for any but the initiated, even among the Irish themselves, to understand. Irish institutions had gone into eclipse, and Irish scholarship was still unborn. The turn comes only by the middle of the seventeenth century, when Ware writes: "I am informed that there are to this Day extant many Volumes, in which the Laws of some of the antient Kings of *Ireland*, before the Arrival of the *English*, are written in the *Irish* Language" (*Works* 2. 69).

128. "*Iriach*." ROLAND SMITH (in a communication to the editor) notes the superiority of the spelling "*Eriach*" in Ware's text of the *View* and adds: "On the legal use of *éraic* or *éric*, sometimes rendered 'wergild' . . . see Pedersen, *Vergl. Gramm. der Kelt. Sprachen*, II, 597, and Thurneysen, in *Studies in Early Irish Law* (Dublin 1936), p. 71. Atkinson, in his 'Glossary to Brehon Laws' (*Ancient Laws of Ireland*, VI, 184, 311-12) fails to make a distinction between *coirpdíre*, which is a fixed payment for homicide, and *éraic*, a variable compensation for any crime." [See *Ancient Laws of Ireland* 1. 8, 3. lxxxix-xc. The incorrect form "*Breaghe*" in BM Additional MS 22022 may be a scribal error for "*Ireaghe*."]

131. TODD. *Sept* is *family*. So, in Moryson's *Itinerary*, fol. 1617. Part second, p. 1. "The Oneale, a fatall name to the chiefe of the SEPT or *family* of the Oneales, etc." See also Percy's *Reliques of Anc. Poetry*, 4th edit. vol. i, p. 119. And the *Hist. of the Gwedir Family*, note in p. 66.

136-46. See 385-402.

147-82. JONES (*Spenser's Defense*, p. 195). Spenser and Bodin also agree in the opinion that the sovereignty of the Prince rests upon a contract of permanent validity. [See Bodin's *République* (liv. I, ch. 9, pp. 126, 129, 139): "la souueraineté n'est limitee, ny en puissance, ny en charge, ny à certain temps"; "le peuple, ou les seigneurs d'vne Republique, peuuent donner purement, et simplement la puissance souueraine, et perpetuelle à quelqu'vn, pour disposer des biens, des personnes, et de tout l'estat à son plaisir, et puis le laisser à qu'il voudra"; and England, he notes, has a sovereign in this sense.]

152-6. MORLEY. It was in 1541 that Henry VIII. elevated Ireland from a lordship into a kingdom, gratifying at the same time the great Irish chiefs by giving them rank as earls. Ulliac de Burgh was made Earl of Clanricarde, Murrough O'Brien Earl of Thomond, O'Neill Earl of Tyrone.

RENWICK. Sir Anthony St Leger was Deputy 1540-1556, with intervals; the Parliament met in 1542 [*i. e.*, 1541].

EDITOR. For the act which created Henry and his heirs kings of Ireland see *All the Statutes*, ff. 95ᵛ-96ᵛ; *The Statutes of Ireland*, pp. 183-5; Maxwell, pp. 101-2; *C. C. MSS. 1515-1574*, p. 183. Spenser probably used the account given by Stanyhurst (Holinshed, vol. II, *The Chronicles of Ireland*, pp. 102-3) rather than the shorter version of Campion (p. 122). Neither of these mentions a reservation of "former priviledges and seigniories" by the Irish chieftains; O'Neill, the only great noble who did not attend the parliament, was the only one who might claim to have reserved his privileges (*State Papers, Henry VIII* 3. 306-8). See 3585-9 and note.

164-71. So the anonymous author of *The History of Sir John Perrott* (p. 142) refers to "the ill-affected Subjectes, who being lyke to Coltes not well ridden, when they finde the Rider not to carrie a straight, even Hand, and a suer Seate, will strive to take the Head, and runne away with theyr Rider, or to cast hym out of his Seate." Ralph Byrchensha (*A Discovrse Occasioned vpon the Late Defeat, Giuen to the Arch-rebels, Tyrone and Odonnell*, 1602, sig. C2ʳ) writes that the Irish

> like yong colts and heifers loue to fling,
> That without bits, and bridles, and strong hand,
> Will not be held in peace or rest to stand.

170. "to Colte." *NED* cites this as the first occurrence of the verb.

173. "forslacked." TODD. *Delayed.* See F. Q. v. xii. 3.

COLLIER. *Postponed*, or here, *neglected*.

183-201. BRADNER (*Edmund Spenser*, p. 46). [Spenser] saw clearly that the attempt to combine the medieval, almost primitive, clan organization of the native Irish chiefs with a secure and efficient Tudor bureaucracy was doomed to failure. A complete overthrow of the Irish feudal system was necessary if the English were to retain peaceful control. [The term *feudal* cannot properly be applied to the Irish system of clan ownership.]

EDITOR. Spenser's account of tanistry is fuller and more complete than that of any English contemporary; except for Davies (*Discoverie*, pp. 167-8) and Moryson (*Shakespeare's Europe*, pp. 194-5), writers mention the institution hastily if at all (*e. g.*, Tremayne, p. 1). In describing tanistry as a law of succession, however, Spenser overlooks the wider implications of the law: if the chiefs held their lands for lifetime only, it is because the clans were regarded as the real possessors of the lands; originally, even *tanist* was apparently the name of a whole class of persons, so little sense did the clan economy have of individual ownership or privilege (see Hogan, *PRIA*, Archaeology 4. 244-7). It was the policy of the Tudor monarchs to break down the clan economy by compelling the Irish to surrender lands held under the system of tanistry and regranting them to the chieftains as their personal inheritances, held in return for submission to the Crown. The result was confusion and conflict since the chieftains, who profited enormously by the change, were inevitably opposed by their clansmen, who lost just as enormously. See Davies, *A Letter to Salisbury* (1610), p. 384; Butler, pp. 208-37.

205-16. Spenser's account is corroborated by modern archaeology in almost every detail (see Joyce, *Social History* 1. 45-50); and this is probably due to the survival of the rites down to the time the *View* was written. On the false report of Turlough Lynagh O'Neill's death in May, 1590, his tanist, Hugh O'Neill, immediately set off for the inaugural stone at Tullahog near Dungannon; there, when Turlough had actually died in 1595, Hugh made himself O'Neill, a deed of some notoriety since he had promised the government not to take that title (*C. S. P. Ir. 1588-1592* 152. 41. 1; *1592-1596* 183. 19). Spenser may have had in mind this inauguration ceremony when he has Glauce turn Britomart thrice in either direction (*F. Q.* 3. 2. 51. 1-5); superstition is involved in both cases.

221-37. Keating (1. 67, 69) defends tanistry as a safeguard against the disadvantages of being governed by children in their minorities; but in the Elizabethan period it is said to have placed the captainships in the hands of those who had the power to exploit the lowly (Hamilton, pp. 84-8).

237-8. Edward O'Reilly finds no evidence in the Brehon laws that land was appropriated to the tanist as tanist (*TRIA*, Antiquities 14. 204).

239. A *cutting* was the levying of a tax (*NED*, def. 5), a *spending* the supply of some produce or commodity (*NED*, def. 2. b). The *View* seems to give the first examples of both words.

241-8. WARE. See whether it may not be more fitly derived from *Thane*, which word was commonly used among the *Danes*, and also among the *Saxons* in *England*, for a noble man, and a principall officer.

MORLEY. *Tanistry* and *Tanist*, to represent the custom of appointing an able-bodied heir to the government, and the name of such an heir, who becomes thereby the second person in the land, are names derived from the Irish ordinal number *tánise* meaning second; and that ordinal was formed from the root of the numeral two (*masc.* dá, *fem.* dí, *neuter* dán). The Irish cardinal numbers one, two, three, four, five, six, for example, were óin, dá, trí, cethir, cóic, sé, and their ordinals were cétne, tánise, tris, cethramad, cóiced, sessed. Thus *tánise* or *tánaise*, meaning simply second, *tanise rig* (second king), was the name given to the appointed heir. With addition of the final *t*,—as it is used to represent an abstract conception, as in theft, thrift,—such heir came to be called the tanist, and tanistry, by help of another suffix, became the name for the old national custom.

DRAPER (*MLN* 41. 127-8). Spenser's curious etymology of *tanistry* ... was perhaps suggested by Camden, with whose work Spenser was undoubtedly familiar. Camden divides the word *Britannia* into the aboriginal proper noun *Brith-* and the supposedly Greek *-tania*, "country." To support this theory, he cites *Mauritania, Lusitania, Aquitania*; and he explains the use of *-tania* among the Celts as a borrowing from Greek traders. Spenser, doubtless cognizant of these statements in Camden, associated tanistry with the group of proper names mentioned by the historian; but apparently because the word seemed to him essentially Celtic, he appears to have discarded Camden's theory of a Greek origin, and to have substituted in place of it the opinion that it is a word immemorially belonging to the "barbarous" peoples of western Europe. [See Draper, *MP* 17. 479-80; Covington, *SP* 19. 246-7.]

RENWICK. Camden, *Britannia*, tr. Holland, 1610, p. 27 [Latin ed. of 1590, p. 28]: "... TANIA: which betokeneth in Greek, a region ... MAVRITANIA, LVSITANIA, and AQVITANIA ... of *Mauri* they framed *Mauritania*, as one should say, the country of the *Mauri* ... of *Lusus* ... *Lusitania*, as it were *the land of Lusus*."

ROLAND SMITH (*JEGP* 42. 506). Ir. *tanaistecht*.... As in *coshery*, the suffix -*ry* is English.

[Camden's etymology may have been derived from the forged books of Berosus, really by Johannes Annius, where the name of Lusitania is traced to one Lusus (*Berosi Sacerdoti Chaldaici, Antiquitatum Libri Quinque*, 1545, ff. 90ᵛ–91ʳ).]

249. The discussion dropped at 185 is here resumed.

263-81. JONES (*Spenser's Defense*, pp. 196-7). Here Spenser apparently has in mind the authority of Bodin's *monarchie seigneuriale*, described in the following passages from the *Republic*:— (1) "puisque le consentement de tous les peuples a voulu, que ce qui est acquis par bonne guerre, soit propre au vainqueur, et que les vaincus soient esclaves des vainqueurs, on ne peut dire que la Monarchie ainsi establie soit tyrannique: veu mesmes que nous lisons, que Jacob par son testament laissant a ses enfans une terre qu'il avoit acquise, dist qu'elle estoit sienne, par ce qu'il l'avoit acquise à la force de ses armes." (2) "Et ne doit pas la monarchie seigneuriale estre appellee tyrannie: car il n'est pas inconvenient, qu'un Prince Souverain, ayant vaincu de bonne et juste guerre ses ennemis, ne se face seigneur des biens et des personnes par le droict de guerre, gouvernant ses sujets comme esclaves, ainsi que le pere de famille est seigneur de ses esclaves et de leurs biens, et en dispose à son plaisir" (Book II, Chapter 2, p. 204 [ed. of 1576, pp. 238, 235]). Moreover Bodin agrees with Irenaeus that the *monarchie seigneuriale* is more stable than that based upon contract, as will appear in the following passage: "Et la raison pourquoy la Monarchie seigneuriale est plus durable que les autres, est pour autant qu'elle est plus auguste, et que les sugets ne tiennent la vie, la liberté, les biens (Spenser's "theyr lives, theyr landes, and theyr libertyes"), que du Prince souverain, qui les a conquetez à juste tiltre" (Book II, Chapter 2, p. 204).

COVINGTON (*UTB*, Studies in English 4. 32) believes that in attacking the act of royalization Spenser is delivering a commonplace of English discussions of Ireland.

RENWICK. By Act of the Irish Parliament 33 Henry VIII (1542 [*i. e.*, 1541]) s. 1, c. 1, the royal title Lord of Ireland was changed to King of Ireland. Spenser follows the argument of the Act: "Forasmuch as the King ... and his

COMMENTARY

grace's most noble progenitors, Kings of England, have bin Lords of this land of Ireland, having all manner kingly jurisdiction, power, pre-eminences, and authoritie royall, belonging or appertayning to the royall estate and majestie of a King, by the name of Lords of Ireland ..." (Quoted from *The Statutes at Large ... Ireland*, Dublin, 1786)

EDITOR. At the time of the act of royalization it was generally felt to be a necessary measure (*State Papers, Henry VIII* 2. 480; *C. C. MSS. 1515-1574*, pp. 141-2; *Letters and Papers, Henry VIII* 16. 166); but the King himself took discreet measures to show that the title had long been his by right of seven historical claims (Alice S. Green, in *A Miscellany Presented to Kuno Meyer*, pp. 278-85). At the beginning of the seventeenth century Sir John Davies still defended the act as an expedient measure (*Discoverie*, p. 246).

272. RIEDNER (p. 121) is unable to trace this reference in either the *Orator* or the *Tusculanae Disputationes*, both of which Cicero addressed to Brutus.

RENWICK. I have not found this.

[Spenser may have in mind the words of Alorcus to the Saguntines in Livy 21. 13: "cum omnia victoris sint."]

282-5. Henry himself wrote to the Deputy and Council of Ireland in 1541 (*State Papers, Henry VIII* 3. 333): "We wolde you shulde not overmoche presse them in any vigorous sorte, but only to persuade them discreatly, uppon consideration that the landes, they have, be our propre inheritance, besides our right and title to thole lande, and what honor, quiet, benefite, and commoditie, they shall have by suche an ende to be made with Us, and what daunger may com to them, if they embrace not this our especial grace shewed unto them, tenduce them gently to condescende to that, which shalbe reasonably desired of them."

308-25. This continues the discussion in 94-117.

310. RENWICK. The *positive* law is "The law of man (the which sometime is called the law positive)" as distinguished from the law of God and the law of reason. (C. St German, *The Dialogue* in English, 1530 — here from the edition of 1593.) [Positive laws are so called because formally imposed (*NED, positive*, def. A. I. 1).]

325-41. RENWICK. Bodin *de la République*, V. 1 [ed. of 1576, p. 518]: "L'vn des plus grands, et peut estre le principal fondement des Republiques, est d'accommoder l'estat au naturel des citoyens, et les edicts et ordonnances à la nature des lieux, des personnes, et du temps." In the same chapter Bodin discusses the possibility of changing natures by laws; but his development and examples are different from Spenser's in each place. Sir Thomas Smith's chapter "That the common wealth or policie must be according to the nature of the people," in *de Republica Anglorum* (which E. K. cited in *The Shepheardes Calender*) may also be in the background.

EDITOR. See Jones, *Spenser's Defense*, p. 201. In his commentary on Aristotle's *Politics* Louis le Roy writes (*Les Politiques*, 1600, liv. II, chap. 10, p. 146) that Solon "ne retrencha ... pas le mal au vif, ny ne remua pas l'estat en la sorte qu'il eust esté le plus expedient: craignant que s'il attentoit de remuer et tourner sans dessus dessous tout le gouuernement de la ville, il n'eust pas puis apres assez de puissance pour la rasseoir et restablir en la forme qui seroit la meilleure." It is interesting that Harvey wrote in his *Letter-Book* (p. 79): "You can not stepp into a schollars studye but (ten to one) you shall litely finde open ether Bodin de Republica or Le Royes Exposition uppon Aristotles Politiques"; and Harvey noted in the margin of one of his books: "Malim esse Spartanus miles, quam Atheniensis Rhetor. . . . Attica Lingua; Lacedaemonijs manibus pedibusque; geritur Res" (*Marginalia*, p. 145). The contrast between the two cities is developed in an entirely different way by Beacon, who, using the passage quoted from Le Roy, has Epimenides reprove Solon (p. 6): "you did not change the whole state thereof [Athens], but altered onely that which you thought by reason you might perswade your Citizens vnto, or els by force you ought to compell them to accept; and framed your lawes to the subiect and matter, and not the matter and subiect vnto your lawes, as sometimes Lycurgus did in his reformation of *Sparta*. . . . For this cause the first institution of *Athens* being meerly popular, corrupt and vnperfit, coulde never after by any lawes made for the reformation thereof, be defended from the tyrannie of such as did aspire vnto the principalitie." But later on (p. 20) Beacon seems to approve of the doctrine that laws should be fitted to the times and the people.

351-4. PADELFORD (*JEGP* 14. 399) cites this passage to show that Spenser believed in the divine right of kings: "Such is the reverence held by the commonalty for the sacred person of the sovereign, that his mere presence is often of more avail than a whole army of men of common clay; he is, in truth, the most stable factor in government." [Machiavelli (*Il Principe*, cap. 3) recommends that a king should inhabit newly conquered states; see also René de Lucinge, *The Beginning, Continuance, and Decay of Estates*, trans. Sir John Finett, 1606, pp. 74-81, and Davies, *Discoverie*, pp. 217-9.]

355-60. Sir Philip Sidney writes in 1577 ("Discourse of Irish Affairs," *Works*, ed. Albert Feuillerat, 1912-1926, 3. 49-50): "For untill by tyme they [the Irish] fynde the sweetenes of dew subjection, it is impossible that any gentle meanes shoolde putt owt the freshe remembrance of their loste lyberty," etc.

361-3. JONES (*Spenser's Defense*, pp. 201-2). Spenser and Bodin agree that those who have put themselves beyond the pale of the law cannot in justice appeal to it. . . . "Des loix humaines," Bodin writes, "ont toujours separé les brigans et corsaires, d'avec ceux que nous disons droits enemis en fait de guerre: qui maintiennent leurs estats et Republiques par voye de justice, de laquelle les brigans et corsaires cherchent l'eversion et ruine. C'est pourquoy ils ne doivent jouyr du droit de guerre commun à tous peuples, ny se prevaloir des loix que les vainqueurs donnent aux vaincus." ([*République*] Book I, Chapter 1, p. 1 f.) [See also a later passage in the *République* (liv. IV, ch. 7, p. 508): "quand le peuple est vne fois eschaufé, ayant les armes au poing, il est bien difficile de l'arrester."]

364-8. In Holinshed (vol. II, *The Conquest of Ireland*, p. 59) Hooker translates a similar opinion from Giraldus Cambrensis: "this people is a craftie and a subtile people, and more to be feared when it is peace, then when it is open warres: for their peace indeed is but enimitie, their policies but craft, their friendships but coloured, and therefore the more to be doubted and feared."

368-9. GREENLAW (*MP* 7. 196) compares this opinion with Machiavelli's *Principe*, cap. 5: "in verità non ci è modo sicuro a possederle, altro che la rovina. ... la più sicura via è spegnerle, o abitarvi."

370-1. RENWICK. Richard de Clare, Earl of Pembroke, called Strongbow, was invited to Ireland and established Norman-English there, 1168 [*i. e.*, 1170].

EDITOR. Strongbow undertook the conquest of Ireland at the invitation of Dermod MacMurrogh, King of Leinster, whose daughter Eva he married (see note on 3642). One of Spenser's sources for the conquest must have been John Hooker's translation of the *Expugnatio Hiberniae* of Giraldus Cambrensis (Holinshed, vol. II, *The Conquest of Ireland*, pp. 1-59); and he almost certainly knew Stanyhurst's Latin redaction of the *Expugnatio* (*De Rebvs*, pp. 59-218; see notes on 1602, 1933-5). But Giraldus will not account for all the racial data which Spenser supplies on the period of the conquest.

379-82. Sir John Davies denies that Ireland was really conquered in the reign of Henry Second (*Discoverie*, pp. 14-24), and later historians support this opinion rather than Spenser's. The Anglo-Norman Conquest extended along the coast from Larne to Cork and inland as far as the south bank of the Shannon in Munster and nearly to the Shannon in Leinster (Bagwell 1. 56-7).

382-402. Henry Second established English law during his visit to Ireland in 1172 (see Matthew Paris, *Historia Anglorum*, ed. Sir Frederic Madden, 1866-1869, 1. 371). By the sixteenth century, however, English law had been promulgated only in the twelve counties of Dublin, Kildare, Meath, Uriel (*i. e.*, Monaghan and Louth), Carlow, Kilkenny, Wexford, Waterford, Cork, Limerick, Kerry, and Tipperary (Davies, *Discoverie*, p. 121); in addition the five Irish septs of the O'Neills, O'Connors, O'Briens, O'Melaghlins, and MacMurroghs enjoyed the legal system of their conquerors (Harris, Ware's *Works* 2. 88). The Irish were repeatedly denied the benefits of English law (see, for example, Richard Cox, *The History of Ireland*, 1689-1690, 1. 74-5). "The Irish generally, were held and reputed *Aliens*, or rather enemies to the Crowne of *England*; insomuch, as they were not only disabled to bring anie actions, but they were so farre out of the protection of the Lawe, as it was often adiudged no fellony to kill a meere Irish-man in the time of peace" (Davies, *Discoverie*, p. 102).

407-21. COVINGTON (*UTB*, Studies in English 4. 29-30) points out that in this passage Spenser does not rely on Holinshed, and he suggests oral tradition as a possible source.

EDITOR. Spenser, however, may combine recollections of various annals and tracts he has read. The *Breviat of Ireland* by Patrick Finglas and a fifteenth-century letter from the citizens of Cork, which Campion and Holinshed quote and to which the *View* presently refers, both describe the revival of Irish power during the Wars of the Roses (see notes on 1964-76, 1976-91); and Davies, making use of Finglas, gives an account similar to Spenser's (*Discoverie*, pp. 90-2; see also E. C. S., pp. 47-8, and Davies, *A Speech on the Irish Parliament*, p. 398).

Actually the Irish had begun to regain their lost power in the thirteenth century, long before the Wars of the Roses (Butler, p. 163). The revolt of Murrogh en Ranagh which Spenser describes in a moment (465-89) must also have occurred before the Wars of the Roses; and, while this mistake may be due to a confusion of Edward Third with Edward Fourth (443), Spenser also speaks of the Irish invading the English Pale with the Scotch under Edward Bruce (522-36), long before the Wars of the Roses.

416. "white meates." MORLEY cites the *Promptorium Parvulorum*: "Whytmete, Lacticinium," food in which milk has the chief place.

RENWICK. Milk, cheese, and such like.

424-9. COVINGTON (*UTB*, Studies in English 4. 18). In none of Spenser's acknowledged sources could he have obtained all these data. Some of the places mentioned were quite obscure—as for instance "Polmonte" and "the Briskelah"—and were not to be found in printed works. The inference is then that Spenser's sources were Irish writings, or Irish traditions, or traditions among the English resident in Ireland. Possibly he drew upon all three.

425. "Slewlogher." RENWICK. Slieveloughera, in north Kerry, mentioned in *Faerie Queene* IV. xi. 41. [These mountains, which are about twenty-five miles west of Kilcolman, are mentioned as a retiring place of the Irish in 1986, where the reference may be due to a misrecollection of a fifteenth-century document (see note on 1976-91); but in the Elizabethan era they continued to be a refuge for rebels and outlaws (*i. e.*, *C. S. P. Ir. 1574-1585* 105. 25).]

425. "Arlo." RENWICK. The glen of Aherlow in the Galtee Mts., 20 miles or so NE. of Kilcolman, and a famous resort of outlaws; see *Astrophel*, 96, *F. Q.* VII, vi. 37 ff. [In *As.* Arlo is a wood, in *F. Q.* the mountain peak of Galteemore (see Judson, *Spenser in Southern Ireland*, pp. 48-54). Aherlow wood still offered protection to outlaws in Spenser's time (Holinshed, vol. II, *The Supplie of Irish Chronicles*, p. 178).]

425. "the bog of Allon." The "fennes of Allan" in *F. Q.* 2. 9. 16. 2 are probably the peat bogs of all central Ireland; here, where Spenser is dealing with Munster, he may have in mind a branch of them which still cut across Co. Tipperary in the eighteenth century (Arthur Young, *A Tour of Ireland*, ed. Constantia Maxwell, 1925, p. 129).

426. "Cullvers." RENWICK. The Curlew Mts. between Leitrim, Roscommon, and Sligo, with an important and difficult pass fortified in 1590.

ROLAND SMITH (*JEGP* 42. 511). There can be little doubt that "Curlews" (Ir. *Coirrshliabh* [*na Seghsa*]) was intended.

[The passes of the Curlews still afforded opportunities for ambush in the seventeenth century. See Gainsford, pp. 146-7.]

426. "Moneroo." RENWICK. Or *Monterolis*: tribal name of south Leitrim.

GOTTFRIED (*ELH* 6. 124-5) identifies "*Mointerolis*" in Ware's text as a tribe of eastern Leitrim and distinguishes it from "Moneroo," which may be

COMMENTARY

the townland of Monerew in eastern Mayo (Y. M. Goblet, *A Topographical Index of Parishes and Townlands of Ireland*) or a scribal misreading of "O'Connor Roo," the name of a family in Co. Roscommon.

ROLAND SMITH (*JEGP* 42. 511-2). ["*Mointerolis*"] is not, as Gottfried assumes ... a tribe-name plural. His sentence should read: "the 'Mointerolis' is easily identified with the territory of the MacRannalls in *southern Leitrim*" .... It is possible that Spenser wrote "Moneroo" .... But it is extremely doubtful that Spenser *intended* "Moneroo" or "Mon(e)roe" (Ir. *Móin ruadh*, "Red bog"), as no place of this name near the Curlews or the O'Rourke country was well known in Spenser's day.... Ware's "Mointerolis," on the other hand, is not only a natural and reasonable emendation; Muinter-Eolais is the only region comparable with the Curlews and the O'Rourke country that is mentioned prominently in the documents of the period.

426. "Orourks Countrie." RENWICK. North Leitrim, roughly.

427. "Glanmalor." RENWICK. The O'Byrne stronghold in the Wicklow Hills. [Spenser mentions this mountainous region of Co. Wicklow again (see 3664-5 and note). Under 1274 Clyn lists an "interfectio Anglicorum apud Glandelory" (p. 9); and on 6 June, 1308, Dowling reports (p. 18), "In Glyndelory alias Glynmolowra, Johannes Wogan justiciarius Hibernie in fugam coactus per Hibernicos rebelles ibidem, et Johannes de Sancto Howgelyn, Johannes Northon, Johannes Brereton et plures alii fuerunt interfecti. Downlowan, Typper, et plures alie villae cremate fuerunt per eosdem rebelles."]

428. "Shillelah." In the summer of 1581 Spenser probably visited this town with Lord Grey (*C. S. P. Ir. 1574-1585* 83. 45, 84. 12).

428. "the Briskelah." COVINGTON (*UTB*, Studies in English 4. 18) identifies this as an obscure place in Co. Tipperary.

GOTTFRIED (*ELH* 6. 130) points out that neither Covington's suggestion nor Ware's reading, "*Brackenah*," the name of an equally obscure district in Co. Wexford (*C. C. MSS. 1603-1624*, p. 321) will answer for Leinster; and he identifies "the Briskelah" as a region near Tullow on the Carlow-Wicklow border, repeatedly mentioned in Sir William Russell's campaigns against Feagh MacHugh (*C. C. MSS. 1589-1600*, pp. 252, 253, 256, and *C. S. P. Ir. 1592-1596* 190. 44. 12; *1596-1597* 195. 20, 196. 31. 6, 197. 13. 8).

ROLAND SMITH (*JEGP* 42. 512-3). Gottfried's identification with western Wicklow near Tullow and Knockloe is more satisfactory than Covington's "obscure region in Tipperary" .... Although the name is undeniably Irish, it is surprisingly infrequent in Irish documents; in the absence of further evidence, it can only be vaguely located as somewhere near the Carlow-Wexford border between Shillelagh and southern Carlow.

428. "Polmonte." GOTTFRIED (*ELH* 6. 131-2). "Polmonte" can be placed in southern Carlow, but the name seems to have designated equally a river, a barony, and a passage through the hills [Baptista Boazio, smaller map of Ireland, ed. dedicated to James First; Dowling, p. 11; Harris 1. 51].

ROLAND SMITH (*JEGP* 42. 513). Ir. *Poll in móintighe*, apparently "the Hole in the Moor." It appears in a marginal note which serves to date *Egerton 1782*, an early sixteenth-century manuscript [see Standish H. O'Grady and Robin Flower, *Catalogue of Irish Manuscripts in the British Museum* 2. 260]. From numerous entries in Ryan's *History of Carlow* Poulmounty is shown to have been the seat of the Kavanaghs . . . at least as early as 1399 and as late as 1662.

429. "Tirconell." The modern county of Donegal (anonymous *Description of Ireland*, p. 29).

429. "ffertellah." GOTTFRIED (*ELH* 6. 119) notes that this name, omitted or miscopied in some manuscripts, offers difficulty: an actual barony of Fertullagh belonged to the Tyrell family, but in West Meath, not Ulster (anonymous *Description of Ireland*, p. 107); Spenser may have intended Fermanagh, the county immediately south of Tyrone, but a name more suitable for confusion with Fertullagh is "Ferto" or "Fertoghe," a family settled at the north end of Co. Down in a region which might naturally be listed between Tyrone and "the Skottes" (*C. C. MSS. 1575-1588*, p. 437; *1589-1600*, pp. 93, 299).

ROLAND SMITH (*JEGP* 42. 514). This place-name . . . . is probably one more indication that Spenser never revised his *View* to the point where he was ready to publish it. . . . In addition to Gottfried's desperate guess at "Fertoghe" in northern Down, one might cite from the "Inquisition of the Earl of Tyrone's Lands" in 1588 [*C. S. P. Ir. 1586-1588* 135. 24, a townland] "called le upper *Fertouaghe*." [But it is improbable that Spenser would list a townland co-ordinately with the region (Tyrone) of which it was a subdivision.]

429. "the Skottes." RENWICK. The quasi-permanent settlement of Highland Scots in NE. Antrim.

443-63. WARE. It was not *George* Duke of *Clarence* here spoken of by the author, but *Lionell* Duke of *Clarence*, third sonne of King *Edw.* the 3. who married the Earle of *Vlsters* daughter, and by her had the Earledome of *Vlster* [Marginalium: *De hac re vide Camd. Britan. pag.* 336. [ed. of 1590, pp. 361-2] *et annal. Hib. ab eo edit. ad an.* 1367]. and although *Edw.* the 4. made his brother the Duke of *Clarence*, Lo. Lieutenant of *Ireland*, yet the place was still executed by his Deputyes (which were at severall times) *Thomas* Earle of *Desmond*, *Iohn* Earle of *Worcester*, *Tho.* Earle of *Kildare*, and *William Shirwood* Bishop of *Meth*, the Duke himselfe never comming into *Ireland* to governe there in person.

RENWICK. Lionel Duke of Clarence was created Earl of Ulster, 1347; married Elizabeth de Burgh (*not* Lacy), daughter of William de Burgh 3rd Earl of Ulster, 1352; appointed Lieutenant in Ireland, 1361.

EDITOR. Spenser probably confuses Lionel's marriage to the heiress of the de Burghs with an earlier marriage, between a de Burgh and the heiress of the Lacys, by which the de Burghs acquired Ulster (Campion, p. 70; Camden, *Britannia*, pp. 710-1); but the confusion of Edward Third with Edward Fourth and of Lionel with George Duke of Clarence is more serious since it leads Spenser to place the rebellion of Murrogh en Ranagh, who died in 1383, in the fifteenth century (465-89 and note on same) and to date the recovery of the Irish as late

COMMENTARY

as the Wars of the Roses (407-21). Lionel Duke of Clarence, the governor to whom Spenser really refers, ruled Ireland, for the most part in person, from 1361 to 1366; his death in 1368 was brought on by nothing more sinister than an intemperate consumption of Italian food. Sir John Davies denies that Lionel redeemed much of Ireland (*Discoverie*, pp. 35-6); but he seems to have recovered large parts of Co. Cork as well as north Munster and the coast of Ulster from Dundalk to Carrickfergus (Butler, pp. 7-8, 110-1, 127, 133; Curtis, *JRSAI* 47. 165-81, 48. 65-73). Spenser must have had access to some manuscript account of Lionel, such as the *Book of Howth* (*C. C. MSS. Miscellaneous*, pp. 167-8). See also O'Flaherty, p. 369.

452. " glennes." TODD. That is, dales or vallies; here spelt in the original edition *glynnes* perhaps in conformity to the Irish pronunciation. So *pen* was accustomed, in the same country, to be pronounced *pin*. See *Castle Rackrent, an Hibernian Tale*, etc. p. 77. [The context shows that Spenser knew the meaning of the word, although E. K. apparently does not when he glosses *S. C. Ap.* 26, " of the glenne, that is, of a country Hamlet or borough."]

454-5. " the Castle of Clare in *Thomond*." WARE. The County of *Clare* was anciently accounted part of the Province of *Mounster*, whence it hath the name of *Tuadhmuan*, or *Thomond*, which signifieth north *Mounster*, and hath at this day its peculiar Governour, as being exempted from the Presidencies of *Mounster* and *Connaght*. [The Castle of Clare stands on the north side of the Shannon estuary.]

456. " Mortimors Landes." Spenser later writes that the great Mortimer assumed the Irish name MacNemara (2058-60); and a manuscript account of Connaught and Thomond, drawn up in 1574, lists " Tullaghnenaspule, containing the Mac Nemaries' otherwise Mortimers' country, in which the Baron of Inshyquyn and Donell Reogh Mc Nemare are chief " (*C. C. MSS. 1601-1603*, p. 472). Hogan notes several families of MacNemaras in Co. Clare (anonymous *Description of Ireland*, p. 124); Speed prints " McNemaries " just west of Killaloe (*The Theatre of the Empire of Great Britaine*, 1614, map of Munster).

463-5. See 3590-3607 and note.

465-89. COVINGTON (*UTB*, Studies in English 4. 30) suggests that Spenser may have found an account of Murrogh en Ranagh in some Irish source and that, although the names and other details seem to be confused, he may have had in mind the Irish leader Art MacMurrogh " Comhanach."

RENWICK. Spenser exaggerates Morrough " en Ranagh " O'Brien's rebellion of 1382. The Four Masters do not record Morrough's being called King. He died of plague in 1383. The fact is not recorded by Camden; Spenser may have learned it from local tradition.

EDITOR. The Four Masters record under 1382, " A plundering army was led by Murrough O'Brien into Desmond, and totally devastated it"; under 1383, " Murrough na-Raithnighe O'Brien . . . died of it [the plague] " (4. 689, 691). Murrogh's death is likewise assigned to 1383 by *The Annals of Ulster* (ed. B. MacCarthy, 1887-1901, 3. 12-3); and he is included in an ancient genealogy of the O'Briens (*Caithréim Thoirdhealbhaigh*, ed. Standish H. O'Grady, 1929,

1. 181, 2. 191). Edmund Curtis identifies him as the leader of a great raid on Munster and Leinster, whom the Parliament of Tristeldermot bought off in 1377 (*A History of Mediaeval Ireland*, 1938, p. 243; see Berry 1. 472-5). Thus there can be no doubt that Spenser's Murrogh en Ranagh really lived in the second half of the fourteenth century, although Spenser places him a century later. For this chronological error see note on 443-63.

466-7.   DRAPER (*MP* 17. 480). The rendering of *Morrice* for *Murroghe* is not actual translation, but rather the adoption of a similar English name as an equivalent. Compare the familiar use of *Charles* for *Cathair* or of *Dennis* for *Diarmuid*. The rest of the expression, however, seems to be accurate translation: *-en-* can regularly be a preposition with genitive force; and *Ranagh* is an altogether possible phonological descendant of *raithneach, -nige*, meaning *fern*.

479.   "Insheginn." Today Inchiquin is a ruined castle in Co. Clare (see George U. MacNemara, *JRSAI* 31. 204-27, 341-64).

479-80.   WESTROPP (*JRSAI* 46. 8). The statement about "Killaloe, at first called Clariford," is monumental in its ignorant assertion.

480.   Mourne was once a preceptory of the Knights Templars, the ruins of which are still standing three miles south of Mallow in Co. Cork (Murray, *Handbook for Ireland*, seventh edition, p. 368; Courtnay Moore, *JCHAS*, Second Series, 6. 210-4). "By an inquisition taken at Cork, Nov. 4, anno 1584, Ballynamony [Mourne] was found to be an ancient corporation" (Charles Smith, *The Ancient and Present State of the County and City of Cork*, 1815, 1. 173).

480.   Buttevant, the town nearest to Kilcolman, is described affectionately in *Col.* 111-5.

488-9.   Spenser forgets that Holinshed calls Gurmundus and Turgesius, who lived long before the English conquest, kings of all Ireland; and Holinshed also writes that before 1095 "Ireland was bestowed into two principall kingdomes, and sometime into more, whereof one was euer elected and reputed to be cheefe, and as it were a monarch, whome in their histories they name *Maximum regem*, that is, the greatest king, or else without addition, *Regem Hiberniae*, the king of Ireland," and that "There was alwaies one principall gouernor among the Irish, whom they named a monarch" (vol. II, *The First Inhabitation of Ireland*, pp. 55-6, 59; *The Conquest of Ireland*, p. 8).

515-53.   COVINGTON (*UTB*, Studies in English 4. 27-8) believes that Spenser used the detailed account of the Scotch invasion in Holinshed. "Buchanan's narrative is very brief; Camden gives no account of this period of Irish history. Campion may have been consulted by Spenser, but there are no indications that he was."

RENWICK. For this history of Edward Bruce's invasion, 1315, see Holinshed and Camden [Campion?].

EDITOR. The Scotch invasion, the most important event in Irish history between the Anglo-Norman conquest and the sixteenth century, is described by Spenser as a phenomenon similar to the raids of Murrogh en Ranagh. This lack

COMMENTARY 293

of proportion, as well as the carefulness with which he explains what he means by the Scotch invasion, betrays the unfamiliarity of Spenser and his readers. The only mediaeval source which treats it at considerable length is John Barbour's *Bruce* (books 14-18), probably unknown to Spenser. Among sixteenth-century printed sources, Polydore Vergil mentions the invasion, very briefly; but the manuscript *Book of Howth* might have furnished Spenser with a much fuller account (*C. C. MSS. Miscellaneous*, pp. 131-46).

520-2.   Edward Bruce landed with six thousand Scots at Larne in Antrim, 26 May, 1315 (Armstrong, p. 73).

521.   In Holinshed reference is made to "the wild Scots, otherwise called the Redshanks, or rough footed Scots (because they go bare footed and clad in mantels ouer their saffron shirts after the Irish manner)"; and they are "esteemed by some to be mingled of Scots and Picts" (vol. I, *The Description of Britaine*, p. 14; vol. II, *The First Inhabitation of Ireland*, p. 52). *Redshank* is an equivalent for *Pict* in many writers of the period (Bede, *The History of the Chvrch of Englande*, trans. Thomas Stapleton, 1565, *passim*; Humphrey Llwyd, *The Breuiary of Britayne*, trans. Thomas Twyne, 1573, f. 48r; Campion, p. 4); and Spenser probably has in mind Picts as distinct from Scots.

522.   The defection of the Lacys is briefly described in Holinshed (vol. II, *The Chronicles of Ireland*, p. 68) and in the *Book of Howth* (*C. C. MSS. Miscellaneous*, pp. 133, 141). The family, which was suspected of treason at the beginning of the invasion and later pardoned, finally deserted to the Scots (Colvin, pp. 45-6).

523-4.   "scattorlinges." TODD. See the note on F. Q. ii. x. 63. He uses *scatterlings* for *ravagers* again in this View of the State of Ireland [1088].

525-30.   The English Pale, which came into existence at the end of the thirteenth century, originally comprised the counties of Antrim, Down, Armagh (in part), Louth, Meath, West Meath, Dublin, Kildare, King's, Queen's, Carlow, Kilkenny, Tipperary, Waterford, Wexford, and Wicklow (in part); later it was reduced in size. An act of 1475 refers to a dike around Dublin; in 1494 the Parliament of Drogheda provided for a new dike and ditch along the borders of the counties of Dublin, Meath, Kildare, and Louth which faced the Irish; and the region within became known, for the first time, as the *English Pale* (Morrin in *Calendar of the Patent and Close Rolls* 2. xxxi; Hardiman in *Statute of Kilkenny*, pp. xxv-xxix, 4; Bagwell 1. 123). *Pale* merely means a limit or boundary (*NED*, def. 2. c); Spenser is mistaken in 913-5, where he associates the word with *palatine*.

526.   "the pointe of Donluce." JENKINS (*PMLA* 53. 351) believes that Spenser was present when the castle of Dunluce, on the point, was stormed, in the autumn of 1584, by the forces under Lord Deputy Perrot. [See the anonymous *History of Sir John Perrott*, pp. 158-60, 227-8.]

527.   "Knockfergus." Another name for Carrickfergus on the east coast of Co. Antrim.

528. "outboundes." NED defines this as a plural substantive meaning "outward bounds" and cites the *View* for the first occurrence of the word.

531-4. *The Annals of Clonmacnoise* says of the Scots, under 1315: "they did not leave neither field of corn undestroyed nor towne unsacked nor unfrequented place (were it never soe little nor soe desert) unsearched and unburnt" (quoted in Armstrong, p. 88). See also Clyn, p. 12; *The Annals of Logh Cé*, ed. William M. Hennessy, 1871, 1. 595, 597.

534-5. Bruce passed through Belfast in the campaign of 1317 (Armstrong, map opposite title). In the spring of 1316 he "took the Green Castle, and put his ward there"; it was also visited by the Scots in 1317 (*Book of Howth, C. C. MSS. Miscellaneous*, p. 131; Orpen, p. 179; Armstrong, map). At Kells in Meath Bruce overcame the English in a great battle on 6 December, 1315; Holinshed tells how he "burnt Kenlis in Meth" (vol. II, *The Chronicles of Ireland*, p. 66; see the *Book of Howth, C. C. MSS. Miscellaneous*, pp. 131, 183); the campaign of 1317 also took him through Kells in Co. Kilkenny (Orpen, p. 191; Armstrong, map; Colvin, p. 39). "Beltalbot" is probably Belturbet in Cavan. Castletown in Louth lay close to Bruce's route in 1317 (Armstrong, map). The *Book of Howth* reports that the Scots burned the church bells of "new Town in Lexe," *i. e.*, Queen's County (*C. C. MSS. Miscellaneous*, p. 134). All of these places except Belturbet were within the English Pale of that period.

536-9. The posterity of the Audleys continued in Lecale, Co. Down, at the end of the sixteenth century (anonymous *Description of Ireland*, p. 9). There were also Talbots in the counties of Louth, Dublin, and Meath (anonymous *Description*, pp. 4, 37, 38, 43, 92-5, 99-100). The name "dutches" causes difficulty since it does not seem to occur in Irish records; the name *Touchet*, which occurs at this place in other manuscripts than the Ellesmere, is also doubtful since the barons of Audley, already included in the list, were Touchets by family; it is possible that Spenser wrote "Tuites," the name of an influential family in Meath (anonymous *Description*, pp. 90, 96, 103-4, 107). The Chamberlains were still among the gentlemen of Co. Louth (anonymous *Description*, p. 5). Duffrin in Co. Down was the original seat of the Mandevilles, although in Spenser's day the only surviving branch of the family was settled in Co. Waterford (anonymous *Description*, pp. 10, 162-3); Sir Thomas Mandeville and his brother were slain by the Scots at Down or Carrickfergus in 1316 (Holinshed, vol. II, *The Chronicles of Ireland*, p. 67; the *Book of Howth, C. C. MSS. Miscellaneous*, p. 135; Armstrong, pp. 93-4). William Savage was likewise slain by the Scots, in 1317 (Clyn, p. 13), but the eclipse of the family was really effected by the O'Neills at a later period (Davies, *Discoverie*, pp. 197-8; anonymous *Description*, p. 10); the poor descendant, who dwelt in the Little Ardes, east of Lough Strangford, rather than the Ardes, farmed out his lands to more enterprising Englishmen (*C. S. P. Ir. 1592-1596* 167. 54; *C. C. MSS. 1589-1600*, p. 93). Of the six families listed by Spenser only the Mandevilles and Savages appear to have been rooted out by the Scots in any real sense. He may have recollected the names of the Savages, Chamberlains, and Audleys from a list of decayed English families, unconnected, however, with the Scotch invasion, in Holinshed (vol. II, *The Description of Ireland*, p. 39).

COMMENTARY

539-53. Edward Bruce was crowned King of Ireland at Dundalk on 1 or 2 May, 1316, and reigned more than two years until he was slain at the battle of Faughart on 14 October, 1318; Spenser's underestimate may be due to the dating of the battle a year too late by Holinshed (vol. II, *The Historie of Scotland*, p. 221) and Camden (*Britannia*, ed. of 1594, p. 667; date not included before 1594). The account of the battle in the *Book of Howth* (*C. C. MSS. Miscellaneous*, pp. 143-6) did not supply Spenser with the description of the survivors' ruthlessness, and it points out that Bermingham was made commander immediately before the battle, not sent by Edward Second to be general.

557-9. Patrick Finglas writes at the beginning of the sixteenth century, " The Erle of *Ulster* might dispend a Yere in that Lond above thirty thousand Marks " (Harris, *Hibernica* 1. 52; see also *C. C. MSS. 1515-1574*, p. 7). In a passage based on Campion, Holinshed explains: " in the time whilest sir Henrie Sidneie was gouernour there, when the countie of Vlster was auouched to belong vnto the crowne: it was prooued in open parlement, that the reuenues of that earldome, in the daies of Edward the third were reckoned, and found to amount vnto the summe of one and thirtie thousand marks yearelie" (vol. II, *The First Inhabitation of Ireland*, p. 72; Campion, p. 35; see also Campion, pp. 70-1, where the revenue of Ulster is a straight thirty thousand marks). Camden writes of Ulster, " suis Comitibus olim triginta millia Marcarum dependit " (*Britannia*, p. 711). Campion, Holinshed, and Camden are undoubtedly Spenser's " good recordes," but the revenues of which they speak were paid in the reign of Edward Third, long after the Scotch invasion.

558. A mark was valued at 13s 4d.

559-72. Spenser probably visited Ulster with Grey in August, 1581 (Judson, *Life*, pp. 99-100; *C. S. P. Ir. 1574-1585* 85. 5); but his enthusiasm may also be colored by Camden's description of the province (*Britannia*, pp. 706-9, quoted by Gottfried, *ELH* 6. 121). Lynch attaches special importance to this passage: " Praeterea Spenserus scriptor post homines natos cum a Cambrensi discesseris Hibernis injuriosissimus, ut qui infimae plebis, et flagitiosorum hominum sordibus nationem universam illiniat ad invidiam genti conflandam, et avitas possessiones abripiendas, in Ultoniae laudes orationem effundens, soli tantam esse ubertatem ait, ut e quovis ei semine mandata, messis copiosa proveniat " (2. 124).

562-4. The lakes of Ulster, with their ships and islands, may have formed a knot of images from which Spenser drew the lake, boat, and isle of Phaedria in *F. Q.* 2. 6. 9-13.

586-7. RENWICK. Thomas Fitzgerald, called also Fitzgarret, 10th Earl of Kildare, rebelled and was executed, 1535 [*i. e.*, 1537. Campion describes his rebellion (pp. 117-21), and Stanyhurst gives an even fuller account (Holinshed, vol. II, *The Chronicles of Ireland*, pp. 89-97). Kildare's sister Elizabeth was Surrey's Geraldine (*Tottel's Miscellany*, ed. Hyder E. Rollins, 1928-1929, 2. 70-5). He was known as Silken Thomas " for that his followers had silk frienges about their head peeces " (Dowling, p. 35).]

587-612. RENWICK. Besides the Desmond war, Grey had to deal with a rebellion in the Pale, led by William Nugent and Lord Baltinglas.

On 29th March, 1581, the Papal Nuncio in France reported to the Vatican: "Yesterday by letters from friends I had more certain confirmation of the affairs of Ireland, that the Catholic party there is equal in strength to the enemy, and very constant: and with them is joined an English Lord called Valtinglas (Baltinglas) and one they call the great Onello (O'Neill) has finally taken up arms on the side of the good." (Vatican Archives, *Nunziature, Francia* 15. 88vo.) A letter from London, 15th March, 1581, states, "Quantum ad Hiberniam iam omnes illius gentis Comites et Reguli usque ad unum a Regina deficierunt . . . solus Hormundanus Comes pertinax adhuc Reginae partibus adheret." (*Ibid*, 94). Grey's march on O'Neill, and his strict dealing in the Pale, certainly saved a very difficult situation.

EDITOR. See Judson, *Life*, pp. 84-5. For Spenser's further defence of Grey's conduct and character see 3302-96. For Grey's part in the political allegory of *F. Q.* see Book V, Appendix II, pp. 299-335. Men of a devout or military character, like Captain William Piers and John Hooker, were admirers of Grey (*C. S. P. Ir. 1586-1588* 126. 87; Holinshed, vol. II, *The Supplie of the Irish Chronicles*, p. 177). Lodowick Bryskett, Spenser's friend, wrote while Grey was still in office: "Her Majestie had never here a more willing, a more zealous, nor a more sufficient minister for suche an enterprise than this L. Deputie, nether was there ever any here more lykely to prosper in any action that he shall take in hand, as a man living in the feare of God, and so consequently assured of his blessing"; and he reiterates his praise in later letters (Plomer and Cross, pp. 23-4, 30, 39).

588.   MORLEY. Arthur Lord Grey of Wilton, in whose service Spenser first went to Ireland.

593-8.   So Artegall is described in *F. Q.* 5. 12. 18. 5-9:

>   As when a skilfull Marriner doth reed
>   A storme approching, that doth perill threat,
>   He will not bide the daunger of such dread,
>   But strikes his sayles, and vereth his mainsheat,
>   And lends vnto it leaue the emptie ayre to beat.

597 n.   RENWICK (*View*, p. 323). The *nose* of a ship is good enough 16th century English, and the metaphor is much improved.

600 n.   "blatter." TODD. To *rail* or *rage*. Thus the *Blatant* Beast is described with various *barking* tongues, F. Q. vi. xii. 27.

MORLEY. Patter, babble (from the noise of rain).

NED defines the word as *talk idly, babble*, but notes that its use is influenced by its phonetic resemblance to *batter, chatter, blast*, etc. [This reading seems preferable to "batter" in the Ellesmere MS: Envy and the Blatant Beast pursue Artegall in *F. Q.* 5. 12. 28 ff.; "envye" would naturally "blatter" against Lord Grey here.]

600-1.   See 3289-3428.

611 n.   "checked." COLLIER. Ought we not to read *choked* for "checked?"
—"*choked* with their owne venome."

617-8.   The O'Byrnes and O'Tooles dwelt in the Wicklow Mountains south of Dublin (anonymous *Description of Ireland*, p. 36) ; see 1428-32. Spenser discusses Feagh MacHugh in 3617-3749.

619.   For the Cavanaghs see anonymous *Description of Ireland*, pp. 50, 56; *View* 1432-3.

619-21.   RENWICK. *Leix*: Queen's County.   *Offaly*: King's County.

EDITOR. In 1556 Philip and Mary instructed Lord Deputy Sussex to shire Leix and Offaly, and the new names were given with reference to these monarchs; before settlements were made, however, the O'Moores were expelled from Queen's and the O'Connors from King's; later the O'Moores succeeded in returning (Falkiner, *PRIA* 24. 182; Maxwell, pp. 229-32; anonymous *Description of Ireland*, pp. 76-8, 81; Dunlop, *EHR* 6. 61-96). The county of Meath is sometimes more properly known as East Meath, to distinguish it from West Meath, mentioned immediately by Spenser; the two were divided by an act of the Irish Parliament in 1543 (*The Statutes of Ireland*, pp. 238-41).

621-2.   The O'Reillys dominated Co. Cavan; the O'Kellys lived along the Shannon in the counties of Galway and Roscommon, whence they could easily cross into West Meath (anonymous *Description of Ireland*, pp. 9, 117, 134-6, 153).

637.   "in godes name."   See Spenser in Letter III 32 and Harvey in Letter II 5.

648-62.   JONES (*Spenser's Defense*, p. 205) parallels this passage to one in Bodin's *République*, liv. IV, ch. 7, and to the statement in Bodin's *Methodus ad Facilem Historiarum Cognitionem*: "Jurisprudentia est ars tribuendi suum cuique, ad tuendam hominum societatem." [Another passage of the *République* seems to offer a closer parallel (liv. II, ch. 5, p. 257): "non seulement le suget est coulpable de leze maiesté au premier chef, qui a tué le Prince souuerain, ains aussi qui a attenté, qui a donné conseil, qui la voulu, qui la pensé. . . . Et combien que la mauuaise pensee ne merite point de peine, si est-ce que celuy qui a pensé d'attenter à la vie de son Prince souuerain, est iugé coulpable de mort, quelque repentence qu'il en ait eu." This theory was carried into practice in 1586 when Mary of Scotland was condemned for the intention of treason against Elizabeth; and Spenser's account of the affair in *F. Q.* 5. 9. 40-41 emphasizes the point.]

653-5.   RENWICK. Spenser's *devise or purpose* echoes the *compass or imagine* of the Statutes of Treasons, e. g. 2 Eliz. *c.* 6. [See *The Statutes of Ireland*, pp. 286-7. The penalty was confiscation of goods and imprisonment for life.]

659-60.   So Harvey writes (*A New Letter of Notable Contents*, 1593, sig. C3r): "Howbeit as in some publique causes, better a mischief, then an inconuenience: so in many priuate cases *better an inconuenience, then a mischief.*"

660.   "*Ius Politicum.*"   Political Law.

668-75.   So in 1578 Sir Henry Sidney writes (*Letters and Memorials* 1. 241-

2): " soch Parcialitie and affectionate Dealings were found in the Juries, as were the Matter never so playne and evident, the Evidence never so full and apparaunte, if it touched any of their Freindes ... no Inditement would be found, no, though the Partie made submission and confessed the Fault: And, on the other Syde ... were the Evidence never so weake, the Proffe never so slender, the Jurie would fynd it." In 1612 Barnaby Rich gives the same picture of Irish juries (*Remembrances*, pp. 139-40; *A Catholicke Conference*, ff. 1v–2r). E. S. (ff. 13v, 19r-v) points out that the whole country joins together in any suit of law against an Englishman; on the other hand, an Irish defendant will confess his crime to a priest, who draws up a certificate which is given to the Irish jurymen, and if the crime is against an English heretic, the defendant is allowed to deny what has been confessed.

670-2. Queen Elizabeth used to say "That the *Irish* were so allyed in kindred the one with the other, and she hauing neuer a Cosine in the Country, could neuer get her right" (Rich, *Description*, p. 30).

699. NED. Quirk. ... Of obscure origin and history; app. native in western dialects. ... 1. A verbal trick, subtlety, shift or evasion; a quibble, quibbling argument.

ROLAND SMITH (*JEGP* 42. 505). The word seems to have been learned in Ireland, where Ir. *cuiridh*, "a turn, twist" ... would have sounded like *quirk* in 1590. [But *NED* cites English examples of *quirk* in Spenser's sense from 1565, 1566, and 1583; moreover *turn* or *twist*, the meaning of the Irish term, does not fit the context.]

705. "cautelous." TODD. *Cautious*. See the Gloss. Urry's Chaucer, in V. *Cautele*.

COLLIER. The word occurs more than once in Shakespeare, and is found in nearly all the writers of the day.

728-32. JENKINS (*PMLA* 53. 360). The fact that the Anglo-Irish lords controlled Irish juries is evinced by an incident in connection with Spenser's neighbor, Lord David Barry. In February, 1586, a tenant of Lord Barry was brought before Norris' court at Cork for horse-stealing. Though sitting on the bench as one of Her Majesty's justices, Lord Barry packed the court with Irish and saved his tenant's life. ... Spenser's survey of Irish laws, courts, and police in the *Veue* is thoroughly competent because his remarks arise from the experience of numerous court-trials.

729-30. TODD. "*Hinds*, which they call churls," as he presently explains the word [3201-2].

EDITOR. Spenser later discusses the churls more fully and sympathetically (2528-84). They were excluded from military employment and, as noncombatants, were at the mercy of their armed chieftains (Ware, *Works* 2. 157-9; Butler, p. 301). Sir William Gerrard calls them "poor wretched creatures in person, and as miserable for want of substance to yield them meat and clothes"; yet he prefers them to the gentlemen and rogues of the Pale (*C. C. MSS. 1575-1588*, p. 477).

COMMENTARY

739-40. An act against wilful perjury had been passed by the Irish Parliament on 14 May, 1586, during Perrot's government (Carte Manuscripts in Bodleian Library, vol. 61, f. 7ʳ; *The Statvtes of Ireland*, pp. 383-6).

741-5. "Every Nation, land, and Countrie, by the nature of the place, the climate of the heaven, and the influence of the starres hath certaine vertues, and certaine vices, which are proper, naturall, and perpetuall unto it" (*The Civile Conversation of M. Steeven Guazzo*, trans. George Pettie, 1925, 1. 64).

748-50. Spenser may remember what Chaucer has to say on the Flemish love of drink in the Pardoner's Tale.

761-4. RENWICK. This is scarcely accurate: 35 peremptory challenges were (and are) allowed in trials for treason, 20 in trials for felony. [A *peremptory challenge* or *exception* is an objection to a juryman, allowed to a prisoner without his being required to show cause (*NED*, *peremptory*, def. 1). Spenser plays on the term in *F. Q.* 3. 8. 16. 6.]

770. TODD. *Garran* is an Erse word; still retained in Scotland, says Dr. Johnson. It means a *strong* or *hackney horse*: See Shaw's Galic Dictionary.

COLLIER. The etymology seems to be Ger. *Gorr*, *equus*. Richardson shows that the word "garran" was also used by Whitelock and by Sir William Temple, but in both authors with reference to Ireland.

MORLEY. *Garrons*, working horses; old Irish *gerrán*, a work horse, a hack.

ROLAND SMITH (*JEGP* 42. 504). Ir. *gearran*.

[Hooker gives the meaning "cariage horsses" (Holinshed, vol. II, *The Supplie of the Irish Chronicles*, p. 156); the real meaning of the Irish *gearran* seems to be "*equus castratus*, a gelding, from *gearr*, to cut" (Joyce, *Social History* 2. 410; see also *State Papers, Henry VIII* 3. 590).]

775-94. Lord Deputy Sussex attacked this evil in 1562, calling it "the root of all other mischief in this realm" (*C. C. MSS. 1515-1574*, p. 342). Sir John Davies, however, describes the execution of one receiver together with a thief (*Letter to Salisbury* (1607), p. 359).

810-1. JENKINS (*PMLA* 53. 352). As secretary to [Sir John] Norris, who represented County Cork in the Irish parliament of 1585, Spenser was soon back in Dublin for its opening on April 26. That he attended many of the parliamentary sessions is evinced by [the present passage].

JUDSON (*Life*, p. 116) feels that Spenser here expresses his personal interest in the program of legislation Perrot introduced in 1585 and that he may have regretted its failure.

EDITOR. In the Irish House of Lords on 10 May, 1585, during Perrot's government, an act for the trial of accessaries was "dasshed" after the third reading (Carte Manuscripts in Bodleian Library, vol. 61, f. 2ʳ).

818-30. Several acts against such "Coullorable conveyaunces" had been passed by Irish parliaments in the fourteenth century (Berry 1. 271, 289, 383; *Statute of Kilkenny*, p. 79).

819-20.   "Closse and Coullorable conveyaunces." See *Hub.* 855-6.

830-3.   RENWICK. This manoeuvre was discovered by Wallop: see his letters in *Cal. S. P. Ir.*, 109. 60, 124. 47, 124. 13. His production of the evidence in the Parliament of 1586 forced on the Act 28 Eliz. c. 5, by which Desmond's lands were attainted. [The attainder of Gerald FitzGerald, fifteenth Earl of Desmond, who had been in open rebellion for several years before his death in 1583, offered peculiar difficulties. Wallop was finally able to produce written evidence that Desmond had purposed treason in September, 1574, at the time when he enfeoffed John FitzGerald of Cloyne and others with the whole of his Munster estates (*C. C. MSS. 1515-1574*, pp. 481-3; *1575-1588*, p. 425).]

834-9.   See *The Statvtes of Ireland*, pp. 403-8. The first reading of the act of attainder against Desmond and of an act against fraudulent conveyances by those attainted of treason occurred on 29 April, 1586; the final assent of the Irish Parliament to both acts was given on 14 May, 1586 (Carte Manuscripts in Bodleian Library, vol. 61, ff. 4ᵛ and 7ʳ).

840-1.   JENKINS (*PMLA* 53. 352). On February 27, 1586, Spenser was once more in Dublin and he again, taking the account of Irenaeus as the experience of the poet, attended the turbulent session of the Irish parliament which lasted almost a month in the spring of 1586. So tired of the stormy disputes which raged over the confiscation of the lands of the Earl of Desmond does Spenser seem to have been that on July 18, when he penned at Dublin his well-known sonnet to Harvey [" Haruey, the happy aboue happiest men "], he appears to have been very envious of his old friend, who is sequestered from the world in his scholarly retreat at Cambridge. [See also Jenkins, *PMLA* 47. 116-7; Routledge, *EHR* 29. 116; Judson, *Life*, p. 119.]

842-6.   For example, the parliament of 1586 had to pass a special act providing that all conveyances made after 1579 by James Eustace, Viscount Baltinglas, and his brothers must be registered and that those made with treasonable intent be confiscated to the Crown (anonymous *History of Sir John Perrott*, pp. 252-66).

853-4.   RIEDNER (p. 119). Ich konnte bis jetzt diese Stelle bei Caesar nicht finden.

RENWICK. Spenser probably remembers vaguely a passage he looked up for his historical remarks, *de B. G.* VI. 14: " In primis hoc volunt persuadere, non interire animas . . . atque hoc maxime ad virtutem excitari putant metu mortis neglecto." [The omissions in some of the manuscripts at this point may indicate that Spenser did not include the reference to Caesar, or included it only tentatively.]

857-69.   Moryson writes (*Shakespeare's Europe*, p. 232): " nothing was more frequent, then for Irishmen, in the tyme of our warr with Spayne, to liue in Spayne, in Rome, and in their very Seminaryes, and yet by these and like Crafty Conveyances to preserue to them and their heyres, their goods, and lands in Ireland, yea very spirituall livings for life, not rarely graunted to children for their

COMMENTARY   301

maintenaunce in that superstitious education, most dangerous to the State." Anthony Standen writes from Spain, 8 September, 1592, that among the Irish entertained in that country were Viscount Baltinglas, Thomas and John Lacy, John Lutterel, and Richard Stanyhurst (Birch, *Memoirs* 1. 82).

878. "knightes service." NED. The military service which a knight was bound to render as a condition of holding his land. [See *F. Q.* 3. 1. 44. 8-9.]

880. "lewdelye." TODD. *Ignorantly.* The word is repeatedly used by Spenser in this sense; as it had been by Chaucer. And thus, in our translation of the Acts of the Apostles, Ch. xvii. 5. we have "certain *lewd* fellows of the baser sort."

896. See 4651-71.

904-8. Sir John Davies traces these special privileges rather to the fact that individual nobles, not the king, had conquered and settled the counties palatine at their own charge (*Discoverie*, pp. 154-5).

907. "wilde Irishe." For a history of this term see Snyder, *MP* 17. 687-725.

913-9. DRAPER (*MP* 17. 474-5). The derivation of *palentine* from *pale* seems to be the merest popular etymology. NED. quotes from Hatz. Darm. a fifteenth-century use of the LL *palatinus*, used as an adjective to mean *of or belonging to the palatium, or palace*, and used as a noun to mean *an officer of the palace, a chamberlain*. The correct derivation was not unknown to scholars of Spenser's own day [see Selden, notes on Drayton's *Polyolbion*, Song XI]. . . . The reference to *Palsgrave*, however, is significant. NED. traces this back to a MHG *pfalzgrâve* and that to an OHG *pfalzengrâvo*, derived, in turn, from *pfalenza*, *palace*, and *grâvo*, *count*. NED. adds a valuable and suggestive note, that the Latin *palatium* appears to have been altered in Teutonic lands to *palantium. . . . unless Spenser spelled his word *palentine* [see 904 n, 911 n, 913 n, 915 n] in order to force the similarity with *pale* (and I think him not above doing that sort of thing), then his is one of the last uses of the word with the old, traditionally Germanic spelling and pronunciation. . . . *Palsgrave* is, indeed, a cousin of *palentine*; but, though Spenser realized the similarity of meaning, I doubt whether he understood any etymological relationship. As for the derivation from the Latin deponent, *palor*, Spenser even seems dubious; and, indeed, he might well have been. [*Palor* means *to wander up and down* and has nothing to do with *palatine*. See Falkiner, *PRIA* 24. 174.]

916. "outrunne." The first example NED cites of this word in the sense of "To run beyond a fixed limit or point" (def. 3) is dated 1655.

919-29. Ulster and Meath were established as palatines at the time of their conquest; Carlow, Wexford, Kildare, Kilkenny, and Leix (Queen's) became palatines in the reign of John, when they were distributed among the five granddaughters of Strongbow; Edward First converted Kerry into a county palatine; and in 1328 Edward Third gave the Butlers, along with the title of Ormond, the palatinate privileges of Tipperary (Davies, *Discoverie*, pp. 137-9; Falkiner, *PRIA*

24. 169-94). By 1596, however, the old palatine system remained in Tipperary alone, and not all of Tipperary was under the jurisdiction of the Earl of Ormond; mingled with the palatine lands was the so-called "Countie of the Crosse" of Tipperary, under the jurisdiction of the Crown (anonymous *Description of Ireland*, p. 207). For the disorders fostered by Ormond's privileges in Tipperary see *C. S. P. Ir. 1574-1585* 94. 84, *1596-1597* 191. 37. 8; *C. C. MSS. 1589-1600*, p. 493; E. S., f. 17r.

919-23. So Hooker calls Ulster "the receptacle and place of receipt of all the preies and spoiles from out of the other prouinces" (Holinshed, vol. II, *The Supplie of the Irish Chronicles*, p. 113). Co. Tyrone and Munster were likewise styled receptacles for marauders (*C. S. P. Ir. 1588-1592* 163. 29, 144. 56).

925-9. Thomas Butler, tenth Earl of Ormond, "the Lorde of the libertye," was the only head of a great Anglo-Irish family who consistently preserved his loyalty; and he enjoyed the peculiar favor of Elizabeth, if not of the newly arrived English officials. Spenser later alludes to difficulties between Ormond and Grey (3319-24) and apparently praises his loyalty (2943-8). See also *Ded. Son.* 7.

930-8. The privileges of Irish "Corporacions," *i. e.*, cities, originated in their early charters: those of Dublin in 1171 or 1172, of Limerick in 1197, of Waterford in 1206, of Drogheda in 1229, of Cork in 1242, and of Galway in 1396 (Bagwell 1. 73-5). Of the five which Spenser lists at least three seem to have been included or assumed in almost every charter: that the city shall not be subject to any other government than its own, that it shall not be deprived of its franchises, and that all taxes and fines imposed on it shall return to it. Fynes Moryson shows that the last privilege is abused by Waterford (*Shakespeare's Europe*, p. 217). The privilege of not being charged with any garrison is more difficult to trace; Waterford could not be forced to receive the king's forces, and some charters, *e. g.*, that of Athboy, stipulated that the king's officers could enter the city only in order to approve the standards of measure in use there (*Shakespeare's Europe*, p. 217; *Calendar of the Patent and Close Rolls* 2. 454); Spenser later proposes to place garrisons in Waterford and Cork (4273-6), without considering that such a privilege would be infringed. The right to buy and sell with thieves and rebels is probably the rarest of the five which Spenser lists; the charter which Henry Fourth gave to Youghal in 1404 grants such a right, but only on account of what the city has suffered from the war and with no promise that it will be renewed beyond the period of the war (*Calendar of the Patent and Close Rolls* 2. 97; *The Council Book of the Corporation of Youghal*, ed. Richard Caulfield, p. xxvii); Henry Eighth specifically commanded Galway not to trade with Irish rebels (*C. C. MSS. 1515-1574*, p. 92; *State Papers, Henry VIII* 2. 310-1); Limerick, on the other hand, believed that it had a well-established right to do so (*State Papers, Henry VIII* 3. 110). In October, 1592, the commissioners for Munster called attention to the excessive privileges, some of them the same as those noted by Spenser, which were enjoyed by the cities of that province (*C. S. P. Ir. 1592-1596* 167. 8. 2).

948. Yet *The Statvtes of Ireland, Beginning the Third Yere of K. Edward the Second*, ed. Richard Bolton, 1621, is a small folio of 445 pages; and it includes only the general statutes.

COMMENTARY 303

952-62. Sir John Davies (*Discoverie*, pp. 100-32) explains at some length that the laws made after the conquest of Ireland applied only to the English dwelling there and not to the Irish, although they repeatedly sought them for themselves. In 1621 Richard Bolton (*The Statvtes of Ireland*, sigs. A4v–A5r) writes: "although the same be not in expresse wordes repealed by any later Act, yet (in mine owne opinion) many of those Stat. and especially those concerning Marchiors, and all Statutes that make markes of differences between the *English* and *Irish*, as that of shauing the beard vpon the vpper lippe, and the distinctions betweene *Irish* enemies and *English* rebells, and of persons amesnable and not amesnable to the Lawe, are by implication and good constructions of the Statutes of 33. *H. 8. 3.* and 4. *Ph. and Ma.* and 11. *Eliz.* repealed as absolutely as if the same had beene by plaine and expresse words."

952-4. RENWICK. 25 Henry VI *c.* 4. repealed 1634. [See *All the Statutes*, f .3v; *The Statvtes of Ireland*, p. 9; Berry 2. 89. This early act applied only to Englishmen; a later act of 28 Henry Eighth forbids the mustache to all subjects (*The Statvtes of Ireland*, pp. 129-30; see *State Papers, Henry VIII* 2. 215, 309).]

954. TODD. He presently explains the reason of their wearing saffron shirts etc. [See 1893-6.]

RENWICK. 28 Henry VIII *c.* 15. [See *All the Statutes*, ff. 67v–71r; *The Statvtes of Ireland*, pp. 129-30.]

955. RENWICK. 25 Henry VI *c.* 6. repealed 1634. [See *The Statvtes of Ireland*, p. 10; Berry 2. 91. The law excepts knights and prelates from the restriction.]

955 n. TODD. See Cotgrave's Fr. Dict. "*Petrinal*, a horsemans peece, a petronell." Hence the soldier, who served with a *petronell*, was called *poictrinalier*. It appears to have been much the same as our *blunderbuss*. See the Fr. *Encyclopedie*, in V.

MORLEY. *Petronels*, horse-pistols, from Spanish *petrina*, a belt around the breast, in which they were carried.

RENWICK (*View*, p. 323). The reading *pettorells* ... makes it clear that the meaning is "peitrel," a horse's breastplate, not "petronel," a pistol, as has been suggested.

955-7. RENWICK. 33 Henry VI *c.* 2. [See *The Statvtes of Ireland*, p. 22; Berry 2. 339. This law is listed in the table of contents of *All the Statutes*, but f. 10, on which it should occur, is missing in the Cambridge University Library copy.]

957-8. RENWICK. 5 Edw. IV *c.* 4. [See *All the Statutes*, f. 18r; *The Statvtes of Ireland*, pp. 37-38; and Berry 3. 292-5. This act applied only to the English and the Irish dwelling with the English. A later act, 10 Henry Seventh, required bows to be used by all subjects in Ireland (*All the Statutes*, ff. 27v–28r; *The Statvtes of Ireland*, pp. 59-60). For the efforts of Henry Eighth to popularize the bow and arrow in Ireland see *State Papers, Henry VIII* 2. 213, 483, 508. Under Elizabeth a concerted movement in the same direction was made in England (see *Egerton Papers*, ed. J. Payne Collier, 1840, pp. 217-20; Millican, pp. 54-64) ; and it may have taken some courage on Spenser's part to criticize a statute which commanded bows and arrows.]

958-9.　　RENWICK.　10 Henry VI. [Renwick's previous reference to an act of "10 Henry VIII *c. 9*" does not fit any of the statutes named by Spenser. For 10 Henry Sixth see *All the Statutes*, sig. A1ᵛ; *The Statvtes of Ireland*, pp. 427-8; Berry 2. 45. In 1367 the famous *Statute of Kilkenny* (pp. 55, 57, 59) contained a stipulation to the same effect.]

960-1.　　RENWICK.　35 Henry VI *c.* 3. [See *All the Statutes*, f. 12ʳ; *The Statvtes of Ireland*, p. 25; Berry 2. 449. This act forbids distraints by those not amenable to English common law (*i. e.*, those dwelling in districts governed by Irish law), whereas the acts described below (972-94) apply to distraints by those subject to English common law.]

960-1.　　"distraine." *NED* (def. 8). To levy a distress .... Originally in order to compel the defaulter, by detention of the thing seized, to pay money due or perform an obligation; but in later use including the power to obtain satisfaction by sale of the chattels.

971.　　"behooffullye." MORLEY. Advantageously, from First-English *behóf*, behoof, advantage.

972-94.　　RENWICK. Spenser's historical explanation is wrong, but his argument is sensible. Distraint was the regular process of Celtic law in Ireland, where courts did not exist, as in England, for redress of grievance. The statutes make exception of "such as are not amenable to common law," but by 1596 the distinction between those to whom Irish law was applicable and those to whom English law had been extended was difficult, especially given the theory that the royal law was for all Ireland, and the phrase must have created confusion. The reference to the later statute is not clear: there were two, 35 Henry VI *c.* 3 and 15 Edw. IV *c.* 1, but the second merely repeats the substance of the first. It is clear that Spenser understood the Irish procedure: the publicity of the distraint and the presence of witnesses were essential to its legality. [For 35 Henry Sixth see *The Statvtes of Ireland*, p. 25, and Berry 2. 449; for 15 Edward Fourth see *All the Statutes*, f. 23ʳ, and *The Statvtes of Ireland*, p. 47. There is a real distinction between the two laws: the later includes nothing about those amenable or not amenable to common law, since, apparently, it deals only with the former (see note on 960-1). A large section of official opinion was opposed to the leniency with which Spenser wishes to handle restraints (see *HMC*, Report XV, part 3, p. 26; *C. C. MSS. 1515-1574*, p. 342; *Analecta Hibernica* 2. 179).]

989-92.　　JENKINS (*PMLA* 53. 359). Spenser possibly has in mind the hazards he encountered when he took possession of the lands of Kilcolman, for the penalty of distraining another's property was death.

998.　　"to violente a medecine." GREENLAW (*MP* 7. 196, 199-200) derives the phrase and the figure from Machiavelli's "medecine forti" (*Il Principe*, cap. 3).

　　JONES (*Spenser's Defense*, p. 210) cites other examples of the medi-

COMMENTARY

cine metaphor from the works of Michel l'Hôpital, Agrippa D'Aubigné, and Jean Bodin.

1020-3. Bodin is far less rigid on this point (*République*, liv. I, ch. 11, pp. 198-9). Spenser may have in mind Buchanan's observation: " Lex enim quasi pertinax et imperitus quispiam officij exactor, nihil rectum putat, nisi quod ipsa iubet. . . . Lex surda, inhumana, inexorabilis est" (*De Ivre Regni apud Scotos*, 1583, sig. a6ᵛ).

1023-34. RENWICK. 3 Edw. II *c*. 1; 18 Henry VI *c*. 3; 28 Henry VI *c*. 1; 10 Henry VII *c*. 18: the second of these makes the offence treason, the third, felony.

EDITOR. See *All the Statutes*, f. 30ᵛ; *The Statvtes of Ireland*, pp. 14, 64-5; Berry 1. 520-1, 1. 573, 2. 31, 2. 168. Coynye and livery are said to have been originated by the first Earl of Kildare in order to victual the English army which opposed the Scots of Edward Bruce (Davies, *Discoverie*, pp. 190-1). Like Spenser, Sir Henry Sidney, the most far-sighted of the Elizabethan governors, believed in the utility of the illegal custom (*C. C. MSS. 1575-1588*, p. 38); but in general it was attacked (Holinshed, vol. II, *The Conquest of Ireland*, p. 43; *All the Statutes*, f. 162ᵛ; *The Statvtes of Ireland*, p. 320; Beacon, p. 77; Tremayne, p. 6). Later in the *View* (2481-2517) Spenser may be accused of some inconsistency when he objects to that form of cess which amounts to billeting, or coynye and livery combined.

1026-34. JENKINS (*PMLA* 53. 359). Spenser here probably has in mind Lord Roche's killing of a fat beef of his tenant, Teig Olyve [O'Lyne?], because Spenser took lodging in Teig's home on his way from the sessions at Limerick.

1029-30. The lack of inns resulted from the chaos which followed the Anglo-Norman Conquest; for anciently the Irish are said to have had free public hostels, called *brudens*, at the crossroads (Joyce, *Social History* 2. 166-75).

1039-47. MORLEY. Livery, fully and rightly explained by Spenser, is *livrée*, a delivery.

DRAPER (*MP* 17. 474). The origin of this word seems to be neither English nor Irish. The English, who seem to have brought the word into Ireland, got it from OF *livrer* (*to give, to deliver*), whence, in turn, it comes from the VL *liberare, to set free*. *Livery*, in the sense of a servant's garments, is derived from the French *livrée, a gift of clothes*, from the same VL root. Spenser is right in suggesting a relationship with *deliver*, the source of which seems to be *deliberare, to give over*. . . . Spenser was right in associating these various derivatives from VL *liberare*; but he either did not realize or he did not bother to put down the French and Latin sources.

1048-54. MORLEY. " Coigny" for man's meat is probably from the Irish *coic*, a cook, derivative from " coquus," with the flexional *n*, or *cucenn*, a kitchen, from " coquina."

DRAPER (*MP* 17. 477-8). The term is a very old one. It appears in Irish literature long before Spenser's day, and seems to be present even in a doubtful passage in old Irish law. The regular sense in these cases is *to billet*. . . .

[NED] derives it from OI *condem, condmin, to billet.* Professor Robinson suggests rather the related *condmad* or *condmedim.* In short, Spenser is correct in that he understood what was probably the chief meaning of the word in his day, and in that he assigns an Irish derivation. The knowledge of the former he doubtless gained from his official position, for the word was in vital use in the law of his day; the etymology was probably not much more than a reasonable guess. Of ancient Brehon Law, per se, he seems to have known little, and of ancient Irish culture, nothing.

ROLAND SMITH (*JEGP* 42. 503). Ir. *coindmhedh, coinnemh.*

[Long after the *View* was written, Ware still accepts the derivation of *coynye* from English *coin* (*Works* 2. 77).]

1054. "spendinge." See note on 239.

1062. "Cuddie." RENWICK. The chief's right to a "night supper" from his tenant.

ROLAND SMITH (*JEGP* 42. 503). Ir. *cuid oidhche,* "night supper." See A. S. Green, "Irish Land in the Sixteenth Century," Ériu, III, 184, where the word is incorrectly derived.

EDITOR. The tenant gave an evening meal to his lord four times every quarter; in the case of the Earl of Clancar the cuddy might be a meal actually served at the tenant's house, or it might be paid either in food or money (Butler, p. 20; Bagwell 1. 131; Ware, *Works* 2. 76; *C. S. P. Ir. 1588-1592* 144. 84; *C. C. MSS. 1589-1600,* p. 72).

1062. "Cossherie." RENWICK. The right to certain feastings at various times, for the chief and his followers.

ROLAND SMITH (*JEGP* 42. 503). Ir. *cóisir, cóisirecht.*

EDITOR. The term is frequently defined as the general right of an Irish landlord to exact entertainment for himself and his followers (*NED*; Bagwell 1. 131); but Elizabethan writers generally limit *coshery* to its original meaning of *feast* (Dymmok, p. 9; *C. C. MSS. 1601-1603,* p. 456; Moryson, *Itinerary* 3. 164). The most picturesque description of such a feast is given by Stanyhurst (Holinshed, vol. II, *The Description of Ireland,* p. 45), who compares it to Dido's banquet and indeed uses *coshery* in his translation of the banquet scene in the *Aeneid* (*The First Fovre Bookes of Virgils Aeneis,* ed. Edward Arber, 1880, p. 40). See also Rich, *Description,* pp. 39, 41.

1062. "bonnaaght." RENWICK. The right of quartering troops on the tenant, or payment in lieu thereof.

ROLAND SMITH (*JEGP* 42. 502). Ir. *buannacht.* . . . Strictly speaking, *bonagh* means the billeted soldier; *bonaght* refers to the billeting. [*Buanacht* usually refers to the tax levied for the maintenance of soldiers (O'Reilly and O'Donovan, *NED,* Bagwell 1. 131); for the two kinds of buanacht see Dymmok, p. 2.]

1062. "Sragh." RENWICK. A money rent.

COMMENTARY 307

ROLAND SMITH (*JEGP* 42. 506). Ir. *sraith* [tax, fine]. . . . [*C. C. MSS. 1589-1600*, p. 71] defines *shraughe* as a "yearly rent in sterling money." [In *State Papers, Henry VIII* 3. 595 the term is glossed as "an exaction for the lord's expense of attending parliaments and councils."]

1063. "forehin [*i. e.*, sorehin]." RENWICK. Meat and drink for the galloglasses.

ROLAND SMITH (*JEGP* 42. 505). Ir. *sórthan, sóraoin*, "notice" . . . . In [*C. C. MSS. 1589-1600*, p. 72]: "*Sorren*: a charge set upon the freeholders' lands for a number of galloglasses for certain days in a quarter." Also in 1589 Sir Warham Sentleger defines the term [*C. S. P. Ir. 1588-1592* 164. 84]: "*Sorowhen* doth warrant the Lord to come once in every fourteen days with all his company, without limitation, to the lands charged therewith, and to take meat and drink for him and his company from the freeholders and inhabitants of the said lands for the space of twenty-four hours." [Dymmok (p. 9) defines sorehin as a money payment; but it was sometimes paid in food (Butler, p. 200). See note on 4642.]

1066. RENWICK. Cf. Ralegh, *Prerogative of Parliaments* [*Works*, ed. Thomas Birch, 1751, 1. 242]: "Defend me, and spend me, saith the Irish Churl."

ROLAND SMITH (*JEGP* 42. 505-6). The usual Irish saying was *Caith agus cosain iad*, "Spend them and defend them" . . . . See, for instance, Robert Payne's *Brife Description of Ireland*, published in 1590: "They haue a common saying which I am perswaded they speake vnfeinedly, which is, *Defend me and spend me*: meaning from the oppression of the worser sorte of our countriemen" (. . . pp. 3-4). [See also Moryson, *Shakespeare's Europe*, p. 483. It is perhaps significant that in the order of *spend* and *defend* the *View* is closer to the Irish proverb than are the other English versions.]

1069. RENWICK. Eudoxus is quoting the common (and still valid) legal maxim *Volenti non fit injuria*.

1078-9. See 659-60.

1080-6. RENWICK. 11 Eliz. *s*. 1. *c*. 4 enacts: "That from henceforth, five persons of the best and eldest of everie stirpe or nation of the Irishrie, and in the countries that bee not as yet shire grounds, and till they bee shire ground, shall be bound to bring in to be justified by law, all idle persons of their surname, which shall be hereafter charged with any offence."

[See *All the Statutes*, f. 154ᵛ. Sir Edward Fitton complains to Burghley in 1571 that the Government is driven by weakness to revive the recently forbidden custom of "Kylcolgashe" (John T. Gilbert, p. 177); but in 1582 Perrot recommends that kincogish be put in execution (E. C. S., sig. C2ᵛ). The man who answered for his family was not the "Chiefe," as Irenius explains the Irish custom, but a member of the non-noble yet free and propertied class (Joyce, *Social History* 1. 158).]

1083. "septe." MORLEY. Clan; equivalent to sect, or division.

1119-24. WARE. I conceive the word [*kincogish*] to be rather altogether *Irish*. *Kin* signifying in *Irish*, the heads or chiefe of any septs.

MORLEY. Perhaps the Irish word here is cocrich, a boundary or bounded district, and "kin-cogish" is the district of men of one kinship or blood alliance.

DRAPER (*MP* 17. 478-9). At first sight one might suppose that *kin-* was related either to the English *kin* or perhaps to the Celtic *cineadh* or *cinne*, meaning tribe or clan.... As a matter of fact, *kin-* seems to be none of these things. [In *The Ancient Laws of Ireland* 6. 137] ... the term is translated "crime of relative"; *cin-* means *crime*; and *-cogish* is an anglicizing of the word *comfocus*, *relative*.... the custom and the name that designated it seem to have been in use in Ireland from early antiquity down at least to the latter seventeenth century. Spenser apparently understood the actual working of the law.

RENWICK. The etymology is false, as Ware points out.

ROLAND SMITH (*JEGP* 42. 504). Ir. *cin cómfhocais*, "liability of kindred."... Renwick's reliance upon Ware has nothing to recommend it, for Ware's etymology ... is quite as false as Spenser's. [But see Joyce, *Social History* 1. 158.]

1121-3. RENWICK. The Law of Alfred equivalent to *Kincogish* I cannot find, unless this be a vague reminiscence of the communal responsibility of the Tithing, as explained by Camden, quoting from William of Malmesbury in his chapter on *Britanniae Divisio*: see [4471-4502, 4786-4804] and our notes thereon.

1131-41. RENWICK. Spenser was deeply interested in Irish history, but he realised that entanglement in the usual labyrinth of citation and argument would be detrimental to his main purpose. He uses historical notions only as heads under which to arrange the customs which are his real subject, and contents himself with as much argument as seemed necessary, and a promise, repeated in the close of the book, to return to the antiquities of Ireland in another work. That he accepts some fables need not surprise us: Hiberus is cited in the Act of attainder of Shane O'Neill in 1569, and, on the other side, one writing in 1591 to the Archbishop of Tuam about a proposed landing of Spanish troops to help the Irish, recommends that the mixed force be commanded by a Spaniard, not by the renegade Englishman Stanley, "in respecte of affinitie sythence *Hyberus a quo dicitur Hibernia* of old tyme." (*S. P. Ir.* 159. 48) If the letter is a forgery as is suspected, the point is only reinforced. Generally, Spenser belonged to the newer sceptical school, and was applying the latest methods as laid down by Jean Bodin—indeed, modern methods, though his judgment of authorities was that of his time and not of ours. His citations are often inaccurate, like those of many contemporaries: in the book that was to be, we should certainly have had many more of them — we miss Nennius, Giraldus Cambrensis, William of Malmesbury, Polydore Virgil, and a dozen others that would have been forced on him. As it is, he relies almost entirely on George Buchanan's *Rerum Scoticarum Historia*, 1582, and Camden's *Britannia*, 1586-87-90-94, and on Holinshed. But even here we have, I suspect, a revised version of matter that may have been intended for the Antiquities of Ireland.

COMMENTARY

1136-7. TODD. Since Spenser wrote this View of Ireland, the Antiquities of the Country have been explored and elucidated, by men "of sound judgement and plentiful reading," with so much patience and precision, as to afford the curious "most pleasant and profitable" information indeed. When I mention the extremely valuable and important researches of the Royal Irish Academy; the labours of an Usher, a Ware, a Leland, a Walker, a Vallancey, a Ledwich, a Beaufort, an O'Halloran, an Ouseley, an Archdall; (to which might be added the ingenious disquisitions of many others;) I point out to the reader the true sources of elegant gratification in regard to the knowledge of Irish history, and topography, customs, and manners.

1151-60. WARE. Touching the *Scythians* or *Scotts* arrivall in *Ireland*, see *Nennius* an ancient *Brittish* author (who lived in the yeare of *Christ* 858.) where among other things we have the time of their arrivall. *Brittones* (saith he) *venerunt in 3. aetate mundi in Britanniam, Scythae autem in 4, obtinuerunt Hiberniam.* [*Marginalium*: *A regione quadem quae dicitur Scythia: dicitur Scita, Sciticus, Scoticus, Scotus, Scotia.* Tho. Walsingham, *in Hypodigmate Neustriae, ad an.* 1185.]

RENWICK. The Scythian and Spanish origin of the Irish is in nearly all the chronicles. Camden, p. 121 [*Britannia*, Latin ed. of 1590, pp. 56-7]: "That these Scots came out of Scythia, the Irish Historiographers themselves doe report ... But the Scots should lose part of their honor and dignity, unlesse they bee brought out of Spayne into Ireland. For, this they both themselves, and their Historiographers labour to proove with all their might and maine; and good reason (I assure you) have they so to do. Unlesse therefore wee find Scythians in Spaine, all our labour is lost ..." And so on.

1152 n. WARE. The discourse from the word *Scythians* ... unto the end of the parenthesis ["I earst spoke)"] ... is wholly to be crossed out, as being then agreeable to the best MS. Copie, onely after *Scythians*, add, which.

TODD notes that the passage is omitted from the manuscript belonging to the Marquis of Stafford [*i. e.*, the Ellesmere MS. See Appendix III, section C for the inclusion of this passage in the Public Record Office MS and for Ware's manuscript sources].

"*Gathelus.*" MORLEY. *Gathelus* or *Gadelas*, or *Gaedhal*, was said to have lived in the time of Moses. His father Niul had married a daughter of the Pharaoh who, in pursuit of the Israelites, was drowned in the Red Sea. He called her Scota, because he was himself a Scythian; they had a son called Gaodhal, as being a lover of learning, from *gaoith*, which is learning, and *dil*, which is love. So the old Irish clergy invented men to account for names of tribes, and gave a founder to the Gaedhels, or Gaels.

"our vaine *Englishmen* ... *Brutus* of *England*." The legend that the British race, like the Roman, was of Trojan origin and took its name from a certain Brutus, the descendant of Aeneas, stems from Geoffrey of Monmouth. Early in the sixteenth century Polydore Vergil denied its truth (*Historia Anglica*, 1651, lib. I, pp. 25-7); but a number of defenders of Geoffrey appeared in the succeeding generation. John Leland replied in 1544 (see Greenlaw, *Studies in*

Spenser's Historical Allegory, pp. 11 ff.) ; during the reign of Edward Sixth Sir John Price wrote another refutation (*Historiae Brytannicae Defensio*, 1573) ; and still a third was the work of Humphrey Llwyd, or Luddus, the Welsh scholar (*Commentarioli Britannicae Descriptionis Fragmentum*, 1572, ff. 7ᵛ–8ᵛ; trans. Thomas Twyne as *The Breuiary of Britayne*, 1573, ff. 6ʳ–9ᵛ; see also Caradoc of Llancarfan, *The Historie of Cambria*, trans. Humphrey Llwyd, 1584, pp. 2-4). It is not surprising therefore that Holinshed accepts the story of Brutus and recounts it at some length (vol. I, *The Historie of England*, pp. 7-11). But a reaction set in with the Scotch historian George Buchanan, who attacks the national vanity which believes such tales (lib. II, f. 13ʳ). Richard Harvey, the brother of Gabriel, it is true, defended the Trojan origin of the British race with some heat (*Philadelphus*, 1593, p. 1) ; Camden, however, who was the most judicious of English historians in the sixteenth century, honestly admitted that there was no real evidence to support the theory (*Britannia*, p. 6). — Spenser's contribution to this complicated quarrel is interesting: One E. S. wrote a little book *De Rebvs Gestis Britanniae*, probably published in 1582, which accepts the popular story of Brutus as the founder of Britain (f. 2ʳ⁻ᵛ) ; the possibility that E. S. was Spenser has been considered and declared doubtful by Carpenter (*Manly Anniversary Studies*, 1923, pp. 64-9; *Reference Guide*, p. 132; see also Millican, pp. 93, 186). In 1590, in any case, Spenser gives ninety-one lines to the Brutus legend in the first installment of *F. Q.* (2. 10. 9. 6-13. 9, 3. 9. 46. 1-51. 6), lines based on Geoffrey, Holinshed, Hardyng, and Camden (Harper, pp. 47-53, 168-71). The present passage of the *View*, which denies the Brutus legend, is undoubtedly Spenser's, although he must have intended to discard it from the final text (the Gathelus story is repeated in 1302-5). Harper (p. 21) offers a possible explanation: "the omission of the passage in the best manuscript suggests that Spenser did not wish to commit himself to any such expression of doubt [in the historicity of Brutus]." Whatever the reason for its omission, the passage reveals either that he had a change of heart on Brutus between 1590 and 1596 or, it is more likely, that for Spenser, as for many other people, the truth of poetry was not the truth of prose.

"*Albany*." This occurs as a variant of *Albion* in *F. Q.* 2. 10. 38. 4 and 4. 11. 36. 7. See Camden, *Britannia*, p. 63.

1159. "*Scuttenlande.*" This spelling seems to reflect the Dutch term for both Scyths and Scots: "Germani inferiores *Scythas* et *Scotos* vno nomine *Scutten* appellant" (Camden, *Britannia*, p. 56; see also Hanmer, *The Chronicle of Ireland*, 1633, p. 6). *Scutten* was said to be a verb meaning *to shoot* (Lambard, *A Perambulation of Kent*, 1596, p. 2; Harris in Ware's *Works* 2. 17).

1169-80. MORLEY. The two branches of the Celtic stock, the Gaels and Cymry, are supposed to have occupied of old the lands north of the Black Sea, the Cymry on that side of the Don occupied by the Κιμμέριοι of Aeschylus, where the Crimea retains signs of their name, the Gaels on the other side, known in Europe afterwards as Gauls. Canon George Rawlinson, in his edition of Herodotus, supports the belief in an original identity of the words Scyth and Scot. . . . Spenser's theory of the origin of the Irish accords with the best knowledge of his time. Scotland was called Albine — Shakespeare's Albany in "Lear" — from its mountain heights, by those who approached it on the north, the word being akin to Alp.

COMMENTARY 311

RENWICK. Buchanan, *Historia*, fol. 18 vo. [ed. of 1583, f. 16ʳ]: "Scoti enim omnes Hiberniae habitatores initio vocabantur . . . Principio autem cum vtrique, id est Hiberniae incolae, et coloni eorum in Albium missi Scoti appellarentur, vt discrimine aliquo alteri ab alteris distinguerentur, initio coepere alteri Scoti Ierni, alteri Scoti Albini vocari: ac paulatim vtrinque cognomenta loco nominis vsurpata efficerunt, vt vetus nomen Scotorum prope obliuioni daretur: ac non ex vsu loquendi, sed annalium memoria repeteretur." Richard Stanyhurst, *Description of Ireland*, in Holinshed's Chronicle, p. 2 [ed. of 1586, vol. II, *The First Inhabitation of Ireland*, p. 52]: "as Scotland is named Scotia minor, so Ireland is tearmed Scotia maior." So also Camden [*Britannia*, p. 63]. Stanyhurst is probably the source to which Camden and others refer when they speak of Irish chroniclers: he was Irish born, and claimed knowledge of Irish chronicles. [See also Stanyhurst, *De Rebvs*, p. 17.]

1170. George Buchanan, the great Scotch humanist, is mentioned at several other places in the *View* (1216-27, 1398-1401, 1689-93, 1759-61, 1824-5); and Spenser frequently uses his *Rerum Scoticarum Historia* without referring to it.

1196-1203. During the reign of Henry Eighth the Irish Council refused to accept the writings of Irish bards and chroniclers as historical evidence (*State Papers, Henry VIII* 3. 479). Buchanan had no faith in the word of the bards (lib. II, ff. 12ʳ, 14ᵛ; Mezger, *Archiv* 150. 234); and Stanyhurst has a more extensive attack on them (*De Rebvs*, pp. 54-8). Rich (*Description*, p. 3) writes: "there is nothing that hath more led the Irish into error, then lying Historiographers, their *Croniclers*, their *Bardes*, their *Rythmers*, and such other their lying Poets." Spenser shows an independent mind in defending Irish records with such persistence (1228-32, 1256-60, 1292-5); and he may remember that Sir John Price (*Historiae Brytannicae Defensio*, 1573, pp. 9-10) argues in favor of the evidence supplied by the bards, who belong to a continuous tradition.

1202-3. WARE. Of the ancient Bards or Poets, *Lucan* makes this mention in the first booke of his *Pharsalia* [1. 447-9]:

> *Vos quoque qui fortes animas, belloque peremptas*
> *Laudibus in longum vates dimittitis aevum,*
> *Plurima securi fudistis carmina Bardi.*

Concerning the *Irish* Bardes see [2256-2345]. The word signified among the *Gaules* a singer, as it is noted by Mʳ *Camden* and Mʳ *Selden*, out of *Festus Pompeius*, and it had the same signification among the *Brittish*. Sʳ *Iohn Price* in the description of *Wales*, expounds it to bee one that had *knowledge of things to come, and so* (saith he) *it signifieth at this day*. taking his ground (amisse) out of *Lucan's* verses. Doctor *Powell* in his notes upon *Caradoc* of *Lhancarvan* saith, that in *Wales* they preserved Gentlemens armes and pedegrees. At this time in *Ireland* the *Bard*, by common acceptation, is counted a rayling Rimer, and distinguished from the Poet.

1210. The "properties of natures," or inherent qualities, are contrasted with the "vses," or qualities determined by external relations.

1214-5. JONES (*Spenser's Defense*, p. 204) traces Spenser's "probabilitye of thinges" to Bodin's "assensio probabilis" [*e. g., Methodus ad Facilem Historiarum Cognitionem*, 1572, p. 63].

1215-1330 n. "ffor it is certaine ... instruccion." See 1256-60 and note.

"amongest which was sent ouer vnto them *Patricius* commenlye called St *Patricke*." Holinshed has nothing to this effect in his account of Patrick (vol. II, *The First Inhabitation of Ireland*, p. 53). As Renwick notes (*View*, p. 264), this passage in the Public Record Office MS must later have been revised with Holinshed at hand.

"Nowe from the Scythians .... Iryshe." See 1260-83.

"for the Sowtherne ... Galls." See 1286-8.

"for they saye that ... inhabit it." See 1302-5 and note.

"as maye appeare ... reade in." See 1402-5 and note.

"lykewise the Easterne Coaste and parte of the Sowthe towardes Englande I suppose to haue been peopled from the Brittons." ROLAND SMITH (*MLN* 59. 473). Spenser here follows Camden (*Britannia*, ed. 1590, p. 682; ed. 1594, p. 646): *ita ex Britannia nostra primos incolas commigrâsse in aperto est*.

"fyre is in Welshe Tane: in Iryshe Tuinnye." SALESBURY explains Welsh "*tan vn or pedwar element* Fyre." [See also Humphrey Llwyd, *Commentarioli Britannicae Descriptionis Fragmentum*, 1572, f. 78ʳ.] MEREDITH HANMER (*The Chronicle of Ireland*, 1633, p. 11) identifies British "*Tan*" with Irish "*Tine*."

ROLAND SMITH (*MLN* 59. 473). "Iryshe Tuinnye" represents a reasonable attempt on Spenser's part to indicate the pronunciation of Ir. *teine*, the common word for "fire," which is cognate with W. *tân*, "fire," Spenser's "Welshe Tane." See further the comment on *teine* in *NED*, s. v. *Beltane*.

"an heigh lande in Welshe and Iryshe Tarbert." ROLAND SMITH (*MLN* 59. 473-4). Spenser seems erroneously to have associated *tarbert* with Ir. *torr* = W. *twr*, "heap or pile," hence his rendering "heigh lande." He may have drawn his assumption from Camden's "LITTVS ALTVM, vbi nunc TARBARTH, id est Britannicè *terra minùs profunda*" (*Britannia*, ed. 1594, p. 635). But Ir. *toirbheart, tairbheart* ... means "isthmus" or "neck of land." Two places named Tarbert must have been known to Spenser. The first, now Belturbet, appears three times in the *View* [535, 3098, 3992]. ... But nearer to Spenser at Kilcolman was Tarbert in Munster, a seignory on the Shannon, Co. Limerick, which was constantly under dispute or discussion among the Munster undertakers.

"Curve Cosh eribord, is bothe Welshe and Iryshe." ROLAND SMITH (*MLN* 59. 474-6). *Curve Cosh eri* (sic?) *bord* appears to be a list of four Irish words. (1) *Curve* is perhaps Spenser's anglicized spelling for Ir. *cuirm*, a common word for "ale," cognate with W. *cwrw*, earlier *cwrf, cwrwf, cwryf* .... Again, it may be that Spenser's attention was drawn to the Welsh *cwrwf* while reading Camden. The first three editions of the *Britannia* (cf. ed. 1590, p. 21) have: "*Cervisiam ad Keirch*, i. auenam, è qua potum illum Britanni multis in locis conficiunt." But the 1594 edition adds to this (p. 20): "vel potius ad *Cwrwf*, i. quam *Alam* [English "ale"] dicimus." (2) *Cosh* stands for Ir. *cos*, g. *coise*, "foot," cognate with W. *coes* .... *Cosh* appears in the Irish place-name *Cois Máighe*, Spenser's "our rich Coshma,/ Now made of Maa," *CCCHA* 522. ... (3) *Eri* offers several possible solutions, from which it is impossible to select the word Spenser intended. It is most likely that he was thinking of Eire ..., the name for Ireland, and what has generally been considered its Welsh cognate *Iwerddon*. ... He may have meant W. *eira*, "snow" = Ir. *oidhre*, which however means "ice." It is conceivable that he had in mind Ir. *áirem*, later *áireamh*, "number," cognate with W. *eirif*; if so, he should have anglicized it *eriv*. It is not likely that he intended *Cosheri*, which is elsewhere in the *View* spelled *Cossherie, Cossirh* [1062], as Ir. *cóisir* (*JEGP*, XLII, 503) has no Welsh cognate. ... (4) Ir. *bord*, "table," is W. *bwrdd*.

"also it appearethe ... even to." See 1446-51 and note.

"And lykewise kinge Arthure ... contained." See 1439-40 and note.

"as maye bee proved ... shewed." See 1428-37 and note.

"Marh in Saxon is a horse, marrah in Iryshe is a horseman." SALESBURY explains W. "*march* A horse." [See also Meredith Hanmer, *The Chronicle of Ireland*, 1633, p. 8.]

ROLAND SMITH (*MLN* 59. 476). This statement is substantially correct. "Marh in Saxon" is OE. *mearh*, g. *mēares*; "marrah in Iryshe" is Ir. *marcach*, g. *marcaigh*, ... There is no OE. word cognate with Ir. *marcach*, which is inadequately represented by Spenser's "marrah."

"to ryde in Iryshe is *gemanus* and so in saxon, or a commen person." ROLAND SMITH (*MLN* 59. 477). There is some confusion here. The lacuna in the MS suggests that "to ryde" may belong with the preceding portion of the text. Was Spenser thinking of OE. *gemǣne, gemāna, gemǣnnes*, "common, community"? .... If so, there is no Irish cognate. ... Ir. *giománach*, "horseboy," is, as I have already pointed out (*JEGP*, XLII, 503, s. v. *cuille*), borrowed from English yeoman, which may be what Spenser intended by "a commen person."

"But as for that ... truthe." See 1326-30.

"no more then theye ... Indians." Spenser probably refers to such works as *The Pleasant Historie of the Conquest of the Weast India* by Francisco López de Gómara, published in the English translation of Thomas Nicholas in 1578.

"But the Iryshe doe ... of Spaine." See 1151-60, 1152 n, and notes.

"the French also ... Troians." See Ronsard's *Franciade*, 1572.

1220-2. MEZGER (*Archiv* 150. 233-4) notes that this list has, for the most part, been copied out of Johannes Boemus, whose *Mores* (p. 7) opens with a citation of the following authorities: "historiae pater Herodotus, Diodorus Siculus, Berosus, Strabo, Solinus, Trogus Pompeius, Ptolemeus, Plinius, Cornelius Tacitus, Dionysius Afer, Pomponius Mela, Caesar, Iosephus: et ex recentioribus nonnulli, Vi[n]centius, Aeneas Syluius." [This list by Boemus, to whom Spenser refers at 1521, 1898, and 1927, includes all the authorities Spenser lists except Llwyd and Buchanan, the two of whom we can be most certain that he made a first-hand use. The names of Trogus Pompeius and Pomponius Mela probably coalesced into

"*Pompeius mela,*" which appears in some manuscripts, although it has been corrected in the Ellesmere text. It is safe to add that Spenser must have used a Latin text of Boemus since the English translation of William Watreman renders the name of Tacitus as "Cornelius the still" (*The Fardle of Facions*, 1555, sig. A1r).]

1220. "*Caesar.*" RIEDNER (p. 120) traces the reference to a brief description of Britain and Ireland in *De Bello Gallico* 5. 12-13. [There is now good reason for thinking that Caesar did not write this description. Spenser refers to Caesar again in 853, 1240, 1922, 1926, 2122; but Caesar's contribution to Spenser's information on Ireland is negligible.]

1220. "*Strabo.*" Spenser refers to Strabo at 1262 and 1438, but neither reference can be traced.

1220. "*Tacitus.*" Spenser's later reference to Tacitus is not made at first hand (see 1289 and note).

1220. "*Ptotolomie.*" Ptolemy may have supplied Spenser with a few names (see note on 1402-5), but he is not referred to again in the *View*. See *F. Q.* 5. Pro. 7. 6.

1220. "*Plinie.*" At two places the *View* may perhaps use material from the *Historia Naturalis* of the Elder Pliny (see notes on 1437-8, 2003-5); but he affords nothing on the early history of Ireland.

1220. "*Solinnus.*" The *Collectanea Rerum Memorabilium* of Solinus contains (in chap. 24) a description of the warlike customs of the early Irish which is paraphrased in the *Book of Howth* (C. C. MSS. *Miscellaneous*, pp. 34-5), referred to by Campion (pp. 15-6), and quoted by Camden (*Britannia*, p. 712). But neither of two later references to Solinus in the *View* (1760 n, 1773) can be traced.

1221. "*Pomponius Mela.*" Spenser refers to Mela again at 1276-7, but the reference was probably secured at second hand.

1221. "*Berosus.*" RIEDNER (p. 60). Ich konnte in den Antiquitates des Berosus nichts darüber finden.

RENWICK. Priest of Babylon: Spenser may have read the fragments of his writings, but does not use them here. [In addition to genuine fragments of Berosus, Johannes Annius in the sixteenth century forged *Berosi Chaldaici Antiquitatum Libri Quinque*. Holinshed (vol. I, *The Description of Britaine*, p. 9) accepts the forgery as authentic; Camden (*Britannia*, p. 11) questions it. But neither the true nor the false Berosus contains anything on the history of Ireland.]

1221. "*Vincentius.*" RENWICK. Vincent of Beauvais, author of *Speculum Maius*, 13th century. [The possibility that Vincent contributed anything to the *View* is a slim one; see note on 1519-25.]

1221. "*Ænaeas Syluius.*" The Italian humanist Eneo Silvio Piccolomini (1405-1464), honored later in life as Pope Pius Second, was the author of *Commentarii Rerum Memorabilium* which Harvey admired (*Marginalia*, p. 95); but the *View* contains no decisive evidence of Spenser's familiarity with the *Commentarii*.

1222. "*Lluddus.*" RENWICK. Humphrey Llwyd (1527-68), author of *Angliae ... Descriptio*, 1573 [*i. e.*, *Commentarioli Britannicae Descriptionis Fragmentum*, 1572], translated by Twyne as *The Breviary of Britayne*, and heavily attacked by Buchanan. [Buchanan writes (lib. I, f. 2ᵛ): "cum tam anxie se torquet, quomodo Luddum scribat, Lhuydumne, an Lludum, an vero Luddum, quorum nullum nec Latinis literis exprimi, nec ore latiali efferri, nec ab auribus latinis sine fastidio audiri potest." But Harvey (*Marginalia*, p. 164) and Camden (*Britannia*, p. 61) praise Llwyd as an antiquarian. The *Commentarioli*, a treatise on British rather than Irish history, can have been of little assistance to Spenser in writing the *View*; there seems, however, to be definite evidence that he used Llwyd's work (see note on 1431-2).]

1222. "*Buckhanan.*" See note on 1170. Spenser's debt to Buchanan is real, as many of these notes can testify.

1223. WARE. *Bede tells us that the Picts were a colony of Scythians, who first comming into Ireland, and being denyed residence there by the Scots, were perswaded by them to inhabit the North parts of Britaine. But Mʳ Camden, out of Dio, Herodian, Tacitus, etc. and upon consideration of the customes, name and language of the Picts, conceives not improbably, that they were naturall Britons, although distinguished by name* [*Britannia*, p. 49].

EDITOR. Hector Boethius calls the Picts "Agathirsanis," who were banished from Sarmatia to Denmark and came thence to Scotland (*The History and Croniklis of Scotland*, trans. John Bellenden, 1540, sig. B1ᵛ); Llwyd suggests that they were emigrants from Scandinavia (*The Breuiary of Britayne*, trans. Thomas Twyne, 1573, f. 36ʳ); and Buchanan gives them a German homeland (lib. IV, f. 28ʳ). Although Spenser seems almost to identify the Picts with the Scots in this passage, he later distinguishes between them (1690-3), as Holinshed does (vol. II, *The First Habitation of Ireland*, pp. 50-1).

1228-32. Campion, in his preface "To the Loving Reader," also defends the Irish chronicles as a source of information on the period before the Anglo-Norman conquest. Buchanan prefers the chroniclers to the bards but feels no respect for them as assistants to the historian (lib. II, f. 12ᵛ).

1240-1. WARE. *Concerning them I finde no mention in Caesar's commentaryes, but much touching the Druides, which were the Priests and Philosophers,* (or *Magi* as *Pliny* [*Marginalium: Hist. nat. lib. 16. cap. 44.*] *calls them) of the Gaules and British. Illi rebus divinis intersunt,* (saith he [*Marginalium: De bello Gallico lib. 2.*]) *sacrificia publica ac privata procurant, religiones interpretantur. Ad hos magnus adolescentium numerus disciplinae caussa concurrit, magnoque ij sunt apud eos honore.* etc. *The word Droi had anciently the same signification* (as I am informed) *among the Irish.*

RIEDNER (pp. 120-1). Wir sehen, dass Spenser in seinen Zitierungen recht irrt; dennoch darf angenommen werden, dass ihm die Lektüre Caesars wohl vertraut war, gehörte dieser Schriftsteller ja damals schon zur Schullektüre.

RENWICK. Not in Caesar; but cf. Buchanan, "Aut quis pro certo tradet, quod a tam incertis auctoribus acceperit?" [lib. II, f. 12ᵛ]

EDITOR. Ware's quotation from Caesar on the druids is really from *De Bello Gallico* 6. 13. Spenser may remember Holinshed's remark that Caesar found bards on his first arrival in Britain (vol. II, *The Historie of England*, p. 3) or Sir John Price's identification of the bards as the ancient druids (*Historiae Brytannicae Defensio*, 1573, p. 11). In any case, Caesar's description of the druids contains no attack on their veracity.

1251.   Learning "softens manners, nor suffers them to be wild."

RIEDNER (p. 106) traces the quotation to Ovid, *Epistolae ex Ponto* 2. 9. 48 [quoted, as an example, in William Lily's *Brevissima Institutio sev Ratio Grammatices*, 1567, ed. Vincent J. Flynn, 1945, sig. E2ᵛ].

1256-60. Bede describes the attendance of English scholars at the early Irish schools (*Ecclesiastica Historia* 3. 27); but Spenser probably derives his information from Camden, who notes that the Saxons had their alphabet from the Irish (*Britannia*, pp. 684-5). The derivation of the Anglo-Saxon alphabet from the Roman-Irish is accepted by modern scholarship (Joyce, *Social History* 1. 407). For a summary of early Irish learning see James Ussher, *Veterum Epistolarvm Hibernicarvm Sylloge*, 1632.

1261-83. SOUTHEY (p. 210). Surely their letters were from their first Christian teachers—or from the Romanized Briton.

JOYCE (*Social History* 1. 407). Spenser here mixes up the original letters of the pagan Irish [the Ogham alphabet] with those brought over by St. Patrick and his fellow-missionaries.

[Spenser seems to have devised his elaborate theory for himself; but the resemblance of the Greek and Irish letters has often been observed (*e. g.*, Ware, *Works* 2. 22-3).]

1262-8.   RIEDNER (p. 63).   Dieses steht im 3. Buche der Geographica, welches von Spanien handelt. . . . Kap. 6. [*i. e.*, Strabo 3. 1. 6]

RENWICK.   Strabo, *Geographia*, III. i. 7 . . . . IV. i. 5; also Buchanan, Book II *ad init*.

EDITOR. Spenser borrows the whole passage from Buchanan (lib. II, f. 12ʳ): "Galli primum characteres literarum a Massiliensibus Graecis accepere, quibus vterentur ad rationes conficiendas, et literas inter se missitandas: Graecis quidem figuris elementorum, sed sermone Gallico. . . . In Hispania vero Graecis, et ante eos Phoenicibus, qui interni maris occupauerant litora, et vnis e Barbaris (vt Strabo scribit) Turdetanis fuit quidem literarum vsus: sed veteris memoriae scriptor, quod adhuc sciam, extitit nemo." See Mezger, *Archiv* 150. 234.

1268-78. RIEDNER (p. 124). Pomponius . . . Mela stammte aus Tingentera in Spanien; im 3. Buche der "Chorographia" beschreibt er die aüssere Küste Spaniens und sagt er daruber im 1. Kapitel Nr. 11 folgendes: "partem quae prominet Praesamarchi habitant, perque eos Tamaris et Sars flumina non longe orta decurrunt . . . cetera super Tamarici Nerique incolunt in eo tractu ultimi . . ." Spenser hat wohl diese stelle im Auge; von einer Abstammung von den Kelten in Frankreich kann ich in Melas Berichten nichts finden.

COMMENTARY 317

Renwick. The method of arguing from the names, and some of the examples, are Buchanan's. . . . Pomponius Mela *de Situ Orbis*, III. i; quoted by Buchanan. I cannot find the *Regnie*, who seem to stand for Mela's *Gronii*; but MSS read thus, or nothing.

Editor. The whole passage has been taken over directly from Buchanan (lib. II, f. 15r): " Ephorus, teste Strabone, Galliae longitudinem ad Gades vsque porrexerit, et certe totum latus Hispaniae ad septentriones versum populorum, et gentium nominibus diu Gallicam testata est originem . . . . Sunt etiam a Celtis, aut Celtiberis oriundi Celtici ad Anam fluuium, Ptolomaeo Betici cognominati, et Celtici alteri in Lusitania Anae propinqui: et, si Pomponio Melae homini Hispano credimus, a Durij fluminis ostio ad promontorium vsque, quod siue Celticum, siue Nerium vocant, Celtici colunt cognominibus distincti, nempe Gronij, Praesamarci, Tamarici, Nerij: ac caeteros quoque Galaecos a Gallica origine non abhorrere nomen gentis indicat." See Mezger, *Archiv* 150. 234.

1273. "*Galdumo.*" What place Spenser had in mind is uncertain.

1282. "pricke." The point used above Irish letters to indicate aspiration.

1289. Ware. *Cornelius Tacitus* in the life of *Iulius Agricola* [cap. 11] saith thus. *Silurum colorati vultus, et torti plerumque crines, et positus contra Hispaniam, Iberos veteres trajecisse, easque sedes occupasse fidem faciunt.* This he speaketh touching the Silures which inhabited that part of South-Wales, which now we call Herefordshire, Radnorshire, Brecknockshire, Monmouth shire, and Glamorganshire. And although the like reason may be given for that part of Ireland which lyeth next unto Spaine, yet in *Tacitus* we find no such inference. *Buchanan* indeed upon the conjecture of *Tacitus* hath these words [*Marginalium*: *Rer. Scot. lib.* 2]. [f. 15v: " C. Tacitus occidentale latus Britanniae, siue Albij a posteris Hispanorum coli certa, vt ipsi videtur coniectura affirmat."] *Verisimile a[utem] non est Hispanos relicta a tergo Hibernia, terra propiore, et caeli et soli mitioris, in Albium primum descendisse, sed primum in Hiberniam appulisse, atque inde in Britanniam colonos missos.* Which was observed unto me by the most learned Bishop of Meth, Dr *Anth. Martin*, upon conference with his Lordship about this point. One passage in *Tacitus* touching Ireland (in the same booke) I may not heere omit, although it be *extra oleas*. *Quinto expeditionum anno* (saith he) *nave prima transgressus, ignotas ad tempus gentes, crebris simul ac prosperis praelijs domuit, eamque partem Britanniae quae Hiberniam aspicit, copijs instruxit, in spem magis quam ob formidinem. Siquidem Hibernia medio inter Britanniam atque Hispaniam sita, et Gallico quoque mari opportuna valentissimam imperij partem magnis invicem usibus miscuerit. Spatium ejus si Britanniae comparetur, angustius, nostri maris insulas superat. Solum caelumque et ingenia, cultusque hominum haut multum a Britannia differunt, melius aditus portusque per commercia et negotiatores cogniti. Agricola expulsum seditione domestica unum ex regulis gentis exceperat, ac specie amicitiae in occasionem retinebat. Saepe ex eo audivi Legione una et modicis auxilijs debellari, obtinerique Hiberniam posse, idque adversus Britanniam profuturum, si Romana ubique arma, et velut e conspectu libertas tolleretur.*

Riedner (p. 123). Die Frage, ob Spenser den Tacitus gelesen hat, wird dadurch schwankend; doch glaube ich aus den bestimmten Worten des Dichters schliessen zu dürfen, dass ihm Tacitus nicht nur dem Namen nach bekannt war.

RENWICK. Tacitus, *Agricola*; quoted by Buchanan.

[It should be noted how the original statement of Tacitus has been twice blurred: Tacitus writes that a Spanish people probably settled in southwestern Britain; Buchanan, referring to Tacitus, also suggests that they settled in Ireland; and Spenser, using Buchanan, cites Tacitus as his authority for saying that they settled in southwestern Ireland. See also Mezger, *Archiv* 150. 234.]

1302-18. RENWICK. These tales, seemingly invented by Fordun and Hector Boece, are discredited by Buchanan and Camden. The curious will find them in Holinshed's chapter on the First Inhabitation of Ireland.

ROLAND SMITH (*JEGP* 43. 400). One cannot help being struck by the canniness with which Spenser, who had before him in Holinshed and Camden six of the seven invasion stories, selected and arranged his material. In placing the Gathelus legend before those of Nemed and the sons of Dela and Mil, he had no precedent except the LG [the Irish *Leabhar Gabhála*], unless he took his clue from Boece's Scottish chronicle in Holinshed. Where he shows other signs of direct borrowing from an R¹ version of the LG [not used by Giraldus, Campion, Stanyhurst, or Camden], it seems less likely that he drew upon Boece. That he did not blindly follow Campion, Holinshed, or Camden, but apparently weighed his numerous sources with some care, is to be seen in his better spelling of *Nemed* (rather than *Nemodus* or *Nimeth*) and in his preference for the "fowre sonnes of Mylesius King of Spayne" rather than the "foure brethren Spaniards" of his contemporaries. Moreover, Spenser's omissions are significant. He avoids mentioning the Holinshed accounts of (1) Cesara, a *fabella* which was condemned not only by Camden but as roundly by Campion . . . and of (2) Partholon and (3) the Tuatha Dé Danann . . . . Can Spenser's skill in condensation and elimination have been purely accidental, or did he rely upon a capable assistant (perhaps his bardic tutor) conversant with Irish letters and lore, as Sir James Ware relied upon Dubhaltach Mac Firbhisigh? We shall probably never know, but it seems likely, in view of Spenser's "characteristic uncritical use of his material, of hasty reading, and . . . of defective memory" [Covington, *UTB*, Studies in English 4. 24], that he was not without the help of a competent guide trained, no doubt, in the bardic traditions. [Such a guide may have translated Irish poetry for Spenser (see *View* 2338-9), who, however, placed little trust in his judgment since he calls these legends "meare fables and verye Milesian lyes" (1315-6).]

1302-5. ROLAND SMITH (*JEGP* 43. 397) notes that Spenser's version of the legend of Gathelus is closer to the version of Hector Boethius found in Holinshed [vol. II, *The Historie of Scotland*, pp. 29-31] than to the version of Buchanan [lib. II, f. 14ᵛ], which Covington believed to be Spenser's source [*UTB*, Studies in English 4. 22. It should be noted, however, that Buchanan's version resembles Spenser's in taking Gathelus and his followers no further than Spain, as well as in treating the story as a worthless fable. See also Stanyhurst, *De Rebvs*, p. 245, and Holinshed, vol. II, *The First Inhabitation of Ireland*, p. 49.]

COMMENTARY 319

1305-9. Spenser probably uses the version of the Nemedus story which Stanyhurst quotes from Giraldus Cambrensis (*De Rebvs*, p. 239): there, as in the *View*, Nemedus and his sons are said to have ruled 215 years; in Holinshed (vol. II, *The First Inhabitation of Ireland*, p. 49) and Campion (pp. 24-5) they are said to have ruled 216 years; in Camden (*Britannia*, p. 681) they are said to have been driven out immediately after their arrival. Standish O'Grady dates the advent of the Nemedian divinities in 1700 B. C. (*Early Bardic Literature, Ireland*, pp. 63-4).

1309-12. WARE. The Irish stories have a continued succession of the Kings of Ireland from this *Slanius*, untill the conquest by King *Henry* the second, but very uncertaine, especially untill the planting of Religion by S. *Patrick*, at which time *Laegarius*, or *Lagirius* was Monarch.

COVINGTON (*UTB*, Studies in English 4. 23) suggests that Spenser found the legend of Dela's sons in Holinshed [vol. II, *The First Inhabitation of Ireland*, p. 49].

EDITOR. Holinshed dates the interval between the races of Nemedus and Dela from 2533 to 2714 of the creation. Spenser seems rather to have used the version of the Dela story which Stanyhurst takes from Giraldus Cambrensis (*De Rebvs*, p. 239), in which the interval is given as two hundred years. Standish O'Grady dates the arrival of the sons of Dela, or Firbolg divinities, in 1525 B. C. (*Early Bardic Literature, Ireland*, pp. 64-5).

1312-8. ROLAND SMITH (*JEGP* 43. 396) notes that Spenser is indebted to Camden's " nugae Milesiae" [*Britannia*, pp. 15, 508, 678] for his "Milesian lyes" and (*MLQ* 3. 547-57) shows that the legend of Milesius and his sons may well have been the source of the story of the sons of Milesio in *F. Q.* 5. 4. 4-20. [See also Gough in commentary on *F. Q.* 5. 4. 7. 3, Book V, p. 194.]

EDITOR. The assumption that Spenser must have found the legend of Milesius in an old Irish, rather than in a contemporary English or Latin, source (see note on 1302-18) is not well-founded. Stanyhurst, following Giraldus, writes (*De Rebvs*, pp. 244-5): " demum aduenerunt de Hispaniae partibus, in sexaginta nauium classe, quattuor nobiles Milesij regis filij, qui et statim totam insulam, nemine rebellante, sibi vendicauerunt. . . . A nomine vero praedicti Heberi, secundam quosdam, Hibernienses nomen traxerunt: vel potius, secundum alios, ab Hibero, Hispaniae fluuio, vnde prouenerant." The Milesians are now supposed to have been the ancestors of the Irish Celts and to have landed in Ireland between 1700 and 800 B. C. (Hyde, pp. 16-8). The Latin adjective *Milesius*, derived from the name of a Greek collection of scandalous tales, originally meant *ribald* (see Ovid, *Tristia* 2. 413-4); later it took on the meaning of *fabulous*, which it has in Camden; but Spenser's pun seems to be original.

1349-52. So Buchanan writes (lib. II, f. 16^v): "Gothi obscura diu natio diluuij instar breui tempore Europam, Asiam, Africam inundarunt." Spenser also uses the flood image to describe a barbarian invasion in *F. Q.* 2. 10. 15. 3-5.

1358. " Barbarians." Apparently the Berbers.

1362. RENWICK. *Elizabeth* should of course be *Isabella*; but all MSS except BM. *Addl.* 22022 read thus. [In the sixteenth century the two names were interchangeable; see, *e. g.*, Birch, *Memoirs* 1. 202.]

1366-9. Bodin observes (*Methodus ad Facilem Historiarum Cognitionem*, 1572, p. 584): "Hispani principes summum nobilitatis fastigium a Gothis repetunt, qui omnium opinione barbarissimi putantur." Spenser's attack replaces another passage, which he apparently deleted (see 1152 n); the method of his attack parallels that of Buchanan in the case of the Brutus legend (lib. II, f. 13ʳ) — the pretensions are ridiculed rather than disproved: like Brutus, the Spaniards are not worthy of being sought for ancestors.

1383-1451 n. ROLAND SMITH (*JEGP* 43. 396). Spenser's confidence in the Carthaginian origin of the Irish, which appears in the P. R. O. MS . . . , was apparently shaken before he wrote his later version, in which he stresses their Scythian origin. It seems likely that Spenser wrote the P. R. O. version before he became familiar with Camden's arguments in the *Britannia*, which convinced him (apparently) of the Scythian origin of the Irish. [But the Public Record Office MS, in one of the passages peculiar to it (see 1215-1330 n), declares that Ireland was planted principally by the Scythians and Africans, and it includes the long discussion of Scythian customs that remain among the Irish (1515-1852).]

ROLAND SMITH (*JEGP* 42. 506-8). It is interesting to note, . . . that of the five names chosen for analysis by Spenser, the first three are Munster names and the last two belong to Connaught. . . . The family names . . . are those which represented much of the strongest resistance to the English invaders, both in Spenser's Munster and in Bingham's Connaught. The source of Spenser's military proposals for the garrisoning of Ireland may well have caused the names of Orourke and Oflahartye to linger unpleasantly in his memory.

"Maccartye, seemes to haue . . . . Carthage." ROLAND SMITH (*JEGP* 42. 506) notes the prominence of the MacCarthys (Ir. *MacCárthaigh*) in Kerry and Cork, particularly the MacCarthy Reagh (Florence MacCarthy), the MacCarthy More (the Earl of Clancar [see 4262-8, 4546-8]), and MacCarthy of Muskerry. [Spenser's curious Carthaginian etymology may have been suggested by John Twyne (*De Rebvs Albionicis, Britannicis atque Anglicis*, 1590, pp. 110-11), who equates *Car* in *Carthage* with *caer* in Welsh.]

"for *y*: and *g*: . . . . *forgett*." William Lambard (*The Perambulation of Kent*, 1576, p. 205) calls attention to this "misrule" in Old English words.

"whence Comes *Odriscoll?* . . . . letter." ROLAND SMITH (*JEGP* 42. 506-7) notes that the best-known O'Driscoll (Ir. *O hEidirsceóil*) was Sir Finnin, who does not seem to have aroused English suspicion. [The O'Driscolls seem to have been established in Co. Cork (anonymous *Description of Ireland*, p. 186). There is nothing in Polybius or Livy on the Carthaginian name *Dursica*.]

"as for Osullivant . . . Sullevant." ROLAND SMITH (*JEGP* 42. 507) places this family in Cork and Kerry and points out that O'Sullivan More and O'Sullivan Beare were branded as traitors. [See anonymous *Description of Ireland*, p. 168.]

"Brourke." ROLAND SMITH (*JEGP* 42. 508). It is possible that . . . "Brourke"

... may stand, not for Orourke, but for Bourke. In that event, Spenser gives us another name of an Irish chieftain capable of striking terror into the hearts of the English. [The passage which follows makes it clear that "Orourke" is intended.]

"Orourk surelye commes ... magnus." ROLAND SMITH (*JEGP* 42. 507). [Roderick] appears however, to be neither Spanish nor Scythian, but Scandinavian (ON. *Hróth-rekr*). With the Irish form (*O Ruadraic, O Ruaidhri*) compare Roderick (*Ruaidhri*) as a given name. [Olaus Magnus (*Historia*, sig. 3^r) mentions "Rodericus," twenty-eighth king of the Goths and the Swedes; since Olaus calls the Goths European Scythians, it is clear why Spenser believes *Roderick* a Scythian, rather than a Scandinavian, name. He would be confirmed in this by the story of "Rodorike a Scithian prince" in Holinshed (vol. II, *The First Inhabitation of Ireland*, p. 50; Campion, pp. 30-1).]

1385. *Monument*, "Anything that by its survival commemorates a person, action, period, or event" (*NED*, def. 4). "Optimi scriptores quo maior fides scriptis haberetur e publicis monumentis ea se collegisse aiunt. sic Amianus se Gallorum antiquitates e publicis illorum monumentis in lucem eruisse profitetur" (Bodin, *Methodus ad Facilem Historiarum Cognitionem*, 1572, p. 60). See *Epith*. 433.

1392-9. RENWICK. Buchanan, fol. 21 vo. [lib. II, ed. of 1583, f. 16^v]: "Nec Scotos a Brittonibus toto sermone, sed dialecto potius discrepasse arbitror, vti posterius dicam, cum nunc etiam tam in sermone consentiant, vt eodem aliquando vsi fuisse videantur." He expands this in the following pages, and is followed by Camden, and by Meredith Hanmer. [See also Buchanan, lib. II, ff. 17^r–18^r. Camden, after establishing the connection of the Britons with the Gauls, asserts, on linguistic grounds, the common origin of the Bretons and Britons and identifies the surviving Britons as the Cornish and Welsh (*Britannia*, pp. 11, 16-7, 48).]

1399-1401. RENWICK. Buchanan fol. 22-24; copied by Camden.

EDITOR. Spenser has in mind the passage which begins: "Iam tandem eo ventum est, vt ex opidorum, fluminum, regionum, et alijs id genus nominibus linguae inter Gallos, et Britannos communionem, atque ex ea veterem cognationem demonstremus"; but the list of about two hundred names which follows includes places scattered all over Europe, not in Scotland alone (lib. II, ff. 18^v–20^v). Camden lists more than forty words, not names, common to the Gauls and the Britons (*Britannia*, pp. 16-23).

1402-5. RENWICK. Camden, in his description of County Wexford. [Camden, on the authority of Ptolemy (1. 2), places the Cauci and Menapii in Leinster (*Britannia*, p. 694); but neither Ptolemy nor Camden mentions the Venti as inhabitants of Ireland. See Ware, *Works* 2. 17, 60.]

1408. "Tanais." MORLEY. The River Don.

1411. "*Celtica*." See *F. Q.* 2. 10. 29. 5.

1412-4. DRAPER (*MP* 17. 484-5). The source for Spenser's opinion was probably Buchanan's *Rerum Scoti[c]arum Historia*. There is a word *gall*, meaning *foreign*, in Irish; and the introduction of the *-u-* may show either that Spenser took advantage of Elizabethan license in spelling to enforce his etymologies, or that he was trying to reproduce an Irish dialectic pronunciation *goul*, or merely that he had chanced upon that spelling in Irish. A relation, moreover, to the *Gaul* of Continental Celtic is generally accepted by scholars; but his idea of a Gaulish invasion, unless we liken it to Rhŷs's second Celtic invasion, seems, rather than anything else, a figment of the legendary histories of Ireland.

COVINGTON (*SP* 19. 244-5) points out that it is improbable that Spenser used the spelling "*Gaull*" and that Buchanan and Campion, whom Spenser must have read, use the spellings respectively "Gald" [*Historia*, lib. II, f. 18^v] and "*Ghalt*" [*Historie*, p. 14].

RENWICK. Buchanan *ut sup.*, and Camden [Campion?].

[Buchanan supplied Spenser with the etymology: "Vox enim Galle, aut Gald, non est minus apud eos significans quam apud Graecos et Latinos Barbarus, apud Germanos Walsch" (lib. II, f. 18^v).]

1415-9. RENWICK. From Camden, *passim*. [Camden gives the locations of the three peoples on widely separated pages but in the same order (*Britannia*, pp. 152, 204, 217).]

1430-3. KEATING (1. 31). I am surprised how Spenser ventured to meddle in these matters, of which he was ignorant, unless that, on the score of being a poet, he allowed himself license of invention, as it was usual with him, and others like him, to frame and arrange many poetic romances with sweet-sounding words to deceive the reader. [See also O'Flaherty, p. 367.]

WARE. In *Richard Creagh's* booke *de lingua Hibernica*, there is a very plentifull collection of Irish words, derived from the Brittish or Welch tongue, which doth much strengthen the Authors opinion, in houlding that the *Birnes*, *Tooles*, and *Cavenaghs*, with other the ancient inhabitants of the easterne parts, were originally Brittish Colonyes.

COVINGTON (*UTB*, Studies in English 4. 15-6) suggests that Spenser's genealogies are probably derived from the Irish chronicles.

1430-1. KEATING (1. 29). He says that "tol" and "hilly" are alike, and that it is from it the Tooles are named; I allow that "tol" and "hilly" are equal, yet "tol" and "Tuathal" are not like each other, for it is from the name of a warrior called Tuathal they are (called): wherefore the opinion of Spenser is false.

DRAPER (*MP* 17. 482-3). O'Toole almost certainly does not come from *tol* or even from the Welsh at all. Professor Robinson says that the immediate source of O'Toole is Ua Tuathail, which is a familiar family name. . . . *Toll*, in varied forms, occurs in all the insular Celtic languages, and regularly signifies a *hole* or *perforation*. [See 3639 n and note.]

RENWICK. *Tol*: modern Welsh *tol*, high.

[The meanings "hillye Countrie" and "hillye" (3639) which Spenser gives to the British, or Welsh, word "*Tol*" involve some mistake. It is

COMMENTARY 323

possible that, having read the translation of Welsh *bryn* as *hill*, he carelessly assigned that meaning to *tol* and gave a wrong meaning to *bryn* in his next statement. See note on 1431-2.]

1431-2. KEATING (1. 29). He says that "brin" and "woody" are alike (in meaning); I allow that "brin" and "woody" are the same, yet it is not from this word "brin" the Byrnes are called, but from the name of a young warrior called Brannút.

DRAPER (*MP* 17. 482). He seems to think that [*brin*] has this meaning in Welsh; but I have found no trace of it.

RENWICK. *Brin*, modern Welsh *bryn*, a hill, *not* "woody".... Spenser may have got the hint for this from the Book of Howth, "*Bren* is an ancient name of English; the 30 cap. of Fabian." (*Cal. Carew MSS.* [*Miscellaneous*] p. 245) But if so he did not verify the reference, for the name *Brenne* in Fabyan is only the anglicised form of *Brennus*. O'Donovan, in a note in his translation of the Four Masters, remarks on this passage, stating that the O'Byrnes and O'Tooles came from Kildare. (vol v, 1712)

[Spenser may well have known the correct translation of Welsh *bryn* as *hill* since it is so defined in William Salesbury's *Dictionary in Englyshe and Welshe*, 1547 (reprinted 1877), and in Llwyd's *Commentarioli Britannicae Descriptionis Fragmentum*, 1572, ff. 46^r, 77^v; but the correct translation may have been given to *tol* by mistake. See note on 1430-1.]

1432-3. KEATING (1. 29). He says that "caomhan" and "strong" are alike, and that it is from it the Cavanaghs are named. My answer to him is, that "caomhan" is the same as a "mild" or pleasant person, and that the Cavanaghs were so named from Dómhnall Caomhanach, son of Diarmuid of the foreigners. The epithet adhered to Domhnall himself from his having been nurtured in Kilcavan, in the lower part of Leinster; and it is from the Kinsellachs they are by descent.

DRAPER (*MP* 17. 481). I have been unable to find any such word in Welsh, or, for that matter, in Irish or Scotch Gaelic.... Professor Robinson suggests that [*Cavanagh*] may be related to the Irish *cabán*, a *hollow* or *cavity*, and that it is probably a family name of local origin.

ROLAND SMITH (*JEGP* 42. 507) notes that Spenser's etymology is fantastic and cites Woulfe, *Sloinnte Gaedheal is Gall*, p. 234, who traces *Kavanagh* to the personal name *Caomhan*, mod. *Kevin*.

1434-7. DRAPER (*MP* 17. 482-3). In Spenser's *cummurreeih* ... I can find no Irish word or cry to be compared with it. Professor Robinson suggests that if Spenser or his informant knew it only in written form, he might have confused the Welsh word with some Irish derivative of *cobair*, *help*, a confusion that might arise from the common interchange of *mh* and *bh*. The *Dictionary* of the Irish Text Society gives a *cumarać*, *strong*, *powerful*, *capable*: perhaps he had this in mind; or perhaps he was simply drawing again on his imagination. He seems to suggest that there is some relation between this *cummurreeih*, Irish or Welsh, and the Welsh *cummeraig*.... this is an older spelling of the Welsh *cymreig*, the source of our *Cymric*.... but of the Irish war cry no certain trace remains.

RENWICK. The word ["*Cummericke*"] had become a technical term: cf. statute 18 Henry VI. *c*. 2 against "such as put themselves into Comrick, or that do take any to Comrick" [*The Statvtes of Ireland*, pp. 4-5]. Spenser takes it as a form of *Cymbri*, or as Camden spells it, *Cumeri*.

ROLAND SMITH (*JEGP* 42. 503). Neither of Draper's guesses is a good one: Spenser's *Cummericke* is no ghost-word, and may be found in Dinneen [*Irish-English Dictionary*, 1927] at p. 223, s. v. *Coimirce, comairce, comraighe*. It means what Spenser said it meant. See also the two entries in Hogan, *Onomasticon Goedelicum*, s. v. *Comrach*.

1437-8. WARE. *Iris* is by *Diodorus* called a part of *Brittaine*: but *Ireland* by neither of them *Britannia*. [See Riedner, pp. 60, 63.]

RENWICK. The citation of Diodorus and Strabo is unfounded.

[Strabo deliberately distinguishes Ierna, or Ireland, from Britain (*Geography* 4. 3-4). Spenser may have in mind a remark of Stanyhurst's: "Non sum autem nescius, Britanniae significatione ipsam Hiberniam a quibusdam vetustis scriptoribus fuisse comprehensam, vt testis est Plinius" (*De Rebvs*, p. 251); all that Pliny says is that England was called Albion, "cum Britanniae vocarentur omnes de quibus mox paulo dicemus," *i. e.*, the other British countries (*Historia Naturalis* 4. 16).]

1439-40. WARE. Concerning King *Arthur's* conquest of Ireland, see *Geffry* of Monmuth, and *Matthew* of Westminster, at the yeare 525. where he is said to have landed in Ireland with a great army, and in a battle to have taken King *Gilla-mury* prisoner, and forced the other Princes to subjection. In our Annals it appears that *Moriertach* (the sonne of *Erca*) was at that time King of Ireland, of which name some reliques seeme to be in *Gilla-Mury*, *Gilla* being but an addition used with many names, as *Gilla-Patrick*, etc. But in the Country writers (which I have seene) I find not the least touch of this conquest.

RENWICK. See Holinshed's chapter on the First Inhabitation of Ireland.

EDITOR. In Holinshed see in particular vol. I, *The Historie of England*, p. 91; vol. II, *The First Inhabitation of Ireland*, p. 49; vol. II, *The Conquest of Ireland*, p. 36. The same stories appear in Campion, pp. 28-9, 71; Stanyhurst, *De Rebvs*, p. 249. The Elizabethan accounts stem from that in Giraldus Cambrensis, *Expugnatio Hibernica* 2. 6. In the sixteenth century Arthur's dominion over Ireland was emphasized since the Tudors regarded themselves as his descendants (Millican, pp. 49-50; see also pp. 42-3). The story of Gurgunt in *F. Q.* 2. 10. 41 Harper (pp. 97-8) believes to be founded on Geoffrey of Monmouth rather than Holinshed; but the present reference to Gurgunt points rather to Holinshed. For Irish refutations of the two legends see Keating 1. 13-7 and Lynch 2. 82, 3. 2-16.

1445-51. KEATING (1. 25). This is not true for him [Spenser], because the old records of Ireland are opposed to that, and, moreover, British authors themselves confess that the Saxons did not leave them any ancient texts, or monuments, by which they might know the condition of the time which preceded the Saxons.

COMMENTARY

RENWICK. Bede [*Ecclesiastica Historia*], IV. xxvi; quoted by Holinshed under the year 684. (1807 edition, I, page 634 [ed. of 1586, vol. I, *The Historie of England*, p. 125]..) . . . . Holinshed, I, 698 [ed. of 1586, vol. I, *The Historie of England*, p. 162]: "Edgar . . . was ruler and souereigne lord ouer all the kings of the out Iles that lie within the seas about all the coasts of the same Britaine euen vnto the realme of Norwaie. He brought also a great part of Ireland vnder his subiection, with the citie of Dublin, as by authentike recordes it dooth and may appeare." [It is more likely that Spenser remembered the stories of Egfrid and Edgar from Camden (*Britannia*, p. 685), where they are separated by an interval of only a few lines (see Covington, *UTB*, Studies in English 4. 25). Edgar appears again in *S. C. Sept.* 151-3 and E. K.'s gloss.]

1452. "rippinge." TODD. This *discovery* of ancestors etc. *Ripping* is metaphorically used. To *rip*, is to break open stitched things.

1469-71. See note on 370-1.

1471-3. WARE. King *Henry* the 2. gave to *Richard Strong-bow* Earle of *Striguil* or *Penbroke*, all Leinster, excepting the city of *Dublin*, and the Cantreds adjoyning with the maritime townes and castles [*Marginalium: Gir. Camb. Hib. expugn. lib.* 1. *cap.* 28.]. Vnto *Robert fitz Stephen*, and *Miles de Cogan* he granted the Kingdome of Corke, excepting the Citty of Corke, and the *Ostmans* Cantred [*Marginalium*: *Vid. Rog. de Hoveden pag.* 567, *edit. Franc. et Camd. Brit. pag.* 739.]. And unto *Philip de Bruse* the Kingdome of Limericke [*Marginalium*: *Rog. de Hoveden ibid.*]. But in a confirmation of King *Iohn* to *William de Bruse* (or *Braos*) Nephew to this *Philip*, wee finde that hee gave to him onely *honorem de Limerick, retentis in dominico nostro* (as the words of the Charter are [*Marginalium*: *Chart. an.* 2. *Io. in arce Lond.*]) *civitate de Limerick et donationibus episcopatuum et abbatiarum, et retentis in manu nostra cantredo Ostmannorum et S. insula*. Among other large graunts (remembred by *Hoveden*) which this King *Henry* gave to the first adventurers, that of Meth to Sr *Hugh de Lacy* is of speciall note. The grant was in these words.

HEnricus Dei gratia Rex Angliae, et Dux Normanniae et Aquitaniae, et Comes Andegauiae. Archiepiscopis, Episcopis, Abbatibus, Comitibus, Baronibus, Iustitiarijs, et omnibus ministris et fidelibus suis Francis, Anglis et Hiberniensibus totius terrae suae, Salutem. Sciatis me dedisse et concessisse, et praesenti charta mea confirmasse *Hugoni de Lacy* pro servitio suo, terram de Midia cum omnibus pertinentijs suis per servitium quinquaginta militum sibi et haeredibus suis, tenendum et habendum a me et haeredibus meis, sicut *Murchardus Hu-melathlin* eam tenuit, vel aliquis alius ante illum vel postea. Et de incremento illi dono omnia feoda quae praebuit, vel quae praebebit circa Duveliniam, dum Baliuus meus est, ad faciendum mihi servitium apud civitatem meam Duveliniae. Quare volo et firmiter praecipio, ut ipse *Hugo* et haeredes sui post eum praedictam terram habeant, et teneant omnes libertates et liberas consuetudines quas ibi habeo vel habere possum per praenominatum servitium, a me et haeredibus meis, bene et in pace, libere, et quiete, et honorifice, in bosco et plano, in pratis et pascuis, in aquis et molendinis, in vivarijs et stagnis, et piscationibus et venationibus, in vijs, et semitis, et portubus maris, et in omnibus alijs locis, et alijs rebus ad eam pertinentibus cum omnibus libertatibus, quas ibi habeo, vel illi dare possum, et hac mea charta confirmare. *Test. comite Richardo filio Gilberti, Willielmo de Braosa, etc. Apud Weisford.*

But above all other graunts made by K. *Henry* the 2. that to his sonne *Iohn* is most memorable. *Deinde* (saith *Hoveden* [*Marginalium*: In He^{nr}. 2. pag. 566.]) *venit rex Oxenford, et in generali concilio ibidem celebrato constituit Iohannem filium suum Regem in Hibernia, concessione et confirmatione Alexandri summi Pontificis.* By vertue of this graunt both in the life time of his father, and in the raigne of his brother king *Richard*, he was stiled in all his charters *Dominus Hiberniae*, and directed them thus, *Ioannes Dominus Hiberniae, et comes Morton. Archiepiscopis, episcopis, comitibus, baronibus, Iustitiarijs, vicecomitibus, constabularijs, et omnibus ballivis et ministris suis totius Hiberniae, salutem.* Thus we have it frequently (although sometimes with a little variation) in the Registers of Saint *Mary* Abbey, and *Thomascourt* by *Dublin*. How the Earle in Leinster, and *Lacy* in Meth, distributed their lands, (besides what they retained in their owne hands,) is delivered by *Maurice Regan*, (interpreter to *Dermot Mac Murrough* King of Leinster) who wrote the Historie of those times in *French* verse. The booke was translated into *English* by Sir *George Carew* Lo. President of *Mounster*, afterwards earle of *Totnes*, and communicated to me, by our most reverend and excellently learned Primate. There wee finde that the Earle gave to *Reymond le Grose* in marriage with his sister [*Marginalium*: *Consul. Gir. Camb. Hib. expugn. lib. 2. cap. 4*], *Fotherd, Odrone*, and *Glascarrig*, unto *Hervy de Mount-marish*, hee gave *Obarthy*, unto *Maurice de Prindergast, Fernegenall, which was afterwards conferred upon Robert fitz Godobert but by what meanes he obtained it* (saith Regan) *I know not.* Vnto *Meiler Fitz Henry* he gave *Carbry*, unto *Maurice Fitz Gerald* the *Naas Ofelin* (which had beene possessed by *Mackelan*) *and Wickloe* [*Marginalium*: This Maurice soone after deceasing at Wexford, king *Iohn* then earle of *Moreton* confirmed to his sonne *William Fitz Maurice cantredum terrae quem Makelanus tenuit, illum sc. in quo villa de Naas sita est, quam comes Richardus dedit Mauritio patri ipsius Willielmi.* Thus the charter. *habetur in rot. com. placis an.* 10. Hen. 6. *in turri Birminghamiano;*], unto *Walter de Ridelesford* he gave the lands of *Omorthy*, unto *Iohn de Clahul* the marshalship of Leinster, and the land betweene *Aghabo* and *Leghlin*, unto *Robert de Birmingham Ofaly*, and unto *Adam de Hereford* large possessions. What these possessions were, are thus noted in the Register of *Thomascourt* abbey, where speaking of the Earle, *Postea Lagenia perquisita, erat quidam juvenis cum eo quem multum dilexit, et dedit eidem pro servitio suo terras et tenementa subscripta, viz. tenementum de saltu Salmonis, Cloncoury, Kill, Houterard, et tenementum de Donning cum omnibus suis pertinentijs.* Thus the Register. This *Adam de Hereford* was founder of *Saint Wulstan's* Priory neere *Leixlip* in the county of Kildare. But we proceed with *Regan*. Vnto *Miles Fitz David* who was one of his cheife favorites, he gave *Overk* in Ossory, to *Thomas le Flemming, Arde*, to *Gilbert de Borard, Ofelmith*, to a knight called *Reinand* he gave 15. knights fees adioyning to the sea, and to one *Robert* (who was afterwards slaine in Connaght) the *Norragh*. What partition *Lacy* made in *Meth*, he thus delivers. Vnto his speciall friend *Hugh Tirrell* he gave *Castleknock*: and unto *William Petit Castlebreck*. I have seene an ancient deede made by Sir *Hugh de Lacy* to this *William Petit* wherein among other things he graunts unto him *Matherethirnan cum omnibus pertinentijs suis, exceptis Lacu et villa quae dicitur Dissert, etc.* Vnto the valiant *Meiler fitz Henry* (sayth Regan) *he gaue Mag-*

herneran the lands of Rathkenin, and the cantred of Athnorker. Vnto Gilbert de Nangle all Magherigallen, unto Iocelin the sonne of Gilbert de Nangle, the Navan and the land of Ardbraccan: unto Richard de Tuite he gave faire possessions, unto Robert de Lacy Rathwer, unto Richard de la Chappell he gaue much land, unto Geffry de Constantine Kilbisky and Rathmarthy: Vnto Adam de Feipo, Gilbert de Nugent, William de Misset, and Hugh de Hose, he gaue large inheritances. In Lacyes graunt to Feipo, we finde that he gave him Skrine, et praeterea (sayth the deede [*Marginalium: Magn. regest. mon. B. Mariae iuxta Dublin. fol* 76.]) *feodum unius militis circa Duvelinam, scil. Clantorht et Santref.* etc. In his graunt to *Gilbert de Nugent,* (the originall whereof I have seene, with an impression upon the seale, of a knight armed and mounted,) he gave to him *Delvin, quam in tempore Hibernicorum tenuerunt O-Finelans, cum omnibus pertinentijs et villis, quae infra praedictam Delvin continentur, excepta quadam villa Abbatis Fourae nomine Torrochelasch pro servitio 5. militum.* Thus the Charter. To *Misset* hee gave *Luin,* and to *Hussey* or *Hose Galtrim. Regan* proceeds. *Vnto Adam Dullard hee gave the lands of Dullenvarthy, unto one Thomas he gave Cramly, Timlath-began northeast from Kenlis, Lathrachalim, and Sendevonath, and unto Richard le Flemming he gave Crandon at 20. Knights fees.*

1480. "meare." In the sense of *pure, unmixed,* without implied disparagement (*NED,* def. 1. b).

1515-9. MORLEY. *Boolies,* herdsmen's huts in the hill pastures; old Irish bó, a cow or ox, bóchaill or búachaill, a herdsman.

ROLAND SMITH (*JEGP* 42. 502). Ir. *Buaile, buala.* [Hardiman translates *buaile* as a *dairy-house* (*Statute of Kilkenny,* pp. 42-3). The custom goes back to the earliest times since it is mentioned in the gloss of the *Senchus Mor,* the great compendium of Brehon Law (Joyce, *Social History* 2. 283). In a communication with the Editor, Professor Smith calls attention to two articles on the *buaile* by Pádraig Ó Moghráin (*Béaloideas* 13. 161-71, 14. 45-52) ; Smith, unlike Ó Moghráin, believes that the word in the sense in which Spenser uses it was already established among the Irish in 1596.]

1519-25. RENWICK. Olaus Magnus, (1490-1568), published *Historia de Gentibus Septentrionalibus,* 1555: an *Epitome* published by Plantin, 1570, was and is more easily found. One might think Spenser was confusing *Suecia* (Sweden) with *Scythia*; but the Scythians were for these men a vague "northern nation," whom the modern northern nations represented well enough. Johannes Boemus, *Mores, Leges, et Ritus Omnium Gentium,* ed. of 1561, p. 114 [lib. II, cap. 9; ed. of 1571, p. 148]; speaking of the Scythians: "per solitudines et inculta vagabatur loca, armenta pecoraque prae se agens." Of the Tartars, p. 125 "armenta pascere, obscuri nominis inter Scythas."

EDITOR. Olaus (Praefatio, cap. 7) identifies the Goths of Sweden as European Scyths; but he says nothing specifically on boolies. Boemus may have supplied the reference to the Tartars: "Non in villis aut vrbibus, sed in campo veterum Scytharum ritu sub tabernaculis habitant: pastores enim sunt plerique omnes. In hyeme manere in planitia solent, in aestate vero pascuarum vbertatem sectantes in montibus degunt" (p. 164); but Spenser may have read the parallel statement in Vincent de Beauvais (*Speculum Historiale*, 1474, vol. III, 29. 71). Herodotus seems to have been the first to describe the wandering pastoral life of the Scyths (4. 46); see also Pomponius Mela (*The Rare and Singuler Works*, trans. Arthur Golding, 1590, book II, chap. 1, p. 38) and Trogus Pompeius (*Thabridgment of the Histories*, trans. Arthur Golding, 1564, book II, f. 9ʳ).— Gainsford may have had this passage in mind when he wrote of the Irish (p. 147): "the inhabitants remoue their cabbins, as their cattle change pasture, somewhat like the *Tartarians*."

1525. "white meates." See note on 416.

1532-50. AODH DE BLÁCAM (*Gaelic Literature Surveyed*, pp. 129-30). We can imagine Spenser, riding from Kilcolman, coming upon some upland *buaile*, and curling his city-bred lip at the coarse realities of rural life and the rough gaiety of the stocaghs. Here was he, within arm's length of a life as yet unfettered by the law of supply and demand—a life exuberant, pastoral, full of song, such as he loved to imagine when he sat pen in hand—and the son of the journeyman clothmaker could not reconcile himself to his environment. So mysterious is the psychology of genius. [Southey comments on Spenser's attack, "This effect is not perceived in Switzerland." (p. 211); but most of the English officials in Elizabethan Ireland would probably have supported Spenser's opinion (*e. g.*, C. S. P. Ir. *1598-1599* 202. 4. 83). See 4909-37 and note.]

1535. See *F. Q.* 6. 8. 35. 1-3. Bryskett writes to Walsingham of "stelthes and spoyles" (Plomer and Cross, p. 35).

1546. MORLEY. *Malign*, now limited in sense to speaking ill, when used as a verb, was applied first to malicious action. The "gn" in malign representing geno, gigno; malignity, ill nature.

1555-6. The description which Boemus gives (p. 149) of the mantles the Scythians make out of the skins of their enemies may have suggested Spenser's parallel.

1556-8. TODD. "In Terconnell the haire of their head growes so long and curled, that they goe bare-headed, and are called *Glibs*; the women, *Glibbins*." Gainsford's *Glory of England*, 4to. Lond. 1618, p. 151.

COLLIER. Todd seems to have forgotten that the "hairy glib" has been mentioned by Spenser in his F. Q. B. iv. c. 8. St. 12, . . . where see the note. [See also 1656-63 and note.]

MORLEY. "Glib" is the old Irish word for a lock of hair.

1562. RENWICK. *Elias mantle*: 1 Kings, xx. 19 [19. 13, 19?]; 2 Kings ii. 8, 13-14.

1562-3. RIEDNER (p. 60). Die Geschichte der Chaldaeer bringt Diodorus in Buch II, Kap. 19 ff.; von Mänteln erwähnt er nichts.

RENWICK. I can find nothing to the purpose.

1563-4. RIEDNER (p. 46). Die Kleidung der Ägypter beschreibt Herodot im II. Buch (Kap. 36 u. 37) seiner Historiae; von den Mänteln sagt er aber nichts.

COMMENTARY 329

RENWICK. Of the Egyptians, Herodotus [2. 36] says only that "the men go in two garments, the women in one." (B. R.'s translation, 1584) Spenser may be confusing them with the Babylonians: "Their vsuall custome is to go clothed in two garments, one of linnen downe to the feete, another of wollen drawne vppon the same: aboute their shoulders they cast a cloake of whyte colour." [Herodotus also writes of the Egyptians (2. 81): "they wear a linen tunic fringed about the legs, and called *calasiris*; over this they have a white woollen garment thrown on afterwards."]

1564-5. RIEDNER (p. 57). Konnte ich darin diese Stelle nicht finden. Man wird zunächst an die berühmteste Elegie des Kallimachus, "das Haar der Berenike," denken, die uns nur durch die klassische Übersetzung des Catull erhalten ist. Nun bestehen zu diesem Gedichte keine direkten Scholien, sondern nur indirekte, d. h. solche zu anderen Schriftstellern, in denen Kallimachus genannt wird, oder in denen auf Grund der Ähnlichkeit mit Catulls Text gewisse Stellen auf Kallimachus zurückgeführt werden; auch von diesen geht keine auf den Vers, der für unsere Untersuchung in Betracht kommen kann (non prius unanimis corpora conjugibus tradite, nudantes rejecta veste papillas, Vers 80).

RENWICK. I can find nothing to the purpose.

EDITOR. Spenser's allusion may be explained as a confused recollection. In the *Hymns* Callimachus twice calls Artemis "Χιτώνη," Goddess of the Mantle (1. 76, 3. 225); in a third place (3. 11-2) her mantle itself is described: "ἐς γόνυ μέχρι χιτῶνα ζώννυσθαι λεγνωτόν," "give me to gird me in a tunic with embroidered border reaching to the knee" (trans. A. W. Mair, Loeb Classics edition, p. 61). For the word "λεγνωτόν" in this passage there is the Greek scholium: "Τὸ ἔχον ὦαν· τουτέσι τὸ ἀπολῆγον τοῦ ἱματίου. Λέγναι γὰρ, αἱ ὦαι, τὰ λώματα, οἱ κροσσοί. ἅπερ Ὅμηρος θύσανοις καλεῖ. Τῆς ἑκατὸν θύσανοι παγχρύσεοι." (*Callimachi Cyrenaei Hymni*, ed. Henricus Stephanus, 1577, p. 13), *i. e.*, "That which has a hem. That is the edge of the mantle. For λέγναι are hems or fringes or tassels, which Homer calls θύσανοι: a hundred tassels of solid gold were on it [*Iliad* 2. 448]." In his note on *F. Q.* 2. 3. 26-27 Upton suggests that the description of Belphoebe may be related to the passage so annotated in Callimachus; in fact, one of the phrases describing Belphoebe (*F. Q.* 2. 3. 26. 8-9),

       and all the skirt about
  Was hemd with golden fringe,

is close to the scholium already quoted. Spenser may have remembered the scholium on the mantle of Artemis in Callimachus; remembered also that Berenice, the Egyptian queen, was the subject of a well-known poem by the same Callimachus; and through a confusion of the two recollections concluded that the Greek commentaries on Callimachus gave evidence that the Egyptians wore mantles.

1566-7. RENWICK. *Venus* appears with a "mantle lined with stars" in Botticelli's picture of her birth, but I have not found the authority for this beautiful astronomical notion. [Aphrodite was represented in antiquity with stars on her garment (Charles Daremberg and Edmond Saglio, *Dictionnaire des Antiquités Grecques et Romaines*, fig. 7383). See also *F. Q.* 3. 1. 36. 2.]

1567-9. WARE. As the *Romans* had their gowne called *toga*, so the ancient outward vestiment of the Grecians was called *Pallium*, by some translated a Mantle, although it be now commonly taken for a Cloake, which doth indeed somewhat resemble a Mantle. By these different kinds of habit, the one was so certainly distinguished from the other, that the word *Togatus* was often used to signifie a Roman, and *Palliatus* a Grecian, as it is observed by *Mr Tho. Godwin* [*Marginalium*: *Romana histor. antholog. lib. 2. sect. 3. cap. 7.*] out of *Sigonius* [*Marginalium*: *De iud. l. 3. cap. 19.*]. *Togati* saith he) *pro Romanis dicti, ut Palliati pro Graecis*. But that *the ancient Latines and Romans used it*, as the Author alledgeth, (out of I know not what place in *Virgil*) appeareth no way unto mee. That the Gowne was their usuall outward garment, is most certaine, and that commonly of wooll, finer or courser, according to the dignity of the person that wore it. Whence Horace [*Marginalium*: *Satyr. 3. lib. 1.*],

——————*Sit mihi mensa tripes, et*
Concha salis puri, et toga quae defendere frigus
Quamvis crassa, queat——————

And from this difference betweene the ancient Roman and Grecian habit, grew the proverbs, *modo palliatus, modo togatus*, and *de toga ad pallium*, to denote an unconstant person. [Spenser's "*Pallia*" is not a Greek word, but the plural of *pallium*, the Latin name for the Greek mantle, especially the rectangular himation.]

1569-73. WARE. *Euanders* entertainment of *Æneas*, is set out in the 8. booke of *Virgils Æneis*, but there we have no such word as *mantile*. In his entertainment of *Dido* we have it, but in another sence.

Iam pater Æneas, et jam Troiana iuventus
Conveniunt, stratoque super discumbitur ostro,
Dant famuli manibus lymphas Cereremque canistris
Expediunt, tonsisque ferunt mantilia villis.
[*Marginalium*:] *Æneid. lib. 1.* [699-702]

RENWICK. This is not in Virgil, nor have I found it. Spenser is thinking of *Æneid* VIII. 175-183, and of a phrase from the description of Dido's feast, I. 702: "tonsisque ferunt mantelia villis," where *mantelia*, however, means *napkins*. [See also Riedner, pp. 70-1.]

1569-70. William Lily uses the phrase "*Vergilius poetarum doctissimus*" (*Brevissima Institutio sev Ratio Grammatices*, 1567, ed. Vincent J. Flynn, 1945, sig. E4v). The standard discussion of Vergil's learning was in Macrobius (*Saturnalia*, especially Libri 4, 5, 6).

1576-81. Spenser may remember that Hector Boethius speaks of the mantles of the ancient Scots (*The History and Croniklis of Scotland*, trans. John Bellenden, 1540, intr. sig. D1r). See also Stowe, *The Chronicles of England*, 1580, p. 9.

1585-7. MEZGER (*Archiv* 150. 232-3) suggests that Spenser may have read a translation from a tenth-century poem by Cormacan Eigeas, which contains the lines:

COMMENTARY

> We were a night at the cold Aillin;
> The snow came from the north-east;
> Our *only* houses, without distinction of *rank*,
> Were our strong leather cloaks. . . .
> Our *only* shelter, our *only* woods
> Were our strong leather cloaks.

[*The Circuit of Ireland*, ed. John O'Donovan, 1841, pp. 37, 45. See 2338-9.]

1593-1645. RENWICK. An unnamed writer in the year 1589, gives nine reasons for abolishing the Irish habit, of which we need quote only the eighth: "The mantle servinge vnto the Irishe as to a hedghogge his skynne or to a snaile her shell for a garment by daie, and a house by night it maketh them with the Contynuall vse of it, more apt and able to liue and lie out in bogges and woodes, where their mantle serveth them for a mattras and a bushe for a bedsteede, and thereby are lesse addicted to a loyall dutifull and Civill lieffe." (*S. P. Ir.* 144. 57 ii)

EDITOR. The use of the mantle by the Irish goes back at least to the seventh or eighth century, when *The Book of Kells*, which includes pictures of the garment, was illuminated; and in Irish literature allusions to the mantle date from the same period (Joyce, *Social History* 2. 193-9; O'Curry 1. ccclxxxix). Lynch (2. 202) describes the advantages of wearing a mantle, and in 1598 it was even proposed to dress English soldiers in it (*C. S. P. Ir. 1598-1599* 202. 3. 55). For the appearance of the mantle see two illustrations from Derrick's *Image of Irelande* (1581), reproduced in Renwick's edition of the *View*, op. pp. 66, 268; also Dürer's drawing of Irish soldiers and peasants (1521).

1602. "Tabernacle." From the Latin word for *tent*; later, through association with Biblical usage, a *dwelling-place* (*NED*, def. 3). See 2 Sam. 7. 6. So Stanyhurst writes of the Irish soldier, "humum pro cubili, arbustum pro tabernaculo habet" (*De Rebvs*, p. 52).

1606. "thicke woods." Edgeworth (*Castle Rackrent*, 1800, p. 8) humorously suggests that these words read "black bogs."

1609-13. See *F. Q.* 2. 9. 16 on the Irish gnats.

1618. "hansome." MORLEY. Handy, serviceable.

1629. "skeane." TODD. "*Sword*; skian, or skeine." See Walker's Memoir etc. (mentioned in the note on *arms and weapons* below [1755-6],) p. 115.

COLLIER. A "skean," or "skena," was a *short sword, dagger*, or *knife*, and seems to have been a weapon particularly Irish. See the note on "Romeo and Juliet," A. ii. Sc. 4. Shakespeare's Works, by Collier, 1858, vol. v. p. 141.

ROLAND SMITH (*JEGP* 42. 505). Ir. *scian*, "knife." [The Irish used this weapon not only for direct thrusts but for flinging from a distance (*C. C. MSS. 1589-1600*, p. 381).]

1631-44. Spenser may have the mantle in mind when he describes Excess in "garments loose, that seemd vnmeet for womanhed" (*F. Q.* 2. 12. 55. 9). Irish women, according to Fynes Moryson (*Itinerary*, part III, p. 180), "goe naked in very Winter time, onely hauing their priuy parts couered with a ragge of linnen, and their bodies with a loose mantell, so as it would turne a mans stomacke to see an old woman in the morning before breakefast." Derrick, on the other hand, describes the beauty and the loyalty of the younger ones (sigs. B4v–C1r).

1632. "*monashul.*" RENWICK (*View*, p. 308) identifies "*Beantoolhe*," the reading of Additional MS 22022, as a synonym of "*Monashut*," the reading of the Rawlinson MS.

HULL (*PMLA* 56. 578-9) points out that "*Beantoolhe*" stands for Irish *bean t-siubhail, a vagrant woman*, and that "*monashul*" (*mná siubhail*) is the plural of the same word; he believes that Spenser probably wrote "*Mona-Shul*" and "*Mona-shules*," as the Ware text reads [but see 2385 n], and that these were corrupted to "*Monashut*" and "*Monashite*" by English copyists, while the scribe of the Additional MS substituted the correct singular "*Beantoolhe.*"

1635. RENWICK. A *safegard* was an outer skirt for riding and travel.

1639-44. Rich (*Description*, p. 36) writes: "to speake truth of our Gentle-women of *Ireland*: that be of *Irish* birth, they haue little practise, either in pride or in good huswiferie; for they are for the most part alwaies busied in taking their ease."

1641. "louse." MORLEY. Be free from encumbrance or employment; old French leisir, later loysir. [But *NED*, under the verb *louse* (def. 1. a) cites the present passage as meaning "to clear of lice." Stephen Batman notes that in Ireland "the men are not free from lice, which cometh of sluttish and filthy vse" (*Batman vppon Bartholome*, 1583, f. 231v). Moryson says of the Irish, "vpon euery hill they lye lowsing themselues" (*Shakespeare's Europe*, p. 483).]

1644-5. The use of the mantle, except for certain legitimate purposes, had been forbidden to all subjects by an act of 28 Henry Eighth (*The Statvtes of Ireland*, pp. 129-30).

1647-50. Spenser seems to have a confused memory of the well-known anecdote of Diogenes: "One day, observing a child drinking out of his hands, he cast away the cup from his wallet with the words, 'A child has beaten me in plainness of living.' He also threw away his bowl when in like manner he saw a child who had broken his plate taking up his lentils with the hollow part of a morsel of bread" (Diogenes Laertius, *Lives of Eminent Philosophers*, trans. R. D. Hicks, Loeb Classics edition, 2. 39). The same story is paraphrased by Erasmus (*Apophthegmes*, trans. Nicholas Udall, 1542, f. 90r-v).

1656-63. The glib is described in Holinshed (vol. II, *The Conquest of Ireland*, p. 55): "their beards and heads they neuer wash, clense, nor cut, especiallie their heads; the haire whereof they suffer to grow, sauing that some doo vse to round it: and by reason the same is neuer kembed, it groweth fast togither, and in processe of time it matteth so thicke and fast togither, that it is in steed of a hat, and keepeth the head verie warme, and also will beare off a great blow or stroke, and this head of haire they call a glibe, and therein they haue a great pleasure." The Irish made the retention of the glib a point of national honor (see Maxwell,

p. 351). In *F. Q.* 1. 9. 35. 4-6 and 5. 9. 10. 6 Despair and Malengin seem to wear glibs. See note on 1556-8.

1663. The use of the glib had been forbidden, along with the mantle, by an act of 28 Henry Eighth (*The Statvtes of Ireland*, pp. 129-30).

1671-6. RIEDNER (pp. 60, 46) finds nothing in the section which Diodorus devotes to the Scythians (2. 43 ff.) on their cries, and notes that while Herodotus writes of the cries of the Scythians and Persians (4. 59-82, 1. 131-40), he does not report what Spenser does.

RENWICK. I can find nothing to the purpose in either Diodorus or Herodotus.

1676. "the Irishe Hubub." MORLEY. The old Irish battle shout, "abo," is in our word "bugaboo," where bug is the old word for a cause of terror, a spectre, as bugbear, a spectre in form of a bear. This word "bug" and the cry "abo" may be akin.

ROLAND SMITH (*JEGP* 42. 504). Ir. *ábobú*. ... Very Irish is Spenser's "many bagpipes shrill, And shrieking Hububs," *F. Q.*, III, x. 43. For a full list of these clan war-cries, see *CSPI*, 1601-03 Addenda, p. 683; and Ware's list in "The Antiquities of Ireland," ch. XXI (ed. Harris, *Works of Sir James Ware*, Dublin 1764, II, 162-65). [Derrick gives the variant form "Bohbowe" (sig. G4r), and Sir Henry Sidney describes the cry as "Bowes, Bowes," apparently associating it with the weapon (*Letters and Memorials* 1. 150). See also Moryson, *Shakespeare's Europe*, p. 484; Barnaby Rich, *The Irish Hvbbvb*, 1617, pp. 1 ff.]

1677. "kerne." See note on 2223-4.

1677-80. WARE. Herodotus in the description of that battle hath no such thing. [See also Riedner, p. 47.]

RENWICK. Herodotus records the battle in which Cyrus was slain, I. 214; but says nothing about calling on the king's name. [See *F. Q.* 2. 10. 56. 4, 4. 11. 21. 5. Tomyris was Queen of the Massagetae, not the Scyths.]

1683-4. ROLAND SMITH (*JEGP* 42. 504). Ir. *lámh dhearg abú*. ... Spenser, whose explanation is quite correct, may well have had in mind Tyrone's encounter near Dundalk in 1595 with Sir Henry Bagenall, whose "little band . . . was charged at the sword's point, to the cry of *Laundarg-abo*" (Wiffen, *Russell Memoirs*, II, 29); cf. Bagenall's letters in *CSPI* 1595, pp. 319-22. [Upton connects this cry with the babe called Ruddymane in *F. Q.* 2. 2. 3-10 and refers the reader to Camden's *Annales* under 1567 for the anger and bloodiness of the O'Neills (see *F. Q.*, Book II, p. 400); but this complicates the interpretation of Ruddymane whose hands are said to remain bloody as the symbol of his mother's chastity. The badge of the O'Neills displays a hand cut off at the wrist (see *JRSAI* 14. 498, 20. 282).]

1685 n. RENWICK. O'Brien's war-cry and its meaning were added by Ware: the MSS leave blanks. It may have slipped Spenser's memory.

ROLAND SMITH (*JEGP* 42. 504). Ir. *lámh láidir*, "powerful hand, violence."

1687. RENWICK. *Cromabo* was the Kildare Fitzgeralds' war-cry, from the castle of Crom. Statute 10 Henry VII *c.* 20 forbade the using of the words *Cromabo* and *Butlerabo*. [The act forbade all private warcries of this kind (*All the Statutes*, f. 31ʳ⁻ᵛ; *The Statvtes of Ireland*, p. 66).]

1689-96. TODD. The vulgar Irish suppose the subject of this war-song to have been *Forroch* or *Ferragh*, (an easy corruption of *Pharroh*, which Selden, in his notes on Drayton's Polyolbion, says was the name of the war-song once in use amongst the Irish kerns,) a terrible giant, of whom they tell many a marvellous tale. See Mr. Walker's *Hist. Mem. of the Irish Bards*, notes, p. 96; and Mr. Warton's note on *Sir Ferraugh*, F. Q. iv. ii. 4 [Book IV, p. 174].

DRAPER (*MP* 17. 484). As to the actual war cry, Keating [1. 43] derives it from *faire, faire ó, watch, watch O*, or *ó faire, O take care*. It may be related to *ferrac, -aig, force* or *violence*; and Professor Robinson suggests a relation to *fear, man*, or *rí, king*, in some combination. As for Fergus or Fearghas, Macbain gives OI *Fergus* perhaps from **ver-gustu-s, super-choice*. Spenser's use of the name is interesting as lending a little more credibility to his having browsed in the legendary history of Ireland.

COVINGTON (*SP* 19. 245-6) shows that the reading "*Farrih*" in Additional MS 22022 makes Spenser's derivation from *Fergus* seem to be more fanciful than it actually was and that "*Ferragh*" is closer to the actual cry.

ROLAND SMITH (*JEGP* 42. 504). Quite as plausible [as *ferrach*] is the derivation from *feargach*, "fierce, strong, lusty," Dinneen, p. 438. Compare the O'Brien *lámh láidir*, with its similar signification, which Spenser has just explained.

1690-3. RENWICK. Buchanan, Book IV, fol. 33 vo. [This passage (ed. of 1583, f. 28ᵛ), however, describes the struggle of Fergus, the first king of the Irish-Scots, not against the Picts but with the Picts against the Britons. Spenser's error, it is possible, may stem from some reference like the following in Thomas Lanquet's *Epitome of Cronicles* (1559, f. 46ᵛ): "Fergus, sonne of Ferquard, kynge of Irelande, who ayded the Scottes agaynste the Pichtes, and was the first kyng of Scottes."]

1700. MORLEY. Richard Stanihurst, the translator of Virgil, published at Antwerp in 1584 a book, *De Rebus in Hibernia Gestis*. He had been at work on it since the close of his college days. Though born in Dublin, he was bred in England, and held the opinions prevalent in England upon Irish policy. Afterwards he became a Roman Catholic, and is said to have wished to recant the errors in his Irish Chronicle.

RENWICK. Richard Stanyhurst (1547-1618), son of the Recorder of Dublin, wrote (besides a notorious translation of Virgil) a Description of Ireland published in Holinshed's Chronicle. [On his later career see Rich, *Description*, pp. 1-2, and *The Irish Hvbbvb*, 1617, p. 3; for his literary work see St John D. Seymour, *Anglo-Irish Literature 1200-1582*, 1929, pp. 145-65.]

1703-14. RENWICK. The reference here is to his history *de Rebus in Hibernia Gestis*, published by Plantin, 1584, p. 43: "Totus autem tam equitatus, quam peditatus, quoties ad manus, et pugnam venitur, alte voce, PHARRO, PHARRO, inclamat. Verum a rege Pharaone, Gandali socero, an ab alia caussa clamor iste natus sit, parum ad rem attinet explicare." The same is in Campion's history [pp. 27-8].

EDITOR. The theory of an Egyptian origin of the Irish can be traced back as far as an eighth-century life of St. Abban (O'Flaherty, p. 347); it is mentioned repeatedly in the mediaeval *Book of the Taking of Ireland* (ed. R. A. Stewart Macalister 1. 39 *et passim*); and a large rock at the eastern end of the Slieve Mis Range near Tralee is known as Scota's grave, proof of the tale's entrenchment in folklore (*JRSAI* 39. 56). In the sixteenth century the Gathelus-Scota story was accepted by Hector Boethius (*The History and Croniklis of Scotland*, trans. John Bellenden, 1540, 1. 1-2) and, to some extent, by Campion (pp. 13, 27-8); it was condemned by Polydore Vergil (*Historia Anglica*, 1651, lib. III, pp. 71-3), Llwyd (*Commentarioli Britannicae Descriptionis Fragmentum*, 1572, f. 31^v), and Buchanan (see note on 1302-5). In the passage quoted by Renwick it will be noted that Stanyhurst does not support the Egyptian origin of the Irish war-cry. In Holinshed (vol. II, *The Description of Ireland*, p. 9) it is true that Stanyhurst writes that Scotland was "named Scotia, in reuerence of Scotach the wife of Gathelus"; but when we turn to the long discussion of the Scota legend in his *De Rebvs* (pp. 17-8), which Spenser almost certainly must have known, we find that Spenser has entirely misrepresented Stanyhurst's point of view. Stanyhurst concludes: "hoc totum, tamquam vanam poetriae fabellam Georgius Buchananus, et ante illum Humfridus Lhuidus, cuius modo mentionem feci, reijcit et respuit. Et si vero Hector Boethius huius seu rei factae, seu fabulae non est architectus, tamen totam narrationem mendaciunculis, more suo, perspergit." Later Hanmer (*The Chronicle of Ireland*, 1633, pp. 4-7) quotes Stanyhurst against the Scota etymology.

1707. "bowe hand." *NED* (def. 1). The hand which holds the bow in archery, i. e. the left hand. Hence (*wide*) *on the bow-hand*, wide of the mark.

1714-6. DRAPER (*MP* 17. 475-6). His etymology of *Scot* seems fanciful. He takes it from the Greek "scotos," which he defines as "darkness." At least he seems right in that it is very likely not a Gaelic word. It first appears in inscriptions and authors in late classical Latin. The Irish form, *Scot,* plural, *Scuit*, seems to have come from this source. . . . The Greek word for *darkness*, to which Spenser refers, was written with an -*o*-, not ω; and one has no reason to suppose either that there is any connection between that classic Greek word and the medieval Greek with an -ω-, or that Spenser knew anything about the latter. In short, his derivation is probably guessed from a chance similarity.

COVINGTON (*SP* 19. 247). The derivation is indeed fanciful; in fact, I believe it was too fanciful even for Spenser. Surely if the sentence is read in its context it will be clear that in this passage Spenser is trying to make a joke; the only one in the "View," and, as might be expected, a rather feeble one.

DRAPER (*MLN* 41. 128). The curious etymology of *Scot* from the Greek word for darkness or obscurity, may well have come from Holinshed, who declares [vol. I, *The Description of Britaine*, p. 6]: "They [the Scotch] were also called Scoti by the Romans, bicause their Iland and original inhabitation thereof were vnknowne, and they themselues an obscure nation in the sight of all the world." Camden also refers to this etymology. Indeed, far-fetched classical etymologies, as the earlier pages of Camden attest, were commonly accepted even by the most critical Elizabethans; and the fact that Spenser seems to use this etymology to make a rather strained pun at the expense of Stanyhurst, whose Egyptian theory he was attacking, does not, I think, disprove his belief in the derivation of Scot from the Greek.

RENWICK. The play of words on σκότος is in Camden, and in Stanyhurst's own book: " Subinsulsa est eorum opinio, qui verbi vim ad Graecas litteras reuocantes, a vocula σκότος, quod obscuritas tenebris fuerit opacata, insulam nominari confirmant." (*de Rebus in H. G.*, *p.* 17)

EDITOR. Spenser playfully derives *Scota*, not *Scot*, from σκότος. How carelessly he attacks Stanyhurst is revealed by the occurrence in *De Rebvs* of the very etymology which he adapts as a weapon against Stanyhurst; but he undoubtedly is imitating the passage in Camden (*Britannia*, p. 55) where the same etymology is made into a punning attack on Buchanan: " Proximum a Pictis locum inter Britanniae gentes Scoti sibi vendicant, quorum ἔτυμος, et origo, ita σκοτίζεται, et caligine circumfusa latet, vt ipse perspicacissimus Buchananus vel parum viderit, vel sibi viderit, intusque cecinerit."

1718-9. RENWICK. The *matters of more weight* were those of religion: Stanyhurst went over to Rome in 1580, and was still a fugitive abroad. Spenser probably had his opinion about his poetry also.

1726. "Platforme." MORLEY. Used here as, "plot," for scheme or plan. So the Maid of Orleans in *Henry VI.*, Part I., Act ii. scene 1, counsels against the English—

"To gather our soldiers, scattered and dispersed,
And lay new platforms to endamage them."

1728-9. Stanyhurst describes the keening in two different works (Holinshed, vol. II, *The Description of Ireland*, p. 44; *De Rebvs*, pp. 47-8). Camden (*Britannia*, p. 719) writes: " Funus autem tantis vociferationibus prosequuntur, vt viuos et defunctos conclamatos esse existimes." Barnaby Rich (*The Irish Hvbbvb*, 1617, p. 4) calls the keening " Such a brutish kinde of lamentation, as in the iudgement of any man that should but heare, and did not know their custome, would thinke it to be some prodigious presagement prognosticating some vnlucky or ill successe, as they vse to attribute to the houling of dogges, to the croaking of Rauens, and to the shrieking of Owles, fitter for Infidels and Barbarians, then to be in vse and custome among Christians."

COMMENTARY 337

1730-2. RENWICK. Jacob, not Joseph: *Genesis*, l. 3: "The Egyptians bewayled him seuentie dayes." The Geneva Bible has the side-note: "They were more excessive in lamenting then the faithfull." [Spenser's mistake is probably due to the occurrence of Joseph's death in the same chapter of Genesis (50. 26). See Herodotus 2. 85.]

1736-8. RENWICK. 1 *Thessalonians*, iv. 13: "I would not brethren, haue you ignorant concerning them which are asleepe, that ye sorow not euen as other which haue no hope." Side-note [Geneva Bible]: "We must take heede that we doe not immoderately bewaile the dead, that is, as they vse to doe which thinke that they are vtterly perished."

1738-9. RIEDNER (p. 60). Von den Scythen (Βιβλιοθήκη Buch II. Kap. 43 ff.) berichtet Diodorus in seiner Bibliothek solches nicht, wohl aber von den Ägyptern (Buch I. Kap. 72); hier schildert er die übertriebenen Trauerfeierlichkeiten beim Tode eines Königs.

RENWICK. Not in Diodorus.

1755-6. TODD. This subject is illustrated, with great care, in the following work: "An Historical Essay on the Dress of the ancient and modern Irish; to which is subjoined a Memoir on the Armour and Weapons of the Irish. By Joseph Corper [*i. e.*, Cooper] Walker, Esq. M. R. I. A." Dublin, 1788.

1756-8. RENWICK. Olaus Magnus, VIII. xi, mentions various kinds of swords used by the Goths, including broad two-handed ones. [See also lib. VIII, cap. 23. For Olaus (Praefatio, cap. 7) the Goths are European Scyths.]

1759-60. RENWICK. Buchanan, fol. 9 [lib. I; ed. of 1583, f. 7ᵛ]: "Sunt qui gladiis latis, aut securibus pugnant."

EDITOR. The English version of the *Scotorum Historiae* of Hector Boethius which appears in Holinshed gives the old Scots long (in the Latin "oblongum"), not broad swords (vol. II, *The Description of Scotland*, p. 21); Stowe, however, tells us that the sword used by the Scots is "verie brode" (*The Chronicles of England*, 1580, p. 9). "Ia: de Breȳ" remains a mystery to me.

1760 n. RIEDNER (p. 126) finds nothing of this in the *Collectanea Rerum Memorabilium* of Solinus.

RENWICK (*View*, p. 325). [Philip] Flatsbury, mentioned in T [the Trinity College MS], was secretary to the Earl of Kildare in the 1530's, and left historical notes used by Hooker (Holinshed, vol VI) among others.

1762-70. WARE. The originall of the very name of *Scythians* seemeth to come from *shooting. vide Selden, annot. in Poly-olb. (ex Gorop. Becan. Beccesel. et Aluredi leg.) pag.* 122.

RENWICK. Olaus devotes two chapters, VII. i and ii, to bows and arrows, but his description of northern archery is very different from this.

EDITOR. The Goths or European Scyths, writes Olaus, "certa telorum genera ferrea unius et dimidiae palmae, medio ligno abietino, medioque ferro acutilissimo confecta, secum ad multa millia in bella comportunt"; "talemque uim habet eius uigore emissa ferrea sagitta, ut uirum lorica, ac duplici thorace munitum, uelut mollem ceram penetrare consueuit" (lib. VII, cap. 13, p. 229; cap. 2, p. 221). See also Buchanan on the weapons used in the Scottish islands (lib. I, f. 7ᵛ). In *F. Q.* 2. 11. 21. 1-4, it will be remembered, Maleger is armed with bow and arrows.

1771-4. RENWICK. Olaus says nothing about broad shields; nor does Solinus. [Joyce explains that "The most ancient [Irish] shields were made of wicker-work, covered with hides: they were oval shaped, often large enough to cover the whole body, and convex at the outside" (*Social History* 1. 124).]

1774-8. RIEDNER (p. 63). In Herodians Τῆς μετὰ Μάρκον βασιλείας ἱστορίαι (1. 8) konnte ich darüber nichts finden.

RENWICK. Herodianus was translated by N. Smyth about 1550, but the reference probably comes from Buchanan's quotation of the passage, fol. 30 vo [lib. III; ed. of 1583, f. 26ʳ]: "loricae, ac gale[a]e penitus ignorant vsu." So also Llwyd [*The Breuiary of Britayne*, trans. Thomas Twyne, 1573] fol 88. [See Mezger, *Archiv* 150. 234.]

EDITOR. The passage from Herodian quoted by Buchanan and Llwyd refers to the Britons, not the Scyths or Scots; and those writers, like Nicholas Smith in his translation (*The History of Herodian*, p. xliiii), Camden (*Britannia*, p. 32), and John Twyne (*De Rebvs Albionicis, Britannicis atqve Anglicis*, 1590, pp. 64-5), refer the passage to the Britons. But in Holinshed (vol. II, *The Description of Scotland*, p. 23) Herodian's description, translated out of Hector Boethius, is applied to the Picts: "as for iacke, shirt of male, or helmet, they made no regard of them, bicause they would trouble them in swimming"; and it will be remembered that in one place (1223) Spenser seems to identify the Picts with the Scots.

1776. "beare of a good strocke." So in Holinshed (vol. II, *The Conquest of Ireland*, p. 55) it is said that the matted hair of the Irish "will beare off a great blow or stroke."

1778-82. Olaus Magnus (lib. VII, cap. 6, p. 224) describes the battle customs of the European Scyths: "fit, ut dum in hostem non secus quam graues, et luctuose tempestates uno impetu deferuntur, ferociterque irruunt, uel facultatem inueniant cedendi, sternendi, capiendi, aut omnia in hostilibus castris confundendi, prout natura loci concedit. Populoque mos est, tumultuaria atque cursoria pugna dimicare." The last statement is closest to the description of the Irish method of attack which appears in the *Book of Howth* (*C. C. MSS. Miscellaneous*, p. 5); but Spenser's description seems almost to have been modeled on Derrick's (sig. G1ʳ):

> Now warlicke raie thei leaue,
>   and on a heape thei clunge,
> Supposyng safer for to bee,
>   as better foes repunge.
> And with a mightie crie,
>   our hoste their doe inuade.

COMMENTARY

See Derrick's note on these lines and Joyce, *Social History* 1. 142-3, 148-9. M. M. Gray (*RES* 6. 414-6) compares the Irish manner of fighting with the attack on Alma's House by Maleger and his band in *F. Q.* 2. 9. 13-16, 2. 11. 5-46.

1791-1802.   WARE.   Not he [Plutarch], but *Herodotus* in the life of *Homer*.

RIEDNER (pp. 47-8). Es existieren 9 Vitae Homeri. Die erste davon trägt den Namen des Herodot, ist aber eine Fälschung aus der Zeit nach Strabon. Die Schrift Πλουτάρχου περὶ τοῦ βίου καὶ τῆς ποιήσεως Ὁμέρου ist aus zwei Schriften zusammengesetzt, von denen die erstere sicher nicht von Plutarch herrührt, und auch die zweite nur Excerpte aus Plutarch enthält. Spenser bezeichnet diese als seine Quelle. Die Vergleichung ergibt jedoch, dass der Dichter dem pseudoherodotischen Texte folgt.

RENWICK. Not in Plutarch, but in the pseudo-Herodotean Life of Homer, xxxvii. T. C. D. MS. reads *Heroditus*.

EDITOR. See *Homeri Opera*, ed. David B. Munro and Thomas W. Allen, 5. 216-7, for the passage in question. It may be translated as follows:

> Further, that Homer was an Aeolian, and not an Ionian or a Dorian, may be deduced partly from his words and partly by means of the following conjectures. For it is likely that so great a poet, who desired to describe the peculiar customs of men, should have invented those which he thought most praiseworthy or have recalled those of his own people. Now, fairly considering his poems, you may judge of this. For when he had some sacrificial rite of this kind to report, he either, as it were, invented one which was quite admirable or chose one which agreed with the customs of his country. So indeed he says: "They first drew back the victims' heads, and cut their throats, and flayed them, and cut out the thighs and covered them with a double layer of fat, and laid raw flesh thereon" [*Iliad* 1. 459-61, trans. A. T. Murray, Loeb Classics ed.]. In these verses there is no mention of the loins [ὀσφύος], which were used in the sacrifices of all peoples except the Aeolians, who did not burn the loin [ὀσφύν]. In the following verses, moreover, he reveals what one who was an Aeolian born would use as the rites of his people: "And the old man burned them on billets of wood, and made libation over them of flaming wine; and beside him the young men held in their hands the five-pronged forks" [*Iliad* 1. 462-3]. For only the Aeolians fixed the intestines on five spits when they roasted them; the rest of the Greeks used three.

1795.   "ὀφυν."   See Appendix III, section C.

1805-13.   WARE.   Lucian hath it, *by the sword and by the wind*. Somewhat may be gathered to this purpose out of the *Vlster Annals* [*Marginalium*: An 458.], where *Laegarius* (or *Lagerius*) a heathen King of Ireland, being taken prisoner by the *Leinster* men, is said to have bin released upon an oath, which was *per solem et ventum*.

RENWICK. Lucian — otherwise quoted accurately enough — says the oath was by the sword and the wind, not the fire. [See also Riedner, pp. 64-5.]

EDITOR. An inscription of Harvey's in one of his books shows that he wagered Spenser a copy of Lucian in December, 1578 (*Marginalia*, p. 23). In Lucian's *Toxaris* the speaker of that name, a Scythian, says, "I swear by Wind and Scimetar"; and he goes on to explain that these are invoked as the causes of life and death, not as the avengers of perjury (*Dialogues*, trans. F. G. Fowler, 3. 57). Leagaire, in the story mentioned by Ware, was destroyed, after he broke his oath, by the offended elements; and Spenser seems to have transferred to the Scyths the worship of fire and sword which was an important part of Irish paganism (Joyce, *Social History* 1. 286-8, 290-3).

1813-6. RENWICK. For a modern trace of this, see *Grace for Light*, in Moira O'Neill's *Songs of the Glens of Antrim*.

1818-21. Spenser may have in mind what Herodotus (4. 184) writes of one of the North African tribes: "The Atarantians, when the sun rises high in the heaven, curse him, and load him with reproaches, because, they say, he burns and wastes both their country and themselves." See Pomponius Mela, *Chorographia* 1. 8.

1821-5. TODD. See Mela, lib. 11 [*i. e.*, 2], cap. 1. Other nations also observed this custom. See Herodotus, l. 1. c. 74 [*i. e.*, 70].

RIEDNER (p. 47) connects this passage with that in Herodotus.

RENWICK. Herodotus, IV. 70; the citation of Buchanan is inaccurate.

EDITOR. The next sentence (1825-6) reveals that Spenser has in mind the account of the Scythian blood-oath in the *Toxaris* of Lucian: "At length a friend is accepted, and the engagement is concluded with our most solemn oath: 'to live together and if need be to die for one another.' That vow is faithfully kept: once let the friends draw blood from their fingers into a cup, dip the points of their swords therein, and drink of that draught together, and from that moment nothing can part them" (*Dialogues*, trans. F. G. Fowler, 3. 56). See also Solinus 15. 16 and Boemus, pp. 150-1. If Buchanan mentions no such custom among the Scots, Giraldus Cambrensis writes of the Irish (*Topographia Hibernica* 3. 22): "Ad ultimum vero, ad majorem amicitiae confirmationem, et quasi negotii consummationem, sanguinem sponte ad hoc fusum uterque alterius bibit. Hoc autem de ritu gentilium adhuc habent, qui sanguine in firmandis foederibus uti solent"; and there is good historical evidence for the use of the blood-oath in Ireland (Joyce, *Social History* 2. 510-2). Camden seems to have supplied Spenser with the parallel between Irish and Scyths: "foedus mutui sanguinis haustu sanciunt... syluestres Scoti et Hiberni, vt olim Scythae" (*Britannia*, p. 57).

1825-32. RENWICK. *The same book* is Lucian's *Toxaris*. [Toxaris explains (*Dialogues*, trans. F. G. Fowler, 3. 62):

> When a man has been injured by another, and desires vengeance, but feels that he is no match for his opponent, he sacrifices an ox, cuts up the flesh and cooks it, and spreads out the hide upon the ground. On this hide he takes his seat, holding his hands behind him, so as to suggest that his arms are tied in that position, this being the natural attitude of a suppliant among us. Meanwhile, the flesh of the ox has been laid out; and the man's relations and any others who feel so disposed come up and take a portion thereof, and, setting their right foot on the hide, promise whatever assistance is in their power: one will engage to furnish and maintain five horsemen, another ten, a third some larger number; while others, according to their ability, promise

heavy or light-armed infantry, and the poorest, who have nothing else to give, offer their own personal services. The number of persons assembled on the hide is sometimes very considerable; nor could any troops be more reliable or more invincible than those which are collected in this manner, being as they are under a vow; for the act of stepping on to the hide constitutes an oath. By this means, then, Arsacomas raised something like 5,000 cavalry and 20,000 heavy and light armed.]

1834-6. Olaus (lib. VIII, cap. 2, p. 242) writes that the Goths used to swear by the name, not the hand, of their kings: "per nomen eorum, quoties ardua subesset causa, iurare solebant." Camden describes the Irish custom (*Britannia*, p. 715): "Tertio, vt iuret per manum Comitis, vel Domini sui, vel potentis alicuius, nam si periurus conuincatur, per priora duo [*i. e.*, oaths by altar or by saint] infamiam subeat, si hoc tertio peierabit, grandem summam pecuniarum, et vaccarum extorquebit potens ille, quasi suo nomini maxima ex periurio illata fuerit iniuria." See also Ware, *Works* 2. 155-6.

1837-40. TODD. "Among these humors of Melancholy, the phisitions place a kinde of madnes, by the Greeks called *Lycanthropia*, termed by the Latines *Insania Lupina*, or *Wolves furie*: which bringeth a man to this point, (as Attomare affirmeth) that in Februarie he will goe out of the house in the night like a wolfe, hunting about the graves of the dead with great howling; and plucke the dead mens bones out of the sepulchres, carrying them about the streets, to the greate feare and astonishment of all them that meete him: And the foresaide author affirmeth, that melancholike persons of this kinde have pale faces, soaked and hollow eies, with a weak sight, never shedding one tear to the view of the world, etc." *The Hospitall of Incurable Fooles*, (a translation from the Italian [of Tommaso Garzoni],) 4to. 1600, p. 19.

RENWICK. Camden, in his chapter on Tipperary. I find no evidence for Scythian lycanthropy, but Olaus Magnus, XVIII. 32-33, discusses the subject.

EDITOR. Spenser may remember what Herodotus (4. 105) reports of a people neighboring the Scythians: "Both the Scythians and the Greeks who dwell in Scythia say, that every Neurian once a year becomes a wolf for a few days, at the end of which time he is restored to his proper shape." See also Mela 1. 1. Camden writes (*Britannia*, pp. 695, 716): "Quod vero nonnulli Hibernici, et qui fide digni videri volunt, homines quosdam in hoc tractu quotannis in lupos conuerti affirmant, fabulosum sane existimo, nisi forte illa exuberantis atrae bilis malitia, quae λυκανθρωπία medicis dicitur, corripiantur, quae eiusmodi phantasmata ciet, vt sese in lupos transformatos imaginentur"; "Lupos sibi adsciscunt in patrimos, quos *Chari Christ* appellant, pro eis orantes, et bene precantes, et sic se ab illis laedi non verentur." Similar legends are common in the old Irish romances (Joyce, *Social History* 1. 299-300).

1841-2. Herodotus (4. 61) writes of the Scyths: "If they do not happen to possess a cauldron, they make the animal's paunch hold the flesh, and pouring in at the same time a little water, lay the bones under and light them." Buchanan (lib. I, f. 7ᵛ) notes the same custom in the Hebrides: "Carnem aqua in omasum, aut caesi pecoris pellem infusa coquunt." Seething in the hide is ascribed to the

Irish by Andrew Boorde, long before Spenser (*The Introduction of Knowledge*, ed. F. J. Furnivall, pp. 131-3), and Moryson speaks of it some years later (*Itinerary*, part III, p. 162). See Derrick's woodcut of an Irish feast, reproduced in Hinton, op. p. 76.

1842-4. At the same place where he speaks of seething in the hide Buchanan writes of the inhabitants of the Hebrides: "in venationibus interim sanguine expresso cruda vescuntur. Pro potu est ius carnium elixarum" (lib. I, f. 7^v). Joyce searched early Irish literature in vain for the custom of drawing blood to make meat puddings (*Social History* 2. 132); but Campion writes with convincing realism, "Their Kyne they let blood, which growen to a ielly they bake and ouerspread with Butter, and so eate it in lumpes" (p. 18; see also Holinshed, vol. II, *The Description of Ireland*, p. 45). For a complete description of Irish culinary art and table manners in the Elizabethan period see Derrick, sigs. E4^v–F2^r.

1845. "davncinge." Joyce, however, writes (*Social History* 2. 445): "There is, in fact, no evidence that the ancient Irish ever danced to music, or danced at all, *i. e.* in our sense of the word 'dancing'; but very strong negative evidence that they did not."

1873. "they." The Gauls and Spaniards.

1880-3. RENWICK. This Statute is already cited [952-4].

1884-6. But the Tartar Mohametans did shave the upper lip (Richard Hakluyt, *The Principal Navigations*, Dent edition, 1. 456).

1893-6. Moryson (*Itinerary*, part III, p. 160) writes that the Irish shirts were "washed in Saffron, because they neuer put them off til they were worne out"; "Their smocks are saffrond against vermine, for they weare them three moneths together," reports Gainsford (p. 151). But Harris believes that saffron was used merely by way of ornament (Ware, *Works* 2. 178).

1896-8. RENWICK. Boemus, III. 23 [ed. of 1571, p. 457]: "Feminae res domesticas, agrorumque culturas administrant."

1900-2. Boemus writes of the Spaniards (p. 457): "Peltas in bello paruas ex neruis confectas, quibus tegatur corpus, habent"; but *peltae* are properly half-moon in shape rather than round. Among the Irish the painting of shields was common in antiquity: Conchubar's, for example, was purple-brown (Joyce, *Social History* 1. 128; see also O'Curry 1. cccclxx).

1903-6. A sculpture in Moone Abbey shows that anciently the Irish women rode across as Spenser says (Joyce, *Social History* 2. 421-2), not astride as Giraldus had reported (*Topographia Hibernica* 3. 26; see also Lynch 2. 150). Moryson makes Spenser's meaning somewhat clearer: "Our wemen riding on horsebacke behynde men, sett with theire faces towardes the left Arme of the man, but the Irish weomen sett on the Contrary syde, with theire faces to the right Arme" (*Shakespeare's Europe*, p. 214).

1909-11. In heraldry *manche* was a term especially applied to the hanging sleeve of the fourteenth century (*NED*, def. 2).

1913-5. TODD cites his note on *Col.* 780 [see *Minor Poems* 2. 480].

MILLICAN (p. 201). The reference . . . may allude to the story as told either in Malory's *Morte d'Arthur* or in the stanzaic *Morte Arthur*, a copy of which was in the possession of one Robert Farrers in 1570. See *Le Morte Arthur*, ed. J. D. Bruce (Early English Text Society, Extra Series, LXXXVIII), 1903, p. vii.

RENWICK. Malory, *Morte Darthur*, XVIII. 8 [*i. e.*, 9], 15. [It is probable that Spenser has in mind the story as told by Malory, who writes that "whan quene Gueneuer wyste that syre Launcelot bare the reed sleue / of the fayre mayden of Astolat / she was nyghe oute of her mynde for wrathe" (18. 15); the stanzaic *Morte Arthur* (ed. Bruce, p. 21) describes the Queen as filled with grief rather than anger.]

1921-4. RIEDNER (p. 120). Dieses scheint sich auf folgende Worte Caesars zu beziehen: "Disciplina in Britannia reperta atque inde in Galliam translata esse existimatur, et nunc, qui diligentius eam rem cognoscere volunt, plerumque illo (= in Britanniam) discendi causa proficiscuntur" (De Bell. Gall. VI. 13, 11).

RENWICK. Caesar speaks only of the Druids (*de B. G.*, VI. 13-14); Buchanan equates the Druids with the Bards. [Buchanan writes (lib. II, f. 17^r): "Idem quoque genus vatum apud Gallos et Britannos in summo fuit honore, quos vtrique Bardos vocabant. Horum et functio et nomen adhuc perseuerat apud omnes nationes, quae vetere Britannorum lingua vtuntur." See 1240-1 and note.]

1924-5. RENWICK. Caesar, *de B. G.* v. xiv, speaking of the Kentish tribes: "neque multum a Gallica differunt consuetudine." [Camden treats the similarity between the customs of the Gauls and the Britons at some length (*Britannia*, pp. 14-6).]

1925-30. RIEDNER (p. 120). Diese Stelle ist bei Caesar nicht zu finden.

RENWICK. Not in Caesar, though he often mentions *maturae, tragulae, pila*. Boemus, III. 22 [ed. of 1571, p. 444]: "gladius longus . . . clypeus etiam longus, hastae ad proportionem [are used by the Gauls]." Boemus reports this of the Spaniards, not the Gauls, III. 23: "gladios ex ferro puro ad palmi mensuram."

1933-5. RENWICK. Solinus, xxii [*i. e.*, xxxiv]. 3: "Sanguine interemptorum hausto prius victores vultus suos oblinunt."

EDITOR. The source of Spenser's information on the Gauls is not apparent; Herodotus (4. 64) notes that the Scyths drink the blood of the first men they slay in battle (see also Mela 2. 1; Boemus, p. 148). The sentence quoted by Renwick from Solinus applies to the ancient Irish, and this is made clear by Camden (*Britannia*, p. 712) and Buchanan (lib. III, f. 25^v) when they quote it. Stanyhurst describes how Dermod MacMurrogh mutilated the head of a decapitated enemy: "stillantes nares, ac cruenta labra, madidis dentibus, corrosit, et sanguinem non solum gustauit, sed etiam exsorbuit" (*De Rebvs*, p. 79; see also Holinshed, vol. II, *The Conquest of Ireland*, p. 6). Spenser may also have had an indirect acquaintance with the stories of Emer and Deirdre, in the Red-Branch

Cycle, who drink the blood that falls from the heads of their slain husbands (Hyde, p. 352).

1937-42. ANONYMOUS (*Dublin University Magazine* 58. 132-3) notes that this passage shows that Spenser was in Ireland before 1580 and that it dates his early trip as of 1577, when Murrogh O'Brien was beheaded at Limerick.

CARPENTER (p. 14). Sp in Ireland 1576-77, possibly as secretary to Sir Henry Sidney, or visiting Bryskett . . . ?

RENWICK. Morrogh O'Brien was beheaded 1st July, 1576 [*i. e.*, 1577]. *Cal. Carew MSS.* 1575-88, *p.* 104.

HEFFNER (*MLQ* 3. 507). We cannot be sure . . . that Spenser's statement, in his *View*, that he was in Ireland in 1577 can be taken literally, but as Carpenter says, it is possible that he was there, and in some way employed by Sir Henry Sidney.

JUDSON (*Life*, p. 46). The detailed account of this horrible event [the execution of Murrogh O'Brien] sounds like that of an eyewitness. Evidently there is ground for believing that Spenser may have been in Ireland on July 1, 1577, three years before he set foot there in the retinue of Lord Grey, although other evidence advanced for his being there at this time crumbles on close inspection, so that the inference must rest on this single passage.

BRADNER (*Edmund Spenser*, p. 22) accepts the inference as "a very reasonable conclusion."

EDITOR. In reporting the execution of Murrogh O'Brien (*C. C. MSS. 1575-1588*, p. 104) Sir William Drury observes that he was an important rebel, that three hundred pounds were offered for his life, and that he was considered the best horseman in Ireland; see also the Four Masters 5. 1699. Southey comments on Spenser's description (p. 211): "The foster mother at the execution!" That Spenser was at the execution is still open to doubt; Ware wrote, "In Hiberniam primùm venit cum *Arthuro Domino Grey*" (*De Scriptoribus Hiberniae*, 1639, p. 137, as quoted in Carpenter, p. 74).

1951-6. The contemporary parallels to this passage are without number. See, *e. g.*, Moryson, *Shakespeare's Europe*, p. 481. A typical representative of such Hibernicized Englishmen would be Sir Edmund Butler, brother of the Earl of Ormond (see *C. C. MSS. 1515-1574*, p. civ).

1957-8. See *F. Q.* 2. 12. 87. 1-5.

1964-76. Patrick Finglas (Harris 1. 41-2), writing long before Spenser, traces the Hibernicization of the great Anglo-Norman families to their feuds, which arose after the departure of the Duke of Clarence in the reign of Edward Third. Tremayne (p. 2) describes how the pride of the English lords led them to adopt Irish customs in order to make themselves strong against one another. Sir John Davies (*Discoverie*, p. 150), the most reliable of contemporary observers, gives a similar account: "these great Estates and Royalties graunted to the English Lords in Ireland, begate Pride; and Pride, begat Contention among themselues, which broght forth diuers mischiefs, that did not only disable the English to finish the Conquest of all Ireland, but did endaunger the losse of what was already gained."

1976-91. RENWICK. Of this letter there is a copy in the Book of Howth, and two among the Carew MSS [*C. C. MSS. 1601-1603*, pp. 441-2; *Miscellaneous*, pp. 23-4, 447]. It was addressed to the Earl of Rutland, then Lord Deputy. Holinshed prints it, vol. VI. 261-2 [ed. of 1586, vol. II, *The Chronicles of Ireland*, pp. 74-5], as from Campion's papers. Campion, however, as printed by Ware in 1633, has another letter, from Richard of York to the Earl of Salisbury, with a conspicuous (though erroneous) heading to the Earl of Shrewsbury [pp. 99-100]. Holinshed prints it with the heading corrected [vol. II, *The Chronicles of Ireland*, p. 78]. So Spenser had access to Campion's papers or to some copy of them. Also he verified his references hastily.

EDITOR. Spenser's indebtedness to Campion was first pointed out by Covington (*UTB*, Studies in English 4. 11-2). The Earl of Rutland, to whom the letter which is the real source of Spenser's information was addressed, was Lord Deputy 1447-1453 and 1457-1459. Renwick fails to note that Holinshed borrows it, as well as the York-to-Salisbury letter, from Campion (pp. 94-6) and follows him in misdating it in the reign of Henry Fourth. Campion's version, which Spenser undoubtedly knew, reads:

> the inhabitants of the county and towne of Corke, being tyred with perpetuall oppressions of their Irish borderers, complained themselves in a generall writing, directed to the Lord of Rutheland and Corke, the Kings Deputy, and to the Councell of the Realme, then assembled at Divelin, which Letter because it openeth the decay of those partes, and the state of the Realme in times past, I have thought good to enter here as it was delivered me, by *Francis Agard* Esquire, one of her Majesties privy Councell in Ireland.
>
> It may please your wisedomes, to have pittie of us the Kings poore subjects, within the county of Corke, or else we be cast away for ever, for where there was in this countie these Lords by name, besides Knights, Esquiers, Gentlemen, and Yeoman, to a great number, that might dispend yearelie 800. pounds, 600. pounds, 400. pounds, 200. pounds, 100. pounds, 100. markes, 20. pounds, 20. markes, 10. pounds, some more, some lesse, to a great number, besides these Lords following.
>
> First the Lord Marquesse *Caro* his yearely revenues was, besides Dorzey Hauen and other Creekes, 2200. pounds sterling.
>
> The Lord *Barnevale* of Bearehaven, his yearely revenues was, beside Bearehaven and other Creekes, 1600. pounds sterling.
>
> The Lord *Vggan* of the great Castle, his yearely revenues was, besides havens and creekes, 1300. pounds sterling. . . .
>
> The Lord *Arundell* of the strand his yearely revenues, besides havens and creekes, 1500. pounds sterling. . . .
>
> And at the end of this Parliament Your Lordship with the Kings most noble Councell may come to Corke, and call before you all these Lords and other Irish men, and binde them in paine of losse of life, lands and goods, that never any of them doe make warre upon another, without licence or commandement of you my Lord Deputy, and the Kings Councell, for the utter destruction of these parts, is that onely cause, and once all the Irish men, and the Kings enemies were driven into a great valley, called Glanehought, betwixt

two great mountaines, called Maccorte or the leprous Iland, and their they lived long and many yeares, with their white meat till at the last these English Lords fell at variance among themselves, and then the weakest part tooke certaine Irish men to take his part, and so vanquished his enemy, and thus fell the English Lords at variance among themselves, till the Irish men were stronger then they, and drave them away and now have the whole country under them, . . . Wherefore we the Kings poore subjects, of the Citty of Corke, Kinsale, and Yowghall, desire your Lordship to send hither two good Iustices, to see this matter ordered, and some English Captaines, with twenty English men that may be Captaines over us all, and we will rise with them to redresse these enormities, all at our owne costs. . . .

1979-80. "The Towre of Englande" may be a misrecollection of the marginalium in Campion (p. 94): "Records of Christ-Church in Divelin." "The Cronicles of Irelande" may be a reference to either Campion or Holinshed.

1997. Spenser's praise of the province in which he dwelt is not altogether inspired by local pride or an awareness of natural beauty. The Golden Vale of the counties of Tipperary and Limerick is the richest soil in Ireland; and during the dearth of 1596 Munster provisioned the rest of Ireland with grain and beef (*C. S. P. Ir. 1596-1597* 191. 20, 194. 37, 194. 57). "Their soile for the most part is very fertil," writes Robert Payne in 1589 (p. 6), "and apte for Wheate, Rye, Barly, Peason, Beanes, Oates, Woade, Mather, Rape, Hoppes, Hempe, Flaxe and all other graines and fruites that England any wise doth yeelde."

1998. "Patchokes." NED. Known only in the passage cited; in which also the reading is uncertain. The first element is app. *Patch* . . . ; the second may be *Cock*, or the dim. suffix -*ock*. . . . A term used by Spenser of the degenerate English in Ireland, either in reference to their character and Habits, their mongrel breed, or their costume: ? a base or mean fellow, ? a ragamuffin. . . . If the word was *patchockes*, it was perhaps the same as Shakspere's "very *Paiocke*" [*Hamlet* 3. 2. 272].

ROLAND SMITH (*JEGP* 44. 292-5) identifies "Patchokes" and Shakespeare's "Paiocke" as the same word, which it is more than likely, he explains (*JEGP* 42. 505), "is an Irish word which Spenser picked up in Ireland. It corresponds phonologically with the Ir. *piastóg*, 'worm, reptile.'"

[The word may be related in Spenser's mind to *puttock*: the besiegers of the House of Alma, who it has been suggested represent the Irish fighters (see note on 1778-82), are described: "Some like to Puttockes, all in plumes arayd" (*F. Q.* 2. 11. 11. 5).]

2003-5. MORLEY. *Messala Corvinus*, who died B. C. 3, was a soldier and scholar who had the favour of Antony and Augustus, and was a friend of Horace, Ovid, and Tibullus.

RENWICK. Solinus, I. 110: ". . . accepimus . . . Messallam certe Corvinum post aegritudinem quam pertulerat percussum proprii nominis oblivione . . ." From Pliny, *Nat. Hist.*, vii. 24. 2, but Spenser probably took it from Solinus, whom he was using for other purposes. [Neither Solinus nor Pliny speak of the great learning of Messala.]

COMMENTARY 347

2006-12. WARE. These families of *Mac-mahones* and *Mac-swines* are by others held to be of the ancient *Irish*. [For a full discussion of the change from English to Irish names see Davies, *Discoverie*, pp. 182-3. See notes on 2006-9 and 2010-12.]

2006-9. RENWICK. Campion, and Hooker (Description of Ireland in Holinshed) have the same story, based on the meaning *Bear's sons*. So also Camden, under County Monaghan. It seems to have been commonly accepted.

EDITOR. Stanyhurst, not Hooker, following Campion (p. 9), refers to the "Fitz Vrsulies, now degenerat and called in Irish Mac Mahon, the Beares sonne" (Holinshed, vol. II, *The Description of Ireland*, p. 39); and Camden takes this over almost verbatim (*Britannia*, p. 706). See also the anonymous *Description of Ireland*, p. 23; Moryson, *Shakespeare's Europe*, p. 195; the *Book of Howth, C. C. MSS. Miscellaneous*, p. 23. But it is significant that these are all English sources; Keating (1. 27), O'Flaherty (p. 365), and modern Irish scholarship accept the Irish origin of the MacMahons (see O'Dubhagain and O'Huidhrin, p. xx; *JRSAI* 46. 8). Spenser carefully specifies that he means the MacMahons "in the Northe," not the MacMahons of Munster, with whom he deals in a moment (2030). Roland Smith (*JEGP* 42. 507) notes that Irish *Mac Mathghamhna* means *Bear's Son* and recalls Spenser's episode of Sir Bruin's wife and the infant saved from the bear in *F. Q.* 6. 4. 17-37.

2010-2. RENWICK. The etymology of the Macswinies seems to be by analogy, the name *Vere* being commonly derived from *verres*, a boar. [Keating (1. 27) and O'Flaherty (p. 367) both deny that the MacSweenys are of English origin.]

2013-5. See *F. Q.* 2. 10. 69. 3-9.

2017-20. RIEDNER (p. 127). Möglicherweise hat Spenser Nepos' "Vitae" gekannt, doch ist es nach diesen nicht richtig, dass die beiden die Perser gegen das eigene Vaterland führten. Alcibiades ging als Verbannter aus Athen nach Sparta, wo er gegen Athen agitierte (Corn. Nepos VII, Alcibiades, Kap. 4); das Misstrauen der Spartaner trieb ihn zu den Persern; auf Veranlassung des persischen Statthalters Tissaphernes führte er die Athener und schlug die Spartaner (Kap. 5); sein wechselndes Schicksal führte ihn nochmals zu den Persern, mit deren Hilfe er den endgültigen Sieg Athens über Sparta herbeiführen wollte (Kap. 9); doch wird er auf Betreiben der Tyrannen in Athen ermordet (Kap. 10). ... von Themistocles hören wir, dass er sich als Vertriebener an den Perserkönig Artaxerxes wandte und ihm seinen Beistand in einem Kriege gegen Griechenland versprach (Nepos II, Themistocles Kap. 10); er kam aber nicht mehr dazu, die Feinde gegen sein Vaterland zu führen. ... Themistocles wählte den freiwilligen Tod, um nicht gegen sein Vaterland ziehen zu müssen (Plutarch, Themistocles, Kap. 31).

2022-8. O'FLAHERTY (p. 368). Haec in praesenti sufficiunt ad omnem fidem historicam Spencero denegandum. Nam Comes ille Oxoniae eximium utriusque fortunae specimen a partu virgineo Anno 1385. Hiberniae sub Richardo 2. Prorex designatus, nunquam tamen in Hiberniam pedem intulit, nec in Anglia morte mulctatus, sed a proceribus proelio devictus, et solum vertere coactus animi moerere in summa penuria vitam extorris finivit inter Ligures in Lovania Anno 1392.

RENWICK. The history of Robert Earl of Oxford is thoroughly confused; he was created Duke of Ireland, but was never there.

2030-1. The MacSweenys dwelt chiefly in Muskerry, Co. Cork; some of the MacMahons in Co. Limerick; and the MacSheehys, one of whom was chief constable of the Desmond Geraldines, in the counties of Cork and Limerick (anonymous *Description of Ireland*, pp. 173, 175, 177-8, 185, 206, 183, 191, 194, 199, 204). The only officially reported detail on the destruction of Kilcolman in October, 1598, is the slaying of one Edmund MacSheehy by an Englishman (*C. S. P. Ir. 1598-1599* 202. 3. 140). The English origin of the MacSheehys is denied by Keating (1. 27); of all three families, by O'Flaherty (pp. 362, 367).

2032-7. WARE. Others hould that he was beheaded at *Tredagh* 15. *Febr.* 1467, by (the command of) *Iohn Tiptoft* Earle of *Worcester*, then Lo: Deputy of Ireland, for exacting of *Coyne* and *Livery*. *vid. Camden Britan. pag.* 738. *edit. Londin. an*; 1607.

RENWICK. Thomas, 8th Earl of Desmond, was executed in 1468. Campion [p. 101] says: "When he had spoken certaine disdainfull words against the late marryage of King *Edward* with the Lady *Elizabeth Gray*, the said Lady being now Queene, caused his trade of life . . . to be sifted . . . Of which treasons he was . . . beheaded at Droghedah." Holinshed [vol. II, *The Chronicles of Ireland*, p. 78] copied Campion: Spenser might get it from either or both. [See also the account by Desmond's grandson and the account in the *Book of Howth* (*C. C. MSS. 1575-1588*, pp. xxxvi-xxxvii, cv-cvii; *Miscellaneous*, pp. 186-7). This Queen Elizabeth was the great-grandmother of her namesake who was ruling England in 1596.]

2040-2. The Four Masters (5. 1653-5) report that in the uprising of 1570 the MacSweenys and MacSheehys assisted James FitzMaurice FitzGerald of Desmond.

2049. The name *O'Hernan* was found in Co. Limerick (*C. S. P. Ir. 1586-1588* 127. 75). In 1592 a certain Nicholas Shynan recovered two ploughlands that had been granted to Spenser (Judson, *Life*, p. 135; Carpenter, p. 35); and in 1611 Spenser's son Sylvanus became embroiled with him in a suit over land (*JCHAS*, Second Series, 2. 527). The anonymous *Description of Ireland* (p. 39) mentions Mangen of Loughton in Co. Dublin; but Spenser is more apt to have known the Ua Mongain, an Irish family of Ross Carbery, west of Cork (*Miscellany of the Celtic Society*, ed. John O'Donovan, 1849, pp. 50-1).

2053. "degendred." TODD. This is the manuscript reading, and confirms the use of the word by Spenser on another occasion. See vol. vi. p. 2 [note on the occurrence of the word in *F. Q.* 5. Pro. 2. 9]. The printed copies read *degenerated*. [See also *H. H. L.* 94.]

2054. "O'Hanlon's Countrie," the seat of that important family, was in Co. Armagh (anonymous *Description of Ireland*, p. 19).

2055-63. TODD. The Manuscripts belonging to the Archbishop of Canterbury

COMMENTARY 349

[Lambeth] and the Marquis of Stafford [Ellesmere] add three "most pittifull examples of this sort," then existing; and the mention of them is made in very severe terms. They are "the Lord Bremingham, the great Mortimer, and the old Lord Courcie."

EDITOR. Ware probably omits this considerable passage out of respect for the great Anglo-Irish families (see Appendix III, section C). The case of Lord Courcy must be an afterthought with Spenser: he promises "two" examples, not three, and the second is called "the other."

2056-8. RENWICK. The Berminghams were Barons of Athenry in Connaught. In 1576 Sir Henry Sidney described the father of Spenser's contemporary as "a poor baron, though the ancientest in this land" (*MSS Carew*, II. 49.) They seem inoffensive and loyal enough, but Camden [*Britannia*, Latin ed. of 1590, p. 704] says "they being now as it were degenerate into barbarous Irishry, scarce acknowledge themselues to haue beene English originally." Maccorish (in some MSS *Noccorish*) seems to be a corruption of the Berminghams' native name, *Mac Feoris, son of Peter*. [See Campion, p. 7; Holinshed, vol. II, *The Description of Ireland*, p. 38; *Letters and Memorials* 1. 105. Edmund Hogan notes, "Edmund, 15th Baron, sat as the *auncientest* Baron of Ireland in the Parliament of 1585" (anonymous *Description of Ireland*, p. 227); this established epithet shows that for "Englande" in 2057 Spenser wrote, or intended to write, "Ireland."]

2058-60. RENWICK. The great *Mortimer* left no descent in Ireland. The only hint I have found is a note mentioning "Macnemaries alias Mortimers country" in *A Description of Ireland*, 1598, ed. E. Hogan, 1878, p. 124: and that might be derived from this. [See note on 456. The connection of the names *MacNemara* and *Mortimer* is further evidenced by a reference to a captain "McNemaries, a Mortymer" (*C. C. MSS. 1601-1603*, p. 450). By "the great mortimer" Spenser probably means Edmund, husband of the heiress of Lionel of Clarence and through that marriage overlord of Connaught and Ulster (Campion, p. 71; Camden, *Britannia*, pp. 705, 711). Spenser's derivation of the MacNemaras, however, is denied by Keating (1. 27-9; see also O'Flaherty, p. 367, and *JRSAI* 46. 8).]

2061-3. RENWICK. The poor estate of the *Courcys* of Kinsale is often referred to; MacCarthy of Carbery held Courcy's land in 1588 (*S. P. Ir.* 134. 98). [The Courcys, who had reached the peak of their fortunes immediately after the Anglo-Norman conquest, when one member of the family became the first Earl of Ulster, were represented in 1571 by "a poore man, not very Irish" (Campion, pp. 70, 7). This Baron of Kinsale, who held the title until his death at an advanced age in 1599, must be Spenser's "olde *Lô Courcie*" (anonymous *Description of Ireland*, p. 229); he managed to keep a certain independence of MacCarthy Reagh, the overlord of the district (Butler, p. 184), but in 1611 it is reported that his heiress married a base, beggarly kern (*C. C. MSS. 1603-1624*, p. 147).]

2073-84. Spenser takes a less prejudiced view of his own race than Stanyhurst, who blames the decay of the Anglo-Irish entirely on their contact with the native Irish (Holinshed, vol. II, *The Description of Ireland*, p. 10).

2092-5. Stanyhurst (Holinshed, vol. II, *The Description of Ireland*, p. 11) observes that a conquest "ought to draw to it" language as well as law and apparel. Spenser's reference to the Romans may have been suggested by Camden (*Britannia*, p. 52), who notes "quantopere Romani laborarint vt Prouinciae loquerentur Latine"; or by Louis le Roy (*Of the Interchangeable Covrse, or Variety of Things*, trans. Robert Ashley, 1594, f. 22ᵛ), who explains, "THE ROMAINS no lesse ambitious in amplifying their tongue then their Empire, constrained the people which they had ouercome to speak Latin." (See also Moryson, *Shakespeare's Europe*, p. 213.) Keating (1. 37) denies that it is just for the conqueror to extinguish the language of the conquered; Lynch (1. 178) denies that the Romans forced the conquered to learn Latin.

2095-7. Spenser overlooks the *Statute of Kilkenny* (pp. 11 ff.), which forbad the English to speak Irish among themselves, and the law of 28 Henry Eighth (*The Statvtes of Ireland*, p. 130), which required every subject in Ireland to speak English and to bring up his children to speak English.

2101-3. Barnaby Rich constantly inveighed against fosterage and intermarriage with the Irish (see *Description*, p. 100; *Remembrances*, p. 128). In 1615 E. S. (f. 11ᵛ) writes: "The fostering of children with Irish Nourses, is a mayne inconvenience both in respect of religion, manners, and languadge; for thereby they grow wholly vp into theire customes, studdy how to cosen the new-come English, build theire howses without Chimneys, come stooping out of theire doores, which they build low to keepe out the troupers horse, denies himself when he is within, and what not?"

2103-17. The fosterage of another's child was undertaken in Ireland for either affection or money; in the second case the rank of the father determined the price according to a scale accepted by Brehon Law; the period of nurture usually extended from birth to marriageable age, fourteen for girls, seventeen for boys (*Ancient Laws of Ireland* 2. xliii-xlvi, 146-93; Covington, *Texas Review* 6. 237-8; Joyce, *Social History* 2. 14-8; O'Curry 2. 355). In a writ of Edward Third it is observed: "homines de genere Anglicano in dicta terra idioma Hibernicum erudiuntur et loquuntur, et infantes suos inter Hibernicos nutriendos ut lingua Hibernica utantur amandantur et lactantur" (*Analecta Hibernica* 2. 267). Camden describes the evil effects of fosterage in detail (*Britannia*, p. 713). See also Davies, *Discoverie*, pp. 178-9.

2103-12. MORLEY. In like manner the Northmen, who came with Rollo into France, lost, after a generation or two, their original language, their children learning the language of French-speaking nurses and mothers.

EDITOR. See E. K.'s remark (*Ded. Epist.* 14) on "their owne country and natural speach, which together with their Nources milk they sucked." In another connection Bryskett (*A Discovrse of Civill Life*, 1606, p. 56) warns that heed should be given to the speech "specially of the nurses, in whose bosoms their children are euer held, and in whose faces their eyes are always fixed; because they note and obserue most what they do or say, hauing lesse regard to others."

COMMENTARY 351

2113. Harvey (*Letter Book*, p. 88) wrote, in a letter which may or may not have been seen by Spenser: "all philosophye saith that the temperature and disposition [and] inclination of the mindes followythe the temperature and composition of the bodye. Galen, etc." The proverb also occurs twice in Lyly's *Euphues*, once in Pettie's *Petite Pallace of Pleasure*, and once in Pettie's *Guazzo* (Morris P. Tilley, *Elizabethan Proverb Lore*, 1926, p. 124); it may be significant that a copy of Pettie's *Guazzo* was in Harvey's possession in 1582 (Moore Smith, *MLR* 28. 80).

2116-7. RENWICK. S. Matthew, xii. 34: "For [out] of the abundance of the heart the mouth speaketh."

2117-30. Spenser's contemporary, William Herbert, places marriage with Irish women first among the causes of the degeneration of the English settlers (*Croftus, sive de Hibernia Liber*, p. 39); but the most famous example of an unfortunate mating of the two races was the marriage of Mabel Bagenal, an English girl, to the Earl of Tyrone (Philip H. Bagenal, *The Vicissitudes of an Anglo-Irish Family*, pp. 51-7). Later in the *View* (4767-76) Spenser proposes that the English and the Irish be closely intermingled, a measure inconsistent with a ban on their intermarriage (see Henley, pp. 186-8).

2121. Tecmessa, the daughter of the Phrygian King Teleutas, became the concubine of Ajax after he had ravaged her father's country; she is among the protagonists of the *Ajax* of Sophocles. Spenser has confused Ajax with his father Telamon, perhaps because the son was frequently called *Telamonius*. See *Gn.* 513.

2121-2. Roxana was a Bactrian princess who fell into the power of Alexander in 327 B.C. and by whom he had a son, Alexander Aegus.

2122. "Cleopatrie." See *F. Q.* 1. 5. 50. 7-8, 5. 8. 2. 6-7.

2134-8. RENWICK. The danger of fostering and intermarriage between English and Irish is one of the commonest of complaints: acts against both were passed, 28 Henry VIII. c. 28; against fostering, 11 Eliz. c. 6. [See *All the Statutes*, ff. 57ᵛ-58ᵛ; *The Statvtes of Ireland*, pp. 427-8; Beacon, pp. 57-8. The famous *Statute of Kilkenny* (pp. 9, 11) made fosterage and marriage between Irish and English illegal in 1367; but similar laws had already been passed in 1351 and 1357 (Berry 1. 387, 412).]

2136-7. "As good neuer a whit, according to the Prouerbe, as neuer the better," writes Harvey (*Fovre Letters*, p. 56); and he repeats the proverb in the margin of the *Parabolae* of Erasmus (*Marginalia*, p. 138).

2138-9. RENWICK. The particular law in Spenser's mind was 28 Henry VIII c. 15. In this, mantles are allowed for travelling. In July, 1596, Wallop recommended the issue of mantles and country brogues to the troops, but was heavily rebuked in August. (*S. P. Ir.* 200. 59, 94.) [A law against wearing Irish apparel was enacted as early as 1297 (Berry 1. 211); and the *Statute of Kilkenny* (p. 13) commanded English clothes for Englishmen. See Maxwell, p. 113.]

ROLAND SMITH (in a communication to the Editor). If a particular document is to be cited, it seems likely that Spenser, as clerk of the Munster

Council, was more familiar with a contemporary document such as the "Munster ordinances proclaimed at Limerick" by Perrot (*Carew MSS* I, 409-412). [But Spenser undoubtedly knew 28 Henry Eighth (see note on 954); and it is unlikely that he would call one of the Munster ordinances a law.]

2147. "Iacke." MORLEY. The old jack, as a coat worn with a coat of mail, has its name ascribed by Ducange to the revolt of the peasantry known as the *Jacquerie* in 1358. Our word jacket, Fr. *jaquette*, is its diminutive.

NED (def. 1. b). A coat of fence, a kind of sleeveless tunic or jacket formerly worn by foot-soldiers and others, usually of leather quilted, and in later times often plated with iron.

2150-2. In Holinshed (vol. II, *The Supplie of the Irish Chronicles*, p. 134) we read of "the Egyptiacall rolles vpon womens heads"; and Moryson explains, "their heads be couered after the Turkish manner, with many elles of linnen, onely the Turkish heads or Tulbents are round in the top: but the attire of the Irish womens heads, is more flat in the top and broader on the sides, not much vnlike a cheese mot, if it had a hole to put in the head" (*Itinerary*, part III, p. 180). The linen turban or *caille* was worn generally by married women and not restricted to those who had cut their hair in sickness (Joyce, *Social History* 2. 215-6). See also *The Council Book of the Corporation of Cork*, ed. Richard Caulfield, p. xvi; *C. C. MSS. 1515-1574*, p. 411; Lynch 2. 168. Spenser may have this coiffure in mind when he describes Disdain in *F. Q.* 6. 7. 43. 5-8.

2152. The pleated Irish shirt is frequently mentioned by Elizabethan writers; see, *e. g.*, Derrick's description (sig. E3ᵛ). A parliamentary act of 1537 condemned it (Maxwell, p. 113); and in 1541 it was provided by ordinance that no lord or nobleman should have in his shirt beyond twenty cubits of linen, no kern or Scot more than sixteen, etc. (*C. C. MSS. 1515-1574*, p. 182).

2154-5. William Herbert likewise notices the fondness of the Irish for their native costumes: "nonnulli illos mores vestitusque Hiberniarum proprios, et quasi essentiales, existimant, et cum Hiberniae incolumitate et prosperitate conjunctos" (*Croftus, sive de Hibernia Liber*, p. 40).

2166-73. RIEDNER (p. 57). Diese Erzählung findet sich nicht bei Aristoteles. Spenser dachte wohl an eine Stelle bei Herodot [1. 155-6].

RENWICK. Not in Aristotle that I can find, but see Herodotus I. 158 [156?], which Spenser has elaborated a little, after the Elizabethan manner.

OSGOOD (*Minor Poems* 1. 392) refers this passage to Plato, *Laws* 3. 694-700, and Aristotle, *Politics* 8. 7. [Both Plato and Aristotle consider the political importance of music, and Plato also mentions Cyrus; but neither tells the story which is in the *View*.]

2171. "gigs." In the old sense of *lively* or *scurrilous songs*.

2177-2210. Scott annotates Derrick's woodcut of a battle between English and Irish soldiers (*Somers Tracts*, 1809-1815, 1. 599): "In the equipment of the Irish horsemen, we may remark the peculiarities pointed out by Spenser; the sliding reins, (or snaffle bridle,) the shank pillion without stirrups, and the fashion of charging the lance over head, instead of couching it like the English cavaliers. Their armour is the chequered quilted jacke, which the same poet likens to a player's painted coat, and open casques, also of a chequered appearance."

2178-86. RENWICK. *Sir Thopas*, 19-24 and 149-154. [Spenser has confused these two widely separated stanzas: in the second only, not the first, the appearance of Thopas as he went to fight the giant is described. See note on 2181-2.]

2181-2. MORLEY. *Shecklaton*, also *siclatoun*. . . . Spenser's explanation of the sort of material represented by this word is probably wrong. The old French *ciclaton*, whatever its origin, was a costly material, named in company with silks and satins, and, as Mr. Skeat observes, it is worn by Sir Thopas before he puts on his raiment of war.

RENWICK. Spenser defines *ciclatoun* wrongly; it was a thin cloth. [*NED* traces *ciclatoun* to Persian *sakarlat*, and defines it as *cloth of scarlet or other rich material*. See *F. Q.* 6. 7. 43. 3-4.]

2184-5. MORLEY. *Cordwain*, Cordovan leather.

RENWICK. He also echoes himself as well as Chaucer: compare "His shoon of Cordewane" (*Sir Thopas*, 21) with "buskins of costly Cordwayne" (*F. Q.* II. iii. 27. 3) and "Buskins he wore of costliest cordwayne" (VI. ii. 6. 1).

2185. "hacqueton." MORLEY. A sleeveless jacket of plate for the war. [Chaucer probably meant "A stuffed jacket or jerkin worn under the mail" (*NED*), since Thopas puts his habergeon on over it. See *F. Q.* 2. 8. 38. 7.]

2185. "habericion." MORLEY. French, from the German *hals*, neck, and *bergan*, to protect, neck armour of chain-mail, hauberk. [*Habergeon* is a diminutive of *hauberk*, and it originally designated a lighter coat of armor (*NED*).]

2187-91. For contemporary descriptions of the Irish horseman see Dymmok, p. 7; Stanyhurst, *De Rebvs*, p. 40. Joyce summarizes modern scholarship on the subject (*Social History* 2. 414-6).

2189. "slydinge Raynes." See note on 2177-2210.

2189. "Shanke pillion." Pommel (*NED*, under *shank*).

2194-9. Stanyhurst, like Spenser, cannot conceal his admiration for the Irish manner of mounting a horse (*De Rebvs*, pp. 40-1): "ferreis scalis (quae a nonnullis, stapides, dicuntur) in equos minime ascendunt: neque huiusmodi nugatoria (sic istorum opinio fert) adminicula phaleris adhaerescere permittunt. Sed eas iubarum setas, quae frontibus imminent, aut equorum auriculas sinistra apprehendunt; atque dum equi, obstipis capitibus quiete inclinant (nam ad talem facilitatem, vt est eorum docilitas, a domitoribus finguntur) equites, etiam loricis aut sagis amicti, mira corporis agilitate, se efferunt, diuaricatisque cruribus, ephippia clitellis non dissimilia, subito occupant. Talis autem ascensio ita in eorum consuetudine versatur, vt non sit tam laudabile illud munus praestare, quam turpe non perficere." In his admiration Spenser seems to have forgotten what he wrote in *F. Q.* 2. 4. 1. 7-8:

chiefly skill to ride seemes a science
Proper to gentle blood.

2200-2. MORLEY. Stirrup, from stigan to mount, is sty-rope, rope to mount by. [For *sty* see *F. Q.* 1. 11. 25. 8.]

2214-20. TODD. See the note on *kern* [note on 2223-4].

MORLEY. *Gallowglas*, "galloglach," the heavy-armed Irish foot soldiers. Old Irish *géillus*, service, *giallaim*, I obey;—whence *gilla*, a servant (Highland *gillie*), a young man in the third of the six ages into which life was divided; —and perhaps *gleic*, wrestling, or *gluaisim*, I pass, move. But more probably the original division is gallog-lach, where lach is the common nominal ending, as in *lucht*, a part or division, *lucht-lach*, a party of people; *tegdas*, a house, *teglach*, the people of the house.

NED. Ir. and Gael. *gall-óglách*, f. *gall* foreigner, stranger + *óglách* youth, servant, warrior. The etymologically correct form *galloglach* appears later than the erroneous *galloglass*, which was prob. the result of the pl. *gallogl(gh)s*. ... The statement, made on etymological grounds by Spenser ..., that the "galloglasses" were originally English mercenaries, seems doubtful; *gall* is used of foreigners or strangers generally, and, although mainly applied to the English in Spenser's day, may not have been so restricted at the time when the compound was formed.

DRAPER (*MP* 17. 485). In general, however, Spenser seems correct as to the meaning of the word: it is a Celtic compound of *gall*, *foreign*, and *oglach*, *a youth*, *servant*, *warrior*.

RENWICK. The etymology is from Holinshed, VI, p. 132 [ed. of 1586, vol. II, *The Conquest of Ireland*, p. 7]: "There are in Ireland three sorts or degrees of soldiers: the first is the horsseman ... the second degree is the Kernaugh, and he also is a gentleman or a freeholder borne ... he is a light soldier on foot; his armor is both light and slender, being a skull, a left gantlet or a target, a sword and skeine, and three or four darts: the third degree is the Galloglasse, who was first brought in to this land by the Englishmen, and thereof taketh his name. For Galloglas is to saie, an English yeoman or serueant; his armor is a skull, a iacke, an habergeon or shirt of male, a sword and a sparre, otherwise named a Galloglasse ax or halbert ... These in all hostings haue attending vpon them a number of boies and kerne, and who doo spoile and kill all such as be ouerthrowne and hurt in the fields."

[See also Holinshed, vol. II, *The Description of Ireland*, p. 45; Dymmok, p. 7; Rich, *Description*, p. 37. Camden describes the wonder which the galloglasses of Shane O'Neill caused when he visited England in 1562: "quos Angli non minori tunc admiratione quam hodie Chinenses et Americanos prosequebantur" (*Annales*, p. 78).]

2218. "*Pedes gravis armaturae.*" "A heavy-armed foot soldier." The regular Latin phrase is *pedes levis armaturae*, a light-armed foot soldier. See Harris, Ware's *Works* 2. 161.

2223-4. TODD. The *kern* is the Irish *foot-soldier*; and is also employed in this sense by Shakespeare. See likewise Gainsford's *Glory of England*, 4to. 1618, p. 149. "The name of *Galliglas* is in a manner extinct, but of KERN in great reputation, as serving them [the Irish] in their revolts; and proving sufficient souldiers; but excellent for skirmish." Again, p. 150. "They [the Irish] are desperate in revenge; and their *kerne* thinke no man dead, vntill his head be off."

COLLIER. In "Macbeth," A. i. Sc. 2, we have both "kerns" and "gallowglasses." See also "Henry VI. Pt. 2," A. iv. Sc. 9.

MORLEY. *Kern*, the light-armed Irish foot soldier, carrying dart and skean; *cearn*, a man; *cern*, victory.

ROLAND SMITH (*JEGP* 42. 504). Ir. *ceithearnach* [soldier].

[For Elizabethan descriptions of the kern see Holinshed, vol. II, *The Description of Ireland*, p. 45; Stanyhurst, *De Rebvs*, p. 42; Dymmok, pp. 7-8; Rich, *Description*, p. 37.]

2230-6. Bale's description of the Irish soldiers (*The Vocacyon of Johan Bale*, 1553, f. 46ᵛ) will serve to represent many similar passages in Elizabethan writers: "Anon after their haruestes are ended there/ the Kearnes, the Galloglasses/ and the other brechelesse souldiers/ with horses and their horsegromes/ sumtyme. .iij. waitinge vpon one iade/ enter into the villages with muche crueltie and fearcenesse/ they continue there in great rauine and spoyle/ and whan they go thens/ they leaue nothinge els behinde them for payment/ but lice/ lecherye/ and intollerable penurie for all the yeare after." Stanyhurst (*De Rebvs*, p. 41) writes of the galloglasses: "Humanum apud illos nihil tam est, quam odium humanitatis." The kern are attacked by Derrick (sigs. D3ᵛ–D4ʳ, E3ʳ ff.) and Grey (State Papers 63. 78. 29, p. 6). Even for Ralegh the galloglasses and kern are "the ministers of all miseryes" (Edwards 2. 16).

2240-3. Similarly Sir Anthony St. Leger praised the Irish: "assuredly, I thinke for ther feate of warre, whiche ys for light scoorers, ther ar no properer horsemen in Christen grounde, nor more hardie, nor yet that can better indure hardenesse" (*State Papers, Henry VIII* 3. 444); and Stanyhurst commends the Irish soldier for the same qualities which Spenser describes (*De Rebvs*, pp. 52-3). The hardships endured by Despair in *F. Q.* 1. 9. 33-36 have been compared to those of the kern (Gray, *RES* 6. 426-8).

2243. "presente." *NED* (def. 4). Having the mind or thought directed to, intent upon, or engaged with what one is about.

2248. "pece." *NED* (def. 11. b). A portable fire-arm, hand gun.

2256-64. TODD. The reader, who would wish for all possible information on this point, cannot attain his object sooner than by consulting "Historical Memoirs of the Irish Bards, interspersed with anecdotes of, and occasional observations on, the Music of Ireland: by Joseph Cooper Walker, Esq. M. R. I. A." Dublin, 1786. I recommend also, as a proper accompaniment to this ingenious work, the *Reliques of Ancient Irish Poetry* by Miss Brooke.

EDITOR. Lucan's lines on the bards (see note on 1202-3) are quoted by both Camden and Buchanan, and Buchanan gives an account of the bards (*Britannia*, p. 14; *Historia*, lib. II, ff. 12ᵛ, 17ʳ); but Spenser can have learned little on this subject from written sources, and little is known today. The bards, originally inferior poets, first came into prominence with the disappearance of the druids in the fifth century; gradually they rose in the social scale until their poetry reached its height in the period immediately preceding the Anglo-Norman conquest; after 1250 there was a decline in spontaneity, though not in technical skill; an account of a late bardic school preserved in the Marquis of Clanricard's *Memoirs* (1744) reveals the almost sacerdotal care with which the poets were initiated in their art; but bards and bardic schools were dispersed by the Cromwellian wars, and by the eighteenth century the name could no longer be correctly applied to any (Hyde, pp. 239-50, 260, 486, 528-30; Eleanor Hull, *A Textbook of Irish Literature*, 1906, 1. 186-93, 2. 154-80; Eleanor Knott in O'Huiggin 1. xxxiii-xlv; Daniel Corkery, *The Hidden Ireland*, pp. 65-7).

2257-8. So it is explained in Holinshed (vol. II, *The Description of Ireland*, p. 45): "Greedie of praise they be, and fearefull of dishonor, and to this end they esteeme their poets, who write Irish learnedlie, and pen their sonets heroicall, for the which they are bountifullie rewarded; if not, they send out libels in dispraise, whereof the lords and gentlemen stand in great awe."

2258-61. According to one tale, when the poet Dallán had threatened to satirize King Mongan of Ulster for having given him the lie, the King offered half his land if the bard would hold his peace; but Dallán was satisfied only with Mongan's wife (Hyde, p. 411). As an example of bardic satire at the end of the sixteenth century see Tadhg Dall O'Huiggin's attack on William Burke (O'Huiggin 2. 112-4).

2261-4. Derrick (sig. F2ʳ) writes of an Irish feast:

> Now when their gutts be full,
> then comes the pastyme in:
> The Barde and Harper mellodie,
> vnto them doe beginne.

In *The Book of O'Connor Don* an Irish contemporary of Spenser's draws a more glowing picture of the same institution: "When seated on the smooth benches of their royal mansions, quaffing their noble banquets of wine, and their harsh, heady draughts; their royal countenances flushed and glowing, as they hearken to verses and poetic lays on their ancestors and forbears, eloquently uttered by declaimers and distinguished bards"; and O'Huiggin similarly describes a Christmas assemblage of bards in the house of Turlogh Luineach O'Neill (O'Huiggin 1. xl, 2. 34-7). See note on "Cossherie" in 1062.

2267-75. This theory, rightly or wrongly, has frequently been traced to Plato (see Allan H. Gilbert, *SP* 36. 1-19). When Spenser expresses the idea in *S. C.* (*Oct.* arg. and 19-24), E. K.'s gloss refers it to the first book of Plato's *Laws*, where there is nothing to the point (see variorum notes on *Oct.* 19-24 and Starnes, *SP* 41. 195). The educational value of poetry, which is a commonplace of Italian critics, is discussed at length by J. B. Giraldi Cinthio (*Hecatommithi*, 1574, vol. II, sigs. 36ʳ-37ᵛ); and the same passage is paraphrased by Spenser's friend Bryskett

(*A Discovrse of Civill Life*, 1606, p. 148). At a slightly earlier period young English critics—*e. g.*, Lodge, Sidney, and Webbe—emphasized the moral value of poetry as part of an effort to win respect for it from a reluctant public; and it is interesting to note that Spenser, while attacking the Irish bards, is careful to state his esteem for poetry as such. See also Hooker's glorification of the British, not the Irish, bards as teachers of virtue (Holinshed, vol. II, *The Conquest of Ireland*, sig. A2r).

2275-8. So Stephen Gosson (*The Shoole of Abuse*, 1579, sig. A7v) writes: "The right vse of auncient Poetrie was to haue the notable exploytes of worthy Captaines, the holesome councels of good fathers, and vertuous liues of predecessors set downe in numbers, and song to the instrument at solemne feastes.... After this maner were ... The *Lacedaemonians* instructed by *Tyrtaeus* verse." References to Tyrtaeus, the Greek poet of the seventh century B. C., occur in Lodge's reply to *The Shoole of Abuse*, in Sidney's *Apologie*, in Webbe's *Discourse of English Poetrie*, and in Puttenham's *Arte of English Poesie* (Gregory Smith 1. 75, 76-7, 152, 158, 234; 2. 18). In Arthur Golding's translation of Trogus Pompeius (*Thabridgment of the Histories*, 1564, book III, f. 23r) Tyrtaeus is also mentioned against the marginalium "The force of Poetrye."

2295-2311. GREENLAW (*MP* 9. 361). As to the bards, contemporary testimony is with Spenser as to the way in which they fomented strife.

EDITOR. Silken Thomas, the young Earl of Kildare who had rebelled in the time of Henry Eighth (see note on 586-7), had been instigated by a bard (Hyde, p. 492). Thomas Smith writes in 1561 (Maxwell, pp. 341-2): "Their first practice is, if they see any young man descended of the septs of O or Mac, and have half a dozen about him, then will they make him a rhyme, wherein they will commend his father and his ancestors, numbering how many heads they have cut off, how many towns they have burned ... and in the end they will compare them to Hannibal or Scipio or Hercules, or some other famous person; wherewithal the poor fool runs mad," etc. The evil influence of the bards is similar to that of the flatterers Bryskett describes (*A Discovrse of Civill Life*, 1606, p. 106). In his portrait of Sansloy (*F. Q.* 2. 2. 18. 3-8) Spenser may have had in mind the young outlaws of Ireland.

2309. "Bardes and rymers." See "wanton Bardes, and Rymers impudent" in *F. Q.* 3. 12. 5. 5.

2310-1. See *F. Q.* 6. 6. 24. 8.

2312-34. RENWICK. Not knowing Irish, I have consulted the erudite: but am told this description might cover many poems, and no one is identifiable.

EDITOR. Spenser's charges against the bards are supported by many English writers of the sixteenth and seventeenth century: for example, Sir Thomas Cusack (Bagwell 2. 65-6), Derrick (sig. F2r-v), Moryson (*Shakespeare's Europe*, p. 199), and Ware (*Works* 2. 126-7); but Hyde (p. 495) declares, after reading hundreds of Irish poems written during this period, that he found many which were intended to arouse patriotism, none which incited to plunder or extortion. Of patriotism there seems to be much in the bardic poems; see, *e. g.*, Angus

O'Daly's "Ode to the Milesians" (Hardiman 2. 280-5). But the "Ode" was preserved in *The Book of O'Byrne*, compiled for the same Feagh MacHugh the suppression of whose outlawry Spenser considers necessary to any settlement of peace (3616-3737); around Feagh and his family, in fact, gathered a whole group of bards, who shared the protection of Glenmalure with his marauders (Standish H. O'Grady and Robin Flower, *A Catalogue of Irish Manuscripts in the British Museum* 1. 498-514; Thomas O'Rahilly, *PRIA*, Archaeology 36. 87, 88-9, 94, 109). Many of the bardic poems that have survived are characterized by a love of destruction. During Tyrone's rebellion Eochaidh O hEoghasa writes to Hugh Maguire, then plundering the region from which Spenser and his family had been driven the year before: "Throughout white-mansioned Munster, courts stripped bare all round about them and themselves clad then in garb of glowing cinders shall (by the act of him that ravages the country of the Gael) abound. As the result of Maguire's circuit many a court on the face of the fair west country's westernmost grasslands is in ignition (the mischief is not new) and many's the territory reft of heir and even of great-grandson" (O'Grady and Flower, *op. cit.,* 1. 452). Tadhg Dall O'Huiggin, the greatest of the bards contemporary with Spenser, can persuade or praise humane conduct (2. 99-100, 168-9); but in his most spirited verses he urges Brian O'Rourke to destroy his enemies (*The Poem Book of the Gael*, ed. Eleanor Hull, pp. 170-1):

> By him be felled their rich fruit-bearing orchards,
> Each open highway clothed with ragged weeds;
> Long ere the harvest-hour their crops be scattered
> By his and Connaught's sons' death-dealing deeds.
>
> Leave hungry famine in Boyne's fertile borders,
> Fir of the spreading-boughs bend 'neath his smart,
> So that a mother on Meath's richest pastures
> Shall munch the morsel of her first child's heart.

See also *A Miscellany of Irish Bardic Poetry*, ed. Lambert McKenna, 2. 13, 2. 92; Quiggin, pp. 115-6.

2319-20. Laoiseach Mac an Bhaird, an Irish bard of the sixteenth century, wrote in praise of Eóghan Bán, "He has no longing for a feather bed, he had rather lie upon rushes" (Maxwell, p. 351).

2320. "slugginge." See *F. Q.* 2. 1. 23. 3, 3. 7. 12. 8.

2320-3. To illustrate the boast there is the description of how Rory Og burnt Naas (Holinshed, vol. II, *The Supplie of the Irish Chronicles*, p. 148): "He in the dead night came to the towne with all his companie, who like vnto a sort of furies and diuels new come out of hell, carried vpon the ends of their poles flankes of fier, and did set as they went the low thatched houses on fier. And the wind being then somewhat great and vehement, one house tooke fier of another, and so in a trise and moment the whole towne was burned; and yet in the towne supposed to be fiue hundred persons in outward appearance, able to haue resisted them: but they being in their dead sleeps, suddenlie awaked, were so amazed, that they wist not what to doo, for the fier was round about them and past quenching, and to pursue the enimie they were altogither vnfurnished, and durst not to doo it, neither if they would they could tell which way to follow him. For he taried verie little in the towne, sauing that he sat a little while vpon the crosse in the market place, and beheld how the fire round about him was in euerie house kindled, and whereat he made great ioy and triumph, that he had doone and exploited so diuelish an act."

2323-5. In 1590 one of the Burkes "abashed not to say to Theobald Dillon, he would for one full year lie every night with his shirt under his wife's head" (*C. S. P. Ir. 1588-1592* 150. 21).

2332-4. In the thirteenth century Giolla Mac Conmidhe received as much as twenty cows for a poem; Tadhg Óg O'Huiggin speaks of the same reward in the fifteenth; at a later period the value of estates allotted to the literati of Tyrconnell amounted annually to some two thousand pounds in modern money (Eleanor Hull, *A Textbook of Irish Literature*, 1906, 1. 215, 2. 155; see also Daniel Corkery, *The Hidden Ireland*, pp. 72-3, and *A Miscellany of Irish Bardic Poetry*, ed. Lambert McKenna, 2. 11). In Spenser's time Tadhg Dall O'Huiggin writes that for one poem he was paid with a dappled steed, a hound, a precious book, and a magic harp (2. 122-3). George Sigerson goes so far as to say (*Bards of the Gael and the Gall*, p. 72), "Had Spenser been an Irish bard, in even a small principality, he would not have died of starvation, but have lived in high honour, with wealth sufficient to tempt confiscation."

2338-9. Henley (pp. 16, 103) suggests that Tadhg, the bard of his unfriendly neighbor Lord Roche, may have assisted Spenser in the study of Irish poetry. Spenser's present statement reveals his interest in Irish poetry rather than his familiarity with it.

2339. "swete witt." See *F. Q.* 3. 11. 32. 3. By *wit* Spenser seems to mean *knowledge* or *learning*.

2340. "invencion." A standard rhetorical term for the "searchyng out of thynges true, or thynges likely, the whiche maie reasonably sette furth a matter, and make it appere probable" (Thomas Wilson, *The Arte of Rhetorique*, 1553, f. 3ᵛ).

2340. "ornamentes." Spenser may have written "argumentes" (see the reading "ornamentes" for "argumentes" in the Rawlinson MS at 2286). Poems which lack "goodlie ornamentes" are not "sprinkled with some prettie flowers"; as Puttenham (f. 115ʳ) says, "This ornament we speake of is giuen to it by figures and figuratiue speaches, which be the flowers as it were and coulours that a Poet setteth vpon his language of arte."

2341. HENLEY (pp. 101-3) suggests that the "prettie flowers" were the sound effects of Irish poetry. [See also Winstanley's note on *F. Q.* 2. 12. 32. But since Spenser had to have Irish poems translated for him, it is unlikely that he refers to the sound effects of the original; probably he has in mind the metaphors and similes which are the most outstanding feature of bardic poetry in translation.]

2342-4. Spenser's observation provoked Standish O'Grady to write: "Reasonable enough from the Spenserian standpoint: Edmund's own Virtue was in or about 1580 beautified and adorned with a grant of 3000 acres in the county Cork" (*A Catalogue of Irish Manuscripts in the British Museum* 1. 341).

2344-5. See the punishment Mercilla metes out to a lewd poet in *F. Q.* 5. 9. 25. 2-9. From 1415 on, a series of statutes and governmental orders was issued against the bards: see, *e. g.*, Eleanor Hull, *A Textbook of Irish Literature*, 1906, 1. 199; *Calendar of the Patent and Close Rolls* 1. 486-7; *C. C. MSS. 1515-1574*, pp. 214-5, 410. But English officials, Sir George Carew and Sir John Perrot, for example, occasionally took the wiser course of hiring Irish bards to write for the government (Hyde, pp. 476-8; anonymous *History of Sir John Perrott*, p. 312); and at least one Irish poem in praise of Elizabeth has been preserved (Standish O'Grady and Robin Flower, *A Catalogue of Irish Manuscripts in the British Museum* 1. 545).

2345-60. Rich notes of horseboys (*Description*, p. 37): "as in *England* we cal them hors-keepers, so in *Ireland* he carries the name but of a horse boy how yong or old soeuer." Sir William Gerrard reported to the Privy Council in 1577-1578 (*Analecta Hibernica* 2. 117): "I told their Honnors the great harme of horseboyes, who comonly came from the Irisherie, and after they were growen able for the swoord they retorned to the Irishe. Theise knewe I sayd all partes of the pale, and ar readye to be guydes to everye spoyle, and as they be charge to the pale whiles they be horseboyes, and conveyers of their goodes whiles they be kerne: so if they in the warrs be maymed or becomme blinde, they contynue to the end to a lyke charge in begginge, and under that coulor ar knowen especially to the rebells." Two horseboys customarily accompanied each horseman (*State Papers, Henry VIII* 3. 444).

2346 n. ROLAND SMITH (*JEGP* 42. 503). *Cuille* [as Additional MS 22022 is read by Morris] is doubtless intended by Spenser for Ir. *giolla* (or *giolla na n-eich*), "horseboy." [Since the Additional MS is an unreliable text and this reading appears in none of the other manuscripts, it is doubtful that Spenser included the Irish term.]

2352. "frye." See E. K.'s gloss on *S. C. Oct.* 14.

2353. "rakehellye." TODD. These *base* or *outcast* horseboys. Fr. *racaille*. See also *F. Q.* v. xi. 44. Gabriel Harvey calls Greene "a *rakehell*, a makeshift, etc." *Foure Letters*, etc. 1592, Sign. A. 2. b. [See *S. C.*, Dedicatory Epistle, section 17.]

2360-9. SOUTHEY (p. 211). This breed exists still.

MORLEY. *Carrows. Cor* in old Irish was a throw, as of dice, or a curved movement, as in dealing round of cards.

ROLAND SMITH (*JEGP* 42. 503). Ir. *cearrbhach* [gambler].

EDITOR. "There is among them a brotherhood of karrowes," writes Stanyhurst, "that proffer to plaie at cards all the yeare long, and make it their onelie occupation. They plaie awaie mantle and all to the bare skin, and then trusse themselues in straw or leaues, they wait for passengers in the high waie, inuite them to game vpon the greene, and aske no more but companions to make them sport. For default of other stuffe, they pawne their glibs, the nailes of their

COMMENTARY 361

fingers and toes, their dimissaries, which they leese or redeeme at the courtesie of the winner" (Holinshed, vol. II, *The Description of Ireland*, p. 45; after Campion, pp. 19-20). See also Rich, *Description*, p. 38; Moryson, *Shakespeare's Europe*, p. 199.

JENKINS (*PMLA* 53. 358) suggests that Brian Carthy, called Brian of the Cards, may have been in Spenser's mind in describing the carrows.

2369-73. Joyce points out that the old Brehon Law looked with disfavor on jesters, buffoons, and montebanks (*Social History* 2. 481-7). "Skelaghes," or story-tellers, were forbidden to come among the English by the *Kilkenny Statute* (pp. 54-7); and Sir John Davies writes of "News-tellers" in the seventeenth century (*Discoverie*, p. 177).

2377-82. RENWICK. This story was quoted recently in an Irish newspaper as still a good and apposite joke. ["Idlenesse, together with feare of iminent mischiefes, which did continually hang ouer their heads, haue bin the cause, that the Irish wer euer the most inquisitiue people after newes, of any Nation in the world" (Davies, *Discoverie*, p. 176).]

2383-7. The treaty which the Queen made with the Earl of Desmond in 1563 puts the control of "rhymers, bards, and dice players, called carroghes," up to the overlords of the districts where they are found (*Calendar of the Patent and Close Rolls* 1. 486); but the severer measure of subjecting them to martial law was proposed by Perrot in 1582 and commanded by the Munster Council in 1603 (E. C. S., sig. C3ᵛ; *Council Book of the Corporation of Kinsale*, ed. Richard Caulfield, p. 303).

2385 n. "*Mona-shules.*" TODD. This is the manuscript reading, and is correct. See *Mona-shul* in [1632]. The printed copies read *Mona-shutes*. *Shuler*, I am told, is a common name for a wandering beggar in Ireland. [Todd's reading seems to come from the Ellesmere MS, to which he had access; but he has added an *s* at the end. See note on 1632.]

"morashites." MORLEY. Men of the morasses or bogs, bog-trotters.

2390-2403. These assemblies were held in part for the enactment of laws (Harris 1. 51). Hooker, like Spenser, emphasizes the treacherous character of the meetings (Holinshed, vol. II, *The Conquest of Ireland*, p. 27): "lightlie and most commonlie there are most treacheries and treasons, most murthers and robberies, and all wickednesse imagined, deuised, and afterwards put in practise among them: and for the most part there is no parlee among them, whereof insueth not some mischeefe." In 1593 it is reported that certain Ulster chieftains and a Catholic bishop have taken a traitorous oath upon a hilltop (*C. S. P. Ir. 1592-1596* 170. 23. 13). One of the articles which the Irish Council imposed upon Sir John O'Reilly in 1584 was that he should "not assemble the Queen's people upon hills, or use any Iraghtes or parles upon hills" (Hardiman 2. 159).

2391. DRAPER (*MP* 17. 485). *Rathe*, also, is a purely Celtic word. Spenser says it means *hill*, and uses it referring to those walled mounds which the ancient inhabitants of Ireland used as fortresses. Spenser seems to have gotten the erroneous sense of *hill* from the fact that these forts were usually upon a barrow or some slight elevation. The ascription to the Danes is noted in NED. as incorrect; and indeed Spenser seems partly responsible for the compounding of the word which has enshrined this bit of pseudo-antiquity in our language. [See 2424.]

RENWICK. Cf. O'Donovan's note in his edition of the Four Masters, vol. V, 1788: "The Oireactas, *anglice* Iraghts, was a meeting, or conference, held by the Irish on hills for the purpose of deliberating about their public affairs, and which frequently ended in a fight."

ROLAND SMITH (*JEGP* 42. 505). Ir. *ráth* [*fort* or *barrow*].

[The Irish word for a meeting-hill was *tulach*; for the meeting itself, *airecht* (Joyce, *Social History* 2. 449).]

2402 n. "tagge." RENWICK (*View*, pp. 326-7). I have preserved [this reading], as it may have some value: I take it to mean *caught by the loose locks of wool*; which is much more striking than the colourless phrase of the rest.

2405. TODD. *Bawn* is evidently used by Spenser for an *eminence*. Of its etymology our lexicographers give no account.

COLLIER. Yet see Richardson's Dict. v. *bawn*, where he shows it to mean a habitation. *Bauen* is "to build" in German.

MORLEY. *Bawns*, high places. "Ban" as in Ban-gor, the high choir; Pan Down, near Carisbrooke.

ROLAND SMITH (*JEGP* 42. 502). Ir. *badhbh-dhún*. . . . For a discussion of seventeenth-century bawns, see *Ulster Journ. of Archaeol.* VI, 125 ff.

[A *bawn* is a fortified enclosure (*NED*). See Thomas Churchyard, *A Generall Rehearsall of Warres*, 1579, sig. Eij^r; Holinshed, vol. II, *The Description of Ireland*, p. 11.]

2408-10. See 2418-20 and note.

2418-20. WARE. *vid. D. Hen. Spelmanni Glossarium* [*Archaeologvs*, p. 314, where, however, *folkmote* is defined as a meeting, not a place of meeting].

COLLIER. Junius gives the etymology of "folk" as A. S. *fylgan*, to follow.

DRAPER (*MP* 17. 473). He derives it correctly from the "Saxon." The obvious source is the OE *folc-mot*, defined in NED. as "a general assembly of a town, city or shire." It appears in OE as a compound of *folc* (*people, nation, army*) and (*ge-*) *mōt* (*meeting, assembly, council*). It is not surprising that Spenser knew at least the meaning of this [term, for it] must have survived in at least occasional legal use down to his own day.

EDITOR. Spenser's etymology may be derived from William Lambard (Αρχαιονομια, 1568, sig. B4r): "*Conuentus* ex omni Satrapia, *Saxonice gemote*, a *gemettan*, quod est conuenire. Id alias *folcgemote* (praeposito *folc* quod populum significat) . . . nuncupatur." Spenser's confusion of the meeting with the place of meeting (he calls the folkmotes *hills* in 2405-10, 2416-7) seems to stem from a confusion of *folkmote*, of which he gives the correct etymology, with *mote*

COMMENTARY 363

from OF *mote*, a *mound, eminence, hill, barrow, tumulus* (*NED*, def. 1, 2); Ireland contains numerous mound fortifications known as *motes* (*JRSAI* 35. 402-6, 37. 123-52). See also *F. Q.* 4. 4. 6. 1.

2422-38. In the eighteenth century Harris noted that the Daneraths were really funeral mounds and fortifications erected before the arrival of the Danes (Ware, *Works* 2. 135-9). The name *Danerath* itself is perhaps of no earlier origin than the *View* (see note on 2391 and *NED* under *rath*).

2426-7. WARE. The like reason may be given for the making of such *Rathes* in *Ireland*, by the *Danes* or *Norwegians. vid. Gir. Cambr. topog. Hib. distinct.* 3. *cap.* 37.

2439-40. Camden describes such a battle monument which the Danes built at Ashdown in Essex (*Britannia*, pp. 351-2); the passage immediately following this description in the editions of 1590 and 1594, it is interesting, concerns Saffron Walden, the home of Gabriel Harvey. See *Am.* 69. 1-4.

2440-7. RENWICK. Holinshed [vol. I, *The Description of Britaine*, p. 124; *The Historie of England*, p. 84] and Camden [*Britannia*, pp. 183-4] cite the tradition that Stonehenge is the burial-place of Ambrosius Aurelius. Camden, speaking of Selbury, says further: " Many of that sort, round and with sharpe toppes are to bee seene in this tract: *Burrowes* they call them and *Barrowes*, raised, happily in memoriall of Soldiers there slaine. For . . . read I have, how an usuall thing it was with the Northerne nations, that everie soldier remaining alive after a foughten field, should carrie his head-peece full of earth toward the making of their fellowes tombes that were slaine." The like is also in Lambarde's *Kent*, and in Olaus Magnus.

EDITOR. In *F. Q.* 2. 10. 66. 6-9 Spenser describes Stonehenge as a group of such monuments for three hundred British lords slain by Hengist. For a similar custom among the ancient Scots see Holinshed, vol. II, *The Description of Scotland*, p. 21. Spenser may also have been familiar with the ancient Irish custom of marking single graves with raths and raising carns, or piles of stones, where a battle had been fought, each stone symbolizing a dead warrior, according to one tale (Joyce, *Social History* 2. 554-62, 577-8; O'Curry 1. cccxxxv-cccxxxix). A group of monoliths near Macroomp in Co. Cork are said to have been erected in memory of a battle fought between Brian Boru and the O'Mahonys of Carbery (Charles Smith, *The Ancient and Present State of the County and City of Cork*, 1815, 1. 178-9).

2444. RIEDNER (pp. 6-7) finds only Joshua 4. 5 and 4. 20 among the " manye places" in the Bible.

RENWICK. The scriptural reference is to *Joshua*, iv., and to places in *Genesis*.

2451-3. MORLEY. *Trevett*, trivet, a three-legged support; alike with tripod, but the *p* has undergone the same change that turned *pod* into *foot*.

EDITOR. For the Welsh *tribedd*, or tripod, stones see *NED* (*trivet*, def. 4); also " trebedd " in William Salesbury's *Dictionary in Englyshe and Welshe*,

1547, reprinted 1877. The giants were supposed to be the earliest inhabitants of Britain (for example, in *F. Q.* 2. 10. 7-9); and Giraldus Cambrensis describes, if not the trivets, the so-called dances or circles of the giants in Ireland (*Topographia Hibernica* 2. 18). Spenser may have in mind Camden's refusal to believe in the circles of the giants as reported by Giraldus (*Britannia*, p. 698).

2461.   Herodotus (4. 71) describes the burial mounds of the Scythian kings.

2481-99.   MORLEY. *Cess*, assessment, with *c* written for *s* in "sess."

DRAPER (*MP* 17. 473). Whether Spenser considered *cesse* an Irish word is doubtful. . . . In the first illustration [2483-90] it appears to mean *billet*, and in the second [2490-9], *tax*. . . . The sense of *billet* may easily have been derived in England or Ireland from the essential and original idea of *tax* or *imposition*. Spenser, so far as he goes, seems to be correct. It is worth noting, furthermore, that, in this sense of *billet*, the word seems to combine the meaning of the Irish *coygnye* and the Romance *liverye*.

EDITOR. Spenser does not observe the *billet-tax* distinction. The first kind of cess he describes [2483-90] consists in billeting the soldiers on the country, but the second [2490-9] consists in "ymposinge" provisions, *i. e.*, buying them for the governor's household or for the soldiers at a fixed rate, the so-called "Queen's Price." *Cess* in this second sense is thoroughly explained by Hooker and Gerrard (Holinshed, vol. II, *The Supplie of the Irish Chronicles*, p. 144; *Analecta Hibernica* 2. 104). When a direct tax replaces either form of cess, Spenser calls it a *composition* (as in 2493).

2491.   An account of the food stuffs consumed by the household of Lord Deputy Sidney has been left by Gerrard; and in the household accounts of Lord Deputy FitzWilliam there are surprisingly large expenditures for food (*Analecta Hibernica* 2. 146, 4. 301-12). The item was an important one in the budget.

2493-4.   A direct tax or composition, as an alternative to cess, was proposed by Sir Henry Sidney in 1577 and adopted for Connaught in 1585, for Munster in 1592 (*Letters and Memorials* 1. 224; *C. C. MSS. 1575-1588*, pp. 405-6, and *1589-1600*, pp. 63-71; *C. S. P. Ir. 1592-1596* 167. 8. 1). Spenser probably refers to the Munster composition as "latelye" instituted.

2500-17.   RENWICK. There are innumerable complaints, not only from Irish and English-Irish, but from officials. A "Declaration of the present state of the English Pale" (B. M., *Titus* xii, 99) complains of soldiers "placinge them selves at their pleasures exactinge meate and drinke far more then competente and Comonly money for them, their Boyes women and Followers much excedinge the peoples habilitye . . . And if they be not satisfyed with meate and money accordinge to their outragious Demandes then do they beate their poore hostes and their people Ransackinge their house." For specific cases, see *S. P. Ir.*, 144. 56, 3; 145. 27, and many orders for restraint of such abuse; also 94. 92, a warrant for execution of certain soldiers for this cause. William Lyon, then Bishop of Ross and Carbery, and certainly at least an acquaintance of Spenser, gives details: "Moreover for the disorder of the Soldiours amonges the people which bredeth great hatred to our nacion, and not without cause. This I can report of my self, for the

COMMENTARY 365

tyme that I lay in Cork . . . the Soldiors that lie there . . . haue horseboyes which goe out into the Contrey . . . and fetche in horse loades of Corne of the pore people day by day, they havinge no other sustenance to releive them and their famelies then their little Corne, about which they haue taken great paynes and travell, and yf they comme to rescue yt from the horseboyes, they fall vpon them, and beate them, and cut them in the heades most lamentable to see. Then comme they and Complayne to the Maior of the Cytie and shewe hym their hurtes: his aunswer is this, you must haue patience for I cannot remedie yt, and yt is true in deede for they esteme no more of the Maior then a man will doe of his horseboy, and their wordes are theis to the Maior, and the best of the towne. Ye are but Beggers, Rascalles, and Traytors, and I am a soldiour and a gentleman. And also I haue sene the poore people come with their heddes cutt, before Sir Warham St leger knight, and my self complaynynge of their grefe, but the soldiors haue Conveyed them selves and their boyes out of the way, for they are lawlesse, and I thinke in Conscience (speakinge yt with grefe of hart) emonges the heathen there is no suche wicked soldiors." (Oct. 9, 1582. *S. P. Ir.* 96. 10 ii)

EDITOR. See also *C. C. MSS. 1589-1600*, pp. 175, 261; Thomas Churchyard, *A Generall Rehearsall of Warres* (*Churchyardes Choise*), 1579, sig. Ee1^r. But Sir Henry Sidney, whom Churchyard addresses, was a staunch defender of cess (Holinshed, vol. II, *The Supplie of the Irish Chronicles*, p. 145; *C. C. MSS. 1575-1588*, pp. 58-64); his son Philip saw in it the only alternative to a thorough conquest (*Works*, ed. Albert Feuillerat, 1911-1926, 3. 48-9); Lord Chancellor Gerrard brought together much historical evidence to justify its use (*Analecta Hibernica* 2. 93-291); and when cess had been abolished in Munster, Chief Justice Saxey lamented that the soldiers were not still charged upon the Irish in order to hold them from rebellion (*C. S. P. Ir. 1598-1599* 202. 3. 127).

2509. Aqua vitae, the Irish *usquebaugh*, *i. e.*, whiskey, was already regarded as an unfortunate invention, for in 1571 Perrot stringently limited its manufacture in Munster (*C. C. MSS. 1515-1574*, p. 411); but Camden explains that the Irish product is superior to the English and that in Ireland it is used against dysentery and colds (*Britannia*, pp. 679-80).

2521-7. See 2961-9.

2522-5. Sir William Herbert uses a similar figure to express a similar idea (*C. S. P. Ir. 1586-1588* 135. 59).

2528-84. RENWICK. Another commonplace. Sir Richard Grenville, writes to Walsingham, 14th Oct., 1589, mentions "the Inconveniences that do growe by the vncerteyne course that the Lordes and Captaines holde in settinge their Landes to their Tenantes, who hold the same not above 4 yeares, and so wander from one place to another, which course being redressed, and they comaunded to sett their Landes as the vndertakers muste doe, wold do muche good to breede Cyvilitie generally, in the Countrey. For wheras nowe the poore man is never certaine to enioye the fruites of his owne labour, and knoweth not in certeyne what his Lorde will haue of him. For feare, he must depende on him and followe all his actions be they good or badde, where otherwais, if the poore Tenaunte held his lande by lease for his lief or for xxi yeares, at a certeyne rente then were he sure of his charge and that the overplus were his owne, So wold he depende on her Maiestie and her Lawes to be defended againste the oppressions which nowe too comonly every lorde vsethe." So also Bryskett, 92. 29 [in 1582; see Plomer and Cross, p. 38], declares he had warrant to hold certain disputed lands, "and to take the best order I could for preserving them from lyeing wast, which in this countrey is a thing sone brought to passe and comonly sene, onlesse great dilligence be vsed in keping the tenauntes at May, who never have but one yeres estate in their farmes, and are free to departe every yere if the list." In Dec., 1598, Justice Saxey of Munster reports that the Churl "by whom the Lord and cheiffe gentleman doth live, is apt to followe his Lord in all Rebellion and Mischeife, And the reason thereof is, That the Irish Tenantes have theire estate but from yeare to yeare, or at moste for three yeares, In regard of which short and weake state, they have not any care to make any strong or defensible houses or buildinges, to plant or to enclose . . . they possesse nothinge which they maye not with ease Carrye or Drive awaye or convert into money." The remedy is that leases be for at least 21 years or three lives, with all rents and services agreed and recorded in writing, "And then the Tenauntes would be encouraged to build strongly, to plant and to enclose," and would not follow his lord easily into mischief. (MS *Titus* B. xii, fol. 92 vo. [also *C. S. P. Ir. 1598-1599* 202. 4. 9. 1]) So also an anonymous *S. P. Ir.* 79. 55: "It were very Necessary by Order to Constraine euery Lord when he letteth his Land to let the same by writing or before Sufficient Wittnesses publiquely, at which time he should [declare?] all the Covenants of their Agreement beyond which he should by noe means exact vpon a Penalty, also that he should demise the same, for a Terme, as for years or Lives whereby the Tennant might be incouraged to build a Dwelling house in some decent order, where now they Live brutishly all in a Cott or rather a Stye, more like beasts then men. And thus the Lords Revenue, and the Tennants Wealth would be certaine, and he comforted to proceed in his Industrious Labours, when he might hope to enjoy of Benefitt thereof." So also others.

EDITOR. See also *C. S. P. Ir. 1592-1596* 171. 21; Dymmok, p. 5; Tremayne, p. 2; E. S., ff. 17^v, 23^v; E. C. S., sig. C3^{r-v}. Spenser's picture of the Irish land system is necessarily inaccurate and incomplete. He overlooks the class of *freeman* tenants, who shared in the lands of their tribes and owned their buildings (*Ancient Laws of Ireland* 2. xlvi-liii, 194-341; O'Curry 1. clxxxviii-cxc; Joyce, *Social History* 2. 195-6); he limits his description to the *fuidir* class, who did not belong to the tribes whose lands they rented, and he confuses the true fuidir, who rented at the will of the chieftain, with the peasant who rented from year to year in order to avoid any permanent obligation of this kind (O'Curry 1. cxxv-cxxvii). Sir John Davies, writing shortly after Spenser, blames the oppression of the tenantry on the Elizabethan policy of surrender and regrant, which gave the largest landholders a royal warrant for their property at the same time that their tenants had no official authorization (*Discoverie*, pp. 273-6); and it has even been said that the English themselves introduced tenants-at-will in order to facilitate the seizure of land (Green, *Ériu* 3. 174-85).

2536. "Coynie and liverye." See notes on 1039-54.

2542. To *hover* is to *linger* or *hesitate*. See *F. Q.* 3. 10. 23. 2.

COMMENTARY 367

2546-8. An anonymous writer later pointed out that the rebellion of 1598 was partly caused by the absolute power of the Irish landlords over their tenants (Chambrun MS, Folger Shakespeare Library, f. 236^v).

2567-8. "hansome." MORLEY. Handy, convenient.

2570. "fine." NED (def. 7. a). *Feudal Law.* A fee (as distinguished from the rent) paid by the tenant or vassal to the landlord on some alteration of the tenancy, as on the transfer or alienation of the tenant-right, etc.

2575-9. So Andrew Trollope writes in 1581: "at night the Mr., Mrs., or dame, men servants, women servants, gesse [guests], strangers, and all, lye in one lytle rometh not so good or hansume as many a hoggescote in England" (*C. S. P. Ir. 1574-1585* 85. 39). William Lithgow describes the Irish farmhouses a generation later (*The Rare Adventures and Painefull Peregrinations*, 1906, p. 374): "There Fabrickes are advanced three or foure yardes high, Pavillion-like incircling, erected in a singular Frame, of smoake-torne straw, greene long prick'd truff, and Raine-dropping watles. Their several Roomes of Palatiat divisions, as Chambers, Halls, Parlors, Kitchins, Barnes, and Stables, are all inclosed in one, and that one (perhaps) in the midst of a Mire; where, when in foule weather, scarcely can they finde a drye part, whereupon to Repose, their cloud-baptized heads." These cabins, according to Gainsford (pp. 147-8), are "wonde with rods, and couered with turffs, as well as they can, bringing their cattle euen within their houses, lying altogether in one roome both to preuent robberies of *Kern*, and spoile by Wolues." Spenser himself had already described an Irish hovel in *F. Q.* 3. 7. 6. 1-3.

2583. "Lewre." JOSEPH WRIGHT (*English Dialect Dictionary*, 1923). LURE, *sb.*² Sc. ... The udder of a cow or other animal.

NED notes the term is now obsolete except in Scotland.

2588-98. In 1596 Bishop William Lyon wishes "that it might please Her Majesty that order may be taken, that no lord, gentleman, or freeholder, let his land but for 21 years, and to condition with his tenants to enclose with quickset and ditch such portion of land as he shall take by lease, according to his ability, every year a portion, and to make lanes, and gates in the lanes, whereby, if any rebellion or spoiling be, they shall not be able to carry away the prey suddenly, but that they shall be met withal" (*C. S. P. Ir. 1596-1597* 191. 8. 1). At the same time Lyon discusses the deplorable state of religion, the subject to which Spenser immediately turns (see 2614-21 and note); it is possible that the poet and the bishop had talked over these subjects before Spenser left Ireland in 1595 or 1596.

2590. "empeachement." MORLEY. Hindrance.

2609-10. See *F. Q.* 4. 2. 34. 3.

2612. "it selfe beinge but one." It will be remembered that in *F. Q.* 1 the name of Una, or Truth, means *One*.

2614-21. RENWICK. This has more bearing on our notion of Spenser. His complaint is not so much that the Irish are Papists, as that they are not even good Papists. This is somewhat the attitude of William Lyon, who says, writing to

Hunsdon, July 6, 1596: "A great part of the people of this kingdom are no better than mere infidels, having but a bare name of Christians, without any knowledge of Christ or light of his truth, in that I myself have examined divers of them, being sixty years of age and upwards, and have found them not able to say the Lord's Prayer, or the articles of the Christian faith, neither in English, Latin, nor Irish." (*Cal. S. P. Ir.*, 191. 8.) [See also Hooker's attack in Holinshed, vol. II, *The Supplie of the Irish Chronicles*, p. 140. Tremayne (p. 4), like Spenser, is willing to grant Catholicism some credit for fostering a kind of religion, at the same time that he attacks the irreligion of the Irish Catholics.]

2628. The dwelling of Até is "Hard by the gates of hell" in *F. Q.* 4. 1. 20. 1.

2633-7. COVINGTON (*UTB*, Studies in English 4. 28-9) believes that Spenser's account of Patrick follows that in Holinshed.

RENWICK. This is (more or less) Camden's version: Holinshed rightly states that Palladius left Ireland before his death.

EDITOR. In Holinshed (vol. II, *The Description of Ireland*, p. 53) it is said that Palladius was transferred to Scotland before his death, and it is probable that Spenser has in mind the version of Camden (*Britannia*, p. 683); but Camden specifically says, on the authority of Nennius, that Palladius died in Britain. It is worth noting that one of the ancient lives of Palladius does say that he was martyred in Ireland (*Catholic Encyclopedia*). Cf. James Ussher, *Britannicarum Ecclesiarvm Antiquitates* [1639], pp. 798-814; *The History of the Church of Ireland*, ed. Walter A. Phillips, 1. 77-103, 376-8.

2640-1. See Revelation 17. 1-4. The Whore of Babylon is the subject of *Th. W.* son. 13; and Spenser again describes her in the form of Duessa in *F. Q.* 1. 7. 16-18. The cup of fornication may likewise have suggested the cup which Excess holds in *F. Q.* 2. 12. 56.

2651-2. See Revelation 22. 1. *Th. W.* son. 10, reworked as *Bel.* 2 son. 12, deals with the River of Life; and it will be remembered that Red Cross is restored in *F. Q.* 1. 11. 29-30 by falling into the Well of Life.

2674-7. Machiavelli develops the same theme: "dove sono l'armi e non Religione, con difficoltà si puo introdurre quella" (*Discorsi sopra la Prima Deca di Tito Livio* 3. 11). The phrase "quiett times" may also reflect Machiavelli's famous observation that the flood of Fortune can be withstood only by the construction of dikes and canals "quando sono tempi quieti" (*Il Principe*, cap. 25).

2686-98. JONES (*Spenser's Defense*, p. 184) points out the similarity of this idea to Bodin's theory (*République* 1. 1) that the first duty of the Republic is to provide the necessities of life. [See the converse observation in *B. N.* 332-3.]

2688-95. See Osgood's note on *F. Q.* 2. 11. 20-23.

2694. "recured." MORLEY. Recovered.

2706-22. RENWICK. *S. P. Ir.* 160. 4. 1 consists of 20 pages of such charges, backed by depositions, against Myler Magrath, Archbishop of Cashel. There are

COMMENTARY 369

others in addition; but Magrath held his see 51 years. Cf. 165. 32, against Loftus of Dublin, probably by Barnaby Riche. Hanmer's character in England, before he became Archdeacon of Cork, was bad; and there is only too much other evidence. Cf. *Cal. Carew MSS*, 1579, 203; and *Cal. S. P. Ir.* 131. 64. *S. P. Ir.* 79. 55 remarks " Altho for the most parte the Incumbentes are vnlearned, yet might they be Inforced to read the Lords Prayer, and the Beleife in Inglish " And Sir Edward Phyton, (130. 55): "The Churchmen collect their tythes with most rygor and neyther give foode temporall nor spirituall as is reported." Most of the complaints come from laymen: the clergy content themselves with demanding High Commission Courts.

EDITOR. Sir Henry Sidney (*Letters and Memorials* 1. 25) even doubted if the Anglican clergy christened the children in Ireland, and he attacked the corruption of the Irish Church in a preamble to an act of Parliament in 1569 (Richard Mant, *A History of the Church of Ireland*, 1840, 1. 286). See also William Lithgow, *The Rare Adventures and Painefull Peregrinations*, 1906, pp. 378-9.

2709-22. Spenser probably had an intimate knowledge of Irish priests: while William Lyon was Bishop of Cork, Cloyne, and Ross, he reported that a William McDermott had been deprived of the vicarage of Kilcolman four months earlier (Carte Manuscripts in the Bodleian Library, vol. 55, f. 584ᵛ); this may be the layman William Sheyne, vicar of Clonfert and Kilcolman, who was deprived in 1591 "propter defectum sacrorum et manifestum contumacium" (MS. E. 3. 14, Trinity College, Dublin, as reported by W. Maziere Brady, *Clerical and Parochial Records of Cork, Cloyne, and Ross*, Dublin, 1863-1864, 2. 248-9). Sheyne's predecessor John William Y Rhuwden, appointed 2 July, 1584, was a " scholar," *i. e.*, something less than a cleric (Brady, *loc. cit.*).

2716-7. Public services in English were held for the first time in Ireland at Christ Church Cathedral, Dublin, on Easter, 1551; at the same period the English *Prayerbook* was introduced, but the act of 1560 which established its use in Ireland provided that the new services might be said in Latin by priests ignorant of English (J. T. Ball, *The Reformed Church of Ireland, 1537-1889*, pp. 36, 56-7). Latin itself was not understood by many of the English and understood to only a small extent by many of the Irish (*C. S. P. Ir. 1598-1599* 202. 4. 57). In 1615 E. S. (f. 16ᵛ) writes: "these Preistes for the moste part, being men vtterly vnlearned, and knowing no part of the function, but the name, and to runne over a short masse in false lattin (and that without booke) many of them beinge not able soe muche as to read, the *Romaine* custome of secrecy in the *Sacrament* is aswell, as the Romayne languadge vnknowne to them."

2725-39. Miler Magrath, the outstanding example of the corruptness of the Irish bishops, held twenty benefices in his own hands, and twenty-six more belonged to his relatives, many of them Catholics (see note on 2706-22; Bagwell 2. 360, 3. 465 and 468-9; John T. Gilbert, pp. 180-1; Ware, *Works* 1. 539; *C. S. P. Ir. 1588-1592* 160. 28). Shane O'Neill's horsemen composed the greater part of the Armagh Cathedral chapter (Bagwell 2. 355); and Sir John Davies writes in 1604 that most of the churchmen are serving men and horseboys who hold two or three benefices apiece, although they remain poor through having precontracted the profits to their patrons (*C. S. P. Ir. 1603-1606*, p. 143). See also Moryson, *Shakespeare's Europe*, p. 288.

2742-7. RENWICK. Statute 28 Henry VIII *c.* 15. 7 deals with the provision of English-speaking clergy, and may have been in Spenser's mind: I have found nothing nearer his statement. [See *All the Statutes*, f. 69ʳ⁻ᵛ. Following an act of 1360, the Kilkenny Statute of 1367 made it illegal for any Irishman to be admitted to a church benefice among the English; in 1485 Irish clerks were admitted to benefices in the diocese of Dublin, and with the Reformation Irishmen had to be accepted in order to maintain the supply of clerks; but when an Englishman offered himself for a place held by an Irishman, the latter was deprived (Berry 1. 420-1; *Kilkenny Statute*, pp. 47-9).]

2752-7. " Ministers were hardly founde, so as many great congregations euen among the English wanted Pastors, and the Bishopps were forced for the most part to tolerate ignorante persons, men of scandalous life, yea very Popish readers, rather then Parishes should want not only diuine seruice but the vse of baptisme, Buiriall, Mariage, and the lords Super. . . . Many who came ouer out of England, if they taught well in pulpitt, gaue ill example in life" (Moryson, *Shakespeare's Europe*, p. 288).

2765-9. The meanness of the parochial benefices had originally been due to the preponderance of the monasteries, but the suppression of the latter did not increase the revenues of the parishes (J. T. Ball, *The Reformed Church of Ireland, 1537-1889*, pp. 77-9); in fact, the secular church was deprived of great properties during the reign of Elizabeth (Richard Mant, *A History of the Church of Ireland*, 1840, 1. 279-80).

2772-7. Bale (*The Vocacyon of Johan Bale*, 1553) gives a long account of how the Irish laymen and priests persecuted him, killing his servants and threatening him until he fled the country in disguise. During the eighteen years that he was Bishop of Kildare, Robert Daly was three times turned out of his house "in a manner almost naked"; and the third outrage is thought to have been the cause of his death in 1582 (Ware, *Works* 1. 391). Barnaby Rich (*Remembrances*, p. 140) tells how a minister of Waterford was beaten on the way to church and almost lost his life. See Moryson, *Shakespeare's Europe*, p. 287.

2787-8. WARE. *Trinity* Colledge by *Dublin*, which was founded by *Queene Eliz* 3. *Martij* 1591. The 13. of the same moneth, its first stone was laide by *Thomas Smyth* then Mayor of *Dublin*, and the 9. of *Ian.* 1593. it first admitted Students.

MORLEY. Trinity College, Dublin, was just founded when Spenser wrote this View of Ireland. Its origin was a grant made by Elizabeth, in 1591, of the Augustine Monastery of All Saints for a Church of England College. Its first stone was laid on the first of January 1593, and it began work in the same year.

EDITOR. Not Elizabeth, but the city of Dublin granted the All Saints property on which the college was built; the first stone was laid on 13 March, 1592, and the college began work on 9 January, 1593, with Burghley as its first

COMMENTARY 371

chancellor; in 1594 "the new college" is described as a three-story brick building (Bagwell 3. 470-2; *Calendar of the Patent and Close Rolls*, 2. 345-7; W. Urwick, *The Early History of Trinity College*, Dublin, 1892, pp. 12, 15; *C. S. P. Ir. 1588-1592* 163. 9, *1592-1596* 175. 50). The strongest motive for founding the college was the strengthening of Irish Protestantism; among the "grave fathers" planted there Spenser undoubtedly included Adam Loftus, the first provost, and Walter Travers, the adversary of Richard Hooker, who succeeded Loftus as provost in 1594. The earliest endowment of the college was a fund of more than two thousand pounds, one hundred of which Sir Thomas Norris collected in Munster (Urwick, *op. cit.*, p. 95); it is quite possible that Spenser was a contributor.

2800-2. Sheriffs, sub-sheriffs, and seneschals had the reputation of buying their offices and then reimbursing themselves by extorting money from the weak and poor (see, *e. g.*, *C. S. P. Ir. 1596-1597* 191. 8. 1, *1598-1599* 202. 4. 9. 1; Chambrun MS, Folger Shakespeare Library, f. 237^{r-v}). Barnaby Rich (*Remembrances*, p. 131) cites an example of corrupt victualers: "in the late raygne of our most gracyous Quene duringe the tyme of Tyrones rebellyon one Newcome that cam into Irelande a poore servynge man (neyther of reputation nor any great acounte) yet atteyning to be vytualer to the Army, he sodaynely begane to buyld, to purchase, and so to florysh, that euerry man could say it could not be but by abusynge the Quene."

2802. "Senescalls." TODD. *Governours*. See F. Q. iv. i. 12, v. x. 30, vi. i. 15, 25.

COLLIER. The etymology of "seneschall" has given trouble, but it is from Gothic words meaning *seniors* and *servus*.

2804-10. In 1584 Lord Delvin called attention to the plots which the captains devised at the time of their discharge in order to continue the war against the quiet Irish (John T. Gilbert, p. 189). In 1595 Sir John Norris warned Cecil: "whilst those that have the chiefest disposition of things here, care not how long the war last so they may make their profit . . . you can look for no other success but an unprofitable expense, and a lasting rebellion" (*C. S. P. Ir. 1592-1596* 182. 5).

2812-7. RENWICK. Robert Gardener, Chief Justice, notes, Jan. 4, 1589, the abuse of "A common alowance for head silver to suche as bringe heades never examyninge or knowinge whose heades whither of the best or worst, so no safty for any man to travell. a strange course in a Christian estate." (*S. P. Ir.* 150. 4). [Moryson blames the Anglo-Irish who "being in the States pay, lest they should be held altogether vnprofitable, and to purchase reward of seruice, would sometymes kill a poore Rebell, or bring him aliue to the State, whose reuenge they feared not, yea perhapps a Rebell of note to whome the cheife Neighbor Rebells bore malice, and so cast him into their hands. And this done they vsed to triumphe as though they had done a masterpeece of seruice" (*Shakespeare's Europe*, pp. 206-7).]

2818-31. Moryson describes the lack of co-operation between governors in similar terms (*Shakespeare's Europe*, pp. 190-1).

2840-65. Froude traces the perennial failure of English rule in Ireland to sudden variations in policy (*The English in Ireland in the Eighteenth Century*, 1872-1874, 1. 36-7). The inconstancy of the English administration, Greenlaw has suggested, may have been in Spenser's mind when he wrote the Mutabilitie Cantos of *F. Q.* (*MP* 9. 365).

2840-58. RENWICK. Spenser is thinking mainly, perhaps, of Grey and Perrot, but the thing was unavoidable under the service conditions. There was bickering between Perrot and Fitzwilliam in their turn.

EDITOR. For Perrot see 3404-33 and notes on same. In direct contravention of the policies of his predecessor Grey, he forbade Archbishop Loftus and other churchmen to bring the Papists of the Pale to a better conformity, so encouraging them that they could not be reclaimed; he discharged all Papists held at Waterford; and he saw to it that no condemned Papists were executed (*C. S. P. Ir. 1588-1592* 154. 37, 161. 19). The favor he showed to Irish Catholics was in turn condemned by his successor FitzWilliam (*C. S. P. Ir. 1588-1592* 144. 6, 150. 44). In *B. N.* 99-103 Spenser cites the changes which followed the government of Lord Deputy Russell to illustrate the same point.

2885-8. "Great was the credit of the Giraldins euer when the house of Yorke prospered, and likewise the Butlers thriued vnder the bloud of the Lancasters" (Holinshed, vol. II, *The Chronicles of Ireland*, p. 78). But the alternations from one family to the other were not frequent: the Lord Lieutenants, Deputies, and Justices were Butlers, with only short intervals, from 1420 to 1452 and FitzGeralds of Kildare, with only short intervals, from 1454 to the reign of Henry Eighth (*PRIA*, Archaeology 36. 218-38).

2890-2. COVINGTON (*UTB*, Studies in English 4. 33-4). Spenser here, apparently, recollected that the name "Banno" was anciently applied to Ireland, and assuming that it was related to the verb "ban," "to curse," he used it to enforce his point, that the country was under a curse. Recollecting also that Ireland had been called "Sacra insula" [by Camden], he assumed that "sacra" in this connection had its alternative meaning, and so made the two words equivalent to "Banna." This treatment of his sources is quite characteristic of Spenser.

RENWICK. Camden, *Ireland*, p. 62, has the form *Banno*, as also Hanmer [*The Chronicle of Ireland*, 1633, p. 16]. The form *Banna* is commoner. The MSS vary.

EDITOR. Camden (*Britannia*, p. 678) is undoubtedly Spenser's source: "Hibernici Bardi in suis cantilenis hanc insulam etiam *Banno* appellitant; ... *Biaun* sacrum Hibernice sonat, et certe hanc SACRUM INSVLAM Festus Auienus vocat in libello cui titulus est ORAE *Maritimae*"; the marginalia "*Bannomanna*" and "*Sacra Insula*" which appear beside this passage in the editions of 1590 and 1594, but not earlier, show that Spenser was using one of those two editions. When he translated "*Sacra*" as "accursed," he probably understood that "*Banno*" really meant *holy*: in *F. Q.* 7. 6. 37. 7 he calls Ireland "this holy Island." — The Irish themselves have associated *Banno* with the legendary maiden named *Banbha* (Keating 1. 141; Ware, *Works* 2. 9-10).

2910-23. Lodowick Bryskett writes of Ireland in 1581 (Plomer and Cross,

p. 18): "The State whereof me thinketh I may well compare, vnto an old cloke or garment often tymes mended and patched vp, wherein now so great a rend or gashe being made by violence, as of late all the world doth knowe, there is now no remedy but to make a newe: for to piece the old againe will be but labor loste, consumpcion of that shalbe bestowed vpon it." "Little is lenity to prevaile," explains Sir Philip Sidney (*Works*, ed. Albert Feuillerat, 1911-1926, 3. 50), "in myndes so possest, withe a naturall inconstancy ever to goe to a new fortune, withe a revengefull hate to all englishe as to their only conquerours, and that whiche is most of all with so ignorant obstinacy in papistry, that they doe in their sowles deteste the presente governement."

2921-2. "*Quem metuunt oderunt.*" "Whom they fear, they hate."

RENWICK. The opening of a line of Ennius, quoted by Cicero, *de Officiis* II. [7.] 23; but Spenser has not heeded Cicero's argument. [Cicero goes on to say that no amount of power can withstand the hatred of the many. See also Erasmus, *Adagiorvm Chiliades*, 1599, col. 1404, under "Oderint dum metuant."]

2922-60. Professor John L. Lievsay has gathered the materials for a study of Richard Beacon's *Solon His Follie* (1594), a dialogue concerning the reformation of Ireland, written by one who was associated with Spenser on the Council of Munster; for the suggestion that *Solon His Follie* may be in some way connected with the *View* I am indebted, both here and elsewhere, to Professor Lievsay's generosity. The possibility of a connection between the two works is more evident, I think, in the present passage of the *View* than in any other; compare with it the following quotations from Beacon:

> such common-weales which in al the parts thereof are found corrupted and declined from their first institution, maie not by profitable lawes made and established as occasion shal them require, be reformed. [p. 8]
> If the necessity of forces be great to effect a reformation, (as it plainely appeareth by that which hath bene said) in such common-weals especially where the manners of the people are found corrupted, then much greater is the necessity thereof, when reformation is to be made of a common-weale, gained by the sword and conquest, as also corrupted in manners; for that the people having here sustained many iniuries by force and violence, whereunto the conquerour is drawne oftentimes by their disobedience, maie not at anie time after with newe benefites, offices, and rewardes, be reconciled and pacified: neither shall we finde here profitable lawes, or any sufficient meanes to effect a reformation, without sufficient forces, to repell all daungers, and difficulties: all which *Salamina* [Ireland] may well witnes vnto the worlde. [p. 42, misnumbered 32]
> it seemeth that good lawes are not sufficient to render a common-weale, happie and prosperous. . . . Noe surely, no more then a medicine well prepared may cure the diseases of the body, if the same be not rightly applied. [p. 78]

For further information on Beacon see Judson, *SP* 44. 165-8.

2924-33. JONES (*Spenser's Defense*, pp. 211-2) traces the conservatism of Eudoxus to "the opinion of Bodin expressed in the third chapter of the fourth book of the *Republic*, which bears the title, *Que les changemens des republiques et des loix, ne se doivent faire tout à coup.*"

EDITOR. Bodin writes (*République*, liv. IV, chap. 3, pp. 451-2): "il vaut beaucoup mieux entretenir le malade par diete conuenable, qu'attenter de guarir vne maladie incurable, au hazard de sa vie. et iamais ne faut essayer les remedes violents, si la maladie n'est extreme, et qu'il n'y ait plus d'esperance. . . . de changer les loix qui touchent l'estat, il est aussi dangereux comme de remuer les fondements ou pierres angulaires, qui soustiennent le fez du bastiment." Sir Thomas Smith, the benefactor of Harvey, writes in his *De Republica Anglorum* (ed. L. Alston, 1906, book I, chap. 5, p. 13): "Certaine it is that it is always a doubtfull and hasardous matter to meddle with the chaunging of the lawes and gouernement"; and it may be significant that E. K. in his gloss on *S. C. Jan.* 10 notes that he has a copy of *De Republica* in manuscript, lent to him by Harvey. In any case the conservatism of Eudoxus is something innate in Spenser; see the Mutabilitie Cantos and *F. Q.* 5. 2. 36. 5-9; also Padelford, *JEGP* 14. 401.

2933.   Bryskett, with whom Spenser may have discussed this point, writes in 1581: "Now is the tyme to goe thouroughe withall, and thoughe the expence seme great; yet better is it to make one great charge for the whole with hope to recover it againe, then to hazard the losse of the whole" (Plomer and Cross, p. 23).

2936-43. In 1592 Ralegh remarks to Cecil of a recent uprising, "yow shall find it but a shoure of a farther tempest" (Edwards 2. 50); and in the following years the English government received innumerable warnings of trouble in the offing. In February, 1596, Wallop writes that the state of the realm was never so dangerous in the memory of man (*C. S. P. Ir. 1592-1596* 186. 52). At the very time the *View* was probably being written in England, Elizabeth's ministers at Greenwich were receiving from Lord Deputy Russell and his advisors the actual news to which Irenius so mysteriously alludes. According to their letter to the Privy Council on 9 July, 1596: "if, by the end of this month, till which time this respite is now granted, the Spaniards come according to their promise and the undoubted expectation of the rebels, as we have many reasons and advertisements to move us to think they will, . . . we see not, nor in our judgments can conceive, how this kingdom should any time be kept against them"; on July sixteenth we are told that Ulster and Connaught are distilling treason into Leinster, and a week later that the Spaniards are expected at the beginning of August; on September twenty-fifth the Irish Council writes that the Spaniards have actually landed in O'Donnell's country, and their letters are endorsed, "Deliver these in haste, haste. Haste, post haste, for life, life. For Her Majesty's most special affairs" (*C. S. P. Ir. 1596-1597* 191. 15, 23, 38; 193. 31). These feverish communications explain the ominous, allusive character of Spenser's words: the bad news of the moment, though not for direct publication, furnished an illustration too apt to be omitted. Tyrone's rebellion, of course, did not break in its gathered power until two years later; but then it completely justified Spenser's predictions.

2943-8.   TODD, COLLIER, and MORLEY identify "one noble persone" as Ralegh, MARTIN (*PMLA* 47. 137-8) as Essex.

COMMENTARY

RENWICK. I take it Spenser means the Earl of Ormond, whose attention might be turned by this compliment from other passages which might not please him.

EDITOR. For Ormond see 925-9, 3318-26, and notes on same. The "one noble persone" must be Ormond, the greatest nobleman of southern Ireland and the one most distinguished by his loyalty to the government: on 6 February, 1597, Robert Cecil calls Ormond "one of greatest trust in her Maiesties kingdome" (Carte Manuscripts in Bodleian Library, vol. 1, f. 46ʳ). The comma Ware placed after "Countrye" in 2945, but which does not occur in the better manuscripts, misled Todd, Collier, Morley, and Martin into identifying "one noble persone" with the commander of a naval expedition.

2945. "the Southe sea." The stretch of the Atlantic immediately south of Ireland (see *C. C. MSS. Miscellaneous*, p. 363).

2945. "ingate." TODD. *Entrance*. Again; "Those two cities do offer an ingate to the Spaniard most fitly" [4292-3]. See also F. Q. iv. x. 12 [and R. T. 47].

2956-60. RENWICK. This was the general opinion. Cf. Grey to Walsingham, Jan. 15, 1581, in Spenser's hand: "Neyther can anye platt take place before force haue playned the grownde for the fowndacion, which onlye for presente muste bee her Maiesties Charge and dispence, A thinge no dowbte for the tyme verye heavie yet in thend will bee broughte in with no smale advauntage beesydes greater honor in case it bee throwghlie followed but one yeare. (Yea halfe I hope in god I mighte saye)" (*S. P. Ir.* 80. 10) Russell, in *Titus B xii*, 171 vo., "The meane to redresse must be the Sword, which is Iustice armed." According to his officer Docwra, Bingham "Founde, and sawe, that Lingring servyce could not but greatly Chardge hir Majestie, and muche encourage the enemye, A softe, kinde of warre that hath bin to, to longe vsed in this Realme." (*Misc. Celtic Soc.*, 1849) [Spenser's opinion was shared by Gerrard, Wallop, Rich, and Davies (*C. S. P. Ir. 1574-1585*, pp. xxxvi-xxxvii, 85. 27; *1599-1600* 206. 119. 1; *Discoverie*, pp. 4-5). The proponents of the sword, however, did not sway Burghley, who advised the Queen to take away the fear of conquest from the Irish and to wink at those disorders which did not offend the Crown (*HMC, Salisbury Manuscripts* 2. 309). See also F. Q. 5. 4. 1, where Spenser expresses the belief that might is necessary to right.]

2957-60. See F. Q. 5. 1. 1. 8-9.

2961-2. See 2521-7. But Irenius there objects to the appointment of a marshal to control the English soldiers who employ the privilege of cess for pillage; Irenius made no objection when Eudoxus had proposed that a marshal be appointed to rid the country of "Iesters, Carrowes, *monashule* and all suche straglers" (2385).

2962. "too violente a meanes." GREENLAW (*MP* 7. 196) refers this expression to Machiavelli's "medicine forti" (*Il Principe*, cap. 3). [But Bodin also speaks of "remedes violents"; see note on 2924-33.]

2965-6. So Beacon writes (p. 113): "where *sanandi medicina* may not prevaile, there *execandi*, is rightly vsed."

2973-9. Perrot had made the same distinction in writing to the Queen in 1582: "I protest it is farre from me to desire any extirpation; but rather that all might bee saued, that were good for the Country to be saued. Yet this I say, Till your Maiesties Sword hath meekened all, I thinke it neither Honour nor safety to graunt mercy to any" (E. C. S., sig. A4ᵛ). In her proclamation of 31 March, 1599, Elizabeth herself denies that in sending an army to repress the Irish rebels "wee intended an vtter extirpation and rooting out of that Nation" (*A Booke Containing All Svch Proclamations, As Were Pvblished dvring the Raigne of the Late Queene Elizabeth*, ed. Humfrey Dyson, 1618, f. 361).

2994. Hugh O'Neill (1540?-1616) became third Baron of Dungannon in 1562, second Earl of Tyrone in 1586, and the O'Neill in 1593. See Sean O'Faolain, *The Great O'Neill*, 1942; Judson, *Life*, pp. 158-9; *View* 3500-3615 and notes.

3005-14. RENWICK. In Sept., 1595, Wallop estimated the army costs at the same figure, £12,000 a month, the ordinary charge being about £8,500. He deprecates the Queen's displeasure — often and forcibly expressed — and defends the expenditure as promoting efficiency and shortening the war. (*S. P. Ir.* 183. 57) [During Elizabeth's reign the cost of the Irish administration mounted steadily: between 1555 and 1565 the average annual expenditure was about £24,000 (*C. C. MSS. 1515-1574*, p. 373); Wallop's accounts for the five and a half years ending Michaelmas, 1584, show charges of £470,000 (*C. S. P. Ir. 1586-1588* 126. 1. 1); the army employed against Tyrone cost £250,000 in the seventeen months ending in February, 1599, and by March the monthly military charge rose to £17,000 (*C. S. P. Ir. 1598-1599* 203. 55, 70); Tyrone's rebellion was finally crushed at an estimated cost of £1,924,000, in a period when the Queen's annual revenues from Ireland were only £30,000 (*HMC, Salisbury Manuscripts* 15. 2; Moryson, *Shakespeare's Europe*, p. 252).]

3017-30. Judson (*Life*, pp. 156-7) points out that Spenser must have been interested in the rebellion of Sir Thomas Norris's company of foot soldiers, on account of lack of pay, in 1590. A memorandum dated November, 1596, observes: "As any treasure is sent over hither, the chief officers are ever first served out of it, besides other defrayments; the remnant, falling out to be small, is commonly shared and assigned for the companies; the which being paid to the captains (who for the most part lie here still in Dublin, pretending to wait and attend for the same), they think such portion too little for themselves, and cease not to murmur thereat"; and a little later an example is cited: "Of all the captains in Ireland, Sir Thomas North hath from the beginning kept a most miserable, unfurnished, naked, and hunger-starven band. Many of his soldiers died wretchedly and woefully at Dublin; some whose feet and legs rotted off for want of shoes; and albeit these poor souls were left thus at random, uncared for and unrelieved, yet were their names still retained in the muster-roll. And, no doubt, pay will be duly demanded in England" (*C. S. P. Ir. 1596-1597* 195. 52, 196. 39). On Lord Burgh's journey to the Blackwater in June, 1597, it is said that almost a thousand soldiers died of famine (*C. S. P. Ir. 1598-1599* 202. 2. 38).

COMMENTARY 377

3041-50. So Tremayne (p. 4) writes in 1573 that in order to subdue Ireland thoroughly an extraordinary contribution will be offered willingly, that the ordinary revenues will not have to be touched, and that the cost of subduing Ireland will not be so great as some men believe.

3054-5. Before 1596 11,000 men would have been considered a very large army in Ireland; yet when Essex entered upon his government in April, 1599, he had forces numbering 19,000 (*C. S. P. Ir. 1599-1600* 205. 38).

3061-3139. In general this plan agrees with the advice of Machiavelli (*The Arte of Warre*, trans. Peter Whitehorne, 1560, f. Ciiij^r): "It is better to conquere the enemie with faminne, then with yron."

3061-6. "These people are verie nimble and quicke of bodie, and light of foot, and for their safetie and aduantage they seeke waies through streicts and bogs" (Giraldus Cambrensis, trans. in Holinshed, vol. II, *The Conquest of Ireland*, p. 56). So Gainsford writes (p. 144): "On the bogg they likwise presume with a naked celeritie to come as neere our foote and horse, as is possible, and then flie off againe, knowing we cannot, or indeed dare not follow them." See also Moryson, *Shakespeare's Europe*, p. 236. Spenser's Guyle fights like the Irish enemy, and Talus issues forth against him like one of the English garrisons which Spenser proposes to use in 3138-9 (see *F. Q.* 5. 9. 5-6, 15-19).

3066-9. So Sir Henry Brouncker writes (*C. S. P. Ir. 1598-1599* 202. 1. 29): "I dare affirm upon my life that there is no other means to save the kingdom than by war, nor no other way to prevail in war than by garrisons."

3083-6. RENWICK. A map of Ireland was available in the atlas of Ortelius (1573), but there were many MS maps. See Dunlop's catalogue in *Engl. Hist. Rev.*, 1905 [20. 309-37].

EDITOR. Although published eleven times between 1573 and 1596 (*Dr. A. Petermanns Mitteilungen* 43. 16, 21), the Ortelius map of Ireland would not give Spenser much up-to-date information: its crude outlines and infrequent place names were largely derived from Mercator's Duisburg chart of 1564. Spenser is far more likely to have used the large map executed by Baptista Boazio, probably in 1578-1580 (see note on 4107-10), the best map of Ireland until well into the seventeenth century. On the smaller version of this map, in the edition dedicated to James First, can be found some 130 of the place names which occur in the *View*.

3087-3102. RENWICK. The strategical scheme first enters here, as a plan of campaign: the scheme of permanent garrisons outlined later is the same in skeleton: as it covers all Ireland its lines will be discussed there. [See 3977-4286 and notes.]

GOTTFRIED (*ELH* 6. 117). A glance at these four positions on a map of Ulster reveals their military significance: forming a quadrilateral around Tyrone, they were intended to block all the channels through which outside support might reach the Earl.... If, therefore, some of Spenser's proposals are almost commonplaces of official opinion, it is not surprising to find that in 1596, the year in which the *View* was written, another plan was submitted for placing more garrisons in nearly the same positions, *i. e.* in Belleek, Ballyshannon, Belturbet,

Lough Foyle, the Blackwater, and Monaghan [*C. C. MSS. 1589-1600*, pp. 199-203].

3089-91. JENKINS (*PMLA* 52. 347) believes that Spenser probably visited the Blackwater with Grey in August, 1581. [See *C. S. P. Ir. 1574-1585* 85. 5 and Spenser's reference to "Swift Awniduff" in *F. Q.* 4. 11. 41. 5. As a convenient place for the garrison he later shows that he has in mind the Blackfort (3992-3).]

3091-3. RENWICK. *Castleliffer* and *Castle Finn* were O'Donnell's chief residences, and important river-crossings. [Castleliffer is the modern Lifford, where the Finn and the Shrule join to form the Foyle, "the Riuer," which flows north into Lough Foyle. Castlefinn lies a few miles west of Lifford. Possibly Grey, and with him Spenser, visited this neighborhood in 1581 (*C. C. MSS. 1575-1588*, p. 323). The military importance of the position is frequently stressed in the State Papers (see, *e. g., C. S. P. Ir. 1598-1599* 202. 2. 52; *1599-1600* 205. 170, 207. 24).]

3093-5. GOTTFRIED (*ELH* 6. 116) identifies "Bundroisse" as Bundoran on the south side of Donegal Bay (see Baptista Boazio's map of Ireland, ed. dedicated to James First; Henley, map facing title; Renwick, *View*, map facing p. 330).

ROLAND SMITH (*JEGP* 42. 508-9). Too great reliance upon maps, both old and contemporary, has led Gottfried into certain errors, including his explanation of "'Bondroise,' " . . . . [which] is more easily accounted for. *Bun Drobhaise* in Irish, it means "mouth of the Drowes" . . . . Bundrowes, as it is commonly spelled, is frequently mentioned in the letters of Sir Richard Bingham [*e. g., C. S. P. Ir. 1574-1585* 111. 81, *1592-1596* 174. 15. Obviously Gottfried has made a bad mistake. The Drowes, which flows into the south side of Donegal Bay a mile from Bundoran, is the "sad Trowis" of *F. Q.* 4. 11. 41. 7. "Fermanaghe" must be some place in the county of that name.]

3097. ROLAND SMITH (*JEGP* 42. 500) calls attention to Sir Richard Bingham's proposal, in 1595, to garrison Belleek and Ballyshannon (*C. S. P. Ir. 1592-1596* 182. 4). [For Bingham's and Sir Conyers Clifford's proposals for garrisoning these places see also *C. S. P. Ir. 1592-1596* 174. 15, *1596-1597* 200. 143, *1598-1599* 202. 2. 21. 2 and 202. 4. 56; Bagwell 3. 256; Martin, *PMLA* 47. 142. Belleek and Ballyshannon lie on opposite sides of the mouth of the Erne.]

3098. "Belterbert" is the modern town of Belturbet in Co. Cavan.

3102-4. Captain Thomas Reade writes to Cecil in 1598, requesting more horsemen since daily experience shows that foot alone are of little avail in pursuing the swiftly fleeing enemy (*C. S. P. Ir. 1598-1599* 202. 4. 19).

3104-28. RENWICK. The permanent problem of victualling troops in the presence of an energetic enemy expert in guerilla warfare was complicated by the nature of the country. Wallop emphasises it often, in the light of such affairs as that of "the Ford of the Biscuits," in July, 1594, when George Bingham was ambushed with his convoy, and lost 56 men killed and 69 wounded. It was not helped by lack of system and of discipline in the services, and by the method of charging the soldier so much a day for rations. This last, especially, as Wallop

COMMENTARY 379

calculated, that the charges were apt to exceed the total pay, was largely responsible for the disorders discussed above. On taking over the victualling in 1595, Wallop tried to decentralise, but not so completely as Spenser suggests. See a long report of his dated 27 Sept., 1595, in *S. P. Ir.*, 183. 5. [For Wallop's efforts in this direction see also *C. S. P. Ir. 1592-1596* 182. 31, 183. 57. In 1586 Captain Nicholas Dawtrey pointed out the danger of victualling the English forces in Ulster from a central storehouse in Carrickfergus; and later he offered to establish storehouses at the Lifford and Bann forts (*C. S. P. Ir. 1586-1588* 126. 93, *1598-1599* 202. 2. 52). In this connection it is interesting to note that at the philosophical banquet described by Lodowick Bryskett (*A Discovrse of Civill Life*, 1606, p. 94) Dawtrey is present along with Spenser and shows a decided interest in good food. Machiavelli cites antiquity in support of a proposal for victualling an army which is similar to Spenser's (*Della Arte della Guerra*, lib. 5).]

3109-14. In actual practice the soldier had other food than bread, beer, and beef: three out of the seven were fish, rather than flesh days, *i. e.*, beef was replaced by butter, cheese, or herrings; and at one time it was proposed to add oatmeal, codfish, bacon, salt pork, and pease to the menu (*C. C. MSS. 1589-1600*, pp. 187-8, 350).

3109-10. So Machiavelli (*Della Arte della Guerra*, lib. 5) recommends that soldiers, according to ancient custom, should bake their own bread.

3114. MORLEY. *Creet*, stock of cattle.

ROLAND SMITH (*JEGP* 42. 503). Ir. *crech, crechadh*. [In a personal communication Professor Smith adds: "More satisfactory than Renwick's definition ["cattle-herd"] . . . is that in *Carew MSS* I, 316: 'creaghes, that is to say, horses, oxen, kine, veals, porks, sheep, goats, &c.' Irish *crech, crechadh*, literally means 'plunder,' hence anything, usually live-stock, taken in a raid. Cf. the verb *crechaim*, 'I rob.'" Maxwell (p. 275) derives "creaghting" from Ir. *caoraigheacht*, which is defined as "a nomadic herd of cattle driven about from place to place for pasture, or in time of war with the forces of their owners."]

3114-6. Each English soldier was supplied with five pairs of stockings, five pairs of shoes, and a cap every year (*C. C. MSS. 1589-1600*, p. 334).

3129-39. RENWICK. For an example of an energetic and well-planned campaign, see Bingham's report of his "journey" against the Burkes, *Cal. S. P. Ir.*, 165. 66. Many cattle were taken, and Docwra reports the result: "These men vppon thier submission were soe Pyned awaye for want of Foode, and soe ghasted with Feare within, vij or viij weeks, by reason, they were so roundlye Followed, without any interim of rest, that they looked rayther like to ghosts then men." (*Op. cit.*, p. 203) [The same strategy was recommended as early as the reign of Henry Eighth (see *State Papers, Henry VIII* 2. 329-30). "I give the rebels no breath to relieve themselves," writes Sir William Pelham to the Queen in 1580, "but by one of your garrisons or other they be continually hunted. I keep them from their harvest, and have taken great preys of cattle from them" (*C. C. MSS. 1575-1588*, p. 293).]

3143-54. The standard opinion is expressed by Machiavelli (*The Arte of Warre*, trans. Peter Whitehorne, 1560, f. xciij^r): "There is nothyng more vndescrete, or more perillous to a Captaine, then to make warre in the Winter, and moche more perill beareth he, that maketh it, then he that abideth it." But in sixteenth-century Ireland it was generally agreed that winter was the best season for pursuing the enemy (*State Papers, Henry VIII* 2. 489-90; *Letters and Memorials* 1. 10; anonymous *History of Sir John Perrott*, pp. 58-60; *C. S. P. Ir. 1598-1599* 202. 3. 142).

3145.   *Glister* is applied to a headpiece in *Mui.* 73 and *F. Q.* 4. 1. 13. 1.

3149-54. Moryson (*Itinerary*, part III, p. 163) notes the dependence of the Irish on their cows: "They feede most on Whitmeates, and esteeme for a great daintie sower curds, vulgarly called by them Bonaclabbe. And for this cause they watchfully keepe their Cowes, and fight for them as for religion and life; and when they are almost starued, yet they will not kill a Cow, except it bee old, and yeeld no Milke."

3158-9.   Derrick (sig. E4^v) describes the preference of the Irish marauders for the night; and Camden notes their pride in committing nocturnal depredations: "Nocte tempestuosissima stertere, et non pedibus viam longissimam noctu conficere, et spoliando omnibus periculis se obijcere, abiecti animi esse dicunt" (*Britannia*, p. 715).

3161-4.   For Feagh MacHugh see 3615-3749 and notes; for the Cavanaghs, O'Moores, and O'Kellys, 617-22 and notes. The Keatings seem to have lived chiefly in Co. Carlow, the O'Dempsys in King's (anonymous *Description of Ireland*, pp. 50-2, 81).

3172-9.   Tyrone himself told Sir John Harington of the hardships he suffered, "comparing himself to wolves, that fill their bellies sometime, and fast as long for it" (*Nugae Antiquae* 1. 248).

3182.   "drawinge sodaine draughtes." Perhaps in the sense of *drawing a net for fish or birds*.

3191-5.   The device was a common one in the Irish wars. Grey, for example, used it with good effect in 1581 (*HMC, Salisbury Manuscripts* 13. 189-90); and in August, 1598, a pardon was proposed which would be effective for twenty days from its proclamation (*C. S. P. Ir. 1598-1599* 202. 3. 55).

3199-3200. The "desmoundes warres" were the series of uprisings led by the Earl of Desmond and his family from the early 1560's until his death in 1583 (see note on 830-3). On April 26, 1581, the Queen published a proclamation granting pardon to all except the leaders of the Desmond rebellion, provided they submitted within ten days (*A Booke Containing All Svch Proclamations, As Were Pvblished dvring the Raigne of the Late Queene Elizabeth*, ed. Humfrey Dyson, 1618, ff. 214-5).

3200.   "raskall." In the sense of *belonging to the rabble*. See *Hub.* 1193, *F. Q.* 5. 11. 59. 8.

COMMENTARY 381

3202. "Churles." See note on 729-30.

3205-13. RENWICK. In the report mentioned above [note on 3129-39], Bingham repeats his conviction that once the chiefs and professional fighting men were checked, the churls would welcome the regime that gave them peace and security. As we have seen, the opinion was common, and there may have been something in it at one time. [See also *State Papers, Henry VIII* 2. 279-80.]

3221-32. Moryson makes a similar observation, but of the Irish soldiers rather than refugees (*Shakespeare's Europe*, p. 206).

3248-70. PADELFORD (*JEGP* 14. 412) calls this "a terrible proposal, uttered with cold deliberateness."

HENLEY (p. 37). "Any stonye heart would have rued the same," but Spenser far from ruing it, proposed later on to repeat the performance in the north, as the most convenient way of disposing of Hugh O'Neill's adherents. . . . So had a gentle poet developed under the tutelage of Lord Grey.

RENWICK (*View*, p. 244). It has proved unfortunate for Spenser that the best-written paragraph in the *View*, and therefore the most quotable, and therefore the only one most people know, is his description of the devastation and famine caused by the Desmond Wars. That paragraph is the best written because it is the one paragraph that is fully charged with emotion; and the emotion is not gloating satisfaction, but horror. As Miss M. M. Gray has pointed out in *The Review of English Studies* (VI. [4] 24) the terrible picture haunted Spenser all his life. It is assumed, and even stated, that he advocated similar treatment for the whole population. The candid reader, however, must not allow the emotion to distract him from the argument. Spenser does not cite this as an example of how to treat the Irish, but as an incidental proof of the common opinion that the campaign commonly held to be a necessary preliminary to reorganization would, if properly followed up, be short. He argues *a fortiori*: if a whole rich countryside could collapse like this, how much more a guerilla army, separated from its women and churls, and living on driven cattle.

HEFFNER (*MLQ* 3. 512-3). It is the general impression that Spenser advocated extermination of the Irish by any means, but principally by starvation. This is literally not true. A passage which has been cited in support of this impression is simply an observation of what Spenser saw in Munster where his feeling at that time was one of horror. This passage should be read, not out of its context, but along with [2954-89].

ONG (*MLQ* 3. 561) notes that in this passage Spenser "calls for a repetition of the Munster horrors."

[For a similar proposal see *C. S. P. Ir. 1598-1599* 202. 3. 185.]

3251. "manuraunce." MORLEY. Cultivation.

3253-70. RENWICK (*View*, p. 230). The Four Masters, whose chronicle gives the Irish side of events, record how Fitzgeralds, Butlers, and English troops raided and counter-raided, until "between them the country was left one levelled plain, without corn or edifices." Almost all Ormond's land "was suffered to remain one surface of weeds and waste. Nor was it wonderful . . . on account of the many times the Earl (of Desmond) had plundered them . . . At this period it was commonly said, that the lowing of a cow, or the ploughman, could scarcely be heard from Dun-Caoin (in West Kerry) to Cashel." (tr. O'Donovan, 1853, v. 1723, 1785). Spenser saw this at first hand, for Grey had to join in the campaign, and his secretary went with him.

EDITOR. In March, 1582, Sir Warham St. Leger wrote that more than thirty thousand had died in Munster in the previous half year; and later he reported that from sixty-two to seventy-two perished daily of famine or the plague in Cork (*C. S. P. Ir. 1574-1585*, pp. lxxxv-lxxxvi; 91. 41, 91. 41. 1). A year later Captain Edward Stanley wrote from Dingle that "the poorest sort hath bene driven to eat the dead men's bodies which was cast away in the shipwreck" (*C. S. P. Ir. 1574-1585* 102. 49. 1). But the most complete and, outside of the *View*, the most vivid description of the famine is given by John Hooker (Holinshed, vol. II, *The Supplie of the Irish Chronicles*, pp. 182-3); among other details he notes, "they were not onelie driuen to eat horsses, dogs and dead carions; but also did deuoure the carcases of dead men, whereof there be sundrie examples: namelie one in the countie of Corke, where when a malefactor was executed to death, and his bodie left vpon the gallows, certeine poore people secretlie came, tooke him downe, and did eat him." M. M. Gray (*RES* 6. 423-4) compares the appearance of the starving Irish to that of Red Cross imprisoned, in *F. Q.* 1. 8. 40-41.

3253-4. JENKINS (*PMLA* 52. 348) notes that Spenser saw the effects of the Munster famine on a journey through the province with Grey in the autumn of 1581.

3257. RENWICK. Spenser disregards the length of the Desmond feud for the purpose of his argument.

3258. See *F. Q.* 3. 9. 39. 6-7.

3259. "glinnes." TODD. That is, dales or vallies; here spelt in the original edition *glynnes* perhaps in conformity to the Irish pronunciation. So *pen* was accustomed, in the same country, to be pronounced *pin*. See *Castle Rack-Rent, an Hibernian Tale*, etc. p. 77.

3260-2. TODD. Thus Shakespeare, in his Comedy of Errors [5. 1. 238-42]:
"They brought one Pinch, a hungry lean-faced villain,
" A mere *anatomy*, a mountebank, etc.
" A needy, hollow-eyed, sharp-looking wretch,
" A *living dead man*."

3263-4. Describing the Ulster famine in the time of Edward le Bruce, Campion (p. 84) speaks of the poor "scratching the dead bodyes out of their graves."

3264-6. Andrew Trollope reported of the Munster famine (*C. S. P. Ir. 1574-1585* 85. 39): "if they can gett no stolen fleshe, they eate if they can gett them, like [leek] blades, and a three-leved grasse, which they call shamrocks, and for want thereof caryon, and grasse in the felds." Campion (p. 18) apparently distinguishes between shamrocks and watercresses, but Stanyhurst explains the first as merely the Irish term for the second (Holinshed, vol. II, *The Description of Ireland*, p. 45). See *JRSAI* 26. 211-26, 349-61; Roland Smith, *JEGP* 42. 505.

3274-5. For "kerne" see note on 2223-4; for "Gallowglasse," note on 2214-20; for "Stocagh," note on 4524; for "horseman," 2177-2210 and notes; for "horsboye," 2345-60 and note.

3293-3302. That policy rather than feeling bred Elizabeth's mercy is certain; if she restrained Grey's severity toward the Irish, she privately applauded his execution of several hundred Spaniards at Smerwick. But Spenser never questions her clemency; for him she is the Mercilla of *F. Q.* 5. 9. 30. 1-3. See also Moryson, *Shakespeare's Europe*, p. 260.

3302-39. GREENLAW (*MP* 7. 196-7) parallels this portrait of Grey with that of Cesare Borgia in Machiavelli (*Il Principe*, cap. 7, 8, 17); both are based on the thesis that cruelty is necessary in order to avoid greater cruelty.

3302-16. RENWICK. A general pardon was sent over in April 1581: the drafts are in *S. P. Ir.* 82. 43-3 [41, 42, 43?]. Grey protested (April 24 and 26) in letters the substance of which is reproduced by Spenser here. Grey declares he never executed any that submitted, but he left a long trail behind him. Among the officials he seems to have been better liked and more respected than any Deputy since Sir Henry Sidney, or any successor during the period. Wallop, Loftus, Brady (Bishop of Meath), and others testify to his qualities, and Ludovick Bryskett's tribute is worth quoting, since only strong feeling could embolden such a minor official to protest so vigorously against the action of the Queen and Council "... his Lordship conceiveth great hope to be discharged: and common brute and reporte maketh it publike. For his owne satisfaction truly I wishe it, and shall thinke him happie, when it shalbe accomplished, But for the State and weale publike I must nedes thinke it the miserablest case that may befall. For if he that hath recovered the State languishing in extremitie of death (as I may say) and hath even in a forced course reduced thinges to that good stay which (God be thanked) they are nowe in, whose Iustice is a terror to the wicked, and a comforte vnto the good, whose sinceritie very envie it self cannott touche, and whose wisdome might, in the oppinion of the wysest that consider his proceedinges, governe a whole Empyre, shall . . . be called away: what can be sayd but that the secrett Iudgement of God hangeth over this soyle. . . ." (*S. P. Ir.* 92. 29)

EDITOR. Captain John Dowdall tells Walsingham in 1582: "My Lord took the course to root out rebellion for ever, if it had been followed, and to have brought this realm into true obedience, but I think he is not well backed in England, as it doth appear by our great wants here. Then by Her Majesty's pardon, given of Her great clemency, was unto them such a relief as if Her Majesty had sent forty ships laden with victuals, it could not have relieved them more" (*C. S. P. Ir. 1574-1585*, p. xciv). The frustration of Grey's plans and his recall are alluded to in the story of Artegall, *F. Q.* 5. 12. 27. See 587-612, 3318-3403, and notes.

3313. "blanked." TODD. *Confounded* or *disappointed*. So Shakspeare, in *Hamlet* [3. 2. 232]:

"Each opposite that *blanks* the face of joy."

3319-24. MARTIN (*PMLA* 47. 141). Spenser, then, is not out of the contemporary tone when he accuses Raleigh of conduct prejudicial to her Majesty's best interests in the Ormonde controversy in Ireland, wherein Raleigh had brought about dissension between Lord Grey and Ormonde, both of whom learned only later that they had been deliberately deceived. This discussion is given to Eudoxus, cleverly enough, who says he cannot forget the unhappy issue of that situation.

RENWICK. The Earl of Kildare was suspected by Grey, and arrested. Spenser is being careful, as Kildare was again in favour; but it seems clear that the families of the Pale were responsible for most of Grey's troubles.

EDITOR. Martin's identification of Ormond as "another noble personage" is probably correct since Ormond was the most important personage with whom Grey came into conflict in the course of his administration and since the results of the conflict were those described by Spenser. On 12 May, 1581, Grey informed Walsingham that there was no help as long as Ormond remained in Ireland; and in the letter, it is significant, were enclosed a copy made under the hand of Spenser from a letter of Ormond's and another document certified by Spenser (*C. S. P. Ir. 1574-1585* 83. 6, 6. 1, 6. 2). Ormond was accordingly relieved of the office of Lord General of Munster; but Grey had won an empty victory since the Queen immediately gave instructions for a general pardon and reduced the size of the army (Bagwell 3. 87-9). Martin's theory that Spenser attacks Ralegh as the source of the trouble between Grey and Ormond, however, is hard to accept. Numerous witnesses, some of them more important than Ralegh, contributed to the articles drawn up against Ormond in March, 1582 (*C. C. MSS. 1575-1588*, pp. 325-7); the iron-fisted Ralegh can hardly have intended to undo Grey's military conquest; if he had fatally deceived Grey, Spenser must have known of it before 1590, when he was on terms of intimacy with Ralegh; and how, in any case, can we explain an attack on Ralegh in 1596, a year after the publication of *Col.*? Spenser, in fact, does not say that one person was responsible for the trouble between Grey and Ormond.

3327-39. RENWICK. Grey's own words confirm Spenser's opinion of him: "I feare I shall doe your Highness litle service emongst [the Irish]; for certeinly a harde and forcible hand, I too well fynd, must bring them to duety, which I confesse, falles not with my nature." (*S. P. Ir.* 78. 29) This after four months only: I take Grey to have been one of those simple, upright, conscientious men who see things black or white, and can be harder than less estimable characters. [Artegall in *F. Q.* 4. 6. 26. 2-3, 5. 2. 26. 1-2, combines the severity and gentleness which Spenser admires in Grey.]

3339-51. WARE. *Consulas* (*si placet*) Camden. *annal. rerum Anglic. et Hiber. ad an.* 1580 [p. 311].

GREENLAW (*MP* 7. 198) believes that Spenser's defense of Grey's conduct in the Pale rebellion follows the lines along which Machiavelli defends Cesare Borgia's extermination of the Romagna nobles (*Il Principe*, cap. 7).

JENKINS (*PMLA* 52. 350-1). During January and February [1582]

COMMENTARY

Spenser was apparently occupied in assisting Grey in amassing evidence against Chief Justice Nicholas Nugent for complicity in the rebellion of his uncle, William Nugent. On April 4 the trial took place at Trim. . . . Spenser together with many of the friends referred to in Bryskett's *Discourse* was undoubtedly present when Grey pronounced sentence and when, two days later, the Chief Justice was hanged. . . . Spenser's defense of Grey in the *Veue* intimates that he and Grey suspected the Chief Justice of far more guile and treachery than they were able to prove.

EDITOR. In October, 1581, informers revealed to the government that a conspiracy involving some hundred gentlemen of the Pale had been on foot for three months; Grey promptly arrested the suspects, and the trials were under way by November twenty-third (*C. S. P. Ir. 1574-1585* 86. 10. 1, 86. 20, 86. 30. 2, 86. 80). In the case of Nicholas Nugent councillors and Grey himself sat in commission with the judges (Bagwell 3. 99); and when the English Privy Council wrote the Deputy to stay the proceedings, he replied that he would let the law take its course (*C. S. P. Ir. 1574-1585* 89. 9). The Queen, apparently influenced by the Earl of Sussex, took grave offence at the executions, according to Camden (*Annales*, p. 311). See also the report of Mendoza, *C. S. P. S. 1580-1586*, pp. 237-8; Judson, *Life*, pp. 104-5.

3346-50. RENWICK. This could not but be true, since the conspirators were members of the prominent families who held all the local and many of the national legal posts.

3355-88. See Appendix III, section D.

3356. HENLEY (p. 140) suggests that Munera's castle in *F. Q.* 5. 2. 4. 5-28. 9 may represent the Fort del Oro at Smerwick. [The fort was erected in 1579, a year before the incident Spenser describes (*C. S. P. S. 1568-1579*, p. 703; *Publications of the Catholic Record Society* 26. 48-56). For a description of it see *JRSAI* 40. 195, 199-203; a photograph of the site appears in Judson, *Life*, op. p. 90.]

3364. "Coronell." TODD. The old word for *Colonel*. See Cotgrave in V. "A *coronell* or colonell."

3366-70. In 1588 Alberico Gentili declares that according to the Law of Nations the lives of captives should not be taken, even though, as at Agincourt, the captors were endangered by being merciful; but he is careful to add that the Law of War does not protect the lives of captives who have violated it (*De Iure Belli*, ed. Thomas E. Holland, 1877, pp. 200-2, 224). Gentili taught at Oxford in the years immediately following Smerwick.

3372. "the Pope." In 1580 he was Gregory Thirteenth.

3376. For the Earl of Desmond see note on 830-3. His brother and co-rebel John was slain and beheaded by enemies in January, 1582, not undeservedly in consideration of the cruelty with which he had murdered his friend Davels three years before (*C. S. P. Ir. 1574-1585* 88. 7, 88. 10. 1; Holinshed, vol. II, *The Supplie of the Irish Chronicles*, pp. 154-6; Bagwell 3. 94).

3404-10. WARE (Osgood copy). *Adam Loftus* Archb. of Dub. Lo. Chanc. and Sir *Henry Wallop* Treasurer at warres. etc.

RENWICK. The *Lords Justices*, Loftus and Wallop, governed from Grey's departure in August, 1582 until Perrot's arrival in June, 1584. They differed as Spenser says, Loftus wishing that Desmond be pardoned, Wallop being harder; they both wished to have Grey back.

EDITOR. Wallop, the first of the two whom Irenius describes, in 1586 leased a portion of the Enniscorthy estate which Spenser had leased for a short time in 1581 (Judson, *Life*, p. 102); Wallop was probably the link between Spenser and Andrew Reade when Spenser acquired Kilcolman in 1589 (Bradner, *MLN* 60. 180-4); and it has been suggested that Sir Sergis in *F. Q.* 5. 11-12 stands for Wallop (Bennett, *The Evolution of "The Faerie Queene,"* pp. 196-9). Where reference is made to him in these notes, it will be seen that Wallop is generally in agreement with Spenser. Loftus, who had become Archbishop of Dublin in 1567 and Lord Chancellor in 1581, was reputed to suffer from avarice and ambition (Ware's *Works* 1. 353). E. C. S., the biographer of Perrot, remarks on the difference in the dispositions of the two men (p. 2). On 5 November, 1582, Loftus writes to Burghley, exhorting him to comfort the famine-stricken people of Ireland; on the same day Wallop writes Burghley on military matters, and he later advises the government to prosecute the war against Desmond as energetically as possible; in 1585 he begs not to be made the colleague of Loftus again, and adds, "he ys a very good precher and petye he ys not imployed only therein" (*C. S. P. Ir. 1574-1585* 97. 16, 97. 17, 98. 15, 102. 54; pp. cxxxiii-iv). In 1594 Lodowick Bryskett was the occasion of another quarrel between Wallop, who recommended him for the position of clerk of faculties, and Loftus, whose candidate was William Ussher (Plomer and Cross, p. 54).

3410-21. Sir John Perrot, Lord Deputy from 1584 to 1588, may have been an illegitimate child of Henry Eighth and so a half-brother of Elizabeth, whom on one occasion he called "a base bastard pisskytching" (Sir Robert Naunton, *Fragmenta Regalia*, 1870, p. 43; *C. S. P. Ir. 1588-1592* 161. 19). His violent temper made enemies of such men as Loftus and Sir Geoffrey Fenton, on whose evidence he was charged with treason in 1591; and he was pardoned by Elizabeth only shortly before his death in the next year (anonymous *History of Sir John Perrott*, pp. 20, 242-5; *C. S. P. Ir. 1588-1592* 157. 9). E. C. S. writes (p. 71):

> Amongst the informations against the Deputy, there was obiected, that hee had taken strict courses in his gouernment, as requiring the Oath of obedience; appointing Officers to looke into mens Patents, Warrants giuen in the late Parliament, to preferre Bills for making the like Lawes, as were in *England* against Recusants. Causing a Bill to be preferred in the first Session, for the suspension of *Poynings* Act, to the hazard of stirring vp a commotion: Vrging that these courses did decline the people from peace to vnquietnesse: Such force had slander got by malicious Enuie, as to make a Bee a Spider, and to worke that honey without, of the flowers of his iudgement and sincerity, he had painfully gathered, to a corrupt poyson, as by the wofull effect, it, in after time, too manifestly appeared.

COMMENTARY

Admiration, however, is expressed for Perrot by John Hooker and Camden (Holinshed, vol. II, *The Supplie of the Irish Chronicles*, p. 134; *Annales*, p. 350; *Britannia*, p. 708); his departure was bewailed by the Irish (Bagwell 3. 167-8); the city of Dublin presented him with a gilt bowl inscribed "*Relinquo in pace*," and he himself declared, "I have lefte all in Peace" (anonymous *History of Sir John Perrott*, pp. 286-8; E. C. S., p. 134). His popularity with the Irish is precisely what Spenser, who favors strong military action, attacks; but if, as has been suggested, Sir Satyrane is intended to represent Perrot, in 1590 Spenser must have thought of him as unwise rather than disloyal (Charles H. Whitman, *A Subject-Index to the Poems of Edmund Spenser*, 1918, pp. 208-9).

3418.   "buxome." MORLEY. Bow-some, pliant, yielding.

3418-20.   RENWICK. The sinister phrase about purposes of his own refers no doubt to the rumours which led to Perrot's trial for treason on his return, that he had designs on more permanent power than that of a Lord Deputy. His real fault was clearly what Camden called "his owne lavish tongue . . . for unadvisedly hee had let flie somewhat against the Princes Majestie."

3426-7.   RENWICK identifies "the nexte after him" as FitzWilliam [Lord Deputy from 1588 to 1594. See *B. N.* 45-56 and note on same.]

3428-30.   RENWICK. Cf. Grey, Aug. 12, 1581: "I know hir Maiesties inclinacion so bente, vppon temporising withe a calme and peceable cours, as I would not enter into a matter of warre, that afterwardes might lacke dew prosecution." (*S. P. Ir.* 85. 13)

3441-54.   Lee (ff. 37ᵛ–38ʳ), himself a captain, points out that the Lord Deputy, the petty clerks, and the merchants make money, under the present system of paying the soldiers, but that the captains, who must furnish their companies before receiving payment, are cheated.

3443-5.   RENWICK. Another commonplace; as Keeper of Musters for Wexford Spenser knew something about it. See Wallop's letter of Aug. 13, 1595 in *Cal. S. P. Ir.* and *passim*.

3463-72.   In 1584 Lord Delvin proposed committing the payment of the soldier to a noble or councillor (John T. Gilbert, p. 192); and in 1587 an order compelled both captain and clerk to swear to the accuracy of their figures and specified a fine of six months' pay for any captain who failed to present a true muster roll of his band (*C. S. P. Ir. 1586-1588* 131. 39). Spenser's scheme overlooks the obvious danger of collusion between captain and paymaster, a form of dishonesty which seems to have occurred later (*C. C. MSS. 1589-1600*, p. 328).

3472.   "*Pagadore*." TODD. Spanish; a paymaster or treasurer.

COLLIER. It does not strictly mean "treasurer," but is the proper term for the *paymaster* of a regiment; from *pagar*, to pay.

[Spenser may recollect the title *pagator exerciti* which Giustiniani held in the list of Spanish and Italian officers spared at Smerwick (State Papers 63. 78. 27). See Appendix III, section D.]

3472-5.   Theoretically each captain led a band of one hundred men, but it often mustered only forty, thirty-five, thirty, or less; in 1595 Wallop wrote that few captains had above forty able Englishmen, and in the next year Russell boasted that he had raised to full hundreds the Irish bands which had been reduced to sixties (*C. S. P. Ir. 1588-1592* 161. 59, *1592-1596* 182. 1, *1596-1597* 191. 51).

3483-5.   Protections were almost universally condemned (*e. g.*, *C. S. P. Ir. 1598-1599* 202. 3. 55, *1599-1600* 205. 72; Chambrun MS, Folger Shakespeare Library, f. 238ᵛ). "The Rebellion was nourished and increased by nothing more," Moryson writes, "then frequent Protections and Pardons, granted euen to those, who had formerly abused this mercy, so as all entred and continued to bee Rebels, with assurance to be receiued to mercy at their pleasure, whereof they spared not to brag" (*Itinerary*, part II, p. 13). See 2853.

3489-90.   "formerlie."   That Spenser intended "formally," as the Gough MS reads, is supported by "Formerly" in *F. Q.* 2. 12. 1. 4, where, as J. C. Smith conjectures, "Formally" seems to have been meant.

3494.   By "the laste generall warrs" Spenser means the Desmond rebellion; see note on 3199-3200.

3500.   "Arch-Rebell."   The same epithet is applied to Tyrone by Essex (*C. S. P. Ir. 1599-1600* 205. 140) and by Ralph Byrchensha (*A Discovrse Occasioned vpon the Late Defeat, Giuen to the Arch-rebels, Tyrone and Odonnell*, 1602, sigs. A2ʳ, B3ʳ, C3ᵛ).

3505-7.   Tyrone made submissions to the English government in 1590, 1593, 1594, and 1595 (Robert Dunlop, article on Tyrone, *DNB*; *C. S. P. Ir. 1592-1596* 183. 108. 1); Sir William Warren described the negotiations undertaken to secure a new agreement in April, September, October, and November, 1596 (John T. Gilbert, pp. 242-52). From then on, Tyrone contrived to hold frequent conferences with English officials, to bargain for short truces or permanent submission; the most notable of these parleys was held with Essex on 7-8 September, 1599 (*C. S. P. Ir. 1599-1600* 205. 164). In 1596 Sir John Dowdall writes that Tyrone only submits in order to gain time; later it is pointed out that the Earl submits regularly in the spring and fall, when the grain is sown and harvested; and the instructions given Lord Deputy Mountjoy at the beginning of his government in 1600 warned him not to be deceived by Tyrone's offers to come in (*C. S. P. Ir. 1592-1596* 187. 19, *1598-1599* 202. 2. 54, *1599-1600* 207. 72).

3507-15.   See *B. N.* 67-75.

3517-8.   In 1593 Ralegh wrote of the greatest king in Christendom: "The Kinge of Spayne seeketh not Irlande for Irlande, but hauinge raysed up troops of beggers in our backs, shall be able to inforce us to cast our eyes over our shoulders, while thos before us strike us on the braynes" (John P. Hennessy, *Sir Walter Raleigh in Ireland*, 1883, p. 180). On 27 September, 1595, Tyrone and O'Donnell address Philip: "Our only hope of re-establishing the Catholic religion rests on your assistance"; on 22 January, 1596, the King replies, "you need not doubt but I will render you any assistance you require"; on 5-6 May, 1596, Cobos, an emissary

COMMENTARY

of Philip's, held conferences with Tyrone (*C. C. MSS. 1589-1600*, pp. 122, 141; *C. S. P. Ir. 1592-1596* 190. 42. 1). At the beginning of December, 1596, Henry Hawkins wrote from Venice that Philip had given the title of King of Ireland to Tyrone, on condition that Spanish garrisons would be received in two of the chief ports (Birch, *Memoirs* 2. 209). At the same time Spanish forces had actually landed in O'Donnell's country (see note on 2936-43). Dymmok (p. 51) traces Tyrone's defection entirely to his oath to support the Spaniards with armed forces should they land in England.

3522-7. O'Donnell, MacMahon, and Maguire were the respective overlords of Donegal, Monaghan, and Fermanagh; of these Hugh Roe O'Donnell was by far the most influential (*C. S. P. Ir. 1596-1597*, p. xxvi). Tyrone, O'Donnell, and Maguire were suspected of joining with treasonable intent as far back as 1593, and in 1595 Burghley noted that Tyrone, O'Donnell, Maguire, and MacMahon should be offered equal terms (*C. S. P. Ir. 1592-1596* 172. 19. 4, notes 1, 2; 183. 68). Three years later Tyrone refused to accept a truce in which O'Donnell did not share (*C. S. P. Ir. 1598-1599* 202. 1. 89).

3529-48. The genealogy of the O'Neills is as follows:

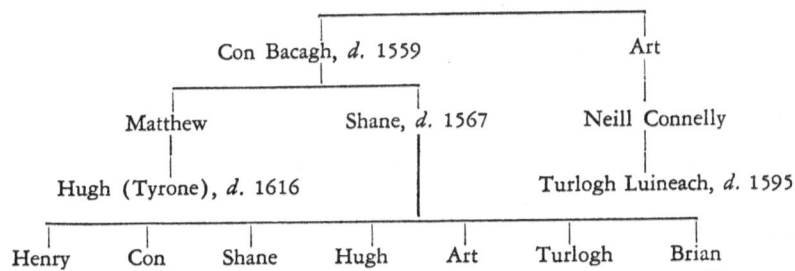

See *A Miscellany of Irish Bardic Poetry*, ed. Lambert McKenna, 2. 360; Paul Walsh, *The Will and Family of Hugh O'Neill, Earl of Tyrone*, p. 64; *PRIA*, Archaeology 40. 132-42; Hamilton, p. 18; *C. S. P. Ir. 1574-1585* 65. 6. 2, *1588-1592* 150. 21.

3529-33. RENWICK. The great Shane O'Neill had 7 sons, two of whom, being legitimate, were valuable according to English ideas. The captaincy was not hereditary, but they had prestige as their father's sons; the notion is as old as 1579 (*S. P. Ir.* 65. 5), and Tyrone kept them close.

EDITOR. Shane O'Neill, who had usurped the captaincy of the O'Neills contrary to the laws of tanistry, excelled in all bestiality and was finally murdered (see Camden, *Annales*, pp. 131-2; *JRSAI* 18. 449-62, 19. 53-8). His son Hugh was hanged, reportedly by Tyrone, in 1590; in 1594 his sons Henry, Con, and Brian are reported to be detained in prison by Tyrone (*C. S. P. Ir. 1588-1592* 150. 21, 29; *Four Masters* 6. 1887; *C. C. MSS. 1589-1600*, p. 94). On 20 December, 1596, Mathias Holmes suggests setting up some of the O'Neills against Tyrone (*HMC, Salisbury Manuscripts* 6. 531), and he probably has the sons of Shane in mind.

3533-8. RIEDNER (pp. 42-3) connects this fable with Aesop 383; "Der Dichter weicht aber von Aesop darin ab, dass er den Hirsch von dem Menschen verfolgt und erschlagen werden lässt." [See Caxton's *Book of the Subtyl Historyes and Fables of Esope* (1484), reprinted David Nutt, 2. 113-4.]

3540-5. RENWICK. Turlough Lynagh, Shane's successor, died in September, 1595, a drunken old man, but O'Neill, and so an obstacle to Tyrone's ambition. Tyrone had himself inaugurated at once, despite his vows never to do so.

EDITOR. Con Bacagh had held both the native title of the O'Neill and that of Earl of Tyrone, bestowed by Henry Eighth; through Con's illegitimate son Matthew, Hugh inherited the Tyrone title in 1586; the title of the O'Neill went first to Con's legitimate son Shane, then to Shane's second cousin Turlogh Luineach, and in 1595 to Shane's nephew Hugh, already Earl of Tyrone. Tyrone, according to Moryson (*Itinerary*, part II, p. 7), "had a troope of horse in Queene Elizabeths pay, in the late warres of the Earle of Desmond, in which and all occasions of seruice he behaued himselfe so valiantly, as the Queene gaue him a yeerely pension of one thousand Markes." Even the astute Wallop at first defended the policy of entertaining Tyrone against Turlogh (*C. S. P. Ir. 1574-1585* 78. 70); Turlogh himself remarked, "They had put up a Whealpe, which they would not be able to pull down soe easily" (anonymous *History of Sir John Perrott*, p. 270).

3543. The letters patent which created Con O'Neill Earl of Tyrone in 1542 provided that the heir of that title should be known as Baron of Dungannon, a castle in Co. Tyrone, a few miles west of Lough Neagh (John J. Marshall, *A History of Dungannon*, pp. 17-8).

3544. "bearde." TODD. To *affront* him. See F. Q. vi. v. 12.

3552. "lifted vp . . . out of the duste." See *H. L.* 177 and notes on 177, 183, *Minor Poems* 1. 517.

3553-5. The allusion is to another of Aesop's fables (see note on 3533-8). In Caxton's version it is called "of the man and of the serpent" (*The Book of the Subtyl Historyes and Fables of Esope* [1484], reprinted David Nutt, 2. 15); but in the Latin of Hieronymus Osius the title "Agricola et Angvis" is closer to Spenser (*Phrygis Aesopi Fabulae*, 1564, f. B4r). In 1583 Ralegh writes to Burghley of Oxford: "I am contente, for your sake, to laye the sarpente before the fire, as miche as in me lieth, that having recovered strengthe myself may be moste in danger of his poyson and stinge" (Edwards 2. 22).

3558-75. In 1596 the employment of three thousand Scots in Ulster was favored by Lord Deputy Russell (*C. C. MSS. 1589-1600*, p. 197); Sir John Norris, Sir Richard Bingham, and other English commanders supported the idea (*C. S. P. Ir. 1596-1597* 191. 45, *1598-1599* 203. 1; Hamilton, pp. 192-7). But Lord Deputy Sidney had endeavored to expell Scotch mercenaries in 1568 (*Letters and Memorials* 1. 35), and Spenser's opinion may be influenced by Grey's efforts to put the Scotch out of Antrim (Hamilton, pp. 97-8). Sir Geoffrey Fenton writes in 1596: "There is so great unlikelihood that the rebels of Ulster can be pulled down by the Scots of Cantire or the Islands, for dogs will not eat dogs' flesh" (*C. S. P. Ir. 1596-1597* 197. 67, 90).

3561-8. WARE. The causes of these feares have been amputated, since the happy union of *England* and *Scotland*, established by his late Majesty.

COMMENTARY 391

RENWICK. In Oct., 1595, Captain George Thornton, an old acquaintance of Spenser, was sent to negotiate with Argyll and Maclean for mercenaries, but nothing was done. (*S. P. Ir.* 183. 77) Turlough Lynagh had married Lady Agnes Campbell, Argyll's daughter [grand-aunt of the seventh Earl of Argyll, who held the title in 1596], and there were many other intermarriages.

EDITOR. In their proposals for hiring Scotch soldiers Russell and the Irish Council were careful "to note . . . that the McConnells have had always friendship with the O'Nelles, both by marriage, fostering, and bonnaught, and therefore not to be trusted to serve her Majesty in this weighty service"; and Sir Nicholas Malby had earlier pointed out the dangers of Turlogh's marriage to a Campbell (*C. C. MSS. 1589-1600*, p. 197; *1575-1588*, p. 297). In addition Turlogh's daughter was affianced to a young MacConnell in 1579; and Tyrone was careful to maintain the Scotch connection by putting his son to foster with Angus MacConnell and promising his daughter in marriage to the Earl of Argyll (*C. S. P. Ir. 1574-1585* 66. 14, *1596-1597* 198. 37). As a result of these alliances the O'Neills could draw on Scotland for an endless supply of soldiers (see, *e. g.*, *C. S. P. Ir. 1574-1585* 50. 4; *1586-1588*, pp. xxvi-xxxiv; *1588-1592* 146. 12; *1592-1596* 173. 94). In 1595, however, a rupture occurred when Tyrone murdered a relative of Argyll's (*C. S. P. Ir. 1592-1596* 183. 77. 1), and this unexpected opportunity was responsible for the English plans to hire Scotch mercenaries and so for Spenser's warning against such a course (see note on 3558-75). The circumstances surrounding this situation are fully described by Eoin MacNeill, *Scots Mercenary Forces in Ireland (1565-1603)*, 1937, pp. 225-300.

3569-73. WARE. *Vide Bed. Eccles. Hist. lib.* 1. *cap.* 1. [See note on 1169-80.]

3585-9. See 152-6 and note on same. Con O'Neill did not vote in the parliament which passed the act of royalization in 1541; but his submission, made in 1542 at the time he was created Earl of Tyrone, contains nothing to show that he reserved all his rights and signories to himself, and he specifically renounced certain of his rights (*C. C. MSS. 1515-1574*, pp. 188-9).

3590-3607. COVINGTON (*UTB*, Studies in English 4. 33). Spenser's source for this passage is uncertain: Holinshed seems to have nothing similar. Camden, however, in his description of the province of Ulster, gives a brief account of its fortunes in historic times, to which Spenser's explanation bears some resemblance. [See *Britannia*, pp. 710-11.]

RENWICK. There is something like this in the Act of Attainder of Shane O'Neill, 1569 [*All the Statutes*, ff. 160ʳ–161ᵛ; *The Statvtes of Ireland*, pp. 315-20], and in Camden; but they attribute the rise or revival of O'Neill's power to the Wars of the Roses. Spenser is making only a vague summary.

EDITOR. See Campion, pp. 100-1. The O'Neills actually founded their petty kingship in the fifth century and gradually enlarged it until it included all central Ulster; in 916 they became kings of that region; and they held the title until 1260, when Brian O'Neill was slain by the English at the battle of Dun (Hogan, *PRIA*, Archaeology 40. 201, 207, 218).

3596-9. See 443-553.

3617-24. JENKINS (*PMLA* 52. 341-7). "Of all the Irish leaders Feagh McHugh appears to approach most closely the wily Malengin of the *Legend of Justice* . . . . throughout Spenser's career in Ireland, no Irish rebel more constantly dogged the poet's footsteps." Jenkins believes that Spenser must have accompanied Grey on his expeditions against Feagh in August, 1580, in June, 1581, and in August, 1581.

EDITOR. In 1575 Feagh MacHugh initiated his career by stealing cattle; in five years he had burned the town of Rathcoole within a few miles of Dublin (Bagwell 2. 311, 3. 81). From then on he harried Leinster and even Meath (*e. g.*, Four Masters 6. 1957, 2007). His depredations were made doubly obnoxious by his insolence (*C. S. P. Ir. 1574-1585* 99. 70, 101. 3, p. lxxxiv); on one occasion he refused a pardon unless the like were also given to Desmond and "religion might be at liberty" (Bagwell 3. 91; *C. S. P. Ir. 1574-1585* 84. 12). Yet in 1594 he is estimated to have no more than a hundred and forty men and to be old and sickly, not to be reckoned with by himself (*C. S. P. Ir. 1592-1596* 177. 34, 180. 22. 3). Lee (f. 16^{r-v}) writes Elizabeth that to deal with Feagh and his adherents is a great dishonor to a prince. As he is here described, Feagh resembles the Ape in *Hub.* 949-1384.

3621. "suffer suche a Caitiffe playe suche Rex." See "suffer none to play the Rex" in Harvey's *Pierces Supererogation*, 1593, p. 72.

3624. "Comericke." MORLEY. Fellowship of warriors; Old Irish, *comrac*, is a coming together, also battle. [See note on 1434-7.]

3634-6. COVINGTON (*UTB*, Studies in English 4. 15-6). This seems to mean that Spenser through association with members of these two important clans was able to secure, and was interested enough to secure, genealogical data from them; and that in addition he consulted historical works for the same purpose. What these were it is impossible to say; but it is probable that detailed accounts of Irish families would be found only in Irish writings,—in particular, in the chronicles.

3636-9. See 1430-2 and notes.

3639 n. DRAPER (*MP* 17. 481-2). The noun *bryn* or *brin* is a common Welsh word meaning *hill*. In Irish, *brinne* means *wood*; but there is *bruinne*, having the original sense of *breast*, and also the tropical sense of *hill* in Irish poetry. Anyone who knew of the *bryn* in Welsh and who ran across *bruinne* in this use, in Irish, might easily associate the two as cognates, as indeed they probably are. The Welsh noun Spenser evidently knew imperfectly, for he gave it as an adjective, but where he picked up knowledge, even as inaccurate as this, is an interesting question. [The question probably applies to the scribe of Additional MS 22022 rather than to Spenser. In any case, the present passage deals wholly with the Welsh word *bryn*, not with an Irish word of similar sound.]

DRAPER (*MP* 17. 483). *Toll*, in varied forms, occurs in all the insular Celtic languages, and regularly signifies a *hole* or *perforation*. . . . The word probably had the meaning of *hollow* and *dell*, and so *valley*, in Irish as well as in Scotch Gaelic; but no such use appears in Welsh; and the sense of *dark* does not seem to occur at all. [William Salesbury's *Dictionary in Englyshe and Welshe*,

COMMENTARY 393

1547 (reprinted 1877), defines Welsh "*twll*" as "a hole" and "*tywyll*" as "Derke"; the scribe of Additional MS 22022, who shows great linguistic independence, has apparently corrected Spenser and then, to be on the safe side, added the meaning of another Welsh word which is similar in sound.]

3640-6. Camden, however, seems to deny that these people were in continuous possession of their lands from before the English conquest (*Britannia*, ed. of 1594 p. 658; passage not in earlier editions).

3642. "Dermotnigald." WARE. *Dermot Mac Murrogh* King of Leinster, who was surnamed [also *added in Osgood copy*] *ni-Gall*, as being a friend to the *English*, and a cheife instrument in inciting them to the conquest of *Ireland*. [See note on 370-1.]

3650-2. Heffner has suggested that this refers to Feagh's recapture of Ballinecor on 10 September, 1596 (*C.S.P.Ir. 1596-1597* 193. 10, 193. 10. 1; see *MLN* 52. 178); but it is more likely that Spenser has in mind a raid by Feagh's henchmen in January, 1595, which the Four Masters describe (6. 1957): "Walter Reagh and some of the sons of Fiagh, the son of Hugh, set out upon a nocturnal excursion (in sleeping time) to Cruimghlinn, near the gate of Dublin. They burned and totally plundered that town [bally], and took away as much as they were able to carry of the leaden roof of the church of the town; and though the blaze and flames of the burning town were plainly visible in the streets of Dublin, Walter escaped without wound or bloodshed." The plural form of "successes" in the Ellesmere and Caius MSS should be noted. See also Appendix III, section B; *C. C. MSS. 1589-1600*, p. 226; *C. S. P. Ir. 1592-1596* 180. 31.

3654-8. See notes on 370-1, 3642.

3659. "*Obrin.*" WARE. Or *O-Birne*.

3660-72. RENWICK. The elective chieftaincy always baffled the English mind. Feagh MacHugh rose to power on the death of Teige Oge O'Byrne in 1578, the head of a different branch of the clan whose fortunes were on the decline as Feagh's rose. (The Four Masters, 5. 1702, 9, 12-13, and O'Donovan's notes) [O'Donovan's note shows that Feagh's grandfather was Shane, the son of Redmond, not of Turlogh. At the beginning of the sixteenth century the O'Byrnes and O'Tooles together commanded less than a hundred horsemen (Harris 1. 44); 130 men are listed as serving Hugh MacShane in 1578 (*C. S. P. Ir. 1574-1585* 63. 2).]

3664-5. In all probability Spenser judged the strength of Glenmalure from personal experience (Judson, *Life*, p. 88). There in August, 1580, Grey suffered a severe defeat at the hands of Feagh and Viscount Baltinglas (Bagwell 3. 60-2), a defeat which Spenser remembers in his reference to the River Avonbeg as "balefull Oure, late staind with English blood" (*F. Q.* 4. 11. 44. 5). In Hooker's account of the affair (Holinshed, vol. II, *The Supplie of the Irish Chronicles*, p. 169) the glen is described as "lieng in the midle of the wood, of a great length, betweene two hils, and no other waie is there to passe through," etc. See also Camden, *Annales*, p. 293. Sir Nicholas White reports, "I was at Ballynecor, Feagh M'Hugh O'Byrne's chief house, standing at the mouth of the Glynn, where law never approached "; although Ballinecor was burned in 1581, Feagh succeeded in re-establishing himself there, and Sir Ralph Lane still speaks of the glen with awe in 1595 (*C. S. P. Ir. 1574-1585* 112. 26. 1, 82. 6; *1592-1596* 178. 43). An Irish manuscript in the British Museum describes Ballinecor as a seat of banqueting and games (Standish H. O'Grady and Robin Flower, *A Catalogue of Irish Manuscripts in the British Museum* 1. 508-9).

3673-80. GREENLAW (*MP* 7. 198), connecting this passage with Tyrone, not Feagh, notes that the terms used suggest a Machiavellian hero.

3685-8. WARE. *Vide Camdeni annales, sub finem anni* 1594.

RENWICK. Russell was pressing Feagh in Feb., 1595, when more serious affairs in Ulster drew him off. He captured [*i. e.*, beheaded] Feagh in 1597. Lord Chancellor Gerrarde wrote as early as 1580, before the rise of Tyrone, "the most who have travelled to seeke refourm and the best experyenced have ever sett downe their plattes to begynne with [the Byrnes and Tooles] to expell them and sett ij or iij Fortes and place Englishe." (*S. P. Ir.* 76. 6)

EDITOR. Sir William Russell was Lord Deputy from 1594 to 1597; his military exploits were long remembered in Ireland, if we may believe William Walker (*A Sermon Preached at the Fvnerals of the Right Honourable, William, Lord Rvssell, Baron of Thornhaugh*, 1614, p. 45), and he is praised by Lee (f. 36ʳ) and Beacon (pp. 43-4). See also *B. N.* 93-8. The expedition of early 1595 to which Spenser alludes is described by the Four Masters (6. 1955-7): "The Chief Justiciary of Ireland, Sir William Russell, marched to Baile-na-cuirre in the month of January, against Fiagh, the son of Hugh [O'Byrne], at the instance of Fiagh's neighbours and acquaintances. Upon their arrival in the neighbourhood of the castle, but before they had passed through the gate of the rampart that surrounded it, the sound of a drum was accidentally heard from the soldiers who were going to the castle. Fiagh, with his people, took the alarm; and he rose up suddenly, and sent a party of his people to defend the gate; and he sent all his people, men, boys, and women, out through the postern-doors of the castle, and he himself followed them, and conveyed them all in safety to the wilds and recesses, where he considered them secure"; Russell lingered ten days at Ballinecor in vain. But not discouraged, he set a price of a hundred pounds on Feagh's head and a hundred and fifty for his capture alive (*C. S. P. Ir. 1592-1596* 178. 44). Expeditions to Glenmalure were sent out in the spring of 1595, the fall of 1596, and the spring of 1597; finally, on 8 May, 1597, Feagh was caught, wounded, and beheaded by Russell's forces (*C. C. MSS. 1589-1600*, pp. 229-30, 249-53, 258-9; *C. S. P. Ir. 1596-1597* 199. 28). See Appendix III, section B.

3690. "maddinge." See note on *Ax.* 231.

3690-2. For the O'Moores and Cavanaghs see notes on 619-21. The lesser branches of the Butler family, who were given to outlawry, dominated Lower Ossory in Co. Kilkenny (anonymous *Description of Ireland*, pp. 67-70). A letter from Archbishop Loftus and Thomas Jones to Burghley, 22 November, 1596, describes the same three families as confederates of Feagh's (*C. S. P. Ir. 1596-1597* 195. 27).

COMMENTARY 395

3703-4. As early as 1542 John Allen proposed to lay waste the lands held by the Cavanaghs, O'Tooles, and O'Byrnes (*State Papers, Henry VIII* 3. 393).

3707-11. Spenser, however, later proposes to interchange the rebels of Leinster and Ulster and to disintegrate the system of dwelling by septs (3859-3901), a plan which overlooks the difficulties mentioned here.

3722-31. RENWICK (*View*, p. 327). Ware says 6 *garrisons*, and adds 50 *horsemen* at Arklow or Wicklow: which, whether it have textual authority or not, corrects the arithmetic. [It is possible that the last two forces were so small that Spenser did not think of them as garrisons.]

3722. In 1594 Lee (f. 34^{r-v}) estimated that a hundred footmen and twenty or twenty-five horsemen could defeat Feagh.

3723-5. Ballinecor lies at the southern end of Glenmalure in the center of Co. Wicklow. See notes on 427, 3664-5.

3725-6. RENWICK (*View*, map op. p. 330) apparently identifies "knocklouh" as some place a few miles east of Tullow. ["Knockloe" House appears in this position on the Ordnance Survey map, in Co. Wicklow close to the Carlow border, an excellent position in which to cut off the O'Byrnes from the latter county. The name may be related to that "Knocklooe" where Cahir MacGerald O'Byrne built a stone castle during the reign of Elizabeth (*Inquisitionum in Officio Rotulorum Repertorium*, ed. James Hardiman, vol. I, Wicklow, inq. 11 James First; *JRSAI* 41. 147-8).

3728-9. On Baptista Boazio's map of Ireland (ed. dedicated to James First) "B. 3. Ca." is marked at the source of the Liffey, not far from the present boundary between the counties of Wicklow and Dublin. See also *C. C. MSS. 1515-1574*, p. 140; *Calendar of the Patent and Close Rolls* 1. 92).

3729-31. Talbotstown, one of the six baronies of Co. Wicklow, stood west of Glenmalure near the border of Kildare (*C. C. MSS. 1589-1600*, p. 189).

3750-1. "atchivinge." MORLEY. Finishing.

3752-6. RENWICK. Gerrarde complains of the difficulty of finding good officers, and of the superseding of experienced captains by new ones. He says Grey objected to this practice; as we might expect of him. [The same opinion was held by Sir John Norris, Sir Geoffrey Fenton, and others (*C. S. P. Ir. 1596-1597* 191. 46. 1, *1599-1600* 207. 89; Chambrun MS, Folger Shakespeare Library, f. 240^r; René de Lucinge, *The Beginning, Continvance, and Decay of Estates*, trans. Sir John Finett, 1606, pp. 41-2).]

3760-8. RENWICK. Contrariwise, Sir Callisthenes Brooke applied for a transfer to the Low Countries, on the ground that he was not learning his profession properly in these guerilla affairs, which required huntsmen, not soldiers.

3772. MORLEY. He who cannot obey, cannot command.

RENWICK. *Parere qui nescit, nescit imperare* is as old as Aristotle's *Politica*, and apparently older still.

3775. "Cuttinge." *NED* defines the adj. (def. 3) as "That is a 'cutter' or swaggering blade" and records no earlier use of it than Richard Harvey's in 1589. [See also Grosart, Harvey's *Works* 3. 132. Spenser may pun, more or less unconsciously, on the terms *cut* and *shuffle* in card play.]

3787-3800. RENWICK. An old story. For the same in England, see Harrison in Holinshed's Chronicle, Harman, and all books on vagrancy and Poor Laws, also *Mother Hubberds Tale*, 183 ff. and our note thereon. Burleigh's view was that soldiering was "a Science no longer in Request then use. For Souldiers in Peace, are like Chimneys in Summer." (To his Son, in Peck's *Desiderata Curiosa*, p. 65) Walsingham had more sympathy: see *The Ruines of Time*, 440-448, which may refer particularly to his support of Bingham. Grey'[s] despatches show his thoughtfulness for the advancement of his captains and for his men. In the Smerwick despatch, for instance, he writes to the Queen: "I most humbly therefore beseech your Maiesty in consideration of your owne servise and compassion of the poore, ragged, and naked creatures to affoord them a thorough pay." He recommends discharged soldiers in several letters, and persistently refused to disband troops after the Munster wars until arrangements had been made for their pay and transport home. [See *Hub*. 193-280 and notes, *Minor Poems* 2. 354-6.]

3810-4. In 1610 Thomas Blenerhasset (*A Direction for the Plantation in Vlster*, sig. B3r-v) outlined a similar plan to settle old soldiers on the excheated lands in Ulster; he proposed to continue their pay and reduce their fees to the Crown since they would make garrisons unnecessary.

3812-3. "husbandes." MORLEY. Husbandmen.

3841-8. Sir William Pelham writes of Munster in 1580: "the poor people that lived only upon labour, and fed by their milch cows, are so distressed, as they follow their goods [*i. e.*, cattle] and offer themselves with their wives and children rather to be slain by the army than to suffer the famine that now in extremity beginneth to pinch them" (*C. C. MSS. 1575-1588*, p. 293; paraphrased in Holinshed, vol. II, *The Supplie of the Irish Chronicles*, pp. 168-9).

3844. MORLEY. "Tag rag" is end and shred, the least and poorest.

NED (*tag-rag*, def. C). Pell-mell; one and all; in a mingled crowd or heap, promiscuously. [See also Holinshed, vol. II, *The Description of Ireland*, p. 25; Harvey, *Pierces Supererogation*, 1593, p. 116.]

3852-7. Sir Humphrey Gilbert would take, as pledges for an Irish leader's good conduct, not those he loved best, but the most powerful men of the same region (Thomas Churchyard, *The Firste Parte of Churchyardes Chippes*, 1575, sig. Q3r); and Sir Thomas Norris felt that children were unsuitable as hostages because, according to the tanist system, they were not the inheritors of lands and signories and most of them were of base birth (*C. S. P. Ir. 1588-1592* 152. 45. 1).

3857-64. GREENLAW (*MP* 7. 197-8) notes that Machiavelli recommends the two policies of disarming and dispersing the conquered (*Il Principe*, cap. 20, 5).

3859-64. SOUTHEY (p. 211). He was for transplanting — as Cromwell did.

COMMENTARY 397

RENWICK. This typical officialism recalls the instructions to Perrot in *S. P. Ir.* 121. 53, that suspected persons "together with the Galloglasses and kerne of those partes neere the attainted lands be first removed (by such meanes as may bee without offence as nere as may bee) to some remote parts provided of some convenient place for habitacion where they may bee imployed in profitable service." Cf. Ralegh, *Maxims of State*: "The safest way is . . . that some good part of the Natives be transplanted into some other place, and our Colonies . . . be planted there in some part of the Province, *Castles, Forts*, and *Havens*." Spenser advocates as a permanent reorganisation the operation carried out as a temporary war measure in South Africa in 1901-2, and for the same reasons that applied there, or anywhere in guerilla warfare in the enemy's country.

3860. "Crete." See note on 3114.

3865. "a godes name." See note on 637.

3867-71. WARE. This carrieth no fit proportion for the transplantation intended by the Author, considering the large extent of *Vlster*, and the narrow bounds heere limited.

EDITOR. Similarly Lord Deputy Sussex endeavored to remove the O'Moores from Leix and the O'Connors from Offaly in the middle of the sixteenth century, but by Spenser's day they had returned (anonymous *Description of Ireland*, pp. 76-7, 86). In 1600 it was proposed to banish them again (*C. C. MSS. 1589-1600*, p. 506); and in 1606 Lord Deputy Chichester, who at one time owned Additional MS 22022 of the *View*, reported that he was in the process of removing the O'Moores and intended to remove the O'Connors (*C. S. P. Ir. 1606-1608*, p. 95).

3887-9. GREENLAW (*MP* 7. 198) points out that colonies were included in Machiavelli's plans for the subjugation of the conquered (*Il Principe*, cap. 3).

RENWICK. The policy of plantation was very old and much discussed; and is too well known to discuss again.

[Spenser proposes a more thorough colonization than Machiavelli, who advizes one or two settlements of the conquerors in key positions. Precedents in Ireland had been the ill-fated colonization of the Ardes by Sir Thomas Smith in 1572 and the division of the Desmond lands in Munster among such undertakers as Spenser himself; but the first settlements for which any large success might be claimed were made in the confiscated lands of the O'Neills during the reign of James First.]

3904-12. RENWICK. This is Spenser's answer to Burleigh's complaint to Wallop, that he marvelled the Council of Ireland could not make that realm self-supporting. (*S. P. Ir.* 178. 67) [Beacon, Spenser's associate in the Council of Munster, offers the same general plan (p. 87).]

3906. "Chieferie." TODD. *Chiefrie* is a small rent paid to the Lord paramount. JOHNSON.

RENWICK. A *chiefery* is a money rent.

3912-7. MORLEY. *Romescot*, or Romeshot. The name was commonly applied to the Peter pence, or tax of a penny on every house formerly paid on Lammas Day to the Pope.

RENWICK. Holinshed I. p. 10 [ed. 1586, vol. I, *The Description of Britaine*, p. 5]: "They planted their forworne legions in the most fertile places of the realme, and where they might best lie for the safegard of their conquests." But *Romescot* is the English name for "Peter's Pence," the Papal tax: Spenser is guessing from the word to the system. [See Spelman, G*lossarium Archaiologicum*, p. 490.]

3915. "Cuttinge." See note on 239.

3923-8. William Herbert illustrates the reasoning which Spenser refutes: "si coloniarum vero loco militum copiae substituantur, majorem in ea re princeps sumptum faciet. Cum in praesidiis id totum sit illi absumendum quod ex ea ditione fuerit prouentus: offenduntur praeterea multo plures, nam tota prouincia castris mutandis laeditur, cuius incommodo caeteris omnibus affectis in omnium etiam odium et offensionem incurrit" (*Croftus, sive de Hibernia Liber*, p. 36). See *B. N.* 156-213.

3933-42. RENWICK. Spenser's plan is an extension of the system already used in some places, that lands were set apart for the maintenance of the garrison, and of the system of composition which was growing, and had been put in practice by Bingham in Connaught, whereby the indefinite cess and tribal dues were replaced by a fixed annual contribution. He puts the maintenance of the garrisons on this as a first charge.

3949. "Cese." Meaning simply *assess*, not *cess* in the special sense.

3950-7. RENWICK. With Spenser's figure compare Cusack's, quoted in a note in Dymock's treatise on Ireland (*Irish Arch. Soc.*, 1843; p. 62): "c and iiijxx and iiij cantredys (undrids other barronys) in Leynster xxxi in Connaght xxxx in Mounyster lxx in Vlster xxxv in Meyth xviii. Every cantred containeth viijxx plowlands (xxx towns) every towne cont. viij plowlands arrabile besyd the pasture of ccc kine in every towne, and none of them shall aneer the other, Sowme of heribie plowland liii.m. and iiijxx.)" In the Book of Howth (*Cal. Carew MSS* vol. 5 [*i. e.*, 6]), p. 27 ff., there are three reckonings, the second a variant of the above. In the Description of Ireland, 1598, (ed. Hogan, 1878) the total is 6814 Townlands, each containing 8 plowlands arable, besides pasture for 300 kine: 54,512 plowlands besides woods. The plowland is 120 acres, of 4 roods by 40, the rood being 21 feet. All these are interconnected, and since the Book of Howth was once in Dublin Castle, and then belonged to Sir George Carew, whom Spenser must have known, we may believe his figures derive from these or related calculations. The basis is the same, though all figures vary. The survey of Ireland was proceeding, but most remained to be done.

EDITOR. The number of acres in a ploughland varied in both England and Ireland (see Sir John Dodderidge, "Of the Dimensions of the Land of England," *A Collection of Curious Discourses*, ed. Thomas Hearne, 1720, p. 68);

some Irish ploughlands contained 440 or more acres (Henley, p. 60; Butler, p. 15; *C. S. P. Ir. 1588-1592* 142. 11). Furthermore the acre itself varied in size since the perch was not a standard measure; Spenser probably specifies twenty-one feet in order to avoid confusion with the English perch of sixteen and a half feet (Joseph Holland, "Dimensions of the Land of England," *A Collection of Curious Discourses*, ed. Thomas Hearne, 1720, p. 65).—This passage is badly confused by Spenser's arithmetic: 9,000 ploughlands of 120 acres each are 1,080,000, not 1,240,000, acres; 46 shillings 8 pence is equivalent to a little more than four pence half-penny, not 1 penny half-penny, an acre; and Ware's correction of "xlvjs viijd" to "40ˢ" seems to have been made in order to secure 18,000 pounds from 9,000 ploughlands. See note on 4047-60.

3964-6. By a "Composicion of Cesse" Spenser means a *composition in place of cess* (see note on 2481-99). Twenty shillings a ploughland is twice as much as the composition paid by Connaught in 1589 (*C. S. P. Ir. 1588-1592* 142. 19).

3977-93. RENWICK. The skill of this disposition of forts and blockhouses may be gathered from our map. The scheme is roughly thus: . . . guard the river-crossings, so as to divide O'Neill from the Scots to north-east, the comparatively quiet region to south-east, the minor chiefs to southward over whom he claimed suzerainty, and from O'Donnell to westward, with whom his predecessor fought but he entered into dangerous friendship: O'Donnell also to be cut off from Sligo and north Connaught and the unruly clans there. [Renwick forgets that according to Spenser's plans O'Neill has already been defeated (see 3776-9), and these garrisons are of a permanent nature. The positions chosen for them suggest a similar plan of Captain Nicholas Dawtrey's for placing garrisons on the Bann, at Lifford, and on the Blackwater, to be supported by the province itself (*C. S. P. Ir. 1598-1599* 202. 2. 53); Dawtrey, it is interesting, was present with Spenser at the discussion recorded in Bryskett's *Discovrse of Civill Life* (1606), and Heffner has shown a financial connection between the two (*MLN* 50. 194). It seems likely that Spenser's knowledge of Ulster geography was obtained from maps and from an acquaintance with military men like Dawtrey.]

3979-84. RENWICK. Strabane was Turlough Lynagh's seat; its strategic value was recognised by Tyrone, who destroyed it lest the English should occupy it. Lough Neagh was called Lough Sidney "by our soldiers" in compliment to Sir Henry Sidney.

JENKINS (*PMLA* 53. 354) believes that toward the close of 1588 Spenser visited Strabane in the retinue of Sir Thomas Norris.

EDITOR. Strabane is only a few miles from Lifford and Castlefinn, where Spenser had placed one of his original garrisons (see 3091-3 and note); but he underestimates geographical difficulties when he proposes to make one force serve both at Strabane and also on Lough Neagh and the Bann, forty miles away, as an equivalent for another of the original garrisons, that on the Blackwater (3089-91). The error may be due to early maps, which show the Foyle as flowing almost due east. Among places on the Bann suitable for wards the castle of "Foane" at the end of Lough Neagh is mentioned in 1579 (*C. C. MSS. 1575-1588*, p. 483). See *F. Q.* 4. 11. 41. 4.

3985-8. RENWICK. Bingham, writing on Nov. 18, 1596, says: "Ballyshannon or Sligo beinge possessed for her Maiestie and Garrizoned with Englishe (which is easie to be done, and the sooner the better), and a reasonable force to prosequute some 3 or 4 monethes, Connaght muste in necesetie submitt themselues to to her Maiesties obediencie, and be deuided from Vlster . . . miself hauinge vrdged to the Lord Deputies diuers times within these iiij yeares the takinge of Ballyshannon in to her Maiesties possession, the same beinge of more Vtilletie then Sligo . . . which beinge once done the Gale of this Rebellion were broken." (*S. P. Ir.* 195. 18) Docwra placed a fort there later on, when he founded Londonderry. A long discussion of this same plan is calendared among Carew MSS, 3. 263. [This second force occupies the position of the third of the original garrisons (see 3093-8 and notes).]

3988-93. The third garrison corresponds to the fourth of those originally planted (see 3098-3102 and note on 3098). O'Reilly's country was Co. Cavan, also known as East Breny (see note on 4220-5). Enniskillen, the stronghold of the Maguires, was built on an island between the upper and lower parts of Lough Erne; its walls are reported to have been seven feet thick; English forces had seized it in February, 1594, and held it until May, 1595, when it was betrayed after a lengthy siege (*C. S. P. Ir. 1592-1596* 173. 35. 1, 173. 19, 175. 47. 1, 179. 82). The Blackfort stood on the south side of the Blackwater, "that Riuer," a few miles north of Armagh; it was completed in 1575, captured by Tyrone in 1595, demolished by him, and rebuilt on the north side of the river (*C. S. P. Ir. 1574-1585* 52. 44, *1592-1596* 178. 53. 2; anonymous *Description of Ireland*, p. 22). The ward Spenser wishes to place here partially replaces the original garrison on the Blackwater (3089-91).

3990. The occurrence of "wardes" and "keyes" together may be a more or less unconscious pun.

3993-4009. At the end of Tyrone's rebellion, Moryson observes, Lord Deputy Mountjoy planned to establish towns around the inland forts, "as was founde by experience in the old Fortes of Lease and Ophalia, and in some newe Fortes in Vlster" (*Shakespeare's Europe*, p. 248).

4006-9. The forts in Leix and Offaly were known respectively as "Protectour" and the "Dingan" (anonymous *Description of Ireland*, pp. 75, 82). In 1553 it was proposed to build market towns around them, and a few years later the act which transformed Leix and Offaly into Queen's and King's Counties established Maryborough and Philipstown, which became market towns in 1567 and boroughs in 1569 (*C. C. MSS. 1515-1574*, p. 241; Maxwell, pp. 233-4; *JRSAI* 7. 367; *Calendar of the Patent and Close Rolls* 2. 219-23). Spenser probably visited Philipstown with Grey in 1582 (*C. S. P. Ir. 1574-1585* 93. 12).

4024. "hundredes." Subdivisions of a county, each with its own court (*NED*, def. 5). In 4799-4804 Spenser distinguishes between two kinds of hundreds, one a division of land, as here, the other a division of men.

4025-9. RENWICK. This plan was as old as Sidney's time and was revived in 1580-81. [In Holinshed (vol. II, *The Supplie of the Irish Chronicles*, p. 181)

COMMENTARY 401

Louth, Down, and Antrim are designated "Old" counties and the rest "New," *i. e.*, formed during the government of Sir John Perrot; but only the three which were long established had any real existence in Elizabeth's reign (Falkiner, *PRIA* 24. 188-9), and this may explain Spenser's proposal to do what had already been nominally performed. For the order establishing Co. Donegal in 1585 see *Inquisitionum in Officio Rotulorum Repertorium*, ed. James Hardiman, 2. xvii.]

4027. "*Colran.*" WARE. This is now part of the Countie of *Londonderry*.

4029-31. The plan to create a governor, or president, and council for Ulster had been suggested years earlier by William Herbert (*Croftus, sive de Hibernia Liber*, pp. 34, 45-6).

4040. "plowlandes." See note on 3950-7.

4040-3. In Holinshed (vol. II, *The Supplie of the Irish Chronicles*, p. 81) Leitrim is called an old county. A commission took in hand the shiring of Galway, Mayo, Roscommon, and Sligo in 1574; in 1576 Sir Henry Sidney completed the division (*C. C. MSS. 1601-1603*, p. 471; *1575-1588*, p. 48; Bagwell 2. 317).

4041. WARE. The county of *Clare* was anciently accounted part of the Province of *Mounster*, whence it hath the name of *Tuadhmuan*, or Thomond, which signifieth north *Mounster*, and hath at this day its peculiar Governour, as being exempted from the Presidencies of *Mounster* and *Connaght*.

4047-60. The reader is perplexed to find that while Sligo and Mayo will yield almost £6,000 and Roscommon £2,400, the three together are expected to give £8,700. Ware changes this to £8,300, the sum of £5,900 (almost £6,000) and £2,400; in fact, "iijC" may easily have been miscopied as "vijC" in 4059. It should also be noted that the rent in Connaught is forty shillings a ploughland "ratablye to the former," additional evidence that the rent in Ulster was intended to be forty shillings too (see note on 3950-7).

4050-1. The Castle, or "House," of Roscommon belonged to the Malby family; and in it Captain Henry Malby was besieged by the Irish for three months in 1596 (*C. S. P. Ir. 1574-1585* 84. 29, *1596-1597* 191. 13. 1; *C. C. MSS. 1589-1600*, p. 222). For descriptions and illustrations of this stronghold see *JRSAI* 20. 346-56, 37. 344. In May, 1596, the English inhabiting Co. Roscommon requested aid against the Irish; and in 1612 a description of Connaught lists in Co. Roscommon "Off Englysh transported out of the pale, the Barron of Dalvin and some of the Nugents, Sr Theobald Dillon, and dyvers others" (*C. S. P. Ir. 1592-1596* 189. 59; *Archaeologia* 27. 127).

4063. Ulick Burke, third Earl of Clanricard, was the most important landowner in Co. Galway (see anonymous *Description of Ireland*, p. 134); but lands of his are not recorded in Co. Leitrim, and Spenser may have confused that name with *Letrim*, a property of the Earl's eldest son, in Co. Galway (*loc. cit.*). The Galway or Uachtar Burkes must not be confused with those of Mayo (see note on 4105-8).

4077-8. The governor of Connaught was officially known as the Lord President.

4088-9. Estimates of the number of arable ploughlands in Ireland vary considerably in the sixteenth century. The *Book of Howth* (*C. C. MSS. Miscellaneous*, p. 28) gives 53,080; E. C. S. (sig. C4v), 53,340; *B. N.* (13), 38,640. Still another sum is obtained by adding up the number of ploughlands assigned to each of the five provinces in the *View* itself: Ulster 9,000, Connaught 8,200, Leinster 9,400, Meath 5,267, and Munster 16,000, the total of which is 47,867.

4097. A noble was worth 6s 8d.

4101. "Chieferye." See note on 3906.

4105-18. RENWICK. Two central garrisons and the usual guard at Athlone, the President's seat, suffice; considerable trust, apparently, being placed in the Earls of Thomond and Clanrickard. MacWilliam Euter was the tribal name of the chief of Burkes of north-west Connaught; MacWilliam Eighter was now Earl of Clanrickard, which hereditary title superseded the tribal one. [The MacCostulaghes were dependents of the Burkes in Co. Mayo, not in Co. Roscommon where they are placed in Renwick's map (op. p. 330; see anonymous *Description of Ireland*, p. 141). "Euter," or *Iachtar*, means *lower* and, in a derivative sense, *northern*, and was thus applied to the Burkes of Mayo (Butler, p. 202).]

4107-10. RENWICK. Garrandough is uncertain: Miss Henley (*Spenser in Ireland* [map op. title page]) identifies it as Corrandoo, a useful central position west of Athlone. [Renwick's own map (*View*, op. p. 330) places "Garendow" twenty miles southeast of "Corrandoo."]

GOTTFRIED (*ELH* 6. 123) adds to these suggestions the townlands of Gariduff and Gariduffe in Co. Galway (see Y. M. Goblet, *A Topographical Index of Parishes and Townlands in Ireland*).

ROLAND SMITH (*JEGP* 42. 509-11). Both Miss Henley's identification with Carrandoo and Renwick's with Garendow are unsatisfactory if only because these places were of no consequence in (or before) Spenser's day and could have had no meaning for him or for his readers. Spenser's Garrandough must be explained in connection with his references to "the Conhors and the Burkes, ... the Kellyes and Macknyrrs." Of these, "Macknyrrs" can be only a misspelling or corruption of "Mackuyrrs" (i. e., Maguires); the variant "Mackmurries" and the more satisfactory "Mackuires" apparently represent efforts to improve the unintelligible form. ... As for the "Kellyes," ... it is clear that Spenser intended the Ui Maine (the Hy-Many or "Kelly Country"). Spenser's Garrandough, then, should be a place (1) of some significance for his Elizabethan readers and (2) within easy striking distance of the four "countries" he names. The only place answering to these specifications is *Cara* (*Caradh, Caraich*) *na dtuath*, explained by Joyce [*Irish Names of Places*, 1875, 2. 452]: "On the road from Rooskey to Drumsna where it crosses an arm of the Shannon between two lakes, there was an ancient weir, very much celebrated, called *Caradh-na-dtuath* [Cara-na-doo], the *caradh* or weir of the three *tuaths* or districts. A bridge now spans the stream on the site of the weir, and it is well known by the name of

Caranadoe Bridge." This Carranadoo, which constituted the northern boundary of the Kelly Country, was no doubt familiar to Spenser not through personal experience but through Sir Richard Bingham, whose operations in northern Roscommon in 1596 must have been fresh in Spenser's memory when he wrote the *View*. Spenser's readiness to identify the Conors, Burkes, Maguires, and Garrandough with Clanrickard is further evidence of his unfamiliarity with the geography of Connaught and Ulster.

EDITOR. Certain objections can be made to Carranadoo as Spenser's Garrandough: (1) Spenser places Garrandough "in the Countie of *Clanriccard*," and by the county of Clanricard he can only mean Co. Galway, a large part of which was called Clanricard and the name of which Ware substituted for "*Clanriccard*" in the text of 1633; but Carranadoo is in Co. Roscommon. (2) None of the better manuscripts read "Mackuyrrs" or some other spelling of *Maguires*, and we cannot assume that Spenser wrote "Mackuyrrs" rather than "*Mackmures*" or "*mackmurries*," as the Ellesmere and Caius MSS read; the Maguires would not be suitable for this passage in any case since, as Spenser goes on to say (4110-2), he has already placed a garrison at Lough Erne, in the heart of the Maguire country, with wards "at fernnanagh at Belicke at Ballyshannō and on the streightes towardes Connaght the which I knowe doe so strongelie Comaunde all the passages that waie as that none Can passe from vlster vnto Connaght without theire leave" (3985-8). (3) Carranadoo was famous in ancient Irish legend as the northernmost point of Hy-Many; but O'Donovan is careful to point out that Hy-Many ended far south of there in the sixteenth century (Four Masters 5. 1435; *Tribes and Customs of Hy-Many*, 1843, p. 134), and there is no evidence that Carranadoo had any significance for Spenser, much less his Elizabethan readers.

It is almost certain, on the other hand, that Spenser had in mind the place called "Garan Dowgh" on Baptista Boazio's large printed map of Ireland, which Dunlop dated 1578-1580 (*EHR* 20. 313) and which the British Museum reproduced in 1939 with the conjecture that it was published about 1600. (The same locality is called "Garandough" on John Speed's map of Connaught in his *England Wales Scotland and Ireland Described*, 1627, sig. Z6^r.) Boazio's "Garan Dowgh" is placed in Co. Galway about ten miles northeast of the city of Galway; in Co. Galway he also places the following names: "Conogher Og" about twenty miles northeast of "Garan Dowgh," "Hugh m^{c}Donnell Okelli" about twenty miles east, "McMarogh" about fifteen miles southeast, and "Earle of Clanrikard" (Burke) about twenty miles southeast. Spenser is far more likely to have found his geographical information on such a map than in ancient Irish works, still unpublished and untranslated in his day.

4117-8. Athlone was in West Meath, although the Castle appears to have been across the Shannon in Co. Roscommon (anonymous *Description of Ireland*, pp. 102, 151).

4130-41. RENWICK. The complaint was old, but the more usual suggestion was that the Lord Deputy should lie in Athlone; thus Wallop, Sherlock (*Titus B xii*) and Power (*ibid*). [Athlone was also suggested for the Deputy's residence by Perrot and Lord Delvin (E. C. S., sig. B4^{r-v}; John T. Gilbert, p. 191). In 1558 Lord Deputy Sussex was instructed to make his residence in several different places, among them Athlone, in the disaffected parts which needed his presence (*C. C. MSS. 1515-1574*, p. 273).]

4134-9. Athy is a city in Co. Kildare, at the approximate center of Leinster. For the O'Moores and O'Connors see note on 619-21; for the Butlers, note on 3690-2; for the O'Dempsys and Keatings, note on 3161-4. The O'Carrols held Ely, a small district of northeastern Tipperary which they refused to cede to the Butlers of that county; the O'Molloys were a family of King's County (anonymous *Description of Ireland*, pp. 87-9, 83-4).

4144 n. "oversene." *I. e.*, neglected (*NED*, *oversee*, def. 6). See *F. Q.* 2. 9. 44. 3.

4144-9. When Elizabeth urged Lord Deputy Mountjoy to move his residence to Athlone, a few years after the *View* was written, the fear of harming the prosperity of Dublin was one of the factors which prevented the change (Moryson, *Shakespeare's Europe*, pp. 192-3).

4158-67. But Sir William Gerrard writes of the same region: "that mountain soil is apt to bring forth such fruit, and as long as those be mountains, how well soever they be governed, and justice executed, yet will the same still breed some thieves" (*C. S. P. Ir. 1574-1585*, p. xxxviii).

4166. An undertaker was "One who undertook to hold crown lands in Ireland in the 16th and 17th centuries" (*NED*, def. 4).

4174-7. Sir William Drury wrote on 6 March, 1579, that he had "erected a newe countie of Fernes," and the next day Sir Edward Fitton speaks of the two new counties of Wicklow and Ferns (*C. S. P. Ir. 1574-1585* 66. 2, 3). By 1598 Ferns had dropped out of the roll of Leinster counties (anonymous *Description of Ireland*, pp. 35, 55); in 1600 Dymmok (p. 12) notes that both Wicklow and Ferns "are yet vnperfett, not having sufficient freholders and gentlemen to chose shriffes and other principall officers or to make a jury for the Queene."

4177. "*Fernes.*" WARE. This is part of the county of Wexford.

4178-9. RENWICK. Arklow was granted to Theobald, the first of the Butlers, before 1189. [For Ormond see note on 925-9.]

4182. Sir Henry Harrington, who came into possession of Newcastle through his marriage to the daughter of Francis Agard, was settled there at least as early as 1580 (*JRSAI* 38. 139; *C. S. P. Ir. 1574-1585* 74. 77). The estate of New Abbey came into his possession a few years after it had belonged to Spenser (Falkiner, *Essays*, p. 14). His famous relative Sir John Harington tells how Tyrone, although an enemy, defended Sir Henry from the charge of cowardice at a recent defeat of the English (*Nugae Antiquae* 1. 251); and Sir Henry Sidney praised him highly in 1580 (*Letters and Memorials* 1. 282).

4182-3. The Castle of Ferns, built in 1173, is described in 1536 as "one of the ancientest and strongest castles within this land" (Dowling, p. 13; *C. C. MSS. 1515-1574*, pp. 97-8). Sir Thomas Masterson, like Harrington, was praised by Sir Henry Sidney in 1580, at a time when he and Harrington seem to have been

COMMENTARY 405

entangled in legal disputes (*Letters and Memorials* 1. 283; *C. S. P. Ir. 1574-1585* 67. 50). Later we hear that his company of foot soldiers are garrisoning the Castle (*C. S. P. Ir. 1574-1585* 88. 40. 2). The present reference introduces a chronological difficulty: in all probability Spenser wrote the *View* in 1596 (see Appendix III, section B); he apparently thinks of Sir Thomas as still alive; but Wallop had reported Masterson's death to Burghley on 15 August, 1590 (*C. S. P. Ir. 1588-1592* 154. 7). Spenser's present tense may refer to the grant, not the grantee, or he may confuse Sir Thomas with his heir Richard Masterson, who seems to have been in possession of Ferns in 1596 (*JRSAI* 40. 313).

4200-9. RENWICK. Here the hills are the danger-point. One garrison holds Feagh MacHugh's stronghold of Ballinecor, two lie to the south of the hills, and two in the plain to westward, at Leix (Maryborough) and Offaly (Philipstown), for police-work like the Connaught forts.

4200-3. The first of the permanent garrisons corresponds to the first of the forces originally used against Feagh; see 3723-5.

4203-5. The second permanent garrison has the same position as the second force originally used; see 3725-6 and notes on same, on 428, and on 619.

4205-6. Ferns, the stronghold of the Mastersons, is a few miles east of the Slaney River in Co. Wexford.

4206-7. Fort Protector at Maryborough in Leix before this time is said to have fallen into extreme decay (*C. S. P. Ir. 1574-1585* 71. 34); see note on 4006-9. For the O'Moores see note on 619-21; for the O'Carrols, note on 4134-9. The reading "*vpper-Ossory*" is a deliberate correction by Ware: not Ossory, but Upper Ossory, in northern Co. Kilkenny, was a region well-known as a home of thieves (*C. S. P. Ir. 1574-1585* 60. 66; see Holinshed, vol. II, *The Conquest of Ireland*, p. 7).

4207-9. The fort called the "Dingan" at Philipstown in Offaly had been a stronghold of the O'Connors when the English captured it in 1537 (*C. C. MSS. 1515-1574*, pp. 122-4); see note on 4006-9. For the O'Connors see note on 619-21; for the O'Molloys, note on 4134-9. The MacCoghlans dwelt in King's County, the MacGeoghegans in King's and West Meath (anonymous *Description of Ireland*, pp. 104, 107-9; *C. C. MSS. 1515-1574*, p. 315). Spenser may recollect services with Grey, who writes in 1581 of a recent campaign he has made against the O'Connors, MacGeoghegans, MacCoghlans, and O'Carrols, and of having hanged Hugh Molloy in Philipstown (*HMC, Salisbury Manuscripts* 13. 189-90).

4212-4. For East and West Meath see note on 619-21. Edward Waterhouse writes on 17 June, 1579, that the Analy has been shired (*C. S. P. Ir. 1574-1585* 67. 9).

4218-9. Camden (*Britannia*, p. 701) quotes the words of Bartholomaeus Anglicus on Meath: "*Camera* vocatur *Hiberniae* vulgariter propter pacem."

4220-5. RENWICK. The dangerous quarter is the north-west, where O'Neill's underlings lie — Maguire, O'Rourke, and so on — towards Connaught and West

Ulster. Annaly is Co. Longford; Brenny, Cavan; Lough Sillon, Lough Sheelin. [East Breny, the country of the O'Reillys, was formed into Co. Cavan and West Breny, the country of the O'Rourkes, into part of Co. Leitrim; the O'Farralls were overlords of Co. Longford (anonymous *Description of Ireland*, pp. 117, 147, 113).]

4223. "that riuer." Presumably the River Inny.

4238-40. The Presidency and Council of Munster were set up in 1570, and Sir John Perrot became the first president (*Letters and Memorials* 1. 48-59; Falkiner, *PRIA* 24. 191).

4242-5. According to the terms of their grant the undertakers were to pay no rent until Michaelmas, 1591, half rent from then until Michaelmas, 1594, and full rent thereafter; the rent from better lands ran as high as four pence an acre; on Spenser's estate the average was one and a third pence an acre (*C. S. P. Ir. 1586-1588* 129. 27; *1588-1592* 144. 21, 22; *1592-1596* 167. 44. 3). In 1592 an attempt was made to levy a composition in addition to the rent, but the commissioners for Munster pointed out that the undertakers were too poor to pay more than the rent (*C. S. P. Ir. 1592-1596* 167. 8. 1); Spenser probably has this incident in mind. For a summary of the undertakers' vicissitudes see Dunlop, *EHR* 3. 250-69.

4256-86. RENWICK. [Munster] faces the Spanish enemy, so four garrisons guard the coast. Two, inland, watch the difficult country between Co. Cork and Co. Limerick, which Spenser knew well, for his home was there. . . . The absence from this plan of mobile field forces working between the garrisons is doubtless due to the mechanical difficulties of supply and transport. [Although Spenser proposes in 4252-3 to use a thousand men in Munster, these six garrisons account for only nine hundred. Of them, five hundred are stationed on the coast and four hundred in the interior; Spenser does not neglect the region in which his property lies.]

4256-9. "The Bantry" is a river and the bay into which it flows in south-western Co. Cork, but the name was also applied to the surrounding region (anonymous *Description of Ireland*, p. 168).

4262-8. RENWICK. Donnell MacCarthy was raiding as early as 1581, and continued some years after 1596.

EDITOR. The depredations of Donnell MacCarthy, the bastard son of the Earl of Clancar, are repeatedly noted in the State Papers (e. g., *C. S. P. Ir. 1574-1585* 118. 21; *1588-1592* 145. 19, 159. 63; *1592-1596* 177. 29). The Earl's only legitimate child was a daughter, but from 1588 on he showed an inclination to make Donnell, the outlaw, his heir (*C. S. P. Ir. 1586-1588* 135. 59; *HMC, Salisbury Manuscripts* 3. 452). Clancar was reported to be sickly on 17 October, 1595; he probably died late in 1596, for Sir Thomas Norris wrote on 14 January, 1597, recommending Donnell, the bearer, as the bastard of "the late Earle of Clancare deceassed" (*JRSAI* 8. 387, 391, 396; *C. S. P. Ir. 1592-1596* 183. 90, *1596-1597* 197. 83; the Four Masters 6. 1993). See Appendix III, section B.

4264-6. JENKINS (*PMLA* 53. 357-8) notes that on 1 July, 1588, Spenser wrote for Sir Thomas Norris a letter detailing the intrigues by which Florence MacCarthy had accomplished his marriage to Clancar's daughter and that the present passage shows Spenser did not recognize the marriage, which would have made Florence Clancar's heir.

4267. "ly in the winde." See *F. Q.* 3. 10. 30. 5.

4268-70. Castlemaine is a port at the mouth of the River Maine. North of the river lies Kerry, where the Earl of Desmond exercised palatine rights until his rebellion; to the south of the river lay Desmond (meaning *South Munster* in Irish), a region now incorporated into Kerry and Co. Cork, which before 1606 had a semi-official status with a sheriff at the discretion of the Lord Deputy (*C. C. MSS. 1601-1603*, p. 175; Butler, pp. 13, 14; anonymous *Description of Ireland*, pp. 169-70).

4270-3. RENWICK. Kylmore, the Great Wood, lay west of the pass where Charleville is now; it was a notorious haunt of outlaws, and its garrison could also guard the Cork-Limerick road.

ROLAND SMITH (*MLN* 59. 4) places Kilmore immediately to the north of Kilcolman. [Here lay the estate of Hugh Cuffe, for whose possible connection with Spenser see Gottfried, *PMLA* 52. 645-51.]

4277-86. RENWICK. The name Kilpatrick appears only in the late P. R. O. [which, however, Renwick seems to regard as an early manuscript at pp. 262-5] and T. C. D. MSS and in Ware [also in the Ellesmere MS]; the others have blank spaces; and there is no Kilpatrick in the district. Kilpeacon is too far away to be useful, though in the barony; it may be Ardpatrick (Donepatrick in the Munster map in *State Papers of Henry VIII*, vol III), near Kilfinnane. But there was sometimes a garrison in Galbally, at the head of Arlo glen, and Galbally may be meant.

GOTTFRIED (*ELH* 6. 136). Conceivably Spenser is referring to the townland of Kilpatrick in the parish of Lattin, Tipperary, just north of the Galtees [Y. M. Goblet, *A Topographical Index of Parishes and Townlands of Ireland*].

ROLAND SMITH (*JEGP* 42. 514). In referring to "Moscrie Whirke, which is the countrey of the Bourkes, about Kill-Patricke," Spenser leaves no doubt that he means the northern slopes of the Galtee mountains north of Kilcolman. He may have had in mind the well-known legend of St. Patrick's wish to establish a church on the hill now known as Ardpatrick ("Patrick's Height"), where the remains of the round tower and the church (i. e., "Kill-Patricke") still stand. Or in writing "Kill-Patricke," he may have been confusing Ardpatrick with Kilfinnan about three miles to the east, with which it is closely associated [see Lythe's map in *State Papers, Henry VIII*, vol. II, part III].

EDITOR. The sixth garrison is placed at the east end of the Galtee range, by which it was necessary to pass on the most direct route between Munster and the Pale. For Arlo see note on 425. The barony of Muskry Wherk or Querk seems to have been in Co. Tipperary just east of the Galtees (Baptista Boazio's map of Ireland, ed. dedicated to James First; John Speed, *The Theatre of the Empire of Great Britaine*, 1614, map of Munster; Dymmok, p. 18; anonymous

Description of Ireland, p. 208). The connection of this region with the Burkes is corroborated by a list of baronies in Tipperary in 1600: "East Clanwilliam: the Burkes of Muskrie, the Burkes of Onaught, the Burkes of Coshnaie, part of the O'Briens of Arloghe.—50 pl[oughlands]" (*C. C. MSS. 1589-1600*, p. 514). The White Knight, a member of the FitzGerald family known specifically as FitzGibbon, is said to have taken his name from the white hair or the white scarf of an ancestor; his lands lay to the south of the Galtees (Dymmok, p. 68; *JCHAS*, First Series 2. 81; Boazio map; Roland Smith, *MLN* 59. 4).

4281-3. Spenser apparently thinks of Ireland in the position in which it is usually represented on sixteenth-century maps, with the east, not the south, side at the bottom of the sheet, so that one went downwards from Munster to the Pale.

4292-5. JENKINS (*PMLA* 53. 355) notes that a letter from Sir Thomas Norris on 22 January, 1589, which stresses the need of fortifying important places to withstand a Spanish invasion of Munster, is written in Spenser's hand.

EDITOR. In 1587 Fenton directed the fortifying of Duncannon near Waterford; at the same time FitzWilliam was instructed that if the Spaniards attacked, they would first attempt to take the ports of Munster; in 1589 Waterford and Clonmell were reported to have bound themselves to Spain by a new oath (*C. S. P. Ir. 1586-1588* 132. 27, 28, 35, 55; *1588-1592* 141. 40). In 1595 Sir George Carew observes that Munster is Spanish at heart; that Waterford, which he proposes to garrison, offers every convenience to an invader; and that Cork is the next most vulnerable point (*C. C. MSS. 1589-1600*, pp. 129-30). Mountjoy later noted that Cork and Waterford were mutinous and should be garrisoned (Moryson, *Shakespeare's Europe*, pp. 247-8). See also *C. S. P. Ir. 1596-1597* 194. 57.

4307-15. Among the twenty-two places named, Spenser lists only one in Connaught and four in Ulster. He seems to have followed a natural order, beginning with those nearest to Kilcolman; seven of the eight in the first column are in Munster, and none in the last column is in Munster. The mistaken sum of 480, rather than 580, is not necessarily a scribal error; other passages in the *View* reveal that Spenser was careless in his computations. A more modest assessment of soldiers was proposed by Sir Warham St. Leger in 1589: two hundred footmen from Co. Cork, two hundred from the other five counties of Munster, and fifty horsemen from the towns — *i. e.*, sixteen from Waterford, nine from Limerick, nine from Cork, three from Youghal, one from Ross Carbery, two from Kinsale, two from Kilmallock, one from Cashel, one from Fethard, four from Clonmel, one from Dungarvan, and one from Dingle (*C. S. P. Ir. 1588-1592* 144. 80).

4308. Spenser may have visited Mullingar, the chief city of West Meath, with Grey on 4 April, 1582 (*C. S. P. Ir. 1574-1585* 91. 11).

4310. For Kilkenny see *F. Q.* 4. 11. 43. 4 and the reference to Ormond's castle there in *Ded. Son.* 7. 8-12. Spenser may have visited Kilkenny with Grey in October, 1580, and again in September, 1581 (Jenkins, *PMLA* 52. 342-3, 348).

4310. Trim, like Mullingar, Spenser may have seen with Grey on 4 April, 1582 (*C. S. P. Ir. 1574-1585* 91. 11).

COMMENTARY 409

4311. "*Dinglecush*," known today as Dingle, was undoubtedly seen by Spenser if he was with Grey at Smerwick, a few miles away, in November, 1580. See Appendix III, section D.

4312. Kinsale was considered peculiarly vulnerable, and several attempts were made to fortify it (*e. g.*, *C. S. P. Ir. 1586-1588* 126. 71, 78); there the English fought it out with Tyrone and the Spaniards in 1602.

4312. "*Tredagh*," better known as Drogheda, may have been seen by Spenser in the train of Lord Grey on 9 September, 1580 (Jenkins, *PMLA* 52. 342; Judson, *Life*, p. 89; *C. S. P. Ir. 1574-1585* 76. 21).

4312. Of the several towns named Kells, Spenser probably refers to the most important, that in Meath.

4313. Several towns were named Ross; Spenser probably has in mind the most important of them, New Ross, the "Rosseponte" of *F. Q.* 4. 11. 43. 4.

4319-24. This is repeated in the instructions given to Lord Deputy Mountjoy in January, 1600 (*C. C. MSS. 1589-1600*, p. 359).

4325-7. The Dutch hired English mercenaries in considerable numbers at this time; at the beginning of 1596, for example, their States General voted to entertain four thousand English soldiers (Birch, *Memoirs* 1. 389).

4335-61. In 1581 Andrew Trollope emphasized the dependence of the whole population on imported food (*C. S. P. Ir. 1574-1585* 85. 39). In September, 1594, Robert Newcommen asked Burghley for more provisions from England since unseasonable weather had greatly increased the price of corn and other victual; a year later Russell calls attention to the dearth; and in 1596 the situation was made doubly acute by the failure of English crops, especially in Cheshire and Lancashire where the victualers of the Irish administration had been accustomed to purchase their supplies (*C. S. P. Ir. 1592-1596* 176. 30, 184. 10; *1596-1597* 194. 3, 36, 37).

4338-40. RENWICK. In July, 1596, Wallop reported he could buy corn and beeves cheaper in Munster than in England. (*S. P. Ir.* 191. 20) [On 2 October, 1596, Wallop finds that Munster is the part of Ireland in the most favorable condition for provisions (*C. S. P. Ir. 1596-1597* 194. 3).]

4341-4. Some measure against the transportation of grain seems to have been in force since a plea is made in 1592 that corn may be allowed to England (*C. S. P. Ir. 1588-1592* 164. 47); but in the same year Burghley is warned that Irish grain, shipped especially from Waterford and Cork, is being sent to Spain (*HMC, Salisbury Manuscripts* 4. 177).

4350-4. RENWICK. A very brief study of Wallop's correspondence as calendared will make clear the point of this. It is one of his most frequent suggestions.

4382-3. The distinction between "this realme" and "that realme" should be noted. The first must be England itself, which, it was rumored in June, 1595, might be attacked by the Spanish fleet (*C. S. P. V. 1592-1603*, p. 162).

4384.   "quinche." TODD. Stir. JOHNSON.

COLLIER. To "quinch" means here to *move* or *stir*, and as Richardson, quoting this passage from Spenser, tells us, it is probably the same word as *wince*. It is also met with in North's "Plutarch"; but the reference given by Richardson must be an error, if he copied from the first edition of that old translation in 1579, folio. We have not met with it in any other author; but Stephen Gosson seems to use *queatche* either for "quinch" (i. e. *stir*) or for *squeak*:—"They shall lacke customers all the weeke, either because their haunt is unknowen, or the constable and officers of their parish watche them so narrowly that they dare not *queatche*, etc. "School of Abuse," 1579, fo. 18. [See *NED*, *quetch*, def. 4, and *quinch*; also "quich" in *F. Q.* 5. 9. 33. 7.]

MORLEY. Quiver, quake.

4404-8.   See 54-8, 64-8.

4414.   GREENLAW (*MP* 7. 200), citing this as the only example in the *View* of the term *prince* as applied to Elizabeth, believes that it reveals the influence of Machiavelli's *Principe* on Spenser.

JONES (*Spenser's Defense*, p. 213) points out that *prince* was a common term for sovereigns, even when women. [See, *e. g.*, *C. S. P. Ir. 1574-1585*, p. xx. The *View* refers to Elizabeth as the *prince*, not only here, but at 888-98 and 2976-9.]

4420-2.   Spenser admits that in the present case he is breaking with the principle, already twice expressed (325-8, 648-50), that the laws should be fashioned to the people, not the people to the laws.

4429.   "Coulorable Conveyaunces." See note on 818-30.

4443-56.   MORLEY. *Baronets*, lesser barons who did not rank as peers bore that name, as we here see, before 1611, when the name was applied to a new order of hereditary knights established by James I., professedly for the defence of the new plantation of Ulster. The first baronet was Sir Nicholas Bacon, of Redgrave, Suffolk, whose patent was dated May 22, 1611.

RENWICK. I can find no trace of this. The Book of Howth gives a list of Baronets, but they were probably bannerets [*C. C. MSS. Miscellaneous*, p. 23]. The O. E. D. quotes this [the *View*] alone. It may be verbal tradition, not necessarily untrue, since the word was there.

EDITOR. Spenser obviously does not refer to the modern title of *baronet*, established in 1611. In the late Middle Ages *baronet* was sometimes used for *banneret* and even for *baron* (John Selden, *Titles of Honor*, 1614, p. 355; Spelman, *Archaeologvs*, pp. 88-9; Thomas Wotton, *The Baronetage of England*, 1771, 3. 252-3); but the context makes it clear that Spenser did not use the term in either of these senses. Concerning the parliament he mentions and the special meaning he attaches to *baronet* I have found only the following passage in a modern work (*The Baronetage under Twenty-Seven Sovereigns 1308-1910*, Preface signed "A Briton. 1910," p. 2) under Edward Third, 1328:

COMMENTARY 411

1 *February.* Coronation of the King at Westminster. His Majesty being, in course of time, worried by the Clergy in the Parliament of Ireland, the King, as he was advised to do, summoned gentlemen of the best ability to sit as Barons in the next Parliament in order to weigh down the Clergy; and those so chosen were created Barons accordingly. However, after the sessions of the Parliament were over, these men were called upon to sacrifice their Baronial rank and accept, instead, the rank and style of Baronet.

There follows a list of Irish baronets, apparently borrowed from Campion (p. 8) or the *Book of Howth*; and it is likely that the writer has merely combined this borrowed list with the present passage in the *View*, specifying that the parliament of Edward Third was Irish, although Spenser does not say that it was Irish, in order to connect it with the Irish nationality of the baronets on the list.

But since Edward Third had a great deal of trouble with the English clergy in the 1340's, it is a fair surmise that Spenser is referring to events which occurred in England during that period. The numbers of barons summoned to English parliaments from 1340 to 1350 varied between 30 and 56; but in 1342 the extraordinary number of 96 barons was summoned to a council, which has been misnamed a parliament by some writers (Charles H. Parry, *The Parliaments and Councils of England*, 1839, pp. 109-21; Sir William Dugdale, *A Perfect Copy of All Summons of the Nobility to the Great Councils and Parliaments*, 1685, pp. 217-9; Cokayne 1. xxiv). It is quite possible that Spenser has this council of 1342 in mind.

4471-4502. WARE. *De his qui plura scire avet, consulat* D Hen Spelmanni *eq. aur. Archaeologum* [pp. 103, 364-8], *in* Borsholder *et* Hundred.

COVINGTON (*UTB*, Studies in English 4. 37) notes that Spenser probably derived his information from Camden [*Britannia*, pp. 96-7] and Holinshed.

RENWICK. All this is from Holinshed, I. 258, 674; who got it from Lambarde's *Perambulation of Kent* [1576, pp. 20-1], including the citation of Jethro (*Exodus* xviii. 13-26). Spenser probably knew Lambarde's works, and possibly the man. He had read also Camden's chapter *Britanniae Divisio*, with its quotations from William of Malmesbury: see below [note on 4508-9]. Much the same scheme is recommended in S. P. Ir. 121. 54.

EDITOR. William Harrison's account in Holinshed (vol. I, *The Description of England*, pp. 153-4) is undoubtedly Spenser's source:

> This prince therefore hauing made the generall partition of his kingdome into shires, or shares, he diuided againe the same into lathes, as lathes into hundreds, and hundreds into tithings, or denaries, as diuers haue written . . . " by the aduise of his nobilitie, and the example of Moses (who followed the counsell of Iethro his father in law to the like effect). . . . He prouided also that euerie man should procure himselfe to be receiued into some tithing, to the end, that if anie were found of so small and base a credit, that no man would become pledge or suertie for him, he should foorthwith be committed to prison, least otherwise he might happen to doo more harme abroad " [quoted from Lambard]. . . . The hundred and the wapentake is all one, as I read in some, and by this diuision not a name appertinent to a set number of townes . . . but a limited iurisdiction, within the compasse whereof were an hundred

persons called pledges (as I said) or ten denaries, or tithings of men, of which ech one was bound for others good abering, and laudable behauiour in the common-wealth of the realme . . . . the said Alfred caused ech man of free condition (for the better maintenance of his peace) to be ascribed into some hundred by placing himselfe in one denarie or other, where he might alwais haue such as should sweare or saie vpon their certeine knowledge for his honest behauior and ciuill conuersation if it should happen at anie time, that his credit should come in question.

But if Spenser undoubtedly used this source, his memory of it is imperfect. He considers a lathe or wapentake to be half a hundred (4478-9), while Harrison says that a hundred is a subdivision of a lathe and that a hundred and a wapentake are equivalent; Spenser later agrees with the second point (4804-8), but he continues to assume that a lathe is a subdivision of a hundred (4779-84). See also Holinshed, vol. I, *The Historie of England*, p. 118.

4477. A lathe was one of the administrative districts into which Kent was divided, each comprising several hundreds (*NED*). See Holinshed, vol. I, *The Description of England*, p. 153.

4477 n. A rape was one of the administrative districts into which Sussex was divided, each comprising several hundreds (*NED*). See Holinshed, vol. I, *The Description of England*, p. 154.

4477-9. Spenser later (4804-8) describes a wapentake as equivalent to a hundred. William Lambard (Αρχαιονομια, 1568, f. 134^r) explains that the term was used in place of *hundred* in Warwickshire, Lincolnshire, Nottinghamshire, Leicestershire, and Northamptonshire.

4481. "borsholder." MORLEY. From First English *burhes-ealder*, chief of the borough, through the Anglo-Norman *borisalder*. ["The chiefe man likewise of euerie denarie or tithing was in those daies called a tithing man, in Latine *Decurio*, but now in most places a borsholder or burgholder, as in Kent . . . although that in the West countrie he be still called a tithing man" (Holinshed, vol. I, *The Description of England*, p. 154).]

4493-5. WARE. *Livie* [1. 13] speaking of *Romulus* hath it thus, *Populum in curias* 30. *divisit*, etc. *Eodem tempore et centuriae tres equitum conscriptae sunt.* And so we have it in *Sextus Aurel. Victor's* booke, *de viris illustribus urbis Romae. Tres equitum centurias instituit* (saith he) *Plebem in triginta curias distribuit.* [See Riedner, p. 127.]

4508-9. RENWICK. Here Irenius paraphrases the passage of William of Malmesbury quoted by Camden (ed. of 1590, p. 97; Holland, 1610, 158). [See note on 4469-4502.]

4509-13. RENWICK. "Robin Hood" appears so often that it seems a slang term among the officials. St Leger uses it of "a knot of youths," including Donnell MacCarthy, engaged on such an adventure as Spenser describes. (*S. P. Ir.* 80. 65) Donnell seems to have gained prestige and popularity by such affairs. Lord Roche of Fermoy was Spenser's neighbour and enemy; his base sons are still described as

COMMENTARY

Robin Hoods in 1597. (*Cal. Carew MSS.* 3. 227). [See also Moryson, *Shakespeare's Europe*, p. 194.]

4518-28. The ideal of virtuous and gentle discipline which Spenser taught in *F. Q.* was not learned in Ireland, where gentility and discipline were seldom associated. "The people are generally haters of bondage, and beyond measure proud," writes Gainsford (pp. 148-9), "so that the yonger brothers and bastards, who are as deare as the other, scorne all endeuours, but liberty and warre. The Gentlewomen stomach, and in truth vilipend others, who get their liuing by trade, merchandice, or mechanically." Rich says that an Irishman would rather be called a traitor than a churl (*The Irish Hvbbvb*, 1619, p. 48). *Idle-man*, the common term for an impecunious Irish gentleman, was derived from some cognate of German *edel*, or *free-born* (Harris, Ware's *Works* 2. 186). Both Camden and Moryson point out that gentility and thievery were associated in the Irish mind (*Britannia*, p. 714; *Shakespeare's Europe*, p. 483). The cannibals with whom Serena meets in *F. Q.* 6. 8. 35 resemble the Irish gentry in their refusal to live by honest work.

4519. The Welsh, according to Humphrey Llwyd, "nimium de nobilitate generis gloriantes, regis et nobilium famulitio potius quam manuarijs artibus seipsos dedunt" (*Commentarioli Britannicae Descriptionis Fragmentum*, 1572, f. 49^v).

4523. "Churle." See note on 729-30.

4524. "Stocagh." TODD. The word *stocah*, as Dr. Johnson observes, is probably from the Erse *stochk*; but it is hardly used by Spenser in the sense of "one who runs at a horseman's foot, or of a horseboy," as the context clearly proves; it may be in that of "an attendant or wallet-boy." So before: "The strength of all that nation is the kerne, gallowglasse, *stocah*, horseman, and horseboy, etc." [3274-5]. Where the distinction is again preserved.

COLLIER. Richardson has not the word.

MORLEY. Irish, *stocach*, an idle fellow, a lounger; foot servant.

JUDSON (*Life*, p. 81), following *NED*, defines a stokagh as the assistant to a kern. [It is possible that this meaning derives only from the present passage.]

4529-37. See Thomas Smith's account in note on 2295-2311.

4544-6. Maurice, sixth Viscount Roche of Fermoy, is described in 1597 as one "whoe is counted a man of moste Enemys in Munster, ffor in his owne kyndred he hathe manye" (*JCHAS*, Second Series 12. 58). For his character and his litigations with Spenser see Judson, *Life*, pp. 132-5, 162-3. His legal victory over the poet in 1594 may partially explain Spenser's bitter allusion to his bastards. In May, 1597, these young gentlemen are described as "two base sons of the Viscount Roche, which being followed by a rabble of loose people, stand out still" (*C. C. MSS. 1589-1600*, p. 217). Before the end of the same year they are reported to have been "cut off" (*C. S. P. Ir. 1596-1597* 201. 10; *C. C. MSS. 1589-1600*, p. 273). See note on 4509-11 and Appendix III, section B.

4546-7. RENWICK. This second mention of Donnell MacCarthy suggests haste, or compilation. [See 4262-8 and note.]

4562-4. This is not entirely true: in 1558, years after receiving his title, the Earl of Thomond took an oath of allegiance to Philip and Mary (*HMC*, Report XV, part 3, p. 56). In 1611 a more comprehensive measure than Spenser's was proposed: that all Irish subjects above the age of sixteen be compelled to take the oath of allegiance established in England (*C. C. MSS. 1603-1624*, p. 160).

4566. WARE. *Richard the 2.*

RENWICK. There is nothing so definite as this in Holinshed.

EDITOR. Holinshed (vol. II, *The Chronicles of Ireland*, p. 66) contains the following passage on the oath exacted for Edward Second by John de Hotham in 1316: "certeine Irish lords, faithfull men and true subiects to the king of England, did not onelie promise to continue in their loiall obeisance towards him, being their souereigne prince; but also for more assurance deliuered hostages to be kept within the castell of Dublin"; these lords, however, were only eight in number. See also *C. C. MSS. Miscellaneous*, pp. 134, 424; Colvin, pp. 27-8.

4566-9. WARE. This service was performed by Sir *Richard Edgecomb*, being appointed thereunto by a speciall commission from K. *Henry* the seventh. There is yet extant an exact diary of all his proceedings therein, from his first landing at *Kinsale* the 27th of *Iune* 1488. till his departure from *Dublin* the 30th of *Iuly* next. [Edgecomb's diary has been published in Harris's *Hibernica* (1. 29-38); it contains an example of the oath of allegiance administered to various lords (1. 35-6).]

4567-8. "Corporate." Apparently in the sense of *joint*.

4569-73. RENWICK. The *other oath* was that administered by Tyrone to his confederates at Lifford, receiving the sacrament together, Feb-Mar. 1595. (*Cal. S. P. Ir.* 187. 19)

4575-8. In 1562 Lord Deputy Sussex proposed that "Every man shall upon a pain deliver yearly a book of all the men he keeps to the captain of the country, and the captain to the Governor and Council, and every man shall bring forth his man to answer for his offence within the year, and for the lack thereof shall satisfy for the offence" (*C. C. MSS. 1515-1574*, p. 340). This measure is clearly related to kincogish, for which see 1080-6 and note.

4579-89. RENWICK. Drury caused the Munster gentlemen to "book" their men and stand surety for them in 1576. [See *C. S. P. Ir. 1574-1585*, pp. xxxiv-xxxv.]

4589. "vndertaken." Become surety (*NED, undertake*, def. 10).

4607. "Risingout is a certain number of horsemen and kerne, which the Irishrie and Englishrye are to finde in her majesties service, at every generall hostinge" (Dymmok, p. 8).

4609. MORLEY. *Hosting*, muster or review.

COMMENTARY

4610. Spenser apparently refers to the Great Seal of England; but the government of Ireland also had its Great Seal (*State Papers, Henry VIII* 3. 459; *HMC*, Report XV, part 3, pp. 74-5). See 4652-3.

4614-26. RENWICK. Spenser now attacks the feudal lords and gentlemen of the Pale and Munster. Grey found them disappointing from the start: "Once this I can say, since my coming into this Gouernement could I not see any man of those that in defence or offence of priuate quarell would haue fownd an hundreth swordes at his deuotion, that euer yett without pay in this your service would affoord mee a man." Warham St. Leger was very suspicious even of Ormond, whom he accused of slackness and of thinking more of his own interests than of the Queen's. (*Cal. S. P. Ir.* 1580-83, *passim.*) Private feud was outside the official consciousness, and such men could not understand the feud that was a normal and habitual part of life and was therefore not carried to such an extreme as to occupy the whole of life even for a time: whereas rebellion is an abnormality to be suppressed as speedily as possible. There was probably something in the financial argument: St. Leger reckoned the Desmond war was worth £3600 a year to Ormond. (*S. P. Ir.* 80. 29)

4625. "poll." See Pollente who "pols and pils the poore in piteous wize" (*F. Q.* 5. 2. 6. 8).

4642 and 4642 n. WARE. What *Coigny* and *Livery* doe signifie, is formerly expressed see [1039-54]. *Sorehon* was a tax laide upon the Free-holders, for certaine dayes in each quarter of a yeare, to finde victualls, and lodging, and to pay certaine stipends, to the Kerne, Galloglasses, and horsemen. [See note on 1063.]

4648-51. RENWICK. Arundel is mentioned in the letter of the citizens of Cork cited earlier, but his revenue is given there as £1500.

EDITOR. See note on 1976-91. Arundel Castle, now called Rine Castle, stands on the south coast of Co. Cork; the Barrys secured possession of the region by exterminating their rivals (Butler, map op. p. 157, p. 183; Charles Smith, *The Ancient and Present State of the County and City of Cork*, 1815, 1. 30). Although among "the ruined reliques of the ancient English inhabitants," the Arundels continued to be mentioned in documents contemporary with Spenser (*Letters and Memorials* 1. 91-2; *C. S. P. Ir. 1574-1585* 55. 19; *C. C. MSS. 1575-1588*, p. 39 and *1589-1600*, p. 64; *JCHAS*, Second Series 12. 60). David Fitz-James, eighth Viscount Barry of Buttevant, was one of the most powerful nobles of Munster; his estates included 392 ploughlands, at least 50,000 acres, and some of this lay close to Kilcolman (anonymous *Description of Ireland*, pp. 169, 171, 224-5). See the Castle of the Strond in *F. Q.* 5. 2-4.

4651-61. The measure was repeatedly attempted: in 1463 a parliamentary act summoned those who held the king's inheritance in Connaught to produce their titles (*Kilkenny Statute*, pp. 106-7); in 1573 twelve jurors conducted an inquisition of the lands of the Knight of the Valley in Co. Limerick (*C. C. MSS. 1515-1574*, pp. 434-6); in 1588 an examination of tenures is commanded in Connaught (*C. S. P. Ir. 1586-1588* 135. 80); and in 1607 Sir John Davies' *Letter to Salisbury* recounts how a commission, of which he was a member, investigated the tenure of lands in the counties of Monaghan, Fermanagh, and Cavan.

4653-4. RENWICK. Drury was President of Munster, 1576-78.

EDITOR. A large portion of the Munster Council Book is preserved among the Harleian Manuscripts, but the earliest entry dates from 1601 (*Catalogue of the Harleian Manuscripts in the British Museum*, 1808-1812, vol. I, no. 697; *The Council Book of the Corporation of Kinsale*, ed. Richard Caulfield, pp. 301-27). That records of Council business were kept before 1601 is clear; these are believed to have been destroyed in the Four Courts fire of 1922 (Plomer and Cross, p. 44; see *C. C. MSS. 1589-1600*, p. 502).

4660-1. For "Chiefe" see note on 3906; for "knightes service," note on 878. *Soccage* was the tenure of land by certain determinate services other than knight-service (*NED*); *free soccage* involved only small services, while *base* or *common soccage* was equivalent to villenage (*Calendar of the Patent and Close Rolls* 2. 604).

4668. "liueries." The writs by which possession of property is obtained from the court of wards (*NED*, def. 5. b). See *F. Q.* 6. 4. 37. 7.

4669. "alienacions." Transferences of ownership (*NED*, def. 2).

4669-71. Several years earlier concealed lands in Munster are estimated to have an annual yield of £599 17s 10½d (*C. C. MSS. 1575-1588*, p. 395).

4671. "by that which I know in one Countye." Probably Co. Cork, which has been mentioned a little earlier (in 4648) and with which Spenser must have been familiar for more than a decade when he wrote the *View*.

4677-86. For the Tudor policy of surrender and regrant see note on 183-201.

4694-4700. As far back as 1541 the same reasoning is used by an English official (*State Papers, Henry VIII* 3. 326).

4717-31. TODD. In the manuscript belonging to the Marquis of Stafford [the Ellesmere MS] there follow two very severe paragraphs. I prefer the text of Sir James Ware, who professes to follow the *best*, that is, I presume, a *corrected*, manuscript. [See Appendix III, section C.]

4721-31. The English-Irish, according to Moryson, explained their alienation from the English as a result of their being excluded from the Lord Deputyship (*Shakespeare's Europe*, p. 202); but according to earlier writers their government had been marked by maladministration and should never, therefore, be renewed (*State Papers, Henry VIII* 2. 175, 2. 182, 2. 507, 3. 346).

4723-4. ROLAND SMITH (*JEGP* 42. 505, 502) identifies "*Sassona*" with Ir. *Sasanach* [Saxon] but notes that Spenser probably wrote "*Alloonagh*," which is Ir. *Alla-chú*, pl. *Alla-chona*, lit., "foreign dogs," a meaning which better suits the context: "with as greate reproche as they woulde rate A dogge." [But the reading "*Alloonagh*" in Additional MS 22022 is supported by none of the other manuscripts, and the Additional MS is not reliable on the whole; furthermore the

COMMENTARY 417

context does not suggest that the Irish word should have *dog* as part of its meaning. For the Irish expression "Bobdeagh Saxonnegh," Saxon churl, see Holinshed, vol. II, *The Description of Ireland*, p. 44; Campion, p. 14.]

4730. "indignifyed." See *Col.* 583.

4732-3. MORLEY. "Ipsis Hibernicis hiberniores," first said of them, became a proverb.

4733-7. See 9-36 and notes. Cecil writes to Howard in 1600: "It cost me some labour before I went to bed, and I protest it brake my sleep (no easy matter, I thank God) to contemplate how that land of Ire has exhausted this land of promise, for so might it well be called till pride and contempt brought that kingdom to such a confusion as it has been one great work to repair the ruins" (*HMC, Salisbury Manuscripts* 10. 345).

4737-40. See 522-3.

4767-84. This passage is somewhat inconsistent with 1951-2159, where Spenser describes the ill effects of contact between the English and Irish. E. S. (f. 12r) notes that, if the English and Irish are planted together, the English are soon reduced to using the Irish system of barter and trust, rather than money payment.

4780. A *headborough*, however, seems to have been the head of a tithing or frankpledge, rather than of the larger unit, the lathe (*NED*; Spelman, *Archaeologvs*, p. 333). In a moment, also, Spenser implies that a headborough is the head of a pledge of a hundred men, rather than of a lathe (4793-4813). See 4477 and note.

4782. See "Aldermannus Hundredi" in Spelman, *Archaeologvs*, p. 31.

4785-98. RENWICK. Holinshed I. 158, VI. 127: the second passage is connected with the series noted earlier. Some of this seems to come from Lambarde, though not accurately remembered. [See notes on 4024, 4471-4502.]

4786-93. WARE. Cantred is a Brittish word, answering to the Saxon *Hundred*. How much land a Cantred containeth, is variously delivered. Some hould that it contains 100. townes. So *Gir. Barry* or *Cambrensis*, in his itinerary of *Wales*, (*lib. 2. cap. 7.*) *Dicitur autem Cantredus* (saith he) *composito vocabulo tam Britannica quam Hibernica lingua, tanta terrae portio, quanta* 100. *villas continere solet*. The Author here cites a record which makes it containe but 30. towne-lands: and *Iohn Clynn*, (if my copy therein be not mistaken) hath but 20. But another more aunceient MS. sometime belonging to the Friars Minors of Multifernan, hath 30. *Quaelibet cantreda* (saith *Clinne*) *continet xx. (al. xxx) villatas terrae, quaelibet villata potest sustinere* 300. *vaccas in pascuis, ita quod vaccae in x. (al.* 1111.) *partes divisae, nulla alteri appropinquabit, quaelibet villata continet viii. carucatas.* We finde also there the Provinces of Ireland thus divided into Cantreds. *Vltonia continet* 35. *cantredas, Conacia* 30. *Lagenia* 31. *Midia* 18, *et Momonia* 70. See more concerning cantreds in Sir *Hen. Spelman*'s excellent *Glossary* [*Archaeologvs*, p. 137]. As cantreds are diversely estimated, so are also carues or plowlands.

MORLEY. *Cantred* was a word from the Welsh, *cant* (cent), a hundred, and *tref*, a dwelling.

EDITOR. In his *De Hibernia et Antiquitatibus Ejus* (in *A Collection of Tracts . . . Illustrative . . . of Ireland*, 1860, 1. 170) Ware quotes the manuscript of Multifernan on cantreds and villatas, noting that it dates from the reign of Edward First and that at the time of writing (before 1659) it was in Ussher's library; the text, as quoted by Ware, suggests that this may be Spenser's "blacke boke of Irelande." Maria Edgeworth (*Castle Rackrent*, 1800, pp. xlī-xlii) notes: "'According to the old record in the black book of Dublin, a *cantred* is said to contain 30 *villatas terras*, which are also called *quarters* of land (quarterons. *cartrons*); every one of which quarters must contain so much ground as will pasture 400 cows and 17 plough-lands.' . . . The Editor was favored by a learned friend with the above Extract, from a MS. of Lord Totness's [Sir George Carew's] in the Lambeth Library." The *C. C. MSS.* fails to show on which document this information is based; but six volumes of the Carew Papers are now lost (M. R. James, *EHR* 42. 263). It is possible that Miss Edgeworth's friend derived his reference from the Lambeth MS of the *View*, which, however, is not now included among the Carew Manuscripts. For references to a certain Black Book, or different Black Books, see *C. C. MSS. 1575-1588*, p. 332; *HMC*, Report XV, part 3, p. 256; Harris 2. 38. For the cantred and villata see *Letters and Papers, Henry VIII*, vol. II, part 1, p. 372; Dymmok, p. 12; Holinshed, vol. II, *The Conquest of Ireland*, p. 4.

4787. "plowlandes." See note on 3950-7.

4798. "*Franciplegium.*" MORLEY. *Frankpledge*, having pledge or surety for the good behaviour of freemen. [Harrison explains, "these pledges be yet called *Franci plegij* of the word Free burgh" (Holinshed, vol. I, *The Description of England*, p. 154); but Spenser immediately makes it clear that he does not accept this etymology (4808-13). See Spelman, *Archaeologvs*, pp. 296-7.]

4799-4804. RENWICK. Camden as noted earlier, quoting William of Malmesbury. [See note on 4471-4502. Irenius himself uses *hundred* in both senses (see 4024 and 4477).]

4804-8. MORLEY. This etymology is given in the Laws of Edward the Confessor.

EDITOR. Camden (*Britannia*, pp. 97-8) quotes the law:

Cum quis accipiebat praefecturam Wapentachij, die statuto in loco vbi consueuerant congregari, omnes maiores natu contra eum conueniebant, et descendente eo de equo suo, omnes assurgebant ei. Ipse vero erecta lancea sua ab omnibus secundum morem foedus accipiebat: Omnes enim quotquot venissent cum lanceis suis ipsius hastam tangebant, et ita se confirmabant per contactum armorum, pace palam concessa. Anglice enim arma vocantur *thaepun* et *Faccare* confirmare, quasi armorum confirmatio, vel vt magis expresse secundum linguam Anglicam dicamus *Wepentac*, armorum tactus est, *thepun* enim arma sonat, *Tac* tactus est.

See also William Lambard, Αρχαιονομια, 1568, f. 134[r-v]; Spelman, *Glossarium*, p. 563. For other etymologies see Sir Thomas Smith, *De Repvblica Anglorvm*,

COMMENTARY

1583, p. 63; Holinshed, vol. I, *The Description of England*, p. 154. *Wapentake* actually comes from ON *vápnatak*, a taking of weapon (*NED*). Spenser here corrects his original statement that a wapentake contained five tithings, or half a hundred (4477-9).

4805 n.   "sparke."   MORRIS (p. 731).   (? an error for *sparthe*), a battle-axe.

4808-12.   Spenser correctly translates OE *borh* as "a pledge or suertye" (Joseph Bosworth and T. Northcote Toller, *An Anglo-Saxon Dictionary*); but *borough* in *freeborough* is not *borh*. The confusion of *borrow* with *borough* dates from the sixteenth century (*NED, borrow*, def. 3).

4812-3.   RENWICK.   Chaucer, *Squire's Tale*, 596; *Complaint of Mars*, 9. [See also Lydgate's "Complaint of the Black Knight," 12, published in Chaucer's *Workes*, 1542, f. cclxxxvii^v.]

4813.   "borrowe."   TODD cites *S. C.*

COLLIER.   It occurs there twice [*May* 131, 150; *Sept.* 96; E. K.'s gloss on *May* 131]. Our poet also employs it in his F. Q. vol. IV, p. 416 [apparently a reference to Collier's note on *Hub*. 852: "Because a *pledge* or *security*, was anciently given when money was lent, the word 'borrow' became in time applied to the act of obtaining a temporary loan"].

4828-32.   See 4579-4627.

4850-60.   WARE.   *An. 5. Edw 4*. The statute referres onely to the *Irish*, dwelling among the *English* in the counties of *Dublin, Meth, Vriel*, and *Kildare*. *Vriel* called also *Ergallia*, did anciently comprehend all that countrey which is now divided into the Counties of *Louth* and *Monoghan*, although it may be conceived, that *Louth* was onely intended by the statute, because *Monoghan* was then (in a manner) wholly possessed by the *Irish*.

COVINGTON (*UTB*, Studies in English 4. 36-7) points out that this statute is mentioned in neither Holinshed nor Camden and suggests that Spenser consulted official documents [but it is included in *All the Statutes*, London, 1572, ff. 17^v–18^v].

RENWICK.   Statute 5 Edw. IV *c*. 3 enacts: "That every Irishman, that dwells betwixt or amongst Englishmen in the county of Dublin, Myeth, Vreill and Kildare . . . shall take to him an English surname of one town, as Sutton, Chester, Trim, Skryne, Corke, Kinsale: or colour, as white, blacke, browne: or arte or science, as smith or carpenter: or office, as cooke, butler, and that he and his issue shall use this name." [See *The Statvtes of Ireland*, p. 36; Berry 3. 290-1. This statute was made in Ireland, not *England*, as the manuscripts read (4851), so that Ware's emendation is justified.]

4860-4.   WARE.   The custome of prefixing the vowell O to many of the chiefe *Irish* surnames, began soon after the yeere M. in the raigne of *Brien boromha* (the son of *Kennethy*) King of *Ireland*, As for *Mac* in surnames, it beareth no other signification, then *Fitz* doth among the *French*, and (from them) the *English*, and *ap* with the *Welsh*. And although it were more anciently used then the other, yet it varied according to the fathers name, and became not so soone fully settled in families.

RENWICK. The objection to Oes and Macs is not to the personal names, but to the chiefly titles, which carried authority. This was well understood; Bingham's composition for Connaught carried the surrender of titles by 46 Macs and 26 Oes, who received patents according to English law in return. The list is in *S. P. Ir.* 120. 2. On his invasion of Connaught which began the Tyrone rebellion, O'Donnell instituted a MacWilliam among the northern Burkes, a title disused for 10 years before: it was symbolic of his cause and purpose. The reference to O'Byrne is unjustified by history. [Spenser's "Obrien" may refer to Brian Boru, the Irish king of the tenth century; although he did not establish the system of Irish family names, their use became common in his time (Joyce, *Social History* 2. 19). The problem of the *Oes* and the *Macs*, in spite of English efforts to abolish them, continued to be a vexing one (see, *e. g., C. S. P. Ir. 1586-1588* 126. 83; *1592-1596* 189. 31, 48; *1596-1597* 193. 32).]

4867-9. TODD. Another severe remark here follows in [the Ellesmere MS; see note on 4717-31].

4870-83. GREENLAW (*MP* 7. 199) compares this passage with a similar one in Machiavelli's *Principe* (cap. 21), where it is recommended that the Prince encourage his people "nella mercanzia e nell'agricoltura ed in ogni altro esercizio degli uomini." [It is significant, however, that Machiavelli does not specify the intellectual occupations, as Spenser does.]

4879-80. HARDIMAN (*Kilkenny Statute*, pp. 115-7) refutes what he believes Spenser here insinuates, that the Irish did not have trade and markets of their own; he points out that a market town is mentioned in *The Annals of Boyle* under 1231 and that acts were passed in 1429 and 1480 to restrain the commerce of the native Irish.

4880. "Chafferye." MORLEY. From First English "ceapan" (cheapen), to buy, and "faran," to fare or go.

4890-4. So Beacon proposes (p. 103): "Let vs then drawe the people of *Salamina* [Ireland] from the exercise of the warres . . . let vs with the ancient kinges of *Athens*, draw them vnto planting, sowing, and ploughing the land."

4891. "Wars which are cursed by husbandmen." This may be a misrecollection of "bella matribus detestata" (Horace, *Carmina* 1. 1. 24-5).

4895. "stocaghes." See note on 4524.

4905-8. WARE. Anno 25° *Hen.* 6.

RENWICK. Cf. the Notes on Ireland in MS *Titus B xii*, fol. 20 ff.: "(5). The said realm have bene for the more part altogether voyd of good laborers, handy craftes men and men of profitable occupatyons by meanes that the sonnes of laborers of husbandmen and other ther lycke, have not bene brought upe in the occupations, and craftes of ther forfathers but would rather becum karne, evyle Doers, wasters, and idle men . . . for remedy wherof ther hath passed a act at a parliament holden 25 h. 6 ca. 7 . . . Thabuse remayne not with standinge."

COMMENTARY 421

[For the text of the old law see *All the Statutes*, f. 4ʳ⁻ᵛ; *The Statvtes of Ireland*, p. 10; Berry 2. 93. In 1571 Perrot put this law into execution in Munster; in 1584 it was proposed to apply it to the sons of laborers unless their parents were able to keep them in school or put them to some honest occupation (*C. C. MSS. 1515-1574*, p. 409; *1575-1588*, pp. 397-8).]

4909-37. RENWICK. See above [1516-53], Spenser's discussion of "bollying," and cf. Bingham, writing Nov. 18, 1596: "the wastes there noe other then a Tartarian waste which is, if one parte be waste another is inhabited, the manner of they people beinge as it is to remoue with there Cattell from place to place." (*S. P. Ir.* 195. 18)

EDITOR. Giraldus Cambrensis (*Topographia Hibernica* 3. 10) emphasizes the bestiality of the Irish herding life, and Lynch (2. 250) defends it by pointing out the Romans' respect for that occupation. See Spenser's phrase "cowheard vile" in *F. Q.* 3. 11. 39. 3 and his frequent use of *cowheard* for *coward* (*F. Q.* 5. 8. 50. 8, 5. 10. 15. 5, 6. 1. 28. 5, 6. 6. 26. 6, 6. 6. 34. 2, 6. 7. 25. 7, 6. 10. 35. 3).

4912-5. The Ape in *Hub.* 261-90 makes his supposed infirmities an excuse to offer himself for herding rather than husbandry.

4919-22. So Bishop William Lyon, in a document from which quotation has already been made, writes from Cork in 1596: "Forasmuch as the cohabiting and living of men together breedeth love and civility, the contrary of necessity bringeth hatred and barbarousness, and dispersed dwellings abroad, which is a maintenance of idleness and thieves" (*C. S. P. Ir. 1596-1597* 191. 8. 1). See also 5153-66.

4932-4. RENWICK (*View*, p. 243). A phrase in one of Bingham's letters suggests that he had seen the *View* soon after its completion, if not before. Writing to Burghley on Nov. 18, 1596, Bingham says of Connaught that "the wastes there noe other then a Tartarian waste." This erudite touch is unlike his usual soldierly style, and reminiscent of our learned author.

[Spenser has already cited the Scyths and Tartars as herders of cattle in the Irish manner; his information was probably derived, with more or less freedom, from Olaus Magnus and Boemus (1515-25, note on 1519-25).]

4946-58. WARE. How requisite also an Universitie is for the further growth in learning, the judicious well know. This happinesse we now enjoy, to the great benefit of this Land. And although former attempts have beene made for erecting and establishing Vniversities in *Ireland*, yet through want of meanes, which should have beene allotted for their maintenance, they have soone faded. So hapned it with that Academy which *Alexander de Bignor* Archbishop of *Dublin* erected (in *S. Patricks* Church) in *Dublin*, and procured to be confirmed by Pope *Iohn* the 12ᵗʰ. And no better succeeded that which was afterwards erected at *Tredagh* by Act of Parliament Anno 5. *Edw.* 4. (as appeares in the roll of that yeare in the Chauncery) whereby all the like Priviledges, as the Vniversity of *Oxford* (in *England*) enjoyed, were conferred upon it. Besides these wee finde mention of others, farre more ancient, as at *Armagh*, and *Ross-Carbry*, or *Ross-ailithry* as it is called in the life of *S. Faghnan* the Founder, who lived in the yeare 590. *Ipse*

Sanctus (saith the Author) *in australi Hiberniae plaga iuxta mare, in suo Monasterio quod ipse fundavit, ibi crevit civitas, in qua semper manet magnum studium scolarium, quod dicitur Rossailithry, habitabat.* But a further search were fit to bee made touching those of the elder times.

    RENWICK. Another rule often recommended, seldom observed: orders, instructions, and complaints throughout the State Papers. The statute 12 Eliz. c. 1 prescribed a free school in each diocese. [See *All the Statutes*, ff. 176ᵛ–177ʳ; *The Statvtes of Ireland*, pp. 346-7. Elizabeth specifically commanded that the act should be enforced in the see of Limerick; Sir Henry Cowley received an advowson on condition of establishing a school at Carbery; and, to cite one more example of official encouragement, Lord Deputy Perrot was bidden to erect a school at Trim (*Calendar of the Patent and Close Rolls* 2. 42, 23; *C. S. P. Ir. 1586-1588* 129. 46).]

    4947. Since a petty is a small boy at school (*NED*, def. B. 1), a "pettie schollmaster" is the lowliest of his lowly species.

    4949. "elamentes." The actual letters of the alphabet (*NED*, def. 14).

    4961-4. So Perrot writes to Elizabeth in 1582 (E. C. S., sig. A3ᵛ): "The reformation must therefore begin at God. His will and word must be duly planted, and Idolatry extirped. Next, Law must be established, and lycentious customes abrogated."

    4963-4. RIEDNER (p. 16) identifies the quotation as Matthew 6. 33. [The words "righteousnes theareof" follow the Matthew and Coverdale versions; the Tyndale version and the Great Bible read "rightwisnes therof," the Geneva and the Bishops' Bibles "his righteousnes."]

    4976-93. Spenser overlooks his previous opposition to the use of a marshal in 2521-7.

    4976-80. The philosophy of these vagabonds is expounded by the Fox in *Hub.* 129 ff.

    4979. "miche." TODD. The word *micher* is used by Chaucer to denote a thief or vagabond, *Rom. R.* 6541. edit. Urr. And Mr. Tyrwhitt cites the following usage of the verb: "*Mychyn* or pryvely stelyn smale thyngs. Surripio. *Prompt. Parv.*" See also Cotgrave in V. "To *miche*, etre vilain."

    COLLIER. Richardson gives the Fr. *miche* as the etymology, to *mich* being to steal small things.

    MORLEY. To lie hid, skulk. [See *NED*, def. 2, for this meaning, which is suitable to the context.]

    4979. MORLEY. "Carrows," as we have seen, are strolling gamesters. [See note on 2360-9.]

    5002-24. RENWICK. One of the heads of "Russells discourse" in *Titus xii* is "Extortion of Sherifs Sergeants and Cessors." Spenser's idea seems to be, that as the Provost Marshal would be a permanent official, whereas the sheriffs were annual, more control could be exercised both by and over the marshal. His Provost Marshal is really a stipendiary magistrate with wide powers. Gardener complains (*S. P. Ir.* 150. 4) not only of the abuse of martial law, but that sheriffs seek general pardons on demitting office, for all offences committed in connection with it, and by themselves and their assistants, among whom they insert friends and clients in need of shelter from the law. His draft proclamation corroborates Spenser: "By reason of the aucthorytye of execution of marshall lawe by diuerse our late deputyes . . . granted as well to provinciall goverers as to other more inferior gouerners of cuntryes, shryves, senesshalls, captaynes, and officers of lyke sort and that in the tyme of peace . . . wherby som partys so aucthorysed as aforsaid through ignorance of the course of the said Lawe . . . others in ther owne ambition to magnifye the greatnes of ther late purchased credyt, others seking vngodly and vnnaturall revenge, others to enriche them selves with the spoile of our pore subiectes in possessing vnlawfully ther goodes taken into ther handes vpp on the apprehension of any supposed malefactors which they knowe being ons taken cann hardly without great danger by ther wives children or frendes be recouered the rather bicause by no presentment inquyry or other record the certenty or value of the said goodes may be knowen, and yet in truth by no Lawe forfeted or lost, have executed by paynes of death no smale numbre of our said subiectes . . . by meane wherof our said subiectes so executed (not havinge meane to learne nor cause to knowe Lawes vnder which they were not bound to lyve) could neyther have assurance of lyve or lyvinge but most shamfully have bynn murthered . . . " In Nov. 1586, a "notable example" was made of one Henry Eyland, Sheriff of Roscommon, for executions and extortion contrary to law. (*S. P. Ir.* 126. 90) [See also *C. S. P. Ir. 1588-1592* 146. 48, 152. 2, 164. 49. 1; Moryson, *Shakespeare's Europe*, p. 200; Lee, f. 5ʳ⁻ᵛ. E. S. (fols. 21ᵛ–22ʳ) complains that sheriffs blackmail wealthy husbandmen, who are only released from trumped-up charges after they have given one tenth of their beasts.]

5028-30. Spenser has used almost the same words in 2611-4.

5031-43. JONES (*Spenser's Defense*, pp. 159, 202-3) finds that Spenser declares the present passage represents the belief of Grey, whom he is defending from the charge of religious intolerance, and that the tolerance he proposes should be compared with Bodin's *République* [lib. IV, chap. 7].

RENWICK. Here I find one fairly certain trace of Bodin: "Et d'autant que les Atheistes mesmes sont d'accord, qu'il n'y a chose qui plus maintienne les Estats et Republiques que la Religion, et que c'est le principal fondement de la puissance des Monarques and seigneuries, de l'execution des loix, de l'obeissance des subiects, de la reuerence des Magistrats, de la crainte de mal faire, and de l'amitié mutuelle enuers vn chacun, il faut bien prendre garde qu'vne chose si sacree, ne soit mesprisee ou reuoquee en doute par disputes: car de ce point là depend la ruyne des Republiques . . . Ie ne parle point ici laquelle des Religions est la meilleure, (combien qu'il n'y a qu'vne Religion, vne verité, vne loy diuine publiee par la bouche de Dieu:) mais si le Prince qui aura certaine asseurance de la vraye Religion veut y attirer ses subiects, diuisés en sectes et factions, il ne faut pas à mon aduis qu'il vse de force: car plus la volonté des hommes est forcee, plus elle reuesch: mais bien en suyuant et adherant à la vraye Religion sans feinte ny dissimulation, il pourra tourner les coeurs et volontés des subiects à la sienne, sans violence, ny poine [peine?] quelconque: en quoy faisant non seulement il euitera les esmotions, troubles, et guerres ciuiles, ains aussi il acheminera les subiects desuoyés au port de salut." (*de la Republique*, livre 4, ch. 7; ed. of 1593, p. 653) The practical outlook and Christian charity of William Lyon lead in the same direction, and Elizabeth's views were well known; but the passage involves Spenser's character as well. He cannot be called a religious poet, and this passage is a warning against ascribing religious opinions to him. It is clear that he has shed his undergraduate Puritanism: the implications of his declaration of the unity of religion are more debatable. It might be read as meaning that there is only one religion, the Protestant, and that all the Irish must be brought to it. His realism hardly allows of that interpretation, though he might think it desirable. We might be nearer his mind in reading it that all religions are one in their essence, the differences being only external and therefore not to be overemphasised. This is possible, and if he ever discussed religion with Ralegh we may well imagine the discussion taking that line. His experience of government would readily bring him to the Queen's notion, that the question is so ticklish that for the peace of the realm the less prominent is it the better. Or he may have taken it from Bodin without much thought of its implications: which is unlikely. This is not the place to examine Spenser's philosophy—a tangled subject at best—but I may say I suspect Ralegh's influence, or rather, the Renaissance syncretism that produced also the mysterious "atheism" of which Ralegh was a notorious sectary.

EDITOR. Elizabeth discouraged contemptuous references to Roman Catholic doctrines; one Irish bishop was summoned to London on such a charge and only secured a pardon by certifying that he had said nothing offensive (John T. Ball, *The Reformed Church of Ireland, 1537-1889*, 1890, p. 65); in 1602 Mountjoy, as a matter of policy, defended religious tolerance outside of certain towns (*HMC, Salisbury Manuscripts* 14. 240). But Spenser's mildness is a little surprising, in view of what he has already said of Catholicism in 2614-64 and in view of the scorn of Artegall for the temporizing of Bourbon, Henry of Navarre, in *F. Q.* 5. 11. 56. 6-9.

5035. "despised and reiected." See Is. 53. 4 (Geneva version).

5035-9. "These onely titular Christians are so ignorant in their superstitious profession of Popery, that neither they, nor the greatest part of their Priests know, or understand, what the mistery of the Masse is, which they dayly see, and the other celebrat, nor what the name of Jesus is, either in his divine, or humane nature: Aske him of his Religion? he replyeth, what his father, his great grandfather were, that will he be also: And hundreds of better then the common sort, have demanded mee, if Jerusalem, and Christs sepulcher were in Ireland, and if the Holy Land was contiguat with Saint Patrickes purgatory" (William Lithgow, *The Rare Adventures and Painefull Peregrinations*, 1906, pp. 374-5).

5039-43. In a contemporary discourse on Ireland James Crofts asks: "why are not some sent to 'repugne' the Papists' doctrine and stablish and confirm the conscience of men in the true and ancient Catholic faith? On [Or?] why be not some to be found that for a godly zeal will offer themselves to be employed in this service?" (*Analecta Hibernica* 4. 315).

COMMENTARY 425

5046 n.   St. Columba (521-597) founded the monastery of Iona in 563 and from there converted the northern Picts.

5048-53.   The zeal of the Catholic clergy is well illustrated in Richard Creagh: created Papal Primate of Ireland in 1564, he was captured, escaped from the Tower of London, but was later recaptured and imprisoned for eighteen years, until he died of disease and filth or of poison (Bagwell 2. 357-9). In 1628 a college for Irish secular priests was established at Rome, but in 1596 they apparently had no institutions of their own at either Rome or Rheims (Harris, Ware's *Works* 2. 255).

5058-9.   So the Priest boasts in *Hub.* 475-6:
> Beside, we may haue lying by our sides
> Our louely Lasses, or bright shining Brides.

5059-60.   RIEDNER (p. 24) traces the allusion to Rev. 14. 15. [The wording of the Geneva Bible is closest to the *View*: "Thrust in thy sickle and reape: for the time is come to reape: for the haruest of the earth is ripe." Spenser also seems to have in mind John 4. 35: "Lyft vp your eyes, and loke on the regions: for they are whyte already vnto haruest" (Geneva Bible). See Joel 3. 13.]

5061-2.   See Matt. 12. 42: "The quene of the south shall ryse at the daye of iudgement with this generacion/ and shall condemne them" (Tyndale Bible, which is closest to the *View*). See also Luke 11. 31.

5069-75.   On January 10, 1581, Elizabeth issued "A Proclamation for reuocation of Students from beyond the seas, and against the reteining of Jesuites" (*A Booke Containing All Svch Proclamations, As Were Pvblished dvring the Raigne of the Late Queene Elizabeth*, ed. Humfrey Dyson, 1618, ff. 211-2); the proclamation specifically mentions the trouble caused by Jesuits in Ireland. On 6 July, 1596, William Lyon, Bishop of Cork and Ross, writes to the same effect as Spenser in this passage (*C. S. P. Ir. 1596-1597* 191. 8. 1; see also Moryson, *Shakespeare's Europe*, p. 289). The decades immediately following 1596 saw the establishment of Irish Franciscan colleges at Louvain, Prague, Rome, Capranica near Viterbo, and Boulay in Lorraine (Denis Murphy, *JRSAI* 23. 239) and Irish secular colleges at Lille, Tournai, Paris, Rome, and other Catholic centers (Walter Harris in Ware's *Works* 2. 251-61).

5075-6.   There does not seem to have been an Irish statute restraining the students of Catholic universities from entering the kingdom; but Spenser may have in mind the English statute of 27 Elizabeth, which banned all Jesuits and Catholic ecclesiastics from all the Queen's dominions (*Anno xxvii. Reginae Elizabethae*, 1585, sigs. A4r–6v). In that case "theare ordained" should read "heare ordained."

5081.   "Coullorable Convayaunces." See notes on 818-30, 819-20.

5092-5107.   HEFFNER (*MLQ* 3. 514-5) cites this passage as evidence that "if ever Spenser had been a Puritan, he no longer subscribed to that doctrine in 1596." [Spenser was never the kind of Puritan Heffner has in mind.—C. G. O.]

5092-7.   The ruined condition of Irish churches dates back to the beginning of the sixteenth century, when that of Ardagh Cathedral is described (Bagwell 1. 295). In 1572 John Crofton complains that the rebels and Scots have burned the church of Athlone, where he had stored his malt, biscuit, beer, and brewing and baking vessels (*C. S. P. Ir. 1509-1573* 37. 11. 2; Covington, *Texas Review* 6. 240). In 1578 we hear that almost all the churches in the diocese of Ossory are ruined and in 1587 that a hundred churches in the diocese of Leighlin have suffered decay (*C. C. MSS. 1575-1588*, pp. 144, 458). In 1595 Lord Deputy Russell converted Armagh Cathedral into a military storehouse (*C. S. P. Ir. 1592-1596* 181. 5, 28). "The churches in moste places," Sir William Gerrard wrote of this period, "were fallen downe, nothinge remayninge savinge the twoe endes without rooffe: that in some placies within some of those counties I had traveled xen or xij myles and cold not see anye churche" (*Analecta Hibernica* 2. 114). See also Moryson, *Shakespeare's Europe*, p. 289). An act to ensure the repair of parochial churches was proposed but not passed by the Parliament of 1569 (Richard Mant, *A History of the Church of Ireland*, 1840, 1. 291). The instructions of 1588 for Connaught provide that decayed churches be re-edified; in 1592 it is recommended that churches be rebuilt at the charge of parishoners and patrons; in 1594 Elizabeth threatened the Irish bishops with the sequestration of their tithes unless they repaired churches (*C. S. P. Ir. 1586-1588* 135. 80, *1588-1592* 164. 49. 1; *Calendar of the Patent and Close Rolls* 2. 294; anonymous *History of Sir John Perrott*, pp. 192-3; *HMC, Salisbury Manuscripts* 14. 337). Thus considerable, if unsuccessful, efforts had been made to rectify the evil.

5099-5101. TOLMAN (*MP* 15. 554) cites this clause as evidence that Spenser was not so much a Puritan as an earnest Low-Churchman. [The reference is undoubtedly to the Puritans, whose hostility to the comeliness of churches he apparently embodies in the Blatant Beast (*F. Q.* 6. 12. 25. 1-5).]

5100. RENWICK. There seems to be something missing here, but all texts read thus. Spenser's idea seems to be that there is *nothing amiss*, or *nothing contrary to true religion* in the comely order of the Church. [By omitting "And" in 5099 and adding "that" in 5100 the Ellesmere MS straightens out the difficulty.]

5101-5. Since churchwardens were recognized as existing in Ireland by the Act of Uniformity, Spenser may insinuate that these were not all they should have been (Richard Mant, *A History of the Church of Ireland*, 1840, 1. 325).

5106. "Mortmaines." Licenses to allow lands or tenements to be given inalienably to an ecclesiastical corporation (*NED*). See Spelman, *Glossarium Archaiologicum*, pp. 395-6.

5113-6. Elizabeth herself wrote Adam Loftus and Robert Garvey that in consideration of the poorness of the benefices one man should be allowed to hold two or three, provided they totaled no more than forty pounds a year and were within twenty miles of one another (*C. C. MSS. 1589-1600*, pp. c-ci). In his *Letter to Salisbury* of 1607 (p. 378) Sir John Davies likewise proposes to join as many benefices as will make a competent living for one minister.

5116-7. Since "the three sortes of trades" are discussed in 4870-4958, the intervening passage on provost marshals and religion must have been inserted after this transitional clause had been written.

5120-4. RENWICK. The scheme comes from the Statute of Winchester (13

COMMENTARY 427

Ed. I. 2. 5): "Highways . . . shall be broadened . . . so that there be neither dyke, tree nor bush where a man may lurk to do hurt within 200 foot of the one side and 200 foot on the other side of the way . . . etc." (Stubbs, *Charters*, 463-9) *Pace* is a regular form of *pass*, a narrow passage. [See *F. Q.* 3. 1. 19. 7. The English Statute of Winchester was enforced in Ireland after 1308 (Berry 1. 209, 211, 256). Early in the sixteenth century Patrick Finglas (Harris 1. 51) suggested "That the Deputy be eight Days in every *Summer* cutting Passes of the Woods next adjoining to the King's Subgets."]

5124-33. So in 1592 the Archbishop of Cashel proposes that bridges, defended by wards, should be built over the Erne and the Bann (*C. S. P. Ir. 1588-1592* 164. 47). When Spenser describes how Timias is attacked at a ford in *F. Q.* 3. 5. 17-25, he may very well have in mind a similar attack made on Ralegh in 1581, an attack which the present measure would have prevented (see Holinshed, vol. II, *The Supplie of the Irish Chronicles*, p. 173).

5125. "spilt." MORLEY. Destroyed; First English "spillan" meant, to kill.

5133. "stretes." MORLEY. *Straits* were narrow passages, whether of land or water. [See *F. Q.* 6. 1. 13. 2.]

5135. "fortilage." See *F. Q.* 2. 12. 43. 5.

5145-51. A statute of 1458 provides that towns and villages on highways may entrench and wall themselves, but it is specified that traffic must not be interrupted in the manner Spenser suggests (Berry 2. 501, 503).

5151-66. In 1567 Sir Henry Sidney supports the building of towns as "in Effecte the onelie Monumentes of Obedience, and Nurceries of Civilitie in this Countrie" (*Letters and Memorials* 1. 20-1). At the time the *View* was written, it is suggested that market towns be built every six or eight miles with villages in places most convenient (*HMC, Salisbury Manuscripts* 14. 8).

5166-9. *F. Q.* is filled with the misadventures of travelers who lodge abroad in cottages: for example, Una (1. 3. 10-20), Florimel (3. 7. 5-17), and Amoret and Aemilia (4. 8. 23-28).

5176. "garren." MORLEY. The Irish word for a horse put to common work. [See note on 770.]

5178-81. In 1571 Sir John Perrot proclaimed an ordinance to the effect of that here proposed, but only for Munster: that no person should buy any goods or chattels of any country folk, but only in the market place upon the market day or before the high constable, or the petty constable, and two other honest men of the parish (*C. C. MSS. 1515-1574*, p. 410).

5181-4. RENWICK. Camden records under the date 1595: "In the meane time, neuerthelesse, a great quantity of graine was brought into *England* from the *Hanse* Townes . . . which very much abated the price of graine, which by continuall raine in summer, and secret transportation, was growne to that high rate, that some of the baser sort of people at *London* began to rise in commotion." (*Annales*, tr. R. N[orton], ed. of 1635, p. 450) A Proclamation of July 31, 1596, deals with the dearth of corn. (S. T.C. 8257) [Another proclamation, of 2 November, 1596, promises that engrossers and regrators will be prosecuted. In Ireland an act had been passed against engrossers and regrators as early as 8 Edward Fourth (*The Statvtes of Ireland*, p. 43).]

5183. MORLEY. *Engrossing* was buying up in large quantities; *regrating* was selling again in small quantities, at an enhanced price, in or near the same market or fair.

5185-91. RENWICK. I have not found this ordinance for cattle-branding.

5196-5201. The Carew Papers contain a long memorandum of the abandoned towns of Connaught: Inshiquyn, O'Brien's Bridge, Inysh, Qwynhy, Clare, Bonratty, Myllyke, and Loghreogh; their decay is traced in several cases to the policy of the overlord, the Earl of Clanricard (*C. C. MSS. 1601-1603*, pp. 475-6). In an article which will soon be published, Professor Alexander C. Judson calls attention to the fact that Spenser himself had at one time leased the waste town of Old Kilcullen, adjoining New Abbey (see Carpenter, p. 38). The practical side of Spenser's present complaint differentiates it from the description of Verulame in *R. T.* 85-154, but the same antiquarian interest underlies both. See also *View* 478-82.

5205-11. Sir Henry Sidney reports how the tyranny of the Earl of Clanricard had gradually annihilated the town of Athenry (*Letters and Memorials* 1. 28-9, 105; see also note on 5196-5201); but in this case Elizabeth attempted to defeat the greed of the overlord, commanding the re-establishment of the ancient town with a new charter in 1584 (*Calendar of the Patent and Close Rolls* 2. 73-4).

5211-5. RENWICK. According to Camden, Henry "suppressed all Monasteries; perswaded thereto by such as preferred their private and their owne enriching before the honour of Prince and Country." (*Britannia*, description of Bury St. Edmunds)

5245-7. Before the fifteenth century the title of Lord Lieutenant was occasionally given to the actual governor; but from then on, if used at all, it was reserved for members of the royal family under whom the Lord Deputy served as the real head of the Irish government (Bagwell 1. 100-1).

5247-8. TODD. Meaning the Earl of Essex.

C. (*NQ*, Third Series 4. 237). I have a strong impression, or rather conviction, that at the end of his *Treatise on Ireland*, Spenser points at his friend Sir Walter Ralegh, and not at Robert, Earl of Essex; for he distinctly states the head of the Irish government should be one, who knew the country, and *had seen service in Ireland*, as well as in France and Belgium. [C. is misrecollecting 3757-68 which applies only to captains.]

MARTIN (*PMLA* 47. 140). The eye of all England is indeed fixed on Essex at this time and . . . the hope of breaking the power of Spain is the last hope upon which the retaining of Ireland as an English possession may rest.

RENWICK. Probably Essex, now coming to the height of his favour and popularity. If the *View* were written later than June, 1596, we should expect some mention or hint of the Cadiz expedition. The uselessness of Essex in Ireland when he was sent there, is common knowledge.

EDITOR. It should be noted that Spenser proposes the unnamed nobleman, not for the Deputyship, but for the Lord Lieutenancy; Essex at this time was apparently trying to avoid an offer of the Deputyship, which would have compelled him to leave the Court (Birch, *Memoirs* 2. 142). The present passage seems, without question, to refer to Essex immediately after his return from Cadiz in August, 1596, in the period when Spenser wrote his public tribute to Essex in *Proth.* 145-60. See note on 2943-8 and Appendix III, section B.

5256-72. GREENLAW (*MP* 7. 198-9) believes that in this passage Spenser may remember Machiavelli's praise of Cesare Borgia for having bestowed the fullest powers on his governor, Remiro d'Orco (*Il Principe*, cap. 7).

EDITOR. Bryskett writes to Walsingham in 1581 (Plomer and Cross, p. 30): "I cannot lett to say thus much that the confusednes of this State and the disorder is suche, what throughe the vniversall inclinacion of this people to mischiefe, and what throughe the small reputacion which the Governors are brought into emong them for want of countenance and creditt from home," a disadvantage from which Grey in particular is suffering. But the inconvenience did not end with Grey: see William Herbert, *Croftus, sive de Hibernia Liber*, p. 55; anonymous *History of Sir John Perrott*, p. 229; Moryson, *Shakespeare's Europe*, p. 188.

5272-9. RENWICK. Spenser's citation of Machiavelli is either from his unsure memory or scarcely candid. In his animadversions on Livy, I. 24, Machiavelli upholds the usefulness of dictatorship in time of crisis, and praises Venice for ruling through a small council; in II. 33, he points out that Consuls, Dictators and other Roman commanders had full powers in war, but not so " le repubbliche de' presenti tempi, come è la Viniziana e Florentina . . . se gli loro capitani, provveditori, e commissari hanno a piantare una artiglia, lo vogliono intendere, e consigliare."

EDITOR. Spenser undoubtedly has in mind the second passage to which Renwick refers (*Discorsi* 2. 33); but it is hard to see how he has falsified its meaning in any way. He may have been introduced to the *Discorsi* by Harvey, who refers to them in a letter perhaps addressed to Spenser (*Letter-Book*, p. 79). " In general, however," Greenlaw observes (*MP* 7. 201-2), " the debt of the *Veue* to the *Discorsi* is extremely small; it is therefore the more significant that Spenser's only direct reference to Machiavelli is to this work. If he drew directly from a book which in the nature of things had little to contribute to the problem which he had in mind, it is the more certain that he must have known the one book of his time which in subject and in method bore most directly upon such a problem [*i. e., Il Principe*]." But Jones replies (*Spenser's Defense*, p. 210): " Nor when we remember that almost everybody quoted Machiavelli to his purpose, need we suppose that Spenser's approval of Machiavelli's opinion in regard to the power that should be delegated to governors gives support to the theory that the English poet approved in principle the Machiavellian politic."

5284. "These Seneschals, Sheriffs, and others, that should have been the reformers (as it was first purposed) became the only deformers (as they behaved themselves); for, in the choice of them, he was ever thought most worthy for the place that would give most money for the office" (Rich in *C. S. P. Ir. 1599-1600* 205. 72). See also Moryson, *Shakespeare's Europe*, p. 222.

5285. RENWICK. According to Gardener there was a regular trade in pardons. "Item. pardons to hundredes and many more, no persons nor ther offences knowen, procured by base followes lyke somners sekinge who have offended and the pardon for all offences except treason to hir Maiesties personn and forging koynes, so I know not who maye not be a common murtherer and yet often tymes pardoned." (*S. P. Ir.* 150. 4) Many of the other abuses were charged against Fitzwilliam. [See note on 5285-6. "For thes 40 yeares togyther that I have knowne Irelande," writes Rich (*Remembrances*, p. 129), "thys onely portseale of pardons is it that hath set so many rebellyons on foote, and it not yet all owt two yeares agoe synce I sawe 1020 severall mens names conteyned in one pardon." See William Lithgow, *The Rare Adventures and Painefull Peregrinations*, 1906, p. 376.]

5285-6. This must be a pointed allusion to Lord Deputy FitzWilliam, who had recently sold the captaincy of Monaghan for beeves. See *B. N.* 45-56 and note.

5311-5. WARE (*Works* 2. 327). Mr. *Spencer* promised to write a particular Treatise on the Antiquities of *Ireland*. But it is probable he never performed the Task, being prevented by Death. [See 1131-9.]

A BRIEF NOTE OF IRELAND

5-6. "foure partes." Four out of five parts, four-fifths.

11. The figure "2060" is undoubtedly a mistake for 1060: an Elizabethan *1* is easily confused with a *2*; if Ulster had 2060 townlands, the total for Ireland would be 6530, not 5530, in l. 7 above; and the sixteenth-century *Book of Howth* gives Ulster 1060 townlands and Ireland a total of 5530 (*C. C. MSS. Miscellaneous*, p. 28).

13. In *View* 4088-9 all Ireland is said to contain 43,920 ploughlands; the present figure may be lower because it includes only arable land.

14-6. See "euerie of which ploughelandes conteineth sixe score acres after the rate of xxj foote to euerie perche of the saide acre" in *View* 3951-3.

16-23. For similar fabulous accounts of the ancient revenues of Ireland see *View* 557-9 and note.

17-8. Since a noble is 6s 8d, 14,146 pounds would be the tax on 42,438 ploughlands; but see 13 above.

19. A mark was 13s 4d, two-thirds of a pound.

25. "*Out of the ashes.*" See *out of her ashes* in *Bel.* 1. 6. 14, *R. R. Env.* 5.

25. "*wastnes of this your wretched.*" See "Her wretched dayes in dolour

COMMENTARY 431

she mote wast" in *F. Q.* 3. 2. 17. 8; "wast his wretched daies" in *F. Q.* 4. 7. 39. 8; "waste in woe my wretched yeares" in *F. Q.* 4. 12. 7. 7.

25-6. "*this your wretched Realme of Ireland.*" See "that wretched Realme" in *View* 2673; "the wretched Realme of Irelande" in *View* 4882.

26-7. "vouchsafe moste mightie Empresse our Dred soveraigne to receive." See "vouchsafe them to receaue" in *Ded. Son.* 2. 13; "Vouchsafe in worth this small guift to receaue" in *Ded. Son.* 10. 8; "vouchsafe, O dearest dred" in *F. Q.* 1. Pr. 4. 9; "vouchsafe now to receive" in *F. Q.* 2. 1. 16. 3. *Vouchsafe*, which occurs thirty-three times in Spenser's poetry, he frequently uses in the initial position and in direct address. See also "The Most High, Mightie And Magnificent Empresse" in ded. of *F. Q.*; "That soueraine Queene, that mightie Emperesse" in *F. Q.* 5. 1. 4. 5; "most sacred Empresse, my dear dred" in *Am.* 33. 2; "soueraigne dread" in *F. Q.* 1. 2. 25. 4; "dreaded souerayntie" in *F. Q.* 5. 9. 34. 1; *most dreaded sovereign* in *F. Q.* 2. 10. 1. 8, *F. Q.* 6. Pr. 7. 1; *dread sovereign* in *F. Q.* 3. Pr. 3. 5, *F. Q.* 5. Pr. 11. 1, *F. Q.* 6. 2. 37. 6; *sovereign might* in *F. Q.* 7. 6. 33. 5, *Am. Anacr.* 4. 46, *H. B.* 54, *H. B.* 124, *H. H. L.* 4.

27. "the voices of a fewe moste vnhappie Ghostes." See "they spake like ghostes Cryinge out of theire graues" in *View* 3261-2.

28. "buried in the bottome of oblivion." See "in obliuion euer buried is" in *F. Q.* 2. 3. 40. 4.

31. "aduancement of your renowne and glorie." See "glory and aduancement" in *F. Q.* 1. 4. 9. 5; "glory and renowne" in *F. Q.* 2. 7. 11. 9; "glory and renowmed praise" in *F. Q.* 3. 1. 3. 3; "aduance his name and glorie" in *F. Q.* 3. 4. 21. 6; "your glory bee aduaunced" in *F. Q.* 3. 10. 28. 6.

32. "heritable dominion." See "inheritaunce and dominion" in *View* 3572.

33-4. "vnworthinesse of vs wreches." See "vnworthie wretchednesse" in *F. Q.* 1. 3. 1. 3; *unworthy wretch* in *F. Q.* 1. 10. 62. 1, 3. 11. 11. 8; "vnworthy of your wretched bands" in *F. Q.* 6. 8. 7. 6; "Vnworthy in such wretchednes" in *Hub.* 602; *I wretch* in *F. Q.* 2. 1. 56. 1, *Gn.* 329; "Vs wretches" in *H. H. L.* 193.

34-7. Probably a reference to FitzWilliam, who is attacked, without being named, in what follows (45-72).

37. "Pardon therefore moste gracious Soveraigne." See "Thy gracious Souerains praises" in *Ded. Son.* 11. 6; "O pardon me, my soueraigne Lord" in *F. Q.* 1. 12. 33. 4; "O dredd Soverayne! | Thus farre forth pardon" in *F. Q.* 3. Pr. 3. 5-6; "pardon me, most dreaded Soueraine" in *F. Q.* 6. Pr. 7. 1; "thy gratious Lord and Soueraigne" in *F. Q.* 7. 6. 34. 5. See also *B. N.* 246.

37-8. "miserable wreches." See "wretched miseries" in *F. Q.* 2. 10. 62. 3; "wretched woman, miserable wight" in *F. Q.* 5. 10. 21. 3; "wretched and miserable" in *Pet.* 2. 6. 13.

39. "plunged in this Sea of sorrowes." See "plung'd in sea of sorrowes" in *F. Q.* 1. 7. 39. 2.

45-56. Sir William FitzWilliam, who had been Lord Deputy twice, the second time from 1588 to 1594, was still alive in 1598; and this may explain why Spenser does not name him here or in the disparaging references to his deputyship and to "bieves taken for Captenries of Countries" in the *View* (3426-7, 5285-6).

The State Papers give a version of the MacMahon story somewhat different from that in *B. N.* On 7 August, 1589, FitzWilliam writes that the MacMahon [Rossa Bui] has died, that his brothers Hugh Roe and Brian have both sought the title, and that he has settled it on Hugh; on 2 March, 1590, he writes that he opposed the claims of Brian in order to bring Monaghan to the Crown, and on 12 October, 1590, that he has executed Hugh by due course of law; four years later he is charged with having caused this execution because Hugh could not pay him a fine of eight hundred beeves (*C. S. P. Ir. 1588-1592* 146. 5, 151. 2, 155. 8; *1592-1596* 176. 19). One of the Carew Papers, written at the beginning of 1596, adds further details from the account of Brian MacMahon: the succession to the captainship "was granted him, the said Hugh, purposely to draw an interest unto him and his heirs, contrary to the custom of the country, and then by his execution to draw the country into her Majesty's hands, as by the sequel showeth. After whose execution a garrison was placed in Monaghan, the name of McMahowne extinguished, and the substance of the country divided by the said Sir William FitzWilliam between Sir Henry Bagenall, Baron Elliott, Mr. Solicitor (Wilbraham), Captain Henshawe, Captain Willis, the Parson O'Connolan, Hugh Strowbridge, Thomas Asshe, Chr. Flemminge, and divers other strangers, and so the native people for the most part disinherited, and some of those that had portions allotted them were afterwards slain and murdered. . . . Also he saith that the said Hugh Roe McMahowne, for obtaining Sir William FitzWilliam's consent, promised and paid him 500 cows, the Lady his wife 100, and John FitzWilliam his son 100; and that also he paid to divers others in reward, and for charges while he attended the State, to the number of 800 cows" (*C. C. MSS. 1589-1600*, pp. 156-7). For an account of the affair which is favorable to FitzWilliam see Bagwell 3. 201-3.

45. "cause and Roote." See "cause and root" in *F. Q.* 1. 10. 25. 1.

53. HULBERT (*MP* 34. 347). By A. B. must be meant Hugh Roe.

56-88. HULBERT (*MP* 34. 347-9) believes that in this passage Tyrone "is treated somewhat sympathetically" and contrasts this attitude with that of Spenser in *View* 3590-3615. [See Appendix IV; also *View* 2993-4, 3500-3615, and the notes.]

67-75. In *View* 3507-29 it is pointed out that Tyrone is too shrewd to believe that he can safely submit to the English government.

71-5. HULBERT (*MP* 34. 348) notes that in Bagwell's discussion of Tyrone's pretended submission no mention is made of his rejected plea to go to England but that such an offer was known to Captain Thomas Lee; she feels there is a similarity between this section of *B. N.* and Lee's proposals in Tyrone's behalf in 1596.

COMMENTARY

[In his letters written to Cecil on 27 July, 1596, and 30 April, 1597, however, Sir John Norris reports that Tyrone has expressed a willingness to come to England; Norris distrusted both offers and seems to have rejected the second (*C. S. P. Ir. 1596-1597* 191. 46, 198. 128). *B. N.* takes a point of view opposed to Norris's both here and in 93-8.]

75-84. Tyrone's dealings with Spain are mentioned in *View* 3515-9.

79. "with strong feares and vaine hopes to feede his euill humour." See "To feede her foolish humour, and vaine iolliment" in *F. Q.* 2. 6. 3. 9; "To feed her humour" in *F. Q.* 3. 2. 12. 2; "To feede the humour" in *F. Q.* 5. 5. 55. 7; "humor feed" in *F. Q.* 6. 2. 29. 9; "their vaine humours fed" in *Hub.* 822; "To feed on hope, to pine with feare" in *Hub.* 900.

81. "make advantage." See "Making aduantage" in *F. Q.* 2. 8. 25. 2; "to make aduantage" in *F. Q.* 6. 3. 46. 9.

85-6. "conteined in reasonoble termes." See "within reasons rule, her madding mood containe" in *F. Q.* 5. 7. 11. 9.

87-8. "Minister newe matter." "Ministreth matter fit" in *F. Q.* 3. 6. 9. 4.

89. "dauled." Perhaps a scribal error for "danled," *i. e., dandled*; see "dandle theire doinges" in *View* 2807-8. *Dawdle* does not occur in Spenser's poetry and is not cited by *NED* before 1656.

91-2. It is interesting that here, where he is addressing the Queen, Spenser blames the "faintnesse of those which were sett here to followe" Tyrone and that in the *View* (3519) he blames the "greate faintenes in her maiesties withstandinge him."

93-8. Russell, who became Lord Deputy in 1594, soon requested that a military commander with extraordinary powers should be chosen to aid him; and Sir John Norris was appointed to the position in 1595. But before long it became common knowledge that the two were in disagreement. Russell wrote to the Queen on 30 June, 1596: "if your Majesty would vouchsafe me the reading of these few lines, I hope it will appear unto your Highness that the consumption of your treasure to so little purpose and with so slender service performed may not justly be laid to my charge, but unto his [Norris's], who being sent specially to manage this war, and for that cause here remaining about a twelvemonth, hath of that time spent nine months at the least in cessations and treaties of peace, either of his own device contrary to my liking, as ever doubting th' end would prove but treacherous, or else by direction from thence, by what means or upon what advices I know not" (*HMC, Salisbury MSS* 6. 230). Both Norris and Russell retired from office in 1597.

HULBERT (*MP* 34. 350) cites the present passage as evidence against Spenser's authorship of *B. N.*:

> when one considers what we know about the relationship of Spenser to the Norrises, it seems most improbable that Spenser would have recorded such

gossip without indicating the reasons for which it was to be dismissed as the slander of vindictive tongues. From 1584 until his death Sir John Norris was Lord President of Munster, with Sir Thomas [his brother] acting as his deputy; during these years Spenser held official appointments, the dates of which are somewhat difficult to determine, and received the grant of Kilcolman. There is no indication that he was not on the most amiable terms with the brothers. In fact, what evidence we have of Spenser's connection with them gives us reason to believe that it was of a friendly sort—Bryskett includes both Sir Thomas and Spenser in the group of friends who gathered in his house near Dublin; one of Spenser's dedicatory sonnets prefaced to the *Faerie Queene* lauds Sir John; at the very time of the writing of the complaint we find Spenser twice being employed by Sir Thomas to deliver messages to the government. All that we know of Spenser's loyalty (and we must remember that at the time of the writing of the complaint Sir John was dead) makes it unlikely that the slanderous sentence was from his pen.

Hulbert adds: "there is no doubt of Spenser's sympathy with the policy of Sir William Russell and regret that the latter was not given a free hand to carry it into execution." [See *View* 3685-9.]

BENNETT (*SP* 37. 177-200; *The Evolution of "The Faerie Queene,"* pp. 191-205) advances the theory that Spenser revealed his admiration for Norris by praising him as Artegall in *F. Q.* 5. 11-12; in developing this theory, she suggests that Norris, like Spenser, believed in a policy of stern military action and that in 1595 instructions from England forced him, against his better judgment, to establish a hollow peace with Tyrone. But JUDSON (*Life*, pp. 181, 192) notes that in 1590 the dedicatory sonnet to Norris was an afterthought and that by 1596 Spenser's admiration had evidently waned since the *View*, which does not mention Norris, refers respectfully to Russell, then quarreling with him; by 1596, moreover, Norris was committed to appeasement of Tyrone.

EDITOR. As evidence on Norris's policy we have a letter from Anthony Bacon to his mother on 22 October, 1595: "from Ireland there were cross advertisements from the lord deputy on the one side, and sir JOHN NORREYS on the other, the first, as a good trumpet, sounding continually in his letters the alarm against the enemy, the latter serving as a treble viol to invite to dance and be merry upon false hope of a hollow peace" (Birch, *Memoirs* 2. 180). In this quarrel over policies it would be natural for Spenser, who favored strong military action in Ireland, to side with Russell against Norris. The *View*, in fact, specifically praises Russell for his vigorous pursuit of Feagh MacHugh. On the other hand, Spenser's only direct allusion to Norris is in the dedicatory sonnet of 1590; and this, an afterthought like the sonnet to Burghley, may well be perfunctory in character and can tell us little about his feelings several years later. If Spenser felt that Norris's policies and conduct were fundamentally wrong, it would not be out of character for him to criticize them in a document like *B. N.* after Norris had died; in the *View* (3410-28) he criticized the policies and conduct of the dead Perrot. The present passage, therefore, gives me no reason to believe that Spenser was not the author of *B. N.*

99-103. The danger of sudden changes in the policies of the governors is treated more fully in the *View* (2866-92).

COMMENTARY 435

99-101. Thomas, Lord Burgh, who succeeded Russell as Lord Deputy in April, 1597, died in the following October.

103-8. For a similar picture of the gathering rebellion see *View* 2936-43.

105-6. "a moste violent medecyne." See "to violente a medicine" in *View* 998; "too violente a meanes," "the same medicyne," "the moste violent redresse" in *View* 2962-4—passages in which Spenser is expressing the same idea as here.

107-8. "shake of the yoke of there obedience." See "shaken of theire yoke and broken the bondes of theire obedience" in *View* 102.

112-3. "like as a fire the longer it is kept vnder the more violentlie it burneth when it breaketh out." See *F. Q.* 2. 11. 32:

> Like as a fire, the which in hollow caue
> Hath long bene vnderkept, and downe supprest,
> With murmurous disdaine doth inly raue,
> And grudge, in so streight prison to be prest,
> At last breakes forth with furious vnrest,
> And striues to mount vnto his natiue seat;
> All that did earst it hinder and molest,
> It now deuoures with flames and scorching heat,
> And carries into smoake with rage and horror great.

114-7. B. N. may exaggerate the local strength of the rebels. William Saxey and William Weaver estimated that between three and four thousand had entered Munster; on 21 October the Earl of Ormond wrote Cecil that they now numbered above three thousand (*C. S. P. Ir. 1598-1599* 202. 3. 127, 138, 118).

118-22. Captain Richard Tyrrell, a member of an important Anglo-Irish family of West Meath, was one of the chief leaders of Tyrone's forces when they entered Munster early in October, 1598; he is listed among the marauders who spoiled the barony of Buttevant, and so probably Spenser's estate, on the fifteenth of that month (*C. S. P. Ir. 1598-1599* 202. 3. 113; Carpenter, p. 33; Henley, p. 157).

124-5. William Saxey, Chief Justice of Munster, gives examples of the rebels' cruelty: "infants taken from the nurse's breast, and the brains dashed against the walls; the heart plucked out of the body of the husband in the view of the wife, who was forced to yield the use of her apron to wipe off the blood from the murderers' fingers; [an] English gentleman at midday in a town cruelly murdered, and his head cleft in divers pieces; divers sent into Youghal amongst the English, some with their throats cut, but not killed, some with their tongues cut out of their heads, others with their noses cut off" (*C. S. P. Ir. 1598-1599* 202. 3. 127).

131. "melt with remorce." See "melt in teares without remorse" in *S. C. Nov.* 131.

135-6. "become so wretched wightes . . . of the worlde." See "become most wretched wightes on ground" in *T. M.* 312. *Wretched wights* occurs in *F. Q.* 1. 10. 39. 6, 3. 5. 36. 9; *H. H. L.* 239.

139-41.   So in *View* 3255-7 Spenser calls Munster "a moste ritche and plentifull Countrye full of Corne and Cattell that ye woulde haue thoughte they Coulde haue bene able to stande longe."

143.   "stroke stricken."   See "stricken strike" in *F. Q.* 1. 5. 7. 7; "strike in battell stroke" in *F. Q.* 4. 7. 39. 3; "strooke me one stroke" in *F. Q.* 6. 2. 12. 4.

148.   "nation so mightie and puisant."   See the phrase *mighty puissance* in *F. Q.* 2. 8. 42. 9, 3. 3. 28. 1; "puissant Nations" in *F. Q.* 4. 11. 15. 2.

149.   "the lapp of England."   See "the verye lapp of all the lande" in *View* 924.

150.   "a people as the Irish so vntrained in warrs."   In *View* 112-3 Spenser calls Ireland "a nacion ever Acquainted with warrs thoughe but Amongest themselves."   But in both passages the Irish are being accused of barbarism.

156-60.   So in *View* 3923-8 Spenser blamed, in the planting of Munster, the lack of any provision for garrisons and the regard only for "presente profitt."

161.   "trained vpp in peace."   See "trained vp in warlike stowre" in *F. Q.* 3. 2. 6. 3; "in theire owne kinde of milytare discipline traynd vp" in *View* 113-4; "traynd them vp . . . in armes and militare exercises" in *View* 333-4.

163.   "relikes of rebellion."   See "reliques of thoulde rebellion" in *View* 4987.

164.   "Armes and warlike exercises."   See "warlike exercise" in *F. Q.* 4. 7. 3. 4; "armes and militare exercises" in *View* 334.

165-9.   So in *View* 3857-63 Spenser says, "I woulde haue them firste vnarmed vtterlie" and then apply themselves "vnto honest trades of Civilitye."

167.   "trades of life."   The same phrase, with only slight variations in some cases, appears in *Hub.* 398; *Ax.* 156, 199-200, 251, 350; *View* 4871.

169.   "swerved."   *Swerve* is used of unregenerate rebels in *View* 4560, 4976.

171-2.   "there daylie conuersing with them would haue brough them . . . to the liking."   See "bringe them by dailye Conuersacion vnto better likinge" in *View* 4774-5.

175-8.   On the Irish love of liberty see *View* 355-60.

178.   "extreame wretchednes."   See "extreame wretchednes" in *View* 366.

178-84.   See the similar passage in *View* 2916-23.

181-2.   "desire . . . revived and kindled."   See "reuiue desire" in *F. Q.*

COMMENTARY 437

2. 6. 25. 9; "kindled youthfull fresh desire" in *F. Q.* 7. 7. 11. 7; "kindle new desire" in *Am.* 6. 9; "kindlest much more great desyre" in *H. B.* 5; "kindleth loue in generous desyre" in *H. L.* 187.

184-8. See 284-310 and *View* 2910-6, where the same idea is expressed. In *B. N.* 186-7 and *View* 2915-6 Spenser uses the same figure of patching.

186. "plucked downe." See same expression in *F. Q.* 1. 9. 12. 4, 6. 8. 28. 6, 7. 6. 13. 3; "plucke them vnder" in *View* 284-5; "plucke him on his knees" in *View* 3138-9.

188-90. Spenser makes a similar disclaimer in *View* 2973-81. Hulbert (*MP* 34. 351), citing the passage in the *View* but not that in *B. N.*, notes a difference in tone between the two documents.

191-9. HULBERT (*MP* 34. 350). Both documents [the *View* and the complaint in *B. N.* "To the Queene"] likewise agree that Munster should have a garrison and should bear the cost of its maintenance. The complaint, however, estimates that Munster could support three thousand to four thousand soldiers; Spenser [*View* 4234-7] estimates one thousand—a difference in detail which does away with whatever significance one might attach to the fact that they both urge the necessity of a garrison. [In *View* 3904-28 Spenser proposes such a plan for Ireland in general and laments the lack of such a plan for Munster in particular.]

192. "framed and fashoned." See "You frame my thoughts and fashion me within" in *Am.* 8. 9.

203-4. In the *View* (4238-40, 4246-53) Spenser points out the advantage of paying the expenses of the presidency, not by a special imposition, but by a charge of four thousand pounds against the general land tax for Munster.

204. "Sheriffes and Cessours extorcion." See "the extorcion of Shiriffes subshirefs, and theire Baylliffes The Corrupcion of victellours Cessours and purveyours" in *View* 2800-2.

214-5. "power out our moste humble and pittiouse plainte." See "poore my piteous plaints out" in *S. C. June* 80. The phrase *piteous plaint* or *plaints* occurs in *F. Q.* 1. 3. 44. 2, 1. 8. 38. 2, 4. 12. 7. 4, 6. 4. 18. 2, 6. 7. 40. 4; *R. T.* 29, 470; *T. M.* 3, 360.

216-7. "caste your graciouse minde vnto the cairfull regarde." See the phrase *cast his mind* in *F. Q.* 2. 3. 4. 2, 3. 7. 12. 5; "cast in carefull mind" in *F. Q.* 1. 9. 15. 6; "cast in her misdoubtfull mynde" in *F. Q.* 5. 6. 3. 8; "cast | In her conceiptfull mynd" in *F. Q.* 6. 12. 16. 1-2.

222. "sauage wilde." See "saluage wylde" in *Am.* 20. 9.

224-80. The same distrust of what Spenser takes to be Elizabeth's merciful nature appears in *View* 3289-3317.

226. "vile Catifes." See *vile caitiff* in *F. Q.* 2. 3. 7. 4, 2. 9. 13. 4.

230. "base raskalls." See "the base blood of such a rascall crew" in *F. Q.* 5. 2. 52. 5.

231. "late hapened reproche." See "late vile reproch" in *F. Q.* 5. 7. 34. 4.

237-8. "madding minde." See "madding mynd" in *S. C. Ap.* 25; "madding kiddes" in *S. C. July* 87; "madding mood" in *F. Q.* 5. 7. 11. 9; "madding mother" in *F. Q.* 5. 8. 47. 5; "madding multitude" in *Ax.* 231; "maddinge mode" in *View* 3690.

238-9. "stirre vpp your Maiestie nowe to take vengance." See "stird to vengeance" in *F. Q.* 4. 3. 14. 4.

241-2. "perpetuall establishment of peace." See "Long time in peace his Realme established" in *F. Q.* 2. 10. 63. 3.

246. "Pardon therefore moste gracious Soueraigne." See note on *B. N.* 37.

246. "wreched greued wightes." See *wretched wights* in *F. Q.* 1. 10. 39. 6, *F. Q.* 3. 5. 36. 9, *T. M.* 312, *H. H. L.* 239; "grieued wight" in *Gn.* Ded. 11.

247. "true faithfull." See *faithful true* in *F. Q.* 1. 1. 2. 7, 1. 6. 20. 7; "trew and faithfull" in *F. Q.* 3. 5. 12. 8.

251. "hard at hand." See same phrase in *F. Q.* 2. 12. 18. 5, 6. 9. 16. 3.

253. "wonted milde courses." See *wonted course* in *F. Q.* 2. 6. 20. 6, 7. 6. 16. 4.

258. "imbrewed them selues so deeplie in our bloud." The expression *to imbrue in blood* occurs in *F. Q.* 1. 7. 17. 9, 1. 7. 47. 3, 1. 11. 36. 7, 2. 1. 40. 7-8, 5. 1. 16. 4, 5. 2. 52. 4-5, 5. 7. 40. 4-5, 6. 2. 7. 3-4, 6. 7. 23. 6.

262. "presume vpon the pride of there owne strength." See "proud presumpteous" in *F. Q.* 1. 8. 12. 5, 5. 12. 14. 1; "His proud presumed force" in *F. Q.* 2. 6. 30. 3; "proud Knight in his presumption" in *F. Q.* 6. 3. 8. 3.

270. "perceth our very soules." See "through his soule like poysned arrow perst" in *F. Q.* 4. 5. 31. 4.

270-1. "dispose your selfe . . . to any such milder dealing." See "more mildelye disposed" in *View* 3407-8.

271-3. *B. N.*, however, goes on to propose a general pardon in 356-62. See also *View* 5285.

277. "humblie beseeching." See "humbly did beseech" in *F. Q.* 4. 2. 21. 1.

285. In the present case *B. N.*, unlike the *View*, uses *reform* in the sense

of *only partial redress*; but both works propose the complete conquest and reconstruction of Ireland. See the plea for "vniuersall reformacion" in *B. N.* 240.

295-7.   In *View* 2522-5 Spenser calls it evil surgery to cut off every unsound part; but he goes on to explain (2965-6) that he does not mean to spare the unsound parts which cannot be saved and which should therefore be cut off by violent means.

303.   "*milde and gentle intreaty.*" See "mildly gan entreat" in *F. Q.* 5. 5. 47. 9; "myld entreaty" in *F. Q.* 6. 3. 37. 9.

311-27.   In the *View* (2985-3057) Spenser likewise proposes "a stronge power of men" which will economize both money and time.

319.   GERARD BOATE (*Irelands Naturall History*, 1657, p. 182). The Loosness doth also greatly reign in Ireland, as well among those of the countrie as among the Strangers, wherfore the English inhabitants have given it the name of The country-disease.

322-3.   See 339-42 below and note.

328-9.   HULBERT (*MP* 34. 351), noting that the *View* is milder in tone than *B. N.*, writes: "though he [Spenser in *View* 3248-70, 3289-3302] realizes that famine will naturally follow in the wake of conquest and hurry its completion, he bemoans that it necessarily must, picturing so vividly its effect that Eudoxus fears the Queen will never be able to endure the sight of such suffering." [In the *View* Spenser undoubtedly shows that he wishes to spare the innocent Irish all unnecessary suffering; but if any reader doubts that the *View*, like *B. N.*, proposes famine as a means of subduing the rebels, let him read 3129-39, 3149-54, 3172-9, and 3248-70 of the dialogue.]

332-3.   HULBERT (*MP* 34. 352-3) notes that *B. N.* and Spenser do not reveal "the same attitude as to the means to be employed in converting Ireland to Protestantism"; the *View* stresses the fact that Ireland must be made whole in body before it can be reformed in soul (2674-98) and that the religious reformation must be effected by persuasion rather than by force (5031-48). [But the present passage, the only one in which *B. N.* touches on religion, is not concerned with the *means* of securing conformity.]

339-42.   These figures may be compared with those Spenser proposes in the *View* (3054-5), ten thousand foot and a thousand horse for a period of not more than a year and a half.

339 n.   Ralph Byrchensha (*A Discovrse Occasioned vpon the Late Defeat, Giuen to the Arch-rebels, Tyrone and Odonnell*, 1602, sig. C4r) makes the same pun: "There did *Mountioy* tyre this *Tyrone* well."

343-5.   So in *View* 4273-6 Spenser proposes garrisons for Cork and Waterford to protect them against foreign invasion.

347.   "*kery.*" Since Kerry is a part of Munster, the scribe seems to have

misread the name of some other region, perhaps Leix, which is frequently coupled with Offaly.

348-53. HULBERT (*MP* 34. 352) shows that the method of warfare here recommended is diametrically opposed to that suggested in *View* 3059-69. See Appendix IV.

349-50. In *View* 3102-4 it is proposed to attach horsemen to the garrisons of foot since the two are complementary.

355. " blouddie and crewell." See " bloddye and Crvell " in *View* 3351.

356-8. " generall proclamacion be made that all which will . . . submitt themselues absolutelie within ten or twelue daies (the principall excepted)." See " proclamacion weare made generallye . . . that what persons soeuer woulde within xx^{ty} daies absolutelye submitt themselues (exceptinge onelye the verye principall " in *View* 3192-5.

363-8. For a fuller discussion of fraudulent conveyances see *View* 818-54.

APPENDIX I

LETTERS

A.

HARVEY'S LETTERS AND THE PREFACE "TO THE CVRTEOVS BUYER"

[For the text printed in this appendix see "A Note on the Text" at the head of Spenser's Letters.]

[LETTER II]

To my verie Friende,

M. Immerito.

LIberalissimo Signor Immerito, in good soothe my poore Storehouse will presently affourd me nothing, either to recompence, or counteruaile your gentle Masterships, long, large, lauish, Luxurious, Laxatiue Letters withall, (now a Gods name, when 5
did I euer in my life, hunt the Letter before? but, belike, theres no remedie, I must needes be euen with you once in my dayes,) but only forsoothe, a fewe Millions of Recommendations, and a running Coppie of the Verses enclosed. Which Verses, *(extra iocum)* are so well done in *Lattin* by two Doctors, and so well Translated into English by one odde Gentleman, and generally so well allowed of all, that 10
chaunced to haue the perusing of them: that trust mee, *G. H.* was at the first hardly intreated, to shame himselfe, and truely, now blusheth, to see the first Letters of his name, stande so neere their Names, as of necessitie they must. You know the *Greeke* prouerb, πορφύρα ποτί πορφύραν διακριτέα, and many colours, (as in a manner euery thing else) that seuerally by themselues, seeme reasonably good, 15
and freshe ynough, beyng compared, and ouermatched wyth their betters, are maruellously disgraced, and as it were, dashed quite oute of Countenaunce. I am at this instant, very busilye, and hotly employed in certaine greate and serious affayres: whereof, notwithstanding (for all youre vowed, and long experimented secrecie) you are not like to heare a worde more at the moste, till I my selfe see a 20
World more at the leaste. And therefore, for this once I beseech you (notwithstanding your greate expectation of I knowe not what Volumes for an aunsweare)

14 πορφύρα] *HG2SmSe*   πορφύσα *Q*   14 ποτί] περὶ *QG2Sm*   Καδὶ *H*   ποτὶ *Se*
14 πορφύραν] *G2SmSe*   πορφύραυ *QH*

441

content your good selfe, with these Presentes, (pardon me, I came lately out of a Scriueners shop) and in lieu of many gentle Farewels, and goodly Godbewyes, at your departure: gyue me once againe leaue, to playe the Counsaylour a while, if it be but to iustifie your liberall Mastershippes, *Nostri Cato maxime saecli:* and I coniure you by the Contents of the Verses, and Rymes enclosed, and by al the good, and bad Spirites, that attende vpon the Authors themselues, immediatly vpon the contemplation thereof, to abandon all other fooleries, and honour Vertue, the onely immortall and suruiuing Accident amongst so manye mortall, and euer-perishing Substaunces. As I strongly presume, so good a Texte, so clearkly handeled, by three so famous Doctours, as olde *Maister Wythipole,* and the other two bee, may easily, and will fully perswade you, howsoeuer you tush at the fourths vnsutable Paraphrase. But a worde or two, to your large, lauishe, laxatiue Letters, and then for thys time, *Adieu.* Of my credite, youre doubtes are not so redoubted, as youre selfe ouer suspiciously imagine: as I purpose shortely to aduize you more at large. Your hotte yron, is so hotte, that it striketh mee to the hearte, I dare not come neare to strike it: The Tyde tarryeth no manne, but manye a good manne is fayne to tarry the Tyde. And I knowe some, whyche coulde be content to bee theyr own Caruers, that are gladde to thanke other for theyr courtesie: But Beggars, they saye, muste be no choosers.

Your new-founded ἄρειον πάγον I honoure more, than you will or can suppose: and make greater accompte of the twoo worthy Gentlemenne, than of two hundreth *Dionisij Areopagitae,* or the verye notablest Senatours, that euer *Athens* dydde affourde of that number.

Your Englishe *Trimetra* I lyke better, than perhappes you will easily beleeue: and am to requite them wyth better, or worse, at more conuenient leysure. Marry, you must pardon me, I finde not your warrant so sufficiently good, and substauntiall in Lawe, that it can persuade me, they are all, so precisely perfect for the Feete, as your selfe ouer-partially weene, and ouer-confidently auouche: especiallye the thirde, whyche hathe a foote more than a Lowce (a wonderous deformitie in a righte and pure *Senarie*) and the sixte, whiche is also in the same Predicament, vnlesse happly one of the feete be sawed off wyth a payre of *Syncopes:* and then shoulde the Orthographie haue testified so muche: and in steade of *Hĕaŭenlĭ Vĭrgĭnāls,* you should haue written, *Heaŭnlĭ Virgnāls:* and *Virgnāls* againe in the ninth, and should haue made a Curtoll of *Imm̄erīto* in the laste: being all notwithstandyng vsuall, and tollerable ynoughe, in a mixte, and licentious *Iambicke:* and of two euilles, better (no doubte) the fyrste, than the laste: a thyrde superfluous sillable, than a dull *Spondee.* Then me thinketh, you haue in my fancie somwhat too many *Spondees* beside: and whereas *Trochee* sometyme presumeth in the firste place, as namely in the second Verse, *Make thy,* whyche *thy,* by youre Maistershippes owne authoritie muste needes be shorte, I shall be faine to supplye the office of the Arte Memoratiue, and putte you in minde of a pretty Fable in *Abstemio* the Italian, implying thus much, or rather thus little in effect.

A certaine lame man beyng invited to a solempne Nuptiall Feaste, made no more adoe, but sate me hym roundlye downe foremoste at the hyghest ende of the

---

37 to the] in the *H*   39 Caruers] Garners *Se*   40 courtesie:] courtesie? *H*   42 ἄρειον πάγον] *SmSe*   ἀρειονπαγον *QHG2*   43 two] the two *G2*   44 *Dionisij*] *Dionisy H*   55 *Vĭrgĭnāls*] *Se   Virgĭnāls Q*[1,2,4,6] *HG2Sm*   66 foremoste] foremaste *H*

APPENDIX I 443

Table. The Master of the feast, suddainly spying his presumption, and hansomely
remoouing him from thence, placed me this haulting Gentleman belowe at the
nether end of the bourd: alledging for his defence the common verse: *Sedes nulla
datur, praeterquam sexta Trochaeo:* and pleasantly alluding to this foote, which 70
standing vppon two syllables, the one long, the other short, (much like, of a like,
his guestes feete) is always thrust downe to the last place, in a true Hexameter,
and quite thrust out of doores in a pure, and iust *Senarie.* Nowe Syr, what thinke
you, I began to thinke with my selfe, when I began to reade your warrant first:
so boldly, and venterously set downe in so formall, and autentique wordes, as these, 75
Precisely perfit, and not an inch from the Rule? Ah Syrrha, and Iesu Lord, thought
I, haue we at the last gotten one, of whom his olde friendes and Companions may
iustly glory, *In eo solùm peccat, quòd nihil peccat:* and that is yet more exacte,
and precise in his English Comicall Iambickes, than euer *M. Watson* himselfe was
in his *Lattin* Tragicall Iambickes, of whom *M. Ascham* reporteth, that he would 80
neuer to this day suffer his famous *Absolon* to come abroad, onely because *Anapaestus in Locis paribus,* is twice, or thrice vsed in steade of *Iambus?* A small
fault, ywisse, and such a one in *M. Aschams* owne opinion, as perchaunce woulde
neuer haue beene espyed, no neither in *Italy,* nor in *Fraunce.* But when I came to
the curious scanning, and fingering of euery foote, and syllable: Lo here, quoth I, 85
M. Watsons Anapaestus for all the worlde. A good horse, that trippeth not once
in a iourney: and *M. Immerito* doth, but as *M. Watson,* and in a manner all other
Iambici haue done before him: marry he might haue spared his preface, or at the
least, that same restrictiue, and streightlaced terme, *Precisely,* and all had been well
enough: and I assure you, of my selfe, I beleeue, no peece of a fault marked at all. 90
But this is the Effect of warrantes, and perhappes the Errour may rather proceede
of his Master, *M. Drantes* Rule, than of himselfe. Howsoeuer it is, the matter is
not great, and I always was, and will euer continue of this Opinion, *Pauca multis
condonanda vitia Virtutibus,* especially these being no *Vitia* neither, in a common
and licencious *Iambicke. Verùm ista obiter, non quidem contradicendi animo, aut* 95
etiam corrigendi mihi crede: sed nostro illo Academico, pristinoque more ratiocinandi. And to saye trueth, partely too, to requite your gentle courtesie in beginning to me, and noting I knowe not what breache in your gorbellyed Maisters
Rules: which Rules go for good, I perceiue, and keepe a Rule, where there be no
better in presence. My selfe neither sawe them, nor heard of them before: and there- 100
fore will neither praise them, nor dispraise them nowe: but vppon the suruiewe of
them, and farther conference, (both which I desire) you shall soone heare one mans
opinion too or fro. Youre selfe remember, I was wonte to haue some preiudice of
the man: and I still remaine a fauourer of his deserued, and iust commendation.
Marry in these poyntes, you knowe, *Partialitie* in no case, may haue a foote: and 105
you remember mine olde Stoicall exclamation: *Fie on childish affection, in the
discoursing, and deciding of schoole matters.* This I say, because you charge me
with an vnknowne authoritie: which for aught I know yet, may as wel be either
vnsufficient, or faultie, as otherwise: and I dare more than halfe promise, (I dare
not saye, warrant) you shall alwayes in these kinde of controuersies, finde me nighe 110
hande answerable in mine owne defence. *Reliqua omnia, quae de hac supersunt*

81-2 *Anapaestus*] *Anapaestes* H   85 Lo] So *Sm*   88 *Iambici*] *Iambics* G2

Anglicorum versuum ratione, in aliud tempus reseruabimus, ociosum magis. Youre Latine Farewell is a goodly braue yonkerly peece of work, and Goddilge yee, I am alwayes maruellously beholding vnto you, for your bountifull Titles: I hope by that time I haue been resident a yeare or twoo in *Italy*, I shall be better qualifyed in this kind, and more able to requite your lauishe, and magnificent liberalitie that way. But to let Titles and Tittles passe, and come to the very pointe in deede, whiche so neare toucheth my lusty Trauayler to the quicke, and is one of the *praedominant humors* that raigne in our common Youths: *Heus mi tu, bone proce, magne muliercularum amator, egregie Pamphile, eum aliquando tandem, qui te manet, qui mulierosos omnes, qui vniuersam Faeministarum sectam, Respice finem.* And I shal then be content to appeale to your owne learned experience, whether it be, or be not, too too true: *quod dici solet à me saepe: à te ipso nonnunquam: ab expertis omnibus quotidie: Amare amarum: Nec deus, vt perhibent, Amor est, sed amaror, et error: et quicquid in eandem solet sententiam Empiricŵs aggregari. Ac scite mihi quidem Agrippa Ouidianam illam,* de Arte Amandi, ἐπιγραφήν *videtur correxisse, meritóque,* de Arte Meretricandi, *inscripsisse. Nec verò ineptè alius,* Amatores Alchumistis *comparauit, aureos, argenteosque montes, atque fontes lepidè somniantibus, sed interim miserè immanibus Carbonum fumis propemodum occaecatis, atque etiam suffocatis: praeterquam celebratum illum Adami Paradisum, alium esse quendam praedicauit, stultorum quoque Amatorumque mirabilem Paradisum: illum verè, hunc phantasticè, fanaticeque beatorum. Sed haec alias, fortassis vberiùs.* Credite me, I will neuer linne baityng at you, til I haue rid you quite of this yonkerly, and womanly humor. And as for your speedy and hasty trauell: me thinks I dare stil wager al the Books and writings in my study, which you know, I esteeme of greater value, than al the golde and siluer in my purse, or chest, that you wil not, (and yet I muste take heede, how I make my bargaine with so subtile and intricate a Sophister) that you shall not, I saye, bee gone ouer Sea, for al your saying, neither the next, nor the nexte weeke. And then peraduenture I may personally performe your request, and bestowe the sweetest Farewell, vpon your sweetmouthed Mashippe, that so vnsweete a Tong, and so sowre a paire of Lippes can affoorde. And, thinke you I will leaue my *Il Pellegrino* so? No I trowe. My Lords Honor, the expectation of his friendes, his owne credite and preferment, tell me, he muste haue a moste speciall care, and good regarde of employing his trauaile to the best. And therfore I am studying all this fortnight, to reade him suche a Lecture in *Homers Odyss*, and *Virgils Æneads*, that I dare vndertake he shall not neede any further instruction, in *Maister Turlers Trauayler*, or *Maister Zuingers Methodus Apodemica:* but in his whole trauaile abroade, and euer after at home, shall shewe himselfe a verie liuelye and absolute picture of *Vlysses* and *Æneas*. Wherof I haue the stronger hope he muste needes proue a most capable and apt subiecte (I speake to a Logician) hauing the selfe same Goddesses and Graces attendant vpon his body and mind, that euermore guided them, and their actions: especially the ones *Minerua*, and the others *Venus:* that is (as one Doctor expoundeth it) the pol-

112 *reseruabimus*] resuruabimus H   117-63 But .... *valebis.*] om. Sm   119 *mi tu*] mitu H
120 *eum*] cum G2   121 *vniuersam*] vniuersum G2   123 *à me*] àme H   123 *à te*] àte H
126 *quidem*] quidê G2   126 ἐπιγραφήν] Se ἐπιγραφτῶ Q ἐπιγραφτώ H ἐπιγάφην G2
132 *verè*] verie H   140 Mashippe] Mastershippe Se   147-222 *Methodus* .... FINIS.]
om. Q⁶   147 *Methodus*] Methodus, Methodus G2   148 at] om. G2

litique head, and wise gouernement of the one: and the amiable behauiour, and
gratious courtesie of the other: the two verye principall, and moste singular Com- 155
panions, of a right Trauailer: and as perhaps one of oure subtile Logicians woulde
saye, the two inseparable, and indivisible accidents of the foresaide Subiects. *De
quibus ipsis, caeterisque omnibus artificis Apodemici instrumentis: inprimisque de
Homerica illa, diuinaque herba μῶλυ δέ μιν καλέουσι θεόι) qua Vlissem suum Mer-
curius, aduersus Cyrcea et pocula, et carmina, et venena, morbosque omnes prae-* 160
*muniuit: et coram, vti spero, breui: et longè, vti soleo, copiosius: et fortasse
etiam, aliquantò, quàm soleo, cum subtiliùs, tum verò Politicè, Pragmaticeque magis.
Interim tribus eris syllabis contentus, ac valebis. Trinitie Hall, stil in my Gallerie.
23. Octob. 1579.* In haste.

Yours, as you knowe. G. H. 165

Certaine Latin Verses, of the frailtie and mutabilitie of all things, sauing onely Ver- tue: *made by* M. Doctor Norton, *for the right* Worshipfull, M. Thomas Sackford, Master of Requestes vnto hir Maiestie. 170

ἀκροστιχὰ.

Th.	TEmpora furtiuo morsu laniantur amaena,
S	Sensim florescunt, occubitura breui.
A	Anni vere salit, Senio mox conficiendus,
C	Cura, labor ditant, non eademque premunt? 175
F	Fallax, vel vigili studio Sapientia parta:
O	Oh, et magnatum gloria saepe iacet,
R	Res inter varias fluimus, ruimusque gradatim:
D	Dulcia Virtutis praemia sola manent.

158 caeterisque] caterisque H 159 δέ] Se δὲ QG2 159 μιν καλέουσι θεόι] G2Se
μινκαλεουσιθεόι Q μινκαλεουσιθεόι H 161 coram] corana H 162 Politicè] Polliticè
QHG2Se 163 Trinitie] Sm resumes at this point 166-222 Certaine . . . . FINIS.]
om. G2Sm 171 ἀκροστιχὰ] ἀκροσιχὰ Q^{1-5} Se

The same paraphrastically varied by M. Doctor Gouldingam, at the request of olde M. Wythipoll of Ipswiche.

    T.   *TEmpora furtiuo labuntur dulcia cursu,*
    S   *Subsiduntque breuî, quae viguere diu.*
    A   *Autumno capitur, quicquid nouus educat annus:*
    C   *Curta Iuuentutis gaudia, Fata secant.*
    F   *Fallax Ambitio est, atque anxia cura tenendi,*
    O   *Obscurum decus, et nomen inane Sophi.*
    R   *Res Fors humanas incerto turbine voluit,*
    D.   *Dulcia Virtutis praemia sola manent.*

Olde Maister Wythipols
owne Translation.

OVr merry dayes, by theeuish bit are pluckt, and torne away,
And euery lustie growing thing, in short time doth decay.
The pleasaunt Spring times ioy, how soone it groweth olde?
And wealth that gotten is with care, doth noy as much, be bolde.
No wisedome had with Trauaile great, is for to trust in deede,
For great Mens state we see decay, and fall downe like a weede.
Thus by degrees we fleete, and sinke in worldly things full fast,
But Vertues sweete and due rewardes stande sure in euery blast.

The same Paraphrastically varied by Master G. H. at M. Peter Wythipolles request, for his Father.

THese pleasant dayes, and Monthes, and yeares, by stelth do passe apace,
And do not things, that florish most, soone fade, and lose their grace?
Iesu, how soone the Spring of yeare, and Spring of youthfull rage,
Is come, and gone, and ouercome, and ouergone with age?

184 *viguere*] *virguere* H   185 *annus*] *amnu* H   196 be bolde] beholde ?

APPENDIX I   447

In paine is gaine, but doth not paine as much detract from health,
As it doth adde vnto our store, when most we roll in wealth?
Wisedome hir selfe must haue hir doome, and grauest must to graue,   210
And mightiest power sib to a flower: what then remaines to craue?
Nowe vp, now downe, we flowe, and rowe in seas of worldly cares,
Vertue alone eternall is, and shee the Laurell weares.

L' Enuoy.

Soone said, soone writ, soone learnd: soone trimly done in prose, or verse: 215
Beleeud of some, practizd of fewe, from Cradle to their Herse.

Virtuti, non tibi Feci.

M. Peter Wythipoll.

Et Virtuti, et mihi:
Virtuti, ad laudem: 220
Mihi, ad vsum.

FINIS.

¶ TO THE CVRTEOVS
Buyer, by a Welwiller of
the two Authours.

*Vrteous Buyer,* (for I write not to the enuious Carper) it was
my good happe, as I interpret it, nowe lately at the fourthe   5
or fifte hande, to bee made acquainted wyth the *three Letters*
following, by meanes of a faithfull friende, who with muche
entreaty had procured the copying of them oute, at *Immeritos*
handes. And I praye you, interprete it for your good happe,
so soone after to come so easilye by them, throughe my meanes,   10

7 muche] *HG2Se*   muchc *Q*

who am onely to craue these twoo things at your handes, to thinke friendely of my friendly meaning, and to take them of me wyth this Presumption, *In exiguo quandoque cespite latet lepus:* and many pretious stones, thoughe in quantitie small, yet in qualitie and valewe are esteemed for great. The first, for a good familiar and sensible Letter, sure liketh me verye well, and gyueth some hope of good mettall in the Author, in whome I knowe myselfe to be very good partes otherwise. But shewe me, or *Immerito*, two Englyshe Letters in Printe, in all pointes equall to the other twoo, both for the matter it selfe, and also for the manner of handling, and saye, wee neuer sawe good Englishe Letter in our liues. And yet I am credibly certified by the foresaide faithfull and honest friende, that himselfe hathe written manye of the same stampe bothe to Courtiers and others, and some of them discoursing vppon matter of great waight and importance, wherein he is said, to be fully as sufficient and hable, as in these schollerly pointes of Learning. The whiche Letters and Discourses I would very gladly see in Writing, but more gladly in Printe, if it might be obtayned. And at this time to speake my conscience in a worde of *these two following*, I esteeme them for twoo of the rarest, and finest Treaties, as wel for ingenious deuising, as also for significant vttering, and cleanly conueying of his matter, that euer I read in this Tongue: and I hartily thanke God for bestowing vppon vs some such proper and hable men with their penne, as I hartily thanke the Author himselfe, for vsing his pleasaunte, and witty Talente, with so muche discretion, and with so little harme, contrarye to the veine of moste, whych haue thys singular conceyted grace in writing. If they had bene of their owne setting forth, I graunt you they might haue beene more curious, but beeyng so well, and so sufficiently done, as they are, in my simple iudgement, and hauing so many notable things in them, togither with so greate varietie of Learning, worth the reading, to pleasure you, and to helpe to garnish our Tongue, I feare their displeasure the lesse. And yet, if they thinke I haue made them a faulte, in not making them priuy to the Publication: I shall be alwayes readye to make them the beste amendes I can, any other friendly waye. Surely, I wishe them bothe hartilye wel in the Lord, and betake you and them to his mercifull gouernemente, hoping, that he will at his pleasure conuerte suche good and diuine gifts as these, to the setting out of his own glory, and the benefite of his Churche. This XIX. of Iune. 1580.

Your, and their vnfayned

friend, in the Lorde.

36 displeasure] *G2Se* displeasnre *QH*

[LETTER IV]

A Pleasant and pitthy familiar discourse, of the Earthquake
in Aprill last.

To my loouing frende, *M. Immerito.*

*Ignor Immerito*, after as many gentle Godmorrowes, as your 5
self, and your sweete Harte listeth: May it please your Maistershippe to dispense with a poore Oratour of yours, for breaking
one principall graund Rule of our olde inuiolable Rules of
Rhetorick, in shewing himselfe somewhat too pleasurably disposed in a sad matter: (of purpose, to meete with *A coople of* 10
shrewde wittie new marryed Gentlewomen, which were more
Inquisitiue, than Capable of Natures works) I will report you a prettie conceited
discourse, that I had with them no longer agoe, than yesternight, in a Gentlemans
house, here in *Essex*. Where being in the company of certaine curteous Gentlemen,
and those two Gentlewomen, it was my chaunce to be well occupied, I warrant you, 15
at Cardes, (which I dare saye I scarcely handled a whole tweluemoonth before) at
that very instant, that the Earth vnder vs quaked, and the house shaked aboue:
besides the moouing, and ratling of the Table, and fourmes, where wee sat. Wherevpon, the two Gentlewomen hauing continually beene wrangling with all the rest,
and especially with my selfe, and euen at that same very moment, making a great 20
loude noyse, and much a doo: Good Lorde, quoth I, is it not woonderful straunge
that the delicate voyces of two so propper fine Gentlewoomen, shoulde make such
a suddayne terrible Earthquake? Imagining in good fayth, nothing in the worlde
lesse, than that it shoulde be any Earthquake in deede, and imputing that shaking
to the suddayne sturring, and remoouing of some cumberous thing or other, in the 25
vpper Chamber ouer our Heades: which onely in effect most of vs noted, scarcely

---

1-3 A . . . last.] This following Letter of Mr. *Harvey* to Mr. *Spenser*, gives an account of
the Causes of *Earthquakes* according to *Aristotle*, and then proceeds by way of Satyr. F *om. Hu*
6-7 your Maistershippe] *you FHu*   8 graund] *om. FHu*   8 our . . . of] *those we count
inviolable in FHu*   9 pleasurably] *pleasantly FHu*   11 *shrewde wittie*] *om. FHu*   11 which]
that FHu   12-398 I . . . . *Finium.*] *occasion'd by the* Earthquake *you have heard of;
whereof I have undertaken, at the request of a grave Gentleman, to give the Causes. Though FHu*

449

perceyuing the rest, beeing so closely and eagerly set at our game, and some of vs taking on, as they did. But beholde, all on the suddayne there commeth stumbling into the Parlour, the Gentleman of the house, somewhat straungely affrighted, and in a manner all agast, and telleth vs, as well as his Head and Tongue woulde giue him leaue, what a woonderous violent motion, and shaking there was of all things in his Hall: sensibly and visibly seene, as well of his owne selfe, as of many of his Seruauntes, and Neighbours there. I straite wayes beginnyng to thinke somewhat more seriously of the matter: Then I pray you, good Syr, quoth I, send presently one of your seruauntes farther into the Towne, to enquire, if the like hath happened there, as most likely is, and then must it needes be some Earthquake. Whereat the good fearefull Gentleman being a little recomforted, (as misdoubting, and dreading before, I knowe not what in his owne House, as many others did) and immediately dispatching his man into the Towne, wee had by and by certayne woord, that it was generall ouer all the Towne, and within lesse than a quarter of an howre after, that the very like behappened the next Towne too, being a farre greater and goodlyer Towne. The Gentlewoomens hartes nothing acquaynted with any such Accidentes, were maruellously daunted: and they, that immediately before were so eagerly, and greedily praying on vs, began nowe forsooth, very demurely, and deuoutely to pray vnto God, and the one especially, that was euen nowe in the House toppe, I beseeche you hartily quoth shee, let vs leaue off playing, and fall a praying. By my truely, I was neuer so scared in my lyfe, Me thinkes it maruellous straunge. What good Partener? Cannot you pray to your selfe, quoth one of the Gentlemen, but all the House must heare you, and ring Allin to our Ladyes Mattins? I see woomen are euery way vehement, and affectionate. Your selfe was liker euen nowe, to make a fraye, than to pray: and will you nowe needes in all hast bee on both your knees? Let vs, and you say it, first dispute the matter, what daunger, and terror it carryeth with it. God be praysed, it is already ceased, and heere be some present, that are able cunningly, and clearkly to argue the case. I beseeche you master, or mystresse, your zealous and deuoute Passion a while. And with that turning to me, and smiling a little at the first: Nowe I pray you, Master *H.* what say you Philosophers, quoth he, to this suddayne Earthquake? May there not be some sensible Naturall cause therof, in the concauities of the Earth it self, as some forcible and violent Eruption of wynde, or the like? Yes no doubt, sir, may there, quoth I, as well, as an Intelligible Supernaturall: and peraduenture the great aboundaunce and superfluitie of waters, that fell shortly after Michaelmas last, beeyng not as yet dryed, or drawen vp with the heate of the Sunne, which hath not yet recouered his full attractiue strength and power, might minister some occasion thereof, as might easily be discoursed by Naturall Philosophie, in what sorte the poores, and ventes, and crannies of the Earth being so stopped, and fylled vp euery where with moysture, that the windie Exhalations, and Vapors, pent vp as it were in the bowels thereof, could not otherwise get out, and ascende to their Naturall Originall place. But the Termes of Arte, and verye Natures of things themselues so vtterly vnknowen, as they are to most heere, it were a peece of woorke to laye open the Reason to euery ones Capacitie.

I know well, it is we that you meane, quoth one of the Gentlewomen (whom

49 Allin] All-in *Se*   55 your] moderate your *G2*   66 Exhalations] *G2*   Exhaltations *QSe*

for distinction sake, and bicause I imagine they would be loath to be named, I will hereafter call, Mystresse *Inquisitiua*, and the other, Madame *Incredula:*) now I beseeche you, learned Syr, try our wittes a little, and let vs heare a peece of your deepe Vniuersitie Cunning. Seeing you Gentlewomen will allgates haue it so, with a good will, quoth I: and then forsooth, very solemnly pawsing a whyle, most grauely, and doctorally proceeded, as followeth.

The Earth you knowe, is a mightie great huge body, and consisteth of many diuers, and contrarie members, and vaines, and arteries, and concauities, wherein to auoide the absurditie of *Vacuum*, most necessarily be very great store of substantiall matter, and sundry Accidentall humours, and fumes, and spirites, either good, or bad, or mixte. Good they cannot possibly all be, whereout is ingendred so much bad, as namely so many poysonfull, and venemous Hearbes, and Beastes, besides a thousand infectiue, and contagious thinges else. If they be bad, bad you must needes graunt is subiect to bad, and then can there not, I warrant you, want an Obiect, for bad to worke vpon. If mixt, which seemeth most probable, yet is it impossible, that there should be such an equall, and proportionable Temperature, in all, and singular respectes, but sometime the Euill (in the diuels name,) will as it were interchaungeably haue his naturall Predominaunt Course, and issue one way, or other. Which euill working vehemently in the partes, and malitiously encountering the good, forcibly tosseth, and cruelly disturbeth the whole: Which conflict indureth so long, and is fostred with aboundaunce of corrupt putrified Humors, and ylfauoured grosse infected matter, that it must needes (as well, or rather as ill, as in mens and womens bodyes) brust out in the ende into one perillous disease or other, and sometime, for want of Naturall voyding such feuerous, and flatuous Spirites, as lurke within, into such a violent chill shiuering shaking Ague, as euen nowe you see the Earth haue. Which Ague, or rather euery fitte thereof, we schollers call grossely, and homely, *Terrae motus*, a moouing, or sturring of the Earth, you Gentlewomen, that be learned, somewhat more finely, and daintily, *Terrae metus*, a feare, and agony of the Earth: we being onely mooued, and not terrified, you being onely in a manner terrified, and scarcely mooued therewith. Nowe here, (and it please you) lyeth the poynt, and quidditie of the controuersie, whether our *Motus*, or your *Metus*, be the better, and more consonant to the Principles and Maximes of Philosophy? the one being manly, and deuoyde of dreade, the other woomannish, and most wofully quiuering, and shiuering for very feare. In sooth, I vse not to dissemble with Gentlewoomen: I am flatly of Opinion, the Earth whereof man was immediately made, and not wooman, is in all proportions and similitudes liker vs than you, and when it fortuneth to be distempered, and disseased, either in part, or in whole, I am persuaded, and I beleeue Reason, and Philosophy will beare me out in it, it only mooueth with the very impulsiue force of the malady, and not trembleth, or quaketh for dastardly feare.

Nowe, I beseeche you, what thinke ye, Gentlewomen, by this Reason? Reason, quoth Madame *Incredula:* By my truly, I can neither picke out Rime, nor Reason, out of any thing I haue hearde yet. And yet me thinkes all should be Gospell, that commeth from you Doctors of Cambridge. But I see well, all is not Gould, that glistereth. In deede, quoth Mistresse *Inquisitiua*, heere is much adooe, I trowe, and little helpe. But it pleaseth Master H. (to delight himselfe, and these Gentlemen) to tell vs a trim goodly Tale of Robinhood, I knowe not what. Or suer if this be

Gospell, I dowte, I am not in a good beleefe. Trust me truly, Syr your Eloquence farre passeth my Intelligence. Did I not tell you aforehand, quoth I, as muche? And yet would you needes presume of your Capacities in such profound mysteries of Philosophie, and Priuities of Nature, as these be? The very thinking whereof, (vnlesse happily it be *per fidem implicitam*, in beleeuing, as the learned beleeue, And saying, It is so, bycause it is so) is nighe enough, to caste you both into a fitte, or two, of a daungerous shaking feauer, vnlesse you presently seeke some remedie to preuent it. And in earnest, if ye wyll giue me leaue, vpon that small skill I haue in Extrinsecall, and Intrinsecall Physiognomie, and so foorth, I will wager all the money in my poore purse to a pottle of Hyppocrase, you shall both this night, within somwhat lesse than two howers and a halfe, after ye be layed, *Dreame* of terrible straunge Agues, and Agonyes as well in your owne prettie bodyes, as in the mightie great body of the Earth. You are very merily disposed, God be praysed, quoth Mistresse *Inquisitiua*, I am glad to see you so pleasurable. No doubt, but you are maruellous priuie to our dreames. But I pray you now in a little good earnest, doo you Schollers thinke, that it is the very reason in deede, which you spake of euen now? There be many of vs, good Mistresse, quoth I, of that opinion: wherin I am content to appeale to the knowledge of these learned Gentlemen here. And some againe, of our finest conceited heades defend this Position, (a very straunge Paradox in my fancie:) that the Earth hauing taken in too much drinke, and as it were ouer lauish Cups, (as it hath sensibly done in a maner all this Winter past) now staggereth, and reeleth, and tottereth, this way and that way, vp and downe, like a drunken man, or wooman (when their Alebench Rhetorick commes vpon them, and specially the moouing Patheticall figure *Pottypôsis*,) and therefore in this forcible sort, you lately sawe, payneth it selfe to vomit vp againe, that so disordereth, and disquieteth the whole body within. And, forsoothe, a fewe new Contradictorie fellowes make no more of it, but a certaine vehement, and passionate neesing, or sobbing, or coffing, wherewithall they say, and as they say, say with great Physicall, and Naturall Reason, The Earth in some place, or other, euer lightly after any great, and suddayne alteration of weather, or diet, is exceedingly troubled, and payned, as namely this very Time of the yeare, after the extreeme pynching colde of Winter, and agayne in Autumne, after the extreeme parching heate of Sommer. But shall I tell you, Mistresse *Inquisitiua?* The soundest Philosophers in deede, and very deepest Secretaries of Nature, holde, if it please you, an other Assertion, and maintayne this for truth: (which at the leastwise, of all other seemeth maruellous reasonable, and is questionlesse farthest off from Heresie:) That as the Earth, vppon it, hath many stately, and boysterous and fierce Creatures, as namely, Men and Women, and diuers Beastes, wherof some one is in maner continually at variaunce and fewde with an other, euermore seeking to be reuenged vpon his enimie, which eft soones breaketh forth into professed and open Hostilitie: and then consequently followe set battels, and mortall warres: wherin the one partie bendeth all the force of his Ordinance and other Martiall furniture against the other: so likewise within it too, it hath also some, as vengibly and frowardly bent, as for Example, Woormes, and Moules, and Cunnyes, and such other valiauntly highminded Creatures, the Sonnes and daughters of *Mars*, and *Bellona* that nurrish ciuill debate, and contrarie factions amongst them selues: which are seldome, or neuer ended too, without miserable bloudshed, and deadly warre: and then go me their Gunnes lustily off, and the one dischargeth his Peece couragiously at the other: and there is suche a Generall dub a dubbe amongst them, and such horrible Thundering on euery syde, and suche a monstrous cruell shaking of one an others Fortes and Castels, that the whole Earth agayne, or at the least, so muche of the Earth, as is ouer, or neere them, is terribly hoysed, and 170 —————— —————— No more Ands, or Ifs, for Gods sake, quoth the Madame, and this be your great Doctorly learning. Wee haue euen Enoughe alreadie for our Money: and if you shoulde goe a little farther, I feare mee, you woulde make vs nyghe as cunning as your selfe: and that woulde bee a great disgrace to the Vniuersitie. Not a whitte, gentle Madame, quoth I, there be of vs, that haue 175 greater store in our bowgets, than we can well occupie our selues, and therefore we are glad as you see, when by the fauourable, and gratious aspect of some blessed Planet, and specially our *Mercury*, or your *Venus*, it is our good Fortune, to lighte on such good friendes, as you, and some other good Gentlewoomen be, that take pleasure, and comfort in such good things. Wherat Mistresse *Inquisitiua*, laughing 180 right out, and beginning to demaunde I know not what, (me thought, shee made, as if it shoulde haue been some goodly plausible Iest, wherat shee is, and takes her selfe prettily good:) Well, well, Master *H*. quoth the Gentleman of the house, now you haue playde your part so cunningly with the Gentlewoomen, (as I warrant you shall be remembred of *Inquisitiua*, when you are gone, and may happely forget 185 her: which I hope, Mistresse *Incredula* will do sometyme too, by hir leaue:) I pray you in earnest, let vs men learne some thing of you too: and especially I would gladly heare your Iudgement, and resolution, whether you counte of Earthquakes, as Naturall, or Supernaturall motions. But the shorter, all the better. To whom I made answere, in effect, as followeth: 190

Master Hs. short, but sharpe, and learned
Iudgement of Earthquakes.

T Ruely Syr, vnder correction, and in my fancie: The Earthquakes themselues I would saye are Naturall: as I veryly beleeue the Internall Causes thereof, are: I meane those two Causes, which 195 the Logicians call, the Materiall, and the Formall: Marry, the Externall Causes, which are the Efficient and Finall, I take rather of the two, to be supernaturall. I must craue a little leaue to laye open the matter.

The Materiall Cause of Earthquakes, (as was superficially touched in the 200 beginning of our speache, and is sufficiently prooued by *Aristotle* in the seconde Booke of his *Meteors*) is no doubt great aboundance of wynde, or stoare of grosse and drye vapors, and spirites, fast shut vp, and as a man would saye, emprysoned in the Caues, and Dungeons of the Earth: which winde, or vapors, seeking to be set at libertie, and to get them home to their Naturall lodgings, in a great fume, 205 violently rush out, and as it were, breake prison, which forcible Eruption, and

200 was] is *G2*

strong breath, causeth an Earthquake. As is excellently, and very liuely expressed of *Ouid*, as I remember, thus:

> *Vis fera ventorum caecis inclusa cauernis,*
> *Exspirare aliquò cupiens, luctataque frustra*
> *Liberiore frui coelo, cùm carcere Rima*
> *Nulla foret, toto nec peruia flatibus esset,*
> *Extentam tumefecit humum, ceu spiritus oris,*
> *Tendere vesicam solet,* and so foorth.

The formall Cause, is nothing but the very manner of this same Motion, and shaking of the Earth without: and the violent kinde of striuing, and wrastling of the windes, and Exhalations within: which is, and must needes be done in this, or that sort, after one fashion, or other. Nowe, syr, touching the other two Causes, which I named Externall: The first immediate Efficient, out of all Question, is God himselfe, the Creatour, and Continuer, and Corrector of Nature, and therefore Supernaturall: whose onely voyce carrieth such a reuerend and terrible Maiestie with it, that the very Earth againe, and highest Mountaines quake and tremble at the sounde and noyse thereof: the text is rife in euery mans mouth: *Locutus est Dominus et contremuit Terra:* howbeit, it is not to be gainesayd, that is holden of all the auncient Naturall Philosophers, and Astronomers, for the principall, or rather sole Efficient, that the Influence, and heate of the Sunne, and Starres, and specially of the three superior Planets, *Saturne, Iupiter,* and *Mars,* is a secondarie Instrumentall Efficient of such motions.

The finall, not onely that the wynde shoulde recouer his Naturall place, than which a naturall reasonable man goeth no farther, no not our excellentest profoundest Philosophers themselues: but sometime also, I graunt, to testifie and denounce the secrete wrathe, and indignation of God, or his sensible punishment vppon notorious malefactours, or, a threatning Caueat, and forewarning for the inhabitantes, or the like, depending vppon a supernaturall Efficient Cause, and tending to a supernaturall Morall End.

Which End, (for that I knowe is the very poynt, whereon you stande) albeit it be acknowledged Supernaturall and purposed, as I sayd, of a supernaturall Cause, to whom nothing at all is impossible, and that can worke supernaturally, and myraculously without ordinarie meanes, and inferiour causes: yet neuerthelesse is, we see, commonly performed, by the qualifying, and conforming of Nature, and Naturall things, to the accomplishment of his Diuine and incomprehensible determination. For being, as the olde Philosophers call him, very Nature selfe, or as it hath pleased our later schoolemen to terme him, by way of distinction, *Natura Naturans,* he hath all these secondarie inferiour thinges, the foure Elementes, all sensible, and vnsensible, reasonable, and vnreasonable Creatures, the whole worlde, and what soeuer is contayned in the Compas of the worlde, being the workmanship of his owne hands, and, as they call them, *Natura naturata,* euer pliable and flexible Instrumentes at his Commaundement: to put in execution such Effectes, either ordinarie or extraordinarie, as shall seeme most requisite to his eternall Prouidence: and now in these latter dayes, very seldome, or in manner neuer worketh any thing so myraculously, and extraordinarily, but it may sensibly appeare, he vseth the

210 *Exspirare*] Expirare G2   244 thinges,] thinges Q²,⁴

APPENDIX I 455

seruice and Ministerie of his Creatures, in the atcheeuing thereof. I denie not, but Earthquakes (as well as many other fearefull Accidentes in the same Number,) are terrible signes, and, as it were certaine manacing forerunners, and forewarners of the great latter day; and therefore out of controuersie the more reuerendly to be considered vppon: and I acknowledge considering the Euentes, and sequeles, according to the collection and discourse of mans Reason, they haue seemed to Prognosticate, and threaten to this, and that Citie, vtter ruyne and destruction: to such a Country, a generall plague and pestilence: to an other place, the death of some mightie Potentate or great Prince: to some other Realme or Kingdome, some cruell imminent warres: and sundry the like dreadfull and particular Incidentes, as is notoriously euident by many olde and newe, very famous and notable Histories to that effect. Which of all other the auncient Romaines, long before the Natiuitie of Christ, did most religiously or rather superstitiously obserue, not without a number of solemne Ceremonies, and Hollydayes for the nonce, euer after any Earthquake, making full account of some such great rufull casualtie or other, as otherwhyles fell out in very deede: and namely, as I remember, the yeare *Ante bellum Sociale*, which was one of the lamentablest, and myserablest warres, that *Italy* euer sawe: and *Plinie*, or I knowe not well who, hath such a saying: *Roma nunquam tremuit, vt non futurus aliquis portenderetur insignis Euentus.*

But yet, notwithstanding, dare not I aforehand presume thus farre, or arrogate so much vnto my selfe, as to determine precisely and peremptorily of this, or euery the like singular Earthquake, to be necessarily, and vndoubtedly a supernaturall, and immediate fatall Action of God, for this, or that singular intent, when as I am sure, there may be a sufficient Naturall, eyther necessarie or contingent Cause in the very Earth it selfe: and there is no question, but the selfe same Operation in *Genere*, or in *specie*, may at one tyme, proceeding of one Cause, and referred to one End, be preternaturall, or supernaturall: at another tyme, proceeding of an other, or the same Cause, and referred to an other End, but Ordinarie, and Naturall. To make shorte, I cannot see, and would gladly learne, howe a man on Earth, should be of so great authoritie, and so familiar acquaintance with God in Heauen, (vnlesse haply for the nonce he hath lately intertained some few choice singular ones of his priuie Counsell) as to be able in such specialties, without any iustifyable certificate, or warrant) to reueale hys incomprehensible mysteries, and definitiuely to giue sentence of his Maiesties secret and inscrutable purposes. As if they had a key for all the lockes in Heauen, or as if it were as cleare and resolute a case, as the Eclipse of the Sunne, that darkened all the Earth, or at the least all the Earth in those Countries, at Christes Passion, happening altogether prodigiously and Metaphysically in *Plenilunio*, not according to the perpetuall course of Nature, in *Nouilunio:* in so much that *Dionisius Areopagita*, or some other graunde Philosopher, vpon the suddayne contemplation thereof, is reported in a certaine Patheticall Ecstasie to haue cryed out, *Aut rerum Natura patitur, aut Mundi machina destruetur:* as my minde giueth me, some of the simpler, and vnskilfuller sort, will goe nye to doe vpon the present sight, and agony of this Earthquake. Marry the Errour I graunt, is the more tollerable, though perhappes it be otherwhiles, (and why not euen nowe,) a very presumptuous Errour in deede, standing

284 warrant)] warrant *SmSe*

only vpon these two weake and deceitfull groundes, Credulitie and Ignoraunce: if so be inwardly (not onely in Externall shewe, after an Hypocriticall, and Pharisaicall manner) it certainly doo vs good for our reformation, and amendment, and seeme to preache vnto vs, *Paenitentiam agite*, (as in some respect euery suche straunge and rare Accident may seeme:) how Ordinarie, and Naturall so euer the Cause shall appeare otherwise to the best learned: especially, as the Earthquake shall be knowne to endure a longer, or a shorter Tyme, or to be more or lesse generall, in more, or fewer places. Which two differences, touching the quantitie of Tyme, and Place, after I had a little more fully prosecuted, alledging certaine particuler Examples thereof, howe in some places huge Castels, in some Townes, in some great and mightie Cities, in some Shires and Seigniories, and Prouinces, in some whole Countryes, and Regions haue been perillously mooued and shaken therewith: in one place, a long time together: in an other place, not so long, or at seuerall and parted times: in another, very short, as, God be thanked here euen nowe: and finally by the way, shewing a thirde and most notable difference of all, (as well for the present or imminent terrour and daunger, as otherwise) by the sundry *species*, and formes which *Aristotle*, *Plinie*, and other Meteorologicians haue set downe of Experience, as they haue heard, or read, or seen the earth to quake, to sturre, and hoyse vp Houses, Walles, Towers, Castelles, Churches, Minsters, whole Townes, whole Cities, whole Prouinces, without farther harme: to ruinate and ouerthrowe, and destroy some: to yawne and gape, and open lyke a graue, and consequently to swallow vp and deuour other: and sometime also to drinke vp whole riuers, and mightie bigge running waters withall, or to chaunge and alter their common woonted course some other way: to sinke and fall downewardes: to cast out and vomitte vp either huge vaste heapes, as it were Mountaines of Earth, or large Ilandes in the mayne Sea, neuer remembred, or seen before: or great ouerflowing waters, and fountaynes: or hotte scalding sulphurous lakes: or burning sparkles and flames of fire: to make a horrible hissing, gnashing, ratling, or some like woonderfull straunge noyse, (which all Effectes are credibly reported, and constantly auouched, of our most famous and best allowed Philosophers) a fewe such particularities, and distinctions, compendiously and familiarly coursed ouer. The good Gentleman gaue me hartily, as appeared, very great thankes, and tolde me plainly, he neuer either read, or heard halfe so much of Earthquakes before: confessing withall, that he yeelded resolutely to my opinion: that an Earthquake might as well be supposed a Naturall Motion of the Earth, as a preternaturall, or supernaturall ominous worke of God: and that he thought it hard, and almost impossible, for any man, either by Philosophie, or Diuinitie, euermore to determine flatly the very certaintie either way. Which also in conclusion was the verdit, and finall resolution of the greater and sager part of the Gentlemen present: and namely of an aunciont learned common Lawyer, that had been Graduate, and fellow of a Colledge in Cambridge, in Queene *Maries* dayes. Who tooke vpon him, to knit vp the matter, and as he said, determine the controuersie, with the authoritie of all the naturall Philosophers, old or newe, Heathen or Christian, Catholique or Protestant, that euer he read, or heard tell of. There Physickes quoth he, are in euery mans hands: they are olde enough to speake for them selues, and wee are

300 *Paenitentiam*] *Poenitentia* G2

young enough to turne our Bookes. They that haue Eyes and Tongues, let them see, and reade. But what say you nowe, quoth I, to the staying and quieting of the Earthe, beeing once a moouing? May it not seeme a more myraculous woorke, and greater woonderment, that it shoulde so suddainely staye againe, being mooued, than that it shoulde so suddainely mooue, beyng quiet and still? Mooue or turne, or shake me a thing in lyke order, be it neuer so small, and lesse than a pynnes Head, in comparison of the great mightie circuite of the Earth, and see if you shall not haue much more a doo to staye it presently, beeing once sturred, than to sturre it at the very first. Whereat the Gentleman smyling, and looking merrily on the Gentlewoomen, heere is a schoole poynt, quoth he, that by your leaues, I beleeue will poase the better scholler of you both. But is it not more than tyme, thynke ye, wee were at Supper? And if you be a hungered, Maister *H.* you shall thanke no body but your selfe, that haue holden vs so long with your profounde and clerkly discourses, whereas our manner is to suppe at the least a long howre before this tyme. Beyng set, and newe occasion of speeche ministered, our Supper put the Earthquake in manner out of our myndes, or at the leastwise, out of our Tongues: sauing that the Gentlewoomen, nowe and then pleasauntly tyhyhing betweene them selues, especially Mystresse *Inquisitiua*, (whose minde did still runne of the drinking, and Neesing of the Earth,) repeated here, and there, a broken peece of that, which had been already sayde before Supper. With deepe iudgement no doubt, and to maruellous great purpose, I warrant you after the manner of woomen Philosophers, and Diuines.

And this summarily in Effect was our yesternyghtes graue Meteorologicall Conference, touching our Earthquake here in the Country: which being in so many neighbour Townes, and Villages about vs, as I heare say of this morning, maketh me presuppose, the like was wyth you also at London, and elsewhere farther of. And then forsoothe, must I desire Maister *Immerito*, to send me within a weeke or two, some odde fresh paulting threehalfepennie Pamphlet for newes: or some Balductum Tragicall Ballet in Ryme, and without Reason, setting out the right myserable, and most wofull estate of the wicked, and damnable worlde at these perillous dayes, after the deuisers best manner: or whatsoeuer else shall first take some of your braue London Eldertons in the Head. In earnest, I could wishe some learned, and well aduized Vniuersitie man, woulde vndertake the matter, and bestow some paynes in deede vppon so famous and materiall an argument. The generall Nature of Earthquakes by definition, and the speciall diuersitie of them by diuision, beyng perfectly knowen: (a thing soone done) and a complete Induction of many credible and autenticall, both olde and newe, diuine and prophane, Greeke, Lattine, and other Examples, (with discretion, and iudgement, compyled and compared togither) being considerately and exactly made, (a thing not so easily done) much no doubt myght be alledged too or fro, to terrifie or pacifie vs, more or lesse. If it appeare by generall Experience, and the foresayde Historicall Induction of particulars, that Earthquakes, *sine omni exceptione*, are ominous, and significatiue Effectes, as they saye of Comets, and carrie euer some Tragicall and horrible matter with or after them: as eyther destruction of Townes and Cities, or decay of some mightie Prince, or some particular, or generall plague, warre, or the lyke, *(vt supra)* whatsoeuer the Materiall, or Formall cause be, Natural, or supernaturall, (howbeit for myne owne part I am resolued, as wel for the one, as for the other, that these two

I speake of, both Matter and Fourme, are rather Naturall in both, than otherwise) it concerneth vs, vpon the vewe of so Effectuall and substaunciall euidence, to conceiue seriously, and reuerently of the other two Causes: the first, supreme Efficient, whose Omnipotent Maiestie hath nature self, and all naturall Creatures at commaundement: and the last finall, which we are to iudge of as aduisedly, and prouidently, as possibly we can, by the consideration, and comparison of Circumstances, the tyme when: the place where? the qualities, and dispositions of the persons, amongst whom such, and such an Ominous token is giuen. Least happily through ouer great credulitie, and rashnesse, we mistake *Non causam pro causa*, and sophistically be entrapped *Elencho Finium*. Truely, I suppose, he had neede be an excellent Philosopher, a reasonable good Historian, a learned Diuine, a wise discrete man, and generally, such a one as our Doctor *Still*, and Doctor *Byng* are in Cambridge, that shoulde shew himselfe accordingly in this argument, and to the iudgement and contentation of the wisest, perfourme it exactly. My selfe remember nothing to the contrarie, either in Philosophie, or in Histories, or in Diuinitie either, why I may not safely and lawfully subscribe to the iudgement of the noble *Italian* Philosopher, and most famous learned Gentleman, whilest he liued, Lord of *Mirandola*, and Erle of *Concordia*, Counte *Ioannes Franciscus Picus*, in my opinion, very considerately, and partly Philosophically, partly Theologically set downe, in the sixt Chapter of his sixt Booke, against Cogging deceitfull Astrologers, and Southsayers, *De rerum Praenotione, pro veritate Religionis, contra Superstitiosas vanitates*. In which Chapter, (if happely you haue not read it already,) you shall finde many, but specially these three notable places, most effectuall and directly pertinent to the very purpose. The first more vniuersall. *Naturae opere fieri non potest, vt Ostentis, vt Monstris magni illi, seu dextri, seu sinistri euentus portendantur, et ab aliqua pendeant proxima causa, quae et futura etiam proferat. Impostura Daemonum, vt id fiat, videri potest. Sed et plaeraque non monstrosa, non prodigiosa per sese, pro monstris tamen, et portentis, haberi possunt, et solent à quibusdam, quibus Rerum Natura non satis comperta est, causarum enim ignoratio, noua in re Admirationem parit. Propter quam, philosophari homines caepisse, in exordijs primae philosophiae scribit Aristoteles.* Wherein those two seuerall points, *Impostura Daemonum*, and *Ignoratio causarum*, are no doubt maruellous probable, and moste worthy bothe presentlye to bee noted nowe, and more fully to be discussed hereafter: appearing vnto me the verie right principall Causes of so manye erroneous opinions, and fantasticall superstitious dreames in this, and the like behalfe.

The seconde more speciall, as it were hitting the white in deede, and cleauing the Pinne in sunder.

Idem in Terraemotibus etiam, quod in fulguribus, fulminibusque interpretandis, obseruauit Antiquitas. Cuius Rei liber, Graeco eloquio, nuper ad manus peruenit, in Orpheum relatus Autorem: sed perabsurdum nimis, vt quod frequentissimè fit, pro vario terrae anhelitu, pro ventorum violentia, vaporumque conductione, (marke

---

398 Truely] *FHu resume at this point*   400 discrete...generally] Man *FHu*   400 our] *om. FHu*   400 and Doctor] *or Dr. FHu*   400-1 are in Cambridge] *om. FHu*   401 accordingly] *om. FHu*   401-50 and....preferring] *I find nothing to the contrary, but that I may subscribe to the judgment of Picus Mirandula, in the Sixth Chapter of his Book against Astrologers, and prefer FHu*   409 Religionis] Relligionis *QG2Se*   413 illi] isti *G2*

you that?) *ex eo rerum futurarum significationem petere, quorum nec effectus esse possunt, nec causa, praeterquam forte mortis inferendae illis, qui fulmen exceperit, aut qui terrarum hiatu perierit. Sed nec ab eadem proxima deduci causa possunt, à qua et futurae pendeant res, vt supra deductum est.*

And then shortly after, the thirde, moste agreeable to the seconde, as flatlye 435 determining on my side, and as directlye concluding the same position as may be.

Nec sanè Orpheus ille, si tamen Orpheus fuit, vllam affert omninò causam, cur quispiam ex terrae motibus, vrbium, hominum, regionum euenta praesagire possit. Solùm vano narrat arbitrio: si terrae contigerit motus, noctu, si aestate, si hyeme, si aurora, si interdiu, quid portendatur: Quae certè, et saniore possunt arbitrio 440 *refelli, et Experientiae testimonio, vt arbitror, non secus irrideri, ac supra Tagis portenta irrisimus, Haruspicinae Autoris.*

A moste excellent sounde Iudgement in my conceit: and ful wel beseeming so Honorable and admirable a Witte, as out of Question, *Picus Mirandula* had: who being yet scarcely thirty yeres of age, for his singularitie in al kind of knowleege, 445 as wel diuine as prophane, was in Italy and France, as *Paulus Iouius* reporteth, surnamed *Phoenix,* as the odde, and in effecte the onely singular learned man of Europe: and to make shorte: suche a one, in moste respectes, as I woulde wishe nowe to be tempering with this newe notorious incident: staying my selfe in the meane while vpon this probable and reasonable *Interim* of his: and preferring it 450 before al the friuolous coniecturall Allegations, and surmises, that oure counterfaite, and reasonlesse *Orphei* oppose to the contrarye. But, Iesu, what is all this to Master *Immerito?* Forsoothe I knowe not by what mischaunce, these miserable balde odious three halfepenny fellowes, alas, a company of silly beetleheaded Asses, came into my minde, that wil needes be sturring, and taking on in euerye suche rare and 455 vnaccustomed euent, as if they sawe farther in a Milstone, than all the worlde besides, whereas euerie man, that hathe but halfe an eye in his head, seeth them to be more blinde, than anye Buzzarde, or Bayarde, *Scribimus indocti, doctique Poemata passim,* and surely, as the worlde goeth nowe in Englande, rather the firste, for aught I see, than the laste. *O interim miseras Musas, et miserabiles:* Where the 460 faulte shoulde rest, *viderint Oculi, atque capita Reip. Mihi quidem isthic, neque seritur admodùm, neque metitur. Non valdè mea nouos Bibliotheca libros desiderat, seipsa, id est, quos habet, veteribus contenta est. Quid plura? Tu vale, mi Immerito, atque ita tibi persuade, Aliquid esse eum, qui istorum longè est dissimillimus, quos Typographi nostri habent venales maximè.* Commende mee to thine owne good 465 selfe, and tell thy dying Pellicane, and thy Dreames from me, I wil nowe leaue dreaming any longer of them, til with these eyes I see them forth indeede: And then againe, I imagine your *Magnificenza,* will holde vs in suspense as long for your nine Englishe *Commoedies,* and your Latine *Stemmata Dudleiana:* whiche two shal go for my money, when all is done: especiallye if you woulde but bestow one 470

439 noctu] *Se nocti QG2*   450 it] *FHu resume at this point*   451 al] *at Se*   452 and reasonlesse] *om. FHu*   453 mischaunce] *chance FHu*   453 miserable balde odious] *om. FHu*   454 alas ... Asses] *om. FHu*   455-65 that .... maximè.] *om. FHu*   462 Bibliotheca] *Bibliothecae Se*   464 dissimillimus] *Se dissimilimus QG2*   465 Commende] *FHu resume at this point*   466-7 nowe ... longer] *no longer think FHu*   468 then ... imagine] *I fear FHu*   469 Latine] *om. FHu*   470 when ... done] *om. FHu*   470 but] *om. FHu*

seuennights pollishing and trimming vppon eyther. Whiche I praye thee hartily
doe, for my pleasure, if not for their sake, nor thine owne profite. My *Schollers
Loue,* or *Reconcilement of contraries,* is shrunke in the wetting: I hadde purposed
to haue dispatched you a Coppie thereof, long ere this: but, no remedie, hitherto
it hath alwayes gone thus with me: Some newe occasion, or other, euer carrieth me 475
from one matter to another, and will neuer suffer me to finishe eyther one or other.
And truly, *Experto crede,* it is as true a Verse as euer was made, since the first Verse,
that euer was made: *Pluribus intentus minor est ad singula sensus:* whiche my *Anti-
cosmopolita,* thoughe it greeue him, can beste testifye, remayning still as we saye,
in statu, quo, and neither an inche more forward, nor backewarde, than he was fully 480
a tweluemonth since in the Courte, at his laste attendaunce vpon my Lorde there. But
the Birde that will not sing in Aprill, nor in May, maye peraduenture sing in Sep-
tember: and yet me thinkes, *Sat citò, si sat bene,* if I coulde steale but one poore fort-
night, to peruse him ouer afreshe, and coppy him out anewe. Whiche I hope in God
to compasse shortly. But I beseech you, what Newes al this while at Cambridge? 485
That was wont to be euer one great Question. What? *Det mihi Mater ipsa bonam
veniam, eius vt aliqua mihi liceat Secreta, vni cuidam de eodem gremio obsequen-
tissimo filio, reuelare: et sic paucis habeto. Nam aliàs fortasse pluribus: nunc non
placet, non vacat, molestum esset. Tully,* and *Demosthenes* nothing so much
studyed, as they were wonte: *Liuie,* and *Salust* possiblye rather more, than lesse: 490
Lucian neuer so much: *Aristotle* muche named, but little read: *Xenophon* and
Plato, reckned amongest Discoursers, and conceited Superficiall fellowes: much
verball and sophisticall iangling: little subtile and effectuall disputing: noble and
royall Eloquence, the best and persuasiblest Eloquence: no such Orators againe, as
redheaded Angelles: An exceeding greate difference, betweene the countenaunces, 495
and portes of those, that are braue and gallaunt, and of those, that are basely, or
meanly apparelled: betwene the learned, and vnlearned, *Tully,* and *Tom Tooly,*
in effect none at all.

Matchiauell a great man: *Castilio* of no small reputation: *Petrarch,* and
Boccace in euery mans mouth: *Galateo,* and *Guazzo* neuer so happy: ouer many 500
acquainted with *Vnico Aretino:* The *French* and *Italian* when so highlye regarded
of Schollers? The *Latine* and *Greeke,* when so lightly? The *Queene mother* at the
beginning, or ende of euerye conference: many bargaines of *Mounsieur: Shymeirs*
a noble gallant fellowe: all inquisitiue after Newes, newe Bookes, newe Fashions,
newe Lawes, newe Officers, and some after newe Elementes, and some after newe 505
Heauens, and Helles to. *Turkishe affaires* familiarly knowen: Castels builded in the
Ayre: muche adoe, and little helpe: *Iacke* would faine be a Gentlemanne: in no
age so little so muche made of, euery one highly in his owne fauour, thinking no

---

471 and trimming vppon] *of FHu*   472 their] *thine own FHu*   472 nor] *and FHu*
472-85 My .... But] *om. FHu*   485 I] *FHu resume at this point*   485 what ...
while] *all this while, what news FHu*   486-9 That .... esset.] *om. FHu*   490 possiblye
rather more] *perhaps more, rather FHu*   493-8 noble ... all.] *om. FHu*   499 reputa-
tion] *repute FHu*   499 Petrarch] *FHuG2* Petrach *QSe*   500 ouer many] *but some FHu*
501-2 when ... Schollers?] *highly regarded; FHu*   502 when so lightly?] *but lightly. FHu*
503-4 many ... fellowe:] *om. FHu*   505 Elementes, and] *Elements, FHu*   506 builded]
buried *G2*   507 Iacke ... Gentlemanne:] *om. FHu*   508-9 thinking ... own:] *om. FHu*

mans penny, so good siluer as his own: Something made of Nothing, in spite of
Nature: Numbers made of Ciphars, in spite of Arte: Geometricall Proportion sel- 510
dome, or neuer vsed, Arithmeticall ouermuch abused: Oxen and Asses (notwith-
standing the absurditie it seemed to *Plautus*) draw both togither in one, and the same
Yoke: *Conclusio ferè sequitur deteriorem partem.* The *Gospell* taughte, not learned:
Charitie key colde: nothing good, but by Imputation: the *Ceremoniall* Lawe, in
worde abrogated: the *Iudiciall* in effecte disanulled: the *Morall* indeede abandoned: 515
the *Lighte,* the *Lighte* in euery mans Lippes, but marke me their eyes, and tell me,
if they looke not liker Howlets, or Battes, than Egles: as of olde Bookes, so of
auntient Vertue, Honestie, Fidelitie, Equitie, newe Abridgementes: euery day freshe
span newe Opinions: Heresie in Diuinitie, in Philosophie, in Humanitie, in Manners,
grounded muche vpon heresay: *Doctors* contemned: the *Text* knowen of moste, 520
vnderstood of fewe, magnified of all, practised of none: the *Diuell* not so hated,
as the *Pope:* many Inuectiues, small amendment: Skill they say controlled of Will:
and Goodnesse mastered of Goods: but Agent, and Patient muche alike, neither
Barrell greatly better Herring: No more adoe aboute *Cappes* and *Surplesses:*
Maister *Cartwright* nighe forgotten: The man you wot of, conformable, with his 525
square Cappe on his rounde heade: and *Non resident* at pleasure: and yet *Non-
residents* neuer better bayted, but not one the fewer, either I beleeue in Acte, or I
beleeue, in Purpose. A number of our preachers sibbe to *French Souldiors,* at the
first, more than Men, in the end, lesse than Women. Some of our pregnantest and
soonest ripe Wits, of *Hermogenes* mettall for al the world: Olde men and Coun- 530
sailours amongst Children: Children amongst Counsailours, and olde men: Not a
fewe dubble faced *Iani,* and chaungeable *Camelions*: ouer-manye Clawbackes, and
Pickethanks: Reedes shaken of euerie Wind: Iackes of bothe sides: Aspen
leaues: painted Sheathes, and Sepulchres: Asses in Lions skins: Dunglecockes:
slipperye Eles: Dormise: I blush to thinke of some, that weene themselues as 535
fledge as the reste, being, God wot, as kallowe as the rest: euery yonker to speake
of as politique, and as great a Commonwealths man as Bishoppe *Gardner,* or
Doctor *Wutton* at the least: as if euerie man nowe adayes hauing the framing of
his own *Horoscope,* were borne in *decimo coeli domicilio,* and had al the Wit,
Wisedome, and Worshippe in the world at commaundement. *Sed heus in aurem:* 540
*Meministin' quod ait Varro? Omnes videmur nobis esse belli, festīui, saperdae, cùm
sumus Canopi: Dauid, Vlisses,* and *Solon,* fayned themselues fooles and madmen:
our fooles and madmen faine themselues *Dauids, Vlisses,* and *Solons:* and would
goe nigh to deceiue the cunningest, and best experienced *Metaposcopus* in a country:

510-1 Geometricall ... abused:] *om. FHu*   511-2 notwithstanding] *FHuG2Se* not-
withstandiug *Q*   512 draw ... and] *drawing in FHu*   513 *Conclusio ... partem.*]
om. FHu   514 key] *om. FHu*   515 indeede] *om. FHu*   516 marke me] *mark FHu*
516-7 tell ... Battes] *you will say they are rather like Owls FHu*   518-9 freshe span]
spawns FHu   520 muche] *om. FHu*   520-1 the ... none:] *om. FHu*   522 small]
but no *FHu*   522-4 Skill ... Herring:] *om. FHu*   525 nighe] *quite FHu*   525 con-
formable] comfortable *Hu*   525 his] *a FHu*   526-8 and *Non* ... Purpose.] *om. FHu*
529-30 and soonest ripe] *om. FHu*   530 for ... world] *om. FHu*   531-6 Not ... rest:]
om. FHu   532 faced *Iani*] sacred Tani *G2*   536-7 to speake of] *speaks FHu*   537 and
... man] *om. FHu*   538 at the least] *om. FHu*   540 in ... commaundement] *at Com-
mand FHu*   540 heus] heus tu *FHu*   541 Meministin'] Meministi *G2*   541 videmur]
videmus *FHu*   543-4 and would ... country:] *om. FHu*

It is pity faire weather should euer do hurt, but I know what peace and quietnes 545
hath done with some melancholy pickstrawes in the world: as good vnspoken as
vnamended. And wil you needes haue my Testimoniall of youre olde Controllers
new behauior? A busy and dizy heade, a brazen forehead: a ledden braine: a
woodden wit: a copper face: a stony breast: a factious and eluish hearte: a founder
of nouelties: a confounder of his owne, and his friends good gifts: a morning 550
bookeworm, an afternoone maltworm: a right Iuggler, as ful of his sleights, wyles,
fetches, casts of Legerdemaine, toyes to mocke Apes withal, odde shiftes, and
knauish practizes, as his skin can holde. He often telleth me, he looueth me as
himselfe, but out lyar out, thou lyest abhominably in thy throate. Iesu, I had nigh
hand forgotten one thing, that ywis somtime I think often ynough vpon: Many 555
Pupils, Iackemates, and Hayle fellowes wel met, with their *Tutors,* and by your
leaue, some too, because forsooth they be Gentlemen, or great heires, or a little
neater and gayer than their fellowes, (shall I say it for shame? beleeue me, tis too
true) their very own Tutors. *Ah mala* Licentia, *ab initio non fuit sic. Stulta est
omnis iuuenilis* Doctrina, *sine virili quadam* Disciplina. *Quasi verò pauperioribus* 560
*duntaxat pueris, ac non multò magis generosae, atque nobili Iuuentuti conueniat,
pristinae illius Institutionis, atque Educationis seueritas, et ingenuae, et prudentis,
et eruditae, et cum Tutoris personae, tum pupillo, etiam ipsi perquam accommodatae.
Vsque-quaque* sapere oportet: *id erit telum acerrimum. Caetera faerè, vt olim:
Bellum inter Capita, et membra continuatum:* δοκοσοφία *publicis defensa scholis,* 565
priuatis confirmata parietibus, omnibus locis ostentata, Scire tuum *nihil est, nisi te
scire, hoc sciat alter.* Plurimi passim fit Pecunia, Pudor *parui penditur: Nihili
habentur* Literae: *Mihi crede,* credendum nulli: *O amice,* amicus nemo. *Quid tu
interim? Quomodo te inquies, geris? Quomodo? Optimum est aliena frui insania.*
Video: *taceo,* rideo: *Dixi. Et tamen addam, quod ait Satyricus ille:* 570

    Viuendum est rectè, tum propter plurima, tum his
    Praecipuè causis, vt linguas Mancipiorum   Contemnas.

E meo municipio, Postridiè quàm superiores de Terraemotu *sermones haberentur,
id est, ni fallor, Aprilis septimo, Vesperi.* With as manye gentle Goodnightes, as be
letters in this tedious Letter. 575

    Nosti manum tanquam tuam.

POSTSCRIPTE.

    This Letter may only be shewed to the two odde Gentlemen you wot of. Marry
I would haue those two to see it, as sone as you may conueniently.

Non multis dormio: non multis scribo: non cupio placere multis: 580
*Alij alios numeros laudant, praeferunt, venerantur: Ego ferè apud nos, ferè apud
vos* Trinitatem.
Verbum sapienti sat: nosti caetera: et tres Charites habes ad vnguem.

  545 euer do] *do any FHu*   546-7 in . . . vnamended] *om. FHu*   550 of his] os his *G2*
551 his] *om. FHu*   552 withal] *with FHu*   553-70 He . . . . *ille:*] *But FHu*   563 *accom-
modatae*] *accomodatae QG2Se*   564 *Vsque-quaque*] *Vsque quaeque G2*   571 *Viuendum*]
FHu resume at this point   573-83 E . . . . *vnguem.*] *om. FHu*   583 *Charites*] *Charities G2*

[LETTER V]

A Gallant familiar Letter, containing
an Answere to that of M. Immerito, with
sundry proper examples, and some Precepts
of our Englishe reformed Versifying.

To my very friend *M. Immerito*.   5

Ignor *Immerito*, to passe ouer youre needelesse complaint, wyth the residue of your preamble (for of the *Earthquake* I presuppose you haue ere this receyued my goodly discourse) and withall to let my late Englishe Hexametres goe as lightlye as they came: I cannot choose, but thanke and honour the good   10
Aungell, (whether it were *Gabriell* or some other) that put so good a motion into the heads of those two excellent Gentlemen *M. Sidney*, and *M. Dyer*, the two very Diamondes of hir Maiesties Courte for many speciall and rare qualities: as to helpe forwarde our new famous enterprise for the Exchanging of Barbarous and Balductum Rymes with Artificial Verses: the one 15
being in manner of pure and fine Goulde, the other but counterfet, and base ylfauoured Copper. I doubt not but their liuelie example, and Practise, wil preuaile a thousand times more in short space, than the dead Aduertizement, and persuasion of *M. Ascham* to the same Effecte: whose *Scholemaister* notwithstanding I reuerence in respect of so learned a Motiue. I would gladly be acquainted with *M. Drants* 20
Prosodye, and I beseeche you, commende me to good *M. Sidneys* iudgement, and gentle *M. Immeritos* Obseruations. I hope your nexte Letters, which I daily exspect, wil bring me in farther familiaritie and acquaintance with al three. Mine owne Rules and Precepts of Arte, I beleeue wil fal out not greatly repugnant, though peraduenture somewhat different: and yet am I not so resolute, but I can be content 25
to reserue the Coppying out and publishing therof, vntil I haue a little better consulted with my pillowe, and taken some farther aduize of *Madame Sperienza*. In the meane, take this for a general Caueat, and say I haue reuealed one great mysterie

1-299 A . . . . *arise?*] *om. MG1*   1-275 A . . . . therein.] *om.* D   1-4 A . . . Versifying.] Another Letter of Mr. *Harvey's*. *FHu*   6 complaint] complaints *FHu*   7 for of] for *FHu*   7 of the] of your *Sm*   7-8 presuppose] suppose *FHu*   11 (whether . . . other)] *om. FHu*   13-4 for . . . qualities] *om. FHu*   14 famous] *om. FHu*   15 Exchanging . . . with] *changing of bald Rhythms* for *FHu*   15-266 the . . . . mee.] *om. FHu*

vnto you: I am of Opinion, there is no one more regular and iustifiable direction, eyther for the assured, and infallible Certaintie of our English Artificiall Prosodye particularly, or generally to bring our Language into Arte, and to frame a Grammer or Rhetorike thereof: than first of all vniuersally to agree vpon *one and the same Ortographie*, in all pointes conformable and proportionate to *our Common Natural Prosodye*: whether *Sir Thomas Smithes* in that respect be the most perfit, as surely it must needes be very good: or else some other of profounder Learning, and longer Experience, than *Sir Thomas* was, shewing by necessarie demonstration, wherin he is defectiue, wil vndertake shortely to supplie his wantes, and make him more absolute. My selfe dare not hope to hoppe after him, til I see something or other, too, or fro, publickely and autentically established, as it were by a generall Counsel, or acte of Parliament: and then peraduenture, standing vppon firmer grounde, for Companie sake, I may aduenture to do as other do. *Interim*, credit me, I dare geue no Preceptes, nor set downe any *Certaine General Arte:* and yet see my boldenesse, I am not greatly squaimishe of my *Particular Examples*, whereas he that can but reasonably skil of the one, wil giue easily a shreude gesse at the other: considering that the one fetcheth his original and offspring from the other. In which respecte, to say troth, *we Beginners* haue the start, and aduauntage of our Followers, who are to frame and conforme both their Examples, and Precepts, according to that President which they haue of vs: as no doubt *Homer* or some other in *Greeke*, and *Ennius*, or I know not who else in *Latine*, did preiudice, and ouerrule those, that followed them, as well for the quantities of syllables, as number of feete, and the like: their onely Examples going for current payment, and standing in steade of Lawes, and Rules with the posteritie. In so much that it seemed a sufficient warrant (as still it doth in our Common Grammer schooles) to make τῑ in τιμή, and ῠ, in *Vnus* long, because the one hath τίμη δ' ἐκ διός ἐστί, and the other, *Vnus homo nobis*, and so consequently in the rest. But to let this by-disputation passe, which is already so throughly discoursed and canuassed of the best Philosophers, and namely *Aristotle*, that poynt vs, as it were with the forefinger, to the *very fountaines and head springes* of Artes, and Artificiall preceptes, in the *Analitiques*, and *Metaphysikes*: most excellently set downe in these *foure Golden Termes*, the famoussest Termes to speake of in all *Logique* and *Philosophie*, ἐμπειρία, ἱστορία, αἴσθησις ἐπαγωγή: shall I nowe by the way sende you a *Ianuarie gift* in *Aprill:* and as it were shewe you a *Christmas Gambowlde* after *Easter?* Were the manner so very fine, as the matter is very good, I durst presume of an other kinde of *Plaudite* and *Gramercie*, than now I will: but being as it is, I beseeche you, set parcialitie aside, and tell me your maisterships fancie.

---

34 Smithes] Smithies G2   50 followed] followeth Sm   53 ῠ] ū G2   54 δ' ἐκ] δ' ἐη H   54 διός] Sm   διος QHG2   Διός Se   54 ἐστί] Sm   ἐστὶ QH   ἐστὶ G2   ἐστι Se
58 Analitiques] Analilitiques G2   60 ἱστορία] SmSe   ισορια QH   ιστορια G2   60 αἴσθησις] αἰθησις H   αἰσθησις Se   61 ἐπαγωγή] Sm   ἐπαγωγὴ QG2   ἐπαγωγὴ H   ἐπσγωγή Se

APPENDIX I

A New yeeres Gift to my old friend Maister

George Bilchaunger: In commendation of three most precious Accidentes, *Vertue, Fame,* and *Wealth:* and finally of the fourth, *A good Tongue.*

VErtue *sendeth a man to* Renowne, Fame *lendeth* Aboundaunce,   70
Fame with Aboundaunce maketh a man thrise blessed and happie.
So the Rewarde of Famous Vertue makes many wealthy,
And the Regard of Wealthie Vertue makes many blessed:
O blessed Vertue, blessed Fame, blessed Aboundaunce,
O that I had you three, with the losse of thirtie Comencementes.   75
Nowe farewell Mistresse, *whom lately I loued aboue all,*
These be my three bonny lasses, these be my three bonny Ladyes,
Not the like Trinitie *againe, saue onely the Trinitie aboue all:*
Worship and Honour, first to the one, and then to the other.
A thousand good leaues be for euer graunted Agrippa.   80
For squibbing and declayming against many fruitlesse
Artes, *and* Craftes, *deuisde by the* Diuls and Sprites, *for a torment,*
And for a plague to the world: as both Pandora, Prometheus,
And that cursed good bad Tree, *can testifie at all times.*
Meere Gewegawes and Bables, in comparison of these.   85
Toyes to mock Apes, and Woodcockes, in comparison of these.
Iugling castes, and knicknackes, in comparison of these.
Yet behinde there is one thing, worth a prayer at all tymes,
A good Tongue, *in a mans Head,* A good Tongue *in a woomans.*
And what so precious matter, and foode for a good Tongue,   90
As blessed Vertue, blessed Fame, blessed Aboundaunce.

L'Enuoy.

Maruell not, what I meane to send these Verses at Euensong:
On Neweyeeres Euen, and Oldyeeres End, as a Memento:
Trust me, I know not a ritcher Iewell, newish or oldish,   95
Than blessed Vertue, blessed Fame, blessed Abundaunce,
O blessed Vertue, blessed Fame, blessed Aboundaunce,
O that you had these three, with the losse of Fortie Valetes,

           He that wisheth, you may liue to see a hundreth
           Good Newe yeares, euery one happier, and   100
           merrier, than other.

Now to requite your *Blindfolded pretie God,* (wherin by the way I woulde gladly learne, why, $Th\bar{e}$, in the first, $Y\bar{e}$ in the first, and thirde, $H\bar{e}$, and My, in the last, being shorte, $M\bar{e}$, alone should be made longer in the very same) Imagin

---

80 *thousand*] HG2SmSe   *thousaud* Q   93 *what*] *that* Sm

me to come into a goodly Kentishe *Garden* of your old Lords, or some other Noble 105
man, and spying a florishing Bay Tree there, to demaunde *ex tempore*, as followeth:
Thinke vppon *Petrarches*

Arbor vittoriosa, triomfale,
Onor d'Imperadori, e di Poete:

and perhappes it will aduaunce the wynges of your Imagination a degree higher: 110
at the least if any thing can be added to the loftinesse of his conceite, whom gentle
Mistresse Rosalinde, once reported to haue all the *Intelligences* at commaundement,
and an other time, Christened her,

Segnior Pegaso.

Encomium Lauri. 115

WHat might I call this Tree? A Laurell? *O bonny Laurell:*
Needes to thy bowes will I bow this knee, and vayle my bonetto:
Who, but thou, the renowne of Prince, and Princely Poeta:
Th'one for Crowne, for Garland th'other thanketh Apollo.
Thrice happy Daphne: *that turned was to the* Bay Tree, 120
Whom such seruauntes serue, as challenge seruice of all men.
Who chiefe Lorde, and King of Kings, but th'Emperour only?
And Poet of right stampe, ouerawith th'Emperour himselfe.
Who, but knowes Aretyne, *was he not halfe Prince to the Princes.*
And many a one there liues, as nobly minded at all poyntes. 125
Now Farewell Bay Tree, *very Queene, and Goddesse of all trees,*
Ritchest perle to the Crowne, and fayrest Floure to the Garland.
Faine wod I craue, might I so presume, some farther aquaintaunce,
O that I might? but I may not: woe to my destinie therefore.
Trust me, not one more loyall seruaunt longes to thy Personage, 130
But what sayes Daphne? Non omni dormio, *worse lucke:*
Yet Farewell, Farewell, the Reward of those, that I honour:
Glory to Garden: Glory to Muses: Glory to Vertue.

Partim Ioui, et Palladi,
Partim Apollini et Musis. 135

But seeing I must needes bewray my store, and set open my shoppe wyndowes,
nowe I pray thee, and coniure thee by all thy amorous Regardes, and Exorcismes of
Loue, call a Parliament of thy Sensible, and Intelligible powers together, and tell
me, in Tom Trothes earnest, what *Il fecondo, e famoso Poeta, Messer Immerito,*
sayth to this bolde Satyriall Libell lately deuised at the instaunce of a certayne 140
worshipfull Hartefordshyre Gentleman, of myne olde acquayntaunce: *in Gratiam
quorundam Illustrium* Anglofrancitalorum, *hic et vbique apud nos volitantium.
Agedùm verò, nosti homines, tanquam tuam ipsius cutem.*

108 *Arbor*] *Arbo H*   108 *triomfale*] *Se   tiromfale QHG2   trionfale Sm*   109 *Poete*]
Poeti Sm   116 *WHat*] *G2Se   WAat QH   What Sm*   136 *bewray*] *beuray Sm*   139 *fecondo*]
secondo Se   139 *e*] *et QHG2SmSe*   139 *Messer*] *Mester Sm*   142 *quorundam*] *quorundum H*
143 *Agedùm*] *Agedium H*

APPENDIX I 467

Speculum Tuscanismi.

Since Galateo *came in, and* Tuscanisme *gan vsurpe,*   145
Vanitie aboue all: Villanie next her, Statelynes Empresse.
No man, but Minion, Stowte, Lowte, Plaine, swayne, quoth a Lording:
No wordes but valorous, no workes but woomanish onely.
For life Magnificoes, not a beck but glorious in shew,
In deede most friuolous, not a looke but Tuscanish alwayes.   150
His cringing side necke, Eyes glauncing, Fisnamie smirking,
With forefinger kisse, *and braue* embrace to the footewarde.
Largebelled Kodpeasd Dublet, vnkodpeased halfe hose,
Straite to the dock, like a shirte, and close to the britch, like a diueling.
A little Apish Hatte, cowched fast to the pate, like an Oyster,   155
French Camarick Ruffes, deepe with a witnesse, starched to the purpose.
Euery one A per se A, his termes, and braueries in Print,
Delicate in speach, queynte in araye: conceited in all poyntes:
In Courtly guyles, a passing singular odde man,
For Gallantes a braue Myrrour, a Primerose of Honour,   160
A Diamond for nonce, a fellowe perelesse in England.
Not the like Discourser *for Tongue, and head to be found out:*
Not the like resolute Man, *for great and serious affayres,*
Not the like Lynx, *to spie out secretes, and priuities of States.*
Eyed, *like to* Argus, Earde, *like to* Midas, Nosd, *like to* Naso,   165
Wingd, *like to* Mercury, *fittst of a Thousand for to be employde,*
This, nay more than this doth practise of Italy *in one yeare.*
None doe I name, but some doe I know, that a peece of a tweluemonth:
Hath so perfited outly, and inly, both body, both soule,
That none for sense, and senses, halfe matchable with them.   170
A Vulturs smelling, Apes tasting, sight *of an* Eagle.
A spiders touching, Hartes hearing, might *of a* Lyon.
Compoundes *of wisedome, witte, prowes, bountie, behauiour,*
All gallant Vertues, all qualities of body and soule:
O thrice tenne hundreth thousand times blessed and happy,   175
Blessed and happy Trauaile, Trauailer *most blessed and happy.*

    Penatibus Hetruscis laribusque nostris Inquilinis:

    Tell me in good sooth, doth it not too euidently appeare, that this English Poet wanted but *a good patterne* before his eyes, as it might be some delicate, and choyce elegant Poesie of good *M. Sidneys,* or *M. Dyers,* (ouer very *Castor,* and *Pollux* for such and many greater matters) when this trimme geere was in hatching: Much like some *Gentlewooman,* I coulde name in England, who by all Phisick and Physiognomie too, might as well haue brought forth all goodly faire children, as they haue now some ylfauored and deformed, had they at the tyme of their *Conception,* had in sight, the amiable and gallant beautifull Pictures of *Adonis, Cupido, Ganymedes,* or the like, which no doubt would haue wrought such deepe impression in

---

149 *life*] like H   155 *Hatte*] Flatte G2   171 Eagle.] Eagle, $Q^{5,6}$ SmSe   174 *gallant*] HG2SmSe   gallaut Q   175 *thousand*] om. Sm   180 *Sidneys*] SIDNEY Sm   180 ouer] our ?

their fantasies, and imaginations, as their children, and perhappes their Childrens children too, myght haue thanked them for, as long as they shall haue Tongues in their heades.

But myne owne leysure fayleth me: and to say troth, I am lately become a maruellous great straunger at myne olde *Mistresse Poetries*, being newly entertayned, and dayly employed in our Emperour *Iustinians seruice* (sauing that I haue alreadie addressed a certaine pleasurable, and Morall Politique Naturall mixte deuise, to his most Honourable Lordshippe, in the same kynde, wherevnto my next Letter, if you please mee well, may perchaunce make you priuie:) marrie nowe, if it lyke you in the meane while, for varietie sake, to see howe I taske a young Brother of myne, (whom of playne *Iohn*, our *Italian* Maister hath Cristened his *Picciolo Giouannibattista*,) Lo here (and God will) a peece of hollydayes exercise. In the morning I gaue him this *Theame* out of *Ouid*, to translate, and varie after his best fashion.

> *Dum fueris foelix, multos numerabis Amicos,*
> *Tempora si fuerint nubila, solus eris.*
> *Aspicis, vt veniant ad candida tecta columbae?*
> *Accipiat nullas sordida Turris Aues?*

His translation, or rather Paraphrase before dinner, was first this:

1.

Whilst your Bearnes are fatte, whilst Cofers stuffd with aboundaunce,
Freendes will abound: If bearne waxe bare, then adieu sir a Goddes name.
See ye the Dooues? they breede, and feede in gorgeous Houses:
Scarce one Dooue doth loue to remaine in ruinous Houses,

And then forsooth this: to make proofe of his facultie in Pentameters too, affecting a certaine *Rithmus* withall.

2.

Whilst your Ritches abound, your friends will play the Placeboes,
If your wealth doe decay, friend, like a feend, will away,
Dooues light, and delight in goodly fairetyled houses:
If your House be but olde, Dooue to remoue be ye bolde.

And the last and largest of all, this:

3.

If so be goods encrease, then dayly encreaseth a goods friend.
If so be goods decrease, then straite decreaseth a goods friend.
Then Good night goods friend, who seldome prooueth a good friend,
Giue me the goods, and giue me the good friend, take ye the goods friend.
Douehouse, and Louehouse, in writing differ a letter:
In deede scarcely so much, so resembleth an other an other.
Tyle me the Doouehouse trimly, and gallant, where the like storehouse?
Fyle me the Doouehouse: leaue it vnhansome, where the like poorehouse?
Looke to the Louehouse: where the resort is, there is a gaye showe:
Gynne port, and mony fayle: straight sports and Companie faileth.

203 *Aues?*] aues. Sm   213 Placeboes] Place-boes H   221 Good] Sm   God QHG2Se
224 *much, so*] much H   226 *Fyle*] Tyle Sm

Beleeue me, I am not to be charged with aboue one, or two of the Verses: and a foure or fiue wordes in the rest. His afternoones *Theame* was borrowed out of him, whom one in your Coate, they say, is as much beholding vnto, as any Planet, or Starre in Heauen is vnto the Sunne: and is quoted as your self best remember, in the Glose of your *October*.

> *Giunto Alessandro ala famosa tomba*
> *Del fero Achille, sospirando disse,*
> *O fortunato, che si chiara tromba*
> *Trouasti.*

Within an houre, or there aboutes, he brought me these foure lustie Hexameters, altered since not past in a worde, or two.

> **Noble** Alexander, *when he came to the tombe of* Achilles,
> *Sighing spake with a bigge voyce: O thrice blessed* Achilles,
> *That such a Trump, so great, so loude, so glorious hast found,*
> *As the renowned, and surprizing* Archpoet Homer.

Vppon the viewe whereof, Ah my Syrrha, quoth I, here is a gallant exercise for you in deede: we haue had a little prettie triall of your *Latin*, and *Italian* Translation: Let me see now I pray, what you can doo in your owne Tongue: And with that, reaching a certaine famous Booke, called the newe *Shephardes Calender*: I turned to *Willyes*, and *Thomalins Emblemes*, in *Marche*: and bad him make them eyther better, or worse in English verse. I gaue him an other howres respite: but before I looked for him, he suddainely rushed vpon me, and gaue me his deuise, thus formally set downe in a faire peece of Paper.

1. *Thomalins Embleme.*

Of Honny, and of Gaule, in Loue there is store,
The Honny is much, but the Gaule is more.

2. *Willyes Embleme.*

To be wize, and eke to Loue,
Is graunted scarce to God aboue.

3. *Both combined in one.*

Loue is a thing more fell, and full of Gaule, than of Honny,
And to be wize, and Loue, is a worke for a God, or a Goddes peere.

With a small voluntarie Supplement of his owne, on the other side, in commendation of hir most gratious, and thrice excellent Maiestie:

232 Sunne]   same *H*   233 Glose] Close *SmSe*   234 ala] a[l]la *Sm*   a la *Se*
244 I,] I Q^{1-5} 245 your] *G2SmSe*   you *QH*   259 and] *G2*   than *QHSmSe*

> *Not the like* Virgin *againe, in Asia, or Afric, or Europe,*
> *For Royall Vertues, for Maiestie, Bountie, Behauiour.*
> *Raptim, vti vides.*

In both not passing a worde, or two, corrected by mee. Something more I haue of his, partly that very day begun, and partly continued since: but yet not so perfitly finished, that I dare committe the viewe, and examination thereof, to *Messer Immeritoes* Censure, whom after those same two incomparable and myraculous *Gemini, Omni exceptione maiores,* I recount, and chaulk vppe in the Catalogue of our very principall Englishe *Aristarchi.* Howbeit, I am nigh halfe perswaded, that in tyme *(siquidem vltima primis respondeant)* for length, bredth, and depth, it will not come far behinde your *Epithalamion Thamesis:* the rather, hauing so fayre a president, and patterne before his Eyes, as I warrant him, and he presumeth to haue of that: both *Master Collinshead,* and *M. Hollinshead* too, being togither therein. But euer, and euer, me thinkes your great *Catoes, Ecquid erit pretij,* and our little *Catoes, Res age quae prosunt,* make suche a buzzing, and ringing in my head, that I haue little ioy to animate, and encourage either you, or him to goe forward, vnlesse ye might make account of some certaine ordinarie wages, at the leastwise haue your meate, and drinke for your dayes workes. As for my selfe, howsoeuer I haue toyed, and trifled heretofore, I am nowe taught, and I trust I shall shortly learne, (no remedie, I must of meere necessitie giue you ouer in the playne fielde) to employ my trauayle, and tyme wholly, or chiefely on those studies and practizes, that carrie as they saye, meate in their mouth, hauing euermore their eye vppon the *Title De pane lucrando,* and their hand vpon their halfpenny. For, I pray now, what saith *M. Cuddie, alias* you know who, in the tenth *Æglogue* of the foresaid famous new Calender?

> *Piers, I haue piped erst so long with payne,*
> *That all myne Oten reedes been rent, and wore,*
> *And my poore Muse hath spent hir spared store,*
> *Yet little good hath got, and much lesse gayne.*
> *Such pleasaunce makes the Grashopper so poore,*
> *And ligge so layde, when winter doth her strayne.*

> *The Dapper Ditties, that I woont deuize,*
> *To feede youthes fancie, and the flocking fry,*
> *Delighten much: what I the bett for thy?*
> *They han the pleasure, I a sclender prize.*
> *I beate the bushe, the birdes to them doe flye,*
> *What good thereof to Cuddy can arise?*

266 Something] *FHu resume at this point*   266-8 more . . . thereof,] *I have attempted in that kind, and would commit FHu*   269 after] *with FHu*   269 same . . . and] *two FHu*   270 *Omni . . . vppe] I recount FHu*   271 very principall Englishe] *principal FHu*   271-5 Howbeit . . . therein.] *om. FHu*   275 Hollinshead] *SmSe*   Hollishead *QHG2*   276 But] *D resumes at this point*   276 Ecquid erit pretij] *om. FHu*   277 Catoes . . . prosunt] *ones FHu*   277 and ringing] *om. FHu*   278 and . . . him] *you FHu*   279-80 account . . . drinke] *some certain account FHu*   279 at] *SmSe*   at at *QH*   or at *G2D*   280-1 howsoeuer . . . toyed, and] *however I have FHu*   281-2 and I . . . fielde)] *om. FHu*   283 trauayle . . . chiefely] *time wholly FHu*   283 and practizes] *om. FHu*   284 mouth] mouths *FHu*   284 euermore] *more FHu*   285 pane] pare *H*   285-99 For . . . . arise?] *om. FHu*

APPENDIX I

But Master *Collin Cloute* is not euery body, and albeit his olde Companions, *Master Cuddy*, and *Master Hobbinoll* be as little beholding to their *Mistresse Poetrie*, as euer you wist: yet he peraduenture, by the meanes of hir speciall fauour, and some personall priuiledge, may happely liue by *dying Pellicanes*, and purchase great landes, and Lordshippes, with the money, which his *Calendar* and *Dreames* haue, and will affourde him. *Extra iocum*, I like your *Dreames* passingly well: and the rather, bicause they sauour of that singular extraordinarie veine and inuention, whiche I euer fancied moste, and in a manner admired onelye in *Lucian, Petrarche, Aretine, Pasquill,* and all the most delicate, and fine conceited Grecians and Italians: (for the Romanes to speake of, are but verye Ciphars in this kinde:) whose chiefest endeuour, and drifte was, to haue nothing vulgare, but in some respecte or other, and especially in *liuely Hyperbolicall Amplifications*, rare, queint, and odde in euery pointe, and as a man woulde saye, a degree or two at the leaste, aboue the reache, and compasse of a common Schollers capacitie. In whiche respecte notwithstanding, as well for the singularitie of the manner, as the Diuinitie of the matter, I hearde once a Diuine, preferre *Saint Iohns Reuelation* before al the veriest *Maetaphysicall Visions*, and iollyest conceited *Dreames* or *Extasies*, that euer were deuised by one or other, howe admirable, or superexcellent soeuer they seemed otherwise to the worlde. And truely I am so confirmed in this opinion, that when I bethinke me of the verie notablest, and moste wonderful Propheticall, or Poeticall Vision, that euer I read, or hearde, me seemeth the proportion is so vnequall, that there hardly appeareth anye semblaunce of Comparison: no more in a manner (specially for Poets) than doth betweene the incomprehensible Wisedome of God, and the sensible Wit of Man. But what needeth this digression betweene you and me? I dare saye you wyll holde your selfe reasonably wel satisfied, if youre *Dreames* be but as well esteemed of in Englande, as *Petrarches Visions* be in Italy: whiche I assure you, is the very worst I wish you. But, see, how I haue the Arte *Memoratiue* at commaundement. In good faith I had once againe nigh forgotten your *Faerie Queene:* howbeit by good chaunce, I haue nowe sent hir home at the laste, neither in better nor worse case, than I founde hir. And must you of necessitie haue my Iudgement of hir in deede? To be plaine, I am voyde of al iudgement, if your *Nine Comoedies*, whervnto in imitation of *Herodotus,* you giue the names of the *Nine Muses*, (and in one mans fansie not vnworthily) come not neerer *Ariostoes Comoedies*, eyther for the finenesse of plausible Elocution, or the rarenesse of Poetical Inuention, than that *Eluish Queene* doth to his *Orlando Furioso*, which notwithstanding, you wil needes seeme to emulate, and hope to ouergo, as you flatly professed your self in one of your last Letters. Besides that you know, it hath

300 But] *FHuMChG1 resume at this point*   300-3 and . . . happely] *but perhaps may FHu*   302 wist] writ *M*   wilt *Se*   303 dying Pellicanes] his dying Pellicane *FHu*   303-5 and purchase . . . him] *om. FHu*   305 passingly] *passing FHu*   306 sauour] fauour *Se*   306 singular] *om. FHu*   308 and fine] *om. FHu*   309 to speake of] *om. FHu*   309 verye] *om. FHu*   310 and drifte] *om. FHu*   311 queint] *om. FHu*   312 in . . . leaste] *and FHu*   313 and . . . capacitie] *of common Capacities FHu*   313-5 In . . . once] *I have heard FHu*   316 or Extasies] *om. FHu*   317-8 soeuer . . . otherwise] otherwise they seemed *FHu*   319 verie . . . moste] *most notable and FHu*   322 than] then *M*   324 wel] *om. FHu*   326-30 But . . . . plaine] *om. FHu*   329 than] then *M*   332 (and . . . vnworthily)] *om. FHu*   332 neerer] *as near FHu*   333 finenesse] finesse *HCh*   334 Inuention . . . Eluish] as the Faëry *FHu*   334-6 Furioso . . . Letters] *om. FHu*

bene the vsual practise of the most exquisite and odde wittes in all nations, and
specially in *Italie*, rather to shewe, and aduaunce themselues that way, than any
other: as namely, those three notorious dyscoursing heads, *Bibiena, Machiauel,* and
Aretine did, (to let *Bembo* and *Ariosto* passe) with the great admiration, and 340
wonderment of the whole countrey: being in deede reputed matchable in all points,
both for conceyt of Witte, and eloquent decyphering of matters, either with
Aristophanes and *Menander* in Greek, or with *Plautus* and *Terence* in Latin, or
with any other, in any other tong. But I wil not stand greatly with you in your
owne matters. If so be the *Faerye Queene* be fairer in your eie than the *Nine* 345
Muses, and *Hobgoblin* runne away with the Garland from *Apollo:* Marke what I
saye, and yet I will not say that I thought, but there an End for this once, and fare
you well, till God or some good Aungell putte you in a better minde.

And yet, bicause you charge me somewhat suspitiouslye with an olde promise,
to deliuer you of that iealousie, I am so farre from hyding mine owne matters from 350
you, that loe, I muste needes be reuealing my friendes secreates, now an honest
Countrey Gentleman, sometimes a Scholler: At whose request, I bestowed this
pawlting bongrely Rime vpon him, to present his Maistresse withall. The parties
shall bee namelesse: sauing, that the Gentlewomans true, or counterfaite Christen
name, must necessarily be bewrayed. 355

To my good Mistresse *Anne:* the
very lyfe of my lyfe, and onely
beloued Mystresse.

GEntle *Mistresse Anne, I am plaine by nature:*
  I was neuer so farre in loue with any creature. 360
Happy were your seruant, if hee coulde bee so Anned,
  And you not vnhappy, if you shoulde be so manned.
I loue not to gloze, where I loue indeede,
  Nowe God, and good Saint Anne, sende me good speede.
Suche goodly Vertues, suche amiable Grace, 365
  But I must not fall a praysing: I wante Time, and Place.
Oh, that I had mine olde Wittes at commaundement:
  I knowe, what I coulde say without controlement:
But let this suffice: thy desertes are suche:
  That no one in this worlde can loue thee too muche. 370
My selfe moste vnworthy of any suche foelicitie,
  But by imputation of thy gratious Curtesie.
I leaue to loue the Muses, since I loued thee,
  Alas, what are they, when I thee see?

338 than] then *M*   340-1 and wonderment] *om. FHu*   341 reputed] *om. FHu*
342 of matters, either] *om. FHu*   344-403 But . . . . euer.] *om. FHu*   349-546 And
. . . . G.] *om. ChMDG1*   353 bongrely] Q^8Se bnngrely $Q^{1,2,4-6}$ vnngrely *H* bungrely *Sm*
356-480 To . . . . steade] *om. Q^1*   356-403 To . . . . euer.] *om. Sm*   364 Anne,] Anne. Q^8

APPENDIX I

Adieu, adieu pleasures, and profits all: 375
  My Hart, and my Soule, but at one bodyes call.
Woulde God, I might saye to hir: My hart-roote is thine:
  And, (ô Pleasure of Pleasures) Thy sweete hart-roote mine.
Nowe I beseeche thee by whatsoeuer thou louest beste,
  Let it be, as I haue saide, and, Soule, take thy reste. 380
By the faith of true Loue, and by my truest Truely,
  Thou shalt neuer putte forth thy Loue to greater Vsurie.
And for other odde necessaries, take no care,
  Your seruaunts Daemonium *shall ridde you of that feare.*
I serue but two Saints, Saint Penny, *and* Saint Anne, 385
  Commende this I muste, commaunde that I canne.
Nowe, shall I be plaine? I praye thee euen most hartily,
  Requite Loue, with Loue: and farewell most hartily.

Postscripte.

I But once loued before, and shee forsooth was a Susanne: 390
  But the Heart of a Susanne, *not worth the Haire of an* Anne:
A Sus *to* Anne, *if you can any Latine, or Pewter:*
  Shee Flesh, hir Mother Fish, hir Father a verye Newter.
I woulde once, and might after, haue spedde a Gods name:
  But, if she coye it once, she is none of my Dame. 395

Nowe I praye thee moste hartily, Thricegentle Mistresse Anne,
Looke for no long seruice of so plaine a manne.
And yet I assure thee, thou shalt neuer want any seruice,
If my selfe, or my S. Penny may performe thy wishe.
And thus once againe, (full loath) I take my leaue of thy sweete harte, 400
With as many louing Farewels, as be louing pangs in my heart.

  He that longeth to be thine owne
  inseparably, for euer and euer.

God helpe vs, you and I are wisely employed, (are wee not?) when our Pen and Inke, and Time, and Wit, and all runneth away in this goodly yonkerly veine: 405 as if the world had nothing else for vs to do: or we were borne to be the only *Nonproficients* and *Nihilagents* of the world. *Cuiusmodi tu nugis, atque naenijs nisi vnâ mecum (qui solemni quodam iureiurando, atque voto obstringor, relicto isto amoris Poculo, iuris Poculum primo quoque tempore exhaurire) iam tandem aliquando valedicas, (quod tamen, vnum tibi, credo* τῶν ἀδυνάτων *videbitur) nihil* 410 *dicam amplius, Valeas. E meo municipio. Nono Calendas Maias.*

But hoe I pray you, gentle sirra, a word with you more. In good sooth, and by the faith I beare to the Muses, you shal neuer haue my subscription or consent (though you should charge me wyth the authoritie of fiue hundreth Maister *Drants,*)

---

378 *sweete hart-roote*] *sweete hartroote* Q³Se sweet-hartroote G2 393 *hir Mother*] *hir, Mother* Q³Se 404 *God*] *FHuSm resume at this point* 404 (are wee not?)] *om. FHu* 405 *yonkerly*] *om. FHu* 406-7 *or . . . world.*] *om. FHu* 407 *naenijs*] *naenijs,* Q⁶ *nanis Sm* 408 *solemni quodam*] *solenni FHu* 410 *aliquando*] *om. FHu* 410 *credo*] *credo, Se* 410-1 *nihil . . . Valeas.*] *Vale F Vale. Hu* 411 *E*] *E. G2* 411-546 *Nono . . . . G.*] *om. Hu* 411-532 *Nono . . . . time.*] *om. F*

to make your *Carpēnter* our *Carpĕnter,* an inche longer, or bigger, than God and his
Englishe people haue made him. Is there no other Pollicie to pull downe Ryming,
and set vppe Versifying, but you must needes correcte *Magnificat:* and againste
all order of Lawe, and in despite of Custome, forcibly vsurpe, and tyrannize vppon
a quiet companye of wordes, that so farre beyonde the memorie of man, haue so
peaceably enioyed their seuerall Priuiledges and Liberties, without any disturbance,
or the leaste controlement? What? Is *Horaces Ars Poëtica* so quite out of our
Englishe Poets head, that he muste haue his Remembrancer, to pull hym by the
sleeue, and put him in mind, of, *Penes vsum, et ius, et norma loquendi?* Indeed I
remember, who was wont in a certaine brauerie, to call our *M. Valanger* Noble
M. Valanger. Else neuer heard I any, that durst presume so much ouer the Englishe,
(excepting a fewe suche stammerers, as haue not the masterie of their owne
Tongues) as to alter the Quantitie of any one sillable, otherwise, than oure common
speache, and generall receyued Custome woulde beare them oute. Woulde not I
laughe, thinke you, to heare *Messer Immerito* come in baldely with his *Maiēstie,
Royāltie, Honēstie, Sciēnces, Facūlties, Excēllent, Tauērnour, Manfūlly, Faithfūlly,*
and a thousande the like: in steade of *Maiĕstie, Royăltie, Honĕstie,* and so forth?
And trowe you anye coulde forbeare the byting of his Lippe, or smyling in his
Sleeue, if a iolly fellowe, and greate Clarke, (as it mighte be youre selfe,) reading
a fewe Verses vnto him, for his own credite and commendation, should nowe and
then, tell him of, *bargaīneth, followīng, harrōwing, thoroūghly, Trauaīlers,* or the
like, in steade of, *bargăneth, follŏwing, harrŏwing,* and the reste? Or will *Segnior
Immerito,* bycause, may happe, he hathe a fat-bellyed Archedeacon on his side, take
vppon him to controll Maister Doctor *Watson* for his *All Trauaīlers,* in a Verse so
highly extolled of Master *Ascham?* or Maister *Ascham* himselfe, for abusing
Homer, and corrupting our Tongue, in that he saith:

Quite throŭghe a Doore flĕwe a shafte with a brasse head?

Nay, haue we not somtime, by your leaue, both the Position of the firste, and
Dipthong of the seconde, concurring in one, and the same sillable, which neuer-
thelesse is commonly and ought necessarily to be pronounced short? I haue nowe
small time, to bethink me of many examples. But what say you to the second in
Merchaūndise? to the third in *Couenaūnteth?* and to the fourth in *Appurte-
naūnces?* Durst you aduenture to make any of them long, either in Prose, or in
Verse? I assure you I knowe who dareth not, and *suddāinly* feareth the displeasure
of all true Englishemen if he should. Say you *suddaīnly,* if you liste: by my *cer-
taīnly,* and *certaīnty* I wil not. You may perceiue by the *Premisses,* (which very
worde I woulde haue you note by the waye to) the Latine is no rule for vs: or
imagine aforehande, (bycause you are like to proue a great Purchaser, and leaue
suche store of money, and possessions behinde you) your *Execūtors* wil deale
fraudulēntly, or *violēntly* with your *succēssour,* (whiche in a maner is euery mans
case) and it will fall oute a resolute pointe: the third in *Execūtores, fraudulēnter,
violēnter,* and the seconde in *Succēssor,* being long in the one, and shorte in the

415

420

425

430

435

440

445

450

455

---

417 Versifying] Vesifying H   417 you] om. H   423 et ius, et] and ius, and Sm
424 Valanger] SmSe   Valanger. Q²⁻⁶   Valanger, HG2   429 Messer] Mester Sm
435 Trauaīlers,] om. Sm   448 you I] SmSe   you I I Q²⁻⁶ HG2   449 liste] like Sm
450 perceiue] preceiue Se   454 fraudulēntly] fraudulently Sm   454 violēntly] violently Sm
455 Execūtores] Execŭtores H   455-6 fraudulēnter, violēnter] fraudulēter, violēter Q²⁻⁶ HG2Se
fraudulenter, violenter Sm

other: as in seauen hundreth more: suche as, *disciple, recited, excited: tenement, orătour, laudăble:* and a number of their fellowes are long in English, short in Latine: long in Latine, short in English. Howbeit, in my fancy, such words, as *violently, diligently, magnificently, indifferently,* seeme in a manner reasonably 460 indifferent, and tollerable either waye, neither woulde I greately stande with him, that translated the Verse.

Cur mittis violas? vt me violentiùs vras?
Why send you violets? to burne my poore hart violently.

Marry so, that being left common for verse, they are to be pronounced shorte 465 in Prose, after the maner of the Latines, in suche wordes as these, *Cathedra, Volucres, mediocres, Celebres.*

And thus farre of your *Carpenter,* and his fellowes, wherin we are to be moderated, and ouerruled by the vsuall, and common receiued sounde, and not to deuise any counterfaite fantasticall Accent of oure owne, as manye, otherwise not 470 vnlearned haue corruptely and ridiculouslye done in the Greeke.

Nowe for your *Heauen, Seauen, Eleauen,* or the like, I am likewise of the same opinion: as generally in all words else: we are not to goe a little farther, either for the *Prosody,* or the *Orthography,* (and therefore your Imaginarie *Diastole* nothing worthe) then we are licenced and authorized by the ordinarie vse, and 475 custome, and proprietie, and Idiome, and, as it were, Maiestie of our speach: whiche I accounte the only infallible, and soueraigne Rule of all Rules. And therefore hauing respecte therevnto, and reputing it Petty Treason to reuolt therefro: dare hardly eyther in the *Prosodie,* or in the *Orthography* either, allowe them two sillables in steade of one, but woulde as well in Writing, as in Speaking, haue them 480 vsed, as *Monosyllaba,* thus: *heavn, seavn, a leavn,* as Maister *Ascham* in his *Toxophilus* doth *Yrne,* commonly written *Yron:*

Vp to the pap his string did he pull, his shafte to the harde yrne.

Especially the difference so manifestly appearing by the Pronunciation, betweene these twoo, *a leavn a clocke* and *a leaven of Dowe,* whyche *lea-ven* admitteth the 485 *Diastole,* you speake of. But see, what absurdities thys yl-fauoured *Orthographye,* or rather *Pseudography,* hathe ingendred: and howe one errour still breedeth and begetteth an other. Haue wee not, *Mooneth,* for *Moonthe: sithence,* for *since: whilest,* for *whilste: phantasie,* for *phansie: euen,* for *evn: Diuel,* for *Divl: God hys wrath,* for *Goddes wrath:* and a thousande of the same stampe: wherein 490 the corrupte *Orthography* in the moste, hathe beene the sole, or principall cause of corrupte *Prosodye* in ouer many?

Marry, I confesse some wordes we haue indeede, as for example, *fayer,* either for beautifull, or for a *Marte: ayer,* bothe *pro aere,* and *pro haerede,* for we say not *Heire,* but plaine *Aire* for him to (or else *Scoggins Aier* were a poore iest) 495 whiche are commonly, and maye indifferently be vsed eyther wayes. For you shal as well, and as ordinarily heare *fayer,* as *faire,* and *Aier,* as *Aire,* and bothe alike: not onely of diuers and sundrye persons, but often of the very same: otherwhiles

467 *Volucres*] Sm *Volucrĕs* Q^{2-6} HG2 *Volŭcres* Se   480 of] Q^1 *resumes at this point*
486 yl-fauoured] yl fauoured $Q^{2,4-6}$ 492 many?] many: G2   494 *haerede*] *haeredè* Q^1
495 to (or] to, or Q^3 to, (*or* Se

vsing the one, otherwhiles the other: and so *died*, or *dyde: spied*, or *spide: tryed*, or *tride: fyer*, or *fyre: myer*, or *myre:* wyth an infinyte companye of the same sorte: sometime *Monosyllaba*, sometime *Polysyllaba*.

To conclude both pointes in one, I dare sweare priuately to your selfe, and will defende publiquely againste any, it is neither Heresie, nor Paradox, to sette downe, and stande vppon this assertion, (notwithstanding all the Preiudices and Presumptions to the contrarie, if they were tenne times as manye moe) that it is not, either Position, or Dipthong, or Diastole, or anye like Grammer Schoole Deuice, that doeth, or can indeede, either make long or short, or encrease, or diminish the number of Sillables, but onely the common allowed, and receiued *Prosodye:* taken vp by an vniuersall consent of all, and continued by a generall vse, and Custome of all. Wherein neuerthelesse I grant, after long aduise, and diligent obseruation of particulars, a certain Vniform Analogie, and Concordance, being in processe of time espyed out. Sometime this, sometime that, hath been noted by good wits in their *Analyses*, to fall out generally alyke: and as a man woulde saye, regularly in all, or moste wordes: as Position, Dipthong, and the like: not as firste, and essentiall causes of this, or that effecte, (here lyeth the point) but as Secundarie and Accidentall Signes, of this, or that Qualitie.

It is the vulgare, and naturall Mother *Prosodye*, that alone worketh the feate, as the onely supreame Foundresse, and Reformer of Position, Dipthong, Orthographie, or whatsoeuer else: whose Affirmatiues are nothing worth, if she once conclude the Negatiue: and whose *secundae intentiones* muste haue their whole allowance and warrante from hir *primae*. And therefore in shorte, this is the verie shorte, and the long: Position neither maketh shorte, nor long in oure Tongue, but so farre as we can get hir good leaue. Peraduenture, vppon the diligent suruewe, and examination of Particulars, some the like Analogie and Vniformity, might be founde oute in some other respecte, that shoulde as vniuersally and Canonically holde amongst vs, as Position doeth with the Latines and Greekes. I saye, (peraduenture,) bycause, hauing not yet made anye speciall Obseruation, I dare not precisely affirme any generall certaintie: albeit I presume, so good and sensible a Tongue, as ours is, beeyng wythall so like itselfe, as it is, cannot but haue something equipollent, and counteruaileable to the beste Tongues, in some one such kinde of conformitie, or other. And this forsooth is all the Artificial Rules and Precepts, you are like to borrowe of one man at this time.

Sed amàbo te, ad Corculi tui delicatissimas Literas, propediem, quam potero, accuratissimè: tot interim illam exquisitissimis salutibus, atque salutationibus impertiens, quot habet in Capitulo, capillos semiaureos, semiargenteos, semigemmeos. Quid quaeris? Per tuam Venerem altera Rosalindula est: eamque non alter, sed idem ille, (tua, vt ante, bona cum gratia) copiosè amat Hobbinolus. O mea Domina Immerito, mea bellissima Collina Clouta, multò plus plurimùm salue, atque vale.

513 alyke:] *G2* alyke? *QHSe* alyke, *Sm*   529 ours] our *Sm*   533 Sed] *F resumes at this point with new heading* POSTSCRIPT.   533 amàbo] amăbo *Q²,⁴⁻⁶*   533 te] ite *Se* 533 quam] quă *G2*   qua *Sm*   534 interim illam] enim istam *F*   534 exquisitissimis] exquisitissimus *H*   534 impertiens] impertias *F*   535 capillos . . . semigemmeos.] Capillos—*F*   537-46 O . . . . G.] *om. F*

APPENDIX I

You knowe my ordinarie *Postscripte:* you may communicate as much, or as little, as you list, of these Patcheries, and fragments, with the two Gentlemen: but there a straw, and you loue me: not with any else, friend or foe, one, or other: vnlesse haply you haue a special desire to imparte some parte hereof, to my good friend *M. Daniel Rogers:* whose curtesies are also registred in my Marble booke. You know my meaning. 540

Nosti manum et stylum. 545

G.

541 there] these *H*   541 one] *om. Sm*   543 curtesies] curteries *H*

B.

THE EARTHQUAKE

Although Spenser merely alludes in passing to the earthquake of 6 April, 1580 (Letter III 15-20), that august event was in good part responsible for the publication of his correspondence with Harvey. On the first title page it is specified, along with "our English refourmed Versifying," as a leading subject of the volume; and Harvey's discussion of it monopolizes more than a quarter of the whole. Nor is this emphasis hard to understand in view of the great interest which the earthquake aroused at the time.

On the two days which followed the earthquake five items dealing with it were entered in the Stationers' Register (Arber 2. 367-8); and during the next three months at least a dozen more pamphlets and ballads on the subject were listed there. One of those which are not extant today is given, under 25 April, as "*per* Elderton A ballat intytuled. *quake. quake. yt is tyme to quake. when towers and townes and all Doo quake*" (Arber 2. 369; Rollins, *SP* 17. 224); as Nashe later pointed out (*Strange Newes*, sig. D4ᵛ), Harvey refers disparagingly to this work in Letter IV (369-73), which he pretends to have written on 7 April (573-4).

At least five of the earthquake pamphlets, aside from Harvey's letter, have survived:

Thomas Churchyard, *A Warning for the Wise*, 1580. [Entered in the Stationers' Register 8 April, 1580 (Arber 2. 368). Sigs. D2ʳ–D3ʳ contain a sixty-six line poem on the earthquake by Richard Tarlton.]

T[homas] T[wyne], *A Shorte and Pithie Discourse*, 1580. [Entered in the Stationers' Register 11 April, 1580 (Arber 2. 368); written, according to title page, on 13 April.]

Anthony Munday, *A View of Sundry Examples . . . Also a Short Discourse of the Late Earthquake,* [1580]. [Entered in the Stationers' Register 27 April, 1580 (Arber 2. 369). The earthquake is treated very briefly, sigs. D3ᵛ–D4ʳ.]

Arthur Golding, *A Discourse vpon the Earthquake,* [1580].

Abraham Fleming, *A Bright Burning Beacon*, 1580. [Published after the pamphlets of Churchyard, Twyne, and Golding, which are mentioned on sig. A4ᵛ.]

Churchyard's account seems to have been written immediately after the event and to have supplied most of the observations on the effect of the earthquake which were used by the later writers (see note on Letter III 15-7). All five of these pamphlets stress the religious significance of the earthquake; their general point of view is well represented by the words of Golding (sig. B1r-v):

> although there bee peraduenture some, which (to keepe them selues and others from the due looking back into the time earst mysspent, and to foade them still in the vanities of this worlde, least they should see their own wretchednesse, and seeke to shunne Gods vengeance at hande) wil not stickke to deface the apparant working of God, by ascribing this miracle to some ordinarie causes in nature: yet notwithstandding to the godlie and wel-disposed . . . it must needes appeare to bee the very finger of God, and as a messenger of the miseries due to such defects.

But the religious interpretation which is common to the five pamphlets is repudiated by Harvey. He centers his formal discussion on the idea that, although a divine purpose underlies every natural occurrence, he cannot presume to determine precisely what God intended by this event (Letter IV 219-304, 373-452); and when he derides "some of the simpler, and vnskilfuller sort" (293-4) and "oure counterfaite, and reasonlesse *Orphei*" (451-2) who will read religious meanings into the earthquake, there is no doubt that he is referring to such pamphleteers as Churchyard, Twyne, Munday, Golding, and Fleming. He pretends to write on 7 April, before their pamphlets were published; but he can hardly have composed the whole of his long letter in one day, and, as we have seen in his allusion to Elderton, he must have at least revised his letter after 25 April; we know, in any case, that it was entered for publication on 30 June, long after the pamphlets of Churchyard, Twyne, and Munday must have been published. Predating his reply to them would be an obvious controversial device and would serve to sharpen the impression of a learned independence of mind: if he answered the simpler sort, it was only by accident.

One of these writers, Thomas Twyne, was not an unlearned hack, however. His translations of Dionysius Periegetes' *Surueye of the World* (1572) and Humphrey Llwyd's *Breuiary of Britayne* (1573) were in Harvey's own library (*Marginalia*, pp. 159-64). His *Discourse*, although it agrees with the popular theory that the earthquake was the sign of God's wrath against sinners, also contains a learned discussion of it as a natural phenomenon (sig. A1r-v):

> following *Aristotle* as cheefe in this behalfe: wee must vnderstand, that the efficient causes of an Earthquake are three, to wyt, the Sun, the other sixe Planets, and a spirite or breath included within the bowelles of the earth: and the materiall cause one, which is an Exhalation, that is to say, a certaine ayre, breath, or smoake drawne out of the earth, which of nature is hot and drie.

This passage is parallel to a section of Harvey's letter (193-228) which also alludes to Aristotle and seems, characteristically, to refine on Twyne's explanation: instead of two kinds of natural causes, the efficient and the material, Harvey sets up four kinds of causes, two of them natural (the material and the formal causes) and two of them supernatural (the efficient and the final causes); and he further complicates this scheme by describing the sun, stars, and planets as secondary efficient causes.

In effect, Harvey demonstrates that his own learning is far more ponderous than Twyne's.

Why Harvey might wish to depreciate the *Discourse* in this very indirect way one can only guess. In addition to his desire to combat the popular religious interpretation, a clue may lie in Twyne's dedication, "To the right honorable my very good Lord, Philip Howard Earle of Arundell": if Moore Smith is right (*NQ*, Eleventh Series, 3. 261-3; *Gabriel Harvey's Marginalia*, p. 16), Arundel was the young noble whose dishonest advances to Mercy Harvey, in the winter of 1574, were disdainfully recorded by her brother Gabriel in his *Letter-Book* (pp. 143-58).— It is probable, in any case, that Harvey's discussion of the earthquake was intended to have a controversial interest, with which the publication of Spenser's letters is thus entwined.

C.

THE AREOPAGUS AND ENGLISH VERSIFYING

Discussion of the Areopagus has dealt chiefly with its existence or nonexistence as an organized literary group. This question does not seem to have arisen before 1862, when Fox Bourne (ed. 1891, p. 200) announced:

> The Areopagus was a sort of club, composed mainly of courtiers, who aspired to be also men of letters, apparently with Sidney as its president, to which were admitted other men of letters—Spenser in particular—who hardly aspired to rank with the courtiers. It seems to have had Harvey as a corresponding member and counsellor-in-chief.... Dyer and Greville were evidently busy members.... Who were the other members of the club we know not.

CHURCH (pp. 24, 29), SCHELLING (*Poetic and Verse Criticism*, pp. 26-9; *English Literature during the Lifetime of Shakespeare*, pp. 25-6), SPINGARN (p. 300), UPHAM (pp. 25-30), DODGE (pp. xiv-xv), MACINTIRE (*PMLA* 26. 500-27), HIGGINSON (pp. 257-86), and HOLLOWELL (*PQ* 3. 52) all accept the existence of the Areopagus as an organized group, which included, besides Sidney and Dyer, their literary associates Spenser, Harvey, Drant, Greville, Daniel, Fraunce, the Countess of Pembroke, *etc.*, the names varying according to the predilections of each scholar. The most extreme claims for the Areopagus have probably been made by FLETCHER (*JEGP* 2. 429-53), who asserts:

> What we know of the *Areopagus* is derived from references and allusions to it in the Spenser-Harvey letters of 1579-80. There we hear of Dyer and Fulke Greville as members besides Sidney and Spenser and the non-resident Harvey. [The present editor has been unable to trace the name of Greville in the Spenser-Harvey letters.] The only business of the club directly dwelt on between Spenser and Harvey is the experimentation with classical metres.... It is certainly hard to conceive the authors of the *Shepheards Calender* and the *Fairie Queene*, of the *Defense of Poesie* and the *Arcadia*, in the very years in which those works were being planned and executed, finding no more fruitful basis for conversation and coöperation than the "Dranting" of English verse;

and Fletcher devotes the remainder of his article to a series of parallels between the work of Sidney and Spenser, *i. e.*, the Areopagus, and the work of the Pléiade, parallels which are intended to prove that an English literary club was formed by Sidney on the model of the well-known French group. MAGNUS (p. 33) is a school unto himself among those who believe that the Areopagus was an organized society: he identifies Harvey, whom he finds a narrow classicist, as the leader and law-giver of the côterie.

But the importance attached to the Areopagus has dwindled since the appearance in 1909 of an article by MAYNADIER (*MLR* 4. 289-301). He observes that the Areopagus is mentioned only in the Spenser-Harvey letters; that, unlike the Pléiade, it did not arouse contemporary comment, even by Nashe, who might be expected to mention it in his attacks on Harvey; that Greville does not mention it in his life of Sidney; that Harvey was probably not a member, much less a leader of the group; that the whole Areopagus consisted of two or possibly three men, if Spenser was included; that the tone of Spenser's and Harvey's references to it is one of raillery; that their use of the Greek, rather than an Anglicized form of the name suggests that it was not taken seriously; and that, while Sidney, Dyer, and Spenser must have had serious talks on poetry, their meetings were probably casual.

This view is accepted by WALLACE in the most reliable life of Sidney (pp. 229-30) and by SARGENT in the most reliable life of Dyer (pp. 59-61). LONG (*Anglia* 38. 174-7), FULTON (*MLN* 31. 372-3), JUSSERAND (2. 355), and JUDSON (*Life*, p. 61) subscribe to it. FAVERTY (*PQ* 5. 280) notes the use of "Areopagites" in Thomas Newton's dedication of *Seneca His Tenne Tragedies* (1581) and concludes: "the word *Areopagus* was applied in the latter half of the sixteenth century to any group of persons which arrogated to itself the province of a judiciary body. Spenser and Harvey use it in this manner, engaging in pedantic pleasantry." [See also Harvey's use of "Areopage" in *Pierces Supererogation* (1593), pp. 113-4.]

Whatever the organization and the membership of the Areopagus, its sole business, as far as Spenser and Harvey testify, was "our English refourmed Versifying," *i. e.*, the composition of English poetry in quantitative meters and without rhyme. This movement, it is generally agreed, stems from a long passage in Ascham's *Scholemaster* (1570) in which he declares (f. 60^r): "now, when men know the difference, and haue the examples, both of the best, and of the worst, surelie, to follow rather the *Gothes* in Ryming, than the Greekes in trew versifiyng, were euen to eate ackornes with swyne, when we may freely eate wheate bread emonges men."

The course of the movement from 1570 to the first years of the seventeenth century has been summarized by SCHELLING (*Poetic and Verse Criticism*, pp. 92-3), by SPINGARN (pp. 298-301), and, most thoroughly, by GREGORY SMITH (1. xlvi-lv): The hexameters which Ascham himself, Thomas Watson, and Thomas Blenerhasset had written in the middle of the century had been accentual rather than quantitative; but under the tutelage of Thomas Drant, apparently late in the 1570's, Sidney and Dyer began to experiment with quantitative, unrhymed English poetry. Spenser underwent their influence for a while; Harvey remained on the periphery of the group, maintaining, against the authority of Drant, that the natural pronunciation of spoken English should not be violated in quantitative verses. In his *Discourse of English Poetrie* (1586) William Webbe supported, without critical understanding, the system of Drant. But Harvey's, rather than Drant's, ideas on prosody were

APPENDIX I 481

adopted by Richard Stanyhurst in his translation of four books of the *Aeneid* (1582) and by the author (apparently George Puttenham) of *The Arte of English Poesie* (1589); the latter, in fact, practically returns to the idea that the meter of English verses should be accentual. The last important name connected with English versifying is that of Thomas Campion, whose *Obseruations on the Art of English Poesie* (1602) argued for unrhymed, quantitative poetry, although he did not recommend the purely artificial quantities of Drant; in the same year Daniel's well-known reply to Campion, *A Defence of Ryme*, marks the end of the neo-classical experiments of the Elizabethan period.

Since the beginning of the nineteenth century, when the English versifying of the Elizabethans came to the attention of scholars, it has frequently met with scorn. TODD (1. xxxi) calls it " an attempt, which, however once the favourite employment of our poets in the age of Elizabeth, will be always too repulsive to gain many admirers or imitators; requiring, as it generally requires, a pronunciation most dismal, most unmusical, or most ridiculous." HALLAM (2. 230-1) develops the same idea:

> An injudicious endeavour to substitute the Latin metres for those congenial to our language met with no more success than it deserved; unless it may be called success, that Sidney, and even Spenser, were for a moment seduced into approbation of it . . . . as most imitations of Latin measures, in German or English, begin by violating their first principle, which assigns an invariable value in time to the syllables of every word, and produce a chaos of false quantities, it seems as if they could only disgust any one acquainted with classical versification.

CHILD (1. xx-xxi), HALES (p. xxvii), CHURCH (pp. 18-9), SCHELLING (*English Literature during the Lifetime of Shakespeare*, pp. 47-8), DE SELINCOURT (p. xxi), and JUSSERAND (2. 355) all express their contempt for a movement which engaged the support of Sidney, Spenser, and Campion. SAINTSBURY (2. 171-5), after blaming the whole thing on Cambridge, elaborates his abuse in such observations as the following: "Ascham's own remarks on what we shall not imitate him by calling his 'foul wrong way' were, as we have seen, confined to generalities, and the examples which he gives . . . are of no special interest, though they illustrate his own frank admission of the hobbling of the spavined jade, with which he wished to corrupt our English stud." As a consequence of this contemptuous attitude CRAIK (1. 20-1), FOX BOURNE (pp. 201-3), and GROSART (Spenser's *Works* 1. 70) prefer to think that Spenser did not take English versifying seriously. [Note, however, that he planned "to sette forth a Booke in this kinde," the *Epithalamion Thamesis* (Letter III 57-8); and although the "*Iambicum Trimetrum*" (Letter I 85-106) is playful in tone and subject matter, Spenser seems to take the technique of the poem seriously.]

But since the time of Grosart most of the scholars who have written on English versifying have tried rather to understand it than to denounce it or to apologize for Spenser's connection with it. DODGE (p. xv) and THOMPSON (pp. 208-9) observe that, given the apparently hopeless condition of English poetry in the 1570's, it was natural for scholarly writers to experiment with classical versification. HOLLOWELL (*PQ* 3. 51-7), following the same line of thought, finds that their verses sound harsh to us because our ears are not so well trained as theirs were to enjoy Greek and Latin poetry. STONE (pp. 118-23) traces their failure, not to the imitation of classical poetry, but to a misunderstanding of English quantities and a confusion of quantity with accent; and WILLCOCK (*MLR* 29. 1-17; Willcock and Walker, pp. lxvii-lxxii) shows how the principle of poetic accent, which had not at first been recognized by the English versifiers, was gradually clarified through their discussions. Harvey's part in the movement has been diversely assessed by BERLI (pp. 80-93), who finds a strong quantitative element in some of his verses, and by YOUNG (*Life and Letters* 4. 492-6), who believes that Harvey's criticisms deterred Spenser from further quantitative experiments. Perhaps the most important contribution to the understanding of English versifying has been made by MCKERROW (*MLQ* 4. 173-8) in his demonstration that to Spenser and other members of the group " quantity was not an affair of pronunciation, of actual length in time; it was merely that conventionally established attribute of a syllable that determined where it could be placed in verse"; this curiously artificial conception, he shows, eventually led Harvey and Puttenham to substitute accent for quantity in imitating classical meters. But curious as some aspects of English versifying are, it had results which are not contemptible. According to RENWICK (*Edmund Spenser*, pp. 104-5) it taught Spenser that English was less tractable than Latin in its word order; in spite of the awkwardness of the poems it fathered, RUBEL (pp. 119-20) believes that it added rhetorical variety to all English poetry; and MORLEY (*English Writers* 9. 73-5) associates it with blank verse, which was the outcome of the same desire to find for the poet a more dignified medium than those which already existed.

SPENCER (*ELH* 12. 257-8). The general impression we get of most English poetry in the 'sixties and early 'seventies is that of dullness, flatness and cowardice; it is as if the writers did not dare to vary from the iambic foot for fear of losing their sense of rhythm altogether. . . .

If English poetry were ever to have any music in it, if the rhythm of the lines were rightly to echo the rhythm of the thought, if there were ever to be any of that essential *drama* in English verse technique, by which a resolved conflict occurs between the basic metrical pattern and the necessary rhythm of the meaning—if all this were to happen, the situation which existed before 1576 had drastically to be changed. The practice of verse technique needed a violent wrench to get it out of its dusty rut. And this wrench, this virtual dislocation was, I suggest, largely accomplished by the experiments in classical meters. To a modern reader the prolonged discussion between Spenser and Harvey as to whether the second syllable of "carpenter" should be long or short, or whether "heaven" is a monosyllable or a disyllable, seems a waste of time, but actually it was not. What such discussions did was to make people *think* about words; in order to "versify," words had to be broken up, each syllable had to be weighed and considered, and new rhythmical combinations had to be found which were as far removed as possible from the unthinking jog-trot of the prevalent iambic habit.

GREGORY SMITH (1. liv-lv). We must not, however, fail to observe that this criticism of rhyme and rhythm is touched by the shyness which characterizes all the critical work of the age. If Drant did seek to establish a tyranny, he has been badly served by history. Harvey, whom posterity would make godfather to every pedantry, and in this manner to the most ridiculous of codes, is careful to disclaim any "general certainty." "Credit me," he says, "I dare give no precepts nor set down any certain general art." Stanyhurst tells us that his preface was written to explain his own verses, not to publish a "directory" to the learned. Puttenham gently persuades to discipline by showing the discredit of a rhymer "that will be tied to no rules at all," and, after showing the danger of inventing a new prosody and the folly of thinking that it will please everybody, proceeds to his account, only that the subject may be "pleasantly scanned upon." If the details of this controversy are less important to us than the general principle for which the writers strove, that general principle is in its turn of subsidiary interest in the history of criticism to the temper in which it was presented and handled. And here as elsewhere the Elizabethan critics showed something of the true classical spirit, not less in the manner of their argument than in their predisposition to certain lines of thought.

D.

PUBLICATION AND RECEPTION

The Spenser-Harvey correspondence was entered in the Stationers' Register on 30 June, 1580, under the title "*three proper and wittie lettres passed betweene twoo vniuersitie men touchinge the earthequake*" (Arber 2. 373). Spenserian scholars from Todd to the present have generally assumed that the separate title pages of "Three Proper, and Wittie, Familiar Letters" and "Two Other, Very Commendable Letters" indicate that two separate volumes of letters were published in 1580; actually, as Johnson has indicated (pp. 10-11), the five letters were published in one volume, with continuous signatures. The last two letters must have been added as an afterthought since they were written earlier than the three which precede them and since they are not mentioned on the first title page or in the preface "To the Cvrteovs Buyer."

This preface states that the publisher secured the letters, through intermediaries, from Spenser; but another provenience and a reception which was not creditable to Harvey are indicated by the references which his enemies later made to the volume. The evidence which they as well as Harvey supply may conveniently be quoted:

LYLY, or another (*Pappe with an Hatchet*, 1589, sig. B3r). One will we coniure vp, that writing a familiar Epistle about the naturall causes of an Earthquake, fell into the bowells of libelling, which made his eares quake for feare of clipping; he shall tickle you with taunts; all his works bound close, are at least six sheetes in quarto, and he calls them the first tome of his familiar Epistle.

GREENE (*A Qvip for an Vpstart Courtier*, 1592, sig. E4r, as the passage appears in the Britwell-Huntington copy) has John Harvey describe his eldest son: "he is a Ciuilian, a wondrous witted fellow, sir reuerence sir, he is a Doctor, and as *Tubalcain* was the first inuenter of Musick, so he Gods benison light vpon him, was the first that inuented Englishe Hexamiter: but see how in these daies learning is little esteemed, for that and other familiar letters and proper treatises he was orderly clapt in the Fleet."

HARVEY (*Fovre Letters*, 1592, pp. 18-9). Signor Immerito (for that name will be remembred) was then, and is still my affectionate friend, one that could very wel abide Gascoignes Steele glasse, and that stoode equallie indifferent to either part of the state Demonstratiue [Harvey's difficulties at Cambridge]: many communications, and writings may secretlie passe betweene such, euen for an exercise of speech, and stile that are not otherwise conuenient to be disclosed: it was the sinister hap of those infortunate Letters, to fall into the left handes of malicious enemies, or vndiscreete friends: who aduentured to imprint in earnest, that was scribled in iest, (for the moody fit was soone ouer:) and requited their priuate pleasure with my publike displeasure: oh my inestimable, and infinite displeasure. When there was no remedie, but melancholy patience; and the sharpest parte of those vnlucky Letters had bene ouerread at the Councell Table: I was aduised by certaine honourable, and diuers worshipfull persons, to interpretate my intention in more expresse termes: and thereupon discoursed euerie particularitie, by way of Articles or Positions, in a large Apology of my duetiful, and entier affection to that flourishing Vniuersitie, my deere Mother: which Apology, with not so few as forty such Academicall Exercises, and sundry other politique Discourses, I haue hitherto suppressed, as vnworthie the view of the busie world, or the entertainement of precious Time.

HARVEY (*op. cit.*, pp. 20-1). Happy man I, if these two be my hainousest crimes, and deadliest sinnes, To bee the Inuentour of the English Hexameter, and to bee orderlie clapt in the Fleete for the foresaide Letters: where he that sawe mee, sawe mee at Constantinople [*i. e.*, anywhere]. Indeede Sir Iames Croft (whome I neuer touched with the least tittle of detractions) was cunningly incensed, and reincensed against mee: but at last pacified by the voluntarie mediation of my honourable fauourers, M. Secretary Wilson, and Sir Walter Mildmay: vnrequested by any line of my hand, or any woord of my mouth. . . . And that was all the Fleeting, that euer I felt; sauing that an other company of speciall good fellowes, (whereof he was none of the meanest, that brauely threatned to coniure-vpp one, which should massacre Martins witt, or should bee lambackd himself with ten yeares prouision) would needs forsooth verye courtly perswade the Earle of Oxforde, that some thing in those Letters, and namely the Mirrour of Tuscanismo [Letter V 144-77], was palpably intended against him: whose noble Lordeship I protest, I neuer meante to dishonour with the least preiudicial word of my Tongue, or pen.

NASHE (*Strange Newes*, 1592, sigs. G1r–G2r). *Signior Immeritò* (so called, because *he was and is his friend* vndeseruedly) was counterfeitly brought in to play a part in that his Enterlude of Epistles that was hist at, thinking his very name (as the name of *Ned Allen* on the common stage) was able to make an ill matter good.

I durst on my credit vndertake, *Spencer* was no way priuie to the committing of them to the print. Committing I may well call it, for in my opinion *G. H.* should not haue reapt so much discredite by beeing committed to Newgate, as by committing that misbeleeuing prose to the Presse.

. . . . for an Author to renounce his Christendome to write in his owne commendation, to refuse the name which his Godfathers and Godmothers gaue him in his baptisme, and call himselfe *a welwiller to both the writers*, when hee is the onely writer himselfe; with what face doe you thinke hee can aunswere it at the day of iudgement? . . . .

The sharpest part of them were read ouer at Counsell Table, and he referd ouer to the Fleet. . . .

A recantation he was glad to make *by way of articles or positions*, which hee moderates with a milder name of an *apologie*, and that recantation purchast his libertie.

NASHE (*Haue with You to Saffron-Walden*, 1596, sig. L2r-v). In the yeare when the earth-quake was he fell to be a familiar Epistler, and made *Powles Churchyard* resound or crie twang with foure notable famous Letters: in one of which hee enterlaced his short but yet sharpe iudiciall of Earth-quakes, and came verie short and sharpe vppon my Lord of *Oxford*, in a ratling bundle of English Hexameters. How that thriu'd with him, some honest Chronicler helpe me to remember, for it is not comprehended in my braines Diarie or Ephemerides.

NASHE (*op. cit.*, sig. M3v). I had forgot to obserue vnto you out of his first foure familiar Epistles, his ambicious stratagem to aspire, that whereas two great Pieres [apparently Oxford and Sidney] beeing at iarre, and their quarrell continued to bloudshed, he would needs vncald and when it lay not in his way steppe in on the one side which indeede was the safer side (as the foole is crafty inough to sleepe in a whole skin) and hewe and slash with his Hexameters, but hewd and slasht he had beene as small as chippings, if he had not playd ducke Fryer and hid himselfe eight weeks in that Noblemans house, for whome with his pen hee thus bladed. Yet neuerthelesse Syr *Iames a Croft* the olde Controwler ferrited him out, and had him vnder hold in the Fleete a great while, taking that to be aimde and leueld against him, because he cald him his olde Controwler, which he had most venomously belched against Doctour *Perne*. [See Letter IV 547-54. Croft held the position of "controller," *i. e.*, steward, of the Queen's household.] Vppon his humble submission, and ample exposition of the ambiguous Text, and that his forementioned *Mecenas* mediation, matters were dispenst with and quallified, and some light countenance like sunshine after a storme, it pleased him after this to let fall vppon him, and so dispatcht him to spurre Cut backe againe to Cambridge.

NASHE (*op. cit.*, sig. T4r). The Compositor that set it [the preface "To the Cvrteovs Buyer"], swore to mee it came vnder his owne [Harvey's] hand to bee printed.

[From these quotations, as well as internal evidence, it is usually assumed that Harvey, rather than Spenser, was responsible for the publication of the letters. See Jones, *Handbook*, pp. 389-91; Judson, *Life*, p. 60.]

JACKSON (3. 1015). The letters seem to have originated from Harvey's failure to obtain the oratorship of Cambridge University. [But Spenser speaks of Preston, Harvey's rival for the position, as "your verie entire" friend in Letter I 83-4.]

BRADNER (*Edmund Spenser*, p. 26). After the *Calendar* came out, Spenser and Harvey, who corresponded frequently and met occasionally in London, began to concoct a publicity scheme to build up a demand for their respective works. This took the form of a series of letters which they would pretend were published without their permission.

E.

THE IDENTITY OF E. K.

See *Minor Poems* 1. 645-50. The theory that E. K. is Spenser himself has recently received two new recruits, D. T. Starnes (*SP* 41. 181-200) and Raymond Jenkins (*SAB* 19. 147-60, 20. 22-38, 20. 82-94; *SP* 45. 76-9).

STARNES rests his case on a number of parallels, in style and subject matter, between E. K.'s contributions to the *S. C.* volume and Spenser's accepted works. Robert W. Mitchner (*SP* 42. 183-90), however, has shown that more than half of these parallels do not constitute evidence that Spenser, rather than some one else, was E. K. [Mitchner, in the opinion of the present editor, destroys the cumulative force of the arguments used by Starnes.]

JENKINS (*SAB* 20. 91-2). The upshot . . . is that Spenser is E. K.: The instances in which Spenser and Harvey endeavor to publicize themselves and make game of their readers by mystifying hoaxes and pseudonyms; E. K.'s unstinted praise of and uncanny familiarity with the published and unpublished works of Spenser and Harvey; biographical evidence that Spenser was in London when the *Calender* was in press; the fact that Edward Kirke is never mentioned by Spenser and neither Edward Kirke nor E. K. by Harvey; the many patent advantages of the anonym E. K.; the ingenuity of the poet in appearing to make the editorial role of E. K. consistent; the palpable blinds of E. K.; the common sources of Spenser and E. K. in contemporary Latin dictionaries and in Badius' gloss on Mantuan; the striking similarity of two passages in reference to Petrarch and to Cicero in the Spenser-Harvey Letters and in E. K.'s Gloss; the identical error of Spenser and of E. K. regarding the signs of the zodiac; the reappearance of themes and stories in E. K.'s Gloss in the poetry of Spenser; the identical errors in classic myth in the *Calender*, in other poems of Spenser, and in E. K.'s Gloss; the identity of learning and of literary convictions of both Spenser and E. K.; the correct glossing by E. K. of learned, dialectal, and obsolete Middle English words as well as neologisms of the poet; the mistaken definitions and false etymologies of Spenser and E. K. Everything assigned to E. K. in the *Calender* is, quite as much as the twelve eclogues, the unmistakable projection of the mind of Edmund Spenser. [Jenkins uses every possible argument in favor of identifying E. K. as Spenser; but he omits, or dismisses as deliberate subterfuge on Spenser's part, all the evidence against such an identification.]

[See also Judson, *Life*, pp. 39-40.]

APPENDIX II

AXIOCHUS

PADELFORD (*Axiochus*, pp. 1-29, with some of the typographical corrections made by Freyd, *PMLA* 50. 908). In the *Catalogus Bibliothecae Harleianae*, published by Thomas Osborne in 1744, for which Dr. Johnson wrote the Preface and the Latin descriptions of books, appears the following entry (vol. 3, p. 365, no. 6218): "Dialogue concerning the Shortnesse and Uncertainty of this Life, by Plato, translated by Edw. Spenser 1592." This was the first mention of a work which now proves to be of great moment to students of Spenser. Fourteen years later John Upton brought out his edition of the *Faerie Queene*, and in the course of the Preface (p. ix) remarked: "'Tis not my design to enter into any minute inquiry of his other writings; for that shall be kept for a third Volume; which will contain his Pastorals, Sonnets, etc., together with his View of the State of Ireland, and a translation of a Socratic dialogue, entitled Axiochus or of Death; which is not taken notice of by any Editor of any part of his works." Unfortunately Upton died in 1760 and the projected volume did not appear. [But see note on F. Q. 4. 1. 40. 9 in Book IV, p. 172.]

The next mention of the *Axiochus* is in the list of "Ancient Translations from Classic Authors," which Steevens incorporated in his edition of Shakespeare, 1773. It is entered (1. E_8 verso) as, "Axiochus, a Dialogue, attributed to Plato, by Edm. Spenser, 4to, 1592." Then in William Herbert's edition of Joseph Ames' *Typographical Antiquities*, London, 1785-1790, under the list of books printed in Scotland there appears the following (vol. 3, p. 1512): "1592. Plato's Axiochus: on the shortness and uncertainty of life. Quarto." Contrary to Herbert's usual practice, the name of the printer, etc., is not given and it therefore seems likely that he himself never examined the book with care, if indeed he actually saw it. This work may conceivably be a different translation from the one noted by the Harleian Catalogue, Upton and Steevens, though the sub-title would suggest identity. So much for eighteenth century notices.

In 1805 H. J. Todd published his eight volume edition of *The Works of Edmund Spenser*, and in the Preface (p. clxxii) made the observation: "I should have added, to the present collection, the translation of Axiochus attributed to him, if my endeavours to obtain it had been attended with success." Seemingly all trace of the book had disappeared by that time.

Malone's *Shakespeare*, 1821, vol. 2, p. 274, n. 6, mentions "a translation of Axiocha's Dialogues (*sic*), attributed to Plato, by Spenser, . . . published in 1592." It seems to be an imperfect recollection of Steevens' entry by the younger Boswell who edited this issue of Malone.

The next scholar to mention the *Axiochus* was J. Payne Collier. In the Preface (p. cxlviii) to his edition of the *Poetical Works*, published in 1862, he remarked as follows: "It is also said that another prose work by our poet has not survived, viz. a translation of the Greek Dialogue called 'Axiochus,' on the brevity and uncertainty of human life. If it were ever printed no copy of it is now known,

487

and even the manuscript of it has entirely disappeared. We doubt its present existence."

[Buck (*PMLA* 23. 99) is the next to refer to the work:] "The translation of Axiochus . . . has been assigned to Spenser on insufficient grounds. Until more proof than mere tradition, and the slenderest at that, is adduced, it had better be left as it is, unnoticed."

In the chapter on Elizabethan "Translators" contributed by Charles Whibley of Jesus College to Volume Four of the *Cambridge History of English Literature*, there is the following brief mention of a translation of the *Axiochus* (p. 5): "Of Plato, to be sure, there is little enough. Besides Sir Thomas Elyot's *Of the Knowledge which maketh a wise man* (1533), distantly inspired by the philosopher, immediately suggested by Diogenes Laertius, there is but a version of the *Axiochus*, a doubtful dialogue." In the accompanying Bibliography, the entry appears (p. 439): "Axiochus, a Dialogue, attributed to Plato, translated by Edm. Spencer. Edinb., 1592. This was translated also by A. Munday." An inconsistency is here to be noted between text and bibliography, as the former speaks of one translation, and the latter allows for two, one by Edm. Spenser and one by Munday. The Spenser item is worded as in Steevens's bibliography, save for the mention of Edinburgh as the place of publication. It is almost a certainty that Whibley had not seen the book, and that for his bibliography he pieced together the entries of Steevens and Herbert.

[Carpenter (p. 130)] refers to Upton's remark; quotes the entry in the *Cambridge History*; and notes the following item in [Arber 2. 610] under date of 1 May, 1592: "Cutberd Burbee. Entred for his Copie vnder the hande of master *Watkins Axiochus of Plato* . . . vjd." He also records the following title [see Arber 3. 336]: "P. de Mornay. *Six Excellent Treatises*, 1607," accompanying it with the note: "Contains a translation of the Axiochus, probably the one in question. Copy in the Newberry Library. I plan to reprint this text." Professor Carpenter's untimely death prevented the carrying out of this proposal. He was mistaken, however, in his conjecture that this translation was the one entered by Burbie in 1592.

[In 1931 Padelford secured from W. Heffer and Sons a copy of the *Ax.* of 1592, each leaf inlaid in folio size and the whole bound in at the end of the 1679 folio edition of Spenser's *Works*. He was unable to identify the writer of most of the eighteenth-century manuscript notes in the *Works*; a few, in both *Ax.* and *Works*, are in the hand of one H. Atterbury, during or after whose ownership the volume was bound together in its present form. It came to Heffer from a Shropshire library.]

The *Axiochus* itself is a crude piece of printing. The paper is coarse and thin, the types are well-worn, and the inking is uneven, the dauber having forced an excess of ink on to the margins of the text. The whole equipment of the printer was obviously crude, as any one can see by glancing at the reproductions. Although Heffer described the book as a duodecimo, it was undoubtedly issued as a quarto. This is proved by the facts that there are four leaves to the signature, that the chain-lines run horizontally, and that on leaves A_2, B_2, and C_2 there is a portion of a water-mark—the upper part of a fleur-de-lis—on the inner margins, one fourth of the way up from the bottom. Steevens describes it as a quarto. As the title-page shows, the book was printed in London, and I am unable to throw any light on Herbert's entry of an *Axiochus* under books printed in Scotland. . . .

The publisher was Cuthbert Burbie. This Cuthbert Burbie was not the brother of Richard Burbage, the great Shakespearian actor, as Collier was led to believe, but, as we know from the Stationers Register, the son of Edmund Burbie, a husbandman, of Ersley, Bedford. Presumably Cuthbert came to London when rather young, for he professes to have been a school-fellow of Benedic[t] Barnam, to whom he dedicated the book. Here again search has failed to disclose what school this was. It *may* have been the Merchant Taylors School, for seemingly Burbie's own son attended there. At least, a Cuthbert Burbie appears in the Register of the school, born, according to the entry, in January, 1608 [?], and we know that one of Burbie's two sons was named after his father. The Register, however, does not contain the names of Cuthbert Burbie, Sr., or of Barnam, and it is hardly likely that so pushing a man as Burbie, who must have been somewhere near Spenser's age, since Barnam, his school-fellow, was born in 1559, would have neglected to advance his own prestige by playing up the poet as an "old boy" of his own school. Whatever his education, on December 25, 1583, Burbie was apprenticed to William Wright, the stationer, and served him for eight years, taking up his freedom on January 13, 1592.

He was very obviously an ambitious man, his long apprenticeship had made him thoroughly familiar with the publishing business, and straightway upon his release he launched out on an aggressive publishing career which won him admission to the Livery on July 1, 1598, and, before his early death, which occurred between August 29 and September 16, 1607, an influential voice in the affairs of the company. . . .

He gained his freedom, as stated above, on January 13, 1592. On April 28th he entered his first book: *The firste Sermon of Noahs drunckennes. A glasse wherein all drunckardes may behold their beastlines.* Three days later, on May 1, he entered the *Axiochus of Plato,* and on May 19, *A Direction for Travellers.* With these three books, so varied in appeal, he started his career.

He must have regarded the publication of the *Axiochus,* bearing the name of Spenser, as a veritable triumph. In 1590 Ponsonbie had brought out the first three books of *The Faerie Queene,* and, eager to take advantage of the poet's great popularity, published in 1591 the *Complaints* volume, followed shortly by the *Daphnaïda.* The oft-quoted foreword to the *Complaints* . . . . discloses the difficulty which Ponsonbie met in trying to assemble those minor poems and pamphlets which Spenser left scattered among his friends when he departed for Ireland some eleven years before. Yet Ponsonbie intended to persist in the quest, and to publish other volumes as he was able.

Now what better fortune could have befallen a novitiate, eager to start on a publisher's career, than to gain possession of one of those very pamphlets for which Ponsonbie was searching? The Earl of Oxford himself, the patron of poets, whom Spenser had praised in one of the sonnets to noblemen annexed to the *Faerie Queene* "for the love which thou dost beare To th'Heliconian ymps," may have supplied the copy, which would perhaps explain the inclusion under the same cover, of the *Axiochus* and an address to the Queen by Oxford's page.

That Burbie printed the poet's name on the title-page as "Edw. Spenser" rather than "Edm. Spenser," and as "Edward Spenser" in the address "To the Reader" is not surprising, in view of the fact that Spenser's full name had not appeared in any of his works published prior to 1592. From the title-page of the 1590 *Faerie Queene*, the author's name is omitted altogether, but in the Dedication to Elizabeth and in the "Letter of the Authors," it appears as "Ed. Spenser." On the title-pages of the *Complaints* and the *Daphnaïda* and in the Dedication of the *Daphnaïda* it appears as "Ed. Sp." and in the Dedication of the *Complaints* merely as "E. S." Indeed as late as 1599 the commendatory sonnet beginning "The antique Babel, Empresse of the East," prefixed to the English translation of "The Commonwealth and Government of Venice," is signed "Edw. Spencer."

Unfortunately the "sweet speech or Oration, spoken at the Tryumphe at White-hall before her Maiestie, by the Page to the right noble Earle of Oxenforde" is missing [from Padelford's copy of *Ax*. The "Tryumphe at White-hall" can hardly have been that held on 15/16 May, 1581. Oxford took part in tilts on 16 May, 1571; 22 January, 1581; and 17 November, 1584.

Benedict Barnam, to whom Burby dedicated *Ax*., was educated at St. Alban's Hall, Oxford, was a liveryman of the Drapers' Company, became a London alderman in 1591, served as sheriff in the same year, and belonged to the Society of Antiquaries. He died 3 April, 1598, at the age of thirty-nine. One of his daughters married Mervin, Lord Audley and Earl of Castlehaven; Alice, the second, married Bacon.] Burbie properly regarded Barnam as a man of sufficient consequence to lend dignity to his undertaking.

When did Spenser make the translation and what induced him to undertake it? Presumably it was one of the "pamphlets" written before the poet's departure "over seas" in 1580, or he would have been able to furnish his own printer with a copy. Again, it is a moral dialogue and associates itself with the Old Testament translations mentioned by Ponsonbie. Moreover a middle aged poet would hardly have set aside the writing of his *magnum opus* to do an exercise in prose translation, however well he might be able to execute it. Translation was, rather, one of the disciplines by which the poet prepared himself for more ambitious literary work. Finally, as we shall see later, there are stylistic qualities that point to early authorship.

In the choice of this particular dialogue for translation, Philippe du Plessis de Mornay and Sir Philip Sidney may have influenced Spenser, directly or indirectly. [Mornay, a young Huguenot noble, was in England in the spring of 1572 and from May, 1577, to June, 1578. During the second visit he became a warm friend of Sidney's. His *Discours de la Vie et de la Mort*, translated into English by Sidney and the Countess of Pembroke, was published by Ponsonby in 1592.]

Whether or not Spenser met Mornay depends on Spenser's whereabouts from May, 1577 to June, 1578. He had not yet come into the employ of Sidney's uncle, the Earl of Leicester. But he of course knew the *Discours*, and in the following year when, as we know, Spenser and Sidney were thrown together, he must have learned that Sidney intended to translate it. Moreover Mornay may well have been engaged in translating the *Axiochus* while in England, since his residence there gave him leisure for study and writing, and he may thus have influenced Spenser to undertake an English translation. Be that as it may, Spenser's translation shows no indebtedness whatever to the French version, which was very literally rendered, though with important omissions.

APPENDIX II 491

[Mornay's translation was published in 1581 and again in 1595. In 1607 appeared an English version which was made from Mornay's; this may have been the work of Anthony Munday; it has no connection with Spenser's English translation of 1592.]

Although, as suggested above, Mornay's interest in the *Axiochus* may have prompted Spenser to make an English version, no such hypothesis is necessary, for though the fact has escaped historians, the *Axiochus* was extremely popular in the sixteenth century. Indeed it is probably safe to say that no other Greek work was more frequently translated or more widely read. By most scholars it was attributed to Plato, although its authenticity was already being questioned. Thus Marsilio Ficino, as early as 1497, assigned the dialogue to Xenocrates. Modern scholars are agreed that the authorship is unknown. It may be based upon an earlier dialogue by Aeschines.

Prior to 1592, the *Axiochus* had appeared in a Latin text translated by the eminent Dutch humanist, Rudolphus Agricola (Roeloff Huysman), first published in 1477, with subsequent editions in 1493, 1506, 1511, 1515, 1518 (two), and 1532; in another Latin text translated by Marsilio Ficino, in editions of 1497, 1498, 1507, 1510, 1515, 1516, 1532, and 1549; in a third Latin text translated by Wilibaldus Pirckheymer, published in 1523; in a French version of approximately 1537-9, translated, according to La Croix du Maine, by Guillaume Postel . . . ; in an edition of the Greek and Latin, the work of Joachimus Perionius, an Italian humanist, published in 1542, and subsequently in 1543 and 1545; in a second French translation by Etienne Dolet, which appeared in *Le Second Enfer*, 1544; in an Italian translation by Don Giovanni Vincentio Belprato, Count of Aversa, 1550; in another version of the Greek and Latin, prepared by Rayanus Welsdalius, which appeared in 1568; and finally in Mornay's translation of 1581. It is thus seen that, despite the silence of historians of literature on this point, the dialogue was extremely popular in the sixteenth century. Indeed, in England it was seemingly used as a school text, for the particular copy of Perionius from which I have worked shows the Greek heavily larded with cribs and one of the margins is decorated with that type of aimless drawing which a tired schoolboy employs to relieve the ennui of a weary task.

[Padelford has compared Spenser's translation with Agricola's (1518), Ficino's (1497), Pirckheymer's, Postel's, Perionius's (1542), Dolet's (1840), Belprato's, Welsdalius's, and Mornay's (1581).]

The comparison proves beyond any question that Spenser employed the text of Welsdalius and that he relied upon the Latin rather than the Greek. This does not necessarily mean that he ignored the Greek which appeared in parallel columns, but there is not a single phrase or word in which he followed the original at the expense of the Latin [but see notes on 17-8, 185-97, 204). . . . To be sure, each of the Latin translators after Agricola was influenced by the work of one or more of his predecessors, so that Spenser's version sometimes recalls the phrasing of Agricola, Ficino, Pirckheymer or Perionius, but in all such instances Welsdalius obviously exerts the immediate influence. There is no evidence that Spenser had seen the Italian version or any one of the French versions. Indeed, the translations of Postel and Dolet were probably rare, even in the sixteenth century. The fact that Dolet's translation furnished the basis for the unwarranted charge of atheism, one of the three grounds on which the author was arrested in 1544, and condemned and executed in 1546, probably implied the speedy suppression or disappearance of *Le Second Enfer.*

[Padelford quotes seven short passages from the *Ax.* of 1592, followed in each case by the equivalent passages in the Greek, as printed by Welsdalius, and in the nine translations named above.]

These passages, chosen more or less at random, leave little if any room for doubt, first that Spenser used Welsdalius' edition, and secondly that he translated from the Latin rather than the Greek. But still more convincing evidence of the first conclusion is furnished by the sub-title which immediately precedes the text in Spenser's version: "a Dialogue of Death, being both short and very Elegant," for this is an exact translation of the sub-title — both in the Greek and Latin — employed by Welsdalius . . . , a sub-title which is not to be found in any other version.

A comparison of the Latin version with the English will show how much Spenser improved upon his original. It is hardly an exaggeration to say that he transformed a rather uninspired dialogue into a prose poem of beauty and feeling, rapid, imaginative, and musical. Prosaic and unadorned statements are reclothed with colorful phrasing, at times perhaps somewhat too ornate, and the literal and matter-of-fact, through personification and verbs of action, changed into the metaphorical and picturesque. Moreover alliteration, antithesis, and balanced phrasing are constantly employed, and the sentences, often long, are yet clear and flowing. Though handled with an ease, fluency and assurance which bespeak a thorough command of the original, the English version is so amplified and embellished that at times it amounts almost to a paraphrase.

For the student of Spenser it is interesting to note how many characteristic words and phrases are to be found in this dialogue that keep echoing throughout the poetry. [For the examples Padelford cites see the commentary of the present edition.]

The attentive reader will detect passages which fall into rhythmical patterns, notably the iambic five-stress verse, a characteristic which the *Axiochus* shares with the *View of the Present State of Ireland.* [See Osgood in Appendix V.] It is . . . further evidence, if such were needed, of the Spenserian authorship of the *Axiochus.*

It has been remarked above that the translation was probably an early undertaking. To be sure, the alliteration, the antitheses, the balanced sentences, and the tendency to overdecoration are Euphuistic, and the first part of *Euphues* did not appear until 1579; but it must be remembered that Lyly only "hatched the egges that his elder friendes laide," for Lord Berners, Cheke and Ascham all made use of parallelism, repetitions and rhetorical questions, and George Pettie, in *The Petite Pallace of Pettie his Pleasure* (1576), employed, as J. W. H. Atkins (*Cambridge Hist. of Eng. Lit.* 3. 348) observes, "all the structural, and most of the ornamental, characteristics of Euphuism."

But the strongest evidence of early authorship is furnished by the translation of the snatches of poetry. [See note on 188-93.]

The fickleness of fortune, the hardships of the earthly pilgrimage, the grim certainty of death were constantly recurring subjects in Tudor literature. They were the dominant themes of those religious and moral treatises that bulked so large in the output of the press, and they persistently intruded even into the literature designed to entertain, revealing how such considerations engrossed the minds of men. The recovery of the writings of the Stoic philosophers, however, introduced a fresh point of view and inculcated in the morally serious an attitude of heroism in confronting the issues of life and death that Christian doctrine, as currently expounded, was neglecting to cultivate. The appeal of the *Axiochus* was of such a character. The treatise of Mornay *Concerning Life and Death* went even further, and harmonized Stoic philosophy and Christian precept. It is interesting to reflect upon the extent to which the translation of the *Axiochus* in his formative years may have influenced the future outlook of the poet. Be that as it may, this youthful exercise reveals habits of phrasing which persist to the very last cantos of the *Faerie Queene*.

DAVIS (*MLR* 30. 519-20). The evidence for assigning this work to Edmund Spenser amounts, perhaps, to seventy per cent.... The lack of any reference to the translation in the Spenser-Harvey correspondence and in Ponsonby's enumeration of Spenser's lost works render the evidence for amending Burbie's title-page [to read *Edmund* Spenser] still inconclusive.

BUYSSENS (*Revue Belge de Philologie et d'Histoire* 14. 132-3) notes that *Ax.*, in spite of its subtitle, does not really deal with the idea, fashionable in the sixteenth century, of the shortness and uncertainty of life. He is not convinced that the recovery of the Stoic writings of antiquity inculcated an attitude of heroism and moral seriousness which Christian doctrine neglected; Protestant readers were already acquainted with 1 Corinthians 15. 55, and many of Calvin's ideas which were impregnated with Greek thought were known in England. "Nous ne nous rappelons pas avoir rencontré chez Spenser aucun passage rappelant les idées de l'Axiochus, à savoir, que nous ne devons pas craindre la mort parce que nous avons une âme immortelle qui par la mort quittera ce monde de misères pour un monde de félicité. [But see *Doleful Lay* 61-96.] Si Padelford connaissait un tel passage il le citerait, au lieu d'ajouter cette phrase creuse: 'It is interesting to reflect upon the extent to which the translation of the Axiochus in his formative years may have influenced the future outlook of the Poet.' Cette influence n'est pas perceptible; d'ailleurs, ce dialogue n'a rien de transcendent ni même de particulier."

FREYD (*PMLA* 50. 903-8) refuses to accept Spenser as the translator of the *Ax.* for the following reasons: The reference of Upton in 1758 is not evidence for Spenser since Upton is unreliable; the reference of Steevens in 1773 is too slipshod to be trusted; Herbert does not assign the translation to Spenser; Todd in 1805 (Spenser's *Works* 1. clxxiii) doubted the attribution to Spenser; the reference in Malone's *Shakespeare* in 1821 is muddled and signifies nothing. From 1590 to the end of Spenser's life Ponsonby was his only publisher; since Burby pirated the *Ax.*, we are not to accept his word on the name of the translator, whether Edward or Edmund Spenser. The only positive evidence in behalf of Edmund Spenser is the marginalium by H. Atterbury, otherwise unknown [see note on "*To the Reader*" 3]. Osgood [see Appendix V] notes that the iambic five-stress pattern appears not only in *Ax.*, but in many other prose works by various authors; and his failure to find such a pattern in Spenser's letters is evidence against regarding *Ax.* as an early work of Spenser's. "Spenser himself never attempted to imitate *Euphues*," as the translator of *Ax*. does. The scraps of verse in the translation bear no resemblance to Spenser's early poetry. No evidence has been offered of the influence, Stoic or otherwise, which the dialogue exerted on Spenser. Thus there is no good reason, either external or internal, for ascribing the translation to Spenser. On the other hand, an obvious candidate is Anthony Munday, who called himself a servant of the Earl of Oxford; who frequently used a pseudonym; who was interested in sophistical paradoxes like that in *Ax*. and wrote other books which were published by Burby; who, unlike Spenser, knew no Greek and therefore would be more apt than Spenser to use the Latin of Welsdalius; who was capable of imitating the Spenserian phraseology which appears in *Ax*.; and who, like the translator of the dialogue, habitually doubled the letter *o* in certain words.

PADELFORD (*PMLA* 50. 908-13) replies to the argument in behalf of Munday's, rather than Spenser's, authorship: that the name of Edward Spenser on the title page and in the preface "To the Reader" is presumptive evidence in Spenser's favor; that since the "Sweet Speech" is not extant [but see below], it is idle to conjecture on its authorship; that the epithet "servant" proves nothing on the translator's connection with Oxford; that we do not know when Munday began writing pageants; that the publication of his *Gerileon in England* (1592), although pertinent, is outweighed by other evidence; that Spenser's poetry does contain Euphuistic elements; that if a predilection for doubling *o* is the mark of Munday's authorship, he wrote much of Spenser's poetry as well as the original version of Sidney's *Arcadia*; that Osgood has detected the Spenserian cadence in *Ax*.; that in translating works similar to *Ax*., Munday employs a bungling, jerky style quite unlike that of *Ax*.; that the verse scraps in *Ax*. resemble Spenser's contributions to *Th. W*. in the awkward handling of accent; that *Ax*. is Stoic in its "attitude of heroism in confronting the issues of life and death" and that both Hughes and Renwick have pointed out a strong Stoic element in Spenser's poetry.

JACKSON (3. 995-8) describes a copy of *Ax*., in the Carl H. Pforzheimer Library, which contains the "Sweet Speech" as well as the dialogue, and he gives an excellent facsimile reproduction of the former. Failing direct testimony, he accepts Padelford's case for Spenser as translator of *Ax*. The "Sweet Speech," however, cannot have been written by Spenser since he was not the servant of Oxford and since he was not in England on 22 January, 1581, when the "Sweet Speech" was spoken at a tournament at Whitehall. It must have been the work of either Munday or Lyly. Freyd's arguments in behalf of Munday are not convincing; the easy rhythm and the marked Euphuism of the "Sweet Speech" point rather to Lyly. It is probable that the manuscript of *Ax*. was no longer in Spenser's possession when Ponsonby published *Comp*. in 1590; that Burby found it in transcript; and that to fill out the volume he added to it a trifle by another author, the "Sweet Speech," which is not mentioned in the prefatory matter of the volume or in the Stationers' Register and which is printed on a separate sheet.

SWAN (*ELH* 11. 161-81), building on the evidence supplied by Jackson, arrives at somewhat dissimilar conclusions. He points out that for Burby to issue a work of Spenser's was an unusual procedure; that Burby, from the time he began to publish in 1592, was engaged in numerous illegal transactions and was apparently "a questionable opportunist"; that the printers of the volume, Danter and Charlewood, likewise did illegal work; and that therefore we should demand more reliable proof of authorship than a mere ascription by the publisher. The "Sweet Speech" was certainly written for a tourney held at Whitehall on 22 January, 1581, when Spenser was not in England; furthermore, the style of the "Sweet Speech" is Euphuistic, and "Spenser and Harvey were rather vocal in their condemnation of the euphuistic fashion of composition." Munday, on the other hand, was a prolific writer of pageants; he twice signed himself the *servant* of Oxford and dedicated several volumes to him; he had long and friendly associations with Burby; a dozen of his works were printed by Charlewood, the printer of the "Sweet Speech" in the *Ax.* volume. Furthermore, Munday made a practice of dedicating books to wealthy middle-class people like Benedict Barnam and died a member of the Drapers' Company, of which his father, Barnam, and Barnam's father had all likewise been members; in the enlarged editions of Stowe's *Survey of London* (1618, 1633) Munday added significant references to Barnam and his family. The dedication of *Ax.*, which "was written either by the publisher or by the author," refers to familiarity with Barnam "when sometimes wee were Schollers together"; since Burby was eight years younger than Barnam, he cannot have gone to school with him; Spenser was about seven years older than Barnam; but Munday and Barnam, who seem to have been born within a year of each other, may well have been scholars together, and therefore Munday is probably the author of the dedication. Both the dedication and the address to the reader, which was probably by Burby, admit the inferiority of *Ax.*, "a concession which would have been unlikely and would hardly have seemed to them necessary if Spenser had really been the author." Lyly, moreover, is not so likely a candidate as Munday since he made no other separate translations, had few business connections with Burby, and was six years older than Barnam. Probably, Swan believes, Burby printed *Ax.* with the connivance of its real translator, Munday, who was contented to make a deal; and later when it became apparent that the printed *Ax.* did not make a large enough volume, the "Sweet Speech," also by Munday, was added to it.

EDITOR. My decision to include *Ax.* among Spenser's prose works primarily rests, not on the title page and the preface which ascribe the work to Edward Spenser, but on its resemblance to Spenser's poems and to his *View*. Padelford cited only a fraction of the verbal parallels which demonstrate that the author of those works was almost certainly the translator of *Ax.*; and since the effectiveness of the parallels depends on the number of them which occur in one short translation, many which were not quoted by Padelford have been included in the commentary of the present edition.

The verbal evidence that Spenser translated this dialogue is not, I believe, disqualified by any of the arguments advanced in favor of Munday. The parallels between *Ax.*, published in 1592, and the *View*, written in 1596, dispose of Freyd's suggestion that in *Ax.* Munday may have copied Spenser's phraseology. Swan has brilliantly demonstrated that Munday was in all probability the author of the "Sweet Speech" and of the dedication to Barnam, but it does not follow that he was also the translator of *Ax.* The dedicator was not necessarily either the publisher or the translator; given Munday's intimate connection with Burby, he may very well have written some of the prefatory matter for Burby's piratical publication of Spenser's translation, especially if Munday's own "Sweet Speech" was appearing in the same volume. It is significant that, according to Swan's account, the *Ax.* was set up by one printer; the prefatory matter and the " Sweet Speech," all or part of which were probably Munday's, by another printer. Furthermore, in view of his character as a publisher, Burby's ascription of *Ax.* to Spenser may have no independent value; but we are not justified in assuming that it must be wrong or that it does not serve to corroborate the internal evidence of Spenser's translatorship.

[In an unpublished criticism of the previous two paragraphs Swan argues that, whether or not Munday translated *Ax.*, the verbal parallels with Spenser's accepted works are of little significance since many of them can also be traced in other Elizabethan writers. But no one other Elizabethan writer, so far as I know, supplies so many or such significant parallels with *Ax.* as Spenser does.]

APPENDIX III

A VIEW OF THE PRESENT STATE OF IRELAND

A.

GENERAL CRITICISM

WARE. [See Appendix III, section E.]

KEATING (1. 3, 5). There is no historian of all those who have written on Ireland from that epoch [the Norman invasion] that has not continuously sought to cast reproach and blame both on the old foreign settlers and on the native Irish.

Whereof the testimony given by Cambrensis, Spenser, Stanihurst, Hanmer, Camden, Barckly, Moryson, Davies, Campion, and every other new foreigner who has written on Ireland from that time, may bear witness; inasmuch as it is almost according to the fashion of the beetle they act, when writing concerning the Irish. For it is the fashion of the beetle, when it lifts its head in the summertime, to go about fluttering, and not to stoop towards any delicate flower that may be in the field, or any blossom in the garden, though they be all roses or lilies, but it keeps bustling about until it meets with dung of horse or cow, and proceeds to roll itself therein.

O'FLAHERTY (*Ogygia*, trans. James Hely, 1793, 2. 285, 288). Spectatum admissi risam teneatis amici? .... We cannot but admire the poet's knowledge in domestic affairs! We are astonished at the politician's puerility in history! So Cicero very justly compares those who are unacquainted with the historical transactions of former ages to children.—However, it is not my design at present to refute the false and calumnious assertions of this writer.

TODD (1. cxxiii). The *View of the State of Ireland* exhibits Spenser as a most interesting writer in prose, as well as a politician of very extensive knowledge, and an antiquary of various and profound erudition. It was probably composed at the command of the queen.

CHURCH (pp. 173-5). It is full of curious observations, of shrewd political remarks, of odd and confused ethnography; but more than all this, it is a very vivid and impressive picture of what Sir Walter Ralegh called "the common woe of Ireland" .... Throughout the work there is an honest zeal for order, an honest hatred of falsehood, sloth, treachery, and disorder. But there does not appear a trace of consideration for what the Irish might feel or desire or resent .... where the spirit was to come from of justice, of conciliation, of steady and firm resistance to corruption and selfishness, he gives us no light. What it comes to is, that with patience, temper, and public spirit, Ireland might be easily reformed and brought into order: but ... he too easily took for granted what was the real difficulty. His picture is exact and forcible, of one side of the truth; it seems beyond the thought of an honest, well-informed, and noble-minded Englishman that there was another side.

GROSART (Spenser's *Works* 1. 216-7). This *Veue of Ireland* is a treatise that, had Spenser left no other evidence behind him of statesmanship, of governing faculty, of mastery of a complex problem, of the courage of his opinions, and it must be added of his "thoroughness" of resolve to reduce Ireland into allegiance to England, this should have established all these. The style of his prose is inartificial, not at all laboured. It rises and falls with its passing subject. It has imaginative gleams. It is occasionally perfervid. Every page witnesses to profound research, wide personal observation and inquiry, and sagacious sifting of evidence. It is pleasing to find him with a ready ear for any old ballad or legend or local folk-lore or folk-speech. Let Irish patriotism bray as it may, the *Veue of Ireland* is a noble book by a "Welwiller" in the deepest sense to Ireland.

SECCOMBE and ALLEN (1. 201). The style of the dialogue is flawlessly clear, and the tendency frankly instructive: there is no florid ornament, no playing with words; the poet here shows himself master of a method of prose exposition, which gains in impressiveness from the fact of its simplicity.

MERRILL (pp. 64-5). Spenser's *View* . . . is constructed in so regular a way that it very closely illustrates the typical method of procedure of rather weighty expository dialogues, and invites comparison with the more substantial essay or treatise. The reader who loses himself—happily, to be sure—in the mazes of *The Faerie Queene*, finds here a discourse so clear and coherent in its thought and arrangement that it might seem almost mechanical, were it less filled with an evident earnestness, sincerity, and depth of feeling. . . .

Save for their eager interest in the sufferings of Ireland, no touches of personality distinguish the two speakers. No touches of setting localize the conversation; there is, in a word, no attempt at the dramatic. Hence the method of dialogue was, apparently, chosen only to make the plan seem more appealing, and the discussion perhaps less technical. Spenser does not seek to avoid the firmer structure of the essay; the main lines of his development would be the same in essay-form; but within those larger divisions, he feels, it would seem, that matters of detail are brought out more clearly and naturally through question and answer. And so one speaker questions the other, and the exposition is given by way of answer.

Though it is entirely possible that such a conversation might take place between two high-minded men, keenly interested in the welfare of Ireland, the lack of personality in the speakers almost necessarily occasions a lack of inevitableness in the form. The warmest lover of Spenser must regretfully admit this, with all high appreciation of the glow of sympathy that animates this work.

WARD (7. 239-40). Though some of the historical and philological information may be questionable, the essay furnishes constant proof, not only of a careful study of the people itself, but, also, of a genuine interest in the associations which have always meant so much for its life—conveyed in ballads and legends and folk-lore of all sorts. . . . The style of the essay is businesslike, and the dialogue form is used with ease; though there is far too much talk about the method of conducting the discussion—always a tedious ingredient in any kind of discourse.

APPENDIX III 499

DE SELINCOURT (p. xxxvii). Written with a wide knowledge both of the antiquities of the country and its laws and customs, and a full appreciation of its present condition, this pamphlet is as able a plea as could well be penned for a policy of resolute and remorseless suppression. In its lack of sympathy with the Irish, and its failure to understand the real causes of their disaffection, it is typical of the view held by all Elizabethans and by most English statesmen since.

COVINGTON (*UTB*, Studies in English 4. 37-8). It would seem safe to conclude that Spenser's knowledge of Irish history was fairly wide, although not profound or exact. Its range embraced ancient, medieval, and contemporary Ireland. While in matters of detail, Spenser was often inexact and careless, he displays occasionally indications that he possessed a knowledge of minutiae not to be gained from general reading. His chief reliance for the whole field of Irish history was inevitably Holinshed's *Chronicles*, the one outstanding historical authority for the British isles. But he read—if not always carefully—nearly all the available books on Ireland. Occasionally he adduced facts from more than one authority into a single passage. Besides printed works in English and Latin, he probably made some use of Irish writings, and drew upon Irish legends and traditions. Toward these he was critical, and attempted to discriminate between fabulous narrative, and fact buried in legend. But even legendary material in English histories and chronicles he seems to have accepted as sober fact. Furthermore, he regarded all his historical data from an English point of view. Finally, while at times his adherence to his sources, particularly to Holinshed, is rather close, he seems generally to have depended upon his memory—which was not infallible—for his facts.

LEGOUIS (pp. 22-3). That the poets' poet was in many respects a practical man, by no means unable to cope with crabbed and even ugly problems of his day, we have a ... proof in his *View of the Present State of Ireland*, a pamphlet much in the vein of Machiavelli, which might have won full praise from the notorious Florentine historian. Whatever we may think of the system of pacification recommended by Spenser, of the conquest by sword and famine that he advocates, he shows himself a keen observer of men and customs throughout the book; he aims at efficiency; he never lets himself be disturbed by imagination or feeling. He appears as a close reasoner whose arguments are based on facts and experience, whose plans are developed by means of statistics. Surely, we have here the work of a clearminded, cool-tempered man of action.

Yet, even here the idealist may still be detected. He betrays himself by his very pitilessness; are not often idealists, when they have to deal with human problems, the most unfeeling of men? With their eyes lifted up to the glorious vision that shines in the distance they will run towards it, never caring if they must cut their way through poor suffering human flesh. To purify Ireland from its evils, Spenser would not have hesitated to exterminate the natives. Do not imagine, however, that he utters such ideas with the passion and vehemence of a fanatic. He remains collected and dignified all through. The contrast between the mercilessness of his schemes and the well-bred elegance of his style is perhaps the most characteristic feature of his pamphlet. The thoroughness of his politics was not at all extraordinary for the time, but they seldom found such a gentlemanly, courteous expression.

JONES (*Handbook*, pp. 377-84). The *View* is of interest for both its form and its content. Written in very competent prose, it is perhaps the best example of the expository dialogue in sixteenth century English literature. . . . While the *View* lacks any such picturesque setting or dramatic characterization as we find, for example, in the Platonic dialogues, the author holds our attention throughout by virtue of his lively and varied interest in his subject. The questions and objections of Eudoxus, though contributing little to our information, are not perfunctory, and indeed serve well to point the many topics and exhibit the structure of the work as a whole. The composition is methodical. . . . In the *View* Spenser is both tolerant and uncompromisingly ruthless, both critical and credulous. . . . The contradiction between theory and practice . . . extends to Spenser's historical method.

DAVIS (*Spenser*, p. 74). Seeing that Spenser had nothing to gain from the publication of the *View*, which was not written until ten years after the death of Grey, his treatise must be read not as the special pleading of a sycophant but as a reasoned statement of opinion, supported by first-hand acquaintance with Irish conditions and by such knowledge of law as would be expected of a civil servant in his particular position. The delusion that it was possible to impose upon disunited tribal communities humanistic notions of loyalty to an undivided state was shared by the great majority of ministers in Ireland throughout the sixteenth and seventeenth centuries. The defence of politic expediency by the champion of Platonic justice is not more anomalous than the persecution of heretics by the author of *Utopia*; in each case such inconsistency is the inevitable outcome of contemporary thought and conditions.

RENWICK (*View*, pp. 240-51). Spenser would have been almost unique among his fellows if he had not produced his "platt" for at least a province, and the *View* is distinguishable only by its greater length and more systematic development, its completeness, and the greater skill and stronger literary intention of the writer.

The business of a provincial official is, to show an orderly population, good crops, and a self-supporting administration: how to procure these is the subject of the *View*. Spenser is not merely cursing the Irish and wishing to reproduce English machinery of government: he is critical of the whole regime; Irish, English-Irish, and English alike. And whatever his immediate incentive to write, he was doing it with a considerable body of official information and official opinion before him. He did indeed consult the files and statutes like a good civil servant, but though the Secretary had to know his minute-book, the Black-Book of the Council of Munster, none of his posts trained him to construct a scheme of taxation for the whole of Ireland. That kind of military budget was more Sir Henry Wallop's business. Again, Spenser says he is "no martial man," but he has the strategic geography of all Ireland in his head, he lays down a military plan on almost classic lines, has views on organisation, and knows the grievances of both officers and men. If this plan was Grey's, Spenser had it on paper, or he had a marvelous memory. His relations with the lawyers may have been closer, but his unprofessional survey of courts, laws, and police is thoroughly competent. It is to Spenser's credit that he sets forth his matter so clearly, but that matter was not merely the passing impression of an intelligent minor official or the gossip of the clerks. Some of his points of policy were subjects of legislation as far back as the third year of Edward

II, they can all, or practically all, be paralleled in some official letter or other in his own time, and many of them are commonplaces. . . .

. . . . Spenser was not a pure intelligence any more than another, but a man of his time, his experience a part of him. For all his advocacy of a well-prosecuted campaign, for all the sixteenth-century carelessness of human life accentuated by service in a country where human life has never been highly regarded, for all his English inadaptability to other modes of living, the common impression of Spenser, that he calls only for blood and wishes all the Irish dead, is a misrepresentation.

. . . . Spenser was really interested in Ireland. He liked the country, found in the churls the makings of a good peasantry, and, however much he disapproved of the fighting castes, he praised their gallantry, military aptitude, and horsemanship. The Roman missionaries were emissaries of Antichrist, but he admired without reserve their courage and devotion. To Irish history and poetry he condescends with all the superiority of a humanist, but though these lie outside the great European tradition in which he had been bred, he recognises their value. He condemns the bards, but not for writing bad poetry; and he contributes to Irish history his collections from the most approved historians and anthropologists, and the most modern method of interpretation. In whatever colours he painted Irish life, his outlines tally with those we can construct from Irish sources. It was his business to know it, and however antipathetic both professionally and temperamentally, he knew it pretty well. For Spenser had struck roots. . . . In the state of Ireland he found a conspicuous example of instability. He loved peace, and there was no peace in Ireland. But here at least something could be done. The *View* was a contribution to the problem of government, but the administrative projects, even the dull details of finance, could further the progress of Ireland towards the ideal of *The Faerie Queene*.

For that ideal, war and the routine of government had to be endured. That Spenser's plan is that of the service he belonged to, is beside the point: it is only since Shelley that the poets have been expected to be in opposition. That he did not imagine that English social and political ideals might not appeal to other peoples, only proves him a true Englishman. . . .

The *View* itself is another matter [than Spenser's poetry]. It was a political document of practical and immediate intention, and as such it was recognised by the cautious Warden of the Stationers' Company who refused to take the responsibility of an unconditional entry in the Register, and by the authorities who apparently forbade its printing. Many manuscripts must have circulated, until Sir James Ware printed it in Dublin, dedicating it to Wentworth—not yet Earl of Strafford—then Lord Deputy. That Strafford's policy, if we include those parts of it that his selfish master hindered him from carrying out, agreed so closely with that detailed by Spenser, may be only that it was the traditional policy of the Irish executive, kept alive in the offices—and indeed *ex Hibernia semper aliquid veteris*—but the *View* was printed in 1633, and, of the antiquated Statutes ridiculed by Spenser, three were repealed in 1634. Strafford was too intelligent to neglect this piece of evidence on Irish affairs, but he might have gone beyond it, for he was a statesman, and this is the work of an official — or, as I have suggested, of several officials. Gladstone, if he ever saw it, would scarcely understand it: Disraeli, who is more likely to have met it, might smile grimly and quote himself, " In England, where society was strong, they tolerated a weak government; in Ireland, where society was weak, the policy should be to have the government strong." But John Nicholson would understand parts of it, and Marshal Lyautey, and M. Stalin. It exposes the ideas of men whose business it is to show results, and require only enough political theory to make them feel secure in mind. If then we recall Spenser the poet, it is to praise him that amidst such influences as produced the *View*, he should have retained so human an ideal as he expressed in *The Faerie Queene*, and, indeed, as appears in many places even here; to be glad that his studious turn of mind forced him continually to seek the larger world he could find only in his books; and, most of all, to rejoice that the poet in him was never killed, but remained to do his poet's office of testifying to those things which outlast all the schemes of the politicians.

BLACK (p. 249) calls the *View* "the most valuable contemporary analysis of Irish society in the sixteenth century."

GOTTFRIED (*Transactions of the Wisconsin Academy of Sciences, Arts and Letters* 30. 327-8). In the beginning . . . the *View* served as an authoritative summary of all that was known about contemporary Ireland. On Brehon law, tanistry, kincogish, and a whole body of native institutions; on the galloglas, kern, bards, carrows, landlords, tenants, all the classes of Irish society; on the corruption and incompetence of English officials, high and low; on Tyrone and Feagh MacHugh, rebels of recent memory, and the best plans of campaign against them; on the distribution of permanent garrisons and the apportioning of composition money for their support; on the civil redivision of Irish communities, on the reformation of the Irish church, on the increased powers of the governor; on these and a hundred other issues the *View* offered the most up-to-date and often the most practical information. Even today, although Spenser's material of this kind may now be supplemented and corrected from many other sources, the dialogue retains its value as the most complete picture an Elizabethan has left us of contemporary Ireland; it is, in short, an historical document of the first importance.

But this does not mean that Spenser was in any real sense an historian. What he saw around him with his own eyes and gathered from the words of his fellow officials, perhaps just because it filtered through a layer of contemporary prejudice, he reports vigorously and well; what, on the other hand, he read at haphazard and hastily transcribed from the records of the past, he presents without judgment or accuracy. And the distinction between the two sides of the *View*, the contemporary scene and the material which for Spenser belonged to the historical past, is not merely an affair of his relative success in this passage or that: the dialogue itself underlines the difference. Although the discussion of history is widely distributed, the greater part of it appears in the first half of the *View*; when "antiquities," as they are called, are specifically introduced near the beginning, we are told to expect only such as have a bearing on the present customs of the Irish; and at the close the promise of a second dialogue on antiquities alone shows that in his own mind Spenser thought of them as a subject apart from the evils of Elizabethan Ireland. Furthermore, their connection with contemporary customs is stated and repeated rather than proved; with the possible exception of those which support the Tudor claims upon the Irish crown, none of the antiquities are essential to

APPENDIX III 503

Spenser's real business, the suffering and reformation of the country; some of them, for instance those dealing with the mantle, offset or actually conflict with his picture of a barbarian world; and the deletion of two fairly long historical passages which have survived in single manuscripts [see footnotes on 1152, 1215-1330, 1383-1451] confesses the irrelevance of much similar material. We can only conclude, therefore, that the antiquities are a completely separable element, a kind of historical decoration on the façade of the *View*; if they are also flimsy in character, they cause no weakening of its broad and solid structure.

JENKINS (*PMLA* 52. 352). These harrowing and disillusioning experiences under Grey influenced both the work and character of the poet. They account for the fact that Spenser in the *Veue* exhibits a thorough familiarity with the topography of Ireland. Much of the advice in the *Veue*, especially that concerning the planting of garrisons, depends upon personal observation under Grey. It would now seem possible to take for granted that Irenaeus is not merely Spenser's mouthpiece but the poet himself, and that almost every observation of Irenaeus is from the poet's first-hand experience.

JENKINS (*PMLA* 53. 362). The advice of the author of the *Veue* is therefore not that of the student only but also that of a man "not without experience in the service of the wars." The *Veue's* completeness and systematic development, qualities which make it the most significant Elizabethan document on Ireland, were possible because it is the product of the poet's varied labors and associations with English leaders as secretary, Clerk of the Council of Munster, landowner, and traveller. Considering that Spenser during these hectic years was both witness and actor in some of the world's sternest work, we marvel that the poet in him was never killed. Amid the influences which produced the *Veue* he continued confident that his humane ideals would outlast the plots and schemes of all politicians.

ROLAND SMITH (*JEGP* 42. 515). Investigation makes it more and more evident that Spenser's was something more than an Undertaker's knowledge of Ireland, but that his first-hand familiarity was limited to those portions of Leinster and Munster he was closely connected with. For the rest of Ireland he relied upon his reading and maps and hearsay. His poet's calling led him to a tolerable if not exhaustive acquaintance with native customs and bardic poetry, and his litigation with Lord Roche seems to have caused him to look beneath the surface of the Brehon laws. But if he had finished the projected work on "the Antiquities of Ireland," it is doubtful if it would have been much more than an amusing curiosity. His failure to produce it has meant no great loss to scholarship.

B.

THE DATE AND PLACE OF COMPOSITION

TODD (1. cxxi-cxxviii). That this treatise was finished in 1596, is proved by the date which Sir James Ware has prefixed to it in the first edition of it in 1633, . . . and by the concurrent dates of four manuscripts, which I have inspected [*L, E, D1, C*; but *E* is undated. Todd has also been told that *T* bears the date

1596.]. . . . This treatise . . . wears the appearance of having been composed in England in 1596. [Todd quotes the opening sentence as evidence. See also Grosart (Spenser's *Works* 1. 216).]

CHILD (1. xlvi). This treatise was probably composed in Ireland, and, receiving afterwards a few finishing strokes in England, presented in the earlier part of 1596 to the Queen and the most considerable persons of the court . . . . the work is too elaborate to have been written, as Todd supposes, in the first half of that year.

COLLIER (1. cxxvii-cxxviii). We are led to believe that it was composed in England. . . . At the same time there is nothing to show positively that this "View of the State of Ireland" was not written in that Country, and afterwards sent over to this. That Irenaeus had lately come from Ireland, and was therefore more competent to the task he had undertaken, might be merely a convenient fiction.

JONES (*Handbook*, p. 377). By internal evidence Spenser's *A View of the Present State of Ireland* may be dated 1594-1597. Sir William Russell, alluded to in the dialogue as "the honorable gentellman that now governeth there" [3685-6], served as Lord Deputy in Ireland from August, 1594 to May, 1597.

DAVIS (*Spenser*, p. 53). During his stay in London [in 1596] Spenser was probably completing his *View of the present state of Ireland*, which internal evidence proves to have been written in England some time during the deputyship of Sir William Russell (1594-7).

MARTIN (*PMLA* 47. 137-43) is satisfied that the *View* was written in midsummer, 1596, since 2943-8 refers to the as yet uncompleted Cadiz Expedition of Essex in June and early July of that year [but see note on the same passage]. In support of this explanation he also cites 5247-8 as an allusion to Essex at the time of the Cadiz Expedition.

RENWICK (*View*, pp. 223-4). The date of the *View* is easily determined. It was written in England, as the opening makes clear [4-5], and England is referred to as *here*, Ireland as *there*, with a consistency difficult to preserve if the placing were imaginary [see, *e. g.*, 5248-70]: the Lord Deputy at the time of writing was successor to Sir William Fitzwilliam—Sir William Russell [see 3685-8], who held office from 1594 to 1597. Spenser was in England in 1589-91, 1596, and 1599. Seven manuscripts are dated: one 1590 [*D2*], one 1598 [*H1*], both of which dates are impossible—the second may be the date of the copy—and five (three, if we dismiss two which seem to be copies of a third), 1596 [*C, R, L, D1, T*]. The *View*, then, was written during his second visit, when he published *Colin Clouts Come Home Againe*, the second edition of *The Faerie Queene*, *Fowre Hymnes*, and *Prothalamion*.

We do not know when Spenser arrived, but the second part of *The Faerie Queene* was entered on the Stationers' Register on 20th January, 1596, and that publication was presumably one of his first cares—the first part had been entered within two months of his arrival in 1589. *Colin Clouts Come Home Againe*, which is not in the Register, is dated 1595, and since Ponsonby dated his books from January and not from March, and since the variants in the first edition demand the author's presence during the printing, we may believe that Spenser was in London before the end of 1595. In the *View* Tyrone is spoken of as "in arms" [2994]; he submitted after a fashion in April, 1596. Again, we might have expected some reference to the taking of Cadiz in June, especially as Essex is—somewhat doubtfully—alluded to near the close [5247-8]. That is not very cogent, and Spenser probably shared the general scepticism as to Tyrone's reliability, but such hints lead us to date the *View* early in the year. . . . I suggest that Sir Richard Bingham had read it by November [see note on 4932-4]. Different parts may have been written at different times, but in any case we are safe in thinking that 1596 was the date of the *View* as we have it.

GOTTFRIED (*MLN* 52. 176-80) gives additional evidence for believing that the *View* was written in 1596. Spenser's visit to England extended at least until 1 September, 1596, when he dedicated *F. H.* from Greenwich. The allusion to Essex at the close of the *View* probably refers to the Cadiz Expedition of the summer of 1596 [see note on 5247-8], although Heffner believes that the passage might equally apply to the Island Voyage of 1597. Spenser mentions the depredations committed by two bastards of Lord Roche's [4544-6], depredations confirmed in another document which can be dated May, 1597; the execution of one of Roche's sons is reported on 11 October, 1597 (*C. C. MSS. 1589-1600*, p. 217; *C. S. P. Ir. 1596-1597* 201. 10). Spenser speaks of what may happen after the anticipated death of the Earl of Clancar [4264-7], who is known to have been ailing in October, 1595, and whose death probably occurred at the end of 1596 since it is referred to in a letter from Ireland on 14 January, 1597 (*C. S. P. Ir. 1592-1596* 183. 90, *1596-1597* 197. 83). The *View* commends an unsuccessful attempt by Lord Deputy Russell to capture Feagh MacHugh [3685-8] on 16 January, 1595; the passage was written before Russell's soldiers slew Feagh on 8 May, 1597 (*C. C. MSS. 1589-1600*, p. 225; *C. S. P. Ir. 1596-1597* 199. 28). Heffner likewise identifies Feagh's "late good successes" [3650] as his recapture of Ballinecor on 10 September, 1596; but the context suggests that Spenser may have in mind the raid on Crumlin in January, 1595 (*C. S. P. Ir. 1596-1597* 193. 10, 193. 10. 1; the Four Masters 6. 1597 [see note on 3650-2]). In any event, it is almost certain that Spenser wrote the final portions of the *View* in the second half of 1596 [if we accept the Cadiz Expedition and the death of Clancar as terminal dates]. A possible discrepancy should be noted: in one passage a grant is mentioned which "theare is" of the Castle of Ferns to Sir Thomas Masterson [4181-3], whose death is reported on 15 August, 1590, and whose heir, Richard Masterson, seems to have been in possession of the Castle in 1596 (*C. S. P. Ir. 1588-1592* 154. 7, *JRSAI* 40. 313); but since all the other evidence points to 1596 as the year in which Spenser wrote, it may be assumed that his present tense applies to the grant, not to Sir Thomas Masterson, or that he was not aware of the death of Sir Thomas.

C.

THE TEXT

THE PRESENT EDITION

Spenser's *View* presents textual problems which are far more difficult to solve than those which complicate the study of any of his other works; it is quite possible that in this case we may never know exactly what he wrote. His dialogue, which had been composed in 1596, was entered in the Stationers' Register on 14 April, 1598;[1] for some reason publication did not follow, and it was only in 1633, thirty-four years after Spenser's death, that the first edition was printed. Today there are at least fifteen manuscripts extant, and more of them may at one time have existed or may still exist; presumably, during the period when the *View* remained unprinted, interest in its contents led to the hasty production of many copies. Most of the fifteen manuscripts available for use in the present edition must have been made by 1633; but none of them is known to be in Spenser's hand, and none of them gives an entirely satisfactory text. Furthermore, the better manuscripts reveal that the text of the first edition is very imperfect; and the later editions either reprint the text of the first or are primarily based on inferior manuscripts.

In view of these difficulties the following plan has been adopted in the present edition: The text of the most nearly satisfactory manuscript available is reproduced without other change than the expansion of most of the abbreviations and the omission of marginalia as well as many deleted words. To correct its errors and deficiencies, as well as to supply additional information on the *View*, a complete collation of this text with the wording of three other texts and a selected collation with the spelling and punctuation of the same three texts are given in the footnotes. The footnotes likewise include significant variants which occur in twelve other manuscripts. This plan should enable the reader, if he wishes, to make a thorough survey of four of the most important texts and to find whatever is important in the others; at the same time he will not be compelled to face the whole overwhelming mass of variants which was spawned by scribal carelessness.

For the basic text of the *View* it has been decided to use Ellesmere MS 7041, now in the Henry E. Huntington Library: although this manuscript contains a fair number of scribal errors, it furnishes the most nearly complete text which is available; it has never hitherto been published; and its history can be traced, back through the Ellesmere and Bridgewater collections, to Sir Thomas Egerton, who may have acquired it through his marriage to Alice Spencer, Spenser's Amaryllis, or to whom it may have been directly presented by Spenser himself.[2] For full

---

[1] Arber 3. 111.

[2] The manuscript contains marginal notes in Egerton's hand, and four pages of his notes are laid loosely in the volume. Some of Egerton's books apparently came into his possession through his marriage to Alice Spencer (J. Payne Collier, Preface of *A Catalogue . . . of the Library at Bridgewater House*, London, 1837). The presence of the manuscript in the Bridgewater Collection is noted by Todd in 1805 (Spenser's *Works* 1. cxxi) and by Collier in 1862 (Spenser's *Works* 1. cxxvii n).

collation with the wording of the Ellesmere MS three texts have been chosen: MS 188. 221 in Gonville and Caius College, Cambridge, one of the most satisfactory texts, although it omits two considerable passages; MS Rawlinson B 478 in the Bodleian Library, a careless text but not without importance since this was the manuscript submitted for publication in 1598;[3] and the first printed edition, which was apparently based on more than one manuscript, which was badly doctored by the editor, Sir James Ware, but which has an historical interest as the standard version of the *View* from 1633 until the last third of the nineteenth century. Of the twelve remaining manuscripts, those of which a limited use is made in the footnotes, the most valuable is that in the Public Record Office (State Papers 63. 202, Part 4, item 58); certain passages in it, which do not appear in any of the other manuscripts available, may have been derived from a first sketch of the *View* which Spenser later revised; the present edition includes all of these passages.

The Genealogy of the Manuscripts

Certain demonstrable relationships exist among the following manuscripts:

A   British Museum, Additional MS 22022.
C   Gonville and Caius College, MS 188. 221.
D1 Cambridge University Library, MS Dd. 10. 60.
D2 Cambridge University Library, MS Dd. 14. 28(1).
E   Henry E. Huntington Library, Ellesmere MS 7041.
F   Folger Shakespeare Library, MS 6185.
G   Bodleian Library, Gough MS, Ireland 2.
Ho the Arthur A. Houghton MS.
H1 British Museum, Harleian MS 1932.
H2 British Museum, Harleian MS 7388.
L   Lambeth Palace, MS 510.
N   National Library of Ireland, MS 661 (Gurney MS).
P   Public Record Office, State Papers 63. 202, Part 4, item 58.
R   Bodleian Library, MS Rawlinson B 478.
T   Trinity College, Dublin, MS E. 3. 26.

E and *C*, the two manuscripts which seem to come closest to Spenser's completed text, are clearly related in origin. At eight of the points at which new pages begin in *E*, there are also page divisions in *C*:

$11^v/12^r$] 26/27 *C* $29^v/30^r$] 64/65 *C* $80^r/80^v$] 168/169 *C*
$16^v/17^r$] 37/38 *C* $35^v/36^r$] 77/78 *C* $95^r/95^v$] 197/198 *C*
$27^v/28^r$] 60/61 *C* $77^v/78^r$] 164/165 *C*

Moreover, these two manuscripts agree in many readings which do not occur in the other available texts. For example, *E* and *C* alone read:

---

[3] On the last page Thomas Man, Warden of the Stationers' Company for 1597-1598, notes over his signature, "Master Collinges I pray enter this Copie for mathew Lownes to be prynted whenever he do bringe other attoryte."

35 rather *for* rather then [4]
638 proposed *for* purposed *or* promised
693 Inhabitaunce *for* inhabitantes
1780 Comminge *for* rvnninge
1842 *blank space for* boyle *or* draw
2227 and vild *for* wylde *or* and wilde
2409 moote *for* meete
2524 recured *for* recouered

2710 peculier *for* particuler
3228 advicement *for* advertisement
3274 Accion *for* Nation
3708 drawinge *for* dryvinge
4217-8 plowlandes *for* poundes
4433 freholdes *for* freeholders
5226 devised *for* deliuered
5241 grauer *for* greater *or* greate

To this group may be added another which also reveals the close relationship of the two manuscripts. Frequently, where the wording of *E* has been corrected, either by the scribe or an early reader, the words originally written were clearly those which appear in *C*. The following readings, to illustrate, are common to *C* and the uncorrected text of *E*:

588 Graie] *om.*
853 Cesar] *om.*
854 saith] *om.*
1017 Eud:] *om.*
1815 honor] haue
2049 *mangan*] *mangnan*
2122 and ... Cleopatrie] *blank space*

2367 hvrte] harte
2489 in vyllages] *blank space*
2877 Cvrrye] Carrye
3125 Rysing out] *blank space*
3742 espeialles] especialls
3943 cuttinge] *blank space*
5193 that] *om.*

The most interesting example of this relationship occurs in the Greek word which *E* reads "ὁφῠν" (1795) and *C* "ὁφύν" and which the other manuscripts either omit or include in such forms as "Οχε," "οφιχο," and "οφχε." [5] Since Spenser himself translates this as "Chinebone," it is clear that he has in mind the word "ὀσφύν," *i. e.*, back or loin, in the Greek text he is following, although either he or a scribe has dropped the σ. *E* and *C*, in any case, are much closer to what Spenser must have written than are any of the other manuscripts; and, in spite of the opportunities for variation in transcribing Greek handwriting, they alone agree on the letters which form the word.[6]

The evidence cited might suggest that *E* was copied directly from *C*, or *C* from *E*; but neither of them can actually have been the source of the other. *C* omits two considerable passages, one of them more than two pages long, which are included in *E* (875-940, 954-62); *E*, on the other hand, omits two passages, one of thirteen and one of twenty-two words (4877, 4985), which are included in *C*. Moreover, a fair number of small mistakes which occur in *C* and *E* do not appear, respectively, in *E* and *C*. The only possible conclusion, therefore, is that the two manuscripts derive, not one from the other, but both from a common source; in fact, it is probable that they were copied from the same manuscript.

The two passages which *C* omits are indicated in *C* itself by blank spaces, and

---

[4] The numbers which accompany these and subsequent readings from the text of the *View* refer to lines of the present edition.

[5] Renwick transcribes "οφεα" in *C* (*View*, p. 326) and amends the text of *R* to read "ὀσφύς" (pp. 75, 306). For the present transcription I am indebted to Professor V. B. Schuman of Indiana University.

[6] Professor D. D. Griffith of the University of Washington notes that Professor Heffner intended to use this word to determine the relative values of the manuscripts.

the longer of these ends at a page division (37/38) and just at the point where a new page begins in E (16ᵛ/17ʳ). Both of the passages may be omitted without damaging the argument, and it is likely that they were marked for omission, perhaps by Spenser himself, in the manuscript from which E and C were made; that the scribe of C therefore omitted them but left blank spaces so that they could be added later if necessary; and that the scribe of E preferred to include them from the first. E and C contain further evidence of having been copied from the same manuscript: Where E reads "sorte" (981) and C "Chorte," the other texts have what must be the correct word "Churle"; probably the scribe of the manuscript used by E and C wrote "Chorle," but his *l* must have been easily mistakable for a *t*; as a result C has the impossible form "Chorte," and E kept the *t* but attempted to make sense by changing the word to "sorte." In the same way, where the other manuscripts read "seated," C has "seate" and E "state" (1317); probably their source spelled the word "seatd"; yet the final *d*, as often happened, had exactly the appearance of a final *e*, and therefore the scribe of C wrote "seate," while the scribe of E tried to correct the word by making it "state."—These cases, of course, are concerned with probability rather than proof; but they serve to make it clear how close is the connection between E and C.

* * *

The most valuable of Renwick's contributions to the text of the *View* is his theory that P contains fragments of an early, unrevised version of the dialogue. He writes of the passages in P which correspond to 1169-95, 1215-1330, and 1383-1451 in E:

> It will be noticed that (1) the reference to St Patrick is quite wrong, and that the additional points are either irrelevant to the main argument or are better dealt with otherwise: they are such things as would be altered on revision. It is difficult to believe that they are additions by another hand; the only motive would be the filling-up of missing pages, and the intrusive matter is too intricately mixed with regular text to allow of that: nor are they mere additions. (2) The reference to "all those families which you name" shows that something has already been cut out. (3) The passage from "For yf ther were anie such notable transmission ..." to "... anie such Gathelus of Spaine" is, though differently introduced and in a different place, the passage on page 27 of Ware's edition [footnote on 1152] which he directed to be "crossed out, as being then agreeable to the best MS Copie." The Caius and Bodleian MSS [C and R] have a blank space just after the tale of Morrough O'Brien's execution [1942], which may be due to an inadvertence in the archetype; but the scribes are at pains to leave it: the Caius and P. R. O. MSS [C and P] are connected by identical omissions in another part [875-940, 954-62]. I surmise that Spenser originally wrote more history, and then cut it down, after the work was completed, to preserve the balance of the whole; and that copying from his MS began before it was finally fair-copied, so that some partly-revised matter was included in the P. R. O. MS, a scrap of it in Ware's, and a blank page or so was left at the end of the section. The mysterious *Africans* who appear in the final text (and trouble some of the copyists who find no reason for their presence [1466, 1588]) are a vestige of the original longer version.
>
> In the P. R. O. version, again, there is "hither" meaning "to Ireland" (so also in Caius and T. C. D. [C and T], but "thither" in the rest), and a

"here" or two, which suggests that Spenser had written his first version in Ireland; and not in dialogue form, since he speaks of "the reader." He had drawn upon Campion's MS . . . and the Book of Howth, both of which were in Ireland. The revision was done with Buchanan, Camden, and Holinshed at hand; Spenser needed to go no further for most of his citations of other authorities. He had indeed looked up Solinus and Pomponius Mela, and he had read Boemus, Lucian, and the *Libellus de Vita Homeri* recently, but Olaus Magnus, Herodotus, and Diodorus Siculus were vague memories cited somewhat at random. The conjecture may be permitted that Spenser brought with him from Ireland some historical notes—there are parallels enough among the Harleian MSS—which he used for the *View* and then revised in a library. Even as it is, there are blank spaces in all texts, and plain errors of fact, that suggest that another revision was intended.[7]

The carelessness which Renwick cites as proof that *P* contains fragments of an earlier version is revealed by other details: in the first paragraph of the passage which corresponds to 1215-1330 in *E*, Irenius declares that the Britons and the Gauls, as well as the Scythians and the Africans, peopled Ireland; yet Eudoxus immediately asks if all Ireland was peopled by no other nation than the Scythians and the Africans. This mistake, the spaces left for omitted names, and the absurd Carthaginian etymologies which occur in *P* alone, along with the evidence cited by Renwick, leave no doubt that we are dealing with a partially unrevised text.

In revising, however, Spenser did more than cut out historical material, as Renwick suggests. The passages 1169-95, 1215-1330, and 1383-1451 are twice as long as those which they replace in *P*; if the discussion of the Africans has been omitted, Spenser has added a list of his sources and a much fuller discussion of the Gauls. The expansion of some sections may also have been offset by abridgment elsewhere: at least six of the manuscripts contain the blank space which, as Renwick notes, occurs immediately after the account of Murrogh O'Brien's execution (1942); but since *P* is one of these manuscripts, it is possible that the text at this point had already been abridged before *P* was copied.

Although *P* represents an early, partially revised text, it also has affiliations with several of the later manuscripts. The existence of a general group to which it belongs is indicated by readings like the following, which it shares with *E*, *C*, *G*, and *T*:

> 1638-9 her mantells . . . Combred [*om. in others*]   2714 Common *for* other
> 3954-5 which shall . . . rented [entred *T*] *for* I will rate

Certain readings in *P* are common to some but not all members of the group:

> 1774 *blank space E C P* [*om. in others*]
> 2186 belonginge] appertaining *G P T*
> 2262 vsuall songe *for* vsuallie sounge *E C G P*
> 2623 Iawes *for* handes *E C P*
> 2730 pleasethe him *for* he listeth *E C G P*
> 4784 pillowe *for* piller *E P T* [pilloe *or* pillre *C*]
> 4944 one *for* acte *E C P T* [8]

---

[7] *View*, pp. 263-5.
[8] It should be noted that *T*, although it gives a careless text in general and may be a late

APPENDIX III   511

In a number of cases C and P have the same or similar readings which appear in no other texts:

    443 iiijth] seconde *C P*
   1675 Habbub] h *and blank space C   blank space P*
   4790 mayntaine] conteyne *C P*
   5183 theareof] therof to sell the same againe *C P*

And P omits the two long passages which C omits (875-940, 954-62).

But P is more extensively related to G than to any other single manuscript, as a few of the readings which appear only in these two will serve to illustrate:

    522 of the lacies and] *om.*
    599 xiij] 14
  2004 sicknes] sickness they say
  2423-4 as . . . danes] *om. and inserted after* arose *in 2426*
  2713 goe like laye men, live like laye men] *om.*
  3163 ketinges and Kellies] ketis
  3281-2 And on And . . . vnspente] *om. and* whatsoeuer they leave unspent
       inserted after likewise *in 3283*
  3484 for . . . daies] *om.*
  4110 *Loughearne*] Logh carne
  4384 quinche] quitch

P, then, stems from an earlier draft of the *View* than do any of the other manuscripts, and yet it is closely related to E, C, T, and particularly G.[9] It would seem to follow, as a corollary, that E, C, T, and G stem from a draft of the *View* which was closer to what Spenser actually wrote than were the drafts on which were based those manuscripts which apparently have no connection with P.

            *   *   *

If anything can be asserted about the remaining manuscripts, it is that R, L, and D1 form a closely related group.[10] The readings which they have in common,

---

copy, is perhaps related to *E*: these two manuscripts, and only these, read "Herodetus" in 1791 and omit thirteen words in 4877; on the other hand, *T* includes twenty words *E* omits in 4985. Unlike *E*, *T* is dated "1596" at the end of the text.

[9] *G*, the Gough MS, is important, not only for its connection with *P*, but also because it seems to have been prepared for publication (see Heffner, *MLQ* 3. 509-11). Heffner, however, once noted that both handwriting and spelling indicate that *G* is a late copy; and it lacks more than one seventh, the whole final section, of the *View*.

[10] *R*, *L*, and *D1* all have the date "1596" at the end of the text. The back cover of *L* contains the note "This is m^r Thomas Perrins boke Concerning Ireland" and several more words, which are indecipherable. The names "Iohēs: Panton Lincoln." and "Richard Bagnett his Booke" are written on the first leaf of *R*, and at the top of the first page of the manuscript appears "Io: Panton 1596." The latter signature is almost identical with that of a certain John Panton which occurs frequently among the Ellesmere MSS in the Huntington Library, and there can be no doubt that *R* at one time belonged to him. Panton's admission to Lincoln's Inn is recorded: "1594 May 29 John Panton, of co. Denbigh, at request of Sir Thos. Egerton, Master of the Rolls"; in the meeting of the council of Lincoln's Inn on 3 November, 1594, it was decided: "At the request of Thomas Egerton, knight, Master of the Rolls, Mr Panton, a gentleman of this Society, attending ordinarily upon the said M. R., whereby he cannot continue in commons, shall have a special admission" (*The Records of*

and which appear in none of the other manuscripts, are numberless; and it is characteristic of this group that the evidence consists almost entirely of omissions and obvious mistakes. To cite only scattered examples:

118-9 it ... vnknowen./] *om.*	2958 boughes] lawes
467 fearne] farme	3483-4 That ... to] *om.*
860-1 dislike ... of] *om.*	4072 two thowsande] iij^m
1148 derived] deuided	4308 *Corke.*—l] *Corck* 100
2029-30 remayned ... is] *om.*	4860 Oes] Othes
2402 advantage] tagge	4861 mackes] markes
2634 *Paladius*] *Pallidus*	5289 exportacion] expectacon

The great number of their common mistakes makes it almost certain that all three manuscripts were directly copied from a single source or that one of them was the immediate source of the other two. Renwick, in fact, believes that both *L* and *D1* were transcripts of *R*;[11] Heffner, on the other hand, was convinced that *R* was transcribed from *D1*.[12] Since neither Heffner nor Renwick supports his opinion with evidence, it will be worth while to consider the relevant passages.

In a few cases *R* gives readings which are inferior to those of *D1* and which might therefore be taken to prove that *R* was copied from *D1*:

1596 an] *om. R*   an *D1*
3656 to *strangbow*] to Stanbowe *R*   to Strangbow *D1*
4162 breede] bread *R*   breede *D1*
4886 are] care *R*   are *D1*

Similarly, in two passages *L* and *D1* agree in readings which are superior to *R*'s:

3772 nescit] *om. R*   nescit *L D1*   4224 kepe] *om. R*   keepe *L D1*

But it is not necessary to assume that an inferior reading in *R* proves that *R* was copied from *D1* or *L*. The mistake which *R* makes in each of these cases is obvious

---

the Honorable Society of Lincoln's Inn, *Admissions*, 1896, 1. 117; *ibid.*, *The Black Books*, 1898, 2. 39). The references to Panton among the Ellesmere MSS show that he was the confidential agent of Egerton (see, *e. g.*, MS 208), and this suggests a possible connection between *R* and *E*, Egerton's own manuscript of the *View*; but neither can have been copied from the other.—It is also probable that *R* may at one time have belonged to Sir James Ware, the first editor of the *View*: in 1686, when Henry Hyde, Second Earl of Clarendon, was Lord Lieutenant of Ireland, he purchased Ware's manuscripts, and in 1697 Clarendon's library contained a manuscript listed as " *Edm. Spencer's* present State of Ireland, 4to." (*Catalogi Librorum Manuscriptorum Angliae et Hiberniae*, 1697, vol. 2, part 2, p. 12). After Clarendon's death in 1709 his collection was divided, part of it, through Richard Rawlinson, reaching the Bodleian in 1755 (*DNB*, article on Ware by Norman Moore). MS Rawlinson B 479, which immediately follows *R* in the Bodleian catalogue, was drawn up by Ware and can be clearly identified as the item which follows the manuscript of the *View* in the Clarendon catalogue of 1697 (*loc. cit.*; *Catalogi Codicum MSS Bibliothecae Bodleianae*, Part V, 1862). Furthermore, many of the Rawlinson manuscripts containing Irish material are known to have once belonged to Ware (William Dunn Macray, *The Annals of the Bodleian Library*, Oxford, 1868, pp. 175-6). But, if it is likely that Ware owned *R*, he does not seem to have used it in preparing the text he published in 1633.—For the unsuccessful attempt to publish *R* in 1598, see the first part of this appendix.

[11] *View*, p. 307.
[12] *MLQ* 3. 509-10.

APPENDIX III

and could easily be corrected by the copyist of *D1* or *L*, working from *R*; in fact, "kepe" (4224) is omitted in *L*, as in *R*, but added later, and the incorrect reading "care" (4886) appears in *D1*, as in *R*, but is corrected to "are." On the other hand, there is irrefutable evidence that *R* preceded *L* and *D1*.

L and *D1* omit the following passages which occur in *R*:

2524-5 afterwardes . . . happelye	5216-7 of which . . . Townes
2764 or . . . wringe him	5278-9 they haue . . . happie
2951 nor . . . them	

These omissions reveal, not only that *L* and *D1* are subsequent to *R*, but that *L* is probably copied from *D1* or *vice versa*; in fact, the omission of the following passages in *D1* and not in *R* or *L* indicates that *D1* is subsequent to *L* as well as *R*:

131-2 him . . . vnto	3895-6 thoroughe . . . Countrye
431-9 that . . . gotten	3902-3 *Eudox*: . . . same/
661-2 And . . . iuste	4416-7 and . . . for the Englishe
1317 of . . . state	4772 maye dwell togeather
2179-80 wheare he describeth	5029-30 and . . . thearein

The derivation of *L* from *R* and of *D1* from *L* is confirmed by a large group of such readings as these:

660 *Ius Politicum*] Ius Pollicium *R L*   in pollicie *D1*
952 idle] *om. R L*   gone *D1*
1082 kincongishe] *Kincougish R L*   Kincorgishe *D1*
2066 Lordes] Lords *R*   Lo: *L*   Lord *D1*
2891 *Banno*] Ranno *R L*   Ramo *D1*
3012 Twelue thowsand] 12000 *changed to* 2000 *R*   2000 *L*   200 *D1*
3664 *Glan*] Glan *R*   Slan *L*   Shane *D1*
4262 Ragtaile] ragtayle *R*   roughtayle *L*   roughe tayld *D1*
4309 *Fedard*] Eederd *R*   Eedred *L D1*
4675 drawne] drawen *R om. L*   taken *D1*
4883 reforme] refore *R*   restore *L D1*
4948 Churche] churge *R*   charge *L D1*
5247 ey] key *R L*   Leige *D1*

Furthermore, it is not hard to see why the careless copy *L* was made from the careless copy *R*, and the careless copy *D1* from *L*. *R*, it has already been pointed out, was submitted for publication in April, 1598. At the time, as far as we know, Spenser was not in England, a circumstance which accounts for the attempt to print the *View* from an inferior manuscript. Then, after the dialogue had not been printed, apparently because the authorities had refused permission, or perhaps because Spenser himself had intervened at this point, there must have been a demand for the handwritten text; and thus it is quite natural that the very copy which had been submitted but not printed should be hastily transcribed and the second copy just as hastily transcribed again.

*   *   *

A, *H2*, and *N* form another group of closely related texts.[13] Out of a great many readings which are common to these three manuscripts, and which appear in none of the others, the following may be selected as illustrations:

326 not] *om.*
763-4 and . . . Cawse] *om.*
854 death] danger
1076 Prince] kinge
1570 greate] Auntient
1915 *Guenover*] *Guenora*
1930-2 But . . . people] *om.*
2187 had] had not

3047-8 Chardge . . . infinite] *om.*
3542 Lenagh] *Oneale*
3859-60 that . . . Leinster] *om.*
4090 43920] 43920000
4166-7 So . . . enoughe] *om.*
4528 moreouer] euermore
5237 obsereued] observe

Although *A*, *H2*, and *N* are obviously related to one another, the available evidence does not establish a direct connection between any two of them. *A* is probably a late copy, as Renwick points out;[14] the blank spaces it leaves for many of the proper names and the peculiar phonetical spelling of many of the Irish names it does include show that it can hardly have been the source of *H2* or *N*. Since *H2*, on the other hand, arranges the list of garrison towns (4307-14) in an order unlike that of any other text, it can hardly have been the source of *A* or *N*. And *N* contains a good many readings which are unlike those in the other two. The only safe conclusion seems to be that all three manuscripts stem from one source or from related sources which have been lost.

Furthermore, the source or sources of *A*, *H2*, and *N* must in some way have been connected with *R*, *L*, and *D1*. The two groups have in common a fair number of readings which do not occur in other manuscripts. For example:

908 thinhabitance] the inhabytantes
1243-4 the Irishe] Ireland
2444-6 as . . . stones] *om.*
3549-50 *Eudox*: . . . vndewtifull] *om.*

3735 And as for] or
4571 bene] beinge
5044 which . . . faithe] *om.*
5045-6 to the . . . did] *om.*
5102 grauest] greatest

What, then, it may be asked, is the relationship of the two groups of manuscripts? An answer is suggested by the passage "Hills . . . these" (2417-21), which *R*, *L*, and *D1* omit; part of the same passage ("apointed . . . is," 2417-8) is omitted by *A*, *H2*, and *N*, and they offer a garbled version of the rest; the logical conclusion seems to be that *R*, *L*, and *D1* omit the whole passage because *R*, the first of the group, is trying to correct the obviously faulty text which has survived in *A*, *H2*, and *N*. Thus it is fair to say that *R*, *L*, and *D1* probably represent a modified version of the type of text which is more accurately reproduced in *A*, *H2*, and *N*.

* * *

Only four manuscripts remain for discussion, and two of them are very closely

---

[13] The name of Arthur Chichester, Lord Deputy of Ireland 1603-1614, is signed at the top of the first folio of *A*. The second flyleaf of *N* is inscribed: " *Bartho: Canham*, geserycke [?] *Anno: Domine.* 1625."; and at the end of the text there is the date " 1597."
[14] *View*, p. 308.

APPENDIX III 515

related. *D2* and *F* have a large number of variants in common.[15] To cite a few representative cases:

42 evills] thinges	3264-6 And . . . time] *om. and inserted after* graues *in 3262*
488 and . . . kinge] *om.*	3562-3 *Mackonells*] *Mack honets*
1024 or twoo] and lawe	3743-4 so . . . baytinge him] *om.*
1440 Gurgunt] *Bargunt*	4050 at vj^m] a 7000
1851 reduced] deducted	4312 *Kelles*] *Rells*
2296 partes] persones	4740 Irelande] England
2419 *Folkemotes*] talkemottes	4947-50 adioyninge . . . Scholmaster] *om.*
2925 newe] good	5046 *blank space*] *Golmithe*

The number of the readings common to *D2* and *F* indicates that one manuscript must have been copied directly from the other; there is, in fact, decisive evidence that *F* derives from *D2*, at least in many passages:

466 Thomonde] *Toomonde D2   Tarmound F*
1276 *Praesamarci*] *Praesamarchi D2   Samarchi F*
1521 *Boemus*] *Bormus D2   Boru F*
3542 *Lenagh*] *Renagh D2   Kennaugh F*
4042 *Letrim*] *Lyretrime D2   Liretrin F*
5135 fortilage] forte. villadg *D2*   ford village *F*

H1 and *Ho*, the only manuscripts not yet considered, are largely mavericks. *H1* contains a great many unique mistakes; in particular, it confuses *the* and *they* far more often than do the other manuscripts; and at the end, unlike the others, it contains an exact date, "10^m die Maij anno domini 1598," probably the date on which this copy was completed.[16] If *H1* has a peculiar resemblance to any group of texts, it is to *D2* and *F*:

8 diuerse] manie *F H1*	1712 approvaunce] apparaunce *D2 F H1*
212 some] one *D2 F H1*	3279-80 and Consume in] at *D2 F H1*
592 righte] *om. F H1*	3690 Liex] Lax *D2 F H1*
1143-4 some other time] *om. D2 F H1*	4311 *Ardie*] *Hardie D2 F Hrdie H1*

The evidence does not reveal the precise relationship of *H1* to *D2* and *F*; we know only that *F* was copied from *D2* and that *H1* probably belongs to the same branch of the textual family as they do.

---

[15] Three leaves of *F* are missing (see footnotes on 241-302, 2624-2806). The manuscript is one section of a folio volume which contains a great deal of miscellaneous material on Ireland and which seems to have been connected in some way with the second Earl of Essex; the inner side of the front cover of the whole book contains the note " Die Veneris Iuly 1°, 1601 per me Richardū Greenen." Heffner identifies Greene as the secretary of Essex (*MLQ* 3. 509).

[16] Since *D2* is dated " 1590 " at the end and *F*, which is copied from *D2*, is dated " 1597 " at the end, it is probable that the scribe of *F* intended to show that he completed this copy in 1597.

The genealogy of *Ho* is even harder to determine.[17] At one point (1798) it contains a blank space which appears in only *E* and *P*, at another (4429) a blank space which appears in only *E*; and the words which *E* omits at 4877 occur as exactly one line in *Ho*, a circumstance which might seem to indicate that the scribe of *E*, when he skipped this line, was copying from *Ho*. But since the text of *Ho* is marked by many erratic variants which occur in none of the other manuscripts, it is safe to say that none of them can have been copied from it; and in so far as *Ho* has an affinity with clearly defined groups of manuscripts, it is with *R L D1* and *D2 F* rather than *E C G P T*.

The connection of *Ho* with *R*, *L*, and *D1* is demonstrated by readings which are found in these four manuscripts, and only these. For example:

992-3 Or . . . felonye,] *om.* 2601 well wott] will note
1564 *Herodotus*] Herodus   3356 Smerwicke] Senawicke

Yet *Ho* cannot have been copied from *R*, *L*, or *D1* since it includes the following passages which they omit:

860-1 dislike . . . of   3946-9 rise . . . maie
3061 that . . . be   5110-1 since . . . mayntenaunce

Similarly, *Ho* departs in many cases from the variants which are characteristic of *D2* and *F* as a group; yet a relationship to them and their associate *H1* is revealed in cases such as these:

198 is] his *H1 Ho*   1725 affectacion] affection *D2 F Ho*
619 Carlo] *Carle D2   Earle and*   4108 Clanriccard] *Clarinam D2   Clau-*
   blank space *F   Carles Ho*   *roinam F   Clanriuan H1   Clan*
                                    Rinane Ho
728 saie] sweare *D2 F Ho*   4208 maccachegan] *Machaghegan D2*
                              F Ho
1270 Cales] Cadiz *D2 F H1   Cades*   4813 borrowe] *Burrowe H1 Ho*
   Ho

This evidence obviously does not show exactly what position *Ho* occupies among the other texts. But it suggests one broad deduction: if the groups *R L D1* and *A H2 N* are undeniably related and if *Ho* has a clear resemblance to both *R L D1* and *D2 F H1*, it is quite possible that all ten of these manuscripts form a larger group, stemming from one source which is distinct from that which underlies the group *E C G P T*.

Printed Editions of the *View*, 1633–1934

When Sir James Ware published the first edition of the *View* in 1633, he indicated, in a marginalium on the second page of the Preface, the manuscript on which his text was based: "*Ex Bibliotheca Reverendissimi in Christo patris D.* Iacobi

---

[17] *Ho* contains two bookplates, reading " *Ex libris Bibliothecae Domesticae Richardi Towneley de Towneley In Agro Lancastrensi Armigeri Anno Aetatis: 73 Domini: 1702*" and "*William Horatio Crawforde* Lakelands Cork." It belonged to Sir Israel Gollancz and reached the Houghton collection via the Rosenbach Company in New York (Johnson, p. 53).

APPENDIX III 517

Vsserij *Archiep. Armachani.*" We know that after Archbishop Ussher's death in 1656 the officers of Cromwell's Irish army purchased Ussher's library and that it was deposited, five years later, in Trinity College, Dublin;[18] from this it is natural to assume, as Johnson seems to have done, that in *T*, the manuscript which now belongs to Trinity College, we have the source of the first printed edition.[19] But the assumption is discredited by the fact that no copy of the *View* can be traced in the seventeenth-century list of the manuscripts, among them Ussher's, at Trinity;[20] and a comparison with all the available manuscripts reveals at once that Ware's text is just as close to several other copies as to *T* and even closer to some of them than to *T*.

With *A*, *H2*, and *N*, for example, *W* (*i. e.*, Ware's text) shares some readings which do not appear in the other manuscripts:

840 wronge] wrought	3021 soulde] due
1387-8 for . . . manye] *om.*	3974-5 theare excheate] be there escheated
2977-8 her Chiefe] the chiefest	

But the evidence for this relationship almost entirely disappears in the later sections of the dialogue, where it seems to have been replaced by a connection with the *C G P T* group:

4083 for] to be *C G W*	4670 lx^m] fortie Thowsand *C P T W*
4144 neuer sene] oversene *C G P T W*	5051 travell] traveillinge *C P T W*
4386 established] setled *C G W*	5171 wheareas] when as *C P W*

W shows most affinity to *G* and *P* in this group, as the following readings which are peculiar to these three texts will demonstrate:

568 and Skotlande] *om.*	2945 Quene] Queene, and
1740 Scottes//] *Scots* at this day, as you may reade in their Chronicles.	3111 drinke] Beere
1842 *blank space*] draw	3622 bolde] bad
2292 lewde] bad	3785 stonie] strong
2556 former] firme	3894 planted] placed

In a limited number of cases *W* agrees with *G* alone among the manuscripts, or agrees with *G* where it does not altogether agree with *P*:

91 perhaps] *om. W G*
1209 likenes] likewise *W G*   lykelynes *P*
1878 then] (all Sea men being naturally desirous of new fashions,) then amongst *W G*   all sea men beeinge more naturallye desirous of new fashions then amongst *P*
2901 nexte] now *W G*

But in a great many details the text of *W* is closer to *P* than to any other manu-

---
[18] W. Urwick, *The Early History of Trinity College, Dublin*, 1892, pp. 93-4.
[19] Johnson, p. 53.
[20] *Catalogi Librorum Manuscriptorum Angliae et Hiberniae*, 1697, vol. 2, part 2, pp. 16-48. See Renwick, *MLR* 29. 448.

script. The following readings will serve to represent the large number of those which appear only in *W* and *P*:

22-3 or appointment] appointed
207 the fote of a man] *om.*
448 Lacie] the Earle of *Vlster*
554-9 and . . . warrs] *om.*
867 secretelye] privily
1573 *mantilia*] *Humi mantilia*
1813-21 likewise . . . scourge] *om.* and *inserted after* likewise *in 1825*

2358 and souldiours] *om.*
2690-1 advizement] advertizement
3100-1 and outgadders] *om.*
3276 livinge] being
4613 hostinge] hostage
4851 *blank space*] Edward the fourth
5289 exportacion] transportation

It would, however, be dangerous to assume, without further evidence, that Ware actually made use of *P* in drawing up his text. He includes part of one of the unrevised passages which characterize *P*, but includes it at a different place and later, apparently on second thought, notes that it "is wholly to be crossed out, as being then agreeable to the best MS. Copie";[21] and Ware, besides differing from *P* in numerous readings, does not include six-sevenths of the unrevised material which appears in *P*. It is clear that he used more than one manuscript of the *View*; but it is quite possible that he based his text on one manuscript which was closely related to *G* and *P*, a manuscript which is not among the fifteen available for the present edition.

In a large number of cases Ware departs from all available manuscripts, and some of these readings are obvious scribal errors. Twice, for example, "*Iren.*" replaces "*Eudox.*" (941, 4119), and the misinterpretation of handwriting probably accounts for such mistakes as:

611 Choked] checked
762 xxxvj] 56
1276 *Tamaricj, Nerij*] *Tamari, Cineri*
1401 three hundrethe] 500

3045 finall] small
4060 viij^m—vij^c] 8300
4936 heardinge] hardening

Besides noting eight "Faults escaped," Ware himself made at least two changes in the text while it was being printed (footnotes on 1152 and 2783). But of far more importance than these errors and corrections are the readings, peculiar to *W*, which seem to reveal that for reasons of his own he deliberately altered Spenser's text.

Ware's very considerable knowledge of Irish antiquities undoubtedly led him to alter the spelling of "*Iriach*" (128) to "*Eriach*"; to fill in the war cry of the O'Briens, "*Laun-laider*," which the manuscripts left blank (1685); to refer a certain law of the time of Edward Fourth to "*Ireland*" rather than "*Englande*" (4851); and, at one point, to make the original text more accurate by inserting three words in brackets (4789). Similarly, he changed geographical names: the "Cullvers" (426) became the more recognizable "*Curlues*," and "*Clanriccard*" (4108) was given its accepted name of "*Galway*"; probably because he could not find a suitable "Moneroo" (426), he replaced it with "*Mointerolis*"; and "Briskelah" (428, 4204), a name which Spenser used correctly, Ware for some

---

[21] *View* (in *The Historie of Ireland*, Dublin, 1633), p. 121. See footnotes on 1152 and 1215-1330.

reason altered to the unsuitable "*Brackenah*." His general information serves to correct "the faire maide of Asterothe" (1914) to "the faire maide of *Asteloth*"; where the manuscripts add up six garrisons as "fowre" (3723), he reads "6." The purpose of all these changes was obviously to make the text of the *View* express what Spenser intended to write.

In a much larger number of cases, however, Ware made textual changes for a purpose which was much less scholarly: he deliberately softened or omitted passages which might be offensive to Irish and, more particularly, Anglo-Irish feelings in his own time.[22] The cumulative effect of these emendations is astonishing:

E	W
6-7 that salvage nacion [Ireland]	that nation
299-300 they [Irish customs and laws] be muche more vniuste	they be more unjust
577 soe manye evills, as everye daie I see more and more throwne vppon her [Ireland]	so many evills as I see more and more to bee layde upon her
668-73 all the ffrehoulders of that realme are Irishe which . . . make no more scruple to passe againste the Inglishman or the Quene thoughe it be to straine theire oathes then to drinke milke vnstrained	most of the Free-holders of that Realme, are *Irish*, which . . . make no more scruple to passe against an Englishman, and the Queene, though it bee to strayne their oathes, then to drinke milke unstrayned
677-81 now that the Irishe haue stepped into the romes of the Inglishe whoe are now become soe hedefull and provident to kepe them out from hence forthe that they make no scruple of Conscience to passe againste them it is good reason that either that course of the lawe for trialls be altered or other provision for Iuryes be made/	now that the Irish have stepped into the very roomes of your English, wee are now to become heedfull and provident in Iuryes.
726-7 the evidence beinge broughte in by the base Irishe people wilbe as deceiptefull	the evidence being brought in by the baser *Irish* people, will bee as deceiptfull
852-4 they [the Irish rebels] shall lose nothinge but themselves wheareof they seme surelye verye Careles like as all barbarous people are, as Cesar in his Comentaries saith verye fearlesse of death	they shall lose nothing but themselves, whereof they seeme surely very carelesse.
1200-1 [Ireland] havinge bene allwaies without Lettres	having bin in those times without letters
1249-50 they [the Irish] are so barbarous still and so vnlearned	they are so unlearned still

[22] See his preface (section E of this appendix), where he apologizes for Spenser's seeming aspersions.

E	W
1326-8 beinge, as they [the Irish] are nowe accounted the moste barbarous nacion in Christendome they to avoide that reproche woulde derive themselves	they derive themselves
1479 the moste parte of them [the Anglo-Irish] are degenerated	some of them are degenerated
1650 they [the uses of the Irish mantle] be all to bad intentes	they be most to bad intents
1656-8 for the Irishe glibbes I saye that besides theire salvage brutishnes and loathly filthines which is not to be named they are fitt maskes	for the *Irish* glibbes, they are as fit maskes
1776-7 [the Irish method of going to battle] is mere salvage and *Scythyan*	is meere *Scythian*
1861-2 [the Irish follow] the manner of all barbarous nacions	the maner of many Nations
1953-4 the Englishe that weare are now muche more Lawles and Licentious then the verie wilde Irishe	some of them are now much more lawlesse and licentious then the very wilde *Irish*
1993 they [the Anglo-Irish] are nowe growen to be allmoste as lewde as the Irishe	they are almost now growne like the *Irish*
1998-9 [some of the Anglo-Irish are] degenerate and growen to be as verye Patchokes as the wilde Irishe	degenerate
2013 Coulde they [the Anglo-Irish] euer Conceaue anye suche divillishe dislike	Could they ever conceive any such dislike
2050-1 Other great howses theare be of the olde Englishe in Irelande which thoroughe licentious Conuersinge	Other great houses there bee of the *English* in *Ireland*, which thorough licentious conversing
2054-63 [some of the Anglo-Irish] are now growne as Irishe as Ohanlans breeche, (as the proverbe theare is) of which sorte theare are two moste pittifull ensamples Aboue the reste, to witt the Lo. Bremingham, whoe beinge the moste anciente Baron I thinke in Englande is now waxen the moste Salvage Irishe naminge him selfe Irishlike, maccorishe. and the other is the great mortimer whoe forgettinge how greate he was once in Englande or Englishe at all is nowe become the moste barbarous of them all and is Called *macnemarra* and not much better then he, is the olde	are now growne as *Irish*, as *O-Hanlons* breech, as the proverbe there is.

APPENDIX III

E	W
Lb Courcie whoe havinge lewdlye wasted all the Landes and Seigniories that he had and aliened them vnto the Irishe is himselfe now growen quite Irishe	
2066-7 the [Anglo-Irish] Lordes and Chief men wax so barbarous and bastardlike	the Lords and cheife men degenerate
2070 [Anglo-Irish customs] are verye bad and barbarous	are very bad
2073 [Anglo-Irish customs are] verye brute and vncivill	very uncivill
2125-6 how cane suche matchinge [of the English and Irish in marriage] but bringe forthe an evill race	how can such matching succeede well
2149-50 his [the Irishman's] thinne breche	his trouse
2464-6 it is verye inconveniente that anye suche shoulde be permitted speciallye in a people so evill minded as they [the Irish] now be and diuerslye shewe themselues	it is very inconvenient that any such should be permitted.
2617-8 as that ye woulde rather thinke them [the Irish] *Atheists* or infidles but not one amongest a hundred	that not one amongst a hundred
2622-69 *Eudox*: This is trewelie a moste pittifull hearinge [there follows a violent attack on the Irish Catholics which is too long to quote] . . . . But if this Ignorance of the people be suche a burthen vnto the Pope is it not a like blott to them that now houlde that place in that they which now are in the lighte them selues suffer a people vnder theire Chardge to wallowe in suche deadlie darkenes? ffor I do not see that the faulte is Chaunged but the faultes master/	*Eudox.* Is it not then a little blot to them that now hold the place of government, that they which now are in the light themselves, suffer a people under their charge, to wallow in such deadly darkenesse.
2716-7 the [the Irish priests] Christen, yeat after the popishe fashion and with the Popishe Latine ministracion.	they Christen yet after the Popish fashion
2890-2 enemyes of bothe, And this is the wretchednes of that fatall kingedome [Ireland] which I thinke thearefore was in olde time not Called amisse *Banno* or *sacra Insula* takinge *sacra* for accursed/	enemies of both.
3163-4 [among other Irish outlaws] the ketinges and Kellies, or suche like	or such like

E	W

3339-41 in that last conspiracye of the Englishe pale thinke youe not that theare weare manye more guiltye then that felte the punishment? or was theare anie allmoste Cleare from the same?

in the last conspiracy of some of the *English* Pale, thinke you not that there were many more guiltie then they that felt the punishment?

3898-9 if theare weare Englishe shed amongest them [the Irish] and placed ouer them

if they were *English* well placed among them

4136-8 he [the Lord Deputy] mighte easelye ouerloke and somtimes ouerreache the moores/ the Butlers the dempsies the ketins the Connours

he might easily overlooke and sometimes over-reach the *Moores*, the *Dempsies*, the *Connors*

4264 donell maccartie whom it is mete to foresee to cutt of

Donell Mac Carty, whom it is meete to foresee to

4292-5 those two Cities [Waterford and Cork] aboue all the reste doe offer an Ingate to the Spanniarde moste fittlye and allso the inhabitantes of them are moste ill affected to the Englishe gouernment and moste friendes to the Spanniarde/

those two Citties, above all the rest, doe offer an in-gate to the *Spaniard* most fitly:

4537-9 this [outlawry and rebellion] happens not onelye in the sonns of theire gentlemen but often times allsoe of theire noble men speciallye of theire base sonns as theare are fewe without some of them

this happens not onely sometimes in the sonnes of their Gentle-men, but also of their Noble-men, specially of them who have base Sonnes

4543-8 freholders which are not tractable to theire bad wills. Twoe suche Bastardes of the L. *Roches* there are now out in mounster whom he doethe not onelye Countenance but allso priuilye maynteigne and relieue nightelye amongest his Tenantes., suche another is theare of the Earle of *Clancares* in desmounde and manye other in manye other places/

Free-holders, which are not tractable to their wills.

4712-3 the rude Irishe ... are now become somwhat more Civill

the rude *Irish* ... are now become more civill

4716-31 they [the Anglo-Irish nobility] are muche more stubborne and disobedient to lawe and gouernement then the Irishe be, and more malicous againste the Englishe that dailye are sente ouer/ [the attack is too long to quote in full] .... bothe discontente and vndewtifull/

they are more stubborne, and disobedient to law and governement, then the *Irish* be.

APPENDIX III 523

E	W
4732-3 the englishe Irishe theare shoulde be worse then the wilde Irishe	any *English* there, should bee worse then the *Irish*
4767-8 Irelande is full of her owne nacion that maye not be roted out	*Ireland* is full of her owne nation, that ought not to be rooted out
4859-60 [the Irishman] shall in shorte time learne quite to forgett his Irishe nacion	in time learne quite to forget his *Irish* Nation
4866-9 what other order will ye take for theire [the Irish] manner of lief for all this thoughe perhaps it maie kepe them from disobedience and disloyaltye yeat will it not bringe them from theire Barbarisme and salvage life/	what other order will you take for their manner of life?
4882 the wretched Realme of Irelande	the Realme of *Ireland*
4956 theire owne [the Irish] brutishe behaviour	their owne behaviour
5035-9 for this I knowe that the moste of the Irishe are so far from vnderstandinge the Popishe Religion as they are of the Protestantes profession and yeat dothe hate it thoughe vnknowen even for the verye hatred which they haue of the Englishe and theire gouernement	And
5053-4 our Idle ministers	some of our idle Ministers
5058-9 [the English ministers will not] be drawen forthe from theire warme nestes, and theire swete loues sides	bee drawne foorth from their warme neastes

This distortion of what Spenser felt and wrote about Ireland is important inasmuch as Ware's text was republished in all the editions of the *View* which appeared before the last third of the nineteenth century.

* * *

Ware's text of the *View* was reprinted, with some modifications of spelling and punctuation, in the following editions:

Edmund Spenser, *Works*, 1679.
Edmund Spenser, *Works*, ed. John Hughes, 1715. Reprinted 1750.
Edmund Spenser, *A View of the State of Ireland*, Dublin, 1763.
Edmund Spenser, *Works*, ed. Henry John Todd, 1805. Reprinted 1856 and again at later dates. (Todd printed Ware's text but also consulted MSS E, C, L, D1, and a transcript of part of T.)
Sir James Ware, ed., *Ancient Irish Histories*, Dublin, 1809.
A Collection of Tracts . . . Illustrative . . . of Ireland, Dublin, 1860.
Edmund Spenser, *Poetical Works*, ed. John Payne Collier, 1862.
Henry Morley, ed., *Ireland under Elizabeth and James I*, 1890.

In 1869, for the first time since 1633, there appeared a text of the *View* which was directly based on manuscript sources: in the Globe Edition of Spenser's *Works* (frequently reprinted since 1869) Richard Morris published the text of *A*, which he supplemented, where he felt it necessary, with readings from *H1*, *H2*, and *W*. Alexander B. Grosart's edition of Spenser's *Works* (1882-1884) included a careless transcript of *L*, which was assumed to be a peculiarly authoritative text. The two most recent editions of the *View* are edited by W. L. Renwick; the text of the first of these (in Spenser's *Works*, 1930-1932) is based on *R*, corrected, apparently, with readings from *C*, *D2*, and *W*; the second (*A View of the Present State of Ireland*, 1934) is likewise based on *R*, which Renwick chose because it was the manuscript intended for publication in 1598, but he corrected and completed this text with many readings from *C*, and in an appendix he provided a selection of variants from *A*, *C*, *D1*, *D2*, *H1*, *H2*, *L*, *P*, *T*, and *W*. None of the modern editions which are directly based on manuscripts, however, not even Renwick's, gives a complete, accurate record of any single manuscript or a selection of variants which is wide enough to serve the needs of an advanced and conscientious student. None of them forestalls a new, perhaps no luckier, attempt to gladden such a reader.

D.

SMERWICK

[Spenser's discussion of the massacre at Smerwick (3355-88) raises two important questions: was he present at Smerwick on 9 November, 1580, during the parleys he describes? and is his defense of Grey's honor founded on fact?]

HENLEY (pp. 29-30) notes that Spenser may not have been present at Smerwick since there are discrepancies between his account and that of Grey himself [*C. S. P. Ir. 1574-1585* 78. 29], who writes that his long parley took place with the campmaster Alessandro, not Don Sebastian, and that the besieged acknowledged they had been sent by the Pope, not that they were adventurers.

JENKINS (*TLS* 32. 331) believes that Spenser was present at Smerwick. A letter from Grey to Burghley, written from Limerick, 28 November, 1580 (British Museum Add. MS. 33924, f. 6), is in Spenser's hand and therefore reveals that he was with Grey on the Smerwick campaign. Another letter, from Clonmel, 30 November, 1580 (*C. S. P. Ir. 1574-1585* 78. 68), is likewise in Spenser's hand. [Jenkins has published a photographic reproduction of the first of these two letters in *PMLA* 52. op. 338, 339.]

RENWICK (*View*, pp. 285-9). It may serve to insert here the relevant part of Grey's despatch of 12th November, written " In campe at Smerwicke " in Spenser's most careful and beautiful Italian hand. Grey had an interview with Alexandro Bartoni, the Campmaster, and a Spanish captain, who explained that the expedition was sent by the Pope; when Grey had made clear his opinion of the Pope, " theyr fault therefore sawe to bee aggrauated by the vilenesse of their Commaunder, and that at my handes no condition of composition they were to expecte, other then that simply they should render me the forte, and yield theyr selues to

APPENDIX III 525

my will for lyfe or death: with this answere he departed; after which there was one or twoo courses two and fro more, to haue gotten a certeinty for some of their liues, but fynding that yt would not bee, the Coronell him self about sunne [*i. e.,* Sunne] setting came forth, and requested respitt with surceas[s]e of armes till the nexte morning, and then he would giue a resolute answere; fynding that to bee but a gayne of tyme for them and losse of the same for my self, I definitely answered I would not graunt yt, and therefore presently either that he tooke my offer or elles retourne and I would fall to my busines. He then embraced my knees, simply putting him self to my mercy, onely he prayed that for that night hee might abyde in the Forte, and that in the morning all should be putt into my handes: I asked hostages for the performance; they were giuen. Morning come I presented my companies in battaile before the Forte: the Coronell comes forth with x or xij of his chiefe ientlemen, trayling theyr ensignes rolled vp, and presented them vnto mee with theyr liues and the Forte: I sent streight certein gentlemen in to see their weapons and armures layed downe and to gard the munition and victaile there lefte for spoile: Then putt I in certeyn bandes, who streight fell to execution. There were 600 slayne; munition and vittaile great store, though much wasted through the disorder of the Souldier, which in that furie could not bee helped. Those that I gaue lyfe vnto, I haue bestowed vpon the Capteines and gentlemen, whose seruice hath well deserued: ... Your Maiesty at this service had here but 800; they haue [putt] out of a Forte well fortefied, better victailed, excellently stored with armure [? and] munition, 600 whereof 400 were as gallant and goodly personages, as of any [...] I euer beheld. So hath yt pleased the Lord of hostes to deliuer your enemies into [? your] Highnes handes." (*S. P. Ir.* 78. 29)

.... The Colonel was Sebastiano di San Joseppi, whose papers form the volume *Inghilterra* 2 of the series *Nunziature* in the Vatican Archives. According to a list of prisoners (*S. P. Ir.* 78. 28) his secretary was "Austin Brano," [*i. e.,* "Brauo,"] an Italian. "Signior Ieffrey" — in MS Harl. 1932 [*H1*], *Iaguas*, in Addl. 22022 [*A*], *Iacques*—I cannot identify, unless Spenser were trying to recall, and his copyists to transmit, the name of Paulo Giustin[i]ani (Iustiniani in the prisoner-list), the paymaster of the force, who was afterwards sent to Rome on a fruitless quest for ransom-money. San Joseppi was an Italian professional soldier, the first of his papers being his commission as "commissary, vulgarly *pagatore*" to Thomas Stucley. After Stucley's death at the battle of Alcazar, a plan was hatched in Spain by which Stucley's scheme of a descent on Ireland should be revived, with San Joseppi in command. After the collapse of the enterprize, he seems to have been blamed for his conduct, especially by one Fra Matteo d'Oviedo, who had sailed with him from Spain, for his papers include testimonials from his officers, and, luckily, a draft report and defence endorsed to the Papal Secretary of State. From this I translate the relevant portion as he first wrote it, his alterations being only verbal and for brevity's sake or to avoid offence at headquarters.

The troops in the fort being demoralised by the English bombardment and refusing to fight, "we held a council, the campmaster, 'Olivero Plunquetto,' some others and I, and it was resolved to treat for surrender to the enemy on some honorable terms, upon which a parley was held; however, he would never hear of any terms of surrender, except that he would have us at his discretion. I hearing this and knowing what would follow, confessed myself and communicated, making my officers do the same, with firm purpose to let myself be cut in pieces before surrendering. And this done I went to all the soldiers, telling them the answer from the Viceroy's side, which meant nothing other than their death." They replied that they preferred death to the miseries they had endured. " I seeing no further means of holding out, and the enemy being greatly reinforced by the arrival of the Earl of Ormond with 1500 soldiers, with great grief I have to tell Your Lordship that we were forced to surrender to the Viceroy at his mercy, which was that, entering the fort, he had all the soldiers cut to pieces, and also a few sailors who were in the ship." San Joseppi complains of Fra Matteo; of Desmond and his brother Sir John, " feeble subjects having little experience, I say none, of war," who gave neither help nor favour; of his troops, Biscay men " the most useless for soldiering that ever I saw "; of the reinforcements from Spain that never arrived; of one " Macamur " an Irishman introduced by Desmond as a principal man of these parts from whom they would draw supplies, but who provided neither horses, men, nor timber, and deserted to Grey, to whom he betrayed the weak points of the fort; and of the Irish, especially the priests, who accompanied the force from Spain, but were " full of ambition, interested, and wished to get money and to domineer over the enterprize like men without minds." But neither in this defence nor in his correspondence with Giustiniani and others is there any complaint of Grey's alleged treachery.

The Papal Nuncio in France, who was the regular channel for English and Irish news, heard of the disaster on 15th Dec., through the English Ambassador, clearly in terms of Grey's despatch. On the 29th he learned from London, where the prisoners were, that it was " caused by the failure of the relief which the Catholics expected from the Earl of Desmond, who was near at hand but either could not or would not come to close quarters." On 26th Jan., 1581, the *pagatore* (Giustiniani) arrived on his way to Rome, and reported the ill behaviour of the Biscay men, who would not fight " however the Colonel beat some and killed some to give them force." On 19th Feb., " There passed here an Italian soldier in very poor state, who says he was in Ireland with the rest when Smerwick was taken ... who gave me an account of that success little differing from that which I have already written," except that the promised help from Spain did not arrive, and that Desmond's following was no more than 50 or 100 gentlemen of the country. On 8th May, however, he reports that Grey could not rely on the Irish—including, presumably, the English-Irish — " who do not trust him since under parole he so maltreated those Italians and Spaniards of Smerwick" (*Nunz. Francia*)

The story of Grey's perfidy, then, was an English or Irish rumour, and, incidentally, achieved its purpose. Whatever we may think of the massacre, the attack on Smerwick was a very well-conducted though risky affair. The staff work was excellent, since according to San Joseppi the navy arrived on 27th October and the land forces on the 28th, and the bombardment was skilfully directed and intensely maintained. The calumny may well have been invented by Grey's enemies to diminish the credit to which he and Wynter, the Admiral who cooperated with him, were certainly entitled.

RENWICK (*View*, pp. 244-6). What horrifies us in this story is the slaughter: we need not assume that its authors enjoyed it, or that Grey's reported tears were hypocritical. In any case Spenser's only concern is to point out, first, that this was not a massacre like that of the people of Haarlem, or done in a fit of ill-temper.

APPENDIX III 527

These Italians and Spaniards were filibusters, indefensible in any court martial: they were indeed disowned by Pope and King. Also Grey was in a tight corner. Mendoza, the Spanish Ambassador, reported that Grey suspected the garrison's attempts to parley "in the fear that it might be a stratagem to keep him in check until Desmond arrived, since it was impossible for any soldier to believe that there could be so few brave men in the fort, which they had been strengthening for two months, as to surrender without striking a blow . . . The Englishmen there say that if the fort had held out for four days, the Viceroy's retreat would have been cut off, and the Queen's ships could not have held their own, to the great peril of the English in Ireland." (*Cal. S. P. Spanish*, vol. 3, no. 57) Five hundred prisoners (or six, acording to Grey) could not be brought off in the face of a strong enemy, through 100 miles of difficult country, in a wet November, by a force whose reliable strength was eight hundred; and Grey adopted the solution which Henry V adopted at Agincourt and Napoleon was to adopt at Acre. The characters of all three may be stained; but it meant, at the time, balancing the lives of five or six hundred foreign filibusters against all Ireland. Any court chosen from the most high-minded commanders of sixteenth-century Europe would certainly have declared unanimously that Grey's action was justified by the laws of war; the Spanish Ambassador and the Papal officials report the massacre without any trace of surprise or emotion, and the Colonel of the fort took it [as] a thing to be expected, as is clear from his report. . . .

The second point entails a conflict of evidence. Grey was accused of massacring troops who had surrendered upon promise of life. Our court of commanders would certainly have declared that Grey would have been unjustified in granting any terms short of surrender at discretion. In any case, his report written at the time — by Spenser's hand — before any accusation was made, agrees with Spenser's evidence sixteen years later, and, what is quite conclusive, with the report of the commander of the fort, Sebastiano di San Joseppi, to the Vatican, and with those of his commissary Paulo Giustin[i]ani and of another of his men, unnamed, to the Papal Nuncio in France. Who invented the tale of Grey's perfidy I do not know. Mendoza, the Spanish Ambassador in London, who mentions it first, was quite capable of it; captured officers may have found it necessary to explain away their surrender of the fort with a strong relieving force in the vicinity, and their return without their men; the Nuncio heard it in Paris seven months later, evidently from Ireland: Grey had enemies enough, and the story was told and remembered. But no statement can stand against the independent statements of the two men who spoke together that November day; and Spenser's truth is as clearly vindicated as his courageous loyalty is clearly displayed.

ALFRED O'RAHILLY divides the evidence relating to the massacre into four categories (1) the contemporary English version, which corroborates the Irish tradition that Grey used torture and acted with the approval of Elizabeth; (2) the Irish version, which, although unreliable for such details as numbers, is accurate in all essentials where it differs from the English version; (3) the evidence of a third party, that contained in the Vatican Archives; and (4) the suppressed evidence which can be arrived at by inference from the first three. He quotes voluminously from all the documents which contain accounts of the massacre. From them, as well as by inference, he concludes that Grey violated his promise to spare the lives of the garrison: (1) Irish, Spanish, and Roman authorities, as well as the Anglophile Thomas Russell (writing in 1638), agree that Grey broke faith. (2) Rumors to this effect circulated in England, witness the uneasiness of Spenser, Moryson, and other defenders of Grey. (3) Sir Richard Bingham [*C. S. P. Ir. 1574-1585* 78. 32], in tracing the massacre to unlicensed soldiers and sailors, uses a clumsy lie to hide the official responsibility, a responsibility revealed by the torturing of some members of the garrison and the sparing of others. (4) Since those saved were not all officers, they were obviously spared by agreement with Sebastian. (5) Mendoza, Russell, Matthew of Oviedo, Nicholas Sander, Desmond, and the English Catholics were all convinced of Sebastian's cowardice. (6) Sander, Don Philip O'Sullivan Bear, and Dominic O'Daly report that Oliver Plunckett was tortured for trying to foil the treachery of Sebastian. (7) "Now, once we admit that Sebastian was a coward and a traitor, it is clear that the only way in which he could carry out his treachery was to secure terms from Grey in order to induce the garrison to capitulate—with the private understanding that he and his chosen few should be spared and that no others would live to tell the tale." (8) The evidence given in Sebastian's behalf by other prisoners is open to suspicion. (9) Grey's account is false in failing to mention the hanging of women and the torture of men and in pretending that he saved "the captains and gentlemen" for ransom. (10) Grey, however, kept faith with Sebastian's men when he spared them. Thus the British defence of Grey is without foundation, and Sebastian's account, on which Renwick depends, is false: "It is so hard for Spenser's editor to believe that the poet should combine with Grey and the Italian to hide the infamy which saved Ireland for the Empire."

JENKINS (*PMLA* 52. 343). That Spenser was present at this massacre is attested by the statement of Irenaeus in the *View*: "my selfe beinge as neare them as anye" [3361]. Further proof of Spenser's presence on this occasion is the letter aforementioned, written in his secretary hand for Grey from Limerick on November 28, only nineteen days afterward. Since Wallop reported that communications between Dublin and Limerick were kept up only by "simple fellows that pass afoot in nature of beggars," we cannot imagine how Spenser could have been in attendance upon Grey at Limerick unless he had accompanied him throughout the journey.... It is indeed probable that Spenser penned this letter [that of 12 November, calendared as *C. S. P. Ir. 1574-1585* 78. 29].

JUDSON (*Life*, p. 92). "Because Spenser's account of the affair is inaccurate in certain respects, the value of his defense has been questioned. When, however, we recall that sixteen years had passed, we are prepared for discrepancies. Moreover, our knowledge of Grey makes a different conclusion almost impossible. Stern he was, even at times pitiless, but shifty and dishonorable he surely was not." Judson goes on to show that the Smerwick episode is represented, allegorically, in the duel between Grantorto and Artegall [*F. Q.* 5. 12. 14-23].

EDITOR. It may be useful to analyze Spenser's defense of Grey's conduct and to compare it with other accounts of the parleys which were held on the afternoon of 9 November, 1580, and of the massacre performed the next morning.

Spenser makes the following points: (1) Grey neither promised life to the occupants of the fort nor gave them hope of life. (2) When their secretary, an

APPENDIX III 529

Italian named Geoffrey, sued for grace, he was refused it. (3) Later their colonel, Don Sebastian, came to beg that they might have their arms, or at least their lives, according to the custom of war and law of nations; but Grey denied them arms or life, on the ground that neither custom nor law could be observed toward unlawful enemies, and added that, if they were lawful enemies, they should show commission from the Pope or King Philip; on the reply that they were only adventurers in the service of the Irish, the Deputy refused to give any terms and left them to submit to his discretion or not; then Sebastian yielded all to Grey's mercy. (4) In order to prevent them from rejoining the rebels and to frighten the Irish from importing foreign aid in the future, the Spaniards were executed. To take up each point in turn:

(1) The English officers whose eye-witness reports of the Smerwick affair are preserved in the Public Record Office are all agreed that the fort was surrendered absolutely and without conditions (State Papers 63. 78. 25, 27, 29, 30, 32, 38); in his letter to Walsingham (78. 30) Grey circumstantially describes how the issue was settled in a council of the English leaders before the parley with the enemy; San Joseppi, the commander of the fort, corroborates the English version, as Renwick shows; and the accounts of both Hooker and Camden are in agreement with it on this point (Holinshed, vol. II, *The Supplie of the Irish Chronicles*, pp. 171-2; *Britannia*, p. 690; *Annales*, pp. 295-6). On the other hand, Mendoza writes Philip on 11 December, 1580, that the besieged were promised their lives (*C. S. P. S. 1580-1586*, p. 69); on 9 January, 1581, Nicholas Sander, the Papal Nuncio to Ireland, who was not in the fort during the siege and massacre and who cannot have met any of the survivors, speaks of a written safe-conduct which Grey gave San Joseppi but later retrieved (P. F. Moran, *History of the Catholic Archbishops of Dublin, since the Reformation*, 1864, 1. 423-4; Wainewright, *Publications of the Catholic Record Society* 26. 57); and Peter Lombard (*The Irish War of Defence*, ed. Matthew J. Byrne, pp. 10, 12), Don Philip O'Sullivan Bear (*Ireland under Elizabeth*, trans. Matthew J. Byrne, pp. 23-5), and Dominic de Rosario O'Daly (*The Geraldines, Earls of Desmond*, trans. C. P. Meehan, 1847, pp. 86-8), all Irishmen writing years after the event, go so far as to say that the English besiegers initiated the parley by promising to allow the garrison free passage. Partisanship, of course, may vitiate the evidence on either side; nevertheless probability favors the version of the English officers, who wrote from Smerwick itself, at the time of the event, and for the private information of their own government; Grey, at least, must have known that he had nothing to fear from the scrupulosity of Elizabeth (see John P. Hennessy, *Sir Walter Raleigh in Ireland*, 1883, pp. 212-3). The evidence, therefore, corroborates Spenser's initial statement.

(2) But his reference to an Italian secretary named Geoffrey is almost certainly wrong. The only secretary included in the extant lists of the Spanish and Italian leaders is Agostino Bravo, and there is no one in the lists whose name resembles *Geoffrey* (State Papers 63. 78. 27, 28; see also *Publications of the Catholic Record Society* 26. 46-7). Before San Joseppi's parley with Grey, however, the Italian campmaster, Alessandro Bartoni, and a Spanish captain, Antonio Ortiguéira, did confer with the English commander (State Papers 63. 78. 27, 29, 38; Moran, *op. cit.*, 1. 423).

(3) In regard to San Joseppi's parley with Grey, Spenser makes a second and

more crucial mistake: it was in speaking to Bartoni and Ortiguéira, and not in his meeting with San Joseppi, that the Deputy explained why he refused to make any terms with the invaders (only the unreliable account of O'Sullivan Bear agrees with the *View* that San Joseppi was present at the more important of the two conferences). In his letter to the Queen (State Papers 63. 78. 29) Grey himself gives significant details on the first meeting: that when he expressed surprise to find people of a king at peace with Elizabeth maintaining rebels against her, Ortiguéira replied that they had been sent, not by Philip, but by the governor of Bilboa; that Bartoni added that the Pope had commissioned them all to defend the Catholic Faith; and that the Deputy thereupon attacked the Pope, denying that he enjoyed any rightful sovereignty. The report which Mendoza sent to Philip on 11 December also declares that the besieged acknowledged that they came by order of the Pope (*C. S. P. S. 1580-1586*, p. 69); and the Venetian ambassador in France transmits the same detail to his government (*C. S. P. V. 1558-1580*, pp. 651-2). Thus, it is clear that Spenser makes a third mistake when he asserts that the invaders said they had no commission from either Pope or King but were only adventurers in the service of the Irish. As Spenser writes, however, Grey refused to make any terms with them, and San Joseppi surrendered to him without condition.

(4) None of the English officers mentions either of the reasons offered by Spenser for the massacre; Bingham, in fact, suggests that it happened by accident (State Papers 63. 78. 32). But Camden justifies it on grounds of expediency: that the English were surrounded by 1500 rebels and themselves only equal in number to the garrison, that the English soldiers would have rebelled if they had not been supplied from stores in the fort, and that there were no ships to convey prisoners away by sea (*Britannia*, p. 690; *Annales*, pp. 295-6).

From this analysis it is safe to say that the other documents on Smerwick substantiate Spenser's defense of Grey's honor; but the inaccuracies in Spenser's account, I feel, still make it impossible to say with certainty that he was present at the siege.

E.

PREFATORY MATTER FROM WARE'S EDITION, 1633

[Marginalia are reproduced in square brackets.]

TO THE RIGHT HONORABLE THOMAS LO. VISCOVNT WENTWORTH, LO. DEPVTY GENERALL OF IRELAND, *LO. PRESIDENT OF HIS MAIESTIES COVNCELL ESTABLISHED IN THE NORTH PARTS OF ENGLAND, AND ONE OF HIS MAIESTIES MOST HONORABLE PRIVIE COVNCELL.*

RIGHT HONORABLE,

THE sence of that happy peace, which by the divine providence this Kingdome hath enjoyed, since the beginning of the raigne of his late Majestie of ever sacred memory, doth then take the deeper impression, when these our halcyon dayes are compared with the former turbulent and tempestuous times, and with the miseries (of severall kindes) incident unto them. Those calamities are fully set out, and to the life by Mr Spenser, with a discovery of their causes, and remedies, being for

APPENDIX III

the most part excellent grounds of reformation. And so much may be justly expected from him in regard of his long abode and experience of this Kingdome. In these respects, and for other good uses, which the collections (now communicated) doe afford for matter of history *and* policy, *I am incouraged to dedicate them to your Lordship, and humbly to desire your favourable acceptance of them, and of*

Your Lordships ever

humbly devoted

IAMES WARE.

THE PREFACE.

HOw far these collections may conduce to the knowledge of the *antiquities* and *state* of this Land, let the fit reader judge: yet something I may not passe by touching Mr *Edmund Spenser* and the worke it selfe, lest I should seeme to offer injury to his worth, by others so much celebrated. Hee was borne in *London* of an ancient and noble family, and brought up in the Vniversitie of *Cambridge*, where (as the fruites of his after labours doe manifest) he mispent not his time. After this he became Secretary to *Arthur* Lord *Grey* of *Wilton*, Lord Deputy of *Ireland*, a valiant and worthy Governour, and shortly after for his services to the Crowne, he had bestowed upon him by Queene *Elizabeth*, 3000. acres of land in the Countie of *Corke*. There hee finished the later part of that excellent poem of his *Faery Queene*, which was soone after unfortunately lost by the disorder and abuse of his servant, whom he had sent before him into *England*, being then *a rebellibus* (as *Camdens* words are [*Annal. rer. Anglic. et Hibern. pag. 729, edit.* 1625.]) *e laribus ejectus et bonis spoliatus.* He deceased at *Westminster* in the yeare 1599. (others have it wrongly 1598.) soone after his returne into *England*, and was buried according to his owne desire, in the collegiat Church there, neere unto *Chaucer*, whom he worthily imitated, (at the costes of *Robert* Earle of *Essex*,) wherupon this Epitaph was framed,

> Hic prope Chaucerum *situs est* Spenserius, *illi*
> *proximus ingenio, proximus ut tumulo.*
> Hic prope Chaucerum Spensere *poeta poetam*
> *conderis, et versu quam tumulo propior.*
> *Anglica te vivo vixit plausitque poesis,*
> *nunc moritura timet te moriente mori.*

As for his worke now published [*Ex Bibliotheca Reverendissimi in Christo patris D. Iacobi Vsserij Archiep. Armachani.*], although it sufficiently testifieth his learning and deepe judgement, yet we may wish that in some passages it had bin tempered with more moderation. The troubles and miseries of the time when he wrote it, doe partly excuse him, And surely wee may conceive, that if hee had lived to see these times, and the good effects which the last 30. yeares peace have produced in this land, both for obedience to the lawes, as also in traffique, husbandry, civility, and learning, he would have omitted those passages which may seeme to lay either any particular aspersion upon some families, or generall upon the Nation. For now we may truly say, *jam cuncti gens una sumus*, and that upon just cause those ancient statutes, wherein the natives of *Irish* descent were held to be, and named *Irish* enemies, and wherein those of *English* bloud were forbidden to marry and commerce with them, were repealed by act of Parlament, in the raigne of our late Soveraigne King IAMES of ever blessed memory [*Vid. lib. Statut. Hibern. edit. Dubl. an.* 1621. *pag.* 427.].

His proofes (although most of them conjecturall) concerning the originall of the language, customes of the Nation, and the first peopling of the severall parts of the Iland, are full of good reading, and doe shew a sound judgment. They may be further confirmed by comparing them with *Richard Creagh's* Booke *de lingua Hibernica*, which is yet extant in the original manuscript, and althogh mixed with matter of story, leaning too much to some fabulous traditions, yet in other respects worthy of light.

Touching the generall scope intended by the author for the reformation of abuses and ill customes, This we may say, that although very many have taken paines in the same subject, during the raigne of Queene *Elizabeth*, and some before, as the author of the booke intituled *Salus populi* [*Floruit sub initium reg. Edw.* 4], and after him *Patrick Finglas*, cheife Baron of the Exchequer here, and afterwardes cheife Iustice of the common pleas [*Floruit sub Hen.* 8.], yet none came so neere to the best grounds for reformation, a few passages excepted, as *Spenser* hath done in this. Some marginall notes I have added, although not intending any, untill the fourth part of the Booke was printed.

APPENDIX IV

A BRIEF NOTE OF IRELAND

ANONYMOUS (*Dublin University Magazine* 58. 143-4). Our next trace of the poet is as the writer, soon after his arrival in London [in December, 1598], of two treatises on the insurrection, for the instruction of the Secretary of State. These able documents, besides disclosing intimate knowledge of the causes which incited Tyrone, gave masterly advice as to the best mode of suppressing revolt. Though the writer was not a martialist, few were better qualified to counsel the government. . . . The two manuscript State Papers written by Spenser immediately before his death, are still unpublished. One is lengthy, and adds to the proofs his printed treatise gives of his consummate abilities.

GROSART (Spenser's *Works* 1. 230-5). That [Spenser] so arrived [in London in December, 1598] in no panic-terror or as having lost his head, is proved by a State-Paper addressed by him to the Queen direct, and not one line of which ever has been printed. It was prepared—as the commencement shows—in Cork, after the "escape" from Kilcolman. That alone witnesses to solidity and courage. It was delivered doubtless by Spenser himself in London to the Secretary of State, along with the "Dispatch" of Norreys of 9th December. This all-important Paper, and the others accompanying, are in the well-known handwriting of SIR DUDLEY CARLETON, and all are carefully noted by him as written by Spenser (spelled "Spencer"). There comes first "A briefe note of Ireland"—most noticeable for its very commonplace of topographical information. The pulse of the man who wrote it was not fevered. Next a Letter or rather State-Paper "To the Queene." Finally, "Certaine Pointes to be considered of in the recovery of the Realme of Ireland" . . . . The "Certaine Pointes" are very much a condensation of the *Veue of Ireland*, and tell us that whatever of sorrow and disappointment had come upon its writer, he was lion-hearted still, and bated no jot of hope or resolution. . . .

This enumeration of (mostly) the margin-notes [in "*To the Queene*"], gives only a meagre idea of the fulness and fearlessness of statement, the firmness and vigour of argument, or the fluent and nervous though quaint English of this most noticeable State-Paper.

This direct Address to the Queen and its accompanying elucidative Statement headed "Certaine pointes to be considered of in the recovery of the Realme," practically adumbrates that *Veue of Ireland* which only eight months before he had "entered" for publication. . . .

I am free to confess that after the pathos and desolateness of the opening of the great State-Paper addressed to the Queen, it is profoundly satisfying to have the high note of the "Certaine pointes to be considered of in the recovery of the Realme."

Its date is to be specially remembered. It could not have been later than the first week of December 1598; for Spenser left Cork for London on 9th December.

HENLEY (pp. 165-6). This unworthy document with its angry whining tone was his last contribution to the subject of Irish affairs. One can excuse and sympathise with the anger, but the exaggerated commiseration of himself and the other sufferers repels, especially when it is remembered how little thought he had for the agonies of those they had supplanted. One would have expected a manlier tone from one "not without experience in the service of the wars" [from the recommendation that Spenser be made Sheriff of Co. Cork, 30 September, 1598, in *Acts of the Privy Council* 29. 205].

RENWICK (*View*, pp. 329-30). The only evidence for attributing [B. N.] to Spenser is that it is endorsed "by Spenser" in a later hand. That there are similarities in its policy to some part of the View is not surprising, since I have shown that policy to be widely held, but I do not accept it as his. Its execrably highflown rhetoric might be set down to emotional excitement, but Spenser's style, in verse and prose, however decorative, is always controlled and never florid. He does not express emotion in that way, and though hysteria may play queer tricks, it is a large assumption that it would so completely destroy the training and habit of a lifetime. What is more cogent, the writer deliberately attempts to exalt Ormond [Russell?] at the expense of Norreys, the Lord President of Munster. Norreys indeed, a sick man at the time, showed neither skill nor resolution, and a sufferer might think little of him, but I see no reason why Ormond should deserve any manifestation of partizanship at Spenser's hands, then or at any other time.

HEFFNER (*MLN* 52. 58) notes that Renwick does not seem to be aware of the copy of part of *B. N.* in Harleian MS 3787, 21, f. 184, which ascribes the work to Spenser and contains verses on Tyrone [see *B. N.* 339 n] which date the document as of late 1598 or early 1599.

HULBERT (*MP* 34. 345-53), like Renwick, has challenged the attribution of *B. N.* to Spenser. She calls attention to the fact that it really consists of three separate documents, of which only the first is properly "*A breife note of Ireland*"; and the whole of this, she believes, deals with matters not touched on in the *View*. The second document, "*To the Queene*," differs from the *View* in treating Tyrone

somewhat sympathetically; Fitzwilliam is condemned severely for his defrauding the Earl of land and, in consequence, of the allegiance of the McMahon; the blame for the Earl's disloyalty is laid, in part, on the influence of other discontented Irish noblemen and the King of Spain and, in part, on his own will, and there is a suggestion that, had the Queen been more diplomatic in handling the Earl, she could have kept him from open rebellion [see *B. N.* 45-98]. . . . Spenser views the Earl of Tyrone in an entirely different light. He is to Spenser a combination of treachery and cunning [see *View* 3551-5]. . . . So far from thinking of him as an important chieftain deprived wrongfully of land and subjects, Spenser regards him as the "most out-cast of all the O'Neales [then, and] lifted by her Majestie out of the dust, to that he hath now wrought himself unto" [*View* 3551-3]. As for his claim to Monaghan, Spenser makes clear his attitude through his mouthpiece Irenaeus [see *View* 3590-3611] . . . . Eudoxus' reply [see *View* 3612-5] . . . is surely an indication that Spenser sympathized with Fitzwilliam's efforts to recover Monaghan for the crown. In addition there is no suggestion in *A view of* . . . . *Ireland* that the actions of Fitzwilliam, the Earl's fear for his freedom and life, and the persuasions of the Irish nobles had any part in shaping the Earl's course; the origin of Tyrone's defection lay, according to Spenser, in that

APPENDIX IV 535

mistaken policy which led England to support the Earl against Tirlogh Luineach and thereby unwittingly to place power and strength in the former's hands [*View* 3542-5].

Hulbert also notes that the author of the second part of B. N. takes a view of Sir John Norris which Spenser could not have taken [see note on 93-8]. Of the third part, " Certaine pointes," she writes:

> when the agreements [with the *View*] which Grosart sees are examined, they will be found to consist merely in this: that in both documents the writers advocate force, as did Sidney and Norris and probably many another Englishman of the day [see note on B. N. 328-9]. Then, when one compares in detail the two plans, one fails to see how Grosart could call such agreement " thorough and exact." For example, both documents suggest that, before the opening of hostilities, a general pardon be extended to all who wish to submit to the crown; but " Certaine points " limits the extent of the pardon to ten or twelve days; Spenser would have it held open twenty days [see note on B. N. 356-8]. Again, the plots differ in their estimates of the time and the number of troops needed for the subduing of Ireland: " Certaine points " states that it will take ten thousand men one-half year, three thousand men two years; Spenser holds that ten thousand men and one thousand horse will not take "above the space of one yeare and a halfe " [see note on B. N. 339-42]. In particular the method of warfare to be pursued, as indicated in " Certaine points," is diametrically opposed to that suggested by Spenser. " Certaine points " condemns that method of conquest which consists in the placing of garrisons and in repeated attacks by them in certain territories; it urges instead a steadily pursued campaign which is " to be begune in Mounster and from thence to proceede to the rest throughe Kery and Offalye." Spenser's plan uses garrisons; the kind of warfare suggested by " Certaine points " is criticized as futile and dangerous [see note on B. N. 348-53]. . . . Before leaving a comparison of these three documents and *A view of . . . . Ireland*, it should be noted that there is no mention in them of Spenser's elaborate plan to keep Ireland peaceful after the conquest by means of garrisons placed in each county [province?], whose support he plans for in great detail by means of a " cesse " [composition? See *View* 3904-4400].

Hulbert points out, in conclusion, that while many of the differences between B. N. and the *View* might be explained as changes in Spenser's opinions, two of them preclude any possibility of a common authorship: the opposite methods of warfare proposed and the strikingly dissimilar attitudes to Tyrone.

> Particularly is this second difference difficult to comprehend if we insist that the documents are Spenser's, for it is almost unbelievable that, after the burning of Kilcolman by Tyrone's men, Spenser would abandon the stern censoring of Tyrone which we find in the *View* to adopt the sympathetic attitude toward him which is characteristic of the second of the three documents. And, of course, the moment we are convinced that even one difference between the *View* and the three documents has weight, then all the other dissimilarities in matter and attitude become additional testimony in support of the hypothesis which that single difference suggests.

HEFFNER (*MLQ* 3. 512). This document has been questioned by Mr. Renwick and others. Mr. Renwick points out that the style is high flown and totally unlike

Spenser's other prose. He finds it impossible to believe that Spenser would have attacked Norrys and upheld Ormond. These do not seem to me strong enough reasons for denying Spenser's authorship. In the first place, the document is addressed to the Queen, and it was customary to write to her in a much "higher style than was used in ordinary discourse." There was even a distinction in handwriting. Most of the memorials to Queen Elizabeth were in the italic rather than the secretary hand. It must also be remembered that if Spenser wrote "A Brief View [Note?] of Ireland," he wrote it at a time when he was in a highly disturbed and emotional state. He had just seen everything that he owned destroyed, and it is possible that he took part in the fight at Kilcolman. Certainly many of his friends and tenants were destroyed by the rebels. Calmness was not to be expected. His attitude toward Norrys at this particular time would be hard to determine. My main reason for ascribing this document to Spenser, however, is that it is so ascribed in two manuscript versions. One, in the Public Record Office at London, is well known and is printed in Grosart's edition. In the British Museum, however, is a manuscript copy of the first [last?] part of this treatise, endorsed "Spenser's Discourse Briefly of Ireland." Thus, for the first part at least, we have two independent ascriptions to Spenser. The Harleian manuscript was, as will be shown, certainly written in 1599, and refers to Essex's expedition against the Irish rebels [see "A Peere of Ingland" in *B. N.* 339 n].

JUDSON (*Life*, p. 200). Perhaps this document—really three documents, different from each other in tone—is the joint work of several refugees, and its endorsement a result of Spenser's having brought it to England along with Norris's dispatches.

EDITOR. Certain points emerge from these discussions. (1) *B. N.* must date from the last three months of 1598, when the condition of the Munster undertakers was most hopeless. (2) *B. N.* is really three documents, the title "*A breife note of Ireland*" applying only to the first of them. But since we need a name for the whole and since it is customary to call the whole *A Brief Note*, it seems best to retain that general title. (3) The three documents differ decidedly in tone and purpose, and the dissimilarity may indicate that *B. N.* had more than one author (both *I* and *we* occur in it). But since, if such is the case, there is no way of determining where each author's work begins and ends, it has seemed best to print the three documents together, as they occur in the original manuscript.

In the fourth place, I feel sure that Spenser is the chief, if not the sole, author of *B. N.* The evidence for his authorship is external as well as internal: the manuscript among the State Papers is endorsed in a contemporary hand as "*A breife discourse of Ireland. by Spencer*"; this authorship is accepted in the contemporary copy of part of *B. N.* in the Harleian MSS; and it is hard to find a motive for wrongly ascribing to Spenser, in 1598 or 1599, a governmental document which there was no likelihood of publishing. What is more important, there is the best internal evidence that Edmund Spenser, the poet and author of the still unpublished *View*, wrote at least a good part of *B. N.*: single parallels to his accepted works prove little, but it is inconceivable that in the few pages of *B. N.* another man than Spenser should happen to produce all the parallels, in both phraseology and thought, which are noted in the commentary of the present edition.

APPENDIX IV 537

This conclusion is not shaken, I believe, by any of the arguments advanced against Spenser's authorship. The "execrably highflown rhetoric" which, for Renwick, distinguishes the style of *B. N.* from that of Spenser's works is at times a mosaic of Spenserian phrases and constructions (see particularly 25-44); it is easier to believe that Spenser was overemotional during Tyrone's rebellion than to deny that *B. N.* expresses hysteria in precisely the form which would be most natural to Spenser. For Renwick's statement that *B. N.* attempts to exalt Ormond at the expense of Norris I am unable to find any evidence; if by "Ormond" he means Russell, the attitude of *B. N.* is not inconsistent with Spenser's (see note on 93-8).

Of the various differences between *B. N.* and the *View* Hulbert only asserts that two are crucial evidence against Spenser's authorship of *B. N.* The first of these, in regard to the advisability of pursuing the enemy in the open or of first establishing garrisons in his country, is a clearcut difference. But it concerns a method, not a principle, and a method in the military sphere, where Spenser, who was not a soldier, might very well change his opinion to accord with the advice of others. Furthermore, the military situation had been radically altered between 1596 and the end of 1598; Tyrone, who had gathered a large, well-armed force, was no longer "a flyinge enemye" of the kind Spenser described in the *View* (3061-2); he had taken the initiative and would have to be defeated in the field.

The second of the two differences on which Hulbert rests the case against Spenser's authorship is not clearcut. She feels that *B. N.*, unlike the *View*, is sympathetic to Tyrone because it explains how the conduct of various parties, including FitzWilliam and the Queen, has driven him to rebellion. But a similar effort to explain the motives which underlay Tyrone's dealings appears in the *View* (3505-27). Specifically, *B. N.* does not say that FitzWilliam defrauded Tyrone of land or that it would have been wrong to convert Monaghan into a county, and so remove it from the overlordship of Tyrone, by honest means; *B. N.* rather attacks FitzWilliam for his treachery to Hugh MacMahon, which gave Tyrone and other Irish lords good reason to expect that they might be robbed, imprisoned, and murdered in the same way; and it goes on to say that it would have been politic to accept the Earl's offer to come to England, whether or not he was sincere in making it. The only sympathy shown for the enemy, if it can be called sympathy, lies in explaining his natural reaction to the dishonorable conduct of the English Deputy, an explanation which is not out of line with the *View*; Spenser's dialogue urges, as a corollary to the vigorous prosecution of the war against the Irish rebels, a thorough reformation of greedy and incompetent English magistrates (2820-85, 5282-91), and it alludes to the misdemeanors of FitzWilliam in particular (3426-7, 5285-6). *B. N.* touches on other sides of Tyrone's career than does the *View*; it would be hard to say that it reveals more sympathy for him. As for the burning of Kilcolman by Tyrone's men: Tyrone himself was, of course, not present on that occasion and had no more immediate responsibility for it than for all the similar depredations committed against other Munster colonists; yet Hulbert would surely grant that *B. N.* must have been written by one or more of the Munster colonists. And which of the Munster colonists, in a document addressed to the government, would use the phraseology as well as the ideas of Edmund Spenser?

APPENDIX V

VERSE IN SPENSER'S PROSE

OSGOOD (*ELH* 1. 1-6) notes that in the *View* he has found some six hundred examples of four, five, six, and seven-stress iambic verse. He cites the following passages as illustrations of this tendency [those preceded by * are iambic meter in Todd's text but not in *E*]: 5 so . . . soyle, 340-1 the . . . Civilitye, *368-9 of plantinge . . . pollicies, 452-3 Corners . . . foote, 563 and . . . seas, 1221 *Vincentius*, *Æneas Syluius*, 1223-4 an . . . learned, 1226 set . . . Ancientes, 1228 Besides . . . themselues, *1228-9 perhaps . . . Artes, 1231 some . . . Antiquitye, 1232 maye . . . out, *1308-9 And . . . out, 1348 an . . . thinges, 1453-4 I . . . travell, 1454-5 to him . . . purpose, 1457-8 that . . . Countrye, 1528 greate . . . grasse, 2339-40 they . . . ornamentes, 2341 yet . . . flowers, *2342-3 which gaue . . . abused, 2344-5 This . . . reformacion, 2736-7 a . . . excuse, 3293 do . . . Comiserate, 3552-4 to . . . releived, 3554-5 sone . . . his, 3608 no . . . warr, 3822 Continueweall . . . obedience, 4165 the widenes . . . pasturage.

In the earlier prose of Spenser's letters Osgood does not observe the same tendency. But he cites the following examples of it from *Ax.*: 350 hee . . . body, 351-3 no . . . where, 354 where . . . run, 357-8 trim . . . cates, 360-1 are . . . payned, 362 being . . . Sunnebeames. In *B. N.* he finds these iambic verses: 25-6 *of this . . . Ireland*, 26 moste . . . soveraigne, 27-8 of whome . . . left, 28 lie . . . oblivion, 29-30 which . . . remote, 33 one . . . shed, 132-3 brought . . . land, 134-7 nowe . . . commiserate.

BIBLIOGRAPHY

This list intends to give, in general, only fuller titles of articles cited by author and of books cited repeatedly in the Commentary and Appendices.

EDITIONS

LETTERS

Quarto. See facsimile title page in text.
Haslewood. Ancient Critical Essays upon English Poets and Poësy. Ed. Joseph Haslewood. London, 1815.
Grosart. The Works of Gabriel Harvey. Ed. Alexander B. Grosart. London, 1884–1885.
Gregory Smith. Elizabethan Critical Essays. Ed. G. Gregory Smith. Oxford, 1904.

AXIOCHUS

Quarto. See facsimile title page in text.
Padelford. The Axiochus of Plato Translated by Edmund Spenser. Ed. Frederick Morgan Padelford. Baltimore, 1934.

A VIEW OF THE PRESENT STATE OF IRELAND

Ware 1. The Historie of Ireland. Ed. Sir James Ware. Dublin, 1633.
1763. A View of the State of Ireland. Dublin, 1763.
Ware 2. Ancient Irish Histories. Ed. Sir James Ware. Dublin, 1809.
1860. A Collection of Tracts . . . Illustrative . . . of Ireland. Dublin, 1860.
Morley. Ireland under Elizabeth and James I. Ed. Henry Morley. London, 1890.
Renwick. A View of the Present State of Ireland. Ed. W. L. Renwick. London, 1934.

COLLECTED EDITIONS

Folio 3. The Works of That Famous English Poet, Mr. Edmond Spenser. London, 1679.
Hughes. The Works of Mr. Edmund Spenser. Ed. John Hughes. London, 1715.
Todd. The Works. Ed. Henry John Todd. London, 1805.
Child. The Poetical Works. Ed. Francis J. Child. Boston, 1855.
Collier. The Poetical Works. Ed. John Payne Collier. London, 1862.
Morris. The Works. Ed. Richard Morris and John W. Hales. London, 1869.
Grosart. The Complete Works in Verse and Prose. Ed. Alexander B. Grosart. London, 1882–1884.
Dodge. The Complete Poetical Works. Ed. R. E. Neil Dodge. Cambridge (Mass.), 1908.
De Selincourt. The Poetical Works. Ed. J. C. Smith and Ernest de Selincourt. London, 1912.
Renwick. The Works. Ed. W. L. Renwick. Oxford, 1930–1932.

MISCELLANEOUS

All the Statutes. " In this volume are contained all the Statutes from the tenthe yere of king Henrie the sixt, to the xiiii. yere of our moste gracious and soueragne lady Queene Elyzabeth, made and established in her highnes Realme of Irelande." 1572.
Analecta Hibernica. 1930–1931.

Ancient Laws of Ireland. Ed. Alexander G. Richey and others. 1865–1901.
Anonymous. The Description of Ireland. Ed. Edmund Hogan. 1878.
———. Edmond Spenser — the State Papers. Dublin University Magazine 58 (1861). 131-44.
———. The History of Sir John Perrott. Ed. Richard Rawlinson. 1728.
Arber, Edward, ed. A Transcript of the Registers of the Company of Stationers of London; 1554–1640. 1875–1894.
Armstrong, Olive. Edward Bruce's Invasion of Ireland. 1923.
Atkinson, Dorothy F. Edmund Spenser, A Bibliographical Supplement. 1937.
Bagwell, Richard. Ireland under the Tudors. 1885–1890.
Banks, Theodore H. Spenser's Rosalind: A Conjecture. PMLA 52 (1937). 335-7.
Beacon, Richard. Solon His Follie. 1594.
Bennett, Josephine Waters. The Allegory of Sir Artegall in F. Q. V, xi-xii. SP 37 (1940). 177-200.
———. The Evolution of "The Faerie Queene." 1942.
Berli, Hans. Gabriel Harvey. 1913.
Berry, Henry F., ed. Statutes and Ordinances, and Acts of the Parliament of Ireland. 1907–1910.
Birch, Thomas. The Life of Mr. Edmund Spenser. The Faerie Queene by Edmund Spenser (1751). 1. i-xxxvii.
———, ed. Memoirs of the Reign of Queen Elizabeth. 1754.
Black, J. B. The Reign of Elizabeth. 1936.
Bodin, Jean. Les Six Livres de la Republique. 1576.
Boemus, Johannes. Omnium Gentium Mores, Leges et Ritus. 1571.
Bourne, H. R. Fox. Sir Philip Sidney. 1891.
Bradner, Leicester. Edmund Spenser and the Faerie Queene. 1948.
———. Spenser's Connections with Hampshire. MLN 60 (1945). 180-4.
Buchanan, George. Rerum Scoticarum Historia. 1583.
Buck, Philo M. Add. MS. 34064 and Spenser's Ruins of Time and Mother Hubberd's Tale. MLN 22 (1907). 41-6.
———. Spenser's Lost Poems. PMLA 23 (1908). 80-99.
Burges, George, ed. and trans. Axiochus. The Works of Plato (Bohn Classical Library). 6. 39-56.
Butler, William F. T. Gleanings from Irish History. 1925.
Buyssens, E. Review of The Axiochus of Plato Translated by Edmund Spenser. Revue Belge de Philologie et d'Histoire 14 (1935). 131-3.
C. The "Arcadia" Unveiled. NQ, Third Series 4 (1863). 237.
Caldwell, James Ralston. Dating a Spenser-Harvey Letter. PMLA 41 (1926). 568-74.
Calendar of Letters and State Papers Relating to English Affairs, Preserved Principally in the Archives of Simancas, 1568–1579, 1580–1586. Ed. Martin A. S. Hume. 1896.
Calendar of State Papers and Manuscripts, Relating to English Affairs, Existing in the Archives and Collections of Venice, 1592–1603. Ed. Horatio F. Brown. 1897.
Calendar of State Papers, Domestic Series, 1581–1590. Ed. Robert Lemon. 1865.
———, 1591–1594, 1595–1597. Ed. Mary A. E. Green. 1867–1869.
Calendar of State Papers, Foreign Series, 1579–1580, 1583 and Addenda. Ed. Arthur J. Butler and Sophie C. Lomas. 1904–1913.
Calendar of State Papers Relating to Ireland, 1509–1573, 1574–1585, 1586–1588, 1588–1592, 1592–1596. Ed. Hans C. Hamilton. 1860–1890.
———, 1596–1597, 1598–1599, 1599–1600, 1600, 1600–1601. Ed. Ernest G. Atkinson. 1893–1905.
———, 1601–1603. Ed. Robert P. Mahaffy. 1912.
———, 1603–1606, 1606–1608, 1608–1610. Ed. C. W. Russell. 1872–1874.

BIBLIOGRAPHY 541

Calendar of the Carew Manuscripts, 1515–1574, 1575–1588, 1589–1600, 1601–1603, 1603–1624, Miscellaneous. Ed. J. S. Brewer and William Bullen. 1867–1871.
Calendar of the Patent and Close Rolls of Chancery in Ireland, of the Reigns of Henry VIII., Edward VI., Mary, and Elizabeth. Ed. James Morrin. 1861–1862.
Camden, William. Annales Rerum Anglicarum et Hibernicarum Regnante Elizabetha. 1615–1625.
———. Britannia. 1590.
———. The Historie of the Most Renowned and Victorious Princesse Elizabeth. Trans. W. Norton. 1630.
Campion, Edmund. A Historie of Ireland. Ed. R. Gottfried. 1940.
Carpenter, Frederic Ives. A Reference Guide to Edmund Spenser. 1923.
Church, R. W. Spenser. 1879.
Churchyard, Thomas. A Warning for the Wise. 1580.
Clyn, John. Annalium Hiberniae Chronicon. Ed. Richard Butler. 1849.
Cokayne, George E. The Complete Peerage. Ed. Vicary Gibbs. 1910–1940.
Colvin, Caroline. The Invasion of Ireland by Edward Bruce. 1901.
Covington, Frank F., Jr. Another View of Spenser's Linguistics. SP 19 (1922). 244-8.
———. Elizabethan Notions of Ireland. Texas Review 6 (1920–1921). 222-46.
———. Spenser's Use of Irish History in the Veue of the Present State of Ireland. UTB, Studies in English 4 (1924). 5-38.
Craik, George L. Spenser, and His Poetry. 1845.
Curtis, Edmund. The Viceroyalty of Lionel, Duke of Clarence. JRSAI 47 (1917). 165-81; 48 (1918). 65-73.
Davies, Sir John. A Discoverie of the State of Ireland. 1612.
———. A Letter to Robert Earl of Salisbury (1607). Ireland under Elizabeth and James I. Ed. Henry Morley. Pp. 343-80.
———. A Letter to Robert Earl of Salisbury Concerning the State of Ireland (1610). Ireland under Elizabeth and James I. Ed. Henry Morley. Pp. 381-90.
———. A Speech on the Irish Parliament. Ireland under Elizabeth and James I. Ed. Henry Morley. Pp. 391-409.
Davis, B. E. C. Edmund Spenser. 1933.
———. Review of The Axiochus of Plato Translated by Edmund Spenser. MLR 30 (1935). 519-20.
Derrick, John. The Image of Irelande. 1581.
Devereux, Walter B. Lives and Letters of the Devereux, Earls of Essex. 1853.
Dowling, Thaddeus. Annales Breves Hiberniae. Ed. Richard Butler. 1849.
Draper, John W. More Light on Spenser's Linguistics. MLN 41 (1926). 127-8.
———. Spenser's Linguistics in the Present State of Ireland. MP 17 (1919–1920). 471-86.
Dunlop, Robert. The Plantation of Leix and Offaly. EHR 6 (1891). 61-96.
———. The Plantation of Munster. EHR 3 (1888). 250-69.
———. Sixteenth Century Maps of Ireland. EHR 20 (1905). 309-37.
Dymmok, John. A Treatice of Ireland. Ed. Richard Butler. 1842.
Eccles, Mark. Spenser's First Marriage. TLS 30 (1931). 1053.
Edwards, Edward. The Life of Sir Walter Raleigh. 1868.
Falkiner, C. Litton. The Counties of Ireland. PRIA 24 (1902–1904). 169-94.
———. Essays Relating to Ireland. 1909.
———. The Parliament of Ireland under the Tudor Sovereigns. PRIA 25 (1904–1905). 508-41, 553-66.
Faverty, Frederic E. A Note on the Areopagus. PQ 5 (1926). 278-80.

Fleming, Abraham. A Bright Burning Beacon. 1580.
Fletcher, Jefferson B. Areopagus and Pléiade. JEGP 2 (1898–1899). 429-53.
Four Masters, The. The Annals of the Kingdom of Ireland. Ed. and trans. John O'Donovan. 1856.
Freyd, Bernard. Spenser or Anthony Munday? — A Note on the Axiochus. PMLA 50 (1935). 903-8.
Fulton, Edward. Spenser, Sidney, and the Areopagus. MLN 31 (1916). 372-4.
Gainsford, Thomas. The Glory of England. 1618.
Galway, Margaret. Spenser's Rosalind. TLS 46 (1947). 372.
Gilbert, Allan H. Did Plato Banish the Poets or the Critics? SP 36 (1939). 1-19.
Gilbert, John T. Account of Facsimiles of National Manuscripts of Ireland. 1884.
Golding, Arthur. A Discourse vpon the Earthquake. 1580.
Gottfried, Rudolf B. The Date of Spenser's "View." MLN 52 (1937). 176-80.
―――――. The Debt of Fynes Moryson to Spenser's View. PQ 17 (1938). 297-307.
―――――. Irish Geography in Spenser's View. ELH 6 (1939). 114-37.
―――――. Spenser as an Historian in Prose. Transactions of the Wisconsin Academy of Sciences, Arts and Letters 30 (1937). 317-29.
―――――. Spenser's View and Essex. PMLA 52 (1937). 645-51.
Gray, M. M. The Influence of Spenser's Irish Experiences on The Faerie Queene. RES 6 (1930). 413-28.
Green, Alice S. Irish Land in the Sixteenth Century. Ériu 3 (1907). 174-85.
Greene, Robert. A Qvip for an Vpstart Courtier. 1592.
Greenlaw, Edwin A. The Influence of Machiavelli on Spenser. MP 7 (1909–1910). 187-202.
―――――. Spenser and the Earl of Leicester. PMLA 25 (1910). 535-61.
―――――. Studies in Spenser's Historical Allegory. 1932.
Hales, John W. Edmund Spenser. The Works of Edmund Spenser (1869). Pp. xi-lv.
――――― and Sidney Lee. Edmund Spenser. DNB. 1909.
Hallam, Henry. Introduction to the Literature of Europe, in the Fifteenth, Sixteenth, and Seventeenth Centuries. 1872.
Hamer, Douglas. Review of The Axiochus of Plato Translated by Edmund Spenser. RES 12 (1936). 84-6.
Hamilton, Lord Ernest. Elizabethan Ulster.
Hardiman, James. Irish Minstrelsy, or Bardic Remains of Ireland. 1831.
Harington, Sir John. Nugae Antiquae. Ed. Thomas Park. 1804.
Harper, Carrie A. The Sources of the British Chronicle History in Spenser's Faerie Queene. 1910.
Harris, Walter. Hibernica. 1747–50.
Harvey, Gabriel. Fovre Letters. 1592.
―――――. Letter-Book (1573–1580). Ed. E. J. L. Scott. 1884.
―――――. Marginalia. Ed. G. C. Moore Smith. 1913.
―――――. The Works. Ed. Alexander C. Grosart. 1884–1885.
Heffner, Ray. Review of W. L. Renwick's Edition of Spenser's View of the Present State of Ireland. MLN 52 (1937). 57-8.
―――――. Spenser's View of Ireland: Some Observations. MLQ 3 (1942). 507-15.
Henley, Pauline. Spenser in Ireland. 1928.
Herbert, Sir William. Croftus, sive de Hibernia Liber. Ed. W. E. Buckley. 1887.
Herodotus. The History. Trans. George Rawlinson. 1858–1860.
Hewlett, James H. Interpreting a Spenser-Harvey Letter. PMLA 42 (1927). 1060-5.
Higginson, James J. Spenser's Shepherd's Calender in Relation to Contemporary Affairs. 1912.

Hinton, Edward M. Ireland through Tudor Eyes. 1935.
Hogan, James. The Irish Law of Kingship. PRIA, Archaeology 40 (1930–1932). 186-254.
Holinshed, Raphael. Chronicles. 1586–1587.
Hollowell, B. M. The Elizabethan Hexametrists. PQ 3 (1924). 51-7.
Hulbert, Viola B. Spenser's Relation to Certain Documents on Ireland. MP 34 (1936–1937). 345-53.
Hull, Vernum. Edmund Spenser's Mona-Shul. PMLA 56 (1941). 578-9.
Hyde, Douglas. A Literary History of Ireland. 1901.
Jackson, William A. The Carl H. Pforzheimer Library, English Literature 1475–1700. 1940.
James, M. R. The Carew Manuscripts. EHR 42 (1927). 261-7.
Jenkins, Raymond. A Note on E. K. SP 45 (1948). 76-9.
———. Spenser and the Clerkship in Munster. PMLA 47 (1932). 109-21.
———. Spenser at Smerwick. TLS 32 (1933). 331.
———. Spenser: the Uncertain Years. PMLA 53 (1938). 350-62.
———. Spenser with Lord Grey in Ireland. PMLA 52 (1937). 338-53.
———. Who Is E. K.? SAB 19 (1944). 147-60; 20 (1945). 22-38, 82-94.
Johnson, Francis R. A Critical Bibliography of the Works of Edmund Spenser Printed before 1700. 1933.
Jones, H. S. V. A Spenser Handbook. 1930.
———. Spenser's Defense of Lord Grey. University of Illinois Studies in Language and Literature 5 (1919). 151-219.
Joyce, P. W. A Social History of Ancient Ireland. 1920.
———. The Wonders of Ireland. 1911.
Judson, Alexander C. The Life of Edmund Spenser. 1945.
———. Spenser and the Munster Officials. SP 44 (1947). 157-73.
———. Spenser in Southern Ireland. 1933.
Jusserand, J. J. A Literary History of the English People. 1926.
Keating, Geoffrey. The History of Ireland. Ed. and trans. David Comyn. 1902–1908.
Kuersteiner, Agnes D. E. K. Is Spenser. PMLA 50 (1935). 140-55.
Lee, Thomas. A Briefe Declaration of the Gouerment of Irelande. 1594. Ellesmere MS 1731, Huntington Library.
Legouis, Émile. Spenser. 1926.
Letters and Memorials of State. Ed. Arthur Collins. 1746.
Letters and Papers, Foreign and Domestic, of the Reign of Henry VIII. Vol. II, Part 1. Ed. J. S. Brewer. 1864.
———. Vols. XVI and XVII. Ed. James Gairdner and R. H. Brodie. 1898–1900.
Liber Munerum Publicorum Hiberniae. 1852.
Long, Percy W. Spenser and Sidney. Anglia 38 (1914). 173-92.
———. Spenser and the Bishop of Rochester. PMLA 31 (1916). 713-35.
Lyly, John [?]. Pappe with an Hatchet. 1589.
Lynch, John. Cambrensis Eversus. Ed. and trans. Matthew Kelly. 1848–1851.
Macintire, Elizabeth J. French Influence on the Beginnings of English Classicism. PMLA 26 (1911). 496-527.
McKerrow, R. B. The Use of So-Called Classical Metres in Elizabethan Verse.—I. MLQ 4 (1901). 172-80.
MacNemara, George U. Inchiquin, County Clare. JRSAI 31 (1901). 204-27, 341-64.
Magnus, Laurie. English Literature in Its Foreign Relations. 1927.
Martin, William C. The Date and Purpose of Spenser's Veue. PMLA 47 (1932). 137-43.
Maxwell, Constantia, ed. Irish History from Contemporary Sources (1509–1610). [1923.]
Maynadier, Howard. The Areopagus of Sidney and Spenser. MLR 4 (1909). 289-301.

Merrill, Elizabeth. The Dialogue in English Literature. 1911.
Mezger, Fritz. Kannte Spenser Irische Gedichte? Archiv 150 (1926). 232-3.
——————. Spensers Quellenangaben. Archiv 150 (1926). 233-4.
Millican, Charles Bowie. Spenser and the Table Round. 1932.
Mitchner, Robert W. Spenser and E. K.: an Answer. SP 42 (1945). 183-90.
Morley, Henry. English Writers. 1887–1895.
Moryson, Fynes. An Itinerary. 1617.
——————. Shakespeare's Europe. Ed. Charles Hughes. 1903.
Munday, Anthony. A View of Sundry Examples. [1580.]
Murphy, Denis. The College of the Irish Franciscans at Louvain. JRSAI 23 (1893). 237-50.
Nashe, Thomas. Haue with You to Saffron-Walden. 1596.
——————. Strange Newes. 1592.
——————. The Works. Ed. R. B. McKerrow. 1904–1910.
O'Curry, Eugene. On the Manners and Customs of the Ancient Irish. 1873.
O'Dubhagain, John, and Giolla na Naomh O'Huidhrin. Topographical Poems. Ed. John O'Donovan. 1862.
O'Flaherty, Roderic. Ogygia. 1685.
O'Huiggin, Tadhg Dall mac Cairbre. Bardic Poems. Ed. and trans. Eleanor Knott. 1922–1926.
Olaus Magnus. Historia de Gentium Septentrionalium Variis Conditionibus. 1567.
Ó Moghráin, Pádraig. More Notes on the Buaile. Béaloideas 14 (1944). 45-52.
——————. Some Mayo Traditions of the Buaile. Béaloideas 13 (1943). 161-71.
Ong, Walter J. Spenser's View and the Tradition of the "Wild" Irish. MLQ 3 (1942). 561-71.
O'Rahilly, Alfred. The Massacre at Smerwick (1580). 1938.
O'Rahilly, Thomas. Irish Poets, Historians, and Judges in English Documents 1538–1615. PRIA, Archaeology 36 (1921–1924). 86-120.
O'Reilly, Edward. An Essay on the Nature and Influence of the Ancient Irish Institutes. TRIA, Antiquities 14 (1825). 141-223.
—————— and John O'Donovan. An Irish-English Dictionary. 1877.
Orpen, Goddard H. Ireland under the Normans. 1920.
Orwen, William R. Spenser and Gosson. MLN 42 (1927). 574-6.
——————. Spenser and the Serpent of Division. SP 38 (1941). 198-210.
——————. Spenser's "Stemmata Dudleiana." NQ 190 (1946). 9-11.
Osgood, Charles G. Spenser's English Rivers. Transactions of the Connecticut Academy of Arts and Sciences 23 (1920). 67-108.
——————. Verse in Spenser's Prose. ELH 1 (1934). 1-6.
Padelford, Frederick M. The Political, Economic, and Social Views of Spenser. JEGP 14 (1915). 393-420.
——————. Spenser or Anthony Munday?—A Note on the Axiochus. PMLA 50 (1935). 908-13.
Payne, Robert. A Brife Description of Ireland. Ed. Aquilla Smith. 1841.
Plomer, Henry R., and Tom Peete Cross. The Life and Correspondence of Lodowick Bryskett. 1927.
Puttenham, George. The Arte of English Poesie. 1589.
Quiggin, E. C. Prolegomena to the Study of the Later Irish Bards 1200–1500. Proceedings of the British Academy 1911–1912. Pp. 89-143.
Rathborne, Isabel E. The Meaning of Spenser's Fairyland. 1937.
Renwick, W. L. Edmund Spenser. 1925.
——————. Review of Francis R. Johnson's A Critical Bibliography of the Works of Edmund Spenser Printed before 1700. MLR 29 (1934). 448.

BIBLIOGRAPHY

Rich, Barnaby. A New Description of Ireland. 1610.
———. Remembrances of the State of Ireland. Ed. C. Litton Falkiner. PRIA, Archaeology 26 (1906–1907). 125-42.
Riedner, Wilhelm. Spensers Belesenheit. 1908.
Rix, Herbert D. Rhetoric in Spenser's Poetry. 1940.
Rollins, Hyder R. William Elderton: Elizabethan Actor and Ballad Writer. SP 17 (1920). 199-245.
Routledge, F. J. The Journal of the Irish House of Lords in Sir John Perrot's Parliament. EHR 29 (1914). 104-17.
Rubel, Vere L. Poetic Diction in the English Renaissance. 1941.
S., E. A Suruey of the Present Estate of Ireland. 1615. Ellesmere MS 1746, Huntington Library.
S., E. C. The Government of Ireland vnder the Honorable, Iust, and Wise Gouernour Sir Iohn Perrot Knight. 1626.
Saintsbury, George. A History of English Prosody. 1906–1910.
Salesbury, William. A Dictionary in Englyshe and Welshe. [1547.]
Sandison, Helen E. Spenser's "Lost" Works and Their Probable Relation to His Faerie Queene. PMLA 25 (1910). 134-51.
Sargent, Ralph M. At the Court of Queen Elizabeth. 1935.
Schelling, Felix E. English Literature during the Lifetime of Shakespeare. 1910.
———. Poetic and Verse Criticism in the Reign of Elizabeth. 1891.
Seccombe, Thomas, and J. W. Allen. The Age of Shakespeare. 1904.
Smith, G. C. Moore. Gabriel Harvey's Letter-Book. NQ, Eleventh Series 3 (1911). 261-3.
———, ed. Gabriel Harvey's Marginalia. 1913.
———. Printed Books with Gabriel Harvey's Autograph or MS. Notes. MLR 28 (1933). 78-81.
Smith, G. Gregory, ed. Elizabethan Critical Essays. 1904.
Smith, J. C. Edmund Spenser. Encyclopaedia Britannica, fourteenth edition. 1929.
Smith, Roland M. Hamlet said "Pajock." JEGP 44 (1945). 292-5.
———. The Irish Background of Spenser's View. JEGP 42 (1943). 499-515.
———. More Irish Words in Spenser. MLN 59 (1944). 472-7.
———. Spenser and Milton: an Early Analogue. MLN 60 (1945). 394-8.
———. Spenser, Holinshed, and the Leabhar Gabhála. JEGP 43 (1944). 390-401.
———. Spenser's "Stony Aubrian." MLN 59 (1944). 1-5.
———. Spenser's Tale of the Two Sons of Milesio. MLQ 3 (1942). 547-57.
Snyder, Edward D. The Wild Irish: A Study of Some English Satires against the Irish, Scots, and Welsh. MP 17 (1919–1920). 687-725.
Southey, Robert. Commonplace Book. Ed. John W. Warter. 1849–1851. Third Series.
Spelman, Henry. Archaeologvs. 1626.
———. Glossarium Archaiologicum. 1664.
Spencer, Theodore. The Poetry of Sir Philip Sidney. ELH 12 (1945). 251-78.
Spingarn, Joel Elias. A History of Literary Criticism in the Renaissance. 1899.
Stanyhurst, Richard. De Rebvs in Hibernia Gestis. 1584.
Starnes, D. T. Spenser and E. K. SP 41 (1944). 181-200.
State Papers, Henry VIII. Part III. 1834.
Statute . . . Enacted in a Parliament Held in Kilkenny, A. Ed. James Hardiman. 1843.
Statvtes of Ireland, The. Ed. Richard Bolton. 1621.
Stone, William Johnson. Classical Metres in English Verse. 1901.
Swan, Marshall W. S. The Sweet Speech and Spenser's (?) Axiochus. ELH 11 (1944). 161-81.

Thomas, Sidney. "Hobgoblin Runne Away with the Garland from Apollo." MLN 55 (1940). 418-22.
Thompson, Guy Andrew. Elizabethan Criticism of Poetry. 1914.
Tolman, Albert H. The Relation of Spenser and Harvey to Puritanism. MP 15 (1917-1918). 549-64.
Towry, M. H. A Note on Spenser's Twenty Lost Works. The Bibliographer 1 (1881-1882). 129-30.
Tremayne, Edmond. Discourse at the Request of S^r Wa: Mildemay. 1573. Ellesmere MS 1701, Huntington Library.
Twyne, Thomas. A Shorte and Pithie Discourse. 1580.
Upham, Alfred H. The French Influence in English Literature. 1908.
Venn, John and J. H. Alumni Cantabrigienses. 1924.
Wainewright, John B. Some Letters and Papers of Nicholas Sander. Publications of the Catholic Record Society 26 (1926). 1-57.
Wallace, Malcolm W. The Life of Sir Philip Sidney. 1915.
Ward, A. W. Historical and Political Writings. Cambridge History of English Literature (1907-1927). 7. 212-63.
Ware, Sir James. The Whole Works. Ed. Walter Harris. 1739-1764.
Webbe, William. A Discourse of English Poetrie. 1586.
Welsdalius, Hermannus Rayanus, ed. and trans. Platonis Axiochvs. The Axiochus of Plato Translated by Edmund Spenser (1934). Pp. 61-80.
Westropp, Thomas J. The President's Address. JRSAI 46 (1916). 2-26.
Willcock, G. D. Passing Pitefull Hexameters. MLR 29 (1934). 1-19.
——— and Alice Walker, eds. The Arte of English Poesie by George Puttenham. 1936.
Young, G. M. A Word for Gabriel Harvey. Life and Letters 4 (1930). 492-6.

INDEX

In the case of the Commentary and the Appendices, this index is selective. No useful purpose would be served by listing all references to such works as the *Calendars of State Papers* or all cross-references to Spenser's own works; and some names which have no bearing on the poet or his writings are likewise omitted.

Absalom of Thomas Watson, 443
Abstemio, Lorenzo, 442-3
Academy of Athens, 31
Accent in English verse, 16, 264, 480-2
Accessaries, trial of, 70-1, 299
Acheron, 36
Achilles, 469
Adonis, 467
"*Ad Ornatissimum Virum* . . . G. H.," 8-11, 255-9, 444
Aemilia, 427
Aeneas, 99, 330, 444
Aeneas Sylvius, see Piccolomini, Eneo Sylvio
Aeneid, 444
Aeolian, 107, 339
Aeolus, 9
Aeschines, 491
Aesop, 167, 389-90
Aetolian, see Aeolian
Africa, 91, 470
Africans, 84-5, 92, 96-7, 100, 104-5, 111, 320, 509-10
Agamedes, 31, 272
Agard, Francis, 345, 404
Agricola, Rudolphus, 270, 491
Agrippa, 444, 465
Aherlow, 57, 194, 288
Airechts, 361-2
Ajax, 351
Alban-Scots, 83
Albany, 82-4, 86, 310-1
Albion, 82
Albyne, see Albany
Alcibiades, 116, 347
Aldermen, 212-4, 417
Aldred (Alfred), 201
Alexander Aegus, 351
Alexander the Great, 119, 351, 469
Alfred, 81, 201-2, 308, 411-2
" All barbarous people are . . . verye fearlesse of death," 72, 300
Allen, Bog of, 57, 288
Allen, J. W., 498
Allen, John, 395
" All inovacion is perillous," 147, 373-4
" All is the Conquerours," 52, 285
" All men be lyars," 87
" All men . . . loue libertye," 211

Alloonagh, 210, 416-7
All the Statutes, 282, 303-5, 307, 334, 351, 370, 391, 419, 421-2
Alps, 11, 258
Alured (Alfred), 81, 201-2
Amaryllis, 506
Amazon's Pillar, 28
Amor, 9, 16, 444, 467
Amoret, 427
Amphiaraus, 32, 273
Anacreontic epigrams by Spenser, 265
Analitics of Aristotle, 464
Analy (Co. Longford), 191-2, 405-6
Ancient Laws of Ireland, 281, 350, 366
Anglofrancitali, 466
Annals of Boyle, 420
Annals of Clonmacnoise, 294
Annals of Logh Cé, 294
Annals of Ulster, 291, 339
Anne, Mistress, 472-3
Anne, St., 472-3
Annius, Johannes, 284, 314
Anno xxvii. Reginae Elizabethae, 425
Anonymous, 344, 533
Anticosmopolita, or Britanniae Apologia, 460
Antiope, 270
Antiquities of Ireland, 81-2, 95, 97, 109-10, 230-1, 308, 430, 502-3
Antony, 119
Antrim, Co., 184, 290, 401
Ape in *Hub.*, 392, 421
Aphrodite, 329
Apollo, 9, 31-2, 36, 259, 272, 275-6, 466, 472
Apparel, 99-102, 111, 120-3, 351-3
Aqua vitae, 365
Aquilo (North Wind), 9
Aquitania, 51, 283-4
Aragon, 91
Arber, Edward, 477, 483, 488
Ardee, 195
Ardes, 61, 294, 397
Ardpatrick, 407
'Αρείῳ πάγῳ, see Areopagus
Areopagites, 31, 480
Areopagus, 6, 251, 442, 479-80
Aretino, Pietro, 460, 466, 471-2
Argive nun (Cydippe), 32
Argus, 89, 467

547

Argyll, Archibald Campbell, seventh Earl of, 168, 391
Ariosto, Lodovico, 471-2
Aristarchi, English, 470
Aristippus, 10, 259
Aristophanes, 472
Aristotle, 121, 352, 395, 453, 456, 458, 460, 464, 478-9
Arklow, 174
Arklow, Barony of, 190, 404
Arlo, see Aherlow
Armagh, city, 61
Armagh, Co., 184
Armenians, 217-8
Arms and manner of fighting, 106-7, 111-2, 120-4, 151, 337-9, 535, 537
Armstrong, Olive, 293-4
Army, cost and size of, 149-51, 245, 374, 376-7, 439, 535
Arsacomas, 108-9, 341
Ars Poetica of Horace, 474
Artaxerxes, 116, 347
Artegall, 296, 383-4, 424, 434, 528
Artemis, 36, 275-6, 329
Arthur, 85, 95, 324
Arundel, Philip Howard, Earl of, 479
Arundel Castle, 415
Arundel of the Strand, 207, 345, 415
Ascham, Roger, 6, 252, 443, 463, 474-5, 480-1
" As good neuer a whitt as neuer the better," 120, 351
Ashdown, 363
Asia, 116, 470
" As Irishe as Ohanlons breeche," 117
Assemblies, 128-31, 361
Asshe, Thomas, 432
Asteroth, Fair Maid of, see Astolat, Fair Maid of
Astolat, Fair Maid of, 111, 343, 519
Atarantians, 340
Athboy, 61, 302
Athena, 466
Athenians, 28, 54, 286
Athens, 29-30, 33, 54, 116, 285-6, 347, 442
Athlone, 188, 402-4
Athlone, Castle of, 188, 403
Athy, 188-9, 404
Atrebatii, 94, 322
Atterbury, H., 269, 488, 493
Audleys, 61, 294
Aurelius, Ambrosius, 363
Autrian, see Antrim, Co.
Avonbeg, River, 393
Awniduff, River, 378
Axiochus, 27-38 *passim*

B., A., see MacMahon, Hugh Roe
Babylon (Rome?), 11, 258
Babylonians, 329
Bacchus, 37
Bacon, Anthony, 434
Bacon, Sir Francis, 490
Badius Ascensius, 486
Bagenal, Sir Henry, 333, 432
Bagenal, Mabel, 351
Bagenal, Philip H., 351
Bagnett, Richard, 511
Bagwell, Richard, 287, 293, 302, 306, 357, 369-71, 378, 384-5, 392-3, 401, 425, 428, 432
Bale, John, 355, 370
Ball, John C., 369-70, 424
Ballashaine, see Ballyshannon
Ballinecor, 172, 174, 191, 393-5, 405, 505
Ballinecorrih, see Ballinecor
Ballyshannon, 152, 183, 377-8, 400
Baltinglas, James Eustace, Viscount, 295-6, 300-1, 393
Bán, Eóghan, 358
Bande, River, see Bann, River
Banks, Theodore H., 249, 267
Bann, River, 182-3, 399
Banno (Ireland), 145, 372, 521
Bantry, 193, 406
Barbarians, see Berbers
Barbary, 111
Barbour, John, 293
Bards, 84, 86-7, 110, 112, 124-7, 203, 219, 311, 315-6, 343, 355-61
Barnam, Benedict, 23, 489-90, 495
Baronets, English, 200, 410-1
Barrows, 130, 363
Barry, David FitzJames, eighth Viscount Barry of Buttevant, 207, 298, 415
Bartholomaeus Anglicus, 405
Bartoni, Alessandro, 524-5, 529-30
Batman, Stephen, 332
Battle monuments, 130, 363
Beacon, Richard, 286, 305, 351, 373, 376, 394, 397, 420
Beantoolhe, or Beantoolne, 101, 128, 332
Beards, 75, 110-1, 303, 342
Bede, 95, 293, 315-6, 325, 391
Belfast, 61, 152, 294
Belgae, 94, 322
Belgia, 93-4
" *Bella execrata Colonis*," 216, 420
Belleek, 152, 183, 377-8
Bellona, 452
Belprato, Count Giovanni Vincentio, 270, 491
Beltalbot, see Belturbet
Belturbet, 61, 152-3, 183, 294, 312, 377-8
Bembo, Cardinal Pietro, 472
Bennett, Josephine W., 266, 268, 386, 434
Berbers, 91, 319
Berenice, 99, 329
Berkshire, 94

INDEX 549

Berli, Hans, 482
Bermingham, Sir John, 61-2, 295
Bermingham, Lord, 117, 349, 520
Berosus, 86, 284, 313-4
Berry, Henry F., 299-300, 303-5, 351, 370, 419, 421, 427
" Better is a mischief then an inconvenience," 66, 80, 297
Bias, 32, 273
Bibiena, Cardinal Bernardo, 472
Bible, 105, 130-1, 137, 140, 218, 221, 328, 331, 337, 351, 363, 368, 422, 424-5, 471
Bilboa, governor of, 530
Bilchaunger, George, 465
Bingham, George, 378
Bingham, Sir Richard, 320, 375, 378-9, 381, 390, 396, 398, 400, 403, 420-1, 505, 528, 530
Birch, Thomas, 251, 266, 301, 320, 409, 429
Biscayans, 526
Bishops, 140-1, 229, 368-70
Biskellagh, see Briskelagh
Biton, 32, 272
Blácam, Aodh de, 328
Black, J. B., 502
Black Book of Ireland, 212, 418
Blackford, see Blackfort
Blackfort, 183, 378, 400
Blackwater of Ulster, River, 152, 183, 378, 399-400
Blatant Beast, 296, 426
Blenerhasset, Thomas, 396, 480
Boate, Gerard, 439
Boazio, Baptista, 289, 377-8, 395, 403, 407-8
Boccaccio, 460
Bodin, Jean, 278, 281, 284-6, 297, 304-5, 308, 311-2, 320-1, 368, 373-5, 423-4
Body to be cured before soul, 139, 368
Boemus, Johannes, 97-8, 111-2, 313-4, 327-8, 340, 342-3, 421, 510
Boethius, Hector, 106, 315, 318, 330, 335, 337-8
Bolton, Richard, 302-3
Booking, 205-6, 214, 414
Book of Howth, 291, 293-5, 314, 323, 338, 345, 347-8, 398, 402, 410-1, 430, 510
Book of Kells, 331
Book of O'Byrne, 358
Book of O'Connor Don, 356
Book of the Taking of Ireland, 335
Boolies, 97-9, 217-8, 327-8, 421
Boorde, Andrew, 341-2
Borgia, Cesare, 383-4, 429
Borh, 213, 419
Boroughs, 212-3, 419
Borsholders (tithingmen), 201-4, 212, 214, 411-2
Boswell, James, the younger, 487
Bourbon, 424

Bourne, H. R. Fox, 251, 479, 481
Bows and arrows, 75, 303-4
Bracknagh, 57, 191, 289, 519
Bradner, Leicester, 259, 282, 344, 386, 485
Brady, Bishop Hugh, 383
Brady, W. Maziere, 369
Branding of cattle, 226
Bravo, Agostino, 525, 529
Breaghe, 47, 281
Brehon laws, 47-8, 53, 280-1, 306, 327, 350, 361, 503
Brehons, 47-8, 280-1
Brehoone, see Brehon laws and Brehons
Bremingham, Lord, see Bermingham, Lord
Brenningham, Sir John, see Bermingham, Sir John
Breny, 192, 400, 406
Bretons, 93, 321
" *Breȝ., Ia: de*," 106, 337
Brian Boru, 363, 419-20
Bribes, 229-30, 236-7, 430, 432
Brief Note of Ireland, manuscripts of: Harleian MS 3787, p. 184—233, 534, 536; State Papers 63. 202, Part 4, item 59—233, 533-4, 536
Brins, see O'Byrnes
Briskelagh, 57, 191, 288-9
Britain, 11, 51, 85, 93-5, 315-8, 324, 368
Britannia, see Britain
British customs, 112-3
British language, 85, 93-5, 170-1, 322-3
Briton, A., 410-1
Britons, 85, 94-6, 137, 170-1, 309-11, 315-6, 321, 334, 338, 343, 510
Britons of France, see Bretons
Brittany, see Britain
Bromley, 466 (?)
Brooke, Sir Callisthenes, 395
Brooke, C. F. Tucker, 263
Brouncker, Sir Henry, 377
Bruce, Edward, 59-62, 169, 210, 288, 292-5, 305
Bruce, Robert, 60-1
Bruin, Sir, 347
Bruse, Philip de, 325
Bruse, William de, 325
Brutus, Marcus Junius, 52, 285
Brutus of England, 82, 86, 309-10, 320
Bryn, 94, 170-1, 323, 392
Bryskett, Lodowick, 278-9, 296, 328, 344, 350, 356-7, 366, 372-4, 379, 383, 385-6, 399, 429, 434
Buanacht, 79, 306
Buchanan, George, 83, 86, 93, 103-4, 106, 108, 292, 305, 308, 310-1, 313, 315-22, 334-8, 340-3, 355-6, 510
Buck, Philo M., 250, 266-8, 488
Bundrowes, 152, 378
Burby, Cuthbert, 21, 488-90, 493-6

Burges, George, 270-1, 274-6
Burgh, Elizabeth de, 290
Burgh, Thomas, Lord, 238, 376, 435
Burghley, William Cecil, Lord, 375, 389, 396-7, 409
Burke, 320-1
Burke, William, 356
Burkes of MacWilliam Eighter, 187, 401-3
Burkes of MacWilliam Euter, 187, 402, 420
Burkes of Munster, 194, 408
Burrows, Lord, see Burgh, Thomas, Lord
Butler, Sir Edmund, 344
Butler, Theobald, 404
Butler, William F. T., 283, 288, 291, 298, 306-7, 349, 399, 402, 407, 415
Butlerabo, 103, 334
Butlers, 114, 145, 172-4, 188-9, 301-2, 372, 394, 522
Buttevant, 59, 292, 435
Buyssens, E., 276, 493
Byng, Thomas, 458
Bynneman, Henry, 3, 13
Byrchensha, Ralph, 282, 388, 439
Byrnes, see O'Byrnes

C., 428
Cadiz, 88, 317
Cadiz Expedition, 428-9, 504-5
Caesar, Julius, 72, 86-7, 112, 119, 300, 313-6, 343, 519
Caithréim Thoirdhealbhaigh, 291-2
Caldwell, James R., 249, 261-2
Cales, see Cadiz
Calixenus, 33, 274
Callias, 30, 272
Callimachus, 99, 329
Callirrhoe, 27, 269
Callisthenes, 29
Calvin, John, 493
Calypso, 9, 259
Cambridge University, 5, 451, 453, 456, 458, 460-2, 481, 484-5, 531
Camden, William, 93, 109, 263, 280, 283-4, 290-2, 295, 308-12, 314-6, 318-22, 324-5, 333, 336, 338, 340-1, 343, 347-50, 354-6, 363-5, 368, 372, 380, 384-5, 387, 389, 391, 393-4, 405, 411-3, 418-9, 427-8, 497, 510, 529-31
Campbell, Lady Agnes, 391
Campion, Edmund, 280-2, 287, 290, 292-3, 295, 314-5, 318-9, 321-2, 324, 335, 342, 345-9, 361, 382-3, 391, 411, 417, 497, 510
Campion, Thomas, 481
Cancii, see Cauci
Canham, Bartholomew, 514
Canopus, 461
Canterbury, Archbishop of, 348-9
Cantreds, 212, 218, 417-8

Captains, English, 143, 164-5, 175, 371, 376, 387-8, 395
Captains, Irish, see Lords, Irish
Caradoc of Llancarfan, 310-1
Carew, Sir George, 326, 360, 398, 408, 418
Carleton, Sir Dudley, 533
Carlingford, 61
Carlow, Co., 64, 173-4, 190, 289-90, 301
Carns, 130, 363
Carpenter, Frederic I., 310, 344, 348, 428, 435, 488
Carranadoo, 402-3
Carrows, 127-8, 148, 219, 360-1, 422
Carte MSS, Bodleian Library, 299-300, 369, 375
Carthage, 92
Carthaginians, 90-2, 320, 510
Carthaye, 92
Carthy, Brian, 361
Cartwright, Thomas, 461
Cashel, 195
Caspian Sea, 98
Castiglione, Count Baldassare, 460
Castlecliffer, see Castleliffer
Castlefinn, 152, 378
Castleliffer, 152, 378
Castlemaine, 193, 407
Castle of the Strond, 415
Castletown, 61, 294
Castor, 467
Catherlagh, see Carlow, Co.
Catholic, 334, 336
Catholic Church, 136-8, 221-2
Catholic colleges on Continent, Irish, 222, 425
Catholic emissaries in Ireland, 221-2, 425
Cato, Marcus Porcius, 10, 442, 470
Catullus, 329
Caucasus, 11, 258
Cauci, 93, 321
Caune, 94-5, 323
Cavan, Co., 64, 152-3, 183-4, 297
Cavanaghs, 64, 94-5, 152, 154-5, 172, 174, 178-9, 190-1, 290, 297, 322-3, 395
Caxton, William, 390
Cecil, Sir Robert, 375, 417
Cecrops (Argus), 89
Celestine I, Pope, 137
Celtica, 93-4, 317
Celts, 88, 316-7, 319
Centaurs, 34
Ceres, 11, 260
"*Certaine Latin Verses,*" 445
Cess, 131-3, 305, 364-5, 399, 535
Chaldees, 99, 328
Chamberlains, 61, 294
Chambers, R. W., 278
Chambrun MS, Folger Shakespeare Library, 367, 371, 388, 395

INDEX 551

Charites, see Graces
Charlewood, John, 494-5
Charmides, 27, 269
Chaucer, 121, 213, 299, 353, 419, 531
Chichester, Lord Arthur, 397, 514
Chiefery, 180, 187, 397
Child, Francis J., 249-50, 259, 261, 267-8, 481, 504
Christ, 137, 218, 221, 455
Christ Church, Dublin, records of, 346
Christendom, 82, 84, 90-2, 137, 166
Christianity, 92, 130
Christian princes, 241
Christians, 109
Christian Stoicism, 493
Church, R. W., 253, 258, 479, 481, 497-8
Churches, repair of, 223, 425-6
Church livings, 223-4, 426
Church of England, 139
Church of Rome, 221-2
Churchwardens, 223, 426
Churchyard, Thomas, 263, 362, 365, 396, 477-8
Churls, 68, 78-9, 118, 133-5, 156, 203, 298, 365-6, 381
Chylde, Machabyas, 259, 466(?), 476(?)
Cicero, 52, 260, 266, 273, 285, 373, 460, 486
Cineri, 88, 518
Cinthio, J. B. Giraldi, 356
Circe, 445
Clancar, Donnell MacCarthy, Earl of, 193, 204, 320, 406-7, 505, 522
Clan MacCostulagh, see MacCostulaghs
Clanricard (Co. Galway), 187, 403
Clanricard, Ulick Burke, third Earl of, 186, 401-3, 428
Clanricard, Ulick Burke, first Marquis of, 356
Clan system, 282-3
Clare, Castle of, 58-9, 291
Clare, Co., 58, 185, 291-2, 401
Clarence, George Plantagenet, third Duke of, 58, 169, 290
Clarence, Lionel Plantagenet, first Duke of, 290-1, 344, 349
Clarence, Earl of, see Clancar, Donnell MacCarthy, Earl of
Clarendon, Henry Hyde, second Earl of, 512
Clarifort (Killaloe), 59, 292
Cleobis, 32, 272
Cleopatra, 119
Clergy, 138-42, 221-4, 368-70, 424-6
Clerks' fees, 75, 303
Clifford, Sir Conyers, 378
Clinias, 27-8
Clonmel, 195, 408, 524
Clyn, John, 289, 294, 417
Cobos, Alonzo, 388-9
Cocytus, 36
Cogan, Miles de, 325

Cokayne, George E., 411
Colina Clouta, see Rosalind
Colin Clout, see Spenser, Edmund
Colin Clouts Come Home Againe, 249
Collier, J. Payne, 259, 282, 297-9, 328, 331, 355, 362, 371, 374, 387, 410, 413, 419, 422, 487, 489, 504, 506, 523
Collins, John, 507
Collinshead, see Spenser, Edmund
Colonels, English, 165-6
Colonies of English, new, 179-80, 184, 189, 209, 211-2, 397-8
Colrane, Co., 184, 401
Columba, St., 221, 425
Colvin, Caroline, 293-4, 414
Comedies, nine English, of Spenser, 459-60, 471-2
Comedies of Ariosto, 471
Comhanach, Art MacMurrogh, 291
Commentaries of Caesar, 72, 300, 519
Commentaries on Callimachus, Greek, 99, 329
Commonalty, organization of Irish, 201-3
Common Law of Ireland, 46-75
Common people, vices of the, 33
Complaints, 251-2, 267
Composition, 132, 182, 185-7, 190-3, 197-8, 240, 364, 398-9, 406, 535
Comraighe, 95, 323-4
Comric, 95, 170, 323-4, 392
Connaught, 57, 59, 83, 115, 151-2, 162, 170, 183-8, 197, 235, 320, 349, 364, 399, 401-3, 415
Connors, see O'Connors
Conquest gives just title to monarch, 52, 284
Controller, Spenser's old, see Perne, Andrew
Conveyances, fraudulent, 71-3, 222-3, 245, 299-301
Cope, Alan (Nicholas Harpsfield), 278
Cork, city, 114, 194-5, 302, 325, 345-6, 364-5, 408, 439, 522, 533
Cork, Co., 193, 207, 291-2, 320, 345-6, 416, 531
Cork, Kingdom of, 325
Corkery, Daniel, 356, 359
Cornishmen, 93, 321
Corporate cities, Irish, 75, 77, 194-6, 302
Corrandoo, 402-3
Coshery, 79, 306, 313, 356
Council Book of Munster, Old, 207, 416, 500
Council Book of the Corporation of Cork, 352
Council Book of the Corporation of Kinsale, 361, 416
Council Book of the Corporation of Youghal, 302
Council of England, Privy, 210-1, 385, 484-5
Council of Ireland, 201, 227, 238, 311, 361, 374, 397
Council of Munster, 192, 351-2, 361
Council of Ulster, 184

Councilors (members of the English Privy Council?), 44, 147
County of the Cross (Tipperary), 302
Courcy, Lord, 117-8, 349, 520-1
Court, English, 6-7, 254, 460, 463
Covington, Frank F., Jr., 284, 287-9, 291-2, 318-9, 322, 325, 334-6, 345, 350, 368, 372, 391-2, 411, 419, 426, 499
Cowley, Sir Henry, 422
Cox, Richard, 287
Coynye and livery, 78-80, 133, 207, 305-6, 348, 364
Craik, George L., 252, 266, 268, 481
Crawforde, William H., 516
Creagh, Richard, 322, 425, 532
Croft, Sir James, 484-5
Crofton, John, 425-6
Crofts, James, 424
Cromabo, 103, 334
Cross, Tom P., 416
Crumlin, 393, 505
Cuddeehih, see Cuddy, Irish custom of
Cuddy in S. C., 470
Cuddy, Irish custom of, 79, 306
Cuffe, Hugh, 407
Culvers, see Curlew Mountains
Cumeraigh, see Comraighe
Cummericke, see Comric
Cummurreeih, see Comric
Cupid, see Amor
Curius Dentatus, Manius, 10, 260
Curlew Mountains, 57, 288, 518
Curtis, Edmund, 291-2
Curve Cosh eribord, 85, 312-3
Cusack, Sir Thomas, 357, 398
Customs of Ireland, 81-136
Cydippe, 32, 272
Cynosargus, 27, 38, 269
Cyrus, 103, 121, 333, 352

Dallán, 356
Daly, Robert, 370
Damon, 27
Danaus, daughters of, 37, 277
Daneraths, 130, 363
Danes, 51, 130, 363
Dania, 51
Daniel, Samuel, 479, 481
Danter, John, 494-5
Daphne, 466
Daremberg, Charles, 329
D'Aubigné, Agrippa, 304-5
David, 461
Davids, 461
Davies, Sir John, 280-3, 285-7, 291, 294, 299, 301, 303, 305, 344-5, 347, 350, 361, 366, 369-70, 375, 415-6, 426, 497
Davis, B. E. C., 264, 493, 500, 504
Davison, Francis, 255

Dawtrey, Nicholas, 379, 399
De Arte Amandi of Ovid, 444
De Arte Meretricandi, 444
Dearth of provisions, 196-7, 226, 409, 427-8
Death, 27-38, 72, 300, 492-3
Deirdre, 343-4
Dela, sons of, 89, 318-9
Delos, 36
Deluge, 131
Delvin, Sir Christopher Nugent, Baron, 371, 387, 403
Delvin, Sir Richard Nugent, Baron, 401
Demosthenes, 460
De Rebus Scoticis of Buchanan, 103-4
De Rebus Gestis Britanniae, 310
Dermotnigald, see MacMurrogh, Dermod, King of Leinster
Derrick, John, 331-3, 338-9, 342, 352-3, 355-7, 380
Description of Ireland, 290, 294, 297, 302, 320, 347-9, 380, 394, 397-8, 400-8, 415
Desmond, 193, 204, 291, 407
Desmond, Gerald FitzGerald, fifteenth Earl of, 71-2, 162, 300, 361, 380, 382, 526-8
Desmond, James FitzMaurice FitzGerald of, 348
Desmond, John FitzGerald of, 162, 385, 526
Desmond, Thomas FitzGerald, eighth Earl of, 116-7, 348
Desmond War, 63, 156, 158, 165-6, 380-2, 388
Despair in *F. Q.*, 333, 355
Deurmuid negalh, see MacMurrogh, Dermod, King of Leinster
Devil, 136, 461
Devising death of prince a capital crime, 65-6, 297
Dillon, Sir Theobald, 359, 401
Dingan, Fort, 183-4, 191, 400, 405
Dinglecush (Dingle), 195, 409
Dio Cassius, 315
Diodorus Siculus, 95, 99, 103, 105, 131, 313, 324, 328, 333, 337, 510
Diogenes, 102, 332
Diogenes Laërtius, 332
Dionysius Periegetes, 478
Dionysius the Areopagite, 442, 455
Discourses of Machiavelli, 229, 429
Disdain in *F. Q.*, 352
Distraining, 76-7, 304
Divine right of kings, 286
Docwra, Sir Henry, 375, 379, 400
Dodderidge, Sir John, 398
Dodge, R. E. Neil, 249, 251-3, 261, 268, 479, 481
Dolet, Etienne, 491-2
Donegal, Co., 57, 184, 290, 401
Donergall, see Donegal, Co.

INDEX

Don Sebastian, Colonel, see San Joseppi, Colonel Don Sebastian di
Douai, 222
Dowdall, Sir John, 383, 388
Dowling, Thaddeus, 289, 295, 404
Down, Co., 184, 290, 400-1
Draco, 29, 271
Drant, Thomas, 7, 16, 253, 443, 463, 473-4, 479-82
Draper, John W., 283-4, 292, 301, 305-6, 308, 321-4, 334-5, 354, 361-2, 364, 392-3
Drapers' Company, 490, 495
Dreames, 17-8, 251-2, 266-8, 459, 471
Drinking of blood, 112, 343-4
Drodagh, see Drogheda
Drogheda, 75, 116-7, 195, 302, 348, 409
Drogheda, Parliament of, 293
Druids, 315-6, 343, 356
Drury, Sir William, 207, 344, 404, 414, 416
Dublin, Castle of, 235
Dublin, city, 61, 64, 75, 171, 185, 188-9, 192, 195, 293, 299-300, 302, 325-7, 392-3, 404
Dublin, Co., 173-4, 189-90
Duessa, 368
Dugdale, Sir William, 411
Dundalk, 61-2, 195, 295
Dungannon, 390
Dungannon, Baron of, see Tyrone, Hugh O'Neill, second Earl of
Dunlop, Robert, 297, 377, 388, 403, 406
Dunluce, Castle of, 293
Dunluce, Point of, 61, 293
Dürer, Albrecht, 331
Dursica, 92, 320
Dutches (Tuites?), 61, 294
Dyer, Sir Edward, 6-7, 16-7, 250-1, 442, 462(?), 463, 467, 470, 477, 479-80
Dying Pellicane, 17, 252, 267, 459, 471
Dymmok, John, 281, 306-7, 353-5, 366, 389, 404, 407-8, 414, 418
Dyson, Humfrey, 376, 380, 425

Earthquake of 6 April, 1580, 15-6, 263, 449-50, 457, 462, 477-9, 485
Earthquakes, causes of, 450-9, 478-9; differences between, 456; staying of, 457; to be treated by learned writer, 457-9
East Meath (Co. Meath), 191-2, 297
Eccles, Mark, 258-9
Edgar, King, 85, 95, 325
Edgecomb, Sir Richard, 414
Edgeworth, Maria, 331, 418
Edmundus, see Spenser, Edmund
Education, 216, 218, 421-2
Edward, King of Ireland, 61
Edward the Confessor, 47, 418
Edward I, 301
Edward II, 58, 60-2, 204-5, 210 295, 414, 500-1

Edward III, 200, 288, 290, 295, 301, 344, 350, 410-1
Edward IV, 58, 116, 214, 235, 288, 290, 348, 419, 518
Egerton, Sir Thomas, 506, 511-2
Egerton Papers, 303-4
Egfrid, King of Northumbria, 95, 325
Egyptians, 99, 104-5, 108, 328-9, 335, 337
Egyptian word, 104
Eigeas, Cormacan, 330-1
Einstein, Lewis, 251
Elderton, William, 457, 477
Eleusina, 37, 277
Elias, see Elijah
Elijah, 99, 328
Elizabeth, Queen, possible meeting of Spenser with, 6, 250; proposed marriage to Anjou, 15(?), 263; may alter laws of Ireland, 53; suffers in Irish trials, 66; revenues concealed from, 67, 73, 207-9; loyalty of Ormond to, 147; cost of army to, 149-54, 160, 176-7, 181, 198; clemency of, 159, 238-9, 241-2, 376, 383, 385, 387; reversed Grey's strong methods, 159-60, 383; unwise handling of Tyrone, 166-8, 237, 433, 534, 537; defied by Feagh MacHugh, 170; grants to Sir Henry Harrington and Sir Thomas Masterson, 190; appeal of Munster undertakers to, 236-42; Irish priests speak dishonorably of, 242; Mary of Scotland's plan to kill, 297; remark on Irish family ties, 298; Irish poem in praise of, 360; treaty with Desmond, 361; pardons Perrot, 386; rewards services of Tyrone, 390; term *prince* applied to, 410; encouragement to Irish education, 422; religious views of, 424, 426; efforts to have Irish churches repaired, 426; commands re-establishment of Athenry, 428; John Harvey's poem on, 469-70; said to have commanded *View* to be written, 497; *View* said to be presented to, 504; approved massacre at Smerwick, 527, 529; bestowed 3000 acres on Spenser, 531; style of addresses to, 536
Elizabeth, Queen of Castille, see Isabella, Queen of Castille
Elizabeth, Queen, wife of Edward IV, 116-7, 348
Elizeus, see Ilissus, River
Elliott, Baron John, 432
Ely, 404
Elysian Fields, 37
Emer, 343-4
Enclosure of land, 135-6, 367
"*Encomium Lauri*," 466
Endoxus, 43
England, easily subjected to Norman Law, 46-7; civility of, 47, 54, 118, 201-3; kings

of, 48-9, 52, 62, 73-4; laws of, 48, 53-4, 56, 81; fraudulent conveyances to support refugees from, 72-3, 222; wardships and marriages in, 73; customary services in, 79; Church of, 139; Roman conquest of, 180; colonists to be sent from, 184; hundreds, parishes, and wards in, 184; want of storehouses in, 197; baronets in reign of Edward III, 200, 410-1; Alfred's organization of, 201-3; nobles without followers to command, 205; Great Seal of, 206; dearth now in, 217, 226, 427-8; churchwardens in, 223; confiscation of monasteries by Henry VIII, 227; low state of learning in, 459
England, Tower of, see London, Tower of
English, 94, 96-7, 474
English chronicles, 85, 201-2
English customs, 113-22
English-Irish, 113-20, 206-12, 344-51, 416-7, 519-23
English language, 16, 23, 81, 92, 122, 320, 350, 369, 473-6
Englishmen wear hair long, 102
English Pale, 57, 60-2, 74, 115, 154-5, 183, 194, 196, 225, 293-4, 364, 408
English to be preferred to Irish livings, 140-1, 370
Engrossing, 226, 427-8
Enniscorthy, 386
Enniskillen, 183, 400
Ennius, 10, 260, 266, 373, 464
Ephialtes, 33, 274
Epicharmus, 30, 272
Epithalamion Thamesis, 17, 266, 470, 481
Erasmus, 260, 332, 373
Eriach, see Iriach
Erne, Lough, 183, 187-8
Essex, 449
Essex, Robert Devereux, second Earl of, 228, 245, 374, 377, 388, 428-9, 504-5, 515, 531, 536
Ethiopians, 108
Eudorus, 43
Eudoxius, 43
Eudoxus, 43-231 *passim*, 278
Euphuism, 492-5
Euripides, 32, 273
Europe, 100, 459, 470
Euryptolemus, 33, 274
Eva, daughter of Dermod MacMurrogh, 171, 287
Evander, 99, 330
Every people with its peculiar vices, 68-9, 299
Examination and regrant of tenures, 207-9, 415-6
Exceptions peremptory in trials, 69, 299
Excess in *F. Q.*, 331, 368
Exchequer of Ireland, Black Book of, 212
Eyland, Henry, 423

Fabricius Luscinus, Gaius, 10, 260
Fabyan, Robert, 323
Faerie Queene, 17, 260, 266-8, 471-2, 531
Falkiner, C. Litton, 297, 301-2, 401, 404, 406
Farreels, see O'Farralls
Farrih, see Ferragh
Fathers of the Church, 221-2
Faughart, Battle of, 295
Faverty, Frederic E., 480
Fear, 29
Fearnemunnaghe, see Fermanagh (city?)
Fenton, Sir Geoffrey, 386, 390, 395, 408
Feragus (Fergus), 103-4, 334
Ferdinand, King of Aragon, 91
Fergus, 103-4, 334
Fermanagh (city?), 152, 183, 378
Fermanagh, Co., 184, 290
Ferns, Castle of, 190, 404-5, 505
Ferns, city, 191, 405
Ferns, Co., 190, 404
Ferragh, 103-5, 334
Ferraugh, Sir, 334
Fertoghe, 290
Fertouaghe, 290
Fertullagh, 57, 290
Festus, Sextus Pompeius, 311
Fethard, 195
Feugh, see O'Byrne, Feagh MacHugh
Ficino, Marsilio, 270, 491
Finglas, Patrick, 287, 295, 344, 427, 532
Fitton, Sir Edward, 307, 369, 404
FitzGerald of Cloyne, John, 300
FitzGeralds, 114, 117, 145, 372
FitzGeralds of Kildare, 334, 372
FitzGerret, Thomas, see Kildare, Thomas FitzGerald, tenth Earl of
FitzStephen, Robert, 325
FitzUrsulas, 115-6, 347
FitzWilliam, John, 432
FitzWilliam, Sir William, 163, 236-7, 364, 372, 387, 430-2, 534, 537
Flatsbury, Philip, 106, 337
Fleet Prison, 483-5
Fleming, Abraham, 477-8
Flemings, 69, 299
Flemminge, Christopher, 432
Fletcher, Jefferson B., 479-80
Florence, 229, 429
Florimel, 427
Flower, Robin, 290, 358, 360, 394
Foane, 399
Folkmotes, 129-30, 362-3
Folly to be mingled with wisdom, 10-1
Fordun, John, 318
Forehin, see Sorehin
Fosterage of English with Irish, 117, 119-20, 350-1
Four Masters, 291, 344, 348, 381-2, 389, 392-4, 403, 406, 505

INDEX 555

Fox in *Hub.*, 422
Foyle, Lough, 152, 182, 377-8
Foyle, River, 152, 378, 399
France, 8, 88, 93, 128, 175, 258, 316-7, 443, 459
Franciplegiums, 212-3, 418
Fraunce, Abraham, 254-5, 479
French language, 460
Frenchman, jest of a, 128
Frenchmen, 86
French soldiers, 461
Freyd, Bernard, 487, 493-5
Froude, James A., 371-2
Fulton, Edward, 480
Furies, 37

G., see Harvey, Gabriel
Gabriel, see Harvey, Gabriel
Gainsford, Thomas, 288, 328, 342, 355, 367, 377, 413
Galateo of Giovanni della Casa, 460, 467
Gald, 94, 321-2, 354
Galdumo, 88, 317
Galen, 351
Galicia, 88
Gallia, 93
Gallic customs, 112-3, 343-4
Gallic language, 93, 316-7
Galloglasses, 122-4, 158-9, 307, 354-5, 397
Galtee Mountains, 288, 407-8
Galway, city, 195, 302
Galway, Co., 185-7, 297, 401-3, 518
Galway, Margaret, 267
Ganymede, 467
Garandough, 187, 402-3
Gardener, Robert, 371, 423, 430
Gardens of Athens, 28, 270
Gardiner, Bishop Stephen, 461
Garendow, 402
Gariduff, 402
Garrisons, 132, 151-4, 173-5, 180-3, 187-8, 190-6, 240-1, 245, 377-8, 398-400, 402-3, 405-8, 436-7, 439, 535, 537
Garzoni, Tommaso, 341
Gascoigne, George, 484
Gathelus, 82, 85-6, 89, 309-10, 318, 335, 509
Gauls, 84-5, 88-90, 92-4, 96-7, 100, 110, 112-3, 311, 315-7, 321, 342-3, 510
Gauls (France and northern Italy), 8
Gemanus, 85, 313
Genius in *F. Q.*, 276
Gentili, Alberico, 385
Gentlemen, Irish, 156-7, 203, 413
Geoffrey, Signor, 161, 525, 528-9
Geoffrey of Monmouth, 309-10, 324
George, St., 245
Geraldine (Elizabeth FitzGerald), 295
Geraldines, see FitzGeralds

Gerrard, Sir William, 278, 298, 360, 364-5, 375, 394-5, 404, 426
Gervasius Tilburiensis, 280
Getes, 93, 217-8
Giants, 89, 131, 364
Gibraltar, Strait of, 88
Gilbert, Allan H., 356
Gilbert, Sir Humphrey, 396
Gilbert, John T., 307, 369, 371, 387-8, 403
Gilt bridles and peitrels, 75, 303
Giovio, Paolo, 459
Giraldus Cambrensis, 286-7, 308, 318-9, 324-6, 340, 342, 363-4, 377, 417, 421, 497
Giustiniani, Paolo, 387, 525-7
Glaucon, 27, 269
Glaunmaleerih, see Glenmalure
Glenmalure, 57, 171-2, 174, 191, 289, 358, 393-5
Glibs, 99, 102, 106, 110-1, 328, 332-3, 338
Goblet, Y. M., 288-9, 402, 407
Gobrias, 36-7
Gobrias, grandfather of Gobrias, 36-7
God, 454-5
Golden Vale, 346
Golding, Arthur, 264, 357, 477-8
Goldingham, William, 441-2, 446
Gollancz, Sir Israel, 516
Gómara, Francisco López de, 313
Gospel, 137, 221, 461
Gosson, Stephen, 6, 251, 357
Goths, 84, 91, 93, 217, 319-21, 327, 337-8, 341, 480
Gottfried, Rudolf B., 288-90, 377-8, 402, 407, 502-3, 505
Governors of Ireland, see Lord Deputies, Lord Justices, and Lord Lieutenants
Graces, 12, 444, 462
Granada, Kingdom of, 92
Grantorto, 528
Gray, M. M., 339, 355, 381-2
Great Britain, 95
Great Seal of England, 206-7, 415
Grecia, 107
Grecians, 471
Greece, 36
Greek alphabet, 88, 316
Greek commentaries on Callimachus, 99, 329
Greek examples, 457
Greek language, 23, 25, 104, 458, 460, 464, 472, 475
Greek prosody, 264-5, 480
Greeks, 16, 88, 99, 107, 316, 330, 476, 480
Green, Alice S., 285, 306, 366
Greencastle, 61, 294
Greene, Richard, 515
Greene, Robert, 483
Greenlaw, Edwin A., 249, 279, 287, 304, 309-10, 357, 372, 375, 383-4, 394, 396-7, 410, 420, 429

Greenwich, 505
Gregory XIII, Pope, 161-2, 385, 461, 524, 527, 529-30
Grenville, Sir Richard, 365-6
Greville, Sir Fulke, Lord Brooke, 479-80
Grey, Arthur, fourteenth Baron Grey de Wilton, 63-4, 159-62, 173-4, 289, 295-6, 344, 355, 372, 375, 378, 380-7, 390, 392-3, 395-6, 400, 405, 408-9, 415, 423, 429, 500, 503, 524-31
Griffith, D. D., 508
Gronii, 317
Grosart, Alexander B., 250, 260-2, 267-8, 396, 481, 498, 524, 533, 535-6
Guazzo, Stefano, 299, 351, 460
Guilles, 127, 360
Guinevere, 111, 343
Gurgunt, 95, 324
Gurmundus, 292
Guyle (Malengin), 377

H., see Harvey, Gabriel
H., G., see Harvey, Gabriel
Hack writers on earthquake of 1580, 457, 459
Hakluyt, Richard, 342
Hales, J. W., 255, 262, 264, 267-8, 481
Hallam, Henry, 481
Hamer, Douglas, 272
Hamilton, Lord Ernest, 389-90
Hampshire, 94
Hanmer, Meredith, 310, 312-3, 321, 335, 369, 372, 497
Hannibal, 91
Hardiman, James, 293, 327, 361, 420
Hardyng, John, 310
Harington, Sir John, 380, 404
Harman, Thomas, 396
Harold II, 47, 280
Harper, Carrie A., 266, 310, 324
Harpsfield, Nicholas, 278
Harrington, Sir Henry, 190, 404
Harris, Walter, 287, 289, 295, 310, 342, 354, 361, 363, 393, 413-4, 418, 425, 427
Harrison, William, 280, 396, 411-2, 418
Hartlib, Samuel, 252
" Haruey, the happy aboue happiest men," 300
Harveius, see Harvey, Gabriel
Harvey, Gabriel, referred to as: G. H., 5, 8, 15, 441, 445-6; G., 5-6, 477; Harveius, 9, 11-2; Angel Gabriel, 11, 463, 472; H., 12, 15, 450-1, 453, 457; Hobbinol, 471, 476;—references to letters from, 5-8, 17, 252, 255; co-operation in editing S. C., 5, 249; preferment of, 6, 10, 442; criticism of verses by, 7, 16-7; Stoic calm of, 9-10; Cato of our age, 10, 442; popularity of, 11; legal studies, 15, 262-3, 468, 473; writing poetry, 15; reference to his "*Satyricall Verses*," 17, 265-6; letters awaited from, 17; ambition to be public orator of Cambridge, 250; connection with Sidney, 250; opinion of Drant, 253; connection with Preston, 254; connection with Still, 254; allusion to trip of, 259; on Aristippus, 259; on Cicero, 260; letters longer than Spenser's, 261; praised by Webbe, 262; letter to Sir Thomas Smith, 262-3; fellow of Trinity Hall, 263; possibly added material to letter of Spenser's, 263; his phrases used by Spenser, 265, 297, 351, 392, 397; depreciation and praise of *F. Q.*, 267, 471-2; on difference between Athens and Sparta, 286; admirer of Aeneas Sylvius, 314; praise of Llwyd, 315; wagers Spenser a copy of Lucian, 339; his copy of Pettie's *Guazzo*, 351; his copy of Smith's *De Republica Anglorum*, 374; knowledge of Machiavelli's *Discorsi*, 429; ashamed of verses, 441; important affairs of, 441; books and writings in his study, 444, 459, 478; his "*These pleasant dayes, and Monthes, and yeares, by stelth do passe apace,*" 446-7; praise of his writings, 448; not privy to publication of Letters, 448; visit at house in Essex, 449-57; references to his *Schollers Loue, or Reconcilement of Contraries* and *Anticosmopolita, or Britanniae Apologia*, 460; flattered by Perne, 462; not ready yet to draw up rules for English versifying, 463; his "New yeeres Gift to my old friend Maister *George Bilchaunger*," 465; his "*Encomium Lauri*," 466; his "*Speculum Tuscanismi*," 467, 484; intends to study for material rewards, 470; his "To my good Mistresse *Anne*," 472-3; replies to other pamphleteers on earthquake, 478-9; dislike for Earl of Arundel, 479; relation with Areopagus, 479-80; ideas on English versifying, 480-3; hand in publication of Letters, 483-5; imprisoned in Fleet, 483-5; condemnation of Euphuism, 495
Harvey, John, brother of Gabriel, 468-70
Harvey, John, father of Gabriel, 483
Harvey, Mercy, 479
Harvey, Richard, 310, 396
Hasdrubal, 90, 92
Haslewood, Joseph, 261
Hawkins, Henry, 389
Headboroughs, 212, 214, 417
Heaven, 218
Heberus, 90, 308, 319
Hecaërgus (Apollo), 36, 275-6
Hecuergus, see Hecaërgus
Heffer and Sons, W., 488
Heffner, Ray, 233, 344, 381, 393, 399, 425, 505, 508, 511-2, 515, 534-6
Helicon, Mount, 11
Hell, 37, 137, 368
Hengist, 363

INDEX 557

Henley, Pauline, 351, 359, 378, 381, 385, 399, 402, 435, 524, 533-4
Hennessy, John P., 529
Henry II, 55-6, 96, 118, 171, 180, 206, 287, 319, 325-6
Henry IV, 302, 345
Henry VII, 204-5, 414
Henry VIII, 48, 52-3, 227, 282, 284-5, 302, 428
Henshawe, Captain, 432
Herbert, Sir William, of sixteenth century, 351-2, 365, 398, 401, 429
Herbert, William, of eighteenth century, 487-9, 493
Hercules, 37
Hermogenes, 461
Hernan, see O'Hernan
Herodian, 106, 315, 338
Herodotus, 99, 103, 107, 131, 313, 328-9, 333, 337, 339-41, 343, 352, 364, 471, 510-1
Hertfordshire gentleman, 466
Hewlett, James H., 249
Hexameter, English, 483-5
Hibernia, 90, 308, 319
Higginson, James J., 479
Highways and bridges, 224-5, 426-7
"*Him loued highest* Iupiter *and* Apollo *deare*," 32, 272-3
Hipponicus, 30
History of Sir John Perrott, 282, 293, 300, 360, 380, 386-7, 390, 426, 429
Hobbinol, see Harvey, Gabriel
Hobgoblin, 472
Hogan, Edmund, 349
Hogan, James, 282, 291, 391
Holinshed, Raphael, 17, 266, 278, 280-2, 286-8, 292-6, 299, 302, 305-6, 308, 310-2, 314-6, 318-9, 321, 324-5, 332, 334-8, 342-3, 345-50, 352, 354-8, 360-5, 368, 372, 377, 382-3, 385, 387, 391, 393, 396, 398, 400-1, 405, 411-2, 414, 417-9, 427, 470, 499, 510, 529
Holland, Joseph, 399
Hollowell, B. M., 479, 481
Holmes, Mathias, 389
Holy Writ, see Bible
Homer, 32, 107, 259, 272, 329, 339, 444-5, 464, 469, 474
Hooker, John, 278, 286-7, 296, 299, 302, 337, 347, 357, 361, 364, 368, 382, 387, 393, 529
Horace, 259-60, 330, 420, 474
Horseboys, 127, 140, 148, 158-9, 203, 216-7, 245, 360, 364-5
Horsemen, 121-2, 158-9, 245, 352-4, 378, 440
Hotham, John de, 414
Houghton, Arthur A., collection of, 516
Houses, Irish, 135, 366-7

Hoveden, Roger of, 325-6
"*How wretched a thred of life haue the gods spun*," 32, 272
Hubbub, Irish, 103, 105, 333
Hughes, John, 258, 523
Hughes, Merritt Y., 494
Hulbert, Viola B., 432-4, 437, 439-40, 534-5, 537
Hull, Eleanor, 356, 359-60
Hull, Vernum, 332
Hundreds, 201-2, 212-4, 400, 411-2, 417-8
Huns, 91, 93
Husbandry, 215-8, 420
Hyde, Douglas, 319, 343-4, 356-7, 360
Hy-Many, 402-3

"*Iambicum Trimetrum*," 7-8, 254-5, 442, 481
"*If so be goods encrease, then dayly encreaseth a goods friend*," 468
Iliad, 272-3, 329, 339
Ilissus, River, 27, 269
Immerito, see Spenser, Edmund
Immerito, Domina, see Rosalind
Immortality, 29-30, 35-6
Inchiquin, 59, 292
Incredula, 449-57
Indians, 82, 86
Inns, 78, 120, 225, 305
Inny, River, 192, 406
Inquisitionum in Officio Rotulorum Repertorium, 395, 401
Inquisitiva, 449-57
Ipswich, 446
Iraghts, see Airechts
Ireland, natural wealth of, 43, 62, 115, 158, 189, 295, 346; evil destiny of, 43-4, 63, 145, 210, 236, 278, 417; the evils which afflict, 45-146; evils in the laws of, 45-81; evils in Common Law of, 46-75; a warlike nation, 47, 55, 64-5, 132, 197, 239, 280, 436; Henry VIII made king of, 48-9; parliaments of, 48, 52, 70-2, 199-201, 282, 284-5, 292-3, 297, 299-300, 349, 391, 411; Anglo-Norman conquest, 55-6, 96, 118, 171, 180, 206, 287, 325-7, 393; recovered by Irish in fifteenth century, 56-9, 226, 287-8, 290-2; rebellion of Murrogh en Ranagh, 58-9, 290-2; kings of, 59, 61-2, 292, 295; Scotch invasion, 60-2, 210, 288, 292-5; revenues and size, 62, 181-2, 185-7, 190, 191-3, 235, 295, 398-9, 401-2, 430; Kildare's Rebellion, 63, 295; Desmond War, 63, 156, 158, 165-6, 295, 380-2, 388; evils in Statute Law of, 75-81; evils in customs of, 81-136; nations which first inhabited, 82-96; legendary invaders of, 82, 85-6, 89-90, 104, 309, 312-3, 318-9; used letters before England, 85, 87, 316; other names for, 83-4, 95, 145, 311, 324, 372; evils in

religion of, 136-42; conversion to Christianity, 137, 368; evils in English administration, 142-6; military reformation of, 146-98, 243-5, 373, 438-9; to be reformed by force, 146-8, 243-4, 372-4, 438-9; ready for rebellion, 147, 374; map of, 152, 377; Pale Rebellion, 160-1, 295-6, 384-5; Tyrone's hope to become king, 166, 388-9; records of, 181, 185, 191-2, 398; Lord Deputy to be stationed at center, 188-9, 403-4; final settlement of, 198-230; oaths of loyalty taken earlier, 204-5, 414; Tyrone's Rebellion, 236-42, 374, 376, 435
Iremus, 43
Irenaeus, 43, 278
Irenis, 43
Irenius, 43-231 *passim*, 278
Iriach, 47, 281
Irin (Ireland), 83-4
Irish alphabet, 87, 316-7
Irish chronicles, 84-7, 89-90, 104, 110, 114, 311, 315, 322, 346, 392
Irish conversing with English, 75-6, 304
Irish craftiness, 55, 286-7
Irish customs, 81-136
Irish desire for news, 128
Irish dislike of work, 203, 413
Irish hate of English, 125, 141-2, 146-7, 221, 240
Irish language, 81, 85, 93, 118-20, 312-3, 322-4, 350
Irish love of liberty, 55, 125, 240, 286, 413, 436
Irish manner of fighting, 151, 377
Irish names, 214-5, 419-20
Irish poetry, 124-7, 355-60
Irish-Scots, 63, 83, 86, 106, 112, 334
Irish women, 101-2, 111, 331-2, 342, 351
Isabella, Queen of Castille, 91, 320
Islands of the North, 85, 95, 325
Island Voyage, 505
Italian language, 460, 469
Italian master, 468
Italians, 161, 471, 526-7
Italy, 8, 88, 229, 258-9, 443-4, 455, 459, 467, 471-2
Itonian Gates, 270

Jack, leather quilted, 120-2, 352-3
Jackson, William A., 485, 494
Jacob, 337
Jacques, 161
James, M. R., 418
James I, 530, 532
Jani, 461
Jenkins, Raymond, 249, 252, 262, 265, 293, 298-300, 304-5, 361, 378, 382, 384-5, 392, 399, 406-9, 486, 503, 524, 528
Jesters, 128, 219, 361

Jethro, 202, 411
Jews, 99
John, King, 301, 325-6
John, St., 213, 471
Johnson, Francis R., 483, 516-7
Jones, H. S. V., 278-9, 281, 284-6, 297, 304-5, 311-2, 368, 373-4, 410, 423, 429, 485, 499-500, 504
Jones, Thomas, 394
Joseph, 105, 337
Jove, 466
Joyce, P. W., 283, 299, 305, 307-8, 316, 327, 331, 338-42, 350, 352-3, 361-3, 366, 402-3, 420
Judson, Alexander C., 249-50, 254, 258, 261, 263, 288, 295-6, 299-300, 344, 348, 373, 376, 385-6, 393, 409, 413, 428, 434, 480, 485-6, 528, 536
Juno, 32
Jupiter, 32
Jupiter, planet, 454
Jupiter's kingdom, 36-7
Juries, 66-8, 297-8
Jusserand, J. J., 480-1
Justinian, 468
Juvenal, 462

K., E., 6-7, 18, 252, 262, 265, 267, 285, 291, 325, 350, 356, 419, 486
Kearrooghs, see Carrows
Keating, Geoffrey, 283, 322-4, 334, 347-50, 372, 497
Keatings, 154-5, 188-9, 380, 521-2
Keening, 105, 336-7
Kells, in Meath, 61, 195, 294, 409
Kellys, see O'Kellys
Kentish garden, see Bromley
Kerke, Mistress, 7, 12, 252
Kerns, 103, 123-4, 127, 158-9, 203, 206, 216-7, 352, 354-5, 397
Kerry, Co., 193, 245, 288, 301, 320, 407, 439-40, 535
Kilcolman, 288, 292, 304, 312, 328, 348, 359-60, 369, 386, 407-8, 415, 434-5, 533, 535-7
Kilcullen, Old, 428
Kildare, Co., 64, 173-4, 190, 301
Kildare, Gerald FitzGerald, eleventh Earl of, 384
Kildare, John FitzGerald, first Earl of, 305
Kildare, Thomas FitzGerald, tenth Earl of, 63, 295, 337, 357
Kilkenny, city, 195, 408
Kilkenny, Co., 64, 172-3, 190, 301
Kilkenny, Statute of, 299-300, 304, 350-1, 361, 370, 415
Killaloe, 58-9, 292
Kilmallock, 195
Kilmore, 193, 407
Kilpatrick, 194, 407

INDEX

Kincogish, 80-1, 205-6, 307-8, 414
King of Asia (Artaxerxes), 116, 347
King of Egypt's daughter (Scota), 89
King of Spain, 89-90, 162, 166, 198, 237, 388-9, 527, 529-30
King's Co., 64, 184, 190, 245, 297
Kings of England, 48-9, 52, 62, 73-4, 114, 169-71, 206-7, 209, 235
Kings of Ireland, 48-9, 52-3, 59, 61-2, 210, 284-5, 292, 295, 319, 339, 389
Kings of Scotland, 103
Kinsale, 195, 409
Kinsale, Baron of, 349
Kirke, Edward, 486
Knight of the Valley, 415
Knockfergus (Carrickfergus), 61, 293
Knockloe, 174, 191, 395, 405
Knott, Eleanor, 356
Kuersteiner, Agnes D., 252, 268

Lacedaemon, 54
Lacedaemonians, 54, 69, 125, 286, 357
Lacy, heir of, 58, 290
Lacy, Hugh de, 61, 325-7
Lacys, 60, 210, 293
Laërtes, 9
Lambard, William, 280, 310, 320, 362-3, 411-2, 417-8
Lancaster, House of, 56, 145, 372
Lancelot, Sir, 111, 343
Landlords and tenants, 78-9, 133-5, 207, 306-7, 365-7
Lane, Sir Ralph, 394
Language, 118-9, 350
Lanquet, Thomas, 334
Larne, 293
Lathes, 201-2, 212, 411-2
Latin examples, 457
Latin language, 23, 119, 140, 350, 369, 457, 464, 469, 472-5
Latin prosody, 264-5, 474-6, 481
Latin proverb, 90
Latins, 99, 475-6
Laundargabo, 103, 333
Launlaider, 103, 333-4, 518
Law of Nations, 161, 385
Law of War, 385
Laws of England, 48, 53-4, 56, 201-2, 208, 287
Laws of Ireland, 45-81, 199-221, 303
Laws to be clear and immovable, 78, 305
Laws to be fashioned to suit those whom they govern, 54, 65-6, 68-9, 285-6, 410
Layarrigabowe, 103
Leabhar Gabhála, 318
Leagaire, King, 339-40
Learning, 218
" Learninge . . . *Emollit mores nec sinit esse feros*," 87, 316

Lee, Sir Sidney, 262, 267
Lee, Thomas, 387, 392, 394-5, 423, 432
Legouis, Émile, 499
Leicester, Robert Dudley, Earl of, 5, 12(?), 15(?), 18(?), 249, 258, 261, 263, 268, 444(?), 460(?), 468(?)
Leicester House, 12, 261
Leinster, 57, 59, 115, 151, 170-1, 178, 183-4, 187-91, 235, 292, 321, 325-6, 405, 503
Leitrim, Co., 185-6, 288-9, 401
Leix (Queen's Co.), 64, 172, 245, 297, 301, 439-40
Leix, Fort of (Fort Protector), 184, 191, 400
Leland, John, 309-10
Letrim, 401
Letters, Spenser-Harvey, in Folio of Spenser's *Works* (1679), 251, 253; in Hughes edition of Spenser's *Works* (1715), 251, 253
Levant Sea, 92
L'Hôpital, Michel, 304-5
Lievsay, John L., 373
Lifford, 399
Lily, William, 260, 316, 330
Limerick, city, 112, 195, 302, 325, 344, 524, 528
Limerick, Co., 193
Limerick, Kingdom of, 325
Lincoln's Inn, 511-2
Listrim, see Leitrim, Co.
Lithgow, William, 367, 369, 424, 430
Little Ardes, 294
Livery, see Coynye and livery
Livy, 229, 285, 320, 412, 460
Lluddus, see Llwyd, Humphrey
Llwyd, Humphrey, 86, 293, 310, 312-3, 315, 323, 335, 338, 413, 478
Lodge, Thomas, 357
Loftus, Archbishop Adam, 163, 369, 371-2, 383, 386, 394
Lombard, Peter, 529
London, 7, 15, 23, 263, 457, 486, 505, 527, 531, 533
London, Tower of, 114, 346
Long, Percy W., 258, 260, 480
Longford, Co., 64, 191-2, 406
Lord Deputies, 48, 63-4, 114, 132, 143-6, 159-63, 188-9, 201, 206, 227-30, 236-8, 290, 364, 371-2, 416, 428-9
Lord Justices, 114, 163, 228, 386
Lord Lieutenants, 114, 228, 290-1, 428-9
Lord Presidency of Connaught, 186, 188, 402
Lord Presidency of Munster, 188, 192-3, 240, 406, 437
Lord Presidency of Ulster, 184, 195, 401
Lords, English, 56, 114-8, 206-11
Lords, Irish, 47-51, 79-81, 105, 203-9, 227, 357, 365-6, 413, 415
Louth, Co., 64, 182, 184, 400-1
Louvain, 222, 425

Love, 7-9, 16, 259, 444, 469, 472-3
Low Countries, 175, 196, 227, 395, 409
Lower Ossory, 394
Lownes, Matthew, 507
Lucan, 311, 355-6
Lucian, 107-9, 339-41, 460, 471, 510
Lucinge, René de, 286, 395
Luineach, Turlogh, see O'Neill, Turlogh Luineach
Lusitania, 51, 283-4
Lycanthropia, 109, 341
Lyceum of Athens, 31
Lycurgus, 54, 69, 286
Lydgate, John, 419
Lydians, 121
Lyly, John, 351, 483, 492, 494-5
Lynch, John, 295, 324, 331, 342, 350, 352, 421
Lynosargus, see Cynosargus
Lyon, Bishop William, 364-5, 367-9, 421, 424-5
Lythe, Robert, 407

Mac, 92
"Macamur," one, 526
Mac an Bhaird, Laoiseach, 358
MacCarthy, 92, 320, 349
MacCarthy, Donnell, 193, 204, 406, 412, 414, 522
MacCarthy, Florence, 320, 407
MacCoghlans, 191, 405
MacConmidhe, Giolla, 359
MacConnell, Angus, 391
MacConnells of Scotland, 168, 391
Maccorish, 117, 349
MacCostulaghs, 187, 402
McDermott, William, 369
MacGeoghegans, 191, 405
Machiavelli, Niccolò, 229, 279, 286-7, 304, 368, 375, 377, 379-80, 383-4, 394, 396-7, 410, 420, 429, 460, 472, 499
MacHugh, Feagh, see O'Byrne, Feagh MacHugh
Macintire, Elizabeth J., 251, 479
McKerrow, R. B., 264, 482
Macknihmarrih, see MacNemara
Macknyrrs, 187, 402
Maclean, 391
MacMahon, Brian, 166-7, 389, 432
MacMahon, Hugh Roe, 236, 432, 537
MacMahon, Rossa Bui, 432
MacMahons of Munster, 116-7, 347-8
MacMahons of Ulster, 115-6, 236-7, 347, 432, 534
MacMurrays, 187, 402-3
MacMurrogh, Dermod, King of Leinster, 171, 287, 343, 393
MacMurroghs, 403
MacNeill, Eoin, 391

MacNeills, 168
MacNemara, 117, 291, 349, 520
MacNemara, George U., 292
Macray, William D., 512
Macrobius, 330
Macroomp, 363
Mac's, see O's and Mac's
MacShane, Hugh, see O'Byrne, Hugh MacShane
MacSheehy, Edmund, 348
MacSheehys of Munster, 116-7, 348
MacSweenys of Munster, 116-7, 348
MacSweenys of Ulster, 115-6, 347
MacTurlogh, Shane, see O'Byrne, Shane MacRedmond
MacWilliam Eighter, Burkes of, 187, 401-3
MacWilliam Euter, Burkes of, 187, 401-2
Magnificat, 474
Magnus, Laurie, 480
Magrath, Archbishop Miler, 368-9, 427
Magueeirhe, see Maguires
Maguire, Hugh, 166-7, 358, 389
Maguires, 187, 402-3
Mahometans, 110, 342
Malby, Henry, 401
Malby, Sir Nicholas, 278, 391
Maleger, 338-9
Malengin, 333, 377, 392
Malone, Edmund, 487, 493
Malory, Sir Thomas, 343
Man, Thomas, 501, 507
Manche, 111, 342
Mandeville, Sir Thomas, 294
Mandevilles, 61, 294
Mangan, 117, 348
Man's supernatural knowledge, 35
Mant, Richard, 369-70, 426
"*Mantilia sternunt*," 99, 330
Mantles, 99-102, 120, 328-32
Marh, 85, 313
Markets, 225-6, 420, 427
Marot, Clément, 265
Marrah, 85, 313
Marriage of Elizabeth to Anjou, 15(?), 263
Marriage of English with Irish, 117, 119-20, 350-1
Mars, 452
Mars, planet, 454
Marseille, 88
Marshall, John J., 390
Marshals, 128, 133, 148, 219-21, 375, 422-3, 426
Martial law, 165-6, 219-20, 361, 422-3
Martin, Bishop Anthony, 317
Martin, William C., 374-5, 378, 384, 428, 504
Mary I, 297, 456
Mary, Queen of Scotland, 297
Maryborough, 183-4, 400, 405

INDEX 561

Massagetae, 333
Massilians, 88, 316
Masterson, Richard, 405, 505
Masterson, Sir Thomas, 190, 404-5, 505
Matthew of Westminster, 324
Maxwell, Constantia, 297, 332-3, 351-2, 379, 400
Maynadier, Howard, 480
Mayo, Co., 185, 187, 401
Meath, Co., 64, 191-2, 297
Meath, province, 58, 152-3, 191-2, 235, 301, 325-6, 405-6
Medici, Catherine de', 460(?)
Mela, Pomponius, 86, 88, 313-4, 316-7, 328, 340-1, 343, 510
Menander, 472
Menapii, 93, 321
Mendoza, Bernardino de, 385, 527-30
Mercator, Gerhard, 377
Merchant Taylors' School, 489
Mercilla, 360, 383
Mercury, 445, 467
Mercury, planet, 453
Merrill, Elizabeth, 498
Messala, Marcus Valerius Corvinus, 115, 346
Metaphysics of Aristotle, 464
Meteorologica of Aristotle, 453
Methodus Apodemica of Theodore Zwinger, 444
Mezger, Fritz, 311, 313, 316-8, 330-1, 338
Michel Angelo, 18, 268
Midas, 467
Mildmay, Sir Walter, 484
Milesian lies, 90, 318-9
Milesio, 319
Milesius, 89-90, 318-9
Milesius, sons of, 89-90, 318-9
Millican, Charles B., 303-4, 310, 324, 343
Miltiades, 33
Milton, 260
Minds of men, not country, alter manners, 211
Minerva, 444
Mingling of English and Irish, 113-21, 211-2, 417
Minos, 36
Miscellany of Irish Bardic Poetry, 358-9, 389
Mitchner, Robert W., 486
Modoham, see Monaghan, Co.
Mointerolis, see Muinter-Eolais
Molloy, Hugh, 405
Monaghan (city?), 152-3, 183, 377-8
Monaghan, Co., 183-4, 236-7, 430, 432, 534, 537
Monashul, 101-2, 128, 332, 361
Monerew, 288-9
Moneroo, see Muinter-Eolais
Mongan, King of Ulster, 356
Moore, Courtnay, 292
Moore, Norman, 512

Moores, see O'Moores
Moors of Africa, 91-2, 105, 108
Moral justification for poetry, 124-5, 356-7
Moran, P. F., 529
More, Sir Thomas, 500
Morley, Henry, 278-83, 288, 296, 299, 303-5, 307-10, 321, 327-8, 331-4, 336, 346, 350, 352-5, 360-4, 367-8, 370, 374-5, 379, 381, 387, 392, 395-6, 398, 410, 412-4, 417-8, 420, 422, 427-8, 482, 523
Mornay, Philippe du Plessis de, 488, 490-1, 493
Morrice of the Fern, see O'Brien, Murrogh en Ranagh
Morrin, James, 293
Morris, Richard, 261, 419, 524
Morte Arthur, stanzaic, 343
Morte d'Arthur of Malory, 343
Mortimer, Great (Edmund Mortimer?), 117, 349
Mortimer's Lands, 58, 291, 349
Moryson, Fynes, 279, 281-2, 300-2, 306-7, 331-3, 342, 344, 347, 350, 352, 357, 361, 370-1, 376-7, 380-1, 383, 388, 390, 400, 404, 408, 413, 416, 423, 425-6, 429-30, 497, 528
Moses, 202, 411
Mountjoy, Charles Blount, eighth Lord, 388, 400, 408, 424, 439
Mourne, 59, 292
Muinter-Eolais, 57, 288-9, 518
Muiopotmos, 266
Mullingar, 195, 408
Multifernan, MS of, 417-8
Munday, Anthony, 263, 477-8, 488, 491, 494-6
Munera's castle, 385
Munster, 57-9, 83, 115-7, 154-5, 158, 178, 180-1, 184, 187-8, 192-4, 196, 204, 235, 238-41, 245, 291-2, 300, 302, 320, 346, 364-5, 401, 406, 408-9, 416, 421, 427, 435-7, 503, 535-7
Munster, desolation of, 158, 238-9, 358, 381-2, 396, 435
Munster, Old Council Book of, see Council Book of Munster, Old
Murphy, Denis, 425
Murrogh en Ranagh, see O'Brien, Murrogh en Ranagh
Muscovites, 217-8
Muses, 12, 466, 471, 473
Muskry Wherk, 194, 407-8
Mutability in English administration, 145, 162-3, 228-9, 238, 371-2
My Lord, see Leicester, Robert Dudley, Earl of
My Slomber, 6, 251-2

Naas, 358-9

37

Naples, 258-9
Nashe, Thomas, 250, 259, 477, 480, 484-5
Naso, see Ovid
Nativity of Christ, 455
Nature, 31
Naunton, Sir Robert, 386
Nemedus, 89, 318-9
Nemedus, sons of, 89, 318-9
Nennius, 308-9, 368
Nepos, 347
Neptune, 8-9
Nerii, 88, 316-7
Neurians, 341
New Abbey, 404, 428
Newcastle, 190, 404
Newcommen, Robert, 371(?), 409
Newry, 195
Newton, Thomas, 480
Newtown, 61, 294
"New yeeres Gift to my old friend Maister George Bilchaunger," 465
Nine Muses, see Comedies, nine English, of Spenser
"*Noble* Alexander, *when he came to the tombe of* Achilles," 469
Noblemen, Irish, see Lords, Irish
Norman Conqueror, see William the Conqueror
Normandy, 46, 53
Norman law, 280
Norris, Sir John, 237-8, 299, 371, 390, 395, 433-4, 534-7
Norris, Sir Thomas, 371, 376, 396, 399, 406-8, 433-4, 533, 536
Northern Irish, 104, 106, 108-9, 112, 168
Northern nations, 82, 84, 91-2, 100, 108
North of Ireland, 58, 60-2, 82-5, 94, 104, 115, 168-70, 177-8
Northumberland, 95
Northumbrians, 95
Norton, Thomas, of Cambridge, 441-2, 445
Norway, 95, 325
Norways, see Norwegians
Norwegians, 217-8, 363
Nugent, Nicholas, 384-5
Nugent, William, 295, 384-5
Nugents, 401

Oath of allegiance to prince, 204-5, 414
Oaths, 107-9, 339-41
O'Brien, 103, 171, 215, 333-4
O'Brien, Murrogh, 112, 344, 509-10
O'Brien, Murrogh en Ranagh, 58-9, 288, 290-2
O'Briens, 58, 64, 518
O'Brin, see O'Brien
O'Byrne, 393, 420
O'Byrne, Cahir MacGerald, 395
O'Byrne, Feagh MacHugh, 64, 152, 154-5, 170-5, 178, 190, 289, 297, 358, 392-5, 505
O'Byrne, Hugh MacShane, 171-2, 393
O'Byrne, Shane MacRedmond, 171, 393
O'Byrne, Shane MacTurlogh, see O'Byrne, Shane MacRedmond
O'Byrne, Teige Oge, 393
O'Byrnes, 64, 85, 94, 170-1, 178-9, 289, 297, 322-3, 392-5
O'Carrols, 188-9, 191, 404
O'Connolan, Parson, 432
O'Connor Oge, 403
O'Connor Roo, 289
O'Connors, 64, 187-9, 191, 297, 397, 402-3, 405
O'Curry, Eugene, 331, 342, 350, 363, 366
O'Daly, Angus, 357-8
O'Daly, Dominic de Rosario, 528-9
O'Dempsys, 154-5, 188-9, 380
O'Donnell, Hugh Roe, 166-7, 378, 388-9, 399, 420
O'Donovan, John, 323, 362, 393, 403
O'Driscoll, 92, 320
O'Driscoll, Sir Finnin, 320
O'Dubhagain, John, 347
Odyssey, 259, 273, 444
Oebalian Mountain (Vesuvius? Taÿgetus?), 11, 261
"*Of all that in the earth are ordained by nature*," 32, 272-3
O'Faolain, Sean, 376
O'Farralls, 104, 192, 406
Offaly (King's Co.), 64, 245, 297, 535
Offaly, Fort of (Fort Dingan), 184, 191, 400
Officials, English, 142-6, 371-2, 537
O'Flaherty, 92, 320
O'Flaherty, Roderic, 280, 291, 322, 335, 347-9, 497
Og, Rory, 358-9
O'Grady, Standish, 290, 319, 358-60, 394
O'Hanlon, 117, 348
O'hEoghasa, Eochaidh, 358
O'Hernan, 117, 348
O'Huidhrin, Giolla na Naomh, 347
O'Huiggin, Tadhg Dall mac Cairbre, 356, 358-9
O'Kelly, Hugh McDonnell, 403
O'Kellys, 64, 154-5, 187-9, 297, 402-3, 521
Olaus Magnus, 92, 97-8, 106, 109, 321, 327, 337-8, 341, 363, 421, 510
O'Lyne, Teig, 305
O'Mahonys, 363
"*Omne tulit punctum*, qui miscuit vtile dulci," 11, 260
Ó'Moghráin, Pádraig, 327
O'Molloys, 188-9, 191, 404
O'Moores, 64, 154-5, 172, 174, 188-9, 191, 297, 397
"One hand rubbeth another," 30, 272

INDEX 563

O'Neill, 58, 103, 167-70, 391
O'Neill, Brian, 391
O'Neill, Con Bacagh, see Tyrone, Con Bacagh O'Neill, first Earl of
O'Neill, Hugh, see Tyrone, Hugh O'Neill, second Earl of
O'Neill, Matthew, 389-90
O'Neill, Moira, 340
O'Neill, Shane, 354, 389-91
O'Neill, Shane, sons of, 167-8, 389
O'Neill, Turlogh Luineach, 167, 283, 296, 356, 389-91, 399, 535
O'Neills, 168, 333, 389, 391, 534
Ong, Walter J., 381
Ὀφυν, see Ὀσφύν
Opis (Artemis), 36, 275-6
O'Rahilly, Alfred, 527-8
O'Rahilly, Thomas, 358
O'Reilly, Edward, 283, 306
O'Reilly, Sir John, 361
O'Reillys, 64, 192, 297
O'Reilly's Country (Co. Cavan), 183, 400, 406
Origins of the Irish race, 82-97
Orlando Furioso, 471
Ormond, Thomas Butler, tenth Earl of, 74-5, 147, 160, 190, 296, 301-2, 375, 382, 384, 415, 435, 526, 534, 536-7
O'Rourke, 92, 320-1
O'Rourke, Brian, 358
O'Rourke's Country, 57, 289, 405-6
Orpen, Goddard H., 294
Orphei, 459, 478
Orpheus, 458-9
Ortelius, Abraham, 377
Orthography, 442, 463-4, 475-6
Ortiguéira, Antonio, 529-30
Orwen, William R., 251, 268
O's and Mac's, 215, 419-20
Osborne, Thomas, 487
Osgood, Charles G., 266, 352, 425, 493-4, 538
Osius, Hieronymus, 390
Ὀσφύν, 107, 339, 508
Ossory, 191, 405
O'Sullivan, 92, 320
O'Sullivan Bear, Don Philip, 528-30
" *O Tite, siquid, ego, Ecquid erit pretij?* " 17, 266
O'Tooles, 64, 85, 94, 170-1, 178-9, 297, 322-3, 392-5
Oure (Avonbeg), River, 393
" Our life is a Pilgrimage," 28
Outlaws, thieves, and rebels, 98, 100-2, 126, 135, 154-5, 172, 219-21, 286, 357-9, 380, 422
" Out of the abundance of the harte the tonge speakethe," 119, 351
Ovid, 87, 261, 316, 319, 444, 454, 467-8

Oviedo, Fra Matteo d', 525-6, 528
" *Ovr merry dayes, by theeuish bit are pluckt, and torne away,*" 446
Oxford, Edward Vere, seventeenth Earl of, 484-5, 489-90, 494-5
Oxford, Robert Vere, ninth Earl of, 116-8, 347-8

Padelford, Frederick M., 269-74, 277, 286, 374, 381, 487-95
Palatine, earl, 74
Palatines, county, 74-5, 301-2
Pale, see English Pale
Pale Rebellion, 160-1, 295-6, 384-5
Palladius, 137, 368
Pallia, 99, 330
Palsgrave, 74
Pamphilus, see Spenser, Edmund
Pandora, 45, 465
Panton, John, 511-2
Papists, 136-8, 367-8, 372, 424, 521, 523
Paradise of Adam, 444
Paradise of Lovers, 444
Pardons and protections, 144, 155-7, 160, 165-7, 177, 229, 242, 245, 380, 383-4, 388, 430, 535
" *Parere qui nescit*, nescit *imperare*," 175, 395
Paris, 527
Paris, Matthew, 287
Parliament of England, 200, 410-1
Parliament of Ireland, 48, 52, 70-2, 199-201, 282, 284-5, 292-3, 297, 299-300, 349, 391, 411
Parry, Charles H., 411
Parthians, 103
Pasquil, 471
Passion of Christ, 455
Patrick, St., 85, 137, 221, 245, 312, 316, 319, 368, 509
Paymasters to be instituted, 164-5, 387
Payne, Robert, 307, 346
Pegaso, see Spenser, Edmund
Pelham, Sir William, 379, 396
Pembroke, Mary Sidney, Countess of, 479, 490
Penelope, 9
Penny, St., 473
People to be fitted to laws, 199, 410
Perionius, Joachimus, 273, 491
Perjury in Irish trials, 68-9, 299
Perne, Andrew, 462, 485
Perrin, Thomas, 511
Perrot, Sir John, 71, 163, 293, 299, 307, 351-2, 360-1, 365, 372, 376, 386-7, 401, 403, 406, 421-2, 427, 434
Persians, 88, 103, 333, 347
Peter, St., 138
Petrarch, 460, 466, 469, 471, 486
Pettie, George, 351

Pforzheimer, Carl H., library of, 494
Phaedria, 295
Pharaoh, 104, 334-5
Philip II, 162, 166, 198, 237, 297, 388-9, 527, 529-30, 534
Philipstown, 183-4, 400, 405
Phillips, Walter A., 368
Phoenician alphabet, 88
Phoenicians, 88, 316
Piccolomini, Eneo Sylvio, 86, 106, 313-4
Pico della Mirandola, Giovanni, 458-9
Picts, 86, 103-4, 293, 315, 334, 338
"Piers, I haue piped erst so long with payne," 470
Piers, William, 296
Pirckheymer, Wilibaldus, 270, 491
Plantation of Munster, errors in, 239-41
Plato, 23, 27, 269, 272, 352, 356, 460, 487, 491
Plautus, 461, 472
Pléiade, 480
Pliny, Elder, 86, 313-5, 324, 346, 455-6
Plomer, Henry R., 416
Plowlands, 181, 235, 398-9, 402
Plunckett, Oliver, 525, 528
Plutarch, 107, 339, 347
Pluto's kingdom, 36-7
Pluto's palace, 36
Pollente, 415
Pollux, 467
Polybius, 320
Pompeius, Trogus, 313-4, 328
Ponsonby, William, 489-90, 493-4, 504
Pope, see Gregory XIII, Pope
Popes, 138
Portugal, 88, 92
Postel, Guillaume, 491
Poulmounty, 57, 288-90
Powel, David, 311
Power, Sir Henry(?), 403
Praesamarci, 88, 316-7
Preston, Thomas, 7, 254, 485
Price, Sir John, 310-1, 316
Priest in *Hub.*, 425
Probability of things, 84-5, 311-2
Prodicus, 30-1, 34, 272
Prometheus, 465
Proserpina, 11, 260
Prosody determined by custom, 473-6
Protections, see Pardons and protections
Protector, Fort, 183-4, 191, 400, 405
Protestants, 221-2
Provisioning of garrisons, 153, 196-7, 378-9
Ptolemy, Claudius, 44, 86, 279, 313-4, 317, 321
Ptotolomy, see Ptolemy, Claudius
Punic Wars, 90-2
Puritans, 223, 425-6
Puttenham, George, 265, 357, 359, 481-3

Pyrenees, 11, 258
Pythian Apollo, 31

Quantity in English verse, 16, 264, 465, 473-5, 480-2
Queen Mother, see Medici, Catherine de'
Queen's Co., 64, 172, 184, 190, 245, 297
"*Quem metuunt oderunt,*" 146-7, 373
Quiggin, E. C., 358
"*Qui monet, vt facias, quod iam facis,*" 12, 261

Ralegh, Sir Walter, 307, 355, 374, 384, 388, 390, 397, 424, 427-8, 497
Rapes, 201, 412
Rathcoole, 392
Raths, 128-30, 361-3
Rawlinson, Richard, 512
Reade, Andrew, 386
Reade, Thomas, 378
Records of Dublin, see Records of Ireland
Records of Ireland, 181, 185, 191-2, 398
Red Cross, 368, 382
Redshanks, 60, 168, 293
Reformation in laws to follow use of force, 147, 373
Regan, Maurice, 326-7
Regni, 88, 94, 317, 322
Regrating, 226, 427-8
Religion, 136-42, 218-9, 221-4, 244, 367, 422-4, 426, 439
"Religion nedethe quiett times," 138, 368
Rent (tax) to support garrisons, 181-96, 398-9
Renwick, W. L., 259-430 *passim*, 482, 494, 500-2, 504-5, 508-10, 512, 514, 517, 524-9, 534-7
Revelation of St. John, 471
Rhadamanthus, 36
Rheims, 221-2, 425
Rhetorical figures, 254-5, 261, 452
Rich, Barnaby, 298, 306, 311, 332-6, 350, 354-5, 360-1, 369-71, 375, 413, 429-30
Richard II, 116, 347, 414
Riedner, Wilhelm, 285, 300, 314-8, 324, 328-30, 333, 337-40, 343, 347, 352, 363, 389-90, 412, 422, 425
Ringler, William A., 251
Rix, Herbert D., 255, 261
Robin Hood, 202-3, 412-3, 451
Robinson, F. N., 306, 322-3, 334
Roche, Maurice, sixth Viscount Roche of Fermoy, 204, 305, 412-3, 503, 505, 522
Roche, two bastards of Lord, 204, 412-3, 505, 522
Roderick, 92, 321
Rogers, Daniel, 477
Rollins, Hyder E., 295, 477
Roman Empire, 100

INDEX 565

Romans, 82, 86, 90-1, 99, 119, 180, 202, 229, 330, 350, 429, 455, 471
Rome, 11(?), 221-2, 258, 300, 425, 455
Romescot, 180, 398
Romulus, 202, 412
Ronsard, Pierre de, 313
Rosalind, 5(?), 7-9(?), 17(?), 249, 267, 466, 476(?)
Roscommon, Co., 185, 297, 401
Roscommon, House of, 185, 401
Rosenbach Company, 516
Ross (New Ross?), 195, 409
Rosseponte, 409
Routledge, F. J., 300
Roxana, 119, 351
Roy, Louis le, 285-6, 350
Rubel, Vere L., 482
Ruddymane, 333
Ruines of Time, 268
Russell, Thomas, 528
Russell, Sir William, 172, 237, 289, 372, 374-5, 388, 390-1, 394, 409, 422, 426, 433-4, 504-5, 534, 537
Rutland, Edmund Plantagenet, third Earl of, 345

S., E., see Spenser, Edmund
S., E. (not Spenser), 298, 310, 350, 366, 369, 417, 423
S., E. C., 287, 307, 361, 366, 376, 386-7, 402-3, 422
Sackford, Thomas, 445-6
Sacra Insula (Ireland), 145, 372
Saffron, 75, 111, 303, 342
Saffron Walden, 363
Saglio, Edmond, 329
St. Leger, Sir Anthony, 48, 282, 355
St. Leger, Sir Warham, 307, 365, 382, 408, 412, 415
Saintsbury, George, 253, 255, 481
Salesbury, William, 312, 323, 363-4, 392-3
Salisbury, Richard Neville, first Earl of, 345
Sallust, 460
Salus Populi, 532
Samuel, 99
Sander, Nicholas, 528-9
Sandison, Helen E., 268
San Joseppi, Colonel Don Sebastian di, 161-2, 524-30
Sansloy, 357
Sargent, Ralph M., 251, 480
Sassonas, 210, 416-7
Satherlagh, see Carlow, Co.
Saturn, planet, 454
Satyrane, Sir, 387
Satyricall Verses, 17, 265-6
"*Satyricus ille*," see Juvenal
Savage, Lord, 61, 294
Savage, William, 294

Savages, family, 61, 294
Saxey, William, 365-6, 435
Saxon alphabet, 87, 316
Saxon king, see Alfred
Saxon language, 85, 129, 213, 312-3, 362-3
Saxons of England, 85, 87, 93-6, 129-30, 212, 316, 324-5
Schelling, Felix E., 253, 264, 479-81
Scholemaster of Roger Ascham, 252, 463, 480
Schollers Loue, or Reconcilement of Contraries, 460
Schuman, V. B., 508
Scoggin, John, 475
Scota, 89, 104, 309, 335-6
Scotch chronicles, 105
Scotch customs, see Scythian customs
Scotch invasion of Ireland, 60-2, 210, 288, 292-5
Scotia Major (Ireland), 83, 311
Scotia Minor (Scotland), 83, 311
Scotland, 60, 62, 83-4, 93, 168, 311, 335, 368
Scotlands, two, 83-4, 311
Σκότος, 104, 335-6
Scots, 60-2, 83-5, 96-111, 168-9, 210, 309-11, 315, 321, 330, 334, 337-8, 340, 342, 352, 363, 390-1, 399
Scots, district, 57, 290
Scott, Sir Walter, 352-3
Scripture, see Bible
Scuts (Scythians), 83-4, 310
Scuttenland (Scotland), 83, 310
Scylla, 34
Scythia, 89, 91
Scythian customs, 97-111, 113, 320-1, 327-8, 333, 337-41, 343
Scythians (Scyths), 82-5, 87, 89-94, 96-111, 168, 309-10, 315, 320-1, 327-8, 333, 337-41, 343, 364, 510
Seccombe, Thomas, 498
"*See yee the blindefoulded pretie God, that feathered Archer*," see "*Tetrasticon*"
Selbury, 363
Selden, John, 301, 311, 334, 337, 410
Selincourt, Ernest de, 266, 268, 481, 499
Senchus Mor, 327
Senights Slumber, 251-2
Serena, 413
Sergis, Sir, 386
Services due to Irish lords, 79, 306-7
Seymour, St John D., 335
Shakespeare, 346, 354-5
Shannon, River, 59
Sheelin, Lough, 192, 406
Shelley, Percy B., 501
Shepheardes Calender, 5-6, 18, 249, 261, 265, 272-3, 469-71, 486
Sheriffs, 142-3, 220-1, 240, 371, 422-3, 429-30, 437
Sherlock, George(?), 403

Sheyne, William, 369
Shillelagh, 57, 174, 289
Shoole of Abuse of Stephen Gosson, 6, 251
Shraugh, 79, 306-7
Shrewsbury, Earl of, 114, 345
Shymeirs, Monsieur, see Simier, Jean de, Baron de St. Marc
Shynan, 117, 348
Shynan, Nicholas, 348
Sidney (Neagh), Lough, 182-3, 399
Sidney, Sir Henry, 278, 295, 297-8, 305, 333, 344, 349, 364-5, 369, 383, 390, 399-401, 404-5, 427-8, 535
Sidney, Sir Philip, 6-7, 12, 16, 250-2, 286, 357, 365, 373, 442, 462(?), 463, 467, 470, 477, 479-81, 485, 490
Sigerson, George, 359
Simier, Jean de, Baron de St. Marc, 460(?)
Sisyphus, 37
Skelaghs, 361
Slaney, River, 191
Slanius, 89, 319
Sleeves worn long, 111
Sleugho, see Sligo, Co.
Slewlogher, see Slievelougher
Slievelougher, 57, 115, 288
Sligo, Co., 185, 187-8, 401
Smerwick, Fort of (Fort del Oro), 161-2, 383, 385, 387, 524-30
Smith, Charles, 292, 363, 415
Smith, G. C. Moore, 250, 254, 258, 261, 263, 351, 479
Smith, G. Gregory, 249-55, 261-3, 266-7, 480, 482-3
Smith, J. C., 252, 388
Smith, Nicholas, 338
Smith, Roland M., 260, 280-1, 284, 288-90, 298-9, 306-8, 312-3, 318-21, 323-4, 327, 331, 333-4, 346-7, 351-2, 355, 360, 362, 378-9, 383, 402-3, 407-8, 416-7, 503
Smith, Thomas, 357
Smith, Sir Thomas, of Saffron Walden, 285, 374, 397, 418-9, 464
Snyder, Edward D., 301
Social War, 455
Socrates, 10, 27-38 *passim*, 269
Soldiers in time of peace, 176-7, 180, 396
Solinus, Caius Julius, 86, 106, 313-4, 337-8, 340, 343, 346, 510
Solon, 54, 285-6, 461
Solons, 461
Somersetshire, 94
Sophists, 10
Sophocles, 351
Sorehin, 79, 207, 307, 415
Sources of information on Irish history, 84-7, 288, 308, 313-5, 392, 499, 510
Southey, Robert, 316, 328, 344, 360, 396
South Sea (Atlantic), 110, 147, 375

Spain, 82-94, 175, 221, 300-1, 309, 316-9, 433, 525-6
Spaniards, 82-92, 94, 96-7, 105, 161-2, 165, 194, 317-8, 320, 342-3, 374, 389, 408-9, 526-7
Spanish chronicles, 86
Spanish customs, 110-1, 342-3
Spanish insolency, 85
Spanish name, 92
Sparta, 54, 69, 125, 286, 347
"*Speculum Tuscanismi*," 467
Speed, John, 291, 403, 407
Spelman, Henry, 362, 398, 410-1, 417-8, 426
Spencer, Alice, 506
Spencer, Theodore, 482
"*Spende me and defende me*," 79, 307
Spens, Janet, 266
Spenser, Edmund, referred to as: Immerito, 8, 11-2, 17, 255, 261, 441, 443, 447-9, 457, 459, 463, 466, 470, 474, 483-4; Edmundus, 11, 261; Edward Spenser, 21, 25, 43, 269, 489-90, 493-5; E. S., 41, 43, 231; Pamphilus, 444; Pegaso, 466; Collinshead, 470; Colin Clout, 471;—references to his works: *Shepheardes Calender*, 5-6, 18, 249, 261, 265, 272-3, 469-71, 486; *My Slomber*, 6, 251-2; *Epithalamion Thamesis*, 17, 266, 470, 481; *Dreames*, 17-8, 251-2, 266-8, 459, 471; *Dying Pellicane*, 17, 252, 267, 459, 471; *Faerie Queene*, 17, 260, 266-8, 471-2, 531; *Stemmata Dudleiana*, 18, 268, 459-60; *Colin Clouts Come Home Againe*, 249; *Complaints*, 251-2, 267; *Senights Slumber*, 251-2; Anacreontic epigrams, 265; lost sonnet, 265-6; *Muiopotmos*, 266; *Visions of Bellay*, 266; *Theatre for Worldlings*, 266, 272; *Ruines of Time*, 268; *Teares of the Muses*, 268; "Haruey, the happy aboue happiest men," 300; Comedies, nine English (*Nine Muses*), 459-60, 471-2;—verses by: "*Iambicum Trimetrum*," 7-8, 254-5, 442, 481; "*Ad Ornatissimum Virum* . . . *G. H.*," 8-11, 255-9, 444; "*Tetrasticon*," 16, 265, 465; "*That which I eate, did I ioy, and that which I greedily gorged*," 16, 265; "*How wretched a thred of life haue the gods spun*," 32, 272; "*Of all that in the earth are ordained by nature*," 32, 272-3; "*Him loued highest Iupiter and Apollo deare*," 32, 272-3; "*What thinkest thou of him*," 32, 272-3; "*Thomalins Embleme*," 469; "*Willyes Embleme*," 469; "*Piers, I haue piped erst so long with payne*," 470;—publication of *S. C.*, 5-6, 249; defers to Harvey's judgment, 5-6; love (for Rosalind?), 5, 7-9, 17, 249, 259, 444, 449, 466, 476; audience with Queen, 6, 250; familiarity with Sidney and Dyer, 6; English versifying in quantitative meters,

INDEX 567

6-8, 16-7, 264-5, 480-2; affection for Harvey, 7-8, 12, 253; prospective trip to Continent, 8-9, 11-2, 249, 258-9, 444-5; without worldly fortune, 11; fear of obscurity, 11; last visit with Harvey in Westminster, 16, 265; will discuss antiquities of Ireland later, 81-2, 230-1; sources of information on Irish history, 84-7, 288, 308, 313-5, 392, 499, 510; perhaps present at execution of Murrogh O'Brien, 112, 344; praise of Munster, 115, 158, 239, 346; has had Irish poems translated, 127, 357-9; not much conversant with religion, 136, 221; perhaps present at Smerwick, 161, 524-30; has seen Old Council Book of Munster, 207; knowledge of Co. Cork, 208, 416; concocted Letters with Harvey, 249, 262; use of Latin, 250; E. K. as a mask for, 252, 262, 486; first marriage, 258-9, 267; dates of Letters, 261-2, 267-8; identification with Irenius, 278, 524-30; historical method, 287-8, 290-1, 292-3, 308, 312, 347-8, 398, 499, 501-3, 509-10; accompanies Grey, 289, 295, 378, 382, 384-5, 392-3, 400, 405, 408-9, 503, 524-30; accompanies Perrot, 293; experience of court trials, 298; in Dublin for Parliament, 299-300; hazards in taking Kilcolman, 304; involved with Lord Roche, 305, 413; possible authorship of *De Rebvs Gestis Britanniae*, 310; ignorance of Ireland, 322, 497; scorn for rural life, 328; feeble joke by, 335-6; clerk of Munster Council, 351-2; personal experience of Irish priests, 369; pitiless proposal to starve Irish, 381; letters in hand of, 384, 406-8, 524; careless computations of, 395, 399, 401, 406, 408, 430; accompanies Sir Thomas Norris, 399; rent paid by, 406; religious views of, 423-6; spoliation of Kilcolman, 435; references to letters from, 441-2, 471; not perfect in English versifying, 442-3; connection with publication of Letters, 447-8, 483-5; promising writer, 448; controlled by Perne, 462; one of best English critics, 470; is expected to earn fortune with poetry, 471, 474; and the Areopagus, 479-80; translator of *Ax.*, 487-96; prose style of, 492, 498-500, 533-8; condemnation of Euphuism, 495; value and limitations of *View*, 497-503, 531-2; aspersions on Irish, 497, 531-2; pitilessness, 499, 501; Grey's influence on, 503; *View* composed in 1596 in England, 503-5; Ware's biographical sketch of, 531; unmanliness of *B. N.*, 533-4; authorship of *B. N.*, 534-7
Spenser, Edward, see Spenser, Edmund
Spenser, Sylvanus, 348
Spingarn, Joel E., 479-80
Srag, see Shraugh
Stafford, George Granville Leveson-Gower, second Marquis of, 348-9
Standen, Anthony, 301
Stanley, Edward, 382
Stanyhurst, Richard, 104-5, 278-9, 281-2, 287, 295, 301, 306, 311, 318-9, 324, 331, 334-6, 343, 347, 349-50, 353, 355, 360-1, 383, 481, 483, 497
Starnes, D. T., 262, 356, 486
Starving of enemy, 154, 158-9, 244, 377, 379, 381, 439
State Papers, Public Record Office, 355, 430, 507, 529-30, 533, 536
Stationers' Register, 477, 483, 488-9, 494, 501, 504, 506
Statute Law of Ireland, 75-81
Statvtes of Ireland, 282, 297, 299-300, 302-5, 324, 332-4, 350-1, 391, 419, 421-2, 428, 532
Steevens, George, 487-8, 493
Stemmata Dudleiana, 18, 268, 459-60
Still, John, 7, 254, 458
Stocaghs, 158-9, 203, 216-7, 413
Stoic influence, 492-4
Stoic wisdom, 9
Stone, William J., 481-2
Stonehenge, 363
Storehouses needed, 197, 409
Stowe, John, 261, 263-4, 330, 337, 495
Strabane, 182, 399
Strabo, 86, 88, 95, 313-4, 316-7, 324
Strafford, Thomas Wentworth, Earl of, 501, 530-1
Strait of Gibraltar, 88
Strongbow, Richard de Clare, Earl of Pembroke, 55, 96, 171, 287, 325
Strowbridge, Hugh, 432
Stubbs, William, 427
Stucley, Thomas, 525
"*Stultorum omnia plena*," 10, 260
Sty, 122, 354
Sullaine, 92
Sullevant, 92
Superstitions, 107-10, 339-41
Surrey, 94
Susanne, 473
Sussex, 94
Sussex, Thomas Radcliffe, third Earl of, 297, 299, 385, 397, 414
Swan, Marshall W. S., 494-6
Swedes, 321
"Sweet Speech," 490, 494-6
Sword to be used against evil men, not whole people, 148, 376
Sword to be used before laws in reforming Ireland, 147-8, 373, 375

Tacitus, 86, 89, 313-5, 317-8

Tadhg, bard of Lord Roche, 359
Tages, 459
Talbots, 61, 294
Talbotstown, 174, 395
Talus, 377
Tamarici, 88, 316-7
Tanais (River Don), 93, 321
Tane, 85, 312
Tania, 51, 283-4
Tanistih, see Tanists
Tanistry, 49-51, 208, 282-4
Tanists, 49-51, 282-4
Tantalus, 37
Tarbert, 85, 312
Tarlton, Richard, 477
Tartars, 98, 217, 327-8, 342, 421
Taÿgetus, Mount, 11(?), 261
Teares of the Muses, 268
Tecmessa, 119, 351
Telamon, 119, 351
"*Tempora furtiuo labuntur dulcia cursu*," 446
"*Tempora furtiuo morsu laniantur amaena*," 445
Tenants, see Landlords and tenants
Terence, 472
"*Tetrasticon*," 16, 265, 465
Thames, River, 17
"*That which I eate, did I ioy, and that which I greedily gorged*," 16, 265
Theatre for Worldlings, 266, 272
"The minde followethe muche the Temparature of the bodye," 119, 351
Themistocles, 33, 116, 347
Theodorus Siculus, see Diodorus Siculus
Theramenes, 33, 274
"*These pleasant dayes, and Monthes, and yeares, by stelth do passe apace*," 446-7
"The wiseman shall rule even over the starres," 44, 279
"*Thomalins Embleme*," 469
Thomas, Sidney, 267
Thomas of Walsingham, 309
Thomond (Co. Clare), 58, 291, 401
Thomond, Murrogh O'Brien, first Earl of, 414
Thompson, Guy Andrew, 265, 481
Thopas, Sir, 121, 353
Thornton, George, 391
Three Castles, 174, 395
Thurles, 59
Tilley, Morris P., 351
Timias, 427
Tipperary, Co., 74, 194, 288-9, 301-2
Tithingmen, see Borsholders
Tithings, 201, 213
Titius, 37
Titus, 17, 266
Todd, Henry J., 249-55, 261, 263, 265-8, 281-2, 291, 293, 296, 298-9, 301, 303, 309, 325, 328, 331, 334, 337, 340-1, 343, 348-9, 354-5, 360-2, 371, 374-5, 382-3, 385, 387, 390, 397, 410, 413, 416, 419-20, 422, 428, 481, 483, 487, 493, 497, 503-4, 506, 523
Tol, 94, 170-1, 322-3, 392-3
Tolman, Albert H., 426
"To my good Mistresse *Anne*," 472-3
Tomyris, 103, 333
Tooles, see O'Tooles
Tooly, Tom, 460
"To the willinge theare is no wronge done," 79, 307
Touchets, 61, 294
Towneley, Richard, 516
Towns to be built or restored, 183-4, 188, 193, 225-7, 427-8
Towry, M. H., 266
Toxaris of Lucian, 107-9, 339-41
Toxophilus of Roger Ascham, 475
Trades, three kinds of, 215-8, 420-1
Transplantation of Irish, 178-9, 395-7
Transportation of grain, 196, 409, 427-8
Traueiler of Jerome Turler, 444
Travers, Walter, 371
Treason, 79-80
Tredagh, see Drogheda
Tree of Knowledge, 465
Tremayne, Edmond, 305, 344, 366, 368, 377
Trim, 195, 408
Trinity College, Dublin, 142, 370-1, 517
Trinity Hall, Cambridge, 5, 445, 462
Triptolemus, see Euryptolemus
Tristeldermot, Parliament of, 292
Trivets, 131, 363-4
Trojans, 86
Trollope, Andrew, 367, 382, 409
Trophonius, 31, 272
Troth, Tom, 466
Trowis, River, 378
Truth, Plain of, 36
Tuinnye, 85, 312
Tuites, 294
Tully, see Cicero
Turgesius, 292
Turkish affairs, 460
Turler, Jerome, 258-9, 444
Tuscanism, 467
Twyne, John, 320, 338
Twyne, Thomas, 263, 477-9
Tyrconnell (Co. Donegal), 57, 290, 359
Tyrone, Co., 57, 184, 290, 302
Tyrone, Con Bacagh O'Neill, first Earl of, 282, 389-91
Tyrone, Hugh O'Neill, second Earl of, 149, 152, 166-70, 237-8, 245, 283, 333, 351, 376-7, 380-1, 388-91, 394, 399-400, 404, 409, 414, 432-4, 439, 505, 533-5, 537
Tyrrell, Richard, 238, 435
Tyrtaeus, 125, 357

INDEX 569

Ua Mongain, 348
Ulster, 57-8, 62, 82, 115, 151-4, 162, 166-70, 177-9, 181-5, 187-9, 197, 235, 290-1, 295, 301-2, 349, 377-8, 382, 390-1, 396-7, 399-401, 403
Ulster, Earldom of, 58, 235, 290, 295
Ulster, Earl of, 349
Ulster, William de Burgh, third Earl of, 58, 290, 518
Ulysses, 9, 11, 259, 444-5, 461
Una, 367, 427
Undertakers of Munster, 192-3, 236, 238-42, 406, 536-7
Upham, Alfred H., 479
Upper Ossory, 191, 405
Upton, John, 329, 333, 487-8, 493
Urwick, W., 371, 517
Ussher, Archbishop James, 316, 368, 516-7, 531
Ussher, William, 386

Valenger, Stephen (?), 474
Vandals, 91
Varro, Marcus, 461
Venice, 229, 429
Venti, 93, 321
Venus, 9, 16, 99, 329, 444
Venus, planet, 453
Veres, 115-6, 347
Vergil, 99, 330, 444
Vergil, Polydore, 280, 293, 308-9, 335
Versifying, English, in quantitative meters, 6-8, 16-7, 251-3, 264-5, 442-4, 463-70, 473-6, 480-3
Verulame, 428
Vesuvius, Mount, 11(?), 258, 261
Victor, Sextus Aurelius, 412
View of the Present State of Ireland, manuscripts of: Additional MS 22022—278, 281, 320, 332, 334, 360, 392-3, 397, 416, 514, 517, 524; Cambridge University MS Dd. 10.60—503-4, 511-4, 516, 523-4; Cambridge University MS Dd. 14.28(1)—504, 514-6, 524; Ellesmere MS 7041—294, 296, 309, 314, 348-9, 361, 393, 403, 407, 416, 420, 426, 503, 506-11, 516, 519-23; Folger MS 6185—514-6; Gonville and Caius College MS 188.221—393, 403, 503-4, 507-11, 516-7, 523-4; Gough MS Ireland 2—388, 510-1, 516-8; Harleian MS 1932—504, 515-6, 524; Harleian MS 7388—514, 517, 524; Houghton MS—278, 515-6; Lambeth MS 510—348-9, 418, 503-4, 511-4, 516, 523-4; National Library of Ireland MS 661 (Gurney MS)—514, 517; Public Record Office MS, State Papers 63.202, Part 4, item 58—309, 312, 320, 407, 507, 509-11, 516-8, 524; Rawlinson MS B 478—332, 359, 504, 507, 509, 511-4, 516, 524; Trinity College Dublin MS E.3.26—337, 339, 407, 503-4, 509-11, 516-7, 523-4.—Ware's text of, 278, 281, 288-9, 309, 332-3, 349, 395, 399, 403, 405, 407, 416, 419, 507, 509, 512, 516-24
Villatas terrae, 212, 417-8
Vincentius, see Vincent of Beauvais
Vincent of Beauvais, 86, 313-4, 327-8
Virtue, fame, wealth, and eloquence, praise of, 465
Virtue, praise of, 442, 445-7
Visions of Bellay, 266
Visions of Petrarch, 471

Wainewright, John B., 529
Walker, Alice, 482
Walker, William, 394
Wallace, Malcolm W., 480
Wallop, Sir Henry, 163, 300, 351, 374-6, 378-9, 383, 386-8, 390, 403, 405, 409, 500, 528
Walsh, Paul, 389
Walsingham, Sir Francis, 278, 396
Wapentakes, 201, 213, 411-2, 418-9
Warcries, 103-5, 333-5
Ward, A. W., 498
Wardships and marriages, 73
Ware, Sir James, 278, 281, 283, 290-1, 298, 306, 308-9, 311, 315-9, 321-2, 324-7, 330, 333, 337, 339-41, 344, 347-9, 357, 362-3, 369-70, 372, 375, 384, 386, 390-1, 393-5, 397, 399, 401, 404, 411-2, 414-22, 430, 501, 503, 512, 516, 518-9, 523, 530-2
Warren, Sir William, 388
Wars of the Roses, 56-7, 287-8, 290-1, 391
Waterford, city, 194-5, 302, 408, 439, 522
Waterford, Co., 64
Waterhouse, Edward, 405
Watson, Thomas, 443, 474, 480
Wealth brings friends, 468
Weaver, William, 435
Webbe, William, 262, 265, 357, 480
Welsdalius, Hermannus Rayanus, 269-77, 491-2, 494
Welsh language, 85, 312-3, 320, 322-3, 363-4, 392-3, 418
Welshmen, 93, 112, 203, 321, 413
Western Sea (Atlantic), 110
West Meath, 64, 191, 290, 297
Westminster, 7, 16-7, 252, 265, 531
Westropp, Thomas J., 292
Wexford, city, 195
Wexford, Co., 64, 172-4, 189-90, 289, 301, 321, 404
"*What thinkest thou of him*," 32, 272-3
Whibley, Charles, 488
"Whiles the yron is hote, it is good striking," 6

"*Whilst your Bearnes are fatte, whilst Cofers stuff'd with aboundaunce,*" 468
"*Whilst your Ritches abound, your friends will play the* Placeboes," 468
White, Sir Nicholas, 393-4
Whitehall, 490, 494-5
White Knight's Country, 194, 408
Whitman, Charles H., 387
Whore of Babylon, 137, 368
Wicklow, city, 174
Wicklow, Co., 190, 404
Wicklow Mountains, 289, 297
Wilbraham, Roger, 432
Wild Irish, 74, 113, 115, 209-10, 301
Willcock, G. D., 264, 482
William of Malmesbury, 308, 411-2, 418
William the Conqueror, 46-7, 53, 55-6, 202, 280
Willis, Humfry, 432
"*Willyes Embleme,*" 469
Wilson, Sir Thomas, 359, 484
Wiltshire, 94
Winchester, Statute of, 426-7
Winter, Sir William, 526
Winter the best season for campaigning, 154-5, 380

Withipole, Edmund, 441-2, 446
Withipole, Peter, 446-7
Worcester, John Tiptoft, Earl of, 348
Worthington, John, 252
Wotton, Nicholas, 461
Wotton, Thomas, 410
Wretchedness of life, 31-4
Wright, Joseph, 367
Wyatt, Sir Thomas, 265

Xenocrates, 491
Xenophon, 460
Xerxes, 36, 275

York, House of, 56, 145, 372
York, Richard Plantagenet, third Duke of, 345
Youghal, 195, 302, 435
Young, Arthur, 288
Young, G. M., 482
Young, Bishop John, 466(?)
Your old lord, see Young, Bishop John
Y Rhuwden, John William, 369

Zwinger, Theodore, 444